THE ULTIMATE DICTIONARY OF

DREAM
LANGUAGE

THE ULTIMATE DICTIONARY OF
DREAM
LANGUAGE

BRICEIDA RYAN

BRISTOL
PARK
BOOKS

First Published as The Ultimate Dictionary of Dream Language in 2004
by Ozark Mountain Publishers

First Bristol Park Books edition published in 2013

Bristol Park Books
252 W. 38th Street
NYC, NY 10018

Bristol Park Books is a registered trademark of Bristol Park
Books, Inc.

Published by arrangement with Hampton Roads Publishing Company

ISBN: 978-0-88486-529-2

Printed in the United States of America.

All dream interpretations are subject to the skills of the individual interpreting the dream. The author and Hampton Roads Publishing Company, Inc. are not responsible, based on the definitions given, for the accuracy of the dream interpretations.

This book is dedicated with love to my children Audrena, Andrew, Angelina, grandchildren Andrew, Sophia, Anthony, Alexander Taylor, each member of my family, and especially to my late son, Kirk P. Ryan, who is no longer with us. This book is also dedicated to all those who seek a truthful self analysis of their dreams.

Contents

Dream (Interpretations) Definitions:

Acknowledgments

A special thanks to the Mighty power of God, and for all of the spiritual and psychic guidance opportunity I have received.

I especially want to thank my mother with love, Silvia E. Suncin, the late Kirk P. Ryan Sr., M.S.W., and Juliana Sanchez, for their wonderful kindness and prayers for me. Charlie Simpson, the late Marvin S. Iscoff and the late Donna Carol Ph.D., who were my best friends.

A big extra thanks to Deborah Goggans Ram, who not only had the tenacity, but the determination and driving force to help me see this project through, as well as the massive patience and editing expertise this project required to reach completion.

A warm thanks to Nancy Aldrette for her patience and the word processing and technical skills needed to bring this project to completion.

With deep gratitude, affection and thanks to Frederick George Miller, attorney, who was there for me at a young age. He opened a stage of opportunities, episodes, and impressions that provided the perfect interaction and atmosphere for me in my young life to better recognize and organize perfectly crystalized formed thought processes. This, coupled with my heightened consciousness, awareness and reactive thought processes, allowed me to manipulate and develop precise techniques and methods in order to achieve this project.

A special thanks with love to Stanley Chong Kwong; Don Lastreto, M.D; Alexandra Erlichman Ph.D.; Chris S. Manitas, M.D.; Hozael Mejia; David Moon, Attorney; Yuan Lin; Art Fine; Andrew L. Bull, M.D.; Sarah McIntosh; Robert Hernandez, M.S.W.; Richard Sweet, M.D., Chief of Staff; William Waters, M.D.; Gerardus B. Staal; Mojo Tubutu; Ming Mullins; Robert F. Reyes; Aimel Nicole Anderson; Andy Turner; Terence O Mayo, Attorney; Tony K. Hertier; Steve Bach; Russ. W. J. Gilmartin; Joe & Joe Jr. Martinez; Sylvia Borruso, M.S.W; Maria E. Melendez; Silvia E. Suncin Cammareri; Fernando Jr.; George Julio Suncin; the late Fernando E., the late Maria Luisa and the late Elliot Ney Suncin. And all family members and friends who offered me their love, support, encouragement and good wishes.

I also want to take this opportunity to thank all of those individuals who, throughout the years, shared their dreams with me and allowed me to interpret their dreams. Those dreams were very instrumental in my research, and gave me the chance to compare and compile notes that lend authenticity to this book.

Preface

The Ultimate Dictionary of Dream Language contains a wider usage of word definitions and terms than any one person can dream of experiencing in a lifetime. A great body of information and research has been compiled to build and organize this dictionary through my personal experiences and the personal experiences of others. I have kept dream journals for more than twenty-eight years for the sole purpose of putting together a complete, accurate, authentic and comprehensive dream dictionary. The vast amount of research that I have compiled lends to the authenticity of this material. It is written in the format of a dictionary, including over twenty three thousand five hundred (23,500) entries, with an introduction describing the use of the material as well as full, precise interpretations of your dreams. This introduction also intensively explores Premonitional Dreams, Sexual Dreams, Love, Out of Body Experience Dreams, Deities, Gods, Goddesses & Extraordinary Figures, Spiritual Guides, Channeling, Art Dreams, Low-Awareness Dreams, Past Lives, Reincarnation, Dreams Within a Dream, Recurring Dreams, Nightmares & Sleep Paralysis, Intuition, Numerology, Traces of Dreams, Benefit of Dream Interpretation, Guidelines on Using this Book to Review and Interpret dreams. This book is intended for individuals of all faiths, religions and beliefs. Anyone will gain more knowledge and benefit greatly from this material. This system is clearly a tool that can be instrumental for all who seek a truthful self analysis of their dreams.

Respectfully yours,

Briceida Ryan, San Francisco

Introduction

The phenomena of dreams are psychic experiences. During sleep, our personality is better able to tap into our psychic level. The manner in which you breathe alerts your spirit that your personality is ready to receive the dream images. Once your spirit is activated, you receive messages that are psychic in nature. The spiritual element creates images in the form of a dream for the mind to view. You may then visualize a sneak preview of what is in store for you in the present and the future. This element allows you to interpret a sequence of images, sexual events, thoughts, fantasies, phantoms, symbols, channeling and/or messages. On occasions of illness your spirit and personality will join forces to allow healing to take place during sleep through dreams. You may experience out of body episodes during the dream stage, as well as the opportunity on other occasions to communicate with friends, relatives, and loved ones who have passed away. The function of this interpretation is to create a language that gives your spirit a voice to communicate with your personality and to be understood.

A description of the three components that make up your identity are personality, spirit and psyche.

* Personality - What we know to be our own identity in the outer world. This is the part that responds to outside stimuli; the mind.
* Spirit - The part arising from a divine power; the soul. The divine part of you is your spirit, and once it is activated and desires communication, you receive that communication as a psychic message.
* Psyche - The energy given to you by your spirit. The psychic message is under the direct command of your spirit. It may also be turned on by any divine power at any time. This psychic message will come to you complete with all the necessary ingredients (i.e., how to achieve your goals, how to respond to events, etc.), through dream images. The psyche is the part of your mind that interprets information received from a psychic message, and puts thoughts in your own voice into a message the personality can react and respond to.

Dreaming is a vehicle provided by the spirit to communicate with and allow the personality to receive messages from several different capacities and perspectives. During the dream process, the body is going through restorative sleep and is reenergizing, replenishing and restoring itself. It is a type of nourishment that we only get in our sleeping hours. This nourishment also allows us to own and retain complete confidence, comfort and calm with our spirit and to have the faith to allow our spirit to assist in the process of healing in time of illness. At this time, the spirit may call upon the collective knowledge of other spirits, living or dead, in order to receive information and assistance that will facilitate the healing process. At this point, your spirit will begin a healing process. You will recover from illnesses at different rates, depending on severity, but you do recover. Dreams serve various purposes and give opportunities to take control of your life in the "real world". Only during dream processing does this allow you (your personality) to automatically possess complete confidence.

Dreams provide the opportunity to communicate with the spirits of other individuals, living and dead, who have the expertise to attend to your specific illness. Depending on the nature of the illness and stage of recovery, the assisting spirits vary and seldom do the same caregiver spirits return. This is because our spirit will choose from a pool of resources, therefore, the correct caregiver spirit for each facet of our illness may differ. Not only have I personally experienced this, but this process has been described to me at length by other dreamers as well.

I have documented my dreams for the last twenty-eight years and have interpreted thousands of dreams for others. I encourage any and all who recall a dream, to actively follow up on its meaning. Should you choose to interpret your dreams, then you will be taking steps to receive messages that have been prepared specifically for you. And to receive messages, as well, for your loved-ones, family and friends.

Traditionally, we have been conditioned to ignore our dreams. We have been taught that they are insignificant. I advise you to stress the importance to your children, grandchildren, etc., of recalling and recording each dream from the moment they can verbalize. And to stress to them that dreaming is an essential part in learning to communicate with the spiritual part of themselves.

A spirit is always in a relentless pursuit of pointing and leading us to a more positive way of living life. It forces us to face up to issues that have been left undone, and helps us to prepare for circumstances and situations that are coming up in our future. The spirit reveals to us a positive solution to what seems to be an unworkable circumstance.

Our dreams can be thankful warnings, for we can then take measures of prevention and turn a negative situation into a positive one, completely avoid an issue or handle it from a different perspective so that it will no longer be a problem. You'll want to remember this: you do make and have control of what goes on in your dream process, as well as in your outer world. It is important that you understand this part of your dreams. There are no restraints and no limitations to the possibilities that you can encounter and accomplish in a dream fantasy. If you don't like the direction a dream is taking or are uncomfortable with the dream, act on it as you would in your outer world. That's right, rearrange and change it as you would like it to be. It's an incredible, fantastic connection that does affect your outer world. Dreams also give knowledge about decisions that other people are going to be making about you, for you, or against you in life, once you learn to accurately interpret them. A visiting spirit may enter your dream to see how you will react to a plan they want you to implement of in reality. Depending on how you perform, the visiting spirit may or may not want to be involved with you in reality. You can gain opportunities and greater rewards, and win in your outer world. Because we have a need to determine whether choices we make will be the right ones, and because we want to know the outcome of a situation, our spirit and the spirits of others enter dreams when there is a driving need. Not so much to manipulate others, but to assist the dreamer in making good choices. Dreams are vehicles the spirit uses to allow us to manipulate our environment for our own benefit and for humankind as a whole. An accurate interpretation will also give you the opportunity to manifest what you need and want out of life, because the personality is able to play the role before it actually happens. During the dream, you'll need to change imperfections in order to project what you want to experience in your outer world. Dreams are an optional method to give you the opportunity to rearrange or prearrange your life in order to create your perfect lifestyle.

Now that you know this, make certain that you do not compromise your feelings in your dreams. Be true to yourself and maintain your integrity and valor. Don't wimp out when you are tested or called on to make decisions in your dreams that will affect your outer world and everyday life. Don't allow yourself to be defeated in a dream. Whatever it takes, do what is necessary to win and maintain your point of view when you know it is the right decision. This is something that comes up time and time again with different people who have allowed me to interpret their dreams -- that a person who became manipulated in their dreams, clearly suffered losses in the outer world.

For example: An older gentleman had given a large loan to a young man a few months before who promised to pay him back and never did. That night the older gentleman dreamed that he stepped into an elevator and when he turned around, he noticed a young masked man had followed him into the elevator. The masked man asked him for money, laughing the entire time. The older man became very frightened and immediately reached into his clothing to get his wallet to give to the masked man, pleading, "Please just take my money, but don't do anything to me." The masked man continued to laugh, took the money, and walked out of the elevator. When the older man woke up, he was very shaken about the dream. The next day the young man whom he had previously loaned money to came to him with a sad story. The older man gave him more money. The young man was able to get a second loan because he, as the masked man in the dream, verified that the older man was going to be an easy mark in reality. The evening after the older man had the dream he called me to discuss this dream. I told him that the masked man in the elevator was a friend of his who had come to ask him, through his dream, for some more money. This particular dream demonstrated several occurrences that are typical of the dream state. A spirit (in this case the masked man) entered the dream state of the older gentleman in order to verify and practice a future event, and to receive feedback that would influence his decision-making in the outer world. At any given time anyone's individual spirit may enter the dream of another individual, at will, in order to leave a message or to communicate in some capacity. Although the young man was not the one who experienced the dream, he could in reality sense the older man's willingness to give a second loan because his spirit had entered the dream in disguise.

His spirit disguised his personality's identity for several reasons. One was to avoid detection and recognition since his primary motive was to manipulate and defeat the older man in the dream state. Because the older gentleman compromised and was defeated in the dream, the masked man received the encouragement he needed to approach the older gentleman for a second loan in real life. The young man was also disguised to protect his true personality from embarrassment should his spirit-self be defeated in the dream. The older gentleman would have recognized him as a thief in real life, and his true personality would have suffered humiliation. A disguise was also used to avoid alerting the gentleman to his true motives in the outer world. This allowed the manipulation to freely occur without the distraction or interference of a known element (the older man recognizing the younger man), and to avoid too much personal involvement in the dream. Active involvement by the older man's spirit in the dream would have altered the outcome of the thief's immediate plans. Personal involvement, assertive action, and a proper response in the dream are important for rearranging the outcome of a negative in a dream, in order to enjoy a positive outcome in reality. Dreams offer further examples of ways in which we can rearrange the outcome. They are discussed in more detail on page xvii.

Visiting spirits entering the dream process reveal only what they want you to see. The illusions created by these spirits at that particular time are the only ones we are allowed to be aware of. Although our spirit is aware of the identity of the visiting spirits, it has no voice and therefore no means of verbalizing, and cannot alert us to the dangers, if any, of manipulations that will take place. If the spirit had a voice, it would no doubt alarm and frighten you unnecessarily. Therefore your spirit will leave large clues by way of symbolic representations that are appropriate at that time in the dream. Something about this visiting spirit will be exposed (i.e., mannerisms, personality, speech, clothing, accessories, etc.). Your personality can then visualize and become aware of the identity of the disguised visiting spirit. For example, a faceless or masked spirit may enter our dream but a clue to the identity of this spirit may be offered, such as a piece of jewelry, clothing, etc., that you recognize as belonging to someone you know.

It is possible to become actively involved in the dream state and it is important that you not allow yourself to be manipulated, bullied or pushed around by other spirits' personalities who may choose to disguise themselves and enter your dream state to test the outcome of an upcoming event. These spirits can tap into the psychic part of your personality in a dream to find out whether they can manipulate you in some capacity, or to see if they can verify a plan to see how workable and successful it could be in real life for both the dreamer and for the visiting spirit. Most of the time these dream messages revolve around positive experiences both of you will benefit from. For example, through active involvement during the dream state, the older man had at his disposal, the means to alter both the outcome of the dream and, as a result, alter the events of the following day. Had the older man become assertive and reached for a revolver instead of his wallet during the dream, the young masked man's spirit would have been defeated. This would have resulted in two occurrences. First, the young man probably would not have had the courage to ask for a second loan and secondly, if he did, the older gentleman would have turned down the request.

It is very important for us to really understand the language of dreams. We can accomplish this by practicing each day of our lives to recall our dreams and to actively train ourselves to retain dream messages. Translating the images of dreams into an understandable form is akin to translating a foreign tongue into our native speech. As interest increases, as well as practice, it becomes natural and easy. Through dreams we come close to experiencing the potential of our natural spiritual abilities and activities. Through the language and practice of dream interpretation we learn to discover and retain messages for our present and future. It is essential that we make dream processing a significant part of our daily life.

One thing that is clearly revealed to us is that our spirits are not always aware of the future involvement. For example, if the spirit of the older man had known ahead of time what would occur (i.e., how he would react), it would have been a premonitional dream and would have revealed a complete and exact representation of the future event. Because the image was incomplete and inexact, we know it was created by a disguised visiting spirit rather than an accurate depiction of future events. Future events portended in most dreams will occur within one to three days, or between five to seven days after the dream. All other dreams that depict a future event will leave clues that will allow the dreamer to identify a visiting spirit and to expose actual people or events that will either benefit the dreamer or pose some kind of threat. This is done by introducing known elements into the dream that the dreamer will be able to identify such as jewelry, manner of speech, familiar sounds, etc. Clues are presented in order to identify visiting spirit intruders or to expose actual people and events. Clues may be presented in a dream state as a series of actual known projected events prior to the unknown main event to indicate and specify a time when the main event will occur. They will be presented in short time segments during the dream. An example of this follows:

A wedding will take place in October. This is unknown to the dreamer. The spirit will attempt to focus the personality of the dreamer to this event, but because it has no voice, clues are left instead. Therefore, in a dream, future events that are known to the dreamer will be shown (i.e., planned baseball outing in July, camping trip in August, etc.) in rapid time frames. The final frame may reveal the sound of a wedding march, tied in with a previously known October event. This leads the dreamer to deduce a wedding in October.

Dreams usually do not follow each other in a sequential manner, like chapters in a book. Each dream message is usually complete on the first try. Our imagination works with the spirit so the psychic message brought to us will be complete. The clues presented to you (the series of events before the main event) can then be translated into your own time frames.

An example of a warning from a relative is in the following dream: This dream was told by a gentleman who had taken a job dog sitting for two dogs, a golden retriever and a miniature black collie. He was to dog sit for ten days with the job beginning in five days. Although the collie appeared unfriendly, the owner assured him it wouldn't bite.

That night, his son called with a story of a dream. With no knowledge of his father's proposed job, he recalled a dream in which his father had come to the house with a golden retriever. A black bat flew in and bit his father on the face. He asked his father if he was okay and he replied that it would be all right.

The father knew it was a message because of the presence of the golden retriever (an undisguised clue from the old man's spirit) and the reminder that the dog's owner had used the same words, "It would be all right." The time frame was important because knowledge was needed within five days, and immediate attention was imperative. This dream was part premonition yet contained clues. I want to stress again that any dream that reveals an undisguised spirit must be taken as a premonition, as well as any dream that contains the element of immediacy (between 3-7 days), because beyond that time span it would be necessary that the dream leave time clues. In this case, the father's spirit took the message to the son via the dream, to alert the father's personality.

It is also common that a loved one, whether living or dead, will use its own personality to alert you in a premonitional dream. When the spirit is aware of something that needs to be revealed to the dreamer it will, on occasion, take on the personality of a respected person or a loved one to give the warning or good news to the dreamer. I have had verification of this through my own experiences as well as through the experiences of others.

Premonitional Dreams

A premonitional dream occurs instantly and informs the dreamer of future events. The following is an example of a premonitional dream that I had when my daughter was very young:

I fell asleep one afternoon with my daughter, who was two years old at the time. It was the middle of the day and we decided to take a nap. I thought we both fell asleep. I began to dream that my little girl was going to step off the curb and go across the street just as a huge truck was coming around the corner. I jerked awake and discovered my daughter was not in bed with me. I jumped up and looked out the window. The only thing that came out of my mouth was her name -- I screamed with all my might. She was just stepping off the curb when she stopped and turned around to look at me. At that moment a huge truck came around the corner. Had I not caught her in time she would have been hit. The spirit brought the psychic message in a dream to allow me to prevent that from happening. This is an example of one of many different ways that a dream can be used by the spirit to alert the personality.

A premonitional dream from a loved one who has passed away will give you a message. It is to the point, there are no abstract clues, and there is a sense of immediacy. The following example demonstrates this perfectly:

A father, who had passed away, appeared in his wife's dream and left a message regarding their son saying, "I have gone to the Social Security office and left papers on top of another stack of papers. I don't know why it is taking so long for my son to receive his money." When the mother awoke, she discovered that she did not know that her son was eligible to receive money. She then inquired whether the young boy was eligible for money from social security -- sure enough, he was. The sense of immediacy was apparent in that the father needed to get this message to the mother. If she had not received this message then her son would not have been eligible to claim that money.

In regards to dream content or message, it makes no difference what you've eaten, what time you've gone to sleep or how well you've slept. These factors do not influence the message in the dream. The spirit is only concerned that you look at the message and take care of it immediately. Therefore, your spirit will deliver a message if you nap only a few minutes, or if you sleep for a few hours.

Another issue is the belief that we dream about what we are familiar with. This is not necessarily true. Clues are very important in order to be specific and to be able to identify more precisely what you need to do.

As the previous example demonstrated, the most extraordinary and special type of premonitional dreams are those in which individuals appear after having been deceased for many years. They may appear as mediators between two people when there is a great need or a desire of one person to communicate with the other to resolve a certain situation. Often an extreme urgency is expressed in this type of dream. The message often comes for someone unable or unwilling to communicate (i.e., severe illness, clinical depression, mental disability) and the mediator will reveal how their needs can be met. This individual may not be equipped to express their wants and needs to another person, especially involving matters of the heart. I strongly believe that when you have the honor of being visited by a deceased person, there are certain rules and regulations that must be abided by. They are restricted in the amount of time they can spend with you and as a result they must limit their conversation. Oftentimes, the messages given will consist of short significant clues to steer you in the direction you must go while remaining within the time period allotted to them. These clues will be very inventive and will sometimes be presented in riddles as well as visual charades if they are unable to get the message across in any other way. If they are contacted by you, they may or may not have a little more leeway in complying with your requests.

Still, premonitional dreams may contain helpful messages from live spirits. In other words, people you may or may not know might appear in your premonitional dreams.

An example of the usefulness of premonitional dream is one experienced recently. I had a friend, Justin, many years ago in the 1970's. I also had another friend named Francesca. Neither one knew each other, but I met both of them at approximately the same time. We were very good friends, but as the years went by we drifted apart. Years later I dreamed that I was swimming in the ocean and there was a man swimming in the ocean along with me. Suddenly he was struck on the head by a passing boat. I rushed to help him, but he was unconscious. I knew that I couldn't help him by myself, I needed additional help. I kept saying to myself, "Oh God, please help me. Someone needs to help me." At once there was a woman swimming beside me. It was Francesca. I was surprised when I saw her in the dream -- and that it was she who came to help me pull this body out of the ocean. In the next dream frame, I was in front of a hospital. A very good looking man came out. It was Justin. He was dressed up in a beautiful, dark blue suit and had a fresh haircut. I said, "Oh, wow, am I glad to see you!" He answered, "So am I, in fact I'm glad to even be alive. I was struck on the head while on a water-skiing trip and lost my practice because I was in a coma for three months. I have nothing left; I lost my business and my practice, but I'm glad to be alive. If it hadn't been for my parents who stuck by me, I don't know where I would be now." As he said that, I woke up.

That morning, I thought I should call his parents. I hadn't spoken with them for awhile but I called anyway. When the mother answered the phone, I told her that I had had this dream about her son. She said, "Well, wait a minute, why don't I call him up and have him return your call." He was living in Los Angeles and I was in San Francisco.

He called back, was really happy to hear from me and wanted to know what all this was about. You know how friends are, even though you haven't seen each other for awhile, you pick up where you left off. I told him my dream and to my surprise he said, "Well, I guess that cancels out the water-skiing trip we had planned for the coming weekend. I just got a haircut and I have on a dark blue suit which I purchased for a reception I'm going to right now. I'm very happy that you called and told me about this, because that's the last thing I would want to happen -- to lose my practice and to have to suffer through an accident." He was very grateful about the phone call. This is a perfect example of an individual's (Justin's) spirit being so desperate that an attempt was made. It was successful enough for me to dream and recall the dream completely in order to warn him. I feel that Justin's spirit, through the dream process, may have tried several times to get the message across to Justin's personality but was unable to. I'm convinced that if Justin had been practicing dream processing, he would have been able to assess this information, on his own, from his spirit.

One important clue was that Francesca's role, as a friend, was to encourage a call to Justin because she had offered me assistance in the dream. This prompted me to offer my assistance in reality to Justin. Francesca also appeared because she knew that I would be happy to see her again. Her spirit was eager to make contact with me and assure me that Justin and I would feel the same in reality after talking to each other. That was another way of exploring different capacities that the spirits use. That's the one way the psyche cleverly plays a big role along with the spirit. The teaming up of these two forces utilizes the ability of the imagination to see. We follow the movements of each image and each detail with our eyes. This component of the imagination displays images that enable us to record what we see and recall in our dreams.

Unlike the straightforward premonitional dream previously discussed, there are those that may also contain clues. Premonitional dreams may be partially straight forward and contain subtle clues as well. It is imperative to pay attention to these clues because they often point out a particular time, date and activity. They are also important for other reasons. For example, people who have passed away and come to you in a premonitional dream with clues usually come when there is an urgent message for you or a close member of their family. The message brought will have a direct impact on your life and the messenger's goal is that you try to turn a negative experience into a more positive experience or to capitalize on an opportunity otherwise missed. Clues in premonitional dreams specify details, such as the date, time, whether or not you are on the right track, or are going in the right direction. The clues left behind are pointers to guide you to the right decision. Sometimes you'll have to choose from many different options. For example, you may have ten choices presented to you and all ten have been lined up in front of you for a decision. The clues that have been left in your dreams will enable you to pick one of the ten different opportunities for the exact, specific one you are supposed to choose. No matter how direct the message, you need to choose which option, decide what day, whether the opportunity is to be seized, or if it is too premature, etc.

To give you an example, I had been looking for a medical facility for several months for a project I needed to complete. I had been interviewing several facilities unsuccessfully. I woke up one morning and knew, because of a premonitional dream, that the correct decision would be made that day. The important clue in this dream was an unknown person asking, "Did you see the black gypsy lady?" That day I had an interview with three different women who were representing their facility. The exciting part was that one of the women to be interviewed by me was a black woman with her hair fixed in a gypsy style. She made a reference to me that she was a Creole woman. There was an immediate flashback to the premonitional dream. So, I assumed that out of the three facilities, the one I should pick was the one represented by the Creole woman who wore a gypsy hairstyle. I have to admit that all of them were professionals. It was a very close margin, but I'm very happy I made the choice that I did, because it was later proven that this was the perfect choice. Clues are an important aspect of dreams because they give the dreamer the tools to specifically identify what they need to do.

Sexual Dreams

Sexual dreams are those that contain sexual expressions when one is in the dream state. At this time the personality gets to analyze its love potential and experience the spirit. This releases all negativity and all tension in consciousness, allowing us to experience the ecstasy one only feels when we are participating in sexual activity. Sexual dreams are also reciprocal. Although the other individual's personality is unaware of its participation in a sexual dream, he or she may be more open to you in real life without knowing why. After all, we are the judicator in this part of our life, if we decide that this is something we want to explore in our outer world. The spirit part of us connects with the other person and we can actually see the connection in the dream state in the form of an aura that leads to that person. Psychics and clairvoyants can easily see this connection. This resembles, at first, a very long umbilical cord. In actuality, it is more of a beam of light than tangible matter, and this wonderful light goes to that other being. Sometimes we will find that, because of this high level of ecstasy and intensity, you can actually feel the other person in a concrete three-dimensional way. It is like the person is really there next to you. The light resembles a long, hollow umbilical cord with a light running through it. It is the same light as an electrical discharge or a strong fluorescent light -- a white color. Once people connect to one another, the excitement creates a mixture of different colors and sparks of light going through it, resembling a diamond with little sparkles. This light umbilical cord connects to the other body through the navel area when we are in love. When two people in love are exercising sexual intercourse, it seems as though the light going through the umbilical cord sparkles with tiny different colored lights. People will also experience different situations that occur while in love, and I believe that the force of this connection plays a role in this. I find that people in a relationship in which one of them no longer wants to be involved will pull and try to split apart. The person wanting to remain in the relationship will then feel tugging and pulling -- the splitting apart of the relationship -- from the stomach area. Once the split has occurred you will no longer dream of being connected through the lighted umbilical cord. There will be a disconnection of the umbilical cord from the abdominal region, and this will result in that "butterflies in the stomach" feeling one has when they are no longer wanted in a relationship. At this time the person will feel a disconnection -- it happens quickly -- and both individuals will still have the memories of that connection. It will feel as though one has experienced mourning. They are feeling sad or have a sense of loss as if they have lost someone to death. These people will then have the need to go through a grieving period until they are able to take charge of their feelings and go on with their lives. They do need that period of adjustment. Both parties will feel it, but the person desiring to remain in the relationship will sense it more than the person who has tugged away and split apart the relationship. Other people have also experienced the form of this light in a non-sexual way. To most of us this connection is invisible, but it can be sensed in times of distress. At times people seem to know when something is really wrong with a close loved-one, (lovers, husbands, wives, children, etc.) and will feel jumpy or feel butterflies in the stomach and have the sense that something is wrong and not know why. It will later be revealed in a dream as well as in reality that a loved one suffered a stressful situation. It is also possible that when someone is truly infatuated, this connection will be attempted through the spirit even if the other is unaware of the infatuation. When the connection is being attempted they will either show interest or be repelled. This differentiates love from being in love. People are very lucky when they have this exquisite force of light invading the body. We call this force love and it enables us to experience being in love. The reason we are all here on this earth is to learn to give and receive love, unconditionally. Through this light umbilical cord we do receive the gift of love. This may occur in dreams as well as reality. It is a gift from a Divinity that we receive unexpectedly throughout life just as we receive the gift of genius of thought, talents, and creativity.

Love as it Relates to Dreams

Love is a gift that needs to be acknowledged and respected. It needs to be viewed and received as a blessing. Love is an emotional gift that one receives from a Divinity. Many people have expressed to me that they don't know what love is, have never experienced love, and don't know if they will ever be in love, although they long for this feeling. Some people may go through their whole lifetime without ever experiencing this emotion. If we are lucky enough to have been chosen to feel the spirit of love, we should be thankful. Once the spirit of love between a couple is abused due to mutual disrespect and petty emotional game playing, it never fully returns. Although couples or loved ones may make up for a wrong, it will never be the same. We simply keep the traces of what we were feeling. Although we attempt to recreate the feeling of love, we can only mimic past feelings because we miss them and wish we still had them. We need to learn to give and receive love, and to communicate love in a more equal and balanced way. We must do everything necessary to ensure longevity of love rather than deplete love. This will ensure that two people can become one, still have separate lives yet survive as one. We need to nourish that feeling and work at it constantly and consistently. Some people are blessed and receive the gift of love more than once. Others, however, will go through life without ever receiving this blessed gift. Whenever love comes, we need to work as a team to keep it alive. When a connection between two people takes place, there is a strong possibility that both parties will experience a deep love for one another. As remarkable as it may seem, you can experience the deep intensity of love in dreams even if you have never experienced this feeling for someone in reality.

Out of Body Experience Dreams

At some point or another you will begin having out of body experiences in dreams. At this point we feel the speed of the spirit traveling in time and from place to place very rapidly. It's a magical experience and difficult to express in words. The body feels very rigid and stationary. Although the spirit doesn't leave the body unattended for very long, it does travel rapidly and accomplishes a great deal in a short period of time. At this time, two special things are occurring. The personality, mind and the spirit are one. Although the body is unable to move and is in a fixed position, the personality has a clear knowledge and memory that the spirit is out of body. Not only have I experienced this myself, but I have had detailed conversations with others who have encountered this phenomenon. There is also the recognition that the spirit is still connected to the body by the illuminated umbilical cord. Although in some cases we have no factual depiction of each event that has occurred, we do awaken with an instilled sense of confidence, and the knowledge necessary for enriching our lives and achieving our goals.

At times, we are invited to participate in the excursion. The body remains behind yet you may feel all of the sensations of travel. Sometimes the events seen are accurately occurring in the here and now, and at other times they are a very accurate depiction of the future. When it comes to assuage loss or longing for another, the spirit will visit another individual geographically. The strength of love between the couple assures that the process of out of body travel becomes simpler and quicker. This has been my personal experience as well as the experience of others who have discussed this phenomenon with me.

Deities, Gods, Goddesses & Extraordinary Figures

The appearance of a deity within a dream leaves us with the feeling of being surrounded by a close light, originating either from the side or directly in front of the face. There is the sense of a voice coming from this light. Visual effects may simultaneously appear in order to arouse the dreamer's curiosity and distract the dreamer from seeing the source of the light. This visual effect is typically an extravaganza of sight and sound, magical and rich enough to hold the dreamer's attention. For example, a waterfall may appear and the dreamer may have no knowledge of its origin. As the dream progresses, it gradually becomes larger and larger. The colors of plants and birds will be intense and rich. The dreamer, therefore, never sees the source of the voice.

You may feel during the dreams about any deity, that you are in a light sleep. It almost feels as though your eyes blink to keep out the light. The voice emanating from the light seems to be male, although there is no real recollection. There is also a sense of having a real conversation. Upon awakening, the gist of the conversation will be recalled in the dreamer's own voice. A higher power/ deity may appear to us at any time. Following the dream, there is a feeling of having a knowledge not present before.

There appears, also, to be a time span following these dreams when the dreamer senses that it's all right to share the dream with another person. The dreamer may sense permission to speak about it immediately but at other times will feel that they should wait before telling anyone.

Each time I have interpreted a dream about a deity, the same experiences were recalled. The dreamer sensed a lightness born of the union of the personality and the spirit. This leads to greater clarity in the outer world. These people seem to be able to make decisions in life based on a sense of balance and order from certain experiences and expressions they have gained from the dream experiences. If you are touched by a divine spirit, the sensation of having been touched remains on your skin long after awakening, perhaps even months afterward.

A divinity may also appear during a time of illness. When this occurs, there is often a remarkable, miraculous recovery. Once you are cured, this illness will never come back and you will be even healthier than before.

When you have dreams about a deity, you will usually have a sense of detailed information about a situation that you previously did not have, and you will feel a sense of excitement and wonder for a long period of time. Most of the time you will have no recollection of how you received this information, although you will recall having had this dream. Sometimes you will retain a very detailed memory of the dream.

When I say extraordinary figures, I mean the divine: Jesus Christ, Jupiter, Venus, a high priestess, Buddha, goddesses, etc. When you dream of such figures, you will obtain information that you did not have before, and you will become knowledgeable about something of which you had no prior knowledge. You will be able to recall all the occurrences in detail and everything you said word-for-word in most cases. You may also be left with a feeling that allows you to intuit about the consequences of your present situation and how to respond even if you do not recall the exact words of the conversation. When a special deity appears in one of my dreams, I acknowledge this by thanking them. I am thankful that I have spent time in their company. After the dream, there is, in reality, a sense of excitement in life that remains a long time afterward.

Because these figures walked the Earth years ago, they understand the emotional trials of each day and empathize with the human plight. They come into a dream to show compassion. When they appear, they are often recognized by their attire. Sometimes, however, they do not appear in the way we typically imagine them (i.e., robes, wings, etc.). We have seen many depictions of the appearance of these figures, and the miracles affiliated with the attire at the time the miracles were performed. This may be a large clue when it appears in a dream. We need to pay close attention to the clothing and look for the miracle performed at the time. This is particularly true of the Virgin Mary. She appeared in many different styles of attire in different parts of the world at different times. The miracle associated with a particular style of dress may indicate to you the miracle that could be associated with you as a gift. Consider it a clue only if the miracle could be associated with events occurring at this particular time in your life.

Jesus Christ, saints, Buddha, goddesses, gods, and other extraordinary figures appear as they are, levitate above the ground and will converse with you. The conversation will be vividly recalled. Jesus will appear when a particular knowledge needs to be imparted, not necessarily when a crisis in life is occurring. The saints, various angels, goddesses, gods and other divinities appear when the dreamer is in a very stressful situation or is suffering deep emotions because of someone else's illness or irresponsibility. They will appear to warn the dreamer of a situation that will leave them unfairly punished. This may be a scam, fraud or a trap created by a relentless enemy who will do harm to you. Or they may warn you that something will happen that will deeply affect your life. They will appear also to warn of a misdiagnosed illness so the dreamer may find a proper cure. When you see a saint, this is a sign that it is not your time to die. They want to stress that you experience life as it should be, and therefore, will warn of an impending but preventable accident that will leave you incapacitated. They will step in to ask specific questions and you will be willing to give answers. Any question you ask of them will also result in a quick and true answer. Angels may appear during a severe illness or when you are about to be placed in a situation you have no business being in or when you are being steered off track. They appear especially when you will be placed in a life threatening situation. This will give you the foreknowledge to take steps to avoid this event. I have found this to be true in my case and in discussions with others who have also experienced this.

Dreams about gods and goddesses involve a transformation of some kind. You will usually focus on an object that attracts attention (i.e., a butterfly with brilliant colors). The object will then transform into the god/goddess itself. It is imperative that you pay close attention to all events, objects and clues presented in these dreams. Many of the clues will be revealed through symbols and letterings in the background scenery.

A good example of such a dream was one in which a man was staring at a calm and serene ocean. The ocean transformed itself into a Goddess clothed in blue green opalescent attire that reflected everything in the scene. The man's focus, through the reflection, was guided to an entrance on which a word was imprinted. He looked up the word to find the meaning of this dream. Be aware that many clues will be represented in these dreams, especially symbols, words and letters.

Upon awakening, you will be filled with the knowledge and skills that will assist you in bringing your plans, creative ideas and projects to perfection. You will also be equipped with the confidence, determination, courage and staying power needed to accomplish these tasks. You will develop perfectionism and will emanate charisma.

Dreams associated with ancient gods and goddesses are often associated with luck. You can be certain that after their appearance, something extraordinary and lucky will occur within a short time. Luck is a gift coming through psychic energy whether through dreams or intuition. The energy of luck will manifest itself through hunches that may result in fortuity one way or another in the outer world.

Spiritual Guides

After keeping a dream journal for a while, you will notice that from time to time familiar people will appear in dreams who are totally unknown to you in real life. You may see the same person from dream to dream and soon learn to recognize them, although you never see them in the "real world". Guides in the real world enter your dreams in order to discuss or relay a message.

Verification of this was provided to me in May of 1995 upon completion of this book. I dreamed that I attended a reception in which over seven hundred people were present. I was given a special gift that allowed me to see in all directions, through people and objects, and with special clarity. It became apparent to me that we were together for the purpose of celebrating the completion of a major achievement. Each person in my dream was recognizable to me as someone who had entered my dream state in the past, and had created a dream scenario that helped me to ascribe definitions to the words used in this dictionary. Because some of them consistently appeared to me in a dream state, I became aware that they were my spiritual guides, not only during a dream but also in my outer world. They recruited some guides to create dream scenarios and other guides volunteered to do the same. This allowed me to place definitions to the words needed in this dictionary in order to complete this project. The most lasting impression of this dream was that I was able to thank each individual guide. We were all clothed in the same manner indicating that we were each committed to bringing this book to a unified completion. The dream concluded with each of us meditating in an open space. I still retain a vivid and accurate memory of this dream as well as a strong sense of thankfulness to all who helped in bringing this about.

I was also told about a dream in which a woman stated that someone in her dream informed her that she was her spiritual guide. She said that she was relaxing by a pool and noticed a woman walking in a way that implied she wanted to go unnoticed. The woman in the dream also made it clear that she did not wish the dreamer to speak to her. She crept close to the dreamer and whispered in her ear that there was a conspiracy against her that would ruin her both emotionally and financially. She then placed her finger in the pool. Drops of blood came out of her finger turning the pool reddish pink. Reflected in this water were the faces of the people who were going to commit this crime against her, and the manner in which it would be committed. After this dream, the dreamer was able to prevent this event from occurring. She also recalled that this woman had appeared in other dreams. This verifies that guides are far more aware of what is going on in our everyday lives, because they have been appointed to help oversee our affairs. They use dreams as vehicles to communicate messages to us.

Their function seems to bring information about things you desire to know in everyday life. This can be anything from giving you an address of an old friend, a bargain for an object you desire, or good news such as the birth of a child. They want to make everyday life more enjoyable.

Channeling

When we respond to our dream language we respond to our own divinity. As I have stated before, dreams have very different capacities from which we can communicate. People who have died will visit in dreams. However, I also know that people who have passed away don't make it a habit of hanging around and coming to see you every chance they get. They will come to see you when they have an urgent need to communicate a message regarding a situation you should or should not pursue. They will also come when you have an urgent need to see them. The spirit of another individual may also enter a dream to thank the dreamer for a favor extended to someone special to them. In either case, they won't stay long. Those who have died suddenly (i.e., by murder or suicide) will visit someone in a dream within twenty four hours. It's very immediate. They will appear only if it is necessary to communicate a specific message, then leave. People who have known for awhile that they were going to die and are prepared for it, will visit a person in their dreams after the eighth day and before the fifteenth day. These people are very happy and look comfortable in their surroundings. The dreams occur during the hypnogogic or hypnopompic state of sleep (the stages of sleep between sleep and wakefulness) and are referred to as channeling dreams. This has been my experience and others have communicated to me that this has been their experience as well.

Art Dreams

When we are experiencing clarity and sanity in our lives, we are better able to tap into our dream processes for ideas, creativity and thoughts. The clearer we are, the easier it is to receive these gifts. These gifts may be demanded, asked for, pled for, and, in some cases, simply given to us by our Divinity, our spirit, other spirits, etc. These gifts may be made tangible in the outer world by the activity of mental inventiveness and intelligence coupled with an acute clarity of thought.

Whether in the arts, scientific endeavors or in everyday life, dreams are like gold mines, and our life allows us to maximize this resource. It is important that when you dream, you get up and jot it down before it disintegrates even if it occurs in the wee hours of the morning. I had an experience with a woman who asked five of us, as artists, to create a design or logo for her new shop three days before it was due. I was unable to come up with anything and wasn't going to submit an idea. Then I had a dream. Because I was a professional dream interpreter, I was better able to use a visual image that was displayed in the dream. I arose from the bed as soon as I had that dream and I drew the image. Mine was picked out of five others who had also submitted theirs. I don't believe that mine was chosen because I was a better artist than my colleagues, but because my spirit did some investigative work, sensed what this lady wanted as a design in her shop, and displayed it in my dream. This, to me, is a primary example of how the spirit can go out and do investigative work. The spirit can bring information to us through our dream process so we can better address and assess opportunities. We can evaluate and choose from different alternatives displayed in our dreams. Dreams are like computer terminals. We can become professionals by learning to use sequences of events and symbols as keys to unlock and transform these images into a language that allows our spirit to communicate with us directly.

Low-Awareness Dreams

These dreams occur to an individual who is presently performing evil deeds in the outer world. The individuals often display immorality, depravity and wickedness and cause misery, disarray, addictions and suffering to themselves and others. They tend to be evil because they choose this over righteousness. These people often have dreams of weeping sounds, souls that are crying, or whipping sounds that come from behind them and voices that emerge distorted, as though they originated from the underworld. Descriptions and explanations of these dreams are gruesome. I know this is factual and consistent because I received a message from behind me, in a dream. I was given the message to warn a friend of the necessity to alter a destructive lifestyle. Once the individual has been warned and doesn't heed that warning, it seems as though they experience years of negativity, anguish and, in some cases, death as the outcome. To experience a dream of this type is a definite warning. There is a need to restore order instead of continuing the abusive behavior they are putting themselves through or are experiencing with people around them. This person needs to make a change -- a real turnaround. There is a need to make changes within the personality and lifestyle. When we are experiencing clarity and sanity in our lifestyle, the cleaner and richer the resources we can tap into in our dream state. In the case of an attempted demonic entry, there is an automatic awakening switch that quickly brings the dreamer out of the dream state because the dream itself is so uncomfortable. This serves to safeguard privacy so the dream process is not used for evil purposes.

Past Lives, Reincarnation and Dreams Within a Dream

If you have experienced past lives through reincarnation, you will have dreams that show you your previous lives. Each person in the dream will be familiar to you and you will often recognize yourself as one of the players in the dream.

People who experience this phenomenon describe it as passing through a solid illuminated area. You will also be shown something that interfered with your growth during a past life, whether this was an untimely death, poor choices, overlooked opportunities, etc., so that these events will not be repeated in this life. You may be shown a lavish lifestyle that you once enjoyed and will be able to regain in this lifespan.

The time and place of the past life will be verified in some way through depicted world events, styles of dress, etc. You will be left with a sense of excitement and a heightened intensity for the need to bring about positive, dynamic changes in your life. The events depicted in the dream will seem as fresh to you as if they occurred that day, and you will be able to accurately recollect the dream years later. For example, you may recognize your face and voice from a previous life, and gain a sense of being connected to each of your previous selves. You will also see a thin line connecting your selves through the umbilical areas.

A dream within a dream is important because the spirit is attempting to force you to pay attention to a dream message you previously ignored. This will force you to realize that this is the second time a message was presented. For example, you will have a conversation with someone in the dream in which you state that you had this dream before, or you will recall while dreaming that you have had this dream before, but this time the dream will be a lucid dream. (In a lucid dream the dreamer becomes aware they are dreaming, and realizes they can change the outcome.)

Recurring Dreams, Nightmares and Sleep Paralysis

Recurring dreams can go on for years, but as the event that the dream is representing gets closer in time the dream frame appears larger and closer to you. This allows the personality to know the event is forthcoming. For example, a recurring dream about a particular house may reveal a small house from a distance to a young child, yet each occurring dream thereafter will reveal a larger home at a closer distance. Finally, as an event is about to occur in reference to this house (perhaps a move or a visit), the frame looms large.

These dreams are always pointing to a major event in our lives that may represent a drastic change. You have prior notice of this and can alter the outcome if it is a negative event. Although many of these dreams appear bad, they may be presented in a graphic way in order to be remembered and to stress importance.

Do not confuse nightmares with low awareness dreams. Nightmares are simply a bad piece of theatre developed by the spirit to dramatize an impression by presenting a shocking scenario in an attempt to get a message across to the personality. There is a sense of urgency in the spirit's need to communicate and to ensure that you do not forget this message once you are awake. Most of the time this is a good message that you will be presented with opportunities and benefits you should not miss.

This dream may also represent something that you or someone you recognize in the dream has no business getting involved with. You have prior notice of this, can diffuse this situation and take steps to allow only positive expressions in your life. Make sure that you alert anyone you recognize to do the same.

Nightmares imply that it is urgent for you to attend to some issue. We should be honored and thankful that we have prior notice and can attend to either a positive or a negative message.

At some point in each person's life an experience will occur that is very frightening. This could be sleep paralysis and takes place during the dream stage, at the point of trying to awaken and most commonly during nightmares. This feeling is one of total physical paralysis when the dreamer feels they are desperately struggling to move. This experience is a warning that this will indeed occur in reality, though not in a real physical sense, unless you are aware of your circumstances now. Be acutely aware of what is unfolding that will have a serious effect on your future. This will take place because of any one or a combination of the following situations:

Interference from someone who will steer you in the wrong direction.

The control that someone assumes over you (i.e., parents, a loved one, etc.).

The leverage that someone will gain by using your words to put you at a disadvantage.

Someone who is in a position of authority who will make decisions for you (i.e., your boss, law enforcement officers, etc.).

You will not know the extent of damage that this person can cause because of their control. This dream is asking you to muster the courage and confidence needed to make sure you take the right steps to prevent a situation from developing that could seriously affect your future. Do not leave yourself vulnerable to this because you will be left with no recourse except to abide by the rules that others place on you. This will leave you with the unbearable feeling of emotional depletion and the feeling that you are caught up in a seemingly inescapable web. This dream is a sneak preview of how you will feel if you do not take steps to turn this around and to ensure that you experience only positive expressions in your life.

Intuition

Intuition during waking hours is equivalent to dream processing during sleeping hours and much needs to be said about this process. Everyone has an intuitive sense, much like we all have a beating heart, however, we are not always aware of it. We can become more aware of our intuitive sense through practice and knowledge in the same way that people can alter blood pressure through biofeedback.

Most people ask the question, "How do we know when intuition is occurring?" The main aspect of intuition is that it comes as a flash without being willed. We also have no attachment connected with the feeling we are experiencing. This is far different from inviting thoughts in because of anxiety over current events, or certain matters that we mull over in the attempt to understand them.

When we have an intuitive thought, oftentimes, in the midst of a thought process, we will have a flash of clarity or knowledge that is wholly unrelated to the original thought. We have absolutely no control over these intrusive intuitive moments nor do we will the feelings they generate. This flash is an attempt to deliver a message, either positive or negative, that we need to act on. In short, the way we know that it is intuition is that we have no control over it and no association with the thought that comes over us.

When you use your intuition, it is by virtue of a process that you are completely unaware of. It begins by you, or rather your spirit, receiving a message from another spirit. This message is called a psychic message, because it is received by your psyche. Your psyche is the part of your mind that receives messages, while your personality is the part of your mind that decides how to act. Within the psyche there is an intuitive or receptive element. This intuitive or receptive part deciphers the message into a thought in your own voice so you may act accordingly. Say, for example, that you are about to cross the street. You look both ways, there's no oncoming traffic. But before you take a step off the curb you hesitate because of some little voice you hear or feeling you get that makes you pause for a moment. And in just that moment a car comes speeding around the corner. You didn't see it, or hear it, but you had a feeling from somewhere inside you that encouraged you to wait. This is the end result of your intuitive process. You were unaware of the communication between yourself and your spirit but there was a message communicated to you that was translated into a language which you could understand and act from.

The intuition is only active when there is a psychic message in our environment that needs to be interpreted for our personality. Our spirits are not always aware of the next situation that may occur in our lives to the extent that we would always know when to keep from stepping off the curb. This is the reason the personality and spirit are caught off guard in some instances. For example, clairvoyants and psychic readers are sometimes accused of not knowing things they should be aware of. The reason is that this information was not given to them to respond to. When there is no psychic message received, we will still be able to act, but only after and not before the actual event, because the primary job of the intuition is to be under the spirit's command during our waking hours, and to guide us to a more positive lifestyle and to the path of our correct destiny. Some people tend to have a stronger sense of intuition while some people seem to have very little or none. This occurs simply because those people with a higher sense are more willing to be receptive. If desired, others may learn to increase their potential. Some people develop intuition in all levels of consciousness (sight, touch, taste, hearing and smell), while others develop only in some.

Our spirit will also ask us to question irrational impulses and behaviors. There are times when we feel compelled to do something out of the norm (use a drug, go to an unfamiliar place, compulsive gambling, etc.). These are times when we may demonstrate obsessive behavior, breeding jealousy and envy and feel almost possessed to do something. The spirit asks us to question these behaviors. This is apparent because these typically result in negative outcomes and interfere with our clarity. Once rid of this behavior, we achieve greater clarity and become more receptive.

At times our spirit will direct us to a dream definition that indicates this is the time to demand what we need from our higher power. Often times we will feel as though our needs are being taken care of when this is not the case. We need to emphatically state our needs again to ensure that they are not overlooked by someone that God has directed to handle these needs. I've noticed from personal experience that intuition picks up accurately translated information perhaps 70-80% of the time. The remaining times, the information is either ignored or lost in translation. Therefore, it is important that we become more attuned to our senses.

A clairvoyant, medium or psychic reader will respond to a psychic message that is being released by the spirit of the individual receiving the reading. Messages coming to the psychic reader may also be brought by her spirit, another person's spirit, or God. These spirit messengers alert her psyche and enable her to complete the reading. The psyche has to be turned on by a divine power or by the spirit or other spirits, living or dead, who will help the personality to complete the reading in full. When the spirit puts out a psychic message that we fail to interpret that portends a negative event, we may feel jumpy in the abdominal region. To sum up, the spirit communicates with us during the day through the psychic intuitive element. During sleep, the spirit uses the psyche through dream imaging displays to communicate. When another spirit has a gift of ideas, etc., for us, that spirit will use the psyche to turn on the intuitive sense. The intuition then goes through some translation process of thought that the personality understands and then we will turn the gift of thought into something tangible in our world.

If our spirit becomes uncomfortable or alarmed in the presence of a certain person or activity, it can be felt turning, tugging or curdling inside the stomach. Should the spirit be aware that something very good will happen, you will feel a giggle deep inside the stomach area (where an individual carries their spirit) before it occurs.

Numerology and Dreams

Numerology often reveals its messages in dreams. The study of numerology has been around for centuries. The ancient Greeks, Chinese, Romans, Aztecs and Druids worked with numbers and applied them to events in their everyday lives. The study of numerology in the European culture was founded by Pythagoras, a Greek philosopher and mathematician. He stated that numbers were the principles that guided the universe, limiting and giving shape to matter. The important underlying tenet of Pythagoreanism was the kinship of all life, and this principle permeated religious and scientific teachings as well as the lives of ordinary people, even to this day. (Encyclopedia of World Biography, 1973). Astrologers, numerologists, tarot card readers, etc., have all applied the use of numbers to their own systems to uncover hidden definitions to enhance readings and pinpoint specific information. These systems have been useful for predicting future events and to pinpoint exactly the direction being taken by the spirit and the personality.

In 1990, I experimented a bit with numbers I saw appearing in dreams. Although I had never played a gambling game, I chose to test these numbers with Lotto. Unfortunately, not all six numbers were chosen at any one time, but did come up in a consistent enough way to keep winning. I was off one week by one digit as a result of my own faulty transcription. Had this error not occurred, I would be a multi-millionaire.

When you are recording numbers from your dream, whether for gambling purposes, for a numerology reading or for another purpose, be sure to include the date the dream occurred. For example, May 10 would translate into a 5 and 10. If desired, large numbers over three digits may be rounded to smaller numbers: for example, 5023 = 10. This is especially important if you only need a single digit. It is also important to use each component of the number. For example, if you dreamed of the number 405, use both 4 and 5. Likewise, if you dream of the number 43 look up both 40 and 3. Likewise, any set of words used in this dream (i.e., loose screw, muddy shoes, black purse, etc.) needs to be broken down into separate words and both words looked up separately.

Birthdays (yours and your loved ones) are fortunate, as well. More fortunate are dreams that fall on a particular day of the month that has a special meaning for you, as well as the numbers 1, 3, 5, 6, 7, 8, 10, 11, 12, 13, 14, 15, 17, 23, 25, and 28. It is also beneficial to look up the astrological sign of the birthday, whether yours or anyone else's. A dream about a birthday cake also signifies that you need to look up the particular astrological sign of the person celebrating their birthday.

On other days (6, 7, 10, 12, and 17) dreams may come to pass immediately, and if they represent a desire, it is best to keep these dreams to yourself until they come to pass. This way the dream can reach fruition without interference from the outer world's atmosphere.

You may also want to record the numbers from your dreams for interpretation by a numerologist. Take care to recall each number whether it is obvious or obscure (numbers as a clock, dates, etc.). These will point to important clues in your life, etc. The spirit will also present to you a number of consecutive episodes in a dream that are similar yet slightly different. These repeating patterns are represented by events involving people you don't know, and imply that a similar episode will occur to you in the immediate future. You are being given prior notice so you can handle this appropriately in your outer world.

Traces of Dreams

If people would take the time to practice and respond to dream languages, they would find that it is equivalent to responding to a divine part of us.

Practicing and remembering to recall your dreams each time you are awake enables you to flex the area of the brain where dream information is stored. By demanding this information from the brain upon awakening, the brain will be alerted to store the information for longer periods of time. This allows us time to retrieve and reconstruct the dream.

Immediately upon awakening, the spirit, personality and psyche are joined and almost full memory of the dream is possible. After awakening, however, we begin to lose control of the psychic part of ourselves and the dream becomes repressed in our memory. If we choose to jot the dream down we have time to retain it before it disappears. Traces of the dream, however, remain throughout the day. Have you ever forgotten a dream but still felt happy or sad during that day because of the feelings it left behind, and/or have an irresistible impulse to share and talk about the dream with someone? The spirit is still seeking a way to deliver a message to the dreamer (personality) that will benefit them.

Traces of dreams also leave behind automatic flashbacks that will lead us back to a forgotten clue. This leaves us with the feeling of experiencing déjà vu and may occur within a day, a week or several months later.

Benefit of Dream Interpretation

The understanding of dreams will allow us many benefits and advantages. These are as follow:

* Dreams allow us to verify and safeguard our future through interpretation.
* Understanding our dreams allows us to facilitate facing up to our own anxieties and confronting them easily and confidently.
* They allow us the opportunity to express our needs to other people's spirit in a safe place.
* Dreams alert us of those things we need to be watchful of, and of the actions and reactions towards us from others in real life. The results of this are fewer conflicts and greater benefits in our life for all parties involved.
* The spirits of other people have entry into our dream state. They come in to present plans in order to gauge our reaction to situations, then leave with a confirmed knowledge of what our true reactions will be in the outer world. Each one of us has knowledge of the entry mechanism into each other's dream processing state and spirits may use it freely and at will. Because we know this, our active participation is important in dreams.
* Through studying dreams, our spirit allows us to practice consolidating and organizing plans, projects and undertakings. We will then see what the result will be in the outer world and determine how to put our plans into practice in the best possible way.
*When we lack the courage to make someone aware of romantic feelings, we are able,

through dreams, to get a clue of the reaction of the other person.

* Dreams will show us what is occurring in the world at large, but may also be used as clues to authenticate when concurrent events take place. For example, if you dream of finding a particular item and also dream of a plane crash, the day you see the crash in the media is the day you will acquire this item.

* We will always get an accurate response to any question we ask in our dreams.

* While the dreamer is ill, our spirit produces joyful and happy images to show compassion to the personality. In cases of serious illness, the spirit will seek assistance from either a living or deceased spirit connected with a needed medical specialty to achieve complete recovery.

* Dreams allow us to experiment sexually and to benefit from all aspects of this expression and experience.

Unlike the usual progression we see in a typical dream (such as previously described), the God, channeling, premonition, out of body, and some sex dreams are different. These usually occur during the hypnogogic or hypnopompic sleep states (the stages of sleep between sleep and wakefulness). In some God or sexual dreams a 3-D effect may occur.

Guidelines on Using This Book to Review and Interpret Dreams

You have taken the first step by arming yourself with a good dream interpretation book and now need a dream journal to record your dreams. When you awaken remain perfectly still and recall as much as you can, then organize the images in your mind from beginning to end. The more you practice, the better you will be at retaining and retrieving information.

While you are trying to retrieve as much information as you can, the dream will move very slowly and start to disappear, but should linger long enough in the memory for you to jot it down. After you have recalled your dream, you must organize it so you can record and analyze it in its entirety.

It is important that when you are in the process of reviewing your dreams, you take care not to underestimate the definition or to limit the possibilities of translation. Always look at a grander and broader view than the translation reads and different ways to apply the definitions from different perspectives. Do not automatically assume that a suggested urge be adhered to. It is important that you assess to ensure that you want to express this experience during this time in your life, especially with dream fantasies that involve romance. It is also important that everyone, male or female, who is going through the change of life (or menopause) immediately write down each dream upon awakening. This is particularly important if you are suffering from hot flashes, because you will retain an acute memory of the dream during the flash but it will disappear in its entirety once it has passed.

You may also find that on occasion, two words that seem to be the same but spelled differently will have different definitions.

One example of taking a broad view is the interpretation which reads that a con-artist, devious person, a conspiracy etc., will soon enter your life. Do not limit the possibility of who this person is. It may be someone new who will enter your life, or could be someone you are familiar with who will take on these characteristics. The person involved may not know this is where they are headed, or that they will implicate you in a conspiracy. Your spirit is alerting you that a scheme will take place and that this person at this time may not be aware of it. Even if they are, do not expect that they will hint at a conspiracy. You may not be directly harmed by this individual, but by those who are involved with them or their situations. Our spirit will introduce a word to us through a visual object or name (i.e., banana, witch, Frank Sinatra, etc.) that serves to attract our attention. The definition given to the word in no way implies that that object is negative or positive in reality, but is merely leading us to a message our spirit wants us to attend to. Consider also that when a suggested procedure is viewed in a dream and is introduced to you as a choice to consider in reality, you must always seek a second opinion and/or review your options to ensure whether or not you feel these are the best choices for you.

Sometimes a message will seem too far fetched to be realistic. It will seem this way because you have yet to experience it and cannot conceive of its actuality. You must make sure that you do not dismiss it. You must become more tenacious in translating the message. It is important that you assess/view it from different perspectives. For example, the definition may read that you will relocate. This may not be something you have even considered. Examples of a possibility that may occur following this kind of dream definition is that someone may come to you with a brochure depicting an area they plan to move to, and you will begin to review this as a possibility for yourself. You can now make plans, become organized and disciplined for a future move; may also become very excited about the move and later dismiss the idea, or you will become engaged in daydreaming about the move and in your mind you actually did move. You must carefully assess your options in order to make the proper choice.

A definition of a dream may read that someone desires you and you will, within three days, surrender to them. In reality someone may have pursued you for some time but you have not become involved yet. At this point you must make assessments to avoid a weak moment to keep yourself from surrendering in reality. Your spirit will try to alert you to a time period when you could be more vulnerable, so you can become firmer and refuse to accept unwanted involvement.

Some dreams leave you with a great sense of exuberance similar to what occurs in the aftermath of some sexual dreams. You may become careless and vulnerable because you will spend time mentally rehearsing the dream fantasy and have a freak accident. In other words, you do not focus on what you should be doing.

It is important to take each translation seriously and carefully look at all the implications it may have for you. Take a broad view and look at each interpretation from different perspectives. Ensure that you want to express the experiences and impressions during the particular time frame indicated.

Everyone has the potential to have dreams of great magnitude. For example, let's assume that you dream of **driving** a **red Ferrari** with the numbers **seven** and **nine** displayed on the **license plate** down **Palmetto Street**. You enter an **apartment building** where you **unlock the door** with a **key ring containing many keys**. You then speak with **three men** who tell you that they are **triplets**. After this you open another **door** and see **three identical women** who inform you that they are also **triplets**.

You would then write down the dream and look up the important words as illustrated above for the proper meaning of this dream.

By looking up definitions on a daily basis you will see that it's less costly than a trip to a psychic reader. In fact, it's almost free, just the cost of this dream interpretational book, a small effort on your part and some time will make a big difference in your life.

May all your dreams take place in the hollow of your Higher Power's hands, and may you experience tangible results from your creativity.

Thumbs up!

A

A You will discover that you possess an unexpected level of power and authority in an area you did not suspect. You will become acutely aware of this within three days. Because of an extraordinary set of circumstances that will occur, you will be able to visualize new lifestyles that you will be eager to adopt as your own. This will bring you a new set of friends and a new source of income. This new way of living will agree with you and cause you to flourish in all areas you desire. You will also be very successful when dealing with any emotional issue. Keep all communications open with others in order to quickly and completely resolve all stressful issues.

aardvark Avoid all family disputes and attempt to get along with all family members, especially older ones.

Aaron *(from the Bible)* Leave yourself open to hear a message or to gain the expertise needed to enhance your career for the next three days. This message will come from an unexpected source and will lead to a brilliant lifestyle that will enrich you throughout life. Expand your horizons.

abacus Do whatever is necessary to steer your life in a more positive direction. Review your friends and lifestyle and let go of all immoral friends and those with loose morals because they will only lead you to a lifestyle of wickedness.

Abaddon *(place of the dead/angel of hell)* Motivate yourself in such a way that you do not forsake your desires and your deep emotional feelings. Do what you can to connect with those feelings that are important to you. Develop tenacity, do not abandon your deepest wishes, and do not allow yourself to be forced into making promises you are unable to keep. Do not compromise your feelings.

abalone There will be an additional family member *(baby)* unless precautions are taken for the next week.
to eat abalone You will receive a gift of jewelry within two days.
divers, or diving for For the next two days be cautious and careful of the choices you make. Make no decisions that will restrict you from moving forward. Remain alert and carefully think through all alternatives.
the shell of Your relationship with another needs to have some excitement added. With some effort on your part, you can replace what is missing. You will also have the enthusiastic support of a special person. Once this process has begun you will experience a greater closeness than ever before.
abandon *to abandon yourself, self hatred* For the next

few days avoid placing yourself in any situation that could lead to a crippling accident. You have prior notice of this and can take steps to prevent this.
to see another acting in a hateful manner toward themselves You will need to take care of all valuable personal paperwork within the week (i.e., deeds, insurance, etc.). Make this a priority or it will lead to a problem in the future. Take the proper steps now to ensure a future of prosperity and a stress free life.

A-battery Within a two day period, make sure you realize that you are not obligated to behave in the way someone else wishes you to, and make sure that no one controls you. You will be able to permanently rid yourself of someone who feels as though they have power over the way you behave, your manner of speaking, or your way of thinking. You will be able to accomplish this with very little stress or anxiety because of your tactful and easy manner. You are headed in the right direction for a prosperous future.

abattoir The person you wish to become involved with on a certain project is not reliable and is not interested in your plans or goals although they will lead you to believe they are. Get on with your plans and look for another person to assist you. Focus on creating a stable financial base within three days.

abbé Meditate in your favorite form and, within five days, demand from your spirit what you need. Eat healthy food and drink plenty of water. You will enjoy prosperity in your life and many blessings will come to you and your family. You will also experience pleasure with the person you most desire.

abbess *if she seems interested in you* You will have much luck while traveling and will meet a person who will expose you to other avenues and more opportunities in life.
if you are ignored by her Do not become easily swayed by others for the next few days.

abbey You will be able to withstand anything and there is nothing you cannot achieve. You must look for ways to quickly achieve your goals.

abbot You will be able to defeat a tough adversary within a four day period if you do not allow your business plans to be known.

abbreviation Within two weeks, you will travel to a distant city to attend a special event. You will enjoy yourself immensely and have a safe return.

abdicate Practice more common sense when dealing with certain situations that will occur within the next few days.

abdomen *your abdomen* You will be performing physical labor, without pay, for another. Be clear whether you choose to render some of your services for free.

a*nother person's abdomen* Within a few days you must allow someone else to express their point of view. This will lead to a clearer mutual understanding and mutual happiness.

pain in You must guard your life for the next few days. You will be shocked by the appearance of a deranged person when you venture into an unfamiliar place.

someone else's pain in You should set aside more time within the next two months for natural creativity and the expression of ideas. Greater rewards will come as a result of a creative thought.

hair on or unfamiliar markings You should back off from the advice of others for the next few days. After this you will have more clarity of thought and the organizational skills needed to implement your thoughts. Powerful results will be the outcome.

abduct *to dream of kidnapping someone* You will be hearing from someone who is a fugitive. This person will reveal this secret to you within two weeks. Remain uninvolved. If you are considering a kidnapping in reality, seek professional help and refrain from this act.

abductee *to a UFO or any other form* Regardless of how many physicians you consult to determine what is taking place with you physically, you will be told that nothing is organically wrong with you. This dream is letting you know that in spite of your feelings that something is wrong, nothing is, and you need to be happy with this fact. Healing will quickly come to you if you start treating your physical complaints from a different perspective. Redirect your thinking patterns and work to change your attitude. Stop treating your body in an unreasonable way. Do what you can to schedule in more physical exercise, change your diet, and make alterations in the way you think in order to remove any form of stress. Reschedule your life to lessen physical demands on your body and remove yourself from anyone who makes you feel uncomfortable and adds extra stress. You can easily turn this into a positive situation by redirecting the way in which you live your life. It will take time but you will recover and be healthier than you were before you began this new regimen. Also take steps to change any negative event in this dream and make sure you experience only positive expressions in your life. You are headed for a prosperous future and many blessings will come to you and your family.

abduction *to dream of being kidnapped* You will meet someone, within the next week, with tremendous wealth who will come into your life and will be interested in involving themselves with you in some capacity. It will be up to you to determine the level of commitment you want. This person is very loyal and will stay with you for a lifetime. Take the proper steps to ensure that you are not abducted, in reality, within two days. This is preventable.

if you recognize the person This implies that someone with similar traits as the one you recognize will enter your life and want to become involved in some capacity. This person is extremely wealthy and it is your choice whether you choose to become involved or not. If there is some neg-

ative aspect to this person, you can take steps to remain uninvolved.

if you do not recognize this person Any clue you can pick up from this person's behavior will offer you a premonition of something that you will experience within two days. If this is a negative situation, take steps to prevent its occurrence in reality. If positive, make sure you bring it to its full potential. Many blessings are with you and you are headed for a brilliant future.

knowledge of an abduction Don't fight someone else's battles; it is better to give moral support in private. This is especially important for the next two days. Also, take steps to keep this dream from becoming a reality and if you do have knowledge of an abduction, seek professional help.

Abednego *(from the Bible)* You need to be more persuasive with a person you are now dealing with. You will have to convert them to your point of view in order to receive benefits. Act quickly on this; it must be done within a four day period.

Abel *(from the Bible)* Someone will be watching you closely and secretly, *(i.e., an inspector of some sort)* and will appear unexpectedly. Be alert to this and make sure you do not perform any illegal or illicit activity, especially for the next week.

ablution *to use or see the liquid used in the religious ceremonies* You will have the physical and mental capacity to complete a difficult task.

abnormality Do not behave in an uncertain and unsure manner when in the presence of someone who is interested in involving you in a certain situation. Deal with this in a direct manner and get on with your life.

aboard *to go aboard a ship or train* Someone will ask to move in with you temporarily, without pay, until they are financially secure. The results will be satisfactory if you choose to allow this. This will occur within a week.

ABO blood group You will be dealing with a personal issue that will demand the expert handling of a professional. Don't waste time and seek immediate help from someone who is qualified to provide this assistance. You will be completely satisfied.

abolition Be confident and do not question anything that works to your favor for the next three days. Accept whatever comes your way as your good fortune. You will achieve prosperity on every level of your life. Any opportunity presented to you will be very fortuitous during this time period, and it would be to your benefit to render a positive response. This is an extremely lucky cycle for you.

A-bomb Within three days someone will put you into a position of potential danger. Problems will arise at a place that you frequent. This evil person has not yet given you any sign of their evilness, but upon getting closer to you they will remove the mask of normalcy. It would be an irresponsible act on your part if you allow yourself to be preyed upon. You have prior notice of this and have the choice of whether you want to allow this person's involvement in your life. Otherwise, you are headed for a very prosperous future.

abominable snowman You will have an irresistible urge for sexual contact with a person you will meet within two days. This will lead to a successful long-term relationship, if you choose to pursue it.

aborigine A mystery that has been bothering you for some time will be cleared up shortly. Everything that has been puzzling you will suddenly become clear and you will fully understand what has been going on.

abortion *someone else having an abortion* You must be careful not to assume responsibility for someone else's problems. Someone may insist that you take on a burden within two days. Be firm in your refusal.

to work in an abortion clinic Someone will pretend to go along with your ideas in order to undermine you and gain privileged information to sabotage your plans. Be wary of this for the next three days.

to have an abortion You will enjoy prosperity in each phase of your life. Freedom from anxiety is yours and you will soon be rid of all long standing burdens. Take steps now to avoid any negativity that has been portended in this dream. Do this within the week.

abracadabra All business transactions that involve travel will be very successful for you and will allow you to develop a better lifestyle than you ever anticipated. Good luck is with you.

Abraham *(or Abram, from the Bible)* Someone you do not know will defend you in a time of crisis. Within two weeks someone from an agency or in a position of authority will relentlessly help to resolve your problems.

abrasion You will receive a call from someone, within three days, who lacks the courage to express their wish to rekindle a relationship. If you choose to reconcile, make sure you give this person a little push and you will reunite in a more loving and stronger relationship. Good luck is with you.

Absalom *(from the Bible)* You will have an opportunity to buy property at a fantastic bargain. Move on this quickly.

abscess *to see an abscess* This dream indicates riches.

in any other form A priceless collection will be damaged within ten days if you do not take steps to prevent it. Otherwise, this is a lucky cycle. Make sure everything you own is immediately insured.

absence *to dream of someone you have not seen in a long time* A faraway friend has a profitable enterprise

(marketable product). You will receive a call from this friend. As a result of this call, it will occur to you that it would be profitable to start the same enterprise in your region. This hunch is correct, go for it. Look forward to this within four days.

absentee ballot Within three days, your abilities will be unexpectedly tested and challenged by someone in a position of authority. Because you have prior notice of this, you will be able to handle yourself appropriately.

absent friend *to be reunited with long lost friend* Do not let your imagination take control, especially for the next four days. The absent friend you dreamed about may represent someone with a similar personality whom you will be dealing with within the next three days, or may be someone you have not seen in a long while whom you may not wish to deal with. You have prior notice of this so if this person has any personality trait, character flaw, etc., that you disliked in the person you dreamed about, take steps to avoid them completely. If this person has a delightful way about them, make it a point to become better acquainted. During this time period, any negotiation you have with others will also result in success because of your communication skills and all conversations that deal with negotiations will have successful results.

to run into an absent friend whom you have not seen in a long time Think back to the time in your life when you were familiar with this person. Any good and positive behavior you were practicing at the time should be repeated and all negative aspects of your life need to be avoided during this cycle. This dream also implies that this person is someone you will want to see or will run into accidentally within five days, or you will run into friends of this person who will talk about this person to you. You will be made aware that this person wants to contact you, and there may be an important reason why you need to connect at this point in your life. Alert this individual to any negative event viewed in this dream so they can take steps to prevent it. You will also run into many other people, other than this individual, whom you have not seen in some time. You will have an enjoyable time during this cycle because you will receive many invitations to a number of events from people you have not seen in a while. You will experience a tremendous amount of joy and will broaden your horizons. This will lead to extra advantages and opportunities. Take steps to keep any negative event in this dream from occurring and make sure you only experience positive expressions in your life. You are definitely headed for a brilliant future.

absent without leave (AWOL) A problematic situation will arise within five days. Although you will feel compelled to become involved and offer assistance, refrain from this involvement. You will not have the emotional resources to cope with this issue extensively. Do not allow yourself to feel guilty, each person is able to handle only so much.

being an AWOL or of someone else being an AWOL Within three days, you will gain the freedom you have long desired. You will be able to express yourself on any level and will explore new dynamic dimensions that will bring you prosperity and happiness.

absolute *to be absolutely certain of something in a dream* This is a great cycle for you to accomplish almost anything you desire. You will be able to handle difficult situations easily and see drastic changes in your life. Motivate yourself to accomplish those things you desire in your life, especially for the next five days.

abstinence *any type* This dream implies the death of a distant relative. You will hear of this within four days.

abstract art Someone will be very happy with your attitude toward them. As a result of your treatment, this person will create many festive occasions for you. You will also develop the strength, tranquility and clarity of thought to make positive changes in your life that will benefit those who are close to you. Make sure you do not involve yourself with anything that seems too serious and avoid all situations that make you uncomfortable.

abundance *an abundance of anything* A long forgotten wealthy friend will renew a friendship. Accept any business association with this person and expect success and luck out of this relationship. This will occur within a three day period.

abuse *(i.e., sexual, physical, verbal or mental)* Be clear about how you respond to others and do not send mixed messages, especially for the next week.

drug abuse You need to be consistently aggressive in your actions, especially when you know you are right. This is particularly important for the next three days. This behavior will bring you closer to your goals, retain happiness and gain honor.

abyss You should not allow arguments to start between you and a friend for the next few days. A difference of opinion will cause both of you to feel depressed.

you are falling into an abyss Someone will cause you emotional pain. Take protective measures for the next three days.

someone else falling You will find bargains over the next few days if you shop alone.

acacia Someone will flirt openly with you in an unexpected place at an unexpected time. If you choose to pursue this route, romance will blossom and you will get exactly the response you are seeking from a romantic situation.

academy The opportunity you have been waiting for will arise within two days. You will make a new start in all areas of your life. All old burdens and issues that have been dragging you down will come to a halt. Major changes will add a new excitement and new dimensions to your life and you will develop and execute plans in all phases of your future.

You will be extremely lucky in matters of the heart. Any union will be blessed.

Academy Award You will have a date with someone within four days whom you don't know yet. This person will be very pleasing and this outing will lead to a deeper relationship, if you choose.

to attend the event You will enjoy mental peace and tranquility for a long time to come.

to receive an award Because of an unexpected declaration of love, you will experience a feeling of exuberance and excitement. If you choose, this can develop into a relationship of any capacity and will lead to mutual fulfillment.

platform Develop the motivation to make something happen. You will be able to ask the key questions to gain the information you need to determine what is important for you to do. Wonderful events will occur if you permit what is destined to happen.

to give an award You will be in contact, within two days, with someone who will be able to work successfully with you. This person will be easy to work with, energetic and have great organizational skills. This will be a great cycle for both of you.

acappella *to perform* Victory and joy will come to you because you will be engaged to marry if you choose to pursue an ongoing relationship.

to hear acappella music You should begin to watch your behavior immediately, because you will be looked at as though you are under a microscope.

Acapulco *a reference of any kind* The arrival of a long anticipated event will occur shortly. This dream may also be used as a reference point in time. If you dream of this city and see its name used in any context, the dream message will occur on this day.

Acapulco gold Someone who is special to you will become more attentive, show more affection and will offer you more respect, love and loyalty than you ever thought possible. This will be a very tenuous and fragile cycle for both of you. Be very considerate of this person's open display of affection and make sure you show affection in return. This person is seeking verification of your feelings. The following week will be a very lucky cycle for love.

accelerator Stay calm and collected for the next three days. A situation will come up during this time period that you will be tempted to become involved with. Do not allow yourself to become so upset with the problems of others that you attempt to take on their problems. Once you become involved it will be very difficult to become disentangled. You are only seeing the tip of the iceberg. Stay uninvolved.

to accelerate Move quickly with your ongoing project in order to achieve success.

to have difficulty with an accelerator Someone will apologize to you within two days for their evasive behavior. This person will go to great lengths in their attempt to repair this relationship. Reconciliation is in your hands.

to see others use an accelerator Watch your behavior around others and stop leaning on them so hard. Back off.

accent *someone with an accent* You will meet someone out of the blue and experience instant love. This person will be kind hearted and generous and will remain to build a long term relationship. You will meet this person within two days.

accessory You will have a problem within two days with someone who is totally inconsistent. This person has a problem being on time and returning calls in a timely fashion. Do not become upset with this behavior; remain calm.

accident You have three days to avoid any negative event you have seen in this dream or to alert anyone else involved to avoid an accident. For this time period, staying accident-free should be a priority. For the next five days, you will also feel an unusual urge to aggressively seek someone to be that special person in your life. This cycle is the perfect time for this. You will have many admirers to choose from and, if you choose, you will find that one person to spend many pleasurable moments with for as long as you wish.

accident prone any form For the next four days, alter your schedule and route to throw off someone who is stalking you. This person has robbery in mind and will be carefully observing your routine.

accolade Within three days, you will accidentally break an expensive piece of hardware or tool. Do whatever you can to prevent this and to avoid having to replace what you break.

accordion You will be dealing with someone who habitually buys time by putting you off a few hours, days, or weeks until the time is right for them. This person will be unable to become involved in any capacity until it suits them. Be clever when speaking to this individual in order to set an exact schedule. This will prevent disappointments.

to play Stick to your own opinions and be firm.

to play without sound Compromise with family members and support all group decisions.

someone else playing Guard your health and watch what you ingest in order to avoid food poisoning, especially for the next two days.

to buy or sell Someone you care for will unexpectedly depart to another state. This will happen within two days.

accountant Be aware of something that is draining you financially that should be cause for concern now. Seek ways to generate extra income within a two week period because money that you expect during this time period will not arrive in a timely fashion.

accounts and account books You will be falsely accused and feel you must run from the law. Take measures to prevent this and keep your priorities straight.

accursed Someone you depend on for a solution will let you down at the last minute. Make alternative plans in order to be prepared for this event.

accuse *if wrongly accused* You will be successful in your undertakings and are on the right path.

to accuse someone You will meet an individual who will assist in a crisis situation within three days.

to hear an accusation You will be given an expected expensive gift within four days.

AC/DC This is a very lucky omen and you will experience a stress-free and tranquil cycle. This is also a good time to re-interest yourself in those opportunities that you once had an interest in. You will now find new opportunities open to you.

ace This implies triumph over anything you desire You will receive prompt relief from an unbearable situation. Move quickly.

ace bandage Avoid a lawsuit by quickly taking care of needed home repairs.

acetone Someone whom you have a deep love and respect for will move out of your life. Otherwise, good luck is coming your way.

ache *to experience an ache* Do not associate with people who have beliefs counter to your ideas, especially for the next two days.

to see someone in pain Protect your reputation from gossip. Guard yourself for the next two days.

achievement *having an accomplishment* This dream implies that you need to be patient and persevere.

Achilles *(Greek mythology)* You will have a fantastic job opportunity handling other people's money. This will start within four days. Proceed with confidence.

Achilles' heel For the next two days you will have a need to clear up a long standing problem with another person. Be sure you have a solution before you approach this individual. You will reach a satisfactory solution.

Achilles' tendon You will have an enlightened, fruitful conversation with someone within three days who will present you with certain facts that will allow you to focus on important details that you would otherwise overlook.

acid Don't allow someone special to slip away from you because of your inconsistency or your abusive manner, especially for the next three days.

acid head Develop and detail the ideas you plan to implement for better results.

acidophilus milk Make sure, for the next two days, you do not allow the hasty actions or words of other people to leave you feeling uncomfortable. Do not lose confidence in your ideas and plans. Remain focused and retain control over your decisions.

acid rain Do not allow curiosity to take control and do not venture into the unknown. There is a thin line between curious inquiry and active involvement, and you are approaching this line. Step back! What you are being told is misleading. This applies to any strange meeting which may take place in any capacity within the next three days.

acne *any form* You will meet a wonderful person within two days and will be given the opportunity for a romantic and lasting affection.

acolyte You will become independently wealthy. Relentlessly pursue your goals to make them a realization. You will receive a hint of this over the next two days.

acorn You and a special person are looking for changes to improve your relationship. You are now open to conversations and new ways to demonstrate love. You will both seek out methods to bring in a new closeness that will benefit the union. This will serve to improve the relationship in all aspects. If you choose to pursue this, the other person will be more than eager to go along with this process. You will experience longevity in this relationship. You will also receive news of a pregnancy within the next three weeks.

acorn squash In four days you will receive services from an agency that you will be dissatisfied with. Continue your search for an agency that will satisfy your needs. Do not give up and you will be successful. You will also have the opportunity to invest in a short-term project that promises to yield a great deal of money. This is a once in a lifetime opportunity. Do not allow it to slip away.

acquaintance Within three days you will be offered a special opportunity. Not only you, but everyone else will benefit and profit from this. Your involvement and expertise are the ingredients needed to set plans into motion and bring it to the highest potential. Go for it.
 to run into an acquaintance you have not seen in a long time Think back to the time in your life when you were familiar with this person. Any good and positive behavior you were practicing at the time should be repeated, and all negative aspects that were occurring need to be avoided during this cycle. This dream also implies that this person is someone you will want to see or will run into accidentally within five days. You will run into friends of this person who will talk about this person to you. You will be made aware that this person wants to contact you. There may be a reason why you and this person need to connect at this point in your life. Alert this individual to any negative event viewed in this dream so they can take steps to prevent it. You will also run into many other people whom you have not seen in some

time. You will have an enjoyable time during this cycle because you will receive many invitations to a number of events from people you have not seen in a while. You will experience a tremendous amount of joy and will broaden your horizons. This will lead to extra advantages and opportunities. Take steps to prevent any negative event in this dream from occurring and make sure that you only experience positive expressions in your life. You are definitely headed for a brilliant future.

acre This dream is a very lucky omen, especially for family unity and harmony. Do everything you can to help.

acrobat A trap has been set to sabotage a project so that a deadline will not be met. You have time to prevent this. Expect it to occur within two days. You are also loved beyond your imagination.

acrophobia You should begin afresh with finances. Stop spending and bank more.

Acropolis You will soon have the opportunity to experience a fantastic, unplanned sexual encounter with a business acquaintance if you choose to pursue this option.

acrylics Stop placing so many limits on yourself. Take steps to add more enjoyment to your life. You are being overprotective of yourself and this is depriving you of life's enjoyments.

actor Circulate for the next seven days in order to meet a wealthy individual eager for a relationship. This will lead to a wonderful union, if you choose.
 if you are the actor Within three days, you will develop a sense of urgency to attract the attention of someone you desire. Follow your hunches. You will find, in this person, a similar lifestyle and ideas. If you choose to pursue this, it is possible to establish a relationship in this cycle. You will find this person to be very demonstrative and affectionate and you will both have a great deal of love to share with each other. This dream is also asking you to face facts and stop looking at everything through rose colored glasses. You are making it easy for someone to lie to you because you give the impression that you prefer not to deal with cold hard facts. Change this behavior and face situations head on.
 an unknown actor Beware of something you desire, it will only bring trouble. Resist all irresistible urges and impulses, especially for the next three days.

actress *to be an actress* A formerly disinterested person will now become interested in a relationship. This will become a passionate experience. Move quickly to ensure success and keep up your appearances.
 to see a well known actress You will experience a new freedom within two weeks due to an unexpected and unusual circumstance. This will help you to get beyond a certain situation that has limited your capacity in some respect. This has left you with a feeling of despair and a depletion of ener-

gy and motivation. During this time frame you will get beyond all of this and experience a new sense of freedom and liberty on each level of your life. You will feel uplifted and enjoy a new lease on life. Anything you felt was impossible is now possible. Proceed with confidence. You will also receive good news and will be involved in a gift giving celebration. You are headed for a prosperous future and many blessings will come to you and your family.

to admire any (unknown) actress Someone who is presently away from home will need to be hospitalized for a few days. Alert all those that this may apply to in order to prevent this occurrence.

Acts *(from the Bible)* *any form, to read, quote, etc.* You will be chosen to be the representative of a conservatorship for someone unable to handle their finances. This will not be a burden to you.

acupressure *any form* You will need to avoid exercise that may lead to a collapsed or punctured lung within three days. Someone will also diplomatically drop subtle hints about a particular area of dissatisfaction in their life. This individual feels they are stonewalled and cannot get through this situation. You will have the conviction and compassion to do this for them and it will lead them to a better lifestyle if you choose to take the initiative. Many blessings are with you.

acupuncture A person you are going to visit unexpectedly will not be home. If you wait, the person you have gone to visit will be very happy that you did. You also need to do everything necessary to avoid any negative event foreseen in this dream that involves you or anyone else you recognize, and bring to fruition anything positive for yourself or anyone you recognize.

acute panic attack Be extremely aware of what will be unfolding in your life for the next two weeks. Think very carefully and clearly about the way you are stepping into a subtle lifestyle change that is being created by someone else or by yourself. This lifestyle seems to be developing on its own with no control from you. Be very alert to this and take steps to gain control over your life and to eliminate the stresses that will be placed on you. You have to be more aware of what is developing and remain alert, especially for the next month. Steer yourself around disguised demands that will feel, at the time they are being made, not as demanding as they will be. The responsibility that you will assume will put a tremendous amount of strain and pressure on you. You will find it a very tedious chore to meet everyone's demands and needs. At the time this is going on you will have no concept of the pressure you are under, and will be doing this as a matter of routine because you want everything to run smoothly and easily. You will not have the time to think about any of this while it is going on. You will finally reach a point of being overextended and will become emotionally and physically fragile, but will continue to proceed in the same fashion. The more you give of yourself, the more others will take. You will reach the point of not having

anyone to talk to about this pressure you are under, and will not have anyone to turn to for help to relieve this stress. You will begin to find this subtly destructive lifestyle intolerable. You need to take steps to stop what you are doing before it becomes a problem, so that you do not find yourself in this situation eight months from now. This lifestyle may lead to illness and it will take you a long time to recover from this. Seclude yourself from these demands at this time in order to refocus and to have time to think and develop a creative idea and bring it to tangible form. This idea will leave a mark on the world and you are destined to bring it about. Do not allow anyone to pry into your affairs or to question your reasons for this sabbatical. Steer yourself away from the subtle demands of others and their projects for at least eight months. Make sure you limit all stress and keep your life simple. If you allow yourself to get to this point, use all the support systems (i.e., crises lines, support groups, self help groups, hot lines, self help books, etc.) at your disposal as well as any professional help you may need. Make sure you eat properly and get plenty of rest. Think defensively (i.e., comedy club, comedy videos, etc.) in order to create the perfect lifestyle for yourself. Do not be so restrictive with your inner child. Let your creative thoughts flow and support your ideas. You will put yourself on the perfect path for a brilliant future. Also, any negative event witnessed in this dream that could become a reality needs to be prevented and anyone you dreamed about whom you recognize needs to be forewarned to do the same. Take steps to ensure you only experience positive events in your life.

ad *want ad* Take steps to keep anything negative in this dream from occurring. Place a want ad for anything that could enhance your life. This is a medium you can use to enhance your life and bring you more prosperity. You can also use this to advertise for a special partner in your life. This is a special cycle for you and many unusual situations can occur by you placing an ad. Many blessings are with you and your family and you are headed for a very prosperous future.

Adam *(from the Bible)* You should buy a gift of appreciation for a special person within two days. This gift will be welcomed beyond your imagination. You will also experience unexpected success in those areas of your life you most desire. Many blessings are with you and your family.

if Adam is joined by Eve You will suddenly find yourself sexually attracted to someone who, until now, you never noticed. It will be a successful union.

Adams apple Reassure someone who is special to you of your love.

add Play a numbers game. A child will also ask for money within seven days but will be unable to repay the loan.

adder Do not place bets on a sporting event for the next three days. You will lose.

addict Someone will need money. Be firm when you refuse to help them out. An unexpected problem will also arise. Handle it now before it gets blown out of proportion.

address *any numbers* These numbers are lucky and may be used in games of chance for a seven day period.

a building with an address This is leading you to an area of opportunity and prosperity. The address in the dream may also be leading you to an item you have desired but have been unable to find. The item may be picked up as a bargain.

a strange address or house with a strange address You will be able to locate an old acquaintance who recently moved to this area. Recall anything connected to this dream that is negative or distasteful about this house or address to ensure you experience nothing negative in reality. You can turn any negative event to a positive situation within three days. Also warn anyone you recognize in the dream to take the same steps.

if the address is not attached to the building (envelope, yellow pages, etc.) You will realize your highest ambitions. This address may be a place where an acquaintance has moved whom you have been attempting to locate, or a place where you may find prosperous opportunities that will open your future and bring you a more improved lifestyle. If this address pointed to a distasteful moment or a negative event, it can be avoided by keeping a clear memory of this address and place in your mind. For the next three days avoid unfamiliar surroundings and take steps to protect yourself. Many blessings are with you and the numbers recalled in the address are lucky for games of chance.

in any other form For the next two days you will find that other people will feel a need for nourishment, attention and affection from you. You may also come into contact with someone who will approach you with benefits in some form. Make sure you are on your best behavior and do everything you can to demonstrate the nurturing aspect of your character to others. If you choose to involve yourself, this will ensure that other people will feel secure and comfortable enough around you to include you in their plans, whether financial, romantic or in any other capacity. Within this time period you will also be intently seeking a specific address. At this time closely attend to any address given to you by another person. This location will bring you benefits. Any negative event depicted in this dream needs to be avoided. Many blessings will come to you and your family. You are headed for a prosperous future.

address book You will have very intuitive thoughts and this intuition will be accurate in every way. You will also develop the skills needed to diffuse negative thoughts and attitudes at the exact time that you need this skill. You will no longer have to deal with the negativity that is holding you back. Proceed with confidence and calmness no matter what is occurring in your life right now. You are headed for a life filled with enjoyment with interesting and influential people.

ade For the next three days, make sure you do not become involved in any situation that involves gossip and backbiting. Avoid any behavior that could result in you being accused of slander. Anything in this dream that foretells a negative event needs to be avoided or changed. All positive events need to be incorporated into your life.

adenoid You are placing trust in a deceitful person who will eventually injure you emotionally. Protect yourself for the next three days.

adhesive You will need a confident attitude in order to ask for a special favor. This attitude will yield better results.

adhesive tape Carefully think over and detail each move prior to a special event taking place. This will occur within seven days and it is important that you act appropriately.

ad lib Someone who has a hard time controlling their jealousy will attempt to involve you in their life. Since you have prior notice of this, you can decide how to limit your involvement with this person.

administration *to attend meetings at large administrations for any reason* Congratulations, you will recover from a long illness and will feel better and younger than you did prior to the illness. Your financial situation will also heal.

administrator Get all the facts on another's situation within two days so you can be more responsive to this other person and their point of view.

admiral A vendor will set prices higher because of the manner in which you are dressed. Be sure you do not pay a higher price for something you can get for less.

admire *to admire* You will receive a gift from a distant place. Your life will run smoothly for a long time to come.

to be admired You will enjoy success regarding an ongoing project and you will receive greater rewards than expected.

in any other form Within two weeks you will unexpectedly advance to a higher place in life than you ever envisioned. You will experience an abundance of productivity, increased income, productive conversations, and will be surrounded by loyal and affectionate people. Others will express a desire to become a part of your goals and will wish to assist you, to teach you the wisdom they have acquired, and whatever else you desire to learn. This will be especially important within five days. You are headed for a brilliant future and will enjoy an abundance of health within a shorter period of time than you expected.

adobe You will achieve sudden wealth. You will also receive good but unusual news about a friend within two days.

adobo All plans set into motion within the next three days should be put into writing to ensure that all details are carried out accurately.

adolescent There is no rivalry for your loved one.

adopt *to adopt* A troubled relationship will change into a loving, long lasting union.

to give up for adoption You are promised that you will have a comfortable life, complete with all of the material wants, domestic help, and luxuries you desire. This will come about because of actions taken within three days that will point you toward a brilliant future. You will also enjoy health and long life.

adoration *any form* A well organized idea will bring rapid rewards.

adornment Within two day's time, you will receive a gift of mental inventiveness from the gods. Motivate yourself to use this gift in those areas of your life you desire. You will also see improvements and great changes in your sex life and enjoy health and tranquility. Drink plenty of water and eat healthful foods.

adult Avoid at all costs, any angry situations between you and another person. Angry words can neither be taken back nor forgotten. At the first sign of an argument, politely back down.

to see an adult behave in a strange manner toward young children Get a grip on your temper and do whatever you can to control yourself. A distasteful situation will occur that will make you suspicious and jealous of another person in some capacity. If you are not careful you will develop an uncontrollable rage that will drive you to do something you will later regret. Do not allow this emotion to develop and do not feed into your suspicions. The moment you sense this rage developing, turn to a professional who can help you to overcome it and to prevent any situation you will have deep regrets about later in your life.

adultery *to catch a friend in the act of adultery* Suppress timely information in order to be a winner.

to be accused of adultery Do not be misled by appearances. Any negative event witnessed in this dream needs to be prevented in reality.

to accuse someone of adultery Do not become stagnant in a love relationship. Add excitement quickly.

Advent Find the information needed to quickly finish a job.

Advent Sunday Someone will go to great lengths to get you involved in a business arrangement. After all the small problems are worked out by communicating openly and by meeting with this person, you will find yourself receiving greater wealth than your partner. This opportunity will come to you within the week.

adventure *to have an adventure* Your instincts are correct.

adventurer(s) Do not surround yourself with known dangerous adversaries. Play it safe for the next seven days.

adversary Someone who has openly threatened you will cause injury to you soon. Be careful for the next two days.

advertisement Within three days, your abilities will be tested and challenged by someone in authority at an unexpected time. Because you have prior notice of this, you will be able to behave in an appropriate manner.

advice This implies that you will be able to arrange events to your advantage in order to increase your financial status. You can begin this process within seven days.

advocate A child engaged in adult play may become seriously injured within two days. This can be prevented.

Aeneas *(Greek and Roman mythology)* The form of birth control you use will be unreliable. If you are attempting to avoid pregnancy, use more caution.

aerialist Be careful; don't lose your keys.

aerie You will be unexpectedly surprised by an out of town invitation. This will be a safe, enjoyable trip if you choose to take it.

aerobatics Actively pursue someone you are interested in, and if you choose, this will be the beginning of an awesome relationship.

aerodynamics An early settlement of a bequest made to you will be reached.

Aesop *(Greek fable writer)* Do not mix business with pleasure for the next three days. It will backfire.

afar *seeing something at a distance* You should avoid putting out extra cash for the next few days.

affair *to be told by someone that they are having an affair* You will be successful with a new project.

to be caught having an affair You will acquire fame and riches through your undertakings.

to ask about someone having an affair You will hear news of someone you know developing a serious illness.

affection *affection toward you* You will acquire wisdom and will eagerly and willingly learn from someone else. This will lead, in later years, to riches and success.

to demonstrate affection to someone else Someone will show innocent affection toward you. This is a big surprise and will catch you very much off guard. This will be such a surprise that it will take you a couple of days to recover from it. You will also experience many thrilling moments with the person of your choice.

in any other form Within a two week period you will suddenly rise to a higher plateau in life than you ever expected. You will see an abundance of productivity, increased income, productive conversations, and be surrounded by those who will be loyal and affectionate toward you. Other people will express a wish to become a part of your plans, wish to assist you, and will teach you the knowledge they have acquired. This will be especially important for the next five days. You are headed for a brilliant future and will enjoy an abundance of health within a short period of time.

affliction *an affliction causing pain* Another's careless-ness will cause you hardship within the next few weeks. Avoid this.

    someone with an affliction The truth you have been waiting for will soon come to you.

affluence A proposal of yours will be accepted shortly.

afghan *any form* Find alternative plans. The one you have in mind will not be successful.

Afghan hound This is an extremely lucky omen. Someone will quickly come to your assistance regarding a particular situation that you wish to quickly resolve. You are deeply loved and appreciated by those you care about. You also need to avoid all accidents and illnesses for the next three days that are within your power to prevent.

afraid Someone will go to great lengths to create a relation-ship between you and a special person. You are destined to enjoy a beautiful, full blown relationship that will blossom within a few days and will bring you a great deal of joy. You will be able to connect emotionally with another person so successfully that this person will respond in the manner you most desire. Also you are headed in the right direction and it is important that you express yourself in a focused and detailed manner, in all matters of personal interest. As a result, you will be able to achieve a great deal and will have many successes in your life. You will magically possess the inner strength to handle any situation and enjoy much tran-quility in your life. An unexpected favor will also be granted to you. You will need to put yourself in the position to speak with powerful, influential people. State your needs directly and clearly. Because of this, you will immediately be grant-ed the money you requested from a certain person. You will enjoy victory in those areas of your life that you deem to be most important now. You can also expect to hear good news within the week and you are headed for a brilliant future, so pay close attention to all conversations over the next three days. All negative messages and events occurring in this dream can be altered and all positive messages can be pro-moted. This is a very lucky dream for you.

    to be afraid You will soon have the knowledge to make the correct decision. Someone longs to be with you but is anxious about putting their passion into words. You will soon learn the identity of this person.

A-frame Do not make promises to be somewhere at a spe-cific time unless you intend to be there. Think ahead before you make this promise and take steps to ensure that you will be there.

Africa *any form* A debt will soon be repaid to you. This dream may also be used as a reference point in time. If you dream of this country and see its name used in any context, the dream message will occur on this day.

African lily Someone will attempt to pull you into an in-volvement before you are ready. Follow your instincts and go for this relationship. It will be successful.

African violet You and a special person are looking for changes to improve your relationship. You are now open to conversations and new ways to demonstrate love and to bring in a new closeness that will benefit the union. This will serve to improve the relationship in all aspects. If you choose to pursue this, the other person will be more than eager to go along with this process.

afro *any form* You will receive a sought after commitment in a relationship and will receive a large sum of money. If you choose to pursue this, it will be a permanent relationship and many blessings will come to you. You are headed for a brilliant future.

Afro-American A business trip will take longer then ex-pected. Take an extra supply of necessary items. You are in a prosperous cycle and are headed for a brilliant future.

afterbirth You will have to deal with a minor family prob-lem connected with finances within two days. Handle this calmly.

afterlife *to have a discussion about life after death or to experience this in a dream* This indicates that you are living too much in the past. You need to focus on the present and add enjoyable activities in order to enjoy yourself now.

afternoon You will be invited to an enjoyable dinner within two days.

aftershave Do not lie to anyone simply to satisfy your sexu-al urges, particularly for the next two days. This individual may not handle the emotional let down easily.

aftershock A financial situation will arise within a few weeks. You need to be aware of this and take steps to pre-pare for it.

against *any form* Be very aware for the next three days. Move forward with a certain person only with extreme cau-tion. The person you will be dealing with, and who you are beginning to develop some sense of closeness, will lead you to believe you can confide in them fully and can depend on their loyalty to you. This person is very crafty and skilled in creating illusions. They will lead you to believe in future occurrences and events that will never take place, and have a hidden agenda that involves pursuing you for reasons known only to them. This individual will go to great lengths to create an atmosphere that will leave you trusting them totally with no suspicions of their devious plans. This person is very charming and charismatic, and if they think you are becoming suspicious, they will create a crisis to divert you. By the time you realize what is happening, you will be suffering deep emotional disappointments, disillusionments and you may suffer financially. It will take a long time for you to recover from this and get back to normalcy. You have prior notice of this and all the ammunition you need to make sure it does not take place. Practice common sense and you will be very successful in diffusing this issue. Do not compromise and do not allow this person to pry into your affairs. Refuse to become involved. You will have the confidence to put yourself on the path toward a prosperous future. Many blessings are with you and your family.

Agamemnon *(Greek mythology)* Don't allow laziness to let an opportunity slip through your fingers. This opportunity will present itself to you within four days.

agape *yourself standing with your mouth wide open* Someone will come into your life within three days eager to have a friendly relationship. As time passes you will begin to receive mixed messages. This person will hint at a romantic involvement but is only playing games with you and wasting your time, because they are seeking only a short term relationship. Do not expect more than this. Enjoy yourself and get on with your life. Do not compromise your own desires especially during this time frame, and you will be able to grasp deep emotional fulfillment. You will enjoy future prosperity.

someone else agape Don't let your business plans become known to others or you will be defeated. Quickly process these plans in order to bring them to reality.

agate Do what you can to help someone special feel more secure in your relationship. Your behavior toward them will make them feel sure of your affections. Your hunches are also right on target and you can, for the next three days, rely on your intuition. You will experience victory in those areas of your life you most desire and in areas you least expect. Many blessings will come to you and your family.

age *your age (any form)* Do not waste your time trying to determine the perfect time to make an important move. Proceed with confidence and do not wait for situations or other people to dictate your timing. Move on this quickly and you will find that everything will fall into place as it should. If you recall the numbers in the dream, use them for games of chance. Any negative event in this dream can be avoided if you take steps now.

someone else talking about their age You are overlooking an important matter that needs to be handled within three days.

to see yourself aging You should take some time off for yourself. Enjoy the marrow of life and focus on things that will bring enjoyment to your life, and make it a point to look at things more optimistically. You will, within seven days,

put yourself on the correct path toward a brilliant future.

to see someone else aging Your judgments in all matters are on target. You are headed for a very prosperous future and many blessings are coming to you and your family.

in any other form For the next seven days, focus on bringing a relationship to the level you desire. This is the best cycle for you to concentrate on this. You can use this cycle to change other levels of your life that you are not very happy with. You will also have the opportunity to meet someone who is far wealthier than they appear. This person will be eager to bond with you on any level you desire. You will find that you will have many things in common with this individual. You are definitely headed for a brilliant future. Many blessings will be with you and your family.

agency You will need to discuss finances with that special person in order to reach an agreement. This will allow you to avoid future pressures before the end of the week.

someone representing an agency Avoid harassment for nonpayment of bills by doing whatever is necessary to ensure timely payments.

county agency You will suddenly recover from a long illness and feel healthier than before becoming ill. This is also a very prosperous time for you.

Agent Orange An unexpected change in your life will create stress within two days. Find a way to alleviate this.

aggression *any form* Someone feels passion toward you. You will learn of this and your days will become brighter. This will result in a positive outcome.

agnostic Be careful of a fight that may break out in the streets (i.e., civil wars, domestic disputes, etc.) for the next four days. Avoid this scene completely.

agony *someone in agony* A misfortunate person will come for help within four days. This person, with your assistance, will shortly be on their feet and you will be rewarded for your kindness.

to be in agony An acquaintance will suffer emotional troubles. Try to find assistance for this person within a two day period.

agree *any form* You will develop an enormous strength that will enable you to communicate an unusual situation to another person and get the relief and support to handle this issue appropriately. You will also be in full control and disciplined in your refusal to overindulge in food, alcohol, etc.. Any negative event that you dreamed of can be avoided in reality. Good luck is with you.

agreeableness *a person being overly agreeable* You will receive a big surprise and unexpected news about your family and career that will bring you profound joy.

being overly agreeable You will receive good news from a powerful person about your goals.

agreement An ongoing union will become a marriage.

agriculture For the next few days do not allow yourself to become fixated on one plan. Make sure you have alternatives in case one does not work to your satisfaction. Do not restrict yourself. Good luck is with you.

A-horizon You will receive the nurturing that you have been longing for and will also find spiritual nourishment in ways you never expected. This will begin to evolve within three days. Many blessings will come to you and your family.

ahoy You will need to stop overextending yourself for others.

aid *to receive aid* You need to take more control over money situations and the possessions you have previously allowed another to handle.

to aid someone else You own something that has more value than you are aware of. Another person is aware of the worth and will attempt to persuade you to give it up within three days. Prevent this.

to ask for aid and not get it Do whatever is necessary to grow at the same or more rapid pace as those around you. Keep growing and learning in order to keep up with those who are important to you. Within three days it will become clear to you why this is necessary.

AIDS You don't have to accept unacceptable behavior from another. It is also important to pay close attention to details about your health. Be very careful and protective of yourself for the next three days. Treat your health as a precious commodity, and take steps to avoid exposure to a contagious disease. You also have detailed reliable information about a certain situation and this information should be used to encourage definite improvements. Motivate groups of activists in order to focus them on certain situations that will take on a life of its own. This will bring about major improvements for all of those involved. You are in a prosperous cycle and are headed for a brilliant future.

air *air is breathed from an oxygen tank* You need to demonstrate more patience toward someone slower than yourself for the next two days.

to breathe or to see anyone else breathe out fog in cold weather Within a three day period you will enter a very lucky cycle and anyone involved in your life will share your luck with you. You will be offered services that will enable you to achieve success on a far greater level than you ever hoped for concerning anything that is important to you or that you place a high priority on. For this three day time period you can expect a number of amazing and wonderful connections that will allow you to grasp and achieve your goals. You can also expect a big merger to take place that will promote a synergism between you and those you will be working with to bring you to a higher plane than you ever hoped for. This dream also implies that you will attend a very joyous event, will enjoy an educational experience that

will bring you big benefits, or attend a gathering and meet one person who will show an avid interest in you. Also in your ongoing interests and will offer you major assistance. You can expect a long period of tranquility following this and will enjoy a brilliant future. Any negative event associated with this dream concerning you or anyone else can be prevented. Forewarn the other person of this event and take steps to prevent it.

if the air is clear and clean Your love relations will blossom and will become healthier, and more prosperous.

if the air has been sprayed by you (i.e., hairspray, deodorizer, etc.) Rethink your decisions, check for errors and begin again.

if air has been sprayed by another (toxins, pollutants) Be sure that all fires have been extinguished and all lights have been turned off (especially car lights). You will also receive an expected sum of money within two days.

if the air seems to be polluted Stop playing with the idea of cheating someone out of their money.

if the air seems smoky or dark Someone will cheat you out of money within two days.

if the air has a floral scent You will enjoy a good sex life.

if the air has a foul odor Your auto may break down. Immediately check the car for any needed repairs.

air bag An undercover inspector will be scrutinizing your behavior. Make sure that you behave in a totally appreciative manner, especially for the next seven days.

air brakes You will be accused of being untrue within two days. Do not allow this to happen.

airbrush You will be able to stop an abusive habit. The stronger the intensity of colors from the airbrush the greater the ability you will have to resist this habit. Look up the color for a more complete definition of this dream. Good luck will be with you.

air conditioning Do not forget a special celebration because this will lead to misunderstandings and disappointments. This will be very important for the next seven days. You will also have the time to turn any negative event viewed in this dream to a positive situation or to avoid it completely. Alert anyone you recognize in the dream to do likewise.

aircraft *to see one flying* You will be a winner if you relentlessly pursue what is righteously yours. Be aggressive in areas that you are taking for granted. It is especially important to display this manner for the next seven days and you will definitely have the financial stability you desire.

to see one on land Be affectionate to someone who is special in your life. Be reassuring to this individual around others in order to display that special something you have together. Good luck is with you.

aircraft carrier Focus on your priorities and respond to them immediately in order to put yourself on the path of prosperity.

Airedale terrier Make it a point to clarify a specific situation or behavior that someone else finds questionable within three days, or take the necessary steps to avoid all questionable behavior entirely.

air force A person of your choice will surrender their heart and love to you within four days.

air gun You are in a position to be hurt romantically. You need to make your feelings clear and avoid any problem area in the relationship in order to avoid a painful breakup. Do this as quickly as you can.

airline Celebrations will take place regarding a gift of property. This will occur within a few weeks.

airmail You will recover money from an unexpected source within ten days.

airplane *to ride on one* An anticipated upcoming event will bring a joyful reunion.

to see someone else in an airplane Guard your emotions. Someone you are attracted to is leading a very busy life. This individual wants to be with you but is unable to. Keep busy and remain patient. This person will come to you at the first opportunity.

to see an airplane explosion You will hear of a freak accident that will involve a friend. This person will die if precautions are not taken. Alert anyone this may apply to.

fall out of an airplane This dream implies that you need to be very careful for the next three days about pleasure seeking expenditures. This behavior could become a bad habit.

in any other form You will be very successful in diffusing a plot that someone has devised against you and it will be impossible for it to be carried out. This plot involves someone who wishes to bring discomfort and chaos into your life. You will effectively use any power you possess in a responsible and efficient manner. During this cycle you will experience many wins and victories and the kindness you have paid others in the past will be repaid. You will receive many gifts and some major victories. You are headed for a brilliant future.

airport *to go to an airport* You are attracted to a very busy person who seemingly has no time to fit you into their life. In reality, this person is trying to find a way to see you. You will receive verbal verification of this within the week.

to meet someone in an airport You will be called upon within four days to be of assistance to a family member. This will be a safe and successful trip.

in any other form You will enjoy the deeper involvement that another person will extend to you. This individual will show more understanding and deeper feelings toward you. You will receive verbal verification of this person's feelings within five days.

air raid You will lend a sympathetic ear to someone who is depressed within two days.

airsick You will miraculously recover from an illness.

aisle *church aisle* Your body language will lead someone special to you to feel uncomfortable because you will create an atmosphere conducive to jealousy.

grocery aisle Don't lose your baggage.

Ajax *(Greek mythology)* To dream of him implies that you should not set up a meeting in an unfamiliar or strange place.

Alabama You will experience new dimensions in your life that are open for exploration. Take steps to do this in spite of anything else that may be going on in your life. You will be able to take these opportunities to align yourself with those people and situations in such a way that everything will work out exactly as you have envisioned. Move on this within three days. You are headed for a prosperous future. This dream may also be used as a reference point in time. If you dream of this state and see its name used in any context, the dream message will occur on this day.

alabaster Protect your privacy against inquisitive people.

Aladdin Keep your immune system healthy. It will also be a good idea to play lotto for the next seven days.

Alamo Research the locale carefully prior to relocating to a new neighborhood. This dream may also be used as a reference point in time. If you dream of this place and see its name used in any context, the dream message will occur on this day.

alarm Don't over-exercise for the next few days. Also be extremely careful for the next two days so that you do not leave yourself open to another individual who could bring you physical or emotional harm. Be extremely cautious and alert to anything that seems unusual and out of the ordinary. Protect yourself in any way you can.

Alaska You will give a much desired present to a relative. You are also deeply loved by those around you. This dream may also be used as a reference point in time. If you dream of this state and see its name used in any context, the dream message will occur on this day.

Alaskan Malamute Make a request for assistance regarding a plan you wish to put into action within three days. In addition, someone who has turned you down in the past will have a change of heart. It will be much easier for this person to come around if you make the first move. Good luck is with you.

albacore Within five days it would be to your advantage to take the time to research the character of someone you will be dealing with. Gather this information as tactfully as you can and keep it to yourself. Good luck is with you.

albatross An older person who is ill will recover quicker with tender loving care.

albino Any negotiations regarding business will be very unlucky. Someone will attempt to undermine you in a business deal. Be careful.

album *photo album* For the next few days, protect yourself in every way. There is a danger that you are unaware of. Guard your health.

album cover A successful, intelligent person will give the impression of being simple. Do not underestimate this person or treat them poorly as they will be of assistance later. This is especially important for the next four days.

Alcatraz (*the prison*) Within the week, do not involve yourself with any unusual or out of the ordinary situation that limits your ability to escape at a later time. You will feel as though all of your daytime hours are spent on the situation that you have become involved with. Step back and clearly think over this involvement. Proceed with caution. This dream may also be used as a reference point in time. If you dream of this place and see its name used in any context, the dream message will occur on this day.

alchemy Do not fear. Your love for someone is mutual.

alcohol Do not cause your family to suffer needless anxiety. Keep them aware of your schedule.
    to be an alcoholic Do not keep your feelings to yourself.
    to see an alcoholic Express yourself lovingly and quickly.
    to attend an AA meeting Someone needs your immediate romantic attention, don't waste time.

ale A new acquaintance will suddenly become dangerous and may injure you. This could be avoided by paying attention and taking preventive measures.

Aleister Crowley (*Executive Director/Master of the 78 cards of the book of Egyptian Tarot*) Within the month you will be thrust forward with massive, deliberate and brilliant clarity of thought. You will be able to manifest and master the abilities to make improved changes that will profoundly and vastly affect your life as well as the lives of others. These changes will endure for a lifetime and you will leave an unusual legacy that others will enjoy and reap benefits from for self improvement. Many blessings are with you and you are headed for a fantastic future.

Alexander the Great You will recover rapidly from a nervous condition. Emotional and mental well being will be yours. A wish will be granted within two days.

alfalfa You will purchase a desired piece of property. This will be a lucky move.

algae Control your actions around someone younger than yourself. Your reputation is at stake.

algebra Take care of pressing matters now or you may find yourself picketed or protested against.

Algonquin You will find yourself paying too much attention to a stranger whom you would be better off having no involvements with. This person is evil minded. Get on with your life without this person in it. Otherwise, good luck is with you.

alias Someone dangerous to you will be released from jail in two days. Take precautions.

Ali Baba If you desire, the person who is most special to you will remain with you for a lifetime. You will have more moments of enjoyment together than stressful times. You will enjoy a life together filled with love and joy. Many blessings are with you. This dream is an omen of health.

alibi A proposed marriage will turn out badly. Reconsider. The other partner has a dark unrevealed side.

Alice in Wonderland Victory will come to you in those areas of your life you most desire. This will lead you to make grand emotional changes and you will enjoy greater stabilization in your life.

alien An anticipated trip will be dull and uneventful. You may want to change plans.

alimony Consider reconciliation and reinvolvement with another. Feelings will now be mutual. Find some quiet time for the next two days to think of ways to resolve the conflict.

Allah Do not ignore the irrational behavior of another. Get completely away from this person for the sake of your health.

allegation *to contend with allegations in a dream* Discourage any meeting from taking place in your home. Find an alternative place.

allegiance A loved one is experiencing difficulty in financial and career negotiations. Give moral support and be tactful in all dealings with this person. Attempt to head this off with a warning within a few weeks.

allegory To hear a symbolic story within a dream implies that a sudden move will be initiated by a family member.

allergy Be wary of anything involving the occult. Do not leap into the unknown. You will also suffer injury from a traffic accident. Make no sudden moves; watch your step. This can all be prevented by being cautious.

alley cat Don't become involved in an active debate. This will lead to disagreement and hatred. Remain calm and avoid all disputes for the next three days. An unexpected event will occur that will leave you financially well off for years.

alligator You are about to make a large decision that will anger many people. You will be protested against. Rethink your move and decide on a better solution.

alligator pear Do whatever you can to express the hidden desires that you have for another. This will be possible within two days.

allowance You will be invited to appear at several different social functions. You will enjoy an open reception by others and will be very popular. You will also meet someone, during this social cycle, who will play a primary role in your life. Take steps to maintain a healthy cardiovascular system by eating the right foods, exercising, and by maintaining a stress free lifestyle.

in any other form Prepare yourself for any impending test. It is also important not to be reckless with money.

All Saints Day Many blessings are with you and your family. You are also entering a very lucky seven day cycle.

All Soul's Day You will leave a creation as a legacy that will serve all mankind. As a result, you will become very well known for this. Expect this to begin developing within three weeks. Many blessings are with you and you are headed for a brilliant future.

allspice The next week will bring you much luck. Be sure to handle a special request with care and you will be able to successfully deal with it.

all star Set yourself on the path toward a higher education by using any means you can. Once you take this path, your life will undergo dramatic changes for a long time to come.

alma mater Do not allow events from the past to ruin the present, especially for the next three days.

almanac This dream is lucky for you. You will describe a goal to an acquaintance and through this person's enthusiasm, you will find a financial backer.

almighty Stolen or lost property will be recovered.

almond You will be celebrating the fact that a loved one has surrendered to a commitment.

alms This dream is connected with sorrow and pain. You will need an attorney to claim a rightfully owned inheritance.

alms house An inebriated friend will create a scene within two days. Do whatever you can to motivate this person to seek professional help.

Aloe vera An older, wealthy, and beautiful woman will come into your life and brighten your horizons.

aloha Within the week, someone who feels a deep gratitude to you for being there in a time of need will express their feelings of thankfulness. You will be overcome with emotion over this person's words of gratitude.

alone *to be alone or to sense aloneness in someone else* Avoid water related accidents.

aloof *to experience aloofness in yourself or others* Your behavior will cause you to lose the respect of friends.

alpaca Your bad treatment of others will slowly disappear. This will mark the end of all past hassles and trials and will mark the beginning of a new life and unexplored avenues. Experience this change with a flair of glamour.

alphabet You will need to find intimate times with someone special. Build up your immune system and that of your family with a healthier intake of food.

alphabet soup Do not waste time when coming to a major decision, especially for the next five days. You will be glad that you did.

alps Make sure you have enough money to cover all expenses for the next two days in order to avoid embarrassment.

altar *to see altars* You will be able to think clearly and arrive at the successful conclusion to a problem.
to see an altar and receive communion You will soon learn of the birth of twins.

altar bar Someone who is special to you will be unfaithful.

altar boy Approach others with confidence in order to work on a solution to a stressful situation. The solution will be satisfying for everyone involved.

altar girl Do not commit yourself to seeing anything through to the end, for the next three days. This would be a big mistake. You will be unable to complete it during this cycle.

alternator You will become involved with someone whom you would normally never consider. Deep affection will quickly develop between both of you. If you choose to pursue this, the outcome will be wonderful. This will be a very good cycle for you.

aluminum Within three days, you will hear the words you have been waiting to hear from someone special to you.

Alzheimer's disease After a break up with your beloved, a reconciliation will immediately occur.

amaryllis You will express greater love for yourself. A business deal will also cause you to lose some money within two days. Back off from this deal.

Amazon You will meet a deceitful and wicked person within two days. This person does not appear to be dangerous but has psychopathological tendencies. This dream may also be used as a reference point in time. If you dream of this river and see its name used in any context, the dream message will occur on this day.

ambassador Someone will confide in you that they lack the finances to meet family needs. This person will recover quickly from financial problems.

amber Keep your relationship trouble free. Do not look for reasons to cause trouble within the union, especially for the next two days. This dream is a very lucky omen. You will enjoy health and financial security. Do not allow small problems to rob you of all your enthusiasm for life. You must also make an attempt to get out and enjoy nature. Take a walk in the country, enjoy fresh air and beauty. Live life to the fullest and you will be richer in a spiritual sense.

ambidextrous You will be mentally sound and will enjoy physical health. Your psychic abilities will be enhanced and you will be enlightened to new facts. This will begin to take place immediately.

ambrosia *(Greek & Roman mythology)* You will elope if this is your desire.

ambulance You will be in the company of someone today who will, at every opportunity, become argumentative, and create problems over trivial issues.

with flashing lights You will need to be very overprotective of yourself for the next few days. Avoid injury to the body, drug overdose, a toxic atmosphere, and food poisonings. Keep your eyes open for any potential freak accidents.

if you recognize someone in the dream This is the person who will need emergency assistance within a few days. Do this person a service by alerting them to the danger of an accident prone cycle.

if you do not recognize someone in this dream You will give emergency assistance to someone within a few days. This will require a heroic action on your part. You must also make sure you prepare yourself so that you will have the money to cover any expenses that may occur over the next month.

to drive an ambulance You are unknowingly allowing a troublesome situation to develop that needs to be aggressively attended to. Discipline and structure yourself in order to grasp each situation before it disperses to the point of chaos. Once it reaches this point you will lose the ability to begin again. Push yourself now in order to resolve each issue and do not allow yourself to get bogged down with extraneous matters that are out of your control. Also make sure that you do not allow yourself to be the major cause of problems. Focus on the aspect of your behavior that leads to this and do nothing that will cause problems with the law.

ambush Someone will offer assistance to you but after realizing that they are involved too deeply, this person will make an impossible demand of you in order to forcefully back away from the problem without losing face. Therefore do not involve someone in a personal issue without leaving an escape hatch for them.

amen You will receive a positive answer to a seemingly impossible request.

America *any form* You will receive the love you request. Within two days you will enjoy physical and emotional pleasure. This dream may also be used as a reference point in time. If you dream of this country and see its name used in any context, the dream message will occur on this day.

American cheese An invitation that you make to someone will be accepted and this individual will quickly fall in love with you. If you choose, this is the right cycle to make a romantic overture. You will also enjoy an abundance of health and prosperity. You are on the path for a brilliant future.

American Indian This dream represents luck for you. It is also a reminder that you have committed yourself to two concurrent events. One of these commitments is far more important and crucial to you. Attend to this as soon as possible.

American Sign Language Think carefully prior to signing an agreement committing yourself to anything. Be very aware of your fluid, food and medicine intake. Be very aware of your health and take steps to protect yourself during this cycle. You will also regret overindulging at a celebration. Be aware of this for the next three days. Make sure also that you deal only with facts, and do not allow your imagination to make any situation more or less than it really is. This dream is a very lucky omen.

amethyst For the next seven days you will possess an overwhelming sense of being solidly grounded, balanced and confident. As a result of this, you will be able to handle those situations that need this aspect of your personality. Work on those areas of your life that you choose to make changes in. You will have victory in all areas. You will also experience a new freedom within two days due to an unusual occurrence that will help you get beyond a certain situation that has limited your potential in some respects. This issue has led you to feelings of discouragement and despair in the past. You will find the courage, motivation and energy to remove whatever is limiting you. You are headed for a brilliant future. Many blessings are with you and your family.

amino acid Do not allow yourself to become a referee between two angry people. If you do, you will be physically and verbally abused by both people. The moment you sense this developing, make sure that you leave the area. Expect this to occur within three days.

Amish An agreement with another person has been reached but the financial aspects have yet to be settled. It is important to fix a solid dollar amount in your mind and stay as close to that amount as possible.

ammonia For the next few days watch your speed while driving.

ammunition You will be suspicious of some people who are close to you. Follow your instincts because these people are deceitful. This is especially important for the next three days.

amnesia *to know someone who suffers from amnesia* You will rapidly gain wealth with a friend's help. You will also receive a cold shoulder from a friend within two days and later realize they are your enemy.

amnesty *grant amnesty* Steer clear of someone you know with deep emotional problems or your life will be miserable.

amoebae You are headed in the wrong direction. Slow down and focus on what you are doing. This implies also, that someone has devised a plot to lure you into a secluded area for the sole purpose of committing bodily harm. Be very cautious for the next three days, and take steps to avoid this situation at all costs.

amorous *to feel* Your love life will be very successful.

Amos *(from the Bible)* You will feel the loss of love from someone you care about. The love is there but stress and anxiety will prevent it from being demonstrated. Show patience and support toward this person for the next two days.

amphibian Someone is plotting your death. Within a few days this person will become known to you and it will be someone you least expect. Do not allow your suspicions to become known, but do protect yourself and leave the area.

amphitheater Think carefully and prepare yourself. Within four days you will have a conversation with someone who is involved with you on a certain issue. This planning will allow you the time to gather all those involved to make plans on how to put a lid on this issue in order to prevent a negative event from taking place. Alert everyone involved. Many blessings will come to you and your family.

ampicillin Within three days, you will find someone who is willing to support you financially. This will be almost as though they wish to adopt you. If you desire this, take steps to actively seek it out. This offer will come with no strings attached and will make many of your dreams a reality.

amplifier Do not offer assistance so readily and do not allow yourself to be taken advantage of. Be especially careful of this for the next seven days.

amputate *any form* Do not allow circumstances to stand in the way of your goals.

Amtrak Stay in control, avoid anger and do not allow yourself to become someone else's emotional yo-yo.

amusement park Find a peaceful spot to release stress. Within two days you will have a delightful invitation from a wonderful person whom you have always admired. You will have an awesome time.

anaconda Take steps to prevent water damage to your property for the next few days.

anal *any reference* You will soon marry the person of your dreams.

analgesic Pay close attention to any situation that comes up within the next two days. This situation will throw you off track but you will somehow feel you are on the right path. Take the time now to revise your plans in order to point yourself in the right direction. It is important that you do this within five days.

analyst You are creating pain for someone who is special to you for your own amusement. Seek counseling immediately.

anarchist During the next two days, a violent, hostile takeover of a building or mall will take place. Be careful of your surroundings in order to avoid involvement or injury.

anatomy *any form* Keep your affairs private.

ancestor Be cautious with explosives and fire this week.

anchor Jealousy between couples will occur within two days unless schedules are organized and time is accounted for. Spend quality time with that special person. This is also a lucky omen.

anchor person For the next five days you will have luck doing things on your own. Follow your own counsel.

anchovy An old relationship will be renewed.

Andes You will spend your life with a free spending socializer. You will enjoy this immensely. This dream may also be used as a reference point in time. If you dream of this mountain range and see its name used in any context, the dream message will occur on this day.

andiron Your partner will organize finances with you in the manner you choose.

Andrew *(from the Bible)* A relentless secret admirer will abruptly stop the pursuit. Your own interest will now become apparent to this person. Have no fear, the admirer is still interested in you.

Androcles *(Roman mythology)* An urgent debt will be unexpectedly paid, just in time.

android You will receive the guarantee you need concerning a new business deal.

anemia *any form* You will hire a new assistant to ease your workload and will be pleased with the outcome.

anemone You will arrive at a plan to stabilize your financial security.

anesthesia An opposite sexed person from the past will reenter your life within three days. You will find a renewed interest and attraction for this person and you will both enjoy each other's company.

angel When you dream of an angel there is reason for rejoicing because they appear to give you important information that you need. There are several reasons why an angel will appear in a dream. One is to warn you that a trap is being laid for you without your knowledge and that someone intends to inflict harm on you in either an emotional or physical way. This damage will affect your life deeply. Another reason an angel may appear is to alert you that you may be misdiagnosed for a particular illness, scheduled for an unnecessary operation, or be given a medication that is not needed. You must be careful to avoid overmedication in any form. Angels also appear to warn you to anticipate unexpected accidents and unforeseeable circumstances in your life. This could be anything that could cause you to be impaired in some way or cause your death. There is something you need to be acutely aware of so you can be alert enough to avoid it. You may also be in danger of becoming involved in something that could throw you completely off track. It would then be impossible to achieve your goals. Be aware also that you may be unwittingly doing something that will steer someone else off track. You will need to be aware of this in order to bring this person back on the right path. You are being told to be the person to inspire someone to head in the right direction. This cycle involves the three day period commencing from the time you have this dream. You will experience an excitement for a long time to come as a result of this dream, and you will be able to successfully tackle each major issue in your life. You are on the path toward a brilliant future. For greater definition to this dream, look up St. Michael.

to see a baby angel You must give moral support to a young child and will need the assistance of an agency to ensure the well being of this child (i.e., motivate yourself to develop a deep interest in this child and actively seek out healthy recreational activities for them, etc.).

yourself as an angel Watch your prescription medications. Avoid taking the wrong medication or taking medications incorrectly. For the next two days do whatever is necessary to protect your health.

death angel This dream is a very lucky omen. Do not take life for granted, or live it as though it is a rehearsal for something else. Take steps to enjoy life to the fullest. Within three days you will have the occasion to demonstrate your love for those you are close to. Many blessings will come to you and your family for a long period of time.

angel dust Make sure that your involvements do not pose a risk for you.

angelfish You will have no difficulty processing paperwork through an agency in order to further your plans.

angel food cake Tutors are needed in order to be successful in school.

anger *to see yourself angry* Within two days you will be of assistance to someone in a depressed state and you will be rewarded for your kindness.

someone is angry at you Do not set yourself up for disappointment by listening to a habitual liar.

anger in another form A mail order will be unsatisfactory upon delivery. Choose an alternative method of purchase.

angina Do what you can to avoid involvement with an unreliable person. This individual is very lax and comes and goes at will. In spite of their reassurances of promptness, this person never arrives when they are expected. Avoid dealing with any new person for the next three days.

angle What you set into motion within a few days will be successful only if you are relentless and consistent in your efforts.

angler fish A special situation involving finance and love will occur between you and someone else. If you choose to pursue this, you will not only benefit financially but will find deep permanent love. Do not allow this to slip through your fingers. Good luck is with you.

Anglican *to dream of this church in any form.* The babysitter you hired may not be the best one for your child.

Anglo Saxon Within three days, someone will be very eager to grant your desires. Use this cycle to ask for what you need and your wishes will be granted.

angora You are being misled by a romantic interest. This person is fickle and deceitful.

anguish *any form* Avoid dropping something on your foot. This will result in a severe injury.

animal *a variety of animals together* A plan you are implementing will leave a mark on this world.

a group of animals eating You will receive a call from an acquaintance. They will shame you and blame you for a fault they committed in order to save face.

animal with aggressive attacking behavior in any form. You are involved with someone who is gun shy about commitment. Be patient. If, within the next three days, you begin to make demands that this person be more committed, demonstrative, and giving, you will drive this person away. You will regret this action.

an attempted bite You are wanted sexually.

to be chased by an animal Your atmosphere may be toxic for the next few days. Take steps to protect yourself.

to chase an animal Reassess your priorities.

a deceased pet This dream is a lucky omen for you and all those who are interested and involved in your immediate situation. You are in a powerful seven day cycle for achievement and for accomplishing everything you attempt. You will also develop more integrity. People in your life will demonstrate greater love and affection toward you. Do nothing to slow down the momentum of those feelings toward you. Everything in your life will flow more smoothly and you will be blessed with better health and more tranquility.

dead Keep a close watch on the safety of pets. Make sure also that you do not allow curiosity to take control against your better judgment, and make sure you do not jump into the unknown. You are walking a thin line between simple curiosity and becoming actively involved in something you have no business being involved in. Stay out of this situation. You are being misled by others who desire your participation. You have prior notice of this and can avoid all negative involvements, especially for the next three days.

if you recognize the dead animal Do what you can during this time period to prevent this animal's untimely death.

animal decapitated Think carefully about an invitation you have received. The person issuing the invitation expects more than you are willing to give. A tactful conversation will put an end to this expectation.

to see an animal bleeding/injured A cluster of events will occur one after the other with each bringing you a tremendous amount of joy, wonder and awe because things are happening so quickly. You will also possess a powerful energy that you are going to be able to direct and control. At the same time that these other events are taking place you will be able to bring other people under your complete control. Because you have prior notice of this you will be able, within the week, to direct this energy in such a way to successfully complete anything you wish in a superb way. If you give assistance to the animal in the dream, you will be assisting someone close to you in some capacity. You will be able to overcome any difficult obstacle and it will now be very simple to deal with it. Your intuition will be right on target and follow your hunches about a new relationship. Many blessings are with you and your family.

pregnant animal Read between the lines to determine what is not being said.

to feed animals Make sure you do not become too

friendly with someone who pretends to be your friend but, in reality, will stab you in the back. Within two days you will be able to determine who this person is. Take steps to discourage this friendship and go on with your life.

to hunt It will be demanded that you handle a distasteful family situation. Handle it quickly.

large animal Within three days, you will begin a cycle that will bring you financial security. Expect grandness. Whatever you see larger than life in a dream, is something you need to focus on in reality. If it is negative, take steps to alter the outcome. If it is positive, promote it to the fullest. You will also become very clear in the manner in which you can help someone who greatly desires you. You will gain the knowledge of what to do in order to make this person comfortable enough to express their future needs and plans. This cycle will allow you clarity of thought and the ability to bring ideas into reality, including the ability to tackle big ideas and projects. This dream is a good luck symbol.

an animal in mud in any form You will soon have to replace old equipment with new. Since you know this ahead of time, start putting money aside now to make these purchases easier on your budget.

any animal hissing A big celebration will occur within the week that will result in rejoicing for everyone involved. For the next three weeks you will enjoy an abundance of health, tranquility and spiritual healing. This dream is also a promise that you are destined to bring an idea, project or plan to completion during the last half of March and for the entire month of April. This project will reach a grander scale than you ever hoped and will take on a life of its own that will easily allow you to go through each channel needed to complete this process. This blessing will be a cause for a big celebration for everyone involved. You are on the path toward a brilliant future. For the next six weeks, make sure that any negative event portrayed in this dream is avoided or altered in reality, and warn anyone else involved to do the same. Pay attention to what is being hissed at and this will offer you a clue to other meanings to this dream.

animus You will fall in love with another person's physical beauty. The feeling will be reciprocated.

anise Beautify your physical appearance.

ankle A person of the opposite sex will feign affection and love while giving subtle mixed messages of an impending break-up. This person will also badmouth you to others while pretending to be nice in order to avoid hurting you. This individual is treacherous and is a master of inducing others to fall neurotically in love with them in order to achieve an emotional high. Do not pursue this person, follow, or harass in any way because the final move will be a restraining order against you. This will further humiliate you and enhance the other person's ego.

anklet You will buy something on term conditions or layaway. This object will more than triple in value over the long run.

to see someone else wearing an anklet Timely knowledge gained from another will be accurate.

anniversary You and your loved one will enjoy yourselves for the next few days. This will be similar to a second honeymoon.

announcement *someone making an announcement* Keep all information of your relationships to yourself.

announcer When you relocate choose an alternative mover because those you hired will be unable to complete the job.

annulment A renter will promise funds for an extended stay. Do not count on this person staying for the agreed upon time span.

anonymity Love yourself and stop taking health risks.

anorexia *any form* Keep your opinions of another person to yourself otherwise this person will hear of them from someone else and become angry. This situation will backfire. Prevent this from occurring.

answer If you receive an answer to a question in a dream, this implies that you will soon become financially secure.

ant Expect a pleasant surprise. You will also realize your ambitions about writing a book. You will find a reputable publishing house that will publish your book. Within a five day period you will also be given a gift of greater healing and richer psychic powers by the gods. You will then be able to develop greater organizational skills to use your talents in a dynamic way. This gift will be wisely used by you. Many blessings will be with you for a lifetime and you are on the path toward a brilliant future.

red ant You will soon come to grips with an important career matter. Carefully scrutinize the plans you hope to execute in order to determine their workability and to decide whether you choose to put them into action. This dream is a very lucky omen and each plan will work out exactly as you wish once you have taken the time to review them.

to see yourself or anyone else bitten by a red ant This dream is an omen of victory. You will enjoy great clarity of thought and this will lead you to riches. You will also enjoy a romantic interlude if this is something you choose. Any negative event seen in this dream may be altered or avoided in reality.

anthill Apply more diligence to your work for quicker results.

antacid Stop being so impulsive.

Antarctic You will experience mental inventiveness for the next few days. Record your ideas on paper. This dream may also be used as a reference point in time. If you dream of this country and see its name used in any context, the dream message will occur on this day.

anteater You will be adored and loved in a physical way and will enjoy each moment. You will also gain access to some very privileged information within three days. Explore ways in which you can utilize this information.

antelope A project you are presently working on will give you stability for the remainder of your life.

antenna Receive another person's point of view and opinions. Do not share them with anyone, simply listen and stay out of trouble. Do not spread another's ideas around.

anthill Apply more diligence to your work for quicker results.

Anthony *(a saint)* An old unhealed injury will remarkably be cured. This applies to old festering emotional wounds as well.

anthrax For the next two days, control your moods and do not allow them to destroy an ongoing situation. This situation will never get the chance to develop if you continue your present behavior. Allow it to develop in the manner in which it was intended.

anthropologist You will receive emotional fulfillment from that special person.

antiaircraft Devise a means to bring in extra income as soon as you possibly can because you will need a greater cash flow within three weeks. Good luck is with you for this time period.

antibiotic Prevent the destruction of a functional love relationship by not becoming over demanding.

Antichrist Protect your property from fire.

anticipation You will experience happiness because of family tranquility.

antidepressant Become aware of someone who is very conniving and evil minded. This person will be someone you least expect and they will do everything in their power to cause you emotional harm. Do not place yourself in a situation that will leave you open to be taken advantage of. Become overprotective of yourself and your belongings for the next five days.

antidote Add more water to your diet.

antifreeze Slow down, you are moving too fast and are heading in the wrong direction. A love relationship will become too overwhelming to another person. Back off and look at alternative behaviors.

antihistamine If you are considering committing a murder, get professional help.

antipasto You will attend a wedding within a few weeks and have a wonderful time.

antique *collectibles in any form* You will be able to hold your own in a debate and persuade another to your point of view.

antique clothes Play a very active part in satisfying those emotional feelings you have. Make sure you provide yourself with what you want on an emotional level. Within five days, you will be able to visualize the path you need to take for a brilliant future. Good luck is with you.

antique shop It is an extremely lucky omen to dream of an antique shop in any form. Pay attention to the events in this dream and you may be led to an item you desire. Consider the possibility of adding this item to your possessions in the future. This dream is bringing to your attention the fact that there is something on display in this shop that you will be dealing with, in some context, within the week. Take every necessary step to avoid repeating any negative event that occurred in this dream, and explore the possibility of bringing all positive aspects of this dream to full bloom. You will be amazed at the level of strength and confidence you will develop during this time period when dealing with a personal situation. Somehow, your communication skills will develop to the point where your words will flow and leave others with a sense of well being, as a result of your ability to interact with those you need to treat in a special way. You are headed for a prosperous future.

antiquity Within two weeks, you will be presented with many opportunities that you can focus on in order to bring about an improved standard of living. Within this time frame you will also need to be very focused. Analyze the moves you are about to make especially regarding those personal issues that need your immediate attention. Your involvement will bring prosperity to your life. This dream may also be pointing out certain items you may be involved with, within this two week period or that you may consider purchasing for yourself.

antiseptic Keep all of your desires for love from your admired for the next few days. Keep this secret to yourself, until a relationship has begun.

antisocial *any form* At the next social event that you attend, be careful not to ruin your clothes with a spill.

antitoxin Step back and review your options before you agree to anything. You are feeling too unsure of yourself now to make a rational decision without reviewing all of your options.
anus A wealthy person will fall in love with you. This will be a successful union.

anvil Within a few months you will become responsible for the education of a young child.

anxiety An admirer of yours desires to see you and needs affection from you. Make a point to see this person within two days.

anxious *to be anxious to complete something* Be prepared for something remarkable and peculiar to take place within three days. At the time this is occurring, you will have the clarity of thought you need to take you through the steps to get through this cycle comfortably. Your curiosity will be at a peak during this time frame. Discipline yourself and be very firm so you do not let your curiosity get the better of you. You will also enjoy an abundance of health during this cycle.

aorta All surgical procedures will have successful results.

Apache You will experience more financial security from now on.

apartheid You will purchase a new automobile. The funds to purchase it will come as a gift from a relative.

apartment You will desire to renew, remake and beautify your surroundings as well as yourself.
    to help someone find an apartment Help a young person by being a good listener.
    to look for an apartment This dream is an extremely lucky cycle. Anything you once felt was impossible is now possible. This is the perfect time to reinvolve yourself in a specific plan that, at one time, was going nowhere. You will achieve amazing results. Any negative event you see in this dream can be altered. Forewarn anyone you recognize to take steps to prevent this occurrence in reality. This is especially important for the next three days.

apathy Watch out for a dangerous fall in a seemingly safe area for a two day period.

ape Do not be talked into a family reunion at your place, a fight will break out. Stay away from all reunions for now.

aphid Do not spread yourself so thin emotionally as a result of a love relationship, especially for the next two days.

aphrodisiac You will become mesmerized by someone of the opposite sex within three days. All of your desires will be fulfilled.

Aphrodite *(Greek mythology)* All problem areas in a relationship will vanish and you will enjoy domestic tranquility. Prosperity and financial security will be yours. You are entering a great cycle for accomplishing almost anything you desire, especially those things you originally felt were not possible. Expect this to take place within five days. Any negative event portended in this dream needs to be avoided.

Take steps to experience only positive expressions in your life.

apiary Refuse to accept defeat. Boldness leads to success.

apocalypse Keep your secrets to yourself.

Apollo *(Greek and Roman mythology)* A family member will lose money on a trip. Warn this person. The trip will be otherwise safe and successful. Any request you make for the next three days will be granted. This dream is an extremely lucky omen.

apology *to apologize to someone* Search for moral support and a goal for your life.
    to be apologized to You will be given financial assistance from afar.

apostle Tension will heighten between you and someone special to you. You must also make a point of not hurting the feelings of a friend or partner.

apostrophe Pay attention to your appearance. You are being closely watched for the next seven days and your appearance will create an impression.

apothecary You will be introduced to a group of powerful people through an influential person. This will result in social rewards and alliances.

Appalachian Mountains Your desires for love will be fulfilled within three days. This dream may also be used as a reference point in time. If you dream of this mountain range and see its name used in any context, the dream message will occur on this day.

appaloosa Be careful of any statue or porcelain object you own. Carelessness will result in breakage.

apparition Be extra careful for a few nights. You may encounter an intruder in your place of residence or a peeping Tom. Don't stay alone.

appeal *to make an appeal* Reread a contract you are preparing to sign. Agreeing to it will be an unwise move.
    to be appealed to Check the safety of your transportation. Make repairs, if needed.

appearances *if you have a messy appearance* You will lose out financially. Be careful.
    if your appearance is good You will travel to an unusual destination but the return will be safe.

appendicitis *to experience* Take precautions in high places for the next two days. A fall would be deadly.
    someone else experiences appendicitis You are considering relocation. Rethink this move.

appetite *to have an appetite* You will enrich the world through a new line of research or a new project.

appetizer Stress the feelings you are having toward that special person within two days. Speak up for your sexual rights.

applause You and someone special to you will develop new and interesting ways to make money within three days.

apple *green apple* Your life will be enhanced by another for the next few days. You will share mad money.
    yellow apple Someone is attempting to deceive you and lead you down the wrong path.
    red apple You will be promised undying love. This promise will be kept.
    in any other form Stop overextending yourself at work and show greater affection toward that special person.

applecart Within five days, you will gain emotional fulfillment because you will grasp your highest ambitions. Many blessings will come to you and your family.

apple cobbler You have the ability to transfer real estate into a real profit. This is the right time for this.

apple pie For the next three days you will be immersed in the feelings of love and the proof of genuine love from another will soon be revealed to you. This person will be a part of your life for a long time to come.

appliance Avoid traffic violations for a few days.

application You will experience emotional and physical fulfillment with a new love relationship within the week.

appliqué You will find success with a contract you are preparing to sign.

appointment Within three days you will learn that a situation has been resolved in your favor.

appreciation *to be appreciated* Make sure your transportation system is in working order so you will not be forced to take advantage of a special person.

apprehension *to have* Medical assistance will be required following an emotional upset concerning a family member. Try to ease this situation if you are present.

apprentice Faulty wiring will cause an appliance to catch on fire. Check all appliances and machinery, etc., for the next two days.

approval *to gain* Reward your sweetheart with a gift.
    to give A good friend will try to start an argument. At the first sign of this, back off.

apricot *any form* You will marry soon and experience tranquility if you choose to accept this option. This dream also implies that you will enjoy an abundance of money and health within seven days.

April You will soon be free of a long standing burden related to the illness of another. After this burden is lifted do not allow yourself to take on another burden. Take care of your needs.

April Fools Day Work quickly for the next two days to improve all those situations that require immediate attention. Use this cycle to improve each situation for the better.

apron An anticipated lease renewal will not come through. Make alternate plans for living quarters immediately.

apron string For the next two days, it would be a bad idea to invest too heavily in the advice of others.

aquamarine Within two days you will be given the gift of mental inventiveness and clarity by the gods. Put this gift to use and you will see an immediate improvement in your circumstances. Your sexual drive will improve and you will gain strength and the ability to rejuvenate certain vital organs *(i.e. liver, kidneys, spleen, heart)*. You will prosper in each area of your life for the upcoming month. Drink plenty of water and eat healthful foods.

aquarium Do not become anxious about changes within the relationship. Face them head on. Take steps to ensure a healthy blood pressure rating for yourself and your loved ones.

Aquarius A good friend who was born under the sign of Aquarius will be ready to assist you financially. Between January 20th and February 18, a long awaited event will occur and will be celebrated. You will experience physical and financial abundance. Unusually good changes in family and love relationships will occur. You will be very surprised that someone special to you (a spouse, boyfriend, etc.) will, without any prompting from you or anyone else, take greater responsibility in keeping the union together and will become more responsible regarding financial matters. This person will also grant you respect and love with genuine sincerity. Those people you are reaching out to, who can help you to reach your goals successfully, will assist in such a way that everything will fall into place perfectly. This cycle will bring you a tremendous amount of luck. Go for what you want most from life and you will soon be harvesting a very strong, very secure financial foundation. You will meet many new people who will bring you immense joy once you move into this new dimension of your life. Good luck is with you.

Arab Release painful emotional feelings. You need to be clear of these because you will soon meet someone whom you need in your life.

Arabian Nights *any form* Someone special to you will request several passionate nights from you. Be prepared.

arachnid *to see many spiders crawling around* Anxieties experienced in a relationship are the result of possessiveness and jealousy by both partners. Let these anxieties go in order to enjoy a fulfilled union.

Arbor Day Prior to engaging in a sexual liaison, someone will promise you undying love. Afterwards, this person will disappear and reappear from time to time for the sole purpose of sexual gratification. If you want a deeper commitment, avoid involvement with this person. You will be very vulnerable to this for the next three days.

arboretum Have patience with another person who lacks the expertise you have. In time, this will work out.

arc Express your feelings to that person who is important to you.

arcade This dream is a lucky omen. Gamble with your lucky numbers for success.

arch Make sure you appreciate the efforts of your loved ones. Take steps to do something special to demonstrate your appreciation, especially for the next three days.

archangel A long time stressful situation will be eased with the discovery of a successful solution. This will occur within two days.

archbishop You will express yourself accurately during a court appearance. This will result in victory.

archer This dream is a very lucky omen. You will become acutely aware of the issues in your life that require immediate attention. This cycle demands that you be very specific about your needs. You will find that you are very well loved by others.

architect You will choose the correct piece of property to buy from many that are offered to you.

Arctic Avoid an argumentative person. This dream may also be used as a reference point in time. If you dream of this place and see its name used in any context, the dream message will occur on this day.

Arctic Ocean The menu chosen for an upcoming event will not be healthy for each guest. Revise. This dream may also be used as a reference point in time. If you dream of this ocean and see its name used in any context, the dream message will occur on this day.

area code Use the numbers you dreamed about in any manner, they are lucky for you. The numbers seen will also be close to the price given for an object of desire. While bargaining keep close to the figures you dreamed about.

arena A deceitful person is plotting your murder. Take aggressive, protective measures. Do this immediately.

Argentina You will receive a gift of emeralds. This dream may also be used as a reference point in time. If you dream of this country and see its name used in any context, the dream message will occur on this day.

Argonaut *(Greek mythology)* Pawn shops or brokers will yield lucky finds for the next few weeks. You are loved beyond your imagination and you will receive verification of this soon.

argument You will be under pressure for a few days due to an excessive work load. You will see yourself clear of this and will be able to withstand this while it is occurring.

to argue You will receive a small valuable gift within seven days from someone who cares deeply for you.

argumentative person *to dream of dealing with one* Be very cautious about where you are allowing someone to lead you emotionally. Although the words of love may not be used at this time, this person will mislead you into believing they care deeply for you for reasons known only to them. You will be treated to romantic outings and will be given gifts and flowers, etc. As a result, your feelings will grow deeply for this person, but if you allow lovemaking to take place you will not connect on a deep level. This person will try very hard, but you will not be kissed or touched in any way that implies that you are loved. Do not put yourself through this emotional upheaval. Get on with your life without this person, because they have a hidden agenda that involves you doing something for them that only they are aware of. This situation will only bring you unhappiness. Otherwise, you are on the path toward a prosperous future that will begin within the week.

argyle Do whatever you can to avoid creating feelings of suspicion and jealousy from others because of the way you conduct yourself. This will backfire within two days.

aria Do not injure the feelings of someone special to you. Be especially wary of this for the next two days.

Aries This dream is a perfect example of the spirit trying to connect with the personality via this dream. The purpose of this is to relieve some of the anxieties connected with certain issues you are feeling some concern about. You are probably already beginning to see some of these changes and feeling a need to clarify and be certain of some of the processes that will occur over the next few months. Your progress on a particular project has already begun a rapid thrust forward. As a result, you will definitely find acceptance with a certain agency, organization, firm, etc., and you will be placed in the position you are looking forward to most in life. A big movement is being made in this direction and you will need

to jump on this opportunity. You will be deeply motivated to pursue this, and this motivation will stay with you for the next two months. You will also develop great clarity about the new dimension you are pointing yourself toward. This will bring you tranquility and pleasures beyond belief. In the past you have felt it was beyond your ability to move in the direction you chose, but now that you have this confidence in your abilities, you will move quickly and achieve what you are after. In other areas of your life, you are becoming very organized and eager to unclutter your surroundings and your life. You are looking forward to opening up your living quarters and developing an office area. You have a strong desire to have your surroundings become cleaner, more organized and orderly. You are visualizing things from a different perspective and deciding the best place to display your talents in order to make the changes you desire. Because of the fulfillments of your goals, and acceptance into the career you want, it will be evident to you that, in spite of anything else that is going on in your life, you will look at other areas of your life from a different perspective. You will be very surprised that someone special to you will take greater responsibility in keeping the union together and will become more responsible regarding unusual matters, will grant open respect and love with genuine sincerity. Within six months, you, your children, family members, or others who are close to you will also develop a new sense of spirituality, whether through baptism, a choice of religious affiliation, religious training (catechism), etc. You will be looking for a spiritual cleansing in more ways than one. You may also be eager to give up harmful personal habits such as smoking, drinking or poor eating habits. You will also feel a need to show some tangible evidence of this new sense of spirituality such as lighting candles, prayer, attending services, or worship in your own way. Go for what you want most from life and you will have secure financial foundation. Good luck is with you.

aristocrat You are involved in a relationship with someone who, because of past hurts, is unable to express emotions. You may feel rejected and unloved as a result of this. If you choose, this is the perfect cycle to move on with your life. You will be emotionally equipped to handle this with few, if any, negative repercussions.

Aristotle *(Greek history)* Beware of your attitude in a relationship. It may create distance between you and that special person because of their feelings of rejection. Be watchful of this for the next two days.

arithmetic Use the numbers to play any numbers game; they will be lucky for you. You may also need to speak to a counselor about your childhood in order to heal yourself emotionally.

Arizona You will get a job requiring travel. You will enjoy this for many years if you choose to go in this direction. This dream may also be used as a reference point in time. If you dream of this state and see its name used in any context, the dream message will occur on this day.

ark Become involved in a new organization and familiarize yourself with their functions. You will be exposed to many new opportunities.

Arkansas You will be very excited about a new product that will enter the market in about three weeks that will assist you greatly on the project you are now working on. This will allow you to achieve your goal in a much more efficient manner. This dream may also be used as a reference point in time. If you dream of this state and see its name used in any context, the dream message will occur on this day.

Ark of the Covenant Someone possessing skills you lack will be able to assist on a project.

Arlington Be cautious about feeling overly friendly to a neighbor. This dream may also be used as a reference point in time. If you dream of this city and see its name used in any context, the dream message will occur on this day.

arm *amputated arm* An acquaintance of yours has become free with money. Attempt to stop this behavior in yourself and steer clear of this person. Any negative event you dream about concerning an amputated arm needs to be prevented in reality. If you recognize someone from this dream who shares the same negative omen, take steps to warn this individual of the dream so they can take the necessary precautions.

hairy arms Do not make a bigger commitment to any business relationship than you intend, especially for the next three days. Also, protect your luxury items from theft.

arms with unusual markings (i.e., tattoos, burn marks, scar, etc.) For the next two days you will be extremely lucky in matters pertaining to love and entertainment. Someone will surprise you by requesting that you spend time with them. You have long desired to be with this person. If you wish, you will have many mutually fulfilling moments and will be able to bring this relationship to the level you desire. If this arm has a tattoo, look up the symbol for a deeper meaning to this dream. Proceed with confidence.

arm injury Use body language in order to convey love in a relationship in order to make your partner feel secure.

an arm placed around your shoulder Be watchful for the safety of children in order to prevent a kidnapping, especially for the next three days.

to place your arm around another shoulder You will receive some signed papers that you have waited for, for some time.

broken arm Take steps to avoid the deep depression that will come about due to the kidnapping of a child. For the next three days be acutely aware of the child's whereabouts to prevent this. It would be a good idea to practice child safety until your child is grown.

underarms You will soon be attending an event. Everyone is looking forward to seeing you but think carefully about who you will be taking. This person's attitude will be

very offensive to many people and will cause eyebrows to be raised. Do not try to fit someone into surroundings where they do not belong. Think about this ahead of time so that you can handle this properly.

armadillo You are dealing with an irrational, hot tempered individual. Following a disagreement, you will have the impression that all is well. Be careful, this person has the potential for going off half cocked and may return to kill you. Avoid all initial disagreements and find immediate refuge.

Armageddon *any reference* You need to meditate in your favorite form.

armchair You will be led into believing another wants a solid relationship with you. Once you decide to commit, the other individual will back off and quickly leave the relationship. Get on with your life, this person will not be fully committed and will be uneasy with close relationships. If possible, do not even involve yourself, you will be left at the most vulnerable time.

armoire Do not look at anyone in a threatening or intimidating manner. This will backfire.

armor You have an in-house administration problem. You will need legal representation in order to receive promised wages. This can be avoided by putting all agreements in written form.

armored car Be cautious and do not become too friendly with a married neighbor.

armory Do not take the law into your own hands. Handle each situation legally and in the proper manner, especially for the next three days.

armpit Be watchful of animals and be careful not to run over someone's pet.

armrest For the next few weeks protect your property from a squatter.

arm wrestling You may be juggling two jobs and after a time will find you have overextended yourself. Do not allow the second job to interfere with your ability to handle the primary position. Be sure that you can handle both before you take on that second job.

army Within a few weeks, you will encounter someone eager to put you down. This will occur at a travel destination. Watch out for this.

aroma Pay closer attention to children in order to better meet their needs.

arousal *any form* Someone is losing sleep over a relationship with you. This person feels as though it is ending and is attempting to keep it alive. You are deeply loved. If you want this relationship, take steps to keep it alive.

arrest *any form* Take preventive measures with your health. Watch your intake of food and be careful not to over-indulge in anything that will be harmful to your body. Take care of yourself.

arrival *late arrival* Avoid losing an important item. This lost item will be quickly recovered by another person who will arrive at your place without notice. Also, someone lacks the courage to tell you of their loss of romantic interest in you. Get on with your life. This person is incapable of commitment.

arrow Do not allow yourself to be pushed around emotionally for the next two days by someone who takes your generosity for granted.

arrowhead Do not put yourself in any position to incur bodily injury. Be very protective of yourself for the next two days.

arrowroot For the next four days, work to build a strong base and longevity with those who are involved in a project you are working on.

arsenal All things you desire in a love relationship will be granted within four days.

arsenic Stay away from a known habitual liar. This will lead to difficulties within three days.

arsonist A mischievous person will unintentionally set you back several weeks on a project. Avoid this person until the project is completed.

art Within a few days, you will learn through a conversation that someone is very interested in becoming involved in a project you are working on. Take down all the necessary information for future contact and make plans to move ahead on this immediately. A joint effort will be very successful. Also make a conscious effort to remember the art work. This will lead you to more meanings of this dream. If the message is positive, work to give it life. If the message is negative, work to change the outcome and what it represents.

art deco You will suffer embarrassment within a few days if you run short of funds for necessities.

Artemis *(Greek mythology)* This dream implies that you will be surrounded by many powerful and influential people within the week. You are destined to become involved with one other person. This will be an opposite sexed person and will be in a capacity you desire. Leave yourself open to circulate and to expose yourself to situations where you have the opportunity to meet this person. Conversations will easi-

ly flow between you and a sense of closeness will quickly emerge. This will allow a relationship to develop if this is something you choose. This person will be well established in their career and will be more secure financially than you expected. You are both destined for a wonderful and tranquil life, and will enjoy an abundance of health as well as a prosperous future. Take steps to avoid or to change the outcome of any negative situation in this dream and forewarn anyone you recognize in the dream to do the same.

artery You will go from one extreme to another in your search to fulfill a desire in your life. This is a good cycle for you to make changes.

arthritis You will be led on by someone with different sexual preferences than you who lacks the courage to be honest with you. Don't force yourself on this person.

Arthur, King Your purposes will be helped by compromise. Kindness and a pleasing manner will work to your advantage for the next five days.

artichoke Get to the heart of a matter and quickly tie up all loose ends.

artifact For the next three days, you will experience many temporary delays on a project that you are attempting to conclude. Accept this calmly and go on about your business in a stress free manner.

artificial respiration *any form* You are interested in someone and the feeling is not mutual. A third party will eagerly and happily convey this information to you.

artillery Your cash flow will stop for a few months in the near future. Put extra funds ahead now in preparation for this.

artist You have been asked out by someone who is very eager to see you. They will do everything within their power to convince you to become involved with them. Maintenance of this relationship will take a great deal of effort on your part, and you will have to work to keep communication open. This person is very busy and finds it difficult to spend time with you. The pursuit is yours now. Make use of appointment books and calendars in order to schedule your time together.

painting a nude model Do not go out with someone purely for sexual pleasure for the next two days. You will decide later that this person is not as attractive to you. This could be a dangerous situation because this individual will later feel used. Avoid this behavior.

Aryan *any form, language or race* You will need to find refuge from stressful situations. This stress arises from another person's behavior or situation.

asbestos You will be charged for services you never received within the week. Be very sure of what you are paying for in advance.

ascetic A job you have applied for will be sabotaged by another. Look for alternative employment immediately.

ascot You will unexpectedly find yourself in a secluded spot with another person and will result in a highly charged romantic evening. This will lead to a relationship of substance and strength.

asexual Carry yourself with confidence for the following few weeks. You need to give others a better impression of yourself because of an upcoming opportunity.

ash You will feel a deep acute pain for a very ill family member. Healing will occur within six weeks.

ashtray At one time in your life you were involved with someone who mistreated you in such a way that you decided to get on with your life without this person. This individual will, within five days, reenter your life with verbal verification that they would like to become reinvolved with you in some way. This will be very appealing to you and you will be offered a proposal and plans about sharing your life together. You will, however, be bothered with flashbacks of what once was. This dream is letting you know that you do not need to lose sleep over this because you can have a good life together. This person will now be sensitive to your needs and is responsible and reasonable. You can proceed with confidence in a new relationship and it will be as solid and as permanent as you desire. You are definitely headed for a brilliant future and anyone else involved will benefit from this union.

Ash Wednesday You will be handling more responsibility at your job within a few weeks. You need to determine whether the stress of a promotion is worth it.

Asia You will be able to meet work deadlines successfully. This dream may also be used as a reference point in time. If you dream of this continent and see its name used in any context, the dream message will occur on this day.

aside Do not allow the opinions of others to confuse you. Trust your intuition, especially for the next few days.
   to put anything aside Do everything necessary to enjoy everything life has to offer in the best way you can.

ask *to have someone ask something of you* You will be required to appear in court for someone else as a witness. This time period will also be financially advantageous and will be emotionally rewarding to you as well.
   to ask of someone else You will be dealing with wealthy business people and asked to join their firm. You will also have the verification of someone's deep love within three days. This will bring you much joy because you have long desired this individual. You will devise plans for the future

that you will find mutually satisfying. Any negative event foretold in this dream can be prevented or altered in reality. You have three days to make these changes and to alert anyone you recognize in this dream to make the proper changes in their life. Proceed with confidence. Good luck is with you.
   to ask someone to come to you but they refuse to Be very careful for the next five days. Someone you have asked to leave your life will break their promise to leave you alone and will begin to impose themselves on you. Prepare yourself in order to avoid being trapped into committing to something you do not want. You will need to be emotionally equipped to handle this delicate issue. Organize your thoughts and feelings and you will be successful in getting your point across in a way that will not be offensive, and in a way that will leave no room for misunderstandings. Proceed with caution and you will be able to resolve this delicate situation.

asp False conclusions will be reached by someone about you. Stay calm. This will allow you to relax enough to clear up the conflict and retain order. After several distasteful moments, the other person will apologize to you.

asparagus Continue working on your plans because they will bring you success. Someone will also request private time with you to express loving sensual private moments together. If you choose to go along with this request, you will enjoy yourself immensely. Eat healthful foods and drink plenty of water.

aspen Do not give anything of value away and don't allow yourself to be talked out of any of your belongings.

asphalt Do not referee a fight between two angry people. You will be physically and verbally abused. The moment you see a situation like this developing, leave the premises.

asphyxiate *any form* Do not rent out your property to anyone for the next few days. The potential renters are destructive of other people's property and are often in trouble with the law.

aspirin Enjoy a fruitful conversation with another about your skills and this will boost your business profits.

ass Someone will attempt to cause you to lose face in front of others within the next two days.

assassin Do not force yourself on another person who is not interested in you, especially for the next three days.

assault *to be assaulted* Your self confidence is a source of irritation to another. Stay with those who like you.
   to assault You will realize your dreams.
assembly line Within five days, bring a certain issue to the attention of others who are unaware of it and insist on a resolution within an agreed upon time. This will be brought

about very successfully.

assets *to dream your assets are being taken* Someone you care about is relocating to another state for job reasons. This person lacks the courage to tell you and will leave with no word. Discuss this issue now and encourage this person to talk about the move and to leave a forwarding address.

assistance *to ask for and receive* Someone wants you to become sexually involved with them and for the next two days this person will go to great lengths to satisfy both of you. This will be a wonderful time for you. Any question you expect to receive a positive answer to, will be granted. Luck is with you.

to ask for assistance and fail to receive it Do whatever is necessary to grow at the same or a more rapid pace as those around you. Keep growing and learning in order to keep up with those who are important to you. Within three days it will become very clear why this is necessary.

to give Focus and work on creating a more stable foundation for yourself. Within two days you will gain the clarity needed to point yourself in the right direction to achieve this. This will stand for a lifetime.

to receive government assistance Be very attentive because an unusual occurrence will develop regarding a person, project or position that will lead to a financial windfall. You may marry someone who will leave you with a monthly pension, develop a project that will deliver you monthly royalties, or secure a position that will offer you monthly provisions for a lifetime. You are in a sound position to receive this in the near future. Develop your curiosity, especially for the next week, to ensure that you do not miss out on these benefits. You will receive an abundance of health, many blessings and are headed for a brilliant future.

assistant Take steps to resolve any internal issues you have with a particular authority figure. Come to grips with your feelings and move on with your life. You will find life much easier because you no longer have to deal with extraneous emotional issues.

to have an assistant You need to be careful around water and electrical wires.

aster Within three days, many powerful friends will rally around you and offer their assistance in a time of need. You will get a quick response to this stressful situation.

asteroid You will be accused of rape within three days unless you control your forcefulness. You must also be prepared to handle an unexpected situation that will arise within two days concerning a crisis between another person and their family. This needs immediate attention. Handle it with tact and the result will be successful.

asthma You will become lost when taking a trip to the country and will have to stop and seek directions. Prepare your route ahead of time in order to avoid this.

astonishment *to be astonished* You will unintentionally see someone nude.

astringent Do not deprive yourself of the enjoyment of doing something delightfully different simply because it seems outrageous or unusual. Add new and healthy elements to your life for your own pleasure.

astrodome All business dealings for the next two days will be very advantageous to you. Whatever route you opt for will provide you with a brighter future than you ever envisioned. Good luck and many blessings are with you.

astrologer Follow the advice given to the word. If you cannot recall the advice, have your chart read. You will need this important information now to prepare yourself for the upcoming months.

astronaut Be careful of products used on the hair because they may result in hair loss.

astronomy Someone from another state will ask you to move in with them.

asylum *any form* Your intuition about someone special is correct and you will enjoy victory in all phases of your life.

Athena *(Greek mythology)* You will receive a gift of jewelry from a special person within seven days. It is essential that for the next week you devote your time to the pursuit of creating excitement and generating a greater interest regarding a new situation. You will be able to gain more success regarding a new product, plan, idea or conversation. You will gain excellent feedback that will bring about more productivity and fun. You will also create a non-stressful outcome to what is a priority to you now. You will be able to bring everyone involved together in building a common understanding. Any negative situation dreamed about needs to be altered and steps taken to experience only positive situations in your life.

athlete You will become famous as a sports figure if you get the proper training. This process will begin within seven weeks if you pursue this goal.

Athletes' foot Because of rapid life changes, be careful of all new undertakings in order to avoid major mistakes.

Atlantic Any proposal you are considering will be accepted within seven days. This dream may also be used as a reference point in time. If you dream of this ocean and see its name used in any context, the dream message will occur on this day.

Atlantis You will travel to foreign lands. This dream may also be used as a reference point in time. If you dream of this place and see its name used in any context, the dream message will occur on this day.

atlas Through an acquaintance, you will meet someone new. This person will share a mutual friend who was lost to death or relocation. Through this person you will experience a new world of friends and experiences and this will lead to greater health and happiness.

atmosphere Be watchful of falling objects from high places.

atom You will be dealing with a very immature person for the next four days. This person has a very subtle way of handling this immaturity. Choose your words carefully when talking to this individual. The situation could be dangerous and you will be dealing with a deranged person if you push the wrong way. You will handle this successfully by being cautious.

atomic bomb Within three days someone will put you into a position of potential danger. Problems will arise at a place that you frequent. This evil person has not yet given you any sign of their evilness, but upon getting closer to you they will remove the mask of normalcy. It would be an irresponsible act on your part if you allow yourself to be preyed upon. You have prior notice of this and have the choice of not allowing their involvement in your life. It is also important not to neglect someone who admires and looks up to you. You may soon need help from this person. Otherwise, you are headed for a very prosperous future.

atomic energy You will find a large sum of money within seven days.

atrium Question the reasons for your inability to resolve certain problems. Once you have isolated the reason you will find personal empowerment. After a two day period you will be able to successfully tackle those issues. Good luck is with you.

atrocity *any form* Protect your body, especially the legs and sexual organs from insect bites for the next two days.

attaché case A current idea will become a reality and you will profit from it with the help of an older relative.

attack *to attack* Stand up for yourself when necessary.
to be attacked Someone you are relying on will be insincere with their promises. Find an alternative mode of transportation. Any negative event witnessed in this dream needs to be prevented in reality.

attendant *any form* Listen to and follow your doctor's advice.

attic You will hear of a friend's engagement.
attitude *any attitude* You will receive gifts of fur within two days. You must also not allow anyone to injure the feelings of someone who is special to you.

attorney Someone you are beginning to feel a bond with will be a waste of time. This person is incapable of sharing real emotion.

attraction *for someone* An unexpected stranger may make your life uncomfortable for a few hours. Be watchful for this.
someone is attracted to you You will enjoy prosperity in your undertakings as well as a wealth of happiness and health. Someone with a great sense of humor will enter your life within three weeks. This will lead to a strong romantic relationship if you choose to let this happen.

auction You will soon meet a person with a great sense of power and authority.
public Keep all new interests to yourself. When you do decide to reveal them, explain them in such a way that no one will mistake what you are talking about.

auctioneer Do not become involved in problematic family issues at this time. It will take much longer to resolve than expected.

audience You will soon enjoy a great sex life. Try to simplify your life as well.

audit Someone at your worksite will injure your feelings because they are in a bad mood. Be watchful of this.

audition Be flexible with a family member's projects.
to be in Have an intimate conversation with someone. Expect, within seven days, an unusual set of circumstances to occur. These circumstances will dramatically raise your standard of living. You are headed for a prosperous future.

auditorium *something occurring on stage* You must be adventurous and take small risks in order to achieve your goals.

August A young member of your family will marry a much older person. They will enjoy happiness and financial stability. In August, loose ends will be tied up on projects and your goals will be realized. You are headed for a brilliant future.

auld lang syne You will marry the person of your choice within six months and share a deep love.

aunt Your moods and behavior are being watched by another. This will lead to a spending spree paid for by this person and to a long term relationship. You are headed for a brilliant future if you choose to become involved.

aura *yours* Trust your intuition and do not rely on anyone else. Any negative event witnessed in this dream can be changed or avoided. You are headed for a brilliant future. Proceed with confidence.

someone else You will win theatrical acclaim and become legendary.

Australia Someone will depend on you for transportation after the offer of one ride. Make it known that you will not be taken advantage of. Your time is your own. This dream may also be used as a reference point in time. If you dream of this country and see its name used in any context, the dream message will occur on this day.

author You will cultivate an original idea developed by an ancestor but never acted on. This will become a gold mine.

authority A much younger person will become deeply attracted to you. It is your choice to decide if this relationship is for you.
authority over another Think before you speak. You will regret rash statements.

autobiography Someone will demonstrate possessiveness over you. Tell them to relax until they know you can be trusted. This will occur within two days.

autograph Do not attend any event for the next two days where there will be guests you clash with.

autoharp Develop an extra source of income as soon as you can. You will need a greater cash flow next month. Good luck is with you.

automat Someone special to you wants you to take the time out to make love. Do this within the week.

automatic pilot Someone will disapprove of your behavior and will expect improvements and an explanation for your actions within the week. You can prevent this occurrence.

automobile For a more detailed definition refer to car.
to be in one Do not waste time on your projects. Focus on them and get to work.
to fall from one You will clash with someone in authority within two days. Avoid this.
to see another fall out Someone will share a secret with you. Keep it to yourself.
to hit or run over someone Be careful for the next three days. Someone answering a help-wanted ad will be very wicked and dangerous but will appear normal.
you are run over You will fall in love with a younger person. You will be happy if you choose to pursue it. Any negative situation can be avoided, especially for the next three days.
to hear backfire from an automobile Do not jeopardize your reputation by taking on a new project.

autopsy Someone you want to meet will arrive at a later time than planned. Wait for this person.

autumn Within two days you will be offered an annuity plan that will provide you with a monthly income.

avalanche The love you want from another is doubtful. They are involved in another relationship you may be ignorant about. Within two days make it your business to learn the facts, then get on with your life.

Avalon You will be able to communicate with those you feel are too intimidating to approach in a very successful way. Good luck is with you.

avarice Do not do anything underhanded or deceitful. Take every step necessary to rid yourself of this behavior. This will lead to nothing but trouble for you.

Ave Maria *to hear the song or the words* You will express your love as if you were on a honeymoon. If you choose to experience this, the opportunity will be yours within three days.

avenge *any form* Someone falsely believes you are wealthier than you are. Make it clear that your money is for your living expenses.

aversion *any form* You will hear news of a premature birth that can still be avoided.

aviary You will invest too much time, money, and effort on a do-it-yourself project.

aviator *to be* Concentrate on your plans for the next few days and check for errors.
to be with an aviator You have a friend whom you share much with but it would be a mistake to rely on this person for business assistance.

avocado You will enjoy yourself with friends at a stadium event and you will share great food and visual stimulation.

avocado seeds An unassuming yet influential person will take interest in your welfare.

avoid Someone is trying to avoid you. Do not make painful accusations.
yourself or anyone else avoiding anything The friend of a special person will proposition you. Do not allow this to get out of hand or it will result in a shameful situation.
avoiding someone You are beginning to grow closer to a certain individual who will lead you to believe that you can fully trust in them and can rely on their loyalty. For the next three days, make sure you move forward only with extreme caution. This person is very cunning and a master of deception and will have you believing in future occurrences and events that will never take place. This person has a hidden agenda that involves pursuing you for reasons known only to them. They will go to great lengths to create an atmosphere free of suspicion, but if you begin to suspect their devious plans they will create a crisis to distract you. It will take a

long time for you to recover from this and get back to normalcy. You have prior notice of this and everything you need to make sure this does not occur. Practice common sense and you will be very successful in diffusing this. Refuse to become involved, do not compromise and do not allow this person to pry into your affairs. You will have the confidence to put yourself on the path toward a prosperous future. Many blessings are with you and you family.

avoidance *trying to get close to someone in any form but they avoid or ignore you* Be very wary for the next five days. Someone you have asked to leave your life and who has promised to leave you alone will break this promise. Take the time to prepare yourself in some way to avoid being pinned down by this person, and make it clear that you want nothing to do with them. You will need to be emotionally equipped to handle this delicate issue. Organize your thoughts and feelings and do not allow anyone to think that you are willing to commit to something you are unwilling to, and make sure there are no misunderstandings. You will be successful in getting your point across in a way that will not be offensive. Proceed with caution and you will be able to handle this delicate situation.

Avon Within three days, you will receive some unusual offers from a person you least expect.

awake *you have been awakened or that you have awakened someone else* Within three days, you will enjoy a growth of maturity and will be able to handle yourself regarding a burdensome responsibility in a way that you felt was impossible. You will enjoy a new clarity of thought and will make good use of your resources like never before. This will allow you to successfully complete your tasks.

away *to hear someone tell you they are going away* This person will in actuality, go away. You will hear of this within two days.

if you do not recognize the person This dream implies that you will finally be rid of your nemesis within four days.

to hear the phrase Someone will attempt to involve you in a ménageátrois. If you become involved, it will work out for both of you because the relationship with the third party is over and you will be together for many years. Since you have prior knowledge of this, you may want to arrange it so the split comes before you are involved. You will gain more knowledge of this within four days.

to tell someone you are going away If you sense hurt feelings from this person, you may want to consider whether you should leave this individual in reality. This dream will determine whether you will be able to make a clean break and how to make it so. Also, do not overindulge in alcohol or food. Restrain yourself in this upcoming situation. Wait until you are certain of what is correct.

if you do not recognize the person you are leaving Become aware, suspicious and investigate more of the events in your surroundings over the next few days. Expect the unexpected.

to walk away This is a great cycle for you to accomplish almost anything you desire. You will be able to handle difficult situations easily and see drastic changes for the better in your life. Motivate yourself to accomplish those things you desire in your life, especially for the next five days.

to step away from someone or to see someone step away You will delight a relative by fulfilling a request. This favor is, to you, not that big but will thrill this family member. Be aware also that the person you are stepping away from represents someone who has an urgent need to talk to you. You are trying to remain detached but this dream is requesting that you become more compassionate.

awesome *any form* You will win money. Play your favorite numbers in a game of chance. Within seven days you will also express unusual feelings in an unusual way to someone else.

awkward *to be in an awkward situation* Take steps to avoid any accident that could lead to a broken leg. Your reputation is also in danger because you will be led to believe an untruth.

awl Within a few days, you will achieve the reconciliation you have been striving for and the results will be successful. Avoid playing hard to get. If you handle this properly, all those loving, close feelings will return.

awning This will be a very lucky cycle for you. This cycle will continue for some time. It is also important for you to roll up your sleeves and get to work on a long standing unresolved personal issue. Resolve it completely now.

AWOL *refer to absent without leave* Within seven days you will have to begin choosing people carefully for their loyalty. Relentlessly seek out and connect with these people. Work to get your point across in a very persuasive manner until they are swayed to your point of view. This is the perfect cycle to do this regarding an important upcoming situation. Seek out these people until you achieve success. It will be a big advantage to you to have this support and it will benefit all concerned. You are headed for a brilliant future and good luck is with you.

ax *to see blood on the blade* This dream implies that your success will come quicker than expected. This also implies that you will be given a blessed gift of mental inventiveness and intelligence.

struck by an ax Confirm that there are no obstacles between yourself and someone who is eagerly attempting to communicate with you.

axis Get your legal affairs in order.

axle Walk for exercise instead of engaging in a more strenuuous fitness program.

azalea Use discretion in romantic affairs until the relationship is solid. Then you may be more open about your relationship.

Aztec Require references when hiring someone for a new project. Be optimistic and you will be successful in finding the right person.

B

B This is a tremendously prosperous cycle for you. This time period is perfect for developing the habit of treating yourself like the precious commodity that you are. Focus on the resources that offer you the means to grow in a profound way. Treat yourself to the assistance that will enable you to bring back that sense of normality and balance. Motivate yourself to explore new avenues and facets of your life in order to move ahead. This cycle also offers you the opportunity to take small risks for the chance of a great payoff. This dream will leave you with a sense of excitement about the future. You are definitely headed for a brilliant life. Good luck is with you.

Baal Do not waste your time speculating about another person. Within the week, you will learn all the facts about this individual and the facts about their involvement with a certain situation.

babble You will enjoy a fantastic sex life and a wonderful love relationship.

Babel *(tower of)* Get accurate information before you judge another person. You are relying on hearsay alone and will later find out that your information is inaccurate. Think before you act in order to avoid an embarrassment. This dream may also be used as a reference point in time. If you dream of this Biblical site and see its name used in any context, the dream message will occur on this day.

baboon Be careful when around an older evil, deceitful, woman concerning your business and love affairs. Although this woman appears friendly, do not put your trust in her. She enjoys discord within family settings.

babushka For the next three days you will have an overwhelming feeling that something suspicious is going on. Do not allow anyone to convince you that you are paranoid or attempt to water this situation down. This dream is telling you that your spirit is sending you an increased awareness about something you need to attend to. This will enable you to handle each situation in an appropriate manner, and will

be assurance that you could not have done anything differently. You have prior notice of this and will be able to take the right steps to deal with this issue now.

baby *to be called baby or babe* Be wary of fast talking friends.

in your arms The person who is deeply in love with you misses you intensely.

abandoned baby Show your interest to someone who may be unaware of your feelings. Bring enjoyment to your inner child.

bald baby You will experience good luck and great success in all of your endeavors.

baby's first step A business meeting will open up opportunities via connections with influential people.

bottle fed Do whatever is necessary to devise a clever idea or solution that will allow you to work independently on a situation that will develop within three days. This will enable you to work without outside interference. These thoughts will come to you with great clarity and you will be able to resolve this situation with success.

to change any garment Although you will soon hear what you do not want to hear, do not allow this to change your attitude and drag you down. Do whatever is necessary to maintain a positive attitude.

breast feed a baby Take the steps you need with a co-worker to receive the assistance and services you need. This action will uncover a secret within your working environment.

crying baby A hot financial tip will lead to riches.

distressful baby A failing romantic situation will be renewed. Look for reconciliation and be sure you do not neglect those who are special to you.

happy baby You will have the courage to make the correct move romantically and to ask that your needs be met. You will get what you need.

first born Take steps to enjoy life to the fullest. You will find pleasures that you have never experienced in your life. The best is yet to come.

newborn baby You will be offered an invitation for an intimate dinner and conversation by someone who does not look as though they have the wealth that they, in reality, possess. You have the opportunity now to deepen the relationship if you choose. This dream is a very lucky omen and you are headed for a brilliant future. If this dream portends any negative event involving a newborn, you have the time to either alter the outcome or to avoid the situation altogether. Make sure any infant you know has nothing but positive experiences in their life, especially for the next five days.

nude baby Do what you can to feel happier about your life. Appreciate life and consistently and persistently do what you can to enjoy it.

sick baby Confront job difficulties and you will receive great financial rewards within two days.

twin babies You will win a promotion. You will also be facing two difficult decisions. These will be successfully resolved if you remain true to yourself and do not compromise your integrity.

skinny baby Do not behave in a suspicious manner to others. You will never be able to erase doubts if you do. Be cautious of your behavior now.

in any other form This dream is a promise that the situation you are presently working on will work out to your satisfaction within seven days. It also implies that you need to move rapidly in order to benefit from this lucky cycle.

baby bottle *if the bottle is empty* Your love will be needed immediately by someone who is special to you.

if full You will be treated like royalty by the person you most desire.

baby buttocks You will have many passionate moments with the one you desire.

baby car seat Do not allow your carelessness to create a strange occurrence that could result in harm to you or to someone else.

baby carriage or stroller You will handle a delicate situation by using gentle persuasion.

baby carrier Within five days you will experience many events that will bring grand and prosperous changes to your life. Your life will improve immensely.

baby clothes Postpone decisions for a few days. You will find a better solution to your problems.

baby crib Do not become desperate over another's problems. Do not be lured in, in spite of the temptations to become involved. This will occur within four days. You will also enjoy longevity. Improve your diet in order to enjoy a healthy life.

baby diaper *to change* Someone you admire will not be what you believed them to be.

baby doll Within four days you will be persuaded to enter into a business deal. You will agree to this only if the deal is kept secret. After a week, you will do something to injure this individual's feelings and out of revenge the secret will be told. There are two ways to avoid this. You can refuse to become involved in this business deal and/or you can avoid hurting this person's feelings. You have been forewarned and have the time to make the correct choice.

baby food Do not become overly dependent on a specific person, especially for the next three days. Stop this behavior and strive to be versatile with the resources you have available. Develop a support system and do not allow yourself to put excess strain on one person. You will also attend a special event within two weeks and will be overwhelmed by the magical voice of one of the performers. You will have a sense of awe when in the presence of this performer. You are headed for a prosperous future and many blessings will be with you.

baby formula Someone who holds you in deep regard will fall deeply in love with you. This person needs you to show deep affection and a strong commitment toward them. You will be able to do this as time passes.

baby grand piano Never settle for less than what you want from a situation. Take each step one at a time and refuse to allow yourself to be taken. Clear each step with yourself first.

baby highchair Your maid has good intentions and is trustworthy.

Babylon You will enjoy going out with an attractive date. This dream may also be used as a reference point in time. If you dream of this ancient city and see its name used in any context, the dream message will occur on this day.

baby rattle A slightly older same sexed person will subtly manipulate you out of a portion of money that rightfully belongs to you. It will be difficult to collect because of the manipulative manner of this person. Think ahead and immediately state your requirements fully, precisely, and in detail in order to collect. Put each transaction in writing.

baby relative Praise a loyal friend and show special gratitude toward this person.

Baby's breath Don't put heavy responsibilities on a child or a young person.

baby shoes You and your loved one will suddenly find yourselves bewitched by a magical romantic atmosphere.

baby sitter You will become financially secure by taking on a temporary second job.

baby teething ring You will feel that someone is either keeping secrets or lying to you. This is definitely a figment of your imagination. This person is very loyal and truthful to you.

baccarat Make a note to remember an important upcoming event.

Bacchante Within five days you will have the chance to talk with someone who has a great deal of power and authority. This person will be very eager to join up with you and your associates and you feel gratitude that this person is on your side.

Bacchus *(Greek and Roman Mythology)* Do not allow yourself to be taken advantage of or used as a stepping stone for another's advancement. Do not allow yourself to become vulturized.

bachelor An honest discussion with a relative will help a child regarding his education or learning disability. Special education may be needed.

Bachelor of Arts or Sciences You will shortly be the beneficiary in a property settlement.

Bachelors' button Someone you have known for some time will want to take your relationship to a higher level. It will become more romantic and affectionate. If you choose to pursue this, you will find it to be a wonderful cycle for love. Good luck is with you.

Bach, Johann Sebastian You will receive a gift of many talents from your deity. Develop the most desirable one and you will leave a legacy to this world.

back *human back in any form* This dream is a very lucky omen for you. Try your favorite game of chance. You will also be introduced to an unusual circumstance within seven days that will generate a great deal of excitement and happiness.

markings on your back or anyone else's back (of any form) After marriage you will find that you have a very agreeable mate. Suddenly a new hidden dimension will emerge and your mate's personality and character will be revealed as more dynamic and richer than you ever imagined. This experience will teach you many lessons in life, including prejudgment.

to see someone stabbed in the back by any sharp object Confirm that there are no obstacles between yourself and someone who is eagerly attempting to communicate with you. Do not assume this person is uninterested. Within two days, tactfully open the lines of communication by placing a phone call. You will find that all is well and you will be richly rewarded in an emotional sense by this person. Proceed with confidence.

to be stabbed in the back by any sharp object or to stab someone in the back Your intuition will be sharper for the next two days than ever before. Proceed with confidence. You will achieve victory over any situation, person, agreement, etc., especially if you recognize the person you are stabbing. This dream also implies that someone you know is not being treated right by another person. You will be very instrumental in getting them to look at other people's points of view. As a result, this individual will be less angry and far more willing to work with others, and will develop a more easy going attitude. This will require time, work and patience from you to make this a reality. Victory is coming your way and many blessings will come to you and your family.

in any other form You will finally achieve the reconciliation you have been seeking within four days. This union will be blessed with prosperity and abundances in those areas of your life you most desire. You are entering a lucky seven day cycle.

backache Show compassion toward a special person who is ill.

backboard Do not be taken by surprise for the next two days. Arm yourself with knowledge about a future undertaking.

backbone You will receive an agreeable settlement. You will hear of this within five days and will be overjoyed by the outcome.

backdoor Within three weeks, you will be exposed to some extraordinary activities. These experiences will bring you prosperity and will vastly raise your standard of living.

back down *from any position* Be flexible with family members and their projects.

to sit back down (anyone) Someone has erected unnecessary emotional barriers against you. Self realization will lead this person to tear down defenses. This person's behavior will indicate more openness and willingness to communicate with you. Be patient until this person comes around.

backfield Concentrate and closely attend to all details of financial matters within three days. You will be able to head off trouble by taking care of them now.

backfire Do not jeopardize your reputation on the job with a new project for the next three days.

backgammon A distant friend will supply fresh ideas and you will mutually work to assure the success of these ideas.

backpack Do not ignore your health. At the first sign of trouble, take care of it so you will not lose time from work.

backslide You will be asked out for an intimate dinner and conversation by someone who possesses a great wealth that is not obvious to you. You have the chance now to deepen the relationship, if you choose. This dream is a lucky omen for you and you are headed for a brilliant future. Take steps to avoid any negative event portrayed in this dream, and make sure you experience only positive events, especially for the next five days.

backstage For the next two days you will be asked to handle a certain problem. Make sure you are emotionally equipped to handle this situation and do not overextend yourself. Be acutely aware of the circumstance prior to committing yourself.

backstitch Make sure that your business associates do not take advantage of you, especially for the next two days.

backstroke You will receive a generous loan that you can repay at your convenience.

backtrack A former lover will reappear for reconciliation within three days. Should you pursue this, you will find success.

backwards *to see yourself walking backwards* Have an intimate conversation with someone to expedite a move and a big change. You will be successful.

anything else going backwards You will discover new dimensions and will meet new challenges with a newly hired assistant. At the first sign of trouble, promptly schedule a meeting to avoid trouble.

bacon This dream is a very lucky omen. Make sure that you personally handle all of your own affairs.

bacon and eggs You will discover the extent of another's love for you within five days.

bacteria For the next four days, take steps to avoid becoming involved in another couple's quarrels. This couple will attempt to drag you in.

bad *(slang term)* Think carefully for the next four days and prepare for a conversation with someone who is involved with a certain situation. This will give you the time to get all those involved together to plan how to put a lid on a particular issue and to prevent a negative event from occurring. Alert everyone involved. Many blessings will come to you and your family.

bad news Within three days you will have to deal with someone who has a habit of creating chaos and stressful situations. During this time period, this individual will create a situation that will escalate to the point of never returning to normalcy. Make sure that you plan other activities during this time period in order to avoid this individual. Anything negative witnessed in this dream needs to be avoided. Forewarn anyone you recognize to do the same. Take steps to ensure that you only experience positive events in your life. Look under *good news* for a greater definition of this dream.

badge *any form* You will be arrested today. This can be avoided if you stop all illegal activities.

badger You will have an opportunity to repair a past error. This time it will be handled correctly.

badminton You will meet someone who speaks a language other than that of their ethnic group. You will be enchanted by this person.

bag *to carry* This dream is a lucky omen. Improve your appearance and be responsible for yourself. You may be caught off guard by someone who will want to drop in for the purpose of catching you at your worst.

full You will enjoy good health and much wealth for a long time to come.

empty Maintain good eating habits. You will enjoy good luck and prosperity. This dream implies also that you should be careful not to overlook something important over the next few days.

to carry a clear bag filled with water and any floating object (i.e., goldfish, etc.) This dream is an extremely lucky omen for the next two weeks. Pay close attention to any item floating in the water for an additional clue to this dream. You also need to play a very active part in making sure that your emotional needs are met. Provide yourself with what you need on an emotional level. Within five days you will be able to visualize the path you need to take for a brilliant future. Good luck is with you.

paper bag This dream is a very lucky omen. You should also take steps to improve your appearance.

plastic A cluster of events will begin to occur one after the other at a very rapid pace, and each one will bring you a tremendous amount of joy, wonder and awe. You will also develop a tremendous amount of powerful energy that you can control and direct in the way you see fit. You will also bring others under your direct control at the same time these other events are taking place. You will, because of your advance notice, be able to successfully complete anything you wish in a professional way. You will be able to overcome any difficulty and it will now be a simple matter to deal with any additional issues. Follow your instincts and many blessings will come to you and your family.

medical bag This dream implies that you will be surrounded by a number of powerful and wealthy people. There is, however, another person you are fated to become involved with. This person will be of the opposite sex and this involvement will grow to any level you wish. Leave yourself open for circulation and to issues that will give you the chance to meet this individual. You will enjoy easy conversation and will both gain a sense of closeness. This will allow a relationship to grow quickly. This person is well established career wise and is much wealthier than you ever expected. You are destined for a wonderful and tranquil life, and you will both enjoy a prosperous future as well as an abundance of health. Make sure you alter the outcome or prevent any negative situation that you witnessed in this dream, and take steps to ensure that you only experience positive expressions in your life.

bagel You will visit, for the first time, a big city, all expenses paid, and have a fabulous time and a safe return. This will occur within the month.

baggage Control your temper. Do not give in to emotional stress.

to pack baggage Do not start an argument with another person.

to lose Do not allow others to believe that you will assume their responsibilities.

Baghdad You will become involved in fundraising for a family member. This will be successful. This dream may also be used as a reference point in time. If you dream of this city and see its name used in any context, the dream message will occur on this day.

bag lady You will be lucky for a few weeks, however, a stranger will make your life uncomfortable for two days. Avoid this if at all possible.

bagman Carefully select a treatment method with a doctor to attain the best results. The present method of treatment may be wrong for you.

bagpipe Your money is not being used wisely by another.

Bahai You are not getting the important facts regarding a certain situation from someone who is special to you. This concerns you a great deal. Do whatever you can to get these facts and resolve this issue completely.

Bahamas You will reach success with your goals. This dream may also be used as a reference point in time. If you dream of this island group and see its name used in any context, the dream message will occur on this day.

bail Be more selective with those you confide in. You will have success with your business dealings.

bail bond Someone will try to destroy your character and you will soon be confronted by this person. Attempt to work things out before this occurs.

bail bondsman Find ways to improve your love life while maintaining your professional goals. Do this within two days.

bailiff Pleasurable bad habits will become expensive. Control your obsessions.

bait Within five days, someone very attracted to you will invite you on an outing. Think this through carefully. This person wants more from you than you are able to give. You will have problems enroute but a tactful straight forward conversation will put you both at ease.

bake For the next seven days, remain alert. Someone will attempt, by body language or behavior, to communicate the deep feelings they have for you. This person is interested in becoming involved in your life in any capacity, especially in a romantic way. This cycle is very lucky for love and for all financial transactions.

baked Alaska You will receive a surprise birthday party and a gift from someone you least expect it from.

baked beans A friend who has been led astray will attempt to lead you in the same direction. Be firm in your refusal.

baker Family members are complaining about the lack of time spent at home with the family. You will have to explain what you do when you are away. Do this nicely and tactfully.

baking powder You will hear good news from a friend. Someone you know will also change their place of residence within three weeks.

baking soda Do not take chances with your health. Take extra precautions regarding health issues for the next five days.

balance You will enjoy prosperity and happiness in business and love. Simplify your life.

balance sheet Bargain when purchasing an item. Take precautions with your money.

balcony You will meet someone special within three weeks and both of you will find mutual emotional support.

bald *to dream you are balding* A secret enemy will purposely steer you in the wrong direction regarding your present undertakings.
to see someone bald in a dream who is not bald in real life Guard your finances.
bald baby You will experience good luck and great success in all of your endeavors.
bald older man You will come into unexpected wealth. Games of chance are lucky for you also.
bald older woman Choose your words carefully when talking to a loved one in order to avoid injured feelings.
bald young man An unexpected argument or disagreement will occur with a member of the opposite sex. Someone will also make a demand that you cosign a loan. Don't do this.
bald young woman You will receive a long anticipated desire. Good health is yours.

bald eagle You will experience success with each of your undertakings within three weeks. You will have an independent and wealthy life.

bale *any form* Return affection as warmly as it is given.

ball *to enjoy attending a ball* All of your ambitions will be realized.
to be depressed while at a ball Your death will be caused by a treacherous, irresponsible friend. This can be avoided. Take precautions for the next two days.
ball *to attend a ball game* A friend will unexpectedly come to your aid.
to catch You will enjoy an outing.
to play ball with a young child You will receive more affection than you expected. A seemingly unaffectionate person will surprise you.
in any other form Treat someone who is special to you in a different and better way than you have treated others in past relationships. Pay close attention to the material of the ball as well as the color. Look them up for a more detailed interpretation of this dream.

ball and chain *any form* Someone, within three days, will have an urge to communicate their deep feelings to you and the degree in which they wish to become involved in your life. This individual will attempt to appease you in any way they can. This will involve scheduling special activities, performing chores and doing favors for you. Your every desire will be fulfilled. Openly show your affection and consideration for this person's generosity and efforts. Be very cautious and do what you can to avoid bruising this person's feelings, and do not become suspicious of this person's motives.

ballad Your energy is running low. Do not overextend yourself for the next few days.

ballast You will experience financial destruction if you are not careful about assuming another's loans.

ball bearing A stranger met through a mutual friend will cause future problems and misfortunes. Protect yourself. Within a two day period, you must also make sure that you realize that you are not obligated to behave in the way someone else wishes you to. Make sure that no one controls you. You will be able to rid yourself, on a permanent basis, of someone who feels they have power over the way you behave, your manner of speaking, or thinking. You will be able to accomplish this with very little stress or anxiety because of your tactful and easy manner. You are headed in the right direction and a prosperous future.

ballerina Do not allow another's words to injure your love life, and do not allow another person to talk to you about your beloved for the next two days.

ballet A supervisor wants to give you extra responsibilities that you may not be trained to handle. Do not go in over your head. Carefully scrutinize the job description and request training if needed.

ball game *to see in action* A friend will unexpectedly come to your aid.

ballistic missile For the next five days, focus carefully on developing detailed, well articulated plans that you wish to execute. Allow fate to run its course and you will enjoy a prosperous future. All your efforts will be worth it and you will begin to see positive results within this five day time period.

ball joint Prepare yourself against future losses.

balloon A joker or drunk will get out of hand and ruin a special occasion within three days.
blow up You will need to change plans due to an illness.
to pop You will receive a phone call within two days from someone who enjoys masturbating while on the phone. This person will attempt to introduce you to new forms of sexual activity. It is your choice whether you wish to pursue this or not.
to see a balloon pumped up, explode Do not allow your

feelings or plans to be known to others.

ballot It is important that you demonstrate extreme loyalty for the next five days. You are headed for a brilliant future.

ballpark An unexpected pleasure will thrill you and long awaited reconciliation will occur.

ballplayer Pursue any new positive change.

ballpoint pen This dream is lucky and implies that you will receive an abundance of health, love and wealth.

ballroom A marriage decision of any kind will yield peace and tranquility.

balm Within five days you will have the opportunity to cater to someone from a different ethnic background. Because of your hard work, your ability to handle certain issues with diplomacy and tact, and your willingness to please, doors will be opened to you on a permanent basis. You will, as a result, be offered many new opportunities and an increase in your finances. Good luck is with you.

baloney A phone conversation with an attractive, generous person with a sense of humor, will lead to emotional fulfillment. This will result in lasting happiness that will be yours for a long time to come.

balsa Within five days, you will gather the energy and resources you need to follow your instincts regarding a certain issue you feel should be taking place. Regardless of what others say to you, this situation needs to occur. It will create big changes in your life and the lives of others. Proceed with confidence. Everything will work out as it should.

balsam A roommate will give you notice that they are moving out. Make arrangements now for upcoming bills. Luck is with you.

bamboo Be wary of an evil, older woman. Protect your business and love affairs. This woman is a big gossip.

banana You will hear of lovers who will elope. This dream also implies that you will be asked out for dinner and conversation by someone who is far wealthier than they appear to be. You will have the opportunity at this time to develop a relationship, if you choose. This is a very lucky omen and you are headed for a brilliant future.

banana seat You will experience happiness.

banana split For the next five days, be very aware of the behavior of a young person to determine what they may be doing that would be physically and emotionally damaging to their health. Encourage this person to create a more healthful environment for themselves. This young person will later show a great deal of gratitude to you for taking the time to point them in the right direction.

band *to play in one* You are loved beyond your imagination.

to listen to one You will achieve wealth through someone who is important to you.

bandage While working, attempt to get the most from your time for the next two days.

band aid Within two days, certain situations in your life will change to the point of becoming unbearable to you. You will be able to handle everything calmly and successfully because you have been forewarned that this will occur. Take steps to eliminate stressful situations in your life and keep in mind that you do not have to commit to anything you choose not to.

bandanna An extremely attractive person will fall in love with you.

bandit You will need to borrow money within two days. Ask for this loan from more than one person in order to ensure that you receive enough.

band saw A decision is coming up within three days that should not be postponed. Do not procrastinate. You will lose out if you do not make a quick decision.

bandstand You will inherit a large fortune from your family.

bandwagon Within a three day period, you will be able to show the love you feel for someone in the manner they desire. This will take place in a wild and romantic setting. Good luck will be with you for the next week.

Bangkok Someone will mislead you into believing they accept your viewpoint and are genuinely interested in becoming a part of your plans. Your time is being wasted by this individual. Get on with your life without this person. This dream may also be used as a reference point in time. If you dream of this city and see its name used in any context, the dream message will occur on this day.

bangle Be independent.

banish *any form* Your financial problems will vanish.

banjo You will be asked to join a very respectable social group.

bank *any form* Observe caution in health, financial, legal or tax matters, especially for the next two weeks.

bank account A violent enemy has planned a trap to hurt you within three days. This can be avoided by taking extra precautions. Take steps to watch your behavior patterns so

you do not become an easy target.

bankbook Your lover is reckless, careless and fickle.

banker You will be disappointed by the unexpected reactions from others. Advice received will not be correct and hidden information will now be revealed. You will also hear of a prisoner leaving jail.

bankrupt A close friend will become a financial drain. Be careful.

banner Demand that your needs be met by your loved one. Happiness will be yours.

banquet A distant friend will call you and send a small gift.

banshee You will hear of a friend's death. This will be a sorrowful time for a few days.

bantam Do not accept a hazardous job and do not expose yourself to dangers on the job site for the next two days.

banyan Do not lend money or anything of value to anyone else for the next three days. You will not be repaid.

baptism You will enjoy yourself very much while attending a special occasion and you will feel a release of tension.

Baptist Lingering situations from the past will interfere with the present and hinder your chances for success. Changes will begin within four days. Do not allow the past to interfere.

bar *(saloon)* Guard your cash. This dream is a lucky omen. You will look for a compromise in a love relationship. Also, a close friend will release you from a financial burden.

happy hour You will receive victory and wealth in the direction you are going. You will achieve your goals and will be surrounded by people who love and respect you.

bar stool For the next two days someone will behave toward you in an entirely different manner. This person will be kinder, more punctual and, overall, an improved being. Do not make any comments on this, just enjoy this change.

barkeeper Someone you have known for a while will become the love of your life.

Barabbas *(from the Bible)* Take a risk in a new territory. You will be successful because you will think out each move carefully and in detail.

barb For three days, avoid unusual weather that will catch you off guard. A sudden change of weather will lead to illness.

barbecue You have a very faithful lover. You will also, because of who you are, always be the center of attention to many people. You will be placed in leadership positions whether you wish to or not. This will occur within two days. Accept this with good will. You are loved by many.

barbed wire Too many people are interfering in your life and offering too much advice. Do not sign any important papers until you have more facts.

to see a man cutting barbed wire This dream implies your murder. Be careful for the next seven days and become wary of events in your life. This can be avoided.

barbell Someone you rely on will back out of a commitment within two days. Find alternative assistance.

barber One person is secretly working against you. Be careful what you say to others.

barber shop You are choosing the wrong person to take care of your business. Find a replacement within three days.

barbiturates Someone will purposely misquote you during the next few weeks in order to put themselves at an advantage. You will find a solution to this problem if you are aware. This could be very hazardous to your partnerships if not avoided.

bare *any form* Do not put yourself in a position of disgrace, and do not put yourself in a situation where you will be surrounded by enemies. Be especially careful of this for three days.

bareback Within two days, information received from a referral agency will be greatly appreciated. This information will put you in contact with someone who will assist you in your future plans. Move quickly on this.

barefoot Avoid situations that expose you to bacteria. This may lead to a severe illness. Also, make sure that you realize, within two days, that you are under no obligation to behave in any way other than you choose. Make absolutely certain that you are under no one else's control. You will then be able to permanently rid yourself of someone who feels they have authority over your behavior, manner of speech, thought patterns and ways of reacting. You will accomplish this with very little stress because of the tactful and easy way you handle this situation. You are headed in the right direction and will enjoy a prosperous future.

barfly For the next three days determine the motive for someone's helpfulness. You will learn that this person has had deep feelings for you and this will come as a surprise to you. The feelings are mutual and you are both compatible. Financial success will also come your way.

bargain *any form* You can have full reliance on all decisions you make for the next few weeks.

barge For the next three days take steps to look at things from a different perspective so that resentments do not get in the way of a good time. You will enjoy a different style of life. Good luck is with you.

bar graph For the next three days make sure you do not allow anyone to make plans that involve you that you wish to have no part of. Avoid giving someone else the authority to speak for you or to make decisions for you without consulting you. A situation will take place that will make you feel taken advantage of.

baritone Someone will purposely attempt to steer you in the wrong direction within the next three days. Think clearly and point yourself in the right decision.

to hear a baritone You will meet someone within two days who constantly harasses you. It can be avoided. Stay away from this person.

bark There is clearly too much interference in your life right now. This is keeping you from being aware of the needs of someone who is important to you and deserves to spend private time with you. Take steps to remedy this. You need to share fun time.

barkeeper Someone you have known for a while will become the love of your life.

barker Someone special to you will become ill for a short time. This individual will recover.

barley You have many blessings coming your way.

barmaid Your financial dealings will be very fortuitous.

barman A very close relative will be interested in helping financially. This will occur within three days.

bar mitzvah You will be married to someone with a great profession within three months.

barn You will have an untrustworthy romance. Seek assistance to strengthen your self esteem.

Barnabas *(from the Bible)* Beware of falsehood and deceitfulness in a job situation. Discern the source and provide a solution to this problem.

barnacle Do everything you can, for the next three days, to project a desired image to a special person. Follow your instincts and you will achieve success.

barn dance You will find just the right person to work with you within three days. Proceed with confidence. This person has many creative ideas and wonderful organizational skills that will be a great benefit to you. Good luck is with you.

barn owl Avoid spiteful people for the next two days.

barnyard *if empty* Beware of conspiracy for the next seven days.

if not empty Look up the specific animal for more clues to the meaning of this dream.

bar of soap *to slip on* Take steps to protect your environment and surroundings. Within five days something will occur that will pose a threat to you. This may be something in the line of undetectable toxic fumes that could lead to sickness or death, or you could become the victim of a random murder. You have prior notice of this and can take steps to avoid any danger, secure your environment and make sure you experience only positive expressions.

barometer At the first indication of jealousy and quarrel, make a move to prevent discord in your life. Make it a point, also, to avoid lifting heavy objects.

baron Be careful with sleeping pills and do not depend on sleep inducers.

barracks Make sure that your home is secure.

barracuda You will be invited to an event. Another invited guest has information about you that will be used in a bullying way. You are aware that both of you clash so be prepared to protect your reputation or don't attend at all.

barrel *full* You will finally be asked out by someone you desire. At the specified time, you will become ill. Make sure you stress another time, and get a rain check. Keep this person encouraged.

empty Do not allow yourself to be bullied by another person.

half barrel as a planter Do not become dissuaded from pursuing a good idea.

rolling barrel You will need to go back one step in order to advance five. This can be changed by reviewing your present position.

in any other form A serious move against your co-workers will be made by a supervisor. Co-workers will want you to testify for them Stay neutral for the next three days.

barrette After a hardship, a pot of gold will be awaiting you. Continue a relentless pursuit to overcome this hardship.

barricade Do not handle electrical wires. This will result in a hazardous accident.

barrier reef Resolve all difficulties you may have with your reproductive organs. It is also important to avoid any exposure to sexually transmitted diseases.

barrio Do what you can to stand firm in situations where it is necessary for you to say no. It is important, for the next five days, to stick with your decision in order to protect yourself.

bartender Ideas created between friends will quickly blossom into a successful venture.

Baruch *(from the Canonical Bible)* Within three days, you will be able to bring someone you have long desired close to you in a passionate way.

base Give a friend the benefit of the doubt regarding rumors and gossip.

baseball Prepare for upcoming stressful events and you will handle them with dignity and success. Take steps to maintain your health and do things to add excitement to your life.

baseball stadium Within three days you will develop a glowing aura and an exuberance that will last for some time to come. This will be the result of good fortune and luck. You will exude a charisma and a new love of life. Others will notice this change in you, but it will be difficult to explain this new zest for life.

baseboard You will come to the realization that other people need time to do things on their own. Stop being so demanding of others who need the time to take care of their personal issues. This is very important for the next three days.

basement You sense that a deep secret is hidden from you. Gradually, within the next two days, this mystery will begin to emerge. After you learn the facts it will be such a shock that you will wish you had never heard of it. It is also important to create a more loving, stable environment for your loved one in order to avoid conflict.

basin Be determined to further your education and develop skills. Prosperity is yours. Begin this process within three days.

basket You will be blessed and will experience luck with all of your projects.

basketball You will receive an unexpected surprise.

basket maker An unemployed friend will need your encouragement.

bass You will meet someone within a next few days and find this person is worth your trust.

bass drum Do not volunteer your time for anything. Stay close at home for the next two days.

basset hound Someone will unexpectedly express love for you in a surprising way at a surprising time. This will occur within two days.

bass horn Pay attention to well-meaning criticisms from relatives. There is some truth to these statements and you may be able to better your life by accepting these opinions.

bassinet A seemingly short term gain will turn into a large windfall in the future. This will happen within two days.

bassoon You will win your heart's desire by becoming strong and self confident.

bastard Do not allow another persons' obstacles to hinder your progress.

baste Tie up loose ends regarding your career.

Bastille Day Within three days, set aside the time to determine the vulnerable areas of your life, and prepare yourself in a way that does not leave you open to attack. This can be prevented by watching your behavior.

bat *(baseball)* You will soon realize the importance of another person's input into your ventures.

batboy You will disagree with a co-worker.

batgirl Avoid all confrontations.

bath *to see someone or yourself bathing in mud* Inter-staff problems will escalate within a few days.

to see someone taking a bubble bath Because you put your knowledge into print, you will realize great fame, fortune, and honor.

to bathe with another Ask and apply for a grant. You will receive it.

cold water bath Develop a good rapport with a dependable co-worker.

herb, floral bath Communicate directly with someone in authority for a salary increase and promotion.

hot water bath Take action within two days concerning a situation that needs prompt attention in order to avoid an escalation of the problem.

milk bath Someone will declare undying love and will propose marriage within three days.

steam bath Keep in mind each thing you dislike about a person you are trying to avoid in order to have the courage to go on with your life without this person.

to spray yourself, something or someone with clear water in the tub You will achieve a big victory during this upcoming cycle that will offer you an abundance of new opportunities. Position yourself in such a way, by using whatever power of authority you may possess, to work the completion of an agreement to your favor. This is especially important for the next week. You have a seven day period from the time you have this dream to push this agreement through, and it will be well received by everyone involved. This is the perfect cycle to take care of this task. You are on a victorious path in life and many blessings will come to you and your family.

Turkish bath This dream is an extremely lucky omen and is letting you know you are headed for a brilliant future.

You will have the courage, strength and valor to handle any situation that will come up within two days. Although they may be stressful, they will be quickly resolved.

in any other form You will soon be married.

bathhouse You will use the information you receive very wisely.

bathinette Watch out for animal bites for the next few days.

bathing cap Someone will be upset with you for no reason. Blame this on mood changes.

bathing suit You will admire a beautiful nude within the next few days. This will bring you much pleasure and will be consensual.

bath mat Use common sense and return to basics in order to handle an urgent situation.

bathrobe You will be well rewarded for work well done in the past. The pay off for this work will come now. For the next three days you will enjoy the mobility that this extra money will give you. You will also bond closer to someone you desire and this will lead to a permanent relationship. You are headed for a brilliant future.

bathroom *to walk into* You will enjoy a brilliant future, financial security and a long healthy life.

to use anything but the toilet Sudden changes will occur within relationships for the better. This will happen within two days.

bath salts Act quickly on a situation you need to attend to that involves another individual. Move on this within two days, otherwise you will lose your chance for success.

Bathsheba *(from the Bible)* You will find love with a financially insecure person. Be patient, this person will gain wealth in the future.

bathtub *empty* Another person will cause you hardship through the theft of valuable information and you will need to begin a project anew. This can be avoided if you take immediate steps to make alterations.

full You will be fortunate in trade affairs.

bathtub ring Be cautious about sexually transmitted diseases.

bathtub water *unusual things floating in the water* Make sure that this does not take place in reality. Someone will also be so satisfied and happy with your attitude towards them that they will want to demonstrate their feelings. This person will keep this a secret until you are in a position of privacy and it can easily be revealed to you. You are loved beyond your imagination by people you least expect.

batik *(dying method)* You will enjoy a long and rewarding life.

baton You will be given false information about another person. Check your sources.

batter *(baseball)* You will soon enjoy liberty from financial worry and will enjoy a new love life. This process will begin within three days.

batter *(dough)* Someone you respect and care deeply about will pay you back with ungratefulness within three days. Be advised.

battering ram Warning! Someone will attempt to kill you by using a slow acting, cumulative poison. Be careful and take steps to prevent this from happening.

battery For the next two days, make it very clear to all concerned that you are under no obligation to behave in any way that someone else wishes you to. Make sure that no one has control over you, and you will be able to rid yourself of someone who acts as though they have authority over your behavior, way of speaking, thinking or acting. This will be done with very little stress and anxiety, because of your tact and the way you handle this situation. You are headed in the right direction for a very prosperous future.

batting *(cotton)* Your ability to move quickly in a situation will result in financial gain.

batting average Be more understanding with others.

batting cage You will fall in love with someone you do not know very well. You will find that you have much in common and the love will quickly grow.

batting helmet Be aware of false pride. This will cause your downfall.

battle You and a special person will make plans for your future. You are headed for a brilliant life.

battle ax You will have an opportunity to purchase a ticket for a future space event. The value of this ticket will be worth a fortune by the time it becomes valid.

battle cry You will need to hire an attorney within three days to fight a disputed inheritance. This dispute will occur within a few months.

battle fatigue You will need to associate with a disliked person because of their authority. Set personal feelings aside in order to achieve success.

battle field Another's life will change because of an obsession with you. This person will pattern their life after yours. Be aware of this and set a good example.

battle ship Bring more knowledge into your line of work for greater success. Keep a log.

bay It is essential that you account for your children's actions and whereabouts for a few days.
to see a fisherman in the bay You are headed for a bright future.
land lock You will fail to handle a situation in the correct manner within three days. Do whatever you can now to avoid failure. Regroup and rethink this situation in order to handle this correctly the first time.

bayberry You will experience good health, good fortune and tranquility with your family. A sudden turn of events will bring you great wealth within three days.

bayonet Do not overextend yourself for the next five days. Your energies are low.

bay window You will need a quiet stress free space. Meditate and think through future decisions for the next three days.

bazaar You will experience stressful, annoying situations for a few days. Keep your sense of humor.

bazooka An unfaithful friend will attempt to destroy a relationship that is special to you. Take care for the next two days, to prevent this from occurring. Do not allow yourself to become passive and satisfied with present circumstances, especially in the next seven days. If you make changes in the way your business is going, you will rapidly see an improvement, and things will start going in the direction you want. Otherwise you will also shortly acquire what you most want from life in a very victorious way.

BB For the next five days, make sure that you do not assume an air of indifference with others. This will only lead to confusion and resentments.

beach You will have to ask a deceitful roommate to move out. If you don't, they will eventually cause problems.

beach ball A brilliant future is yours. You will be contacted by someone, within five days, who always brings a wealth of excitement into your life.

beachcomber Listen to a troubled younger person who desires to relocate. You may help to make the move easier.

beach umbrella Stop overworking. Take a few days off for rest.

beacon You will move into a nursing home within three weeks. You will be cared for correctly.

bead You and your family will receive many blessings. You will also reach an agreement within two days with another person and gain prompt completion of a goal.

worry beads You definitely have the capabilities and means to be victorious in situations that will come up within the week that you felt you were unable to grasp. Many blessings are with you and you are headed for a brilliant future.

beadwork Make your sex life with someone special as important as your work.

beagle A decision reached within a few days will be upsetting. Seek alternative decisions.

beak Do not go overboard on a project for the next three days.

pecking beak Do not prolong the finalization of a small business venture.

beaker Do not assume that something will automatically work in your favor because it has in the past. This time the result will be different. Prepare for this eventually within the week.

beam *(of light)* You will achieve the privacy you need. You will also be able to communicate with someone special about your relationship without interference.

bean Do not borrow or lend money.

beanbag A situation may arise that concerns jealousy. Be alert to this and take steps to prevent it.

bean curd For the next three days be very wary of your involvement with family members or you could become embroiled in a tough situation. Do not allow anyone to disturb your equilibrium.

beanie Avoid losing anything that you feel is in jeopardy for the next three days.

beanpole Make a detailed list of the obligations you expect from someone else in order to avoid problems.

bean sprout A request made via mail will result in a positive answer.

beanstalk You will be made an attractive offer for something you own and no longer desire.

bear An acquaintance will exert authority over you to the point of following and stalking you. In spite of this person's overt friendliness, you must put a stop to it before it gets out of hand.

grizzly bear A priceless collection will be damaged if you do not take steps to prevent this within ten days. Any negative occurrence in this dream needs to be avoided in reality. Do everything you can to experience only positive expressions in your life.

teddy bear Within five days express your true feelings to those who are unsure of how you feel toward them. You are deeply appreciated and loved and will experience this more in this time frame. Many blessings are with you and your family. Anything you want to achieve will be accomplished very successfully.

bear cat An unexpected stranger will begin to harass you. The moment this starts, leave the premises and stay clear of this person. Especially for the next two days.

beard *to shave off* You will lose someone you care about to an accident. Warn this person in order to prevent this during the next two weeks.

beautiful beard You will receive a gift of jewelry.

to trim You will suffer emotionally from a nagging, abusive mate. You bring this on yourself and can put a stop to it.

combing a beard Handle your taxes soon.

bearskin This dream is extremely lucky. You will be pursued by many different suitors over the next few days. This will be a fun cycle for you, and you will flit from person to person. This will not be a serious time for you.

beast Control impulsive behavior.

beast of burden If someone is hesitant over an agreement you will be entering within five days. back off. If you do not, problems will arise within two weeks that will be very difficult to get back to a normal status. Otherwise, good luck is with you.

beat *to beat eggs or any mixture* You will hear of a miscarriage. This can be prevented.

to beat someone in a race You will be successful with your ambitions.

to be beaten in a race Avoid any annoying conversation with someone in authority for the next three days.

to beat up someone Good luck, good health and wealth will come to you and your family.

to be beaten - any form Take steps to prearrange and rearrange situations that would lead to a loss of ambition. This is a warning not to be defeated.

beater You will unexpectedly be called upon to defend someone who is special to you.

Beatles, the Take stock of your possessions. Some will increase in value over thirty years and are worth collecting.

beatnik Get a new lease on life. Focus on the positive and redo your appearance. Let go of old negative types.

beauty *any form* You and your business associates will celebrate a business success.

beauty mark/spot *anywhere on the body* You will find a generous, loyal, sexually exciting person to share your life with.

beauty salon You will make progress in a romantic situation.

to work in salon You will receive a surprise invitation within three days.

to have hair cut in salon You are procrastinating an agreement. Stop putting off decisions, the result will be successful.

beaver Be careful when in traffic and around busy intersections for a few days.

bebop Do not become lazy. Bring humor into your work life.

because *any form* Within a five day period, you will gather your resources and the energy needed to follow your instincts regarding a particular situation you feel should be happening. In spite of what others say or do, this situation needs to occur. It will bring vast improved changes into your life and the lives of others. Proceed with confidence. Everything will work out as it should.

bed For the next seven days, focus on bringing a relationship to the level you desire. This is the best cycle to concentrate on this. You will also be asked out for dinner and conversation by someone who is far wealthier than they appear to be. You have the opportunity at this time to develop a relationship, if you choose. This is a very lucky omen and you are headed for a brilliant future.

to make a bed You and someone else will go through great lengths to strengthen the bond between you. You will have many open conversations to improve the relationship. You will feel wonderful about everything that has transpired.

to see a beautifully made bed Be relentless and consistent in developing the closeness you need from someone.

unmade bed Express the feelings you have for someone in unusual ways. This will verify your feelings to a special person. Good luck is with you and, within three days, you will feel loved beyond your imagination.

hot bed Be prepared to determine what you really want from someone you are interested in. Once you reveal your true feelings, you will be able to specify the depth of the relationship. The other individual may want more from this union than you. Be prepared to make compromises for mutual satisfaction if you choose to go in this direction. The more time you spend nurturing this relationship, the greater the passion and the deeper the emotional feelings will be. Take steps to keep any negative event you witnessed in this dream from becoming a reality.

bed in an unusual place You will develop an unusual strength that will allow you to communicate a difficult problem to another person. You will be able to get much off your chest and get to the heart of the matter. This dream also implies that your divinity is with you and you will receive anything you need. Good luck is with you, especially for the next three days.

to be in bed with something unusual Do not waste time waiting for certain information. Use the knowledge you have now to make a decision. Be consistent in your actions.

to be in bed with many people Other people will become very jealous and focused on you. It will become difficult to deflect this focus from you. Act toward others the way you want others to treat you.

to see someone else in bed with you If you see anything negative taking place with you or anyone else in this dream, you have prior notice to make sure you do everything necessary to bring a desirable resolution to ensure you experience only positive expressions in your life. This dream represents a future event that will take place within four days with the person whom you dreamt about or someone who resembles them. You can choose to allow this to occur or dismiss it in reality. This dream is a very victorious omen and implies that within the next two days, no matter what is occurring in your life, you will be able to focus on what you need to be doing in order to reach your goals. You will also be able to use your abilities to pull strings on your behalf. You will develop the confidence you need and will maintain this level of confidence until you succeed. Many blessings will come to you and your family. You are definitely headed for a brilliant future.

to see someone lying down in bed in any unusual position Be extremely aware for the next three days and make sure that you move forward with another person with caution. This person is someone you are beginning to feel some closeness to and will lead you to believe you can fully confide in them and can depend upon their loyalty. This person is also very crafty and skilled at creating illusions and deceptions, and will have you believe that certain events will take place in the future. These events will never take place. A hidden agenda is at play here that involves this person pursuing you for reasons only they are aware of. They will go to great lengths to create a trusting atmosphere. If you do become suspicious of their motives, this person will use their charm and charisma to create a diversion to allay your suspicions. By the time you become aware of what is happening, you will be suffering deep emotional disappointments, disillusionments and financial losses. It will take you a long time to recover and get your life back to normalcy. You have prior notice of this and all the ammunition you need to ensure that this does not occur. Practice common sense and you will successfully diffuse this situation. Do not compromise and do not allow this person to pry into your personal life. You are on the path toward a prosperous future and many blessings are with you and your family. If the person you dreamed of is the same sex as you, the danger of this taking place is closer and far more dangerous.

bed & breakfast Set aside private time for lovemaking and romance.

bed board Your friend will need sympathy for the next few days.

bedclothes Do not go out with someone you do not know well.

bedcover Recycle and renew items for extra cash.

bedding Help a younger person apply for a grant.

bed jacket Be loyal and generous with a loved one.

bed linen Keep doing what you are currently doing. You are very secure and will be more so within a few days.

Bedouin For the next three days, take it easy and place yourself in a stress free environment. You are also being warned not to assume someone else's responsibilities, especially for the next five days.

bedpan Within three days a younger person will experience a temper tantrum because of the theft of one of their valuables. Alert a young person to this in order to prevent this loss.

bedridden A friend will betray you by joining an adversarial group. Avoid this early by choosing an alternative assistant.

bedroom You and a special person will enjoy exciting, sensuous lovemaking for as long as you desire. Good luck is with you, especially for the next two days.

bed sheet Watch out for a depraved individual.

bedsores You will suddenly and unexpectedly become wealthy. The wealth increases with the number of sores seen.

bedspread Do not allow your family to slow down your production by inside fighting. Set a positive example and promote harmony.

bedtime story Take steps for the next two days to ensure the safety of a young child. Make sure this child is very protected. Every conference meeting will also be successful for the next few days.

bed wetter *someone else wets the bed* You will be very excited about the news you will receive within two days. You will also receive a marriage proposal and this will lead to a festive time of preparing for a wedding.
  to wet the bed This dream implies that you may unintentionally sabotage the plans of another. Be acutely aware of what you are doing over the next two days that may affect another person's future.

bee You will experience victory in all phases of life.

beechnut Your application for a job will be turned down within a few days. Seek alternative work.
beech tree Quickly handle upcoming petty situations and move on with your life.

beef A secret admirer will ask for your aid within three days. This person will be kind and sensual.

beefcake *(slang)* Be sure that you take an active role in getting everything you want on an emotional level. Within five days you will be able to visualize the path you have to take for a brilliant future. Good luck is with you.

beef face You will have to deal with an individual who takes pleasure in creating chaotic and stressful situations. Plan ahead. Within three days this person will create a monster situation that will escalate to the point of being completely out of control. Make plans for entertainment to avoid this person and situation for the next three days.

beefsteak tomato You will receive the words of love, in a letter, that you have long waited to hear.

beef stroganoff A big change will occur in your life due to unusual circumstances that will result in an increase in wealth. You will also be able to retain the relationships in your life that mean a lot to you.

beef Wellington You will develop a wonderful work plan while brainstorming with another individual. Both of you are headed for a brilliant and prosperous future.

beehive Someone will become too sexually aggressive. Communication about needs will lead to better understanding.

beekeeper You will receive a letter that will bring you closer to a special person within two days.

Beelzebub *(from the Bible)* Do not become involved in another's emotional problems for the next seven days. Be firm in your refusal to involve yourself.

beep *to hear* You and a special person will discuss plans for the future. Your emphasis should be on maintaining harmony.
  to beep Share money and good news with loved ones. Do not become selfish.
  to be beeped This dream is a warning to be aware of a situation that will arise next month. This situation will require an extra outlay of money. Put money aside now to ease this situation. Good luck is with you.

beeper Your plans will be developed and executed in a very professional way. You will then be able to enjoy more prosperity in your life. Within three days you will also verbalize your detailed thoughts in such an appealing way that someone will be put at ease and feel comfortable in your presence. Conversation will flow easily and you will develop a special closeness. This person will tell you what they have been longing to say to you. You are headed for a prosperous future and will be able to use your communication skills to reach others. Both of you will enjoy a wonderful and tranquil life together if you choose this path. Pay attention to the message on the beeper or to the purpose of being beeped. Listen carefully to the message and take steps to prevent anything negative portended by this dream. Otherwise, you are headed for a brilliant future.

beer *to drink beer* Speak your mind when another person makes unilateral plans that involve you. Attempt to prevent this behavior ahead of time.

to see others drink beer Do everything necessary to avoid a disease due to your carelessness. This can be prevented.

in any other form You believe, or are led to believe, that a sexual encounter with someone you care about will lead to a long term commitment. This will not be the case with this individual. The relationship will not change as a result of sexual intercourse. It is your decision whether you choose to relate to this person only in sexual terms.

beesting Do not waste time with pettiness. Get legal advice.

beeswax Do not overload your schedule for the next few days.

beet Be aware that someone yearns for your love. You must also take care of your circulation, walk, drink extra water and avoid anemia. Do everything necessary to maintain health.

Beethoven A document promising a sum of money will arrive in the mail.

beetle You will enjoy a speedy and profitable reunion with someone special. It is also important to get a checkup to rule out anemia.

beg *to beg for your life* Take every precaution necessary to make sure that you are not leading yourself down a dead end path. This will create a very stressful future. You have prior notice of this and can take the necessary steps to steer yourself toward the correct path. Many blessings are with you and your family.

beggar *you are the beggar* Treat yourself with respect, especially for the next three days so that others will hold you in high regard.

someone else is a beggar Your family will enjoy prosperity. Many blessings are with you and your family.

in any other form You have vastly underestimated a situation that you will become involved in within five days. Move on this before you let it slip away. This will be your golden opportunity.

begonia Listen and show tolerance for another person who is upset.

behavior *to see someone behave in an odd manner* You have been led to believe that you can entrust someone with

heavy responsibilities. Once you allow this person to take on these tasks, you will be let down in a big way. This individual fully believes they are capable of handling these big responsibilities but their ego is larger than their ability. Be aware of this and do not risk anything of importance.

asking someone to stop a certain behavior Within five days you will need to really take a stand in order to put a stop to someone's disagreeable behavior. Limit your involvement with someone or something that you are becoming more deeply involved with. Use any available means to stop this involvement. You will be showered with gifts, but you will need to be firm in your refusal to commit because you will later regret any involvement. You will also experience an abundance of health and a clarity of thought that will allow you to handle this appropriately and with as little stress as possible.

beheaded *any form* Share responsibilities with others. Allow them to be helpful. For a more defined definition, refer to *decapitate*.

beige Do everything you can to bond closer to a special person. Verbalize your feelings and your intentions in order to make this bond permanent. Good luck is with you.

Bel and the Dragon *(from the Canonical Bible)* Within three days, you will receive a very thrilling gift and will also rid yourself of a long term burden that has been weighing you down. Good luck is with you.

belch Give a bit more to your relationships than you receive for the next few days.

belfry Within two days, take time out to choose the right person to delegate tasks to. This person should be someone you can rely on until you resolve an ongoing situation.

bell *to hear continuous bell ringing* Be aware that someone is attempting to catch you off guard for the express purpose of gratifying their emotional needs. Play it safe and take steps to prevent others from taking advantage of you.

alarm Within the next few days do everything necessary to prevent exposure to a virus.

to see someone or yourself playing bells Beware of being struck by falling objects for the next three days.

to pull a bell rope Do not allow laziness to take control of your life. The moment you feel this coming on, push yourself to take care of all necessary chores. Laziness will lead to guilt and regrets.

to stop a bell from ringing Doors that were formerly closed to you are now open. You will be seen by others from a different perspective. Opportunities will start coming in. You can look for this to happen within two days.

bell without a ringer or without a tone Within a few days, a couple you know will begin a fight that could lead to a break-up. This couple will want to involve you. Avoid this situation.

paper bells Someone is in love with you and knows they

should marry you. This person has wasted a great amount of time working up the courage to ask. Nothing you have done has caused this delay. This individual simply has difficulty asking and will decide to go to counseling to alleviate the problem. It is up to you to decide whether you want this union or whether to remain patient. This dream is a lucky omen for you and many blessings will come your way.

in any other form Keep your secrets to yourself for the next few days. You are in a lucky cycle and will receive a romantic offer you cannot refuse.

belladonna Do not risk everything by sidestepping your responsibilities for the next few days.

bell-bottoms You will enjoy a thrilling love affair within three days with someone you desire, if you choose. This dream implies many happy moments.

bellboy You will have a great experience with a sexual partner within two days.

bell jar Take steps to avoid a bad reputation as an exhibitionist.

bellows A warm fireplace and soft music will help to launch a romance.

bell pepper You will enjoy an abundance of health and good luck. Keep your immune system healthy.

bell tower Do not engage in risky affairs behind another person's back, especially for the next three days. Do not become involved in any underhanded activity.

belly *your belly* You will be performing physical labor without pay for another. Be clear whether you choose to render some of your services for free.

another persons belly You must allow someone else to express their point of view, within a few days, for a clearer mutual understanding, and mutual happiness.

hair on or unfamiliar markings You should back off from the advice of others for a few days. After this you will have more clarity of thought and the organizational skills needed to implement your thoughts. Powerful results will be the outcome.

pain in You must guard your life for the next few days. A deranged person may surprise and shock you in an unfamiliar place.

someone else's pain in You should set aside more time for the next two months for natural creativity and the expression of ideas. Greater rewards will come as a result of a creative thought.

belly button When in the company of family members, keep your opinions to yourself, especially for the next two days.

belly dancer Think of a variety of plans and alternative moves to meet your goals. Do not rely on one plan or be-

come locked into one mode of behavior. Develop different perspectives. Do not restrict yourself for the next three days.

belong *to belong* A number of events will occur very rapidly one after the other, and each will bring a sense of joy, wonder and awe. You will also find you possess a powerful energy that you will be able to direct and control. As a result, you will bring other people under your subjugation at the same time that these events are taking place. Within the week you will also bring to completion anything you wish in a successful way, and be able to handle any difficult issue that comes up. Each subsequent problem will be easier to handle. Trust your intuition and many blessings will come to you and your family.

in any other form Someone will misuse your power and authority to commit a horrible act against someone who is important to you, and will then hide behind this authority to successfully get away with this. You have prior notice of this and can take steps to prevent it. This is especially important for the next three days. Otherwise, you are headed for a very prosperous future.

beloved You will enjoy good fortune in all phases of your life.

belt Remain firm in all of your decisions. Maintain a solid center and stay on an even keel.

safety belt Be consistent and persistent in the attitude of love you show toward someone who is special to you. You will be surprised in their change of attitude.

beluga Don't allow jealousy to take control for the next few days. You will have better results without this emotion.

bench You will find your love by advertising and by circulating socially.

work bench Someone with a dynamic reputation will back you up on a business plan. Good luck is with you and you are headed in the right direction.

bench press Avoid animal bites for the next three days.

bend Do not pay too much attention to specific negative aspects of an individual's personality. This will be a distraction and will hinder the progress of a particular situation that needs to be taken care of that involves this person.

bend over You will attend a business meeting within two days and find the other person very pleasant. This meeting will result in a positive outcome.

benediction You will experience exuberant and exciting feelings because of someone's unexpected declaration of love. If you choose, this will develop into a relationship in any capacity you wish and will lead to mutual fulfillment.

benefit Volunteer your services and you will receive rich emotional rewards.

bereave Do not allow criticisms and put-downs to keep you from achieving your desires.

beret Commit yourself to changes in your life. You will come out ahead.

Berlin Become busy for the next two days. Create a bond with someone you feel will be important to you. Build a stronger friendship between yourself and this person. This dream may also be used as a reference point in time. If you dream of this city and see its name used in any context, the dream message will occur on this day.

Bermuda For the next four days work as hard as you can, then relax. Opportunities will fall into place. This dream may also be used as a reference point in time. If you dream of this island group and see its name used in any context, the dream message will occur on this day.

Bermuda grass You will be able to demonstrate the love you feel for someone in the manner they desire within a three day period. This will take place in a wild and romantic environment. Good luck will be with you for the next week.

Bermuda shorts This dream is an omen of health and wealth. Build stronger foundations in those relationships that are important to you. This will motivate all those who are involved to demonstrate more affection toward you.

berry Do not allow those who depend on you to lose respect for you.
  bayberry You will experience good health, good fortune and tranquility with your family. A sudden turn of events will bring you great wealth within three days.
  black berry Do not allow financial stress to upset your relationships. Communicate with those involved within three days.
  blueberry Joy will enter your life within seven days and will be prompted by genuine feelings of love from another.
  boysenberry You will need to visit an ill friend. Love is also in the air. This is a great three day cycle to bring any emotional situation into a proper balance for a successful outcome.
  cranberry This dream is a lucky omen. Take care of your kidneys and drink plenty of water. Be sure not to eat anything that will cause an allergic reaction.
  raspberry You will make the correct decision concerning someone who wants to be close to you. Take this opportunity to allow yourself emotional gratification.
  strawberry A great event will be celebrated within a few weeks. This will be a big surprise to you and will bring you much joy. It will take a great deal of preparation on your part regarding gifts and attire so start planning now.

best man You will know of someone who is being released from jail.

bet *to place a bet* This is a perfect day to try your luck. Play small amounts for five consecutive times for big winnings.

betel nut For the next week advertise your skills in order to increase your earning powers. Do whatever is necessary to inform others of your talents.

Bethlehem You will be liberated from a burden. Happiness and honor will be yours.

betrothal Your company will successfully merge with a large corporation.

bevel You will have an urge to marry. Follow this urge.

beverage *to see a large variety* You will receive large profits from your ventures.

beware A warning in a dream should be taken as a plea for caution in your real life.

bewitch A major situation plagued with problems will miraculously vanish.

Bhagavad-Gita You will receive an unexpected invitation at the last moment. You will enjoy yourself immensely and will share laughter and conversation with others.

bib You will feel an urgency to commit yourself to someone you are interested in. If you choose to take this path, you will enjoy a long term relationship filled with mutual happiness.

Bible You will enjoy good luck, health, happiness and financial security from now on. It is also lucky to keep a Bible open in your house at all times.

biceps A sick family member will rapidly recover.

bickering You will need to warn a pregnant woman to care for herself now in order to have a healthy, trouble free birth.

bicycle The road to success will escalate rapidly. Offer a helping hand to someone in need within the next two days.

bid You will find a believer in your project and receive seed money within three weeks.

bidet Do what you can to space out your commitments. Do not allow them to overlap and interfere with each other.

bifocals Two mutual friends will have a dispute. Walk out before your loyalty becomes divided.

big Whatever you see larger than life, is something you need to focus on in reality. If it is negative, take steps to alter the message. If it is positive, promote it to the fullest.

You will also become very clear in the manner in which you can help someone who wants you and/or needs you in some capacity. Your thinking will allow you to gain the knowledge of what to do to make this person comfortable enough to express their future needs and plans. This cycle will allow you clarity of thought and the ability to bring ideas into reality, including the ability to tackle big ideas and projects. This dream is a good luck symbol.

Big Apple You will enjoy a long and fruitful life.

bigamist Your experience will be in demand to help solve a problem. This problem will be more complex than expected. Refuse to offer assistance.

big band Someone you know with a great deal of power and authority will pull strings on your behalf. Good luck is with you.

big bang theory Do not allow inconsistent behavior to rule your personality, especially for the next three days.

Big Ben Love yourself.

Big Dipper Do not place obstacles in the way of a happy relationship.

Bigfoot Think ahead. If you choose, you will fall in love with a much older person. This could be a fantastic relationship. Remember, also, that peace of mind is dependent on self respect.

big game Within three weeks, you will meet someone who finds it very important to develop a deep personal relationship. This individual needs and wants a strong family relationship. This is a great cycle for putting yourself in circulation and finding this person if you desire this kind of relationship. This individual will be wealthy and will have a tremendous influence over your life. You are headed for a brilliant future, and many blessings will come to you and your family.

big head You will be talking to a bewitching person. Be careful. You may find this person mesmerizing and will go along with plans against your better judgment.

bighorn Business problems will cease within two days if you push yourself to resolve them.

bigot You will personally have to dispose of a decaying animal. Search your premises for a sick or dying animal, and your property for the possibility of any poisonous substances. Take steps to keep these substances off your premises.

biker Do everything you can to avoid the development of any negative situation for the next five days. You do have control over how situations unfold, and you have the ability to maintain them in a positive fashion.

bikini Become part of a team effort.

bile The answer to a mystery that has been plaguing you for a long time will surface shortly. Everything that has been puzzling you will become clear and you will come to a full understanding of this issue.

bill *to receive a bill* The amount you see on the bill represents a particular monetary amount that you will be overcharged. This dream is alerting you to become actively involved in comparing prices when shopping. This extra effort will result in a surprising and pleasing difference in the amount you will pay for certain items. It would be to your advantage to shop around. Within three days someone will also try to trick you in order to gain a financial advantage over you without suspicions on your part. You have enough notice of this and can take steps to avoid this situation. At the same time that these other two events are taking place you will receive an unexpected gift. Although you will wonder why this is being given to you, it will simply be that someone wants to demonstrate their affection toward you. You are headed for a prosperous future and will receive an abundance of health and financial security.

paying bills To dream of paying bills signifies luck. You will also receive a fantastic invitation.

bill (*bird*) Someone is feeling abandoned by you. Act quickly to ensure that this person knows your true feelings and understand how special they are to you. Your actions will bring this person a great deal of pleasure and will be deeply appreciated by them. Put your love into action and anything you choose to develop permanently will occur within five days. A gift will also hasten this development. You are loved beyond your imagination.

billboard Give a helping hand to another person in order to launch them professionally.

billiards Do not overextend yourself. Set limits to prevent fatigue, especially for the next three days.

billiards table Someone you trust will become unintentionally deceitful. Be careful and do not lay the groundwork to easily facilitate this behavior.

billionaire An unknown talent of yours will be requested by another. This talent will blossom and increase the wealth of the other individual and bring success with riches to you.

Bill of Rights This dream is a lucky omen. You must also make sure you are aware of all of your rights. Ensure that, for the next two days, your rights are not violated on any level. Any positive message revealed to you should be pursued and any negative message may be changed or avoided completely.

bill of sale You will feel pain and anguish as a result of a misplaced item.

bill poster Someone will downplay your role to others concerning a project you are involved with.

billy club Within the week, a casual relationship will, if you desire, turn into a deeper commitment. This relationship will develop into a mutually satisfying union.

billy goat This dream signifies riches. The color is of no significance.

Billy the Kid Someone special to you will be quarrelsome for the next three days.

bin Very private behaviors may accidentally occur in public. Avoid this embarrassment and protect your reputation.

bind To dream of binding something together is equivalent to binding someone special closer to you.

binder Ask a special person to include you in ongoing plans. This individual will be more than happy to include you.

bindery You will have a good life with someone special.

bingo You will be lucky and can expect success within your family.

binocular You will receive valuable information within a few days. This information will be used productively for any project you have.

biography Avoid confusion with a special project. Make notes to avoid chaos.

biology Do not buy or impress friends with money. You will need this money and will soon be without resources.

biorhythms You and someone who is important to you are looking for changes to improve your relationship. You are open for conversations and new ways to demonstrate affection to bring a new closeness into the relationship that will benefit this union. If you decide to pursue this, the other person will be more than eager to go along with this process.

biplane Within seven days, someone will try to involve you in a relationship. You will have mixed feelings at first but your uncertainty is unwarranted. You will have a wonderful experience if you choose to pursue this. Involve yourself completely and you will enjoy yourself on any level you desire.

birch Rush important papers to the proper destination.
bird Your wishes will be granted. Pay attention to the bird's color and refer to the color definition.
  in a cage You may be involved in an accident while out

with someone else. This can be prevented.
  to catch You will surrender to a commitment and experience undying love.
  dead bird Do not let your ambitions die.
  to feed You will receive a gift of fragrance.
  bird in flight This dream implies that any idea or plan set into motion over the next two days will be dynamically successful and have a pleasant outcome. The object of your affection will also offer you a pleasant and unexpected surprise. You will have the opportunity, if you choose, to travel the world for many months. Good luck is with you. Proceed with confidence.
  injured bird Within two days you will feel neglected by someone who has promised to call but will not contact you. This person is difficult to contact due to the nature of their work, therefore, prior to this two day period make it clear that you expect promises to be kept and communications to be left open.
  pecking bird Do not prolong the finalization of a small business venture or of any negotiations that you wish to conclude.

birdbath Nourish special friendships.

bird dog Use your imagination. Within three days your mental inventiveness will be stimulated to the point that will allow you to make plans to generate a second income.

birdhouse Do not put anything in writing that may later be held against you.

bird of paradise Do not make promises to call someone unless this is your intention.

bird of prey Some important missing information will become an irritating riddle.

birdseed Within five days, a close friend will contact you with the news that they have come into some power, authority and a great deal of money. This person wishes to have you join them in a joint venture that will bring you lifetime benefits. Good luck is with you.

birdsong You will be paid well for domestic work done for a wealthy older person.

bird watcher You can accomplish a great deal by projecting an interesting image of yourself around influential people. They will be involved in a project you are currently working on and you will enjoy your work on this enterprise.

birth *to witness a birth* You will hear of a birth of twins. Apply yourself and express your ideas graphically within a few weeks. This will give others the chance to really visualize your ideas and this will work to your advantage. A compromise on an agreement will end problems and you will be better off in the long run.
  child birth in any form You will be, within the next five

days, given a gift of greater mental inventiveness by your deity. Put this gift to practical use in order to change your present circumstances. You will experience instant wealth, a brilliant future and have the clarity of thought that you need to correctly direct the fortune you will be coming into. Make sure that anything negative that could become a reality does not occur and take steps to ensure that you experience only positive expressions in life.

still birth Demand assistance from your higher power to handle a difficult situation that you are presently undergoing. Do this by way of your favorite form of meditation. You will be able to resolve this satisfactorily within three days. You have a great deal of power within this cycle for handling difficult situations.

afterbirth You will have to deal with a minor family problem connected with finances within two days. Handle this calmly.

birth certificate What you once felt was impossible concerning a relationship will now be a possibility within the week. This dream also implies that you will receive a gift that you will treasure for life.

birth control Move quickly for the next two days to close an important business deal that you have been trying to conclude.

birth control pills *male or female* Within five days you will be entering an extremely lucky cycle. Everyone involved in your life will share in your luck. You will also be offered services that will allow you to successfully complete your goals, and reach a grander level of achievement than you thought possible, especially with anything you feel is a high priority. You can expect many wonderful and amazing connections that will assist you in meeting your goals. You can also anticipate a mega merger, and the energy generated between you and those you will be working with will promote you to a far higher level of success than you expected. This dream also implies that you will gain benefits by attending a festive event, participating in an educational experience, or by attending a gathering in which one person will show an interest in you and your projects. A long period of tranquility will follow this experience and you will enjoy a prosperous future. Any negative event witnessed in this dream can be prevented, and anyone you recognized in the dream needs to be forewarned to do likewise.

birthday To dream of anyone's birthday signifies a lucky omen. It is also beneficial to look up the astrological sign of the birthday, whether yours or anyone else's, that is celebrated.

birthday cake The opportunities you have been waiting for will come your way within two days. You will enjoy a new lease on life and all issues that have been dragging you down will suddenly come to an end. You will enjoy a new excitement and new sense of confidence. For the next two days, make sure that you demonstrate self reliance and make an

effort to look at both sides of a particular issue. Explore the possibilities of what could unexpectedly take place prior to making any major decisions. You are loved beyond your imagination, are deeply respected and will be surrounded by those who love you. Others will show you their appreciation within the week. A dream about a birthday cake also signifies that you need to look up the particular astrological sign of the person celebrating their birthday.

birthmark You will enjoy the company of someone sweet and agreeable for the rest of your life.

birthstone Direct yourself to the color of the stone for additional clues. You are headed toward a successful future.

biscuit Do not envy another person's career. Make your own success. For the next few days someone will also show a great deal of interest toward you. This person is interested in a fling and nothing else. It is your choice whether you want to pursue this or not.

bisexual Demand that your needs be met as soon as possible.

bishop You will receive accurate professional advice. This will lead to success.

bison Stop harassing others.

bit *(bridle)* Do not involve yourself in any new ventures or investments. They would prove unlucky for you.

bitch *to hear the word* Think ahead. Do not allow someone to place responsibilities and pressures on you that do not belong to you. Take steps to avoid this situation, especially for the next three days. Remain uninvolved.

bitch *to see a pregnant dog* Someone will propose to you and you will be married soon, if you choose. Good luck and a brilliant future are yours.

bitchin *(slang term)* You are making all the right moves and are motivating yourself to achieve victory. A connection you have long wanted to make with a certain person but have been unable to in the past will also be successfully made within the week. Schedule a small vacation to a quiet get away place. This will leave you with many pleasurable memories. All things that you felt were impossible in the past are now possible. You are headed for a brilliant future.

bite Feelings you have for another individual are temporary. Enjoy this feeling while it lasts.

to be bitten by anything You will be made clearly aware of the feelings someone has for you. This individual is hopelessly in love with you. This emotion will come over them very rapidly and they will be unable to contain themselves. This dream also implies that you will rid yourself of the problem of not concentrating enough in your relationships.

You will become very consistent in concentrating and focusing on not only relationships, but on anything else that requires this trait. This behavior will last a lifetime. You are definitely headed for a brilliant future.

to bite someone Make sure that a certain person is very motivated and highly enthusiastic about a certain situation that will come up within three days. Do nothing during this time frame that will diminish these feelings in this person. You will regret any action you take that will dampen the enthusiasm this person had for you or for anything that involves you. You will be able to act accordingly because of your prior notice of this. You are definitely headed for a prosperous future.

to be bitten by another person Make sure that no one else kills the motivation or enthusiasm you have for a certain person or situation.

to see you or anyone else bitten by a bug This dream is an omen of victory. You will enjoy great clarity of thought and this will lead you to riches. You will also enjoy a romantic interlude if this is something you choose. Any negative event seen in this dream may be altered or avoided in reality.

bitter *any form* You will need a support system. Begin work on this now.

bivouac Stop your negative thinking.

blabbermouth For the next five days make sure that you have a camera ready in order to capture precious moments, and make sure that the equipment you are using is in adequate condition.

black *to be dressed in black* An attractive, powerful, highly educated person will become interested in your undertakings. You will be able to empower yourself.

a black coat A secret will be confided to you.

someone clad in black at a wedding Keep your plans simple to avoid disappointment.

a woman in black Maintain your confidence in times of hardship for a positive outcome.

man in black Maintain your confidence in spite of the opinions of others.

many people dressed in black At one time you wanted the impossible in a relationship. This person will suddenly return after a long absence and everything you ever wanted from a relationship will now be possible. You will also see other people you have not seen in a long while who are in no way connected with this love relationship. Luck is with you during this cycle.

in any other form Victory and power are yours in each phase of life that you need them. You are headed toward a brilliant and prosperous future.

black and blue Do not freely donate your time. You need this time for yourself. Within three days, someone will also use your authority as a way to commit an atrocious act against someone who means a lot to you and will later hide

behind your authority to get away with this action. This will cause you deep emotional pain. You have prior notice of this and can take steps to prevent it. Otherwise you are headed for a prosperous future.

black bear Certain issues in your life are evolving to the point of allowing others the chance to take advantage of you and will grow to the point of being intolerable to you. Take control of this and do not allow yourself to lose power. This is particularly important for the next three days.

black belt You will need to see a dentist soon for tooth repair.

blackberry Do not allow financial stress to upset your relationships. Communicate with those involved within three days.

blackbird You will go on a spending spree and find all you need at a low price.

blackboard Do not permit painful feelings from the past to fester and resurface to the point where they hinder the pursuit of your goals. The moment you sense this occurrence get busy in another, healthier area of your life. Do not allow these feelings to block your path. You are headed for a healthy and prosperous life. Something will also occur within in three days that will bring you very exciting news. You will become actively involved in a very exciting and gratifying project.

black book You need to be in touch with current situations that are occurring around you. You will uncover unusual events that will point you in the right direction. Any name seen in the book will be instrumental in pushing you in the right direction.

black box Do not encourage yourself to have a sexual encounter with someone you are currently interested in. You will be very unhappy with the results. Use discipline and control.

black death You will be in the presence of someone who is very inconsiderate of the feelings of others. This person is interested only in their own personal gratification. Do not become involved with this person and get on with your life.

black eye You will be lied to by someone you are deeply involved with on an emotional level. This will occur within three days. It can be prevented.

blackface Turn on the charm. You will be invited to an important event.

black foot You will soon rejoice over a reconciliation regarding someone you know.

black hole Make sure you do not become involved in a situation with two other people who are attempting to manipulate you to gain the upper hand and an unfair advantage over you. Remain mentally alert when dealing with others during this three day cycle.

blackjack Protect your eyesight from strain and flying particles. Any number seen will also be lucky in games of chance.

black lung Motivate yourself for the next three days, in order to put yourself on the right path. This is the best cycle to determine what you need to do and to calmly reach a solution. Be aware also that a promise that has been made to you will not be kept. You will hear of this within three days. Do everything you can to ensure this does not take place.

black magic *to hear the word* Place emphasis on the security of your home. Check all gas fixtures and electrical wiring as well as the wiring in your auto. Be sure to turn off everything after use.

to see yourself involved in black magic Any negative event you dreamed of will be fulfilled accurately in real life if you do not quickly take steps to prevent it. This dream serves as a warning to turn this problem around. You will have plenty of time to do so. This dream also implies that you need to make some dramatic changes in your life. Search for the tools that will allow you personal growth and do not allow your loved ones to outgrow you. Look for ways to get rid of outmoded behaviors and ways of thinking in order to keep those you care about around you. Do not allow yourself to become verbally abusive to others either in public or in private. The help you need will come from private counseling, group therapy and self help agencies. These groups can offer help with a variety of problems such as drugs, gambling, alcohol and sexual abuse. Pay attention to what is going on around you and be compassionate with yourself while you are undergoing these changes. If you pay attention to the message in this dream and make the necessary changes, your life will improve dramatically and you will face a brilliant future.

if you see someone you do not know performing black magic that you have no involvement with This will be someone you need to make a point of avoiding in reality. This person represents someone who has a hidden agenda to cause you physical or emotional harm of some kind. You have prior notice of this and can take steps to avoid this person and this situation altogether.

if you see someone you do not know performing black magic and it involves someone you do know Make sure you alert this person that someone is targeting them for the intent of inflicting emotional or physical harm.

to see someone perform black magic against you Be acutely aware of the identity of the person in your dream. This will be a very immoral and wicked person. If you do not recognize the person they will represent one who will come into your life and cause you great emotional harm. Do everything you can to avoid this individual and prepare to protect everything that is emotionally precious to you. You will have the strength and ability to endure anything you need to handle. Victory will be with you. You must also be very careful when engaged in pleasure seeking activities. Be careful that you do not allow anyone to usurp your power and authority. This person will wish to gain control of something you now control, and will try to manipulate you in order to gain power over you and a certain issue you are now dealing with. Do not fall prey to this and prepare yourself now in order to prevent this. You will be able to handle this successfully. Good luck is with you.

blackmail Follow your children's dreams and keep a constant watch over them for the next few weeks.

black market Prepare for long range plans regarding a specific relationship that is important to you. Do this within four days.

Black Mass *(A funeral mass)* Postpone a visit that you have planned to make.

Black Muslim This will be a very lucky cycle for you. You are loved and appreciated by those you care about and many blessings will come to you and your family.

blackout An evil person will attempt to involve you in their plans. Do not become involved.

black pepper Within a week you will meet an evil stranger. Do not invite this person to your house. Your property will be endangered and this could escalate to physical injury. Beware of this.

blacksmith Your children will need extra protection from illness.

black sun Very bad news will come from a relative within a few days. This will involve the illness of a female relative.

black widow An in-law will approach you romantically. Be firm in your rejection.

bladder You need to eat more vegetables, especially cooked parsley. Increase your intake of water. This dream also implies that, for the next seven days, you will be entering a very lucky cycle.

blade *blood on the blade* This dream implies that your success will come quicker than expected.

to be stabbed in the back with a blade This dream confirms that there are no obstacles between yourself and someone who is eagerly trying to communicate with you.

in any other form You will gain mental inventiveness and intelligence. This is a blessed gift that will be given to you.

blame *any form* You will accidentally be locked out of your hotel room partially or completely unclothed.

blanket   Trust your intuition for a few days and simplify your life. Within three days, the person you most desire will also come to you for a very mutually fulfilling sexual encounter.

wet blanket   Someone who loves you but is not in verbal contact misses you a great deal and has intentions to contact you soon to involve you in an enjoyable event within the week.

blasphemy   This dream implies danger. Protect yourself physically in every way for several days.

blast   Do not make false accusations.

blaze   Never betray a private secret about someone who is important to you.

bleach   Someone will want to move in with you. This will be a happy union.

bleachers   You will encounter a former lover. Instead of speaking, you will both ignore the other. The feelings that were caused by this reaction will remain with you for several days. You may decide to make the first move and change the outcome.

bleat   You will enjoy yourself with neighbors at a barbecue.

bleed   *to cut yourself and bleed*   A friend will become a financial drain.

someone else bleeding   Do not jeopardize your security because of a misunderstanding. You will also receive a financial windfall.

to see an animal bleeding/injured   A cluster of events will occur one after the other with each bringing you a tremendous amount of joy, wonder and awe because things are happening so quickly. You will also possess a powerful energy that you will be able to direct and control. At the same time that these other events are taking place you will be able to bring other people under your complete control. Because you have prior notice of this you will be able, within the week, to direct this energy in such a way to successfully complete anything you wish in a superb way. If you give assistance to the animal in the dream, you will be assisting someone close to you in some capacity. You will be able to overcome any difficult obstacle and it will now be very simple to deal with it. Your intuition will be right on target and follow your hunches about a new relationship. Many blessings are with you and your family.

blemish   You will impress another person with your creativeness. This individual will want to promote your talent to fruition. Discuss your investments with a professional for an accurate prospectus.

blender   A supervisor will focus on your bad work habits. Take steps to improve.

in any other form   Your wishes will be granted.

Blessed Sacrament   This will be a good cycle for prosperity and social events. You will reach your highest ambitions within a three day period. You will also experience new dimensions that are open for exploration. Take steps to explore these new areas in spite of anything else that may be going on in your life. You will be able to connect with those people and situations in such a way that these opportunities will work out exactly as you have envisioned. Move quickly on this. You are headed for a prosperous future and good luck is with you.

blessing   *any form*   An abundance of blessings and prosperity will come to you and your family. You will begin to experience this within seven days.

blight   You will accidentally stumble onto much needed timely and valuable information.

blimp   You will travel to another state for a vacation and have a fabulous time. You will also receive diamonds as a gift.

blind   *to be blind*   You are headed in the wrong direction concerning a family situation. Slow down and reassess your moves, especially concerning one member of the family. You are focusing negatively on one person. Set yourself free of pettiness.

someone else is blind   An acquaintance will be revealed as an evil person and you will take the blame for their wrong doing. This can be prevented.

blind cleaners   This dream is a warning that a very malicious person will approach you and you will erroneously believe that they are very trustworthy. You will get the impression that whatever is discussed will be kept a secret. In reality, this person is attempting to glean as much as they can from you about another person and will then take your words back to the third party. Be very alert to this so you can avoid this completely, otherwise the person you were talking about will attack you verbally. This has the potential for escalating to violence. You have prior notice of this to ensure that it does not occur.

blind date   A long lost friend will return to share their good fortune with you.

blindfold   A job that you will accept will be more hazardous than it appears. Investigate before accepting the job.

blink   *any form*   You will have a thrilling love affair.

blintz   Be keenly aware of your intuitive sense and discipline yourself to use this ability correctly. You will benefit greatly from this ability.

blister   You will be dealing with a hypochondriac. This will be annoying to you, but make it a point to be kind to this person. This situation will last only a short time and you will be able to go on with your life. This person will leave you a large legacy after their death.

fever blister Do not expose yourself to any contagious infections. Drink plenty of water and eat healthful foods.

blizzard Warning! Watch out for broken bones, particularly broken legs.

block You are being asked to remove any mental block that keeps you from moving ahead. You need to clear yourself mentally within the next three days.

to walk city blocks You will be paid all the money that is owed to you in a short while.

cement block Bring together creative people who will become a pool of resources that you can draw information from to help you with your business ventures. The time is perfect for this now and your energies will result in life long riches.

wooden block Within a week an injury will occur to you or your property due to inclement weather. Prepare ahead.

blockade runner When asked for help, be sure that you demonstrate a sympathetic manner. Be very compassionate with someone who finds it difficult to go into detail about their problems but doesn't show any overt distress. Treat this matter seriously. This will occur within three days.

block and tackle Within three days, you will receive some very disagreeable news that will be out of your control.. Remain calm and handle it as best you can.

blond *to dream about a blond* You will receive a thrilling message and a romantic gift.

blood A cluster of events will start to rapidly occur in your life one after the other and will bring you a tremendous amount of joy, wonder and awe. You will develop a powerful energy that you will be able to harness at the same time these other events are taking place. You will also be able to bring others under your subjugation and control. Within the week, you will be able to successfully direct this energy in a way that will help you to complete anything you wish in an exceptional way. You will be able to overcome any difficult obstacle and easily deal with any new issue. Your intuition is right on target. Anything negative portended in this dream needs to be altered or changed to enjoy only positive expressions in your life. Many blessings will come to you and your family.

to cut yourself and bleed A friend will become a financial drain.

to taste or drink blood Think ahead. Someone you meet will subtly manipulate them self into your life. This will be a purposeful act and little by little they will come to dominate you. You will begin to account to this person each detail of your life. You will be amazed that this has happened and will find it difficult to get out of this situation. Watch for this ahead of time and take steps to avoid it.

red blood cells Get an up to date blood analysis within

seven days. You may have a deficiency that needs to be treated in some way. You must also develop a concise plan that will allow you to meet your goals in the shortest possible time with the least amount of hassle. You are headed toward a peaceful and restful cycle.

white blood cells Do everything necessary to remain physically healthy and do not expose yourself to any infectious diseases. Eat healthy foods, drink plenty of water, get plenty of rest and avoid stress. Take steps to avoid any negative event foretold in this dream.

in any other form Your wish will be granted. You will also receive a financial windfall.

blood bank If you are planning surgery within the next few weeks, research the procedure to determine whether it is necessary or if there is a simpler procedure.

to give blood at a blood bank If you are a surgeon or are planning surgery, postpone all medical procedures and reschedule in a few days. Otherwise, question the particular procedures to be used to ensure a successful outcome.

blood cell You are deeply loved and will experience loyalty from, and many happy moments with, someone who is special to you.

blood clot Be very prepared for a remarkable and unusual event to occur within three days. At the same time you will be able to clearly think through the steps you need to take in order to comfortably get through this cycle. Your curiosity will be very strong during this time frame and you must discipline yourself and remain firm so that you do not let your curiosity control you. You will also enjoy an abundance of health during this cycle.

bloodhound Do not reveal your secrets to anyone.

bloodmobile Take every precaution and make sure you do not overextend yourself by attempting to involve someone in your life. You will get mixed messages from this person. It will seem as though they are playing hard to get and at the same time seem to be leading you on. This behavior will continue for as long as you allow it to. Get on with your life without this person in it. Someone else will appreciate your affections.

blood money Do not convince yourself to go out with someone you are not interested in. You are wasting your time and the other person's time.

blood poisoning Stop your selfish behavior toward others. You will also need to learn oxygenating techniques for your body.

blood pressure Something will occur that will leave you ecstatic. Good news will come your way within five days. Have your blood pressure checked, have your iron checked, drink more water, and get a check up.

a blood pressure situation that involves someone else If

you recognize this individual, make it your business to see that this person gets adequate treatment for this ailment. You must also avoid any unnecessary repair work on an electrical appliance.

a blood pressure situation involving you or a loved one This dream implies that you or your loved one needs to have their blood pressure checked. Make sure you treat yourself in such a way that will keep your blood pressure at a healthy limit. Blessings are with you.

blood pudding For the next two days, pay careful attention to what is happening to those around you. You will know ahead of time which situations to prevent. Think of the repercussions that will occur by allowing a certain situation to take place.

blood sausage Within three days, you will receive a very thrilling gift. You will also be able to rid yourself of a long term burdensome situation that has dragged you down for a long time. Good luck is with you and a brilliant future is yours.

bloodstone This dream implies that you will have relief from mental, physical and emotional stress. Eat properly and drink plenty of water. Eat to live, don't live to eat.

bloodsucker Someone will develop a well thought out plan to pull you into a situation that will hurt your feelings deeply. This person does not have the courage to tell you to your face that they wish to end the relationship/friendship and will attempt to get their point across in a very cruel way. Get on with your life without this person.

blood vessel Be very aware of someone who will lie to you and cheat you out of your valuables. You will also become very emotionally involved with this person. Use discipline to stay away from a person like this, especially for the next seven days.

Bloody Mary What you are convinced is a sure thing will, within a few days, turn out to be a risky situation. Think carefully and avoid making a tragic mistake. This situation is not a sure thing.

bloom A love relationship that appears to be ending will suddenly revitalize and blossom. A new zeal will be added. For the next few days it will seem as though you are entering the best part of your life because of this relationship.

bloomer Make it a point to remain calm and centered for the next three days. A situation will arise that will tempt your involvement. Do not allow yourself to become so desperate over another person's problems that you compromise yourself and become entangled in this issue. Once you do, it will be very difficult to pry yourself loose and it will become progressively worse as time goes by. You are now seeing only the beginnings of this problem. Remain uninvolved.

blossom The person you desire will show more affection and love toward you than ever before, especially in public. This will result in the enjoyment of the beauty of life.

blotting paper You will become a codependent in a new relationship. This is not a good situation. Back out if you can.

blouse This dream implies good luck, health and money. A selfless act toward another will also result in an unexpected gift of money as well as a small item of appreciation. This will occur within seven days.

blow *to blow* This dream implies future prosperity and a rapid acceleration toward your goal.

to have difficulty blowing Within seven days a random killing spree will occur within your vicinity. Unless you take precautions you will be one of the victims. Avoid all areas where this is likely to occur during this time period.

blowfish For the next two days make sure you do not deny yourself moments of great pleasure. Do everything you can to bring more tranquility and simplicity into your life.

blowgun Meditate in your favorite form. Add a romantic touch to the way you live your life.

blowtorch You will fall in love with a dynamic person. This will be reciprocal. You will also place yourself in the position of having to settle for less within two days. Do not allow yourself to be cornered and rethink this situation so you will be better able to handle it when it arises.

blow up *to see anything blow up in any way* Carefully read the label of prescription drugs and be aware of possible side effects. Become aggressively involved in researching the medication you take. You may be taking them improperly.

to blow up something Warning! Be careful that you do not become the hostage of a deranged person.

BLT A proposal made by you within three days will be warmly received.

blubber You will receive a generous inheritance. For the next three days, in order to achieve success, you must also skillfully use your gift of tact and diplomacy when involved in any negotiations. Your feelings and the feelings of others could easily be hurt during this time period if you do not use caution. Take it slowly and behave accordingly in order to prevent this.

bludgeon *any form* Warning! Be watchful of a serial killer or someone who will kill many people in a public and violent way within the next three days. Avoid all public places during this time period.

blue You will enjoy health, balance, clarity, peace, blessings, and strength in all areas of your life for the next few weeks.

Bluebeard Attend closely to what someone is trying to tell you for the next three days. You will find it very easy to agree with everything this person suggests but their words will be easily misinterpreted. This will put you at a disadvantage later on. Make sure you have a perfect understanding of what you are agreeing to during this time period.

blueberry Joy will enter your life within seven days and will be prompted by genuine feelings of love from another.

bluebird This dream implies business prosperity for five days. All business negotiations will work to your advantage.

bluebonnet A new and mysterious person will enter your life within three days. This person will share many amusing stories with you that give you many moments of pleasure. You are headed for a brilliant future.

blue book Within five days, you will accidentally stumble across information about another person that will shock you a great deal. Keep this information to yourself.

blue cheese Set limits on the labor you are willing to expend for others.

blue crab Within a few days you will be asked out. If you are expecting this to lead to a deeper emotional attachment, turn this person down. They are only interested in a one night stand.

bluefish You will enjoy tranquility and a peaceful lifestyle with your family for a long time to come. Continue to reach out in a special way to others who are important to you.

bluegill An unusual and extraordinary event will take place that will create unexpected wealth for you. This will develop within three days and will come from a very stable source.

bluegrass Within three days, you will be able to demonstrate the love you feel for someone you care about in the way they most desire. This will take place in a wild and romantic setting. Good luck will be with you for the next week.

blue jay Tranquility will be yours.

blue jeans You are headed in the right direction and will enjoy a brilliant future. This dream is also a promise of wealth in the near future.

blue law Within the week, you will hire someone for repair work and the cost of the job will be much higher than the original estimate. Be sure to put everything into writing.

blueprint This blue print may be a clue indicating where you need to search for specific information. You also need to watch out for a very nosy person. Do not reveal your business to anyone.

blue ribbon Within the week, someone will become aware of you in a very special way. This person will pursue you and become very determined to marry you. This individual will proceed very slowly yet persistently in the direction of marriage. If you choose to pursue this, the relationship will be long lived and you will enjoy prosperity. Follow your intuition. Your hunches will be on target especially for the next three days.

blue sight *(paranormal sight that allows psychics to track down murderers)* Be very careful. You are beginning to adopt a dangerous pattern of thinking that will lead to health problems that have no physical or organic cause. You will consult many physicians who will tell you that they find nothing is wrong with you. Be diligent and take steps now to prevent this from occurring. Act quickly to change your pattern of thinking and your mental attitude. Begin treating your body with respect, increase your exercise level, make lifestyle changes, alter your diet, and reschedule your life in such a way to lessen physical demands on your body. Divorce yourself from anyone who may be making you feel uncomfortable. You can easily avoid this situation by redirecting the way in which you live your life and can avoid a loss of health by practicing this regimen. Take steps to avoid or to alter any negative event in this dream that could become a reality. Do everything you can to experience only positive expressions in your life. You are headed for a prosperous future and many blessings are with you and your family.

blue whale For the next week, you will be motivated to make changes in your life and to work in those areas that will bring you prosperity. This will be a very lucky cycle for you.

blush *to use* Study your lifestyle and surrounding situations in order to make the correct decisions for your future. Do this within a few days. Everyday occurrences hinder you from making good decisions.

to see someone else use blush Budget your money and save for awhile. Make a conscious effort to go without luxuries. You will be glad, next month, that you did.

to blush Within a few days someone will go to great lengths to make you believe what they are telling you. Most of the information this person will give you is incorrect, and this person has no intention of carrying out their plans.

to see someone blush You will meet someone within a few days who will find you irresistible to the point of being unable to contain their excitement around you. This person will talk about many things but will be able to deliver on half of what was promised. It is up to you to sift through the talk and discern what this person will deliver. Move slowly on this.

in any other form A much younger person will fall in love with you.

boar *in the wild* Do everything you can to avoid financial defeat and bankruptcy. Trim your expenses now; start saving.

in any other form You will be lucky in all phases of your life.

board A secretary or someone who works in a similar job will cause problems of jealousy between you and a special person by playing petty games (i.e., not allowing you to speak to someone important on the phone). There is nothing unusual going on between the secretary and this person.

board game An abundance of health and wealth are coming your way within the week. This dream also indicates that a situation will take place within three days that will require aggressive behavior on your part. You will be able to act accordingly and the situation will be resolved quickly.

boardinghouse Do not forget that variety is the spice of life. Enjoy yourself.

boardwalk Enjoy sunsets and stop to smell the roses. You will begin to feel a strong emotional wave that will waste a lot of your time, because you will be totally unaware of the source of this urge. This drive will cause you to focus on bringing something to tangible form and will continue for a three week period. You will be able to determine the source and reason for this feeling during this time period. This drive may be the result of a heightened awareness and a psychic ability that will push you in the direction you need to go. You will somehow comprehend this on an instinctive level although you will have no real proof or verification. You will understand this because of the intense excitement you feel.

boat You will enjoy health, wealth and longevity.

to be on a boat You are headed toward a brilliant future. Luck is with you.

to fall overboard Directly deal with the reasons why you will not commit to a relationship. Do not allow your behavior to destroy a good thing. For the next three days take extra care to preserve this relationship.

a boat in bad weather Watch out for an evil person who has designed an agenda specifically for you. This person does not appear to be evil. For the next three days they will go to great lengths to put you under their control. Avoid any involvement.

love boat For the next few days use diplomacy in all of your dealings. Let issues roll off your back instead of becoming personally involved. Someone will say unkind words to you in front of others. Do not allow these remarks to bother you. Get on with your life and do whatever is necessary to avoid this situation completely.

steam boat Remain optimistic about your future because you are headed in the right direction.

boat on fire The person you are romantically involved with will state, within a few days, the need for a deeper union. This will lead to marriage. Good luck is with you. Pre-pare a surprise romantic outing with this person to encourage this occasion if you choose to take this route.

speed After many years of having another person not speak to you, you will be contacted for a reconciliation. You will enjoy a speedy recovery of a lost friendship.

punt boat Avoid any change that will turn things in a bad way. Keep a watchful eye on work projects to ensure that situations do not turn sour.

tug boat Make it a point to motivate someone to get things moving in the right direction. This will enable you to meet a specific deadline that is particularly important for the next three days.

boat hook Don't waste your time for the next few days with someone who leads you to believe a romance will work. This person is very selfish and this union will not work out.

boathouse Start planning ways to have an extra income. Use your mental resources to plan for a difficult time next month. If you start now you will be able to handle a financial crisis.

boat people Within a few days you will meet someone of a different nationality who will be a true friend for a long period of time. You will find this friendship very enjoyable.

bobbin Teach a young child a hobby or skill that can only be taught by you. This may be an archaic skill that can be passed on from generation to generation.

bobby pin Watch for an upcoming event. Enter this on your calendar. Also, make sure that you do not present a demeanor that discourages others from being open with you. Someone wishes to speak with you but will find it difficult because of your manner.

bobby socks Some happy and long anticipated news will arrive.

bobcat A friend will talk about you behind your back. Watch out for treachery.

bobsled Do not commit anything to writing for the next two days that may be used against you.

bobwhite Do not allow anyone to aim their displaced anger toward you. And do not allow yourself to become sucked into a conversation that could escalate to violence between you and a third party. Don't be lured into expressing anger in return. This should be your main focus for the next three days.

body *to wash your own body* You will reach an agreement for sexual gratification with another person. This will lead to a love relationship and, eventually, to a life long union if you so desire.

to wash someone's body Expect rewards of love, affection, and financial stability.

hairy body Your friends will soon expect you to take the lead. Restrict your responsibilities and stay in the background.

burned body You will be able to verbalize your thoughts in a dynamic manner. This will convince others to join you and cooperate with you until you meet your goals.

dead body You will enjoy victory and the resolution of a large problem. The greater the number of bodies seen, the greater financial rewards for a long term project. Family misfortunes will end and you will shortly receive a large sum of money.

your dead body Investigate the cause of your death in the dream. This is a major clue of what you should avoid in order to prevent your own death. Be alert to the possibility of a vitamin or mineral deficiency caused by improper diet that could lead to system failure, and take precautions to avoid sudden stressful situations that will affect bodily functions. Be careful that you take all medications properly in order to prevent sudden death. You will also be able to purchase what you desire at the price you want. You will be in great financial shape for several years. You also need to avoid all impulsive behavior and curb your sense of urgency for the next week. If it is not curbed, you will become involved in something you have no business being involved with.

your nude body - if it appears healthy You can expect good health for a long time. You will immediately gain a financial improvement in areas where you have been experiencing anxiety. You will also experience an unexpected surprise gift of some sort and the person you least expect will unexpectedly call or visit. This individual will encourage intimacy and quiet moments. If you decide to go along with this, you will enjoy yourself immensely with no strings attached.

your nude body - if something appears wrong or unusual Take steps to prevent any negative aspect you witnessed in the dream. Correct and prevent bad health. Eat healthful foods, and maintain good health. You will have the strength to correct any problem. Many blessings will be with you for a long time.

nude bodies You will enjoy a romantic liaison, if you choose. This is a good cycle for romance. You will also hear of the surgery of an acquaintance. A good rapport will also be developed regarding business affairs.

nude body - old An unexpected surprise gift will arrive.

nude body - young Think ahead in order to avoid a serious problem with a special person. For the next few days discuss changes you are making that will involve your loved ones. Seek a mutual decision.

nude baby Do what you can to feel happier about your life. Appreciate life and consistently and persistently do what you can to enjoy it.

to distinctly recall only the body of someone you recognize Recall the events that occurred when you were associated with this person in reality. Within three days you will be going through similar events with another person. Make sure that you do not repeat any negative events and be sure to repeat all positive events. This dream also implies that situations that were going badly will turn around and yield a positive result.

the feeling of being unable to move your body when trying to awaken For the next seven days you will need to be very attentive and acutely aware of certain events that will begin to unfold and will have a serious and damaging affect on your future. These events will destine you to alter your life and point you in the wrong direction. You must become more assertive and muster the courage and confidence to take the necessary steps to protect yourself from this situation, as well as watching the words you use when speaking to others because your words may be used as leverage against you. Be observant of what is unfolding that will have a serious effect on your future. This will occur because of any of the following situations or a combination:

- The influence that someone will have over you.
- Interference from someone who will steer you in the wrong direction.
- The control that someone in power will exert over you.
- The leverage that someone will gain by using your words to put you at a disadvantage.
- Someone who is in a position of authority who will make decisions for you.

Do not allow yourself to become vulnerable by not acting on your own behalf, because you will suffer emotional depletion as a result and be guided in a direction you have no desire to go. Prod yourself to get your point across to those in authority. And make it a point to avoid everyday stresses caused by the decisions others make for you who have no business being involved. You are in danger of surrendering your control. Avoid unhealthy situations and circumstances and remain suspicious of all changes. Become confident and relentless in correcting those areas of your life that require corrections. You will then be able to put yourself on the right path. You have the power to change any negative aspect of this dream as well as changing your life to encourage positive expressions. Make sure that all of your bases are safely covered. Practice common sense and your plans will be successfully carried out. You will place yourself on the path of prosperity.

to be aware that you are unable to move your body for a short time because of some unusual occurrence Your spirit wants you to see what is in front of you and to make sure you do not overlook anything. Take steps to ensure you are not being narrow-minded about something you are about to involve yourself in, and make sure you get more than one perspective about this issue. Create several alternative ways to deal with this situation. Do not make excuses that will keep you from motivating yourself into moving forward. You will accomplish anything you need at this particular time by being flexible and by looking at things from a different angle. This attitude will offer you many alternatives to deal with this situation. Anything in this dream that was displayed to you is a major clue to what else you need to be doing in your life. If it was negative, take steps to prevent it in reality. If positive, make sure you take steps to promote it. You will be putting yourself in the position for a brilliant future.

to put your body in an unusual position to complete a task Be ready for an unusual and remarkable event to occur. At the precise time that this is going on you will have the clarity of thought you need to take each necessary step to get through this cycle easily and comfortably. You will also need to be very firm and disciplined in order to control your curiosity. Expect to enjoy an abundance of health during this cycle.

to recognize the head on an entirely different body (a man's head on a woman's body or vice versa) You need to be acutely aware of this person because they will attempt to bring some emotional harm to you, either emotional or physical. Do everything you can to keep yourself safe. Get on with your life without this person in it because they are serious. Although this person will present a very kind and nice demeanor, they are very evil and cunning. Within three days make sure you disassociate from this person, move on with your life and take steps to turn this situation around. Make sure you take steps to turn any negative event you dreamed of around so you can experience only positive expressions in your life.

body bag *full* You will unexpectedly receive a large sum of money within a few days.

empty Do not allow yourself to be in an intimate setting with someone you have no wish to be intimate with.

if you suspect your body is in the body bag Investigate the cause of your death in the dream. This will be a major clue of what you should avoid in order to prevent your own death. Be alert to the possibility of a vitamin or mineral deficiency caused by improper diet that will lead to system failure. Take precautions to avoid sudden stressful situations that will affect bodily functions and be careful that you take all medications properly in order to avoid sudden death.

bodyguard Protect your valuables.

body language Be careful not to send mixed signals via body language.

body stocking You have an irresistible urge to beautify your appearance. Go for it.

body surfing Someone will immediately fall head over heels in love with you. This person will do the necessary footwork for you to know them better and to make it easier for them to involve you in their life. They will be very attentive and take steps to appease you in every way. You will enjoy many wonderful moments together. If you choose to take this path, you will have a fantastic time with this person.

bodysuit Tell someone special how much you love them.

bog You will have to deal with a very wicked person within a three day period. This person will do everything they can to twist around the words of another individual to their advantage and will give you conflicting and unreliable information. Be wary of this and do everything you can to avoid this person. Otherwise, you will be entering a lucky cycle within the week as a result of a decision that you make.

bogeyman Make sure the advice you get comes from someone with experience in the particular area that you require assistance.

bohemian Be sure that you fully express yourself and allow your opinions to become known. This will be very important within three days.

boil *water boiling* In the past you were asked to do something distasteful and you firmly refused. This person will again make this request. Control your anger and do not allow yourself to be put off balance. Strongly refuse again. This will occur within three days.

to see something else come to boil Beware of lending money to someone with loose morals. You will not be paid back.

boil *to see a boil or blister* This dream signifies riches. Make sure everything you own is insured.

boiler Watch out for a deranged person, especially in dark unfamiliar places.

bok choy Allow a professional to clear up a confusing situation that will come up within three days. A specially trained person will quickly cut through all of your confusion.

bola You will need to pay close attention to someone else's point of view for the next two days. This will enable you to determine the correct steps to ensure your own happiness.

bolero You will make the right connections with the right person for a particular project or event that you have in mind. This person will prove to be completely reliable.

bologna Do not take life so seriously. Enjoy a favorite sporting event within three days.

bolt Hidden priorities will surface shortly. Be prepared. Do not allow others to take advantage of you.

bolts and nuts This dream is a lucky omen for those who work with this hardware. Your affection, love and sexual favors will be required within a few days. You will be eager to respond.

bombs *to see a city bombed* Be up front about new financial situations (i.e. salary, etc.) at the time of discussion. Anything negative portended in this dream needs to be altered or changed so you can experience only positive expressions in your life.

to be in a bombing situation Stop slaving yourself for others. Take time out for yourself. Anything negative portended in this dream needs to be altered or changed so you can experience only positive expressions in your life.

plastic explosive You are being asked not to put on a persona that confuses others. Too much of a change is too drastic for others to comprehend. Step back and stop confusing others with your behavior. You must also be careful while traveling and avoid any situation that may be hazardous for the next five days. Anything negative portended in this dream needs to be altered or changed so you can experience only positive expressions in your life.

pipe bomb Be careful while traveling for the next two days. Take all precautions to remain safe and to avoid accidents. Anything negative portended in this dream needs to be altered or changed so you can experience only positive expressions in your life.

bombs in any form Be sure to take the proper minerals, drink enough water, eat enough vegetables and increase your calcium. Anything negative portended in this dream needs to be altered or changed so you can experience only positive expressions in your life.

bon bon Someone deeply loves you.

bond Do not embarrass someone else in public.

bond paper A friend of yours will become very wealthy in a short period of time. This person will go to great lengths to include you in their new and exciting lifestyle.

bone Do everything necessary to enjoy the marrow of life. Protect yourself from broken bones for the next two days. Eat foods containing calcium, exercise, drink plenty of water, and avoid medications that interfere with bone production.

broken bones other than arms and legs For the next two days, take precautions to avoid injury due to faulty machinery. Be very careful and stay away from any machinery that is in disrepair.

broken arm You can avoid deep depression and a bitter loss due to a child's kidnapping. For the next three days take major steps to prevent this from happening and be acutely aware of the child's whereabouts. It would be a good idea to practice child safety until your child is grown.

broken leg Do whatever is necessary, for the next four days, to keep your temper under control. A distasteful situation will arise that will render you suspicious and jealous of the behavior of someone close to you. You will also be driven into a murderous rage over this. Take steps to keep this rage from developing and do not cater to this emotion. You are placing too much importance on another and not enough on yourself.

cross bones Do not involve yourself in a risky financial situation. It seems safe but instincts will say otherwise. Follow your hunches. This will occur after a two week hiatus. You have time to research this project.

hip bone Remain in a safe environment for the next five days and take steps to avoid freak accidents. Make sure your home environment is safe during this time frame as well. Take steps to avoid any negative event witnessed in this dream and make sure that you experience only positive ex-

pressions in your life.

tail bone Take steps to avoid or turn around any negative event connected with this dream and make sure you forewarn anyone you recognize in the dream to do the same, especially for the next three days. You will also be surrounded with love and receive verification of this within the week. You are loved, respected and appreciated beyond your imagination.

bone china You will receive a gift of emeralds.

bone marrow Enjoy life to the fullest.

bone meal Within five days, do everything you can to get the best possible medical attention in order to keep a minor ailment from developing into a crisis situation. The moment you sense that something is not quite right with your health, seek professional help.

bonfire This dream is a lucky omen for those in love. You will enjoy a deeper bonding and respect for each other.

bongo You will soon enjoy a performing arts event.

bonnet This dream is a lucky omen, especially when playing games of chance.

bonsai You will go out with a very charming individual but will never hear from this person again. Be aware of this and don't build up your hopes for a downfall.

boo You are deeply loved and respected by someone but are unaware of this feeling. Within a few days this person will find a way to tell you. Do not be surprised.

booby trap Funds will be missing and it will look as though you are the thief. Stay calm even though you are innocent. The truth will be revealed.

book *to dream about this book* (*dream book*) This dream is a good luck symbol. Whatever knowledge or message you have gleaned from this book should be followed. This will render a clue that you need to watch for within the next two weeks. Your intuition and psychic abilities are at a high point. This will be a sneak preview of what is in store for you within the next few months. Follow your hunches. You will also find that, for the next ten days, you will reach your peak and will be so together that you will instinctively know that you will reach the finish line before the race has really begun. You will begin to have feelings of confidence that comes from knowing you will succeed. You will experience the strength that comes from your inner core. Follow your goals as if you were on a mission and this will bring you to a victorious completion. Within this time frame, your sense of ethics and judgment will be intact. You are headed for a fantastic future. If the message is negative, you have time to alter the outcome. If positive, enhance it to the fullest.

black book You need to be in touch with current situations that are occurring around you. You will uncover unusual events that will point you in the right direction. Any name seen in the book will be instrumental in pushing you in the right direction.

blue book Within five days, you will accidentally stumble across information about another person that will shock you a great deal. Keep this information to yourself.

class book Someone will feign a desire to start a family. Do not get your hopes up, this person will not be ready to become a parent.

coloring book You will enjoy many days with your grandchildren.

cookbook Someone who has turned down your request for help on a consistent basis will change their mind and assist you in accomplishing your goals. Take steps to alter or prevent the occurrence of any negative event witnessed in this dream.

Good Book A proposal you will be making within five days will be received with success.

guidebook Meditate in your favorite manner and you will find your path paved with gold. You are headed toward a wonderful future.

paperback book In a short time, your desire to become committed in a relationship will deepen. This desire will be realized and the relationship will last a lifetime.

schoolbook A phone conversation will result in a quarrel. You can prevent this by remaining calm.

song book All legal negotiations will result in your favor. Also, someone who has undergone some distasteful moments in their life will come to you as the first person they will open up to. Display sympathy and understanding toward this person for the next three days.

yearbook Do not allow someone else's influence to cause you to switch gears. Listen to your own counsel and advice, and follow your own hunches. Your intuition is correct. Anything you dreamed of in the yearbook that you perceive as negative must be altered or avoided in reality and make sure all positive things you saw are brought to fruition. You have five days in which to do this. You are headed for a brilliant future.

yellow pages This is an extremely lucky omen and you will be very victorious in anything you are about to involve yourself in for the next seven days. You will need to be persistent in getting the information you need. Any information you need will be easier to come by in this time frame. You will also need to turn around anything negative that you dreamed you saw in the yellow pages and take steps to turn any positive information you received into a reality,. If anyone you recognized was in this dream, advise them to do the same. Many blessings are with you and you will enjoy a very victorious future.

workbook Someone, within five days, will lead you into a new career that will prove to be very successful and will provide a solid foundation for a lifetime. This will be a same sexed person who will be very tenacious in making sure you are headed in the right direction.

in any other form This dream is a lucky omen. You will receive many blessings and will realize all of your goals,

especially if you are working with written material. Any negative event witnessed in the dream involving the written word needs to be changed into a positive event in reality.

bookcase You are having a relationship with someone who is open, demonstrative and loving in privacy. In public and behind your back, this person shuns you, avoids phone calls and makes it clear to others that they want little to do with you. Be aware of this and move on with your life.

book club Someone is very eager to become involved in your life in any capacity. Without your knowledge, this person desires you in a passionate way. Take the necessary steps to either bring this person closer or to avoid the development of a relationship, as you see fit. You are headed for a very prosperous future and many blessings are coming to you and your family.

bookend Attend closely to the physical and emotional state of a young child. Make sure this child's needs are being met, especially for the next three days.

bookie You will soon go out with a well dressed fantastic person. Enjoy yourself.

booklet Make education your priority for now, especially in areas that you wish to develop more skill. Do not neglect these areas and do not be afraid of revealing proper upbringing and charisma as well as the polish you have gained through education. These traits will be admired by a group of influential people.

bookmark You are in a situation that will get progressively worse. Take notes, keep a log or journal. Keep records and protect your interests.

bookshelf Within a few days your partner will refuse to compromise on a business plan.

bookworm Find a private place to meditate in peace. This will allow you to decide what you really want from a specific situation that is causing you dissatisfaction.

boomerang An item purchased at a bargain price will suddenly become more valuable than you ever imagined.

boomtown You will soon acquire your life's desire and this will be a very joyful time for you.

boondocks Pay close attention to your words for the next three days. Words spoken in haste cannot be taken back and this may result in the severing of a close friendship.

boot Make an effort to do your part in a relationship to create balance and equality. Make the union more rewarding for you and for someone special. You will enjoy safe travel.

cowboy boot For the next four days, move with determination. You will achieve great success in the field you are moving toward. Everything you do for the next few days will be extremely lucky.

bootee Research carefully the benefits that are due you. You will get a full picture of what you are owed within five days. Within the month, you will purchase what appears to be an insignificant item at a low price. In reality, this item is priceless. Good luck is with you and opportunities will abound for you this month. Motivate yourself to take advantage of these opportunities.

bootleg Be careful not to lose a good luck charm or trinket. Also, do not place yourself in a situation that will leave you trapped and defenseless, especially for the next three days.

booth Do not allow another person to put you in a position of humiliation. Break this cycle immediately.

bootstrap Restrictions will be placed on you because of something you will do this coming week. Be acutely aware of cause and effect and avoid committing an act that will produce repercussions.

booze Keep a log or journal of everything you do. This will be useful in the future.

Bordeaux It would be to your benefit to become a team player. It is important that you and everyone you are involved with understand the importance of working together. Success will come to you as a result of this development.

bordello Within two days, you will be dealing with someone who refuses to take no for an answer. Prepare yourself ahead of time about how best to handle this situation, and do not allow yourself to become stressed out because of it.

border *any form* Jealousy will surface in a relationship. Face this issue head on and resolve it as quickly as possible.

borough In order to find love with someone else, you must first learn to love yourself. The confidence and love you have for yourself will quickly attract others.

borsch Your romantic desire will be realized following a romantic dinner date. It is also imperative that you have your hemoglobin checked and take steps to avoid anemia.

bosom Your consistency in a stressful situation will be appreciated. You will persist until you reach a successful resolution.

boss Older people will bring luck to you for the next few days. Make sure any negative event you dreamed of does not occur in reality and take steps to ensure you experience only positive expressions in your life.
  female boss - if she seems interested in you You will have much luck while traveling and will meet a person who will expose you to other avenues and more opportunities in life.
  if you are ignored by her Do not become easily swayed by others for the next few days.

bossa nova Within a three day period, you will find the perfect person to work with. Proceed with confidence. This person has wonderful organizational skills and many creative ideas that will be a benefit to you. Good luck is with you.

Boston You will enjoy many beautiful days with a special person. You will spend these days engaged in activities that you both enjoy. This dream may also be used as a reference point in time. If you dream of this city and see its name used in any context, the dream message will occur on this day.

Boston baked beans You will put yourself in a situation that will result in poor negotiations. For a three day period avoid negotiations of any sort.

Boston brown bread Avoid quarrels for the next three days. Someone also plans to move away and you will decide to give a small going away party. This will turn out nicely.

Boston cream pie Within a three day period you will meet a kind, generous person with a wonderful sense of humor. This person is free to pursue romantically. In a short while they will grow to like you a great deal. Enjoy yourself.

Boston Massacre Do not allow another person to handle your finances for the next three days. You must also make no major changes for this time period.

Boston Tea Party You will hear delightful news from a close friend while enjoying a quiet meal. You will discuss many topics but one bit of information will be especially important. Keep your ears open for the next week.

Boston Terrier Be sure to express the love you feel for someone else. Take each opportunity to tell this person.

botany Shop for the lowest price when buying an item you desire.

bother Within three days you will be in the company of someone who will purposely address you in such a way that you will feel cornered into agreeing to do something this person wants you to do. This individual will do everything in their power to force you to surrender to their wishes, behave in the manner they wish, or speak in the manner they wish. Be extremely aware. This person will be very forceful in trying to get their way. You have prior notice of this and can take the right steps to avoid being placed at an unfair disadvantage.

bottle *odd shaped* You will be marrying soon, if you choose this option. You are headed for a brilliant future.
  empty bottle Take care of your skin and protect it from the elements.

broken bottle Take healthy steps to prevent a premature birth. Avoid all heavy activity for a three day period. Be sure also to fulfill any promise you mean to keep within five days.

full bottle You will enjoy thrilling sexual moments if you choose to go this route.

wine bottle Within two days you will need to take the time to review the whole picture concerning a particular issue that will come up. You will then fully understand what is going on and determine how you feel and how you want to live your life. This should be the single most important issue to you right now. Proceed with confidence. This dream also implies that any request you make, even to someone who does not seem interested in you, will be granted. You can proceed with confidence and can expect an abundance of health.

to pull the cork out of the bottle For the next ten days you will be unbeatable because of your tenacity and relentlessness in pursuing your goals. You are in a very lucky position and you will be celebrating a joyful victory.

in any other form You will enjoy a wonderful outing with a new acquaintance within four days. This will lead to something more meaningful, if you choose this option.

bottlebrush Within five days, you will be able to overcome any long term burden, regardless of anything else that is going on in your life right now. You are headed in the right direction and will be experiencing new pleasures and many joyous social events. Focus on achieving a peaceful and stress free life.

bottle company You will soon receive a gift of richer mental inventiveness and greater intelligence from the Gods. Take the time to use this gift for your own personal benefit and to raise your standard of living to the level you desire. Expect this to occur within four days.

bottle fed *any form* Do whatever is necessary to devise a clever idea or solution that will allow you to work independently on a situation that will develop within three days. This will enable you to work without outside interference. These thoughts will come to you with great clarity and you will be able to resolve this situation with success.

bottle feed Riches and power will come to you within the week as a result of what you are now actively pursuing. Many blessings will come to you and your family.

bottle opener Within three days you will become involved in a very embarrassing situation. Make sure you are keenly aware of your actions during this time period in order to avoid this situation completely.

bottlers Make sure the decisions you will be making about a particular person are not interfered with by others. You will be the one who has the final word. Carefully analyze your thoughts and do not allow others to influence your choices and selections. Do not allow yourself to be manipulated.

Only put into writing those wishes you know will be respected and carried out by others.

bottom *to hit bottom or see someone else hit the bottom* Be suspicious. A certain aspect of a situation that you will be involved with will be corrupted by another individual for purposes known only to them. Be very cautious of those situations that require you to be alert, especially for the next four days.

in any other form Someone will use very subtle and tactful means to trigger guilt feelings to make you feel indebted to them and to get preferential treatment. You know this ahead of time and can avoid feelings of obligations and guilt toward this person. This will be done to provoke some kind of behavior from you that will benefit this person in some way.

botulism You will receive special knowledge, skills or ideas from an older person. This person will take pleasure in helping you to develop skills that they have expertise in. Within the week, you will develop plans that will utilize these skills and lead you to a brilliant future.

bougainvillea Within five days, a close friend will confide a close kept secret to you. This person only wants a listening ear and you can give comfort just by being there. Do what you can within this time frame to allow any romantic situation to flow freely. This will allow you to experience a closer union.

bouillabaisse You will surround yourself with loyal people who love you deeply and will show you much affection, especially for the coming week. Extend yourself to those you care about.

bouillon Pay close attention to future relationships. This attentiveness will prevent an opportunity from slipping through your fingers that may occur only once in a lifetime.

boulder Watch out for a hit and run driver, especially for the next three days.

bounce Do not allow your progress to be blocked by another person.

bouncer Guard your possessions and property. Protect them from damage and theft.

bounty Watch your pets and protect them from accidents and illnesses.

bounty hunter You will overlook an important situation within three days. Check your schedule and make an effort not to forget anything on the third day.

bouquet You will travel within three weeks to a place you have always wanted to visit. This will be a thrilling experience for you. Take care of your body. Relax through massage and treat yourself well.

to smell a bouquet You will receive a proposal for marriage. It is your option to accept or refuse.

to catch the bouquet Advertise for a mate in order to increase your chances of meeting the ideal person. This small risk will result in a beautiful relationship.

bourbon Watch your speed and be careful of traffic violations.

boutique The person who loves you misses you intensely. Within a week this person will let you know the extent of their love.

boutonniere The advice you will receive from someone who cares deeply for you will be completely accurate. Follow this advice for your own well being.

bow You will undergo pressure from someone within the next day or two because you will stand up for your rights and will refuse to compromise your principles. Take steps to remain calm through this time period. Otherwise, you are headed for a prosperous future.

hair bow In the next few days an extremely attractive and much younger person will verbally communicate to you that they are hopelessly in love with you. You are to follow your instincts on this and anything you choose to do will be correct. You are also going to have an abundance of health and many joyful events.

bow and arrow You will have serious financial difficulties that you can overcome by carefully watching what is currently happening career wise.

bowel Take steps to keep your life running smoothly.

bowie knife Take steps to draw a special person closer to you. This will be a very important issue for you for the next five days. Good luck is with you.

bowfin fish Make sure that you get to the meat of a certain issue. Once you determine the missing element, you will be able to resolve this matter in an appropriate way.

bowl You will attend a special function that will allow you to associate with people who will be important regarding your business ventures.

of any food Make it a point to come up with a clever idea or plan that will make it possible for you to work alone on a particular situation without having to depend on others for their help. This plan will come to you with great clarity and you will be able to conclude this situation successfully.

bowlegs You will hear of the birth of twins.

bowling You will attend a very special event within five days. That event will last only a short time but will seem longer because of your enjoyment.

bowling pins Someone with an uncontrollable urge to spend time with you will go to great lengths to convince you to see them. If you choose to go in this direction, you will enjoy yourself immensely and will experience many unusual and delightful moments. Many blessings are with you and you will experience much luck during this seven day cycle.

bowstring Someone is very eager to grant you a favor. Make your request within five days and your wish will be granted.

bow tie Do not become involved in scams and get rich quick schemes. You will be let down.

box Someone will apologize to you for a long absence and strange behavior. This person will be very loving and affectionate toward you.

full Within a three day period, you will begin to change your viewpoint concerning a certain issue. In the past you held this point of view because of someone else's influence. Remain focused on your own goals and desires and do not allow someone else to interfere and stand in your way. This will be a productive cycle for you as long as you stay away from outside interferences.

to open an empty box You will have the necessary strength to ask meaningful questions and will receive timely answers.

to open a box that is not empty Whatever you see in the box represents something you may wish to include in your life. Take steps to avoid anything negative you see. Blessings are with you and your family.

box camera Within three days someone will be very happy to grant you your desires. Use this time to ask for what you need and your wishes will be granted.

boxcar This dream is a very lucky sign. Confide to a special person the facts about an illness that causes you pain. This will allow you to seek the proper help. This person will be more considerate and helpful to you.

boxer There is much rivalry among co-workers. Be careful.

boxing glove For the next three days, do everything you can to prevent a break up between you and someone special. During this three day period you will also want information from someone who has extensive expertise in an area that interests you, but they will try to keep this knowledge from you. Do everything you can to either get this information from this person or from an alternative source.

box lunch Take steps to ensure that you avoid friction between yourself and a special person. The head of the house needs to be sure that all their bases are covered, both financially and romantically, especially for the next three days. All potential negative situations need to be taken care of prior to the development of a crisis.

box office Be careful of water accidents.

box seat This dream is an extremely lucky omen for you and you will enjoy an abundance of health and wealth in areas of your life that you least expect, as well as a vast improvement in your sexual drive. You will also be able to tackle big tasks that seemed impossible to you at one time. Proceed with confidence. You are on the path toward a prosperous future.

box spring Carefully examine your plans for the future in order to determine whether they are realistic. This will save you time and energy. Otherwise, you are headed for a brilliant future.

boy You will find a restful, tranquil spot to enjoy with someone special. You will enjoy a long, healthy, wealthy life.

school boy Do not display outbursts of temper in public places.

boycott You will be boycotted because of a decision you will make without consulting others. Be sure you include others in your decision making processes.

boyfriend *to dream that you have a boyfriend whom you recognize and in reality he is not your boyfriend* This represents someone whom you will be dealing with within the next five days. This person will be very romantically drawn to you and will have some aspects of their personality very much like the person you dreamed about. You are being forewarned so you will know what you will be dealing with. If this person possesses a positive trait, or traits that you dislike, you will be able to conduct yourself accordingly. You will have some concept of who this person is based on the character of the person you dreamed of (i.e., their manner of speech, personality, behavior, etc.). This may or may not be the particular person you recognized. This dream also implies that you will receive some important and encouraging news regarding your finances. Prosperity will come to you within two weeks and will vastly improve your standard of living. You are in a very lucky cycle.

to dream of a boyfriend whom you do not recognize and in reality you do not have one Within five days you will meet someone who will be irresistibly drawn to you romantically. This person will leave large clues about certain facets of their personality that you will like or dislike. You will become aware of who they are by their character, speech patterns, etc.. This dream is giving you prior notice of what you will be dealing with and can decide whether you wish to become involved or not based on this person's behavior. Be very wary of any bad aspects of the personality seen in the dream. This dream also implies you are entering a fantastic cycle for social interactions and advantageous business negotiations. Your intuition will be heightened and you will be able to use your common sense and intuition for greater success and to create a perfect lifestyle for yourself. You are

definitely headed for a brilliant future. You will also need to be consistent in those areas of your life that require this trait.

to dream of looking for a boyfriend and being unable to find one This dream implies there is a situation that you need to divorce yourself from. This issue is something that will soon no longer matter. You must move on with your life. You are trying now to get someone to react to this situation in a certain way, but in a few weeks it will no longer make a difference in your life. Some people need to learn to handle certain issues on their own and have their own experiences so they can evolve and grow. Situations constantly change and need to be handled in different ways instead of the same way because of the advice of others. Do not interfere with someone to the point that they become unable to handle issues on their own.

in any other form You will be lucky with a new enterprise and all business negotiations will be successful for the next three days. Someone who needs your affection would also like to see love put into action. Do not act like a parent, be a lover. Pay close attention to the details of this dream. They will lead you to a clue that will point you to an event or something in particular that you will need to explore further. This will give you an advantage that will enhance your lifestyle and put you further on the path you desire. Take steps to prevent or avoid any negative event foretold in this dream, and to ensure you and others experience only positive expressions in your life. You are headed for a brilliant future.

boy scout You will be invited to a large celebration within five days. You will assume that this will be too hectic and will try to talk yourself out of going. Attend for a portion of the celebration. You will enjoy yourself and will make new friends.

boysenberry You will need to visit an ill friend. Love is also in the air. This is a great three day cycle to bring any emotional situation into a proper balance for a successful outcome.

bracelet Have patience with someone who dearly loves you but lacks the courage to pursue that feeling. Have patience and it will work out.

fancy stone bracelet Look up the particular stone for a clear meaning to this dream. This is also the appropriate time to touch base with anyone you have not heard from in some time who is working on a project or a particular situation in which you need to know the status. This will allow you to determine the degree of progress that has been made. You may need to become personally involved to ensure that your plans are shaping up in the manner you desire. It will need only a light push from you to get this rolling again, and it will give you pleasure to know that everything is still intact. Many blessings are with you and you are headed for a brilliant future.

broken Do not allow yourself to develop a sense of responsibility for everyone else's comfort, problems and issues. Within three days you will unexpectedly develop this pattern of attending to everyone else instead of yourself.

Once you involve yourself in this behavior, it will be very difficult to become uninvolved. Many blessings are with you. Proceed with caution.

braces Do not allow another person to harass you into doing something you do not want to do. Watch for this behavior over the next two days.

Brahman Within seven days, someone who feels a deep gratitude to you for being there in a time of need will use this cycle to express these feelings toward you. This person will also bring you a small gift of appreciation and you will be overcome with emotion over this show of gratitude.

braid If you are cautious, you will have success in a risky undertaking.

braided hair Any negotiation that involves travel will be very successful for the next three days.

braids *long* Defend yourself immediately against any accusations. This will not happen for a few weeks so you will have the opportunity to prevent it.

Braille A close relative will pass away. You will be involved in making the funeral arrangements.

brain A gift of mental inventeness will shortly be bestowed on you by the Gods. You will receive an abundance of wealth soon after this. Practice healthy eating habits and don't allow yourself to run on empty.

brakes An unexpected personal problem will arise. Get help immediately and quickly get to the heart of the problem in order to reach a successful resolution.

bran Do not discuss your investments with anyone. It is also important to eat more bran and drink plenty of water.

branch *green and leafy* Avoid buying anything on credit. A roommate will also treat you to dinner.
   dead or wilted You will learn of the unemployment of someone you know.

brand *anything branded or being branded* Do not allow a situation to arise that will cause hurt feelings between you and a younger person in the family.

brand name *to see a label* You will be received more warmly at another person's home than you ever expected.

brand new *any form* An event is scheduled within the week that you should not miss. You will be in the company of two admirers who will subtly attempt to win your affections. Although it is not apparent to you, one of them possesses a great deal of authority and power. You will find both individuals to be very agreeable and charming, and you would enjoy having one of them in your life. You can be

confident that you are on the path toward a prosperous future.

brandy You will have to deal with someone of the opposite sex who is untruthful. Take steps now to avoid this.

brass Someone will treat you to an expensive gift.

brassiere You will be talking long distance to a relative about their health within three days. This dream also implies that you will have an unexpected conversation with someone who lives far away. You will experience a thrill after hearing from this person. At this time, you will discuss mutual interests and they will promise to stay in close contact with you. The excitement that you will feel after this conversation will stay with you for a long time. Use this time period to get your point across although any time spent on the phone with this person will be very enjoyable. Many blessings are with you and your family.

brass knuckles Pay close attention to any negative event portended in this dream and take steps to avoid its occurrence in reality. You must also not allow the opinions of others to interfere in the decisions you will have to make pertaining to an upcoming situation.

bratwurst Within three days, you will have to deal with a very evil person who will do what they can to twist around the words of other people to their advantage. This person will then give you conflicting and unreliable information. Be aware of this and take steps to avoid this person. Otherwise, you will be entering a lucky cycle as a result of a decision you have made.

bravery Ask questions about a particular ongoing situation. Refuse to be stressed out by this issue.

bray Question the reasons for calling others by affectionate terms rather than by their names. Not everyone likes it.

Brazil You will be able to travel extensively and will be exposed to many different cultures and lifestyles. You will enjoy speaking with and getting to know a variety of people from many walks of life. In particular, you will befriend an older same sexed person and will gain from this individual a new and different way of looking at life. This will assist you at a later time in gaining prosperity and in making lifestyle choices. Be grateful because this will lead to a better way of living. You will experience peace, tranquility and joy as a result. You are headed for a prosperous future. This dream may also be used as a reference point in time. If you dream of this country and see its name used in any context, the dream message will occur on this day.

Brazil nut You will need to travel to meet a business associate. This associate will also need to travel a long distance. Arrange a meeting at a halfway point in order to avoid an unnecessary waste of time. This will be a successful meeting.

bread *to cut* Whatever you are waiting for will fall neatly into place.

brown bread Be very receptive to your hunches for the next four days and you will get a sense of what is required to handle a particular situation that will come up in this time period.

cornbread You are worried about one of your children. This child will have a very fruitful life and make a great living by using a part of your inheritance. Your grandchildren will be left financially secure. You are also loved beyond your imagination.

rye bread Make sure that you protect yourself from the weather. Keep warm and do not allow yourself to be caught out in the elements without proper attire. Many blessings are with you and your family.

sweet breads You will enjoy immense wealth and financial security for a long time to come.

wheat bread A business involvement you will have in three days should be kept strictly business. Do not become overly friendly. This behavior would not be appropriate during this time period.

white bread Something unusual will occur within five days. You will locate someone who will be willing to help you and will relentlessly stick to their goals until your needs are met.

in any other form You will receive financial assistance when you need it.

breadbasket For the next two days, make a conscious effort to be kind when you communicate with that special person in your life. Take steps to motivate this person to talk about their feelings, commitments, and plans regarding the future. As a result you will be going in a more positive direction with this person. Good luck will be with you for the next seven days.

break *any form* Resolve differences of opinions by arranging private meetings. The outcome will be successful.

breaker A great future is ahead of you.

breakfast Stop trying to interest someone who is special to you in an exercise plan that they are not interested in.

breast *to see milk flowing from a breast* Discuss sexual problems, tactfully, with that special person in order to enjoy a better and more successful response. For those interested in starting a family, this is a sure sign that this blessed event will occur.

if you recognize someone with milk flowing from a breast This individual will experience a new addition to the family. If this dream portrays any negative aspect associated with the breast, take the steps to prevent this occurrence or to correct any existing problem.

if this dream portrays a healthy breast This dream implies that you will enjoy good health and wealth.

to bare your breasts or to see someone bare their breasts

An event will occur within seven days that you must attend. You will be in the company of two admirers and will have the pleasure of watching both of them subtly try to win over your affections. Although it doesn't show, one of these people possesses a great deal of authority and power. You will find both of these people very agreeable and charming and would enjoy having one of them as a lifetime partner. You can be confident that you will put yourself on the path of a prosperous future.

in any other form Follow your romantic urges. The person you are interested in is highly romantic and sensual. You will be granted the full treatment, with flowers, fireplace, champagne, walks on the beach, etc., if you so desire.

breast feed Take the steps you need with a co-worker to receive the assistance and services you need. This action will uncover a secret within your working environment.

breastplate Do not become involved in any situation that appears overly important for the next three days. This situation is not in sync with your lifestyle although on the surface it appears to be. The temptation to get involved will be there but this would get you off track and will be a much bigger issue than you anticipated. This will affect your lifestyle in the long run.

breaststroke Be more affectionate with those you care about.

breath *any form* Communicate your needs to another without becoming angry. Keep things in perspective for the sake of clarity.

to breathe or see anyone else breathe out fog in cold weather Within three days you will enter an extremely lucky cycle and anyone who is involved in your life will share this cycle with you. You will receive services that will allow you to achieve success on a higher level than you ever hoped for, regarding anything that is important to you and that you place a high priority on. During this time period you can expect many amazing and wonderful connections that will enable you to achieve and surpass your goals. You can also expect a major merger. The synergism that will be working between you and those you will be working with will bring you to a far higher scale than you ever imagined. This dream also implies that you will attend a very joyful event, will have an educational experience that will bring major benefits to you, or will attend a gathering in which one person will show an interest in you and your projects and offer you major benefits. Expect a long period of tranquility following this and a brilliant future. Any negative event associated with this dream that concerns you or anyone you dreamed about can be avoided.

breed *(animals)* Protect yourself from limb severing injuries, especially for the next three days. Be very careful. This is a double warning.

breeze You will have many affectionate moments with

someone special within two days.

brew You will buy beautiful and expensive clothes for yourself in an unexpected shop at an unexpected time. Look for this occurrence within four days.

brewers yeast Do everything you can to prevent a falling out between yourself and a close friend. This other person will stage a power play because you do not have the finances and power they have. You will continually be asked to perform favors for this person. Take them aside to express your feelings. If you do not, you will have to cut this person out of your life.

brewery You will be able to publicly demonstrate your talents this year. Be prepared for an exciting time. Good luck is with you. You must also cleverly do what is necessary within three days to complete a job successfully.

briar For the next four days, do whatever you can to encourage a special person to grow closer to you. Put your love into action and you will be successful in encouraging closeness.

Briceida Ryan *(author of this book)* You will find that, for the next ten days, you will be at the peak of experience and will be so together that you will instinctively know that you will reach the finish line before the race has really begun. You will have the feeling of confidence that comes from knowing you will succeed. You will feel the strength that comes from your inner core. Follow your goals as if you were on a mission and this will bring you to a victorious completion of your goals. Within this time frame, your sense of ethics and judgment will be intact and you are headed for a fantastic future. Make sure that anything negative you dream about you or anyone you recognize does not occur, and take steps to ensure that you experience only positive expressions in life.

bribe Be careful to avoid swimming accidents.

bric a brac Unexpectedly change your plans and you will find this to be a blessing. The alternative plan will be a better choice. Do this within five days.

brick Bring together creative people who will help you to develop a pool of resources that you can draw information from when needed for a business venture. The time is perfect now and will result in life long riches.

brick laying You will run for office in the future and become a great success.

brickyard You will achieve victory and will gain wealth if you keep going in the direction you are headed. You will achieve your goals and will be surrounded by those who love and respect you.

bridal shower You will be attracted to someone. Do not pursue this. This is an unwise decision and this person is not a good partner for you.

bride *in white* Keep information of your inheritance to yourself for a lifetime. Share this information, in time, only with someone special to you.

to see yourself as a bride You will be asked out by someone totally unexpected whom you feel inferior to. You will find many things in common and enjoy a rich sex life.

to dream of a bride with disheveled clothing Take steps to keep your nervous system healthy. This could become a dangerous health risk if you do not take care of yourself.

to kiss a bride Take your best performing co-worker with you on a business trip to expedite the job.

to see a groom kiss the bride Your financial intuition is correct.

to catch the bouquet Advertise for a mate in order to increase your chances of meeting the ideal person. This small risk will result in a beautiful relationship.

to see a bride and bridesmaid together Be tactful when handling the problems that will arise between in-laws and someone special to you.

to see the bride in street clothes You will enjoy a brilliant future.

bridegroom This dream is a lucky omen.

to see a bride and groom dance You will marry soon, have a happy life, and experience health and wealth.

to kiss a bride groom You are depended on to make the correct decision. Proceed on this and you will be successful.

bridesmaid *you are the bridesmaid* You will capitalize on an inherited annuity by making investments. The funds will double.

to kiss a bridesmaid You will enjoy a quick reconciliation with a lover. You will be treated with mutual affection and respect.

to see bridesmaids dancing You will be held spellbound by someone during a candlelight dinner.

bridge You will be asked to offer assistance to a relative who is financially burdened. This will be a cycle that gives you the means and opportunity to help out several relatives in financial distress. You are deeply loved, respected, and appreciated by many people, even those who are unable to verbalize their feelings. You will be able to sense this by their behavior and mannerisms.

to cross a bridge Avoid all problems that would influence the power you have over others with authority.

to drive over or walk on a bridge Be direct with your dislikes.

to go under a bridge A conniving person will forsake you during a business deal. This will occur at the last possible moment. Choose an alternative person to keep this from happening. Expect this to occur within a few days.

to fall off Be careful of injuries to the eye. Guard your eyesight.

a non functioning bridge You are loved by both young and old.

bridge *(card game)* Something that was previously a secret and a mystery will become clear to you

bridle The information you seek will be reliable.

bridle path Do not allow yourself to be cheated in a business agreement. You are asking for less than you should receive.

brie Make sure that you do not overlook any important upcoming events.

briefcase Do not allow yourself to be led in the wrong direction because of a vengeful attitude.

brigade For the next three days, all of your negotiations will be fortuitous. Schedule all meetings and negotiations during this time period to ensure success.

brim *if a cup is filled to the brim* You will gain wealth through marriage if you choose to take this option.
cracked brim A stressed out young person will ask your advice about a love relationship. Within a few days, the problems will work out to this young person's advantage.
hat brim You will receive the verification you need regarding a certain situation that involves the feelings of a very special person. You will soon hear the words of love you have been wanting to hear. This person is very kind, generous and tenacious about having you become a part of their life.

brimstone You will visit a place filled with evil and wickedness. Research your plans before you travel.

brine You will be able to minimize your expenses by making sure all valuable property is properly insured. Follow your intuition. All of your travel arrangements will be successful and you will enjoy a safe, pleasurable trip.

brine shrimp Be aware of the behavior of another person. This individual will start to behave strangely around you and is becoming increasingly more dangerous. Do whatever you can to protect yourself from someone who could cause you harm. Move on with your life as safely as you can.

briquette *unlit* You will encounter an obnoxious, irritating person at a party within three days. You may choose not to attend.
burning briquettes A guarded secret of yours will become known. Problems will develop because of this. This will occur within a few days. Try to keep this from taking place.

bristle *(hair)* You are presently working on two projects. You will find greater success by merging the two into one.

Britain Be relentless in the pursuit of your goals. This dream may also be used as a reference point in time. If you dream of this country and see its name used in any context, the dream message will occur on this day.

British Isles People in authority will promptly respond to your needs. This dream may also be used as a reference point in time. If you dream of this island group and see it used in any context, the dream message will occur on this day.

brittle Do not compromise yourself to those who refuse to see your side.

broadax Be sure you allow the special people in your life the time to take care of their own personal needs without causing them to feel guilty of neglecting you.

broadcast An aggressive sales approach will bring your product to a greater number of people. Act quickly.

broadcloth You will have a wondrous invitation from someone you least expect. Pursue this and you will have a great time.

broad jump Do not jeopardize your reputation by assisting a minor in what could be a dangerous endeavor. Be careful that a kind gesture doesn't put you in jeopardy.

broadsword You will be able to get the necessary answers to questions by finally pinning down a very elusive person. This will be possible within five days.

Broadway This dream promises you that you will enjoy grandness, power and victory in every aspect of your life. It also implies that you will experience exhilarating changes in your lifestyle. You will also meet someone new very soon who has a flair for visual effects. This is the perfect time to add style and drama to your appearance, if this is something you choose. This will result in a very pleasurable meeting and a larger cash flow within five days.

brocade The information gained by accidentally eavesdropping on a group of powerful people will be implemented to your benefit.

broccoli Become territorial and guard your property. Take care of your health and drink plenty of water.

brochure Make education your priority for now. Do not neglect your responsibilities. Do not be afraid of revealing your proper upbringing and charisma as well as the polish you have gained through education. These traits will be admired by a group of influential people.

brogan Take over some of the responsibilities of another person so they may regain health. This will result in greater independence for this person.

brogue Dress in a manner that will impress others.

broiler You previously turned down a request from another person. This person will now make the same request within three days, but with the hidden agenda of starting an argument. Stay calm or this could create an angry situation.

broken *broken arm* You can avoid deep depression and a bitter loss due to a child's kidnapping. For the next three days take major steps to prevent this from happening and be acutely aware of the child's whereabouts. It would be a good idea to practice child safety until your child is grown.

broken bottle This is an alert to those who are pregnant to prevent a premature birth by taking steps to guard their health and avoid all heavy activity for a three day period.

broken cup A lack of communication will cause a major setback. Take steps to prevent this with the person you wish to be in your life.

broken dishes For at least two days avoid taking risks because of your bad temper. This behavior will bring about a permanent split between you and a special person. Remove all communication blocks that will keep this union from growing to a deeper level.

broken drinking glass Think ahead for the next two days. Someone special to you will blurt out a stupidly inconsiderate and insulting remark in front of others. Take this person aside, ahead of time, and subtly express your opinion about this kind of behavior in an unaccusing manner. This will prevent these thoughtless, unintentional remarks from occurring.

broken bones other than arms and legs For the next two days, take precautions to avoid injury due to faulty machinery. Be very careful and stay away from any machinery that is in disrepair.

broken window glass Prevent a falling out between yourself and a dear friend. This other person will pull a power play because you lack the finances and power this person has. They will continually ask you to perform favors for them in order to keep you in control. Take this person aside and express your feelings. If you don't, you will be forced to cut this person out of your life instead of maintaining a friendship.

broken leg Do whatever is necessary, for the next four days, to keep your temper under control. A distasteful situation will arise that will render you suspicious and jealous of the behavior of someone close to you. You will also be driven into a murderous rage over this. Take steps to keep this rage from developing and do not cater to this emotion. You are placing too much importance on another and not enough on yourself.

broken mirror Think ahead. You will be invited to visit a new acquaintance within a three day period and will be terrorized by this dangerous person. This will be a horrifying experience with no possibility of escape. Avoid this by having nothing to do with this new acquaintance and by not going to this person's house. Do not put yourself in the position of being held against your will. This is a life threatening situation.

broken pottery You can avoid many depressing and distressful moments by not going on that trip you planned. Something will go tragically wrong and no one will be there to help you. Take steps to really take care of yourself.

broken car window Remain calm and centered for the next three days. A situation will come up that you will be very tempted to become involved in. Do not allow another person's problems to cause you to become so desperate that you compromise yourself and become entangled in this issue. Once you involve yourself, it will be very difficult to pry yourself loose and it will become progressively worse as time goes by. You are seeing only the tip of the iceberg. Remain uninvolved.

broken anything Do not travel by air for the next three days in order to avoid an air disaster. This is also a warning to friends and relatives who have scheduled air travel during this time period. Take steps to prevent accidents and injuries of any sort within this time frame.

broken crockery This dream implies that unless you do something now you will not receive anything by way of a settlement. Proceed with confidence because whatever you set out to receive will be accomplished if you work at it.

in any other form Something is taking place behind the scenes with another individual for reasons known only to them. This person enjoys creating chaos and distasteful episodes in the lives of others. Become very aware of your surroundings and any unusual episodes in your life. Take steps to avoid this and to bring balance and stability into your life.

broker Stocks are going up. This dream is a very lucky omen.

bromeliad Make sure, for the next three days, that you are not drawn to someone with a secretive, mysterious past. Make sure you do not get involved with this person or with any unusual situation that comes up within the week.

bronchitis Concentrate on your priorities. Eat the proper foods to build up your resistance to disease. Drink plenty of water.

bronco You will need to research an area before you make that trip. Make phone calls and check out the situation there before traveling. You may decide to cancel.

brontosaurus Do not allow yourself to be abused or insulted in public. You will never forgive yourself for allowing this to take place. Avoid any situation within the next few days that could allow this to happen.

bronze You will meet someone of a different nationality, within four days. You will enjoy each other's company and will enjoy doing a variety of things together. This dream is an omen of happiness. Also, you will receive the assistance and encouragement necessary to complete a project.

bronze medal You will make a public appearance this year to demonstrate a talent of yours. Be prepared for an exciting time. Good luck is with you.

brooch Do not mix romance with business for the next five days. If you choose to meet someone for business purposes, keep it strictly business. Romance has its time and place.

brook Motivate yourself to add a number of new events to your life and you will see big improvements within five days. These changes will continue for the next month. Many blessings will come to you and your family.

broom A major change will occur in your life that will be out of your control. Be prepared for this within the week and expect the unexpected.

broomstick Within four days you will finally achieve the reconciliation you have been seeking. This union will be blessed with prosperity and abundances in those areas of your life you most desire. You are entering a lucky seven day cycle.

broth Within the week, someone will start to notice you in a very special way. This person will romantically pursue you and will be determined to marry you. They will move slowly yet persistently in this direction. If you choose to pursue this, the relationship will be long lived and prosperous. Follow your instincts. Your hunches are correct, especially for the next three days.

brothel You need to spend time in a quiet private place with someone special in order to start a fantastic love affair.

brother Your brother's appearance in a dream is a warning to be patient and watch that you don't use words to injure your loved one's feelings. Enjoy a long and happy relationship. Within the next few days a known person or persons with the tendency to be conniving will also enter your life. This person will lead you into uncomfortable situations.
  stepbrother You will enjoy success when bargain hunting.

brother-in-law You are being warned to remain calm, stable and nonargumentative during an upcoming family situation. Take steps to stay out of this situation.

brow Because of the untimely death of someone you know due to a freak accident, you will gain an inheritance.

brown This dream is a lucky omen and refers to a job done well in great haste. During this cycle you will also be gaining strength in all of your internal organs, especially the heart and spleen. Maintain your health. If you choose, this is also the perfect time to spark a romantic interest in someone you desire. Within four days you will meet someone of a different nationality. You will enjoy their company and doing things together. This dream is an omen of happiness. You will get the encouragement and assistance you need to

complete any project.

brown bag You will rejoice when you unexpectedly receive a long desired present. This will occur within three days.

brown bread Be very receptive to your hunches for the next four days and you will get a sense of what is required to handle a particular situation that will come up in this time period.

brownout You will enjoy an abundance of health. You must also prepare yourself for natural disasters by planning ahead and protect yourself in all sexually related activities.

brown recluse spider Do not allow temptations to steer you wrong. You will be tempted to enter into a conspiracy with someone in order to gain access to something you desire. Do nothing that will lead to regrets.

brown rice Be careful of cigarette burns.

brown sugar Be wary of fatigue when it is least expected. Take care of yourself and take steps to fight it off.

brownie Focus on strategy when attempting to secure donations from large corporations, especially for the next two days. Think clearly in order to achieve success.

bruise Be wary of toxins around children in order to avoid accidental poisoning. Otherwise you will have a brilliant future. Take steps to prevent any negative event foretold in this dream to you or anyone you recognize, and experience only positive expressions in your life.
  black and blue Do not freely donate your time. You need this time for yourself. Within three days, someone will also use your authority to commit an atrocious act against someone who means a lot to you, and will later hide behind your authority to get away with this action. This will cause you deep emotional pain. You have prior notice of this and can take steps to prevent it. Otherwise you are headed for a prosperous future.

brunch Someone will show a romantic interest in you. Be aware that this person is lazy and may abuse you financially.

brunette For the next few weeks you will experience a burst of greater creative thought. Be sure to jot down all ideas. You have a brilliant future ahead.

brush Within three days you will be overwhelmed with excitement about something good headed your way. Do not become overexcited about this. Step back, restrain yourself, and make sure this is exactly what you want.
  any kind An urge and yearning for a sexual encounter with another person will be realized within a few days. Surprisingly, this person shares a yearning for you also.
  to brush anything For the next four days you will be in a perfect cycle for uncovering important information about

another person's business. You will discover each important detail during this time. This dream is also a lucky omen for you.

brushing teeth You will be received with open arms due to your dynamic reputation. Others will be very amenable to a certain situation you are introducing within the next three days.

Brussels sprouts Show your affection to someone who thinks you are not interested.

brute A major change will subtly take place in your life for the better. You will then experience more abundances.

bubble Another person demonstrates an enthusiasm and eagerness to be with you. You will then experience a new zest for life.

bubble gum A problem in the family will be revealed to you through a child. This problem will be resolved and each person in the family will receive an abundance of health and blessings.

bubble top Do not become involved in a domestic quarrel.

bubonic plague You are being drawn into the wrong circle of people. As a result, you will begin to experience poor health and will need medical assistance in order to recover. You need to become involved with other friends in a healthier environment.

buccaneer Watch out for snake bites. An unexpected surprise will also thrill you.

buck Help relieve a loved one's stress.

bucket *a full bucket* You will meet that special person through a third party.

an empty bucket Do not allow friends to start a domestic dispute in your house.

to carry a splashing bucket of liquid Do not assume that you will receive help from one who has repeatedly promised to assist you. This help will not come through.

bucket of milk Someone will promise deep love for you and will be willing to commit.

bucket seat You will accidentally find yourself in a dangerous area. Be careful about where you drive to avoid this situation.

buckle Place emphasis on recovering from an illness. Get more rest for at least a month.

buckshot Stay away from nervous people.

buckskin Do not allow someone to impose a particular lifestyle on you by using deception and trickery, and do not allow yourself to be manipulated and controlled by false prom-

ises. Do not delude yourself into being strung along by the illusions of another person.

buckteeth You will take an all expense paid trip to a fantastic city and you will meet someone there for an enjoyable time. This person will be advantageous to you in the future.

buckwheat Do not allow yourself to be brainwashed into joining a cult. Remove yourself from this environment and avoid all people involved in this process for a few weeks.

bud You will be granted your deepest desires.

Buddha This dream is a good luck omen. You will enjoy prosperity, good fortune, health and wealth for a long time to come.

budget You will be married soon if this is the option you choose.

Buffalo Do not talk yourself out of an idea because it seems overwhelming. Proceed with confidence and you will be successful. This dream may also be used as a reference point in time. If you dream of this city and see its name used in any context, the dream message will occur on this day.

buffet Someone will be irresistibly drawn to you and will make their feelings for you known. If you choose this route, you will not only enjoy the refinements in life but a deep abiding love as well. This dream is an extremely lucky omen and many blessings will come to you and your family.

buffoon You and your loved one will enjoy many passionate moments. You must also be careful of burns.

bug This dream is a warning to avoid catching herpes.

lady bug Within five days you will receive the proper medical treatment for a long standing problem and all medical advice will be totally reliable. You will rid yourself of all pre-existing problems and all problems that are developing at the present time. You will also need to take the proper measures to prevent fire on any of your properties.

lightning bug Make sure you make the effort to display special behavior toward someone special that you desire closeness with who is not yet involved with you. During this cycle you will do all of the right things to encourage this. You will be able to have this special person in your life if this is the way you choose to go. Many blessings are with you and your family. You will achieve an abundance of health and prosperity during this cycle.

potato bug Take a very close look at your investments over the next four days. Pay close attention also to someone who is making romantic overtures toward you. It will not be suitable to have a sexual encounter with this person because of the real possibility of contracting a unrevealed contagious disease. Take precautions to protect yourself sexually and financially.

to see you or anyone else bitten by a bug This dream is

an omen of victory. You will enjoy great clarity of thought and this will lead you to riches. You will also enjoy a romantic interlude if this is something you choose.

bug eggs Be very aware and cautious about where you are allowing someone to lead you emotionally. For purposes known only to them, a certain person is leading you to believe that you are loved completely by them. Although words of love may not actually be used at this time all of the trappings will be there such as gifts, flowers, romantic outings, etc. Your feelings for this person will grow quicker and deeper than their feelings. If you allow the possibility of lovemaking, this person will not be able to touch you in any way that implies that love exists and you will feel very empty and cold as a result. It will be impossible to connect with this person on the same level they have led you to believe was there. Instead of putting yourself through this, you have enough advance notice to avoid this scenario completely. Get on with your life without this person and you can avoid the emotional upheaval that will follow. This person has a hidden agenda that involves you performing a task for them that only they are aware of. This situation will only lead to unhappiness. Otherwise, you are headed for a prosperous future that will begin within the week.

buggy You will receive a long desired piece of jewelry as an inheritance. You will receive it as a gift prior to the owner's death.

bugle Someone in your family will win a large amount of money. Everyone will rejoice.

build *to see others build* Someone will be seeking approval from you and will do everything necessary to deepen your involvement with them. If you choose, you will both enjoy a mutually satisfying relationship. You are headed for a brilliant future.

to build something This dream is a very lucky omen for you. You will enjoy an abundance of health and will receive wealth in areas you never expected as a result of an unexpected income. You will be able to accomplish tasks that you felt at one time were impossible. This is a great cycle to tackle those big projects. Proceed with confidence, you are on the path toward a prosperous future.

in any other form You are entering a cycle that will require you to make more time for romance, sex and emotional fulfillment. Set aside time for yourself and, if you choose, you will be welcomed with open arms by someone you desire.

building Someone important to you will appreciate you and show more affection toward you for the next few days. Do not become suspicious of this.

bulb *(light)* *turned off* A physical pain experienced by another will be concealed from you. Be alert to this.

turned on Pay more attention to legal matters. This attentiveness will result in great success. This will be a victorious time for you.

bulb *(flower)* Within the next three days you will overcome difficult obstacles. This dream implies victory in what you felt was impossible in the past. Many blessings are with you and your family.

bulge Creatively inspire children to become involved in their education.

bull Someone you know takes pleasure in provoking arguments. Remove this person from your life.

bulldog Do not make any sudden changes. Stay home and slow down for the next few days. Reschedule all appointments.

bulldozer Conduct research before moving into a new neighborhood.

bullet Someone you know, either by theft or by unfair bargaining, will acquire some of your valuables within three days. Be aware of this. A family member may also avoid a serious operation as a result of a fall, if alerted.

bullet hole Pull yourself together and remain calm for the next three days. A situation will arise during this time frame that you will be tempted to become involved with. Do not allow the problems of others to cause you to become desperate enough to get involved. Do not compromise yourself and do not become entangled in this situation. Once you become involved, it will be difficult to pry yourself loose, and it will become progressively worse as time goes on. You are only seeing the beginning stages of this problem. Remain uninvolved.

bulletin You are too socially active and are ignoring your family and responsibilities. Change this.

bulletin board A family member will attempt suicide unless assistance is given soon. Be watchful of this behavior.

bullet proof Watch out for food poisoning.

bullet proof jacket Within four days take the time to prepare yourself for a conversation with someone who is involved in a particular situation. This will give you time to gather all those involved to discuss ways to keep a negative event from taking place regarding this particular issue. Alert all those involved of the possibility. Many blessings will come to you and your family.

bullfight Be careful of a small deep cut. You will be unaware of the cause but the cut will continually bleed and refuse to heal. Watch out for small sharp objects.

bullhorn Do not give anyone the chance to insult you without reason for the next three days. Otherwise, a lucky occurrence will take place during this time period.

bullion You will achieve success with your ideas and plans and will achieve your goals within five days. Proceed with confidence.

Bull's eye Within the week, you will hear extremely good news and you will also achieve victory in all aspects of your life. This luck will remain with you for the next week.

bullterrier Prior to engaging in sexual play, someone will promise undying love to you. Afterwards, this person will return only for the purpose of sexual gratification. If you wish a deeper commitment, do not become involved with this individual. You will be vulnerable for the next three days.

bully Someone desires you sexually. This person will not openly state their desire but will drop large hints. Relax and face the issue so that this person will discuss their desires with you.

bum Someone you know needs temporary lodging. Do not offer your home. This would be an unwise decision.

bumble bee Your intuitive powers will be at their highest level. Follow all hunches and urges. This dream is also a lucky omen for couples.

bumper Promote yourself in order to achieve your goals. This will happen quickly.

bumper car Make sure you are not placed in the position to suffer terror at the hands of a very dangerous person. This person will mislead you into believing that they either want to view something you are selling or wish to show you something you want to buy. Be very wary of this for the next three days.

bumper sticker Someone in authority will request a favor. This will be repaid generously.

bun You will soon enjoy a gift of an all expenses paid vacation. This will occur shortly.

bundle Long awaited news about your career will arrive and you will celebrate.

bungalow The distasteful feelings you have about another person are accurate. Follow your hunches.

bunion Expect a new addition to the family.

bunk bed Keep your financial affairs from nosy people.

bunkhouse Do not say anything that could be damaging if someone chooses to use it against you. You also need to do everything you can to remain healthy.

bunny Question your drinking habits. Be careful that you do not overindulge.

Bunsen burner You will enjoy prosperity and success with your career.

buoy Someone you know enjoys being with you only to boast about money, belongings, etc. Avoid this person.

burden A long standing burden will disappear overnight.

bureau *(chest of drawers)* Insure all of your property. A financial tip you receive will also be totally reliable.

bureau *(government)* Live within your means.

burglar Someone you know is developing schizophrenic tendencies. This condition is not serious now and the behavior is normal most of the time. This disease will escalate until you are threatened. This person also plots, late at night, the theft of small precious objects. Avoid this person.

burglary Someone who owes you a great deal of money will purposely leave town with no forwarding address or phone number in order to avoid the debt. Take steps to collect the money before this occurs.

burgundy *(color)* You will receive abundances in all phases of your life. This color also indicates that you will gain the advantage in capitalizing on all of your ideas. This color also facilitates the self healing process. Communication with others will be more open. You will relentlessly pursue your goals in spite of barriers. Take care of your teeth and bones.

burgundy *(wine)* Do not compromise your goals.

burial This dream indicates a dynamic and thrilling time in your life. You will meet someone special on a business trip and will enjoy this union.

burlap Be sensitive to the responsibilities of others.

burlesque A very close friend will release you from financial burdens. You must also guard your health. This dream is a lucky omen. You will look also for compromises in an emotionally fulfilling relationship.

burl wood Make education a priority right now and make sure you do not neglect your responsibilities. Do not be afraid of showing your charisma and proper upbringing as well as the polish you have acquired through education. These traits will be admired by people with influence.

burn *to burn yourself* You have sent information to another person in authority. Take care that your plans are not sabotaged by someone who has a conniving personality and make sure the information is not purposely rerouted.

anyone burned by a cigarette Do everything necessary

to make someone aware of the deep passion you feel for them and make certain this person knows exactly how you feel. Make sure romance flows freely during this cycle. This experience will be similar to a honeymoon for the next two months.

unhealed burn marks on the body Respect your health. Someone will also aggressively attempt to schedule a date with you. This person is very tenacious and will offer a fulfilling sexual relationship if you desire.

healed burn marks on the body For the next month, get ready for costly emergency situations such as dental work, auto repairs, etc. Put aside money now for these occasions. Handle each episode with as little stress as possible. Take steps to ensure that any negative event occurring in this dream does not take place in reality.

to see a burning house You will reconcile with someone who is special to you. This will result in a loving, passionate relationship.

to see someone burned alive You will open a small shop. At first it will not be very successful but eventually will grow into a large business.

to see yourself burned alive Be careful not to accidentally overdose on medicine by taking two drugs that should not be combined.

fireplace burning You will enjoy a romantic interlude with a special person.

to smell burning odors Within two days, you will be surprised at someone's request to spend private moments with them. This request will be unexpected and will come after you have repeatedly asked this person to spend time with you and after repeatedly being turned down. Curiosity will lead you to spend time with them. The choice is up to you.

anything burned Do not put yourself in the position of being falsely accused of anything. Think ahead to prevent this.

burner Watch what you put into writing.

burn marks *on wood* Within three days someone will diplomatically drop subtle hints about a particular area of dissatisfaction in their life that they would like to see you become responsible for. This person wants you to take it upon yourself to make the necessary changes to improve their life. They feel they are stonewalled and cannot get through this situation. You will have the conviction and compassion to do this for them and it will lead them to a better lifestyle if you take the initiative. Many blessings are with you.

burp Do not be so quick to react to a situation that will flare up within the week. You will gain more information about this issue as time goes on. As you gain more insight, you will be able to make the correct decisions.

burr Stay calm and centered for the next three days. A situation will arise that will tempt your involvement, but make sure you do not become so desperate over another person's problems that you become entangled in their issues. It will

be very difficult to extricate yourself and this situation will become progressively worse as time goes on. You are now only seeing the tip of the iceberg. Remain uninvolved.

burro Do not make a clown out of yourself in public.

burrow A long overdue apology will arrive from someone who has injured your feelings.

bury You will hear of a bad snowing accident involving an acquaintance. This can be prevented by alerting them.

to dream of being buried alive Someone will treat you in a way that goes far beyond your expectations and will express their feelings in a way you never imagined. You can expect a proposal from this person that will give you a great deal of happiness and will be difficult to refuse. You are on the path toward a brilliant future.

bus *to see yourself or another drive* An overwhelming problem will finally be resolved after much work. You will experience a great deal of satisfaction once it is finally over.

red bus You will do something that will reverse, destroy or slow down the progress of a particular situation. Pay close attention to your behavior for the next five days to determine what you need to change in order to turn this situation around.

school bus Stop being so gullible and stay on top of all situations.

in any other form Within three days you will gain the freedom you have long desired. You will then be able to express yourself on a different level and explore new dynamic dimensions that will bring you prosperity and happiness.

busboy Avoid crowded places for the next few days.

bush This dream is a lucky sign. You will develop a deeper clarity of greater thought and a stronger command that arises from within. This will allow you to express yourself in a straight forward manner. This will occur if you divorce yourself from those whom you associate with on a daily basis. You will then be able to make all the correct decisions that will lead you to a comfortable lifestyle. You are headed for a fortuitous and tranquil future.

dead or wilted You will learn of the unemployment of someone you know.

in bloom All speculations will pay off.

leafy Convince someone who is jealous that you are faithful and that your feelings are for them.

bushel Victory will be yours.

business *any form* You will enjoy an abundance in all phases of your life.

business cards *to receive* Sexual favors will unexpectedly be asked of you.

to give You will open a successful business of your own. This will be a very positive move.

businessman You will find rare antiques at a bargain price if you really search.

business school You will work hard for a long period of time. Your harvest will pay off and you will finally reap many profits.

bust A very intelligent person will unexpectedly come to your aid at the request of another friend. This will occur within three days.

bustle Do not allow someone to abuse you sexually or physically in play. This may, at first, seem acceptable yet will later become abusive. Be firm about setting limits.

busybody Someone who is developing an interest in you will be turned off by your resentments regarding a former relationship. Be very aware of how you sound to others, especially for the next four days.

butcher Do not be unfaithful.

butcher block Be very sensible when you request that someone help you with something they are reluctant to become involved in. This person does not have the courage to tell you this to your face, and will talk behind your back instead. Do not insist on trying to recruit someone who is not interested in helping you. Seek alternatives in order to avoid hurt feelings.

butcher knife Within five days, you will undergo a great deal of pressure for standing up for someone else. Do not compromise your principles but prepare yourself for this pressure and handle yourself with dignity.

butler Your life will change dramatically. You will associate with many influential people and receive many honors.

butt *cigarette with ashes* You will feel remorse for a very sick child. This child will recover after a long time in the hospital.

cigar A close friend will unexpectedly die young. This will cause you deep pain.

butter A family member will undergo surgery within a few weeks. This will result in a successful recovery.

butter bean Do not borrow or lend money, especially for the next three days.

buttercup You will soon find relief for a long term physical pain.

butterfly Someone you meet at a conference, etc., will invite you out. You will have a great time and will be exuberant about this person.

butterfly stroke Within four days you and someone else

will find you have underestimated your relationship. This relationship will go from platonic to romantic, and you will reschedule your life to spend as much time together as possible. This will be an enjoyable time for you.

butter knife Within four days you will have a pleasurable time with a wonderful companion.

buttermilk For the next few weeks, you will be exposed to constant small problems and stresses. Take them a day at a time and they will be successfully handled.

butternut A special person will return to rekindle the relationship within four days. This will be an exciting, passionate time and the union will be a success.

butterscotch You will be invited to a fiesta and will enjoy yourself immensely. This will occur within two weeks.

buttocks You are in a very lucky cycle and will achieve victory in anything you choose to become involved in. You will be very satisfied with the result of your choices. You will also experience loyalty and affection from those around you, especially for the next week. Any negative event foretold in this dream may be changed to produce a positive result.

baby buttocks You will have many passionate moments with the one you love.

beauty marks on buttocks You will gain a new family member through marriage.

clothed buttocks You will take a fabulous vacation with someone in the near future and you will share wonderful memories for years.

itchy buttocks You will marry the person you choose. You will also receive a small inheritance.

your nude buttocks You will receive money from an older relative and be financially secure for life.

someone else's buttocks (nude or otherwise) You will enjoy many happy times with someone who loves you. Someone will also finally come to grips with themselves and make a decision you have long awaited. This decision will have a major impact on your life. You and this person will make mutual plans that will lead to a brilliant future. Expect this to occur within the week.

sores on buttocks The more sores you see the greater and faster your financial gain.

an enjoyable touch on the buttocks You will enjoy many happy years with your loved one.

a distasteful touch on the buttocks Do not undergo unnecessary surgery.

button (*decorative buttons*) *campaign/political buttons or buttons that make a statement of some kind* Within three days you will develop a sense of urgency to attract the attention of someone you desire. Follow your hunches. You will find, in this person, a similar lifestyle and ideals. If you choose to pursue this, it is possible to establish a relationship in this cycle. You will find this person to be very demonstrative and affectionate, and you will both have a great deal of love to share with each other. Also, pay close attention to the message on the button. This will offer you a clue signifying something you will want to embrace in your life, or something you will want to take steps to avoid or alter.

to remove or to have someone remove a button from you or someone else Play it safe and do not allow an opportunity to slip through your fingers. Pay close attention to all future involvements to ensure you do not allow any chances to slip by. This dream is also asking you to face facts and stop looking at everything through rose colored glasses. You are making it easy for someone to lie to you because you give the impression that you prefer not to deal with cold hard facts. Change this behavior and face situations head on. Otherwise buttons represent an extremely lucky omen.

in any other form Within a few days you will have a sudden urge to visit a relative. This relative will give you a cherished object, perhaps an antique.

button *push button* You will need medical attention for the next few weeks. If you visit a doctor at the first sign of illness, you may cut the healing process in half. You will enjoy a successful outcome.

to dream of pushing buttons and successfully open something Someone you know will attempt to reform the behavior of someone else by using their bad temper. Think ahead so you will have a way of counteracting this by using skillful communication to settle everything down once it starts to flare up. You will be able to make others feel more comfortable and more agreeable. Clear thinking and a skillful use of words will diffuse this issue. You will also receive good news during this time period.

to push buttons and be unable to open Be very cautious about where you are allowing someone to take you emotionally. Someone, for reasons only they are aware of, will lead you to believe you are loved completely. Words of love may or may not be used but this person will present a scenario of love (i.e., gifts, flowers, romantic outings, etc.). You will quickly develop strong feelings for this person but if you allow lovemaking to occur, you will not be touched, loved or kissed in any special way that implies you are loved. This individual will try to put on a good act but you will feel cold and empty as a result. Do not put yourself through this emotional upheaval. You have enough prior notice to avoid it entirely. This person has a hidden agenda in mind that involves you doing something for them that only they are aware of. This will only lead to unhappiness. Otherwise, you are headed for a prosperous future that will begin within the week.

button *(clothing)* *any form* You will have to rely on your own conscience and gut level feelings in order to make the correct analysis about a particular situation that will be coming up within three days. This will enable you to make the right decision.

buttonhole You will have an irresistible urge for sexual contact at the wrong place and time. Your partner will be unavailable.

buy *any form* You will be the only one with the opportunity to purchase a certain stock. This will rapidly grow in value. A certain status will be attached to this purchase.

buzz The company you are working for will shortly enter bankruptcy proceedings. Find alternative means for financial security.

buzzard Do not allow others to abuse your generosity.

buzz saw Aggressively handle financial troubles within the family.

bystander Do not waste your time with those who are unworthy of you. Use your life in a meaningful way.

C

C You are contemplating a separation from someone who is special to you. Your image of the future is one of loneliness and despair. In reality, this move will set you free to explore life and develop your creativity in ways never imagined. You must discover the reason behind this faulty thinking and change your view of the future.

cab Do not dwell in the past. As soon as you let go, your life will be altered in a positive way.

cabana An event will occur within two days that is important for you to attend. You will enjoy the pleasure of being in the company of two admirers who will subtly try to win over your affections. Although it is not apparent to you, one of these admirers possesses a great deal of authority and power. Both of them are charming and agreeable and one of them will be perfect as a lifetime partner. You are on the path to prosperity.

cabaret You will dance the night away with wealthy and famous people. If you continue in the direction you are going, you will gain fame.

cabbage Your education and personal development will be a priority now.

cabbageworm Do not allow someone to harass you to the point of giving up something you cherish. Be very firm about putting an end to someone's abusive behavior, especially for the next week.

cabdriver *to be one* someone will attempt to bring an injury suit against you for insurance purposes. Be wary of this for the next three days.

    to have one You are headed in the wrong direction. Rethink your goals, regroup, and maintain your optimism. You will be able to handle everything properly.

cabernet You will be captivated by someone and will shortly enter into a long term involvement. This will be mutually satisfying.

cabin Live within your means in order to gain financial security and to progress at a faster rate.

cabin cruiser Take every necessary step to complete your goals, even if it involves a bit of risk taking. This is the best cycle for you to do this and you will enjoy success.

cabinet Be careful not to break a priceless object.

cabinetmaker Do not push your luck with someone who is important to you. Although this individual is far away, be assured that this person loves you. Your behavior may force an issue to the point of separation. Control your impulsive behavior and seek help to avoid creating an unbearable situation for someone special to you.

cabin fever Someone will promise undying love prior to engaging in sexual pleasures with you. After this is over, this person will disappear and will reappear from time to time only for sexual pleasure. If you choose a deeper involvement, avoid this person. You will be especially vulnerable to surrender for the next four days.

cable *(wire)* Be cautious in unexpected places. You may encounter a life threatening situation.

cable box This dream is an extremely lucky omen but you will need to be very selective about what you are willing to apply yourself to. This regards any project, idea or plan, etc., that others are offering you. Once you have made your choice of the opportunities, give everything you have to this project. Look at everything on a grand scale and take this opportunity to a higher level than the original conception. You will enjoy a burst of creative thought and will succeed on a higher and grander scale than you ever imagined. You are definitely headed in the right direction and are on the path of prosperity and a wealth of opportunities. You will also enjoy an abundance of health.

cable car You will receive many blessings in your life. You will also be influenced by a wealthy and influential person within three days. This connection will make you rich.

cable television Do whatever you can to put your product on the market, it will be tremendously successful.

caboose For the next three weeks, luck will be yours. You are also deeply loved, physically and emotionally.

cacao Do not postpone any pending project, especially for the next five days.

cacciatore Take every necessary step to complete your goals, even if it involves a bit of risk taking. This is the best cycle for you to do this and you will enjoy success.

cactus Your roommate will talk behind your back and spread your personal affairs to everyone. Get a new roommate. This can be prevented. You will also find that someone you feel unsure of has deep emotional feelings for you. This will become apparent to you within five days.

cadaver Do whatever you must to convince someone special to commit to marriage.

caddie Stop being suspicious of someone who is important to you.

cadet Guard your computer software and keep a close eye on all of your computer equipment.

Cadillac An unexpected business offer will be extended to you (i.e., mail centers, Laundromat, etc.) by an unexpected person. If you choose to involve yourself, this enterprise will be very fruitful.

Caesar You will be captivated by someone you feel an intense sexual desire for.

Caesar salad Let a certain person you are interested in make the first move. Once you do this, you will both receive what you want and need for mutual satisfaction. This will occur within two days. You will also, within this time period, receive an answer you have long wanted to hear. A long desired wish will come true.

caesarean section Do not undergo any unnecessary surgery. Research any procedure that is recommended for you.

cafe An insincere person will feign interest in you, yet each time you attempt to set up a date, excuses will be made. Stop this now. You must also make sure you do not become a workaholic. Take time out for recreation with a special person. This is especially important for the next two days.

café au lait You will have a very successful private conversation within five days with someone who will help you to expedite a specific goal you are working on.

cafe curtains Your plans will not work out in the way you wish. Within the week, check out alternative ways of achieving your goals.

cafeteria Do things that are fun for you. Enjoy humorous events.

caffeine You are going too fast in a relationship, slow down.

caftan Make it your business to monitor the consumption level of alcoholic beverages and prescription medications of older adults for the next three days. It is important that you become aware of any abuse, and of the dangerous combination of alcohol and medicine. You will also win over the person you desire most.

cage *with bird* Inspire a sick relative to achieve balance in order to survive and heal.

empty cage An acquaintance will be released from jail.

caiman Other people rely on you to make good decisions and you are the first person many people call on in times of need. Other people think well of you and you are loved by many. You will also be able to accomplish a great deal with very little leg work.

Cain *(from the Bible)* Be careful when handling the financial side of a business. Your partner will be watching for mistakes. Earn the trust of your partner by accurate accounting.

cairn For the next three days, your eagerness, enthusiasm and desire to handle a personal problem for someone else will win them over.

Cajun You are thinking of taking in an infant. Think carefully. You need to be very committed because this child will become very attached to you. This will bring you much joy but remember to cherish the child's feelings.

cake Someone is trying to persuade you to join them in a project. If you do this, it will be very profitable. This will occur shortly.

to bake a cake Show your love and appreciation to someone who is waiting for you to do so.

to buy Be careful in public around someone who has lost control. Be sure this person does not focus on you. This is a dangerous situation.

to eat cake You will find unexpected pleasure for the next few days connected with a pet project.

birthday cake The opportunities you have been waiting for will come your way within two days. You will enjoy a new lease on life and all issues that have been dragging you down will suddenly come to an end. You will enjoy a new excitement and new sense of confidence. For the next two days, make sure that you demonstrate self reliance and make an effort to look at both sides of a particular issue. Explore the possibilities of what could unexpectedly take place prior to making any major decisions. You are loved beyond your

imagination, are deeply respected and you will be surrounded by those who love you. Others will show you their appreciation within the week. It is also beneficial to look up the astrological sign of the birthday, whether yours or anyone else's, that is celebrated.

angel food cake Tutors are needed in order to be successful in school.

cheesecake You are faced with a recurring problem. You will find a solution to keep this problem from reoccurring or at least delay it long enough for you to recover. Play a very active part in ensuring that your emotional needs are fulfilled. Within five days you will also visualize the path you need to take for a brilliant future. Good luck is with you.

cupcake Make your relationship solid on all levels.

hot cakes Open up your communication and show your affection to the one you care about. Put your love into action and give this person evidence of your feeling because this person is feeling very neglected. It is important that you do this within three days. Take any negative situation in this dream and turn it into a positive. Make sure that you experience only positive expressions in your life.

marble cake Make it a point to enjoy more of what nature has to offer. Get back to basics and enjoy what is around you. Love yourself, pamper yourself and treat yourself to marvelous events.

pound cake You will shortly be celebrating your own wedding.

seed cake Do whatever is necessary to prevent a premature birth. Warn others if it is appropriate.

shortcake Special knowledge that you have acquired and recorded needs to be protected until it is copy written. This will be a special gold mine for you. Hasten the copywriting process.

sponge cake For a two day period, stay within the boundaries of your neighborhood. You will be in danger otherwise.

upside down cake Stop shortchanging yourself and limiting yourself so much. Try to involve yourself in pleasurable events more and deprive yourself less. You are being too overprotective and this is keeping you from enjoying life.

wedding cake You will receive a wonderful answer to a difficult situation within two days.

wheat cake Within the week you will have the chance to begin all over again. This time you will definitely be able to get it right. Good luck is with you.

yellow cake Relax, certain situations that will soon evolve will fall in your favor. Go for it and do not question this development.

cakewalk You will unexpectedly run into a former love. You were not ready to make a commitment the first time you were involved, but you are now willing to commit and work to make the relationship grow. This individual has also recently come into a great deal of money.

calamari Encourage an older person to seek more enjoyment and to put excitement into their lives.

calamine Take care not to lose time because of sabotage. This will result in an over funded project.

calcium Someone wearing a wedding band is not really married. Find a way to find access to this person in order to become involved in some facet of their life. This will result in a romantic situation, if you desire. You are headed for a brilliant future. Eat healthily, drink plenty of water and take steps to ensure a good intake of calcium.

calculator You have an idea you feel is brilliant. Go for it and do not let anyone stop you. This idea will be a success.

caldron Keep up your house and work at finding the correct foods to remain healthy.

calendar This dream is a lucky omen in all phases of your life. Pay attention to the dates and months seen. Your calendar may be full and it is important that you make a list so that you will not miss a single event of immediate importance. You will have time to avoid an unfortunate event witnessed in the dream and you must alert anyone else to do the same. Make sure that you encourage any positive event to make it a reality. Pay particular attention to the date of the fortunate event and move on this because it will bring you future prosperity.

calf Make a point of seeking out a much needed friend to assist you in making a timely payment. You will also enjoy a lucky and climatic love affair.

calfskin Your instincts will tell you not to go into a particular situation. Follow this feeling or you will later regret it.

calico You will be shattered over a romantic affair. Someone important to you wants to separate from your relationship.

California Someone you have just met will promise undying love to you. This individual is serious about this. Go for it. This dream may also be used as a reference point in time. If you dream of this state and see its name used in any context, the dream message will occur on this day.

California condor You will get an unexpected call within five days from someone who will request your company for a day's outing. You will find enjoyment and amusements at various events but you will not see this person again for a long time to come.

California poppy The opportunity you have been waiting for will present itself within two days. You will enjoy a new start in all areas of your life. All old burdens and issues that have been dragging you down will end. Major changes will add new excitement and new dimensions to your life. You will also develop and execute many new and exciting plans.

call *to call* Be careful not to hurt the feelings of someone who is dear to you.

to receive a call This dream is lucky, listen carefully to the words you hear and follow this advice.

a call from the dead This dream is a very lucky omen.

to call out someone's name whom you recognize This name represents a certain person whom you should have by your side when a particular situation starts to develop that could easily get out of control. With this person on your side you can prevent an abusive episode in the nick of time.

to call out someone's name whom you do not recognize For the next three days, make sure that you do not go anywhere, especially if you are going out with someone, or will meet with someone you do not know well, without the company of someone else. This could easily turn into an abusive episode and by having someone else present, you can avoid this.

calla lily A family member needing an organ transplant will shortly receive the needed organ.

call box *working properly* The hopes you have harbored for something to occur will take place within five days. Many blessings are with you and you are headed for a brilliant future.

working improperly Get as much accomplished within the next two days as you can, in order to stay ahead of your work schedule and to accomplish everything in a timely fashion. Many blessings are with you and your family.

call girl You will become quickly involved with someone you have just met. This person is demonstrative and loving and this will be a happy union.

calligraphy You will merge your talents with someone from a distant country. This will result in a successful business venture and financial security for some time.

calliope A lawsuit will result in your favor.

call letters You will soon be laid off from your job. Seek alternative employment.

callus Someone you know slightly will seek more familiarity. Avoid this. This person tends to attract problems.

calmness Either help out a senior citizen who needs extra help for the next few days, or find help through an agency.

calorie Do not waste time running errands for others. Your time is valuable. Budget time for yourself.

Calvary Do not alienate yourself from a frank and candid friend. This person is simply being helpful.

calypso You will visit a carnival, have a wonderful time and experience treasured memories for some time.

Cambridge Ask yourself why you cannot find a resolution

to a particular situation. Within two days, you will gain the knowledge and power to clear up this problem and finally be relieved of this burden. Good luck is with you. This dream may also be used as a reference point in time. If you dream of this city and see its name used in any context, the dream message will occur on this day.

Cambridge University You are dealing with a personal issue that will require special handling from an expert. This will be resolved satisfactorily within the week. This dream may also be used as a reference point in time. If you dream of this university and see its name used in any context, the dream message will occur on this day.

camcorder You are beginning to grow weary of something that is occurring in your life and you are anxious to communicate to someone else exactly what you are tired of. Be very clear about what you want changed, the behavior you want to stop or anything new you want to introduce into your life. Be very clear in determining who the person is who is responsible for your frustrations and take steps to get your point across.

film projector You will definitely develop a support system and the network of knowledge you need to place yourself in a comfortable lifestyle. During this seven day cycle you will have many opportunities to celebrate and enjoy joyful occurrences. Prepare yourself for some unexpected happy news that will come to you during this time period. You are headed for a brilliant future and you will feel as though everyone is on your side and supporting your goals.

camel Someone you meet within a few days will alter your life completely. You will enjoy a wonderful future because your merged talents will work magic.

camel hair Someone who is behaving irritably toward you is only seeking affection. Do not lead this person on if you do not feel affectionate toward them, and do not allow yourself to become involved with this individual. This situation will begin to evolve within a few days.

camellia Within two weeks you are destined to meet a loving, generous, and kind person. This person will bring much joy to your life and you will see a dramatic improvement in yourself and your life. It is your choice to pursue this involvement or to let it go. Good luck is with you.

Camelot This dream is an extremely lucky omen. Anything you desire from a relationship, in any capacity, will be possible. This dream may also be used as a reference point in time. If you dream of this place and see its name used in any context, the dream message will occur on this day.

cameo Within two days, make sure that everyone involved knows your feelings about a certain individual. This will clear up any misunderstandings and will ensure that this person will be treated with the proper respect.

camera You will enjoy a happy family reunion.

surveillance camera Be very attentive because an unusual occurrence will develop regarding a person, project or position that will lead to a financial windfall. You may marry someone who will leave you with a monthly pension, develop a project that will deliver you monthly royalties, or secure a position that will offer you monthly provisions for a lifetime. You are in a sound position to receive this in the near future. Develop your curiosity, especially for the next three days, to ensure that you do not miss out on these benefits. You will receive an abundance of health, many blessings will come to you, and you are headed for a brilliant future. Make sure you do not put yourself in the position to be viewed by a surveillance camera doing something you don't want to be seen doing. Make sure that any negative event witnessed in this dream is prevented in reality.

cameraman A friend of yours will be involved in a snowmobile accident. This can be prevented by issuing a warning to this individual.

camisole Remove all precious jewelry when cleaning and performing heavy chores. This will protect your jewelry from loss or damage.

camp You will be approached for a large business venture. Do not be intimidated by the size. It will be a success.

campaign Go for that big goal you are thinking about pursuing. Victory will be yours.

Campbell, Joseph You will find that, for the next three months, you will be at the peak of experience and be so together that you will instinctively know you will reach the finish line before the race has really begun. You will have the feeling of confidence that comes from knowing you will succeed. You will feel the strength that comes from your inner core. Follow your goals as if you were on a mission and this will bring you to a victorious completion of your goals. Within this time frame, your sense of ethics and judgment will be intact and you are headed for a fantastic future.

campfire Do not restrict yourself regarding a romantic relationship.

camphor tree Slow down and reassess your thoughts in order to act in an appropriate manner. Do not allow your own assumptions to lead you to make a poor decision. This dream is also a very lucky omen.

camp meeting Someone is plotting your injury or death through an automobile accident. Watch for this over the next three weeks.

campsite Be careful not to develop a lice infestation.

campus Use blueprints or visual aids to clarify an idea to someone else. Move quickly and the project will be a success.

camshaft Copyright all ideas created within your company by other people under the company's name.

can Collect all outstanding debts within seven days.

six pack of cans Do not overextend yourself. Budget your time.

smashed A problematic situation will arise within five days. Although you will feel compelled to become involved and offer assistance, refrain from this involvement. You will not have the emotional resources to cope with this issue extensively. Do not allow yourself to feel guilty, each person is able to handle only so much.

to be handed a can Someone will unexpectedly come to you with an exhaustive, plentiful wealth of greater ideas. You will welcome these ideas because they will offer resources and a means to redirect your life in a more positive and prosperous fashion. This will occur within five days.

to hand someone a can Within three days, you will be aggressively pursued by a married person. In spite of temptations, stay uninvolved and resist all enticements. You will soon find someone to make a life with who is more suited to you.

to drink from a can You will be surprised and elated when someone expresses their deep feelings for you. This person is someone you have admired but felt was unreachable. Expect this within five days.

to drink something distasteful from a can All negotiations conducted within a three day period will not work to your advantage. This is because one person will purposely attempt to stymie all progress. Expect this opposition and find ways to work it to your advantage.

to open a can You will experience a wonderful, unexpected surprise within three days. Good luck will be with you for the next seven days.

crushed cans Someone is feeling very abandoned by you. You must quickly let this person know that they are very special to you and give them a tangible representation of your appreciation (i.e., flowers, a gift, etc.). This will catch them off guard and also let them know that you are deeply involved with them. Put your love into action and words in order to create a deeper bond between you. This is a wonderful time to put love into your life on a permanent basis. You are headed for a very prosperous future.

Canaan Put everything into writing and make sure that you have guarantees. This dream may also be used as a reference point in time. If you dream of this Biblical site and see its name used in any context, the dream message will occur on this day.

Canada You will be taking on a large project and will recall a past conversation with an individual who revealed information that may be helpful to this project. A joint venture will yield much success. Be open to this for the next few weeks. This dream may also be used as a reference point in time. If you dream of this country and see its name used in

any context, the dream message will occur on this day.

canal You and a special person will undertake a risky venture. This will be successful and will yield wonderful results. Others will join in and add to the success.

canary You will achieve victory in all phases of your life.

to hear one sing You will marry soon, if you choose.

to see one fly You will learn of another person's pregnancy.

canary yellow This dream is a very lucky omen and love will come your way from someone you least expect if this is something you choose to have in your life.

canasta Social events will help your business ventures.

cancan Do not lend money to someone who is clearly not in need of it. Within five days, an unknown individual will also play matchmaker. This person will attempt to introduce you to someone they know in the hopes that you will enjoy a good time together. If you choose to pursue this, you will have a wonderful time. Any negative event portrayed in this dream needs to be avoided, and any positive event needs to be promoted.

cancer *(the disease)* Hard work and consistency will pay off. Protect your belongings and plants from rust. Take steps to avoid any negative event witnessed in the dream and make sure that you experience only positive expressions in your life. You will also be dealing with someone, within three days, who is very knowledgeable of your likes and dislikes, and is also very aware of the lifestyle choices and the kind of situations that you reject. This person will use many tactics of persuasion to lure you subtly into a lifestyle that you are against. Their intent will be to get you to do something that you are against and will offer you gifts, vacations, etc, to win you over. It may take a great deal of time and many offers but you will do what this person wishes if you are not careful. You have prior notice of this and can take the necessary steps to keep this from taking place. Otherwise, you are on this path toward a brilliant future.

Cancer *(the Zodiac sign)* Someone who holds you in high regard will fall deeply in love with you. As time goes by, you will need to continue showing a deep commitment to this person. You will share many affectionate moments together and will both be very excited about this new development. Your fantasies and desires will become yours in this time period. You will enjoy the experience of your life filled with thrilling and pleasurable moments if you do not deprive yourself of this experience. You are headed for a very prosperous and brilliant future.

candelabra For the next two days, you will deeply miss a special person. This person has been only able to show love through actions. Upon returning, this person will be more verbally expressive with their feelings of love.

candidate *to be a candidate* Check all of your precious stones against loss. You may have a loose stone in your setting.

candle Within three days you will receive a positive response to a request that you expected a negative response to. Also, if you choose, romance will work in your favor for the next month. By having prior notice of this, you will be able to actively do your part to bring this about quickly. This will also allow the person you are interested in to respond in an appropriate manner. You will be able to develop a strong support system and are headed for a brilliant future. Many blessings are with you and your family.

lit candle An unexpected answer to an invitation will arrive. You will expect a negative reply and will receive a positive one.

unlit candle Do the best you can on a new job.

to attempt lighting a candle A great surprise is in store for you.

to see yourself or someone else walk with a lit candle For the next three weeks you will enjoy an abundance of health, tranquility and spiritual healing. Within the week a celebration will take place that will bring rejoicing to everyone involved. This dream is also a promise that for the last two weeks of March and for the entire month of April, an idea, project or event will be brought to full bloom. It will take on a life of its own and will reach a grander scale than you ever thought possible. You will be able to easily carry this through any channel it needs to go to complete this process. You will be blessed by this and it will be a big cause of celebration for you and for each person who participated in this process. You are headed for a brilliant future.

sconce with candles Do not misinterpret another's actions toward you. You will think this person is romantically interested in you but they are not, and you will later be embarrassed if you continue to believe this is the case.

Candlemas You will finally receive the marriage proposal you have long waited for. Happiness will come to everyone who hears of this. Good luck will be yours, and riches and joy will fill your life.

candlestick Separate lies from the truth in order to move ahead.

candlewick You will be appointed to a position of power that you have long desired. You will enjoy a wonderful life and will experience much happiness.

candy Sexual favors will be needed from you immediately. Give attention to this facet of your life. Within this week long cycle, you will also be able to successfully resolve any problematic situation you are presently working on.

cotton candy You are doing what you can to better your life. Within two weeks something important, such as a new career, will enter your life. This will result in success and abundance.

candy cane You will enjoy many nights of passion.

candy counter Be very aware that several issues will occur over the next five days. Motivate yourself to accept one opportunity that will unexpectedly be offered to you. Think quickly and act quickly because the person offering you this opportunity will only be in a specific place at a specific time and will be in the mood to give you this chance only once. If you do not respond in a positive fashion you will miss out. Tactfully work out any aspects of this proposal that you do not agree with so that it works out well for both of you to proceed on. In spite of any differences in lifestyle, this is a workable situation.

candy striper For the next few days, take pains not to forget an event and a gift for a special person. If you forget, they will be deeply hurt.

cane Do not put yourself in the situation to be sexually abused by a persistent person.

canister Do not take on extra financial responsibilities or expenses.

canker sore You will experience a sudden increase in wealth.

cannibal Do not rely on the promises of others. You will be disappointed and misunderstandings will arise. You must also not pay attention to what others think you deserve financially. Make it clear that you deserve what you are asking for.

cannon Give a small unexpected gift to someone you appreciate.

cannonball Take care of your sexual organs.

canoe This is not the time to be confused. Take advantage of all opportunities offered in life now.

Canonicals You will rapidly and unexpectedly recover from a long illness and will feel better than you did before becoming ill. This will be a very prosperous cycle for you.

can opener For the next three days, you will feel very competent and will develop the confidence to squeeze all you can from your talents and intelligence in order to make your mark in the world. Riches will come your way and you will be treated very kindly by others. Many blessings are with you.

canopy Take a practical approach to solving a relative's health problem.

cantaloupe You will have a very profitable venture.

canteen Do not jeopardize your career by allowing your

obsessions to take control of you.

Canterbury Within three days, an interested person will have the opportunity to be close to you and will reveal that they want something more than friendship. After this, the relationship will move rapidly ahead and will provide mutual satisfaction and happiness. This dream may also be used as a reference point in time. If you dream of this city and see its name used in any context, the dream message will occur on this day.

Canterbury Tales Within a few days you will need a great deal of discipline and control in order to avoid sexual and physical contact with another person. Be ready to switch gears the moment this situation begins to develop. This will not work out well for you.

cantina For the next week, follow your instincts. You can fully rely on your hunches. A situation will come up that will involve someone in your private life. Be careful, this person is not the right person to involve in this issue.

canvas You will meet an artist on a daily stroll. This person will become a lifelong friend and will also paint a flattering portrait of you that will win compliments for years.

canyon Counsel an in-law who may be mishandling finances. Your advice will be greatly appreciated.

cap You will be lucky in love for the next five days.

cape Your frank manner will create discord between you and someone who is important to you. Take steps to change your behavior.

Cape Cod This dream is an omen of victory. You will receive the assistance needed to advance in the right direction. Goals that were unattainable for you in the past are now within your reach. This is also informing you that someone new will enter your life and passionate love will come your way if you choose to pursue this. You will find your life will become very interesting within five days. This dream may also be used as a reference point in time. If you dream of this Cape and see its name in any context, the dream message will occur on this day.

caper For the next four days, you will be very lucky in receiving the services you request. The assistance will come very quickly and you will successfully meet your needs.

capital Be tactful and polite while turning down a request from an influential person.

capital punishment Do not become unwittingly caught up in the stressful situations of someone who is undergoing a miserable time. Make private time for yourself.

capon Think before you speak.

cappuccino Within two days you will become very aware of an emotional hang up you need to work on. You will develop the strength and tranquility to rid yourself of this burden and develop a lifestyle free of hang ups. Go for it.

Capricorn You will reach an agreement with a special person about both of your needs in a relationship. This is a sign of victory in many areas of your life.

capsule Be wary of thieves. Also, watch your food intake and drink plenty of water.

captain Within a few weeks, someone special will want to leave the relationship. Prepare for this now by being good to yourself, then the disappointment will not be so bad. Couples counseling will not work.

captured Someone else will seek credit for your work. Be prepared for this and do not allow it to occur.

car *to fall out* You will clash with someone in authority.

another person falls out someone will shock you with a secret. Keep this secret to yourself.

to hit or run over someone Be careful for a few days not to unintentionally injure someone with a car.

to be run over or hit You will fall in love with a younger person. This will be a happy union, if you choose to pursue this.

to be followed or chased in a car Get away from someone who is dangerous to you. This person appears to be harmless but your instincts will tell you otherwise. This individual will attempt murder. Do not let them know that you suspect this.

to escape from someone attempting to run you over with a car A certain individual will go to great lengths to create a relationship between you and another person. It is your destiny to enjoy a beautiful, full blown love relationship that will blossom within a few days and bring joy into your life. This is the perfect cycle to emotionally connect to another person. You will be so successful that this individual will respond to you in the exact manner you desire. This dream also implies that you are headed in the right direction in life, and you will be able to express yourself fully regarding all matters of personal interest. You will be able to focus yourself in a very detailed manner and as a result you will be able to achieve a great deal and enjoy many successes in life. You will magically possess the strength and courage to handle each issue in your life and you will be able to enjoy peace and tranquility. An unexpected favor will also be granted to you but you will need to put yourself in the position to talk with powerful and influential people. State your needs clearly and directly and you will immediately be given the money you request from a particular individual. You will achieve victory in those areas of your life that you consider to be the most important, and you will also hear some good news within the week. You are on the path toward a brilliant future. Pay very close attention to all conversations for the next three days and make sure that all negative events and messages foretold in this dream do not become a reality. Take steps to ensure that all positive messages are fulfilled.

to follow or chase someone in a car Riches will be yours in all of your ventures.

to see someone drive your car Either you or the company you work for has placed an advertisement. Be aware that if you are the interviewer, someone answering this ad will be a very dangerous individual. Take extra precautions for the next seven days against a deranged person.

to be carsick You are wasting time on a project that needs to be expedited. Look around and pinpoint the one thing that needs to be done now.

to look for your car and be unable to find it This dream implies that you will gain instant wealth at a time when you least expect it. Doors that were once closed to you will now be open. You will be able to handle some very tough tasks that will be coming up within the week. Other people will then see you in a different light and you will enjoy more opportunities and achieve success.

to see your car in the garage Your beloved needs more attention from you and doesn't know how to ask. They will angrily provoke you in order to make up after a fight. This will result in a more loving feeling afterwards but it is better to avoid this by being more loving to start with.

to see your car parked You can accomplish much by projecting an interesting image of yourself around an influential person. This person will be connected to a project you are presently working on and will also influence your life. You will enjoy working on this project. Maintain an interesting demeanor to ensure continued interest from this person.

to have difficulty parking a car A sudden strange event will occur to you and your loved ones. This may be distasteful for a few moments.

to easily find parking Victory is yours. A target group will be very happy to support you on a specific quest.

to see your car towed away You will become instantly wealthy at an unexpected time and doors that were closed to you in the past will now be open. You will be able to tackle any difficult task coming up within the week. As a result, other people will begin to view you in a completely different light. You will be able to seize new opportunities and achieve success.

many empty cars parked on the street You will do away with a lifestyle that handicaps you because of past hang ups and mental barriers. This attitude will keep you from achieving the financial prosperity you are capable of. Many blessings are with you and you are headed for a brilliant future. Proceed with confidence.

to see a luxurious car Your project is moving rapidly ahead. This will bring profitable results.

to view an auto accident Take steps to avoid injury to yourself or others. Avoid driving accidents for the upcoming week.

to be in a vehicle that rolls over in an accident Situations that were going badly will turn around to a new positive approach within three days.

to be involved in the buying or selling of a car Two peo-

ple will be interested in you at the same time. Both would be a wise choice but one of them will be better to become involved with than the other. Pursue the one you feel is too good to be true. You are definitely headed for a brilliant future.

to hear backfire Do not jeopardize your reputation on the job with a new project.

to live out of a car Luck will be with you for a very long time. Money will also be lost through some kind of sham. Be very protective of yourself for the next three days.

to dismantle or start a car Within two days, it will be necessary to have a conversation with certain people in order to make the proper requests and connections before a certain situation begins to develop. This will keep everything from falling apart before it takes off. Stay ahead of yourself and you will be able to make the proper adjustments in time. Focus on this now and everything will fall into place successfully. Good luck is with you and your family. You are headed for a brilliant future.

to be the one who hits and runs with a car Do not treat someone you care about in such a way that will drive them away. You must also make sure that for the next two days you are not involved in a hit and run accident.

to be the victim of a hit and run Be very cautious with your involvement with others. You are in danger of contracting a sexually transmitted disease. Take precautions to avoid this and any other negative event seen in this dream. Make sure that you only experience positive expressions in your life.

if you recognize the hit and run driver Alert this person so they can keep this incident from occurring within two days. Good luck is with you. You also need to make sure that any negative incident you dreamed of does not become a reality and take steps to enjoy only positive experiences in your life.

boxcar This dream is a very lucky sign. Confide to a special person the facts about an illness that causes you pain. This will allow you to seek the proper help. This person will be more considerate and helpful to you.

car dashboard Become firm in your refusal to allow a friend to tell you what you should or should not do with others, especially for the next three days.

police car You have overlooked an urgent matter that needs to be taken care of. This matter is of acute importance and needs to be attended to now. If you see another person connected with this dream, this person has an urgent need to discuss an important matter with you. It is important that you meet with them to find out what they have in mind. Do this in such a way to avoid any subtle manipulation.

if you recognize the person in the police car This implies immediate danger from the person you see in the car. This will be something in the nature of acquaintance rape and you will contract a sexually transmitted disease. Take extra precautions against this personal violation.

if you do not recognize the person in the police car You will be stopped for a minor traffic infraction. For two weeks, take extra precautions while driving in order to prevent this.

if you are driving the police car You are unknowingly

allowing a troublesome situation to develop that needs to be aggressively attended to. Discipline and structure yourself in order to grasp each situation before it disperses to the point of chaos. Once it reaches this point you will lose the ability to begin again. Push yourself now in order to resolve each issue. Do not allow yourself to get bogged down with extraneous matters that are out of your control. Stay focused. You must also take steps to keep from being the major cause of problems. Focus on the aspect of your behavior that leads to this. Do nothing that will cause problems with the law.

police car with flashing lights A danger that you are now aware of will become far more dangerous in a short while. If you know you are in a dangerous area, remove yourself from this vicinity immediately. Cover all bases to prevent any attack from a dangerous individual in any circumstance at any time. Within three days, take extreme preventive steps. This is a very dangerous situation that can be avoided.

to steal a car You are becoming very tired of something that is taking place in your life and you are anxious to communicate to someone about it. Be very clear about what you want this particular person or yourself to change, the behavior you wish to start or stop, or anything new that you wish to bring into your life.

to have your car stolen Someone will use you and take advantage of you without your knowledge. This person will use deception and dishonesty in a particular situation with you as an innocent unwilling participant, and you will be cheated in the long run. Pay close attention to your present situations and be acutely aware of the actions of others in order to avoid this.

to polish a car Maintain a low profile and keep your mind on routine tasks. Maintain a constant vigilance against any errors that could occur in any capacity for the next three days. Handle any mistake immediately so that everything can fall into place correctly. Because you have prior notice of this you can take steps to avoid unnecessary problems. Many blessings are with you and you are headed for a brilliant future.

broken car window Remain calm and centered for the next three days. A situation will come up that you will be very tempted to become involved in. Do not allow another person's problems to cause you to become so desperate that you compromise yourself and become entangled in this issue. Once you involve yourself, it will be very difficult to pry yourself loose and it will become progressively worse as times goes by. You are seeing only the tip of the iceberg. Remain uninvolved.

to see yourself or anyone else fog up a car window by heavy breathing Within the week you will be entering an extremely lucky cycle and anyone involved in your life will share this luck. You will also be offered services that will help you to successfully accomplish your goals and reach a higher level of success than you thought possible. You can expect to make many amazing and wonderful connections that will assist you in grasping and meeting your goals. You can also expect a mega merger and the synergism working between you and others that will bring you to a higher level

of success than you ever anticipated. This dream also implies that you will receive many benefits by attending a festive event, an educational event, or an event in which one person will take an interest in promoting you and your plans. Following this you will enjoy a long period of tranquility and enjoy a prosperous future. Anything negative witnessed in this dream may be changed, and you must make it a point to forewarn anyone you dreamed about to do the same.

car seat Do not allow yourself to be doubted after telling a true but unbelievable story.

baby car seat Do not allow your carelessness to create a strange occurrence.

bumper car Make sure you are not put in the position to suffer fear and terror at the hands of a very dangerous person. This person will lead you to believe they either want to look at something you want to sell, or you should look at something they have that you wish to purchase. Be extremely cautious of this for the next three days.

electric car This implies that within the week you will develop a sense of urgency about something that needs to be accomplished with someone else's help. This could involve the loan of a large sum of money or a big favor that needs to be performed immediately and hassle free. This request will be so large that it will be difficult for you to imagine that it would be granted to you. Follow your intuition and it will guide you to the person who will come through for you. Proceed with confidence and explore each option until you determine which one is perfect for you. Once you have reached an agreement, act on it immediately so that this issue can be concluded before they have a change of heart. Many blessings are with you and you are on the path toward a prosperous future.

to see yourself or anyone else sleeping or resting in a car You will be very excited about the opportunity to purchase land at a low price. This property will quickly increase in value.

town car Do not allow pride to stand in your way of accepting a gift of money, especially for the next two days. This dream is an extremely lucky omen for you.

to see a junked car An unusual occurrence will make you feel inferior to someone else. You will feel that someone much older than you is in much better physical shape. This person has a great deal of stamina and you feel you are letting yourself down. Don't be so hard on yourself but take it as a reminder to begin exercising in small easy steps. Remember that everyone has different levels of energy.

car honk All negotiations that you are involved in will be extremely successful. Someone new will enter your life and will, if you choose, become a lifelong friend. This person is very charming and will share many wonderful stories with you. They will also give you an important message that will offer you a different viewpoint of a certain project or concept you are presently working on. You will be able to use this knowledge to improve your lifestyle. Expect this to take place within three days. Something unusual will also occur within four days. You will find someone who is willing to help you, and will relentlessly stick to their goals until your needs are met.

to honk at someone Be wary of someone who has led you to believe you can confide in them. Do not depend on this person's loyalty, they will let you down. Do not become involved with gossips.

to be honked at Don't allow yourself to get caught up in game playing. Someone will attempt to draw you on a path that will lead to discomfort and stress. Work to keep this from occurring, especially for the next three days. You must also make sure that any negative aspect of this dream does not become a reality and take steps to enjoy only the positive aspects of life.

car tape deck The next three days will be an important time to connect emotionally with another person. Be very clear about the message you want to communicate before you speak. You will be able to make this connection so successfully that this individual will respond in the manner you most desire. If this message is negative you have enough time to ensure that you only experience positive events in your life.

car wash Beware of tricky deals, do not allow yourself to be taken advantage of in love matters. Someone you care about may use this love against you during the next few days. Also, within two days, you will notice something missing in a conversation you will have with another. Because of this, you will find it difficult to reach a much needed decision.

sports car Proceed with confidence, your ideas and projects will meet with success and you are headed in the right direction. Relentlessly and consistently pursue this goal. Within three days, a very successful person will go to great lengths to change their life in order to be with you. Work together in order to synchronize your plans and to make things run smoothly. It is your choice to pursue this relationship or not.

to run out of gas Make sure you do not develop a defeatist attitude when working on a specific situation. Proceed with confidence and you will definitely get over this feeling and emerge victorious. All negative messages and events occurring in this dream need to be altered and all positive messages should be promoted. This is a very lucky dream.

tail light Within three days someone will be very eager for you to sign some papers. Regardless of how wonderful you think this move would be, do not sign. They will not offer you any advantage, but you will not know this until a later time when it is too late to change paths. Take all the necessary precautions and do not sign these papers.

in any other form Someone you know will be very eager to help you out with any means they have available, whether this is an emotional or financial matter. Within three days someone will also tell you what you need to do next involving a situation which is of concern to you. You will arrive to a decision that will bring you to a more secure lifestyle in either the emotional or financial sense. Move ahead with confidence and everything will come together just as you have envisioned. Use this cycle to bring about changes in certain areas of your life that need to be changed in order to ensure the perfect lifestyle. Look up the make of the car for more meaning to this dream.

carafe Someone is seeking information about you. This is a dangerous situation. If you desire love from someone, you must first learn to love yourself. The confidence and love you have for yourself will attract others to you.

caramel Be wary of jealous impulses and possessive behavior.

carat You will shed tears of joy over good news. You and your family members will share happiness in abundance. Wealth will be yours. Keep your eyesight healthy.

caravan The answer you have been seeking will soon be revealed to you.

caraway Lighten up in a romantic situation and take better care of yourself in order to relieve some of the stress.

carbon You will be clear about the changes you plan to make in your life within a few days. You will know which direction to take.

carbon dioxide A snow skiing accident will take place involving you or someone you know. This can be prevented.

carbon paper Do whatever is necessary to protect yourself against a conspirator. You will be successful.

carburetor Concentrate on a potential relationship. This person lacks the staying power to be in a commitment. You may want to back off.

carcass A business acquaintance will suffer a breakdown. This person will direct attention to you and create a stressful time at work. At the first indication of mental illness in another person, do what you can to avoid this person's daily focus. This will occur within a few weeks.

carcinogen You may be considering going off to war. If you choose this option, you will return home safely.

card *(playing cards)* Follow your intuition. You are entering a cycle of greater mental clarity that will last for seven days. This will allow you to make good decisions.

face card You are handling a particular situation in the wrong way. Within three days you will make an incorrect decision regarding this situation. It is also important that you challenge yourself to grasp the opportunities and positions that are coming your way. Right now you feel as though you will be unable to handle this task but you will gain the confidence and determination you need to win this position and succeed. Good luck is with you.

to deal cards Do not allow the inconsideration of another to cause you distress. Someone within the next three days will put into writing words that completely contradict everything you believe in and have verbalized. Regroup and remain calm throughout this in order to handle this situation correctly. If you are playing solitaire, you will be married and have many wonderful years together.

deck of playing cards You will quickly get the money you need to pay all of your outstanding debts.

someone else with a deck of cards You will soon make future plans with a special person and will make arrangements to live together.

trump card Within a two week period you will unexpectedly rise to a higher level in life than you ever envisioned. You will experience an abundance of productivity, an increased income and productive conversations. You will be surrounded by very loyal and affectionate people and others will express a desire to be a part of your plans and goals. These people will wish to assist you and to impart the wisdom they have acquired as well as anything else you wish to learn. This will be of special importance to you for the next five days. You are headed for a brilliant future and will enjoy an abundance of health in a shorter period of time than you expected.

card *(greeting cards)* You will need to quickly decide whether you wish to commit to a relationship. Another individual may become interested in your partner and attempt to move in. If you don't commit now, you will lose the relationship. If you do, it will be a successful union.

cardamom Do not take unnecessary prescription drugs. Double check to ensure that you are taking the correct medications. Mistakes can be made.

cardboard You are asking another for the impossible. Control yourself and stop this behavior.

card file Do nothing for the next few days that will result in a restraining order against you. Control your behavior.

cardigan Think carefully for the next few days about an undesirable situation that could easily take place. Do what you can to prevent this occurrence. You will also have many moments of anguish during the next few weeks due to the lost address and phone number of a friend who has recently relocated. Put each phone number and address in a safe place.

cardinal A friend will be prosecuted by the law and you will feel remorse over this.

cardiogram A professional person will have sexual dealings for you.

card table Within a few days, someone will come into your life for the sole purpose of acquiring a large sum of money from you. Avoid this person at all costs.

care *any form* You are making all the correct moves and are motivating yourself in such a way to achieve victory. You will also finally make a connection with a certain person you have had difficulty pinning down. During this time period all things you felt were once impossible to achieve are now possible. Schedule a mini-vacation to a quiet stress free locale in order to clear your head. You will be left with many pleasurable memories. You are headed for a brilliant future.

career Do not become suspicious of a special person. You will be surrounded by loyal, trusted people, especially for the next seven days.

careful *to be careful* Think ahead for the next four days in order to prepare yourself for an important conversation with someone who is involved in a certain situation. This will allow you the time to get everyone involved together and determine how to put a lid on a particular issue that could trigger the occurrence of a negative event. Many blessings will come to you and your family.

to see someone else being careful Within five days you will finally overcome a long term situation that has become burdensome. Relentlessly work on any issue that needs to be taken care of. You are headed in the right direction and will experience the freedom that comes from ridding yourself of this burden. You will also experience many social events in the near future. Proceed with confidence. Good luck is with you.

in any other form Control your temper and do what you can to get a grip on your emotions. A distasteful situation will arise that will make you suspicious and jealous of another person. If you are not careful this will create an uncontrollable situation that will lead to an action you will regret for a lifetime. The moment you notice this anger start to develop, seek professional help in order to avoid regrettable action.

caretaker An exciting, climatic love relationship is in store for you.

cargo Watch out for broken glass and windows. Do everything necessary to avoid breakage.

carhop You will have bad luck for a few days. Take care of yourself.

Caribbean You will be invited to a wedding that will take place in a garden setting. Place a great deal of emphasis on your attire and on your choice of a gift. You will have a wonderful time. This dream may also be used as a reference point in time. If you dream of this place and see its name used in any context, the dream message will occur on this day.

caribou You will experience sorrow over the illness of a female family member. She will recover soon.

caricature You will marry a professional comedian and experience life long happiness. If you choose this route, do everything necessary to make it happen.

Carlos Santana A fantastic future is in store for you, especially for the next two weeks. You will be thrust forward into a life filled with an abundance of prosperity. This will seem to be almost magical to you and you will experience special qualities and abilities.

carnation Follow your instincts. You will feel comfortable in another person's surroundings. These instincts are correct and the relationship will be successful. Refer to the color for a more detailed definition.

carnival You will take a senior citizen on a mini vacation. This person will have an enjoyable time. If you choose to do this, the inspiration will be there for the next seven days.

carnivore Be careful when preparing food for a large group of people. Unintentional food poisoning may result.

carob Within three days you will be given a gift of greater mental inventiveness by the Gods. Put this gift to use in changing your present circumstances. Your sex life will improve dramatically. Protect your health, drink plenty of water and get plenty of rest.

carol A supposedly good investment will not be good. Protect your finances.

carotene Eat more fruits and vegetables. Get more rest. Drink plenty of water and find a peaceful, restful place to spend more time.

carousel You will celebrate an unexpected reunion within a few weeks.

carp Do not let pride keep you from accepting a last minute invitation. You will enjoy yourself.

carpenter You will receive wise counsel when it is sought. Relatives will also call with good news.

carpet *to see soiled carpet* Set aside time for dancing and enjoying life. You will also see a dream preview of what will happen to a relative if a problem is left to develop. Help in every way you can.

to clean or shampoo a carpet Get to the meat of a particular situation. Once you define what the missing element is you will be able to handle yourself in the appropriate way to take care of this issue.

magic carpet This is an extremely lucky omen. For the next month you will enjoy an abundance of health and financial security because unusual circumstances will take place that will allow this to occur. Do not limit and deprive yourself of unique experiences and involvements that will come up within five days. Enjoy your life fully, eat healthy foods, drink plenty of water and get plenty of rest. Life will reward you handsomely not only in a financial sense but spiritually as well.

in any other form This is a very lucky omen for you and signifies that you will receive a financial windfall. Within a

two day period your drive, determination and courage will also motivate you to break through any mental or physical barrier that stands in the way of moving forward. Once you are rid of those aspects that hold you back, you will be able to bring any new project into tangible form. You will be welcomed by those you care about with open arms. You are headed for a brilliant future and many new opportunities are headed your way.

carpet bagger Avoid diseases as best you can.

carpeting You will enjoy fantastic companionship for the next two days.

carpet sweeper Take steps to ensure your safety and the safety of others. Be especially alert to the potential of accidental drownings for the next two days.

carpool Someone will make detailed plans to involve you in their life. This person will invite you to lunch and will go to great lengths to take advantage of your innocence. Do not become involved with this person. Also, if you suspect anger in another, do not assume this person will confront you with the problem. Meet this issue head on and resolve it.

carport Your venture will move rapidly forward. You will prosper and better times are ahead.

carriage You will receive a long desired piece of jewelry as an inheritance. You will receive it as a gift prior to the other person's death.

horse carriage Someone who demonstrates a small liking for you will suddenly develop a deep emotional love.

baby carriage You will handle a delicate situation with gentle persuasion.

carrier *baby carrier* Within five days you will experience many events that will bring grand and prosperous changes to your life. Your life will improve immensely.

person who is a carrier - any form You will be able to successfully carry out anything you attempt. This will be a very prosperous cycle for you. Apply yourself to those areas of your life that will bring you more prosperity.

carrot You will hear false news. The person relaying this news is incorrect in their assumptions. You must also take care of your eyes and drink plenty of water.

carry *to carry or to see someone else carry a person* Within the next five days someone will plot to violate your rights simply to satisfy their own emotional gratification. This person will attempt to manipulate you into being involved in a situation that will become increasingly distasteful as time goes by. This will be in either a sexual context or some other capacity. This involvement will go against your better judgment and your will. Do not allow yourself to be placed in a position that will require you to compromise yourself in order to get out safely. This is preventable. Good luck is with you.

to be carried by someone Be very attentive because an unusual occurrence will develop regarding a person, project or position that will lead to a financial windfall. You may marry someone who will leave you with a monthly pension, develop a project that will deliver you monthly royalties, or secure a position that will offer you monthly provisions for a lifetime. You are in a sound position to receive this in the near future. Develop your curiosity, especially for the next week, to ensure that you do not miss out on these benefits. You will receive an abundance of health, many blessings, and are headed for a brilliant future.

to carry anything Take special care to avoid hurting the feelings of someone who is in the early stages of falling in love with you. Practice caution when speaking to this person because you will fall in love also, and if feelings are hurt, you will be mistreated due to old resentments.

carrying charges A problem is coming your way. This can be prevented before it occurs. If left to develop, it will take a long time to resolve.

carrying on Another person is overly concerned about your well being while ignoring their own needs. Take care that this person does not overextend themselves.

carry out order Your suspicions are unwarranted.

carry over Make sure you are not caught in a stage of undress in a public place.

car seat Do not allow yourself to be doubted after telling a true but unbelievable story.

baby car seat Do not allow your carelessness to create a strange occurrence.

car seat cover Be very patient for the next three days with a special person who is unable to verbalize their true feelings. You are loved beyond your imagination. This cycle will bring much love and appreciation from others.

carsick Do not be so impulsive in love matters.

cart Beware of a dog attack by a loose rabid dog.

cartel Do not become trapped alone in a dark area within the next few weeks.

cartilage You are thinking of hiring a certain individual. Consider alternatives. You will regret hiring this person.

carton Someone is purposely avoiding you and doesn't want you to find out.

cartoon You have found a good solution to a long standing problem and will experience much happiness. The solution will arrive in three days.

cartridge Be sure to fully express your opinions to others. This will be very important to you for the next three days.

cartridge belt Take precautions to avoid accidentally poisoning yourself or any member of your family. Exercise extreme caution for the next three days. You will unexpectedly find yourself in an unusual situation with a very dangerous person. Be acutely aware of your surroundings in order to avoid this situation completely. You have prior notice of this and can take steps to prevent it.

cartwheel Back off from hasty moves.

carve *any form* You will be led to believe that a certain person desires romance. If you respond, this individual will begin to back off and withdraw from you. This is a warning to take the friendship for what it is and expect nothing more.

car wash Beware of tricky deals and do not allow yourself to be taken advantage of in love matters. Someone you care about may use this love against you during the next few days. Also, within two days, you will notice something missing in a conversation you will have with another. Because of this, you will find it difficult to reach a much needed decision.

Casablanca You will enjoy a healthy, wealthy life. This dream may also be used as a reference point in time. If you dream of this city and see its name used in any context, the dream message will occur on this day.

Casanova Someone will go to great lengths to convince you to spend time with them. If you choose to do this, you will enjoy each moment and will experience many unusual and delightful times. Many blessings are with you and you will experience much luck for the next week.

cascade Victory is yours.

case Display your imagination

to build up a (legal) case against someone A treacherous deceitful person will leave your life and you will enjoy new freedom.

a case against you A disease may develop out of your own carelessness. Take steps to prevent this.

cash *any form* You will be asked to travel abroad for business purposes.

cash crop Allow others to express their own point of view for the next two days. You will then enjoy mutual happiness and understanding.

cashew nuts Bewitching magical moments will take place between you and your loved one.

cashier You will find exactly what you seek at a public auction.

cashmere You will find a great business partner.

cash register You are deeply loved. A potential thief is also spying on you and your belongings. Take steps to prevent theft.

casino Play your numbers in a game of chance. You will be a winner.

casket Someone is yearning to be only with you. You will soon learn of this and be happy.

cassava Be kinder to yourself. You have been placing too many demands and pressures on yourself. For the next three days, enjoy life and take pleasure in the simplicity of life. Good luck is with you.

casserole Stop approaching someone romantically who does not feel the same way you do.

cassette You will become a millionaire early in your life-time.

cassock You will have a fire on your property within a few days. Take steps to prevent this.

cast You will feel disappointment with a new love affair. Be patient and this person will make it up to you.

castanets You will experience sudden trouble with room-mates because of their partying lifestyle.

castle You will have a loving and patient lover. Lucky you. Also, every person who is involved in a certain situation will be more than eager to cooperate with you, and everyone involved will enjoy success within two weeks. Things will fall into place exactly as you desire. Move ahead on your plans and ideas. This dream is a lucky omen for you and many blessings will come to you and your family.

castor oil You will see an improvement in your finances and this will bring relief from all your problems. You will also be able to settle disputes quickly.

castrate During the next few days take care that you do not become intoxicated.

cat Someone has led you to believe that you may become more familiar with them but they do not want you to behave in an overly friendly fashion in public. You will be made to look bad and this person will ignore you in front of others. This will occur within two weeks.

to hear a cat purr Another person will make it seem to others as though you are coming on to them. They will want it to appear this way for their own ego. There are no genuine feelings for you.

to hear a cat fight Horseplay with someone special may turn into a real argument. Avoid this situation.

to hear a cat and dog fight You will be sorrowful to hear about an injured friend.

to kill a cat Avoid mechanical work unless you work under adequate lighting.

to feed a cat Watch your behavior around a young child. Always behave properly.

cat food For the next four days, restrain yourself from demanding that someone behave in a manner you expect them to. This will not work out well for you.

cat scratching Your feelings will be hurt because of your insistence that you be treated better. Avoid this.

cat jumping A special person in your life will act jealous. Answer questions, be calm and let it go. This person needs to satisfy their suspicions.

cat running You will be called to witness for the defense in a jury trial.

bear cat An unexpected stranger will begin to harass you. The moment this starts, leave the premises and stay clear of this person. Especially for the next two days.

Persian cat You will see someone you are acquainted with in a different setting than you are normally accustomed to. Although this person knows you, you will be snubbed. Do not take this personally. Wait until this person speaks first.

Russian blue Within three days you will overwhelm someone with an unusual gift they do not expect. You will feel joy that you were able to grant someone's desire. You will also have a strong desire to relocate. This cycle is perfect to find an alternative place to live. Good luck is with you and many blessings will come to you and your family.

tabby cat Do whatever is necessary to keep your health up to par. Check your vital signs, eat healthy foods and drink plenty of water.

wild cat Someone will attempt to manipulate you to get what they want. This will be done in a very subtle fashion and they will try various ways to achieve their goals. This person will use trickery and conspiratorial means to succeed. This person is desperate and will latch on to anyone who makes themselves vulnerable and easy prey. It is extremely important that you do not allow yourself to become a target because after you become involved it will be too late. This will be a very draining, controlling and demeaning situation. You have prior notice of this and can take steps to keep this from taking place. Many blessings and good luck are with you.

cat and dog fight Within five days you will do something that will deeply disappoint another person. This will result in an argument between both of you. Watch your behavior closely during this time period in order to avoid this argument.

to see a cat bleeding/injured A cluster of events will occur one after the other with each bringing you a tremendous amount of joy, wonder and awe because things are happening so quickly. You will also possess a powerful energy that you are able to direct and control. At the same time that these other events are taking place you will be able to bring other people under your complete control. Because you have prior notice of this you will be able, within the week, to direct this energy in such a way to successfully complete anything you wish in a superb way. If you give assistance to the animal in the dream, you will be assisting someone close to you in some capacity. You will be able to overcome any difficult obstacle and it will now be very simple to deal with it. Your intuition will be right on target so follow your hunches about a new relationship. Many blessings are with you and your family.

to see a cat hiss A celebration will take place within the week and will be a cause for rejoicing for everyone involved. You will enjoy an abundance of health, tranquility and spiritual healing for the next three weeks. You will also be able to bring an idea, project or event to full bloom. This project will advance to a higher level than you ever hoped for. This process will occur during the last two weeks of March and for the entire month of April. It will take on a life of its own and will easily go through each channel you have to take it. This will be a blessed event and will lead to a big celebration for everyone involved in this process. You are headed for a brilliant future. Any negative event in this dream needs to be prevented, especially for the next six weeks and anyone you dreamed of needs to be warned to do likewise. Pay attention to what the cat was hissing at. This will offer you a more detailed meaning to this dream.

alley cat Don't become involved in an active debate. This will lead to disagreement and hatred. Remain calm and avoid all disputes for the next three days. An unexpected event will occur that will leave you financially well off for years.

to dream of a deceased pet This is a lucky omen for you and for all those interested and involved in your immediate situation. You are in a powerful seven day cycle for achievement and for accomplishing everything you attempt. You will also develop more integrity. People in your life will demonstrate greater love and affection toward you. Do nothing to slow down the momentum of those feelings. Everything in your life will flow more smoothly and you will be blessed with better health and more tranquility.

catacomb You will soon marry the person you desire and you will be happy for many years.

catalog Expect the unexpected for the next few days. This will be a fabulous opportunity. You will also be reunited with an old friend who will offer you an unexpected treat.

catamaran Financial improvements are on the way. You will rise above your problems.

catapult You will enjoy a good job while pursuing a career change. This career change will be successful and lead to greater levels.

cataract A secret admirer will soon approach you and let you know their feelings.

catastrophe A misdiagnosis will be made confusing two similar symptoms (i.e., Huntington's chorea and a stroke,

etc.). This will result in improper medication and treatment. Take care of this now. Take charge of your body and develop a sense of spiritual healing. You will improve in a short period of time.

Catawba Do not direct angry words at another person. You will never be able to take these words back and this will lead to permanent, painful feelings.

cat burglar Take steps to guard your possessions and your life for the next three days. Be careful.

catcall Believe in yourself. Love yourself. Pamper yourself. Relax.

catch *to catch anything* This dream implies that you will enjoy good luck. Also do not expose yourself to any contagious diseases.

catcher Drive carefully and avoid any infraction that can lead to a traffic ticket.

to see You will purchase a long awaited for item at an affordable price. This dream is a lucky omen.

"catch up" *to catch up with someone* Within three days your fantasies will be played out. You will have the experience of your life, filled with joyful, thrilling and pleasurable moments. Do not deprive yourself of this as it will bring you a tremendous amount of joy.

in any other form Actions and deeds make more of a difference than mere talk, in anything you apply yourself to, especially for the next two days.

catechism You will buy a beautiful embroidered item.

catering *if you are catering* You will have kitchen damage by fire. Take steps to avoid this.

if someone else is catering You will receive a mystery envelope containing beautiful touching words. The sender will be anonymous.

caterpillar A sudden reciprocal sexual attraction will develop between you and another person. Words will be unspoken until the other person returns from a trip. Communication will then come alive and this will result in a loving satisfying relationship.

catfish A quick reaction will prevent a minor issue from becoming a crisis.

cat food For the next four days, restrain yourself from demanding that someone behave in a manner that you expect them to. This will not work out well for you.

catgut You will be pleasingly surprised with a new friend. Extra money will also arrive within a few days.

cathedral A new friendship will turn out to be an error and it will sour quickly. Be aware of this ahead of time.

catheter Face up to problems that will arise in an ongoing situation. Although it may be painful to face up to these problems, this step will allow you to move on with life.

Catholic You will have problems with money that is owed to you. This money will be tied up for a while. Be relentless in your pursuit and it will shortly come your way. You must also recheck all addresses and insure all money being sent out so that it will reach the proper destination.

cat litter Someone is mentally devising a plan to deceive you within the next three days. Become very aware of the behavior of others during this time frame. Do not allow yourself to be deceived.

catnip A lover will soon return from a long trip. This will be a happy reunion.

CAT scan Someone in the medical profession will soon fall deeply in love with you.

Cat's cradle You will experience a great increase in wealth within two weeks.

Cat's eye This dream is a very lucky omen. You will demonstrate remarkable clarity of greater thought. Communicate those feelings you have kept to yourself to the person you are interested in. This individual can then be made aware of your interests and involve you in their life. Knowledge of your feelings will please your object of interest and draw you closer. Move on this as soon as possible. Good luck is with you. Eat healthily, drink plenty of water and get plenty of rest.

Cat's paw Trust your instincts. Dig deeply to uncover the information you need about another person.

catsup You will need dental work. Research will provide the name of a dentist who will do the work at a low cost.

cattle You will soon hear good news that will bring you a great deal of satisfaction. This will involve whatever is most important to you at the moment.

Caucasian *to hear the word* You will enjoy a vacation on water.

caul This is a good luck symbol in all matters dealing with paperwork, especially for the next two days. You will enjoy a brilliant future.

cauliflower You will enjoy a pleasurable surprise, new friends and extra money. Take care of yourself, eat well and drink plenty of water.

caulk Do not be taken in by what appears to be a bargain and is not.

caution *to see the sign* Information that you will stumble on accidentally will be a passkey to great benefits. Good luck.

to be cautious You will be suspected of thievery. Be careful and check this out.

cavalry A cowardly person will not be straight forward with you about their opinions. This person will hide behind others and will have other people tell you what they think. This will occur frequently. Don't concern yourself about this.

cave The situation you are trying to keep secret will soon be out in the open if you are not careful to prevent it. This will occur within a few days.

cave in A close friend will go to jail for murder.

caveman Do not wrongly lead people to believe you are a selfish person. Someone will also love you passionately for a long time to come.

cavern Don't expose yourself to another person's infections. Be good to yourself.

cavewoman You will meet an aggressively loving, passionate person. This will be a refreshing change. Keep up your appearance and be prepared for any adventure within the next two days.

caviar Don't allow others to kill your visions.

cavity You are involved in a relationship with someone who wants to separate. Try to deal with your emotions in a calm and dignified manner. Within a few days, this person will desire a reconciliation. You are also spending too much money and are expending too much energy on friends. Watch this.

cayenne pepper This dream implies good luck and good fortune. Keep your cardiovascular system healthy and drink plenty of water.

Cayuga Join forces with another person and opportunities will rapidly expand. Both of you will benefit from this. Good luck and many blessings will come to you.

CB radio During a time of total chaos, someone will suddenly appear to rescue you. This person will be almost an angel in disguise.

C.D. Get to the source of an issue. Once you determine the missing element, you will be able to handle yourself appropriately regarding certain situations.

C.D. Rom drive A time filled with passionate lovemaking is coming your way.

cedar Do not allow your emotions to carry you away.

ceiling You have not been doing well financially. Your future will suddenly open up and finances will improve. This will create a new life for you.
to dream of repair work on the ceiling This dream is even more fortunate. Finances will improve more rapidly.

celebrate Legal litigations will turn to your favor. Do not overspend.

celebrity You have been putting off placing one phone call because you are feeling intimidated. This call will change your life for the better. Make the effort to place that call.

celery A friend will be a financial drain. You must also watch your blood pressure levels and your intake of sodium.

celibacy Stop being so stubborn. This behavior will get you nowhere.

cell Beware of a conspiracy.

cellar Do not push a deranged person too far. This person will become violent.

cello Within a few days, you will be confronted by a powerful enemy. Take steps to prevent this.

cellophane Within a few days you may suffer financial embarrassment. This can be prevented.

cellular phone During a time of total chaos, someone will suddenly appear to rescue you. This person will be almost an angel in disguise.

Celt You will be asked to help another person reform their ways within a few days.

Celtic knot Be very cautious of someone you are affiliated with who will try to pull the wool over your eyes within three days. This person will cleverly create a plan to manipulate you into committing to something they wish you to do. Make sure that you are extremely aware of this because this will only cause you a great deal of discomfort and irritation. You have prior notice of this and can take steps to protect yourself. You will otherwise receive abundances in your life due to opportunities that will be presented to you at this time.

cement Someone will confide in you their thoughts of suicide. Help this person in any way possible.

cement block Bring together creative people who will be able to draw from a pool of resources the information you need for a business venture. The time for this is perfect now and will result in life long riches.

cemetery You will enjoy success while bargain hunting.

This dream is also a promise of a long and happy life and success with a new venture.

census Big advantages will come to you after signing a contract.

cent Take care that you do not get dandruff. Visit a dermatologist if necessary.

centaur This dream is a good omen. You will enjoy good health and will become rich with the help of someone else's skills.

center *any form* Stay open to receive any information you can use. This information will lead to a rise in status.

centerfold Do not become involved in anything negative that regards business ventures.

centerpiece You will fall in love with someone of a different religious belief. This will, however, result in a happy union.

centipede You are strongly seeking friendship and companionship with someone who does not want you around. This person does not like you. Stay away to avoid injured feelings.

Central America A beautiful romantic setting with fine dining and dancing will be yours. This is a very romantic and loving cycle for you. Good luck is with you. This dream may also be used as a reference point in time. If you dream of this place and see its name used in any context, the dream message will occur on this day.

central nervous system Within three days, someone will enter your life eager to have a friendly conversation. As time goes by, you will begin to receive mixed messages and this person will begin to hint at a romantic involvement. Be aware that they are wasting your time because they are seeking only a short term relationship. Expect nothing more than this. Do not compromise your own desires and you will be able to enjoy deep emotional fulfillment. Enjoy yourself and get on with your life. Expect prosperity in the future.

centurion Take the initiative to promote a particular situation that needs to be attended to but is being ignored by others. Investigate this situation carefully so you can present it to others in such a way that will entice them to become involved. Schedule a meeting to determine a way to make this situation a workable reality. You must also clearly define your limits within this group to avoid overextending yourself and to ensure that each person shares equally in the work.
centurions on horseback Any request you make will be successfully fulfilled. Everything will work out exactly as you have envisioned.
to see centurions behaving in a distasteful way Be very watchful. A conniving and hypocritical person will expose

you to emotional harm when you least expect it. Play it very safe and take every precaution to protect yourself, especially from the unknown.

century Prepare ahead for any property fire. Insure all property and take steps to prevent this situation. This will happen within a few days.

century plant You will find inspiration for a new idea that will later bring you large profits. This will occur shortly if you choose to pursue this. You will also learn of someone's engagement.

ceramic People are expecting more from you than you are aware of.

cereal You will win the admiration of someone you desire in a sexual way.

cerebral palsy You are thinking of lending money to a friend. This friend will be unable to repay you and this will result in a loss of friendship. This will happen within a few days.

ceremony *graduation* Force yourself to explore other facets and avenues in life.
wedding You will enjoy a brilliant future.
funeral or wake This dream is a very fortunate omen. Someone will come into money and this person will be eager to share their good fortune. Your plans and ideas will also pay off. This will occur within the week.

certificate You will acquire some information about a relative. This information is private and the person prefers that you keep it to yourself. It is better that they don't know you have this information.

certificate of deposit Within seven days you will be chosen for a sought after position. Demonstrate that you have a sense of humor and common sense.

certified public accountant (CPA) You will soon be hired to oversee the growth of a new facility and the utilization of its services. You will be blessed in each decision. Take this job.

cervix Be tactful in order to avoid a quarrel. You also need to make sure that you do not neglect needed repairs.

cesspool Within a few days make sure that all written material intended for a person in authority is given to this person. It may be taken or hidden purposely. Find a more reliable method of transferring information.

Chablis Make more of an effort to build trust and to bond with that special person in order to promote stability and peace of mind. It is important to do this within three days.

cha cha A same sexed person will lead you to a lifestyle

that will be very satisfying. Security will be yours within five days.

chaff Do not make a move regarding a certain situation for a few days until you have more facts.

chafing dish You will be experiencing domestic problems. Support will shortly come from other family members.

chain You will have the opportunity to show passion toward someone you desire. This will result in a more passionate way of living life.
gold chain A failing relationship will suddenly revitalize.
silver chain Do not alienate yourself from your only support system.
binding chains Brainstorming with a group of people will cost you dearly within the next seven days. Develop your ideas on your own. You will be successful.

chain gang You will receive a special invitation from a casual acquaintance and your suspicions will be aroused. Trust your intuition and tactfully decline.

chain letter A solution to a difficult situation will be found within two days. Any negative event seen in this dream can also be prevented.

chain link fence Do not allow yourself to become sleepy or to lose your sense of alertness in a hazardous area. Be very careful in this environment for the next four days in order to prevent accidents.

chain saw Gain a fresh start with an ongoing negotiation.

chair You will have greater success this time around. This dream is a lucky omen. Project a good impression in front of a large group of people. You have a potential ally who deals with contracts and business dealings.
arm chair You will be misled into believing that someone wants to build a solid relationship with you. Once you decide to commit yourself, this person will back off and leave the relationship. Go on with your life because this person will not commit fully and will be very uneasy with close relationships. If at all possible, do not even involve yourself because you will be left at a vulnerable time.
broken chair You will need to have a private but necessary meeting with an associate.
rocking chair Place emphasis on work during your peak energy times.
wheelchair For the next four days you will be able to affect changes that will vastly improve your life. All of your goals will be realized in the exact manner that you have planned. This dream is a very lucky omen.

chairlift You will reach a decision to separate from someone you care about.

chairman Your skills need to be developed and you need to seek more training to refine these skills. This will be a short term program but will work wonders.

chaise lounge You are neglecting a special talent. Place more emphasis on the development of this talent.

chalet Be practical and use common sense when handling responsibilities.

chalk Seek agreement with others regarding an emotional situation. This will successfully resolve a problem. This dream is also alerting you that within three days you will be dealing with a certain person who is very aware of your likes and dislikes and knows the kind of lifestyle and situations you are against. This individual will use many different subtle methods of persuasion and will be able to develop a plot that will lead you into the lifestyle that you are against almost before you are aware of what is happening. The intent is to lead you into doing something that goes against your principles, and many different tactics will be used to accomplish this. These methods may be as varied as gift giving, vacations, etc., and it may take several offerings and a great deal of time for this person to win you over but you will end up doing what this person wishes. You have prior notice of this and can take the appropriate action. Be sure that you know exactly what you will or will not do. Otherwise, you are headed for a brilliant future.

chalkboard Talk face to face with someone about a financial situation before it becomes a crisis.

chalice Reassure a person who is deeply in love with you that you are determined to grow within the relationship and that you will do whatever is necessary to create stability, both emotionally and financially.

chamber Conversation with an associate will bring out unexpected issues. You will be able to work together to resolve these issues.

chambermaid Within the next few days, you will have a few bad moments. Be prepared for this and you will handle it well.

chamber music Do not lose out by saying the wrong thing to a colleague who is working with you on an important endeavor. Do not allow this to occur.

chameleon Spend more time and be friendlier to a child. This will give the child an emotional lift.

chamois Do not allow a co-worker to become counterproductive.

chamomile *(tea or in any other form)* You will soon buy a desired item. Your nervous condition will also disappear. Find something to soothe your stomach and do things for yourself to relieve stress. This dream is a lucky omen.

champagne Offer your time and assistance to a young relative. This person will remember your help and will be inspired for a lifetime. You will be rewarded for your patience and generosity at a later time.

champion Do not become careless with your status in life. Your careful behavior will benefit you professionally as well as emotionally.

chance *"give me a chance", "let's take a chance", "if I only had a chance", etc.* Someone will want to become involved in your life within seven days. This individual wants this very much, but has many things to take care of first in order to have the time and energy to devote to a real relationship and to be able to support both of you. If you are interested in this relationship, be patient and give this person time to take care of these things. Meanwhile, you can spend moments together when this person has free time. Take it easy, everything will fall into place better than you have envisioned. Many blessings are with you and you are headed for a brilliant future. Taking a small risk within three days will also lead you to a prosperous, brilliant future. An opportunity that you are excited about and have been long awaiting will present itself to you. You now have the means to grasp it and you will have a new start in all areas of your life. All old burdens and issues that have been plaguing you will come to an immediate halt. Drastic changes will occur and leave you with a new exciting zest for life.

change Someone you have shared many wonderful moments with and have deep respect for will enter your life in order to receive assistance in making a transition in some aspect of their life. This person is asking for your involvement in their life. If you choose, you will both become involved in many new experiences you have never considered before. While this person is making these changes, you will be swept into making wonderful changes for yourself. This opportunity will present itself to you within seven days.
to dream of many coins Step back and determine what you are trying to prove and to whom. By doing this, you will be able to develop a plan that will get you exactly what you are trying to accomplish. Good luck is with you.

changeling Do not place so much importance on another person that you overextend and abuse yourself emotionally and mentally, especially for the next five days. Take steps to change or avoid any negative event connected to this dream.

channel For the next five days, pay close attention to the events occurring in your life and take time to regroup. Restrain all impulsive behavior and curb your sense of urgency. Do not become involved in anything you have no business being involved in. Many blessings will come to you and your family.

channeling You will have many accurate intuitive thoughts and will also develop the skills needed to diffuse negative thoughts and attitudes at the exact time that you need this skill. Proceed with confidence and calmness no matter what is occurring in your life right now. You are headed for a life filled with enjoyment with interesting and influential people.

chaparral Do not allow yourself to be manipulated by friends and family members into doing something that goes against your sense of ethics. Practice discipline, and do not abuse yourself by over partying and overindulging in alcohol. You will be encouraged to do this. You are in a very healthy cycle.

chapel You will invite someone to your home for an extended visit. While there, this person will spend very little time with you. You will feel taken advantage of and used because this person will spend time making phone calls and running errands. In reality, this person very much wants to spend time with you and chose to stay with you because you are special to them, but they need to accomplish as much as they can in a short period of time. Enjoy the visit and do not allow yourself to feel hurt and used for the next four days. Someone is also feeling very abandoned by you. Act quickly to make sure that this person knows how special they are to you. Do whatever you can to give them an adequate description of your true feelings for them. You will bring this person a great deal of pleasure and it will be deeply appreciated by them. Put your love into action and anything you want to develop on a permanent basis will occur within five days. This dream also implies that a gift of any kind will enhance this development. You are loved beyond your imagination.

chaperone Someone is anxious to see you but is hesitant about letting you see their true emotions. This person will ask to see you within the week but will instead see you within a two day period. Do not allow yourself to be caught off guard. Their enthusiasm will lead to a phone call and a request to drop by at a moment's notice. Make sure that your physical appearance is up to par. This is a lucky cycle for you.

chaplain You are entering a very lucky cycle and will achieve victory in anything you choose to become involved with. You will be very satisfied with the results of your choices. You will also enjoy loyalty and affection from those you care about, especially for the next week. Take steps to avoid any negative event represented in this dream.

chapped *in any form* By asking questions, being suspicious, and by developing a certain degree of objectivity, you will be so successful in diffusing a plot against you that it will be impossible for it to be successfully carried out. This plot will involve someone who wishes to create chaos and discomfort in your life. You will be able to use what authority you have in a responsible, efficient and effective way. You will also, within two days, experience many wins and victories and the generosity you have paid to others in the past will be repaid. Expect to receive many gifts and major wins. You are definitely headed for a brilliant future.

chaps You are headed in the wrong direction and are taking far too many risks. In spite of all guarantees, your plans will not work out.

chap stick Someone will blurt out, in jest, a marriage proposal. Both of you will laugh it off but the seed will be planted. This will later blossom into a real proposal if you desire.

charcoal You will receive a gift of diamonds. You will also hear of an associate who has committed suicide in a violent way. This will occur within the week.

chard For the next five days, avoid people who enjoy provoking anger in others.

charge account For two days do not allow yourself to become anxious when someone speaks to you about a stressful situation. Do not become involved in another person's problems.

chariot You will be able to bring someone closer to you in a passionate way. You have long desired this person and this involvement will bring you a great deal of happiness. If you choose, this person will eventually marry you. Begin work on this situation within two days.

charioteer Within three days, a young person will bring trouble between you and your loved ones. Do not allow this to happen.

charm Someone will promise you undying love prior to engaging in sexual play with you. After this incident, this individual will appear from time to time only for the pleasures of sex. If you choose a deeper involvement, avoid this person. You are especially vulnerable to this for the next four days.

chart A problematic situation will develop within five days. Although you will feel compelled to offer assistance and involve yourself in some way, refrain from this. You do not have the emotional resources to deal with this issue extensively. Do not allow yourself to feel guilty. Each person can handle only so much.

chase Speak up for your rights.
to chase someone in a car Do whatever you can to get away from a dangerous person. This person could kill you. Keep quiet about leaving.
to be chased in a car Be patient and allow a relationship to grow.
bicycle chase A young person will show you a new way to do a do it yourself project.
motorcycle chase Concentrate on making a relationship more functional. You will be rewarded with a nice gift.
to chase after a bus or train, etc. You will receive information about another person that is false.

foot chase Don't be so pushy.

to chase after a boat or train Speak to an associate or co-worker in order to speed up work. Your product will be much in demand within a few weeks.

to chase and catch whatever you are chasing Because of your easy going personality, others enjoy your company. Set boundaries early in order to avoid hurt feelings. There are times when you need private time and there are times when others unknowingly overstep boundaries.

to chase and be unable to catch whatever you are chasing Ask questions about any suspicions you may have. It is important to clear up all suspicions prior to making decisions that lead to major changes in your life.

to be chased on foot and not be caught Put aside some time within three days to clear your head and to put yourself through some greater mental gymnastics. This will allow you to pinpoint the suspicions you feel about another person and determine whether they are valid. You will understand then how to go about resolving this issue. If you motivate yourself now, you will be successful. This is the best cycle to find the answers you are seeking. You are headed for a very prosperous future.

to see someone or something chased on foot Several unexpected events will take place concurrently and you will receive a flood of invitations that you will be able to choose from. It is important that you attend one specific function because it will be far more glamorous and exciting than the others. Be sure to prepare yourself for this ahead of time. This function will require formal attire and you will want to look your best. You will meet many influential people who will become life long friends. You will enjoy yourself tremendously and win a door prize at this function. You will also become aware during this time period that the person you most desire feels the same about you. You will have affectionate feelings toward one another and you will both be very excited about this new development. You are headed for a very prosperous and brilliant future.

to be chased on foot and caught or to see someone chased and caught You will be in the presence of a certain person within a few days who will promise you many things in a desperate attempt to keep you from separating from them. This individual is, in reality, going through many transitions and stresses in their life and it will be impossible for them to deliver on these promises. Although you are able to see through this ploy, back off from making any decisions if you are interested in this person. They will quickly recover from this episode and within two weeks will be in great emotional and financial shape. They will then be able to deliver on these promises. Everything will work out exactly as they have envisioned and you will both enjoy an abundance of health and a brilliant future. Take steps to avoid or alter any negative event witnessed in this dream and forewarn anyone you recognized to do the same. Do everything you can to make sure that you only experience positive expressions in your life.

chasm Do not become too overpowering to someone special. Tone down your attitude.

chassis You will be given the gift of healing and receive psychic abilities from your higher power. You will enjoy a tremendous amount of order in your life. You will put this gift to good use and blessings will be with you for a lifetime.

chastisement A young child needs encouragement. Help to point this person in the right direction.

chastity Prepare to meet an intelligent person within a few days. This person will be a potential mate, if you desire.

chastity belt Do not start revising your plans at this particular time, this is not the best cycle for you to do this. Otherwise, this will be a very enjoyable five day cycle. Trust your hunches and go with what you feel.

chat Your love relationship is fortunate and will continue to be so.

chateau Keep yourself respectable. Others will notice this attitude.

Chaucer Strange uncontrollable desires will bring you ruin within seven days. Do whatever is necessary to control these urges.

chauffeur *driving your car* Someone answering a help wanted ad appears normal but is, in fact, very dangerous. Prepare yourself and be cautious.

driving his own car Your project is moving ahead and will yield great profits.

chauvinism You will have to travel to a foreign country for business purposes. After a week or so, you will want to stay and begin a new life. This will be an exciting, exuberant time for you.

cheap A career move at this time will be very fortunate. It is important that your physical appearance is at its best.

cheapskate You will finally, within two days, pull yourself away from a long term tortuous situation. Good luck is with you.

cheat *to be* Do not allow small problems that make you irritable stand in the way of meeting a very intelligent person. This person is a good listener and you will share many moments of laughter.

to deal with a cheat Put emphasis in how you word things to achieve success.

catch a lover cheating You will meet someone within the next few days with the qualities of a life long mate.

to be caught cheating on a mate You are working on a long project. Discipline yourself to complete it.

check Pay close attention to the numbers on the check. This is the amount you will soon receive. You may also use these numbers in a game of chance. If you are planning to buy a particular item, focus on the amount given in the dream as a bid for the item. You must also push to meet a deadline.

rubber check Be very careful not to say something at the wrong time. You may blurt out something you have no business saying out loud.

to be the recipient of a government check Be very attentive because an unusual occurrence will develop regarding a person, project or position that will lead to a financial windfall. You may marry someone who will leave you with a monthly pension, develop a project that will deliver you monthly royalties, or secure a position that will offer you monthly provisions for a lifetime. You are in a sound position to receive this in the near future. Develop your curiosity, especially for the next week, to ensure that you do not miss out on these benefits. You will receive an abundance of health, many blessings and are headed for a brilliant future.

checkbook This is a lucky sign. The figures shown closely represent the amount you will have in your checkbook. It is also important to develop activities that you and your family can do together for fun.

checkerboard A newcomer to the area possesses magical qualities Through a conversation with this person, you will both work out a new endeavor and do well.

checkers You will be asked to reveal your sources of information within the week. Do not reveal this to anyone.

checking account This is a lucky omen. The numbers seen will be lucky in games of chance. Do not allow others to waste your time.

checkmate What appears promising will turn out not to be. Revise it in order to have a successful outcome.

checkup What appears to be promising will turn out not to be. Revise your plans to achieve a successful outcome.

cheddar cheese A new person will unexpectedly appear in your life. This person will be a fast talker but will inspire you in the future because your creative juices will start to flow. You may never see this person again but the energy created by them will carry over to success.

cheek Review old forgotten ideas and, with a little inspiration, they will make you rich.

cheek bone Love yourself and be good to yourself.

cheer You will capitalize on another person's influential position while working on a new endeavor. You will be pointed to a path of success.

cheering *rhythmic* For the next three days be very cautious of who you are dealing with and go forward with someone only with extreme caution. You are beginning to feel close to a certain person who will lead you to believe you can fully confide in them and can depend on their loyalty to you. This person is skillful at creating deceptions and illusions and will lead you to believe that certain events will take place in the future that will never occur. They have a hidden agenda that involves them pursuing you for purposes known only to them, and will do everything in their power to create an atmosphere that will be free of all suspicions. This person is very charming and charismatic and will create chaos to divert you if they sense you are being suspicious. By the time you realize what is happening you will be suffering deep emotional disappointments, disillusions and you may suffer financially. It will be a long time before you recover from this and get back to normalcy. You have enough time and all the ammunition you need to make sure this does not occur. Use common sense, refuse to get involved, do not compromise yourself and do not allow anyone to pry into your affairs and you will be able to successfully diffuse this. You are headed for a prosperous future and many blessings will come to you and your family.

cheering section Certain situations will start to develop within three days that are important not to make worse by dwelling on. Motivate yourself to get busy on new projects that you need to focus on.

cheerleader Do legwork in order to capitalize on an opportunity you have worked on for a while. Move quickly on this because there is a deadline.

cheese Someone you have known for a while, whose personality complements yours, will begin taking the relationship to a different level by asking you out. If you choose, relax and this will be a lovely union.

cheese box Within a five day period, someone will make plans to violate your rights for their own gratification. This person will try to persuade you into becoming involved in a situation that will become increasingly distasteful to you, sexually or in any other capacity. This situation will go against your sense of ethics and your better judgment. Do not place yourself in any situation that will require you to compromise your morals in order to remain safe. You have prior notice of this and can take steps to prevent it. Good luck is with you.

cheeseburger You will surrender to the union of a wonderful marriage. This is someone you will be proud to be married to if you choose this option.

cheesecake You are faced with a recurring problem. You will find a solution to keep this problem from reoccurring or will at least delay it long enough for you to recover. Play a very active part in ensuring that your emotional needs are fulfilled. Within five days you will also be able to visualize the path you need to take for a brilliant future. Good luck is with you.

cheesecloth Pay careful attention to what people are saying about an agreement you will be making. What is expected of you now is not what will be expected of you later. Think ahead.

cheetah A recurring problem will arise again in a few days. Take care of this promptly and do not waste valuable time.

chef Prepare ahead for a private conversation with a person who handles situations very cleverly. Use this conversation to make a special agreement or arrangement within the next few days. This will be a fortunate meeting.

chemical Gather knowledge ahead of time in order to make an important decision. Do not be afraid to make this decision. It will result in success and you will be admired greatly.

chemical warfare Do everything you can, for the next two days, to bring happiness to your home life. This change will create a deeper love for you and will bring you happiness.

chemist Strengthen your talents. You will then be able to sell yourself in a simple, straightforward manner. This will be a fortuitous cycle for you.

chemotherapy Do not allow flashes from the past to ruin the present. Focus on the good things, not the bad. Good times will come to you soon.

chenille Devise a clever plan or idea that will make it possible for you to work alone on a particular situation without depending on other people for their help. These ideas will come to you with great clarity and you will be able to successfully conclude the situation.

Cherokee Two people who are closely related to each other will become attractive to you. Both will approach you at the same time. Be careful who you choose, and once the choice is made, remain loyal. You will have a wonderful time.

cherry A married person will be attracted to you. Do not encourage this person's behavior. Keep the situation as it is. This person's mate is very jealous and will try to kill you.
   sweet cherry Someone desperately wants to see you in order to demonstrate their affection for you. This individual will contact you very soon.

cherry bomb Within five days, you will receive news that will be difficult to comprehend. Do not involve yourself or volunteer your assistance.

cherry, sour You will live a long and healthy life. Maintain healthy eating habits and drink plenty of water. Blessings are with you.

cherry tomato Do everything necessary for the next seven days to bond closer to a special person. Make this bond permanent.

cherub Pay close attention to everything concerning your real estate.

Cheshire cat Someone will cause you a great deal of personal stress. At first this person will appear to be very kind but will later require a great deal of personal attention. Be careful about where this situation is leading in order to avoid a bitter argument at a later date.

chess Someone will, within a few days, raise your hopes over a long desired promise. You will be let down within the next two weeks. This person is not interested in you. Go on with your life.

chessboard Do not betray your sources of information under any circumstances. Do not allow outside pressure to turn you into a traitor.

chessmen Within seven days someone will attempt to discourage you from your interests by giving you the runaround. Do not allow this to occur.

chest *your chest* Bond more closely with those people who are close to you.
   unusual markings Do not expose yourself to any virus that will cause illness.
   someone else's chest Avoid any shameful activity with the opposite sex that you will regret.

chest *(of drawers)* A financial tip you receive will be totally reliable. Make sure also that you insure all of your property.

chestnut You will be offered assistance within a few days. There will be strings attached to this offer. This is neither good nor bad and it is your choice to go along with it or not.

chevron *to see this shape* All of your plans will work out exactly as you have envisioned. You will be in a good cycle for the next seven days to ensure the success of your goals. Good luck is with you.

chew Do not allow anyone to know about a plan you have until it has been implemented and you know that it will work.

chewing gum Do not become confused about what to do regarding a specific situation. Seek professional help to steer you in the right direction.

Cheyenne Love your family. Foster unity and look for ways to maintain happiness.

Chicago This dream is a fortuitous omen. Think ahead. Time taken off now will be needed later for an important matter. Conserve your time and energy for this event. This dream may also be used as a reference point in time. If you dream of this city and see its name used in any context, the dream message will occur on this day.

Chicano Give immediate attention to an important issue that others consider unimportant. Attend to it now or it will continuously come back as an irritant. You will gain extra advantages and benefits in the long run.

chick Others need to know where they fit into your life. Someone is attempting to convey deep feelings to you. You are in an invigorating cycle of life.

Chickasaw Remain calm and centered for the next three days. A situation will develop that will tempt you to become involved. Do not allow the problems of another individual to cause you to become so desperate that you compromise yourself and become entangled in this situation. Once you become involved, it will be very hard to pry yourself loose, and this situation will grow progressively worse as time goes by. You are seeing only the tip of the iceberg. Remain uninvolved.

chicken You are a visionary and see the future clearly. Take the lead and point others in the proper direction. You are now making decisions using your mental clarity. Take advantage of this cycle in all areas of your life.

to eat chicken Do not be too proud to receive a gift or a grant of money from someone who truly believes that you deserve it. You are headed for a brilliant future.

prairie chicken You will receive an unusual gift within three days that you do not really like. Exchange this for something more to your liking.

chicken feed Think ahead. Someone you hire to do repairs has bad intentions. The cost of repairs will be more than you agreed to.

chicken hawk Your lack of confidence will prevent you from accurately stating your opinions and feelings to others. This mental barrier will ultimately keep you from fulfilling your potential and will create physical problems. Work on carrying yourself with the confidence and assurance you need to break through this block. Within three days, your attempt will be successful.

chicken pox Surround children with amusing stories and loving, light entertainment.

chicken wire A cowardly person feigning friendship is planning, with another person, to murder you. Find out who this person is and seek immediate help. This will occur within two months if you do not take precautions.

chickpea You will enjoy profitable negotiations for the next three days.

chicory You will be resolved of all conflicts for the next week by maintaining a cheerful and kind demeanor.

chief Have all phases of one set of repairs completed before another begins.

chiffon Many temporary delays will set you back on a project you will be working on for the next few days. Do something else for a while then come back to the original project.

chigger Don't become an emotional extremist.

Chihuahua Someone you know will extend a large loan to you. You will attempt to pay them back rapidly but you will hear complaints about the manner of repayment. Think ahead. You may not want to take out a loan and have to deal with this issue.

child You are thinking of revising and merging your business into a large corporation. Your ideas are good. Go for it and you will be victorious.

children You will be more effective if you brainstorm with a clever person. You will mutually arrive at successful new ideas.

step child You will be directly involved with a lazy person who, on the surface, appears energetic. Be wary of this; it will affect your life greatly.

to kiss a child Within a few days you will experience great happiness because you will be able to do what you want and will gain a certain freedom. You will also be treated better by others. You will receive more affection, consideration and respect.

a child in distress Someone is feeling abandoned by you because you are not giving enough affection and love. Do something special for those who love you within the next week.

to see an injured child If you recognize this child become aware that it needs to be heavily protected for the next four days from physical harm. Make sure all bases are covered. Create a protective haven.

to see a child you recognize drowning You need to be very protective of any child you recognize in order to ensure that their needs are being met. It is important that you make sure that this child is carefully watched to ensure that this does not occur. Be sure that you warn the custodian of this child so they can take all the necessary steps to prevent this incident. For the next three days any quick decision you make will lead to riches.

if this child is unfamiliar to you Take care of yourself, especially for the next four days. Do not be so strict with yourself, but do not leave yourself open to gullibility in certain situations.

group of children Someone will communicate their eagerness to grant you a favor. This person is in the position to win influence on your behalf. Go for it, you are in a great cycle.

possessed or accompanied by evil spirits For the next three days make sure a child is kept in a protective environment. Shield this child and take precautions to ensure that any illness does not develop into a crisis. Protect them from undue stress and cruelty from others and ensure that all vital needs are met.

if a child is a demon This dream implies that this child needs more protection health wise. You will be able to turn this child's life around in a more positive fashion. Be careful of the people this child associates with and provide only positive role models. Guard them carefully for the next ten days.

if you do not recognize this child Become more lenient with your inner child and add more excitement and enjoyment to your life. It is important that you do this within three days. You must also not allow a small problem to escalate to the point of a crisis. Work to maintain a stress free environment. You have the time to keep any negative situation from developing by changing your behavior and manner of speaking to others.

if you recognize the child This child will need supervision and discipline in order to prevent problem behaviors. Make sure also that food allergies are not present that may cause personality disorders. Be alert for food poisoning.

children that are accompanied by ghosts Within three days make sure this child has a protective environment. Protect them from illnesses and the escalation of a pre-existing illness. Protect this child from unusual and unbearable stress, outside peer pressures, cruel remarks, and ensure that all their needs are met. Be very watchful over this child for the next three days.

child birth Apply yourself and express your ideas graphically within a few weeks. This will give others the chance to visualize your ideas and this will work to your advantage.

Children's underwear For the next four days think carefully and plan what you will say to someone who is involved in a certain situation. This will buy you the necessary time to gather everyone involved and to decide how to put a lid on a particular issue that would lead to a negative occurrence. Many blessings will come to you and your family.

Children's voices You will need more privacy in order to accomplish what needs to be taken care of.

Chile *(Coast of South America)* Within a two week period you will rapidly advance to a higher plateau in life than you have ever anticipated. You will enjoy an abundance of productivity, an increased flow of income, productive conversations and more affection from others. You will be surrounded by loyal people and others will be eager to be a part of your plans and join your work force. You are headed for a brilliant future and will enjoy an abundance of health. All of this will occur in a shorter span of time than you ever expected. This is the best time to travel to a different continent and to return safely. This dream may also be used as a reference point in time. If you dream of this country and see its name used in any context, the dream message will occur on this day.

chili A close friend, who is a musician, will be killed due to

mistaken identity within a two week period. If you know who this person is, warn them. Also, you have recently left a relationship. Take this freedom and allow your creativity to flow. Create a stress free environment for yourself.

chili con carne You will go along with another's idea because your judgment is not accurate. Recheck this. This idea will not work out well.

chili dog Do not push a person to behave in a romantic fashion if this person resists you. This person is simply unable to express themselves this way. In a short time this person will learn to surrender and express their feelings this way.

chili powder A close person will suggest lifestyle changes. This will surprise you but go along with it and you will be happy with the change.

chili's *(chili peppers - firecracker)* Think ahead. You have a relative who is very fond of you but lives far away. This person will be getting rid of property but will feel you are uninterested in it. Make your feelings known quickly.

chili sauce Demands and conflicts will mount for the next few days. Be firm and work to resolve these situations to avoid becoming overwhelmed.

chime Someone will attempt to bring an injury suit against you in order to collect the insurance. Be very wary of this for the next three days.

to have a chime You are headed in the wrong direction. Rethink your goals and take the time to regroup. Maintain your optimism. You will be able to handle everything properly.

chimney Watch out for a faked accident created for the purpose of a lawsuit against you.

chimney sweep Do not abruptly take on any strenuous athletic recreational pastimes for the next week. You may be out of condition and this could lead to injury. Make sure you are in good health prior to taking up any new pastimes.

chimpanzee Stay away from those who enjoy prolonging family situations for the pleasure of creating discord.

chin Treat your time as a precious commodity. Set limits in order to use your time wisely and not waste precious moments.

China This dream implies that exciting experiences will be coming your way and you will experience prosperity on many levels of life. This will allow you to navigate through the luxury and riches of beauty from an area that is presently unknown to you. Enjoy your journey with confidence. This dream is an omen of victory. It may also be used as a reference point in time. If you dream of this country and see its name in any context, the dream message will occur on this day.

China Wall This is a very victorious omen and implies that within the next three months, no matter what is occurring in your life, you will be able to focus on what you need to do in order to reach your goals. You will also be able to use your abilities to pull strings on your behalf. You will develop the confidence you need and will maintain this level of confidence until you succeed. Many blessings will come to you and your family. You are definitely headed for a brilliant future.

chinchilla For the next two days, do not allow yourself to become involved in political debates while at an outing. This will escalate to angry outbursts.

Chinese *Chinese person* This dream is an extremely lucky omen for you as well as for anyone who is involved in your life at this particular time. You will be provided services that will enable you to achieve a higher level of success than you ever imagined. Expect amazing and wonderful connections that will enable you to reach and achieve your goals. You can expect a mega merger. This dream also implies that you will either attend a joyful event with people of this ethnic group, experience an educational event taught by someone of this culture, or referring to this particular culture. This will be of major benefit to you. Or you will attend a gathering in which one member of this group will show an interest in you and your projects and offer you major benefits. You can expect a long period of tranquility following this and you are headed for a brilliant future. Anything negative portended in this dream must be prevented in reality. Take steps to forewarn anyone you dreamed about to do the same.

in any other form (i.e., anything of Chinese orientation) Receive a reading in any form. This dream is lucky for you. All forms of gambling are also lucky during this cycle.

Chinese Checkers You will have luck at the horse races for the next few days.

Chinese food Within a three day period, an old friend will contact you. You will enjoy wondrous times and the friendship will rapidly become a love affair.

Chinese lantern Be careful not to slip and fall for the next few days.

Chinook Do everything necessary to improve the environment in your community. Don't be afraid to lead and inspire others.

chintz Develop a healthy environment for an older person in order to prevent falls.

chip *(poker)* Do not become involved in useless arguments. Other people will refrain from offering their help. Otherwise, this dream is a very lucky omen, especially for the next five days.

chip *(potato)* Someone you know needs a special treat for a past kindness. This person was there when you needed help and now you can repay this with a kindness.

chipmunk Someone you have relied on to perform a service will be embarrassed. They are unable to because of their lack of expertise. To avoid telling you this person will set an outrageous price that you are unable to meet.

chipped beef Drive defensively in order to avoid an accident for the next few days.

Chippewa All negotiations conducted within a three day period will not work to your advantage. One person will purposely attempt to stymie all progress. Expect to come up against opposition and find ways to work it to your advantage.

chisel Do not use shortcut methods to rush an important project or carpentry work. A thorough approach will result in a successful project.

chitterlings Hire an assistant whom you can use to advance your projects to a successful completion. Do this by building this person's skills.

chives Do not ignore the rights of others.

chlorine When laundering, take care to wash clothes that bleed in separate loads.

chocolate *to receive* You will become clear in how to help someone who desires you. You will find ways to make this person feel comfortable enough to verbalize their feelings, hopes and plans. This cycle will spur you to tackle big ideas and projects. Go for the golden opportunity. Blessings and luck are with you.

to drink You will be harassed by the police because of another person's lifestyle and carelessness. This will occur within a few days and will result in an enormous amount of property damage. This is not within your control. Stay calm and it will eventually work out. Take it slowly and proceed in a step by step fashion. You will be able to put your life back in order.

to eat Someone loves you very deeply.

in any other form You will be given a gift of greater mental inventiveness by the gods. Put this gift to practical use in order to change your present circumstances. Sexual favors will also be passionately requested from you. Maintain healthy eating habits and drink plenty of water. Chocolate is lucky in matters of love. You will experience much passion and lovemaking and both of you will cater to each other's needs.

chocolate chip cookies Do not conduct business with the person you are considering doing business with. For the next seven days stay alert to this situation in order to avoid it.

Choctaw You will be captivated by someone and will soon enter into a long term relationship. This will be mutually satisfying.

choir *to hear a choir* Get help from an associate who has expertise about the project you are working on. This information will be reliable.

to see yourself in a choir This dream is a lucky omen. You will have a conversation with someone you do not know well and you will express your business goals. You will find that you share the same goal. You will develop a partnership in business and complement each other completely.

choke *to choke up on feelings or to see anyone else choke up on feelings* You are finding that you would rather live in a style that goes against your principles and ethics rather than face up to your feelings of disillusionment. You will find that you have completely different feelings about an aspect of your life than you originally thought. Although this awareness will stir up painful feelings you will find the strength to prepare yourself to face up to these conflicts in emotion. Remember that it is always easier to maintain the status quo than to make painful changes. But you will heal quickly and move toward a more dynamic, positive way of life. You are headed for a prosperous future.

to choke Make sure that anything negative you dream of does not occur and take steps to ensure that you experience only positive expressions in life. This dream also implies that you will experience riches that will come from an unusual and unexpected source. Nothing you can do can spur this on. This event will occur naturally and will be out of your control and lead to instant wealth. You will experience a brilliant future and have the clarity of greater thought that you need to correctly direct the fortune you will be coming into.

to choke someone else You will have the feeling that something is wrong with you physically but after consulting a number of physicians you will find there is nothing organically wrong with you. Be assured that healing will quickly occur if you start treating your physical complaints from a different perspective. Change your attitude and thinking patterns and remove anything that may have harmful affects on your physical well-being, whether this involves a change of diet, a lessening of stress or the addition of physical exercise. Reschedule your life in order to lower the physical demands on your body, and take yourself away from anyone who makes you feel uncomfortable and puts extra stress into your life. You can easily turn this into a positive situation by changing the way you live. It will take some time to recover and you will be healthier than you were before you started this new regimen. Take steps to change any negative event in this dream and do everything you can to experience only positive expressions in your life. You are on the path toward a prosperous future and many blessings will come to you and your family.

in any other form You will become wealthy overnight.
choke collar *if you see someone wearing a choke collar*

This dream implies that this person is a workaholic and you will be dealing with this individual or someone who fits this description within three days. If this is someone you know and typically brings you some kind of discomfort, you have time to prepare yourself in order to handle this smoothly and easily. Move on with your life with confidence.

if this is someone you recognize who brings you many pleasant times Prepare yourself with a special gift for this person within three days. You are definitely headed for a brilliant future.

in any other form You are becoming a workaholic. Try to control this and spend more time with your family. Provide yourself with more amusing things in your life.

choked up *speechless or to have trouble swallowing* Do not allow someone who puts on airs to put you in the position of feeling inferior or defeated in some way. Do not place any importance on this issue and go on with your life without letting this situation disturb you. Look for other things to do that will separate you from this vicious person. Once you take yourself away from this environment you will be able to see clearly and will be able to introduce enjoyable things into your life. You have prior notice of this so you can avoid getting emotionally caught up with it. Many blessings will come to you and your family.

choke up a process For the next few days take steps to keep your feelings and emotions under control. You will find you have been left out of a situation or a particular group that you wanted to be included in, and are wasting far too much time getting emotionally caught up in this. Do not feed into this because your involvement was simply not meant to be. Focus on other matters that are important for you to attend to.

choking sounds *to hear someone or yourself making choking sounds* You will be talking to someone within three days who has undergone so much stress that they are unable to verbalize their feelings about what has occurred. This has been a very humiliating experience for this individual. Be supportive and patient until they are over this crisis and can be more involved in your life.

if you do not recognize the person making these sounds You will unexpectedly hear of someone going through this stressful experience.

if you do recognize this person Make it a point to warn this person that something stressful is coming their way so they can be prepared to deal with it, or can take steps to avoid it entirely. They can expect it to occur within three days.

cholera The advice of a close friend will lead you to the proper information to file a claim against someone in authority for money owed to you.

cholesterol Doubts about someone involved in a current dispute will dissipate after you receive facts during a one on one conversation. Other issues will also be cleared up. Take care of yourself and drink plenty of water.

chop Do not violate another person's rights.

chopsticks You will encounter someone whom you have not seen in a long time. This person will treat you to an enjoyable brunch.

chop suey Within a three day period, an old friend will contact you. You will enjoy wondrous times and the friendship will rapidly develop into a love affair.

choral A close relative will call from a distant city and discuss the way they are feeling. You will be asked to join this relative and another close relative for an enjoyable time in a distant city. Eat a balanced diet and drink plenty of water.

chord Within a few days, you will be surprised by an unprovoked verbal attack. The moment you suspect this will occur, stop it.

chore Do not be so strict with yourself. Give in to your loved one with emotional displays.

chorus Avoid those who enjoy provoking arguments and are critical of others.

chow Someone important to you will become verbally abusive. Watch for this and stop it the moment it first starts to evolve.

Chow Chow Someone is undergoing emotional turmoil because of their inability to express their deep hidden feelings for you. Develop a softer demeanor in order to allow this person to gain the courage to express their feelings. Create a safe, comfortable environment for this person for the next four days.

chowder A friend from far away will send a small gift to you.

chow mein Within a three day period, an old friend will contact you. You will enjoy wondrous times and the friendship will rapidly develop into a love affair.

Christ Your thoughts will be magically illuminated and you will be able to clearly communicate ideas that will enhance your life. You will feel solid and whole and will be able to handle problems quickly and confidently. Others will see these changes. You will be blessed for many years and the knowledge you have gained will always remain with you. You will be able to tap into this greater knowledge for future benefits.

Christ carrying the cross, on the crucifix or being crucified Make sure that you are not symbolically crucified by others who are plotting to do this. Someone you least expect will attempt to cause you extreme emotional harm in order to seriously damage your well being. You will be able, with this prior notice, to take the necessary steps to protect your-

self in all capacities. Make sure all bases are covered and you will be able to handle this situation victoriously. For the next two weeks the powers of your higher power will be with you.

christen Do not waste time speculating about the money needed to launch a project. This enterprise will not work out. Move on to something else.

Christian This dream is telling you to go full speed ahead and you will achieve victory. Many blessings will come to you and your family. Any negative event witnessed in this dream may be avoided in reality.

Christianity You will enjoy good fortune and blessings for many years to come.

Christian Science Do not remain in a situation that continues to create resentments. Good luck will be with you for the next two weeks.

Christmas A new opportunity will present itself and you will now have the means to grasp it. You will make new starts in life in those areas that you desire changes in. All old issues and burdens that have been plaguing you will come to an immediate halt. Major changes will occur and leave you with a new zest for life. All negotiations taking place within the week will be highly successful and everyone involved will help bring these plans to completion. A mystery will also finally surface. You will receive one thrilling gift that will come to you no matter what time of the year you have this dream. It is very fortuitous to dream about Christmas.

Father Christmas Advertise for the specific services you need to have performed. Within two weeks, you will find just the right person to confidently complete the tasks you need to accomplish in the manner you wish. This dream also implies that within three days, a promise that was made to you some time ago will be fulfilled.

Christmas card Unbeknownst to you, someone will play cupid. The person they have in mind for you will be wonderful. If you choose to pursue this, you can look forward to delightful and major events in your life. Many blessings will come to you and your family, and you are entering a very lucky cycle.

Christmas tree *any form* Within a two week period you will suddenly rise to a higher position in life than you ever anticipated. You will enjoy an abundance of productivity, increased income, and productive conversations. You will also be surrounded by people who will be loyal and affectionate towards you. Other people will also express their desire to be part of your plans, to offer their assistance and teach you the knowledge they have acquired. You will find this to be especially important for the next five days. You are headed for a brilliant future and will enjoy an abundance of health within a short period of time.

Christmas tree lights Your intuition is right on target and you will be receiving unspoken verification that your hunches about love and affection are correct. Someone will promise deep love for you and will be willing to commit. This commitment will bring a long lasting love. You are headed for a brilliant future if you choose to accept this commitment. All things you felt were impossible are possible now.

chrome You will experience a burst of creative energy and will be able to develop many profound ideas. This is the perfect time to take control of and promote these ideas.

chromosome Have a much needed private conversation with an associate as soon as possible.

Chronicles *(book of the Bible)* Focus on the benefits that are owed you that you may not even be aware of. For the next three days, investigate this thoroughly to ensure that you receive what you are entitled to receive. You are headed in the right direction.

chrysanthemum Inspire an older person to include more activities in their life and to develop a more dynamic exciting lifestyle.

chuckle In spite of obstacles and setbacks, persevere in your goals and you will find success.

chuck wagon Use more discretion regarding your personal affairs for the next few days.

chum You will have a deep urge to investigate a particular issue. You would be better off leaving this situation alone.

church Within three days you will meet someone with a bad reputation in business. Keep away from this person.

Churchill, Winston You will be approached by someone with a novel situation they feel you can handle. Back off, and refuse to accept any new projects for the next seven days.

church key Make sure that the information you send reaches the person it is intended for in a timely fashion. If you do not take important steps to ensure this, the recipient will wait a long time for this much needed information. You will also receive an invitation to celebrate the wedding of someone you know.

churchyard Explore better ways of making a living.

churn Stay away from someone you know who tends to create problems out of nothing.

chute Do not postpone pending projects.

chutney Carefully watch young children around alcohol. Make sure they do not accidentally partake of alcoholic beverages. A relative will also have dental problems. Do whatever you can to offer assistance.

cider Within three days, carelessness will result in an injury caused by a fall. This can be prevented.

cigar This dream is a good luck omen. Do not waste time on a new routine.

to light one from another You will suffer pain and anguish over an inheritance left to you. You will need to hire an attorney to claim it.

to light someone else's cigar Be careful of injuries to the eye.

to be burned by a cigar What seems to be a romantic possibility now will disappear unless you move quickly.

cigarette *to dream of smoking* Do not allow a lack of self confidence and determination to keep you from bringing a certain issue to completion within five days. Do not create barriers that will hinder your progress. Push yourself to take care of this and proceed with confidence. This will result in a feeling of accomplishment and well being. You will invest wisely and this will result in prosperity.

to light someone else's cigarette You will join a military camp.

cigarette with ashes You will feel remorse for a very sick child. This child will recover after a long time in the hospital.

to be burned by a cigarette Due to misidentification, you will be falsely accused of creating an accident. This can be prevented.

to see someone else get burned Do everything necessary to make someone aware of the deep passion you feel for them and make certain this person knows exactly how you feel. Make sure romance flows freely during this cycle. This will be similar to a honeymoon experience for the next two months.

to light one cigarette with another You will travel to a foreign land due to the career move of someone special to you.

to see someone else smoke Your trust in a friend will result in a big loss. Reevaluate your judgment. You will also need to carefully consider the path you need to put yourself on in order to go in the direction you choose. You will then be able to reach your goals.

in any other form You will, within two days, move ahead rapidly with anything you desire. You can expect to find success with this.

cigarette lighter Prepare yourself carefully so that when you meet with a certain individual in three days, you will be able to draw the truth from them with a minimal amount of stress. This will enable you to get to the bottom of a certain situation that you have a great deal of curiosity about.

cigarette pack An opportunity that you are excited about and have been long awaiting will present itself. You now have the means to grasp it and you will have a new start in all areas of your life where you desire changes. All old burdens and issues that have been plaguing you will come to an immediate halt. Drastic changes will occur and leave you with a new exciting zest for life.

empty pack Someone will come into your life now who at one time had decided they were not interested in a relationship with you in any capacity, although this was not apparent to you at the time. This individual now has had a change of mind and will seek the possibility of becoming a part of your life on some level. It will now be your choice whether you want to get involved with this person. You will also hear some terrific news and will receive a small present. This will be a pleasurable cycle for you.

cinder You will learn of a dear friend's death.

Cinderella You will enjoy life long contentment as a result of your employment for domestic work with a kind person at a high salary. After this person's death you will receive a large annuity. Actively seek this position.

cinema A dear friend will want to confide a long kept deep secret to you. This person wants only to tell it once and never have it brought up again. Listen carefully and quietly and be discreet. This will occur within a few days.

cinnamon You will be loved for the remainder of your life and both of you will enjoy much happiness.

circle Your ability to understand will bring you much profit.

circuit breaker Someone you know enjoys provoking anger in you simply to watch your reaction. Avoid this person.

circuitry Be careful not to injure a pet with your car.

circular A flea market will yield a wonderful gift for a loved one if you search carefully.

circular saw A physical sport will result in injury within a few days. Take steps to prevent this.

circumcision Keep your eyes open for the potential sexual abuse to a child for the next few weeks. You may be able to intervene and prevent this.

circus Someone you desire romantically and physically has a contagious disease. Do what you can to avoid physical contact with this person until you have more information.

cistern Take steps to protect all of your valuables and do not become overly friendly with strangers.

citadel You will enjoy an evening of dancing and entertainment.

citizen Your family will shortly experience a prosperous time. You also need to recheck a planned jobsite. It could

be hazardous to workers. If so, choose a different site.

Citizen's arrest Be careful of sharp objects and knife cuts. Be alert also to the behavior of a loved one. This person may need help for the next few days.

city Maintain your composure during a delicate period in order to buy time for a compromise. This dream also implies that you can expect grand changes in your life in any way you desire.

city blocks You are associating with a very imaginative person. This person lacks the funding to put this imagination to good use. You will be able to help and your assistance will benefit both of you.

to walk city blocks You will shortly be paid all the money that is owed to you.

city hall Keep your papers and bookkeeping in order. You can then determine and monitor what is being spent on another person's care.

city slicker Think ahead, you will be arrested for theft within a few days. This can be avoided.

civil defense You will let go or fire someone with a bad temper within a few days.

civil disobedience Pay attention to a young child's physical and emotional well being.

civilian You will notice that someone special to you has a new, more positive way of handling things. Do not be intimidated by this as it will work more to your advantage in future negotiations.

civil liberties Be aware of what a young child is ingesting. Take steps to prevent poisoning due to the ingestion of toxins or spoiled food.

civil marriage Two of your friends will be moving in together. This will be a good arrangement.

civil procession You will be taking huge steps to raise your standard of living. This will be accomplished by focusing on your goals in a grand way. Expect this to come about within three days due to an unusual and joyful circumstance. Everyone involved in this will enjoy beautiful expressions of joy and tranquility. Many blessings will be with you and your family.

hostile in any form You will receive a verbal threat that will affect you tremendously. Either this person is sure of who they are talking to or is mistaking you for someone else. In either case, this is an extremely dangerous situation to be involved in for the next three days. You need to increase your awareness in order to stay safe and clear of anyone's focus who has an evil intent. Because of your prior notice of this you will be able to avoid harm. Use any person you have at your disposal to make sure that you remain safe.

civil rights Ask for special consideration. It will be granted.

civil war Prepare for the occurrence of an earthquake within a two day period.

claim You are asked to go on a trip. Make a decision quickly or another person will be asked in your place.

clairvoyant *to see* Follow the advice given carefully because each word will come to pass. A negative message can still be changed and prevented.
if you are clairvoyant You will hear a shocking secret within the family. Keep this to yourself.
to be talking to a clairvoyant If you do not receive a message, find someone who can give you a prompt reading.
a clairvoyant in any other form This dream is a lucky omen and you will have victory with all of your ventures.

clam *to eat* You will enjoy the finest things in life and have sufficient funds to cover your expenses. This has been a concern of yours for some time.
in any other form You will be lucky in love and finances.

clambake You will receive a pleasant surprise and good news from friends. You will also receive extra money.

clamp Do not put undue pressure on someone unwilling now or in the future to commit to a relationship. Back off.

clamshell Be aware of emotional upsets while at an event you are in charge of, especially those involving entertainment. Be watchful and try to prevent this from occurring.

clan What appears to be a quick and easy way to make money will become a nightmare. You will regret your involvement in this decision if you do not take steps to remain uninvolved. Expect this within four days. You are also headed in the wrong direction, career wise. Back off and start from a different direction.

clandestine You will be charged for an item you did not receive or for unrendered services. Be alert to this for the next few days.

clansman Do not push away friendships because of the manner in which you treat others. Be especially careful of this over the next few days.

clap *(slang for gonorrhea)* Be good to yourself and reward yourself with a small gift.

clap *(to clap hands)* An overenthusiastic friend will be all fired up over taking a wonderful trip. Do not allow yourself to become caught up in the excitement. The trip will not take place and you could suffer disappointment if you do not

prepare ahead of time.

clapboard Watch out for a deadly bite in any form.

claret This dream is a very lucky omen. Look up the specific color of the wine for more detailed clues.

clarinet You have a brilliant idea. Follow this and you will be very successful.
to see another play or to hear one Recheck an address. You will be asked to pick someone up and will go to the wrong place. Make sure that you have the proper directions so you will arrive in a timely fashion.

clasp You will have a memorable time on a romantic date.

class Someone is aggressively pursuing you in a romantic way. This person is interested only in a short term sexual affair. It is your choice whether or not to pursue this. Think ahead.

class action suit Speculations in investments will pay large dividends.

class book Someone will feign a desire to start a family. Do not get your hopes up. This person will not be ready to become a parent.

classical A fantastic person will request your company on a venture. This will be very successful.

classmate You are interested in purchasing a musical instrument within a few days. This will not work out. Be sure to check refund policies at the time of purchase.

classroom Someone you care deeply for will lead you to believe they desire a long term relationship. You will be disappointed because this person will let you down at the last moment. Think ahead.

claustrophobia You will have a fantastic time in a new city. Each moment will produce wonderful memories. You will enjoy a safe return.

claw Watch out for dangerous falls. Take extra precautions to protect yourself for the next two weeks.
to be clawed It will soon become clear that someone has deep feelings for you and is hopelessly in love. This emotion will develop very rapidly and this person will barely be able to contain themselves. You will finally be rid of the character trait of not focusing enough on your relationship. You will then become very consistent in giving your time not only to those relationships that are important but also anything that requires this behavior. Expect this change to last a lifetime. You are on the path toward a brilliant future.

claw hammer You will finally enjoy victory over an unbearable situation and will soon be free of this burden.

clay *to see an object made from clay* You will get what you want from a love relationship.

to work with You will receive a large settlement after winning in a financial dispute.

to dream of a clay statue falling apart at a touch Do not allow anyone to shatter your dream or visions.

clay pigeon Watch out that you do not harass a noisy neighbor. Tolerate this person and do not make demands.

clean Information you received about a plan is incomplete. Dig deeply to uncover accurate information about a situation involving your new plans to ensure a positive outcome. You will also ask for services on credit within three days. You have every intention of paying this person but situations will arise that prevent this. Do not take on any credit for the time being.

clean and jerk You will enjoy a fantastic sex life with a great partner.

cleanliness You will be able to draw a seemingly disinterested and elusive person toward you. For the next four days this person will demonstrate a greater enthusiasm and more affection toward you.

cleanser Maintain your sense of humor.

clean shaven The person you are interested in romantically is not of the same sexual orientation as you.

clearance sale You will receive good news from an old friend whom you have not seen in years.

cleat Within three days, you will be pursued aggressively by a married person. In spite of all temptations, resist all enticements and remain uninvolved. You will soon find someone to make a new life with who is more suited to you.

cleavage You will achieve a very special goal. Someone with extensive knowledge and experience in a certain field will extend a training program and mentorship once they are aware of your interest. This will be free of charge and will occur within seven days. This will offer you a lifetime of benefits and financial security.

cleaver You will be given the gift of greater mental inventiveness and intelligence. This is a blessed gift.

blood on the blade This dream implies that your success will come quicker than expected.

to be stabbed in the back with a blade Confirm that there are no obstacles between yourself and someone who is eagerly trying to communicate with you.

cleft palate Be careful to prevent the loss of limbs or serious injury to the limbs.

Cleopatra You will be making dramatic changes in your life soon. For example, you will move to a larger house or from the suburbs to the city. This will leave you feeling emotionally fulfilled.

clergy That special person thinks only of you.

clerical collar Do not watch your pennies so closely. Loosen up a bit.

clerk You will have to replace a broken appliance within a few weeks. You will find a good used one at a bargain price.

click You will become prosperous when you least expect it as a result of the success of an ongoing project.

click beetle Control yourself morally around a young child.

client Do not allow yourself to be cheated in business dealings. Use caution.

cliff *any form (to be on the edge of something you can fall from, i.e., cliff, building)* This dream is a warning to you to remain calm, stable and non argumentative during an upcoming family situation. Take steps to stay clear of this situation.

to climb up This represents a progression toward your goals. You will be able to realize your ambitions within three days, free from all obstacles.

to climb down Look for another job and make changes for a better life.

anything climbing down This represents a negative forthcoming event that may be changed in reality. You will also hear from someone you have desired to get in touch with. Expect this within four days.

to fall down You will hear of the death of a male member of the family.

climb over This is a very lucky cycle for you. Anything you choose to accomplish will come to a quick and successful resolution within three days. Anyone you wish to bring closer will comply. This is a very lucky cycle and will remain lucky for the next seven days.

in any other form Either you or someone you recognize from this dream is coming dangerously close to mishandling a situation in such a way that will drastically change the way one of you lives. This will result in stagnation. Within three days you or this other person will need to come to grips with what you are about to undertake. Make sure it is not mishandled to the point of a financial collapse. You have prior notice of this and can take steps to prevent it and to warn anyone you recognize from the dream. Many blessings are with you and you are headed for a prosperous future if you heed this warning.

climax Your deepest desires will be granted and you will enjoy a long and healthy life. You will also achieve success in all of your ventures.

climb Someone who is sexually interested in you will give you a small expensive gift.

to climb up You will recover quickly from a serious illness. A business proposal will also be brought to your attention within two days. This will be luckier than you ever imagined and it will bear fruit for you.

to see someone climb over a fence You and the person you recognize going over the fence will motivate yourselves in an unusual way that will enable you to get in touch with an, as yet, unknown person. You and the person in this dream will both have this experience although they will be totally unconnected. Conversations will flow easily between you and the person you have yet to meet, in a delightful way. You will both have the feeling that you have not experienced this in a long time, if ever. The person you will meet possesses an artful sense of timing as well as the unusual ability to sense the feelings of other people. They are capable of bringing pleasure to others and of fully committing themselves. They are also able to put themselves in a subservient role, tastefully and within limits, as well as having the capability of pampering others to the extreme, but not overly so. You will find this to be very delightful and will never have a distasteful moment. If you choose to have a relationship, it will grow as much as you want and will be a mutually satisfying and nurturing union. Expect this to occur within three days and alert the person you dreamed about to expect this as well. You are headed for a brilliant future.

clinic A creative service you are performing from your home will yield great financial success within seven days.

women's Any negative event you saw in this dream needs to be altered in reality. You have plenty of prior warning to ensure that you experience only positive events in your life. Anyone you recognize in this dream should also be forewarned to avoid any negative message that is connected to this clinic. Within a few days, you will be in the company of someone who will promise many things in order to keep you interested in them. This individual is desperate to keep you from separating from them. In reality, they are going through many transitions and undergoing a great deal of stress in their life and it will be impossible for them to deliver on everything they want. This person will quickly recover from this and within two weeks will be able to deliver on the promises they made. Although you can now see through these promises, hold back if you are interested in this person because they will be in great danger both financially and emotionally in the future. Everything will work out exactly as they have envisioned. You will both enjoy an abundance of health and are headed for a brilliant future.

in any other form This dream is a warning that a very malicious person will come to you with a very trustful demeanor and will lead you to believe that anything you tell them will be kept strictly confidential. In reality, this person is pumping you for information about a third party for the express purpose of carrying your words back to them. Be alert to this situation because they will confront you with what you have said about them and this could escalate to a violent episode. You have prior notice of this and can take steps to ensure that it does not happen. Trust no one and keep your feelings about others to yourself. Any negative event you saw needs to be altered in reality.

clinician You will take a lot of pressure for the next two days because you will stand up for another person's rights.

clip Be diplomatic when dissuading the friendship of someone who periodically pops into your life. If you do not, you will have to associate with this person for a long time. You do not need this type of friendship. Be firm and do this within two days.

clipboard You will meet an influential person at a friend's house. This person will spot an ability within you that will be beneficial to their business. You will be asked to work for this person temporarily at a high salary. This is a solution to your financial problems and will benefit both of you. Expect this within five days.

clipper You will enjoy a fantastic sex life. Within four days you will begin to see an improvement.

clipper ship This is not the time to divulge your plans to someone else. Within two weeks do everything you can to keep personal and business affairs a secret. You will also be going through a very enjoyable cycle for the next seven days. Trust your hunches and go with what you feel. You can expect a prosperous future.

clitoris Someone will be eager to be with you in a sexual way within three days. This person will go to great lengths to ensure that you are both satisfied and fulfilled.

cloakroom You will overhear a conversation that contains information about another person. This information will shock you. Keep this to yourself, especially for the next three days.

clock All negotiations will have good results for the next week. Think ahead, someone you hire to do repair work will give you a different estimate than was originally agreed upon. Get this in writing within two days and refuse to accept verbal agreements. It is also important that you do not behave rudely or continually check the time when in the presence of another. This person will be insulted. Otherwise, this dream is a lucky omen.

to hear a clock tick This dream indicates that you should not waste time when pursuing a project.

to look at a clock and note the time This is a lucky omen. If you have an important event scheduled within the week, attempt to schedule it at the time you dreamed about for greater success. Any hurdle you wish to resolve will be worked out in this time frame and an anticipated great event will occur at this specific hour. An unexpected romantic interlude will also occur within five days and will leave a lasting memory.

clock radio You need to help someone who is suffering from a mental illness. You will do this by seeking alternative treatments and medications as soon as possible.

clockwork You will spend more money on a special event than you imagined. Prepare a budget for this within the month.

clog Make sure that you have good air circulation. Take steps to ensure this.

cloisonné Convince family members to unite. Aim for more closeness.

clone You will find the solution, with medical assistance, to recurring pain within the week.

close You will nurture love to full bloom within three days with the person of your choice. You are loved far more than you can imagine. Do not deprive yourself of the deep feelings that are being offered to you. You will experience a great love and appreciation from others within the week.

to have something or someone close to you or to someone else that makes you feel uncomfortable You will begin to undergo a strong emotional pull that will take up a lot of your time because you will have no idea where this drive comes from. This urge will cause you to focus on bringing something into reality. It will continue for two weeks and you will continue to feel this deep emotional craving. During this time period, you will uncover the root and reason for this feeling and will start acting on it. You have prior notice of this and if you feel this is socially unacceptable you will have the time to seek professional help. This will allow you to come to grips with your desires and to live in peace with them. Start seeking help the moment you sense this starting to develop. You are destined to find the perfect person to help you during this time period. It will be properly addressed and you will gain a healthy control of your emotions.

for you or someone else to be close to a finish line or the conclusion of something Make sure that any negative event does not become a reality and take steps to ensure that you experience only positive events in your life. You will also come to sudden wealth from an unexpected and unusual source that will take place without any action on your part. You will have the wisdom and foresight to correctly direct this fortune into a comfortable lifestyle and enjoy a very prosperous future.

to hear that you or someone else is moving closer to a certain situation or area A number of delightful events will start occurring one after the other at a rapid pace and this will leave you with a sense of awe, wonder and joy. You will also discover within yourself a powerful energy that you will be able to direct and control. You will, because you have prior notice of this, be able to direct this energy to successfully complete anything you wish in a superior way. You will also be able to overcome any difficult obstacle and it will now be an easy matter to handle any new problem that comes up. Your intuition is right on target and many bless-ings are with you and your family.

to draw the edges of something together closely (i.e., incision)/to pull closer to another person/to have another person pull you closer to them Within two weeks, you will unexpectedly advance to a higher plane in life than you ever anticipated. You will enjoy an abundance of productivity, productive conversations, and an increase in your income. You will be surrounded by loyal and affectionate people who will express a wish to be a part of your plans and who will offer their assistance. These people will be willing to teach you the knowledge they have acquired as well as anything else you wish to learn. This will be very important to you within the next five days. You are headed for a brilliant future and will enjoy an abundance of health. This will occur in a shorter period of time than you ever anticipated.

to be unable to get close or not allow yourself to get close to anyone Remain alert and guard those things you feel very passionate about, especially for the next three days. This will ensure that you will enjoy a prosperous life.

to see something up close This dream is a promise that everything will work out if you just give it time and take calculated risks. Good luck and many blessings are with you, especially for the next three days.

to dream of trying to get close to someone in any form but they refuse to come to you Be very wary for the next five days. Someone who has promised to leave your life at your request will fail to keep their promise. Take the time to prepare yourself for this to keep from being pinned down by this individual. Make it very clear to them that you want no involvement. Organize your thoughts and feelings and do not allow anyone to think you will commit to something you are unwilling to. Be sure that you are not misunderstood. You will successfully get your point across in an inoffensive way. Proceed with caution and you will be able to handle this delicate issue.

close *(shut)* *to close something* Within five days you will be dealing with a certain individual who will mislead you into believing that they are respectable, professional, stable in their career, financially secure and lead a very credible lifestyle. This person will be very eager to involve you in their life in some capacity. Because of their believability and the comfort you feel in their company you will also want to become involved with them. This person will give you every indication that you will have easy access to them at any time you choose. You will be given phone numbers, company addresses, etc. as assurance. If you take the time to track this person down, you will find that it is impossible to reach them at their company or any of the phone numbers. It will take days for this person to return any calls. It will dawn on you that this person has a far less impressive lifestyle than they have led you to believe and if you involve yourself in any capacity you will suffer disappointment. Become very shrewd and disciplined to keep this person from violating your emotions or insulting your intelligence. You will be able to handle this successfully. You are in a lucky cycle and will enjoy a prosperous future.

to try to close someone or something out You will uncover a mysterious and deep plot that another person or persons have devised to use against you. You have enough notice to take the necessary steps to turn this around to a positive experience. Do not allow yourself to fall prey to anyone else for reasons known only to them. You are otherwise headed for a prosperous future.

to close a window to keep something or someone out Be keenly aware of where you are allowing someone to lead your feelings. This person will, for reasons known only to them, mislead you into believing that they are completely in love with you. Words of love may or may not be used at this time, but an atmosphere of romance will be created by this individual (i.e., flowers, gifts, romantic outings, etc.). Your feelings will grow very deep for this person but if you allow this individual to make love to you they will not touch you in a way that suggests love. You will feel very empty and cold as a result. You will not be able to connect on the level of love you felt was there and you will not be loved, touched or kissed in any way that is special although this person will make an attempt to fulfill this need. Rather than put yourself through this, you have enough notice to avoid this scenario completely. Get on with your life without this person and the emotional upheaval that will go along with this situation. A hidden agenda is at play here that will require you to do something for this person that only they are aware of. Avoid this because it will only lead to unhappiness. Otherwise, within the week you will start on a path toward a prosperous future.

closeout You will uncover a mysterious plot that someone has conspired with others against you. You have prior notice of this and can take the necessary action to turn this around into a positive experience. Do not become prey to anyone else for their own hidden reasons. Other than this situation, you are headed for a prosperous future.

close quarters You will be very shocked to discover that someone has developed a very mysterious and deep plot against another person. Do not become involved. You will hear about this within three days.

closet Think ahead, you will have an unplanned opportunity to speak in private to someone within the week. Move quickly to communicate those important words to this person you have wanted to say in order to quickly conclude an ongoing situation as well as ensuring that you are included in an upcoming one.

close to This dream is alerting you that you will have major doubts about certain plans, projects, etc., that you are dealing with for the next three days. You will feel as though they are spiraling downward, malfunctioning, or failing in some way. You will have the strength to get through this and the result will be completely opposite to what you thought it would be. Move forward and everything will turn out exactly as you hoped they would and you are headed for a brilliant future.

closet queen An unusual, extraordinary event will take place that will make you unexpectedly wealthy. This will

develop and occur within three days. This money will come from a very stable source.

close up You will become aware that someone you know will try to reform someone else's behavior by using temperamental and heavy handed methods. Think ahead. You will be able to counteract this by thinking clearly and by using your communication skills. You will be able to make others feel more comfortable and more agreeable and successfully diffuse this situation. You will also receive good news during this cycle.

clot You will emerge victorious from a depressing time because you will reach for and grasp your goal. You will reap what you sow. You must also prepare yourself for a remarkable and unusual event that will take place within three days. You will concurrently be able to think through each step you need to take to comfortably get through this cycle. Your curiosity will be especially keen during this three day period and you must be firm and disciplined in order to keep your curiosity at bay. You will also enjoy an abundance of health during this cycle.

cloth This dream is a lucky omen. You will have an abundance of life's pleasures for several months. Someone you have not noticed is eagerly trying to attract your attention for the purposes of asking you out. If you choose to pursue this, it will be a successful relationship.

sack cloth Your wishes will be fulfilled.

clothes *fashionable clothes* An old friendship will develop romantically within four days. If you choose this path, you will enjoy a long relationship. Sophistication, honor and elegance are yours for the asking.

soiled clothes Beware of someone with immoral conduct. Be sure that you do not become influenced by this person.

flashy clothes An old friend will become affectionate and will come on to you sexually. This promises to be a long relationship, if you choose.

to have your clothes stolen You will gain love and will receive a marriage proposal.

to steal clothes Take steps to avoid burn injuries.

to borrow clothing Prioritize your responsibilities.

damaged or burned clothes You will unexpectedly receive a large amount of money from an unexpected source.

embroidered clothes You will enjoy a long, healthy and prosperous life.

gold lame or gold embroidered clothes You will enjoy a brilliant future.

disheveled clothing You will find a home of your own.

to fold clothes Within the week you will be developing a creative project that will lead, in less than a year's time, to a profitable money making venture. The more clothes folded indicates the faster that this will take place.

folded in a stack You will quickly reach a cherished goal. This will create a feeling of fulfillment. Within two days you will also feel overjoyed by the good news you hear.

in a pile or scattered on the floor Within five days someone will start creating an unusual scenario that will allow them to violate your rights for the sole purpose of satisfying their own emotional gratification. Be acutely aware of this to avoid being caught off guard. This person will do everything in their power to cause you to fall into their trap. You have prior notice of this and can take steps to guard against this distasteful situation. Proceed with confidence. Good luck is with you.

clothes in a hamper Someone is making a big issue out of a small situation. Take an active personal role in handling this responsibly before it becomes too large to easily control. Take care of this within four days.

on a hanger Move forward with a certain person only with extreme caution, especially for the next three days. You will be dealing with someone whom you are beginning to develop a sense of closeness to. This individual will mislead you into believing you can fully confide in them and that their loyalty to you is absolute. You will also be led to believe that certain events will occur in the future that will never take place. This person is a master of deception and illusion and will go to great lengths to create an atmosphere of trust but, in reality, has a hidden agenda that involves pursuing you in some way. Because of their charm and charisma they will, if they believe you are becoming suspicious, create a crisis as a diversion. By the time you realize what is going on you will be undergoing deep emotional disappointments, disillusions and financial hardships. You will return your life to normalcy but it will take you some time to recover. You have all the ammunition you need and the necessary time to keep this from taking place. Use your common sense, do not become involved, do not compromise, and do not allow this person to pry into your affairs. You will be very successful in diffusing this issue. You are headed for a prosperous future. Many blessings will come to you and your family.

to dream that you cannot find some of your clothes due to misplacement, etc. This dream is a very lucky omen but you need to be very selective about what you are willing to apply your energies to. This will be regarding any project, certain ideas, plans, etc., that will be offered to you by others. Once you have made a choice from the many opportunities you will be offered, make sure you have given yourself a chance to explore as many of them as possible and then apply yourself fully to this project. Approach everything on a grand scale. You will enjoy a burst of creativity that will enable you to succeed at a higher level than you thought possible. You are headed in the right direction and are on the path to prosperity. Expect to gain a wealth of opportunities and an abundance of wealth.

to be reluctant to remove clothes This dream serves as a warning that you will be overcome by guilt about something you will do that you were against from the start. This situation will come up within two days and you will need to take a stand against it. Look carefully at everything you are tempted to become involved with on any capacity. You will also enjoy an abundance of health during this cycle, but you need to take all the necessary steps to avoid involvement in anything you should not become involved with.

wrinkled clothes Be prepared, for the next three days, for something remarkable, peculiar and unusual to take place. You have the clarity of greater thought to take you comfortably through this time period. Your curiosity will also be very keen during this cycle. Be very firm, discipline yourself and do not allow your curiosity to take control. You will enjoy an abundance of health during this time period.

for someone else to be reluctant to take off their clothes This dream is a warning that you will be stricken with guilt about something you will do that you were opposed to. This will come up within two days and you need to take a stand against it. Look more carefully at what you are willing to involve yourself in. Also, you will enjoy an abundance of health during this cycle but you need to take steps to avoid becoming involved in something you should not become involved with. Also, make sure that anything negative connected to this dream does not become a reality.

underclothes You will be speaking with someone you are interested in being involved with. Make sure you handle yourself in a straightforward manner. Let this person know what is distasteful to you, and what you are willing to do so you can work together for a mutually fulfilling relationship.

in any other form You will experience victory in those areas of your life that you most desire. All those things you felt were impossible are now within your grasp and you are headed in the right direction, especially for the next two weeks. Trust your intuition; your hunches are right on target.

clotheshorse You will reach your goals and achieve prosperity.

clothesline Come to a decision with that special person about what you want and need from life. For the next three days, all business proposals presented to you involving another person will provide you with a brighter future than you have ever envisioned. All conversations will bring a new closeness that will be a benefit to everyone involved in the process. Good luck and many blessings are coming your way. You are on the path toward an abundantly prosperous future.

clothes moth You will have riches connected with your career.

clothespin Your partner will soon have a financial boom and you will both share in this abundance. A distasteful and uncomfortable situation is also rapidly coming your way. Within three days, you will need to take steps to avoid this. Begin taking action the moment you see the situation start to develop, because it will quickly escalate and be hard to handle once it has gotten out of control.

wooden Within three days you will meet with a very elusive person. Tell this person exactly what you need and want out of this meeting. Use this cycle to accomplish this task.

clothes tree Stay on the good side of the law. Do not put yourself in the position to be incarcerated.

clothing store Within the week, you will develop a feeling of being solidly grounded and will enjoy a new sense of balance and confidence. As a result, you will be able to tackle issues that require this aspect of your personality. Use this cycle to change those areas of your life you desire to make changes in. You will have the chance to bring prosperity into your life at the level you desire and are on the path toward a brilliant future.

cloudburst Stay longer and work to develop roots in a relationship. Allow growth.

clouds *beautiful clouds* You are making the correct decisions and are heading in the right direction.
dark clouds Be friendlier and bond closer to those who are important to you.

clove Think ahead and do not allow yourself to be intimidated by another to the point of stagnation. Tear down those walls of intimidation in order to better your life.

cloven hoof A very dangerous situation will arise within five days. You will be physically injured because of someone else's unusual behavior. Be prepared to protect yourself at all costs. You have prior notice of this and can take steps to prevent it.

clover That special person is faithful to you.
sweet clover You will have a very happy and mutually satisfying sex life.

cloverleaf Push yourself to think positively. Force yourself to include romance in your life while you still have the opportunity to choose from a variety of people. This will allow growth in you life.
four leaf You will secure a position of power in a large corporation. This dream is a very lucky omen and will bring you honor.

clown Do not ask too much of a young person. This person will be unable to handle this much responsibility.

club You will enjoy good fortune and an end to all obstacles in the pursuit of your ventures. You will soon receive some beautiful messages in your dreams. Follow these messages to enhance your life. You will achieve the life you want for yourself and for your family.

club *(dance)* You will be paid for escort services and this will be very profitable.

clubfoot You will suffer sadness over the break up of two companies seeking a merger. You will discover later that this was a better alternative.

clubhouse Blessings will come your way. You are deeply loved by a new acquaintance.

club member You will be involved in an angry stressful situation and will receive unexpected help to overcome this problem.
to be a club member Communicate with others and make it easy for someone to communicate their loving feelings to you. This dream is a lucky omen and you will enjoy a successful outcome.

club room You will go from rags to riches within a few years and this will be as a result of much help from others.

club sandwich You will become heir to a large inheritance before this person passes away.

club soda You will be invited to a social function and will meet new friends who will invite you to more events. You will enjoy a full social life.

clue You will find a lost object and will be highly rewarded.

cluster headache Do not focus on someone else's problems for the next seven days.

clutch Avoid air travel for the next few weeks.

Clydesdale Do not present a confusing and suspicious manner toward others. You will also enjoy yourself immensely at a performance of some kind. You will enjoy popularity and party invitations will run rampant. Good luck is with you.

Clytemnestra *(Greek mythology)* Be very cautious and avoid any area that could expose you to explosions. Avoid any situation that may put you close to one.

coach Do whatever is necessary to prevent crop damage.

coachman Protect your plants in any way possible for the next few weeks.

coal Do not expose yourself to a virus.

coal oil Avoid dealing with caustics that can damage your skin.

coast Trust your heart and express your deepest emotions to another.
scenic This dream is lucky and will bring an abundance to the family.

coaster Do not allow another person to put you on an emotional roller coaster. Avoid this unhealthy relationship.

coast guard Practice preventive medicine and drive carefully.

coastline *(rocky seaweed covered)* Become assertive in your approach to bring a particular individual closer to you.

Behave in such a way that this individual will feel comfortable enough in your presence to say those words you have longed to hear. Many blessings come to you and your family, and you are headed for a prosperous cycle.

coat *black coat* You will enjoy an invitation to a festive elegant event. This dream is a lucky omen.

coat of many colors Someone will want to confess a problem behavior to you.

mink coat You will become attracted to someone whose sexual appetite is a lot greater than yours. This individual will go to great lengths to involve you in their life in an excessive manner. Think carefully about this situation in order to act in the most appropriate manner so you do not miss out on this person's love and affection. But you must also get the message across clearly that their sexual appetite is much larger than yours. This individual will quickly take steps to accommodate you in order to keep the relationship mutually satisfying.

top coat Make sure you are self reliant for the next two days and that you take the time to look at both sides of an issue. Explore the possibilities of what could unexpectedly take place before you make any major decisions. You are loved beyond your imagination, are deeply respected and will be surrounded by those who care a great deal about you. Other people will show their appreciation for you within the week.

torn You have been dealing with a situation that has been tearing you down emotionally. This situation will soon revert to a more normal and stable situation. You will feel relief from this burden. All mysteries surrounding this situation will be revealed. Good luck will be with you for some time.

white coat You will enjoy an unexpected love affair with a fantastic person. This affair will blossom if you choose.

in any other form Force yourself to finally complete a project. You are also deeply loved and appreciated by those around you.

coat hanger Do whatever you can to build a strong foundation on which to base a relationship. You will finally find the solitude you have long desired.

coat of honor/arms Do not allow your honor and principles to be tarnished.

coattails Do not allow interference from others to bias a decision. Do not ask others for their opinions.

cob Someone is trying to provoke you to fight. Avoid this person.

cobbler *(fruit)* You have the ability to transfer real estate into a real profit. This is the right time for you to accomplish this.

peach It is important for you to plan ahead for yourself and your family. Additional expenses will arise in the future.

cobbler *(shoe)* You will unexpectedly discover a cure for a long term illness.

cobblestone You will become a victorious, powerful person. This dream is a very lucky omen.

cobra A secretary or someone in a similar capacity will play petty games to promote jealousy for their own gratification. Do not concern yourself, nothing is really happening between this person and the person you care about.

cobweb *to brush aside* A fantastic new job opportunity is in the works.

to see Do not overindulge in anything.

cocaine Be aggressive and go after what you want. You will be successful.

cock Devote more time to an emotional relationship. This is an extremely lucky omen as well for money and love. You are definitely headed for a brilliant future.

cockapoo You will immediately find what you are searching for.

cockatoo Keep your own counsel.

cocker spaniel Protect your pets from fire. Take steps to prevent fires and take precautions to ensure that pets are safe.

cockfight Within a few days you will be a witness to an unexpected fight between two men. Stay away from the situation.

cocklebur You are planning to start a costly project without the necessary funds to back you up. You will, however, locate the necessary funding through an ongoing government project and will work closely with another person who complements your talents. You will enjoy a profit from this project. Begin this process within the week. This is the perfect cycle for success.

cockpit In the past you asked a close friend to give you a job. This person was in a position of power and could have granted you this wish but didn't. This person will shortly apologize for this oversight. You will also see in a dream a preview what will happen to a relative if a problem is left to develop. Help in any way you can.

cockroach You will receive sudden wealth for work well done. This is for a creative job and there is high demand for the finished product.

cocktail Do not insist on special privileges and considerations from yourself. Watch out for subliminal messages.

cocktail glass Make sure that you take all necessary steps to ensure a good outcome to any negative event witnessed in this dream, and do everything possible to only experience positive events in your life.

cocktail lounge This dream is a lucky omen. You will find stabilization of family problems and issues. Guard your cash. A close friend will also release you from a financial burden.

cocktail party Within three days you will be very clear about the changes you want in your life, the behaviors you wish to put a stop to, and anything new you wish to introduce into your life. Any negative event seen in this dream may be altered or avoided in reality.

cocky Be very careful and aware of someone you are associated with who will try to pull the wool over your eyes. This person will develop a clever plan to get you to commit to something they want without arousing suspicions. This plan, which is only known to this individual, will cause you a great deal of discomfort and irritation. You have prior notice of this person's intentions and need to do whatever you can to protect yourself. Otherwise you will receive abundances in other areas of your life due to opportunities that will be offered to you at this time.

cocoa You will be granted a favor by another.

cocoa butter Do not disassociate from an issue too soon. Stay until a successful resolution is reached. You will receive gratification from the stabilization of these issues.

coconut For the next few days do not believe everything you are told.

coconut milk *any form* Force yourself to make positive physical changes. You will shortly encounter a highly intelligent person who appreciates aesthetic beauty. This person will open doors for many exciting avenues that will lead to real life changes.

coconut oil Take care of yourself and do whatever you can to stay healthy.

coconut palm You will enjoy peace of mind and spirit and will receive happiness.

cocoon You will wish to purchase an item and another person will offer to buy it for you. Rely on yourself. You may lose out if you wait for another person.

cod Avoid doing anything in darkness. Use plenty of light.

code You will enjoy yourself immensely at a comedy club.

cod liver oil You will enjoy a sexual liaison with someone you have desired for a long time.
coffee Trust your instincts regarding a love affair. You will soon receive a marriage proposal if this is what you desire.

coffee cake This dream is a very lucky omen. You will have changes in your thought processes that will bring more improvements to your life. You will see these improvements in your behavior, and gain peace and greater tranquility within the next three days.

coffee maker During your quiet times you will be able to develop successful plans.

coffee pot Someone will blow the whistle on another's secret activities. You will come to hear of this soon.

coffee roll Everything will turn out better than you have anticipated. Any negative event can be avoided and it is important that you take steps to ensure that you only experience positive expressions in life.

coffee shop/house You will enjoy brunch with someone you have wished to spend time with. This will develop into a greater relationship. Within two days you will also begin to feel younger, will develop a new vigor and greater self esteem.

coffee table You will be used as a sounding board for another person's conflicts. Be aware of this and be patient. After talking for some time, this person will begin to gain clarity and find solutions to these conflicts. This dream is also letting you know that each of your requests will be granted. Pay attention also to any negative event witnessed in this dream and take steps to prevent it.

coffin You will attend an event that will rapidly turn sour because of words spoken by you at the wrong time and place. Prevent this.
    to see a corpse in coffin Within a month, you will receive a marriage proposal from someone who is in a different age group. This union will lead to becoming a beneficiary of this person's wealth.

cog You will love and enjoy the company of the same person for a lifetime.

cognac Within three days you will meet someone who is attracted to you. This person is seeing someone else therefore will be going through a juggling act. Ultimately, you will make more demands on this person. This will result in them choosing the other person.

cohabitation t*o ask someone to move in with you or to be asked to move in with someone* Take the most profitable course of action and you will find that your plans will be grander and come from a much improved and higher level. Your enterprise will be respected by others.
    to be asked to move out You will enjoy a mature growth of spirituality and also be able to handle a pressing responsibility in a way you were unable to do before. Within this three day period, you will be able to make clear choices and

make good use of your resources in order to complete your tasks.

coil Take caution with your surroundings. Someone is plotting your murder.

coin *gold* You will receive a marriage proposal.

silver You will be asked to join a company as a staff member.

foreign You will soon receive congratulations on past accomplishments and for work well done.

to find coins Completed hard work will bring you satisfaction and you will reap on abundance of prosperity in areas that you most desire.

coins *many coins* Step back and determine exactly what you are trying to prove and to whom. By doing this you will be able to develop a plan that will get you exactly what you are trying to accomplish. Good luck is with you.

cola *coca* You will attend an event and dance to your heart's content.

colander Transportation problems will come up soon. Take precautions to prevent this.

cold *to dream of anyone having a cold* Someone is very attracted to you. This person has sexual problems in connection with you due to their own fears. This problem did not exist before. They fear losing control and surrendering to you. Eventually, with patience, this problem will dissipate. It is your choice whether you choose to coach this person. Anything negative happening to you or anyone else you recognize should be changed to a positive situation. Do whatever is necessary to keep up your immune system to avoid catching a cold.

cold *(weather) to see yourself or someone else with the feeling of being cold* Do whatever is necessary to avoid anything negative happening to you or to anyone else you recognize from becoming a reality. Within the next five days focus on your private matters. Be more nourishing, kind and affectionate to others in areas you feel you should. This dream implies that within this same time frame you will rise to greater heights in areas you seek changes in. Expect satisfactory benefits to come to you at the nick of time.

in any other form You will gain great health, zest for life and more love and attention from others. Within the next three days do whatever is necessary to avoid anything negative that you saw from becoming a reality. In this same time frame you will also definitely find a solution to a problem. An advice given to you will be totally reliable. Proceed with confidence.

cold cream You will have direct communication with those in authority and in powerful positions.

cold cuts Do not push your luck concerning a job situation.

cold duck A long awaited marriage proposal will finally come. Even if you feel less than exuberant, add excitement to your answer.

cold pack An intoxicated person will spoil a good time. Watch for this in advance and leave the situation. Don't waste time with these people. It is also important not to allow others to dissuade you from pursuing your interests. For the next three days you will be in danger of being talked out of pursuing your goals.

cold shoulder Someone has plotted ways to get what they want and need from you, and you will be drained by this person's constant requests for favors they can do themselves. You must also become aware that you will be spending money on them, a little bit at a time. This money will add up over time. This person is also insincere and unable to be open and upfront with you. This individual is one thing to you and something else to others, and will tell people only what they think people want to hear. You would be better off without them in your life.

cold sore You will receive riches.

cold storage You will receive a gift of vegetables and fruits.

cold sweat Do not allow someone to place undue responsibility on you. Refuse to accept it.

coleslaw You will develop strength of character and a strong backbone. As a result you will achieve success.

colic *to experience* You are in danger. Beware of another person who is planning to physically injure you.

coliseum You are going too fast in a relationship. Slow down and allow the relationship to develop.

collage A secret love affair will be revealed. If you wish to keep it hidden, do everything necessary to conceal it.

collar Do not allow peer pressure to convince you to join a club you feel uncomfortable about. You are unsure of their motives for asking you.

collard greens Someone you hold in high regards will travel a great distance to see you. This will occur within five days. You are on the path toward a brilliant future.

collect *to collect or to see others collect money* You are underestimating a situation that you will be involved with within few days. Move on this before you let it slip through your fingers. This will be a golden opportunity.

collection *of anything* Take steps to ensure that other people value you for who you are instead of the power you possess or because of what you own. You will also enjoy an exotic vacation within two weeks. You will have a safe return.

collectors Someone is feeling very abandoned by you. Move quickly to ensure that this individual knows how special they are to you. This will bring them a great deal of pleasure and it will be deeply appreciated by them. Put your love into action and anything you desire on a permanent basis will occur within five days. This dream also implies that a gift of some kind will accelerate this development. You are loved beyond your imagination.

Collectors' item You are in a good position to demand what you need and want from your divinity. Your wishes will be granted. Within two weeks you will begin the process of reassessing your priorities. You will also make a list of plans that will enable you to live life far better than you are living it now and enable you to go through dramatic changes. Find a peaceful spot to relax and enjoy tranquility.

college You have a loyal, faithful friend. This person will be with you in times of trouble.

collie You will receive advice and sympathy when you need it. This advice will empower you.

cologne You will relocate in the near future and have a wonderful time in your new environment. Love is also in the air. Make sure a former love does not meet your present love.

colon An important foreign person will offer assistance in times of distress. This will happen shortly. The distress will involve paperwork but will be easily resolved.

colonel You will be swept away by the love and affection of another.

colony Do not overindulge in alcohol. Someone will also ask you kindly to forget the past because this friendship was interrupted by a misunderstanding. You will be willing to forget the past, but be sure to set limits on your behavior in order to avoid future misunderstandings.

color *for those who dye hair in reality* If the color of the dye is one that is totally unacceptable to you, be aware that certain chemicals on the hair may produce an unusual discoloration within the next three days.

off-color Someone you do not know well will, within three days, overly demonstrate a display of emotions that will make you feel uncomfortable. Many blessings will come to you and your family.

oil color For the next three days you will be channeling your energies in the right direction. Keep going in the direction you are going. For greater definition, look up the individual colors you saw in this dream.

in any other form Many brilliant colors seen at one time indicate a brilliant future. The color displayed in the dream represents a color you have not considered in the past. This color may be used for hair color, clothing, decorating, etc. Look up the specific color for a deeper, more detailed meaning. Also, bring into your life a series of specific events in order to add spice and zest to your life. You will be in this cycle for three weeks. Use this time to brighten your life. Good luck and many blessings will be with you during this time period.

Colorado Do not deprive yourself of anything you want for the next five days. Go for what you really want. This dream may also be used as a reference point in time. If you dream of this state and see its name used in any context, the dream message will occur on this day.

color blind A friend will be injured by a fall from a horse. This can be prevented by warning this friend.

coloring book You will enjoy many days with your grandchildren.

Colossians *(book of the Bible)* Make sure, for the next three days, that you do not lose your sense of alertness and do not let down your guard. Do not allow yourself to be talked into going somewhere that could represent a hazard to you, and do not become involved with anyone who could accidentally cause you injury. During this time period, it is important that you choose carefully what you will and will not become involved in.

Colossus of Rhodes You will learn of a friend who will be injured by breaking their jaw. Give your services to this friend until they are healed.

colostomy You will, in the near future, control powerful resources.

colt You will develop more power, greater intelligence and a better sense of well being.

Columbus Day You are entering a dynamic, prosperous cycle and are headed for a brilliant future. You can make specific demands from your higher power during this time period and they will come to pass regardless of how impossible they seem. You will also reach mutual agreements and understandings with a special person during this time period involving plans for the future.

column Carefully follow the instructions given with drug prescriptions.

coma You will soon be part of a powerful, professional group.

Comanche This dream is a good omen and you will be in a good cycle for the next two weeks. Focus on benefits that are due you that you may not be aware of.

comb Keep your life and thoughts private for a few days.

combat Within three days a new physician you contact for services will seem very aloof and detached. The moment you notice this, work on getting a different physician.

come If you choose this path, someone you are interested in will be eager to become a part of your life. Let your desires be known. You will enjoy many wonderful moments, sexual satisfaction and a mutually satisfying exchange within seven days. Aggressively pursue this. A little encouragement will allow this person to make the first move. Good luck is with you and your family.

to dream of wanting someone to be close to you in any form but they refuse to come to you For the next five days, be very cautious because someone you have asked to leave your life will go back on their promise to do so. Prepare yourself so you do not get pinned down by this person. Make it very clear that you want nothing to do with them. You will need to be emotionally equipped to deal with this delicate issue. Be sure to organize your thoughts and feelings so you do not allow anyone to pin you down and to think that you will commit to something you are unwilling to. You will successfully get your point across in a tactful way with no misunderstandings. Proceed with caution and you will be able to handle this delicate issue.

comedian For the next few months, greater power, greater intelligence and genius will be yours. Use it in every way you can.

comedy You will have a brilliant idea that will sustain you for some time, if put to use.

comedy club Within five days, a major decision that you are in the process of making will work out successfully.

comet This dream is a very lucky omen. Within two days you will hear a confidential secret about someone else. This will be very unexpected and this person will seek you out to speak to you about this matter. Be sure to keep this to yourself.

comfort *to have someone try to make you comfortable* Make it a point not to miss an event that has been scheduled within seven days. You will enjoy the company of two admirers who will go to great lengths to win your affections. Although it is not apparent to you, one of these people possesses a tremendous amount of authority and power. You will find both of these suitors to be very agreeable and charming and you would enjoy having one of them as a lifetime partner. You can have the confidence that you will enjoy a prosperous future.

comfortable *to make someone comfortable* Within five days you will overcome any long term situation you have been working on that has become a burden. Relentlessly work on any issue that you need to take care of. You are headed in the right direction and will soon experience the freedom that comes from ridding yourself of this issue. You

will experience many social events in the future. Proceed with confidence. Good luck is with you.

comforter *(person who comforts)* Make sure young children are comfortable in warm weather and are protected from the elements.

comforter *(bed cover)* Within three days the person you most desire will come to you for a very mutually fulfilling sexual encounter.

comic Love will come from an unexpected source. This will be a big surprise to you.

comic book An inexpensive collectible hobby will become valuable.

comic strip Do not allow yourself to be alone in an enclosed place with someone whom you know has extreme mood swings. This person could harm you. Be especially wary of this for the next three days.

command *any form* Gain control over your temper and take extra steps to control yourself. An unusual situation will arise that will create suspicious and jealous feelings in you. If you do not take precautions, these feelings will develop into an uncontrollable rage that will drive you to do something you will later regret. Do not feed into these suspicions. The moment you sense these emotions developing, seek professional help.

commander Use discretion in your behavior. Control your actions.

command post You will soon become engaged.

commando Do not allow someone's opinion to bias your decision about an upcoming matter. Watch for this over the next two days and be vigilant about sticking to your own counsel.

commencement You will spend hours in passionate foreplay with someone you desire.

commentator Be aware that you could be lonely and depressed for a long period of time. You can avoid some of this depression by preparing ahead of time. Take walks and window-shop to break this cycle.

commercial A beautiful sight will give you inspiration for a profitable idea. Watch for this.

commissary Do not waste time being kind to an unappreciative person.

commissioner Within three days negotiations will conclude successfully and you will be able to overcome any obstacle.

commitment Go for what you want to do most in life. This will bring you much success.

commode Watch out for and rid yourself of destructive habits. You have the strength to do this now.

common law marriage Do whatever is necessary to avoid being jailed. You will be injured by another inmate.

common sense *someone asks you to use your common sense* This dream implies victory in any area you desire.

commune Do not allow misfortune to control you emotionally. This situation will be short term.

communication It is extremely lucky to dream about communication in any form. Within this cycle, it must be a priority to use your communication skills appropriately and skillfully. This will allow you to change what you really want to change. This ability will allow you to bring prosperity into your life. You must also make sure that you play an active part in satisfying your emotional needs. Within five days you will be able to visualize the path you need to take for a brilliant future. Good luck is with you.

communism Someone will come to you unexpectedly with a wealth of exhaustive, plentiful ideas. These ideas will offer you the resources and a means to redirect your life in a positive and prosperous fashion. This will occur within five days. Do not put yourself down in front of others. Other people see a beauty that you are unable to recognize.

communist You will feel despair over the illness of an older relative. They will soon recover.

community You will run for local office and enjoy great success.

community college Be aware that a young person just beginning to have some freedom may be injured through the use of drugs. You can prevent this.

community property If you recognize this property and sense anything negative, take steps to change the outcome. You must also make sure that important information reaches the proper destination on the first attempt. You are deeply loved by those around you.

commuter Do not waste time by making the mistake of involving a friend in a business deal. This is likely to occur within two days.

compact *(small mirror container, etc.)* This dream is a good luck omen. Within two days, any creative ideas discussed in a group setting will quickly move forward.

compact disc Within two days you will receive a positive response to a request you have long waited for.

compactor Learn from your mistakes and don't dwell on them. Get on with life.

companion An inventive idea will lead to great benefits and financial security. This will occur within five days. Any negative action taking place in the dream may be avoided.

companionship Force yourself to determine what you are not doing to promote a better life. Focus on this and start working on it.

company Decide what you want to reform and act on it to promote a better lifestyle.

compass *drawing compass* Think ahead. Within two months you will be cheated out of a promotion. You have the time to change this and to ensure that it does not happen.
  mariner's compass This dream is an extremely lucky omen. You will enjoy yourself for the next five days and are headed for a brilliant future.

compassion You will receive news of a female family member's death.

compensation Avoid breaking an arm when participating in rough play.

competition *to compete and win* Your life will undergo a major turnover while you deal with a stressful situation. This will work out to our advantage.
  to have a competition You will have difficulty achieving sexual satisfaction. Prevent this by communicating your needs to your partner.

complain *to hear a complaint* Someone wants you sexually and does not know how to ask.
  to complain Someone you know will be hurt badly because of a fall from a high place. Warn anyone you know who works in high places that a fall could occur.

completion *to dream of being anxious to complete something* For the next three days be prepared for a remarkable and peculiar event to take place. At the same time this is going on you will enjoy the clarity of thought needed to take each step you need to comfortably get through this cycle. You must also be very firm and disciplined in order to keep your intense curiosity at bay. Expect to receive an abundance of health during this time period.

complexion You will meet a wonderful person and will be given the opportunity for romantic and lasting affection.
  bad Within three days you will become involved in a tug of war with another person to keep them from doing something you do not want them to do.
  to have a beautiful complexion Follow a diet that prevents the development of kidney stones. Drink plenty of water and keep yourself healthy.

compliment *you give a compliment* Do not allow another person to question your final hiring selections.
to be complimented Concentrate more on romance.

compose Someone in authority will take you under their wing. You will learn the expertise needed to generate wealth. This wealth will stay with you for a lifetime.

composer Wealth will rapidly come to you. You will also be the one who has the last word regarding a particular situation even if it does not seem so at this time. This is just the way things will work during this cycle. You are in a time period that will permit anything you desire to take place. You can confidently expect verification of love from someone you desire. You are deeply loved and will find permanent abiding love within five days with the person you want most in your life. Good luck is with you.

composition A relative's success will result in your wealth.

compost You have been seeing the same person for awhile and you are confused about the nature of this relationship. Others are also confused and will begin asking you questions. Clarify the nature of this relationship for your own peace of mind.

compound Within two days, you will receive a written message that will rekindle a relationship with someone who played an important role in your life. Reconciliations will move quickly ahead.

compress Do not practice deceit with people who do not deserve it.

compulsion Do not expose your skin to oil based toxins, such as poison ivy.

computer This dream is a lucky omen. You will be heir to a large inheritance from someone who will shortly pass away.

conceal You will enjoy domestic happiness.

conceit Do whatever you can to prevent an automobile accident. You have prior notice of this and have the time to take precautions.

concert Do not listen to what others tell you about the person you care about. These people will attempt to break up your relationship. Do not pay attention to them and get on with your life.

concert master Do not waste time trying to seek a meeting with someone you expect can be talked into seeing your side of a story. This will not happen.

concert piano *(grand)* A wonderful person will enter your life for a while, and this will be a great time for you. Enjoy it

while it lasts because this person will soon move away.

concession *(stand or booth)* Do not allow another person to put you in a position of humiliation.

conch shell You will find yourself in a beautiful, unplanned romantic setting. If you choose, this will rapidly develop into a passionate evening.

concord Take a strong stand concerning financial dealings. You deserve more than you are offered. Relentlessly pursue this and you will be successful.

concrete Be watchful for anything that may result in an accident to your legs and feet.

concubine *any form* For the next four days, circulate in select areas and you will be able to determine first hand what needs to be taking place in your life. Any negative event in this dream needs to be avoided in reality.

concussion *to see someone suffering a concussion* Hard work will pay off financially. Also, you will soon be part of a powerful, professional group. Anything negative needs to be changed. Experience only positive expressions in your life.

condemn Stay warm and well covered for the next few days in order to avoid illness.

condensed milk Stop being so arrogant and self righteous. The attitude that you are better than others is the wrong one to display. Listen to what others are saying to you.

condiment You will enjoy a festive happy reunion.

conditioner *(hair)* This is a warning to you that within a three day period you will be associating with someone who is extremely aware of your preferences in lifestyle and the situations you refuse to enter. This person will use methods of subtle persuasion and will formulate a plan to lead you into the lifestyle you reject. Their intent is to lure you into doing something that goes against everything you believe in. This person will use a number of different tactics to get you to do their bidding. This persuasion will be done stylishly and in the manner of gift giving, vacations, etc. It may take a long time and many gifts but you will end up doing as they wish. You have enough notice to handle the situation appropriately. Otherwise, you are headed for a brilliant future.

condom The contraceptive methods you are using will fail. Seek alternative methods. Within five days the barriers you have erected to protect your privacy and well being also stand a good chance of being infiltrated. Take care to strengthen your barriers and keep this from occurring.

condominium Someone you know is actively trying to get your attention. You have never really noticed this person before but the relationship will be very good if you choose to pursue it.

condor Do everything necessary to develop a healthy relationship with the person you care about.

cone This dream indicates harmony. You will feel tranquility with yourself and your relatives during this cycle and you will sleep easier.

Conestoga Do not allow anyone to harass you to the point of giving up something you cherish. Be very firm and put a stop to someone else's abusive behavior toward you, especially for the next week.

Coney Island You and a casual acquaintance will decide to take a short trip. This will be eventful and you will acquire many cute souvenirs. This dream may also be used as a reference point in time. If you dream of this island and see its name used in any context, the dream message will occur on this day.

Coney Island hot dog You will be very surprised and elated when someone expresses their true feelings for you. This will be someone you have long admired but felt was unreachable. Expect this within five days.

Confectioner's sugar Assess your present situation within two days to ensure that you take the correct steps forward.

confections You will be invited out by a powerful, influential person. During a conversation you will learn you have a great deal in common and both of you will want to see more of each other. You will enjoy this wonderful outing.

confederate Do not allow anyone to criticize you in public.

conference table *to be having a meeting* Someone special to you will talk about a staff problem that is irritating and wearing on the nerves. Heed this person's words.

confession Someone will make a confession to you and you will learn that someone you think is a good friend considers you a mere acquaintance. This will shock you but you will recover.
    you confess Take steps to avoid hurting the feelings of another.

confessor You will be wealthy in a short period of time because of an undertaking. You are going in the right direction.

confetti Every day will be like a holiday from now on. You will also be financially secure for a lifetime. Several unexpected functions will occur one right after the other and you will be overwhelmed with invitations that you will be able to pick and choose from. Make certain you do not turn down one particular function because this one will be far more

exciting and glamorous than any of the others. You will be required to dress in formal attire, so be sure you prepare yourself in plenty of time so you will be in your best form. Do not deprive yourself of this event because you will enjoy yourself tremendously and will meet many influential people who will be friends for a lifetime. You will win a door prize at this gathering. You will also become aware during this time frame that someone you deeply desire feels the same way about you. You will enjoy mutually affectionate feelings and will both be very excited about this new development. You are headed for a very prosperous and brilliant future.

confidence man Do not allow yourself to be talked into a one night stand.

conflict For the next two weeks your loved ones will be very agreeable to all your suggestions.

Confucius This dream implies victory and a dynamic international position for you.

Conger Eel You feel a deep emotional love for someone. This person suffers from a mental illness and involvement would mean an unhappy life.

congestion The person you are interested in is of a different sexual orientation than you.

Congo A long time enemy will suddenly become a true friend for life. This dream may also be used as a reference point in time. If you dream of this place and see its name used in any context, the dream message will occur on this day.

congratulations You will receive congratulations and will be promoted to a long awaited position.

congregation Compromise and demonstrations of physical love will be rewarded.

congress You will be elected to the office you seek. This will be an awesome cycle for you.

Congressional Medal Quick decision-making will lead to success. Victory is yours.

congressman A younger person will be instrumental in helping you to quickly achieve your goals.

conifer You will experience an unexpected and wonderful surprise within three days. Good luck will follow you for the next week.

Connecticut You will be able to perform properly in order to meet another's romantic demands for the next three days. This dream may also be used as a reference point in time. If you dream of this state and see its name used in any context, the dream message will occur on this day.

connoisseur You will be involved in a relationship with someone who is not fully committed. This person will run hot and cold and the relationship will become on again off again. You have prior notice and may choose not to get involved.

conquistador You are unsure of the career you want. Eventually you will find success in the public arena.

conscience Follow your conscience. You are in a position of power and will be able to make dynamic decisions.

consecrate Copyright and patent all of your ideas and creations.

conservatory Help a relative decide about the placement of an older person in a nursing home. The decision will be easier to make with your vote of confidence.

consignment shop You will come into riches from an area that was presently unknown to you. Move ahead on this with confidence.

consolation prize You will be a winner in life and will also be granted a long awaited favor.

console table Beware of infections from insect bites.

consommé You will receive a gift of copper jewelry. This will bring you much joy.

consonant Watch your mate carefully. Body language may indicate a health problem. If dealt with soon, it will be cured.

conspiracy Be aware of your surroundings. Focus on what does not seem in place. Pay attention to what is really happening.

constable You will receive good news via mail within two days.

Constantine Think ahead. You are entering a cycle of high energy and creative thought. Take advantage of this time to tackle high priority projects and to tie up loose ends.

constellation Take steps to avoid the company of a suspicious acting person. Your feelings that this person has a hidden agenda is correct. Follow your hunches. You will also receive word that someone desires a total commitment from you in a relationship. If you choose this path, you will enjoy a stable and long lasting relationship.

constitution *(body)* Your complexion will clear up and you will be very happy that everything you tried has worked for improvement.

Constitution *(U.S.)* When choosing from a variety of people who will serve on a board of directorship, make sure you choose those who are loyal to you and your ideas.

construction What you are now taking for granted will be a cause for regret in the future. Take care of your goals and treat your loved ones better. Take nothing for granted.

construction paper New turns of events that take place within two days will affect your romantic life immediately. Make sure you will be doing exactly what you want to be doing.

construction worker Give a delicate situation more time. Compromise more for the next five days. A flexible manner will be more advantageous than you can imagine. Be patient and hang in there until everyone can reach an agreement. This will produce less stress and will work to your advantage.

consultant You are being taken for granted by a young adult in the family. Handle this tactfully and gently. Correct this young person and get on with your life.

consumer *any form* Watch for falling objects for the next three days.

contact lens Take care of your eyes. Make sure you are wearing the correct eye wear. Blind dates are also very lucky.

contagion You will hear of a going out of business sale and you will find bargains here. This will also work to the advantage of the business owner.

container Within three days you will show a renewed interest in an old hobby. This will bring you extra profits in the future and will add enjoyment to your life.
full container The person you are considering involving in a particular situation will work out wonderfully and your project will bear fruit. You are headed in the right direction, especially for the next three days.
empty container Check your sources of transportation to ensure that you are not delayed due to mechanical breakdown. This is likely to occur within three days.
plastic food containers For a two day period, do everything you can to lobby for a connection with those you want to steer in your direction. Relentlessly seek these people and get your point across until you are able to sway them to your position. Your actions will ensure that everything falls into place to your advantage and for everyone else involved. Many blessings will come to you and your family and you are headed for a brilliant future.

contaminant Do not expose yourself to viruses. If you recognize someone in your dream, avoid this person. This is the individual who will expose you to illness.

contamination Within three days, a situation will arise involving two people of equal power who will face off against each other to prove who is the most powerful. Emotions will run high because everyone will be interested in who will be the victor. The older of the two will come out on top and everyone involved will be happy with the outcome. You will also experience a financial windfall and are definitely headed in the right direction.

contentment You will enjoy contentment and a long life.

contest *if you win* You will be a big winner in life.
if you lose Make changes in your plans to ensure that you will be a winner in life.

contestants Be careful of financial fraud and fraudulent promotions.

continent Someone has a deep desire to share their life with you in a special way. This person will welcome you with open arms and everything they own will be at your disposal. You will be well respected and will share your partner's power and authority. You will also have the authority to conduct their affairs when they are unavailable. You will also receive a very special gift within three days. Many blessings are with you and you are entering a very lucky cycle.

continental breakfast You will need to speak with someone special about your needs. This person will be very eager to accommodate you. Do not suffer in silence.

contortionist Bind a special person closer to you.

contraception The contraceptive methods you are using will fail. Beware of this and seek alternative methods.

contract An ongoing union will lead to marriage.

contractor For a three day period do not become involved in any new investments. They will not be profitable.

contradiction Someone will not be agreeable to your desires. Persuasion will change this person's opinion.

contribution A period of slowness and stagnation will be with you for a two week period. Enjoy this stress free time because life will enter a fast-paced, eventful productive period after this.

controller Someone will persistently ask you for money. Be consistent in your refusal to offer a loan.

control cards Your aggressive energy is needed.

control tower Come to the realization that others need time to do things on their own. Do not become so demanding of people who need time to take care of their personal business. This is especially important for the next three days.

in disrepair You need to ensure that you do not create friction between yourself and a special person. The head of the house needs to be sure that all bases are covered financially and romantically, especially for the next two days. All potential negative situations need to be taken care of now before a crisis develops.

controversy Be wary of falling trees in order to prevent injury.

convalescent *if you see yourself in a convalescent hospital* Take better care of yourself and add enjoyable activities to your life. Variety is the spice of life.
to see someone else Be compassionate to an older member of the family. This person may need more variety in their life.

convenience food You will have a profitable future with a new venture.

convenience store Keep your life simple and basic.

convent Do not travel in bad weather. Wait until it improves.

convention Within two weeks you will suffer because someone will intentionally lie to you. This can be avoided if you are watchful of this person.

conversation *any form* This is a lucky cycle. You will enjoy many passionate nights during this time period.

convertible Within a few weeks someone you know will be offered a surprising business opportunity. This person wants your involvement for a little money, a small risk and big dividends.

conveyor belt You will feel overwhelmed by a bad situation that will be made worse if you listen to someone who tends to be an alarmist. Make sure you understand that a small situation has been blown out of proportion. Do everything you can to avoid stress and schedule some private time for a retreat in order to regain tranquility. Make sure nothing disrupts your quiet time for the next four days.

convict Someone is behaving in a secretive manner around you. Do not be suspicious, nothing is going on, this person is only seeking attention.

convulsions Two people are planning to entrap you in order to hurt your feelings. This will be done out of envy and jealousy and will be an embarrassing situation. You have prior warning and this can be avoided.

cook *to see someone else cook* You will hear different advice from different people. Follow your own counsel.

to cook Many people will congratulate you on a victory within the near future.

to see food cooking and to see many dishes You will meet someone who is very compatible to your lifestyle. You will be very happy together and will receive many benefits from this compassionate individual.

cookie You will leave a lengthy meeting and unexpectedly bump into a friend. You will then be asked to join this person for a meal. This will be very pleasant after the long meeting.

cookie cutter Prepare early for the holidays in order to make them pleasant and stress free. Do this even if the last holidays were enjoyable. You will enjoy this year even more.

cookie sheet Make sure that your behavior and mannerisms are not responsible for the break-up of the relationship of someone you know. Become aware of these behaviors and make the necessary changes to prevent this occurrence. This is likely to happen within five days.

cookout That special person is very faithful to you.

cookware Enjoy bargain days.

cooler You are looking to start a new enterprise within a few days. You will make the correct decision and this venture will lead to a miniature gold mine.

coon Take it easy and do nothing for awhile.

coonskin You will be victorious in all of your undertakings.

co-op If you lead your family to believe you will be somewhere, be there. If not, call them and let them know where you are.

coop You will find a small restaurant and this will soon become a favorite spot for you and your family.

cop Be patient with a loved one who is incapable of verbalizing their feelings of love. You are loved beyond your imagination.

cope Maintain your goals, they will soon be granted.

Copenhagen Eat a variety of vegetables, drink plenty of water and exercise. This dream may also be used as a reference point in time. If you dream of this city and see its name used in any context, the dream message will occur on this day.

copier You will decide to hire someone to do extra chores. Your life will become much easier after you cut your workload.

copilot You will enjoy many achievements and will progress rapidly in life. Go full speed ahead and your worries will vanish. Your mind energy will flow during this cycle. Be sure that you maintain a healthy blood circulation. You must also make time to educate yourself in these things you need to better your life. This is the perfect cycle to get that extra training and you will find it easy to grasp your goals.

copper Now is the time to have too much instead of too little. Your friends will offer financial relief. Change your doctor in order to receive the proper help with your allergies.

copperhead Stay away from those you know are your enemies. They are dangerous to you.

copper mine Read sexual materials in order to add more pleasure to your sex life.

copy *to make copies or to see copies made* You will start to change a point of view that you have held for a long time due to the influence of someone else. Stay focused on your own desires and goals now and do not allow interfering statements from someone else to stand in your way. This will be a very productive cycle if you stay away from outside interferences.

copycat Do not do anything for the next few days that can damage a relationship. You know that your plans are wrong and you will be caught.

copyright Protect all of your interests.

coral You will have to deal with someone who is, by nature, very emotional. Within a few days this person will find emotional strength. You will also find that water is soothing and healing for you. Take steps to surround yourself with water. You will receive the positive answer you have long been seeking. If you carry a piece of coral, you will have immediate luck.

Coral Sea You will be very lucky for the next few days.

coral snake This dream implies that a conspiracy between two people is taking place to keep important messages from you. Be alert to this.

cord Watch out for a deranged person who may do you harm. Do not allow yourself to be lured into a lonely, unfamiliar place.

corduroy Keep gossip to yourself and do not become a part of it.

core Enjoy the marrow of life.

coriander Take whatever steps are necessary to maintain a healthy cardiovascular system.

Corinthians *(from the Bible)* Good luck will be with you when you undertake new responsibilities and obligations. You must also carefully attend to the behavior of someone who does not easily show their emotions, but implies through body language that something is wrong. This person is considering suicide and needs help to get back on the right track. You will successfully put a stop to this situation and will be able to help someone who is emotionally vulnerable right now. Expect this to occur within three days.

cork There will be tricky dealings from an unexpected source within a three day period. Otherwise, you are headed for a brilliant future.

to pull the cork out of the bottle For the next ten days you will be unbeatable because of your tenacity and relentlessness in pursuing your goals. You are in a very lucky position and will be celebrating a joyful victory.

corkscrew Do not allow yourself to be taken advantage of financially for the next month.

cormorant *(greedy person)* You will make unwise business dealings. Try to avoid agreeing to anything for the next two weeks.

corn Make decisions quickly.
sweet corn You will enjoy a very romantic, beautiful sex life with music, candlelight, dancing and all of the romantic trappings.

cornball You will be performing work that is easy and nonlabor consuming for the remainder of your life. You will be financially secure with this arrangement.

cornbread You are worried about one of your children. This child will have a very fruitful life and make a great living by using a part of your inheritance. Your grandchildren will be left financially secure. You are also loved beyond your imagination.

corncob You will be lucky in finding the appropriate city to live in.

corncob holder For the next few days, restrain yourself from becoming involved in a situation you have no business being involved in. Use your best judgment.

corncob pipe Your family will enjoy prosperity.

corn dog After having many affairs you will finally find mutual love.

corner *to dream of many people standing at a corner* You will be embarrassed by a date's behavior in public.
to be cornered Within five days, you will be asked to come up with certain documents that will take time to locate. Do everything you can to locate this paperwork and turn it over to the right person in a timely fashion. This will allow everything to run smoothly and easily. Avoid the stress that will result in missing this deadline.

to cut corners You will be moving to an unfamiliar area within two days. You will find this to be a wonderful experience and will meet many new people who will add excitement to your life. The unfamiliarity of this place will wear off in a short time.

to turn corners Keep going in the direction you are now going because you are headed for a brilliant future. You will also hear the words of love you have long been wanting to hear.

to see the corner of any area For the next month only associate with people whom you find a delight to be with. Do not make any allowances for anyone you feel you should see. Only be around those you feel comfortable with. If you do otherwise, you will have many distasteful moments.

cornerstone This dream is a lucky omen.

cornfield You will be suddenly attacked in an attempted mugging. You have prior warning and can prevent this.

cornflakes Make sure you are eating properly and include beans in your diet.

corn flour Be very frank and direct about your needs.

cornflower Someone you know will recover quickly from a long illness.

Cornish game hen Within two days a young child will need extra care and pampering.

cornmeal Keep your plans to yourself. Your speculations are lucky.

cornrow You will enjoy celebrations and happy reunions within a short period of time.

corn silk You will receive some beautiful silk clothing as a gift.

cornstarch Avoid disloyalty to anyone. You are deeply loved. You will also finally receive the apology you have been waiting for.

corn syrup Someone will surrender their love to you.

cornucopia Avoid a separation from someone you care about by using any means available to you.

corn whisky Do not overindulge in anything.

coronary unit You will be purposely given the wrong address, directions and phone number.

coroner You will achieve prosperity in life and will receive a marriage proposal.

corporal Avoid doing anything that will get you into trouble. You will have to accurately explain your actions.

corporal punishment A friend of yours will be tried for murder.

corporation Do not overextend yourself while doing physical exercise.

corpse You will soon receive a sum of money that will increase with each corpse you see. This will occur within a seven day period.

Corpus Christi Within four days you will be asked to show your affections for another person. This individual feels you do not care as much as you do. Explain your feelings to this person because you are adored very much.

corral An argument will be purposely started within three days and the fault will be placed on you. This person has plans and wants to argue in order to prevent you from questioning them. You know this ahead of time so do not allow pettiness to escalate into a fight.

correct *to correct* You need to make a decision when dealing with the opposite sex about a sexual situation. Discussion will lead to a satisfactory solution. Do this as quickly as possible.

corridor Do not allow old hurt feelings to fester and resurface to the point where they keep you from completing your goals. The moment you sense their return, make sure that you busy yourself on another task in order to keep you moving in a healthier direction. You are headed for a healthy and prosperous life. Make sure also that your actions will not be wrongly interpreted. This will occur within seven days.

corrosion You and other family members will become involved in a joint venture. This is an unwise decision and you will lose your investment. Revise your plans and decide on a workable enterprise, regardless of persistent family pressures.

corruption Watch your actions around small children throughout the month. A small child needs more care and protection.

corsage Your relationship will grow into a more caring and satisfying love affair.

corset You will fall in love with someone who possesses great physical beauty.

cortisone You will have true loyal friends around you for a lifetime.

corvette You will enjoy victory in a business partnership. You will also find beautiful leather goods at a bargain.

cosign Do not cosign for anyone unless you have a guarantee.

cosmetic bag Within three days, you will be making a personal decision. You will be moving ahead rapidly because of the success of this decision.

cosmetician You are in a powerful cycle and will receive what you want in a business agreement.

cosmetics Your priority for the next two weeks will be to improve your physical appearance.

cosmic You will enjoy peace and tranquility for the next few days.

cosmonaut You will pay heavily for overextending yourself physically. You will also suffer muscle and joint pain.

Costa Rica You will begin living a luxurious lifestyle within the next two weeks. This will last a lifetime. This dream may also be used as a reference point in time. If you dream of this country and see its name used in any context, the dream message will occur on this day.

costume *to see someone dressed in costume* Do not consider stealing, you will be caught.
to see yourself in costume The person you care about is loyal to you.

costume jewelry An event is scheduled within seven days that you must not miss. You will be pursued by two admirers who will both attempt to win your affections. Although it is not apparent to you, one of them possesses a great deal of power and authority. You will find both of these admirers to be very agreeable and charming and would enjoy having one of them as a lifetime partner. You can be confident that you will put yourself on the path of a prosperous future. Someone you know will also boast about their worth. Ignore this, this person enjoys over-inflating their self worth.

cot Pull yourself back together. For the next week, do not allow bad memories from a past relationship keep you from finding happiness with a special person, if this is what you want. Both of you will be in perfect union this time.

cottage Allow yourself to express your inner feelings for another person. You will find that these feelings are mutual.

cottage cheese Do not spread yourself too thin. You are overextending yourself and lending too much money. This is a very prosperous time for you. You will also experience great happiness over a new birth.

cotton You will enjoy a great future.

cotton ball You will soon purchase a luxury automobile.

cotton belt You will have success at public auctions for the next two weeks.

cotton candy You are doing what you can to better your life. Within two weeks something important, such as a new career, will enter your life. This will result in success and abundance.

cotton flannel This dream indicates wealth.

cottonmouth Do not allow someone to escape punishment who may be a treacherous, dangerous person. Learn all you can about a person's character before you choose to ignore transgressions.

cotton picking You will experience a general abundance of all things in life.

cotton seed You will enjoy a brilliant future.

cotton swabs A situation will occur within three days that will make it necessary for you to determine whether someone working with you on a particular project is keeping up with the pace. This individual may be having you do the work of two people if you are not alert to this. Focus on this so you can get the assistance you need without taking over extra responsibilities. Speak up and let this person know they have to pull their own load. Remain stress free. Many blessings are with you and you are headed for a very prosperous future. You will enjoy a financially secure retirement.

cottontail Prepare your child for life by providing a strong educational background.

couch You will develop a new sales technique that will lead to wealth.

couch potato You will be employed in advertising.

cougar Decide quickly whether you wish to take a certain business trip or someone else will be chosen.

cough Keep your hands clean at all times to avoid contagion. Keep yourself healthy. This is especially important for the next week.

cough drop Find an item made of crystal to add to your collection of belongings. This will make you very happy.

cough syrup You will be performing physical labor without pay for someone else. Make sure that you want to do this prior to committing your time.

counselor Make sure that someone you know seeks counseling to handle stress. This will prevent a serious illness.

count You will get your way with your beloved in all plans and issues regarding love.

countdown Be determined to reach a goal promptly. Set up a work schedule that will ensure dedication.

counter This dream implies power in each phase of your life.

counterfeit Your plans to secretly assist another will not work out.

counterperson Be aware that several situations will take place over the next five days. You will need to motivate yourself to accept one opportunity that will unexpectedly be offered to you. Think quickly so you can rapidly involve yourself. The person offering you this opportunity will be in the specific place and time, and in the frame of mind, to give you this chance only once. If you do not respond positively you will miss out. This will happen soon so motivate yourself to grasp it. Think wisely and quickly and if there is some aspect of this proposal that you do not agree with, you must accept, but at the same time tactfully work out the kinks so it works out well for both of you. In spite of differences in lifestyle, this is a workable situation.

countess Be supportive of a family member who is going through domestic problems. This problem will be quickly resolved and happiness will be restored.

country You will enjoy a new companion and have some of the best days of your life.

country club Information you gain accidentally will be like a gold mine. Do not share this information but use it for your own business purposes.

country music You will have the support you need in dealing with a banking issue.

country rock You will soon receive a large item from a family member who no longer wants to deal with it. This could be a boat or car, etc.

country singer What you felt at one time was an impossibility is now possible. Go for it.

county Handle each issue and piece of paperwork properly in order to avoid bureaucratic red tape.
   to be the recipient of a county check Be very attentive because an unusual occurrence will develop regarding a person, project or position that will lead to a financial windfall. You may marry someone who will leave you a monthly pension, develop a project that will deliver you monthly royalties, or secure a position that will offer you monthly provisions for a lifetime. You are in a sound position to receive this in the near future. Develop your curiosity, especially for the next week, to ensure that you do not miss out on these benefits. You will receive an abundance of health, many blessings and are headed for a brilliant future.

county agency You will suddenly recover from a long illness and will feel better than before becoming ill. This will be a prosperous cycle for you.

to enter a county agency You will need to discuss finances in order to reach an agreement. Avoid harassment for non-payment of bills.

coupe You will be granted a favor.

couple Focus on and deal with your obsessions. Within two weeks you will have control over them.

coupon Take the initiative while seeking financial backing for a project.

courage You will find the solution to a very serious matter in your life within five days. Also, within five days, someone who secretly hates you will try to sabotage your plans by steering a particular situation in the direction that will benefit someone else. You are trying to work things out so that everyone can enjoy a more prosperous future. Although this person knows you are in the right, they will work against your efforts in spite of the destruction it will wreak on others. You have prior notice of this and can take steps to prevent this interference. This individual has no idea of the degree of hardship they will bring to others.

courier A delicate situation that appears to be on a downhill spiral will, within three days, take a rapid turn for the better. You can expect rapid progress. Maintain a calm demeanor. All those involved will have the greater mental acuity to proceed correctly.

court Speak your mind in order to be better understood.

courtesan You will be a great comfort now to someone in need.

courthouse Avoid involvement in a civil suit for the next two weeks.

court martial Take steps to prevent skating accidents for the next two weeks.

courtroom You will attend a family reunion within seven days and will see family members you have not seen in a while as well as others you have never met. You will have a wonderful time.

courtyard You will enjoy a festive occasion, similar to a carnival.

cousin Have your bicycle or motorcycle brakes checked.

cove Go for risky new ventures and investments for the next few days. These will be successful.

coven Do your best to uncover a conspiracy. You are on the right track. Do this quietly and secretly because discovery of your motives will only complicate matters.

coverall For the next week, be consistent in the way you behave in order to avoid confusion. It is very important, during this time period, to avoid sending out mixed messages. Make sure that others are not misled. Good luck is with you.

cover charge You will enjoy an outing with friends and family in a cabin by the woods.

covered wagon Make sure all fires are extinguished.

covers You will be asked to join another person on a trip. The primary reason you are asked will be to help out financially. It is your choice to go or to stay home.

cover up Make sure you do not become involved in a conspiracy.

cow You will come to grips with an important career matter. Examine the plans you hope to execute in order to determine their workability and whether you still want to put them into action. This dream is a good luck omen and each plan will work out to your specifications once they are reviewed.

cowbell Someone will want to possess you totally. This person is generous, affectionate and kind. It is your choice whether to pursue this or not.

cowboy Within four days someone is desperately wanting to see you so they can demonstrate their affection for you. Let this person know how much they mean to you.

cowboy boot For the next four days, move with determination. You will achieve great success in the field you are moving toward. Everything you do for the next few days will be extremely lucky.

cowboy hat Within two days, you will be in touch with someone who will be able to work with you successfully. This person will be easy to work with, energetic and has good organizational skills. This is a good cycle for both of you.

cowhide Avoid jealousy and petty arguments with someone who is special to you. Maintain a peaceful demeanor at all times.

cowl You will enjoy a new assignment, receive a better salary and will gain financial security.

cowlick A priceless collection of yours will be damaged within ten days if you do not take steps to prevent this. This dream is a lucky omen for you.

cow person Do not allow another person to use you to further their career. You will be prosperous and healthy.

coyote Avoid narrow-mindedness and unnecessary worry.

crab Within three weeks an intense situation will develop that will lead to a broken engagement. This can be prevented. If it occurs, the relationship will never be as it was before.

crab apple Someone will attempt to lure a special person away from you. Pay attention to the actions of someone you care about for the next two weeks.

crabgrass Balance work and enjoyment. You are working too hard.

crack *(the drug)* Aggressively pursue your goals to ensure success. Also, aggressively pursue anything of personal importance to you in order to promote a smooth polite handling of events.

cracker You will enjoy luck for the next two weeks. This dream ensures that you will enjoy tranquility in all phases of your life.

cracker barrel You will finally be asked out by someone you deeply desire.

cracker jack A platonic relationship will quickly become a love relationship. Determine ahead of time if this is what you want.

cracker jack prize Believe only what you see.

cracks *to see* This dream is an unlucky omen. Take care of all business affairs for the next week in order to ensure smooth transactions. You may want to cancel all business decisions for this time period.

cradle Do not become desperate over another person's problems and do not allow yourself to be lured into involvement in spite of temptations.

craftsperson Someone will attempt to take advantage of your generosity.

cram Beware of accidents around water.

cramp You will enjoy peace of mind and soul, and will enjoy a clear conscience.

cramps For the next three days make sure you prepare yourself for an unusual and remarkable event. While this is occurring, you will be able to clearly think through the steps to take to get through this cycle comfortably. Your curiosity will be very keen during this time period and you will need to be disciplined and firm with yourself. Do not allow your curiosity to control you. You will receive an abundance of health during this cycle.

cranberry This dream is a lucky omen. Take care of your kidneys and drink plenty of water. Be sure not to eat anything that will cause an allergic reaction.

cranberry juice You will enjoy yourself because you will be able to touch another in an emotional, passionate way. This will occur within three days.

crane *(bird)* Someone new will enter your life with flair and enthusiasm. This will add a new dimension to your life. This new attitude will fit perfectly into your life and will bring you happiness.

crane *(machine)* For major benefits, get into the habit of regularly consulting with others before making decisions, especially when it concerns someone you care about.

crank shaft Someone you care about is ready to separate from a relationship. This person feels you don't care as much about them as you do. Change your attitude and show more affection in order to prevent a permanent split. You are deeply loved and your coldness will hurt this person. If you want this relationship to work, take big steps to revise it.

crap An influential person will inform you of alternative means to achieve your goals.

crapout Do not become bossy with your beloved. A more pleasing demeanor will accomplish more.

crappie Do not start a problem that will lead to the downfall of a relationship. Do whatever is necessary to keep the relationship together.

craps *(the game)* This dream is an extremely lucky omen. You will experience an abundance of health and wealth in areas you never expected. You will also enjoy an unexpected income and be able to take care of those tasks you felt at one time were impossible. This is the perfect cycle to take care of those difficult jobs. Proceed with confidence, you are headed for a prosperous future.

crapshooter A loan you are seeking will be authorized.

crash You will find it difficult to communicate with someone but you will have to respond soon and move on with your life. Do this as quickly as possible. You will also need to take steps to avoid any negative situation connected with this dream and alert anyone you recognize to do likewise. It is especially important to do this for the next three days. Move quickly for the next five days to ensure that anything that requires structure and detail is handled properly. Make sure also that what you hear is consistent with what you think you are hearing. Good luck is with you.

crash dive An unexpected introduction to someone will suddenly lead to a primary relationship. This will occur rapidly.

crash helmet You will receive much love and affection and enjoy a healthy life.

crate You will enjoy romance in a quiet secluded area.

crater Keep the object of your affection interested in you.

cravat You will experience a sudden lucky change for the better.

crave *to crave* Your wish will be granted.

crawfish Give the person you care deeply about a surprise gift.

crawl *to crawl* Take extra precautions to avoid a back injury, especially for the next two weeks.

crayon Advertising will lead to the growth of your project.

crazy *any form* This dream implies genius and a brilliant future.

crazy quilt For the next three days, anything you do with a partner will be a disaster. Back off and regroup, and you will be able to handle this situation with success.

cream For two weeks believe only what you see. Seek the endorsement from another person so you will receive a positive answer to a long held secret desire.

   whipped cream Circumstances will occur that will create a lot of eroticism in your life for the next five days. This may come through books, films or pleasures of the flesh. You will enjoy this time period tremendously. You are headed for a brilliant future and you will enjoy a financial windfall that will come in an unexpected way and from an unexpected place.

cream cheese You will overeat due to the stress of someone else's failure to commit. Control your obsessive behavior and this will lead to normal eating patterns. Watch your weight and cholesterol.

creamery Watch that a young child is not cruelly teased by other children. This child will not tell adults about this teasing and will be very hurt by it.

cream filling Several unexpected events will begin to occur one right after the other, and you will be flooded with invitations to many functions and events that you will be able to take your pick of. It is imperative that you not miss one particular event. This one will be far more glamorous and exciting than the rest. Prepare yourself ahead of time because this will require formal attire and you will want to look your best.

Do not deprive yourself of this enjoyable event because not only will you have a fantastic time, but you will also meet a number of influential people who will become good friends for life. You will also win a special door prize or a gift that you will treasure for a lifetime. During this cycle, you will also be made aware that someone you desire feels the same desire for you and you will share many affectionate moments with each other. You will both feel excitement about this new development. You are headed for a prosperous and brilliant future.

cream puff You will receive much love and many kisses.

cream sauce Someone will declare their love to you.

cream soda You will be invited to many social events.

crease Make sure your brakes are in good working order.

create *to create* Instigate a meeting with someone you feel you need to meet with. This person will work with you to create an unexpected windfall for the future.

creator You will enjoy victory in all phases of your life and your special divinity will always be with you. You and your family will receive many blessings and your ambitions will be realized.

credit Change your attitude about money. You can be your own worst enemy in financial arrangements.

credit bureau Do not allow a large establishment to cheat you. Written financial figures may be incorrect.

credit card Quickly find a practical solution to a problematic situation.

credit rating You will soon experience much love and affection.

Cree Be very aware of the needs of the young people who are in your care now.

creek You need to make roof repairs.

Creek Indian You will soon need to make a positive commitment.

creel Any anticipated event will be a disappointment for the next few days.

creep Do not allow yourself to be defeated. Be determined to avoid career disappointments.

creepy crawlers Within three days several situations will occur that are important for you. Motivate yourself to take advantage of them because they will be once in a lifetime opportunities. Take immediate steps to grasp each chance and do not procrastinate. You are headed for a brilliant future.

cremate You will receive a marriage proposal. Do not let others know of your plans regarding love relationships for the next few days.

crematory Your intuition is correct. Follow your hunches.

Creole You will enjoy some new recipes with a neighbor.

crepe You will receive an unexpected legacy from someone who is making plans for your future. Before passing away this person wants to see what you will produce. You will develop a successful enterprise.

crepe paper Within four days an advertisement you place will yield much desired and welcomed wealth.

crepes suzette Within two days, it will be required that you provide accounts and paperwork from the past. Begin keeping track of all records, making copies and locating old documents and paperwork now. This will alleviate stress and the sense of urgency this situation often triggers.

crescent You and your family will receive an abundance of money as a result of a promotion. This will be a good cycle for you.

crest An insincere person will agree to meet with you at a specified time and place but has no intention of actually meeting with you. Be prepared for this to occur within five days and avoid wasting your time on this.

Crete Find support for new ideas within two days so you can direct your project in the direction you desire.

cretin Someone is anxious to meet you and is in the position to pull strings on your behalf. Do not allow your timidity to keep you from requesting a favor. This will lead to an occurrence that needs to take place in your life.

crevice Tie up all financial loose ends. This will allow you to clearly see your next move.

crew A sense of humor will improve your relationships.

crew cut Compromise to reach agreements for old problems.

crewmen Someone will try to break a warranty agreement within a few weeks. Watch for this and take steps to prevent it.

crew neck Within three days, someone will want to show how deeply they feel for you and how involved they desire to be with you. This person will go through a series of activities, chores and favors, and will behave in a puppet like man-

ner. Your every desire will be fulfilled. Openly show your affection and consideration for this person's generosity and efforts. Be very cautious and do not bruise this person's feelings, and do not become suspicious of this person's motives.

crew sock Within three days, you will experience a deep emotional pain because someone will set up a situation that will cause you to feel betrayed. Avoid painful feelings by taking steps to prevent this situation.

crib Do not become desperate over another's problems. Do not be lured in, in spite of the temptations to become involved. This will occur within four days. You will also enjoy longevity. Improve your diet in order to enjoy a healthy life.

cribbage Do not donate blood for the next two weeks.

crib death Within the next few days you will be dealing with someone who appears to be very nice. In reality, this person is very much the opposite. Guard yourself and take steps to avoid being with this person alone. This person will ultimately try to ruin your life. Anything negative witnessed in this dream needs to be avoided in reality.

cricket This dream represents victory in all phases of your life.

crime A good friend will move to a distant place and become a hermit. Try to talk this person out of this idea.

criminal Do not restrict your enjoyment with others. The person you see in this dream will also attempt to create a disturbance with you. You have the chance now to avoid this situation entirely. Protect yourself. This dream also implies that you should not allow someone to waste your time on nonsense. During this cycle you will have to accomplish things that need to be taken care of immediately.

criminology You will finally get the person you desire to ask you out.

crimson You will need someone to be a liaison in order to have services quickly assimilated. This person will work between two agencies. Business transactions will run smoothly after this is taken care of.

crinoline Do not make lifestyle changes for a couple of weeks.

cripple Wait at least a month before making a commitment to a career or relationship. This will lead to more success and better harmony and success. Take steps to change any negative event and do everything you can to experience only positive expressions in your life.

crisis Someone you know will go through a crisis situation. Do not take it upon yourself to straighten it out.

crisp A friend will suddenly depart to a new town.

critic Do not distance yourself from a loved one because of your method of communication. Communicate in a manner that shows genuine interest in another person's life. It is also important not to be so hard on yourself in times of stress. A hobby will help with this and will yield big profits.

criticism *to be criticized* Be practical and use common sense regarding a new venture.

to criticize You will ask for a favor and will be turned down. Seek alternative action.

croak You will have a wonderful time sampling many different kinds of foods.

crochet Teach a younger person a skill they may never learn from someone else. This will bring much pleasure.

crochet hook Determine what is keeping you from moving ahead in the right direction. This is a great time to work on this aspect of your life. Within two days you will be able to achieve this goal.

crockery *broken crockery* This dream implies that unless you do something now, you will not receive anything by way of a settlement. Proceed with confidence because whatever you set out to receive will be accomplished if you work at it.

in any other form Within the week you will receive a large expected settlement that will come earlier than you anticipated. You are also in a cycle that will bring success for work performed independently. By working steadily and having a detailed plan, success will come. Your life will vastly improve.

crock pot You will be around someone striving for a career in comedy. Encourage this person.

crocodile You will make a career change within two weeks.

crocus Follow your children's dreams and keep a constant watch over them for the next few weeks.

croissant Be patient. You are running on emotional energy and will feel this later on. Slow down and take care of yourself.

Cro-Magnon You will receive a long awaited apology. The reunion that results from this will be pleasant. You will produce a successful enterprise.

crop *any form* You have a brilliant future ahead of you. Your life is undergoing profound changes in terms of health, wealth and money. You will experience an abundance in each of these areas. Someone special to you will notice these changes and love will develop on a deeper level. You will experience great love in your life caused by a major event

you have created. You must also keep a close eye on all plants to ensure that no damage is caused by insects or the elements.

croquet Seek professional help to enable you to break the habit of emotional deprivation. Treat yourself well and stop depriving yourself.

croquette Within a few days, you will meet with someone whom you have not seen for some time, but have always been attracted to. Stop being passive and ask this person to join you for brunch. Do what you can to bring them closer to you. This person holds affectionate feelings toward you.

cross *the shape of the cross in any form* The more you practice optimism the more you are able to achieve this attitude. A variety of people feel love and affection for you and you will receive praise and honor. An abundance of blessings will come to you and your family for a long period of time. An issue will also arise within two weeks involving a sick relative. Clear off all personal responsibilities now in order to be free to offer assistance. You will be under less stress this way. This dream implies luck in all matters and in all levels of your life for a long time.

to see someone make the sign of the cross You will be undergoing a tremendous amount of pressure. You will find the courage and inner strength to endure, to make needed changes in your life, and to rectify wrongs. Many blessings will be with you.

to make the sign of the cross This dream is a lucky omen.

to see someone you recognize carrying a cross The person is overextending themselves and setting themselves up to be emotionally, physically and financially drained. Forewarn this person to guard against this.

to carry a cross Take steps to prevent yourself from being financially, emotionally and physically drained by others. Set limits to keep yourself healthy. Make sure you do not set yourself up to handle the problems of others. Love yourself and do not give anyone the opportunity to drain you, because other people will not set limits on what they will demand from you.

Christ carrying the cross, on the crucifix or being crucified Make sure that you are not symbolically crucified by others who are plotting to do this. Someone you least expect will attempt to cause you extreme emotional harm in order to seriously damage your well being. You will be able, with this prior notice, to take the necessary steps to protect yourself in all capacities. Make sure all bases are covered and you will be able to handle this situation victoriously. For the next two weeks the powers of your divinity will be with you.

in any other form This dream signifies victory. You will make a connection with someone of complementary talents. This merging of talents will lead to a great product or enterprise. Both of you will achieve financial success.

cross *(to cross path)* You will rise above administration problems within two days. Have a conference in order to regroup and brainstorm with others. Good ideas will be generated and energy will be renewed to ensure success.

crossbones Do not involve yourself in a risky financial situation. It seems safe but instincts will say otherwise. Follow your hunches. This will occur after a two week hiatus. You have time to research this project.

crossbow A stressful legal situation involving a lawsuit will be resolved.

cross eye Go after the big project. You will receive support and now have the enthusiasm and expertise to launch this venture.

cross fire A favorable living arrangement will result from a romantic conversation between you and a special person.

crosshatch After failing the first time, regroup and try again. This time you will achieve success.

crossroad You and that special person will have many sensual, magical moments together.

cross stitch Do not rely on a friend to help you with a plan. This plan will work but the friend will let you down. Consider alternative assistance and put finances in order before making a move in order to handle the project alone and efficiently.

crosswalk Prepare, ahead of time, the method you will use to manage a delicate situation. You are being watched by someone in authority and your method of handling this will be important. This dream is also an extremely lucky omen. You will experience an abundance of health and wealth as a result of an unexpected income. You will be able to accomplish tasks at this time that you felt were impossible. This is the perfect time to take on big projects. Proceed with confidence. You are headed for a brilliant future.

crossword puzzle Focus strictly on business for the next three days.

croup Do not allow pettiness to motivate any action or decision.

crouton Discuss your financial status, ongoing investments and future investments with an experienced CPA.

crow Do not accept the responsibilities of another person and be firm in your refusal to compromise your time.

crowbar Future invitations will be very fortuitous for you.

crowd You will receive exactly what you expect from love now. All plans made regarding romance will occur.
to walk through a crowd You will be faced with a variety of chores, tasks, etc. to do for yourself and others. Avoid

the feeling of being overwhelmed and you will, within three days, be able to accomplish these tasks successfully. Within this time frame, you will also do something very special for another person that will help them develop a better outlook on life. This will be something that will help this person spruce up their physical appearance. You are headed for a prosperous future and others will respond very warmly to you. You will experience love from others. Many blessings are coming to you and your family.
others walking through a crowd You will meet someone who has a very busy schedule due to their high position of authority. This is a person of means and very much a workaholic. This person will take the time to do something special for you emotionally and financially. You will be assured that you are a priority in this person's life. Many blessings are with you and you are headed for a brilliant future. Expect this within three days.
large crowd You will receive an unspoken verification that your current hunches about love are accurate. This will lead to romance.

Crowley, Aleister *(Executive Director/Master of the 78 cards of the book of Egyptian Tarot)* Within the month you will be thrust forward with massive, deliberate and brilliant clarity of thought. You will be able to manifest and master the abilities to make improved changes that will profoundly and vastly affect your life as well as the lives of others. These changes will endure for a lifetime and you will leave an unusual legacy that others will enjoy and reap benefits from for self improvement. Many blessings are with you and you are headed for a fantastic future.

crown Someone will confide shocking news about themselves that you will wish you had never heard. This information is false.

crown jewels *any form* Within two weeks, you will unexpectedly rise to a higher plane in life than you had ever envisioned. You will experience an abundance of productivity, an increase in income, productive conversation and be surrounded by loyal and affectionate people. Other people will desire to become a part of your plans, will offer their assistance and also offer to teach you the wisdom they have acquired. This will occur within five days. You are headed for a brilliant future and will enjoy an abundance of health.

Crown of Thorns For the next four days you must be very careful that you do not allow yourself to be vulturized by anyone who will take advantage of you financially, emotionally and physically. Set limits in order to keep others from demanding that their needs be met. Make sure that your needs take priority. Act as though you are on a mini vacation and make sure you do not overextend yourself. One person in particular is very demanding. Watch out for them.

crows foot You will receive an expected pleasant surprise but you will be caught off guard because you did not expect it so soon.

crows nest You will be tearfully happy at the growth of your enterprise.

crucible A friend will be in a very argumentative mood and will disagree with every idea you have. Avoid this person.

crucifix Be very careful you do not allow yourself to be vulturized by others who will take advantage of you financially, emotionally and physically. Set limits in order to keep others from demanding that you meet their needs. Make sure, for the next month, that your needs have priority. Act as though you are on a mini vacation and be certain you do not overextend yourself. One person is particularly demanding. Watch out for this individual.

to recognize the person on the crucifix This individual will be abused by others and needs to be forewarned in order to protect themselves from physical, verbal or emotional abuse from someone they least expect.

to see yourself on the crucifix Someone, unknown to you, is secretly plotting to inflict emotional and physical harm and will plan to catch you unprotected and off guard. For some reason this person has focused on you in order to satisfy their strange obsessions. Protect yourself at all costs and do not allow yourself to be caught off guard in any area where this may occur. There is also a possibility that your food may be poisoned. Remain on guard for at least two weeks.

to see someone you recognize carrying a cross The person is overextending themselves and setting themselves up to be emotionally, physically and financially drained. Forewarn this person to guard against this.

to carry a cross Take steps to prevent yourself from being financially, emotionally and physically drained by others. Set limits to keep yourself healthy. Make sure you do not set yourself up to handle the problems of others. Love yourself and do not give anyone the opportunity to drain you, because other people will not set limits on what they will demand from you.

Christ carrying the cross, on the crucifix or being crucified Make sure you are not symbolically crucified by others who are plotting to do this. Someone you least expect will attempt to cause you extreme emotional harm in order to seriously damage your well being. You will be able, with this prior notice, to take the necessary steps to protect yourself in all capacities. Make sure all bases are covered and you will be able to handle this situation victoriously. For the next two weeks the powers of your God will be with you.

crucifixion You will agree to another's plan and later regret this. You will wish you had stuck to the original agreement. You have prior notice and can prevent this occurrence.

cruise You will be shown something shocking. You will have difficulty believing what you are seeing and because of the strangeness, the event will stay in your mind for some time to come.

crumb What you thought would be a pleasant reunion will be a disaster. Stay calm and do the best you can. This situation is not in your control. Expect this to occur within the week.

crusade Someone will, within five days, conceal information to prevent you from becoming angry. This information is important to you so persist in finding out the truth. You are also placing too much importance on someone who is only interested in playing games. This individual plots the games they will play. Protect yourself.

crush Someone will make a comment within three days that implies they are interested in letting you have something that belongs to them. It is in your best interest to follow this through as soon as it is offered, otherwise this person will quickly change their mind. Take steps to acquire this item before the offer is rebuked. Good luck is with you.

to see someone else crushed A dangerous undertone is apparent in a situation involving a member of the same sex. This situation is dangerous and evil and this person will attempt to catch you off guard in order to gauge your reactions at an unexpected time. Do what you can to protect yourself for the next three days and remain in a safe environment.

crushed Someone is feeling very abandoned by you. You must quickly let this person know they are very special to you. Give them a tangible representation of your appreciation (i.e., flowers, a gift, etc.) You will catch this person off guard and will let them know that you are deeply involved with them. Put your love into both action and words in order to create a deeper bond. This is a wonderful time to put love into your life on a permanent basis. You are headed for a very prosperous future.

crust Push yourself to be successful with new projects.

crustacean Do not allow your inconsistencies to cause a special person to develop negative feelings toward you.

crutch Within a few weeks, the news you receive regarding a close relative will alarm you.

crutches Do not make excuses for those areas of your life in which you are not conducting yourself properly. Face facts and discipline yourself in such a way that you change your personality and become the person you want to be. This is a cycle that will allow you to make these changes easier and quicker if you act now. During this three day cycle, you will want to demonstrate that special personality that you want others to see and that will leave a positive impression on their minds. Prioritize your desires in other areas of your life. This cycle will allow you to accomplish this. Also, any negative event that you do not want to experience in reality can be altered. Make sure you alert anyone you recognize to avoid this event as well. Many blessings are with you and you are headed for a very prosperous future.

cry *to cry* This dream implies victory. All things you thought were impossible will now be possible. Within five days you will also receive a verification of the love someone has for you. This will lead to emotional fulfillment in some capacity.

someone else crying You will enjoy happy reunions. A love reconciliation is also possible during this cycle, if you choose. New financial agreements will be made with a special person. This is a lucky cycle.

baby crying A hot financial tip will lead to riches.

man crying You will be charged for services never received. Be careful of con artists and lawsuit charges. This will occur within a few days.

woman crying You will have to put away money because a situation will arise within a few weeks that will require extra finances.

to see many people crying Take the necessary steps to prevent an untimely death due to unusual circumstances. Take extra precautions for the next seven days.

daughter crying You will be making the wrong decision within two days. In order to avoid a mistake, rethink all of your decisions during this time period. If you dream of any unfortunate situation or illness occurring with your daughter, you must also alert her to this occurrence so she can take steps to prevent it. Expect this to occur within two days.

in any other form You will receive massive support in those areas in which you seek support. Certain situations will take place within five days that are unfolding in a way you neither desire nor expect. Overall, things will develop to your advantage. As a result you will experience dramatic changes and improvements in your life. You will then experience an improvement in your emotional and financial status.

crypt You will harvest an abundance of fruits and vegetables. Much wealth will come from this.

crystal Take care of your eyesight. Drink plenty of water. Take note of the color of the crystal for further information.

crystal ball This dream implies good luck. All pleasant things seen in the crystal ball will occur. Any negative event may be changed. You have the time and the choices to alter negative occurrences.

cub Avoid family disputes.

Cuba Keep your eye on your investments. Do not become careless as they grow. This dream may also be used as a reference point in time. If you dream of this country and see its name used in any context, the dream message will occur on this day.

cubbyhole Someone wants only to be cuddled and held by you.

cube *any form* This implies that you will have a major victory in an area you much desire. This will occur within five days. A cube of ice is a lucky omen. You will soon be victorious in your ventures.

cube steak Something unusual and unexpected will happen within two days. Be prepared. You will receive some positive, exciting, yet shocking news. Good luck is with you.

cub scout For the next month you will enjoy an abundance of energy and health. This dream is a lucky omen.

cuckoo You will enjoy a great dinner with a famous personality.

cuckoo clock You will be victorious in each phase of your life.

cucumber Watch your financial status and especially watch your joint assets.

cud You will fall in love with a much older person.

cuddle If you want to be with someone, act as though you do. Do not become cold and standoffish. This will give the impression of disinterest.

cue Someone is giving the impression that they are disinterested and will display coldness. This person, in reality, is aching for you.

cuff You will marry someone you never expected you would marry.

cuff links You will marry someone you strongly desire.

culottes Watch you appearance. You will shortly receive an unexpected visitor and it is best not to be caught off guard.

cult Beware of an injury to the nose.

culture *any culture* You will thoroughly enjoy yourself at a festive occasion similar to a carnival.

cultured pearl Beautify your complexion and make sure that you do not compromise your virtue under any circumstances.

cup *full* You will gain headway in a present situation by setting up a meeting with those who are eager to hear what you have to say. This will yield a positive outcome.

empty Do not panic in times of distress. Things will work out for the better within a few days.

cracked You will lose a bet.

broken Lack of communication will result in a major set back. Think ahead in order to prevent this.

cupboard Someone wants to spend a romantic evening with you.

cupcake Make your relationship solid on all levels.

Cupid You will fall in love with the person you least expect. You will enjoy a great life and much wealth with this person. You also need to break down any invisible barrier that handicaps your progress toward a more positive and different direction. Do this quickly.

Cupid's bow Strengthen your love relationship on all levels.

curate Someone you desire passionately will want to communicate their eagerness for you. You will be mutually satisfied with this union. Expect this to occur within two days.

curator Do not become a bore with your loved one. They may look elsewhere for excitement. Be creative.

curb Get rid of all negative, argumentative behaviors.

curbstone Dispose of unwanted property at a profit, then use the funds to purchase what you want.

curd You will uncover sought after information.

cure Do not allow brainwashing tactics to affect your state of mind. Do not put yourself in a situation where this is likely to occur. You must also chase away those people with a tendency to use this technique.

curfew You will become more open in your communication of feelings of love for another.

curiosity Slow down before you spend too much on a relationship.

curl You are loved beyond your expectations.

curling iron Perseverance and patience will bring you success and honor.

currant This dream implies victory in all phases of your life. Have faith and confidence in yourself and put out all the right signals indicating that you have faith in those who work with you. Everything will work much better if you demonstrate this faith.

curry This dream implies luck. Let go of the past and create a new life.

curry powder Watch what you say to others. A secret about your loved one may slip out and get back to this person. Avoid embarrassment and hurt feelings.

curse For the next few days, situations in love relationships may be difficult. Be patient, this will pass and wonderful days are ahead.

curt Be aware of someone who is filled with emotion whenever you are around, although they are not fully aware of it. Once you find out who this person is, you will feel very gratified. This person will be a valuable and important person in your life.

curtain call Be wary of cuts and bruises around the eye.

curtains *closed* You are not living up to your full potential in life. You are missing something. Search for this missing element.

half open You are going in the right direction. Enjoy life as much as possible. You will pursue a new avenue that will require more education and you will receive training as you progress toward your new ideas. This will result in a very successful outcome.

open At one time you wanted the impossible in a relationship. This person will unexpectedly return after a long absence and everything you desired from a relationship will now be possible. You will also see others whom you have not seen in a long while who are in no way connected with this relationship. Luck is with you.

in any other form Rally friends to help with a personal project such as painting the house, moving, etc.

curtsy You will be treated royally by someone you meet.

curve Relax; you have a creative spirit that is taking up much of your time but a special person wants to spend some relaxing private time with you. You need to take some time off.

curve ball You will be rewarded abundantly for work well done.

cushion A situation will escalate unless you make an effort to call and straighten things out.

custard A young person will depend on you for direction. Be careful and patient while leading this person in the right direction.

custody Keep love alive in a relationship. Do whatever is necessary to grow closer.

custom You will soon have a lovely quiet home of your own.

cut *on another person* You will enjoy a financial windfall. Do not jeopardize your financial security because of misunderstandings.

to cut yourself and bleed A friend will become a financial drain.

to have your hair cut without your consent in a violent way Because of a disagreement, a contract will suddenly be altered. This could escalate to verbal and physical violence between two people. This will be a very dangerous situation. Avoid this at the first sign of trouble. Remain calm and avoid all behavior that may escalate this. Make sure that all agreements and contracts should be in writing.

hair cut at a salon You are procrastinating an agreement. Stop putting off decisions, the result will be successful.

cut on face Protect your face from all accidents or damage as a result of an automobile accident, the sun, sun tanning booths, lacerations and any number of other causes. Do not spoil a current situation by involving too many people.

cuts of any form on the body A co-worker will become upset about a certain situation. This will result in an outburst of violence. Leave the scene at the first sign of this because it could become a very dangerous situation. Return to work only after an assurance of peace.

to cut food Whatever you are waiting for will fall neatly into place.

to cut anything Be careful of cuts and accidents that could cause lacerations for the next two days.

cut glass Within a week an extremely dangerous, destructive person will enter your home and destroy massive amounts of property. If possible acquire a watchdog.

cuticle Become personally involved for the next two days with situations that you want to fit perfectly into place. You will be successful in this quest.

cutlass Within the week, a very significant situation will occur that will start a series of upwardly spiraling events for the next six months. This will dramatically alter your life for the better but the real significance will not be felt for seven months.

cutlery You will invent an instrument and this will turn your life around.

knife, wood block set Any idea set into motion over the next two days will be tremendously successful and will have a dynamic outcome. Put all new ideas into action.

cutter *(pizza, etc.)* For the next month, it is a good idea to promote group activities. This may be something in the manner of card games, parlor games, etc. Something lucky will also occur within a group situation. You will gain information that will enhance your life.

cuttle bone Love is in the air.

cyanide You will be working in close quarters with a very attractive person for the next few days. Make sure that you do not put yourself in the position to allow an involvement to develop. Keep everything strictly business.

cyborg You will come very close to killing someone who has committed a violent act against a close relative. Seek help. Warn this relative and take steps within a few days to prevent the initial violent act.

cyclist *to be* You will work at silk screen printing and fabric printing. This will generate financial security for you.

cyclone Do not put yourself in an environment that uses explosives. Avoid injury due to fireworks, etc.

Cyclops You will witness a horrifying situation that will linger in your mind for many days. Do everything necessary to take your mind off this.

cylinder Make sure, for the next five days, that you wear the proper attire for the right occasion, otherwise you will be highly criticized and be made to feel very uncomfortable.

cypress You will enjoy a pleasurable time because of a conversation with another person. This person will give you the opportunity to enjoy a wonderful event. Go with this, you will enjoy yourself immensely. You will also experience health and longevity and will win honors in cooking contests.

dead cypress You are overlooking a certain situation. This must be handled within two days in order to have a positive outcome.

Cyprus Within two days you and another person will experience good foresight about something you need to work on together. This individual will help you to avoid making a mistake.

cyst You will receive great news within three days about a windfall you will be receiving. During this cycle you need to aim for love, romance, courtship and all the good emotions you can handle.

cystic fibrosis You have abandoned a situation now that will come up again later. It will be more costly and time consuming to handle this at a later date. Do what you can now to bring this to completion. Each project you undertake will also work to your advantage.

czar You will create an excellent opportunity for yourself and be in a dynamic position to make this project tangible.

Czechoslovakia Do not handle any problems that are not your own. Stay out of the lives of other people. There may be a dangerous overload of bad lifestyles. This dream may also be used as a reference point in time. If you dream of this country and see its name used in any context, the dream message will occur on this day.

D

D You will soon meet someone with a dramatic flair for life. This person is very charismatic and intelligent and you will be eager to see this optimistic person. This individual always lives life to the fullest in a grand way. They will perform a favor for you that will be treasured for a lifetime. You will both share a mutual respect and admiration for life even if you do not see each other as often as you would like.

dachshund You will buy an item for very little money but will receive years of use from this purchase. You will have a good experience buying anything on term payments.

daddy *any form* Stop taking yourself so seriously and stop being so strict with yourself and others. Be less of a parent and more of a lover in a relationship. Too many rules and restrictions spoil a relationship. Take more enjoyment in those loving feelings, and stop depriving yourself.

daddy longlegs This dream is an extremely lucky omen. You will also enjoy a very happy family reunion.

daffodil Someone is very eager to see you and things will work out beautifully. You will get together within a few days and find that you complement each other perfectly.

dagger You and another person will decide mutually to move away from a relationship and go your separate ways. Handle this as calmly as possible. This process will start within the week. This is a good cycle to take care of this.

dahlia Gather friends together for advice and to assist you in times of need. They will be there for you when you need help and to compare notes. The advice given will be invaluable.

daily double This is a wonderful dream to have. It implies that you will be lucky with games of chance for the next few days. You will also exchange wonderful memories with another person.

daiquiri Do not allow other people's problems to spoil your festive mood for the next three days.

dairy Flirt a little and see how rapidly a full blown romance will occur. This is destined to happen within the week and you will be surprised at how rapidly your heart is captivated by another.

dairymaid All business transactions that involve travel will be very fortuitous and will offer a lifestyle that you never anticipated. Good luck is with you.

dairyman Situations will develop within five days that you need to attend to. You will be able to put a stop to any negative aspect of these issues if you become actively involved. This cycle will allow you to deal successfully with all matters that need to be addressed.

daisy Someone will attempt to make up for their lack of interest in the past. This person has been too busy to see you and will attempt to make it up by taking you out, buying flowers and apologizing. This will be a very successful union.

daisy wheel You will have an unexpected opportunity to speak with someone in private within five days. Move quickly in order to communicate the words you have wanted to say that will conclude an important ongoing issue. You will be successful in getting your point across to this important person.

Dakota You will need to use verbal strategy to steer large corporations into donating funds. Choose your words carefully and study the best methods to use. Do this within three days.

Dalai Lama You are taking all the correct steps and are motivating yourself to achieve victory. A connection you have been unable to make in the past with a certain individual will be successfully made this week. Schedule yourself a small vacation to a quiet, out of the way place and you will find this will leave you with many pleasurable memories. All things are possible now and you are headed for a brilliant future.

Dallas Within a few days you will enjoy buying luxurious items for yourself and will enjoy life to the fullest by experiencing the best foods, hotels, etc. Enjoy yourself. This dream may also be used as a reference point in time. If you dream of this city and see its name used in any context, the dream message will occur on this day.

Dalmatian Keep all decisions to yourself until you are absolutely sure of the direction in which you are headed. Work out each detail first. After you are positive of the changes you want to make, bring others into your decisions. You will be very successful. Go with confidence.

dam Make sure you do not spend money that is intended for essentials, especially for the next two days. You will be tempted to do so but will later regret it.

Damascus Do everything you can to bring your family and in-laws closer. Promote family unity by asking each member to plan family events together. This dream may also be used as a reference point in time. If you dream of this city and see its name used in any context, the dream message will occur on this day.

damask You will receive an invitation within a few days. This event will result in chaos. Think carefully about whether you really want to be there.

dame You will be involved in promoting activities for young children in the community. This will bring great emotional rewards and you will be looked upon highly by other people in the community. Be careful not to overextend yourself. Good luck is with you.

Damion and Pythias A long overdue favor requested by you will be finally granted.

damn Spread your responsibilities around. Encourage others to pick up some of the burdens you have been carrying. You will find others will be more than willing to help. Relax for a few days. You are very popular and well liked.

Damocles *(Greek Legend)* During this cycle you can mix business and pleasure successfully.

damp Do not leave young children in the care of an inexperienced caretaker. This person will panic at the moment an infant needs special care. Do not allow this to happen.

damsel An unexpected and unusual occurrence will happen within two days to the object of your affections. Take this time to warn them.

damsel fly Within five days, you will be given an all expense paid trip to a region you wish to visit. This will be a rewarding experience for you.

dance *to dance* You will immediately be granted the money you requested from a certain person. Someone will also go to great lengths to become involved with you sexually. This will bring you a great deal of joy and will occur within three days.

other people dancing Your resourcefulness and consistency will lead to success with all of your ongoing activities.

people who are unable to dance Be open to a business opportunity proposed by an older person. This will lead to future financial security.

to dream that you cannot dance Put yourself in the position to speak with powerful, influential people. State your needs directly and clearly. The response will not be immediate but two people will mull it over and come back to you. These two people will, independently of each other, offer services to help you. These resources will bring your goal to reality.

bride and groom dance You will marry soon, have a happy life, and experience health and wealth.

in any other form This dream is an extremely lucky omen and implies that within two days you will undergo a transformation and develop an inner strength and courage that will drive you to break through any physical and mental barrier that is holding you back from achieving your goals. Once you do this, you will be able to move ahead on any new project that is more to your liking and will bring this to a successful completion. You will also, during this time period, be greeted with open arms anywhere you go and this regal treatment will surprise you greatly. You are headed for a brilliant future and many new opportunities are headed your way.

dance club You will be paid handsomely for escort services. This will be a very profitable enterprise. Expect this to begin within three days.

dance hall Within a few weeks, a big celebration will take place. You will feel, at the time, that this will be too hectic for you. It is a good idea to attend for part of the time. If you decide to go, you will enjoy yourself immensely.

dance school Someone who was in your life in the past and dropped from sight will come back. The relationship will be fresher and brighter and this person will have new ideas to contribute.

dance teacher Within a few days you will become involved with someone and experience a roller coaster effect of emotions. Do not allow yourself to become involved in emotional game playing.

dandelion You are dealing with two separate situations. Both combined will lead you to great riches. You are heading toward a brilliant future. Do some investigative work to ensure this.

dandruff Someone you find attractive and charming will, within two days, involve you in a very dangerous, unfortunate event. This person has a jealous, violent mate who will attack you if they gain knowledge of your involvement. Make it clear that you will not become involved until this person is free. This is a lucky omen and implies riches.

Dane *(people of Denmark)* You will enjoy yourself at an event far more than you anticipated. Expect this within a few days.

danger *to be involved in a dangerous activity and escape* Avoid any explosive disagreements in public with the object of your affections. Your restraint will prevent any gossip about your behavior. Avoid any dangerous activity that you see yourself doing in this dream and schedule peaceful moments in order to alleviate stress.

to be involved in a dangerous activity and not escape Someone who has consistently sought attention from you will become annoyed with you. Although you have clearly stated your lack of interest, this person will still persist. You will then say words that will trigger a response of anger and revenge from this person. Take steps to prevent this. Use soft words that state your desire for friendship and move on with your life.

to see someone in danger and give aid Do everything necessary to rescue a relationship with someone in a distant city. This person feels very neglected by you. You also need to get some much needed rest.

to see someone in danger and not be able to help An unexpected romantic situation will occur and you will feel as though you have to comply with the mood. Be polite but be sure that you do not put out signals of encouragement. Think ahead and guard against sending out mixed messages. Be very clear about what you want now and in the future.

dangle Think ahead for the next two days, someone special to you will unthinkingly blurt out an inconsiderate and insulting remark in front of others. Take this person aside as soon as you can and subtly state your opinion about this kind of behavior in a non-accusing way. This will prevent these thoughtless, unintentional remarks from being said.

Daniel *(from the Bible)* Your educational pursuit will become a big challenge within the next month. Take care of all necessary action now in order to avoid being challenged next month.

danish *(pastry)* Think twice about lending money to people who have always paid you in the past. This time this person will be unable to repay you.

Danube Beware of an upcoming situation. You will have a financial crisis next month and will need to prepare for this. Start setting money aside now. This dream may also be used as a reference point in time. If you dream of this river and see its name used in any context, the dream message will occur on this day.

Daphne *(Greek mythology)* You will develop great clarity of thought within three days that will allow the insight you need to convince another person to express their needs and desires. You will both be able to develop future plans to achieve mutual fulfillment.

dare *any form* You will be able to live up to the plans you have set up for the future.

daredevil Beware of someone who is attempting to take control over you as well as an ongoing project. This will occur within three days.

dark ages Someone will attempt to steer you into a different lifestyle. This will appear alarming and disturbing. Be firm in your decision not to become involved in this lifestyle.

dark horse An unusual occurrence will prevent someone from keeping a date with you. Do not allow this to upset and discourage you but be sure to tactfully and politely demand a rain check for the date. This dream is also a good luck symbol.

darkroom Avoid all thoughts that will take you away from your present life and business dealings. Keep watch on any unusual occurrences for the next three days.

darling *to call someone darling* Someone is looking for more private time with you and is craving attention. You will hear of this within seven days. This is a lucky omen and you will enjoy an abundance of health.

in any other form You will be physically attracted to someone else within a few weeks. Watch your behavior in front of others, this could get you in trouble with your beloved.

darn *(needlework repair)* This week is not the best time to travel. If possible, rearrange all travel plans for a later date.

darn *(the expletive)* Someone who has offered to help you and to become involved in your present undertaking is insincere. Be aware of this in order to avoid disappointment. Choose an alternative person within two days.

darning needle Someone will be entering your life within a few days. This person marries for money and is a con artist. Get on with your life without this person.

dart or dartboard Pay attention to the numbers hit by the dart and look up the numbers for major clues to upcoming events that will occur within three days. Take steps to alter any negative message and expect any positive message to come true. You are also in a cycle that stresses independent work for greater success. Work in a detailed, step by step manner.

if you hit the bull's eye You will hear extremely good news within three days. You will also enjoy victory in all aspects of your life. This luck will stay with you for the next seven days.

Darwin, Charles Never settle for less and refuse to be taken advantage of. Go step by step to ensure that this does not occur, especially for the next seven days. This dream is a good luck omen.

dashboard Become firm in your refusal to allow a friend to tell you what you should or should not do with others, especially for the next three days.

data Do not interfere in other people's lives for the next three days.

data processing Within a few days, you will receive a very significant message through a dream. Be alert to this and follow each message in detail.

date A specific date on the calendar indicates a special event that will occur on this date. This event will bring a special opportunity that will enhance your life in one way or another. This number may also be combined with other significant numbers and used for games of chance. Be sure to mark this date and if you have nothing scheduled, leave yourself available for a good event. You should also have the time to schedule a significant event for the particular date dreamed about. You will be able to achieve a great deal and have many successes on this day. Use it to your advantage. Should the dream offer a clue referring to a negative event, make changes that will alter the outcome.

a social engagement with another person Maintain your sense of humor when someone is making demands of you and your time. Realize this person is placing a great deal of importance on you by desiring to make you a part of their life. Do not become upset at these demands. Good luck is with you.

to recognize your date Your partner, in the dream, is someone who, in reality, desires your company on a date. Any negative occurrence seen in this dream may be altered.

date *(the fruit)* A great amount of work will be coming your way within two weeks. Do not allow this work to pile up. Maintain a steady pace in order to handle this smoothly and efficiently and this will keep down your stress levels.

daughter You can expect, within two days, the events of this dream to become a reality and all words spoken by the daughter in the dream to come true. If this is a negative event, take steps to alter the outcome. Any positive event may be promoted. This also implies that you will reach a desired agreement with someone over the next few days. This will be a wonderful cycle because you will reach a mutual agreement that will ensure all of your plans fall into place.

step daughter Do not allow your indecisiveness to interfere with your determination and slow down your goals.

crying or sick daughter You will be making the wrong decision within two days. In order to avoid a mistake, rethink all of your decisions during this time period. If you dream of any unfortunate situation or illness occurring with your daughter, you must also alert her to this occurrence so she can take steps to prevent it. Expect this to occur within two days.

daughter-in-law A situation regarding a family member needs immediate attention within two days. Make a contribution in effort, finances and time to resolve this issue. You will also be able to pull a special person closer to you emotionally. All negative messages and events occurring in this dream may be altered and all positive messages may be promoted. This is a very lucky dream. If you dream of any unfortunate situation or illness occurring with your daughter-in-law, alert her to this occurrence so she can take steps to prevent it.

dauphin You have greatly underestimated a situation that you will become involved in within a five day period. Move quickly on this before it slips away. This will be your golden opportunity.

David *(from the Bible)* Someone you regard highly will spend time presenting a positive point of view about an upcoming distasteful situation. This advice will be very helpful to you in handling this unpleasant event. Plan on this occurrence within the next three days, and expect the advice to come to you almost immediately following this dream. Pay close attention to ensure that you remember the words spoken prior to the development of the event.

dawn Be aware of your choice of words for the next few days. There is a danger of you blurting out words that will injure someone deeply and that will not be easily forgiven.

day *beautiful day* A destined, beautiful, full blown love relationship will blossom within a few days. Each day you will share deep emotional love and will express mutual goals. This also implies that you are headed in the right direction. Express yourself fully in all matters of personal interest.

daybed Take steps to win over a very powerful and influential person as a friend. You have four days to accomplish this task. Once this person is befriended, the sky is the limit.

daybreak Focus on those issues that require immediate attention. Express your personal needs so you can take care of all situations now instead of waiting until they reach crisis proportions. Do not wait for assistance from others. Handle each problem promptly, by yourself.

daydream Take time out for yourself in order to think creatively and to put your thoughts in order. This will allow you to express yourself in a focused, detailed manner. Concentrate in order to bring your ideas to fruition and within two days you will find you have very concrete, creative ideas. Put those ideas in writing so they will not be lost.

daylight Someone will soon provide you with information you were not aware of. Pay very close attention to all conversations over the next three days and you will glean a wealth of knowledge from words spoken by others.

daylight savings time Begin saving for your future in order to enjoy financial stability in your senior years.

daylily Do what you can to get close to a certain person within the week. You will not be disappointed.

daytime If you are able to recall the exact time, use these numbers for games of chance. You can also schedule an event for this particular time in order to reap greater personal benefits. For the next two days, look for a beneficial situation to occur within the daylight hours.

daze *to be in a daze* Make sure you do not become permanently involved with another person. Your impulsiveness will lead to regret.

DDT Make sure you do not overmedicate yourself in your attempt to recover faster from a particular illness. Proceed with caution.

deacon Meditate in your favorite manner and demand from your higher power what you need in life.

deacon's bench Do not allow feelings of depression to overcome you. This will only restrict you and hold you back. Do not allow old negative feelings and resentments to fester and hinder you from completing your goals. These feelings will keep you from moving in the direction you desire.

dead *to dream of people who have died in reality* This is considered a lucky omen. Consider it an honor to have someone who has deceased visit you in a dream. The message given to you by this person will become a reality. If there is a positive message, promote it to the fullest. If the message is negative, it may be altered or avoided. Do everything you can to experience only positive expressions in your life. The main issue is that when you are visited by a deceased person, you will experience victory due to your valiant integrity when making decisions. You will not compromise your principles. Develop a quiet conviction and be relentless in your pursuit of something that righteously belongs to you. This may be in the form of money, contracts, items, agreements, as well as productive conversation. Do not give up until you succeed. The dream will leave large clues for a dramatic move you are about to undertake. This move will bring immediate and positive changes to your life.

to be deceased Investigate the cause of your death in the dream. This will offer a major clue to what you should avoid in order to prevent your own death. Be alert to the possibility of a vitamin or mineral deficiency caused by improper diet that will lead to system failure. Take precautions to avoid sudden stressful situations that will affect bodily functions. Be careful that you take all medications properly in order to avoid sudden death. You also need to avoid all impulsive behavior and curb this sense of urgency for the next week. Do not become involved in something you have no business involving yourself with..

to dream of a deceased father/mother This dream implies that you are headed toward a fortuitous future. Be courageous and explore several options in order to achieve your goals. You will be successful if you remain practical while taking calculated risks. You will see an immediate improvement in your life.

to talk with a deceased person who is, in reality, still alive If you recognize the person, get in touch with this individual and warn them to guard their health as well as everything that is emotionally precious to them such as reputation, private life, career, etc., from those demonstrating envy. Avoid friction. Warn this person against accidentally overmedicating themselves. They will also be dealing, concurrently, with a number of emotional issues that may drain their strength. Remind them that their faith and strength will get them through. Relentlessly work on any medical problem that comes up before it becomes a crisis.

to have a conversation about someone who has died in reality If this is a positive conversation, you will be successful for the next three days, if you are very detailed in the plans you are about to execute. Train yourself to see the whole picture in order to reap the results of what you are now working toward. You will skillfully use words with enough clarity to complete this task. As a result, you will make yourself available for riches that would otherwise not come to you. Blessings are with you and your family.

to have an untrue conversation about a deceased person You are steering yourself in the wrong direction. Make the effort to determine the cause of this and to determine the direction you want to go. You have been led to believe, by yourself or by someone else, that something is correct, when in actuality it isn't. Dig deeply and make absolutely sure that you are not being misled about an important situation. This dream also implies that certain plans you have made will not work out as you had hoped. Take the proper steps within three weeks to ensure that plans made about a crucial situation will work to your benefit. Focus on your health as well as everyday situations that you take for granted.

to dream of getting married to someone who is deceased This dream is an assurance that your life will turn around and you will enjoy a brilliant future. Enjoy life fully and do not take it for granted. This dream is an extremely lucky omen. Someone will also come into your life within a few days. This person will come on eagerly and will rush you into a friendly relationship. At first you will get mixed messages while on a date. You will feel this person also desires romance. After you begin to respond, this person will back off quickly and withdraw from the friendship. Take this as a forewarning to enjoy the relationship and take it no further.

to talk with a very young deceased person who was much older in reality when they died You need to aggressively pursue what you need in your life and do not procrastinate on any issue you need to take care of. You need to also think back to important events that were occurring during the time period that this person was a part of your life at the age they appeared in the dream. This will supply you with a message of a forthcoming event that will occur within four days. You may want to include this in your present life or take steps to ensure that it does not occur. Focus on your health as well as on everyday situations that you take for granted.

recognizable dead bodies Each dead body you recognize that is still alive in reality represents someone who is living life with a sense of urgency. This person needs to be warned to take steps to calm down this anxiety, impatience and nervousness. These irresistible impulses need to be stopped for the next week. If they are not, this person will become involved in something they have no business being involved with.

the bodies are unrecognizable Each body represents a financial gain of one thousand dollars within the next few days.

dead person who calls or a letter from a dead person Within four days you will consider entering into a business deal. You have spoken to this person before and made it clear that you would enter into an agreement if it involved only the two of you. This individual will not keep their word and will discuss this deal with others.

dead animals Keep a close eye on the safety of a pet. You must also not allow curiosity to take control over your better judgment and do not venture into the unknown. There is a very thin line between mere curiosity and an active participation in something you should not be involved in. Remain uninvolved. You are being misled by others who seek your participation. You have prior warning of this and can avoid all negative involvements, especially for the next three days. If you recognize the dead animal, do what you can, during this time frame, to prevent its untimely death.

a deceased pet This dream is a lucky omen for you and

all those who are interested and involved in your immediate situation. You are in a powerful seven day cycle for achievement and accomplishing everything you attempt. You will also develop more integrity. People in your life will demonstrate greater love and affection. Do nothing to slow down the momentum of those feelings toward you. Everything in your life will flow more smoothly and you will be blessed with better health and more tranquility.

to kill someone or see someone kill someone who is already dead in reality Back off from someone who requires more private time to take care of personal matters and career goals. Stop being so demanding of others, especially for the next three days. Remain relentless in the pursuit of your own goals. You will be in an extremely lucky cycle for the week.

anything you recognize that you see dying Take steps to ensure that this does not occur in reality.

anything else dying Don't let your ambition die and do not allow others to hinder the progress toward your goals or allow yourself to hinder the progress of others. Aggressively act on those aspects of your life that are stagnating and take steps to avoid running into a dead end.

a deceased person who tells you in a dream that in reality they are not dead The person who has come into the dream with this message is telling you there are many ways of experiencing death without really dying (i.e., death of financial security, someone coming into your life who will take over to the point of your experiencing an emotional or spiritual death, etc.). This person will give you a clue to the type, time or place of this death. There is an urgency to this message and you must pay close attention to the decisions you make to keep this death from taking place. They will direct you to the path you should or should not be taking based on the conversation in the dream. Be acutely aware of what may evolve within three days.

deadbeat Expect a good surprise within the next two days.

dead bolt Do not make unkind and unthoughtful remarks to an insecure newcomer. Avoid cruelty to others.

dead end *to see yourself or anyone else run into a dead end of any kind* You are beginning to feel a strong emotional wave that will take up much of your time, because you will have no idea where this drive is coming from. Your urges are causing you to focus on bringing something to tangible form. This feeling will continue for two weeks and you will soon be able to determine the source. At this time you will begin acting on what you feel you should be doing. These strong feelings may be a result of increased awareness and a heightened psychic ability that is driving you to the path you need to take. You will have no tangible proof or verification of this, but your excitement will lead you to know instinctively that by acting on this urge you will reap grander benefits than you ever felt possible. If you deem this to be socially unacceptable or wrong for you, you have the time and advance notice to seek the professional help you need to come to grips with your desires and to live at peace with your urges. This is the perfect cycle to find the right

person equipped to take care of this issue. It will be properly addressed and you will once more gain control over your emotions in a healthy way. You are on the path toward a brilliant future.

dead end street Within three days you will make a decision that will involve you in what later will be a situation with no escape route. Do not make any major decisions for the next few days unless you provide yourself with an escape hatch.

dead letter Avoid heavy labor and excessive demands on yourself for the next two weeks.

deadlock Within the week, a new position will open up and others will expect you to move in quickly. You will be welcomed and the position will prove beneficial, but move quickly.

deadly nightshade Do not openly demonstrate your affections toward someone who does not appreciate it. Be very careful for the next three days in order to avoid disappointment.

deadly sin For the next five days do not divulge your plans to anyone else and keep all of your goals to yourself. This is an extremely lucky omen and you are headed for a brilliant future.

deadpan Stick with your goal until success is achieved.

dead people *to kill someone or see someone kill someone who is already dead in reality* Back off from someone who requires more private time to take care of personal matters and career goals. Stop being so demanding of others, especially for the next three days. Remain relentless in the pursuit of your own goals. You will be in an extremely lucky cycle for the week.

Dead Sea Someone in your life will become more demonstrative in their feelings toward you. You will be very pleased with this. This dream may also be used as a reference point in time. If you dream of this sea and see its name used in any context, the dream message will occur on this day.

Dead Sea scrolls Within a few days, someone will become more demanding of you financially and emotionally. Do not allow this to happen. You are not in a cycle to give at this time. Do everything necessary to remain stress free.

deaf Someone is very eager to inform you of important information you need to know within the next three days. This information has, until now, been concealed from you. This dream also implies that you will give out detailed and accurate information. The person you are imparting information to needs to listen attentively to ensure they catch each detail and nuance of this information. This will prevent later misfortune. This dream is a lucky omen for you.

deal *(cards)* Do not allow the inconsideration of another to cause you distress. Someone, within the next three days will put into writing words that completely contradict everything you believe in and have verbalized. Regroup and remain calm throughout this in order to handle this situation correctly.

dealer Within eight days you will become involved and tangled in a situation you have no business being involved in. Rise above petty activity and protect yourself.

dealership Check all prescriptions carefully and become very knowledgeable about the medications you will be taking.

dean It will become very apparent, within a few weeks, that a group of people you have enjoyed many pleasurable times with are no longer people you feel comfortable with. You will feel as though you have now outgrown these people. Move on with your life but do not burn bridges and do not feel guilty about this.

Dear John letter Someone who has the expertise you need will be more than eager to take you under their wing and assist you in developing this special skill.

death See dead for greater definition

death angel This is a very lucky omen. Do not take life for granted or live it as though it is a rehearsal for something else. Take steps to enjoy life to the fullest. Express love toward those you care about. Within three days you will have the occasion to demonstrate your love for those you are close to. Many blessings will come to you and your family for a long period of time.

deathbed *stranger's* You will hear of someone denying the parentage of a child.
  your deathbed Take every step to prevent any accident or illness for the next three days. Be very aware of food and liquid intake and make sure you take the proper dosage of medications. Pay attention to the cause of your death in this dream and take extra precautions to avoid it.
  someone you know Give warning to this person to take extra precautions with their health and personal environment. Warn this person to be careful of their food and liquid intake and to make sure they take the proper dosage of medications.

death camp A situation will come up within three days that will make it necessary for you to decide whether the person working with you is keeping up their pace. They may be forcing you to work harder because of their own laziness if you are not alert to this. Attend to this now so you can get the help you need without taking over extra responsibilities. Speak up and let this person know they have to do their share. Remain stress free. Many blessings are with you. You are headed for a prosperous future and financially secure old age.

death chamber Do whatever you can to gain knowledge about the character of others that will be of benefit to you. Once you gain this information, keep it to yourself. Do this within three days.

death mask Be very aware of hurricanes and take steps to avoid areas where they may strike.

death rattle Avoid being run over by any vehicle.

death's head moth Within five days you will gain the love of someone who will cherish.

death squad For the next three days you will have to deal with a very desperate person. This person will attempt to involve you in their problems. Take steps to prevent this and do not allow this person to manipulate you.

Death Valley You will receive the promotion you are trying for. Use tact and diplomacy when refusing to take on more responsibility than the promotion requires. This dream may also be used as a reference point in time. If you dream of this desert and see its name used in any context, the dream message will occur on this day.

death warrant Plan your days well ahead of time. This will prepare you to tackle greater opportunities and handle the demands you place upon yourself. Begin this process now to save your energy so you can handle situations in a calm manner as they develop. Budget your energy.

deathwatch A family member will create confusion within the home within seven days. Other family members will become involved and will attempt to arrive at solutions to this problem. You will be asked to become involved. It is better, for the time being, to remain in the background.

death wish You will experience the let down of mental barriers and obstacles in your life within five days. This is also the perfect cycle to rid yourself of unhealthy addictions.

debate *to see another person debate* Someone, within the week, will tell you of suspicions they have and will imply that you have a role in them. This will come as a complete surprise. Remain calm and avoid getting sucked into an argument on this.
  to be in a debate Do not allow silly misunderstandings to crop up. Keep things running smoothly for the next two days. Stay on your toes in order to nip all disagreements in the bud.

Deborah *(from the Bible)* You will finally get the answers you need by pinning down a very elusive person within the next five days.

debt *to owe* A generous person will come to your assistance and rescue you from a financial crisis. This person will relentlessly offer assistance until you are on your feet.

to repay You need, within the next two days, to break out of a routine because you will become irretrievably stuck in the same rut. Devise a new routine and plan new activities.

debutante Be very certain that the information given to you by another person is correct, especially for the next five days. It is preferable to research this information on your own.

decade *any form* Your product will be popular for at least ten years.

decanter A business offer will be extended by an unexpected person. The venture will seem great but in reality will not work out. Move on without accepting this proposal.

decapitate Pay close attention to who or what is decapitated in the dream.

if you are being decapitated You will become very wealthy within six months. This dream also implies victory in achieving a goal. This will come about by working on your goals slowly but surely. Maintain a level of common sense after you achieve your success.

if you recognize the person being decapitated Take the necessary steps to warn this person of a possible negative occurrence within the next few days. You must also not allow anyone to vulturize you in terms of emotion, time and physical energy for the next three days. Set limits on what you are able to handle.

to see an animal decapitated Think carefully about an invitation you have received. The person issuing the invitation expects more than you are willing to give. A tactful conversation will put an end to this expectation.

decathlon Within a three day period your car will turn up missing. Be very cautious about where you leave your belongings.

decay Someone has a serious and important question to ask you and will contact you within three days.

deceit *to hear this phrase* Someone you are passionately in love with will parent a child with someone else unless you take steps to prevent it within three months. It is still possible to maintain a healthy relationship, if this is what you desire.

in any other form For the next month, when you express your interests and feelings with others, express it in such a way that leaves no doubt about what you are talking about. Any deceit occurring in a dream that has a possibility of occurring in reality needs to be prevented.

December An opportunity that will excite you will be presented and you now have the means to grasp it. You will enjoy a new start in life in those areas where you desire change, and all old issues and burdens will disappear. Vast changes that will lead to immediate success will come your way and leave you with a new and exciting zest for life. The

nurturing you have longed for will come to you through spiritual nourishment. Many blessings will come to you and your family.

decibel Do not try to keep up with those who are better off than you. Avoid false pride, this only leads to extra stress.

decimal This represents a monetary figure you need to remember for conducting business transactions. You may use the figures for games of chance. You must also make sure that you maintain absolute loyalty to those who are important to you. You are headed toward a brilliant future.

decimal point Do whatever you can to draw closer to that special person. Make this a permanent bond by verbalizing your feelings and intentions. Good luck is with you.

deck Someone is very eager to include you on a business trip. If you choose to pursue this, you will have a very enjoyable time. Within five days, you will also have the chance to cater to someone with a different ethnic background. Your hard work, ability to handle situations with diplomacy, tact, and eagerness to please will open doors to you on a permanent basis. As a result, you will be offered many new opportunities and will experience an increase in finances. Good luck is with you.

deck *(of cards)* *to play* You will quickly get the money you need to pay all of your outstanding debts.

someone else with a deck of cards You will soon make future plans with a special person and will make arrangements to live together.

deck *(tape deck)* *any form* The next three days will be an important time to connect emotionally with another person. Be very clear about the message you want to communicate before you speak. You will be able to make this connection so successfully, that this individual will respond in the manner you most desire. Pay attention to the message heard on the tape. If this message is negative, you have enough time to ensure that you only experience positive events.

deck chair Someone you have known for a while who has admired you from a distance will become your lifelong love.

deckhand Take over some of the responsibilities for another person so this individual can regain their health. As a result, this person will gain greater independence. Good luck is with you.

Declaration of Independence Your creative and mental energies are high. Share your ideas, in detail, with others so they may utilize your services more effectively.

decompose *worms in decomposing material* This dream implies that you will have victory in that area of your life you deem to be most important to you. You must also remain uninvolved in any quarrelsome situation that will arise within the next three days. Pay attention to the objects being decomposed in this dream. This implies that you are not taking care of these items properly in reality. Take special care that these objects do not become lost to you.

in any other form Do not postpone anything of importance for the next three days. You will be tempted to do so but you will ultimately lose out if you do.

decongestant Express yourself with more confidence and break out of the mold of the ordinary. Have fun being a little outrageous.

decorating A stranger in distress will involve you in a situation that could be very dangerous. Get back-up help instead of assuming the responsibility of another person. This will come about within three days.

decoration A lack of communication will cause you to have a major set back. Take steps to prevent this and to draw closer to the person you desire in your life.

decoration day Give everything you have for the next few days. You will get the job done more quickly and more enjoyably.

decorator Within two days you will receive the gift of mental inventiveness by the Gods. Put this gift to good use and you will see your present circumstances improve dramatically. You will prosper in each area of your life for the upcoming month.

decoupage Do not allow a bad situation from the past to keep you from making that necessary change in your life. It is important to make these changes within the next four days in order to achieve a more prosperous life. Luck is with you.

decoy Do not let others in on secrets. Do not betray the confidence of others and do not compromise your sense of ethics.

deed *to be thankful for a good deed performed for you* You will soon get the promotion that you are seeking and will receive what you want from this promotion.

deed *(legal writ)* You will finally go out on a date with someone you have desired for some time and you will experience many sweet moments. Expect this within three days.

deep *anything* Avoid unnecessary strain to the body. Do not lift anything heavy, especially for the next week. Any negative message will be altered by taking preventive steps.

deep dish pie You will be spending time with someone you have a deep respect for. Afterwards you will realize that you are in love with this person. If you pursue this, the relationship will develop nicely for both of you.

deepen In two days, you will be called by someone who is very eager to see you. You are eager to see this person as well and the visit will be very relaxing and enjoyable.

deep freeze Pay attention to the contents of the deep freeze. Any item that does not belong there represents an occurrence that will have a negative impact on your life. Take steps now to prevent this. Within three days you will also experience unexpected wealth.

to see yourself in the deep freeze Avoid putting yourself in a similar situation (i.e., locked out of the house on a cold day) for the next three days. An unusual situation is also taking place that you are neglecting. Attend to this promptly in order to avert a crisis.

deep fry You will be around someone for the next week who has a problem controlling alcohol and may cause a great deal of embarrassment to you.

deep sea Make sure you do not place yourself in the position to be taken advantage of sexually. You will be able to handle yourself properly.

deep six Referral agencies will be very beneficial for you and will go to great lengths to help you reach your goal.

Deep South Become very aware of someone you least expect who has set a trap to lure you into saying something you will regret. Watch this situation carefully. This dream may also be used as a reference point in time. If you dream of this region and see its name used in any context, the dream message will occur on this day.

deer The person who accepts a date will not show up. You will be invited out again within five days.

deerskin For the next few weeks you will experience several trivial, bothersome situations. You will have the strength to handle each problem. Keep yourself in balance

deerstalker You will accomplish far more by handling things on your own. This is a lucky cycle for taking care of things alone.

deface You will be asked by someone, within four days, to complete an assignment that presents a danger to you. You can avoid this.

default Someone has devised a plot to lure you somewhere for the intent to commit bodily harm. For the next seven days, take special precautions to prevent this occurrence.

defeat *to defeat* Avoid all places where another person who enjoys embarrassing you in public is likely to be, especially for the next week.

to be defeated A tricky situation is developing over the next two days with someone whom you are attracted to. Do not allow this person to play games with you. Move on with your life. Do whatever is necessary to create a positive situation from a negative one.

in any other form Tie up all loose ends and do everything necessary to develop positive negotiations for two weeks. Make sure all bases are covered in order to avoid any defeat.

defecate Your determination will lead you to a great future and your life will undergo a major change in all areas of love, money and health. You will gain a new zest for life and will receive more love and affection from others.

defect *to defect* Do not allow yourself to be spread too thin by catering to the request of others. Take care of yourself and have compassion for yourself.

to help someone else defect Remain uninvolved with any mysterious situation that has been purposely put out there to lure you in. Your curiosity could be your undoing. Remain calm and uninvolved.

in any other form You will gain a position in the public eye. Do not forget others you leave behind. Make time to fit old friends into your new life.

defend You must stop being so possessive. Watch your attitude and do not destroy a wonderful friendship. Whatever you see yourself defending in a dream needs to be guarded in reality. Take steps to cover all bases regarding an ongoing situation.

defendant Pay close attention to your surroundings. Someone will intentionally attempt to steer you in the wrong direction. Be very clear about what you want and take steps to prevent this from occurring. It would be very detrimental to your welfare.

you are the defendant Take steps to prevent being a defendant in reality. This dream contains major clues that will keep you from becoming involved in something that will create problems for you. You are also too lenient and allow too much interference in your private life. Become aware of the needs of a special person so you can set aside private time to spend with them. This is a cycle that requires you take these steps.

if you recognize the defendant Take the time to carefully scrutinize all important papers. It is also important to view them from a different perspective, especially for the next three days.

defense Take your time with paperwork. Think carefully and be detailed when taking care of important work.

deflate *to deflate* You will be lied to by someone who will attempt to build up your hopes with false statements. Avoid disappointment by not paying attention to their statements.

defogger Be very cautious with your behavior for the next three days. You could inadvertently be cruel to another person.

defoliant For the next two days, do not take any risks that

could result from your bad temper. This behavior will bring about a permanent split between you and someone special to you. Remove all blocks in communications that keep this union from growing deeper.

deforestation Within three days you will have to deal with a very evil person who will twist around the words of others to his own advantage. This person will give you conflicting and unreliable information. Be aware of this and do everything you can to avoid this person, otherwise you will be entering a lucky cycle within the week resulting from a good decision that you will make.

deformity You have the time to prevent any illness or accident that will create a deformity similar to that presented in you dream. This dream also implies victory. You will acquire what you desire within a two week cycle. This will be a joyous time for you.

defrost For the next five days, do not place yourself in the position that allows another person to gain enough power over you to mistreat you in public.

defrosting package Someone has purposely taken a stand against you for no reason. You have not spoken to them for some time and this person will soon begin to reconnect with you.

defuse You will enjoy many peaceful and tranquil moments in life, but for the next two days take precautions and make sure that you do not put yourself in danger. Remain in a safe place and guard your life.

degenerate You will receive the money you are expecting within two weeks.

if you recognize the degenerate This person or someone with a similar personality will cause you disappointment if you do not take steps to prevent this.

if you are the degenerate Do not become intimate with anyone you have no desire to be intimate with. Follow your instincts.

degraded Do everything necessary, for the next three days, to alter your regular schedule in order to throw off a stalker with murderous intentions. You have prior notice of this and have time to prevent it.

degree For the next seven days, take steps to be especially nice to someone special.

dehydrate Take steps to protect your well being and be sure you are maintaining a healthful diet. You must also make sure you do not become deficient in vitamins, minerals and important electrolytes.

to be dehydrated Do everything necessary to avoid exposure to a virus.

someone you know is dehydrated Alert this person to the need of a proper diet. Do not waste time. Focus on ways to bring balance into your life in the areas you desire.

someone you do not know is dehydrated Do not allow jealousy to take control in any area of your life. By refusing to allow this in your life, you will prosper in ways you never imagined.

deice For the next week, do not deprive yourself of something that will give you many pleasurable moments. This will give you memories you will treasure for a lifetime.

deity You are headed for a brilliant future. Good luck is with you, especially for the next week.

dejá vu The experience of dejá vu that you have in the dream will occur in reality within four days. You will also enjoy luck and good health for a long time. Follow your hunches; your instincts are on target.

Delaware You will enjoy an abundance of health and will begin to enjoy this improvement within seven days. This dream may also be used as a reference point in time. If you dream of this state and see its name used in any context, the dream message will occur on this day.

delegate Become better organized. Pleasure seeking will lead you on a dangerous path. A situation will arise within three days that will be highly dangerous if you do not stop this pleasure seeking habit. Take care of yourself.

deli You will be rescued by someone within three days. This person will offer financial aid in the nick of time and will be eager to continue this help until you are on your feet.

delicacy Within three days you will need to express more love and affection to a loved one. The messages you have been giving out have been cold and hurtful. Avoid a separation by working at becoming more loving and demonstrative.

delight A promised situation will come to pass. For the next five days, you will also be surrounded by people who will express their deep love for you. You are headed in the right direction and your future will be very prosperous.

Delilah *(from the Bible)* You will have the intuitive thoughts you need to overcome a difficulty in your life and be able to deal with this in a confident way. Stay balanced and you will keep a major disappointment from coming your way.

delinquent For the next three days, take extra precautions while traveling to prevent an avoidable accident.

delirium Do not allow yourself to become unconsciously manipulated for the next seven days. Become very aware of the negative game playing of others in order to keep your own thoughts from becoming negative. You must also control your own reaction to negativity.

deliver For the next three days, all of your thoughts will be focused on one specific person. If you choose, make the first move and you will find a mutual sexual desire. Don't waste time.

to have anything delivered to you You will gain the power to make desired changes in your life. You will also quickly receive the money you have been expecting. Live life to its fullest. These changes will begin to take place within two days.

to deliver Within three days, understanding and a deep closeness will develop between you and someone who is important to you. Listen to what you are being told and keep communications open.

general delivery You will be very instrumental in pointing out the needs of a young person to an adult in charge of this young individual. Do this within four days. You also need to assign tasks only to those who have the specific knowledge to handle the job.

delivery room One of three things will occur after dreaming of a delivery room. You will begin receiving money from a billed source. But because of circumstances over the next week, you will receive less than anticipated. Be patient, but relentless. In time you will receive the full amount. You may also be required to perform physical labor without pay. You must also be very aware that someone you have put out of your life and has promised to leave you alone will break this promise within three days. Prepare yourself in such a way that it will be difficult for this person to pin you down. Make it very clear that you want nothing to do with them. Prepare yourself emotionally to deal with this delicate situation. Organize your thoughts and feelings so you will not be misunderstood and make sure you are not willing to commit to something you are unwilling to. You will be able to get your point across in a tactful way without offending anyone. Proceed with caution and you will successfully handle this delicate situation.

to see a delivery You will hear of a birth of twins. Apply yourself and express your ideas graphically within a few weeks. This will give others the chance to really visualize your ideas and this will work to your advantage. A compromise on an agreement will end problems and you will be better off in the long run.

to be in a delivery You will be, within the next five days, given a gift of greater mental inventiveness by your deity. Put this gift to practical use in order to change your present circumstances. You will experience instant wealth, a brilliant future and have the greater clarity of thought that you need to correctly direct the fortune you will be coming into. Make sure anything negative you dream of does not occur, and take steps to ensure that you experience only positive expressions in life.

dell Do not waste your time on a romantic involvement that is being pushed on you by someone else. This will not work out the way in which you imagined.

delphinium Do not put yourself in the position to suffer hurt feelings because you have said the wrong thing at the wrong time. Watch your behavior.

delta *(the symbol)* You will enjoy victory in a desirable special situation within the next seven days. Luck is with you.

delta *(levee)* You and your family will enjoy an abundance of health, wealth and tranquility.

deluge *(flood)* For seven days, a variety of equally troublesome situations will arise. Work at your top level on each of these issues to ensure that they are successfully resolved. Remain flexible, calm and relaxed while handling each experience. Your life will soon reach a balance once more.

delusion Pay attention to the events of this dream. Any negative occurrence may be altered and result in a positive outcome. Any positive situation may be embraced. Someone will also attempt to lure you into a romantic situation. Do not let your guard down because you will suffer disappointments. If you choose to pursue this situation, it will take years to bring this to the level you desire. Get on with your life without any involvement in an impossible situation.

delusional *to become delusional* Within the month you will finally realize your ambitions. You will be able to complete a major portion of the work that is necessary to finish. You are headed toward a brilliant future.

deluxe Within the month you will receive an item of luxury that you have always desired but felt you would never be able to afford. This cycle will place you in the lap of luxury and elegance. You will also find that a number of people will feel an urgency to speak to you about their deep feelings for you. You are esteemed and honored by many.

demagogue Set limits to what you are willing to do. Make sure your limits are stated clearly to those you are working with to offset later disappointments. Do this within two weeks.

demand *to demand and receive what you are demanding* Specifically demand from your higher power what you need to point your life in the right direction. You will receive clarity of greater thought. Once you take this step, opportunities will present themselves and you will turn your life around in a positive fashion. Your special deity is with you.

to demand and have your demands refused You will learn an unexpected truth about someone from another person. This involves shocking behavior against the person you are speaking to. Lend an ear and do whatever is necessary to steer this person toward the help they need. At the moment this individual is not thinking clearly and needs you to motivate them into seeking immediate help.

to have demands placed on you and you refuse to comply You will receive an excited reaction from someone about a well thought out plan you are thinking of instigating. You will be very eager to have this plan accepted by others.

This will occur within three days.

to have demands placed on you and you comply A situation you are working on will rapidly accelerate toward success. Dispel all your doubts. You will receive a rapid response to all your needs for the next two days.

in any other form Help others who are in unstable situations to bring a balance and more prosperity to their lives. Do this within two weeks. Encourage others to use this cycle to bring about positive changes. Promote these changes and the resulting stability will make everyone's life easier.

demented Within the month you will finally realize your ambitions. You will be able to complete a major portion of the work that is important for you. You are headed toward a brilliant future.

demerit Do not overlook situations, for the upcoming week, that need immediate attention. Take these matters seriously and do not ignore important details.

Demeter *(Greek mythology)* You will request an important favor from someone who will offer it free of charge within five days. This service will change your life significantly. Take advantage of this. The opportunity for this free service will never come again and you will save a great deal of money if you act now. You are headed for a brilliant future. Anything negative portended in this dream needs to be changed. Take steps to experience only positive expressions in your life.

demigod Each event connected to this dream that is positive needs to be converted into a reality as quickly as possible. Each negative event may be altered. This dream is a lucky omen for you and you will magically possess the inner strength to handle forthcoming situations. You will enjoy prosperity, balance and tranquility in your life. Luck will be with you, especially for the next seven days.

demitasse Trust your instincts, especially for the next three days, regarding matters of love. You will quickly receive a proposal that you will find very attractive regarding present involvements in your life. Approach this in a positive fashion.

democracy Do everything possible to communicate, within the week, your plans to a specific person and you can expect action from this individual. Open communication will bring everything together more rapidly.

democrat You will enjoy good luck throughout the next month.

democratic convention Within seven days, an unusual occurrence will prevail. You have the time now to think of any situation that has the potential for development and the time to take steps to prevent an unfortunate circumstance.

demolish *to see something demolished* Use a great deal of discipline and control for the next week to avoid a sexual encounter with someone you do not desire. Be sure that you steer clear of any situation that may allow this to occur.

demolition Within the week, someone will go to great lengths to create a situation that will break up a relationship between you and a special person. Be very aware of what is happening and take steps to prevent it.

demon You will be pursued by someone who needs you by their side on a permanent basis, if you choose to follow this path.

if you dream of a demon Within ten days you need to rid yourself of everything that could result in a self-inflicted injury. Stop putting yourself in a position that allows others to inflict cruelty. Take yourself from all stressful situations. The next ten days will put you in the best cycle for self healing.

to be chased by a demon An organization is attempting to undermine your efforts. This group owes you and is attempting to keep what is rightfully yours. Make yourself aware of behind the scenes events and do not allow yourself to be manipulated. Relentlessly pursue what is rightfully yours even if it takes longer than anticipated.

to be pursued and not be able to escape You must be aggressive and use valor and integrity to handle an upcoming negative situation. You have enough prior notice to turn this situation to your advantage.

to outwit a pursuing demon You will enjoy victory in all phases of your life. Do whatever is necessary to maintain a stress free life for the next ten days. Be relentless in your pursuit of your goals. This cycle is special and lucky for you. Be sure that you eat healthful foods.

if a child is a demon This dream implies that this child needs more protection health wise. You will be able to turn this child's life around in a more positive fashion. Be careful of the people this child associates with and provide only positive role models. Guard them carefully for the next ten days.

to dream of a demon laughing at you Time is running out for you. You are in danger from a very evil person. Although this person has not yet demonstrated any sign of their evil nature, they will remove their mask of normalcy once you grow closer to them. You will need to investigate to determine who this person is. This will take place within four days. Do not allow this person to get close to you and take steps to protect yourself.

demonstration Whatever you see demonstrated in this dream will occur in reality. Anything positive may be promoted. All negative messages may be altered. This dream also implies that you need to subtly encourage the person you are interested in. Make a romantic overture within three days. This cycle is perfect for this.

demonstrator Be very aware for the next three days. Take extra care to make the correct decisions in any situation that is important to you.

den For the next two days, make sure that all machinery is operating properly and there are no faults that will create hazardous conditions for you.

denim You are headed in the right direction and will enjoy a brilliant future.

Denmark Within the week, you will be invited to a yacht party. Everyone will enjoy themselves immensely. You will also meet a dynamic person who will become a lifelong friend. This dream may also be used as a reference point in time. If you dream of this city and see its name used in any context, the dream message will occur on this day.

den mother Within two days, be sure that everyone involved in your life fully understands exactly how you feel about a certain person. This will clear up any misunderstandings and ensure that everyone treats this person with the proper respect. Find the time to relax and take time out to pamper yourself, especially for the next three days.

dent For the next three days, take care not to blurt out a planned secret event and spoil the surprise.

dental floss Be prepared to handle an unexpected situation that will arise within the next five days. This will consist of a domestic crisis within another family and will require tact, diplomacy and calm to resolve this successfully. Also, floss your teeth properly and on a daily basis.

dental hygiene A very spoiled person will create a scene within three days. Be alert to this behavior in order to avoid a very nasty and obnoxious moment. Attend to this person carefully and listen to each word they are saying.

dental hygienist You will be unable to repay money that you will ask to borrow in five days. Do not embarrass yourself by putting yourself in the position of being unable to repay someone in a timely fashion.

dentist *to see a dentist working on your teeth* You need to visit a dentist prior to it becoming a necessity. You will also receive a gift in a short period of time.

denture For the next three days do not act like a penny pincher in front of someone else. This person will be very turned off by this attitude and will be convinced that you are like this all of the time.

Denver A family member will be very eager to come to your aid in a financial matter, especially for the next seven days. All you need to do is ask. This dream may also be used as a reference point in time. If you dream of this city and see its name used in any context, the dream message will occur on this day.

deodorant Do everything necessary to rid yourself of all damaging behavior. Within seven days you will discover something new inside of you that will facilitate this change. Be very acutely aware of any new behavior you pick up. You will have the inner strength you need to crush destructive behavior.

department For the next two days, steer clear of someone who has an irrational temper. You will be successful in keeping this person out of your life for this time period.

department store For the next seven days, develop more affectionate, loving feelings toward someone special. Treat this person with extra kindness. Your disinterested behavior will destroy the love someone feels for you if it is not changed immediately. The upcoming cycle is perfect for correcting all past mistakes.

departure *to dream of someone leaving and returning at a later time* Be very aware that someone you have asked to leave your life who has reassured you they will leave you alone will, within five days, break this promise. Prepare yourself to avoid being pinned down by this individual and make it clear you do not want anything to do with them. Organize your feelings and thoughts and do not allow someone to feel you are willing to commit to something you are unwilling to. Make sure you are not misunderstood. You will be able to get your point across in a way that will not offend. Proceed with caution and you will be successful in dealing with this delicate situation.

dependent Any negative event associated with this dream may be changed to alter the outcome. All positive events may be promoted and included in your life. You must also make sure that you do not allow anyone to abuse you physically or verbally while engaged in sexual play. This may appear innocent now but will become serious at a later time. Be firm about setting limits. You will be in a very good cycle for the next seven days. Luck is with you.
Someone is dependent on you Someone who has not previously been interested in a relationship will now come to you eager to discuss love and affection. This will come at a time when you have lost interest in this person. Make an effort now to rekindle this feeling. You will find a great deal of satisfaction from this relationship if you make this effort within three days.
to be dependent on someone else Over the next three days, carefully go over all insurance forms and determine what is lacking. If it is necessary to include something, contact the proper representatives and make additions to ensure proper coverage.

deportee *someone else is* You will learn of a friend's violent death.
to be Make sure you are not placed in the position to be falsely accused due to a mistaken identity. Be very cautious you do not become involved in unusual situations for the next seven days.
depose *to depose* Within three days, you will be dealing

with a very deceitful person. Remain alert, do not believe anything they say and make an effort to steer clear of this individual.

deposit Within two days you will receive a satisfactory answer to a question you have posed to someone else.
to make a deposit You will be very shocked upon discovering a deep and mysterious conspiracy that someone has plotted against someone else. You will hear about this within three days and you must remain uninvolved.

deposit slip For the next three days, make sure you do not put yourself in the position of having to take a very unpleasant trip that will lead to many distasteful moments. Do everything you can to prevent this.

depot This dream is a very lucky omen, particularly if many people are present. Follow your hunches, your intuition is correct.

depot *(bus)* Allow yourself plenty of time to keep an important appointment.

depot *(train)* A project you are now involved with needs alterations and more detail in order to assure success.

depraved You will receive the money you are expecting within two weeks.
if you recognize the degenerate This person will cause you disappointment if you do not take steps to prevent it.
if you are the degenerate Do not become intimate with anyone you have no desire in being intimate with. Follow your interests.
if you find amusement in this dream This dream is an extremely lucky omen and you will find the strength to tackle a difficult situation within three days. The rest of this cycle will be filled with enjoyable times and happiness, and you will enjoy much tranquility.

depressant You are about to make a big mistake. You care deeply about someone who cares a great deal about you but you want the relationship to develop faster than it is. Because of this, you will become very demanding and will try to rush things. Take the time to develop your personality in order to project a more positive image and this person will eventually grow into the relationship. You will then be able to reach a mutual understanding.

depressed This dream implies that within three days you will be in the presence of a certain person who will speak to you in a way that will corner you. This person will go to great lengths to pin you down, and you will agree to do anything they wish, behave in a manner they desire or verbalize statements they wish. Be very wary of this because this person will be very forceful in trying to get their way. Take the appropriate steps now to avoid being placed at a disadvantage.

depression Within the week, someone responding to a want ad will be the perfect person you are looking for regarding a particular project. Any negative event associated with this dream may be changed to alter the outcome. All positive events may be promoted and included in your life. Also, do not allow anyone to abuse you physically or verbally while engaged in sexual play. This may appear innocent now but will become serious at a later time. Be firm about setting limits. You will be in a great cycle for the next seven days. Luck is with you.

depressor *tongue* Within two days you will reach a decision about a career matter. Carefully investigate the plans you hope to execute to determine their workability and to decide whether you wish to put them into action. This dream is a lucky omen and each plan will work out exactly as you wish once you have taken the time to review them.

depth perception All private information you seek will be easily obtained within the next seven days. Follow your hunches. You will have good luck for a very long time.

deputy Check all matters relating to leases and make sure nothing is overlooked. Anything you see the deputy doing in this dream may manifest itself in reality. If this is a negative message, take steps to alter the outcome. If it is positive, take steps to promote it.

derail Within two days, you will experience the beginning of something new and different concerning trade agreements and consignments. You will find that, in the near future, this will be a profitable business situation.

deranged Pay attention to the identity of the deranged individual.
if you recognize the person Be suspicious and cautious when working with this person, especially when dealing with finances and important paperwork. This is particularly important for the next seven days.
if you do not recognize the person Do not allow yourself to become involved in a quarrel between two angry people. You will be physically and verbally abused as a result. The moment you realize this situation is developing, take yourself away from the area.
if you are deranged Within the month you will finally realize your ambitions and be able to complete a major portion of the work that is necessary. You are headed toward a brilliant future.

derby *(hat)* You had a successful profitable idea in the past. With a few alterations, you will find success with the same idea now. Begin work on this within seven days.

derby *(race)* This dream is a good luck omen. Look carefully at situations that are developing now between you and another person. This will give you the guidance you need to correctly handle any new situation.

derelict Within three days, you will be able to convince a very difficult person to look at your point of view and to come to a mutually beneficial agreement. Move quickly. This cycle is good for producing wonderful results.

dermatitis Become very aware for the next three days of your involvements with family members and do not become involved in a difficult situation. Do not allow others to disturb your balance.

dermatologist Make sure you carry yourself properly so you won't have to justify your actions later on. Be very aware of your behavior for the next three days.

derrick Be very wary of an evil person who will attempt to change your life. This person will attempt to involve you in a very distasteful and degrading situation. Be very alert to all new acquaintances and situations for the next three days.

derriere *(buttocks)* You are in a very lucky cycle, will achieve victory in anything you choose, and be very satisfied with the result of your choice. You will also experience loyalty and affection from those around you, especially for the next week. Any negative event foretold in this dream may be changed to produce a positive result.

derringer Make sure that you do not allow anything unusual to occur at an unreasonable hour.

dervish Do whatever is necessary to prevent a financial drain on your resources. Maintain balance and order in your life. Meditate in your favorite form and do not take any financial risks for the next four days. Good luck is with you.

descendent Do not sign any important papers for the next five days and make sure you go over each document carefully to eliminate any mistakes.

describe *to have something described to you* Check for the connection in this dream to reality. If it is a negative situation, you have time to alter the message. You will also plan to come into an agreement with someone within three days and this will fall into place exactly as you wish.
to describe to someone else All paperwork connected with government agencies will not turn out well. Do everything necessary now to ensure that this works to your advantage.

desecrate Make the first move to bring positive attention your way. This will ensure that you get the promotion you desire. If you keep a low profile, the promotion will be denied to you. Make this move within three days. Good luck is with you.

desert You will be successful with an ongoing project depending on how aggressively you pursue this goal over the next three days. Take steps not to allow unusual and irregular circumstances to interfere with the natural flow of this work. A former lover will also seek you out for the apparent purpose of renewing the relationship. The hidden agenda is to victimize and abuse you because of the resentments harbored from a past relationship. Refuse to become reinvolved.

deserted *(area)* *to be in one* Someone will spend your money without asking you. Take steps to prevent this.

to be deserted You will be sexually aroused by someone you do not know. This person has an air of mystery about them. If you make a move within three days, you will be able to involve yourself romantically. This will be a successful match.

to desert someone Do not expose yourself to a rare illness. It is especially important for the next three days to be extra cautious.

design *to design* Express boldness by taking action for the next three days.

someone else designs Avoid all people who appear to be opportunists and do not allow them to take advantage of you.

to see any design The symbol in the design represents a clue to either a positive situation that should be promoted or a negative situation that needs to be avoided. Complete all projects prior to beginning new ones and attempt to complete all ongoing projects within three days.

designer You will enjoy many wonderful moments with a date whom you hoped would be romantic. If you choose, this relationship will develop to the level you desire and be emotionally and romantically fulfilling for as long as you want. You are headed in the right direction.

desire What you desire in a dream is what you need to work at acquiring in reality. Begin work on this within three days.

to have someone discuss their desires with you Pay attention to what this person is saying. Their records will yield clues to what is happening in your life. This dream also implies that you will gain the position you want within the family in a few days.

desk Do everything necessary to get together a group of people for an amusing outing such as a comedy club, etc. Start adding pleasurable get-togethers to your life.

desktop Do not allow yourself to become overly picky and a nuisance to others. Make certain you also avoid an irritating person for the next three days. This person will be a big nuisance during this time period.

desperado Within the next three days make sure you do not push a certain person the wrong way. By using tact you will successfully handle any situation that arises.

if you recognize the desperado You will be able to accomplish a desired reconciliation regarding an ongoing situation. If you take advantage of this cycle and work toward this goal you will achieve success.

if you are the desperado This will be a very lucky cycle for you. You will be able to spark an interest in others concerning something you choose to interest them in. You will also be the object of much affection. Do everything necessary to create a simple, stress free lifestyle.

despot Each positive event connected to this dream needs to be converted into reality as quickly as possible. Each negative event may be altered. This dream is a lucky omen and you will magically possess the inner strength to handle forthcoming situations. You will enjoy prosperity, balance and tranquility in your life. Good luck will be with you for the next seven days.

dessert Conduct yourself in such a manner that proves you to be a delightful lover instead of a parent.

dessert spoon Pay close attention to your financial affairs. Stocks will rise and all things associated with your finances will improve. This is the perfect time for investing and you are headed for a very prosperous future.

dessert wine Expect someone to relate an important message to you within the week. This message will contain knowledge that will enable you and your family to develop a new and better lifestyle.

destination *any form* A business meeting will result in agreements in your favor and be a dynamic success. This will occur within three days.

destiny *if someone is talking about your destiny* Locate any positive message and work to bring it to fruition. Any negative message will be changed if you take steps to alter it. It is also imperative that you be very graceful and diplomatic for the next three days. Someone will perform a priceless favor for you that will dramatically improve your life. Good luck is with you.

to discuss another's destiny Inform this person, of the issues discussed in the dream. This will give them time to develop the positive and to alter the negative. You also need to be very determined to resolve an ongoing situation, especially for the next four days.

destitute Someone will begin to behave differently toward you. You will see greater kindness, punctuality and respect. This will puzzle you until you learn that this individual has been working on self-improvement. Expect this behavior to be permanent. Good luck is with you.

destroy *to destroy* Refrain from extreme behavior. Review all ongoing situations calmly and in detail. It is especially important to address this within two days. Be very careful not to destroy something you hold close and dear to you by the manner in which you behave and communicate.

to see someone else destroy Make it a point, over the next few days, to demonstrate extra kindness to someone who needs this in their life. Pay attention to what is destroyed and take steps to ensure this does not happen in reality.

destroyer This dream is a very lucky omen. Stressful situations and long standing burdens will be lifted. A solution for a difficult situation will be found within three days. You will find tranquility and health and will benefit financially from this.

detective *to be a detective* Do not back away from a project merely because it appears overwhelming. Encourage yourself to work on this task until completion.

to be arrested by a detective Within three days you will commit an act that will lead to your arrest. Do not put yourself in the position to commit a crime.

to speak to one Children in the family should be protected against kidnapping, especially for the next four days.

if you recognize the person the detective is speaking to Warn the person you dreamed about not to commit a crime in order to avoid arrest.

detective story A mystery will be solved within the week.

detector Do not allow yourself to get caught up in the glitter and glamour that someone else projects. This person has a tendency to be irresponsible and within three days will glamorize a situation that will not work out in the way they present. Back off and make your own decisions. You are entering a cycle that promotes good health.

detention home Plan your schedule in such a way that you are able to accomplish as much as possible in the least amount of time.

detergent Offers will be made within four days. Make sure all details that are important to you are included. Everything will then fall into place nicely.

dethrone Anyone connected with this dream should strongly heed the reason for the dethroning. It is possible to keep these events from taking place to retain the respect of those you care about. You will also be captivated by the charm and physical appearance of someone within three days. This will ultimately result in a long and mutually satisfying relationship, if you choose this option.

detour Be sure you do not take the wrong path in life. When taking road trips, make an extra effort to carefully map out your destination. You must also avoid all stubborn behavior that will cause others to become uncomfortable. This is especially important for the next seven days.

detox Be very careful for the next five days not to involve yourself with outrageous situations and unusual behavior. This is crucial. Any involvement will change your life and you will regret it at a later time.

Detroit You will be given a prepaid extended vacation. This will occur within the month. Luck is with you. This dream may also be used as a reference point in time. If you dream of this city and see its name used in any context, the dream message will occur on this day.

deuce You will enjoy a variety of lifestyles, festivities, and points of view. Good luck is with you. Games of chance are lucky. For two days, you will have fun, luck and happiness.

Deuteronomy You will have many blessings for a long time to come.

develop *to develop film* You will decide on a way of handling something that will work well for you although it appeared at first that it would not. This will prove to be the perfect solution to an important issue. Do not allow others to intimidate you because of your personal viewpoints. Try new things and you will notice a big difference in your life.

developer This dream is a warning to those who are pregnant. They should take precautions against a premature birth by guarding their health and avoiding all heavy activity for a three day period.

Devil Anything negative that occurs in this dream will be fulfilled accurately in real life, if you do not quickly take steps to avoid it. Make sure you only experience positive expressions in your life. You need to take all necessary steps to avoid a problematic situation that is unfolding that you have no business being a part of. You must make sure all your bases are safely covered so you can protect everything that is emotionally precious to you. You can do this by making sure you do not put yourself on the path of destruction. During this time period, someone will also enter your life who is very immoral and wicked. This person will cause you great emotional harm. You have prior notice of this and will need to take every step to avoid this individual completely. You will have the ability and strength to endure anything you are required to handle. Make corrections in those areas of your life that require changes and do everything within your power to make sure problematic areas are rerouted, and to ensure you set yourself on the righteous path you should be headed toward. Dramatic positive changes will be easier to accomplish at this time. Search for tools that will allow personal growth and do not allow loved ones to outgrow you. Find ways to shed outmoded ways of thinking and behaving in order to keep your loved ones around you. Stop being so verbally abusive to others in public and private. The necessary help will arise from private counseling, group therapy and self help. These groups will help with a myriad of problems such as drug, alcohol, sexual and gambling abuse. Attend to what is going on around you and be compassionate to yourself while you are making changes. If you pay attention to the warning this dream is delivering and make the necessary changes, you will find your life will change dramatically and you will face a brilliant future. Because this dream serves as a warning, you have prior notice to turn your life around in a dramatic way, filled with tranquility, peace and joy.

to dream of the devil laughing at you Time is running

out. You are in danger from a very evil person. Although this person has not yet demonstrated any sign of their evil nature, they will remove their mask of normalcy once you grow closer to them. You will need to investigate to determine who this person is. This will take place within four days. Do not allow this person to get close to you and take steps to protect yourself.

devilfish Do everything you can to separate yourself from a stressful situation.

Devil's advocate Do not put yourself in any situation where you will feel tempted to accept someone's dare, especially for the next three days. Avoid all negative challenges.

devil's food cake You will become deeply involved with someone for sexual pleasures for a long period of time, should you choose to take this path.

Devil's Island A love that you felt was over will rekindle within two days due to a new situation. This will bring you much happiness and will last a long time. This dream may also be used as a reference point in time. If you dream of this prison and see its name used in any context, the dream message will occur on this day.

devil's tattoo *(rapid drumming of the fingers or feet)* Be very alert for the next week. Someone will subtly attempt to bring an unusual opportunity to your attention in an attempt to involve you. Jump at the chance for involvement. This will bring wonderful financial opportunities and benefits to you.

Devonshire cream Proceed with confidence. You will achieve success with your plans and ideas and within five days you will reach your goals.

devotion Demonstrate your feelings toward someone who cares for you.
    to have someone show devotion towards you Within seven days you will be emotionally satisfied because you will have realized your ambitions.

devour Do everything you can, for the next two days to avoid miscommunication between yourself and a loved one. Carefully watch your words for this period of time.

dew Get in touch with your feelings and instincts. If you feel someone is going to deceive you, this will be a likely event within two days. You have time to change what you feel will happen.

dew drop This dream is a lucky omen. A special event will provide the opportunity of a lifetime and enable you to make special changes in your life. Go for it.

diabetes Take care of yourself and eat properly. Blessings will be with you for a very long time.

diabolical Anything negative that occurs in this dream will be fulfilled accurately in real life if you do not quickly take steps to avoid it. This dream is alerting you to a problem that needs to be turned around into a positive situation. Because this dream serves as a warning, you have the time to turn the situation around. This dream also implies that you need to make dramatic changes. Search for tools that will allow personal growth and do not allow loved ones to outgrow you. Find ways to shed outmoded ways of thinking and behavior in order to keep your loved ones around you. Stop being so verbally abusive to others in public and in private. The necessary help will come from private counseling, group therapy and self help. These groups will help with a myriad of problems such as drugs, alcohol, sexual and gambling abuse. Attend to what is going on around you and be compassionate to yourself while you are making these changes. If you pay attention to the warning this dream is delivering and make the necessary changes, you will find your life will change dramatically and you will face a brilliant future.

diagnosis This dream is strongly connected with events in reality. Each negative message may be changed by taking the necessary steps now to alter the outcome. All positive messages may be included in your life. For the next seven days you will be in a perfect cycle to promote prosperity and balance to your life.

diagnostician Pay close attention to the diagnosis given. This will serve as a clue to an event that you either desire or can work toward preventing in reality. Expect this to occur within seven days. You must also make sure that money you want to keep from others is kept in a safe and secure place. If you do not, this money will be spent little by little until it is depleted. Eat well, take care of yourself, get enough rest, drink plenty of water and meditate in your favorite form. You will find tranquility for the next month.

diagram Pay close attention to what is being demonstrated to you through this dream. If this is a negative message, take steps to change the outcome. If the message is positive, make an effort to promote and foster this event. This is a very lucky dream. Do not waste time with those who are not worthy of your time and make sure you spend time with people who show a deeper appreciation for you.

dial Someone will put you in a position to be cheated out of a lot of money. Be very aware of situations over the next two days. This can be prevented.

dialect Avoid food poisoning for the next few days.

dialysis Someone you care a great deal about will move to an area that is costly to communicate via phone. As a result, you will suffer a deep emotional loss. Expect this to occur within three days and prepare yourself for this loss.

diamond You will have unusual creativity and a clarity of greater thought that will, along with your imagination, enable you to reach through mental barriers and allow you to reach your inner spirit. As a result, you will be able to reach your goals swiftly and enjoy more mental healing and greater tranquility. You will have an abundance of health and do away with the lifestyle that keeps you from having the material wealth you desire. Good luck is with you.

diamondback Do not allow others to dissuade you from pursuing your interests. This is especially important for the next two days.

Diamond Head You will see many improvements over the next month because new activities and events will add a new desired dimension to your life. You are headed for a very prosperous future beginning within two days. This dream may also be used as a reference point in time. If you dream of this beach and see its name used in any context, the dream message will occur on this day.

diamond ring This dream is a very lucky omen. Do not take for granted anyone who has deep feelings for you. Treat a special person with love and care. This dream is a promise that if you do not have someone in your life and are seeking one, you will have someone special in your life, if you choose, for a lifetime. You will have victory in matters of finance and love, and your plans will work out exactly as you desire. If you choose, you can turn a union into a marriage in a short period of time. Take care of your health and drink plenty of water.

to lose the stone Maintain your tranquility and peace regarding special relationships for the next seven days. You will then avoid a traumatic breakup.

to receive You will be given exactly what you need from a special person in a special relationship. This union will be mutually satisfying.

to give This dream will portray an event that will occur in your life within two weeks. Give another person exactly what they need and want from you. Do not deprive yourself of what could be a wonderful working relationship with others. Good luck is with you.

broken ring Make sure you do not put yourself in a financial bind. Think clearly so you will be able to enjoy the luxuries you want. Budget now in order to avoid a financial crisis next month. Good luck is with you.

to have a ring stolen Someone you revere and hold in high esteem will be caught in a degrading, unusual circumstance. Your opinion of this person will lessen and you will feel great disappointment. This will occur within five days. Also, be careful not to lose anything of value for the next five days.

to find a diamond ring Within three days, someone will seek you for the intent of involving you in a permanent union. You will have lengthy conversations expressing your plans for a future together. This will be a cycle for romance and a special excitement stemming from your new plans. You will feel more attracted to this person than you ever have before.

to find an exact duplicate of a ring you were given in the past Someone will enter your life possessing traits similar to the person who originally gave you the ring. Make sure you treat this new person with greater kindness and understanding than you treated the original giver of the ring. This new person will either have emotional hang-ups or delightful traits similar to the first giver. Look at the total picture and decide whether you wish to pursue the relationship. If you do, take steps to avoid repeating old patterns of behavior. You will be deeply loved in spite of any hang-ups.

Diana *(Roman mythology)* Because of someone's unexpected declaration of love for you, you will gain a feeling of excitement and exuberance. If you desire, this can develop into a relationship in any capacity you wish and you will find mutual fulfillment. Within five days, you will also reach a wonderful conclusion when deciding on a new lifestyle. You will be introduced to new people and be exposed to new and different experiences that are far better than you ever expected. Peace and tranquility will be yours for a long time to come.

diaper *rolled up* The person you are interested in will not live up to your expectations. This will bring you disappointment over the next three days.

soiled You will soon see definite improvements in love and financial matters. You will have a great deal of luck for the next three weeks.

changed diaper Someone will unexpectedly come to visit. This person will also bring good news.

neatly folded diapers A new romance will turn out exactly as you envision it. You will have assurance of this within three days.

diaper bag Go to great lengths to get the best possible medical attention within five days in order to keep a minor illness from reaching emergency proportions. The moment you sense that something is wrong with your health, seek the proper help.

diaper pin Take extra precautions when transferring money from one location to another. Insure all money against loss for the next seven days. Good luck is with you during this cycle.

diaphragm When someone speaks down to you, take steps to turn those negative remarks into positive statements while this person is still in your presence. This dream is a lucky omen. A new blessed event will occur for those who are interested. For those who are not, be alert to the possibility of a new addition to the family and take steps to prevent it. Within four days, a solution that you want to put into practice regarding a problematic situation within the family will be a failure. Do not depend on this device to prevent pregnancy for the next few days. Otherwise, any blessings are with you and you are headed for a very prosperous future.

diarrhea Within five days, unusual events will begin to take place and will result in great riches in a short period of time. You will be able to accomplish a great deal during this cycle.

diary Any advice written in the diary should be followed. Any negative message needs to be changed to your benefit and any positive message may be promoted to the fullest. For the next three days you develop well thought out plans that you can implement to bring a positive change to your life.

dice You will enjoy a fantastic sex life soon. Do everything you can to live your life as fully as you can. Plan new and exciting activities to become involved in.

Dickens, Charles All of your plans will work to your advantage for the next three days.

dictaphone For the next three days avoid the company of someone you will meet. This person has a bad reputation in business and in keeping their word.

dictator Do not deprive yourself of an encounter that will give you special moments that you can recall at a later time. This encounter will also offer you new ways to share your life with another. You will have this opportunity within three days.

dictionary Dig deeply to find the proper words to communicate your interests, needs and wants to another person. Specify what you need from the relationship. This will enable the other person to become involved in the relationship, to better fulfill their needs and wants, and ultimately create a more mutually fulfilling union. This dream is a lucky omen, particularly in matters of love and education.

die You will meet someone of a different nationality within four days and will enjoy each other's company and doing a variety of things with each other. This dream is an omen of happiness. You will receive the assistance and encouragement you need to complete any project.

diesel Watch your behavior with another person. Offer more kindness and less cruelty. This is very important for the next three days.

diesel engine Your situation will change within two months and you will find it necessary to relocate. Do not panic. You have enough time to make plans and will enjoy your environment far more than you realize.

diet *to diet* Someone will grant you exactly what you want within three days.

someone else on a diet You will be unable to win the love of someone you adore. In three days you will sense a difference in attitude with this person. Do everything necessary, during this time frame, to improve relationships. This relationship can still be salvaged should you desire.

dietitian Do not allow yourself to be cheated in a business deal. You deserve to receive more than you are asking for.

dig *to see someone dig* Someone will go to great lengths to destroy your relationship. This hypocritical person is only out to injure you and your beloved.

to dig Do not ignore anyone who seeks your involvement in their life. Avoid evasiveness.

digest Do everything you can to provide yourself with a tranquil, peaceful way of life for the next two days.

digital clock Do not allow someone else to encourage you to be mean to another person. The way this individual speaks to you about someone will encourage cruelty. Be aware of your behavior for the next three days. You will also be in a very lucky cycle for the next two weeks.

Dijon mustard Within three days, someone who is only interested in sexual gratification will promise you undying love. Be wary of this, it will only be a one night stand.

dike Your intuition is correct. Follow your hunches and urges and you will have a great amount of luck by doing this.

dill Do not put yourself in the position to become physically injured. Be very careful for the next three days.

dill pickle Someone will be very interested in you sexually. This person is also interested in a relationship and is possessive in a pleasant way. Pursue this for the next five days and it will develop into a strong union if this is what you choose.

dim *any form* You will be dealing with a hypocritical person for the next seven days who will go to great lengths to steer you in the wrong direction. Do everything within your power to prevent this occurrence.

dime You will recover a lost item within two days. You will also be offered an opportunity. Do with it as you choose. This dream is a good luck omen.

dime store You will be able to regroup and refocus within two days and will break through a major difficulty. Everything will work out as you envisioned.

dimples This dream implies the birth of twins.

din Do not create needless stress and chaos. Watch your behavior for the next two days.

dine This dream is a very lucky omen and you will recover quickly from financial difficulties. You will have the chance to do this within the week.

diner Within three days you will be able to convince someone with a high mental intellect to join you on a project. The agreement will benefit both of you. Luck is with you.

dinette Make sure you do not make any major decisions

while under stress. A troublesome situation will arise that will force you to make a decision without thinking. Be sure to think this through carefully.

dinghy Good luck is with you.

dingo You will be able to resolve an important issue that you have lost the confidence to handle. Within two days, you will regain confidence and successfully resolve this.

dinner An unfamiliar person will demonstrate unusual affectionate behavior towards you. This will please you and you will take steps to continue this situation. This will occur within three days. Do everything you can to encourage this.

to have dinner with someone at a well dressed table You will become involved, if you choose, with someone you will meet in the next three days. This person will be very wealthy but married. This person will claim the marriage is over when, in fact, it is still strong. You will be very much a secret to the world and this situation will never change. It is your choice to pursue it or not.

dinner jacket You are involved in a relationship that will not grow because the other party refuses to allow it. For the next three days, open all lines of communication that will enable this person to open up to you. This is the perfect cycle for this.

dinner theater You will enjoy pleasurable moments for the next seven days with company you enjoy. You will be enjoying peace, quiet and tranquility. It is also important that you do not plan a strategy of revenge on another person. It will only waste your time and cause regrets later.

dinnerware Within five days, you will realize an agreement will never be reached within a group of people. Don't waste your time. Find an alternative method to meet your goals.

dinosaur Don't overwhelm yourself with negative mental tapes that will keep you from taking on a big idea. Go for it and you will be successful. Make sure also that your environment is safe and be sure to drink plenty of water.

diorama You are well on your way toward developing plans for your independence. This cycle promotes confidence, physical and emotional healing, and financial improvements. You are now making the right moves to ensure a bright future. This will be a prosperous cycle and you will be able to make improvements in your life in those areas you most desire. Many blessings are with you and your family and all requests made to your special deity will be granted.

dip You will receive a surprising proposal of marriage within five days. You will accept it and be wed in a short while.

diplomat Keep a close eye on all expected mail. An important piece of paperwork will be intercepted by someone else. Keep watch for the next two days.

dipper Within four days you will receive news that will be difficult for you to even comprehend. Don't even try, most of it is untrue. Get on with your life.

dipstick Do not allow violence to erupt within the next four days because of the stubbornness of another individual. You have enough prior notice to avoid any involvement with this person.

directions *to ask for directions* A series of events will start occurring one after the other that will bring you a great amount of joy, wonder and awe, because they will take place so quickly. You will possess a powerful energy that you will be able to direct and control. You will also be able to bring others under your control at the same time that these events are taking place. Because of your advance notice, you will be able to direct this energy in any way you choose for the next week. You will overcome any difficult obstacle and be able to effectively deal with any new issue. Follow your instincts. Many blessings are with you and your family.

to give or leave someone directions All negotiations will be extremely successful. Also, a new person will enter your life who will be a friend from the very beginning. This person will be very charming and will share many wonderful stories with you. They will tell you something that will be an important message to you. This message will give you a different way of looking at a certain project or concept that you will be working on. You will be able to use this knowledge to improve your life in many ways. This will occur within three days and, if you choose, this person will be a friend for life.

director A behind the scenes event is taking place with another individual for reasons known only to them. This person enjoys chaos and will go to great lengths to create distasteful episodes in the lives of others. Become very aware of your surroundings and pay special attention to any unusual episodes in your life. Take steps to avoid this and make sure that you bring balance and stability into your life.

director's chair Be very pragmatic when you make a request of someone who is reluctant to involve themselves in a particular situation. This person does not have the courage to tell you this to your face but will instead talk behind your back. Your feelings will be hurt if this gets back to you. Do not insist on recruiting someone who is not interested in helping you. Seek alternatives.

dirge Within five days you will need to alert a friend to the possibility of an accident that will occur while on a short vacation trip. This event is preventable if you take steps to give ample warning.

dirt In the next three days you will become insecure with a new relationship and will develop mixed feelings. Proceed with confidence and affection. This relationship will be a success.

dirt bike Within seven days, someone will lose something of value that belongs to you. Take extra precautions to keep this from occurring.

dirt farmer Within four days, divorce yourself from a certain situation that has become very trying for you. This issue will only lead to a dead end.

dirty *any form* Make it a point to participate with others in order to bring greater success to your ongoing projects. This will be especially important for the next five days. Certain issues will also require more personal involvement during this time period. Any negative event in this dream can be prevented.

dirty linen You can expect each of your plans to work to your specifications for the next seven days and you will experience many positive changes in your life during this time frame.

dirty old man You will have the strength to regroup and to make a move toward someone you desire in order to push things along in the direction you want to go romantically. This person is not aware of your feelings as yet. Good luck is with you.

dirty pool Someone you are interested in involving in a project will be rude and disgusting. You will, however, find that this person is organized and performs exceptional work. They will be a real asset to you. Go for it.

dirty word *if you are using dirty words* Do not put yourself in the position of being treated indecently in front of others or in private. Be very aware of the behavior other people demonstrate toward you and stop all abuse.

if someone is using dirty words toward you Do not treat others in a disgusting way. This will only embarrass you and cause regrets later.

disability You will need to go to great lengths to let another person know you are interested in them. It will take a little longer for them to become aware of your desire. Luck is with you.

disabled person A priceless collection will be damaged within ten days if you do not take steps to prevent it. Otherwise, this is a lucky cycle.

disappear *any form* This dream is alerting you that anything or anybody seen in this dream that disappears will do so within three days. If this is something you do not want to happen, you must take steps to ensure that it does not take place. You will also reach an agreement with someone that involves the loan of a great deal of money. After this agreement is reached, this individual will pretend as if they have forgotten it. This person will make you out to be a liar and act as though something is wrong with you. As a result, you

will feel shame for bringing this issue up. At the same time that this is going on, you will feel as though a burden has been lifted from your shoulders and you will be able to put yourself on the path toward prosperity. You will enjoy a long and healthy cycle.

disappointment *to see someone's disappointment* A request you have made for a loan to buy a big ticket item will be granted.

to be disappointed You will be asked to perform a favor in exchange for a large amount of money. If you comply, you will be granted the money immediately.

disassemble *anything* Within two days it will become necessary to have a conversation with specific people to make the proper requests and connections for a certain situation to begin to develop. This will keep everything from falling apart before it takes off. Stay ahead of yourself and you will make the proper adjustments in time. Focus on this now and everything will fall into place successfully. Good luck is with you and your family. You are headed for a brilliant future.

disaster Any disaster you see in the dream is preventable in real life. Take steps to do so. Each individual you recognize in this dream should also be alerted to the possibility of this disaster. This dream also implies that a family crisis will emerge and one individual will require immediate financial assistance from other members of the family. This person will need to be surrounded with love and support. Be sure to do your part.

disc brakes Attend to all impending mechanical problems and promptly take care of any needed repairs. Do this now in order to avoid mechanical failure at a more inconvenient time. Also, set limits with those who ask personal questions about your finances and your private life, especially for the next seven days.

disciple Blessings will be granted to you and your family members and you will receive an abundance of health and money. Much needed information will also come to you from an unexpected source within three days.

disc jockey Within four days, you will be invited to join a group. You will find much pleasure and will enjoy many surprise events. Do not allow yourself to be timid; become actively involved.

disco You will be included in secret organizational plans that you have been yearning to be a part of. This will occur within the week.

discount Become involved in new activities. You will meet a number of new people who will be instrumental in helping you to achieve your goals. These new acquaintances will also provide you with variety and new perspectives on how to live your life.

discount house For the next three days ask for special considerations and they will be granted.

discount store You will have a better chance of reconciliation if you make a move within three days. This dream also implies that you will receive a quick response to a request you have made for specific information.

discovery Money you owe will be paid back far easier than you anticipated. Situations will fall into place to enable an adequate cash flow, especially for the next five days.

to be discovered Someone in a powerful position will work for your benefit within five days. This dream is also a very lucky omen.

discrimination Remain on guard and stay alert for the next two days in order to prevent a dangerous accident. Carefully scrutinize each new situation and you will succeed in preventing this occurrence.

discus Mental pain and anguish will disappear overnight. Expect this within the week.

disease Do everything possible, within five days, to get the best medical help possible, in order to keep a minor illness from escalating into a crisis situation. The moment you feel that something is wrong, seek professional help.

disembowel Be very careful when traveling for the next seven days to avoid accidents.

disfigure Develop compassion and sympathy for yourself while going through an emotional crisis. Treat yourself gently and add pleasure to your life. This crisis will occur within four days.

disgrace Keep all confidential business information from others who will attempt to pry into your private affairs. This is especially important for the next three days.

disguise For the next two days, take steps to avoid injury as a result of using faulty machinery. Be very careful and avoid any equipment that is in disrepair.

to disguise yourself as something different from what you are This dream will offer you an important revelation because your spirit is making you aware you will take on the character or personality of this animal, or anything else you have disguised yourself as within four days. You will either assume a positive power and respect or an attitude that may or may not be to your liking. This is something you must go through in order to manifest something that needs to be brought into balance. Pay close attention to any words spoken at the time of transformation. This will offer you a clue to something you will either want to pursue or to avoid entirely because it will become a reality. You have the time and prior notice to keep anything negative from occurring and to promote the positive. Alert anyone involved that you

recognize so they can either reap the benefits that are coming their way or avoid any negative event. Make sure you do not stray from your priorities or goals until they are successfully achieved. You will enjoy tranquility in the family structure and have a long and healthy life.

to dream of someone else disguising themselves This is letting you know that this person has gone into disguise so they can determine whether any hidden plans they have are feasible, and whether they can carry this plan to their advantage. Do not take this dream for granted because you could be setting yourself up for a painful and humiliating situation. This could also be an event that you should not miss because it could be to your advantage. Take steps to find any important clues that have been left so that within five days you can avoid anyone who could introduce a stressful time to your life. Your spirit will leave you clues to the identity of this individual through their character, manner of speech, clothing, mannerisms, jewelry, etc. Your spirit will heighten your sense of intuition and you will have a sense of who this person is. The spirit itself may have taken on a disguise of its own to alert you to something you may or may not want to experience in your life. Eliminate any negative expression and allow only positive expressions in your life.

to see yourself, someone or something disguising themselves as something magical Look up the particular object for more profound clues to the meaning of this dream. This dream is an extremely lucky omen. For the next month you will enjoy an abundance of health and financial security because unusual circumstances will take place that will allow this to occur. Do not limit yourself or deprive yourself of unique experiences and involvements that will come up within five days. Enjoy your life fully, eat healthy foods, drink plenty of water and get plenty of rest. Life will reward you handsomely not only in a financial sense but spiritually as well.

if this disguise is a form that is not magical in any sense You need to look up the particular animal, whatever or whoever the disguise is, for further clues to the meaning of this dream. If those clues are positive, make an effort to look for this person by way of the clues they leave behind so you can grasp this situation and handle yourself appropriately. If this person is disguised as something that is distasteful to you, you can expect this person to have the power and character of their disguise. Make decisions ahead of time about whether you want to involve yourself with this person or not. You will develop the strength and courage to deal with this for the next three days, and will maintain a stress free environment during this time period. You will be able to handle anything you once felt was an impossible task and will be able to bring this to a successful conclusion. You are headed for a prosperous future and your intuition is right on target.

disgust *to disgust* Take extra steps to avoid making someone uncomfortable in your presence because of your behavior.

to be disgusted Within a seven day period, someone will make you very uncomfortable in their presence while attending a special event. Take measures to avoid this person at the first sign of discomfort.

dish *dirty dishes* Someone will attempt to involve you in some kind of unusual secret. This will be a conspiracy of some kind. Do not become involved. You must also be careful to prevent food poisoning and drink plenty of water.

clean dishes You will receive a small, expensive, luxurious gift.

to wash Someone you know, who has mysteriously disappeared in the past, will unexpectedly reappear within five days. This person will want to become involved in your life. You will be told interesting stories about this missing time period and will find this individual fascinating. They will be in your life for a short time and will then disappear again.

broken dishes Someone will break an appointment with you within the week. Be sure to reschedule. This dream also implies that someone will keep their commitment to you.

to see food cooking and to see many dishes of food You will meet someone who is very compatible to your lifestyle. You will be very happy together and will receive many benefits from this compassionate individual.

in any other form This dream is a very lucky omen. Simplify your life and trust your intuition. Within three days, the person you desire will come to you and you will share a mutually fulfilling love, if you choose to pursue this relationship. Blessings are with you.

dishcloth You will have the courage to display aggression in a situation that requires this behavior. You will need to develop this within four days.

dishpan You will be able to rid yourself of a hang up and alter your life for the better. This will cause another person to become interested in your plans and ideas. Be determined to change in such a way that will allow others to be more comfortable around you.

dishpan hands Do not stay in an area when two people are fighting. Immediately remove yourself from this environment in order to avoid a stressful and shocking scene.

dishrag Make it a point to promote closeness between yourself and your in-laws. Do not distance yourself from them by your manner of communication. You will have the opportunity to accomplish this within two days.

dish soap You will gain financial security because of the high demand for your services. Within four days you will also become aware of the depth of feelings someone has for you.

dishwasher Do not allow yourself to be belittled or manipulated. Stand firm. You will have the strength to do this within five days. If you can bypass everyone with a tendency to treat you this way, do so.

dishwater An older, wiser person will help you get to the heart of a problem very quickly. Within four days you will be able to resolve this issue. Luck is with you. Someone will also express their loving and unusual affection. This will bring you a great deal of joy.

disinfectant Be very careful that you do not expose yourself to a deadly disease for the next four days. This is preventable.

to use disinfectant or see someone use disinfectant You will enjoy an abundance of health and spiritual healing within the week and a celebration will take place that will cause everyone involved to rejoice. For the second half of March and all of April this dream is promising you that a certain idea, project or event you have planned will reach tangible form. This will reach a high level of perfection and will take on a life of its own. You will be able to take this through each channel in a quick and easy fashion in order to complete this process. This project will be a blessing and will be a cause for celebration for you and everyone involved. You are headed for a brilliant future.

disinheritance Do not just imagine fame. Put yourself in the company of others who will steer you in the right direction to achieve your goals. Begin work on this immediately.

dislike Make sure you don't repeat whatever you saw that was distasteful to you or someone you recognize. Be relentless in the next three days in those areas you feel you need to experience changes and put to use the heightened clarity of thought that you experience in this time frame. Thrust forward in the directions you feel you should be moving. Move rapidly in order to benefit from this lucky cycle.

dislocate Think ahead and prepare yourself for situations you will be dealing with in the upcoming month. Make sure all agreements are understood and binding prior to making your next move.

dismembered Do not let circumstances stand in the way of your goals. You will have the strength, for the next seven days, to overcome any situation that threatens to steer you away from your future plans.

dismiss *Someone else is being dismissed* This dream indicates that you will be fired from your present position within five days.

you are being dismissed Your wedding engagement will be broken within seven days.

Disneyland You will be enchanted within five days, with the manner and behavior of a certain individual. This person will treat you in such a way that will encourage you to react to them. You will enjoy and savor each moment of this flirtation. You will also have an opportunity to create a brilliant future.

disorderly conduct A jealous lover will falsely accuse you of disloyalty at an unexpected time. Do whatever you can to avoid a jealous disagreement for the next four days. You will also easily be taken in by a very conniving friend. This person will be very cunning and will go to great lengths to sabotage an important opportunity just prior to your gaining knowledge of it. Since you are aware of this ahead of time, you can determine who this person is and take care of this issue properly. You will successfully turn this around to your advantage.

dispatch You will attend a special event and find your former mate with another person. This will occur within two weeks. You can either attend the event and remain calm or choose to avoid the event.

dispatcher You will attend an enjoyable elegant function and meet a new acquaintance. This person will later provide you with many pleasurable, emotional moments. Take steps not to miss out on this event.

dispensary A relative from a distant city will call and describe what seems to be a mental breakdown. This person is suicidal. Get help in any way you can for this relative. With help they will heal.

disposable You will be unexpectedly invited on a short trip. You will enjoy yourself and have a safe return. You must also be sure to tell the truth at all times to avoid being trapped in a lie. This will occur within three days and will prove to be very embarrassing.

disposable diaper *balled up* Someone you meet will turn out to be very different from what you believed them to be. This will be a great disappointment to you.
in any other form You will enjoy victory in each phase of a new enterprise.

disqualify Focus on benefits that are due you that you have not received and may not even be aware of. Take the time to do the necessary research and learn all you can about special benefits.

disrepair *any form* Something is taking place behind the scenes with another individual for reasons known only to them. This person enjoys creating chaos and distasteful episodes in the lives of others. Become very aware of your surroundings and any unusual episodes in your life. Take steps to avoid this and to bring balance and stability into your life.

disrobe Trust your acquaintances. You are surrounded by those who love you and are loyal to you. You will feel this strongly for next three days.

dissect Take steps to avoid placing yourself in the position of being vulturized and taken advantage of by others for the next three days. This will deplete you of your energies and resources. Keep this from occurring.

dissertation You are putting your trust in a very irresponsi-

ble person who appears to be, initially, a responsible individual. Do everything necessary to disassociate from this person. If possible, avoid placing your trust in this person to start with. You will save yourself much misery.

dissolve *any form* There are those who are eagerly awaiting the time when they can rejoice at your failure. You will, however, enjoy victory against all odds.

distemper Within a five day period, take precautions not to be caught off guard in a dark unfamiliar place. This will cost you your life. Become very protective of yourself and your environment.

distillery Do not allow yourself to be chastised verbally by someone who wants you to enter into an agreement you have no desire to become involved in. Expect this within three days and when it comes up, cut the conversation short because it will escalate into a very violent argument.

distortion *to see something distorted or not in its real form* This implies that within three days a very forceful person will purposely use language in such a way that you will feel compelled to surrender to their wishes, behave in the way they want and speak in the manner they wish. Be very wary of this because this person will do everything in their power to get their way. You have prior notice of this and can take steps to avoid being placed at a disadvantage.

distress *You are in distress* Get some sleep and find some time for peace in your life. Do everything necessary to keep yourself in a safe environment for the next week and be very aware of your surroundings in order to avoid any harm from another person.
someone else in distress You need to carefully guard everything that is emotionally precious to you; your privacy, reputation, children, career, etc.

distributor Make sure you become personally involved in all business and financial matters for the next four days.

district attorney Be very wary of seeking unusual pleasures and of pleasure seekers for the next four days. This could lead to serious complications in your life.

District of Columbia Someone will offer you the funds needed to launch a new project. You will be able to repay the seed money in a short period of time.

disturbance *any form* Someone will require your assistance within five days. It will be your responsibility to make this person more comfortable and successful in life. Luck is with you for a long period of time.

ditch *to fall into one* You will invite someone to your home who appears to be friendly. This person, however, is deranged and will turn on you and attempt to cause you harm. Be especially watchful of this for the next seven days.

in any other form Someone you disliked in the past will reappear and will go to great lengths to reinvolve you in a friendship. This individual has developed worse habits than before. Do not become involved in this friendship.

ditch digger Make sure you are getting the best medical advice possible. If, within the next five days, something does not seem right, work on getting different professional help.

diuretic You will be able to acquire the items you desire at bargain prices for the next three days.

diva Think carefully and make sure you have all your facts at hand before discussing your point of view. This is especially important for the next three days.

divan Be careful and allow no domestic problems to develop over the next four days.

dive *to dive* Focus on any allergies before symptoms develop. Do not let it get out of hand for the next three days. Any negative event seen in this dream may be altered or avoided in reality.

to dive off anything high into the air Someone will go to great lengths to create a relationship between you and another person. You are fated to enjoy a beautiful full blown love relationship that will bloom within a few days. This relationship will bring you great joy. This is the perfect cycle to connect emotionally with another person so successfully that they will respond in the manner you most desire. This dream also implies you are going in the right direction and it is imperative that you express yourself fully in all personal matters. You will be able to focus in a very detailed manner and, as a result, will be able to accomplish a great deal and enjoy many successes in life. You will magically possess the inner strength to take care of any issue and you will enjoy much tranquility in your life. An unexpected favor will also be granted to you but you will need to put yourself in the position to speak with some very powerful and influential people. State your needs directly and succinctly and you will promptly receive any money you request from a certain person. You will enjoy victory in your life in those areas you deem to be most important. You will hear some good news within the week and are on the path toward a brilliant future. Pay very close attention to every conversation for the next three days. Each negative message or event taking place in this dream needs to be altered and all positive messages need to be promoted. This is a very lucky dream for you.

dive bomb Someone is plotting ways to borrow money from you with no intention to repay it. Be alert to this for the next five days and do not lend money to others.

diver Do not lose touch with those who are special to you. Time goes by rapidly and without constant contact, friendships slip away. Make a point to touch base with those you care about on a consistent basis. It is important to begin this within seven days.

any diver with diving gear The seemingly impossible hope of turning a stale relationship into a loving close one bears hope now. Move on this within three days.

any diver without proper diving gear Cover all bases when dealing with situations that are important to you at the moment. Double-check each move in order to bring about a positive outcome. Be aware that a member of the family needs assistance and support in areas that will later give them financial security.

Divine (The) Good luck will be with you for an extended period of time. You are headed for a very brilliant future.

diving board Someone will go to great lengths to hide a shameful act committed while attending an event. This person will never admit the truth. It is preventable if you immediately discuss, in length, the danger of certain lifestyle choices to this person.

diving suit and/or gear You will be tempted to enter into a conspiracy to gain access to something you really want. Avoid doing anything that will later cause you deep regret. This will be a good, lucky cycle for the next seven days.

divining rod Focus on situations you have ignored for too long. Get the assistance you need now to correct anything personal that needs correcting. This seven day cycle will allow you to move quickly in this direction. This dream is a good luck omen.

divorce *to hear this word in a dream* You will soon receive all of the money owed to you. If this dream contains a message of warning pertaining to a separation of emotional significance, take steps to prevent it. You have the time to correct all negative situations.

Dixie Avoid becoming cruelly focused on another person for the next four days. Stop this behavior permanently.

Dixie cup Do not become involved with anything out of the ordinary for the next three days. Stay away from any unusual situations.

DNA Go back, refocus and rethink in order to move quickly ahead. Good luck is with you. Any event witnessed in this dream with negative repercussions may also be turned around to a positive event in reality.

Doberman pinscher Make it clear what you need to do and what another person expects from you, otherwise you will be delivering something other than what this other person needs. There will be miscommunications and you need to be sure you deliver the correct services in order to avoid hostility. Be attentive and put everything in writing for the next five days.

dock *to dock pay* You will gain a salary increase.

dock *to dock a boat* Do everything necessary to quickly complete transactions in order to meet the set deadline.

doctor Anything that appears unusual and out of the ordinary for the next five days will work to your favor. Events will occur one after the other and will give you great pleasure.

to be examined by a doctor Pay attention to the reason you are at the doctor's office in the dream and take steps to ensure this does not occur in reality. Also, make sure you personally handle all of your own affairs so you can get a clear idea of what needs to be taken care of.

to be examined by a doctor and find something wrong Take preventive measures to avoid developing the illness depicted in the dream. Take steps to avoid any preventable accident to yourself and to others in your care. Take steps also to not leave yourself open to emotional pain as a result of someone's lack of consideration.

to witness or hear of someone being examined and finding something wrong If you recognize the person, alert this individual to use preventive measures to ensure that this illness does not occur in reality. Make it a priority to determine your needs and work to fulfill them. Take steps also to avoid becoming involved in a group that creates chaos in the lives of other people. This group is well known for this behavior and it is to your advantage to avoid them. You will experience good luck for the next seven days and you and your family will experience many blessings.

if you dream of a doctor's visit Take each negative message and work to alter the outcome. Each positive message needs to be promoted to the fullest. Do this within seven days.

if you recognize the doctor The message he gives you in the dream will be truthful. Take steps to correct any physical problems within five days.

to dream that you are the doctor Carefully analyze what is bothering you physically and take steps to find the right physician who will provide the right treatment for this ailment. If you dream that you are a specialist, you are doubly ensured you will find success immediately. This does not imply that you will need assistance from the particular specialist you dreamed you were, but rather that you will have a heightened sense of awareness about the particular ailment you are suffering from and the proper treatment you will need.

doctorate You will be buying, within the month, some valuable items. Make sure these items are insured because they will be damaged and will have to be replaced.

document This dream is a good luck omen. Be true to yourself and do not compromise your feelings. Pamper yourself, and be good to yourself. Purchase a beautiful gift and surround yourself with joyous events. Do not deprive yourself of anything you need in life and make sure you do not overlook some small, but important issue. Pay attention to the document in the dream. It will give you a large clue as to what should be avoided or embraced in reality, especially for the next seven days.

documentary Do not allow personal information to leak out to someone you prefer to keep it from. This is especially important for the next four days. Make sure you speak with someone who knows about your personal life and request that they keep this information to themselves.

dodo Make sure you put nothing in writing that you prefer to keep private for the next four days.

doe Do not procrastinate the completion of needed paperwork. Move quickly on this so that you can get on with your life and receive what is rightfully yours.

doeskin Do not push too hard to include someone in your life. Your aggressiveness will cause the other person to back off before they get the chance to know you and realize how good this relationship could be. Be gentle and patient when speaking with this individual.

dog Anything you plan to become involved with, over the next seven days, regarding negotiations will be extremely lucky. A co-worker will also do everything possible to work with you to bring a project to a successful completion. You also need to look under the particular breed for a more profound definition.

white dog This dream implies good news. Someone has very deep feelings for you but lacks the courage to express this verbally. This person will attempt to do this within five days. It is your role to create a comfortable atmosphere for this person and to encourage the expression of these emotions. This will develop into a loving relationship.

black dog Someone's inappropriate behavior will cause you disappointment within two days. You will also receive some bad news within three days.

dog with many strange colors You will be fired from a position you really enjoy.

licking dog Someone will attempt to break an important appointment with you within five days. This will set you back. Be prepared and remain calm enough to find a solution to this problem.

mad dog Do not become involved in squabbles between friends. At the first sign of this, back out of the situation.

hunting dog A friend of yours desperately needs a lifestyle change. Do everything you can to help this person. Be patient and sympathetic.

sleeping dog You will attend an event within five days and strike up a conversation with someone whom you will find very attractive. You will also discover that the feelings are mutual. Wonderful things can come from this relationship. This will be very meaningful and fulfilling if you choose to pursue it.

attacking dog This is a warning that someone you are dealing with has a hidden agenda. This person could cause you bodily harm or death. Be aware of any suspicious person and do everything you can to avoid unusual places and protect yourself.

dog and cat fight Within five days you will do something that will deeply disappoint another person. This will result in an argument. Watch your behavior closely during this time period in order to avoid this.

to see a dog bleeding/injured A cluster of events will occur one after the other with each bringing you a tremendous amount of joy, wonder and awe because things are happening so quickly. You will also possess a powerful energy that you are going to be able to direct and control. At the same time these other events are taking place you will be able to bring other people under your complete control. Because you have prior notice of this you will be able, within the week, to direct this energy in such a way to successfully complete anything you wish in a superb way. If you give assistance to the animal in the dream, you will be assisting someone close to you in some capacity. You will overcome any difficult obstacle and it will now be very simple to deal with it. Your intuition will be right on target. Follow your hunches about a new relationship. Many blessings are with you and your family.

dead dog Watch all pets closely in order to prevent injury for the next five days. This dream also implies that the person you are interested in and who is aware of this interest will begin to show interest in you. Within seven days a beautiful love relationship will begin to blossom.

to kill a dog You will rid yourself of a very deceitful person who has gone to great lengths to undermine you. This person is very much the backstabber and will, within the next seven days, move to a different city and out of your life.

dogfight Make certain that a former lover and a new admirer do not meet. This will result in jealousy and will backfire. You will be physically injured.

dog bite The object of your affections will unexpectedly display rudeness, meanness, and an ill mannered behavior toward you. This person will start a disagreement because of jealousy. Avoid any behavior over the next seven days that will lead to this.

playful dog Do whatever is necessary to cater to the people you love. Let them know how much you love them. Do not erect barriers or limit the time you spend with them. Do not become a parent to your mate or anyone else.

dog that barks continuously Be very careful of the words you use when talking to another person for the next three days. Someone will react irrationally to what you are saying and it will take a long time to calm this person down. Avoid this situation at all costs. Set your goals high and these goals will be met within three days.

jumping Someone you are very fond of was unresponsive to your desires in the past. This will change now. Do not become suspicious. Go along with it.

police dog Stand firm and do not allow others to belittle and manipulate you. Do not compromise your feelings and allow this to continue out of fear of losing a friendship. This person will stand by you.

to see a pregnant dog Someone will propose to you and you will be married soon, if you choose. Good luck and a brilliant future are yours.

watch dog Someone you are working very hard with on a certain project that you both want to complete will be as tenacious as you in reaching your goal. Both of you will experience, in the near future, an increase in finances like you never imagined. You will both flourish because of this project in ways you never envisioned. Many blessings are with you and you are headed for a brilliant future as well as everyone involved in this project.

puppy dog Someone you meet within a few days will fall deeply in love with you. This person is much older than you and will request much of your attention and time. Let this person know early on the degree of your involvement in order to avoid hurt feelings.

to dream of a deceased pet This dream is a lucky omen for you and all those who are interested and involved in your immediate situation. You are in a powerful seven day cycle for achievement and accomplishing everything you attempt. You will also develop more integrity. People in your life will demonstrate greater love and affection toward you. Do nothing to slow down the momentum of those feelings. Everything in your life will flow more smoothly and you will be blessed with better health and more tranquility.

dog biscuit Take the time to enjoy yourself, listen to some good music and relax. You will also be able to acquire some long desired possessions. You will be able to accomplish this within the next five days.

dog chain Avoid the feeling of discomfort that will stem from emotional depletion and a lack of confidence. Learn to get your point across to someone in authority. Push yourself to the point of doing this and you will see very positive results. This cycle will enable you to develop the confidence you need to carry out your goals. This is a very lucky cycle for you.

dog collar Someone will purposely push your buttons in an effort to trigger a violent argument. Take steps to prevent this occurrence for the next two days.

dog days Make sure, within two days, that a certain person knows exactly how you feel about a particular situation. This will prevent a big misunderstanding at a later time. Attend to this as soon as possible.

dog food For the next three days, create an environment of warmth toward others. This will promote tranquility.

doggie bag You will be in a very lucky and fantastic cycle for the next seven days. Ignore someone who is trying to convince you that the person you desire is not the right person for you. Follow your intuitions. Also, pay close attention to the contents of this bag. This will provide you with more detailed clues about a forthcoming event that you will choose to either include or exclude from your life.

doghouse It is necessary to communicate your needs and wants to someone who means a great deal to you. This person will be very attentive to your words and will follow each suggestion. Do this within three days.

dog paddle Tactfully push for the assistance you need to get a project moving in a productive way, especially for the next few weeks. For the forthcoming month demand for your services will exceed your ability to supply unless you are able to be more productive.

dog show Stay in touch with those you treasure as friends and cater to your in-laws as well as your family members. For the next seven days, create a close union between yourself and those you feel close to.

dogsled You will meet an obnoxious, irritating person at a social event within three days. You may choose not to attend.

Dog star You will receive expected documents within four days. Information contained in these documents will be positive rather than negative.

dog tag Do not revise ongoing plans at the moment and do not take on anything new. Maintain a steady course for the next seven days.

dogwood Someone will portray a situation as being far worse than it really is. Do not add additional stress by believing the worst, especially for the next five days.

doily Be very cautious. Someone will attempt to cause trouble between you and a special person. Do everything necessary to protect yourself from this situation.

doll Become very concerned about the behavior and whereabouts of children. You must also carefully watch young adults around alcohol in order to prevent any mishap for the next three days.

dollar For the next five days your plans will work out in the exact manner in which you have anticipated. Proceed with confidence. The dollar amount of the bill is a number to use as a lucky symbol in any way that will benefit you.

stack of dollars This dream implies the amount you will have within seven weeks. Pay attention to whether this stack remains stable, increases or decreases. This foretells your future financial status.

doll collection You will receive news of an unexpected inheritance.

dollhouse The major clue lies with what you see in the doll house. If this portrays a negative event, you have time to alter the outcome. If positive, take steps to enhance the benefits. Within five days you will also find the words necessary to bond a special person closer to you in a permanent way.

dolphin You will experience deep, passionate, emotional love with another person within the week. You are headed in the right direction. You will gain the knowledge and clarity you need to make the right decisions for a long and prosperous life. This cycle will begin in two days and will remain with you for several weeks. Good luck is with you.

dead dolphin You will be divorced within five months if you continue to demonstrate a cold, aloof, behavior. If you want to maintain this relationship you need to change your attitude. Be very cautious when involving yourself in a situation that could be very detrimental to you as well as your family. Make sure you play it safe in every area of your life, especially for the next three days.

dome This dream is alerting you to the fact that someone will visit you and break an expensive item by accident. Be very watchful of your treasures in order to avoid the disappointment you will suffer if one of them is damaged. Watch for this within five days.

domestic *any form* Make sure that all domestic chores are evenly divided. Be patient with each other and make sure that no one is overloaded with work. This is important for the next two days. Good luck is with you and you will enjoy tranquility and peace.

domestic help You will earn your keep for a lifetime as an important staff person to one individual. You will be esteemed and paid well. It is destined that you have this position. Make an effort to seek out this job for the next five days.

Dominican Republic You will receive an unexpected gift and will be invited to a festive event within the week. This will give you great pleasure.

domino The object of your affection is attempting to create an argument for no real purpose. Avoid all disagreements for the next three days. After this time, this person will come out of this argumentative mood.

Donahue, Phil / *famous talk show host* You are in a powerful 10 day cycle for achievement and accomplishing everything you attempt to experience in your present life. People in your life will demonstrate greater love and affection towards you. Good luck will be with you. Everything in your life will flow more smoothly. You will have better health and more tranquility. You are on a path of a very prosperous future.

donation Politely back off from additional demands placed on you by others that you feel you would be unable to meet. Make sure you do not give others the impression that you are willing to carry a heavier load.

Don Juan For the next five days, treat yourself royally and set limits on the amount of time you are willing to waste on things you do not feel like handling. Give yourself wonderful moments that you will be able to share with others and that will give you joy for a lifetime.

donkey You will find yourself unexpectedly lending a helping hand to someone in distress within the week. You will be able to handle this correctly.

Donner Pass You will be introduced to an exciting new venture within the next three days. Become involved in this and you will enjoy each moment. This dream may also be used as a reference point in time. If you dream of this mountain pass and see its name used in any context, the dream message will occur on this day.

donor Someone with a taste for melodrama will provoke an argument to the point of a loud verbal exchange. This person will make sure that others hear and will attempt to place you in the role of a villain. Prevent this embarrassing scene by avoiding this person for the next three days.

Don Quixote You will be entering a lucky cycle for the next month and will be offered many new opportunities. Choose those people you prefer to work with in order to develop a comfortable way of life for the future.

"don't be so mean" *to say or to hear this phrase* Be very cautious about where your feelings are taking you. Someone will, for reasons of their own, lead you to believe you are loved by them. The word "love" may or may not be used at this time, but all of the romantic trappings will be there in the nature of gifts, flowers, romantic outings, etc. Your feelings will grow very deep and strong for this individual, but if you allow lovemaking to occur, this person will not touch you in any way that gives you the impression they care deeply for you. As a result, you will feel very empty and cold. This person will be unable to connect with you, although they will put on a good act. Instead of putting yourself through this, you have enough notice to avoid this scenario entirely. Get on with your life without this person, because they have a hidden agenda that involves you doing something for them that only they are aware of. This situation will only lead to unhappiness. Otherwise, you are headed for a prosperous future.

"don't do that" *to hear the phrase* Within five days you will be involved with someone who will lead you to believe they are a very respected, professional, financially secure person with a stable career and credible lifestyle. This person is very eager to involve you in their life, and because of their believability and the comfort you feel in their presence, you will want to become involved with them. You will be given every indication you can easily contact them at any time. But after checking various phone numbers, company addresses and after leaving messages with a secretary, you will find this person to be very difficult to track down. It will take hours and sometimes days for you to get a return call. It will dawn on you that this person has inflated their status and if you do become involved you will be disappoint-

ed. Develop a shrewd and disciplined attitude in order to keep this person from violating your emotions or insulting your intelligence. Because you have prior notice of this you will be able to handle this with success. You are entering a prosperous cycle and are headed for a brilliant future.

doodle You will develop the confidence and assurance to adopt big plans and ideas. Blessings are with you and your family.

doomsday Do not associate socially with someone you do not know well for the next week. Do not plan to be alone with this person.

door Within four days you will be introduced to a person who will become instrumental to your success. Make sure you expose yourself to different situations and events in order to meet this person.

to walk through the entrance of a door Someone will soon be flirting with you in a romantic way. You will enjoy dancing and dining with this person.

to walk through a closed door or see someone else walk through a closed door This dream is a warning that a very devious person will come and mislead you into believing you can trust them. This individual will have you believe that anything you say to them will be kept strictly confidential, but their true intent is to gather as much information about another person as they can. They will then take what you say back to the person you were talking about and this will lead to the third person attacking you verbally. Be careful, this could escalate to violence. You have prior notice of this and can take steps to ensure that this does not take place.

to hear continuous knocking and no one is at the door Someone is plotting to violate your rights in order to satisfy their own emotional desires. This person will attempt to entice you into a sexual liaison against your better judgment and will. Do not put yourself in a compromising situation. Protect yourself and do not betray your principles.

to answer a door and recognize the person knocking This person is eager to engage in productive conversation and will be open to all of your demands. This is a healthy cycle and good luck will be with you.

if you do not recognize the person knocking If this person speaks to you, recall the message given to you. This will represent a clue to a future event that you may choose to avoid or to incorporate into your life. You will also need to pace yourself and limit the demands and pressures you are willing to accept, especially for the next two days. Simplify your life and learn to enjoy life to the fullest. Within five days, someone will bring satisfaction to the work you want completed. This will be a productive cycle and many blessings are with you.

glass door When you are aware that someone is definitely in the wrong, ignore the behavior in order to keep the issue from escalating into a fight. This will occur within four days. Allow the day to continue stress free. Since you have been given prior notice, you will be able to change the outcome.

backdoor Within three weeks you will be exposed to some extraordinary activities. These experiences will bring you prosperity and vastly raise your standard of living.

revolving door You know someone who has the habit of creating chaos and stressful situations with others. If you know that you will be around this person within the next few days, do whatever you can to stay calm and stress free. Do not allow yourself to get caught up in this person's games.

swinging door Every opportunity will be presented within a few weeks to make a real difference in your life. Take a chance and pioneer new ideas. One of these will make a prosperous and profound difference in your life for a long time to come.

trapdoor Be aware that there is a plot to commit robbery at an event you will be attending within seven days. Each guest will be robbed of cash and valuables. Take steps to alert each guest to this event. This may be prevented or you may choose not to attend.

door with missing hardware Someone close to you will be missing within two days. Take the necessary steps to warn family members to be alert to this, especially if this young person is disabled. This is preventable.

unhung You are being far too strict and demanding with yourself. Start enjoying life. For the next five days do everything you can to avoid blurting out any cruel statement that you will later regret.

broken off hinges All negative messages implied in this dream may be avoided if you take the right steps now. A new person will enter your life and this individual would be someone wonderful to spend your life with. If this is something you want, go for it and you will share many wonderful moments together. Avoid all involvements in family squabbles. At the first moment you notice trouble brewing, leave. Give yourself a treat and live life to the fullest. Maintain a healthy and humorous environment.

to close a door on someone and successfully kick them out You will have a very shocking experience upon discovering a deep and mysterious plot that someone has conspired with another. Remain uninvolved. This will occur within three days. Your hunches and instincts will alert you that something is going on. As a result you will be able to successfully diffuse this. You will be dealing with someone who is very tenacious in having everything go their way. You will be very successful in keeping this person out of your life and will easily disengage yourself from this individual.

to close a door on someone and be unable to keep them out You will discover a mysterious and deep plot that others have conspired against you. You have prior notice of this and can take steps to turn this into a positive experience. Do not fall prey to anyone for reasons known only to them. Use every means at your disposal to make sure that nothing happens to you and make sure you do not become involved with someone who will become an enemy. You will come very close to danger but will come through successfully. Otherwise, you are headed for a prosperous future.

doorbell Certain precautions need to be taken within the next three days. Make sure your residence is secure and that your locks are adequate. Ensure your safety, as well as that of your loved ones.

to ring continuously and no one is at the door Someone is plotting to violate your rights. This person will attempt to entice you into a sexual liaison against your better judgment and will. Do not put yourself in a compromising situation. Protect yourself and do not betray your principles.

doorjamb Do not lose your sense of alertness and do not let down your guard in places that pose a hazard for you. Remain alert in all aspects of your life in order to avoid accidents. This is especially important for the next four days.

doorknob If you choose to go in this direction, you will enjoy an unexpected romantic moment involving candlelight, dinner and dancing. This will occur within five days. This cycle will bring you much luck in love.

any unusual doorknob movement Guard yourself from an unexpected intruder. This person will cause you much distress and many distasteful moments. Be acutely aware of strangers. It is important to keep yourself safe for the next four days.

to see a door knob that appears unlocked It will be very important within a two day period to have a meeting with certain individuals and to make connections and the necessary requests before an important situation starts to develop. This will ensure that it does not fall apart before it takes off. Stay on top of this and you will be able to make the correct adjustments in time. Pay attention to this now and everything will fall into place as you desire. Good luck is with you and your family. You are headed for a brilliant future.

to see a doorknob that appears locked Insist on special privileges and considerations for the next five days and do not allow others to assume you can handle more than you can. Let others know that you need help. This is the perfect cycle to make these requests.

doorman You are very much looking forward to a date with someone. This person will cancel the date due to unusual circumstances. Prepare for this occurrence over the next three days in order not to be caught off guard and make sure that you can request a rain check.

doormat Do not go anywhere with someone you do not know well for the next four days. This could lead to unusual and dangerous circumstances

door prize Play games of chance. You will also receive an unexpected gift and will be extended an invitation to a pleasant event. You will enjoy yourself for the next three days.

doorstep Someone you associate with frequently will go to great lengths to get your attention. This person is interested in you romantically. Take the time to get to know this person and you will find you will become interested as well. This will occur within the next four days.

doorway Take a strong stand against someone spending your money. Do this within five days. You will also have good luck and this will be of help in this decision.

dopey For the next seven days, take steps to keep you and your family safe while participating in water activities in order to avoid accidental drownings.

dormitory Be prepared. Within five days, grand changes will begin to occur that will continue for the next month. You need to take steps to introduce a variety of events into your life and you will see big improvements during this time period. Good luck is with you.

dormouse Someone will enter your life within two days because of your inquiry about a certain situation. This person will provide the knowledge you have been seeking and their expertise and information will prove invaluable to you for a lifetime.

dose Listen attentively to what is told to you. Miscommunication will be a result of not paying attention and you will give faulty information to others. This will lead to interference and the interruption of important matters for the next five days. Pay attention to medications that you are dosing yourself with in the dream. This will be something that should either be encouraged or discouraged in reality.

dot Within three days you will receive a windfall. Whatever is being dotted in the dream will lead to a clue of something you will either want to include in your life or to exclude. You have the ability to change any negative message.

dotted Swiss Within seven days, your friends will approve of and get along beautifully with the person who is most special to you. This will be a stress less cycle for you that will bring you much joy and happiness. A special unity will develop between friends and loved ones.

double Within three days, you will find that you have scheduled two events at the same time. Both are important and both need to be personally attended to by you. Make sure you correct this soon in order to avoid disappointments.

to clearly see two things or people in two places at the same time Your spirit is reminding you that you have committed yourself to two events at the same time. The first thing scheduled is far more important than the second.

double agent Make sure you do not assume an air of indifference with others in your life. This will lead to a quarrel within four days.

double barrel Do everything necessary to avoid exposing yourself to an epidemic. Keep yourself healthy. Anything in this dream that signifies a negative message may be turned around. Do not allow yourself to be caught off guard for the next two days.

double boiler Two different people, within seven days, will approach you to discuss some very troublesome issues. Be prepared to work these situations out prior to their becoming a crisis. Do not allow others to become angry with you and don't allow yourself to be lured into expressing anger in return.

double breasted You will invite someone to share your company but will be unsure of their willingness to accompany you. Put these doubts to rest. You will spend many precious moments with the person you most desire and you will be able to take this to a deeper level of closeness if you choose to pursue this.

double chin You will fall deeply in love with someone whom you normally would never consider becoming involved with. This person is very special and affectionate and this relationship will develop into a deep involvement if you choose to pursue this.

double date A situation you felt had been resolved will resurface within seven days. Regroup and resolve this issue permanently so it will not resurface more complicated than it is now. The events occurring in this dream will potentially occur in reality. Do everything necessary to prevent a negative event from occurring and take steps to promote any desirable occurrence. Do this within five days.

double decker Within three days, you and one other person will be able to develop a wonderful work plan via a brainstorming session. This plan will benefit both of you and bring future prosperity.

double decker sandwich For the next five days, negotiations will work out exactly as you hoped. You are deeply loved by friends and family members.

double dribble For the next three days, you will be treated sexually in the manner you most desire. You will be deeply touched in an emotional way. This individual is offering you a long term relationship if this is what you desire. Many blessings are with you.

double edge Make sure that, for the next three days, you do not involve yourself with someone who enjoys arguing and creating a crisis out of small issues. Do not subject yourself to an abusive situation. Get on with your life without this person.

double helix Someone you offered support to in the past will be very eager to involve you in a venture that you want to become involved in. Expect this within two days. Good luck will be with you on this project.

double jeopardy Stay away from heavy lifting and heavy labor. Do not place so many demands on yourself for the next seven days. Get more rest, eat healthful foods and drink plenty of water.

double jointed Within three days, you will meet with someone you wish to hire for the performance of certain tasks.

This person will be incompetent and will unintentionally destroy equipment. Be very careful who you put in charge of your projects.

double knit This dream is a good luck omen. You will enjoy an abundance of blessings and good health. This will be a good, week long cycle for you and your family.

double park Within seven days, someone will relate an important message to you. Be expecting this. This message will offer ways to drastically improve your life.

doublet Make sure you do not settle for less, especially for the next three days. Do not compromise your desires and go for what you need.

double take You will be involved in business transactions that will involve travel. This will result in great success even if you are not the one actually making the trip. You are entering a very lucky cycle for the next seven days, but you are experiencing too much interference from others especially in matters that require that you, alone, make a decision. Stop asking for the opinions of others. You will be overwhelmed by different pieces of advice that serve only to confuse you. Rely on your own counsel for the next five days.

double time For the next four days, there will be a tendency for situations to become magnified and for tempers to flare. Control your temper for this time period.

double vision With the proper medical help, you will find the solution to a recurring pain within a three day period. Search relentlessly for a solution until you get the proper help. Any negative event in this dream needs to be altered or avoided. Experience only positive expressions in your life.

doubloon You will be vigorously chased by someone who wishes you to enter into a romantic agreement. This person will push for a quick agreement to their terms. If you choose to pursue this, this cycle will bring you many of the wonderful treats love has to offer. Many blessings will be with you for the next seven days. This dream is also a good luck omen.

doubting Thomas Stocks, etc., are going up. This dream is a very lucky omen for you.

douche Within three days, you will learn of the deep feelings another person has for you while in a special setting. This will result in passionate moments if you choose. You will be very surprised at the depth of feeling this person has for you.

douche bag Do not lend any articles of clothing or tools. They will not be returned in the same condition they were loaned out.

dough You will achieve a higher level of power in the areas of your life you most desire. Victory will be yours for the next seven days.

doughboy Arrange your schedule in such a way that enables you to accomplish as much as you can in the time allotted to you. Do this for the next five days.

doughnut Prosperity and abundance will be yours within four days. It is also important that you maintain caution and take steps to prevent sexually transmitted diseases. Take care of your health.

Douglas fir Someone will flirt openly with you in an unexpected place and at an unexpected time. If you choose to pursue this route, romance will blossom and you will get exactly what you are seeking from a romantic situation.

dove You will enjoy victory in all phases of your life, especially in matters of love. Do not waste time deciding to pursue someone you desire. You have taken too long to make a move in the direction you want to go. For the next three days, the cycle will be perfect for you to make a romantic overture.

dead dove Make sure you are not struck by a moving vehicle and take steps to avoid all accidents for the next two days. Take steps also to protect yourself from illnesses for the next two days because the recovery time will be lengthy. Do what you can to nourish yourself, get plenty of rest, drink liquids, and eat healthful foods.

dove cote Any form of reconciliation with another individual is possible if you make a move within four days. This will rapidly develop into a wonderful situation.

dovetail You will be able to perform in the manner another person desires while in a romantic setting and this person's requests will be successfully met by you. This will occur within three days. If you choose to go along with this, you will enjoy a wonderful response from the other person. You will also receive good news via mail within two days.

dowel Do not place yourself in a position where you will be easily blamed if something is missing. Although you are innocent, you will be accused of theft. Make sure this does not take place. Be very protective of the events occurring in your environment to avoid becoming someone's scapegoat.

down You will enter a relationship with someone who demonstrates love and affection toward you only in private. In public and behind your back, this person will attempt to make others believe that you are not involved with each other. Be aware of this before you become too deeply involved. Go on with your life only as friends, if you choose to maintain the relationship.

anything going down that should not be going down Someone will go to great lengths to steer you from your greatest interests. Remain firm and stick to your goals.

downhill Make sure you do not borrow money for the next five days. You will be unable to repay it. Remain financially free for the next month.

down payment Do not allow paint or chemicals to be splattered on your personal items. Be cautious about your environment and wary of any spills, especially chemicals. Also, pay attention to what you are placing a down payment on. If it is something you would choose in reality, go for it. If not, take steps to avoid it in reality.

downpour Everything you once felt was impossible is now a possibility for the next five days and favors will be granted to you readily during this time period. You are going in the right direction and many blessings will come to you and your family.

downshift Someone will go to great lengths to con you out of what is truly yours. For the next five days, be very watchful for this.

downspout Make sure you do not hire anyone to perform a service who does not have the necessary licenses and expertise to adequately perform the job. Check this person's references.

Down's Syndrome Protect your plants for the next five days to ensure their health.

downstage Someone with a dynamic reputation will, within five days, want to back up your business plans. Good luck is with you.

downstairs Do not, for the next four days, put yourself in the position to be investigated and interrogated. Keep yourself clear of any activity that would draw out this type of behavior.

downwind A same sexed person will lead you to a career that you will find very satisfying. This will result in a lifetime of prosperity and security.

downy Make sure that any agreement for services performed on credit is put into writing to ensure that the agreed upon price does not increase, especially for the next three days.

dowry Someone will commit an act that will have severe consequences for them. You will benefit from this person's downfall. Expect this within the week.

doze For the next five days, refrain from performing tasks that will require heavy labor and from strenuous athletic pursuits unless you are in the proper physical condition.

dozen Within two weeks, pleasure seeking activities will become very expensive and will easily develop into a bad habit. Watch your behavior carefully and control your spending.

Dracula Take steps to get more rest, and avoid stressful situations. Pamper yourself, eat healthful foods and drink plenty of water. Give yourself a small gift. For additional information see vampire.

to dream of being a vampire Give others a break. Back away from a certain person and allow them the space to have their own life so they can take care of their own business. You are demanding too much of another person's time.

to recognize someone as Dracula This person will become very obsessive and possessive and will expect you to report each move you make to them. Schedule a talk with this person in order to put this behavior to an end, otherwise you will start to feel smothered and without a life of your own. Do not allow others to direct your life.

draft Do not involve yourself in a risky situation for the next three days. You will regret this.

draft board This dream is a good luck omen. Anything is possible within the week, even those things you felt were impossible before.

draft dodger You are in the position now to demand what you need and want from your spirit. Your desires will be quickly answered. You will also overcome a crisis that will arise within four days. Remain calm and clear headed and you will successfully arrive at a solution.

draftsman Someone is feeling very abandoned by you. Quickly let this person know how special they are to you and give them an adequate description of your true feelings for them. This will give this individual a great amount of pleasure and will be deeply appreciated by them. Put your love into action and anything you want to develop on a permanent basis will become a reality within five days. A gift of any kind to this person will enhance this development. You are loved beyond your imagination.

dragnet You will become interested in someone within the week. You will also be tempted to tell another person about your feelings. If you do, this will be spread around to anyone who will listen. Keep your personal business to yourself.

dragon This dream is a powerful symbol and is a promise that you will grasp the goals you are pursuing. You will be in a very victorious cycle for the next three weeks. The deities are with you.

dragonfly You and the person you want to share your victories with will be successful in those areas you most desire. All of your hopes and plans will work out as you have envisioned.

dragon lizard For the next five days any joint venture you are interested in becoming a part of will have fantastic results and prosperity will come to those involved. One individual will be very willing to give you the money you need within three days.

dragon teeth For seven days, take precautions to avoid freak accidents. Situations that seem the most unlikely are apt to occur during this cycle. Protect yourself from all injuries and accidents.

dragoon Concentrate on your priorities. Drink plenty of water and do what you can to build up your resistance to disease.

drag queen This dream is a good omen. Within seven days, you will be able to turn a very negative, volatile relationship into a loving tranquil one.

drag race Do everything necessary to bring harmony and tranquility into your personal environment. Do not allow yourself or others to bring hostility and disharmony into your life and disrupt your privacy. Don't be you own worst enemy.

drag strip Dig deeply for the reasons why you are reluctant to confront personal issues. It will be required that you explain this behavior within three days. Regroup yourself and you will find ways to release yourself from this burden.

drain *to see anything go down the drain* This dream is alerting you that someone who is indebted to you is having a difficult time financially. Within four days, this individual will go to great lengths to get enough money to pay you. There is a good chance this person will not get the payment to you on time. Be prepared for this but also encourage this person to make a greater effort.

to try to unplug a drain Within seven days, you will reach an agreement with someone to surrender property within a specified period of time. You will have to stay on top of this because this person will attempt to delay handing over this property.

to successfully unplug a drain What you attempt to achieve for the next seven days will result in success.

to be unable to retrieve an object from the drain You will fail to reach an agreement with someone on matters that are important to you. This individual will refuse to concede to any of your requests. This will occur within three days.

to see anything drained Someone special to you is prepared to separate from a relationship. They believe that you are no longer interested. Change your cold, aloof manner and take steps to become more demonstrative and affectionate in order to save this relationship.

to retrieve an object from the drain You will experience prosperity in your life due to an unusual opportunity and you will be able to capitalize on this. Keep your eyes open for any opportunity coming your way. Pay close attention to the object retrieved. If the message is negative, alter the outcome. If positive, include it in your life. This three day cycle will make you very aware of how aligned you are with those you admire.

anything unusual coming up from the drain Pay close attention to what is coming up from the drain. This will provide you with a major clue to the meaning of the dream. When you are required to give explanations and information to someone else, be sure to give only the information required, do not go into lengthy explanations. Do not assume an attitude of guilt and refuse to answer all questions you are unsure of until a later time. By adopting these suggestions for the next three days, you will avoid saying something you regret.

to be drained Do not allow others to manipulate you into spending money. Keep yourself disciplined and organized for at least seven weeks.

drainpipe Do not allow others to sway your decisions on financial affairs. Make sure all agreements are carefully structured and scrutinized for the next three days. Take precautions to ensure that you are not manipulated or undermined during this cycle.

to retrieve anything from a drainpipe You will be able to reconcile with others on those matters that are important to you. You will enjoy success and have many happy moments for the next five days.

in any other form Do not allow anyone to unilaterally volunteer your time for the next three days. You will also experience unusual physical strength and greater communication skills during this time period. Good luck is with you.

drama Someone will demonstrate genuine affection toward you within the week. Show no signs of dislike and aversion toward this person because, in time, you will come to be interested in a meaningful relationship. If you demonstrate dislike at the beginning, they will always feel a hidden resentment.

drape Give yourself time to clear your thoughts. Make sure you have absolute clarity when making decisions.

drapes Praise family members and loved ones who are important to you.

draw *to draw a picture* Pay close attention to what is being drawn. This will provide a major clue to what will be forthcoming in your life within two days. You may either take steps to avoid this event or to promote it to the fullest. This picture may also represent an object you want to possess. This dream also implies that someone from a different ethnic background will be very successful for you to work with. You will both experience an abundance of prosperity. Take steps to improve your appearance.

drawbridge Do everything necessary to keep a relationship intact. Communicate in a manner that will promote unity, especially for the next three days.

drawers Make sure, for the next two days, that you do not omit anything of importance in a negotiation. Think carefully prior to reaching any agreements.

drawing board You will be able to capitalize on another's misfortune and this will lead to prosperity. Within the week you will also achieve prosperity in the areas of your life you most desire.

drawing room You will become successful through the efforts of a third party. The friend of an acquaintance will be able to perform favors for you that will lead to very positive results.

drawstring Do not allow jealousy, envy and ignorance to cloud your decisions and lifestyle.

dray Check first before you volunteer the time or efforts of another individual to a cause, especially for the next three days.

dray horse Do not allow a quarrel to develop between you and a special person. For the next three days, make sure that a disagreement does not occur that could escalate out of proportion.

dread Do not allow someone else to take up too much of your time. Learn to budget your time and use it wisely, especially for the next two days.

dread lock This dream is a very lucky omen. Your intuitions are right on target and you are headed toward prosperity.

dream *to dream of dreaming* Make sure the buck stops with you in personal matters and that you assume responsibility for your personal life. You will also have a sneak preview of forthcoming events. Make sure you promote positive messages and work to prevent any future negative ones. Meditate in your favorite form and trust your instincts.

wet dream Within seven days you will make an emotional appeal to someone who is in the position to help out in any way you wish. This person is able to help out financially and is able to pull strings on your behalf. You will empower yourself, because of this occurrence, in ways that you will find beneficial in your life. Move quickly on this. You will be able to position yourself in life in ways you were never able to before. Many blessings are with you and you are headed for a brilliant future. You are also loved by someone beyond your imagination and will have verification of this within seven days.

in any other form This dream is a sneak preview of what will occur to you or to someone you know within the month. If this is a negative situation, take steps to change it; if positive, take steps to include it in your life. It also implies that you will see great improvements in your life if you actually work to motivate yourself. Good luck and many blessings will come to you and your family. The gods are with you.

dream book This is a good luck symbol. Whatever knowledge or message you have gleaned from this book should be followed. This will render a clue that you need to watch for within the next two weeks. Your intuition and psychic abilities are at a high point. This will be a sneak preview of what is in store for you within the next few months. Follow your hunches. You will also find that, for the next ten days, you will reach your peak of experience and will be so together you will instinctively know you will reach the finish line before the race has really begun. You will begin to have feelings of confidence that come from knowing you will succeed. You will experience the strength that comes from your inner core. Follow your goals as if you were on a mission and this will bring you to a victorious completion of your goals. Within this time frame, your sense of ethics and judgment will be intact. You are headed for a fantastic future. If the message is negative, you have time to alter the outcome. If positive, enhance it to the fullest.

dredge Someone will request their money back after an agreement that they pay for a particular service or item you are selling. This will occur within three days. Be prepared for this. Either refuse to work with this person, set aside the money to give it back, or prepare to negotiate.

dreg Make sure you do not become part of a rumble that will break out in the middle of a social gathering. Avoid large gatherings for the next two days.

drench Someone, within three days, will go to great lengths to draw you closer to them. This will have a positive effect on both of you. Good luck is with you.

to be drenched with anything You will be hearing the words of love you have longed to hear within three days.

dress Your intuition is correct, especially in matters of love. You will get a message from a third person about someone who would like to become involved romantically. This will surprise and please you immensely. You had not thought of this person in this way before but now that the seed has been planted, you find your interest kindled. Within five days, this person will approach you and prior to this, you will enjoy many moments of anticipation.

adorned dress Pay attention to the individual adornment for extra clues. Mingle with new groups to open new doors of opportunity. You will be able to express your ideas better, and will enjoy an improved social life as well as having the chance to attend exciting new functions.

beautiful dress At one time, in the past, you were interested in developing a seemingly impossible relationship but gave it no real thought. Now you are again interested in this person and the feelings are now mutual. Everything you ever wanted from a relationship is now possible. You will also have many admirers who will be interested in you at the same time. For the next month you will date several people and be able to decide who you choose to have a relationship with.

cotton dress You will be using your creative sense to become financially secure. You are headed in the right direction.

evening dress You will receive an unexpected call from

someone who will not immediately identify themselves. It will become apparent this person is an admirer and toward the end of the conversation they will identify themselves. Once you learn the identity, you will be eager to further this involvement.

silk dress A wealthy, professional person will be eager for you to accept a marriage proposal within the next two months.

soiled dress You are headed in the wrong direction and, in spite of all guarantees, you will expose yourself to risks. Reanalyze your decisions and do nothing out of the ordinary for the next three weeks. Make sure also that a garment does not become soiled in reality.

torn dress You will, for the next week, be facing unusual situations that will demand extra time and personal attention. Take steps to eliminate stress in order to remain calm enough to make clear decisions. Take care also not to tear any clothing. Additionally, someone will want to treat you to an outing within the next three days. Take the initiative in offering to treat this person.

unusual colors or materials check the color and material of the dress and look up the meanings for additional clues to this dream.

to be dressed in black An unusually powerful and well educated person will become interested in your personal undertakings. Because of this interest, you will be able to advance yourself successfully. This will occur within three days.

many people dressed in black At one time you wanted the impossible in a relationship. This person will suddenly return after a long absence and everything you ever wanted from a relationship will now be possible. You will also see other people you have not seen in a long time who are in no way connected with this love relationship. Luck is with you during this cycle.

to see men dressed in black Maintain your confidence when others are trying to make you feel desperate, especially for the next two days.

to see women dressed in black Keep your confidence high, in spite of misfortune, and all of your plans will bear fruit.

to see babies dressed in black A family member will be missing and will not be found. Do everything necessary to alert all those concerned to take precautions to prevent this occurrence, especially for the next seven days.

wedding dress A number of unexpected events will occur in a cluster, one after the other and you will receive a flood of invitations to pick and choose from. It is imperative that you accept one specific invitation. This one will be more glamorous and exciting than the others and will require formal wear. Prepare yourself well in advance so that you will look your best. Make sure you do not deprive yourself of this enjoyable event. You will enjoy yourself immensely and will meet many influential people who will become life long friends. You will also win a door prize or receive a gift of some kind. During this cycle you will also become aware that the person you are interested in will have the same feelings for you as you have for them. You will enjoy many

affectionate moments together and you will both be excited about this new development. You are headed for a brilliant and prosperous future.

in any other form A certain person will be very affectionate and eager to help you in any way they can, whether this is an emotional or financial matter. Someone will also tell you the next step to take that will be instrumental in a decision you have to make within a three day period. This decision will bring more emotional and financial security to your life. Act with confidence and everything will fall into place exactly as you have envisioned. Take advantage of this cycle to make changes in other areas of your life that you wish to improve.

dress circle You will need to try a number of ways to meet your goals. It is reachable if you seek several alternative methods.

dressed *to see someone incorrectly or incompletely dressed* For the next three days, do not become any more deeply involved with someone unless you take extreme precautions. The person you will be dealing with will lead you to believe you can depend on their loyalty and that you can completely confide in them. This person is a master of deception and will lead you to believe that certain situations and events will occur in the future but they will never take place. This individual will create an atmosphere free of suspicions and full of trust, but at the same time has a hidden agenda that involves pursuing you for devious reasons known only to them. If you start to develop any suspicions, a crisis will be created as a diversion. This person is charming enough to pull this off with success. Once you realize what is going on you will have suffered financially, and will be totally disillusioned and disappointed. It will take a long time to recover but you will get your life back to normal. Practice common sense and you will be successful in handling this issue. Do not compromise your feelings and do not allow this person to pry into your affairs. You have prior notice of this and all the ammunition you need to avoid it. You are headed for a prosperous future and many blessings are with you and your family.

dresser For the next three days be on your guard because you will be in the presence of someone who will suffer an accident by falling. This will result in a severe injury. You have the opportunity to prevent this occurrence.

dresser drawers Make sure, for the next two days, that you do not omit anything of importance in a negotiation. Think carefully prior to reaching any agreements.

dressing *to see yourself or others dressing* A friendship you have pinned your hopes on will be a disaster. A business partnership will not work out either. Make plans to find an alternative partner.

dressing *salad dressing* Unless you get help now you will be unable to make the grade you are after.

Russian dressing You have greatly underestimated a

situation that you will become involved in within five days. Move quickly and do not let it slip away. This will be your golden opportunity.

dressing gown You will be entering an unforgettable, one of a kind, cycle that will be filled with many social events and functions and a number of different, interesting individuals will be attracted to you. This will be such a positive cycle that each person will be a prize. It is up to you to choose the one you most desire.

dressing room A great event will occur that will be celebrated and talked about for weeks. This will be a very joyful event and will occur in the very near future.

dressing table Within the next two days you will be cornered by someone you have been trying to avoid. Be alert to the possibility of running into this individual and take extra steps to elude this person .

dressmaker Do not push away a loved one because of your behavior. Communicate with this person and express your love with action in order to bring them close and keep them close. Do this for the next month.

dress rehearsal Within three days you will finally rid yourself of a responsibility you have been wanting to be free of.

dress suit Think ahead to your next move and have an overdue conversation with someone to gather much needed information. Pinpoint those people you want to work with based on their response to your ideas. Do this within seven days.

dressy *dressed up* You will be entering an unforgettable, one of a kind, cycle that will be filled with social events and functions. There will also be a number of different, interesting individuals who will be attracted to you. This will be such a positive cycle that each person will be a prize. It is up to you to choose the one you most desire.

dribble Keep your hands off other people's money. For the next three days do whatever is necessary to avoid unusual situations regarding the finances of other people.

drift A group of people will be angry at a decision you make while excluding them from the decision making process. Make sure that for the next two days you include others in your decision making processes.

driftwood Do not push yourself on others for the next three days because other people are not interested in this behavior. You will be able to accomplish a long desired goal. You must also be very cautious and aware of where someone is leading you emotionally. This person will, for reasons known only to them, lead you to believe they are completely in love with you. The word love may or may not be used at this time but all of the romantic trappings will be there (i.e., flowers, gifts, romantic outings, etc.). Your feelings for this

person will grow deep and strong, but if you allow yourself to make love with this person you will find this individual will not be able to touch you in any way that implies that they love you. You will not be able to fully connect and will be left feeling empty and cold. Instead of putting yourself through this emotional pain, avoid this situation entirely. You have prior notice of this and can get on with your life without this person. This situation will only lead to unhappiness. Otherwise, you are on the path for a prosperous future that will begin to evolve within the week.

drill This dream is a good luck omen. Someone is highly attracted to you. Pay particular attention to this for the next two days.

drilling Do everything necessary to develop new friendships. Do not associate only with old friends and do not frequent old habitats. Develop new interests and new social clubs.

drill press Do not pay attention to a known alarmist because this will cause you to become overly stressed about issues of no consequence. Stay calm and in control for the next two days.

drill team Make sure that, for the next five days, you are well protected from fires. Make sure your wiring is not faulty and be careful when operating machinery. Play it safe and keep your loved ones safe as well.

drink *to drink cold clear water* This is an omen of health, wealth and good luck. This cycle will last for two months. It also implies that the person you desire a close relationship with will become committed to you and both of you will develop a close union.

to drink warm water Someone will push just the right buttons to anger you. Do not allow yourself to be baited this way, especially for the next five days.

to drink tainted water For the next seven days you will have to be very relentless and aggressive in pursuing what is rightfully yours.

to drink vinegar Someone will promise you money so you can meet a payment. This money will not come through for you. Make alternative plans to secure this money.

to drink wine You are very much interested in someone who is also very interested in you. This person cannot commit to a traditional relationship due to a busy lifestyle. Rather than do things half way, this individual will not be involved at all until their lifestyle allows it. Sometime in the future this situation will change but until then, go on with your life.

to drink milk You are treating a relationship too lightly. You need to sit down and look at this union a bit more seriously. The other person involved would also like to see you take the relationship more seriously. Demonstrate your feelings and offer a small gift to your loved one in order to keep this relationship going.

to drink chocolate milk You will be harassed by the police because of another person's lifestyle and carelessness. This will occur within a few days and will result in an enormous amount of property damage. This is not within your control. Stay calm and it will eventually work out. Take it slowly and proceed in a step by step fashion. You will be able to put your life back in order.

to drink ice water This dream implies that this seven day lucky cycle will be even stronger than a dream to drink cold water. You will experience an abundance of what you desire.

to drink boiling water Someone will intentionally push the wrong buttons for the purpose of provoking your anger. This will occur within two days. When you see this situation begin to develop, take steps to avoid confrontation.

to drink dirty water For the next seven days be careful not to put yourself in the position to contract a virus or venereal disease. Someone will intentionally try to infect you.

to see yourself or someone else drinking something unusual or that is not meant for drinking purposes Take extra precautions when you transport money from one location to another. The other party will never receive the money. Be very alert to this for the next seven days.

to be unable to quench your thirst Within seven days, someone will purposely lie to you. They will agree to meet you at a specific event and will not show up. Choose an alternative person to go with.

to taste or drink blood Think ahead. Someone you meet will subtly manipulate themselves into your life. This will be a purposeful act and little by little they will come to dominate you. You will begin to account to this person each detail of your life. You will be amazed that this has happened and will find it difficult to get out of this situation. Watch for this ahead of time and take steps to avoid it.

to drink water in any other form You are entering a cycle that will allow you to enjoy advantages for the next seven days. You will obtain victory and put yourself into a powerful position with situations you are now working on. You will be in a lucky cycle for the next seven days.

drinking fountain For the next seven days, you will be in a great cycle to accomplish goals you have long wanted to accomplish.

drinking song Someone you know will be subjected to abuse. Do what you can to intervene and to ensure that this person will not endure further abuse. This will occur within three days.

drip You will receive the sexual gratification you desire. For the next seven days you will enjoy emotional pleasure.

drip dry This is a great cycle to take steps in removing yourself from a very stressful situation.

dripping pan You will volunteer to do the meal planning and cooking for a large event. Another person will intervene and volunteer their services. Be aware that at the last moment this other person will not come through. Be firm in your original offer in order to avoid a disaster.

drippings Do not give in sexually to someone simply because you feel it will make this person feel better. Guard against this behavior for the next seven days.

drive You are moving in the right direction and are making the correct decision in a difficult situation that you will be handling within the next seven days. You must also be aware of other events and symbols connected with the drive for more clues.

drive an ambulance You are unknowingly allowing a troublesome situation to develop that needs to be aggressively attended to. Discipline and structure yourself in order to grasp each situation before it disperses to the point of chaos. Once it reaches this point you will lose the ability to begin again. Push yourself now in order to resolve each issue and do not allow yourself to get bogged down with extraneous matters that are out of your control. Do not allow yourself to be the major cause of problems. Focus on this aspect of your behavior and take steps to change it. Do nothing that will cause problems with the law.

to drive on a road in disrepair Someone you know and deeply respect will pass away within the next two weeks.

drive in You will be permanently free from a long term burden within seven days. You are headed toward a brilliant future.

driver *to see someone drive your car* The person answering an ad in the newspaper is a very dangerous individual. Take extra precautions for the next seven days to protect yourself from a deranged person.

to see someone driving any car other than your own If you recognize whomever you see at the wheel they will be making a dramatic change in their lives. This person will also need assistance from you in order to make this change. You will be an instrument by using the right words to inspire the confidence they need to motivate themselves. You will know of this projected change within the week.

in any other form You will be the target for romantic affection. This will appeal to you for the next two days. If you should pursue this, you will be happy for a lifetime.

driver's license Within three days, you will receive an unexpected gift that will bring you special pleasure.

driver's seat You are fated to meet someone within the week who is loving, generous and kind. If you choose to pursue this, you will experience a new joy and a dramatic improvement in your style of living.

drivers test *to pass a driver's test* A cluster of unexpected events will occur one after the other. You will also receive a flood of invitations that you will be able to pick and choose from. One special invitation you should not miss. This one will be more glamorous and exciting than any of the others and will require formal attire. Make sure you prepare yourself ahead of time so that you look your best. Do not deprive yourself of this enjoyable event. You will not only have a fantastic time but will be able to meet a number of influential people who will become good friends for a lifetime. You will also win a door prize or receive some gifts at this event. During this cycle you will become aware that the person you most desire feels the same way about you. You will have very affectionate feelings toward each other and will be very excited about this new development. You are headed for a very prosperous and brilliant future.

drive shaft Within three days you will have to be prepared to care for an ill parent. With care, this person will recover rapidly. Good luck is with you and many blessings will come to you and your family.

drive through window Focus on someone who carries themselves in a simple and quiet fashion. Do not overlook the importance of this person. This individual possesses a great deal of knowledge relating to an issue you are handling now. Listen carefully to this wealth of information in order to ensure a prosperous outcome.

driveway Do not allow anyone in on your plans for the next two weeks. Be sure to keep your affairs to yourself and trust your instincts. Go for it.

driving range An uncontrollable strange desire will overcome you. For the next two days, take steps to control your behavior. This desire could lead you to commit a regrettable act.

drizzle Put your love into action and show kindness and generosity toward your loved ones, especially for the next four days. Eliminate all hostile behavior.

dromedary Someone will finally come to grips with themselves and reach a decision you have been long waiting for. This decision will have a major impact on your life. Both of you will make plans that will lead to a brilliant future. Expect this to take place within the week.

drone Do not allow yourself to become emotionally caught up in negative game playing. Maintain a positive frame of mind, especially with situations that will be developing over the next three days.

drool For the next four days, you will need to actively change your direction in order to increase your finances. Your original plan will not work out.
to see others drool Someone will, within four days, ask that you enter into a joint agreement. Take advantage of this agreement; the results will be very positive.

droop Do not create chaos out of a small issue, especially for the next three days. This will be a waste of time for you.

drop *to drop* Pay close attention to what you dropped. This will be a clear indication of what will occur in the future.

You also need to speak with someone about your needs. Do not suffer in silence. This person will be very accommodating for the next three days.
to see others drop something Prevent a similar occurrence from taking place in reality. You must also not allow yourself to be persuaded by others to spend your money frivolously. Be determined about what you choose to spend your money on.
to drop something heavy on your foot or to see something heavy drop on someone else's feet Do not allow yourself to be put in a position to be mauled or injured by an animal, especially for the next five days.

drop cloth Leave all investigative work to others for the next three days.

drop cookie A roommate will not be truthful within the next four days. You will gain information that will cast doubts about some of their statements. Pay close attention to what is going on during this time period.

dropkick Do not put yourself down in front of others. This will allow others to mistreat you. Be especially aware of this behavior for the next two days.

droplet Plans for a long desired vacation will begin to take shape within three days. Pursue this and it will become a reality.

dropper You are asking someone to handle a situation that they are not mentally or emotionally able to handle. Think carefully of ways to handle this without this person's involvement.

drops *any form* Someone else will seek credit for your work. Be very watchful of this and take steps to prevent it.

drought Stop speculating. Take all of your plans and work toward detailing and collaborating each phase in order to put these plans into action. This will ensure success and a good income by making sure that all your bases are covered. For the next four days, work out each detail and you will have smooth sailing for the next four months.

drove Within four days, a particular situation will arise more frequently than in the past. You will need to seek immediate assistance. You will find this help to be extremely important during this cycle. Good luck is with you.

drown Within five days, the behavior that another person demonstrates toward you will cause you to feel overwhelmed. Ignore this person and do not allow this to destroy your tranquility and peace of mind. Remain steady and calm. Riches are coming your way and you will experience more prosperity and security. You are headed in the right direction.
to see a child you recognize drowning You need to be very protective of any child you recognize to ensure that

their needs are being met. Be sure that you warn the custodian of this child so they can take all the necessary steps to prevent this incident. For the next three days any quick decision you make will lead to riches.

if the drowning person is an adult Warn this person of the danger of drowning in the near future. This individual will also be coming into riches. You will also be placed in a position of power and will be able to make dynamic decisions that will steer you in the right direction. Any negative event seen in this dream needs to be prevented in reality.

anything drowning This dream is an extremely lucky omen and you are headed for a very prosperous future. You will be undefeatable because of your tenacity. This manner is exactly what you need to realize your ambitions. This dream also implies that someone from the past will drop in on you unexpectedly with joyful news. You will also enjoy positive moments from a date that you hoped would be romantic. If you choose, this relationship will be emotionally and romantically fulfilling for as long as you desire. You are headed in the right direction. Do everything you can to ensure that anything negative you dreamed of does not occur in the next three days. Take steps to avoid or alter this event.

drug Be very aware of any self medication in order to prevent an accidental overdose or an allergic reaction. Make sure also that you relentlessly work to resolve any ongoing situation until it is worked out to your advantage.

drug raid Someone will do everything in their power to lead you in the direction of emotional or physical harm. This will catch you off guard at an unexpected moment. Carefully scrutinize all situations and take steps to protect your environment. Avoid any situation where someone has the opportunity to gain an upper hand, especially for the next seven days.

drug addict Aggressively work with an ill person to ensure that they receive the proper medical attention and assistance. You will succeed because of your relentless pursuit to help this person. Good luck is with you and you will also develop the gift of patience. It also implies that you need to aggressively pursue what you need in your personal life. Do not procrastinate an issue you find important for yourself.

druggist You will receive a job offer that will prove to be too demanding on your time and health. Seek an alternative means of support.

drugs *to handle legal drugs in any form* Do not jeopardize friendships or your career because of your obsessions. You are developing intolerable behavior patterns. Do not become your own worst enemy. Also, be aware that prescribed medications may be wrong for you and will result in an allergic reaction.

in any other form Be very aggressive with upcoming situations. Work to solve problems immediately before any of them reaches a crisis. Aggressive, relentless action is the only way to handle any personal crisis.

drugstore Be aware of your actions and purchases in the drug store. This will be a major clue to future occurrences in your life. You have the time to alter any negative message. It is also important not to become a nuisance to someone else as a response to their behavior. Once you see this pattern begin to develop, back off. This is especially important for the next four days.

Druid Place yourself in someone else's position in order to determine the proper way to behave around them for the next four days.

drum Someone you were very interested in at one time will reenter your life. This person has enjoyed a major triumph in life and has become wealthy. You will be invited to share their new life and a mutual interest will develop. It is up to you how far this relationship will go. This dream is also a warning that you have overlooked an issue that must be attended to. If you do not become aware of this, you will be taken advantage of.

drumbeat You are being told to pursue the big projects. Go for it. This cycle will guarantee your success.

drum majorette You will receive a large grant if you ask for it. It will come to you sooner than anticipated. This will be a very lucky cycle for you.

drummer This is an accident prone cycle. Be very cautious for the next five days. Make sure also that you are not the cause of another's misfortune.

drum roll Within four days, two companions will become involved in a physical fight. Avoid all altercations and avoid the company of these people during this time period.

drumstick Someone will be less than you imagined them to be. This will result in disappointment and will occur within three days. Do not assume a certain behavior from another. This will prevent disappointment.

drunk Avoid all negative situations and make an effort to turn each negative into a positive.

to see yourself drunk Be very aggressive with upcoming situations. Work to resolve problems immediately before they reach a crisis situation. Aggressive, relentless action is the only way to handle any personal crisis. Within three days you will also meet a wealthy individual. This person will quickly become interested in investing in your projects. This will get the ball rolling and you will be able to pay this person back. This will occur in the near future.

to see others drunk Someone you know will be very dishonest with you. This person will try to cheat you out of money and keep information from you. Be very wary of this for the next four days. Speak up for your rights and fight for what you want out of an ongoing situation.

to dream of someone passing out due to drunkenness Within five days you will be entering an extremely lucky cycle and each person involved in your life will share in this cycle. You will receive services that will allow you to complete your goals successfully. You will achieve a higher level of success than you anticipated regarding anything you place a high degree of importance on. You can expect, during this time period, to make many wonderful connections that will assist you in grasping and meeting your goals. You will merge successfully with other people and the synergism created will advance you to a greater level of success than you hoped for. This dream also implies that you will gain benefits by attending a social event, through an educational experience, or by attending a gathering in which one person will demonstrate an interest in you and your plans and offer their assistance in helping you to complete them. A long period of tranquility will follow this and you can expect a brilliant future. Any negative event portended in this dream can be avoided. Forewarn anyone you recognized in the dream to take the appropriate steps.

in any other form Someone is plotting to keep you from getting in touch with someone you are interested in. Pursue other methods of reaching this person and you will find that your object of interest will go to great lengths to maintain contact with you.

dry Protect yourself from fire.

to dry your hair/anything or to see someone else drying anything Someone who harbors a secret animosity toward you will attempt, within a five day period, to sabotage your plans to steer a situation in a certain direction that will benefit others. You are trying to work things out in such a way that everyone involved will enjoy future prosperity. Although this person knows you are right, they will work against you, regardless of the destruction they will wreak on others. They are not aware of the degree of hardship they will bring to others. You have prior notice of this and can take steps to prevent this interference.

to dry off or to see someone else dry off Within three days, a situation will develop between two people of equal power who will face off against each other to prove themselves to other people. Emotions and excitement will run high because everyone will be interested in the one who comes out on top. The older of the two will emerge victorious and everyone involved will be satisfied with the outcome. You will also experience an unexpected windfall and are definitely headed in the right direction.

in any other form You need to be focused and analytical about each move you make. This will allow you to achieve prosperity.

dry cleaners For the next four days you will be unable to draw someone close to you because of your failure to communicate. Make sure when you speak with someone that they understand exactly what you mean. Make sure you are not misinterpreted.

dry dock You will uncover needed information within the next two days.

dryer You will hear the words of love that you have been longing to hear within the next two days.

dry goods You will find it difficult to believe what another person is telling you. This individual is being truthful. Drop your doubts and suspicions.

dry ice You will become very wealthy within the year.

dry rot Someone who has been very supportive of you in the past will suddenly become disinterested in you and your projects. Within four days you will notice this lack of interest. With a little gentle prodding, you will find this person is going through a large personal trial in their life. You will be able to offer assistance simply by listening. Also be sure you are taking precautions to ensure the safety of livestock and pets. Take steps to keep them safe and free of disease. Be sure you prevent dry rot from occurring in the location portended in the dream. You are entering a prosperous and healthy cycle for the next seven days.

dry wall For the next two days it is very important to connect emotionally and verbally with those who are very important in your life.

dual Do everything you can to make that special person in your life feel special. This will keep this person from seeking emotional satisfaction in other areas. This is especially important for the next seven days.

dub You will hear of the birth of twins.

Dublin For the next few days you will have more energy and will demonstrate more pizzazz for life. You are headed in the right direction. This dream may also be used as a reference point in time. If you dream of this city and see its name used in any context, the dream message will occur on this day.

Duchess Your romantic plans will work out the way you have planned.

duck Within two days the person you have made plans with will lack the courage to follow through. Be prepared to accept a breakdown of mutual plans. You will also receive financial assistance from a relative who will be eager to invest in your project. Discuss your enterprise with a family member whom you feel is open to new ideas. This will hasten the process. Good luck is with you. This will occur within seven days.

mandarin duck Avoid people who complain and are constantly miserable. You will have to deal with this within five days. You have prior notice and can make yourself scarce in order to avoid ruining pleasurable moments.

duckbill Avoid anything that will result in a court subpoena, especially for the next three days.

duck feet Be relentless in staying on the right track. Do not give up and do not take short cuts. You are headed in the right direction.

duckling Be aware that someone who lives in your vicinity may be a child molester. Protect young children from perverse behavior.

duckpin An inheritance that you will learn about will cause you a great deal of anxiety before you receive it. Move quickly and do everything you can to protect your interests.

duck soup You will meet someone who will soon be working closely with you. Do not put yourself in the position for anything unorthodox to develop. This is not the right environment for improper behavior.

ducktail Someone will promise to contact you later but you will never hear from this person again. This will occur within two days. You may decide to contact this person instead if you are very interested or you may simply let it go.

duck walk You will allow someone to take over your decision making procedures. This person will make dynamic accurate decisions for you and will work very successfully with you. Watch for this person over the next four days.

duct tape Do not become involved in costly projects for the moment. Any new projects will not work out for you now.

dude *(slang term)* You will be entering a wonderful cycle for the next seven days. Take each goal, idea, plan, etc., and view it on a grander scale. This is the perfect cycle for this. Proceed with confidence.

duel Within a few days you will be offered a position with a large salary. This position will not be the right one for you. Begin looking for an alternative position.

dues Remind yourself that nothing can take the place of your existence. Be aware that to many people you are irreplaceable.

duet *any form* Two separate situations will arise that will require you to make a choice. Your decisions will make a big difference in your lifestyle. One of the situations will yield more benefits and open many doors. Think carefully and choose the one that will bring you more opportunities. Check each decision for the coming month that will affect your lifestyle. Good luck is with you.

duffel bag Within three days you will be able to tap into your inner resources and express the love you have for others. Your relationship will grow to a higher level.

dugout Work to motivate another person in order to get things moving in the right direction. This will allow you to meet a specific deadline. This will be particularly important for the next three days.

Duke Within two days, someone will approach you with confidential and juicy details about someone else. You will feel burdened with this knowledge of personal matters. Think whether you really want privy to this information. If not, politely decline to listen.

dulcimer Get busy for the next two days to develop a network of people you can tap into for information. This will create energy and resources for a fundraising drive you will become involved with. It will be successful.

dumb Carefully check your actions in the dream. If this is a negative message, take steps to alter the outcome. If the message is positive, take steps to promote it to the fullest. Also, make sure you do not put yourself in the position of leaving other people out of future plans, especially for the next two days.

dumbbell Within three days, you will go with someone to a distant place and find yourself driving in circles endlessly with this person. After this individual reveals to you they are lost, you will become very upset. Take steps to avoid this problem. Buy a map and get the correct directions needed to reach your destination.

dumbstruck The information you have been seeking will land directly in your lap. Look for this to happen within three days. This information will fill in many gaps and hasten the completion of a major goal.

dumbwaiter Do not surrender for the next two days to someone who is trying to win you over. This situation is not right for you and never will be.

dum dum bullet Be watchful of a pedophile in your area for the next three days. This person is very interested in photos of young children. Be very aware and make sure you do not inadvertently cater to this behavior. This individual will soon be caught and prosecuted.

dummy You will be dealing with a situation within five days which requires that you remain true to yourself and aggressively pursue what you truly want from someone else. Verbalize your needs and you will have them met.
  to hear this phrase You need to devise a new way of appreciating life. Take steps to get out of your boring rut.

dummy *(mannequin)* You are suffering from a deficiency in your body system. Get a check up to determine what you are lacking and take steps to correct this in order to live a full and healthy life. This will be a lucky cycle for you. Eat well and drink plenty of water. This dream also indicates that a loved one is sorry for the way they have treated you lately. This person is embarrassed but is unable to verbalize their feelings. In time, words of apology will come and you will both work toward adding new joy and happiness to your union.

dump Delegate time out to meet with others about a certain situation that needs to be handled immediately in order to avoid stress. Ensure that important decisions are made within three days involving this group of people to assure that all crises are handled promptly.

dumplings For the next week you need to take extra precautions if you are not ready to add a new member to the family. You will also experience good luck in all phases of your life.

dumpster Take steps to be on time for a performance you promised to attend. Your companion may be late but make it a point to wait. You will enjoy the performance. It is especially important this week to complete this and every other cycle you put into action.

dump truck Within three days, you will hear from a member of the family who will request a special favor from you. This person is undergoing a tremendous amount of stress and will need to leave their child in your care for at least a month. This will allow them to take care of this situation while knowing their child is well taken care of. Do everything necessary to offer assistance at this time. You will enjoy good luck and an abundance of love. You will also receive respect for your sacrifice.

dunce Think ahead and devise a method for dealing with others. Locate the right person to correctly deal with your particular situation and to back you up the entire way.

dunce cap You will enjoy many wonderful private moments over the next few days. Be aware of this and take the time to make sure these moments are captured in memory. Do nothing for the next two days to destroy moments that will improve your relationship with another.

dune Make a list of priorities within the next three days and stay with your choices until successful completion. This dream is also a warning to keep you from straying from your goals and priorities. Someone will also enter your life within three days who will be very eager to have a friendly relationship. You will, however, receive mixed messages as time goes by after this person begins to hint at a romantic involvement. This individual is wasting your time and only playing games. Do not expect anything more than a short term relationship. Enjoy yourself and get on with your life. Do not compromise your own desires during this time period and you will be able to grasp deep emotional fulfillment. You are headed for a prosperous future.

dune buggy Make personal plans and set rules for yourself within three days and you stand to win over an ally whom you have long been seeking support from. This individual also has many powerful connections. This will prove to be a very successful relationship.

dung Within three days, you and that special person will sit down and make plans that will be mutually satisfying regarding how you treat each other. You will learn to respect each other more and to be more loving to each other. You will see an improvement in the relationship after you have come to this decision.

dungarees Within two days you will make a successful appeal to another person by taking an independent approach at the right moment at the right time. The appropriate communication techniques will prove to be very beneficial to you. All of these actions, in combination, will be very successful.

dung beetle Make sure that a group of associates do not take advantage of you, especially for the next seven days.

dungeon Make sure that you and another person do not put yourself in a dangerous position for the next seven days by traveling to places you are unfamiliar with. Guarding your life should be a priority.

dunghill Do not play negative tapes in your mind, and within the week, learn to stop putting your negative thoughts into action. Watch your behavior carefully.

Dunkirk One of your closely guarded secrets will become publicly known and problems will arise because of this. Expect this to occur within a few days and take steps to keep it from taking place. This dream may also be used as a reference point in time. If you dream of this city and see its name used in any context, the dream message will occur on this day.

dunk shot Think carefully about an invitation you will receive within three days. The person giving out the invitation possesses an unusual manner and has an offensive lifestyle. Tactfully decline this invitation.

duplex Do everything within your power for the next week to avoid taking on any unnecessary responsibilities and financial burdens.

duplicate *to see anything duplicated* Within two days, all items you have been wanting to acquire in life will be obtainable. You are headed for a pleasurable, dynamic time in the future and your life will be filled with tranquility and contentment.

duplicating machine This implies that you need to come back to your original idea within two days. Pay close attention to what was being duplicated. This will lead to a large clue of an event that will take place in reality. If it is negative, take steps to alter the outcome.

dusk Make sure all your equipment is in perfect working order. Avoid paying for anything, for the next seven days, until you are sure it will not break down.

dust For the next week, do not allow a situation to develop in a negative way in which you have some control. Make sure you maintain this control in order to have all affairs run smoothly. It is also important that you stop being so forceful in demanding that others do what is distasteful to them. This selfish behavior is becoming old and others will not tolerate it much longer.

dustbin Within three days, a situation will occur that may tempt you to betray another person. Do not become involved in this type of behavior, you will later regret this.

dust bowl Avoid creating suspicion and jealousy.

dust devil Make sure you are aware, for the next seven days, that certain environments may cause a disturbance in bodily functions. Prevent any emergency situations from occurring.

duster Someone you have been a great support to in the past, will give you an unexpected gift of appreciation within seven days.

dusting jacket For the next two days, you will enjoy a cycle that will benefit communication with someone of importance. You can then sort out feelings for mutual help instead of divided interest. Good luck is with you.

dusting powder Prevent the occurrence of accidents for the next three days. Keep yourself safe for this period of time.

dustpan Make sure that if you promise someone you will accompany them on an outing you will follow through. Do not go along half heartedly as this will make the other person feel they have pushed you into this. If you cannot attend joyfully, do not commit to going at all. This situation will present itself within the week.

dust robe/gown Within three days a close relative will diplomatically drop subtle hints regarding a particular area of their life that they feel dissatisfied with, and they would like to see you become responsible for this. This individual desires that you take it upon yourself to make the changes needed to improve their life. They feel trapped and cannot seem to get through this situation. You will develop the conviction and compassion to help them and lead them to a far better lifestyle, if you choose to take the initiative. Many blessings are with you.

dust ruffle Watch yourself closely for the next seven days in order to prevent interference with another person's decision. This will play an important role in how you feel about yourself later. Avoid regrets.

dust storm Create a variety of ways in which to reach your goals. There are many ways to approach a situation.

Dutch This dream is a promise that nothing will interfere with your happiness for the next month. You will be motivated to come up with new and festive ways to enjoy your-self during this cycle.

Dutch cheese This dream is a very lucky omen for you. You will also accidentally overhear a conversation that would hurt someone badly if it is repeated. Make sure you keep this information to yourself.

Dutch door Within three days you will be able to draw someone, whom you have long desired, close to you in a passionate way. This union will bring you a great deal of happiness if you desire to pursue this. You are on the path for a brilliant future.

Dutch elm disease Remain calm and centered for the next three days. A situation will arise that will tempt your involvement. Do not allow someone else's problems to cause you so much desperation that you compromise yourself and become embroiled in this situation. Once you become involved it will be very difficult to get out of it. It will become worse as time goes by and you are now seeing only the tip of the iceberg. Stay uninvolved.

Dutch oven Someone has a strong desire to get close to you. Provide situations and the encouragement that will allow this person to verbalize these feelings and to make the move to get close to you. This is very important for the next seven days.

Dutch treat Within four days, you will hear the words you have been longing to hear from the one you desire. This person will nervously express their need for you to be in their life. Good luck will come to both of you and things will work out well on a mutual basis.

duty *to dream of something that is your duty* Do not allow anyone to create stress and desperation by the manner in which they communicate to you. Maintain control and go on with your life.

in any other form Someone you care deeply for will go to great lengths to provide physical evidence that you are well loved by them. This will be a very successful cycle for you.

duty free Carefully screen all people responding to an ad you placed in the newspaper. This is especially important for the next three days. Each respondent would be fantastic for your purposes but one is especially well-suited.

dwarf This dream is a very lucky omen and this is also a good cycle for romance. Feelings will deepen over the next two days and you will accomplish everything you attempt in the way of love. You will also quickly locate the person who will fit your needs regarding an ongoing project. This person will offer you the assistance you need while remaining in the background. You will know who this person is and will only need to request their input.

dwelling Encourage yourself to become more aggressive and less timid. You will see a great improvement in how situations around you work out.

dye *to dye* Within seven days the object of your affection will lie to you. This will cause a deep hurt. If you can do anything to prevent this, do so.

to dye hair Pay attention to the color of the dye for a more detailed meaning to the dream. This dream may be suggesting a color to experiment with for a new look.

if the color of the dye is totally unacceptable to you Be aware that certain chemicals used on the hair may produce an unusual discoloration within three days. It is also important that you include a variety of new events in your life to add more spice and excitement to your daily routine, especially for the next seven weeks.

Dylan, Thomas Concentrate on your finances and detail each move. Do this in order to avoid money troubles for the next five days.

dynamite *to hear the phrase* Treat yourself with more respect and guard your health. Avoid placing yourself in a situation where you will be exposed to a virus.

to see inactive dynamite Over the next month, you will develop more responsibility. You will rid yourself of a care free, irresponsible attitude and this will aid you in meeting your goals. You will also develop a bond between yourself and a close friend with whom you desire more intimacy.

explosion You will hear of a freak accident involving someone close to you. This person will die. Alert anyone this may apply to. This will be out of your control but you must do everything you can to warn this individual.

if the explosion affects you personally Take steps to avoid this negative situation and for the next three days, do everything possible to keep yourself safe by avoiding unusual and out of the ordinary events. Schedule all events for the time period following this cycle.

dynasty You will experience long desired personal growth and improvements that will be noticed by others. Good luck and an abundance of love and respect will be with you.

dysentery You will suddenly become wealthy within the week. You will also experience a great deal of luck.

dyslexia *to hear the word* Others will attempt to include you in a secret plot. Develop the courage to avoid becoming involved. This is especially important for the next week.

in any other form You will have much sympathy for a family member who will be undergoing a great deal of emotional pain within the week, caused by another's irresponsible behavior. Protect yourself in order to have the strength and peace of mind to be of assistance.

dystrophy All mental pain and anguish will disappear almost overnight. You will be grateful that certain situations have occurred to allow this burden to be lifted. This will happen within seven days. Good luck is with you.

E

E This dream implies that you will be entering an emotional period within three weeks. This will require you to make some stern decisions about someone else's well being who is no longer able to properly care for themselves. It will be necessary to detail your decisions precisely because this individual's life depends on you. This is a delicate situation and it may be necessary to have this person confined to a treatment facility against their will. This will enable this person to receive the proper professional help. Develop a thick skin in order to prevent injured feelings when you are criticized for this decision. The person you are trying to help may also want you to take them in and care for them. Proceed with confidence and do not doubt your decisions. You would be doing this person a disservice if you allow others to change your mind. This situation will be resolved successfully and you will feel pleased that you took control over it. You are entering a cycle that will bring you good health and tranquility and you are headed for a brilliant future.

eager *to be eager* Whatever you see yourself being eager about, you should be enthusiastic about in reality if it is a possible goal. Otherwise take steps to restrain your behavior. You are in a great cycle because everything you previously applied yourself to will now reach fruition. Work well done in the past will yield rewards now.

someone else is eager If you recognize the person, they are eager to communicate feelings they feel are important to discuss with you. This feeling concerns an irresistible impulse to be with you and will be communicated to you within three days.

eager beaver Do everything you can to place some unusual responsibilities that are coming your way in the hands of someone else. If these responsibilities are not delegated to others, you will find yourself overloaded. Do not make yourself responsible for any added burdens or responsibilities.

eagle You will enjoy victory, love, good fortune, health and brilliant ideas. Within a few days you will have the opportunity of a lifetime that will turn your life around completely. You will also have the opportunity, if you choose, to become involved with a very influential and powerful person who is eager to become a part of your life. Take this slowly, gently and in a subtly aggressive way. Your behavior will magically bring forward what you seek in life.

dead eagle This dream implies the death of your vision and an inability to grasp opportunities. Within seven days you will have the opportunity to change this around and bring about grand opportunities.

Eagle scout Within three days your presence will be requested at a social function. If you promised to be there, make sure you attend. A special place will be reserved for your.

ear Make sure you are taking proper care of your ears. This dream also implies that you need to become very aware of what others are saying to you. In addition, you can avoid a distasteful time by not insisting that everything be done your way. Listen to what others have to say. Your insistence that everything be done to your specifications will result in failure.

someone else's ear Revenge will not bring satisfaction. It will only bring a feeling of disappointment and regret. Channel your energy into something more positive.

earache Be very alert of the short comings in someone's behavior. You will desire closeness from this person but they will be unable to provide the degree you desire. Although you will be given the impression this person is willing to commit fully, they have an emotional problem that requires professional help. This is beyond their control.

eardrops Make sure you are channeling your affections in the right direction because someone will be offended and surprised at our actions. Be very aware of this behavior for the next four days and take steps to prevent it.

eardrum Someone you know is going through a difficult time. Take caution when talking to this person in order to avoid making them feel worse. Take special care to watch your behavior for the next three days.

eared seal Be aware that a relationship will grow only as much as the other person allows. This person does not feel as deeply as you. Move on with your life. Become very aware of your behavior for the next two days.

Earl A relative will, within two days, plead for your assistance in handling a situation they have gotten themselves into. Work to resolve this problem and you will enjoy successful results.

early bird This is the cycle to handle things that require urgent handling. Take advantage of this smooth sailing time. This cycle will last for the next three days.

earmuffs For the next three days, ensure that you do not undergo abusive behavior from another person. After you remove yourself from the presence of this individual, you will not be verbally abused again. Do this quickly in order to go on with your life.

earn This dream is a very lucky omen. Pay attention to your vocation in the dream and your earnings. This will indicate what you need to make a reality. Also, make a point of admitting that your actions are wrong when you behave badly. Do everything necessary to correct improper behavior.

earnings This dream is a lucky omen. Do everything within your power to avoid doing anything that will bring you shame.

earphones Pay attention to the message you hear over the earphones. If it is positive, go in that direction. If the message is negative, take steps to alter the outcome. If you recognize the voice, there will be a sense of urgency to the message. Assistance will also be requested by older people. Make sure that you offer your personal help to ensure success. Be especially aware of this for the next three days.

earpiece You will receive gifts of emeralds. Look for this over the next two weeks.

earplugs Make sure you pay close attention to what a close older person is telling you and pay attention to their needs, especially for the next three days.

earring You will enjoy yourself immensely in a wonderful relationship if you choose to take this route. You will experience deep passion from an individual and will fall very much in love. This option will be provided to you within four days. Because of this, you will somehow gain a sense of how to strengthen the bond between you. As a result you will be able to experience harmony and tranquility in your life.

to see earrings being worn You will be involved with someone who will bring humor and passion to a potential relationship. This will deepen to a mutual love. You will have this option within five days.

in any other form Do everything possible to keep a relationship alive if you choose to maintain this union. Bring excitement, laughter, good times, balance and tranquility into this relationship. Good luck is with you. This dream also implies that you need to keep your environment safe in order to avoid injury.

earth Your companion is very honest and truthful with you. You can feel safe in your environment and among friends.

earthenware Supervise your intake of food carefully in order to avoid any system failure or food poisoning for the next three days.

earthling *to hear this phrase* Someone will go to great lengths to pursue you for the purpose of marriage. This person will not use a slow, subtle approach. You will meet them within three days and the proposal will quickly follow. It will be very straight forward and to the point. If you choose to marry, the union will be very successful. Follow your instincts and do not listen to the opinions of others. Good luck will be with you throughout your life.

earth mother You are entering a cycle that will allow you to demand what you want from your deity and your wishes will be granted. Within two weeks you will see the desired changes in your life and will enjoy many tranquil times over the next month. Drink plenty of water and practice a healthy lifestyle.

earthquake For the next month, do everything necessary to keep situations from escalating to the point of a separation in those areas of your life that are important to you, particularly regarding relationships.

earthworm This dream implies that you will enjoy victory in that area of your life you deem to be most important to you now. Also, remain uninvolved in any quarrelsome situation that will arise within the next three days.

earwax Someone is eager to grant you anything you desire within two days. All you need to do is ask.

earwig Someone will attempt to lure you into a situation that you will later feel shame about. Make sure that you carefully watch your behavior and the motives of others for the next two days. You will also finally overcome a long term exhausting burden. You are headed in the right direction as long as you stay focused on your wants and needs, especially for the next seven days.

ease This dream implies that you will be very lucky in all phases of your life for the next three days.

East For the next three days conduct research and develop plans that will bring you greater benefits for the future. You are going in the right direction and are headed toward prosperity.

East Berlin Face up to any changes in a relationship, especially for the next three days. You will find the courage to allow things to fall into place exactly as they are supposed to. You will also receive good news via the mail. This dream may be used as a reference point in time. If you dream of this city and see its name used in any context, the dream message will occur on this day.

Easter Someone who patronizes you to the point of enmity will suddenly disappear from your life. You will feel as though a burden has been lifted. This will take place within three days.

Easter candy It is an extremely lucky omen to dream of Easter candy. You will receive an unexpected gift as well as being granted a favor (financial or otherwise). Make sure also that you play an active role in having your emotional needs met. Within five days you will be able to focus on, and visualize, the path you need to take for a brilliant future. Good luck is with you.

Easter egg Something you felt was impossible in a love relationship will take place within three days. You will finally achieve the union you want. Should you pursue this,

you will achieve marriage. Good luck and many blessings are with you.

Easter Sunday Take time out from your hectic life to meditate in your favorite form. You will find a sense of fulfillment for a long time to come.

East Germany Be sure to take adequate steps, within the next three days, to promote more prosperity and health. This dream may also be used as a reference point in time. If you dream of this country and see its name used in any context, the dream message will occur on this day.

East Indies You will enjoy a festive time with an exotic, charismatic companion who will be in your company for the next two days. This will spur you to sample many exotic lifestyles and to seek festive events that will bring you much pleasure. This dream may also be used as a reference point in time. If you dream of this region and see its name used in any context, the dream message will occur on this day.

easy Many strange situations will occur within three days and you will find the strength to go through them. You will enjoy satisfactory results with each situation as long as you control your emotions.

easy chair Someone is plotting to take your money. This person will request a loan from you with no intention of paying it back. Do not lend money for the next four days.

easygoing Someone you are acquainted with enjoys interrogating you constantly. Within four days this person will begin to question you again. Make it clear that you are no longer willing to go through this harassment. Good luck is with you.

eat Your hunches about the love and affection of another person are accurate. This individual will greet you with open arms. You will receive an abundance of health and are headed for a very prosperous future.

to eat alone Appreciate the efforts of your loved ones.

to eat with family members and/or friends Accept a last minute invitation to enjoy yourself with many easy going, light hearted people. This event will be very memorable.

to eat fat or lard You will become wealthy by way of a windfall. As a result, you will begin to eat ravenously. Become disciplined, eat healthful foods and drink plenty of water and take steps not to gain weight.

to eat chicken Do not be too proud to receive a gift or a grant of money from someone who truly believes that you deserve it. You are headed for a brilliant future.

to eat clams You will enjoy the finest things in life and you will have sufficient funds to cover your expenses. This has been a concern of yours for some time.

to eat fish A mysterious illness you have been dealing with will suddenly disappear. Good luck is with you.

to eat chocolate Someone loves you very deeply.

to eat human flesh or the meat of large animals You

to eat chocolate Someone loves you very deeply.

to eat human flesh or the meat of large animals You will receive a large inheritance just when you need it.

to eat fruit All legal matters will be settled in your favor.

to see others eat Spend more time making young people feel comfortable in their environment.

to eat with strangers Become more protective over your possessions.

to eat yet not be fulfilled Someone who has made you a promise will not come through due to unexpected circumstances.

to eat raw meat Allow someone else to express their feelings about you. You will find that you are well loved.

to eat salt Listen carefully to what others tell you in order to avoid jumping to conclusions.

to eat sugar Be very careful about choosing someone to care for a young infant. Be sure the caretaker is experienced in infant care, especially for the next five days.

to eat at a deli Within a few days, someone will begin to make greater demands on you because they are unsure of your feelings. Take steps to create a greater level of security within the relationship.

to spill your meal You and another person will go down a path that will, unbeknownst to you, be very dangerous because of an unfortunate event that will take place. Speak with this other person in order to reschedule an event you are planning within the next few days. You can avoid this dangerous situation.

eaves A close relative will ask for your assistance in leaving their parent's home. Do everything necessary to help this person get on with their life.

eavesdrop Situations are occurring in your life at the present time that you need to pay more attention to. Unusual issues will start to develop within three days unless you uncover them and put a stop to them before they fully develop.

if you recognize the eavesdropper This person is very curious about your personal life and has a desire to communicate their feelings to you. All meetings, conferences and personal communications will result in major success. You will also be able to meet the romantic demands of another for the next five days. You will have the courage to communicate openly with those who are important to you. You are headed in the right direction. Good luck is with you.

ebony Regardless of any difficulties that are coming from various sources, you will find relief from old burdens and all new issues within the week. You will also hear good news about options you have been desiring for some time. This cycle promotes family harmony. Many blessings are coming to you and your family and you are headed for a prosperous future.

eccentric You will be planning a get away within three days and you will have an irresistible impulse to visit exotic places. If this is possible to do within two months, do so. Also, do not give someone the impression, for the next three days,

that you want to commit to a relationship when, in truth, you are not capable of giving emotionally at this time. Good luck is with you.

Ecclesiastics Make sure all of your immunizations are up to date, especially if you are making travel plans. Many blessings are with you and your family and you are headed for a very prosperous cycle.

echo You are very curious about the unknown. It would be very risky to continue in this way of thinking. Do not involve yourself with the occult. You will be tempted to do so within three days. Pay attention to the message you hear. If it is a positive message, take steps to promote it; if negative, take steps to alter it.

éclair For the next three days, you will experience greater clarity of thought. Use this gift to develop plans that will bring you greater prosperity. Trust your instincts, you are right on target, especially for the next three days.

eclipse Within three days you will attend an event and meet someone whose recent past mirrors a situation you will shortly be encountering. This experience will grant you the opportunity to learn ways to correctly handle this forthcoming situation with calm and balance. Also, do not take chances and risks for the upcoming week that may cause injury to your arms and legs and those of small children.

ecology Do not surrender your feelings to someone for the next three days who is trying to win your favor. This relationship is not the right one for you and never will be.

economy You have good reason to be watchful of those who do not like children and seem intolerant of their presence. They will take any chance to abuse children. Any negative event in the dream foretells a future event. Take steps to prevent its occurrence, especially for the next three days.

Ecuador This dream is telling you that nothing will take your place to your loved ones. You are deeply loved. Verbalize your feelings to those you love. This is especially important for the next three days. You are entering a cycle of abundance for health, love and finances. This dream may also be used as a reference point in time. If you dream of this country and see its name used in any context, the dream message will occur on this day.

eczema For the next three days work on developing the courage you will need to bring someone close to you. You will be able to verbalize the need to bond closer to that special person. This dream also implies that you will receive riches by way of a windfall within five days.

Edam cheese Focus on joyous events and create more festive, joyous activities in your life. For the next two days, look for hobbies and amusements to add spice to you life.

edelweiss Do everything necessary to encourage a special person to grow closer to you. Try to bring more balance into a situation that will be occurring within three days.

Eden Do everything you can within three days to bring a situation into focus. Concentrate on the facts and realities of this situation. This will play an important role in how you feel about yourself. Make sure you make the correct decision now in order to avoid problems later on.

edge *any form (to be on the edge of something you can fall from, i.e., cliff, building)* This dream is a warning to remain calm, stable and non argumentative during an upcoming family situation. Take steps to stay clear of this situation.

margin Be careful of fatigue when you least expect it. Take care of yourself and try to fight off this feeling.

the quality of being sharp or keen Because of your dynamic reputation you will be received by others with open arms and they will be very amenable to a particular situation you will be introducing to them within three days.

to get a word in edge wise Do not involve yourself in domestic quarrels.

edging An event is scheduled within the week that you must make a point of attending. You will be pursued by two admirers and both of them will try to win your affections. Although it will not be obvious to you, one of them possesses a great deal of power and authority. You will find them both very agreeable and both will possess a great deal of charm. You would enjoy having one of them as a lifetime partner and you can be confident you are on the path for a prosperous future.

editor Within four days, devise a plan to choose the perfect liaison. This person will quickly handle your most important tasks and will back you up until your situation is successfully resolved.

editorial Remain true to your priorities until your goals are completed. This is especially important for the next three days.

education Take extra precautions to prevent any negative event from occurring. Also, warn family members to take extra precautions to avoid an unwanted birth.

EEG You will appear to another in the specific way you want to appear, both physically and emotionally. You will adopt an independent manner and this person will be more eager to approach you within three days.

eel Make sure a special person does not divulge private information to another.

effigy Make sure that, for the next five days, any precious moment you wish to capture is photographed or recorded. Take steps to ensure that all equipment used for these purposes is in good working order.

egg(s) *and/or have an egg shape* This dream is a lucky omen. You will enjoy a festive, joyful event. You will be reunited with those you feel love toward and each of you will feel very tranquil in each other's company. You are entering a cycle of abundance in health and finances, and are headed toward a brilliant future.

to cook Your desires will come true.

to beat Take steps to prevent a miscarriage and alert those who are pregnant to take precautions.

nest egg Keep going in the direction you are going. You will enjoy various areas of opportunities within the week and you will experience a brilliant future.

scrambled Someone whom you felt was impossible to become involved with in a love relationship will return after a long absence. A relationship is now a possibility. Blessings are with you.

soft boiled You will feel very sorrowful because a family member whom you love deeply will act nasty for no apparent reason. Try to prevent this for the following week by demonstrating extra kindness toward family members.

sunny side up Your career will improve immensely over the next year.

raw/fresh The opportunity you have been waiting for will arise within two days and you will make a new start in all areas of your life. All old burdens and issues that have been dragging you down will come to a halt. Major changes will occur that will add a new excitement and a new dimension to your life. Blessings are with you and your family.

goose egg You will be loved, cherished and protected for a life time from those you desire.

insect/bug eggs Be very cautious and wary about where you are being led emotionally. For reasons known only to them, someone will lead you to believe you are loved completely by them. Words of love may or may not be used but all the romantic trappings will be there (i.e., flowers, gifts, romantic outings, etc.). Your feelings will grow stronger and deeper than this other person's feelings. If you allow this to develop into lovemaking, you will not be touched in any way that implies that love is present. You will feel very empty and cold as a result and will fail to connect with this person on any level that you felt was there. Rather than putting yourself through this emotional upheaval, you have enough notice to avoid this scenario completely. Go on with your life without this person in it, because they have a hidden agenda that involves you doing something that only they are aware of. This situation will only bring you unhappiness so take steps to avoid it completely. Otherwise, you are headed for a prosperous future that will start to evolve within seven days.

to accidentally drop eggs A person who deeply loves you finds it impossible to verbalize these feelings. This week this person will try very hard to state their feelings toward you.

broken You will find yourself in a vulnerable situation within three days. Someone will attempt to force you to do something against your will that you will find very distasteful. This is a warning to take steps to avoid this situation at all costs.

to have eggs thrown at you To dream of fresh eggs being

thrown at you is a warning that someone new who desires friendship is, in fact, a serial killer. Be aware and stay away from strangers.

to find something in an egg You will be a prize winner within three days.

to find a person in the egg Someone has an urgent need to speak with you. This person has a deep emotional feeling of gratitude and love that they have difficulty verbalizing. This individual is now entering a cycle that inspires the courage to speak. Be gentle, set aside time and leave yourself open to this person for the next seven days and you will feel overwhelming joy after hearing their words.

snake eggs Be extremely aware and cautious about where you are allowing someone to lead you emotionally. Someone will, for reasons of their own, lead you to believe that you are completely loved by them. The word love may or may not be used but all of the trappings will be there (i.e., flowers, gifts, romantic outings, etc.). Your feelings will grow deeper and stronger than this other person's feelings. If you allow the possibility of lovemaking, you will not be touched or kissed in any special way although they will try very hard. You will feel very empty and cold as a result. You will fail to connect with this person on the level they have led you to believe was there. Rather than putting yourself through this, you have prior notice and can avoid this scenario completely. Get on with your life without this person and the emotional upheaval they will cause. This person has a hidden agenda that will involve you doing something that only they are aware of. Avoid this situation entirely, it will only lead to unhappiness. Otherwise you are headed for a prosperous future that will begin to evolve within the week.

egg beater Within the month you will stumble across something of great value. Keep yourself open for this event to happen.

manual You are entering a very lucky cycle within two days, and will undergo a metamorphosis that will result in the development of a steel drive, inner courage and the determination to break through greater mental and physical barriers that may be holding you back. Once they have been overcome, you will quickly bring into tangible form a new project you are very excited about. It will be completed in the manner you desire. You can also expect to be greeted with open arms and placed on a pedestal anywhere you go by those you care about. This will be a big surprise to you. You are headed for a brilliant future and many new opportunities are headed your way.

electric Be very cautious. Someone you have requested to leave your life and has given you this reassurance will break their promise within five days. Take the time to prepare yourself emotionally in order to avoid being cornered by this person. Make it clear that you wish nothing to do with this individual. This is a very delicate situation and you will need to prepare your self emotionally. Organize your thoughts and feelings and do not allow someone to think you are willing to commit yourself to something you are unwilling to do. You will be able to get your point across in a way that will not offend anyone. Proceed with caution.

egg foo yung The person you are making mutual plans with will lack the courage to follow through. This will occur within three days. Be aware of this because you will have to offer encouragement throughout the entire process in order to avoid a breakdown of mutual plans.

egghead You are putting your trust in the wrong person and are allowing them to make decisions for you. This is particularly important for the next three days. This dream is a very lucky omen.

eggnog *to make* For one year, you will enjoy the best time of your life. Initiate any needed changes to ensure success.

to drink You will attend a baby shower.

egg roll You or someone you know will be led to believe you should do something you have different feelings about. This individual fully believes this is the best option for you although they have no idea what the detriments of their choices will be. This will put you or someone else into a dangerous and troublesome area.

egg timer You will become attracted to someone who has a far greater sexual appetite than you. This person will go to great lengths to involve you in their life in some capacity. Think this over carefully in order to behave in the appropriate way. You will not wish to miss out on the love and affection this person has to offer but you must also make it clear that your sexual appetites are different. This person will work to accommodate you in order to keep the relationship mutually satisfying.

ego Think ahead and network with others in order to accomplish your goals. You will be able to utilize your resources and the energy provided by others. Information you have been eager to uncover will, within three days, fall into your lap.

egret Do everything you can to protect children and young adults who require more supervision, especially for the next three days. Take steps to ensure that they do not come to any physical harm. You have prior notice of any problem that could lead to physical harm and can take the appropriate steps to prevent it. Many blessings will come to you and your family.

Egypt You and your family will receive an abundance of blessings. You will also receive an invitation to visit an exotic place and will enjoy yourself immensely. This dream may also be used as a reference point in time. If you dream of this country and see its name in any context, the dream message will occur on this day.

eiderdown A new person will enter your life within five days. Make sure you do not become too involved because this will not be an enjoyable relationship. Go on with your life without this person in it.

eight Within eight days a turn of events will bring grand changes into your life and it will improve immensely. Your intuition is correct. You may also use the number eight for scheduling events and for all games of chance. Good luck is with you.

eight ball You have one talent that you have not developed to the fullest. Use this talent now to reap great rewards.

eighteen Within three days you will successfully complete a long term project. This is a lucky number for scheduling events the next two days.

elbow Within a few days you will seek a job. You will verbally be offered a salary but if this is not put into writing upon acceptance, the pay will be far less than anticipated. Otherwise, good luck is with you.

to elbow someone or to be elbowed Someone will put on airs around you and attempt to impress you with their financial status. This will be done subtly for the purpose of creating envy. Ignore this behavior and go on with your life. Otherwise, this will be a very lucky cycle for the next five days.

elbow grease Plans you have made with a special person need to be shared with others. Exclusions will cause hurt feelings. Include others in your plans, especially for the next two days.

elbowroom Someone who has a tremendous amount of jealousy toward you will attempt to create problems. Avoid anyone who demonstrates animosity toward you for the next two days.

elderberry Become involved with a new group of people and take advantage of new resources of opportunity. This will be possible within two days. Go for it.

elderly Think ahead to the next four days and carefully prepare what you plan to say to someone who is involved in a certain situation. This will give you the time to gather all those involved to discuss how to put a lid on a particular issue in order to keep a negative event from taking place. Alert others to the possibility of this taking place. Many blessings will come to you and your family.

in any other form Think ahead and make it a point to schedule a necessary conversation with certain people within three days. This will allow everyone to discuss ways to put a stop to something that will take place if everyone involved does not take aggressive steps. This situation will hurt everyone involved. Take steps now to put a stop to this and to alert everyone. Otherwise, many blessings will come to you and your family.

El Dorado You will receive long awaited information that will bring you joy and satisfaction. This dream may also be used as a reference point in time. If you dream of this city and see its name used in any context, the dream message will occur on this day.

election Avoid all negative and jealous thoughts toward your neighbor and avoid making any promises you cannot deliver. You will be tested for the next few days to break these patterns.

electric *mobile chair/electric car* Within seven days you will have an urgent need to accomplish something that depends on someone else's help. This could involve the loan of a large amount of money or a big favor that needs to be given immediately with no hassles. This will be such a large request that it will be hard for you to imagine that anyone would grant this. Follow your intuition and it will lead you to the person who will come through for you. Proceed with confidence and explore your options until you determine the perfect one. As soon as an agreement is reached, you need to take immediate action so this issue is concluded before this person has a chance to change their mind. Many blessings are with you and you are headed toward a prosperous future.

electrical wave You will enjoy a lucky cycle for the upcoming month and will experience what you need to improve your life.

electric chair Stop short changing yourself. You are underestimating your abilities.

to be in one Stop being your own worst enemy. Supervise your actions for the next three days in order to handle an ongoing situation in a more positive fashion.

to see someone else in one Be very cautious of a deranged person who may be a serial killer. This person has special designs on you that you are unaware of. You will encounter this person within three days. You will have prior notice of this, therefore take extra precautions to protect yourself.

electrician Within three days someone will want to show how deeply they feel for you and how involved they want to become with you. This person will go through a series of activities, chores and favors and behave in almost a puppet like manner. Your every desire will be fulfilled. Openly show your affection and consideration for this person's generosity and efforts. Be very cautious, do not bruise this person's feelings and do not be suspicious of this person's motives.

electricity This is the time to take advantage of your talents. Do your best to put yourself out there and demonstrate your skills to others for the next three weeks. Luck is with you.

electric plug You will have a conversation with a wealthy, older person. You will be unaware of this person's wealth and will converse about your skills, creativity and ideas. This older person will then, after a three day period, offer to finance your ideas and will put you in touch with those who will assist in launching your plans.

electric wall socket You and someone you recognize in this dream will motivate yourselves in an unusual way that will enable you to get in touch with an, unknown person. You and the person in this dream will both have this experience although they will be totally unconnected. Conversations will flow easily between you and the person you have yet to meet, in a delightful way. You will both have the feeling you have not experienced this in a long time, if ever. The person you will meet possesses an artful sense of timing as well as the unusual ability to sense the feelings of other people. They are capable of bringing pleasure to others and of fully committing themselves. And are also able to put themselves in a subservient role, tastefully and within limits, as well as having the capability of pampering others to the extreme, but not overly so. You will find this to be very delightful and will never have a distasteful moment. If you choose to have a relationship, it will grow as much as you want and will be a mutually satisfying and nurturing union. Expect this to occur within three days and alert the person you dreamed about to expect this as well. You are headed for a brilliant future.

electric wires Victory will be yours within seven days and you will connect with someone who is perfect for the project you are presently working on. Go for it.

to see a man working with electric wires Be very aware of someone who could cause you death. This person kills for pleasure. Take extra precautions to protect yourself for the next three days.

electrolyte Within seven days make sure your body is sufficiently maintained in order to run at a consistent pace. Make sure you have a balance of necessary vitamins and minerals.

electron Someone you know with a mysterious past will want to confess to you. Be forewarned. You will not want to know all of this information. It will be better to refuse to listen and go on with your life as tactfully as possible.

electronic music You will enjoy victory in those areas of life that are most important to you. Within three days, doors of opportunity will open for you. Point yourself toward a more prosperous future.

electronics You need to be less opinionated for the next two days and work to keep the peace.

electronic toys For the next two days, become verbally assertive with a certain individual to prod them to interact with you verbally and emotionally in the manner you expect and deserve. You will be successful in your request. There is a sense of urgency to this. Proceed with confidence.

electron microscope Between now and the next three days, be watchful for a tip that will prove to be very lucky.

electroshock therapy Be very attentive to matters dealing with the law for the next two days in order to avoid having any action taken against you.

elegance Someone will unexpectedly drop by and spontaneously request that you join them on an outing. This will occur within three days. Should you choose to go, you will have a wonderful time. This will bring excitement to your life, particularly because of your companion.

elementary school *to dream of being in your elementary school* This dream is a lucky omen. A hobby, learned in the past, can be used, in conjunction with something else, to create a second income. This idea will come to you within seven days.

to see yourself as a child in elementary school For the next two days, be alert to anything involving your health. All minor problems will have a tendency to escalate during this time period. Take care of all health problems now.

to see an adult you recognize as a child in elementary school Warn this person to take care of all minor health problems now. It is important that these problems do not become life threatening.

in any other form This dream is a good omen.

elephant *to ride* The powers of the gods are with you. You will have the creativity you need to accomplish what you want. Do not talk yourself out of achieving because of your feeling of intimidation. Go for the big plans.

to hear an elephant trumpet You will achieve a great victory within seven days.

two elephants fighting Agreements, disputes and litigations that you will become involved in will result in your favor. You will achieve major victory and will have the courage to stand up for yourself and get your point across.

aggressive This dream is a warning. Someone you are very fond of will become cruel to you. You will request that this behavior stop but over the weeks it will become a habit and will escalate to a point of embarrassment. Do not prolong this. Refuse to accept this behavior or to justify it. Take steps to eliminate this abuse from your life and develop your own personality.

pink elephant Within four days you will receive a very unexpected proposal. This proposition will seem too good to be true and you will be tempted to turn it down because it will seem impossible to accomplish. Take a few days to mull this over and do not close doors or burn bridges. You will want to experiment with this idea at a later time to see if it is a possibility. It will take place as planned and the person who presented this to you will keep each commitment. Good luck is with you.

white elephant This is an exceptionally lucky omen and you will experience a rapid increase in wealth within three weeks due to an unusual occurrence. Success will abruptly come to you at a time you least expect.

elephant trunk This dream is an extremely lucky omen and you will enjoy an abundance of health. You will also receive an unexpected income and as a result will receive riches in areas you never expected. You will also be able to handle certain situations you once felt were impossible. This is the perfect time to tackle those big tasks. Proceed with confidence. You are headed for a very prosperous future.

in any other form You will enjoy a brilliant mentality and charm. You will relentlessly apply yourself toward achieving and grasping a golden opportunity, especially for the next three days. You will be able to handle everything on a grand scale and this will dramatically improve your life. Any person, place, or thing referred to in this dream will be instrumental in bringing you what you most desire. If you do not achieve victory in this dream, for any reason, you must make sure during this time period to observe carefully what is going on around you. Anything you feel is not working the way you wish it to needs to be worked on until you are able to turn it around to meet your specifications. This is the perfect cycle to investigate new areas of opportunity and add new dimensions to your life. Many blessings will come your way and you are headed for a brilliant future.

elevator You will be doting on someone within seven days who will be perfect for you to spend the rest of your life with.

to go down You are about to make a mistake. You are very fond of someone and are becoming impatient because this person is not coming across in the manner you wish them to. You will want to rush this person into a commitment and will, over the next three days, become demanding and mistreat them. Back off and use your time to develop your personality. Demonstrate a warmer, more positive attitude and this person will mature. You will enjoy a more meaningful relationship as a result.

to go up You will enjoy greater clarity of thought, and will finally be able to see your goals manifested. You are headed for a brilliant future.

to push elevator buttons Play an active role in satisfying your emotional feelings. Within five days you will be able to visualize the path to take to ensure a brilliant future. Good luck is with you.

elevator buttons An event is scheduled for the coming week that you should attend. You will be in the company of two admirers who will attempt to win you over. Both will be very charming and agreeable but one of them, unbeknownst to you, will possess a great deal of authority and power. You would enjoy having one of these individuals as a life long partner and you can be confident that you will put yourself on the path toward a very prosperous future.

eleven This dream is a lucky omen and you can use this number in games of chance. Any luxury item you have desired will also be yours within two days.

eleventh hour A certain person is sure you will be able to handle a particular situation they are required to handle. Make sure you do not become involved. This will not work out well for either of you. Otherwise you will be in a very lucky cycle for the next seven days. You will also be so concerned and focused on pressing issues for the next three days that you will find yourself wasting time that you could be spending on more pleasurable undertakings. The intense focus you have will not let you get beyond these issues. Do not deprive yourself of something that could bring you tremendous joy. You are now unable to see what you are doing to yourself and cannot imagine anything that might bring you joy. You will also find you are loved beyond your imagination.

elf Do not allow yourself to become caught up in the glitter of romance or to jump into love without thinking. Allow love to develop slowly and you will enjoy greater success. Don't chase someone away by moving too quickly, especially for the next three days.

Eli *(from the Bible)* This is not the time to make any new plans. Leave things as they are for at least a month. To avoid future confusion, put all existing plans into writing now. This will be a lucky cycle for the next seven days.

Elijah *(from the Bible)* Within seven days you will receive a very luxurious gift. It is also important to avoid a conversation with someone who seems very anxious to impart information to you. Do not become involved, at this time, with someone else's problems. Enjoy your leisure time and make an effort to pamper yourself. This will be a lucky cycle for the next seven days.

Elisha *(from the Bible)* You will be able to bring someone passionately close to you within the week. You will be romanced in a way that pleases you and this could last a lifetime, if you choose to pursue this. Consider this dream to be a very lucky omen for the next seven days.

elixir For the next week control any unusual or irresistible impulse you may experience.

Elizabeth Taylor *(Movie Star)* You will be resilient and determined due to a powerful quality that will arise from within. Unusual circumstances will come up and you will be able to tap into this resource. You will be able to brilliantly see yourself through this situation and anything you felt was impossible is now possible. Expect this within four days. After you overcome this you will enjoy tranquility for a long time. You are headed for a brilliant future.

elk Within seven days you will overcome a long term financial burden and you will find ways to free yourself from this anxiety.

elkhound Do not overtly display emotions toward someone you do not know very well.

elm Someone you know with power and clout will join your group of associates. Look for this person for the next three days and make a point of asking this individual to join you.

El Niño You will be able to find a restful, tranquil spot to enjoy with a special person. You will also have a long, healthy, wealthy life ahead of you.

elope *to see yourself eloping* If this dream represents something you wish to occur, pursue this situation. If this is something you do not wish in your life, take the steps to avoid it.

in any other form Take the necessary steps with others to ensure that the money you want to remain untouched is secured in a safe place. Make sure there are no leaks to an unspecified source who has the connections to take this money without your knowledge or consent. Protect your resources. Be very cautious for the next month.

Elvis Presley Someone will send a message to you (i.e., flowers, gifts, etc.) that they are interested in you. Once you know this person is interested, romance will quickly blossom and you are being told to go full speed ahead. You will achieve success. Regard the power this person symbolizes as the power you will possess for the next five days. Pay close attention to what these people are telling you because this will be an accurate depiction of what will be occurring in reality. If this is negative, take steps to prevent its occurrence in reality. Otherwise, you are headed for a prosperous future. Refer to the definition "to dream about a deceased person" for a greater definition of this dream message. You will find this definition under the word "dead".

embalm You will receive a rare and unusual offering within three days. Pounce on this gift and be grateful that you were offered this prize.

embankment Make sure that you and a special person do not separate for the next week. Take steps by changing your behavior and ways of communicating. Make it a priority to schedule joyful events and to surround yourself with happiness.

embarcadero You will be invited to an event you should not miss because you will enjoy yourself immensely. Place all of your attention on attending.

embargo Within two days you will be asked to deal with unusual demands. Emotionally detach yourself in order to have the clarity to handle this situation.

embarrassment Within a few days, money you have placed in safe keeping will not be as secure as you have led yourself to believe. Rethink your options and place your money into a more secure place. As it is, others have access to your finances without your knowledge.

embassy A love relationship will come to a complete end within two days. There will be no emotional pain experienced by either party as a result of this break-up. You will enjoy a lucky cycle for the next month. You also need to broaden your horizons in business affairs.

ember Keep your relationship trouble free. Do not look for

reasons to cause problems within the union, especially for the next two days. Do everything you can to ensure that each plan set into motion over the next five days will work out exactly as you have envisioned. You will achieve success with all of your goals during this cycle. Good luck is with you.

emblem Pay close attention to the emblem. This represents a forthcoming occurrence that you will want to either encourage or discourage. For the next seven days you also need to treat yourself as a special commodity and monitor your time carefully to ensure that precious moments are not wasted.

embrace For the next three days each thought will be centered on someone you wish to make love to. Force yourself to make the first move. You will arrive at the proper approach and find the feeling is mutual. If you do not make this move you will waste time thinking about your next step.

embroider Do everything necessary to make a newcomer feel welcome. This person will then be able to relax and flow with the group. Do this within two days. You are headed in the right direction. You will also receive a positive response to something you thought would result in a negative response.

embroidery A certain individual will be unable to make the grade. Within four days you will be able to achieve success and capitalize on this person's failure.

embryo Do not make any decisions while under stress for the next four days. You will go to extremes if you do. Give yourself some time.

embryonic sac An overseas business trip will be very successful within the month.

emcee Within seven days someone will seek what you are after in a secretive, underhanded way. Put yourself in control of the situation.

emerald You will develop a deep love for yourself and also fall deeply in love with someone else. If you choose, this will result in a mutually rich relationship and a higher standard of living for both of you. You will experience a deep spirituality and enjoy tranquility. You are entering a cycle of healing and strength, especially regarding your heart, kidney and liver. The clarity you gain during this cycle will enable you to maintain a healthy lifestyle. Eat more vegetables and build up your immune system. Practice patience and foster emotional strength and confidence in all levels of your life. You will begin to see gradual changes within the month.

Emerald Isle For three days be very careful while shopping. Make sure you do not misplace money or purchased items. This dream may also be used as a reference point in time. If you dream of this country and see its name used in any context, the dream message will occur on this day.

emergency Be very aware of the emergency portrayed in the dream. You have the time to avoid this completely or to take steps to change the outcome. This dream is also alerting you that there is someone who is eager to talk to you about their romantic feelings toward you. There is an urgency about this. In addition, within three days, someone you know will undergo a very stressful situation. Suggest that this person schedule time out for themselves.

emery board Put time aside for leisure and use this time only for recreation and enjoyment.

emigrate Become involved in new activities. Do this within a few days and you will find immense enjoyment.

emir Make sure you call for all the information you need prior to visiting an unfamiliar place to avoid disappointment.

emissary Stop pushing another person around, especially for the next three days.

emission A letter that you receive within the next week will bring bad news.

Emmy Within three days, the end will come to something that has created a steady turmoil in your life. This cycle will allow you to experience freedom.

emotion Whatever you experienced in the dream will provide a clue to a future event in reality. For the next three days you must also practice patience when someone is attempting to get their point across to you.
to see someone you know demonstrating an emotion This dream will provide a clue of what to expect from this person within the next seven days. Be especially aware of negative emotions and take all necessary steps to alter the outcome. Promote any positive emotion.

empathy Within three days an argument will break out between you and another person. This can be avoided by practicing constraint and developing an easy going attitude.

emperor You will, within seven days, become involved in some business deals that will require you to travel extensively to other states. You will enjoy this and will welcome the chance you are offered.

emperor penguin A project you have been working on for a long period of time will be completed within seven days. This will be an exciting cycle for you and you will enjoy good luck for a long time to come.

emphysema Make sure for the next three days you do not become irritated at someone. Watch your behavior.

empire Use discretion when making a major decision that involves another person. You will have to make this decision alone and without consulting others.
fallen empire Within three days, a group of people who have been supportive of you will become distant because of your behavior. Watch your actions to ensure that you alienate no one.

Empire State Building This dream is a very lucky omen and also implies that you need to build more strength within yourself and your relationships. At the first sign of discord, become personally involved to ensure harmony within the home. This dream may also be used as a reference point in time. If you dream of this building and see its name used in any context, the dream message will occur on this day.

employ Someone you know is close to physical burn out but will lack the courage to ask for help. Look for signs and take steps to get assistance for this person to ensure they do not become ill.

employee Attitude speaks louder than words. When you notice certain behaviors aimed at you, seek legal counsel and let the law protect you. This will become apparent within three days.

employer Be very flexible when dealing with difficult situations that will arise within the next two days.

employment Someone will lie to you within two days. Be prepared to demand the truth from this person because this is an important matter. You will be very successful.
to be unemployed You will be given the salary and position that you are seeking.
to receive unemployment benefits You will be asked unexpectedly for advice and money. Make sure you give the proper advice although this person will be unable to repay you.
to look for, or any other form Drive a hard bargain for the next few days and stick to your own dollar amounts. Do not compromise if you want to successfully achieve your goals. You will also hear the words you have longed to hear during this cycle.

employment agency Pay attention to the discussion in the dream. This event will occur within seven days. If it is a negative occurrence, take steps to ensure that it does not take place. If positive, ensure that it does. You must also develop compassion for yourself and do not accept more responsibilities than you can handle, especially for the next two days. Take steps to enjoy life. Good luck is with you.

empress Open your eyes when dealing with a certain person and see this person for what they really are. This person is cunning and fickle. You will also develop a special aura that will serve to guide others in their lives. Your charisma and fostering behavior will bring out the best in others and in yourself. Expect great changes in your life within two days.

empty This dream is a very lucky omen. You will reach a decision within seven days and decide to separate from a relationship. Avoid that empty feeling by keeping busy during this time. This is a good cycle to accomplish this. You will also fulfill your ambitions and reach your goals.

empty bag This dream is a good luck symbol. Maintain good eating habits. You will enjoy good luck and prosperity.

emu You will find yourself in a beautiful, unplanned romantic setting. If you choose, this will rapidly develop into a passionate evening.

enamel For the next three days, take it easy, enjoy yourself and play it safe. You are respected and loved by others.

enamelware Be careful that pets do not become injured.

enchant Do not ask for advice. Follow your own instincts and counsel. You are headed in the right direction.

enchantment Imagine what may be accomplished in some of the empty areas of your life. Develop a constructive pastime within three days in order to avoid boredom.

enchantress The person you are interested in has an interest in your best friend. Avoid placing yourself in a position of embarrassment. Step back, allow situations to develop naturally and keep your own feelings to yourself. It will not change anything to speak of them.

encore Within seven days you will be called by someone who appears to be very friendly but is a hypocrite. This person is attempting to become privy to your private life for the purpose of using it against you. Answer no questions that you feel are too personal. Protect your personal and business life.

encounter *if the encounter is distasteful* Accept this as a clue to something you need to avoid in reality. Make it a point to also visit someone within two days who is confined. This individual will appreciate your concern.

if the encounter is pleasant Look for this occurrence in reality. Also, discuss with those who are interested in your welfare each schedule change you make. This will keep another individual in touch with you and will keep them from feeling left out. Do this for the next week.

in any other form You will be dealing with someone who habitually buys time by putting you off a few hours, days, or weeks until the time is right for them. This person will be unable to become involved in any capacity until the time suits them. Be clever when speaking to this individual in order to determine the exact time to make a move. This will keep you from suffering disappointment.

encourage Pay attention to what you were being encouraged to do in the dream. If it is a positive situation, go for it. If not, don't. Within three days you also will put an end to a large problem that has burdened you for some time.

to see yourself or another person encourage someone to make demands, moves, etc. Within five days, someone who secretly hates you will attempt to sabotage a particular situation. This will concern something you are trying to steer in a certain direction for the benefit of someone else. You are attempting to work things out so everyone involved will enjoy a more prosperous future and, although this person knows you are in the right, they will go against you in spite of the hardships it will cause others. You have prior notice of this and need to take every precaution to stop this interference. This person has no idea of the magnitude of destruction they will wreak on others.

encyclopedia Recall the section you were reading. This will offer a large clue to what will occur in reality. If it is a positive message, take steps to make it a reality. If negative, take steps to alter the outcome. Horse racing will also be very lucky for the next seven days. All games of chance will be lucky and all information you seek will come to you quicker for the next seven days.

endangered species Do not give up any privacy and make sure that you guard your wants, needs and comforts in life.

endive Keep information to yourself, especially if it is stressful. If you give this information to anyone over the next three days, the result will be chaos.

endorse Be sure, for the next three days, that you do not behave in such a way that makes you appear unpredictable.

endorsement Be very honest and upfront for the next seven days. Make it very clear what you will and will not agree to. This will prevent any future disagreements.

endowment Do everything you can to get more from life and do not allow your imagination to control you.

endurance A friend will come to your assistance just in the nick of time. This will occur within seven days and you will always have gratitude for this.

enema You're about to make a big mistake. You are very fond of someone who is also very fond of you. This person has not been acting toward you in the manner you wish, therefore you will become pushy and demand that they behave in a more demonstrative way. Do not use this approach. Back off and open up communication by introducing a mutually interesting topic. In time you will have your needs met but a demanding attitude now will drive this person away. Concentrate on enjoying your time with this person.

enemy Your instincts are correct. If you feel as though you are dealing with someone with an attitude, follow your hunches. You are dealing with a very deceitful, hypocritical person. For the next seven days, be aware of this person.

energy *any form* You are channeling your energy in the proper direction. Become very controlled and use this energy to help you realize your ambitions. You will see the results of this determination soon.

enforcement Someone will involve you in some adventurous outings within seven days. You will also find unexpected romance.

engagement *to break an engagement* You will be interrogated by a jealous loved one. Take steps to ensure that this person has nothing to feel jealous about. Tactfully and gently encourage this individual to release the jealousy.

to meet an engagement Someone is feeling very abandoned by you. Act quickly to make sure this person knows how special they are to you. Do whatever you can to give them an adequate description of your true feelings. You will bring this person a great deal of pleasure and this will be deeply appreciated by them. Put your love into action and anything you want to develop on a permanent basis will occur within five days. This dream also implies that a gift of any kind will enhance this development. You are loved beyond your imagination.

to become engaged Do not become shy and insecure in matters of the heart. Someone who is hesitant lacks the courage to express themselves romantically. This person will develop a spark that will push them toward making a move. Be very attuned to this because if you miss your opportunity it may not repeat itself. Help this person along in order to ensure a stress free, easy flowing development toward romance.

someone else becomes engaged If you recognize the person from the dream, this implies that this person has a need to speak with you about an important situation and will contact you within four days. This also implies that within three days a new acquaintance will want to involve you in their strange lifestyle. Avoid this person and go on with your life.

engine Someone you desire passionately will want to communicate their eagerness for you. You will be mutually satisfied with this union. Expect this to occur within two days.

steam engine Do everything you can to tuck away extra money. Practice setting aside petty cash for later emergencies.

V-type engine You will find for the next ten days you will be at the peak of experience and will be so together that you will instinctively know you will reach the finish line before the race has really begun. You will have the feeling of confidence that comes from knowing you will succeed. You will feel the strength that comes from your inner core. Follow your goals as if you were on a mission and this will bring you to a victorious completion of your goals. Within this time frame, your sense of ethics and judgment will be intact and you are headed for a fantastic future.

engineer You will enjoy a candlelit dinner for two, music, romance and soft words. There will be a definite improvement in love matters within seven days.

England Within four days you will need to address an important situation that is coming up. Treat it in the same manner that you would a pleasurable event. Promote growth and wisdom in all situations. This dream may also be used as a reference point in time. If you dream of this country and see its name used in any context, the dream message will occur on this day.

English *any form* You will receive the information you have been long awaiting. Be sure to check with a third person to ensure that the information you have received is current. Add the latest information to the old within seven days.

English Bull Dog Someone with a mysterious lifestyle will attract your interest. Do not become involved with this person. Go on with your life.

English Channel Do everything necessary to display your talents. Make the effort to showcase your skills and allow others to take notice. This will be a very lucky cycle for you.

English horn Demands will be placed on you concerning another person's family. You will find this very distasteful. Tactfully refuse to involve yourself in issues you do not wish to become involved in. Good luck is with you.

English muffin Do not invest in any financial dealings for the next four days. You will suffer big losses.

English saddle Within the month, you will commit yourself to marriage.

English Setter For the next three days, listen carefully to someone who has the experience you lack.

English Spaniel A new person will enter your life within seven days. Beware, this person is a con-artist and there are no limits to the damage they can do. During this cycle, do not involve yourself with any new acquaintances.

English Sparrow Do not give gifts to those you do not know well. You will later regret this move.

engrave Take note of what you saw engraved. This will prove to be a big clue as to what you wish to avoid or to incorporate into your life. You will also achieve a greater level of power as a result of a position you will be appointed to. This will prove to be a great source of income.

enjoy What you see yourself enjoying in the dream will offer a clue to what needs to be included or excluded in reality. You have the power to make the changes you need. You will also have a wonderful time at a performing arts event.

enlarge Do everything necessary to let others know how you feel about certain situations. Keep communications open.

enlighten A long time friend who in the past was struggling financially will now come to you with good news of their increased financial stability. This individual will be eager to share their good fortune with you.

enrich Your dreams and ideas will reach fruition.

enroll You will develop a friendship that will last a lifetime. This individual will also acquire a position of great power. Within seven days, you and this friend will enjoy many pleasurable moments together.

ensemble Do not perform heavy lifting and physically demanding labor for the next week. This is not the cycle to do this.

ensign You will have to choose between two people. Neither one is aware of the other and the one rejected will not understand. Think ahead and plan a way to handle this with tact. This will happen within the week.

enslave A situation will arise within the month that will prove to be greater than you can handle on your own. Be sure you get the proper assistance to take care of this issue. This assistance will ensure a proper resolution to this situation.

ensure This dream is a very lucky omen for you. You will enjoy an abundance of health and receive wealth in areas you never expected as a result of an unexpected income. You will be able to accomplish tasks you felt at one time were impossible. This is a great cycle to tackle those big projects. Proceed with confidence. You will, within the next two days, enjoy a prosperous future.

enter Someone you know will be in trouble for bestowing too much physical attention on you. Once you see this occurring, put a stop to this behavior in order to protect the feelings of a third party. This will happen within seven days.
    to enter Someone will flatter you romantically and you will enjoy yourself while dancing and dining. You do not know this person yet but will within five days.

enterprise A deeper understanding and closer feelings will develop between you and another person. This will begin within three days and will last for a long time.

entertain Do everything you can to acquire more knowledge and training in your field. You will need this within two months. Begin this learning process now.

enthusiasm You will need to focus more on your responsibilities. Encourage yourself to deal with them enthusiastically.

entrails Be sure to eat more fresh vegetables and fruits to ensure that your health is properly maintained. Drink plenty of water and create a stress free environment.

entrance Avoid all group activities for the next seven days. This will be a stressful situation for you and will place far too many demands on your time.

entwine *any form* You will enjoy peace, harmony, tranquility, clarity and many blessings for a long time to come.

envelope An unusual and extraordinary event will occur that will make you unexpectedly wealthy. This will develop within three days. Riches will arrive through a positive situation.
    manila envelope You will make all the correct decisions and will choose the ultimate role to take within the week. You are headed for a brilliant future.

environment Pay attention to what is occurring within the environment. This will offer a large clue of something that needs to be avoided or included in your life, depending on the circumstances. Within two days you will also meet someone who will later prove worthy of your trust.

environmentalist Analyze the actions of the environmentalist to determine what needs to be included or excluded from your life. You are also wasting too much time analyzing another person. This energy is better applied to something you really need to do within the week.

envy Someone will leak very personal information about a situation you are presently involved in. For the next three days, take steps to keep someone from blurting out information that needs to be kept to themselves.

epaulet You will soon receive a gift of greater mental inventiveness from a divinity. Put this gift to good use and bring needed changes into your life. If you desire, you can also make positive changes in your sex life. Protect your health, drink plenty of water and maintain a tranquil, stress free environment.

Ephesians *(book of the Bible)* You are destined to come into riches and are headed for a brilliant future.

epic Do whatever you can to ensure good health. Check all vital signs on a regular basis and drink plenty of water.

epicenter Promote more group activities with the family in order to bring more balance into the family unit. Work to organize family outings, board games and get-togethers within the week.

epicurean Do not make any investments for the time being. This is not a good cycle for this.

epidemic You are becoming very annoyed with the way someone is treating you emotionally. Do not push this person into becoming more committed and more demonstrative toward you. Back off, this person is emotionally unable to handle this at the moment. Within the month, this person will come around on their own.

epilepsy *any form* An earthquake will occur within three days.

Episcopalian Do everything necessary to find some quiet time to meditate in your own way. This will be a delightful time filled with happiness, joy, and good luck for the next seven days.

Epistles Your intuition will broaden and your judgments will be on target for the next seven days. Follow your hunches and meditate in your favorite form. Drink plenty of water and eat healthful foods.

epitaph Beware of danger. You are not fully aware of your surroundings and your judgments are faulty right now. Be very careful for the next three days.

Epsom salts Be very aware of someone who is covertly attempting to gather information about you for their own gratification. This is likely to occur within two days. Prevent any personal information from falling into this person's hands.

equator You will become emotionally fulfilled in the way you want within three days. This dream is a good luck omen for the next week.

equestrian Guard your eyesight. This dream also implies that you will receive a proposal of marriage within seven days. Good luck is with you.

equinox Someone who has treated you in a cold manner in the past will unexpectedly welcome you with open arms. Do not be resentful of past actions against you. This person is serious in their attempt at reconciliation.

erase Recall what you were erasing. This will give you a major clue to the meaning of this dream. You will also receive a unexpected gift of emeralds within three days.

eraser Do not blurt out words that cannot be taken back. These words will always to implanted in someone's memory. Avoid this for the next seven days.

erection Treat yourself with kindness, love yourself, treat yourself to a nice gift and do something that makes you feel good about yourself. Be openly affectionate to someone you know needs your affection. Pay attention to the person having the erection. This individual is interested in you in a variety of ways, both sexually and as friends. They also miss you and would like to communicate with you. There is a sense of urgency about this. If you do not recognize this person, someone will go to great lengths to become romanti-

cally involved with you within three days.

if you are having an erection You will attain your highest ambitions within seven days. You will also experience a variety of different events during this time period.

child's erection The person who is interested in you possesses a very childlike nature.

ergot This dream is a warning that you need to attend to a particular situation to ensure that it doesn't start to spiral downhill. Do what you can to avoid any negative event that will go in a direction you do not wish it to. Pay attention to your hunches. Your instincts will warn you of a certain individual you do not need to associate with. Other people will try to harm you in subtle and crafty ways at a time when you leave yourself unguarded. Protect yourself and everything that you find emotionally precious to you. You have prior notice of this and will be able to conduct yourself appropriately, especially for the next three days.

Erickson, Lief Within three days you will develop a great friendship with someone you will have a nice conversation with. This person will invite you to a distant state to spend leisure time on their property.

Eric the Red You are loved beyond your imagination. Remain calm and do not panic if you do not hear from the person for the next three days. You will hear from them soon.

Erie *(lake)* You need to control your sexual urges for the next three days. This dream may also be used as a reference point in time. If you dream of this lake and see its name used in any context, the dream message will occur on this day.

Erie Canal Do not allow power to go to your head. It will be difficult for others to cope with your egotism. This dream may also be used as a reference point in time. If you dream of this canal and see its name used in any context, the dream message will occur on this day.

ermine You will enjoy good times, joy and happiness for the next month.

Eros *(Cupid, Greek mythology)* You will marry a kind, affectionate and intelligent person and this union will last a lifetime. You will meet this person within the week, and can expect love to develop within the month. Good luck is with you.

erosion Within seven days someone will create problems between you and a special person. This will create discord within the union. Expect this to arise from a visiting friend. You have prior notice of this and can take steps to prevent it.

errand Do everything necessary to remain true to your beliefs and to what you know is true. Do not allow anyone to persuade you to act counter to your beliefs, especially for the next four days.

error For the next week, make sure you take the proper medication for your illness. Self medication may lead to serious problems.

eruption Within three days, you will meet someone new. This will develop into many passionate wonderful moments. This will be a tranquil, peaceful time for both of you and will provide a welcome change in your life.

Esau *(from the Bible)* This dream implies that you will be entering a lucky cycle for at least six months. Within the week you will also learn of an unexpected inheritance.

escalator You will finally be free of a long term burden within seven days. This turmoil was a result of another person's illness but they will rapidly recover. This dream is a good luck omen, especially for the next week.

to go up Trust your intuition. You are right on target concerning matters of the heart. Go the extra mile to make that special person happy. You will enjoy mutual love and fulfillment.

to go down Stop allowing yourself to be put through an emotional roller coaster by another. In order to have a healthy relationship, refuse to take part in this game playing. As soon as you see this start to develop, remove yourself from the area.

escape Within three days, you will aggressively put an end to an ongoing problem. Good luck is with you.

to escape from someone attempting to run you over with anything A certain individual will go to great lengths to create a relationship between you and another person. It is your destiny to enjoy a beautiful, full blown love relationship that will blossom within a few days and bring joy into your life. This is the perfect cycle to emotionally connect to another person. You will be so successful that this individual will respond to you in the exact manner you desire. This dream also implies that you are headed in the right direction in life and you will be able to express yourself fully regarding all matters of personal interest. You will be able to focus yourself in a very detailed manner and as a result you will achieve a great deal and enjoy many successes in life. You will magically possess the strength and courage you need to handle each issue in your life and be able to enjoy peace and tranquility. An unexpected favor will also be granted but you will need to put yourself in the position to talk with powerful and influential people. State your needs clearly and directly and you will immediately be given the money you request from a particular individual. You will achieve victory in those areas of your life that you consider to be the most important and you will also hear some good news within the week. You are on the path toward a brilliant future. You must also pay very close attention to all conversations for the next three days and make sure that all negative events and messages foretold in this dream do not become a reality. Take steps to ensure that all positive messages are fulfilled.

to be involved in a dangerous activity and escape Avoid any explosive disagreements in public with the object of your affections. Your restraint will prevent any gossip about your behavior. Avoid any dangerous activity you see yourself doing in this dream and schedule peaceful moments in order to alleviate stress.

to be involved in a dangerous activity and not escape Someone who has consistently sought attention from you will become annoyed with you. Although you have clearly stated your lack of interest, this person will still persist. You will then say words that will trigger a response of anger and revenge from this person. Take steps to prevent this. Use soft words that state your desire for friendship and move on with your life.

escape artist Be very careful that you do not lose paperwork that is important to you. Take preventive measures against loss for the next three days.

escape hatch You will hear shocking news that a family member will be assaulted during a robbery attempt. Alert other family members in order to prevent this occurrence.

escort You will be eager to join a group you feel is very mysterious. A week after joining, you will find you very much enjoy this group although they have many secrets. You are going in the right direction.

Esdras *(book of the Canonical Bible)* This dream is a promise to you that from this time on you will enjoy everything you need. This will begin to evolve within three days because of an unusual occurrence. Also, someone you know will also be very eager to offer their assistance with any means they have available. This may be either an emotional or a financial matter. Someone will also tell you what you need to do next involving a certain situation you will have to make a decision on within the next three days. This decision will bring you a more secure lifestyle in either an emotional or financial sense. Move ahead with confidence and everything will come together just as you had hoped. Use this cycle to bring about the changes you need in certain areas of your life that need to be changed in order to ensure a perfect lifestyle.

Eskimo A close friend of a friend will become your sexual partner for life.

Eskimo dog Within four days, you will be asked to offer hospice to a relative involved in an emotionally painful relationship. This relative is attempting to make a break from this union. Do everything necessary to facilitate this and to promote self healing.

ESP Any message revealed in this dream signifies a forthcoming event. If it is negative, the result can be altered. All positive messages may be promoted to the fullest. Within seven days you will also receive the gift of mental inventiveness. You may use this gift to manifest your goals. Trust your intuition. Many blessings are with you and this will be a lucky cycle for you. You are headed toward a brilliant future.

espionage No matter what the circumstances, do not become involved in stalking anyone. Control your behavior. Focus your energy on healthy pursuits and avoid jealousy. If you do not, you will run into legal trouble. Be especially careful of this for the next three days.

espresso You will unexpectedly meet someone in a crowded area within three days. You will both feel an instant attraction and this person will ask you out for a small daytime outing. If you choose, this person has the potential to be your partner in life.

esquire You will fall deeply into a reciprocal love within three days. Good luck is with you.

essay Take steps to promote closeness between you and a special person for the next three days.

establishment Seek help for a recently noticed emotional problem. Do this within seven days in order to prevent the escalation of this situation. You will then see many positive changes.

estate Within two days, you will definitely notice a much needed improvement in financial affairs. Financial help will arrive in the nick of time.

estate tax The person you are interested in is not as attentive as you would like. This is not a big problem. Do everything you can to keep from complaining about small issues. This person is destined for a brilliant future and wants you to be a part of it. You will also develop a plan, within the month, that will lead to your own wealth. You will enjoy financial stability. Money will come to you from many different areas and you will enjoy all of it. Many blessings will come to you and your family.

Esther *(from the Bible)* This will be a very lucky cycle for you. A small risk will yield big profits.

etching Within five days, you will receive a positive reply to a request that you expected a negative response. Pay close attention to the particular etching. This will offer you a clue to a forthcoming event you will either want to encourage or discourage. This is a very lucky cycle for you.

eucalyptus Within three days, you must take a reasonable and responsible approach toward handling a difficult situation that involves someone close to you. Your involvement will make a big impact on their life. Strive for better understanding in order to keep this situation from becoming chaotic. This will occur if you do not have a logical way of approaching this. You will have the strength to handle this situation.

eucalyptus oil Within three days, a family issue will be resolved and will no longer be a problematic situation. You will also find that you are deeply loved. This is a good luck omen and this cycle will continue for seven days.

Eucalyptus tree Your intuition is right on target and you will soon receive unspoken verification that your hunches about love and affection are correct. You will be promised deep love and commitment by someone who will be willing to commit to you and this will bring you a long lasting love. You are headed for a brilliant future if you decide to accept this commitment. All things you felt were impossible are possible now.

eulogy You will be very pleased with the person you choose to spend your life with.

eunuch Keep a close eye on your time, money and energy for the next week.

Europe You will be very successful with all legal transactions. All inheritances that are due you will also come your way. This dream may also be used as a reference point in time. If you dream of this area and see its name used in any context, the dream message will occur on this day.

evacuate Do not meet others in secrecy or arrange matters behind the scenes. This will backfire, particularly within the next three days. You will be in a great deal of trouble. Avoid this situation entirely.

evacuee Do not lie in order to gain sexual gratification at someone else's expense. If you pursue this, you will find yourself in big trouble within the week. Control your behavior.

evade For the next five days, be very aware of the behavior of another person around you. This person will focus on you in a public place in an attempt to inflict a violent act. Avoid all public places during this time span.

Evangelical Buy yourself a gift and surround yourself with peace and quiet for the next seven days. This dream is a very lucky sign.

evangelism You and your family will receive peace, joy, blessings and healing for the next month. Meditate in your favorite form and get in touch with the spirit within you.

evaporate Doors that were formerly closed to you will open. Opportunities will present themselves and offer you a variety of ways to make extra money.

evaporated milk This dream is a lucky omen for you. It is also a sign that you are deeply adored by someone special to you.

evening Do not sexually harass anyone. Control your physical urges, especially for the next week.

evening dress You will receive an unexpected call from someone who will not immediately identify themselves. It will become apparent that this person is an admirer. Toward the end of the conversation they will identify themselves. Once you learn the identity, you will be eager to further this involvement.

evening gown Be very aggressive and go for what you want. You will have the exact words necessary to communicate successfully to another. All of your demands and desires will be met within five days. Your determination will create positive changes in each area of your life. You will gain greater health and a new zest for life as well as more affection from others. A prosperous life will be yours.

evening star Become very aware of children and their surroundings to ensure no danger comes to them. You also need to guard your valuables.

Everest, Mount Regardless of a chaotic lifestyle, you will find a way, within the week, to succeed in the situation you are involved in. You will enjoy wonderful times for the next month. This dream may also be used as a reference point in time. If you dream of this mountain and see its name used in any context, the dream message will occur on this day.

Everglades The more outrageous, expensive and elaborate your plans, the more successful they will be. Make a budget and stay with it. Everything will turn out according to plans and you will receive much praise for it. This dream may also be used as a reference point in time. If you dream of this swamp and see its name used in any context, the dream message will occur on this day.

evergreen If you make a commitment within the week, you will be very successful, especially if you give it your personal touch. This will be a very lucky omen for those things you desire.

evict Do not allow yourself to be talked into compromising your feelings. Be sure that, for the next three days, you do not allow this. You will deeply regret it if you do.

evil You are now under a tremendous amount of stress and it will become more unbearable over the next three days. Do everything necessary to alleviate stressful situations. Get more rest, drink plenty of water and find ways to bring more joy into your life.

evil eye Someone will drop in at an unusual time with no prior notice. The strangeness of this situation will alert you. This will be a dangerous person. Do everything within your power to protect yourself. This will occur within three days. If you feel unable to protect yourself in your own home, make sure you find a safe haven.

evil minded Someone will go to great lengths to manipulate you without your knowledge. Within three days this person will attempt to gain access to what is rightfully yours. Do everything you can to protect your interests during this time period.

evil spirit *if you recognize the spirit* Someone you know has a problem they expect you to resolve. This individual feels as though you are somehow responsible for this issue. For the next seven days, avoid this person so that problems do not arise that will have to be dealt with.

if you do not recognize the spirit There are people conspiring against you to gain the upper hand in a situation you are dealing with. Become relentlessly aggressive in pursuing what you want. Keep detailed records and stay on top of each issue.

to drive away an evil spirit Make sure you only experience positive expressions in your life. You will need to take the necessary steps to avoid a problematic situation that is unfolding that you have no business being a part of. You must assert yourself and make sure all of your bases are safely covered so you can protect everything that is emotionally precious to you. You can do this by making sure you do not put yourself in the path of destruction. Also, during this time period, someone will enter your life who is very immoral and wicked. This person will cause you great emotional harm. You have prior notice of this and will need to take every step to avoid this individual completely. You will have the ability and strength to endure anything you are required to handle. Make corrections in those areas of your life that require changes and do everything within your power to make sure that problematic areas are rerouted. Ensure that you set yourself on the righteous path. Dramatic positive changes will be easier to accomplish at this time. Make the necessary changes and you will find your life will change dramatically and you will face a brilliant future. Because this dream serves as a warning, you have prior notice to turn your life around in a dramatic way, filled with tranquility, peace and joy.

eviscerate Make sure, for a three day period, that you are very watchful of your intake of fluids, food and medications. Also, be careful of someone attempting to poison you and become aware of a person who is jealous of you. Your alertness will keep you alive. Be careful.

evolution Think carefully prior to agreeing to anything, signing anything, or committing yourself to anything. Make sure you know exactly what you are doing.

ewe You are adored and deeply loved far more than you have imagined. You will become aware of this within the week.

ex *to dream about your ex* Anything you dream of regarding this ex that is enjoyable will occur within seven days. Look for behavioral similarities from others in your life at this time. Whatever you dislike, be very watchful that this does not occur to you for the next four days. Watch for both things and compare them with similarities in your present life. You have the chance to either promote or keep past episodes from reoccurring. This dream also implies that someone will request to see you within the week. In reality, they will eagerly anticipate seeing you at an earlier time. Their anticipation will drive them to unexpectedly drop in within two days. At the same time this is occurring, you will have an instantaneous attraction with another person who will contradict you about a petty issue. You have prior notice of this so make sure that you do not get sucked into a debate. Proceed with confidence.

to dream of your ex getting married Within the week, several events will occur that you need to expose yourself to. Motivate yourself to take advantage of these situations because they will offer you once in a lifetime opportunities. Mobilize yourself in order to catch each opportunity. Otherwise, you are headed for a brilliant future.

exam *to take* You will be asked in a short while to accompany someone you would like to be with for some relaxation time.

to give an exam You will be carefully scrutinizing the behavior of another. The longer you do this, the fonder you will become of this person. It is also important that you avoid suspicion and jealous feelings from another person. You will enjoy your life immensely for the next few months.

to pass any exam Within three days, you will suddenly be free of a long standing burden. You will not have to go through a difficult and lengthy process to achieve this. One particular invitation will come up that you should not miss. It will be far more glamorous and exciting than the others and will require formal attire. Make sure you plan ahead so you can look your very best. You will not only have a very enjoyable time, but also meet many influential people who will become friends for life. You will win a door prize at this event and/or will receive a gift. During this cycle, someone you desire will also make it clear they feel the same about you. You will enjoy many affectionate moments and you will both be very excited about this new development. You are on the path toward a prosperous and brilliant future.

in any other form It is urgent that you take care of, in real life, whatever you were being examined for in the dream. Within a three day period you will also need to set aside some time to clear your head, and perform some greater mental gymnastics in order to single out and decide how to resolve suspicions you have about a particular person. You will be successful if you motivate yourself now. This cycle is the best time to find the answers you are seeking. You are on the path toward a brilliant future.

examination table Do not overextend yourself in any capacity. Make sure you are doing everything you can to maintain your health. Do not expose yourself to the illnesses of others.

examine *to examine your physical appearance* You will be asked, within three days, to take in a relative for a week or two. Prepare for this event. Also, be sure you do not leave out anything because of your forgetfulness. It will be lost for good.

to be examined by a doctor Pay attention to the reason you are at the doctor's office in the dream and take steps to ensure this does not occur in reality. Make sure also that you personally handle all of your own affairs so you can get a clear idea of what needs to be taken care of.

to be examined by a physician and find something wrong Take preventive steps to avoid coming down with the illness presented in the dream. Take steps to avoid any preventable accident for yourself and others in your care. Do not leave yourself open to emotional pain as a result of someone's lack of consideration.

to witness or hear of someone else being examined and finding something wrong If you recognize the person, alert them to use preventive measures to ensure that this illness does not occur. Make it a priority to determine your needs and work to fulfill these. You must also take steps to avoid becoming involved in a group that creates chaos in the lives of others. This group is well known for this behavior and it is to your advantage to avoid them. You will experience good luck for the next seven days. You and your family will experience many blessings.

Excalibur Become more forgiving and loving toward that special person. You will enjoy much love and affection in return, especially for the next four days.

excavate What you see evacuated is a major clue of something you will either need to avoid or to embrace in your life. You have the choice to alter all future situations. This dream also implies that you will hear bad news within a few days.

exchange *to exchange something or see someone exchange something* Someone you know feels very abandoned. Move quickly to ensure that this person knows your true feelings. This will be deeply appreciated and will give this person a great deal of pleasure. Put your love into action and you will find that anything you want to develop into a permanent relationship will occur within five days. A gift of any kind will hasten this development. You are loved beyond your imagination.

to exchange anything with someone Be sure you actively pursue what you need for emotional fulfillment. Within five days, you will be able to focus on and visualize the path you need to take to ensure a brilliant future. Good luck is with you.

excommunication Become very aware of what you do and do not want from life. Pursue only what you truly want, especially for the next three days. Eat healing foods, drink plenty of water and get enough rest. Many blessings are with you and your family.

excuse Someone will go to great lengths to justify their lazy behavior. Go on with your life and do not allow bad habits to rub off on you.

if you are making excuses You will have strong backing from the majority of a group you are attempting to win over.

execution *if you are being executed* Within three days, you will feel sorrow upon discovering that someone you know is plotting to deceive you. You prefer this person to be straight forward about a situation. You can prevent this by stepping back and rechecking each angle. You can avoid the pain of betrayal by doing this.

to see someone else executed If you recognize this person, they are the one who will achieve a major victory over ongoing situations.

if you do not recognize this person Be wary and determine which situation you are involved in that will leave you open to being taken advantage of. This is an important issue and your awareness of it can prevent its occurrence entirely.

executor For the next five days, be very cautious and do not allow anyone to take advantage of you sexually. Someone will tell you what you want to hear in order to obtain sexual favors. Do not allow this. Any negative event witnessed in this dream needs to be avoided.

exercise *if you are exercising* Flirt openly with someone you are very attracted to. Within three days this person will take the lead in the direction you want to go.

if someone else is exercising Check your tires to prevent a flat. Make sure also that your transportation is reliable in order to prevent mechanical failure.

to dream of doing heavy physical exercise or to see anyone else perform heavy physical exercise Take steps to avoid any deeper involvement with a certain person you are growing closer to unless you use extreme caution, especially for the next three days. This person is very charming and charismatic and will mislead you into believing you can give them your full confidence and rely on their loyalty. This person is extremely crafty and a master of deception and illusion, and will have you believing in future events and situations that will never take place. They have a hidden agenda that involves pursuing you for devious reasons. An atmosphere of total trust will be created but if you become suspicious this individual will create a diversion to distract you. Once you understand what is going on you will be suffering financially, emotionally and will undergo disillusionments and disappointments. You will recover from this but it will take some time for your life to get back to normal. You have prior notice of this and have all the ammunition you need to make sure this does not take place. Use common sense and you will be very successful in diffusing this. Do not become involved with this person, do not compromise, and do not allow this person to pry into your affairs. You are on the path toward a prosperous future. Many blessings are with you and your family.

exhale Take steps to be in the company of those who like you and respect you. Avoid those who only pretend to like you. You can avoid stress by doing this. Clean house and determine who your friends really are.

exhaust *if you are exhausted* You will be attracted to someone who will make romantic advances toward you.

This person can be a mate for life. This person's sex drive is, however, greater than yours. Think carefully before making a decision. Decide within three days the direction you need to be going.

exhaust fumes Be very alert and attentive for the next two days so you will not overlook something that needs immediate attention. You will be able to handle this correctly.

exhaust pipe Someone will ask for your opinion and will later use your words against you. For the next two days, keep all opinions to yourself.

exhibition Acquire a tutor and focus on hiring someone who will teach you what you lack in order to be successful. Do this within the month and you will see major changes in your life. You can also move with confidence regarding all paperwork and contracts you anticipate signing within five days. You will be in a very lucky cycle for the next two weeks.

exhibitionist Use more discretion in all of your relationships until situations are more stable and you can afford to be more open with others. The exhibitionist depicted in this dream has an urgent message to deliver to you in reality. This will occur within five days.

if you are the exhibitionist Be sure to put money aside this month to ensure stability for the following month. Be very aggressive in doing this.

someone else is the exhibitionist Control your possessiveness and your obsessive behavior. Stop making a nuisance of yourself to others immediately.

exit You will be able to ask someone to get out of your life without causing a disturbance you will handle this in a tactful and successful manner. This will occur within seven days. Pay attention to what you are exiting in the dream. If this is something you do not choose to occur, take steps to change the outcome.

to look for a way out Take every precaution you can to keep any negative event in this dream from becoming a reality to you or to someone else. Maintain a low profile and keep your mind on your regular routine tasks. Focus on any mistake that could come up within the next three days. Make sure you take care of all mistakes immediately so that everything will fall into place as you desire. Many blessings will come to you and your family and you will enjoy an abundance of health.

to seek an exit unsuccessfully Take a close look at what is stressing you out and determine whether this has anything to do with what is really going on now. If not, move on with your life and do what you can to eliminate stress. Develop a stress free environment in order to clearly envision the direction you should be going. Practice this attitude and you will begin to better your life immensely.

Exodus *(from the Bible)* Do everything necessary to improve your sex life. Start taking the necessary steps within four days and you will meet with greater success.

exorcism *to see someone exorcised whom you recognize* This person will be very deceitful and hypocritical and will set you up for failure by keeping important information from you. Carefully watch those around you to prevent this occurrence. Do everything necessary to eliminate stress from your life.

if you don't recognize the person Be kind and gentle with yourself. Buy yourself something special. Avoid stress and avoid the company of those whose behavior you find deceitful and evil.

to see a child exorcised Take steps to protect the child from dangerous elements in the environment. Carefully watch other people around this child. You may find that those you trust are not so trustworthy.

to drive away an evil spirit Make sure you only experience positive expressions in your life. You will need to take the necessary steps to avoid a problematic situation that is unfolding that you have no business being a part of. You must assert yourself and make sure all of your bases are safely covered so you can protect everything that is emotionally precious to you. You can do this by making sure you do not put yourself in the path of destruction. Also, during this time period, someone will enter your life who is very immoral and wicked. This person will cause you great emotional harm. You have prior notice of this and will need to take every step to avoid this individual completely. You will have the ability and strength to endure anything you are required to handle. Make corrections in those areas of your life that require changes and do everything within your power to make sure that problematic areas are rerouted. Ensure that you set yourself on the righteous path. Dramatic positive changes will be easier to accomplish at this time. Make the necessary changes and you will find your life will change dramatically and you will face a brilliant future. Because this dream serves as a warning, you have prior notice to turn your life around in a dramatic way, filled with tranquility, peace and joy.

in any other form Be careful to control your stress level in order to avoid illness.

exotic Within four days, you will experience a thrilling moment with another person that you will treasure for a lifetime. Allow yourself to experience the best in life and, remember that most of the best things in life are free.

expansion bridge Be very alert to unusual situations that require immediate attention. Do what needs to be done now to avoid a crisis within two weeks.

experiment You will be required to handle a situation that could become a major problem. Do not allow it to escalate to this point because it will take a long time to bring it back to normalcy. You are emotionally equipped to handle this properly.

expert Make a list of your priorities. You will need this list within the week to ensure that the decision you make is accurate. Focus on and be determined to rid yourself of those things that keep you from moving in the direction you should be heading. This is a great cycle to take on this task because you will easily be able to turn your life toward a more positive direction.

explain *any form* For the next few days make sure that you keep your feelings and emotions under tight control. You will find out that you have been left out of a group or situation that you feel you should be a part of. There is a danger that you will become so focused on this situation that you will get emotionally sucked in. Make sure you do not feed on this because it was simply not meant to be. Do not make matters worse by spending too much time focusing on it. Pay attention to other things that are far more important.

explosion Someone who is very close to you will die in a freak accident. Take the necessary steps to alert those close to you to keep themselves in a safe haven for the next three days.

explosives *to dream of explosives in any form* Someone who is close to you is in jeopardy of losing their life within two days if you do not take the proper steps to warn them. Their death will be the result of a freaky and unexpected situation that will occur when they are traveling. Take every step to warn them. This will be out of your control but you must do everything you can. You will also experience an unusual occurrence within four days that will require you to put everything else on hold until you can rethink and redirect your plans in the way you feel they must go. Make sure your rights are honored and make it a point to pursue a positive attitude. You will see yourself through this issue successfully. You will also be provided with deep passionate love, if this is what you choose.

to see a city explode Be up front about new financial situations *(i.e., salary, etc.)* at the time of discussion.

to be in any setting that includes explosives Stop slaving yourself for others. Take time out for yourself.

plastic explosive You are being asked not to put on a persona that confuses others. Too much of a change is too drastic for others to comprehend. Step back and stop confusing others with your behavior. You must also be careful while traveling and avoid any situation that may be hazardous for the next five days.

pipe bomb Be careful while traveling for the next two days. Take all precautions to remain safe and to avoid accidents.

expression If you recognize the person in the dream demonstrating a certain expression, carefully watch the expression on their face. This will give you a major clue to an impending situation. If this is a negative situation, you have the time to alter it or to avoid it completely. If positive, promote the situation. For three days it is also important to help young children develop self reliance and a questioning attitude. Curiosity is necessary for promoting a quest for knowledge.

extension cord Someone will be eager to comply with your wishes. Do not put off talks with this person about your special needs. This person will be more than happy to do everything necessary to make you happy. You are much loved and appreciated. If you choose, this individual will share great passion toward you within seven days.

exterminator Look for the motive behind someone who doesn't know you well and is overly eager to become your associate. You will be able to make an accurate decision about this person within four days.

extinguisher Someone is reaching out for your help but will be unable to verbalize this need. This will occur within two days. Pay attention to the body language of others and you will be able to offer assistance at the right time. This will result in a successful conclusion.

extortionist *if you are the extortionist* Someone will request your company in the near future. This will be a very exciting time and you will quickly surrender to this person. This will be a mutually satisfying occurrence.

　　someone else is the extortionist You are headed toward a brilliant future.

extra *anything extra* You are being alerted to have an extra set of keys somewhere to be on the safe side in case of a lock out. This dream also implies that you will have extremely good luck, especially during this cycle.

　　in any other form Within seven days an overwhelming sense of balance, confidence and the feeling of being solidly grounded will overwhelm you. As a result, you will be able to handle situations that require this aspect of your personality. Use this cycle to work on those areas of your life that you want to make changes in. You will have the opportunity to introduce prosperity into your life at the level you desire. You are on the path toward a brilliant future.

extra large/XL *any form* An event will occur within seven days that you must attend. You will be in the company of two admirers who will subtly attempt to win over your affections. Both of these people will be very agreeable and charming but one of them possesses a great deal of power and authority. It would be to your advantage to choose one of them as a life long partner. You can be confident that you are on the path to a prosperous future.

eyeball You will be appointed to set up a family reunion. Don't be timid. Go all out and you will be a great hostess. This reunion will be a very special event.

eyebrow Do not treat someone new in the manner you have treated someone else in the past. This person is a different individual. It is important to realize this for the next three days.

eye contact For the next two weeks, take steps to update your address book. Include new friends and all pertinent information. Make yourself more accessible and add more people to your life. You will be entering a cycle that promotes and encourages new friends.

eye drops Follow your heart and you will go in the right direction. This is especially true for the next three days.

eye/eyes You will soon be making big changes to raise your standard of living by focusing on your goals on a grander scale than ever before. A very joyful and unusual situation will take place within three days. Everyone involved in this will experience beautiful expressions of joy and tranquility. Many blessings will come to you and your family.

　　to wink at someone You will enjoy pleasurable moments with a person you desire in your life. For seven days, the cycle will be perfect to bring someone much closer to you. This person is kind, demonstrative in giving and very affectionate. Good luck is with you.

　　to be winked at Pay attention to messages coming from someone else for the next seven days. These messages will offer suggestions that will alter your life for the better. Pay close attention to matters that should not be overlooked. Also, pay close attention to your dreams during this cycle. Your intuition is right on target.

　　expressive eyes Focus on what the eyes are looking at. Turn each negative occurrence into a positive and work to fulfill each positive promise. You will also see a large definite financial improvement within the month. Focus on private matters.

　　to be looked at by expressive eyes Wealth will come to you rapidly and you, as well as your family, will enjoy an abundance of blessings and happiness. Meditate in your favorite form, eat well, and drink plenty of water.

　　bloodshot eyes Within a few weeks you will be planning and eventually take a much needed pleasurable vacation. You will enjoy yourself and have a safe return.

　　with dark circles Someone will lie to you. Be prepared for this and handle yourself appropriately.

　　to cover your eyes Maintain your sense of alertness, especially for the next three days and make sure that you do not let down your guard. Do not allow yourself to be talked into going somewhere or becoming involved in new situations with another person who could inadvertently cause you harm. It is very important, for this time period, to carefully choose what you will or will not involve yourself in.

　　glass eye Guard against any injury to the face, especially for the next two days. This dream is a lucky omen. You and your family will enjoy an abundance of blessings.

　　itching eyes Wealth will come to you in the form of an unexpected windfall. You will fall deeply in love with a very special person and enjoy a wonderful life. You will enjoy many blessings and love. The Gods are with you.

　　pink eye Keep a low profile and keep your mind on regular routine tasks. Focus on any error that could arise within three days and make sure you take care of it immediately so that everything will fall into place as it should. Take steps to avoid any negative event in this dream that involves you and another person. Many blessings are with you and your family and you will enjoy an abundance of health.

iris Someone will challenge you for your position within five days. This person will attempt to grab what is righteously yours. Since you have prior notice of this, you will be able to handle this matter successfully.

red eye Keep a close eye on someone else's health. Continually watch this person to ensure there are no serious health problems. Push this person to get the proper care in order to recover.

hook and eye Someone you know who is very charismatic, confident and has a wonderful sense of humor will do everything in their power to bring you closer to them. This individual will invite you to an enjoyable outing and is planning to ask you to be a part of their life. A variety of things will occur on this outing that will make it clear that you want to make major permanent changes in your life. You will rejoice in these changes. Someone will also request your affection within a three day period. You will be overjoyed at this and more than willing to surrender yourself to this person. Many blessings are with you and your family.

"keep your eyes open" Remain calm and nonargumentative when discussing a delicate situation that will arise with family members. Do what you can to remain uninvolved for the next seven days.

in any other form Pay close attention to what the eyes are focused on. They will lead you to focus on something you will either want to include or exclude from your life. You must also promptly execute those plans you have been considering that will allow you to bring someone into your life. Do this within three days. Do everything within your power also to avoid contracting an infection, especially for the next three days.

eyeglasses For the next five days, avoid eyestrain and all injuries that could lead to eye damage. You need to analyze your relationship with someone who is a special person in your life and well loved by you. This person has deep feelings for you but both of you can do more to bring life to this union.

if you recognize the wearer Someone will lie to you within the week.

with broken lenses or frames Someone you feel a special closeness to is undergoing a great amount of strain that is being placed on them by another person. They will come to you within three days trying to explain this situation but will be unable to state exactly what they are feeling. This person is very much in danger of having their spirit broken because the other party is being irresponsible and abusive in many areas of this person's life. They are feeling controlled and are developing suspicions about the methods being used. Now is the perfect time for this person to act on their suspicions and confront their own inability to move out of this situation. They need to be made aware that the moment they talk with you about this, they must motivate themselves to move on. It takes a long time to break the spirit and this person needs to take steps now to make changes and to reenergize their spirit. What does it take to heal a broken spirit? It takes a long time to get a balanced sense of consciousness

back and a great deal of abuse to destroy it. This individual will discover the extent of the abuse they are under only when it is too late, unless they start making moves right now. Any negative event that can be prevented during this time cycle needs to be dealt with. Also, within three days you will be able to skillfully use your talent for communication to gain someone's attention in an intense way and will have their absolute attention. You will then be able to open their eyes in some way so they can become motivated enough to raise their standard of living to the level they desire. You will also be able to glean the information you need from others by using your communication skills. This information will benefit you greatly and will offer many advantages to both of you. Many blessings will come to you and you are headed for a brilliant future.

eyelash You will be moving from one residence to another within the month. The place you will be moving to will be your place of residence for many years. Luck is with you.

eyelet Bring together those people you need to talk with. Detail each issue on paper and take steps to work together as a group. You will be more successful if you do this within seven days.

eyelid You will have company for a short time and this person will spend a great deal of time complaining, moaning and groaning. Step back from this person and allow them to complain in order to avoid discord. The visit will be only for a short time.

eyeliner Within five days, you will meet someone in a group setting. This person will be irresistibly attracted to you and will be unable to control their feelings toward you. You will be surprised and charmed by their behavior and this will lead to a mutually satisfying companionship.

eyepiece Do not limit your feelings, especially for the next three days. Openly reveal your feelings to others.

eye shadow You will be invited, within two weeks, to a fantastic, elegant event. Do everything you can to attend this event. Put yourself into a festive mood and live it up. You will enjoy yourself immensely.

eyesore You will become very wealthy within the month. This will be the result of a very unusual situation.

eyestrain Protect your valuables for the next week. Make sure they are in a safe place.

eyetooth Do not allow yourself to be bullied by anyone, especially for the next two days.

F

F Your spirit is reminding you that everything you have undergone in life is designed to make you complete as an individual. Remember what you have gone through in the past and use this knowledge to handle the situation when it comes up again. You will then be able to use this experience to improve your life. Take each positive situation and make it better the next time. All events that occur in life work to make you more complete and whole. This dream is a good luck symbol. You will now know your strengths and become aware of the inspiration that arises from your inner god.

fable You were previously in a situation that will come up again within three days. This time commit yourself to seeing it through to completion.

fabric Make sure you conserve your energy in order to meet your needs. Do not expend energy for those who do not appreciate it. Luck is with you.

facade Play a strong role in sustaining a working relationship, especially for the next three days.

face *distorted, ugly face* Within five days, you and another person will agree to participate in a joint venture. This enterprise will never reach fruition and you will lose your investment. Rethink this and choose an alternative co-worker.

to cover your face Do not lose your sense of alertness, especially for the next three days. Do not let down your guard and do not allow yourself to be persuaded into going somewhere that could represent a hazard to you. Remain alert in all aspects of your life. Be careful when involving yourself in new situations with another person who could unwittingly cause something to occur that will cause you injury. It is very important, for this time period, to carefully choose what you will and will not become involved in.

to see the face of someone you know as they were when a baby or far younger than they are in reality Think back to important events that were occurring during the time period when this individual was a part of your life. This will supply you with clues of a forthcoming event that will occur within four days. You may desire to include this in your present life or take steps to ensure that it does not occur. You will also need to focus on your health as well as everyday situations that you take for granted. The person you dreamed about or someone with similar traits will require extra help and protection from freak accidents. This dream also implies that someone has difficulty expressing their true feelings for you. It is important to allow this person to be comfortable enough to open up and express their true feelings. Any negative event depicted in this dream needs to be avoided in reality. Alert those who need to be forewarned of events that were depicted in this dream. Remain alert and open to all messages for the next four days that will bring you good news. Otherwise, you are headed for a prosperous future.

to see the face of someone you recognize as a bit younger than in reality If this individual represents a time period in your life when certain patterns occurred that you do not want to repeat and/or people you do not want to be involved with now, you have prior notice and can take steps to prevent it. This could be the same episodes, or similar events and people with the same characteristics. This could also represent a time period when you enjoyed many wonderful experiences and want to repeat them in your life. Think back to something you want to recreate to gain the benefits and advantages these experiences offered. Make the person you recognized aware of your dream so they can do likewise. You may also, within the month, see this particular person or someone they were associated with during the time period you dreamed about, who will talk about this individual. You may also run into someone who was in your life during this time period whom you may or may not want to include in your life. Any negative situation you dreamed of concerning this person needs to be prevented and any positive expression will become a reality. Your spirit is alerting you that what you dreamed of will occur when you see this person in reality. Your plans will work out on a grander scale than you ever anticipated. You are headed for a prosperous and brilliant future.

to recognize the face of someone who was a minor part of your life You may see this particular person or someone they are associated with during the month who will talk about them. You may also run into someone who was a part of your life during the time period that the person you dreamed about was. It is your choice whether you wish to include this person in your life. Any negative situation you dreamed about regarding this individual needs to be prevented in reality. Any positive expression will become a reality because your spirit is alerting you that what you dreamed about will take place when you see this person in reality. Your plans will work out on a grander scale than you ever anticipated. You are headed for a prosperous and brilliant future.

to see your face or the face of someone you recognize older than in reality Determine how old this person was in order to estimate the time period when the episode you dreamed of will occur. So you can alert this person to any negative event or protect yourself from any negativity. Encourage only positive expressions in your life. This other person's and your highest priority is to live life in such a way to avoid future abusive situations. Make sure you do not cramp your lifestyle and can live life to the fullest. This is the perfect time to schedule amusements and to lessen the stress in your life. You have the chance to go from one extreme to the other and disassociate yourself from stressful episodes in your life. You are definitely headed for a prosperous future. Take steps now to create the perfect lifestyle for yourself and alert the person you dreamed about to do the same. Do this within three days.

to see yourself as a baby or far younger than you are in reality Avoid any accidents and illnesses that are within your power to prevent, especially for the next three days. Also, pay attention to the people who were most important to you during this time frame. Be sure to involve someone in your life who shares similar traits as someone who, in the past, brought you much happiness. Be sure to avoid anyone who shares the same behavior as someone who caused you distress and despair. Any positive experience you had during that time period can be reproduced in the present. Keep all old patterns and hang ups that you were going through during that time period from reoccurring during this cycle.

youthful female face Pay close attention to what you hear over the next seven days. The Gods will use an unexpected person to give you a message but this person will be unaware of the source of this message. These words will greatly improve your existing circumstances.

youthful male face Your plans will work to your advantage in a very surprising way. This will happen within seven days.

dirty face For the next five days take no risks with your bad temper. This may result in a permanent split with a special person. Try, instead, to reach a deeper level of love unless you choose to lose this person.

unshaven face This dream is warning you of a situation that will occur at an unreasonable hour. Take steps to protect yourself from injury at the hands of a stranger and place yourself in a safe haven for the next three days. Do not venture outside during the late hours.

face with a skin rash An unusual circumstance will occur that will provide you with more wealth and a very wealthy, shy person will fall deeply in love with you. Be sure to keep your eyes open for anyone who fits this description if you choose to move in this direction. Take steps to ensure you do nothing that will cause your face to break out, and make sure that you forewarn anyone you recognize to do the same.

to save face For the next seven days the decisions you make will have a profound effect on the direction your life and the lives of others will take. It is a priority that you focus on this.

frowning anxious face The face you dreamed about will offer you the description of a person you will become aware of who will be going through a very anxious time. This may be someone you recognize or represent someone with similar traits. If you do not recognize this person you will know this individual by the clues that are left based on ethic group, age, gender, mannerisms, speech patterns, etc. Within three days you will be dealing with this person. They will hear disturbing information that will affect their life in a substantial way through either the loss of a job, eviction, or something very similar. This dream is telling you to be a good listener and to use words that will motivate this person to proceed with confidence and eliminate stress in their life. Your job will be to uplift and motivate this person. You have prior notice and any negative event that can be prevented during this time cycle needs to be dealt with. At the same time that this is taking place two other people will be undergoing certain situations that will cause them distress. Try to use the right words to motivate and uplift them. Something will also take place in your life that will cause you to experience much joy. This will come about because of a conversation that will provide you with tips that will lead you to get in touch with a certain individual who will follow through for you. This will bring you many benefits. You are headed for a brilliant future and an abundance of health.

beauty mark on face You will meet a generous, loyal and sexually exciting person within seven days. If you choose, this person will be your future mate.

burn marks on face Do not take on any extra burdens for the next two months. Stay far away from the demands of others.

blushing face - if you are blushing in the dream Within a few days someone will go to great lengths to have you believe that they are telling the truth. Most of the information this person gives you is incorrect and they have no intention of carrying out their plans.

to see someone else blush You will meet someone within seven days who will find you irresistible. This person will promise many things but will be able to deliver on only a portion. It is up to you to decide what you will be satisfied with.

scarred face Within seven days two people will attempt to set you up for the intent of injuring your feelings because of their jealousy. You have prior notice of this and can do a great deal to avert it.

scratched face Within five days, you will meet someone who has a very emotional nature. Do not quarrel with this person because it could easily escalate to physical violence. This is preventable.

cut and bleeding face Do not suspect disloyalty from anyone. You are deeply loved. You will also receive the apology you have been waiting for. Protect your face from all accidents or damage. Take steps also not to spoil a current situation by involving too many people.

discolored, pale face Do nothing that is socially unacceptable for the next three days. You will have to explain your behavior.

sorrowful face Give a detailed account of your needs as soon as possible to your deity and to a special saint, goddess, etc., you favor. Have faith and confidence in your request. Assistance will come at an unexpected time but you can be assured that what you receive from your higher power will always be yours and work out better than you expected. Blessings are with you.

face up to Within five days, you will be required to take forceful action to deter someone from making a decision that will be detrimental to them. This person will later be grateful that you intervened.

face down For the next four days, watch your actions carefully. Someone who is interested in you is very fragile due to a recently broken relationship. Any careless conversation between you may result in driving this person away. If you choose, this could become a dynamic union. Handle this person with kid gloves.

two faced Within five days you will visit a place filled

with depravity and wickedness. Carefully research your plans before traveling in order to keep this from occurring.

to make a face Make a demand to your higher powers that they lift the burden you are presently shouldering. Tell them that you have gone through this long enough and are exhausted. You will experience immediate relief and can then move on with your life.

in shadow or hidden by a hat, veil, etc. Within five days you will be dealing with someone who will mislead you into believing they are respected, professional, stable in their career, financially secure and have a very credible lifestyle. This person will be very eager to become involved in your life. Because of their believability and the comfortable feeling you have with them you will, in turn, very much desire to be a part of this individual's life. You will be given every indication that you will have easy access to them at any given time. This person will give you phone numbers, company addresses, etc., that will lead you to believe you can track them down at any time. If you make the effort to get in touch with this person you will find it impossible to reach them and it will take hours or days for them to return your calls. It will dawn on you that this person has misled you into believing they have a higher position in life than they do. If you become involved with them on any level, you will be let down. Be very shrewd and disciplined in order to keep this person from violating your emotions or insulting your intelligence. You have prior notice of this and will be able to deal with this successfully. You are in a lucky cycle and are headed for a prosperous future.

to see your face in profile Stop being so short tempered. You may have a food allergy that causes this. Get a doctor's advice.

to see another's face in profile Be more selective about what you will and won't do for another.

smooth face You will take steps to complement major changes in your life. These changes will also extend to every phase of your life.

in any other form Within three days a situation will arise involving two people of equal power who will face off against each other to prove who is the most powerful. Emotions will run high because everyone will be interested in who will be the victor. The older of the two will come out on top and everyone involved will be happy with the outcome. You will also experience a financial windfall and are definitely headed in the right direction.

face card You are handling a particular situation in the wrong way. Within three days you will make an incorrect decision regarding this situation. It is also important that you challenge yourself to grasp the opportunities and positions that are coming your way. Right now you feel as though you will be unable to handle this task. But you will gain the confidence and determination you need to win this position and succeed. Good luck is with you.

face cream In a short while you will be dealing with a certain person who is associated with an agency that can lead you to resources that will meet your needs. This individual has a great deal of expertise and knowledge of these resources. And is in power because of their ability to procure grants that will meet the needs of those who seek their help. They will decide on their own to do something for you on the side and will have you go through them instead of the agency. This will ensure that they will be paid through the agency as well as through you. Make sure you are not steered from your path and do not compromise your goals because you will miss out on accomplishing what needs to be taken care of. You will become aware of this because of the sense of strangeness that will surround this transaction. This feeling will arise from your heightened sense of awareness and is letting you know that you are on the wrong path. Expect this to occur within three days. You will be able to catch this in the nick of time but since you have prior notice you can take steps now to avoid falling prey to this. Otherwise you are headed for a brilliant future and are destined to accomplish what you set out to accomplish.

face lift You have kept things pending for too long. Within two days, tactfully state what you need. You will have the strength to make these demands now and will be successful in having your needs met.

face off For the next three days, you will need to be sensitive to the feelings of others. You will be in a situation that may lead you to make someone feel better at the expense of another. Avoid this and keep close ties with others at all times.

face powder For the next two days, do not allow others to keep you from voicing your opinion on certain subjects. You have very strong views and you will not have the opportunity at a later date to express them.

facial You will be appointed by the gods to perform a special service for someone in need. This will be an emergency life and death situation and you will be unable to explain the source of this heroic action. This will be happening within seven days. Allow yourself flexibility during this cycle.

facility Do not allow friends and social events to distract you from what you feel is important for you to accomplish. Face up to your commitments.

facing For the next two days, someone will be determined to lead you into certain pleasure seeking activities. Carefully watch your behavior and make sure you do not expose yourself to something you will later come to regret. You have the integrity to protect yourself. Otherwise, you are entering a lucky two day cycle.

factory You will receive more than you anticipated in a business deal. Concentrate for the next four days on ways to accomplish this.

facts Someone will lead you to believe they are interested in a relationship. This person is simply a big flirt and desires nothing else. This will occur within three days.

faculty You will sense a greater loyalty from someone than you ever thought possible. Allow your actions to encourage this behavior for the next four days in order to maintain this level of loyalty throughout your time together.

fad Within five days, someone will be very attracted to you. The primary reason is financial. Be very aware of this person's motives during this time period.

fade Someone is planning to move from your premises within the month. Do whatever is necessary to change your behavior now. This person will change their mind about the move as a result.

fade away *any form* Within four days what you choose to eliminate from your life will subtly and permanently fade away. This will range from bad habits to undesirable people. It is also important that you do not allow resentments to stand in the way of good times.

fade out Someone you want and need in your life will return after a long absence. You will enjoy many moments of mutual happiness.

to fade out During this cycle you will be showing others your very best side when it comes to nurturing others. Within three days you will be surprised that you will have a soothing and calming effect on someone who is not treating you well. You will also enjoy a number of different people who are interested in you. They will come to you at separate times during this time period and will be unaware of each other. You have prior notice of this so that you will be able to handle the demands they place on you and be able to share your feelings and emotions in a profound and touching way. You will be successful in treating each one with equanimity and will be able to fulfill each one's emotional expectations. Go ahead and share yourself with as many people as you wish, because you will be able to handle yourself appropriately, treat yourself with respect and be surrounded by people who love and respect you. You will enjoy an abundance of health and will have a victorious future. Many blessings are with you and your family.

to see someone fade out This dream is a warning that a very malicious person will come to you with a very trustful air, and will lead you to believe anything you discuss will be held in strictest confidence. In reality, this person is attempting to glean as much information from you as they can and will then take what you say back to this individual. Be acutely aware of this so you can avoid this situation altogether, because you will be confronted by the person you were talking about and this could escalate to violence. Keep your opinions and knowledge about this person to yourself.

fail-safe For the next three days, demonstrate your desire to be more helpful to someone who needs motivation. Once you offer help, this person will be more eager to motivate themselves into going in a positive direction.

failure Become more focused on something you desire for the next four days. Avoid putting up blocks that will prevent you from accomplishing your goals.

faint *someone else faints* Someone will do whatever is necessary to steer you in the wrong direction within a three day period. Be very aware of this in order to avoid entrapment and disappointment.

to faint Someone you least expect will behave in an unexpected fashion. This individual will lie to you within three days.

fair *to hear the word* Someone is aware they should be treating you more fairly will come to their senses and start treating you better within three days. Actions will bear this out.

in any other form Within three days someone you least expect will attempt, in a variety of ways, to attract your attention. You will enjoy this. Think ahead and decide whether you want to encourage this. You will drive this person away if you treat them rudely, but if you choose, you may enjoy many wonderful times together.

fair ball Your wish will be granted within three days.

Fairbanks, Alaska You can expect dramatic, positive changes in your life and all travel plans will work out beautifully. Expect these changes within the month. This dream may also be used as a reference point in time. If you dream of this city and see its name used in any context, the dream message will occur on this day.

fair catch Make sure you know who you are abandoning because of your lack of love and affection. Be especially careful of this for the next three days.

fairground For the next four days, any professional service you request will result in a very satisfactory performance.

fair trade Within a few days you will find someone to help you in an ongoing situation that you feel is almost impossible to turn around. This will result in a positive outcome.

fairway You are depending on another person to handle your responsibilities. Learn to depend on yourself and to be responsible for your own life, especially for the next five days.

fairy Listen carefully to the message the fairy brings to you. This message will be instrumental in improving your life, or will represent an important issue you have previously overlooked. It may also point to a negative situation you need to turn around. Take steps to ensure that the result is positive. This dream also implies that you are loved beyond your imagination by someone who is unable to verbalize this love. This person will be able to accomplish this goal during this cycle. Luck will be with you for the following month.

fairyland Proceed with confidence. All of your plans and ideas will meet with success. Those who offer you help will relentlessly pursue your goals with you.

fairy rings Someone you are romantically interested in will state, within five days, a desire to deepen the union they have with you. This person will request to spend more time with you and during this cycle you will both have the opportunity to talk with each other about this.

fairy tale Pay close attention to the words spoken in the dream. They will give you a clue to something that will occur in reality. You must also be keenly aware of someone who is becoming increasingly untruthful and inconsistent and may cause problems with a situation you need to be working on. Make sure you avoid all delays.

faith *to hear this word* You need to develop more faith and confidence in your abilities. This attitude will lead to greater success and more faith in your ideas. Do not compromise your feelings, especially for the next three days. It is also important that you change your routine for the next few days and introduce something new into your life. These changes will bring you much joy and happiness.

faith cure For the next two days, take steps to educate yourself and to gain more information by reading about health issues. Take a more preventive approach in health matters to ensure that you remain healthy.

faithful Remain focused on ongoing personal situations. Do not allow any outside interference to sidetrack you. Make it a point to stop all distractions immediately to ensure tranquility and a successful outcome.

faith healer Become very aware of a situation that will lead you to become angry and to lose confidence in yourself. Be prepared for the next three days to handle this situation effectively.

fake Someone will present themselves to you at a far higher level of authority and position than they possess. Be careful that you are not taken in by promises this person cannot deliver.

falcon Within three days, you will meet someone who will treat you with a high degree of interest. Be very aware of this person. Marriage is in the picture and you will be financially secure for life. If you do not pay close attention, this person may be overlooked.

to see many falcons Whatever is put into motion for the next three days will meet with tremendous success. Take advantage of this cycle.

falconer Become very active for the next four days in creating a bond between yourself and someone who is important to you. This close bond will add an important dimension to your life. Someone you know in the past will also reenter your life and will share their good fortune with you. You will enjoy many wonderful times and entertainments.

falconry Remain focused on a personal situation in spite of what others are doing, in order to achieve success.

Falkland Islands You will have a fantastic time within three days. You will be introduced to someone through a friend and go out together, if you choose this option. Live it up and enjoy yourself. This dream may also be used as a reference point in time. If you dream of this island group and see its name used in any context, the dream message will occur on this day.

fall Be very careful of pleasure seeking activities. This behavior could become a bad habit. Be very aware of this for the next three days.

to see water falling All joint investments made within three days will be very successful. Glorious days are ahead. Enjoy yourself.

to fall down stairs Within three days you will seriously contemplate involving someone else in your life. Resist this urge. This person is ill-mannered and rough and this situation will not change. Avoid involvement and you will spare yourself a great deal of unhappiness.

to fall behind Keep yourself away from hazardous situations in order to avoid unhappiness. You will be in an accident prone cycle for the next three days.

to fall down Avoid paying more than is necessary for anything. You will be caught off guard in a situation and will pay more than you should. Be prepared to avoid this for the next three days.

fall back Someone special to you is ready to separate from a relationship due to the feeling that you are no longer interested in maintaining it. Do everything necessary, for the next two weeks, to renew this union.

to see others fall Be very careful, for the next three days, not to duplicate events seen in the dream. Alert all those involved to prevent any negative event foretold. Give yourself more love, respect and compassion and avoid all preventable injuries. Within three days, an important development will also occur that will be of particular interest to you. Conversation with a special person or with someone you have a special interest in speaking with will lead you to understand that you must compromise in order to ensure that everything falls into place as it should. Compromise only with those who are very special to you and with those you know will be committed to this compromise. Discipline yourself in order to achieve victory in love and financial matters. Without the proper discipline, all of your plans will fall apart.

to fall from something with no knowledge of how the event occurred Prevent the feeling of discomfort that comes from emotional depletion and from lack of confidence. Practice getting your point across to those in authority. Push yourself to do this and you will see very positive results. This cycle will enable you to develop the confidence to successfully carry out your plans. This will be a very lucky cycle for you.

to fall from a high place Be careful, your relationship is in jeopardy. You have prior notice of this and can take steps to rectify it.

to fall from a high place and not hit the bottom Someone will go to great lengths to create a relationship between you and another person. You are fated to enjoy a beautiful full blown love relationship that will bloom within a few days. This relationship will bring you great joy. This is the perfect cycle to connect emotionally with another person so successfully that they will respond in the manner you most desire. This dream also implies that you are going in the right direction and it is imperative that you express yourself fully in all personal matters. You will be able to focus in a very detailed manner and, as a result, will be able to accomplish a great deal and will enjoy many successes in life. You will magically possess the inner strength you need to take care of any issue and you will enjoy much tranquility in your life. An unexpected favor will also be granted but you will need to put yourself in the position to speak with some very powerful and influential people. State your needs directly and succinctly and you will promptly receive any money you request from a certain person. You will enjoy victory in your life in those areas you deem to be most important. You will hear some good news within the week. You are on the path toward a brilliant future. Pay very close attention to every conversation for the next three days. Each negative message or event taking place in this dream needs to be altered and all positive messages need to be promoted. This is a very lucky dream for you.

to fall into a ditch You will invite someone to your home who appears to be friendly. This person, however, is deranged and will turn on you and attempt to cause you harm. Be especially watchful of this for the next seven days.

falling star You will feel much sorrow over the illness and impending death of someone you have known for years and have grown close to. Within the week you will also meet someone who will be very loyal and loving and will be true to your interests. If you choose to add this person to your life, take steps now to pursue this. Good luck is with you.

fallout Do everything you can to keep someone special from slipping away from you because of your lack of involvement.

fall short For the next two days, someone will go to great lengths to destroy the feeling of excitement you have for a new involvement. Follow your instincts and do not allow anyone to keep you from going in the direction you wish to go.

false *to hear the word* What you feel is false in your outer world is truly an opportunity that will provide security for you. Look carefully at this and do not allow a seemingly small opportunity to escape your notice.

false arrest Because of your inability to be completely

truthful and to verbalize your feelings, someone will suffer emotionally. This will result in a verbal confrontation within four days. Check your behavior to ensure that this does not happen and move on with your life.

false bottom Be very aware of your belongings for the next four days. Ensure that they are not lost or stolen from you.

false imprisonment Check the printed media to gain information that is important to you. This information will change your life immensely, particularly if you apply it to your everyday life. This tactic will be very effective for the next four days.

false pregnancy *any form* Someone you are thinking of asking for help will not come through. Come up with an alternative person within four days.

false teeth *to have false teeth* Do everything you can to keep your teeth and gums healthy. This two week period is the best cycle to have any necessary dental work taken care of.

to see someone else with false teeth For the next three days, do not entice someone sexually if you are not interested. This person will be very offended at being rejected.

in any other form Affection coming from another person within the next four days will be false.

falsetto Avoid all suspicions and jealousy.

Falstaff You will hear the words of love you have long awaited within four days. You will be exhilarated by these new events in your life.

fame Be as efficient and as effective as possible when dealing with important situations for the next four days. Ask others to help you recover financially. Money will become an issue within two weeks. You will be successful in getting what you need from others during this cycle. You will also be sent a message via a gift of some sort (flowers, candy, etc.). This person will soon let you know their identity and will reveal their interests in you. Romance will quickly develop from this. You also need to move quickly in an ongoing situation and will experience success.

family Within two weeks, make it a priority to tie up all loose ends in financial matters. This will ensure that you have the financial stability you need for the future.

your family Pay attention to what the family is doing. This will give you a major clue to what you need in your life or what you need to prevent within the next month. You will also be working with someone to develop an idea that will lead to a brilliant future. Other people depend on you to take the lead regarding a major decision that will be made within two days. You will have the strength and the encouragement from others to make the correct decision.

family Bible You will enjoy many blessings and a variety of opportunities for the next two weeks that will greatly improve your life. You will also experience tranquility during this cycle.

family planning Pay attention to the content of the dream. If you recognize the people involved, they will offer you a clue to what will be occurring in the future. If the message is negative, you have the chance to alter it. If positive, take steps to include it in your life.

if you do not recognize anyone in this dream You will be offered a part time job with low pay. If you desire to take this position, the wages will increase dramatically within a few days.

in any other form Create an atmosphere of tranquility in your surroundings.

family room Protect yourself from gossip and do not give anyone anything they can use to gossip about, especially for the next four days.

family tree Keep your sources of information to yourself, particularly if you are going to be paid for them. This is especially important for the next four days.

famine Avoid confusion when developing certain plans by making sure all facets are implemented properly. Be keenly aware of the potential of losing money if this is not handled properly for the next four days.

famous people *to dream of a famous person or to hear the name* Someone will send a message to you via a physical channel (i.e., flowers, gifts, etc.) that implies that they are interested in you. Once you know this person is interested, romance will quickly blossom and you are being told to go full speed ahead. You will achieve success. Regard the power this person symbolizes as the power you will possess for the next five days. Pay close attention to what these people are telling you because this will be an accurate depiction of what will be occurring in reality. If it is negative, take steps to prevent its occurrence in reality. Otherwise, you are headed for a prosperous future.

fan Be certain that you do not overlook an important matter for the next two days. Pay close attention to all upcoming situations.

fan belt Give everything you have for the next two days. This behavior will also give others the motivation to back you up. You will find that your judgment is accurate.

fan club You will win a law suit. By compromising and caring for the feelings of others you will also lead a fuller life.

fancy You will attend a glamorous function within three days and enjoy yourself immensely.

fancy free To use this phrase in a dream implies luck. It is

also necessary to watch your blood pressure.

fandango You will be required to work with someone who is difficult to get along with. Make sure you know exactly what you are required to do before accepting this job to ensure you do not shoulder extra responsibility from this person. Do this within three days.

fang The person you have desired to become close to will now begin to move in this direction. You will see a big change within three days and will receive more affection and appreciation.

fan mail You will be chosen to represent someone regarding their financial estate. This will require extra planning on your part and you must make a special effort to live up to your responsibilities.

fantail shrimp The person you want to approach romantically will, within three days, become very offended. Adjust your behavior, this person is not interested in you.

fantasy You will achieve your highest ambition within three days. You will also have a conversation with another person and will reveal your fantasies. This person will go to great lengths to ensure that your fantasies come true. Enjoy yourself. This will be fun.

far Do not listen to gossip, especially for the next two days. Even if the gossip is not repeated, your participation will be revealed and this will result in hurt feelings.

faraway You will accomplish as much as you want for the next two days concerning a situation you are eager to move on.

fare Maintain an upright lifestyle. Carry yourself with confidence, be true to yourself and show kindness to yourself, especially for the next three days.

farewell *to hear this word* Someone in a far away place has a deep urge to see you. You are being missed.

if you recognize the person This person will soon experience a crisis within the family. You will be asked for assistance and all will work out within a few days.

farm For the next three days do not put yourself in a situation that requires extra physical labor. Maintain your health and do not overextend yourself.

farmer You will be the object of another person's affection for the next three days. The cards are in your hands and you have the choice to pursue this or to let it go.

farmers' cheese Do not allow yourself to be placed in the position to be taken advantage of sexually for the next three days. This person will use subtle coercion in order to get their way. Take steps to ensure that this does not happen.

farmhand You will be verbally threatened by someone within three days. Take steps to avoid a situation where this may occur.

farmhouse Someone will be very eager to grant you what you wish from them. This will be especially true for the next three days.

farmyard Within two days, you will be ecstatic when you learn of someone's true feelings for you. You will finally know where you stand with this person.

far off Business travel will not be productive for you for the next two days. Wait out this cycle for more success.

farsighted This dream is a lucky omen and you will be able to purchase a luxury item you have long desired.

fart For the next two days you will enjoy a period of calmness in your life. You will find relief from your overcrowded schedule due to an unexpected circumstance. Maintain a less stressful schedule from now on.

fascinate You will receive property as a gift and will learn of this transaction with two days.
to be fascinated You will savor the fact that someone will become very excited while in your presence.

fascist A stranger will purposely attempt to start a quarrel with you in a public place. Do whatever you can to protect yourself in unfamiliar public places.

fashion Do everything necessary to spruce up your attire. It is also important that you do not allow yourself to get into a rut. Take time to take care of what you need to accomplish and everything will work to your advantage, especially for the next two days.

fast You are being pursued simply for sexual favors. You will know of this within two days and because you have prior knowledge that this will occur, you may decide whether you choose to go along or whether to dissuade this behavior.
to move fast You will gain a position in the public eye and will be admired and honored by many people.
to see others move fast Do not become involved with any mysterious situation. Play it safe and everything will work out well.
to pull a fast one Do not discuss your financial status with those you do not know well.
to have a fast one pulled on you Take the necessary steps now to build up your finances so that next month you will be able to cover your expenses without stress. You will easily make ends meet.

fast *to fast* Stop demanding so much of yourself, especially in areas where you lack expertise. Be especially wary of this behavior for the next two days.

fastball Do everything necessary to hasten and encourage bonding with someone you are interested in. You will be in a good cycle for this for the next two days.

fastener A beautiful phone conversation will result in a quarrel within two days. Remain calm in order to avoid this. You must also take steps to avoid separating from a wonderful relationship because of this person's failure to repay a loan. Within two days you will be asked to lend money. You can prevent a breakup by refusing to lend money in the first place.

fast food After a friendly get together, several friends will remain at your house overnight. One of the guests will unintentionally expose themselves while sleepwalking. This can be prevented by not having overnight guests for the next two days.

fast food restaurant Several issues will take place within five days and you will need to motivate yourself to accept one particular opportunity that will unexpectedly be offered. Think and act swiftly because the person offering you this clue will be in a specific place at one specific time and in the frame of mind to offer you this chance only once. If you do not respond quickly, you will miss out on this. Think quickly because this will take place very soon. You will need to work out all aspects of this proposal that you disagree with in a tactful way so both of you can proceed successfully. In spite of any differences in lifestyle, this is a workable situation.

fasting day Do not become sidetracked and ignore someone who is very important in your life. Time will slip away before you know it.

fast lane Someone is developing the bad habit of spending your money without asking. Put your foot down the moment you notice this. This person will quickly put you in debt. Handle this matter firmly, tactfully and with calm. Maintain the friendship.

fast talker Someone will go to great lengths to involve you in a romantic relationship. This individual is very possessive. You have prior notice of this and can work out ways to handle a relationship of this type if you choose to become involved.

fast track Within two days, someone will anger easily because you do not express the same ideas and opinions they do. Keep your opinions to yourself and get on with your life.

fat You will have a true sense of being able to communicate with those who are important to you. Conversation will flow easily and beautifully and anything you want to resolve will be handled quickly. Anything you expect a positive answer to will come to pass. You will enjoy a new wealth.
to see a fat person You will hear reports of sexually abused children. If you are the person committing this act, stop now and seek help. If you do not you will be appre-

hended shortly and prosecuted. If you know of someone committing these acts, advise this person to stop now or they will be arrested and prosecuted.

to eat fat Within seven days you will meet someone who will profoundly alter your life. You will have a wonderful time because your talents will complement each other. The meshing of these talents will open up new horizons.

to see others eat fat This dream implies that you will need to work independently for the next three days. This will eliminate unneeded outside distractions. You need to concentrate and develop detailed plans now for a successful outcome.

fatty - to hear the phrase Do not give someone the go ahead to handle a delicate situation until you know them better. This individual is inconsistent and it would be better to consider an alternative.

fatality *to use this phrase* Do everything necessary to develop a close bond between you and a special person. You will also find that a creative idea will develop between you within three days that will provide a friendly working environment and a supplemental income.

fatback Make sure you control all of your impulsive behavior around those who are younger than you, especially for the next two days.

fat cat You will realize that someone has a special need for private time in order to take care of their needs. Do not become so demanding of another that you try to live their life and act like their warden. Back off and give this person the time they need. This will be very important for the next three days.

fat cell Do not allow jealousy and envy to become a part of a special relationship. Control your emotions. Otherwise, you are headed for a brilliant future.

Fates, the You are headed in the right direction and will enjoy a brilliant future.

fathead *to hear this* For the next two days you will speak with someone who has the propensity to build false hopes. Become very protective of yourself in order to avoid disappointments.

father Pay close attention to the words spoken in the dream. They will accurately depict a future event. A warning of a future negative event can spur you to make changes that will alter this outcome. A positive prediction may be fostered. This is especially important for the next five days. A much older person will also enter your life and assist you by lightening your burdens, either financial or emotional. This dream also implies that you will have many avenues during this two week cycle to turn many things in your life around to your advantage.

step father You will soon receive a proposal of marriage from a serious minded and intelligent person who is a fancy dresser, enjoys the finer things in life, and will always be a romantic. If you decide to marry, you will always enjoy romance.

to dream of a living father This dream implies good luck. An unknown person will enter your life and help you to realize your goals.

to dream of a deceased father This dream implies that you are headed toward a fortuitous future. Be courageous and explore several options in order to achieve your goals. You will be successful if you remain practical while taking calculated risks. You will see an immediate improvement in your life. Look under the definition of dead people for a greater definition.

angry father Do not allow anyone to take advantage of you and be protective over your personal possessions. Do not allow yourself to be robbed emotionally or physically.

to see your father at a younger age Watch and protect your health. Eat well, exercise and drink plenty of water.

to dream of your father dying Do not allow anyone to distract you from your ambitions. Do not let your dreams and goals die. Have faith and you will achieve success far quicker than you expected. You must also recall what they were dying of in the dream and take steps to warn them of this.

to dream of a sick father Your plans will not work out in the way you have imagined. Rethink your plans and develop a workable solution.

to dream of being a father when in reality you are not Certain acquaintances will take you down a new path and introduce you to others who possess a high level of expertise and new influences. This will occur within three days. With the help and support of these people, you will achieve your goals easier and faster.

Father *(priest)* Do not allow any personal information about yourself be known in the next few days.

Father Christmas Advertise for the specific services you need to have performed. Within two weeks, you will find just the right person to confidently give you the attention you need to complete the tasks you need to accomplish in the manner you wish. This dream also implies that within three days, a promise that was made to you some time ago will be fulfilled.

father-in-law Pay attention to the events that involve the father-in-law. This will provide a major clue to the situations you either desire in your life or need to exclude. This dream also implies victory with an ongoing project. You will enjoy a variety of many pleasurable moments over the next two weeks.

father's day You will experience great sexual satisfaction with someone you have long desired within three days. This liaison will continue for as long as you desire, if you choose to pursue this option.

Father Time You will find a timely solution to a crucial situation. Move quickly ahead and let go of the past.

fathom Within five days you will be able to purchase an item at a much lower price than you anticipated. The plans you have set into motion will also work out exactly as you have projected. Many blessings are with you. Make sure for the next three days you watch out for dangerous falls.

fatigue A wonderful person will soon enter your life. This person has a stronger sex drive than you and you will be unable to satisfy them. If you choose to become involved in this relationship, inform this person of your limitations and everything will run smoothly. You will be able to discuss ways to handle this situation.

if you are fatigued Take steps to avoid this feeling by protecting your health and by not overextending yourself physically for the next two weeks. Develop a healthy lifestyle.

fatigues *(Army)* Make sure your transportation is in proper repair for the next three days in order to avoid later frustrations and inconveniences.

fatty *to hear the phrase* Do not give someone the go ahead to handle a delicate situation until you know them better. This individual is inconsistent and it would be better to consider an alternative.

fatty acid Within three days, the yearning you feel for another person will be satisfied.

faucet Within three days, negotiations between you and someone in power will result in a successful outcome. Everything will work out better than you have envisioned.

to open a faucet All mysteries will surface within three days. In spite of anything else that may be going on, you may also take steps to improve your physical appearance. You will have verification that you are loved beyond your imagination.

leaky faucet Someone is eager to reconcile but is unable to verbalize these feelings. The reconciliation will take place and will be mutually satisfying for a long time.

to close a faucet You will receive one thrilling gift and for the next three days you will be showered with love by someone who cares a great deal for you.

fault Within three days, a misinterpreted conversation will lead to a misdirected action on your part. This action will cause embarrassment to you later. Be very aware of this in order to prevent future embarrassment.

faulty Do not give someone the go ahead to handle a delicate situation until you know them better. This individual is inconsistent and it would be better to consider an alternative.

faun *(Roman Mythology)* You will be blessed with more strength and spiritual faith. You will enjoy a courage that you never had before and will be able to stand up for your-

self. As a result, you will feel more complete and whole. Good luck is with you.

Faust Someone will approach you with a very problematic situation that they will want you to handle. You will be better off referring this person to someone else although it will appear, at first, like you will have the expertise to handle it. This problem will grow more complicated than you have the ability to deal with.

fava bean Do not allow yourself to become so caught up in small matters that they begin to take up more of your time than you can afford. Look at these problematic situations more pragmatically and learn to deal with them quickly and simply in order to get on with the more important issues of your life. This is especially important for the next three days.

favor Someone will attempt to interest you in helping to finance a business venture. Any joint effort will not work out. Turn down this opportunity.

perform a favor for someone else Someone will apologize to you for their long absence and strange behavior. This person will show great appreciation for the resumption of this friendship.

to receive a favor Someone will grant you a favor when you most need it. This will occur within three days and will result in prompt relief from a burden.

to ask for a favor and not receive it Motivate yourself for the next two days to accomplish your goals. You will be successful at this.

favorite son You now have the time and financial means to do more to enjoy your life. You will find, in this cycle, many low cost trips and entertainments that you can take advantage of and will have a great time.

fawn Within five days, a same sexed person will encourage you to enter a career that you will find very satisfying. This career will provide you with financial security for some time. You will enjoy an abundance of health and good luck is with you. Blessings are with you and your family.

fax Within two days, someone will promise to contact you. But as time goes by you will be puzzled because this person will fail to reach you. Since you have prior notice of this, you can avoid the emotional stress of wondering why you have not heard from this person. This individual will not contact you unless you take the initiative at the first meeting and determine how to get in touch with them. Also, pay close attention to the contents of the fax. This will either give you clues that will enable you to turn your life around in a positive fashion, or foretell an event you will want to alter.

FBI This dream is alerting you that someone with their own opinions will try to impose them on you. Do not allow this to block your original creative way of thinking and make sure that you continue on your present course.

feast Do everything necessary to make yourself more mobile in terms of transportation. Make sure that lack of transportation is not the one thing that keeps you from moving ahead. Do not deprive yourself of the freedom that comes with mobility, especially for the upcoming month.

feather For the upcoming two weeks, base any decision you plan to make solely on facts. Carefully research any upcoming situation in order to make the correct decision. A very wealthy person is also eager to meet with you and will make direct contact within three days. You are headed for a brilliant future. Look up the colors of the feather for additional meanings.

featherbed A successful, wealthy person will be seeking your advice within three days. This person's only fault is jealousy in personal relationships. This individual will be very attracted to you in several ways and if you choose to pursue this you will find a richly rewarding relationship.

featherweight Within four days you will be very enchanted by someone who is not at all what they appear to be. They will seem to be very casual and somewhat rustic but this person is far more educated, sophisticated and wealthy than appearances allow. You will be very happy to learn that this individual has more going for them than you originally believed.

anything that appears to be as light as a feather This cycle promotes a sense of well being and peacefulness with all relationships. Good luck is with you and blessings will come to you and your family.

February During this month you will be able to arrange events in such a way to increase your financial status. You also need to increase your social activities and enjoy more entertaining events. You will receive some exciting news from others who wish to share their excitement with you. Any additional clue may foretell a negative event or a positive omen. You have the time to alter the outcome of any negative event or promote and ensure that any positive event will occur.

feces *any form* Your determination will lead to a better future and you will see an improvement in all areas of love and money. You will gain health, wealth and a new zest for life and will also experience more love and affection from others.

Federal *to be the recipient of a federal check* Be very attentive because an unusual occurrence will develop regarding a person, project or position that will lead to a financial windfall. You may marry someone who will leave you with a monthly pension, develop a project that will deliver you monthly royalties, or secure a position that will offer you monthly provisions for a lifetime. You are in a sound position to receive this in the near future. Develop your curiosity, especially for the next week, to ensure that you do not miss out on these benefits. You will receive an abundance of health, many blessings and are headed for a brilliant future.

Federal Reserve Bank Do everything you can to make another person aware of the deep feelings you have for them. This behavior will allow this individual the chance to respond to you and to let you know where you stand with them. Do not waste time hoping that this person will contact you because you could be enjoying yourself now with this individual. Good luck is with you.

fedora If you choose not be easily found, do not put in a change of address at the Post Office. This action will prevent those you have no wish to be contacted by from locating you. Find ways to achieve peace, tranquility and to enjoy your serenity.

fed up Keep your feelings and emotions to yourself for the next few days. You will be left out of a particular group or situation that you feel you should have been included in. As a result you will become very focused on this issue to the point where you will emotionally feed into it. This will only make matters worse. Focus on other things that are far more important.

fee Be prepared for the occurrence of an unusual and remarkable event within three days. You will be able to clearly think through the steps to get through this cycle at the same time this unusual event is taking place. Your curiosity will be at a peak during this cycle and you will need to be disciplined and firm so you can hold this curiosity at bay. You will enjoy an abundance of health during this cycle.

feed This will be an emotionally nourishing time for you. You will be nurtured by others and also enjoy a greater abundance of good health. You will receive an abundance of joy during this cycle.

to feed animals Make sure you do not become too friendly with someone who pretends to be your friend but, in reality, will stab you in the back. Within two days you will be able to determine who this person is. Take steps to discourage this friendship and go on with your life.

to be fed or to see someone else fed Within the week you will find the motivation to bring more changes into your life. You will put more emphasis on the work you need to accomplish to bring you more prosperity. Many blessings are with you and your family.

feedback Within three days, a situation of a shocking nature will occur. This will involve one family member of the opposite sex who will disappear. Prior notice of this will help you determine who this person is and allow you to warn this relative. This situation can be avoided. You have doubts that you will ever be loved in the manner you desire. Within three days, you will see a change in someone that will erase all these doubts. You will rejoice in the knowledge that this person cares deeply for you.

feeder For the next two days, use your imagination when

planning family outings. Make each event richer and encourage love and sharing within the family unit.

feedlot Do everything necessary to make yourself feel good emotionally. The faster this is accomplished, the sooner you will be able to build your self esteem.

feel/feelings Pay attention to the emotions you are going through in this dream. This will offer you a clue to what should or should not be occurring in reality. Also, keep looking and you will find what you have lost within three days.

to be filled with an emotion Someone will communicate to you, within four days, their eagerness to grant you a favor. Move quickly on this and you will enjoy a great cycle.

demonstrating a feeling This dream will provide a clue of what to expect from this person within the next seven days. Be especially aware of negative emotions and take all necessary steps to alter the outcome. Promote any positive emotion.

in any other form Whatever you experienced in the dream will provide a clue to a future event in reality. For the next three days you must also practice patience when someone is attempting to get their point across to you.

feeler Closely look at the motives behind someone's desire to be close to you and to offer their assistance. This individual is a hypocrite and is only trying to get information on your plans for the purpose of undermining you. Be careful, this could have a major effect on your future prosperity.

feet This dream implies that you need to guard your health. Pay close attention to the condition of the feet seen in this dream. This represents a condition you may want to avoid in reality. If the feet belong to someone you recognize, alert this person to the possibility of a future foot condition they may want to avoid. Do whatever you can to keep yourself healthy and to build up your immune system by eating the correct foods. Educate yourself about the foods you need for your particular system, drink the proper beverages and do everything in moderation.

someone else's feet It is best to seek a professional when planning a trip. This will ensure that you arrive safely with few inconveniences.

webbed feet Be very cautious that children and young adults who are involved in your life do not place themselves in the position to make it difficult for them to follow their chosen path. You have prior notice of this and can deal with emotional hang ups and attitude problems now before they reach crisis proportions and disrupt this young person's future. This person will be very grateful to you at a later date.

feline Someone has led you to believe you may become more familiar with them but they do not want you to behave in an overly friendly fashion in public. You will be made to look bad and this person will ignore you in front of others. This will occur within two weeks.

to hear a feline purr Another person will make it seem to others that you are coming on to them. They will want it to appear this way for their own ego. There are no genuine feelings for you.

to hear a feline fight Horseplay with someone special may turn into a real argument. Avoid this.

to hear a feline and dog fight You will be sorrowful about an injured friend.

to kill a feline Avoid mechanical work unless you work under adequate lighting.

to feed a feline Watch your behavior around a young child. Always behave properly.

feline scratching Your feelings will be hurt because of your insistence that you be treated better. Avoid this.

feline jumping all around, etc. A special person in your life will act jealous. Answer questions, be calm and let it go. This person needs to satisfy their suspicions.

feline running You will be called to witness for the defense in a jury trial.

fellowship Do everything necessary to curb impulsive spending, especially for the next three days.

felon The person you see in this dream will attempt to create a disturbance with you in reality. You have the chance now to avoid this situation entirely. Protect yourself. Also do not allow someone to waste your time on nonsense. During this cycle you will have to accomplish things that need to be taken care of immediately.

felony Dramatic changes will occur with someone you care about. You will find yourself unable to locate the source of this person's irrational behavior and mood swings. For the next four days, make sure you do not push this person the wrong way. If you do, violence will erupt. After this cycle ends, this individual will return to normal behavior, with an explanation for these past altercations.

felt Make time to handle each problem, one at a time and step by step. This will prevent the frustration you will feel if projects build up on each other. Each of these situations are of major importance and need to be handled thoroughly and in a timely fashion.

felt tip pen Someone you have known for a long time will call unexpectedly and ask subtle questions to draw information from you. After a short period of time, this person will bluntly ask you to marry. This will be prefaced by the statements that they have known you for a long time, have no one in their life and you would be a good couple. It is your choice whether to pursue this or not. This person has an income and property but is neither rich nor poor. If you choose this route you will find it is the right and proper path for you.

female Your intuitions about money and love are right on target. Move quickly during this cycle and accomplish what you can. Within the month, a female friend will also surprise you with their ability to cleverly bring to tangible form an invention. This invention will be very simple in form yet very necessary.

to dream you are female when in fact you are male Within five days you will be entering a very lucky cycle and everyone involved in your life will share their luck with you. You will be offered services that will enable you to successfully complete your goals and reach a higher level of achievement than you hoped for concerning anything that you place a high level of importance. During this time period you can expect many wonderful connections that will assist you in meeting and surpassing your goals. You can also expect a mega merger. The energy created between you and those you will be working with will bring you to a far higher level of success than you hoped for. You will gain benefits through attending a festive event, through an educational experience or through a gathering that you will attend in which one person will show an interest in you and your projects. You can look forward to a long period of tranquility following this and will enjoy a prosperous future. Any negative event associated with this dream may be avoided for you or anyone you dreamed about.

feminine   to hear this phrase You will be loved beyond your imagination. This dream also implies that health and luck will be with you.

femme fatale Do your best to get along with your co-workers and do what you can to create a good working environment for the next two days.

fence You will enjoy an abundance of peace and tranquility.

to build a fence Within three days, a new affectionate admirer will approach you. This will be a lasting union if you choose to pursue this.

to pull down a fence Do not gamble with your plans or with people who do not have the experience to implement these plans, especially for the next three days.

to see others tear down a fence You will have a chance, within two days, to reconcile a former relationship. Lose all doubts that it will not work out. It will be a beautiful union.

to climb over You are sexually desired by someone you do not know yet. You will meet this person within three days and will be pleasantly surprised.

to see someone go over a fence You and the person you recognize going over the fence will motivate yourselves in such an unusual way that will enable you to get in touch with an, as yet, unknown person. You and the person in this dream will both have this experience although they will be totally unconnected. Conversations will flow easily between you and the person you have yet to meet, in a delightful way. You will both have the feeling that you have not experienced this in a long time, if ever. The person you will meet possesses an artful sense of timing as well as the unusual ability to sense the feelings of other people. They are capable of bringing pleasure to others and of fully committing themselves. They are also able to put themselves in a subservient role, tastefully and within limits, as well as having the capability of pampering others to the extreme, but not overly so.

You will find this to be very delightful and will never have a distasteful moment. If you choose to have a relationship, it will grow as much as you want and will be a mutually satisfying and nurturing union. Expect this to occur within three days and alert the person you dreamed about to expect this as well. You are headed for a brilliant future.

to climb down from a fence The plans you have made for love will not work out in the manner in which you hoped, especially for the next three days. Do not allow yourself to become disappointed. Merely retrieve what you can from the situation and make new plans.

burning fence Guard yourself for the next three days against automobile accidents.

falling fence Stop putting so much importance on an individual who does not deserve or appreciate it, especially for the next two days.

made of any material other than wood Communicate in such a way that will attract those people you desire to include in your life. Behave in a manner that will promote closeness rather than distance.

fence *(to fence)* **to see yourself fencing with another** Follow the advice you are given by someone else for the next two days. Pounce on this advice and you will find it will work very much to your advantage.

to see others fencing Select a new environment, new people to associate with, and new ways to seek amusement.

sword man Do not make financial loans to a relative, you will not be repaid.

sword play Do not attempt to strike against anyone within the next week. It will backfire.

fence *(to fence stolen goods)* **if you are the person fencing goods** You will have a pleasurable lunch with a new and flirtatious person within three days.

to see others fence stolen goods Someone special will quickly return to you after a quarrel.

fender Do not allow yourself to panic or become frustrated with circumstances that will arise within three days. Remain calm and do not allow these situations to change your mood. Handle these problems calmly and with steadfast clarity.

fender bender You are clearly being asked to avoid any situation that may result in a fender bender. If you recognize the car in the dream as belonging to someone else, make sure you forewarn the owner of a potential accident. You must also do everything within your power to foster an understanding attitude toward others for the next two days. This attitude will help to enlist a conversation with someone who will bring you much needed information.

fennel Pay close attention to your ears and seek medical help immediately at the first sign of any problem, especially for the next two days.

ferment Be very conscious of what you are doing with other people's money. Become very strict regarding your spending behavior, especially for the next three days.

fern Attempt, for the next three days, to be very understanding to a new acquaintance. This person is very kind and generous but is also very shy due to a very harsh and critical upbringing. Be very patient with this individual. You will then have a wonderful friend who is also a genius at turning ideas into money.

ferret Take steps to slow down the development of a relationship until you have a clearer understanding of the events occurring in the life of this other person.

ferris wheel For the next two days your ideas will be very detailed and calibrated. You will be able to use words in such a way that will allow someone else to feel at ease and express their feelings of affection for you. This will result in a desired union. By using your communication skills and clarity of thought, you will be able to successfully implement your ideas concerning money and love. You are headed toward a brilliant future.

ferry Victory will be yours in every aspect of your life. Focus on those things in your life that are more important and that you feel the most urgency about. You will be successful in your accomplishments.

ferryboat This dream is an omen of abundance in health and financial matters. You are going in the right direction.

ferryman You are being too strict with yourself. Add more excitement to your life and develop a sense of spontaneity. A few changes in your routine and manner of dress will bring more joy and zest into your life.

fertility You will enjoy an abundance of health, finances, and emotional stability. Expect dramatic changes to begin within three days.

fertilize Experiment with different ethnic foods and people. Intermixing with different cultures will add excitement and spice to your life. You will also learn something you can use to improve your life.

fescue Within three days you will arrive at a solution to an ongoing problem. You will then be able to move on with your life.

festival Donate money to a family with a number of small children who need financial assistance. Do this within three days.

feta cheese Someone you dearly love will return for a reconciliation. The outcome of this will be good.

fetch *any form* Be careful when operating any form of machinery and protect yourself from accidents.

fetish You will receive the wrong treatment for an illness. Be aware of this, research your symptoms and make sure that you do not take the wrong medication.

fetlock Set firm limits with yourself and do not allow someone to take advantage of you verbally. Separate yourself from this person and allow no contact to be established. Place yourself in a safe haven from all emotional abuse. This cycle will allow you to accomplish the impossible.

fettuccine You will resolve a long standing problem within a few days.

fetus *any form* This dream implies good luck.

feud Watch out for the secretary or someone who works in this capacity who plots to keep your calls from getting through to the person you are trying to reach. You will encounter this within a few days. Control your emotions. This person enjoys creating negative emotions in others.

fever You will receive a gift from a secret admirer within three days.
   someone else has a fever Drink plenty of water, eat healthful foods and take steps to avoid hospitalization because of self neglect. This is likely to occur within two days.
   you have a fever Speak passionately to the person you desire. You will receive a most pleasant response.
   yellow fever This is the wrong time to move on proposals in any capacity. Stay uninvolved and step back, especially for the next seven days.

fever blister Do not expose yourself to any contagious infections. Drink plenty of water and eat healthful foods.

fez Within the week you will become privy to some important and privileged information about certain situations and associates. Handle this information with discretion.

fiancée Develop a more positive attitude and motivate yourself to bring romance into your life while you still have the chance to enjoy life with a special person.

fiat Anything connected with this dream will come to pass within two days. You have the opportunity to alter the outcome of anything you do not choose to incorporate into your life.

fiber The plans you have made will work out the way you expect within two days.

fiberboard You will be expecting assistance from a particular agency but the person assigned to help takes delight in creating a negative environment. Take your business elsewhere.

fiberglass For the next month, all surgical procedures will be successful.

fiber optics Do not allow anyone to steer you from your path of success.

fibrillation Do everything necessary to practice a tolerant attitude for the next seven days. Several situations will arise that will require self control. Remain calm and you will achieve success.

fiction *any form* You will receive sought after approval from a powerful and influential group within three days.

fiddle Within three days, someone you have a great deal of sympathy for will discuss their abusive childhood with you. Time will pass rapidly when in the company of this individual. Make sure you budget your time wisely while remaining gentle and kind.

fiddler *to see a fiddler* You will be unexpectedly proposed to.
to be the fiddler You will spend many passionate nights with someone you desire. You will also be paid a special compliment that will remain with you for a lifetime.

fiddler crab Within three days tell others about the deep feelings you have for a special person.

field Within a few days you will be notified of a family reunion. You will enjoy good food and fun activities. Make sure you do not let anyone feel left out. Mingle and associate with all members of the family.
to play the field Within three days, you will meet someone you will be deeply attracted to. You will continuously think of this person, but the barrier of marriage will stand in the way. This individual will confess their feelings to you and it will be very difficult to stay apart. Stay busy and meditate until you learn more of the status of this marriage.

field corn Someone you did a financial favor for in the past will remember you and send you a beautiful gift.
field of green corn This dream is a lucky omen. Within three days, a politically active group will intervene on your behalf and greatly improve an ongoing situation.
field of dried up corn Make sure that you associate only with people who genuinely care about you. Do not force yourself on someone who is not interested in your friendship. You also need to participate in activities you enjoy.

field day The project you are presently working on will not work out according to plans. Explore different ways of accomplishing your tasks and you will experience success. Do this within four days.

field event Within four days someone will attempt to violate you sexually after luring you to an isolated area. Be very aware of this situation. It is preventable.

field glasses You will set aside a weekend to spend with someone. This person will spend less time with you than

you hoped for because they will stay constantly busy making calls and attending to important paperwork. Do not feel rejected. This person cares deeply for you but it is imperative that they attend to these tasks. Enjoy the visit and do not allow yourself to become resentful. Good luck is with you.

field goal You are in a successful cycle. Be sure to work steadily and have a detailed plan to ensure that you successfully meet your goals.

field hand You are planning to enter into a business agreement within three days. The outcome will be more successful than you anticipated.

field mouse You may unintentionally sabotage the plans of another person. Be very aware of your actions for the next four days and make sure that you do not inadvertently affect the lives of others because of your behavior.

field pea Within three days you will receive news that you will receive something you had not expected to get. Good luck is with you.

field spaniel Do not settle for less and make sure your body language does not give off signals that you will accept less. Refuse, for the next four days, to allow yourself to be taken.

field sparrow For the next five days, do not allow yourself to be talked into making plans for a family vacation.

field trip Make sure that a young member of the family is having their needs met. Make certain for the next four days that this child is being properly taken care of and that no physical abuse comes to them.

fieldwork For the next three days, do not become involved in a family disagreement. Promote unity and peace.

fiery cross Do not allow yourself to build up resentments toward someone because of your feelings of inferiority. Do not focus on bringing this person down to assuage your feelings. This situation will arise within four days.

fiesta What you consider a fine reward will soon be yours. You are headed for a brilliant future if you keep doing what you are now doing.

fife You will be invited on an outing within three days by a very attractive person. You will have the sense that this person is insincere. Disregard these feelings and enjoy the outing. This dream is also offering you a clue to the way someone will behave toward you in the near future. You will be offered an opportunity that will dramatically improve your life and you will enjoy many new and welcomed experiences.

fifteen A great celebration is planned for the upcoming week. You will feel overwhelmed but will enjoy yourself immensely. It is also important that you allow yourself to experience different lifestyles. You will be lucky at games of chance if you use this number.

fifth Demand loyalty from those who will be helping you to develop a personal venture and make sure that you stress the seriousness of this project. You are headed for a brilliant future. Work with this number in any way you deem applicable. This dream is a good luck symbol.

fifth amendment Any decision you are required to make within the next two days should not be postponed. Do not allow yourself or others to procrastinate. It is important that you act in haste.

fifth wheel This dream is a good luck omen. You are headed toward a brilliant future and you are entering a very lucky cycle that will remain with you for a long time.

fifty The ventures you have worked on for a long time will begin to yield results. You will be shown much love by those around you.

fig This dream is a very lucky omen. Revise your diet and avoid fatty foods. You will also see great financial improvements.

fight Lack of communication will result in major setbacks. Take steps to prevent this by touching base with that person you need to be in constant contact with. For the next three days you will be in the perfect cycle to improve communication skills.

to fight and lose Do everything necessary to prevent the sudden disappearance of a family member. Forewarn all those you care about to take extra precautions for the next three days. Make sure the plans you have made are flexible enough to change at the first sign of failure. Make several alternative plans to ensure success.

to win a fight You will enjoy victory in those areas of your life you most desire and have worked for. All of your plans will turn out as you had hoped. You are entering a lucky cycle that will lead to improvements in most phases of your life. Practice, on a continuous basis, turning each negative situation into a positive event.

others fighting Do everything necessary to avoid any accident that will result in a broken arm for the next three days.

women fighting Make sure you take steps to prevent this from becoming a reality. This dream also indicates a need to prevent a premature birth especially for the next four days. Forewarn anyone to whom this may apply to avoid heavy labor and lifting.

a man and a woman fighting Someone you care about will hurt you within three days by unintentionally blurting out an insult in front of others. Prior to this event, take this person aside and make your feelings known about this type of behavior. This will prevent the need for an apology at a later time.

men fighting men Do not ruminate about the past. Old hurts will fester and stand in the way of moving ahead in the future.

animals fighting Within four days, a friendship will break apart due to a power play. You have fewer funds and less prestige than this other person and will be asked to perform numerous favors in an effort, on the part of your friend, to maintain control. Do not allow this behavior to destroy a friendship. Make your feelings known early in order to avoid an altercation.

fig leaves You will receive the financial assistance you need from another person within three days. You are presently doubtful that it will come through but simply asking this person will dispel all doubts.

figure Look up the particular symbol or figure for a more descriptive analysis. This dream usually implies that you are entering a lucky cycle. Someone will also be very motivated to help you once you communicate your needs.

to see a human figure (yours or someone else's) Pay attention to all events connected with this figure. Each negative event may be altered and each positive event may be enhanced by taking action now. You will also be surprised and delighted to learn of another's deep hidden feelings for you. Finances and love matters will improve.

perfect human figure Within five days you will be placed in the position of vigorously caring for someone until they are able to improve their quality of life and physical state to the point of social and personal acceptance. Also for the next five days, you will be so swamped with social activities that you will have to take extra pains to keep your appearance and attire in top condition. This cycle will be very successful for you.

horrifying human figure You are overextending yourself to the point of burnout. Take steps to maintain and improve your health. Eat healthful foods, drink plenty of water and set limits on what you are willing to do for others. All requests made of your divinity, within seven days, will also be granted, no matter how impossible this request seems to be.

melting human figure Someone will finally come to terms with their life and make a decision you have long waited for. This decision will have a major impact on your life. You will both make mutual plans for a brilliant future. Expect this decision within the week.

if you dream of someone you know melting This person is very eager to fulfill your wishes with no limitations.

golden figures Each positive event connected to this dream needs to be converted into a reality as quickly as possible. Each negative event may be altered. This dream is a lucky omen and you will magically possess the inner strength to handle forthcoming situations. You will enjoy prosperity, balance and tranquility in your life. You will also be blessed with the clarity of thought needed to develop a plan and to execute it successfully. This plan will bring about the changes you so desire to experience in your present life. Luck will be with you, especially for the next seven days.

figure eight Within eight days you will be able to win over someone's affections. This will be a genuine, mutual affection and will bring balance and tranquility into your life for a long time to come.

figurehead Within two days, information from an agency you are waiting for will prove to be inadequate. Make sure that any information you receive will provide you with the means to get the best services. Investigate carefully and you will see major improvements in your life.

figure of speech Determine the motives behind someone's overly helpful behavior and agreeable manner. You will learn, within three days, that this individual is in need of a large favor from you. Make it your business to convince this person to open up and state their needs. You will be able to help out with no additional stress to you.

figure skating Within three days, you will be walking a thin line. This will make it very easy for someone to steer you in the wrong direction. Think clearly and pragmatically during this time period and you will be able to stick with your goals.

Fiji This dream is a very lucky omen for love. Within three days you will be able to verbalize your thoughts in such a clear fashion that you will be able to convince someone to open up to you about their feelings. Your actions will allow this person to feel comfortable around you and will result in the start of a warm and loving relationship. This cycle will allow all communication to flow easily and openly. This dream may also be used as a reference point in time. If you dream of this island group and see its name used in any context, the dream message will occur on this day.

filbert nut You will soon celebrate your wedding day.

file Look at life from a variety of perspectives in order to keep resentments from getting in the way of your enjoyment of a variety of lifestyles. Extensively sample different cultures.
to file anything Within three days, you will acquire what you most want out of life. You are entering a very joyous cycle.

file cabinet Take steps to create a bond with someone whom you feel will be important in your life. Follow your instincts and do everything necessary to bring this person closer to you. This friendship will work dynamically to benefit you in many areas of your life.

file clerk Stop analyzing a potential relationship. You risk talking yourself out of enjoying a wonderful outing.

file paper You have too much outside interference in your life right now. Set your priorities and become very aware of the needs of your family. Make an effort to take private time

for yourself in order to focus on what you need to do.

filet The opportunities offered to you will work out beautifully and will fit perfectly into your existing plans in spite of your thoughts to the contrary.

filet mignon Someone is devising a plot to deceive you in an unexpected way and at an unexpected time. This will not be noticed by you until it is far too late. Be very aware of the actions of others during this time period and take steps to avoid any deception.

filibuster Within two days, develop a plan to create a greater flow of income. You will need this extra income within three weeks.

Filipino You will be introduced to your significant other through the friend of a friend. This union will last a lifetime and will be mutually satisfying.

fill *to be filled with an emotion* Someone will communicate to you, within four days, their eagerness to grant you a favor. Move quickly on this and you will enjoy a great cycle.
to fill up For the next three days, you will become aware that someone will constantly interfere with your plans. This will be done unintentionally. Budget your time in order to focus on what you need.

fillet Watch your diet. You are presently eating foods you feel are healthy for you but, in reality, are doing you harm. Investigate your eating habits and research the foods now in your diet. Eliminate all foods that are not healthy. Good luck and a long life will be yours.

filling Anything negative connected with this dream implies a need to turn situations around in order to ensure a positive result. You need to take a strong stand in your refusal to go along with the plans of another. State your mind clearly and refuse to compromise.

filly An advertisement will take an unexpected turn and yield much desired and welcomed wealth.

film Pay close attention to what you are watching. This will lead you to a clue that will portend a future event. If this event is negative, take the necessary steps to avoid it or alter the outcome. If positive, make sure you take the steps to ensure a good outcome. Within five days, you will find yourself working with someone who is surprisingly more sincere, selfless and eager to work with your suggestions than you had hoped. You will find your surroundings pleasing and the performance of tasks will be easier.
to develop film You will decide on a way of handling something that will work well for you although it appeared at first that it would not. This will prove to be the perfect solution to an important issue. Do not allow others to intimidate you because of your personal viewpoints. Try new things and you will notice a big difference in your life.

if you recognize someone in the dream This person represents a particular past event in your life. Recall what was happening in your life at this time. This may be an event you wish to take steps to avoid or something you want to include in your present life.

film projector You will definitely develop a support system and the network of knowledge you need for a comfortable lifestyle. During this seven day cycle you will have many opportunities to celebrate joyful occurrences. Prepare yourself for some unexpected happy news that will come to you during this time period. You are headed for a brilliant future and you will feel as though everyone is on your side and is supporting your goals.

film recorder You are growing weary of something that is occurring in your life and you are anxious to communicate to someone exactly what you are tired of. Be very clear about what you want changed, the behavior you want to stop or anything new you want to introduce into your life. Be very clear in determining who the person is who is responsible for your frustrations and take steps to get your point across.

filmstrip You will learn, within five days, of funeral plans for someone who was very close to you. You will also have the opportunity to marry a very wonderful person, if you choose. This chance will present itself within three days. Good luck and many blessings are with you.

filter Do not allow someone to exploit your time and efforts. This person may not be totally aware of the amount of work you do and this will lead to underpayment and underappreciation. Subtly, point out the amount of work you do for an increase in pay. Good luck is with you. Take advantage of this seven day cycle.

fin Creative ideas that are discussed in a group setting will quickly blossom. Good luck is with you.

find *to search for someone and be unable to find them* Someone you know is desperate to get out of their present living arrangements. This person is unable to help themselves because of physical, emotional or financial reasons. Something is keeping this person from mobilizing themselves to get on with their lives. You will hear about this shortly and this person will come to you for assistance. Within five days you will be able to locate the resources to ease this person's needs and to help them. You will, however, have several discussions with them prior to this. Enter these conversations with caution so you can avoid hurting anyone else's feelings that may be involved. All negotiations you will be involved in whether they involve business, romance or productive conversation will be very successful. You are headed for a brilliant future.

to dream of looking for a boyfriend or girlfriend and being unable to find one This dream implies that there is a situation that you need to divorce yourself from. This issue is something that will soon no longer matter. You must move on with your life. You are trying now to get someone to react to this situation in a certain way, but in a few weeks it will no longer make a difference in your life. Some people need to learn to handle certain issues on their own and have their own experiences so they can evolve and grow. Situations constantly change and need to be handled in different ways. Do not interfere with someone to the point that they become unable to handle issues on their own.

to look for something in particular and find it Within five days you will be very surprised because someone will turn out to be more together than you thought they were. Your original assessment of their character was wrong. You will be joyfully exuberant to discover their true character. You are headed for a brilliant future.

to look for something in particular and be unable to find it You will need advice within seven days. Follow this advice carefully. The information will come to you quickly and you will need to pay close attention. You will need this advice to help structure your plans to accomplish what you desire. If you are unsure of what you are hearing you will need to have it repeated until it is fully understood. You will accomplish what you desire and are headed for a prosperous future.

to look and find what you are looking for (anything, person, etc.) You can expect within the next four days an idea, project or event will be brought to fruition and will reach a higher level of perfection than you ever felt possible. This project will develop a life of its own and you will be able to easily take it through any channel necessary for completion. This will be a blessing to you and everyone involved in this process. An abundance of health, spiritual healing and tranquility will come to you.

in any other form Maintain your composure in delicate situations that will require your personal attention. Compose yourself in such a way that will allow you to buy time until compromises are reached. Because you will take control of the situation, you will come out ahead and experience grand changes in your life.

fine *to use the word* By circulating in select areas, you will be able to see, first hand, what needs to be taking place.

fine *(opposite of coarse)* Do not hesitate to make decisions that are out of the ordinary. These decisions will create changes for the better and will promote a greater prosperity. Go for it.

fine *to pay a fine or be paid a fine* Be very practical and down to earth when dealing with a situation that will arise within three days. You will be called upon to demonstrate valor and confidence and this will allow you to successfully resolve this issue.

fine tooth comb You are headed for a long, healthy, and financially secure life. You are now entering a cycle of prosperity, rejoicing, and tranquility.

finger *in any form* Pay attention to what you are wearing on your finger. If this is something you presently do not own, you will possess this in the near future.

bruised finger Be wary of toxins around children in order to avoid accidental poisoning. Otherwise you will have a brilliant future. Take steps to prevent any negative event foretold in this dream and experience only positive expressions in your life.

cut finger Do not put yourself in a situation that will reflect poorly on your character. Watch your behavior for the next four days.

to snap your fingers Stop being a parent instead of a lover to that special person. Think of ways to add fun and festivity to a relationship.

to break a finger You have a friend who will become a financial drain. Take steps to put a stop to this behavior.

pointing a finger Pay attention to what the finger is pointing at. This will give you a clue to a forthcoming event in your life. This dream also indicates that someone will enter your life who is open for romance.

pinky This dream is a very lucky omen for you. You will win a special prize. Your sense of receptivity is also very strong and your intuition is right on target. Follow your hunches and proceed with confidence.

first finger This is a good time to use your imagination to bring someone closer to you. This is critical for the next two days.

ring finger You will soon find yourself in the position to have to ask for assistance. It will be difficult to ask for help because you know that it will involve a great deal of time from the person giving assistance. This cycle is perfect for getting the help you need without annoying someone else.

to put your finger over your mouth to shush someone or to be shushed by someone This dream is a very lucky omen and implies that you will be in a lucky cycle. You are also being alerted that there is something you need to keep to yourself, especially for the next three days. If you do not, this will result in someone blurting out something that should not be said that they need to keep to themselves. Be aware that someone is keeping something from you that you need to know about. They are waiting for the right time to spring this on you in order to catch you off guard. This will be done for the sole purpose of enjoying your surprised reaction. You will need to do what you can to flush this information out of this person beforehand.

to cross your fingers An event will occur within the week that you should not miss. You will have the pleasure of being in the company of two admirers who will try to win over your affections. Both of these people will be very agreeable and charming but one of them, unbeknownst to you, possesses a great deal of power and authority. You would enjoy having one of them as a lifetime partner. You are on the path toward a very prosperous future.

to drum rapidly Be very alert for the next week. Someone will subtly attempt to bring an unusual opportunity to your attention in an attempt to involve you. Jump at the chance for involvement. This will bring wonderful financial opportunities and benefits to you.

gesture of two fingers over the mouth with the tongue

sticking out Within the week, you will be imbued with a new sense of confidence, balance and a feeling of being solidly grounded. As a result of this, you will be able to handle situations that require this aspect of your personality. Use this cycle to work on those areas of your life that you want to make changes in. You will have the chance to bring prosperity into your life at the level you desire. You are putting yourself on the path toward a brilliant future.

to sign with fingers Think carefully prior to signing an agreement committing yourself to anything. Be very aware of your fluid, food and medicine intake. Be very aware of your health and take steps to protect yourself during this cycle. You will also regret overindulging at a celebration. Be aware of this within the next three days.

deformed or unusually shaped Within five days you will meet someone who appears to have a beautiful, generous, polite and candid demeanor. Do not allow yourself to be deceived by this person because this individual is very devious and hates children although they will lead you to believe otherwise. Be very leery of them and be aware that although they demonstrate a sweet nature, they have a hidden agenda that involves you becoming responsible for each aspect of their life (i.e., financial, emotional, etc.). After you start catering to this person and making sure that their needs are met, they will become aggressive and verbally abusive. You must be very aware of their behavior because they tend to be sneaky and will do things on the sly, especially in regards to your finances. Make sure also, that any negative aspect of this dream that involves your finger is prevented in reality. Otherwise, you are headed for a very healthy long life and will enjoy greater prosperity.

in any other form Within five days, you will finally overcome all long term issues that have become burdens to you. Relentlessly work on any issue that you need to take care of. You will soon experience the freedom that comes from being rid of this issue. You will also soon experience a busy social schedule. Proceed with confidence. Good luck is with you.

finger food Do not allow anyone to handle your finances, especially for the next three days. Remain personally involved in all financial transactions.

fingernails You will hear delightful news within the next two days that will capture your interest. This will involve someone who has just come into town.

unclean and broken nails Do not overlook an upcoming important event that is to take place within three days. Recheck your schedule and be sure to include all important events.

long claw like nails Someone who loves you misses you tremendously. You will learn more about this within three days. Through this relationship you will become empowered in a very beneficial way.

fingernails falling off fingers You will be let down because the hope you had for someone to pay you a certain amount of money by a particular date will not come to be. This person will change their mind about a particular arrangement you have made. Plan on agreements to be broken. Since you have prior notice of this, you will have the opportunity to cover yourself financially.

painted You are beginning to feel a strong emotional urge that will take up a great deal of your time because you have no knowledge of the source of this drive. This drive is causing you to focus on bringing something into tangible form. This urge will continue for a two week period and you will continue to feel this deep emotional drive. Within this time period you will be able to determine the reason and source and begin to act on what you feel you should be doing. This overwhelming urge could be a result of a psychic ability and a heightened awareness that is pushing you in the direction you need to go. Although you have no real proof or verification, you will know on an instinctive level that if you act on this urge you will reap greater benefits than you ever felt possible. You will know this because of the excitement you feel. If you determine that this urge is inappropriate and socially unacceptable, you have enough time and notice to seek out the professional help needed to come to grips with your desires and to live at peace with yourself and these urges. The moment you sense this beginning to develop, seek help. This is the perfect cycle to find the perfect person equipped to handle this event. It will be handled correctly and you will be able to gain control of your emotions in a healthy way. Otherwise you are on the path toward a brilliant future.

finger paint Express your feelings to someone who is unsure about how you feel about them.

fingerprint You will learn, within four days, that someone wants to touch you passionately in the precise manner you wish to be touched. If these are your fingerprints, be careful that you do not commit an unlawful act that will lead to your fingerprints being taken, especially for the next two days.

finish *to finish* Within four days you will meet someone totally different and from a completely different culture. This person will share a gift of creativity that will be of great pleasure to you.

finishing school You will finally be able to introduce your talents to an audience and will enjoy much success. Good luck is with you.

finish line Your passion will be requested and you will be very eager to cater to someone's emotional desires, especially for the next three days. Good luck is with you.

to fail to cross a finish line Make sure that laziness does not take over and control your life. Accomplish necessary tasks now and handle immediately any situation that looks as though it will take a negative turn. If you are working with someone else, take steps to ensure that this person handles important tasks immediately.

to cross a finish line You will have the power in this cycle to victoriously grasp what you need in life.

Finland Any trip to an icy habitat will be fantastic and awesome. This is a good cycle for this. Also a relationship you felt was dying out will reblossom within two days if you express your true feelings. This dream may also be used as a reference point in time. If you dream of this country and see its name used in any context, the dream message will occur on this day.

fir Someone will unexpectedly apologize to you for a past wrong. You will be surprised and glad that this is finally behind you. This will occur within three days.

fire *fire that burns clearly* Your passionate desires will be fulfilled within three days with the person you most desire.

fire that burns smoky You are too eager in your pursuit of the one you most desire. This will create distance between you and this person. Back away, for three days, and you will have a better chance of success.

try unsuccessfully to light a fire You will fail to interest the person you desire. Change your behavior for greater success.

line of fire Make sure for the next five days you do not become involved in a particular situation due to a sense of obligation. You need to get more information before you make any decision. This situation will not be to your advantage and you will be better off not becoming involved.

build a fire Do everything necessary to advertise yourself to the person you desire in order to turn them into a life long mate.

to open fire A promise will be broken within three days. You can prevent this.

to play with fire Do not allow yourself to be placed in the position of having to relate disagreeable news to someone with a bad temper, especially for the next three days.

in any other form You will uncover an unsuspected power in areas you did not suspect. Within two weeks you will become aware of this power and of the high degree of authority you possess. This discovery will motivate you to experiment with different lifestyles and to experience new levels of social functioning. New friends will open your eyes to new experiences and you will be very eager to adopt new ways of living. You will experience gratification in areas you have never experienced before (mentally or emotionally). Doors to greater sources of income from different avenues will also be open to you. Any negative event connected to this dream may be avoided or altered and any positive event may be promoted. You are headed for a brilliant future.

fire alarm Any agreement made with another individual needs to be put in writing to ensure that all details are accurately adhered to. Do this within three days.

fire ant Do not allow yourself to be lured into a love relationship you are not ready for. Make it clear to the other person how you feel in a very tactful and gentle manner.

firearm Do not allow anyone to make unilateral plans involving you that you do not wish to be a part of. Do not give others the authority to make plans for you that you find distasteful. Take care of this problem within four days.

fire away Make sure you do nothing that will result in the loss of your freedom, especially for the next three days. You may be incarcerated for a long period of time.

fireball Take extra precautions in order to avoid any freak accident. Also protect yourself from the threat of bodily injury by another person.

firebird Get a bird's eye view by stepping back and reviewing your options. This is especially important to do within three days.

firebomb Move quickly to head off a situation that is rapidly turning into a crisis. You have two days to take care of this.

fire chief Take the initiative with those who are working closely with you. Become a leader.

firecracker Within three days you will meet someone who will give you the passion you have always desired in life.

fire department Someone will promise you undying love but you will suspect they are interested only in a sexual relationship. Give yourself time to work this through. You will find this person's feelings are genuine and that this individual will wait as long as is necessary for you to feel secure enough to commit to a relationship. You will enjoy a wonderful time within three days with a sexual partner, if you choose.

firedog A situation that has been tearing you apart emotionally will quickly stabilize. Within three days you will find relief from this burden. Immediately following this, you will be offered an all expense paid vacation and life will begin to look up for you.

fire drill You need more practice dealing with a particular situation you are now involved with. Gain more experience and training before you go any further.

fire engine *with siren and lights* Become very protective of someone you are in charge of and responsible for, especially for the next three days. Take steps to ensure that this person does not incur injury, carefully monitor prescription drugs to ensure against accidental overdose, protect the environment against toxins, and guard against food poisoning. This dream also implies that someone has an urgency to express their gratitude to you for work well done.

if you recognize the person driving the fire engine This person needs to take protective measures to guard their safety. Be sure to warn this individual.

without sirens or lights A financial crisis will come up suddenly. Take steps to ensure that you have the funds to cover all emergency needs for the next few days. Start planning for this now. This dream also implies that you are deeply loved by everyone, especially by those you least expect.

to drive You are unknowingly allowing a troublesome situation to develop that needs to be aggressively attended to. Discipline and structure yourself in order to grasp each situation before it disperses to the point of chaos. Once it reaches this point you will lose the ability to start fresh. Push yourself now to resolve each issue and do not allow yourself to get bogged down with extraneous matters that are out of your control. Stay focused and do not allow yourself to be the major cause of unnecessary problems. Focus on the aspect of your behavior that leads to this and do nothing that will cause problems with the law.

in any other form This is a great cycle to tackle any big situation you need to take care of. The outcome will be more favorable if you handle this situation now. Someone will also have a great urgency to talk with you within the next three days to explain, in detail, the facts behind a certain situation they are going through.

fire escape Someone close to you will attempt suicide. Be keenly aware of the behavioral changes of those around you so that you will be able to take steps to prevent this occurrence. This person will be especially vulnerable for the next four days.

fire extinguisher This dream implies that a missing person will be found alive within two days. After it appears that all efforts are exhausted, this person will be successfully located. Don't give up hope.

to extinguish a fire You are adored and loved beyond your imagination. You will see evidence of this within three days.

firefighter Your plans for love will not work out if you continue to follow your present course of action. You will fail to enlist the possibility of love and romance if you do not redirect certain situations. By doing this you will achieve success within three days.

firefly Someone from a distant city will befriend you. You will learn that not only is this person charming and interesting to talk to but also has a great capacity for developing new ideas. You will develop, with this person, a new enterprise that will lead to a future source of income, if you choose to go this route.

fire hydrant Pay careful attention to how you are handling a particular situation. You are unknowingly creating a debt for someone else. It is especially important to attend to this within three days.

fire insurance An earthquake will occur within the month. Prepare yourself ahead of time and make sure that all of your property is properly insured.

fireman/person *if you are unable to clearly see the face* Make sure you are taking proper care of your body. Something may be interfering with your system that is life threatening. Be aware of all medications and potential allergies and guard against all life threatening situations that you may unknowingly create. This is especially important for the next three days.

to see the face of the fireman/person Someone is feigning love toward you but this person is more interested in controlling you and getting what they can from you. This individual will promise a great deal emotionally but will be unable to deliver. Do not compromise your feelings. Stay in control of the situation, especially for the next three days.

to recognize the face Someone will make proclamations of love but you will think this person is only interested in a physical relationship. After you have taken the time to think this through, you will find their feelings are genuine and that this individual will wait until you feel ready to commit to a relationship. You will also enjoy a wonderful time within three days, with a sexual partner, if you choose this option.

fire marks/damage Within three days, a close relative will diplomatically drop subtle hints about a particular area of dissatisfaction in their life that they would like to see you become responsible for. This person wants you to take it upon yourself to make the necessary changes to improve their life. They feel they are stonewalled and cannot get through this situation. You will have the conviction and compassion to do this for them and it will lead them to a far better lifestyle if you choose to take the initiative. Many blessings are with you.

fire opal Someone will enter your life within three days who harbors a great deal of bitterness toward themselves. This person has never been loved in the way they desire. Make sure you do not become a target of revenge for this person. Make it very clear that you wish to continue a friendship but will not be a scapegoat for their misery. This is a good luck omen for those in love, especially if the opal is fiery.

fireplace *without fire* You will soon receive a proposal for marriage. Great plans are in the works for the celebration of this union. This will occur within the month.

with fire Sex will be requested of you and you will be passionately eager to surrender once you know who this person is. You will enjoy many passionate moments with the person of your choice, as well as a lasting union, if you choose this option. Do everything necessary to bring this to reality. This cycle will offer you a green light to bring this about.

fireplug Make sure, within two days, that all of your acquaintances know how you feel about a special person. This will ensure there are no misunderstandings and that no one will mistreat the person you care about.

fire screen Make sure someone does not purposely attempt to block you from pursuing someone you have special feelings for. This will occur within three days.

fire station Do whatever you can to put your feelings of love into action. Leave physical evidence of your feelings in view of the person you care about. This is particularly important for the next three days.

firestorm Do not forget an important event that is planned for the upcoming week. If you do, someone's feelings will be deeply hurt. Prepare a gift in advance and take steps to ensure that everything runs smoothly in order to prevent disappointments.

firewood *lit* Your hunches about someone's romantic feelings toward you will be verified. You will be overwhelmed by love and appreciation from this person.

unlit Focus on and complete a project you are very involved in. This is a good cycle for finally completing this in an accurate and correct manner. You will be very happy with the results.

fireworks You will meet someone, within four days, who is very sharp, well dressed, has a flair for the dramatic, is an interesting conversationalist, generous and well off. This person will want you to join them in their journey through life. If you choose to be with this person, you will enjoy a wonderful future starting with an invitation to a special event. If you go, you will have an awesome time with this person.

firing squad *any form* You will suffer deep emotional hurt within three days. You have prior notice of this and can take steps to prevent it.

first *any form* This dream is an extremely lucky omen and you will be in a lucky cycle for a long period of time. It also implies that you have a good chance of winning at games of chance with small amounts of money. Any enterprise you become involved with over the next three days will be very successful.

first aid Someone will come to you in an attempt to make up for past neglects. Once this issue is resolved you will both enjoy a wonderful friendship.

first base Within the month, you will reach the top of the professional level you are eager for. You will be very practical and your down to earth, simple steps will allow you to grasp this position. Do not allow yourself to lack confidence.

firstborn Take steps to enjoy life to the fullest. You will find pleasures you have never experienced in your life. The best is yet to come.

first class You will be treated like royalty by the person you most desire. You will be happy that you waited patiently, especially for the next three days.

first cousin Do not allow anyone to talk you into spending money that is intended for your essential needs. This is particularly important for the next two days.

first floor Make sure that the young people around you are getting the exercise and proper nutrition they require. These children may be lacking in one of these areas. Take steps to ensure that this is corrected.

First Lady For the next seven days, you will possess an overwhelming sense of solidness, balance and confidence. As a result of this, you will be able to handle those situations that need this aspect of your personality. Work on those areas of your life that you choose to make changes in. You will be presented with the opportunity to bring prosperity into your life at the level you desire. You are on the path toward a brilliant future. This dream is telling you to go full speed ahead and you will achieve victory. Regard the power this person symbolizes as the power you will possess within five days.

first mate Someone you know only slightly will give you a gift purchased in a distant city. You will be overjoyed that this person thought of you and parted with this beautiful item. This will occur within four days.

first time You will experience a big win during this week long cycle that will bring you an abundance of opportunities to choose from. Put yourself in this position by using whatever authority you have at your disposal to complete an agreement in your favor. You will have one week from the occurrence of this dream to become motivated enough to push this agreement through, and it will be well received by everyone involved. You are on a victorious path in life and many blessings will come to you and your family.

fish *in aquarium* Do not become anxious over changes in your relationship. Face these changes head on. You must also do everything necessary to maintain good health and proper blood pressure levels for you and your loved ones.

to fish and come up empty handed You are trying to involve someone in a relationship who is gun-shy. Be patient and do not push this person into a commitment, especially for the next three days because they will balk at this behavior and distance themselves from you. This person will come around in their own time.

large fish Within two days, a fantastic person you care a great deal for will surprise you in their request for private moments with you. You will be very eager to accept this request and this will result in a very enjoyable date.

small fish Do everything necessary not to misinterpret body language and to assume that someone wants you to approach them romantically. This person enjoys playing games and will feign ignorance when you approach them. Be very careful.

fresh Create a beautiful romantic setting for yourself with all of the trappings in order to keep the feelings alive with a certain individual. You will be showered with gifts and attention in return. You are well loved.

salt water fish You will be accused of giving someone the runaround. Your intent was not to give this impression but your actions will be misinterpreted. Take all the necessary steps to keep this from occurring and to avoid hurt feelings.

tropical fish Within the week an abundance of health and wealth will come your way. This dream also implies that a certain situation will take place that will require you to use aggressive behavior. You will act accordingly and this issue will quickly be resolved.

dead fish Do not allow your imagination to recall old tapes that trigger suspicions and jealousies. If you can control your emotions for the next three days, you will find that your doubts are in error and you will be glad you did not make unwarranted accusations. Avoid embarrassment due to your lack of control.

fish trapped in nets Be very careful with a new person in your life. This person will expect more of you than you are able to give. You will be expected to be the answer to all this individual's problems. Be very sure that you do not mislead this person into believing you can give more than you are able to give in friendship. It is also important that you do not restrict yourself with your enjoyment. Treat yourself to a movie, play or other enjoyments.

fish on the line Do not allow someone you do not know very well to involve you in a dangerous unforeseen event. This person has a very violent and jealous mate who will attack you because of a faulty conclusion. Do not place yourself in the position to be injured because of a ménageàtrois situation. This individual is involved with someone other than their mate and, although you are not the one, you will be accused.

to eat fish You will be married in a very short period of time and will enjoy a wonderful future with your mate.

live fish out of water Something will occur that is so unusual and extraordinary that no law of physics can explain it. This will occur within three days and will leave you with a sense of wonder and awe. You will feel as though you have witnessed a miracle with no way of explaining how it all came about. After this takes place you will be able to present yourself to others at your highest level and be able to handle yourself, other people, and situations in the best possible way. You are headed for a brilliant future and many blessings will come to you and your family.

to fish in rough waters Do not allow a dangerous situation to unfold because you become overly confident about what an individual has led you to believe they can do. For the next five days, handle situations promptly and correctly to prevent a chaotic situation from developing.

to catch a fish You will receive good news within five days and be very pleased with the outcome of a business affair you are concerned with.

spoiled fish Be very careful not to lose a priceless possession within the next three days.

fresh water fish Within three days, a major stressful situation will come to an immediate halt because you will find a way to turn this situation to your advantage. You will be able to create a tranquil and peaceful environment for yourself and also hear some surprising good news that will bring you joy for a long time to come. This will be the result of the way you manage certain business dealings.

aggressive fish You are involved with someone who is gun-shy about commitment. Be patient. If, within three days, you begin to make demands that this person be more committed, demonstrative and giving, you will drive them away. You will regret this action.

fish that got away You need to develop the habit, within three days, of tracking down negative situations and resolving them in a positive fashion. This will enable you to keep something you would otherwise lose.

in any other form This dream is an extremely lucky omen. You and your family will experience tranquility and blessings for a long period of time.

fish and chips You will be dealing with two separate situations at the same time. Both are lucky and will bring you prosperity. You are headed in the right direction. Do not lose your confidence and continue doing what you have been doing.

fishbowl Salvage an ongoing long distance relationship. Make sure this person does not feel neglected, especially for the next two days.

fisherman This dream implies riches and health. You are headed in the right direction and will enjoy a brilliant future.

fishery You will enjoy a long healthy life.

fish eye You will see your goals realized.

fish ground Do not allow someone to become involved in your ongoing enterprise if they lack the experience to help out. This will only lead to frustration and a waste of time.

fishhook Do not allow yourself to be lured into doing something other than what you are presently doing. You are headed in the direction you should be going. You will also win a lawsuit.

fishing line Avoid making an error in the direction you are going. Carefully review all of your decisions and make changes that will lead to success.

fishing tackle Prepare yourself now. Within three days, you will be faced with a tremendous amount of work. You need this work very badly and finances will improve dramatically. A family will also need immediate attention within a few days. This will require time and extra finances. Everything will be resolved successfully.

fishmonger Do not interfere in the lives of others, especially for the next three days.

fishpond Someone will demand a great deal of your time and attention, to the point of overwhelming you. This will continue for a few days, then the situation will ease as this person begins to feel more secure with you. Be patient and accommodating until this levels off.

in any other form This dream is an extremely lucky omen. It is also important that you do not venture so quickly into the unknown with someone you have just met. Otherwise, this is a good cycle for romance and love.

fish story You are headed for a brilliant future. The work and ideas you are generating now will provide you with a stable financial base for your retirement years.

fishtail A mystery has had you puzzled for several days but you will uncover the source of the puzzle within two days. Someone has created this situation in order to capture your attention. Once you discover the creator you will be delighted.

fishwife Rise above petty behavior for the next two days and guard against becoming involved in this kind of behavior.

fist Do not allow a rift to occur between you and someone who is close to you because of your actions. Do not put yourself in the position to be gossiped about for the next three days.

fistfight You will be entering a new situation and a new environment. Make sure you have knowledge of all the details surrounding this new circumstance. You may find information that will cause you to want nothing to do with this. Research this within two days.

fit *perfect fit* Take steps to keep anything negative that you dream about from becoming a reality and make sure that you experience only positive events in your life. This dream also implies that you will experience instant wealth that will spring from an unusual and unexpected source. This will be something that will be out of your control and will take place naturally with no help from you. You will enjoy the clarity of thought you need to direct the future. You are on the path for a brilliant life.

fitness Someone will try to control you by creating a big issue out of a small situation. This is done to make you feel like you should be doing more than you are. Make sure you are not manipulated for the next three days.

five This dream implies that your intuition is correct. Develop an optimistic attitude and you will find, within five days, that you will be able to realize the ambitions you thought were impossible to grasp. This number is a good luck omen. Use it for games of chance and invest small amounts of money for big winnings.

five and dime store You possess something that is far more valuable than you imagined. Take care of your possessions and keep them in good shape.

five hundred Any elective surgery intended for self improvement will be a tremendous success, especially for the next month.

five o'clock shadow Do not jump so quickly into the unknown, particularly with situations that will be coming up within three days. Do your research carefully prior to becoming involved in anything new. Make sure you are safe and are headed in the direction you wish to go.

fix Within three days, you will find the solution to an overwhelming problem you felt there was no answer to.

to fix something Be prepared for the next three days for a remarkable and peculiar event to take place. At the same time this is occurring you will have the clarity of thought to take you through the steps to comfortably get through this cycle. You will have a keen curiosity that you must firmly control. Use discipline. You will also enjoy an abundance of health during this cycle.

fizz *to see something fizz* Something will occur within three days that you think will be a disaster. This situation will unexpectedly turn to your favor. You will find success when dealing with desperate situations. Good luck will be with you.

flag *the American flag* Allow the other person to make the first move to settle a grievance between you. This matter will be resolved within a three day period and you will find just the words to clear things up. The other person will be very eager to smooth things over and everything will work out beautifully.

any other flag A significant other will invite you to an elegant event. You will enjoy yourself immensely and will leave feeling refreshed. Go for it.

the flag is up Within two days, you will experience a welcome change of pace. You will be entertaining a great deal, and an aura of romance will enter your life and add just the right touch.

the flag is down Rebel against all thoughts that create a mental block and hinder your progress. You will also hear news of someone passing away.

white flag Move slowly in the direction you will be going for the next three days so you do not miss any important details necessary for future decisions on your behalf.

flag day For the next two days you will need to protect your reputation in those areas where you earn your living. Keep your personal life private.

flag officer For the next two days, keep others from placing unnecessary demands on you. Save your energy for personal entertainment.

flagon You will enjoy many wonderful days with someone special whom you have long desired to share activities with.

flagpole The spiritual nourishment you are asking for will be given to you.

flagship Stay out of the private lives of others and do not let others pry into your private affairs. The use of common sense will benefit you for the next three days.

flag waving Speak what is on your mind, especially for the next two days. Trust, determination, and aggressiveness will put an end to anything that is not in your best interest.

flake *snow flake* Your presence will be requested at many social functions. Your calendar will be crowded and you will enjoy many beautiful times. Good luck is with you.

in any other form Do not expect too much from a young child for the next two days. Change your behavior, this will avert a disaster. You will be respected for a lifetime.

flambé Pay very close attention to what your heart is saying right now. Take a responsive approach and welcome this challenge. For the next two days, the moment will be right to develop a relationship with another person.

flame *blue flame* Get expert advice in order to avoid getting yourself in a tight spot for the next two days.

red flame You will win your heart's desire in love and romance within two days.

in any other form Within two days you will be able to rekindle a love affair because of a new attitude. Push yourself to express yourself during this time period and you will enjoy a long lasting union.

flame eater For the next three days, be very aware that children are very demanding and can put a big strain on another person's time. Be very sure that a child left in the care of another is emotionally able to cope with this situation. If not, you need to find an alternative plan to your present situation.

flamenco dancer You are destined, within two days, to swap ideas with someone who is able to creatively develop new plans. You will be able to mutually develop an idea that leads to prosperity.

flamethrower For the next three days, do not force issues with others.

flamingo Within three days, you will come to terms with your own identity. You will come to realize a part of yourself never seen before that will lead to a sense of pride. This aspect of your personality will carry you through a specific unusual situation within seven days and will result in more self love and appreciation.

flannel Make sure you have all the information before you judge another person. For the next three days you will hear many lies. Be very careful.

flapjack For the next two days you will participate in a major quest. This will motivate others to participate in a significant project and collectively you will be more successful in encouraging others to accept your services.

flapper Do not place yourself in the position to endure the mood changes of another person. Although this individual will not direct their feelings toward you, their mood changes will affect your thinking patterns. Move on with your life without this person in it.

flare Pay attention to what is being illuminated by the flare. This will offer you a clue to what will be occurring in reality. If the foretold event is negative, take the necessary steps to change it. If positive, work to make it a reality. Make it a point, as well to add a bit of pizzazz and glamour to your life in order to accomplish everyday affairs with more ease and grace.

flash Focus on what you need to do to put yourself on the proper course. You are allowing yourself to idle away too much time. Remain focused for greater success, especially for the next three days. You will also be invited to attend an elegant function within five days. You will be very eager and excited to attend.

flashback *to experience a flashback in the dream* Pay close attention to the particular event in the flashback. This will be either an experience you will wish to recreate or one you will choose to avoid. You have the time now to change, recreate and enhance any forthcoming event. This dream also implies that you need to keep your distance from someone who is going to great lengths to get close to you. By doing this, you will keep disappointment from entering your life.

flashbulb Do not allow yourself to fall back into a situation you dealt with in the past. Do not reopen doors to past events you have no business being involved with at the present time. Let the past remain the past.

flash card Pay attention to what was depicted on the flash card. This will offer you a clue that will foretell an event you will either want to enhance or alter. You will also gain the confidence you need to communicate something of importance. You will be able to get your point across to someone special. Your words will be well received and lead to your emotional fulfillment.

flashcube Within three days, you will learn of the death of someone you know. You must also become very consistent and resourceful in your present dealings. Look at situations from different perspectives in order to achieve greater success.

flasher Within five days, you will offer assistance to someone who has requested your help in reaching an agreement with another person. You will not have to go to extremes to complete this task. Good luck is with you.

flash flood Trust your intuition for the next three days and use common sense in all your dealings. Be sure you are giving the right impression to those who are important to you. Do not leave any room for misinterpretation. Good luck is with you and you will have the strength and conviction during this cycle to complete your tasks.

flashlight Someone will eagerly put you in touch with those who can help you in whatever you need assistance with. You will be able to launch your plans in the direction you choose. This will be a very victorious time for you. Make sure you also keep a flashlight on hand. Circumstances will present themselves, within five days, that will necessitate the use of one.

flask You and another person will go to great lengths to arrive at an agreement you can both live with. Good luck is with you. Make compromises in order to ensure that this takes place within five days. This will work very much to your advantage.

flat Within two days, become verbally assertive when discussing your plans with another person in order to make your intentions clear to them. This will allow this individual the opportunity to open up and come to an agreement about what can be mutually accomplished. Everything will work out as planned.
　　anything with a flat design You will definitely get a lucky break. Take all the necessary steps to maintain a relationship at the highest level you can. Do your part to maintain closeness. Love and affection will help you focus on important issues instead of wasting your energy. You are both headed for a prosperous future.

flatbed You will receive a thrilling gift from someone you least expect.

flatcar Participation with others will bring greater success to your ongoing projects, especially for the next three days. Certain situations will also require more personal involvement during this time period.

flatfoot Do everything you can to stop being so mean to others. Nothing gives you the authority to behave in this manner. This behavior is unwarranted and will only lead others to avoid you. You can avoid a lonely life by learning to curb this behavior and by disciplining yourself.

flat rates You will be overcome with excitement within two days over an unexpected gift that you will receive. You can also expect an abundance of health during this time period.

flatter Within three days, you will need to use patience and understanding when a young person comes to speak to you about their first romantic situation. Treat this young person with respect and warmth. This conversation will always be remembered by this youngster.

to flatter someone Because of special circumstances that will occur within two days, you will know who your true friends are.

to be flattered You will receive an unexpected gift that is totally unconnected to any special date.

flatulence For the next two days you will enjoy a period of calmness in your life. You will find relief from your over-crowded schedule due to an unexpected circumstance. Maintain a less stressful schedule from now on.

flatware Take the time you need to look at the whole picture when a certain issue comes up within three days. You will then have the time to clearly understand what is going on and this will allow you to make the way you are living the most important thing right now. Proceed with confidence. You are headed for a prosperous future.

flavor *to taste something that has a flavor other than what is expected* You will have a physical reaction to a prescription medication. Be very aware of any drug that will result in an allergic reaction.

flavoring Within three days, you will enjoy an unexpected improvement in your financial status due to an unforeseen circumstance. Any problem you are seeking a solution to will be resolved.

flax You will enjoy an abundance of health and will be able to use this cycle very much to your advantage.

flaxseed Prepare more nourishing meals, drink more water and seek entertainment that makes you feel good.

flea This dream implies riches.

fleabag Do not put pressure on someone to commit to a relationship they are not ready for, especially for the next two days.

fleabite Within three days, someone will behave in such a way that will create anger and jealousy in you. This will be done on purpose. Since you have prior notice of this, ignore the behavior.

to kill fleas You will receive pleasurable news from a friend and will seek entertainment that will bring pleasure to you.

flea circus Watch out for deadly insect bites for the next five days.

flea market A good friend will request your company on a trip to see a sick parent. The trip will be successful and you will return with wonderful refreshing memories, if you choose to go.

fleece The person who is attempting to start a relationship with you will give the impression this is exactly what they want when, in reality, they simply want a sexual relationship. Afterwards you will not hear from them again. Think carefully before becoming involved.

fleet *(of ships)* Within three days, a natural disaster will occur. Prepare yourself to ensure that you, your family, and your possessions remain safe.

flesh Open communication and show affection toward the person you are emotionally involved with. Put your feelings into action. This person has no clue of your true feelings and is feeling neglected. It is especially important to do this within three days.

decayed flesh You are allowing your loved ones to outgrow you by hanging on to old patterns of behavior you need to outgrow. Bring loved ones closer. Focus on changing your behavior for the next three days.

detached flesh You will be pleasantly surprised within five days, on three separate occasions. The first will be as a result of an unexpected gift, the second after hearing the words you have longed to hear, and the third after learning of an unexpected financial windfall. This is also the perfect opportunity to pursue what you once felt was impossible. All things are possible now.

flesh and blood Become aware of your selfish behavior and take steps to change it within three days. You are purposely depriving someone of the words they long to hear from you.

flesh eater A deep inspiration will come to you and will serve as a great motivator. You will find out within three days that you are better prepared than you thought. You will be more motivated than ever before during this time period.

flesh wound Pay attention to the cause of the wound and take steps to prevent this in reality. If this injury occurred to another in the dream whom you recognize, warn this person to be careful and to avoid this occurrence in reality. This dream also implies that within three days, someone will extend an unexpected kind gesture toward you. Make sure you remain safe.

fleur de lis You will be with a group of friends who will be very eager to attend a big event. As things progress, you will find that expenses will grow at a faster rate than you expected. Make sure you are not talked into spending more than you should.

flex *to flex muscles* Within three days, you will receive many wonderful appraisals for work well done. You will also have a great time in a new city. You will spend only a brief time there on your way somewhere else but the memories will be delightful. You are entering a wonderful cycle.

flicker Information you thought would be impossible to receive will come to you faster than you anticipated. This will occur within two days.

flier Display your charming, proper upbringing and education and you will be admired by influential people within the next five days. Do not allow timidity to hold you back.

flight Within three days, you will need to practice common sense when making a decision concerning sex. This will be an important feature in your life. Do not ignore your feelings. Enjoy life to the fullest but take responsibility for your personal safety.

to see someone else in flight Make sure you keep all personal affairs to yourself when conversing with a new person, especially for the next two days.

if you recognize the person in flight This person is very anxious to help you reach a special goal, especially for the next three days.

to see yourself in flight You will recover your financial status within three days as a result of a windfall that you will receive from a friend. This person has come into wealth and will insist that you share in their good fortune.

to see yourself or someone being lifted by something into the air Make it your business to place yourself into the area it is necessary for you to be in, in order to save a situation in the nick of time. You have prior notice of this and will be able to figure out, just in time, what you need to be doing. This situation will fall into place just as you desire. Move quickly, confidently, and courageously, especially for the next five days.

flight attendant A family member will receive a large financial settlement. You will also be traveling to an unfamiliar city within the week. Make friends with someone there in order to ensure you have help if you need it. Good luck is with you.

flight bag Within three days, you will find a solution to a very critical situation.

flight control Someone is not being honest with you. This person has a contagious disease that you may contract. Be very cautious about exposing yourself to something that could be transmitted to you, especially for the next three days.

flight crew You will enjoy a family reunion with much food and festivities. Do whatever you can to contribute to the fun and food, and be sure to actively participate in the festive mood.

flint Someone with creative talents will fall deeply in love with you. Be prepared for this to occur within five days.

flintlock Be prepared. Within two months you will allow yourself to commit to someone and you will shortly celebrate your own wedding.

flirt Someone will steer you the wrong way emotionally.

This person runs hot and cold because they lack control over their reactions and have no idea of the direction they want to take. Be aware that within three days you will encounter this behavior. Be understanding, remain calm, and get on with your life.

to flirt with someone You will be unexpectedly repaid for a favor performed so long ago that you have forgotten it.

to be flirted Someone will mistake the date of your birth and will give you a present months prior to the actual date. It is up to you whether you want to keep it or to return it with an explanation.

to flirt heavily with someone and have them flirt right back with you An abundance of health, spiritual healing and tranquility will come to you within a three week period. Within the week a celebration will also take place that will cause rejoicing among everyone involved. You can expect an idea, project or event to be brought to fruition. It will reach a higher level of perfection than you ever felt possible. This project will develop a life of its own and you will be able to easily take it through any channel necessary for completion. This will be a blessing to you and to everyone involved in this process and be a cause for celebration for everyone. You are headed for a brilliant future.

float Within three days, you will need to practice common sense when making a decision concerning sex. This will be an important feature in your life. Do not ignore your feelings.

the floatation of anything unusual You will develop a clear idea about what needs to be taking place with a special person. Be clear about the steps you want to take emotionally. Victory is yours and you will successfully accomplish what you set out to accomplish. You will also need to be forewarned to take special precautions to prevent anything you feel should not be floating in water from occurring in reality. This is especially important for the next two days.

to float in air You will be taking big steps that will enable you to raise your standard of living. You will be able to do this by focusing on your goals in a grand way. This will come about because of an unusual and joyful circumstance that will take place within two days. Each person involved will enjoy beautiful expressions of joy and tranquility. Many blessings will come to you and your family.

to see anything unusual floating in toilet water Make sure this does not take place in reality. Also, someone will be so satisfied and happy with your attitude that they will want to demonstrate their feelings, but will keep this a secret until you are in a position of privacy and it can easily be revealed. You are loved beyond your imagination by people you least expect.

to see someone float in air Make sure that you keep all personal affairs to yourself when conversing with a new person, especially for the next two days.

if you recognize the person in flight This person is very anxious to help you reach your special goal, especially for the next three days.

to see yourself in flight You will recover your financial status within three days. You will receive a windfall from a friend who has come into wealth and they will allow some of this to trickle down to you.

flock Quickly return to basics and learn to practice more simplicity in life. Do not needlessly use time for unnecessary tasks.

flog For three days, you and your family will enjoy an abundance of good luck and good health. Victory is yours.

flood You need to focus on what needs immediate attention. You will then be able to reach a very important decision, on a very important matter. Do this within two days. For the next seven days a variety of equally important troublesome situations will also arise. Work at your top level on each of them to ensure they are successfully resolved. Remain flexible, calm and relaxed while handling each experience. Your life will once more reach a balance.

floor Someone will be very offended by your honesty. You will lose a friend, within two days, due to your frankness.

first floor Make sure that the young people around you are getting the exercise and proper nutrition they require. These children may be lacking in one of these areas. Take steps to ensure that this is corrected.

second level The opportunity you have been waiting for will arise within two days and you will make a new start in all areas of your life. All old burdens and issues that have been dragging you down will come to a halt. Major changes will add a new excitement and a new dimension to your life and you will develop and execute plans in all phases of your life.

with a hole knocked in it Within three days you will be dealing with a very evil and conniving person who presents a sweet facade and will give you the impression they will do almost anything to keep you happy. Something, however, about you triggers a desire in them to hurt you. This behavior is a result of their past, the way their mother treated them, etc. You will be able to identify who the person is by traces left in the dream (i.e., appearance, speech, clothing, etc.). This individual will use their charm and winning ways to trick you and purposely screw up your plans. You will eventually figure this out but since you have prior notice of this, you can turn it around so you can handle life appropriately and avoid a great deal of hurt.

floorboard Stop being so short tempered with people who love you.

flophouse Someone will come into your life, within three days, who has a difficult time controlling their obsessive behavior. Do everything you can to set limits way ahead of time in order to avoid hurt feelings later on.

floppy disk Do not agree to something you do not want. Any pertinent information you feel should be entered into a computer also needs to be recorded on a disk and any information you do not want entered needs to be guarded from others. Safeguard each entry from erasure due to a computer virus. Do not allow yourself to become involved in an uncomfortable situation because you were not paying attention to what you were doing. For the next five days, pay close attention to your surroundings and avoid making a mistake in any capacity. This is especially important when dealing with financial matters.

Florida A member of your family will give you an all expense paid vacation. You will learn of this within five days. Good luck will be with you. This dream may also be used as a reference point in time. If you dream of this state and see its name used in any context, the dream message will occur on this day.

Florida Keys You will need to do extra research, within three days, in a new area you will soon become very involved in. Once you become focused on this particular area, structure your activities and gather as much information as you can as soon as you can. This will lead to a rapid acceleration to your goal. This dream may also be used as a reference point in time. If you dream of this island group and see its name used in any context, the dream message will occur on this day.

florist Someone who loves to create envy will flaunt their possessions. Do everything necessary to prevent a feeling of inferiority. Get on with your life.

floss Do not allow your emotions to control you. Meet all issues head on and take steps to resolve them.

flounder Someone will do everything within their power to manipulate you into spending more than you can afford. This dream also implies that victory is yours and good luck is with you.

flour Within three days, you will have to defend someone who will be punished for something they did not do. You will suffer later on if you do not help this person.

flower This dream will be a very lucky cycle for you. You will be making up for a loss of social activity with a wonderful group of people.

to give flowers You will share much laughter with a new group of people you will be meeting within four days. You will cement friendships and enjoy shared hobbies.

to be given flowers You will be able to bond closer with someone you desire for a permanent relationship.

if you remember the person you gave flowers to This person has a great deal of affection toward you and has an urgency to speak with you about their deep feelings.

plastic flowers You will be with that special person for a lifetime and will enjoy each moment. This dream also implies that an unusual event will take place within a few days. This will bring you much joy and happiness.

wild flowers This is the time, within three days, to arrange your life in such a way that you will automatically have the power you need in certain situations and will have your wishes granted in the manner you desire. You will have no limitations, especially for the next seven days.

wind flower Someone will come to your assistance in the nick of time. Help is on the way.

flower bed You will be well rewarded for work well done in the past. This hard work will start paying off now. For the next five days, you will enjoy the mobility this extra money allows you to have. You are headed for a brilliant future. You will also enjoy being entertained by someone you care a great deal about and this will lead to a sense of joy and tranquility.

flower child An event is scheduled for the upcoming week that would be to your advantage to attend. You will be in the company of two admirers and will have the pleasure of watching them try to win over your affections. Although it doesn't show, one of them possesses a great deal of power and authority and you will find both to be very charming and agreeable. You would enjoy having one of them as a life long partner. You are headed for a prosperous future.

flower girl Within three days, you will meet and fall in love with someone who will demand a great deal of attention from you. This person is very generous, affectionate and giving. This relationship will work out very well, if you choose to go in this direction.

flowerpot Protect yourself, and do not allow yourself to be taken in by a scam that requires that you give a small amount of money on a regular basis over a period of time. After this amount is tallied, it will add up to a substantial amount of money.

flower shop Develop a more romantic attitude and go all out for a romantic evening.

flu You need to protect yourself from being exposed to any virus. Get plenty of rest and drink plenty of water for the next five days to build up your resistance. Aggressively take charge of your health because any virus will take a long time to recover from. You will also receive an unexpected wind-fall within seven days.

if you see someone you recognize with the flu Take steps to warn this individual of this possible occurrence in reality.

fluid Pay attention to the color of the fluid and look it up for a major clue to the meaning of this dream. This dream also implies that within three days you will receive a new inspiration that will drive you to create something wonderful in your life.

fluids *(body)* You will enjoy a wonderful night in front of a fireplace with someone you desire after a romantic evening. This dream is also a very lucky omen for you.

fluorescent lamp Within two days someone who wants to have a conversation with you will pin you down in order to force a mutual agreement. You will be glad this took place because it will be more successful than you anticipated.

fluoride Great riches will soon come to you. Make sure you remember your old friends.

flush *to flush* Success, in the areas you choose, will come much faster than you expected. This dream also implies that you are headed toward a brilliant future.

flute Put everything down in detail when you anticipate that changes will be made. Leave nothing for the last minute or to anyone's imagination. Do this for the next few days and you will see many great changes in your life.

flutist Someone is suffering because you do not spend enough time with them. If you desire this person in your life, put your feelings into action.

fly *(flight) to take off or to see someone take off* Do not push yourself on someone who is totally disinterested in you. This person is not interested in developing a relationship. Get busy with something else and move on with your life.

to see someone fly in the air Make sure, when you are talking to someone that you keep all personal matters to yourself, especially for the next two days.

if you recognize the person in flight This individual will be very eager to help you reach a special goal, particularly for the next three days.

to see yourself fly Your financial status will improve dramatically within three days. A friend will receive a wind-fall and this wealth will trickle down to you.

to see anything unusual in flight You will develop a clear idea of the emotional steps you need to take regarding a special person. Victory will be yours and you will accomplish what you set out to accomplish. Take steps to keep anything negative in this dream from becoming a reality, especially for the next three days.

in any other form For the next three days you will have to use common sense when making a decision regarding sex. This is an important aspect of your life and you need to make a point of paying attention to your feelings.

fly *(the insect)* Each goal and ambition you have will be realized. Victory will be yours. The number of flies indicate the degree of achievement.

white fly A certain possession of yours needs to be more protected. Take stock of what you own and make sure that a certain possession does not get lost, stolen or destroyed due to your neglect. Cover your bases for the next three days to make sure that this does not occur.

fly casting For the next three days list your priorities in order to budget your time.

flycatcher Make sure you remain uninvolved in quarrels.

For the next three days, you must also keep the lines of communication open with someone who seems to want out of your life.

flyer You will be gifted with accurate intuitive thoughts as well as the ability to rid yourself of negative thoughts and attitudes. This will come about at the precise time needed and you will no longer be hampered by negativity. Proceed with confidence as well as a calm attitude in spite of anything else that may be occurring in your life right now. You are headed for a full life rich with enjoyment and filled with interesting and influential people.

fly fishing You will find much more enjoyment in life if you add a touch of romance to everything you do. You will also receive a great favor from a very powerful person. Moments of solitude will physically regenerate you and luck will be with you for the next two months.

flying buttress This dream implies that you are moving too fast for the plans you have made. Slow down your pace for at least a week in order to regroup and detail you goals more thoroughly.

Flying Dutchman Prepare ahead for a possible last minute change of plans and you will be able to move ahead and meet your challenges. You will then be able to reap greater benefits.

flying fish A stressful situation will worsen within two days if you fail to keep your promises. This dream also implies prosperity in all levels of your life.

flying fox Someone will attempt to lure you into a secluded place for the intention of causing you harm. Take steps to protect yourself.

flying people Within two days, you will be completely mesmerized by a glamorous, hypnotic person who will unexpectedly enter your life. You will quickly become good friends and find your life filled with social events and exciting activities. The glamour will also rub off on you and you will lead a more exciting life from now on.

flying saucer You will pay a small amount for a ticket to an unusual event or travel, but as time progresses the cost of the ticket will reach immense proportions to those who are just purchasing it. Your ticket will still be valid at no additional cost. The chance to purchase this ticket will occur in the near future.

flying squirrel You are headed for a brilliant future. Within two days you need to involve yourself in many areas that are not ordinary activities for you, and you will be able to pinpoint what you are destined to become involved in.

flypaper Within three weeks begin the process of wiping your slate clean of all debts. Work toward putting your finances in the black. Certain circumstances will arise during this time frame that will enable you to do this.

flyswatter Take some of those tough assignments you are required to do and delegate them to someone else. A team effort will enable projects to be completed on time and in the manner you wish under your supervision. For the next three days you must also give yourself flexibility to handle a number of troublesome issues that are headed your way. Handle each one as it comes up in a very calm manner. Treat each problem as a challenge and you will be successful.

flywheel You will have to set aside some spare time during your busy routine. Certain circumstances will unfold that will require some flexibility in your schedule and this extra time will enable you to successfully complete these tasks. You can also expect a windfall of riches within the week.

foal You will spend beautiful moments with someone you have not seen for a very long time. You will have many wonderful memories that will stay with you for a lifetime. This is a wonderful cycle for you and good luck is with you. Play games of chance and stay organized and focused.

foam Do everything you can to promote group activities and to include people who are important to you in your life. These people are beginning to feel left out. It is important to do this within three days.

fodder Anything that appears unusual or out of the ordinary signifies something you should not become involved with. This situation will arise within three days. This dream also implies that grand changes will bring you prosperity.

fog Do everything necessary to stop focusing on one person whom you are unwittingly cruel and hard on. Take steps to change this behavior.

fog bank Someone who dislikes you is waiting impatiently for you to fail. You can prevent this by correcting, within three days, anything that appears to be headed toward a dead end with your career. Luck is with you to make these changes.

foghorn Make sure you arrive at a planned destination at the appointed time. Failure to arrive on time will lead to anger on the part of the person who awaits you and this will spoil your future relationship.

foil *(wrap)* Within three days, you will be able to successfully express a point of dissatisfaction with someone in power, without any rebuttal.

foil *(fencing sword)* A close male member of your family who lives in a distant city desperately needs your help but has difficulty expressing their needs. Make it your job to reach out to this person and to offer your assistance, especially for the next two days.

fold You will, for three weeks, be developing a creative project that will lead in a year's time to a successful profit making venture.

to see anything folded Your wishes will be fulfilled.

folder Be careful when pleasure seeking. Someone will try to violate your rights.

foliage *dead* You will receive distasteful news about a friend within two days.

folic acid You are headed in the wrong direction romantically. If you become involved with the person you are interested in you will experience cruelty, but will have difficulty leaving the situation. You can avoid involvement. Get on with your life without this person.

folk Be persistent and consistent in areas of your life that require this trait.

folkdance You will receive gifts of flowers from someone whom you least expect within five days.

folklore Express your pleasure verbally to someone else within five days.

folk music You will experience domestic tranquility and prosperity within the family unit. All fighting, and domestic problems will cease for a very long time.

folk song You will join a group of people who will teach you a great deal about yourself. This group will bring you a great deal of joy within five days.

follow You will be introduced to a lifestyle that is totally different from your own. You will experience a wealth of new ideas and impressions of life that will bring you pleasure for months.

to follow someone You have been waiting for help on a particular matter you have been handling. You will receive the help you need within the week. You will then be able to tie up all loose ends.

to be followed Do not allow anyone to put you in the position to experience envy or jealousy. Use this energy for something more productive, especially for the next three days. This person is playing games on purpose.

to dream of following someone and not being able to catch up You need to be brief and to the point and must not allow yourself to be conned by anyone, especially for the next two days.

to ask someone to follow you and they do not Within five days you will be dealing with someone who will mislead you into believing they are well respected, stable in their career, financially secure and enjoy a very credible lifestyle. You will feel very comfortable in their presence and will believe everything they say. This person wants to become a part of your life, would like you to be a part of theirs, and will lead you to believe you will be able to reach them at any time you wish. They will give you several phone numbers, company addresses, etc. But if you try to reach this person, you will find it will take days for them to get back in touch with you. You will not be able to directly contact this person and you will also realize you have been led to believe they have a much more impressive lifestyle than they do. If you choose to become involved with this person you will be in for a big disappointment. Become disciplined and very cunning in order to keep this person from violating your emotions or insulting your intelligence. You will be able to handle this successfully. You are entering a very lucky cycle and are headed for a prosperous future.

followers You will develop the courage to express yourself to a very influential group of people. You will be able to get your point across and gain a greater sense of independence.

follow the leader Immediately contact an attorney about a situation that will develop within two days. This matter is best handled by a legal professional.

follow through Many things are beginning to occur late at night that are strange and unexpected. Be aware of this for the next three nights and do not become involved in anything that could make you a victim of crime.

follow up Follow your instincts and take steps to determine what someone else is planning. It will be to your advantage to get to the bottom of an ongoing situation and resolve it quickly.

fond Someone new will come into your life with some unusual information that will enable you to realize your ideas, ambitions and potential. This information will assist you in furthering your career to the level you desire.

fondle This dream is a lucky omen for you. Carefully guard your cash to ensure against pickpockets.

to fondle someone Someone you have known for awhile will become a special person in your life.

you don't recognize the person you are fondling This person is very eager to communicate with you and desires to experience emotional affection from you. You will have evidence of this within three days.

to recognize the person you are fondling This person, in reality, is very eager to offer assistance and to rush to your aid whenever you need them. Do not deprive or limit yourself emotionally. Enjoy life to its fullest but play it safe at the same time.

to recognize the person who is fondling you This person would like very much to involve themselves in your life and will eagerly come to your assistance when you need them. You will also sense an unusual power you were not aware that you have in certain areas of your life. Once you experience and use this power, it will place you in a very favorable position in life. Go full speed ahead with confidence. Everything will work out beautifully for you.

to be fondled You need to quickly arrive at a plan to ensure that situations are being properly carried through.

font You are in a very good position to demand what you want from your deity. Be direct and specific about your wants and needs. For the next three weeks you will be developing a list of priorities that will serve you as an aid in supervising the way you live your life. Take the time to reflect in peace and tranquility.

food The product you plan to market will be a great success. Move on this quickly in order to benefit from this cycle.

to eat food Whatever you are waiting for will fall neatly into place.

a shortage of food You will be dealing with someone who displays a normal temperament but in the middle of the conversation, this person will start problems with you and everyone else involved. This will lead to a very stressful moment for everyone involved. Do whatever you feel is necessary to spare yourself this distasteful moment.

junk food Do not focus on what is taking place in your life. Focus, instead, on what is not taking place that has not been fully addressed by you.

spoiled food The person you are trying so hard to please will never appreciate your efforts. You are dealing with someone who does not care for you in the manner you desire. Otherwise, you are entering a lucky cycle for the next seven days. Be watchful of the above situation for the next three days.

to find anything unusual in your food Be acutely aware, for the next three days, of someone who will go to great lengths to cause you emotional pain. This will come from someone you least expect. Protect yourself from the unexpected. Guard yourself against accidents and from tainted food.

an abundance of food Within five days, you will experience emotional fulfillment due to the sincerity someone displays toward you. The kindness and generosity shown by this individual will elate you. Good luck is with you. Make sure also that you have an extra supply of food. Guests will drop in unexpectedly and you need to make sure there is enough to go around.

to eat food with other people This is the best time to show others the very best you have to offer and to display your best qualities when it comes to nurturing someone else. This will even come as a surprise to you when, within three days, you will have a calm and soothing effect on someone who is not treating you well. Within three days you will also be dealing with a cluster of people who are interested in you and you will share your feelings and emotions with each of them in a profound and touching way. You are being forewarned about this because you will be caught off guard by the demands these admirers put on you. You will be able to handle this successfully, will treat each one with equanimity, and fulfill each one's emotional expectations. Go ahead and share yourself with as many people as you desire because you will be able to handle this appropriately, treat yourself with respect, and surround yourself with those who love and respect you. None of these people will know each other but

will come to you at separate times, one after the other. You will enjoy an abundance of health and are on the path toward a victorious future. Many blessings are with you and your family.

soul food Within five days you will be given the gift of greater healing and heightened psychic powers by your special divinity. You will develop greater organizational skills and be able to put this talent to use in a dynamic way. You will be able to use this gift wisely and many blessings will follow you for a lifetime. You are headed for a brilliant future.

to spill your food You and another person will go down a path that will, unbeknownst to you, be very dangerous because of an unfortunate event that will take place. Speak with this other person in order to reschedule an event you are planning within the next few days. You can avoid this dangerous situation.

plant food You have all of the information you need to give to a certain person who is seeking advice. When this person comes to you, open up and give them exactly what they need to run their life more efficiently.

food chain Take steps to behave in the appropriate manner toward someone with a conniving nature. You will become more aware of this behavior as time progresses.

food cycle Do not allow yourself to get too deeply involved with a family member who is headed in the wrong direction. If there is anything you can do to help, offer assistance but otherwise do not become involved. It is very important to do this for the next three days.

food poisoning Do everything necessary to avoid eating tainted food. If you dream of someone you recognize with food poisoning, issue the proper warning to them. This dream also implies that you need to stop being so trustful of others and become more watchful for the next three days .

food processor You will hear news of a riding accident that will involve a friend of yours. Warn any friend who enjoys horseback riding of this possibility. This dream also implies that you need to take extra precautions when riding in any vehicle to avoid accidents.

food stamps Take the proper measures to avoid a money shortage for the next three days.

fool Within three days, you will experience a change that will give you permission to express yourself intellectually and creatively. This dream is a very lucky omen.

foolish Within three days you will be approached by someone with a once in a lifetime offer. Together, with a small investment, this opportunity will bring you both a very prosperous future.

fool's gold Someone, within three days, will be very eager to grant you a favor. This person is in the position to pull strings on your behalf. Your life will change for the better.

foot A wonderful older person will do everything possible to ensure your happiness.

best foot forward - to hear this phrase You will be asked, within five days, to do something you felt was next to impossible. You will be able to acquire the proper information to handle this correctly. Success will be yours.

put your foot down - to hear this phrase Organize yourself and do everything necessary to bring success into your life.

under foot - to hear this phrase You will undergo unbearable emotional pain within three days. You will find yourself unable to explain this situation to anyone. At the first sign of stress, remove yourself from the environment and write a letter to those involved in order to clear up the issue.

sole of foot This dream is an extremely lucky omen. Anything you felt was impossible is now a possibility for you within the next two days. Also, prepare yourself for an enormous surprise that will catch you off guard and fill you with enormous joy. Good luck is with you and you will enjoy yourself immensely during this time period.

to drop something heavy on your foot or someone else's Do not allow yourself to be put in a position to be mauled or injured by an animal, especially for the next five days.

foot and mouth disease Rid yourself of self-hatred. Develop a more compassionate attitude toward yourself and plan activities that will bring you joy.

football You will be the object of another's affections. If you choose to allow this to develop, this person will come to love you deeply. This will occur within seven days. Do whatever you can to maintain tranquility and harmony within the family unit, especially during this cycle.

football player Within a three day period, you will be able to detail and calibrate your thoughts in such a way that will enable someone to feel comfortable around you. The conversation will flow and you will both develop a sense of closeness toward each other. This person will speak the words they have been longing to say. You are on the path toward a brilliant future and will be able to reach others through your words. You and this person will enjoy a wonderfully tranquil life, if you choose to go this route.

footlocker Avoid heavy strain and avoid performing any unnecessary tasks. Take time to relax and enjoy tranquility for the next three days.

footloose Watch out for someone who is unable to control their intake of alcohol. This person could cause you embarrassment at a special outing within three days.

footpath Do not place yourself in the position of being taken advantage of sexually. Be very clear about what you want and keep yourself safe. This person has a long history of sexual abuse and of getting away with it.

footprint Within three days, you will come to understand exactly how much someone wishes to see you. This person will ask to meet in five days but will then call and request your presence within two days, then right away. Make sure your physical appearance is up to par and avoid being caught off guard. Otherwise, this is a good luck symbol.

footrace You will accomplish much more on your own than working with someone else's support, especially for the next two days.

to lose a foot race Remain watchful, for two days, of another's violent reactions. Do nothing to provoke this behavior in others.

to win a foot race You will achieve victory in the areas you most desire.

foot soldier Do not allow others to push you into a relationship you do not want. Speak up for yourself.

footstep A casual friend of someone you know will attempt to start an argument with you. Be aware of this and take steps to prevent it.

footstool Get the proper amount of rest in order to avoid becoming a monster and taking it out on your loved ones. Attempt to promote peace between those you care about.

forage Someone will create an atmosphere to arouse your suspicions and make you feel there is something you need to know. Ignore this behavior and find better uses for your time.

forbid For the next three days you will be involved in pleasure seeking activities. This will take you on a dangerous path. A precarious situation will arise as a result of this behavior. Keep yourself safe and find better means of enjoyment.

to be forbidden Make sure your travel routes are well drawn out to ensure a safe trip.

to forbid someone Do not deprive yourself of what could be a beautiful and long lasting relationship.

forbidden fruit Become very aware of the negative game playing of others in order to prevent your own thoughts from becoming contaminated. This is especially important for the next three days.

force Pay close attention to what you are being forced to do in this dream. This implies a forthcoming event that, in reality, you may want to prevent. Make sure you do not place yourself in the position of allowing someone to exert this much control over you. This dream also implies that someone will go to great lengths to create chaos between you and someone else. Be keenly aware of this for the next three days in order to keep this relationship from going sour.

to force someone Practice control and discipline for the

upcoming week in order to avoid forcing yourself on another. Practice this in all areas of your life.

to see yourself or someone else force something to fit Within the week you will find the motivation to bring more changes into your life. You will put more emphasis on the work you need to accomplish in order to bring you more prosperity. Many blessings are with you and your family.

force feed *to be force fed* Conversation for the next two days will be filled with complaints, problems and issues that need to be taken care of. Remain flexible and do what you can to offer assistance in any way you can. Avoid becoming involved in situations that do not involve you, in spite of the insistence of others.

to see someone force fed Be very careful when pleasure seeking and make sure you do not allow someone to give your power to someone else. Someone wants to gain control of a certain situation you are dealing with and they will attempt to manipulate you in order to gain power over you. Make sure that you do not fall prey to this person.

forceps Within five days you will hear unexpected bad news about a friend. This person will commit suicide. If you have any feeling that a friend is in trouble, offer a listening ear and any necessary help to prevent this occurrence.

forearm Someone who has no business doing so will begin to make demands on you. Set this person straight and refuse to accept these demands.

forebrain You are headed for a brilliant future. Do not allow anyone to steer you from your path. Your intuition is right on target.

foreclose/foreclosure Someone with a charismatic, persuasive personality will lead you to believe they are good for the money owed you. This is a large sum of money but you will feel comfortable that they will come through. In reality, this person doesn't have a cent to pay. Do not place yourself in the position of being owed a substantial amount of money, especially for the next three days.

forefather You will be entering a stage of grand self-improvement and will enjoy each moment. You will vastly alter your physical appearance.

foreground Do everything necessary to keep yourself from being corralled into involving yourself in a difficult situation. This will take longer to resolve than you ever anticipated.

forehead You will be given the gift of greater creative and ingenious thought for the next three weeks. Take advantage of this cycle and record each thought. You will be able to develop an idea that will take you on a very prosperous path.

to see yourself or someone else put your forehead against another person Be very cautious and aware of where your feelings are leading you. Someone will, for reasons only they are aware of, lead you to believe you are

loved completely by them. This person may or may not use words of love at this time but will create an air of romance by sending gifts, flowers and taking you on romantic outings. Your feelings will grow deeper and stronger than theirs and if you allow the possibility of lovemaking, you will not be touched in a way that signifies they love you. As a result, you will feel very empty and cold. Do not put yourself through this emotional upheaval. You have prior notice of this and can avoid this situation entirely. This person has a hidden agenda that involves having you perform a task for them that only they are aware of. This will only lead to unhappiness on your part. Get on with your life without them. Otherwise, a brilliant future is ahead of you and this will begin to evolve within the week.

foreign Someone is going to great lengths to prepare a behind the scenes surprise for you. This will occur within three days. Ignore any suspicious behavior that might otherwise cause you to become angry.

foreign person/language This dream implies that a person from this country or who speaks this language will enter your life within the week and will influence you in a manner that will improve your standard of living. Make sure you put yourself in an environment where you will be exposed to someone who speaks this language or is from this country. During this time frame you will become aware of a certain power you never thought you possessed that will lead you to avenues of greater income. You are on the path toward a more prosperous future. Look under person for a greater meaning of this dream.

foreigner You will be able to explain, in detail, a plan you are developing to another person. Move quickly on this. This person will be able to offer the assistance needed to quickly complete your goals.

foreign exchange You will unexpectedly come into a sum of money within three days. Do not assume extra heavy responsibilities because of this money. You will later find them greater than you can handle.

foreign legion Others will strongly back your opinions.

foreign league All meetings and conferences will be very successful for you during this cycle.

forelimb Do not allow the criticisms of others to keep you from moving forward in life. Act on your ideas and ignore the criticisms.

forelock Prepare for an unexpected visit at an unusual time. This will be a very satisfying visit for you. Expect this within three days.

foreman Someone you meet under unusual circumstances will play an increasingly important role in your life. This will be a very pleasing change for you.

foreplay Within two weeks you will become friends with a group of very powerful people. You will remain friends for a lifetime. This dream also implies you need to be good to yourself and to do things that make you feel good. Treat yourself to something special you have always wanted and take yourself to special entertainments. Good luck is with you.

foreskin For the next few days, you will enjoy an increasing amount of satisfaction and will enjoy more love and peace during this period of time. This will be a very tranquil cycle for you.

forest You will be immersed in an idea that you will focus on completely. Your thought patterns will develop in such a way that you will be able to pinpoint exactly what you need to do to successfully execute your plans. This dream is an extremely lucky omen. You will also need to make sure you only experience positive expressions and do what you can to alter any negative event. Warn anyone else involved in this dream to do the same.

to find your way out of the forest Many rejoiceful events are coming up for you within two weeks. Do not ignore a special person whom you can share these moments with. The synergism between you and another person will also be an unbeatable force. The driving force working for you is love. The more hopelessly lost that you dream you are, the greater the love between you.

to walk through a green forest You are definitely headed for a brilliant future. You will be making all of the right decisions for the next three days.

to walk through a dying forest You have been keeping things pent up for too long. You will finally have the courage to communicate your needs to those who are important to you. Do not allow yourself to become so timid that you are unable to voice your needs. Once you speak up, you will be surprised at the quick response you receive.

to become lost in a forest Within three days, you will have to be specific about the amount of time you are willing to devote to a particular situation. Create a stress free environment and allow yourself to be nourished in peace.

tropical rain forest You will enjoy great clarity regarding the new dimension you are pointing yourself toward. This will bring you tranquility and pleasures beyond your belief. In the past, you have felt it was beyond your ability to move in the direction you desired but now you have a renewed confidence in your abilities. You will move quickly and achieve what you are after. Within the week, you will have the feeling of being solidly grounded and will develop a sense of balance and confidence. As a result, you will be able to tackle certain situations that require these traits. Use this cycle to change those areas of your life you want to alter. You will have the chance to bring prosperity into your life at the level you desire. You are headed for a brilliant future.

forest ranger Someone will ask for extra affection from you within three days. As a result, the relationship will develop to a deeper level than you anticipated. This was a pla-tonic relationship at one time but you are now aware that this person desires more. All of your relationships will develop on a deeper level and you will enjoy a greater love, more bonding and encouragement if this is something you desire. Your quality of life will vastly improve and many blessings will come to you and your family.

forge Do not put yourself in the position to be snubbed by someone, especially for the next three days. Be very aware also that a young person whom you are close to is associating with another youngster who poses a danger to them. This young person is cruel and is capable of violence toward animals, etc. Make it a point to keep this young person safe from any violent influence.

forgery Make sure you have not double booked a place for a scheduled event. Recheck the schedule to ensure this place is free to use.

forget You will begin to doubt the person who cares deeply for you. You will have evidence, within three days, of the depth of love this person has for you. You will enjoy a wonderful life together.

forgetful The person you care about will accidentally run into a small goldmine that will lead to sharing a great deal of money. Work together and the money will last for a long time.

forgetfulness Do not allow yourself to accept indolence as a way of life. Force yourself to act on certain situations and do not procrastinate. This is going to be very important, especially for the next five days.

forgive *to forgive someone* Do not place so much importance on someone who is untrustworthy and is trying to confuse you emotionally. Stop catering to someone who is giving mixed signals. Get on with your life.

to be forgiven Be only in the company of those who care about you for the next two or three weeks. Build up your confidence. You will be surprised how quickly joy will return to you.

fork It is very important that you pay attention to requests for information that others make about you for the next days. This is important because unsolicited questions about your personal life may be extracted and recorded on paper and you will be unable to have it retracted. This information will be untrue and will injure you in many areas of your life when you least expect it.

forklift Make sure you are never alone with someone who has a violent and aggressive behavior. You do not know this person but for some reason they will focus on you with violent intent. The moment you sense this situation beginning to develop, promptly remove yourself from the premises.

forked tongue Do not forget those who have cared about

you for many years. Make sure also that you do not fall prey to a con artist, especially within the next two days.

formal *to see people in formal wear* You will soon be dealing with someone who has a strong sexual drive. You will be able to keep up with this person and enjoy this tremendously. You can take this relationship in any direction you choose. A long term relationship would be immensely satisfying.

formal *(party)* *to be a part of the party* You will fall deeply in love and be very eager to make a commitment in a short period of time.

formaldehyde Be faithful to yourself by being true to your goals in spite of the criticisms of others. You will be well rewarded for this.

Formica Someone who has been holding you back from something you love will not behave in this manner anymore. This person will undergo a big change of heart.

formula *(baby)* Someone who holds you in deep regard will fall deeply in love with you. This person needs you to show deep affection and a strong commitment toward them. You will be able to do this as time passes.
   in any other form For the upcoming week make sure you practice tolerance. This dream is a good luck omen.

fornication Your determination will lead you toward a great future and your life will undergo a major change in all aspects of love and money. You will maintain better health and a new zest for life and experience more love and affection from others.

fort Within four days circumstances will change in ways you felt were impossible concerning people in leadership positions. Someone in power will be willing to offer you assistance in ways you desire. You will demonstrate a willingness to adapt to another person's way of life. Good luck is with you.

Fort Knox The person you are requesting financial assistance from would prefer to speak to you in private. It is better to keep information of this loan to yourself if you want the money. This dream may also be used as a reference point in time. If you dream of this place and see its name used in any context, the dream message will occur on this day.

Fort Lauderdale Young children should be encouraged to show more aggressiveness when pursuing what they want, especially educational pursuits. Teach them patience and the ability to keep things simple. This formula will give them the key to grasp success. This dream may also be used as a reference point in time. If you dream of this city and see its name used in any context, the dream message will occur on this day.

fortress Within three days someone will attempt to sway you to their side. This person has a bad temper and a bad disposition. Do whatever you can to avoid involvement with this individual.

Fortuna God *(Roman Mythology)* You will enjoy an enormous amount of productivity for the next thirty days. All business negotiations will be very fortuitous and any sales activity will bring you an increase in revenue. You will also be able to expand your business plans and improve your financial status. Family harmony will be strong during this time period and many blessings will come to you and your family. Eat healing foods and drink plenty of water. Good luck is with you.

fortune You will experience an abundance of health, wealth, love and happiness. This dream is a very lucky omen. You will also receive good news.

fortune cookie Pay attention to any fortune you read. This will represent a forthcoming event. You have ample time to change the result, if you choose. You will also experience many moments of genius and be able to clearly communicate your ideas to others and bring them to fruition. Good luck is with you.

fortune hunter *any form* You will enjoy life long contentment because of the choices you make regarding your career. Focus on these decisions for the next three days.

fortune teller You have the knowledge and means to clearly visualize the direction you wish to take and to make changes regarding those areas of your life that you feel require improvements. This will be a lucky omen for the next seven days. You must also recall what you can of the conversation. This will indicate a forthcoming event in reality. You have the time and ability to either alter the outcome or embrace the event. All things seen in this dream will offer you major clues to future occurrences. If you are left with questions, seek a professional reading.
   to be a fortune teller Follow your own advice and if you recognize the people you gave the fortune to, inform them of the importance of this dream. The outcome of any future event can be changed, if desired. Anything connected to the dream will offer major clues to events that will occur within seven days. Someone you desire will also be seeking a long term commitment in any capacity. Use any means to maintain all relationships and be sure to build up strong foundations. Good luck is with you and many blessings are coming to you and your family.

forty Maintain your sense of humor and you can expect a fantastic sex life. Use this number in ways that are most advantageous to you. Use your mental inventiveness for the next three days.

Forty-five This dream is an extremely lucky omen and within eight weeks you will be rewarded for work well done in the past. During this time period you will be entertained by new people who will come into your life. New doors will also be opened that will bring you a greater source of income. Your new lifestyle will bring you tranquility and greater prosperity. Also make sure during this time frame that you do not bring any of the skeletons in your closet out in the open. Leave well enough alone. Learn to forgive yourself so you can get on with your life. Do not bring more chaos into your life by revealing secret information. You are headed for a brilliant prosperous future. Be sure to use this number in ways that will bring you the most benefits (i.e.., games of chance, etc.)

forty niner Motivate yourself to reveal your true feelings for another. Put your words into action. You will also acquire the information needed to make some meaningful changes in your life. You will experience new beginnings in areas of your life you have never tapped into and will begin to experience a new prosperity within seven days.

fossil Investigate your family tree. Information you uncover about your ancestors will bring you riches. Seek out this information and work toward making this prediction a reality. You are headed for a joyful future.

foster child You will be under a tremendous amount of pressure because you will stand up for the rights of a young child. Follow your instincts.

foster home You need to begin looking for second hand appliances at a bargain price to replace one that has broken down.

foul ball Be wary of any cosmetics for the next three days that may damage the skin, scalp or hair.

foulmouthed Take care to have all necessary dental work completed as soon as possible.

foul shot You will have the courage to keep someone from putting you on an emotional roller coaster. Rid yourself of this manipulation.

foundation This dream is a lucky omen and you will finally find the means to stabilize and resolve a family problem. Everything will turn out better than you anticipated.

foundry Make every effort you can, for the next four days, to behave in such a way that will bring someone you desire close to you. This person is not yet involved with you and at first you will feel they are not interested in you in the way you desire. During this time period, you will also experience an abundance of health, a financial windfall will come your way, and you are headed for a prosperous future.

fountain You are in a very good position to demand what you want from your divinity. Be direct and specific about your wants and needs. For the next three weeks you will be

developing a list of priorities that will serve as an aid in supervising the way you live your life. You will be able to meet you goals with peace and tranquility. Many blessings will be with you and your family. Good luck is with you.

water fountain You will receive good news within three days and be very pleased with the outcome of a business affair you are concerned with. This is a lucky omen for you as well as lucky for love and finances.

fountainhead You will be granted all your requests.

fountain pen This dream is an omen of wealth. You will be celebrating the completion of a major goal within the week.

four Someone you meet, within four days, will have everything needed to excite you sexually. Become determined to win this person over to a deeper relationship. The feelings will be reciprocal. This relationship will offer everything you need and all your friends and relatives will approve of this union. Use this four day cycle to focus on and accomplish anything that is important to you. Use this number to schedule important events and for use in games of chance. This is a very lucky number for you.

4-H Club Within three days ask someone to put in a good word for you. This will result in a very fortuitous connection and will, as a result, set up a series of events that will help you promote your ideas.

Four Horsemen You will be asked out by an admirer within three days. This person will be very kind, generous and sensitive. If you choose to be with this person, you will enjoy many wonderful moments of lovemaking for as long as you choose to be together.

four leaf clover This dream implies intelligence and good luck. You are encouraged to use this spark of intelligence to bring an original idea to full bloom. Do this within two days.

four letter word You have the power to prevent the wilting of a certain relationship. Use spontaneity and humor to bond more closely with another individual. Spend time focusing on how to successfully accomplish this.

four o'clock flower This dream implies a lucky cycle for you. Within two days you will develop the inner strength, courage, steel drive and determination you need to motivate yourself to break through the barriers that are holding you back. Once you get rid of these blocks (whether physical or emotional) you will be able to bring any new project into tangible form and complete it in the manner you desire. You will also be greeted with open arms and placed on a pedestal anywhere you go during this time period. This royal treatment will surprise you greatly. You are headed for a brilliant future and many new opportunities will come your way.

fourteen Someone will, unbeknownst to you, play cupid

with you and another individual. This will result in a wonderful meeting. Look forward to a delightful date within three days. You may also use this number to schedule major events and for use in games of chance.

Fourth of July You are headed in the right direction and within six months you will be better off than you ever imagined. This dream is also a very lucky omen. Use the number four in games of chance. You will have good fortune in all phases of your life.

fox Be very aware of potential damage due to floods, weather conditions, etc. Someone you regard highly will also travel a great distance to see you. This person will present you with a small gift of appreciation and you will experience emotional gratification with this individual. You will enjoy yourself immensely and are headed for a brilliant future. Expect this within seven days.

to kill a fox This dream is an extremely lucky omen. All negative situations that are now plaguing you will evolve into positive situations.

foxglove Someone who has consistently turned down your request for help will have a change of heart and will be eager to assist you in accomplishing your goals.

foxhunt Be very careful of who is in charge of your finances and budget. This is not a good time to trust others. Keep a close eye on everything that is going on in order to avoid later disappointments.

foxtail Someone will lead you to believe they desire more familiarity with you when, in reality, they choose not to be any friendlier with you, especially in public. Do not set yourself up for disappointment and embarrassment by putting yourself in the position to be snubbed.

fox terrier An unknown trouble maker will suddenly become aggressive toward you. Be very aware of other people and of your surroundings for the next three days. Don't allow yourself to be caught off guard.

foxtrot Be very aware of where and how you spend your money. A con artist will attempt to sell you lessons for something you desire to learn. You will only lose your money on this proposition.

fractions Treat your family with love and compassion and stop talking down to family members. Use praise and encouragement instead. Pay attention to the numbers seen in this dream and use them in any way you deem important such as scheduling important events, games of chance or as a fixed price for something you desire to purchase.

fracture Be very aware of your food intake, make it a point to eat healthier and be sure you are taking in all of the minerals your body requires. Take precautions to avoid all accidents that could lead to a fracture. If you recognize another

person with a fracture, alert this person to the danger of an injury.

someone with a fracture whom you do not recognize You will soon grieve over the loss of the spouse of a newly-wed friend due to a freak accident.

fragment Get plenty of rest, be compassionate with yourself and do not allow others to speak abusively toward you.

frame *(picture)* Do not rush into a relationship that seems just right for you. This will not be worth investigating because it will not work out.

frame *(to frame someone)* You will receive a gift of property in a distant vicinity. Good luck will be with you.

to be framed Trickiness and wickedness are traits associated with someone you are attracted to. Don't waste time dwelling on this. Get on with your life without this person.

in any other form You will always be surrounded by members of the opposite sex who will hold you in high regard and treat you with a great deal of respect. This dream will bring you luck for the next two days.

France You will enjoy travel within six months. Begin preparations for this now because this will be a long trip. This dream may also be used as a reference point in time. If you dream of this country and see its name used in any context, the dream message will occur on this day.

frank You will have to be frank with someone who is attempting to get you to discuss your financial status, especially if you do not know this person well.

Frankenstein Someone is pursuing you for the express purpose of sexual pleasure. This person will approach you within three days and will be very candid about their desires. They will also express a desire to keep this liaison private and on a sexual level. It is your choice whether you want to enter into this or not. If you voice your desire for a real relationship this person will surprisingly comply.

Frankfurt If you are considering travel to Europe, this is a good cycle to do this. Within five days, you will be highly inspired and enlightened by a piece of literature that creates new dimensions in the way you perceive the world. When offering assistance to another, make sure you have all the details and information needed and that all referrals check out. This dream may also be used as a reference point in time. If you dream of this city and see its name used in any context, the dream message will occur on this day.

frankfurter Someone you will go out with for lunch will, within three days, disappear from your life for a long period of time. This is due to circumstances beyond anyone's control. Knowing this ahead of time, you can make the most of this luncheon because you may not see this person for another ten years.

frankincense For the next six weeks you will have nothing but pleasure and good luck and you will be granted three of your most desired wishes.

Franklin, Ben Ideas that enter your thoughts over the next seven days will bring dramatic changes to your life. Although you will lack the confidence to push through these ideas when they first come to you, be assured they will work. You will also be invited to a very elegant event by someone who will go to great lengths to have you join them. This individual has a flair for glamour and will provide you with many amusements, understanding, and joy. You are headed in the right direction and your life will be very fruitful. Expect this to occur within the week.

Franklin stove Do nothing to encourage someone for the next three days. You will find they want what you want. Don't allow anyone to change gears for you. Make your own decisions. Within seven days you will also have a wonderful emotional experience that will last for a long time.

Frank Sinatra *(Entertainer)* You will finally be able to acquire long desired possessions. You will be given these by a very kind and generous person. Refer also to the definition of someone who is deceased. You can find this as a subcategory of "dead".

frappe You will be appointed to a position in the public eye. Your life will be completely different from now on. Do not forget your faithful friends.

fraternity Focus on expressing your ideas graphically for the next three weeks. This will give others the opportunity to visualize your plans. Your ability to express yourself will work to your advantage.

fraud Do not allow yourself to be sidetracked from what could be a wonderful opportunity. You will get a second chance for something you strongly desire within four days. Do not ignore your personal yearnings.

Fraulein In order to evolve and grow into the person you want to be, you must be capable of letting go and separating yourself from thoughts and attitudes that have little to do with present circumstances. This is the perfect time to accomplish this. Within three days, someone you admire will mirror their confidence and ability to support you. Pay close attention to this person's manner of behavior. Listen and ask questions. Take the steps to grow at the same rate as your loved ones.

freak Do not expose yourself to the illnesses of others for the next three days. During this cycle, you will find it easier to rise above your present lifestyle. Good luck will be with you.

someone acting freaky - to recognize this person This person is going through this mental attitude in reality and should be alerted to their behavior. Do not allow this per-son's behavior to interfere with your personal life. You must also focus, for the next five days, on bringing a relationship to the level you desire. This cycle will give you the opportunity to accomplish this successfully. You will also be asked out by someone who possesses more wealth than appearances dictate. If you choose, you will have the opportunity to deepen this relationship. This dream is a very lucky omen and you are headed for a brilliant future.

someone you do not recognize acting freaky Pay attention to the behavior demonstrated and make sure it does not happen in reality. Take care of yourself and love yourself. Blessings are with you.

freak accident Make sure you do not become involved in a freak accident or that it does not occur to anyone you recognize in reality.

freak show Do not listen to a habitual liar who will build up false hopes. Avoid disappointments by refusing to be taken in. Within five days, you will also enjoy vast improvements in your financial status. Any negative omen connected to this dream may be altered in reality. Any person you recognize from this dream will be very eager to satisfy any request from you and any unrecognizable person signifies a new acquaintance who will enter your life within two days. This person will profoundly alter your life for the better.

freckles After working for a long time on a specific creation, it will finally become tangible in the way you desire. It will quickly bear fruit and you will soon harvest much wealth as a result of the hard work you have done in the past. You will be in a very lucky cycle for a long time. Many blessings will come to you and your family.

free You will experience a new freedom within two weeks due to an unexpected and unusual circumstance. This will help you to get beyond a certain situation that has limited your capacity in some respect. This has resulted in a feeling of despair and a depletion of energy and motivation. After this cycle has ended, you will experience a new sense of freedom and liberty in each phase of your life. You will feel uplifted, will enjoy a new lease on life and anything you felt was impossible is now possible. Proceed with confidence. You will also receive good news and be involved in a gift giving celebration. You are headed for a prosperous future and many blessings will come to you and your family.

free agent Be aware of someone you know who harbors animosity toward you. This person will reenter your life within three days and is still jealous and still seeks revenge. Do everything necessary to prepare for this situation and move on with your life.

freebase Be more aggressive with what you are currently handling in order to bring it to a successful conclusion. There is a need for more discipline and order in your life. A situation will arise within three days that will require these traits in order to avoid participation in behaviors you find distasteful.

if you recognize others free basing These are people with attitudes and mannerisms you find distasteful. Be sure these attitudes do not rub off on you.

if you do not recognize the free basers By using discipline and establishing order in your life you will be able to enjoy a new lifestyle, healthy social outings, and attend many wonderful social events. This process will begin within three days.

freedom Do everything necessary to set aside more free time to enjoy amusements you normally are unable to do on a regular basis. Within three weeks, it is important to do this. Enjoy yourself and add new entertainments to your life. Do nothing to jeopardize your freedom.

free enterprise You will enjoy intimate, unplanned companionship within three days. This will come as a pleasant surprise to you.

freelance Do not misinterpret another person's actions toward you. This person is not romantically interested in you and a misinterpretation will lead to embarrassment.

freeloader Your attitude of indifference to another will lead to a quarrel within two days. Watch your behavior and make an effort to demonstrate a more loving attitude.

if you are a freeloader Someone with a mysterious lifestyle will attract your interest. This individual is from another country and will bring much delight into your life. Within three days, you will make this person's acquaintance. You will enjoy many pleasurable moments that will last a lifetime.

to see others freeload Challenge yourself to make use of your talents. You will be able to impress others and quickly make a career of these skills. This cycle will be with you for seven days.

free love Do not underestimate yourself. Stop shortchanging yourself and don't become your own worst enemy. Push yourself to become emotionally involved. Within three days, you will enter a very fulfilling cycle and be able to involve yourself in ways that will emotionally enhance your life. Love is waiting for you.

free lunch The head of the household will make an emotional appeal to someone in power. This will bring more abundance of wealth to the family. Move quickly, this cycle will last for seven days. This dream is also an omen of luck for this time period.

Free Mason Information you will receive within three days needs to be checked for accuracy and authenticity. This information will play a major role in your success.

freesia This dream is a very victorious omen and implies that within the next seven days, no matter what is occurring in your life, you will focus on what you need to be doing in order to reach your goals. You will also be able to use your abilities to pull strings on your behalf. You will develop the confidence you need and maintain this level of confidence until you succeed. Many blessings will come to you and your family. You are definitely headed for a brilliant future.

free throw Avoid crowded environments for the next three days.

freeway *with free flowing traffic* You are headed for a brilliant future. You will also be the guest of someone wonderful who will take you to an unexpected function. You will enjoy yourself immensely with this exciting new person.

with bumper to bumper traffic You will have to make extra time in your schedule in order to handle matters coming up within the week. Start clearing up your schedule now so you will have the time to handle these issues calmly and correctly.

anyone speeding on a freeway This dream is an extremely lucky omen and is a promise of health. You will achieve victory in those areas of your life you most desire. Take life slowly for the next week to ensure you do not miss any opportunities you should take advantage of.

to travel on a freeway during rush hour Take precautions to avoid involvement in any careless accident, especially at an upcoming outing.

in any other form Within two weeks, take the time to clear out your schedule. An opportunity will be presented during this time period. You will recognize this opportunity as something beneficial to be involved in and you will have the means to grasp this opportunity. You will experience no extra issues or burdens as a result of your involvement. You are headed for a prosperous future.

freeze A loan made to someone you are close to will lead to a separation due to nonpayment over the next six months. It would be wise to decide against making this loan.

to see someone freeze It is wise not to enter a relationship over the next seven days because it will require you to constantly use tact and diplomacy. You will feel you must always walk on eggs because of this individual's explosive personality. This aspect of this person's character is not revealed to you now and will only emerge once the relationship becomes comfortable. Since you have prior notice of this you may choose not to enter into a commitment.

if you recognize the person freezing Alert this person to avoid any situation that may lead to death by freezing.

if you are freezing Tackle an ongoing distasteful situation in the same way you would treat a pleasurable event. You will find more success this way. Focus on a situation that creates a feeling of being frozen in reality. Work to turn this situation around or to prevent it entirely.

to see anything else freeze Stop being so gullible and get on top of all situations. You also need to prevent anything from being frozen that should not be.

to see anything freeze, then slowly thaw You will be entering a cycle for the next two days in which you will find it difficult to receive services in a fully satisfactory manner.

Specify, in writing, exactly what your needs are. This will ensure satisfaction on your part.

freeze dry Do not make unkind or thoughtless remarks to young children and young adults. These remarks will be remembered for a lifetime. Pay close attention to the freeze dried item you dreamed about. This is something you will be able to use in life. Aim for emotional satisfaction for the next three days.

freezer It would be wise to listen to the advice of someone who loves you. This individual is giving this advice only because they care for you. Any negative event connected to this dream may also be changed or altered.

freight A close friend of yours will soon come into power and authority. You will not be forgotten by this person. Express the desire to share in your friend's new life and you will experience many joyful moments together. You must also not give gifts to those you do not know well. This will only create suspicion, especially for the next three days.

French A long anticipated negotiation that you have worked hard on will be finally brought to conclusion. Everyone involved will reap tremendous benefits from this mutually satisfying agreement. Expect this exciting event to take place within the week.

French bread Be very aware of your surroundings for the next three days. You will be the random target of a deranged person's intent on committing bodily harm. During this time period, play it safe, trust no one and do not allow yourself to be caught alone in any area where you could easily be ambushed.

French Canadian Do not invest in anything for the next two weeks. You will suffer big losses. Play it safe.

French dressing Write down each of your plans in detail in order to plan your future correctly. This is the perfect cycle to accomplish this.

French fries Use your own resources to tackle a major stressful issue. Do not rely on others. This will only prolong the stress. Blessings are with you.

French horn Within three days you will have to deal with a desperate person who will go to great lengths to get their way. Stand your ground and refuse to compromise or take steps to avoid this individual completely.

French kiss Stop wasting so much time analyzing the behavior of another. Don't allow this person to slip away. Use your time to focus on the positive aspects of their behavior instead of the negative. You are headed in the right direction both romantically and in business affairs.

    if you recognize the other person This person is very eager to satisfy your emotional needs. This dream is a lucky

omen that will lead to improvements in matters of love and money.

French knot If you volunteer your services for something that is important to you, you will receive emotional gratification and an increase in status. You are headed in the right direction.

French pastry Do no heavy lifting or heavy labor and decrease the demands you place on yourself, especially for the next week. You will then be able to avoid unnecessary trips to the doctor.

French toast This dream is a lucky omen and implies that you will win the love and respect of the person you most desire. A long term union will be the result. Expect these changes within five days.

French twist Do not allow your imagination and suspicions to run wild. Control your thoughts. Nothing is going on behind your back.

fresco Someone desires you in a sexual way. For the next five days this person will go to great lengths to satisfy your emotional needs. You will be mutually satisfied.

fresh Get more training and education in your field and face up to your responsibilities and obligations. It is important to begin this process within three days.

freshwater For a five day period your thoughts will be illuminated. This will be a gift from the gods. You will be able to precisely detail those things that are important to do in your life and once these plans are set into motion, you will experience grand changes in your way of living. You are headed in the right direction. Eat healthful foods, drink plenty of water and love yourself.

freshwater bass You will meet someone within a few days and find this person is worthy of your trust.

Freud, Sigmund This dream is a very lucky omen. Do not give out information about an ongoing enterprise for at least three days. Take steps to protect your creative ideas.

friar Do not allow yourself to be placed in a situation that will leave you feeling limited and restricted. Break through these restrictions and point yourself in the direction you want to go. You will have the strength and conviction to do this within three days. Good luck is with you.

friction Riches and power are promised to you. This will be in connection with someone you will meet within three days. You will enjoy a good working relationship.

friction tape Do not allow the power you possess to rule you and go to your head. Continue to treat others in a courteous and gentle way.

Friday This dream is a lucky omen. A special event will occur on a Friday. Wonderful and delightful things will start to happen on this day and will last for a long time to come. This day will be a wonderful time to schedule something important that will change your life for the better. This dream also implies that friends will be more than eager to help you reach your goals.

Good Friday Many blessings will come to you and your family and you will achieve victory in those areas of your life that you most desire. You will also be in charge of a large group of people, organization, etc., and you will eventually be paid a large salary for this work. Any negative event you dreamed of occurring on this day can be prevented. Forewarn anyone you recognize in this dream to do likewise. Make sure you experience only positive expressions in your life.

friend *to hear the word* Take steps to protect your eyesight.

to dream of a particular friend The event you see occurring in this dream is an omen of a forthcoming event in reality. If the upcoming event foretells a negative result, take steps to alter the outcome. It is also important to go out of your way to provide a stable environment for fostering friendships. This is particularly important for the next two days.

friendship You will receive shocking good news that will fill you with joy for a long time. This will occur within three days.

frieze You will experience a very unusual occurrence within four days. It will be important to put everything on temporary hold until you can rethink and redirect your plans so they will go in the direction they need to be going. Make sure your rights will be honored and make a point of pursuing a positive attitude while this is going on. You will see yourself through this successfully. You will also experience deep passionate love, if this is something you desire.

frighten You will hear word of an unexpected inheritance within three days.

to be frightened You will receive what you are pursuing within a very short time.

to be frightened by someone you do not recognize You will receive a proposal of marriage within five days from someone you care deeply for. This union will last a lifetime.

to run from someone you do not recognize who frightens you Make sure this dream does not become a reality. Play it safe and do not place yourself in any situation where this could occur. Someone will also attempt to force you to comply with something you find distasteful. This will occur within three days. Although you will be afraid to refuse this demand, you will find the means to do so.

to be frightened by someone you do recognize This person will make a sexual request and you will want to fulfill it, but you will feel a tremendous amount of stress associated with this request. Do not compromise and do only what you want to do. Find ways to release stress and create a tranquil

environment, especially for the next five days. If this person is depicted negatively in the dream, take steps to prevent any negative event from taking place.

to frighten someone else or see someone else frightened Don't place so much importance on someone who is only trying to confuse you emotionally. Stop catering to this individual and sever your emotional ties. Treat yourself well and you will notice a big change in this person's behavior within five days.

to frighten someone you recognize This individual will be eager to offer relentless assistance to help you attain your highest goals.

to be frightened of a shadow A depraved person will attempt to force you into a distasteful sexual act. This act may be filmed or watched by another person. Take steps to prevent any behavior you find immoral or despicable.

frightened Someone will go to great lengths to create a special relationship with you. You are destined to enjoy a beautiful, full blown relationship that will blossom within a few days and will bring you a great deal of joy. You will be able to connect so successfully that this person will respond in the manner you most desire. This dream also implies that you are headed in the right direction and it is important that you express yourself fully in all matters of personal interest. This will allow you to express yourself in a focused and detailed manner and as a result you will be able to achieve a great deal and will have many successes in your life. You will magically possess the inner strength to handle any situation and will enjoy much tranquility in your life. An unexpected favor will also be granted to you. You will need to put yourself in the position to speak with powerful, influential people. State your needs directly and clearly. Because of this, you will immediately be granted the money you requested from a certain person. You will enjoy victory in those areas of your life you deem to be most important to you now. You can also expect to hear good news within the week and you are headed toward a brilliant future. Pay close attention to all conversations over the next three days. All negative messages and events occurring in this dream will be altered and all positive messages will be promoted. This is a very lucky dream for you.

fright wig This dream is an omen of wealth and you can expect grand changes in your life within four days.

frijoles Do not lend money to anyone, especially for the next four days.

frills Do not listen to gossip or allow jealousy to set in. Someone is purposely creating this situation in order to provoke a violent reaction. Don't allow yourself to be baited, especially for the next four days.

fringe You are headed toward a brilliant future. Someone you know will soon come into a great deal of money and will shower you with gifts and invitations to wonderful events. This will occur within seven days.

Frisbee Maintain a stress free life. Many blessings are coming your way and you are headed for a very healthy and prosperous future. You will also be very surprised when you unexpectedly receive exactly what you desire in the form of a gift. Make sure your pets are well taken care of and are not in any area where they could be injured in a freak accident. In one specific area of your life, you will also need to carefully consider the path to take that will lead you in the right direction. You will accomplish what you are after.

frisk *to be frisked* Someone will go to great lengths to lure you to a secluded spot for the purpose of committing murder. This will occur within five days. Take extra precautions to ensure that this does not occur.

to frisk someone An unknown person will unexpectedly begin to aggressively attack you. This will occur in an isolated area within three days. Guard yourself and make sure this does not happen.

frisky Take care of essential matters on your own. You will have greater success this way.

fritter A good friend will unexpectedly become a con artist and will target you as a victim. Do not place yourself in a situation for the next five days, where you can be taken advantage of. Get on with your life without this person.

frivolity Someone you care deeply about and who has been a long time friend will unexpectedly pass away in a preventable freak accident. Do everything necessary to prevent this if at all possible.

frock *beautiful frock* At one time in the past you were interested in developing a seemingly impossible relationship but gave it no real thought. You will become interested in this relationship again but the feelings are now mutual. Everything you ever wanted from a relationship is now possible. There are also several other individuals who will be concurrently interested in you. For the next month you will date several different people and be able to decide who you choose to have a relationship with.

unusual colors or materials Check the color and material to gain additional clues to the meaning of this dream.

torn frock You will, for the next week, be facing unusual situations that will demand extra time and personal attention. Take steps to eliminate stress in order to make clear decisions. Take care also not to tear any clothing. Someone will want to treat you to an outing within three days. Take the initiative and offer to treat this person.

silk frock A wealthy, professional person will be eager for you to accept a marriage proposal within two months.

cotton frock You will be using your creative sense to become financially secure. You are headed in the right direction.

soiled frock You are headed in the wrong direction and, in spite of all guarantees, you will expose yourself to risks. Reanalyze your decisions and do nothing out of the ordinary for the next three weeks. Make sure also that a garment does not become soiled in reality.

adorned frock Pay close attention to the individual adornment for extra clues. Mingle with new groups in order to open new doors of opportunity. You will be able to express your ideas better and will enjoy an improved social life. You will attend many exciting new functions.

frog This dream is an extremely lucky omen. You will receive the emotional and financial support you need and, within five days, your plans will fall into place exactly as you have envisioned.

frog kick Let others know exactly how you feel about a particular situation by opening up the lines of communication and by being honest. Keep these lines open, especially for the next three days.

frog leap Within four days you will receive gifts of diamonds.

frog legs Do not allow your opinions to become known, in spite of how hard others try to convince you to voice them. Your opinions will be held against you and another person will betray you by letting others know what you say. Do not allow this to occur, especially for the next three days. You will also be going through a lucky cycle for the next three weeks. This will be a good time to accomplish as much as you can toward your goals.

frogman Within two days you will reach out for emotional support in a time of need to someone who has led you to believe they will be there for you. This person will be unable to come through. Remain calm and teach yourself to rely on no one but yourself for your emotional needs, especially for the next two days.

front Stop being so stubborn. You are depriving yourself of a very enjoyable situation. Change your behavior and enjoy life. Many opportunities for enjoyment will be lost if you continue this behavior.

frontage road Do not place yourself in a position that will allow a hypocritical person to take advantage of you in any way.

frontal lobe Choose your friends wisely, especially for the next five days. Do nothing that will jeopardize your career.

front burner Make sure you do not reenter a difficult situation that you have managed to break away from in the past. Within a few days you may unintentionally reinvolve yourself in this situation. The distress you experienced in the past will reoccur if you allow this to happen. Go on with your life without further involvement.

frontier You will, within five days, choose a life long partner. Be more assertive during this time period to ensure that you are both headed in the right direction. This dream is a good luck omen for love and finances.

frost This dream is an omen of love. Add more excitement to your life by adding a touch of romance and sex. Actively seek out this aspect of life within five days and you will receive more pleasure and attend more exciting events.

frostbite Do everything you can to protect children and young adults from the negative aspects of bad company. Carefully watch their role models and peer group to ensure they do not cave into negative peer pressure, especially for the next six weeks.

frosting Doors of opportunities that were formerly closed will now open for you. For the next three days, you will be seen by others as having more of a zest for life and more confidence. You will be exposed to more opportunities as a result. Good luck is with you.

froth You have led yourself to believe that social events coming up within three days will be very distasteful. Since you have prior notice of this, you can choose not to attend. If you do choose to go, you will find these events pleasurable and will enjoy yourself immensely.

frown Someone in a position of power will begin displaying a strange attitude toward you. Don't jump to conclusions and don't allow yourself to become stressed because of this. Remain calm and tactful and you will be able to resolve your differences, otherwise this will eventually lead to an altercation and will result in nasty name calling.

to recognize the frowning person This person is feeling neglected by you. This issue can be corrected by open communication and by acting on your feelings. Do this within two days.

if you are frowning The person who is working with you on a project has become very lazy. Work to motivate this person and push them to become more active in the project. You will find that the work output increases.

if you recognize the person you are frowning at This person will apologize, within five days, for their unreasonable behavior.

to dream of someone frowning The face you dream about may be someone you recognize, represent someone you know or will soon meet. They will be going through a very stressful time and will hear disturbing information that will profoundly affect their lives. This situation will be something in the nature of a job loss, eviction, etc. If you do not recognize this person you will, in reality, be able to identify them because of the ethnic group, age, gender, mannerisms, speech patterns, etc., given in this dream. Be a good listener and use words that will uplift and motivate this person to proceed with confidence. You have prior notice that any negative event that can be prevented during this time cycle needs to be dealt with. Concurrently, two other people will also undergo certain situations that lead to their distress. You will be able to use the correct words to motivate and uplift these people. Something will also occur in

your life that will lead to joyful emotions as a result of a conversation that will provide you with tips. This will lead you to get in touch with someone who will follow through and bring many benefits into your life. You are on the path for a brilliant future and an abundance of health.

frozen Inform everyone who feels as though they have control over your finances to back off. This is an omen of wealth and you can expect an increase in finances within five days.

anything frozen that starts to melt You will be entering a cycle for the next two days in which you will find it difficult to receive services in a fully satisfactory manner. Specify, in writing, exactly what your needs are. This will ensure satisfaction on your part. If anything negative was depicted in this dream, take steps to change it or avoid it entirely.

frozen custard Make sure you are well stocked with food. Family members will drop in and you will need to feed them. If you allow others to go hungry, spats will ensue due to cranky feelings. Keep all visits short and festive.

fruit For the next five days do not feel obligated to take on heavy responsibilities simply because you have the funds available. This will turn out to be more than you can handle. You have the choice to refuse any extra burdens.

fruit bat Someone will make a decision that involves you without consulting you. Since you have prior notice of this, develop a curiosity about everything around you. This will ensure that this situation does not happen.

fruitcake Within five days you will put together a very successful and loyal group for plans you are now undertaking. Make sure you become personally involved in each step to ensure success.

fruit cup Someone you will meet under unusual circumstances will play a large but subtle role in your life. This person is generous and kind and will bring you much pleasure in life.

fruit fly This dream is an omen of wealth. A secretary or someone who has a similar role will play petty games to keep you from getting in touch with someone you are trying to reach. They have reached the faulty conclusion that you are interested, romantically, with this person. Do not allow yourself to get caught up in these petty games. Continue to conduct yourself in a professional manner.

fruit tree Someone you desire will verbalize their feelings of adoration and respect for you. Expect to receive this grand display of emotion within three days and you can expect this individual to always have a deep regard for you. You will experience prosperity in areas you least expect but greatly desire.

fry Someone will unexpectedly drop in on you at a very

unreasonable hour within three days. You will experience much love and satisfaction from this visit. Don't allow yourself to be caught off guard.

fryer You will become ill within three days. Do everything within your power to quickly recover your health and do not take this lightly. This could easily develop into something more serious. Good luck is with you.

frying pan You will undergo a difficult situation within three days. Step away from this emotionally, and by the fifth day you will be able to see clearly enough to resolve this issue successfully.

fuchsia *flowering plant* A blessed event will be celebrated within the week. You must also pay close attention to a creative thought. Once put into action, this idea could be a goldmine. Do not take any thought for granted and take steps to promote these ideas. Good luck is with you. You will also enjoy many accurate intuitive thoughts and develop the ability to diffuse negative thoughts and attitudes at the exact time you need this ability. Proceed with confidence and calm in spite of anything else that may be occurring in your life. You are headed for a life filled with enjoyment with interesting and influential people.

color This dream is an extremely lucky omen and this luck will stay with you for the next three months. You will be overwhelmed by the manner in which someone treats you. This individual will be extremely affectionate and you will be verbally assured of their feelings. This could be in any capacity (i.e., gratitude, romantic feelings, etc.). Their unexpected and genuine words will leave you feeling deeply touched. This individual will be very tenacious in their efforts to bring you into their life. You are headed for a brilliant future. Expect this to take place within five days.

fudge Someone will challenge you for your position. Within five days you will eagerly rush to the challenge and come out the winner. This dream is an omen of wealth and health.

fuel Request special attention when needed. Become very verbal, especially for the next three days, in order to keep balance and stability in your life. You must also make sure that everything you own is properly fueled.

fuel oil Use your power and authority to pull strings to benefit another who would not otherwise receive help. Make sure also that any machinery you own has the proper amount of oil, especially for the next five days.

fugitive Do not doubt the loyalty of others. For the next five days it is also important that you make sure you do nothing that will force you to become a fugitive.

if you recognize the fugitive Warn this individual to do nothing that will place them in the role of a fugitive, especially for the next three days. A special person in your life will also make a financial decision that will bring lifetime benefits.

full *any form* You will be totally and emotionally satisfied because of a situation that will arise within three days. Your desires will be fulfilled. You will also experience an increase in financial status. You are headed for a brilliant future.

fullback Don't allow yourself to be tricked by someone who appears nice but is a monster in disguise. For the next two days, avoid all situations that others attempt to involve you in. They will not work out to your advantage.

full blooded You will receive what you request regarding all business transactions for the next seven days.

full moon You will be storing away some beautiful romantic memories within five days. This will involve candlelight, music and a lit fireplace. Enjoy these moments; you will always treasure them.

fume For the next five days, take steps to ensure that your environment is safe. Watch out for leaking gas and toxic fumes.

fun A relative will give you a beautiful gift that you will treasure forever.

fund raising Do not overextend yourself. Take care of yourself and do not allow others to place demands on you that will deplete your energy.

funds Do nothing to jeopardize your freedom for the next five days. Someone will behave in a violent manner toward you. Protect yourself but do not jeopardize your freedom.

funeral This dream is a good luck omen and implies a brilliant future. Someone you know will come into a great deal of instant money. You will be swept into the same circle of friends and enjoy a variety of many wonderful and joyful events. All your plans and ideas will also pay off and lead to an improved and prosperous lifestyle. You will also hear of the funeral of someone who is close to you within the week. This is beyond your control and is simply part of the cycle of life.

funeral director Take it slowly in order to avoid accidents for the next two days.

funeral home Focus on what is really going on concerning a family situation. Take steps to ensure that nothing threatens your family stability. For the next two days, remain focused and clear up each issue that should not be occurring in order to avoid any distasteful event. This may be the result of an unpaid bill.

funeral procession Within three days you will involve yourself with unusual situations that will vastly improve your standard of living. The larger the funeral procession you dream of and the larger the attendance, the more prominence and importance of someone who will pass away within the week. Otherwise, good luck is with you and many blessings will come to you and your family.

fungus Plead with a relative to act on your behalf in areas you need help with. You will find this person to be on your side if you do this within two days.

fun house Let someone know, in a very caring way, that you are not quite ready to become involved. Within two weeks you will feel ready to make a commitment. Assure this person now that you will contact them once you have time for true involvement.

funnel You are spending too much time focusing on and analyzing a particular situation. Within two days, move past this and focus on what you need to accomplish. Stop holding yourself back.

funny Within three days, someone will ease their way into your heart. Before you realize it, you will be in love. You will also be loved deeply in return.

funny book Remain alert. A collectible hobby will prove valuable and will become a treasure to you.

funny farm Make sure you give yourself enough time to arrive at a function in which you will be making a public appearance. An unforeseen situation may prevent you from being there on time. Take steps to ensure that this does not happen.

funny paper Avoid nosy people who are seeking personal, private information from you. Make it very apparent that you are not interested in sharing personal information.

fur Someone will attempt to involve you in an ongoing venture. This project will yield greater benefits than you ever imagined. Good luck is with you.

furlough Someone is attempting to drag you into petty games. If you become involved, this will prove costly to your reputation. Remain alert to this for the next three days.

furnace Divorce yourself from the behavior and demands of others. You will have a smooth three day cycle that will enable you to do this.

furnish You will experience the love you have long been waiting for. You will meet this person through a friend and things will progress rapidly if you choose to go in this direction.

furniture A casual relationship will develop into a deeper commitment. Within three days you will both develop plans that will strengthen and deepen the relationship.

furrier You will visit a distant city within six weeks. While there you will attend a glamorous party and will enjoy yourself immensely. You will also meet someone who finds you exciting. Good luck is with you.

furrow Within two days, you will undergo dynamic changes that will lead to a new way of life. You will finally be lifted from a long standing burden.

furry A close friend will go to great lengths to break up a relationship you have with someone else who is very helpful to you. This sabotage attempt is done out of envy and jealousy and is an attempt to keep you from achieving your goals. Pay close attention to this for the next two days to keep this from happening.

fur seal You need to subject a present situation to many alternative plans. Think carefully and detail each move. The plan you choose within two days will successfully resolve this situation.

fuse Make sure someone who signs a lease agreement with you within five days doesn't back out and leave you to handle the full payment. You will not have the funds to do so. Make it clear at the beginning you cannot handle this alone. Remain firm and things will turn out well. Good luck is with you.

fuselage For the next two days do not become involved in angry verbal exchanges with a cunning individual who is aching for a fight. You have prior notice of this and can take steps to avoid it.

futon Within two weeks, something unexpected will occur that will require you to transfer from one location to another. This will be a very successful move. Good luck is with you.

future This dream implies victory in those areas of your life that are most important to you. Enjoy life, love yourself and take time to admire nature. All negative events in this dream may be altered to change the outcome. You are headed for a brilliant future.

fuzz You will enjoy yourself immensely with friends while participating in recreational events. This is a seven day cycle for fun. Enjoy yourself. You will also hear personal information about someone else. Keep this information strictly to yourself.

G

G You and a close friend will open a place of business. You will develop a mutual respect and will care deeply for each other. You will also take out insurance on each other's life in case something should happen to one of you. After many years of success, your partner will pass away and leave you with an inheritance greater than you ever anticipated. By the time this happens, you will both have families. Take some of the insurance money for yourself and take the rest to turn your business into a franchise, merger, etc.. This will ensure prosperity for your family and your partner's family. You will be entering a cycle within two weeks that will lead you down this path. Since you have prior notice of this, keep your eyes open for this opportunity so it will not be missed.

gabardine Within three days you will purchase an item for a low price, but in a few years this item will be worth far more than you imagined. Keep an eye out for an item of interest so you won't bypass it.

gable Stop taking everything so seriously and stop being so strict with yourself. Avoid parenting yourself and allow the child within you to have more fun. This is especially important within three days when you will be asked to join someone in a fun loving event.

gable roof Take steps to eliminate interference from an authoritative person. Confront the issue within three days and determine what the problem is between you and this individual. Once you are able to do this, you will be able to enjoy other facets of this person's personality.

Gabriel *(from the Bible)* Specifically demand from your deity the assistance you need to lift yourself from a long standing burden. You will receive the proper help immediately after making this request. You will experience more love and appreciation from others and many blessings will be with you. You will be entering, within five days, an easier, more tranquil and less burdensome time in your life.

gadget You will learn, within two days, that someone is completely infatuated with you. You will be overjoyed to learn this and both of you will enter into a mutually satisfying, and physically gratifying relationship. This love will last for a long period of time.

Gaea *(Greek mythology)* A powerful revelation will occur within seven days and will bring a great sense of excitement because it will come directly from someone else's heart. Many blessings will come to you and your family. Any event in this dream that signifies a negative event can be altered or avoided. All positive messages need to be encouraged. Otherwise, this dream is an extremely lucky omen.

Gaelic You will be able to make up for lost time on a major project by stepping back and reviewing an avenue that will break through the barrier that is slowing you down.

gag You will have the right words to convince others to keep information to themselves that they have no business being in possession of. Because of your gentleness and manner of speech, you will be able to keep this information pri-

vate. This will occur within two days.

to see someone gag on a cloth or tape Any idea that is set into motion within two days will be very successful. The outcome will be more successful than you anticipated.

to see yourself gag Do everything necessary to keep your plans private until you are sure they are workable.

gait This dream is an omen of love and an abundance of health. This will come to you within two days and will stay with you for a long period of time.

gala Within three days, a wonderful event will be lavishly celebrated. Make sure you do not forget this event. You have plenty of time to prepare and to go all out for this celebration. You will also receive an affirmative answer to a question you posed some time ago.

galactic Within three days, due to particular circumstances, you will experience the wonderful life another person is enjoying. This is a preview of what you will be able to achieve if you so desire. Good luck is with you.

Galahad Beware of becoming a workaholic. Focus, within three days, on those things in your life you need to make time for and incorporate these activities into your life. Once you do, you will experience a wide range of new and delightful experiences.

Galapagos Islands Someone is feeling very ignored by you. You are not giving them enough love and attention. Perform special little tasks and actively show your love to those you care about within two days. This dream may also be used as a reference point in time. If you dream of this island group and see its name used in any context, the dream message will occur on this day.

Galatians *(book of the Bible)* You are entering a cycle of health, wealth and love. You will enjoy meditating in your favorite form.

galaxy For the next two days, you will hear something you do not want to hear. Do not allow this to affect your attitude or to keep you from moving in the direction you want to go.

gale You will be creating chaos due to your spoiled, selfish behavior. Do everything possible to turn this around in order to create a more constructive way of living. It is important to begin work on this within two days.

Galilee A large group of people will side with you on an important issue. Victory will be yours. This dream may also be used as a reference point in time. If you dream of this sea and see its name used in any context, the dream message will occur on this day.

gall Within two days you will see an abnormal change in someone's behavior patterns. This person will require your help to find treatment for a mental disease. Do what you can to locate the proper medical services for this person.

gallbladder An older member of your family will kindly extend to you an all expense paid vacation anywhere you desire to go. If you sense a negative message in this dream, take steps to change the foretold outcome.

galleon For the next two days, you need to be focused on analyzing and detailing each move you take. Once you do this you will be better able to achieve prosperity in a shorter period of time.

gallery Become more open with your feelings toward friends and family members. Express your feelings of love, especially in public. You are in a two day cycle that will enable you to do this with more confidence. You are headed in the right direction.

galley Join forces with others in order to break through a major obstacle. Within two days you will have a clear idea of how to accomplish this.

gallon Resist all temptation to give up on a certain situation. Someone will provoke you and behave in an argumentative manner to wear you down to the point of giving up. This situation will allow this individual the freedom to pursue their interests. Do not compromise on this and do not give in to your feelings of defeat. Be watchful of this for the next four days.

gallows Think carefully about the revenge you are seeking. This will bring you no satisfaction and you will feel very disappointed by your actions. Let these thoughts go and get on with your life. Within two days you will discover a wonderful alternative to this issue.

gallstones A relationship that is important to you now will grow only as much as the other person allows. Within two days you will have a discussion and arrive at the level on which you both choose this relationship to go.

galoshes Do everything you can to spend quality time with a younger person. Within two days you will be able to arrive at a plan that will allow this.

galvanized steel For the next three days you will bask in the arms of another person and receive deep love and affection, if you choose to take this route.

gamble You will be able to sell anything for the next two days, and be very satisfied with the profit you receive.
to gamble or to see someone else gamble Someone will do everything within their power to change your opinion about a particular selection you have made. Remain firm and do not compromise on your selection. Any negative event you dreamed of needs to be avoided or altered. This is the best time for you to follow your instincts when it comes to gambling.

to place a bet This is a perfect day to try your luck. Play small amounts for five consecutive times for big winnings.

gambler Do not behave in a suspicious manner for the next two days around a special person. You will never be able to erase the doubts created by your behavior.

game Within three days you will be inspired to go for what you really want. By doing this, you will be putting yourself in the position for a much more prosperous future. It is also imperative that you do whatever is necessary to prevent the loss of a valuable item because of the irresponsibility of someone else. You have prior notice of this and can take steps to avoid this loss. This will prevent a feeling of anger and disappointment.

gamecock Someone is acting very stubborn about an issue you would like to see handled. Within three days a violent altercation will occur. You have the time now to ensure that this does not happen.

game fish This dream is an omen that you will have a profitable financial transaction.

gamekeeper Within two days you will become anxious because a relationship is moving much faster than you had anticipated. You are unsure whether you want to slow this relationship or maintain the status quo. Remain calm, enjoy yourself and allow this relationship to continue in the direction it is going.

game plan Do everything necessary to maintain closeness in a relationship with another person. Introduce your relatives to this special person so that everything seems proper and no one feels left out.

gamma rays Within two days someone will come to you solely for the purpose of requesting a large sum of money. This person will be unable to repay this money and your friendship will suffer if you choose to loan the money.

gander Your presence will be requested at many social functions. You are entering a cycle of popularity, health and general good humor. You will be in this cycle for a long time to come.

gang Within a few days you will feel the urge to become committed in a relationship to the point of marriage. Follow this urge. This marriage will be very lucky for you.

gangplank You will have the courage to put your thoughts into action regardless of anyone else's opinion or anything else that is occurring in your life.

gangrene Do not allow yourself to be placed in the position where you have no control over what someone else does to you. Think all decisions over carefully and maintain control over your activities.

gap Do not allow painful feelings from the past to create distance between you and another person within the next three days. You can take steps to prevent this now in order to have a more productive life with this individual.

gape Within two days you will be able to avoid a regrettable involvement. By doing this, you will prevent regrets and pain in the future. Pay close attention to your actions during this time period and you will not have to deal with this failure.

gap toothed Rally together a group of people who will be able to give you financial backing. Work it so that others will have a stake in your plans. This is a wonderful cycle for commitment and you will all prosper in the future as a result of this.

garage Within two days you will have a real urge to change your outer appearance to reflect your personality. Others will notice these changes. Make sure you let those who are concerned with these changes know they stem from a positive outlook and there is nothing to be anxious about. You will also feel a new freedom once you have shed past burdens that have been dragging you down. Good luck is with you.

to notice an unusual occurrence in the garage Resist the urge to bring out any skeleton from your closet and leave things as they are. You will have the courage and strength to execute thoughts and develop plans in the way you desire. You are headed for a brilliant future. Any negative occurrence will imply a future event in your own life. Do whatever you can to keep this from happening. Play it safe. Any positive occurrence foretells an event that will occur within the week. You will also be given the chance to pursue new offers and participate in productive conversations, if you choose to pursue this course.

unusually empty Be careful of personal involvements, especially sexual activities. Play it safe.

unusually filled Delegate tasks, when overextended, to those who are qualified to handle them. During this cycle you will require extra time and flexibility. Simplify your life. Good luck is with you.

garage sale You are denying your feelings by insulating yourself from someone you are destined to surrender to. Go out and live life to the fullest. Within two days you will have the courage to do this and will find you have nothing to regret.

garbage For the next two days be cautious and careful of the choices you make and make no decisions that will restrict you from moving forward. Remain alert and carefully think through all alternatives.

garbage can Someone will come into your life within three days and will be very eager to have a friendly relationship. As time goes by, you will get mixed messages from this person and they will begin to hint at a romantic involvement. This person is wasting your time and playing games because they are seeking only a short term relationship. Do not expect more. Enjoy yourself, get on with your life and you will enjoy future prosperity. Do not compromise your own desires during this three day period. You will be able to grasp deep emotional fulfillment with someone else who is far more nourishing to you.

garbanzo bean You have allowed another person to make a decision for you. This decision will not work out as you had envisioned. Be sure to carefully check this to ensure against any error.

Garcia, Jerry Within one month you will realize what heaven is when you recognize the creative and profound thoughts that are coming from within you. Motivate yourself to develop these thoughts with confidence, neither over nor under doing them. Execute these thoughts on a grand scale and do not allow yourself to develop tunnel vision. Become flexible but not overly so. Do not allow yourself to take today's moments for granted because these moments will be your future memories. Use common sense and get in sync with your health regarding food and beverages. You will victoriously achieve your goals through your journey in life and you are headed for a brilliant future.

garden Within three days encourage a special person to be more confident, self assured and self reliant concerning a special project they are involved in. Do this gently and tactfully. This will convince this individual that they have the skills and confidence to tackle this project and it will blossom as a result.

in poor shape Do everything necessary to put young children and young adults on the right track in life. Find out what is lacking in their life and take action within two days to keep this situation from deteriorating further.

garden apartment Within the week someone will give you the opportunity to purchase property from them at a lower price than you ever anticipated because they are anxious to move out of town. This will prove to be very prosperous for you.

gardener Someone will make an unbelievable request and it will be so outrageous that you will take it as a joke. Take this opportunity seriously and make a point of accepting it within two days. This will be a once in a lifetime opportunity and you will never regret it.

gardenia A new acquaintance will, within a short period of time, offer you the chance of a very promising love affair. This will be financially advantageous to both of you because you have mutually compatible, creative ideas. Within two days, this process will begin. You also will receive some great news within two days. This news will be better than you had ever hoped and will be the result of a small insignificant move on your part. Good luck is with you and many blessings will come to you and your family. You are headed for a brilliant future.

garfish Listen to what others are saying about you. This will give you an idea of whether you are on the right track or need to improve in some areas. You are headed for a prosperous future and good luck is with you.

to eat Within two days you will make a decision about a partnership and the person you choose will be a dynamic team player. You will receive exactly what you need from this individual and will be successful in accomplishing all of your goals.

gargle Make sure you do not confuse love with financial interests.

gargoyle For the next two days, make sure you make your goals a priority. This will ensure that outside events do not interfere.

garland You will become deeply interested in someone new who exhibits a mysterious aura. This person will treat you with the highest level of respect and kindness. Wonderful days are headed your way.

garlic Within two days you will have the courage needed to make powerful changes in your life. This extraordinary inner strength will allow you to confidently make the correct decisions and to see all situations clearly. You will also feel a surge of physical strength, a healthy constitution and blessings will be with you for a long time to come.

garnet You will soon be invited to a wonderful gala affair. Formal wear will be required for this specific event and you will have a wonderful time. You will also receive gifts of money within two weeks and will enjoy a new passion for life. You will be able to make decisions clearly and without hesitation and someone will show a compassionate, generous interest in you. During this cycle you will feel a healthy rejuvenation of your vital organs.

garnish Do not allow anyone to manipulate you out of an item you truly do not want to part with. This will be attempted by someone within two days.

garrison Pay attention to the faces of those occupying the garrison. If you recognize these people, avoid doing business with them. Do everything necessary to protect yourself when engaged in any business transaction for the next four days.

garrote Within two days someone will manipulate you into believing they truly love you. This person is only interested in your wealth and property and will do everything in their power to involve you in a relationship in order to control your finances. Take steps to keep this from occurring.

garter Don't jump to conclusions. Deal only with facts,

especially for the next two days.

garter belt You have consistently refused to go out with or allow a certain individual to visit you. Within two days, this person will unexpectedly drop in on you without prior notice at an unusual time and will refuse to leave. If you choose to allow this person in, you will have a marvelous time. You will dine together and have many amusing moments. This dream is also a good luck omen.

garter snake A friend will introduce you to someone they do not know. This person appears charming but has many hidden hang-ups, and has been involved in many strange situations. Do not become involved with this person if you choose to live a tranquil life.

gas Make sure that, for the next two days, you do not allow someone to bully you or coerce you into spending more money than you can afford. You have prior notice of this and will be able to handle this properly.

to run out of gas Make sure you do not develop a defeatist attitude when working on a specific situation. Proceed with confidence and you will definitely get over this feeling and emerge victorious. All negative messages and events occurring in this dream need to be altered and all positive messages should be promoted. This is a very lucky dream.

gas burner Someone you know is a genius in disguise. This person will drop in to see you within two days. Discuss your goals with this friend and you will receive remarkable feedback. You will then feel empowered and motivated to meet your goals.

gas can The faces connected to this dream belong to people who will be able to open doors and pull strings on your behalf so you will be able to experience a brighter future. Within two weeks you will also be able to cement friendships with new acquaintances and share hobbies, laughter and many social events. You will welcome this change of pace.

gas chamber Remain alert and aware in order to prevent any freak accident that may occur within three days. Make sure you do not suffer bodily injury. Any face you see in this dream represents someone who is dangerous to become involved with. Do everything you can to avoid those people who go to the extremes in eccentricity.

gas furnace Do not become involved in the squabbles of unfamiliar people for the next two days.

gas guzzler For the next two days make it a point not to present stagnated opinions in front of others.

gasket Simplify your life and do what you can to get down to basics in order to achieve success.

gaslight Do not turn your home into a prison for others.

Those you live with feel as though they have no freedom. This will backfire unless you take immediate steps to turn this situation around.

gas log Push yourself harder for the next two days in order to complete your goals.

gas mask Be acutely aware of someone who is in need of help but is unable to verbalize this need. Within two days you will be able to determine what their needs are and be able to relentlessly seek help until their needs are met.

gasoline This dream is a lucky omen. You will be entering a cycle of greater wealth and will have the opportunity to purchase a priceless, one of a kind item that you have desired for some time. Go for it.
to pump gasoline You will be given the authority to develop something that needs to be completed in an entirely different way. Practice leniency with others because those who are working with you need to be allowed the freedom to develop creative ideas. These ideas will assist you in completing your projects.
to run out of gasoline Make sure you do not develop a defeatist attitude when working on a specific situation. Proceed with confidence and you will definitely get over this feeling and emerge victorious. All negative messages and events occurring in this dream need to be altered and all positive messages promoted. This is a very lucky dream.

gasoline pump/meter Within three weeks, riches will start coming to you. This dream is a lucky omen. The numbers you see displayed will be significant to you (i.e., dates, prices, times, lucky numbers in games of chance).

gas works Take the proper steps to ensure that your credit remains intact. You will be tempted to spend more than you should for the next two days.

gate You have to take the initiative to open your own doors of opportunity when it comes to love and business affairs. This is the appropriate time to reenter someone else's life. Use some form of communication to help tie up loose ends with those you want to bring closer to you in any capacity. You have the chance to be victorious if you apply yourself in these matters within the week. Make sure when you do make these attempts you play your cards close to the vest. Each move you make will bring prosperity in return. Many blessings are with you and your family. This is an extremely lucky cycle to enter into areas you feel insecure about.

gatehouse Do not waste your efforts on others who have asked for your time. These efforts will not be appreciated and you will feel like you have been taken for granted.

gatekeeper Within two days an arrogant, demanding, egotistical person will place demands on you that you will feel are impossible to meet. This person will create a horrifying public display that you will want to completely avoid. You

have the time to develop a plan on how to handle this.

gatepost Do everything you can to stop your obsessive attention getting behavior. Other people are very tired of this.

gather *to gather - any form* You are headed for a brilliant future and will be lucky for a long time to come. Make it a point to only be with those who like you and want to be with you. Make sure you work only with those who want to work with you. Don't associate with those who only waste your time, and tell those you care about that you love them.

gaucho Make it your business to determine the needs of children and young adults. Take steps to have these needs met within three days in order to prevent chaos.

gauge Spice up your life by adding more romance, developing your sex life and adding moments of soft communication. This will bring delight to your life. You will be entering a cycle that will allow this to become a reality for you.

gauntlet Within three days someone will ask your opinion but later resent your honesty and frank behavior. Do everything you can to keep this from occurring.

gauze Be alert and take steps to prevent any physical injury. Keep yourself accident proof and stop being so short-tempered. This is especially important for the next two days.

gavel Within three days you will find yourself eager to become involved with someone who attracts you emotionally and romantically. This is the type of person who is difficult to pin down for an ongoing relationship. This person is very busy but eager to be with you. Involve yourself only if you are interested in seeing them when they can schedule time to be with you, otherwise you will be very disappointed at your lack of time together. If you choose to enter this relationship, you will be richly rewarded on an emotional level.

gay Within five days you will be ready to make changes that will profoundly alter your life. You will develop and execute well thought out plans that will fall right into place. You are headed for a brilliant future.
if you recognize someone in the dream who is portraying a gay person but who in reality is not This person urgently needs to see you in order to discuss an important matter about themselves. An honest conversation will resolve all problems with ease, especially if held within three days.

gazebo For the next three days do not allow yourself to become overly suspicious of the behavior of others. Remain calm and relaxed. With time, everything will become clear.

gazelle Include those who are special to you in all decision making procedures. This is especially important for the next three days.

gazette For the next two days use no shortcuts to expedite any project you are handling. This will not work out to your advantage.

gear This is a very lucky omen and you are headed for a prosperous future. Be sure you are not swayed by others from going in the direction you want to go in order to meet your goals. Allow no one to slow you down.

gearbox Be sure that you extend kindness to those who will be coming to you for financial aid within the next two days. This person will be able to repay you.

gearshift The person shifting gears will experience a dramatic change in their lives. Their ideas of what they want and need in their lives will shift drastically. This individual will also want you to extend them a loan with the promise of monthly repayment. This assistance will help them to bring balance into their lives. This dream also implies a change in residence very soon that will be very successful and prosperous.

gearwheel Stop depriving yourself of situations in your life that could be very special to you and will provide special moments that you will carry for the remainder of your life. Bring more social events, exchanges of conversation, and flexibility into your life. You will experience tranquility and blessings will come to you and your family.

gecko This dream is a very lucky omen. Someone is very eager to be in your presence and has a special gift for you. You will be made aware of this within five days.

Geiger counter Take all necessary precautions to ensure your life is not at risk, especially for the next two days. Avoid all risks for contamination, freak accidents or foul play.

geisha Within five days situations will work themselves out in such a way that overwhelming, long standing problems will be resolved with little or no effort on your part. This dream is an extremely lucky omen and you can proceed with confidence.

gel *hair gel* You are being alerted that within three days you will be dealing with a certain person who is very knowledgeable about your likes and dislikes. This individual is also aware of the kind of lifestyle you do not approve of and the situations you are against. They will use methods of subtle persuasion and will formulate a plot to lead you into a lifestyle that you would ordinarily reject. This person intends to lure you into doing something that goes against your principles. Many different tactics will be used in order to get you to do their bidding. This persuasion will be done in a very stylish way through the use of gifts, vacations, etc. It may take several gifts and a great deal of time to win you over, but you will end up doing as this person wants. You have prior notice of this and can take the appropriate steps to handle this issue. Otherwise, you are headed for a brilliant future.

gelatin Do not allow an abusive situation to occur in your presence within three days in which the victim is weaker than the attacker. Restrain from behaving in an abusive way to someone who is weaker than you. Take steps also to improve your nails and hair. Eat properly and drink plenty of water.

gelding Do everything necessary to protect yourself from the environment. Place special emphasis on this in order to improve your health.

gem Expect grand changes in your life. You will receive assistance from another person that will help bring those changes about. This person will take an active involvement in your life to make sure your needs are met. The color of the gem will also give major clues to the meaning of this dream. You are headed for a brilliant future.

Gemini Do what you can to strengthen your financial base. Do not allow any abusive situation to occur that will deplete you or your finances. This dream also implies that someone will intensify their involvement with you for the purpose of maximizing sexual gratification. If you choose to take advantage of this cycle, it will be a dynamic time to benefit in love and finances. Good luck is with you.

gene Within six days you will create a network of people and situations that will transform your plans into tangible form. You are going in the right direction.

genealogist Within the week you will have an incredible need to have something accomplished that needs to be taken care of by someone else. This could be anything (needing money, a favor, etc.,) that needs to be given immediately with no hassles. It will be such a large request that it will be difficult for you to imagine it will be given to you. Follow your intuition and this will give you a clue to who will come through for you. Proceed with confidence and explore your options until you locate the perfect one. As soon as a mutual agreement has been made you need to take immediate action so this issue will be concluded within this cycle before this person has a chance to change their mind. Many blessings are with you and you are headed toward prosperity.

general For the next four days use any resource you can draw from to help you release repressed feelings. No matter what else is going on in your life, deal with these issues first. Do not allow the emotional issues of others to become your issues. You will have the strength and clarity to deal with this for an improved way of life.

general admission Take steps to avoid muscle injury or strain in any form. Take steps to avoid reinjuring an area you have had problems with in the past. Take care for the next four days.

general assembly For the next three days stay away from

someone you do not know well. You will find their conversation and problems very distasteful. Keep this from taking place.

general assistance Do not allow your imagination to make assumptions about what is really going on. Gather the facts and rely only on the facts to base your opinions and decisions, especially for the next four days.

to receive general assistance Maximize your creative powers. You will be able to draw benefits from these and improve your life. You must also avoid putting yourself in the position to give to others more than you first intended. Make it clear from the beginning what your limits are.

general contractor Do not postpone a pending conversation with another person. This person is eager to meet with you to improve and maximize life's opportunities for both of you.

general delivery You will be very instrumental in pointing out the needs of a young person to an adult in charge of this young individual. Do this within four days. You also need to assign tasks only to those who have the specific knowledge to handle the job.

generation Pay close attention to what is being said to you. For the next four days, listen carefully for clues that will enable you to establish a stronger position for yourself.

generation gap A situation will develop within four days. You can keep this from getting out of hand by looking at it from a different perspective. You will then be able to handle it quickly and effectively before it escalates into a major problem.

generator Intensify the way you show love to others. Use actions as well as words to demonstrate love. This will, in turn generate more love and affection from others.

Genesis Within four days you will relentlessly help another person meet their goals. After this tremendous task is accomplished, the gratification shown by this other person will be immensely rewarding. You and your family will receive many blessings and good luck for the next six days.

genetics Within seven days the ideas you have been repressing, need to be presented to another person for processing. Do not cancel any event that requires your presence. Expect great changes in your life.

genitals Take the steps to seek professional help in all matters that need correcting, especially if those issues make you uncomfortable. Do this now in order to satisfy your needs. Learn to love yourself.

genius Within a month someone will give your plans consideration and will bring them into tangible form. Because of their faith in your ideas, they will work to make it a reali-

ty. Dynamic changes will occur in your life that you never felt were possible before.

gentile Within five days someone will be intensely, sexually aroused by you and this person will go to great lengths to become sexually involved with you. Should you choose to go in this direction, you will experience a maximum amount of love for a long period of time.

gentle An older, wiser person will help you to quickly resolve an old troublesome problem. You will feel gratitude that this person was there for you when you needed them.

gentlemen/women You need to require a higher level of efficiency from others. This will help promote your financial security.

geography Within the month someone you least expect who has accumulated a great deal in their lifetime will leave you an inheritance. This will come from a distant place and will surprise you greatly. Any positive message should also be promoted and you have the time to alter any negative message.

geometry Become more focused on the company that a child is keeping. Pay attention to this child's peer group and monitor their friendship until you feel this child has the confidence and wisdom to choose acceptable friends of their own.

Georgia Make sure you decide wisely between two choices you have to make. Gather the necessary information before making this choice and you will be pleased with the outcome. Blessings are with you and your family. This dream may also be used as a reference point in time. If you dream of this state and see its name used in any context, the dream message will occur on this day.

geranium Doors that were formerly closed to you will now be open. You will be seen by others from a different perspective and new opportunities will now become available to you. Good luck is with you.

gerbil You are going in the wrong direction and you will only run into a dead end. Calmly regroup and scrutinize the options you have in order to arrive at the perfect alternative.

germ Do not associate with the wrong person. Certain people have a history that you are not aware of. Retract your involvement, for your own sake.

German You will be happily involved with a particular group, and for the coming month will experience many exotic social events and foods. This will be an exciting time in your life. Go for it.

German cockroach You will receive an inheritance that will bring great wealth at an unexpected time and from an unusual source. This will occur within the coming year.

German Shepherd A blessed event will be celebrated by all within two weeks.

Germany Someone you meet within the week, will play an increasingly large role in your personal interests. You will be very pleased with this turn of events and a closeness will develop between you. You will find this person to be far more affectionate than you ever imagined. This dream may also be used as a reference point in time. If you dream of this country and see its name used in any context, the dream message will occur on this day.

germ warfare Create a stress free environment and get more rest and relaxation in your life. Find healthy amusements, simplify your life, be good to yourself, eat well, and drink plenty of water.

Gestapo You will become involved, within two weeks, with a very controlling person. Do everything you can to distance yourself from this person and do not create patterns you will have difficulty breaking away from.

Gesthemane *(from the Bible)* You will be provided with an unusual opportunity to have your goals met with the help of your acquaintances and friends. This will occur within three days. This dream may also be used as a reference point in time. If you dream of this garden and see its name used in any context, the dream message will occur on this day.

gesture Pay close attention to the type of gesture displayed. If it is negative, you have the time to turn a very dangerous situation into a triumphant one within a two week period. If it is a positive gesture, within the week you will be able to put yourself in the frame of mind to think clearly and bring order into your life. You will be able to rid yourself of things you have no need to take care of. This will result in more tranquility in your life.

geyser This dream is an extremely lucky omen. A secret wish you have been holding close to you will become a reality. Expect great changes in business and love in the ways you desire.

gherkin Become more affectionate to those who seek and deserve your affection. Take steps to fulfill their emotional needs. Good luck is with you for the next seven days.

ghetto All negative messages revealed in this dream may be turned around to your advantage. All positive messages need to be promoted to the fullest. You will also need to focus on the reality behind a family situation. Pay close attention to those things that don't seem quite right in order to prevent a crisis situation. This is likely to occur within seven days.

ghost Pay close attention to what the ghost says. This will

ultimately depict a reality. If this is a negative message, alter the outcome. If it is positive, take steps to promote it to the fullest. You must also push yourself in order to bring a situation to maturity. This will result in dynamic changes in your life.

friendly ghost You will have the opportunity, within four days, to express your hidden emotional desires to others. This will bring you instant gratification. Your affections will be reciprocated.

unfriendly ghost Be very alert for the next two weeks. You will have to take drastic steps to avoid becoming involved in a situation that will cause you a great deal of undue stress. In spite of the pressures from others, remain uninvolved. Seek peace, tranquility and a stress free lifestyle.

if you are the ghost For the next two weeks pay close attention to your surroundings. A stranger will enter your life and seem quite normal and decent. This person is an extremely dangerous necrophiliac. Do not venture into unfamiliar places and make sure you take extreme caution. Trust no one during this time period. Within seven days, you will also have the capabilities to handle what appears to be an unsolvable, unbearable situation. You will be able to resolve this in a satisfactory fashion and banish it from your life permanently. During this cycle, you will have the strength to resolve any difficult situation. Anything you dreamed of that was negative also needs to be turned around into a positive situation.

the ghost of a living person Alert this person to be very aware of their surroundings when in an unfamiliar area, especially for the next two days, and alert them to be careful of any freak accident. Anything negative you dreamed of must be avoided, and alert anyone you recognize in this dream to do the same. You must also make sure you do not make rash judgments about a concept or an individual. Examine everything a bit more thoroughly so you can have a clear picture from which to judge. Remain safe.

children that are accompanied by ghosts Within three days make sure this child has a protective environment. Protect them from illnesses and the escalation of a pre-existing illness. Protect this child from unusual and unbearable stress, outside peer pressures, cruel remarks, and ensure that all their needs are met. Be very watchful over this child for the next three days.

child's ghost that you do not recognize Become less strict with your inner child and bring more joy into your life, especially for the next three days. Live life to the fullest and take steps to enjoy the marrow of life.

ghost town For the next two days someone will do everything in their power to take advantage of your generosity and good intentions. Be alert to this and take steps to prevent it.

ghostwriter Closely examine your options for the next three days in order to avoid future disappointments.

ghoul You will be accepting a mutually satisfying proposal within two weeks.

giant You have a situation that needs to be brought under control and put back into order immediately. It is important to handle this within three days, otherwise it will escalate to the point of being out of your control. Pay close attention to any situation that requires personal handling and do not allow yourself to be caught off guard. Anything that you dreamed of that foretells a negative event needs to be avoided or altered in reality. Take steps to ensure that you enjoy only positive experiences in your life.

giant panda Within three days make it a point to verbalize your needs to a special person. Once this person is made aware of your needs, they will immediately come to your assistance and your needs will be met.

giant sequoia Make it a point to add excitement to relationships that are important to you. An extra effort, on your part, can put back what is missing now. You will also see definite improvements in business negotiations.

gibbon Within three days you will be contacted by someone who is anxious to work something out with you. Do not become involved with this person because, in spite of any excitement connected with these arrangements, things will not work out for you. Set limits now.

Gibraltar This dream is a very lucky omen and implies that a long standing problem will end with a complete and successful resolution within three days. This dream may also be used as a reference point in time. If you dream of this place and see its name used in any context, the dream message will occur on this day.

Gideon's Bible You and your family will enjoy an abundance of health and blessings for the next two weeks.

gift You are completely unaware of someone else's infatuation with you. You will become aware of this within three days. If you desire, this will become a thrilling time for both of you and this will develop into a mutual giving, sensual and loving union. If this is something you want, move quickly.
to receive a gift Any idea or plan set into motion over the next three days will be tremendously successful and result in a dynamic outcome. The more luxurious the gift, the more successful the outcome. Good luck is with you. Also, pay close attention to the gift and the giver. These two pieces of information will provide major clues to what will be occurring in reality.
to give a gift Within two days you will receive help in overcoming what now seems to be an impossible situation. Someone you have been wanting to see for a long period of time will also concede and grant you this wish. Expect this to occur within three days.

gift certificate Someone who has, in the past, treated you with disrespect will come to their senses and treat you as you should be treated. This also implies that, within four days, you will receive large winnings for a small outlay.

gift wrap Someone will take you into their confidence to discuss a situation they find distasteful to see if your advice can ease the problem. You will be very willing and able to offer a different perspective. This will allow this individual the chance to solve the problem on their own. They will become whole and productive again. Your assistance will also benefit you in the near future.

gigolo Within five days someone will express the desire to have you move in with them. Whether you choose to make the move or not, everything will work out well for you. If you choose not to make this move, make sure you keep the option open for a later time.

G.I. Joe All financial negotiations that you will be entering into will work to your advantage for the next week. This is the best cycle for you to move in this direction.

Gila monster Take the time to prepare all papers correctly that need to be personally attended to. Do this immediately and this will ensure you receive what is due you in a timely fashion.

gilded Request any special attention and assistance when needed, and do not allow yourself to be intimidated. Take care of and protect yourself.

gill For the next three days take the proper steps to protect garments from damage, especially the ones you plan to wear during this time period.

gillnet Be very cautious for the next three days when pleasure seeking in order to avoid serious complications. Play it safe.

gilt Someone will request a high level of sexual energy from you. Within three days you will be able to perform at a level adequate to satisfy both your needs. You are deeply loved and adored.

gimlet Do not put on a persona that confuses others. Be consistent in your manner of behaving, especially for the next three days. It will be very important to avoid mixed communications.

gimmick An older, wiser person will rush to your aid when an upcoming problem begins to develop. This person will offer financial help as well as advice once you ask for it. You will resolve this problem successfully and quickly.

gin Unbearable mental pain and anguish will disappear within three days because of plans you set into motion. This will put you on a clear path that will enable you to resolve issues and meet your needs.

ginger You will receive an abundance of luck in those areas of your life you most desire, especially in matters of health. You will be able to create a stress free, peaceful and tranquil environment within three days. You will also travel and return home safely.

ginger ale You will enjoy the fact that you are desperately needed. Your affection will be requested within three days.

ginger beer Become more aware of what your family is trying to communicate to you. They need to feel a greater bond with you and to be made aware of your schedule. This will allow them to feel as though a part of you remains, even if you are not around. Make the effort to spend extra time with your family for the next five days.

gingerbread A family member will take you into their confidence within four days. You will be able to offer assistance simply by listening to what they have to say. Help in every way you can to assist this person in meeting their needs. Good luck is with you.

ginger jar An acquaintance you have not really noticed before has a deep desire for you. This individual is trying to attract your attention. You feel as though this is only a friendly gesture when, in reality, this person is trying to make a romantic overture. Should you decide to follow this up, it will result in a satisfying relationship for both of you.

gingersnap A situation you are considering that will involve another person needs to be acted on within two days. This will ensure that you meet your goals successfully with this person and that you reach a mutually successful agreement.

gingivitis Watch your behavior. You are placing too much importance on another person. Do not overly extend yourself emotionally to this person and allow no one to take you for granted.

gin rummy Follow your instincts when it comes to professional help in order to handle those things that need immediate attention. This is especially important for the next five days.

ginseng Pay attention and think ahead. You need to restrain all impulsive behavior and curb this sense of urgency for the next three days. If you do not, you will be involving yourself in a situation you have no business being in.

giraffe This dream is a symbol of victory especially in romance. Someone you are romantically involved will desire a deeper union. This person will want a deeper level of commitment from you and an affirmation of love. Actively demonstrate your love for them within three days. See 'big' animals for more definitions.

girdle You will find deep satisfaction and will rejoice over a reconciliation.

girl Your determination will lead you to a lifestyle change

for the better. Within three days you will also learn that a much younger person has deep feelings for you and desires an emotional involvement. You will find other people will be more focused on you and will demonstrate a greater love and respect for you.

school girl Within two days your life will become more social and you will have few dull moments.

girlfriend *you have a girlfriend whom you recognize when in reality she is not* This person represents someone you will be dealing with within five days. They will be very attracted to you in a romantic way and will demonstrate character traits much like the person you dreamed about. You are being forewarned in order to be aware of what you will be dealing with. If this individual possesses positive traits or traits you dislike, you will be able to conduct yourself accordingly. You will have some idea who this person is based on the personality you dreamed about (i.e., manner of speech, personality, behavior, etc.). This may or may not be the particular person you recognized. This dream also implies that you will receive some very important and encouraging news concerning your finances. Prosperity will come to you within two weeks and this will vastly improve your lifestyle. You are entering a very lucky cycle.

you have a girlfriend whom you do not recognize Within a five day period you will meet someone who will be very attracted to you romantically. Large clues will be left in this dream about this person's character that you will either find pleasing or displeasing. This may or may not be someone you know in reality. You will become aware of who this person is by their character, speech patterns, etc. You are being given prior notice of the kind of person you will be dealing with and can decide whether or not you wish to become involved based on this person's behavior. Be very wary of bad aspects of their personality. You are also entering a fantastic cycle for social interactions and advantageous business negotiations. Your intuition will be heightened and you will be able to use your common sense wisely. This heightened intuition will lead to greater success and help you create a perfect lifestyle. You are definitely on the path for a brilliant future. You will also need to behave in a consistent way in those areas of your life that require this trait.

looking for a girlfriend and being unable to find one You are involved in a situation you need to divorce yourself from in order to get on with your life. At the moment you are trying to get someone to react to this issue in a certain way but in a few weeks it will no longer matter. Some people need to learn to handle certain issues on their own and to have their own experiences so they can evolve and grow. Situations are constantly changing and need to be handled in different ways. Do not interfere to the point that they become incapable of handling things on their own.

in any other form Do not allow loved ones to slip away because of your inconsistent behavior and abusive manner, especially for the next two days. Create a loving, tranquil environment for yourself as well as for those around you. Pay close attention to the details of this dream. They will give you a clue that will point you to an event or to something in particular you will need to explore further. This will give you an advantage that will enhance your lifestyle and put you further on the path you desire. Take steps to prevent or to avoid any negative event foretold in this dream. Ensure that you and others experience only positive expressions in your life.

Girl Scout For the next three days if you are unwilling to go along with a certain situation, person, belief, etc., clearly and promptly state your mind in order to avoid discomfort at a later time.

give Within the week you will feel amazingly confident, solidly grounded and balanced. As a result of these feelings, you will be able to handle those situations that require this aspect of your personality. Use this time period to work on those aspects of your life you want to change. You have the opportunity to bring prosperity into your life at the level you wish. You are on the path toward a brilliant future.

to give of yourself Before you decide to hold a reunion, make sure any pre-existing animosities have been resolved. Do this to ensure everyone enjoys a peaceful, tranquil, stress free reunion.

to have another give of themselves Within the week you will meet a new person who is full of kindness. In a short time you and this person will enjoy many comfortable, unusual and pleasure filled moments.

gizzard You will be able, within five days, to remove invisible barriers through the use of good communication skills with a person in authority. You will be able to meet situations head on and achieve a mutual goal. This cycle is a good time to conduct verbal negotiations.

glacier You will be entering a very intuitive cycle for the next two days. Follow your hunches, they will lead you in the right direction.

glade Control your impulsive behavior around someone younger than you, especially for the next two days.

gladiator You will find someone irresistibly, sexually attractive and you will learn, within two days, that this person feels the same about you. You will be the one to determine whether you choose to become involved. Joyful days are ahead of you and you are destined for a brilliant future.

gladiola Those areas of work you have applied yourself to will fall into place exactly as you have envisioned and the results will bring you a great deal of excitement. Victory will be yours within three days.

glamour Within three days you will be asked out by an admirer. This person will be very generous, kind, and sensitive. If you choose to be with them, you will enjoy wonderful, mutual lovemaking for as long as you opt to be together.

glance Listen to and demonstrate tolerance toward someone who is upset, especially for the next five days.

gland Within two weeks, you will rejoice over unusual circumstances that will make you a very wealthy person. You will also be traveling extensively for the next few months and will enjoy every minute.

glass For the next three days, practice consistency if you want to successfully achieve your goals. Follow your intuition; your hunches are correct. You also will experience greater clarity of thought and many blessings will come your way. You will enjoy a lucky cycle for the next seven days.

broken drinking glass Think ahead. Within two days, someone will throw out stupid, insensitive, inconsiderate remarks at you in front of others. You have the time now to take this person aside and tactfully request they curb their behavior. This will prevent an unkind and disrespectful remark from occurring.

broken window glass Prevent a falling out between yourself and a dear friend. This other person will pull a power play because you lack the finances and power they have. They will continually ask you to perform favors for them in order to keep in control. Take this person aside and express your feelings. If you don't, you will be forced to cut this person out of your life instead of maintaining a friendship.

to see glass shatter You will need to be aware of another's irresponsibility. This will catch you off guard. Be prepared and do not allow yourself to be taken.

safety glass Someone will give you a container of items to hold for them. When this person returns to pick the items up, you will be accused of going through the container and taking some. Be cautious of this and do not allow this situation to occur.

cocktail glass Make sure you take all the necessary steps to ensure a good outcome to any negative event witnessed in this dream. Do everything possible to only experience positive events in your life.

glassblowing A long lost friend will appear and share their good fortune with you. You will enjoy many wonderful moments and hours of entertainment. Pay close attention to the colors of the glass for additional clues.

glass cutting You are heading in the wrong direction by focusing on a specific family member. Slow down and reassess your thoughts about this person because your assumptions are incorrect.

glasses *(field)* You will set aside a weekend to spend with someone. This person will spend less time with you than you hope because they will stay constantly busy making calls and attending to important paperwork. Do not feel rejected. This person cares deeply for you but it is imperative that they attend to these tasks. Enjoy the visit and do not allow yourself to become resentful. Good luck is with you.

glasshouse Do not place yourself in the position to have your vehicle hijacked. Be especially careful of this for the next two days and make sure all your precious objects are not taken from you without your knowledge.

broken windows in glass house Be very careful and do

not make extra demands on someone who is special to you. This individual feels overwhelmed due to certain situations that are occurring in their life right now and will come to you seeking a listening ear. If you choose to offer your time, this person will be forever grateful to you.

glassmaker For the next two days, do not allow the opinions of others to disrupt your thoughts. Follow your own counsel when it pertains to someone special to you. Take time out to regroup and add some enjoyment to your life.

glass slipper You are destined to meet someone who shares many of the same positive traits as you. This individual is very generous, demonstrative, honest, intelligent, highly educated and also demonstrates a charisma that attracts many people to them. Make a genuine effort to get out into the world and leave yourself open to this meeting. Once you meet this person, they will genuinely desire a lasting union.

to recognize the wearer This is the person or someone who represents the traits of a person who will come to you within four days with the desire to begin a relationship. Depending on the character of the person you dreamed about, you may choose to pursue this or to avoid this relationship altogether. If you choose to go after a relationship because of this person's positive character, you will receive whatever you want. Be assured that what you are given will be given with sincerity. If this person is not of good character, go on with your life without them.

if you do not recognize the wearer The positive actions of this person will be manifested in the character of someone you will deal with within five days. At first these behaviors are not apparent but will be revealed within this time frame. Be aware also that negative behaviors will occur and prepare yourself emotionally in order to handle this in the best possible way. Anything negative seen in this dream needs to be prevented in reality. You have prior notice of this and can handle yourself appropriately. Make sure you experience only positive expressions in your life. Proceed with confidence. You are headed for a prosperous future with many abundances in life.

glass snake Avoid the feeling of being inferior to someone else because of the occurrence of unusual situations. Do not allow an authority figure to bring about a feeling of inferiority. This is especially important for the next two days. Keep yourself balanced, focused and take this time to regroup.

glassware Do everything necessary to make another person aware of your deep feelings for them. This will give them a chance to respond and let you know where you stand. Instead of wasting time hoping this individual will contact you, you could be out enjoying yourself with this person. Good luck is with you.

glaucoma For the next two days, make sure you are emotionally equipped before responding to the request for assistance from another person. You will be overextending yourself during this particular cycle. Be keenly aware of your circumstances prior to committing yourself.

glaze *to glaze anything* Someone, within the near future, will put you in touch with people from a different culture and a different way of life. Under normal circumstances you would never have visited this particular locale or have met these people. You will have an exciting time during this cycle.

glee club Within the week, you will be privy to some privileged information about certain situations and associates. Use this information with care and discretion.

glide *to glide* Focus on plans you expect to put into action in the near future. Determine what you really want and decide whether these plans are workable. You have the time to make alterations in order to ensure their success.

glider You will be able to cleverly make a claim on someone's affections. This will meet with success and you will experience an intense love from this individual. If you choose, this option will be available during this cycle and you will experience passion at its fullest.

gloat *to gloat* This dream offers you a clue to the behavior someone will demonstrate toward you in the future. You will also be offered a once in a lifetime opportunity that will allow you to improve your life immensely. You will also be exposed to many new and welcomed experiences in life.

glob Meet your personal involvements with others in meetings and discussions head on. This will provide mutually satisfying results in situations that demand your personal involvement and close attention.

globe Try to tolerate everything that comes up with others, for the next two days, and do not deprive them of your closeness.

glockenspiel You will have a very lucky experience within five days and this will bring you a tremendous amount of excitement. This cycle will stay with you for a long period of time. Health and happiness will be yours.

glory You will be blessed with more spiritual faith and strength. You will develop a courage you did not have before and will be better able to stand up for yourself. This courage will lead to a feeling of being whole and complete. Good luck is with you.

glossary Any enterprise connected with color, printing on fabric or advertising will be very profitable. You will be lucky with any new enterprise.

glove/gloves Do not allow yourself to become passive and satisfied with present circumstances. If you make the effort to make changes in the way your business is going, you will rapidly see an improvement and a new direction. Things will start going in the direction you want them to go. This is a good omen for love and health.

cotton work gloves A situation will come up within three

days that will make it necessary to determine whether someone who is working with you on a particular problem is doing their share of the work. This person may be, because of their own laxity, having you do the work of two people. Be alert to this so you can get the assistance you need without taking on any extra stress or responsibilities. Speak up and make it clear this person has to pull their own load. Keep your life stress free. Many blessings are with you and you will enjoy a prosperous future throughout your senior years.

rubber gloves You will have a desire to expose yourself to new experiences and new horizons. You will no longer be able to take anything for granted that you may have in the past. You will be emotionally gratified when a golden opportunity presents itself within the next five days. You will grasp victory because you will recognize this opportunity for what it is. You will then be able to pursue your destined future.

glove box Within three days many of your secrets will be revealed. If you have a secret you wish to keep private, take steps to ensure that it remains private. You will also hear from an old friend shortly and will share many fun filled moments.

glove compartment Do not pass the buck when it comes to responsibilities with your family and children. Do everything necessary to ensure that obligations, on your part, are met. If you do not have the necessary education to meet these demands, take steps to rectify the situation.

glow Your intuition is right on target and you are headed for a brilliant future. You will enjoy very good luck regarding all negotiations and love relations.

glowworm Use a friend's discount privileges to purchase something you desire. Your friend will be very happy to work with you on this, especially for the next two days.

glue Within five days someone special to you will undergo a strange occurrence. Alert this person so that they can prevent any strange event from happening.

glue pot Make sure you do not mishandle someone else's property. Within three days, someone will entrust something of value to you. Treat these items as though they were your precious belongings, otherwise you will risk your position of trust.

glue sniffing Whomever you recognize performing this act needs intervention and help for a problem in reality. Also, within three days you will find yourself becoming a referee for two people who cannot reach an agreement to a specific problem. With your help they will find a solution.

glutton Make sure that you are not ignoring a potentially abusive situation involving a much younger person. Do not allow the mistreatment of someone else to continue.

gnat You will be chosen to represent another person regarding their financial estate. This will require special planning on your part. Make a special effort to live up to your responsibility.

gnaw *to gnaw* For the next three days give yourself the flexibility you need to handle a number of troublesome difficulties that are headed your way. Deal with each one calmly as it comes along. Treat each problem as a challenge and you will see this cycle through with success.

gnome Within three days you will have to give out a great deal of information about yourself. This will allow someone to understand you well enough to make a positive decision in your favor. This individual will also be able to pull strings for you. You are headed for a brilliant future. Proceed with the big changes you want to make in your life.

gnomon Within three days you will devise a plan to stash away money for a wonderful vacation. If you choose to do this, you will enjoy yourself immensely.

gnosis You will choose the perfect words to prevent manipulation and an abuse of your generosity. Good luck is with you.

gnu Someone will request to borrow money from you. Take the time to think carefully about this before making a decision and you will be able to prevent later regrets and resentments.

go *any form* Someone will go to great lengths to rekindle a feeling of closeness and will go out of their way to make you happy. If you choose to go this route, you will be spoiled by this person and will enjoy yourself immensely.

goal You and another person will develop a very mutually satisfying union. If you choose, the union will be permanent. The plans you both develop will become a reality and bring many benefits. You will develop a deep love and appreciation for yourself. These feelings will serve to normalize events and make it possible to express yourself fully. Many blessings are with you and your family.

goalkeeper Do not assume that a certain situation will turn out the way you anticipated. Make an effort to ensure the result you get is what you want.

goal line Others will receive you with open arms. Proceed with confidence. You will be strongly backed on a project you are presently working on. Go for it.

goalpost You will be able to purchase the items you have long desired with someone else's money. These items will be presented to you as a gift.

goal tending Any out of town activity scheduled for the purpose of showcasing your talents, wares, or for business negotiations will work to your favor.

goat You will soon be the recipient of a wonderful surprise and also enjoy an abundance of health and finances.

goat antelope Doors that have been closed to you will now be open and people who have consistently turned you down when asked for assistance will now come to your aid. You will have the help needed to successfully complete your projects.

goatee Do not involve yourself in any way with someone who enjoys creating chaos or arguments out of small issues. The moment you find yourself in the company of someone who fits this behavior, remove yourself from their presence.

if you recognize the person with the goatee Think of something you have always wanted to be involved in but have been unable to because of your lifestyle. It is now possible to become involved. There was also someone in your past who will now desire to become involved with you. At the time, because of a busy lifestyle, they were unable to pursue a relationship in any capacity. This person now has the freedom to reinvolve themselves.

goatfish You will begin to receive the payoff from work done well in the past. This is an opportune and fortunate cycle for you.

goatherd Do not allow any mechanical problems to tie you up unnecessarily.

Goat's beard Leave yourself open to more business opportunities by listening carefully to people from different ethnic backgrounds. Your willingness to help others will also be greatly appreciated by others.

goatskin This dream is a very lucky omen and this cycle will be with you for the next month. This is also a lucky omen for healthy reconciliations. You will hear news of a certain couple reuniting that will bring you much happiness. This is a lucky omen and you and your family will enjoy an abundance of blessings and health. This victorious cycle will be with you for seven days.

Goat's milk Do not allow yourself to stagnate to the point of being unable to accomplish simple tasks that need to be handled. Make it your business to break through patterns that are holding you back. Simplify your life, add more joyful activities, get plenty of rest and eat healthful foods. Good luck is with you.

gob If you fail at something on the first attempt, make an effort to keep trying from a different angle. Stay centered and regroup yourself.

goblin For the next two days, carefully watch a newcomer in your life. This person demonstrates the same problems and hang ups as someone you knew in the past. You will have no desire to repeat the same pattern. At the first sign of game playing, exclude this person from your life. Blessings are with you and your family.

go cart Do what you can to arrive at a clever plan or idea that will enable you to work independently on a situation that will develop within three days. This will allow you to work alone without depending on another person's assistance. Clever thoughts and ideas will come to you with great clarity and you will be able to successfully resolve this situation.

God This is a reminder to reaffirm your beliefs and faith. Brilliant events will begin to happen suddenly and surely. Whatever was revealed to you in this dream must not be revealed to another person until it has been manifested in reality. Any message revealed about another person should be given to this individual so they will have time to change any forthcoming negative event or work to enhance any future positive event. This applies to the dreamer as well. You will also receive a sense of optimism and confidence that will allow you to turn your life around. You are headed for a brilliant future. This feeling of excitement will stay with you for a long period of time and will assist you in the task of turning your life around more rapidly. Blessings will be with you and your family.

man of God You are headed for a new and prosperous lifestyle.

Sun God For a very long period of time you will be able to receive and enjoy the finest things the world has to offer. You will enjoy yourself to your heart's content. The gods are with you and you will enjoy good luck.

godchild This is a good time to make decisions that are out of the ordinary. Good luck is with you, especially for the next three days. Pay attention to anything negative that may be occurring in this dream involving you or another person. Take steps to avoid this in reality and alert the other person to do the same. Pay close attention to what the godchild is saying. You have prior notice of this and can handle any situation appropriately.

goddaughter Do not overindulge in anything that will result in improper behavior on your part, especially in public places. This is especially important for the next three days. Pay attention to any negative event in this dream that could occur to you or anyone else in reality. Do everything you can to avoid this. Pay attention to what the goddaughter is saying. Since you have prior notice of this you will be able to handle any situation appropriately.

Goddess This dream is a promise that within eight weeks you will reach a point in your life to make major changes although you may not be aware of it at the time of the dream. You will be destined to bring about a long desired lifestyle and leave old mental and emotional issues behind that stand in the way of self motivation. Your skills of introspection will be heightened and you will be able to clearly see the result of certain decisions. Be sure to put each thought in writing so they will be clearly understood and have an impact on others. You will be very successful in applying this method to something that is important to you. Anything said by a goddess in the dream will also become a reality. You need to do everything you can to keep any negative message from becoming a reality. Make sure you take steps to experience only positive expressions in your life and alert anyone you recognize to do likewise. You are definitely headed for a brilliant future

godfather Make sure, for the next three days, that you do nothing questionable, especially when it pertains to money. Guard your reputation. Pay attention to the words spoken by the godfather and make sure you take steps to alter any negative message. Make sure you experience only positive expressions in your life. You are headed for a brilliant future.

Godhead You are deeply loved.

Godiva You will accomplish much more if you practice projecting a more interesting demeanor around influential people. This will encourage closeness between yourself and these people.

godmother Someone is very eager to have you sign some papers. Do not sign them. Things will not work out in the way you have been led to believe. Pamper yourself and love yourself. You will be asked out by someone who is in a terrific state of mind and you will enjoy yourself immensely. Take steps to experience only positive expressions in your life. Make sure that any negative message given by the godmother is avoided in reality. You are headed for a brilliant future.

Godparent Within three days the person you are interested in will show you a great deal of affection. Anything spoken by the godparent will become a reality. Be sure to take steps to avoid any negative event seen in this dream. Forewarn anyone you recognize from this dream to do the same.

Gods This dream is a promise that within eight weeks you will reach a point in your life to make major changes although you may not be aware of it at the time of the dream. You will be destined to bring about a long desired lifestyle and leave old mental and emotional issues behind that stand in the way of self motivation. Your skills of introspection will be heightened and you will be able to clearly see the result of certain decisions. Be sure to put each thought in writing so they will be clearly understood and have an impact on others. You will be very successful in applying this method to something that is important to you. Anything said by the gods in the dream will also become a reality. You need to do everything you can to keep any negative message from becoming a reality. Make sure you take steps to experience only positive expressions in your life and alert anyone you recognize to do likewise. You are definitely headed for a brilliant future

goggles Be very careful when making travel arrangements for the next few weeks, especially when traveling overseas. Make sure you do not put yourself at risk of contracting a contagious disease that you would not be otherwise exposed to. You will be able to carry out your business plans successfully.

go go dancing Do not implicate yourself in a risky situation that appears to be a sure thing.

goiter Avoid, at all costs, reacting toward someone by using angry words. You will be unable to take back these words and they will only lead to painful feelings that will last a lifetime.

gold or gold color The opportunity and time are ideal now for you to carry out your plans and do something spectacular that will drastically raise your standard of living. You will enjoy a very prosperous lifestyle and everything will go in the direction you want it to. During this time you will be given the gifts of greater thought and greater intelligence that will enable you to correct your path. This will quickly advance you up the ladder to success in those areas that most interest you. You will also be gifted with the ability to act appropriately and to demonstrate charm. You will be honored by others. This dream also implies you will be in a very lucky cycle for the next seven days. You will welcome new changes with an optimistic attitude. Your best days are yet to come and you are headed for a brilliant future.

gold hair Within the week you will be offered a golden opportunity that will come only once in a lifetime. Remain flexible and stay open to this opportunity during this time period. This also implies that you and a special person will be doing whatever is necessary to improve relations between you. You will also adopt new methods for improving your life together and will explore new ways to show mutual respect. You are headed for a brilliant future.

anything that appears gilded You will enjoy a brilliant mentality, charm and will relentlessly apply yourself for the next four days, to achieve and grasp a golden opportunity. This will dramatically improve your life. Any person, place, or thing referred to in this dream will be instrumental in bringing you what you most desire. If for any reason you do not achieve victory in this dream, make sure, for the next three days, to carefully observe what is going on around you. Anything you feel is not going in the direction you desire needs to be worked on until it meets your standards. This is the time to investigate new areas of opportunity and add new dimensions to your life.

golden figures Each event connected to this dream that is positive needs to be converted into a reality as quickly as possible. Each negative event may be altered. This dream is a lucky omen and you will magically possess the inner strength to handle forthcoming situations. You will enjoy prosperity, balance and tranquility in your life. You will also be blessed with the clarity of greater mental inventiveness needed to develop a plan and execute it successfully. This plan will bring about the changes you so desire to experience in your present life. Luck will be with you, especially for the next seven days.

in any other form The opportunity and time are ideal now for you to carry out your plans and do something spectacular that will drastically raise your standard of living. You will enjoy a very prosperous lifestyle and everything will go in the direction you want. During this time you will be given the gifts of greater thought and intelligence that will enable you to correct your path. This will quickly advance you up the ladder to success in those areas that most interest you. You will also be gifted with the ability to act appropriately and to demonstrate charm. You will be honored by others.

gold beads Enjoy life to the fullest and add spice to your life by enjoying a variety of new entertainments.

goldbrick *to have it taken from you* There is a situation that is of utmost importance to you that, for the next two weeks, must not be taken for granted. Do not assume it will work out as you envisioned. Become personally involved in order to ensure this situation works out to your advantage. Once you become actively involved, everything you felt was impossible will be possible for the next seven days. This cycle is perfect for this and you are headed for a brilliant future. This will begin to manifest within three days.

gold bug A very wealthy person will be interested in developing a close friendship. Go for it.

gold certificate Someone who lives far from you will extend an invitation to visit them at their expense. Proceed with confidence, you will have a fabulous time.

gold coast This dream implies luck. You will be able to resolve a troublesome situation very easily and completely within two days. Someone will also be appointed to come and lead you in the direction you should be headed. You will be given excellent advice and are headed for an awesome future. Good luck is with you.

gold digger Do not involve yourself with someone who has an outrageous and unusual idea. This person will attempt to involve you in a situation that will leave you feeling restricted and penned in. Move on without this person.

golden age Do not take life for granted. Take this time to determine what you really want and need from life and go for it. You will also have a variety of people enter your life and offer jobs to you.

golden calf Within two days meet with a person who will offer the correct advice on how best to handle a crisis situation. Don't be taken in by those who are not qualified or experienced enough to give you the correct advice. You will be able to find a satisfactory solution to this issue.

golden eagle An older person will offer you assistance in areas you need it. This individual is very influential, has many connections and is very wealthy. This dream is an omen of abundance in every area of your life, especially health.

golden eye You will unexpectedly receive a gift from someone you deeply love and respect. You are deeply loved by others.

golden fleece Someone who feels abandoned by you will start complaining because you are failing to demonstrate enough affection. Unless you show affection to this person, they will go through an emotional crisis. You have prior notice of this and can change your behavior in a manner you feel is more appropriate.

Golden Gate Bridge You will be treated sexually in just the way you wish by someone special. If you desire, you will also be emotionally touched by this individual. You will make long range plans with them to travel and add spice to your life. You will also share many passionate moments together. You will both be lucky in financial affairs and are headed for a brilliant future. You are well loved. This dream may also be used as a reference point in time. If you dream of this bridge and see its name used in any context, the dream message will occur on this day.

Golden Globe You will have an exciting awesome time within the next two days in a variety of ways.

golden locks Any enterprise you enter into will be successful and will improve your life dramatically.

golden parachute Share your ideas with others and get them involved to achieve faster results in reaching you goals.

golden retriever The person you are interested in will lead you to believe they will contact you at a later date but this person has no intention of contacting you again. Get your point across now while you have their attention and do not allow yourself to be manipulated.

goldenrod Make sure that someone who seeks your advice is directed toward the proper help. This will ensure you do not take on unwanted responsibilities.

golden rule Within a few days your assistance, in terms of energy, time and money, will be needed for a family member who is away from home. Move quickly on this in order to reach a successful conclusion. Do not drag your feet.

goldenseal You are deeply loved and respected by many. Good luck and many blessings are with you.

golden wedding anniversary Break away from your daily routine and make an effort to bring positive changes into your life. Do this quickly and you will be surprised at the social events you will be attending. This will be a good cycle for this.

gold finish Do not allow yourself to be so intimidated that you do not seek special attention and help when you need it. Take care of yourself and protect your needs.

goldfish A very generous person will enter your life and consistently offer financial assistance until you are on your feet.

goldilocks You are entering a three day cycle that will demand you give extra attention to someone you have special feelings for. Demonstrate patience.

gold leaf This dream implies victory when dealing with certain individuals in those areas you felt were impossible. Expect this within three days.

gold medal Dress appropriately and carry yourself with dignity, especially for the next three days in order to win over your competitors.

gold mine You will enjoy victory in all legal matters. You will also sense a good attitude from those you work with. This will make life much easier for you.

gold rush Do not push away someone special because of your behavior and style of communication. Change your behavior.

goldsmith Have all the details and dollar amounts put into writing for a service you will be having done so the job will be done correctly with no added work. Get a firm price.

golf Do not behave in a cruel manner to another person. Change this behavior because this individual will always remember you as a cruel person.

golf club The news you receive within five days is not the news you have been waiting to hear. Prepare for a change of plans.

golf course This is the perfect time to ask for assistance from someone that will take up a great deal of their time. Do it now and this person will agree to your terms.

gondola Run your own errands and deliver your own messages in order to avoid wasting time.

gong Neighbors will complain to you about a certain situation. Be very helpful in normalizing life.

gonorrhea Within a three day period you will be in the presence of someone who will promise you many things in a desperate attempt to keep you interested in them. In reality, this person is going through a number of transitions and it would be impossible for them to deliver on these promises. They will, however, quickly recover from these changes and be able to offer you what they promised. Do not make a move yet, especially if you are interested in them. They will soon be in great financial and emotional form. You will both enjoy an abundance of health and are headed for a brilliant future. Any negative event you saw in this dream also needs to be avoided or altered in reality. Anyone you recognize in this dream needs to be forewarned to do the same. Take steps to ensure you experience only positive events in your life.

goober *any form* This dream implies victory. You are entering a five day cycle that will allow you to make positive changes in your life.

good afternoon *to hear this phrase* Regroup yourself and come to grips with a situation that needs to be understood in order to avoid danger. You have prior notice of this and can take steps to prevent it. Get plenty of rest, drink plenty of water but in moderation and eat healthful foods.

Good Book A proposal you will be making within five days will be received with success.

goodbye *to hear this word* Avoid going anywhere that you feel may include some distasteful situations. Pay close attention to the person saying goodbye. Take steps to prevent this person from leaving in reality, if this is what you choose to avoid. You are in a cycle that will enable you to gracefully avoid all distasteful situations.

good day *to hear this word* Do everything necessary to avoid arguments and the company of someone who enjoys creating discord, especially for the next two days.

good faith Take the time to determine what you really want from someone you are interested in. When you reveal your feelings, specify the depth you wish this relationship to go. Be prepared to compromise in order to create a mutually satisfying union.

Good Friday Many blessings will come to you and your family and you will achieve greater victory in those areas of your life you most desire. You will also be in charge of a large group of people, organization, etc., and will eventually be paid a large salary for this work. Any negative event you dreamed of occurring on this day can be prevented in reality. Forewarn anyone you recognize in this dream to do likewise. Make sure you experience only positive expressions in your life.

good looking You will have the protection and help you need from your special deity to develop an emotional and financial balance. This will be a lucky and tranquil time. You have many admirers but the one you desire most will return your love and affection.

good morning Use prudence when dealing with a senior citizen. You will need to do this within three days.

good news You are entering a very powerful growth cycle and can expect good news to arrive shortly. You will also receive a positive response to anything you hold as your highest priority, especially for the next seven days. Good luck is with you.

good night Think ahead. Do not allow yourself to become involved in a secret that someone is eager to let you in on. You will later feel burdened by this knowledge.

Good Samaritan Be firm when you refuse to comply with

someone who is making demands of you. Their issues are not your responsibility. Expect this within three days.

Good Shepherd Doors and opportunities that were formerly closed are now open. Others will be eager to discuss any situation in order to arrive at a satisfactory solution.

goose Be sure you do not allow anyone to take your generosity and kindness for granted, especially for the next three days.

to goose or be goosed Develop an aggressive demeanor when attempting to bring an individual you desire closer to you. This is a good cycle for you to behave in such a way that this individual will feel comfortable enough to express their true feelings. Many blessings will come to you and your family. You are headed for a very prosperous future.

gooseberry A romantic situation you felt was a possibility will, for the next two days, appear to be an impossible situation. Think ahead in order to avoid a careless and embarrassing move on your part.

goose bumps Someone you consider a friend will become a very cunning enemy. This individual will attempt, without your knowledge, to sabotage a very important opportunity just moments before you receive knowledge of it. You will be able to successfully turn things around to your satisfaction. You have prior notice of this and can make sure you receive the information you need without interruption.

goose egg You will be loved, cherished and protected for a life time by those you desire.

gooseflesh For the next three days you will be very busy. During this time period you will receive a call you should be very attentive to because it concerns certain matters you need to know about. Take the time to accept the calls you need to be responding to.

goose liver Within three days someone who is very special to you will not fully understand what you are trying to communicate to them. Because of this inability to communicate, a large amount of time will be wasted. Be sure you speak clearly and succinctly in order to avoid this.

gopher Take care of yourself, avoid unhealthy relationships and keep yourself from stressful situations, especially for the next two days.

gopher snake Keep all private, personal information to yourself, especially new information that will be coming up shortly.

gorge Think carefully about the changes you are about to make. Be sure to include everyone who will be affected by these changes in the decision making process. This will give you a support system and allow everything to run smoothly.

gorilla Someone will attempt to start trouble at an upcoming event in front of a large group of people. This will result in a spoiled evening for everyone. Be very aware of the people you associate with, especially for the next seven days. Keep to yourself and avoid getting involved in a situation that involves squabbling. This can be avoided.

goshawk For the next three days take steps to become more considerate. A special person will be going through a very emotional time and requires patience and sympathy until they get through this difficult time.

gosling Do not pass judgment on someone and do not criticize anyone. Take steps to change this behavior. You will become more sensitive and practical in your dealings with others.

gospel This dream implies victory. You will be able to purchase a piece of real estate at a very low price because someone is in a hurry to sell.

gossip You are placing too much attention on a stranger and can be easily misled by this person. Get on with your life without this person in it.

gothic Someone has a problem controlling their angry attitude and is constantly making themselves and others miserable. Pay attention and remove yourself from this unhealthy environment. Get on with your life.

gouda cheese For the next three days, any negotiation you enter into will be successful.

gouge Guard everything that is emotionally precious to you such as reputation, career, private life, etc., from others who demonstrate envy. Protect yourself from these people.

goulash Be very diligent and handle your own responsibilities for the next three days. Do not rely on someone less qualified to handle your responsibilities.

gourd Someone whom you disliked in the past will, within three days, reenter your life and try to play a part in it. Do everything necessary to avoid involvement with this person but, at the same time, avoid friction. Go on with your life without this person in it.

gourmet Someone will be interested in becoming romantically involved with you. This person does not speak your language and is unable to make themselves understood. For the next three days, if you choose to pursue this, be more patient and understanding with the person who fits this description. You will enjoy a wonderful life together.

gout It is a good time to plan a comfortable retirement. You will gain important information within three days that will steer you in the right direction.

govern Someone you will meet will want to relate to you on a more personal level than you desire. Be personable and nice to this individual because you will later learn to like them and first impressions are important. Any negative event connected with this dream can be avoided or altered. Make sure you only experience positive expressions in your life.

government Speak up for your rights and do not be afraid to allow the truth to come out. Everything in this cycle will work to your favor. You will be able to get your point across and receive a positive response from others. Make sure you take steps to avoid or alter any negative event seen in this dream. Take steps to ensure you experience positive expressions in your life.

to be the recipient of a government check Be very attentive because an unusual occurrence will develop regarding a person, project or position that will lead to a financial windfall. You may marry someone who will leave you with a monthly pension, develop a project that will deliver you monthly royalties, or secure a position that will offer you monthly provisions for a lifetime. You are in a sound position to receive this in the near future. Develop your curiosity, especially for the next week, to ensure that you do not miss out on these benefits. You will receive an abundance of health, many blessings and are headed for a brilliant future.

governor Do not take up any new athletic past times at the moment. You are out of condition and need to get into proper physical condition first. Stay healthy and avoid injury due to athletics for the next seven days. Any negative event foretold in this dream can be avoided or altered in reality. Make sure you enjoy only positive expressions in your life.

gown Someone who has an extensive amount of experience in a specific field will extend an offer of a training program, free of charge, within seven days. Once you express your interests they will be eager to offer assistance. As a result of this, you will experience a financially secure career.

grab bag This is not a good time to tell someone else your plans. For the next two weeks, keep everything to yourself and do not allow anyone to know the details of what you are planning. You are entering an enjoyable cycle for the next seven days. Trust your hunches and go with what you feel. Be very wary of anyone who is trying to impress you with their financial status. Pay no attention to this behavior and move on with your life without this person in it.

grace Do not allow anyone to dissuade you from pursuing your interests. This is a possibility for the next three days.

grade The physician you are seeking services from will act very detached. The moment you become aware of this, seek a new physician.

grade school This dream is a very lucky omen. It also implies that, within seven days, you will learn of a deep personal matter relating to someone else. This matter will surprise you but it is a good idea to allow this person the chance to discuss this matter with you.

graduate Within three days negotiations will be handled correctly and will result in the removal of a certain obstacle. Plan ahead for ways to handle this.

graduation It would be a good idea not to follow the opinions of another when seeking guidance for a matter you will be dealing with within two days. You will find the right direction. Stick to your own counsel.

graffiti This dream is an extremely lucky omen. The words or symbols you see may represent a large clue to the meaning. This clue will foretell a negative event that needs to be altered or a positive event that needs to be sought after. This dream also implies that any information you sent to another person needs to be received the first time it is sent out. Make sure this happens, especially for the next two days. You are deeply loved and appreciated by everyone around you.

graft Do not settle for less, especially for the next seven days. Do not compromise your desires.

graham cracker You will learn of someone's special feelings toward you. Once you hear about these feelings, set up a special time so both of you can dedicate private moments to set up special plans. Good luck is with you.

grail Blessings and good fortune will be with you and your family for the next two weeks. Do not waste time by making a huge mistake that will involve a friend in a business plan. Do not involve yourself. You will also receive good news within two days. This will be in the form of a positive response you have been waiting for.

grain An inventive idea will promise comfort and be a financial lifesaver.

grain alcohol Do what you can to protect yourself from broken bones for the next three days.

grain elevator This is an extremely lucky omen, especially if the elevator is going up. You are headed toward a brilliant future.

going down Become more resourceful for the next two days and be more flexible to changes.

grain of salt Within two days you will receive a written message that will rekindle an old love, if you choose to take advantage of it. Plans for reconciliation will move quickly.

gram Assess your situation within two days in order to determine your next move.

grammar You will be able to perform in such a way that will meet the romantic demands of another within three days, if this is something you desire. You are headed for a prosperous future.

grammar school The mail you receive within two days will contain good news.

Grammy Now is the perfect time to develop a relationship with that special person. This is a relationship you desired at one time but for some reason was unable to develop due to a difference in lifestyles. This individual will now offer you deep respect, affection and an appreciation of you as a person. This will be a permanent union if you choose to go this route. Many blessings are with you and your family.

grand Events within two days will take a romantic turn and affect your life immediately. Make sure you are doing exactly what you want to be doing.

Grand Canyon Take a close look at those things you want to move forward with on a grand scale. All things that you felt were impossible in the past are now possible regarding business negotiations, as well as romantic situations. Good luck is with you and this is an especially good cycle for all negotiations. Another person needs the time to do things on their own. Try to understand this and stop being so demanding on others who need time to take care of personal affairs. This is especially important for the next three days. This is an extremely lucky omen and you are headed for a brilliant future. All negative events you witnessed in this dream can be avoided or changed to a positive event. Make sure you experience only positive expressions in your life and in the lives of others. This dream may also be used as a reference point in time. If you dream of this place and see its name used in any context, the dream message will occur on this day.

grandchild You are headed for glorious days, good fortune and plenitude. You will enjoy an abundance of happiness. All negative events in this dream can be changed or avoided in reality. Take steps to experience only positive expressions in your life and in the lives of others.

unhappy grandchild Take care not to create friction with a special person in your life. The head of the house needs to make sure all bases are covered, especially for the next two days, when it concerns finances. Anything negative that can be avoided should be within this time frame.

happy grandchild You are loved beyond your imagination by someone who is unable to verbalize these feelings. You will have verification of this within two days.

crying grandchild A child will need extra care and pampering. Be understanding. Make sure this child is shielded from a negative environment.

granddaughter Become personally involved in those situations you want to fall perfectly into place. You will be successful. Make sure you take steps to keep any negative event in this dream from becoming a reality and make sure you alert anyone you dreamed of to do the same. Do everything you can to ensure you experience only positive expressions in your life.

happy granddaughter Make sure for the next five days you wear the appropriate attire for all situations and take steps to ensure you meet this requirement in order to avoid discomfort. All negative events connected with a granddaughter you recognize needs to be altered in reality. All

positive events need to be fostered.

crying granddaughter Someone will communicate with you about a certain situation that will bring you a great deal of joy. Involve yourself with this situation for many pleasurable moments.

injured granddaughter Take steps to avoid this situation in real life. This dream also implies you are overlooking a potentially negative situation that needs to be attended to. Start working on this particular situation within two days in order to turn it around to a positive situation.

grandfather Make sure you have everything you need in order to ensure you will not be delayed due to a mechanical breakdown for the next three days. Take steps to change any negative event to a positive one and make sure you experience only positive expressions in your life. Forewarn anyone you recognize in the dream to do likewise.

Grandfather clock Within three days a recycled hobby you were once interested in will launch a profitable income in the future. Move quickly on this. It will be fun. Any negative event foretold in this dream can be altered or prevented. Take steps to ensure you experience only positive expressions in your life. Make sure you alert anyone you recognized in the dream to do the same.

grand jury Within two months it will be demanded of you that you produce paperwork and statements of accountability. Start digging up old records and begin keeping track of anything you will have to be held accountable for within two days in order to avoid a stressful situation later on.

grand larceny Allow yourself the flexibility you need to calmly go through a chain of events that will be occurring concurrently. Each situation will be difficult and very different from each other. One of them involves an individual who will request very specific assistance from you. Gather yourself and calmly deal with each one as it arises and you will be able to handle each one successfully and quickly. Get back to your normal way of life very quickly. Do everything you can to prevent any negative event you dreamed of from occurring to you or anyone else involved. Make sure you experience only positive events in your life.

grand mal seizure You need to be more concerned about money that someone is wanting from you. Think carefully about this in order to avoid grief later on.

grandmother A particular situation you are thinking of becoming involved in will work out great. This situation will bear fruit for everyone involved. You are headed in the right direction, especially for the next three days. Take steps to prevent anything negative you dreamed of from becoming a reality to you or anyone else. Make sure you experience only positive expressions in your life.

grand opera You will become aware of someone's deep feelings for you. This individual will verbalize these feelings within three days in a special way and in a special setting.

grand piano Someone will get in touch with you within two days to renew the feelings of closeness you once had together. Because of your busy schedules, you have both abandoned those feelings of unity.

Grand prix Control your temper, especially for the next five days, with those who are special to you.

Grand Rapids Do not assume that a particular situation will automatically turn out the way you want it to. Take steps within three days, to ensure the result is one you desire. This dream may also be used as a reference point in time. If you dream of this city and see its name used in any context, the dream message will occur on this day.

grand slam This dream is an extremely lucky omen but it is important that you do not allow your mood to guide your direction. Do not make a mistake by relying on your emotions when you make important decisions. Control your impulsive behavior.

grandson Within two days someone will realize what both of you need to accomplish together in the near future. Because of this you will both be able to avoid committing a big mistake. Do everything you can to alter the outcome of any negative event you dreamed of or avoid it completely. Alert anyone else you dreamed of to do the same. Take steps to ensure you experience only positive expressions in your life.

happy grandson Within three days you will learn of a large windfall that is coming your way. Anything negative you see in the dream connected with a grandson that you recognize needs to be avoided in real life. All positive events need to be incorporated in your life. Also implies that a project or situation you are dealing with now will come up again in the near future when you least expect it. You will have to deal with this now.

crying grandson Make a point of bringing happiness to this child. Within five days you will also be communicating with someone who needs to know quite a bit about you. Be sure you give this individual all the information they require so they can make a decision in your favor.

injured grandson Take steps to avoid this situation in real life. This dream also implies that you are overlooking a potentially negative situation that needs to be attended to. Start working on this particular situation within two days in order to turn it around to a positive situation.

grandstand A certain situation that requires the help of another will work out well because you will be able to choose the right person to work with. You will find this person within three days.

granny knot For the next three days avoid settling for less than you really want. A situation you are leaving, because you think the new path is a better choice, is the wrong move and you will find you are headed in the wrong direction. Think things through carefully before you make any further decisions.

Granny Smith apple You must not allow yourself to stagnate to the point of losing your appreciation of those things you used to enjoy. Make a list of enjoyable things you can do immediately. Push yourself to do these things and you will develop a younger outlook on life. You will enjoy good luck, comfort, tranquility and joy within seven days.

grape You will be sexually active in just the way you want to be and your partner will touch you emotionally in the way you desire. You and this person will make plans for your life and will be together for a very long time to come. This is a lucky omen and implies an abundance of love and money. You will clearly see during this cycle that you are surrounded by those who love you.

grapefruit Build up your resistance and treat your health as a precious commodity. Eat healthful foods and do everything necessary to maintain your health. Pamper yourself and add more joy to your life.

grapefruit juice Be very careful for the next three days not to involve yourself with anything that seems outrageous or unusual. There is an underlying danger in all of this. Your involvement will change your life and you will come to regret this.

grapevine Within three days you will prepare for an all expense paid vacation with another individual. This vacation will last a short time but will make you feel very happy. You will experience warm and exciting moments. Good luck, love and joy is with you. You will receive an abundance of blessings and experience a more spiritual outlook on life.

graph Someone you are interested in who has led you to believe they will contact you for a romantic interlude will let you down. Do not get emotionally caught up in this and prepare yourself so you can handle yourself appropriately.

graphite This dream is a lucky omen. A business enterprise you will become involved in within two days will be very fortuitous and bear fruit. You are going in the right direction. This dream also implies that someone you have been anxious to hear from will contact you soon.

graph paper Come to grips with a situation that requires immediate handling to avoid any complications in the near future. Avoid stress and relentlessly work to alter the course of all negative situations.

grass Within two days an offer will be made to you that is too good to refuse. Jump on this chance. You will also find things you felt were impossible in the past are now possible regarding business and romantic situations. Good luck is with you and you will find this to be a good cycle for all negotiations.

grasshopper This dream is an omen of health. Do everything necessary for the next two days to use your communication skills in a way that will bring someone closer to you. You are headed for a financially secure future.

grass snake Within two days someone will begin to create chaos in your life. This person will catch you off guard and you will become dragged in to this chaos. Do everything you can to remain uninvolved and stress free.

Grateful Dead Within seven days you will realize what heaven is when you recognize the creative and profound thoughts that are coming from within you. Motivate yourself to develop these thoughts with confidence, neither over or under doing them. Execute these thoughts on a grand scale and do not allow yourself to develop tunnel vision. Become flexible but not overly so. Do not allow yourself to take to-day's moments for granted because these moments will be your future memories. Use common sense and get in sync with your health regarding food and beverages. You will victoriously achieve your goals through your journey in life and you are headed for a brilliant future.

grave Do not deprive yourself of special moments with someone who is special to you by making excuses and not allowing yourself to develop the time to spend with them. This will become an issue within three days. Take steps to avoid this problem. You are also going in the wrong direction. Focus on what needs to be done now to set yourself on the right track. Make sure any negative event witnessed in this dream does not become a reality and alert anyone else involved to do likewise. Take steps to experience only positive expressions in your life.

grave digger A health problem could be lessened by reading the proper information. This information will make this issue easier to deal with and will guide you toward proper treatment.

gravel This dream is a good luck symbol, especially regarding love and education. The correct decisions about education will make a big difference in your life.

graven image For the next three days you will be pursued by someone who does not appear to be as well off as they are. This person will be eager to build a close friendship and will also offer financial help. Do not take this lightly.

gravestone Do not constantly replay negative tapes. You are talking yourself out of some great ideas. Go for the impossible and you will be surprised at how quickly you can gather together the tools and knowledge to launch the impossible. This is the perfect cycle for this and good luck is with you. Make sure also you do not allow any negative event seen in this dream to become a reality. Take steps to only experience positive events in your life.

graveyard A situation will come up within two days that you will feel you lack the confidence in handling. Do not allow this feeling to overcome you for you will be able to handle important situations quickly and correctly. Do every-

thing you can to prevent the occurrence of any negative event you dreamed of or to alter the outcome. Take steps to enjoy only positive expressions in your life.

graveyard shift An impromptu party will be thrown. At this festivity you will want to avoid speaking extensively to one individual. Think ahead and take the time to speak with this person and you will find they will become the best friend you will ever have. The relationship will grow only as much as you will allow it to and you will enjoy the best years of your life with this person as a friend.

gravity You will receive what you most desire and a special favor will be granted. Blessings are with you. Any negative occurrence you dreamed of must be altered or avoided in reality. Do everything you can to experience only positive events in your life.

gravy Pain and anguish will disappear within two days because a situation will arise that will alleviate these burdens.

gray whale Do not assume a personality that confuses others. Too much of a change is sometimes too drastic for others to comprehend. Step back and check yourself in order to avoid confusing others about what is going on with you. Also, pay attention to your travels and take pains to avoid accidents.

gray wolf An older wiser person will help you to reach the heart of a problem quickly. Within two days you will be able to easily solve a very complicated problem.

graze Make sure you do not become jealous of someone who is special to you and do nothing that will create envy in others. This dream is a good luck omen.

grease Do not expose yourself to a deadly disease for the next two days. Do everything you can to prevent this now.

grease monkey You will demand a high efficiency from others and this will enable you to gain the financial security you are after. Do not display a disagreeable temperament when making these demands.

grease paint Do not allow anyone to belittle or manipulate you. You will allow this to happen because you do not want to lose this person's friendship. Do not compromise your feelings. This individual will stand beside you but make sure you do not allow them to abuse you any longer.

grease pencil Do everything necessary to promote closeness between yourself and family members as well as others you feel you should be close to. Do not assume an air of coldness or purposely distance yourself from others. This is especially important for the next three days.

greasy *anything greasy* You need to avoid damaging the garments you will be wearing for the next three days. Any negative event portended in this dream must also be avoided or altered in reality. Take steps to experience only positive expressions in your life.

great aunt This dream implies good luck and is an omen of abundance in all levels of your life. You will be introduced to something new and wonderful within a short while. Take steps to keep any negative experience in this dream from becoming a reality. Do what you can to only experience positive events in your life.

Great Britain All special plans you have made, particularly travel plans, will fall into place exactly as you wish and all things you previously felt were impossible are now possible, especially for the next seven days.

Great Dane This dream is an extremely lucky omen. Do not procrastinate paperwork that needs to be handled now. You will then receive what you are after in a timely way.

great grandchild For the next three days, take care you do not blurt out something that should not be repeated in front of others. This will spoil someone else's surprise. Be very careful of what you say in front of others in order to keep a special surprise a secret. Blessings are with you and your family. Make sure you change any negative event in this dream or avoid it entirely. Take steps to enjoy only positive expressions.

great granddaughter Within three days you will have a desire to move to a new location and will excitedly go over your plans for this move. This relocation will be very successful for you. Do not allow any negative event to occur in reality and make sure you experience only positive events.

great grandparents This dream is a very lucky omen. Take the time to meditate in your favorite form and treat yourself in a special way. Enjoy solitude when you most need it. You must also be very alert. If you do not attend to a special plan, it will start to fall apart because of your inconsistent involvement. Be relentless in the pursuit of your goals. Anything negative connected to this dream needs to be changed to a positive event or avoided. Do what you can to experience only positive events.

great grandson This dream is a good luck omen. You will experience an abundance of blessings in all areas of your life, especially regarding health. Become more aware of your stress levels in order to create a stress free environment. This is especially important for the next ten days. Relentlessly take care of each new situation as it comes up during this cycle. Take steps also to alter or avoid any negative event depicted in this dream and do what you can to experience only positive expressions in your life. You will gain through this dream a clue of the positive, prosperous events that will occur during this time frame.

Great Lakes Someone will go to great lengths to get you out of a certain situation you feel is impossible to get yourself out of. Good luck is with you and many blessings will come to you and your family. This dream may also be used as a reference point in time. If you dream of these lakes and see their name used in any context, the dream message will occur on this day.

Great Salt Lake You will soon be given information that you lacked knowledge in. Pay close attention to this conversation because it will not be repeated. This dream may also be used as a reference point in time. If you dream of this lake and see its name used in any context, the dream message will occur on this day.

Great Smokey Mountains You will be able to sway someone regarding a business deal in the direction you wish. Aim for the big issues and proceed with confidence. This dream may also be used as a reference point in time. If you dream of this mountain chain and see its name used in any context, the dream message will occur on this day.

great uncle Within three days you will receive an unusual and unexpected gift that you will not like that much and will want to return. You will exchange this gift for one you are very satisfied with. Anything negative in this dream must be avoided or altered in reality. Make sure you enjoy only positive experiences in your life.

Great Wall of China Allow yourself to think creatively and put your ideas down in an orderly and structured fashion. You will then be able to focus on details. This concentration will allow you to bring your ideas to fruition. Within two days you will find you have well thought out concrete ideas. Jot them down so they will not be forgotten. Blessings will come to you and your family. This dream may also be used as a reference point in time. If you dream of this historical site and see its name used in any context, the dream message will occur on this day.

Greece You will enjoy a wonderful time with a group of people within five days. You will be very popular with everyone. This dream may also be used as a reference point in time. If you dream of this country and see its name used in any context, the dream message will occur on this day.

Greek Orthodox The plans you want to implement within three days must be done very carefully in order to make the correct decisions. Blessings are with you and your family.

green Quickly process what needs to be handled within three days so you can quickly receive what you desire. Whatever you thought was impossible is now possible. Go for it. You are also entering a period where you will feel more youthful, healthier and energetic.

green bean You are placing too much importance on someone else and are overextending yourself emotionally. Avoid disappointments by limiting the time you give to others.

green beret Within three days get the professional help you need to take care of those things that require immediate attention. Do not waste time on this.

green card Make it a priority to join new groups and meet new people. By doing this, new doors of opportunity will be open to you. Express your desires to this group and you will be surprised at how quickly your goals will be accomplished. Instant money and/or a profitable enterprise will also be an option you will want to explore within three days. This will bring you many advantages.

green dragon This dream is a very powerful symbol and you will be victorious in accomplishing the goals you are seeking. The gods are with you and many blessings are coming your way.

greenhouse Within five days someone who once played an important role in your life will seek you out for the purpose of renewing the relationship. If you choose to go with this, you will find both of your lives will be dramatically changed for the better.

green light Take a giant step and view your goals on a grander scale. This will be a tremendously lucky cycle for you.

green onion You will win some money within five days by playing your favorite games of chance.

green pepper You will enjoy an abundance of health and joy. Luck and blessings are with you and your family. All negotiations will also work out successfully if conducted within the week. Love yourself and eat healthy foods.

green snake You are expecting money within two days but this money is already spent in the mind of someone else. Do not allow anyone else to spend your money without including you in the decision making process. You have prior notice of this and can take steps to keep this from taking place. Otherwise, good luck is with you.

green tea You will ask an individual with a higher mental ability to go along with you in a joint effort. You will arrive at a perfect agreement. Good luck is with you.

green thumb Pay close attention to your behavior for the next three days to ensure you stay on the right track. Good luck is with you.

green turtle Drink plenty of water, but only in moderation. You are also finding it difficult to resolve an issue you have lost confidence in being able to handle. You will resolve this successfully within three days after having this dream.

greeting card You must quickly decide whether you want to commit to a relationship. Another person will become interested in the person who is special to you and will try to move in. If you do not commit, you will lose a healthy relationship. If you do commit, you will enjoy a very successful union. You will be asked to make a commitment within five days. This is a fantastic cycle for money and all business transactions. You must also make sure you are not neglecting to send a greeting card to someone during this cycle. You are headed in the right direction.

gremlin Avoid all friction between yourself and a loved one for the next two days. Put yourself out more and attend a special event with this person. Make it a point to make changes that will strengthen this union. This is an excellent cycle for promoting closeness.

grenade A special person is not permitting a relationship to grow as it should. At the first sign of this, open the lines of communication in order to persuade this individual to open up and stop setting so many limits. This is the perfect three day cycle for this.

greyhound Do not continuously run disturbing tapes that prevent you from taking on new ideas. Go for the big ideas. You have no reason to hold yourself back and you will find your ideas will be very successful. Eat healthful foods, make sure your environment is safe and drink plenty of water.

grey squirrel This dream is an extremely lucky omen and you will enjoy an abundance of health and wealth in areas of your life that you least expected. This will be as a result of an unexpected income. You are now able to accomplish those tasks you once felt were impossible. Use this cycle to tackle those big projects. Proceed with confidence, you are headed for a very prosperous future. You must also make sure for the next two days you are safe and avoid all accidents.

grid Do not waste your time developing a strategy of revenge against another. This will not bring you satisfaction and will only lead to later regrets.

griddle You will receive a surprising proposal for marriage within three days. You will accept this proposal and marry within a short period of time.

gridiron Within four days you will receive news that will be difficult for you to comprehend. Do not even try. Most of this information is false and you do not need to waste time being upset with lies.

gridlock Do not allow violence to erupt over a situation that someone else is too stubborn to acknowledge. Do not involve yourself with a stubborn person, especially for the next three days.

grill Within the week someone will lose something of value that belongs to you. Take precautions to keep this from occurring. Otherwise you will become very upset and tempers will flare. Make sure you keep any negative event in this dream from taking place and take steps to enjoy only positive experiences.

grim reaper Within three days you will become unsure

about a new romantic relationship. You will be experiencing mixed feelings and be unsure about which way to go. Proceed with confidence. This promises to be a great relationship. Be kind and affectionate to this individual and the relationship will develop on its own.

grind Someone you want to involve in a project as a co-worker will be rude and unmannered and you will have a feeling of disgust when you are around this person. While at work, however, this person is very organized and will be able to get down to the basics. This individual will be a real benefit to have on your staff. Go for it.

grindstone Luck is with you. For the next three days make sure you do not put yourself in the position of being treated indecently by others either in private or in front of others. Be very alert to the manners other people demonstrate toward you in order to avoid this.

gringo Within two days you will be seeing some good news regarding your financial status. You are headed very quickly toward a brilliant future.

grits Think ahead and be alert. You need to go to great lengths to really let someone know you are interested in them. It takes a while for this person to really understand what is going on with others. Do everything necessary to get your point across even if you have to take unusual steps.

grizzly bear A priceless collection will be damaged if you do not take steps to prevent this within ten days. Any negative occurrence in this dream needs to be avoided in reality. Do everything you can to experience only positive expressions in your life.

groan *to groan* Blessings will come to you and your family and you will all enjoy good health and good financial situations. You will also receive needed information from an unexpected source within three days.

grocer You will be involved in the plans of a secret organization that you have been yearning for. Look forward to this event within seven days.

grocery *any form* A cluster of events will occur one after the other with each bringing you a tremendous amount of joy, wonder and awe, because things are happening so quickly. You will also possess a powerful energy that you are going to be able to direct and control. At the same time these other events are taking place you will be able to bring other people under your complete control. Because you have prior notice of this you will be able, within the week, to direct this energy in such a way to successfully complete anything you wish in a superb way. You will be able to overcome any difficult obstacle and it will now be very simple to deal with it. Your intuition will be right on target. Follow your hunches about a new relationship. Many blessings are with you and your family.

grocery aisle Don't lose your baggage.

grocery cart You will have the support system and the network of knowledge you need to help position yourself in a comfortable lifestyle. During this cycle you will enjoy many opportunities for celebration and joyful events. Prepare yourself for some unexpected joyful news that is coming your way within the week. You are definitely headed for a brilliant future. You will also be left with the feeling that everyone is on your side and is supporting your goals. Also make every effort, for the next four days, to behave in such a way that will bring someone you desire close to you. This person is not yet involved with you and at first you will feel they are not interested in you in the way you desire. During this time period, you will also experience an abundance of health, a financial windfall will come your way, and you are headed for a prosperous future.

grog All of your mental pain and anguish will disappear overnight. Expect this to take place within seven days.

groin For the next week be very careful when making travel arrangements in order to avoid accidents.

groom You can accomplish exactly what you want in a romantic situation. Good luck is with you.

groove Develop compassion and sympathy for yourself for the next four days. You will be going through an emotional situation during this time period. Put enjoyment into your life and treat yourself gently.

grooving/groovy *(slang terms)* Someone is devising a plot to violate your rights for the purpose of their own emotional gratification. This individual will try to manipulate you into getting involved in a situation that will become more disgusting and distasteful as time goes on. This involvement will go against your will and your better judgment. Do not put yourself in a position to compromise yourself. This is preventable. Good luck is with you.

grope *to grope* You will be meeting a very attractive, generous and charismatic person. Your sexual drive, however, is much stronger than this individual's, and a relationship would be unfair. Think this situation through and determine the easiest move. This will occur within five days.

grotto You have the courage to become more aggressive in a situation that requires this trait. You will be able to tackle a very important issue within four days.

ground Within five days you will rid yourself of an emotional hang up and be able to change the way you run your life. This will influence another person into agreeing with plans you are developing. Be determined to change your behavior in order to get this positive response from others.

ground beetle Do everything necessary to promote closeness between yourself and your in-laws and behave in a manner that will bring more closeness to the relationship. You will have the opportunity to accomplish this within two days.

ground control You will achieve financial security because your services will be in demand. Within four days you will also learn of the deep feelings someone has for you.

ground cover Do not allow anyone to belittle you or to manipulate you out of something you do not wish to give up. Stand firm and protect your possessions and position. You will have the strength to do this within five days. It would be better to bypass this situation altogether.

ground crew Take the time to regroup and concentrate. This will help you to quickly get to the heart of the situation in order to make the proper corrections where needed. Do this within four days. Good luck is with you.

ground floor Within four days you will be invited to join someone's social group. This will give you a great amount of pleasure and exposure to a number of events.

ground glass You will receive many blessings and an abundance of health. Good luck is with you. Introduce yourself to new people and bring more spice to your life. Enjoy yourself.

groundhog Someone you very much want to demonstrate an interest in you will do so within the week.

ground squirrel Situations are going to change within three days unless you are willing to adopt another person's ways of living. Because of this you will become very irritated. Do everything necessary to maintain happiness. These situations are beyond your control. Otherwise you are headed for a prosperous future.

groundwater The state of mind of someone you are now focused on is very unhealthy. Be cautious when making decisions with this person.

group You will receive a surprise gift as a prize. Lucky you.

groupie Negative thoughts about another person are unfounded. It is better to focus on more positive things.

group insurance Gather all of the information you need when assuming the supervision of others. Don't waste time. Someone will want to review your method of supervision.

group medicine Talk, for the next few days, will be filled with time consuming problems and trouble. Avoid the problems of others. This will only waste time that is better spent on more important activities.

group therapy Someone you want to request financial help from will want to speak to you in private. This individual prefers to keep knowledge of this loan private. It is best to keep it to yourself until you speak with them, otherwise you will lose out.

grouse Be sure you do not inadvertently blurt out an insult because you do not think ahead. Make sure you do not unintentionally hurt someone's feelings, especially for the next seven days.

grout Do not compromise yourself and make sure you aggressively pursue what it is you are after from someone else within three days. You will achieve victory if you are aggressive in your pursuit.

grove For the next three days make sure you do not put yourself in the position to have to explain an attitude that is not socially acceptable.

grow *to see things grow* The opportunity you have been waiting for will come through within three days. You will have the ambition to start anew in the areas you are interested in. Old issues that have been dragging you down will come to an end. Welcome these changes with enthusiasm. The best days of your life are yet to come.

in any other form You will have more joy in your life by practicing a positive attitude and way of thinking with yourself and others. Anything negative in this dream can be avoided or altered in reality.

growing pains Someone is intentionally plotting to send you on a wild goose chase. Make sure the directions you are given are accurate, otherwise you will find yourself following the wrong ones. Be alert to this within three days in order to complete your tasks without frustrations.

growl *to hear anything growl* You will be in a very lucky cycle for the next seven days.

in any other form Within three days you will have to deal with a personal issue that will require special handling by an expert. Use common sense and be practical in all phases of this matter to ensure a successful resolution.

grown-up *in any form* Do everything necessary to earn big dividends.

growth Relax, bask in love and listen very carefully to the words you hear. You are loved beyond your imagination and will learn of this within seven days.

grub Make sure you are not duplicating someone else's efforts. Check on the work someone else is doing to ensure you are not repeating work already done. It will make a big difference in the amount of time you spend on this.

grudge *any form* Do not allow yourself to become involved in a ménage â trois. Everyone involved in this relationship will be hurt.

gruesome *any form* Plans to pull out of a situation need to be well thought out. Do not make any sudden changes.

guacamole A special person will suddenly be in a rush to consummate the relationship. This will be a once in a lifetime memory.

Guadalajara Within two days you will feel the urgency to consummate a relationship with someone who has caught your interest. If you choose, this relationship will be one of mutual satisfaction with someone who loves to travel, is demonstrative and very giving. Great times are coming. This dream may also be used as a reference point in time. If you dream of this city and see its name used in any context, the dream message will occur on this day.

Guam You will have a grand and wonderful time with many young children. This dream may also be used as a reference point in time. If you dream of this island and see its name used in any context, the dream message will occur on this day.

guaranty Put your affairs in order within two days.

guard You will be easily persuaded by someone who seems very pleasing. In reality this person has a very bad disposition and attitude. Be wary of this because you will be coming into contact with this person in three days. You have prior notice to prevent any negative event you dreamed of from becoming a reality with you or with anyone else involved. Take steps to ensure you experience only positive expressions in your life.

guardhouse You will always be the center of attention in someone else's life.

guardian Do not dwell on the decisions of others. These are out of your hands and out of your control.

guardrail Enjoy a spending spree at someone else's expense who has encouraged you to do so.

Guernsey Someone will demonstrate an interesting display of feelings toward you within two days.

guerrilla warfare Pay close attention to the chemicals you are working with and remind yourself that odorless chemicals can also be deadly.

guess *to guess the right answer* You will be unable to deny yourself emotionally like you have in the past. The potential for emotional fulfillment is now at its peak. Proceed with confidence.
    to be unable to guess the right answer You need to avoid making mathematical errors for the next three days.
    in any other form Another person cannot possibly keep up with your potential. Proceed with confidence. Anything negative you dreamed of needs to be turned around into a positive expression.

"guess who" *to hear this phrase* Within three days you will be more thrilled and overjoyed than you ever felt before because of several unconnected occurrences that will occur almost simultaneously. It will be more successful than you ever thought possible with very little effort on your part. This will be a result of your motivation, being in the right place at the right time, by following your hunches and by paying attention to your perceptions. You will experience much more of this within the month.

guest Be very aware of where your focus is for the next week. You will be very attracted to two separate people and unless you make up your mind quickly, you will be unable to encourage the affection of either one. Arrive at a quick decision. Anything negative connected with this dream needs to be turned into a positive experience.

guide Remind a same sexed workaholic friend that you only live once. Life is not a rehearsal. Remind this individual that they can live a fuller life. Take steps to keep any negative event you dreamed of from becoming a reality.

guidebook Meditate in your favorite manner and you will find your path paved with gold. You are headed toward a wonderful future.

guided missile Do not put in a change of address with the post office if you have no desire to be found. Rent a P.O. Box to keep undesirables away. Any negative event foretold in this dream can be altered or avoided completely. Do everything you can to experience only positive expressions in your life.

guide dog Someone will unexpectedly seem more attentive toward you. Enjoy this and accept it with humor. Take steps to turn any negative event connected to this dream into a positive expression.

guidepost Make an effort to focus more on romance and foreplay.

guild Sharpen your skills and put them to use in new and different ways in order to secure financial stability. Anything negative connected to this dream can be turned around into a positive expression.

guildhall Do not allow family interference to alter the course of your decisions, especially in the near future.

guildsman You will receive a wonderful surprise gift from a distant place.

guilt Promote closeness between you and those who are special to you. Avoid conversations that create distance and look for compromise during this cycle. A special favor will be granted to you within three days. This will be the perfect cycle to tackle those seemingly impossible tasks. The end result will be successful.

guinea pig Someone much younger than you will fall in love with you.

Guinevere Life's finest rewards will soon be yours.

guitar *any form* Within three days you will be able to lay claim to someone's affections and desires. You also need to make sure you avoid or alter any negative event witnessed in this dream.

gulf You will be able to gain the advantage in certain situations by setting up meetings with those you desire to discuss your wishes with. Proceed with confidence. These people are open to discussion.

gull The person who has expressed a desire to contact you will fail to do so due to a very busy schedule. At the first mention of this be sure to determine a way you can make contact. This individual wants to hear from you and by contacting them you will eliminate a great deal of their stress and anxiety.

Gulliver Within five days it will be necessary to express yourself fully to another person. Determine what is keeping you from living life to the fullest and do not allow anyone to block your path.

gully You will soon experience more attentiveness and love from others.

gulp *in any form* You will meet someone who will treat you with a high degree of interest and will pay you a lot of attention. Be very aware of this. This person is married and their spouse is away on a trip. You will be given everything you desire, emotionally and physically until the spouse returns, then you will be forgotten. Do not allow yourself to be taken. Otherwise, good luck is with you.

gum *bubble gum* A problem in the family will be revealed to you through a child. This problem will be resolved and each person in the family will receive an abundance of health and blessings.

in any other form Do not allow yourself to be taken in by someone who presents themselves as an authority figure. Do not believe in promises that this person is unable to deliver, especially for the next two days.

gumdrop Use your mental inventiveness. Be very aware, also, of certain situations that create anger in you. Regroup and remain calm, especially for the next three days. Angry outbursts will only lead you to lose confidence in yourself.

gumbo Remain focused on all ongoing personal issues and do not allow outside influences to sidetrack you from the certainties you feel. Maintain harmony and tranquility and be sure to drink plenty of water.

gumshoe A special person will not support your ideas, especially for the next four days.

gum tree Make sure all people planning to attend a reunion agree to come in a relaxed mood in order to avoid any potential stresses. Many people are invited who do not care for each other. Make sure these differences are resolved prior to the reunion.

gumwood Someone has entered your life with a deep expression of kindness toward you. You have desired this person but feel love is impossible. Now, anything is possible.

gun Keep up with your work schedule and go all out for entertainment and enjoyable events. You will also need to take steps to change the outcome or to prevent, within five days, any negative event in this dream from becoming a reality. Warn anyone else involved of this danger. You are definitely headed for a prosperous future. For the next two days you must also do what you can to keep someone from ill-treating someone precious whom you hold close to you. This will be done subtly and painfully by someone you least expect and will lead to the development of deeply painful feelings and resentments toward this individual. Do everything you can to avoid this scene or to prepare yourself appropriately. You will also enjoy a tremendous victory that is not connected to this scene but will occur within the same time frame.

gunboat Don't panic because of the occurrences of out of the ordinary events. Remain calm, this is a temporary situation.

gunfight Change your attitude and remove that chip from your shoulder. Learn to enjoy life.

gunfire In spite of the number of physicians you see to find out what is wrong with you physically, you will be told there is nothing organically wrong. This dream is telling you that although you feel certain abnormalities are taking place, you have nothing seriously wrong with you. Be happy with this and be assured that healing will come quickly if you start treating your physical complaints from a different perspective. Your attitude and thinking patterns need to be redirected. Stop treating your body in an unreasonable manner and change the way you treat yourself in the form of exercise, lifestyle habits, diet, and stress levels. Reschedule your life to lessen the physical demands on your body and remove yourself from any person who makes you feel uncomfortable and adds extra stress to your life. You can quickly turn this into a positive situation by redirecting the way in which you live your life. It will take time for you to recover and you will be healthier than when you began this new regimen. Take steps to alter any negative event in this dream that could become a reality, and do what you can to experience only positive expressions in your life. You are headed for a prosperous future and many blessings will come to you and your own family.

gung ho You will be able to contact a very elusive person if you act within the next two days. This individual is in a good mood because they will shortly be leaving for a long vacation.

gun lock Think ahead, regroup yourself and remove all invisible blocks to success. You will find success by using diplomacy in your dealings with others.

gunmetal Go all out when planning a romantic date.

gunpowder You will receive a nice gift and all of your wishes will come to pass. You will also be invited to a very elegant formal event. You will enjoy yourself immensely.

gunrunner Divorce yourself from any action taken against another person.

gunslinger Be wary of anyone who is attempting to impress you with their financial status. Ignore this behavior and get on with your life without this person in it. You also need to take steps to avoid any negative event in this dream and do everything you can to enjoy only positive expressions in your life.

guppy You will soon be showered with more love than you have seen before. You have long awaited this demonstration of love from this person. Do not become emotionally attached to them because of their wishy-washy behavior although many benefits can be gleaned from this relationship. It will last a long time.

gurney This dream is very lucky for you and implies that, within two days, you will develop an inner strength and courage that comes from within. You will be motivated by your steel drive and determination to break through all hidden physical and mental obstacles. You will be able to rid yourself of any aspect of your life that keeps you from being thrust forward. Once you remove these blocks you will see a clear path and will acquire the knowledge you need to develop those areas of your life you most desire as well as the perfect lifestyle for yourself. This will be the perfect time period to accomplish this. You will also be greeted like royalty and be placed on a pedestal anywhere you choose to go. You will be very surprised by this treatment. You are on the path for a brilliant future and many new opportunities will present themselves.

guru This is not a good time to mix recreation time with romantic time. Spend your time exclusively with those who need you and do not combine that time with other pleasures.

gush Your relationship will break apart due to your lack of affection and expressions of love toward someone who is special to you. While the original agreement was to keep this union casual, it has developed into something deeper. Change your ways if you desire to keep this relationship. Good luck is with you and this is a very lucky cycle.

gut Be very cautious with self-medications in order to avoid an accidental overdose or allergic reaction.

gutter Remain alert and do not allow yourself to become caught up in any negative game playing. You will be tempted to do so but must remain aloof from this.

guttersnipe Do not create a big problem out of a small issue, especially for the next three days. This will lead to a feeling of dislike from others and a waste of too much precious time.

Guy Fawke's Day Be very aware of someone who acts the role of a chameleon and changes their personality and behavior in order to get what they want. This person will make it a point to be at the right place at the right time and will change each aspect of their personality to suit their purpose. They will do this whether they are acting in good faith or not.

gymnasium Talk with someone who has experience with what you are presently undergoing. You also need to take steps to avoid any negative message foretold in this dream or alter the outcome. Be sure to alert anyone else you dream of to do the same. Make sure you experience only positive expressions in your life.

gymnast An angry past acquaintance is seeking revenge. Make sure you do not become embroiled in a physical dispute in public. This person is very dangerous and is out to hurt you.

gymnastics Someone in your vicinity is afflicted with a mental illness and will lose control. Be careful and keep your distance. You have prior notice of this and can take steps to avoid anything negative you saw in this dream.

gynecology Develop the understanding that you are very important to someone else and that material possessions will never take your place. Your love together will deepen over the years. Good luck is with you. You also need to make sure anything in this dream that was negative does not become a reality and forewarn anyone you dreamed about to do the same.

gypsum Be good to yourself and stop being your own worst enemy. Devise a plan that causes you to focus on the direction you choose to go and one that will allow you to supervise your activities. You are headed toward big problems with the law unless you put this plan into action. Any endeavor you choose to become involved with will also have a more satisfactory outcome than you imagined.

gypsy You will become involved in a new way of living, will sample many new experiences and will love every moment. Take steps to avoid any negative event you saw in this dream and make sure you experience only positive events in your life.

gypsy moth Within seven days you will be in the position to make major changes in your life. Each plan you set into motion will be successful. Good luck is with you.

gyroscope For the next seven days, aggressively motivate yourself to actively change your direction in life in order to better your financial status. Once this is done you will be able to grasp a better position in life.

H

H This dream implies that you know a certain person who can provide you with benefits and opportunities you have not yet focused on. You are wasting time as well as the opportunity to take advantage of the wealth this person is willing to offer you. Wake up and pay attention to the benefits you can gain from this individual. This person will also be a loyal friend for years.

Habakkuk *(Hebrew prophet)* Be very receptive to your hunches in order to avoid being put on an emotional roller coaster by someone. You will find this very distasteful. Within two days you can eliminate this issue and avoid going through this pain.

haberdasher This dream is an extremely lucky omen. Do not allow any unexpected jobs that come your way to put you in a bad frame of mind. Accept what is coming, deal with it and handle it quickly, especially for the next three days. Many blessings are with you and your family.

haberdashery Use your wisdom for the next three days. A wrong decision will be your own doing so choose wisely and be careful when making choices. Do not blame others for a mistake you can easily avoid during this time frame.

habit Do not be so judgmental with others, especially for the next two days.

habitat Someone will call it exactly as they see it. Listen carefully so you can gain the benefit of this person's insight. Be especially attentive for the next three days. This person will blurt out some valuable information that will benefit you greatly.

hacienda Be sure blame is placed on the right source regarding a particular matter. See matters for what they really are. This is especially important for the next two days.

hack Within two days you will need to work on a special appeal for yourself. You will then be provided with the opportunity to be heard.

hacksaw For the next three days be very careful of firearms. Discourage the presence of these weapons in your vicinity and around your friends and family.

haddock You are entering a very lucky cycle. Make the effort to promote closeness with those you care about who live far from you. For the next two days do everything necessary to establish communication with these people. You will also come to grips with an uneasy feeling you have about a special person. You will both then be able to talk through these feelings.

Hades *(Greek mythology)* Let that special person know you have a very high regard for them. During this cycle, an opportunity will present itself that will make this possible. You will be successful for the next five days if you are very detailed in the plans you are about to execute. Force yourself to see the whole picture in order to reap the results of what you are now working toward. You will be able to skillfully use words with enough clarity to complete this task. As a result, you will make yourself available for riches that would otherwise not come to you. Blessings are with you and your family. Any negative event portended in this dream needs to be altered and you need to only experience positive expressions in your life.

hag Within five days a special friend will offer you an opportunity to get away to an unusual hideaway. This will be a wonderful experience that you will enjoy immensely.

Hagar *(from the Bible)* You are contemplating moving to an altogether different geographical area and beginning life over again. These thoughts will begin to develop within the week. If you choose to make this move, your life will change on a grand scale. Good luck is with you.

Haggai *(Hebrew prophet)* Within three days you will have an irresistible impulse to bring more pleasure into your life. This will lead to a more inspired way of living and your health and attitude will take a turn for the better. Many blessings are with you and this time cycle will be very lucky for you for the next month.

hail For the next two days push yourself to bring a certain obligation to completion. You are entering a very lucky seven day cycle.

Hail Mary A younger person will need special attention for the next four days. Make sure any illness they have is treated promptly.

hailstone Do not surrender to an agreement you have been avoiding. Do not compromise and do not agree to anything for the next three days. This will enable you to avoid many distasteful moments.

hailstorm Beware. Unexpectedly dropping in on someone unannounced will not be a good idea and you will not be pleased with what you find. Discourage this move. You will be tempted to do this within two days.

hair Take the time to clear out your schedule and make room for some free time because within the week you will be required to handle additional matters of importance. You will be able to use the free time to handle these matters much easier and with more calm.

gold colored hair Within the week you will be offered a golden opportunity that will come only once in a lifetime. Remain flexible and stay open to this opportunity during this time period. This also implies that you and a special person will be doing whatever is necessary to improve relations. You will also adopt new methods for improving your life together and will explore new ways to show mutual respect. You are headed for a brilliant future

outrageously colored hair Establish a strong outlet for your creativity. It should be a priority for the next three days to promote your talents.

white hair You will have high hopes when a particular person suggests you meet casually for light conversation. You will think this person is over past hurts and has worked through old resentments. Avoid this situation at all costs because within three days you will find these old feelings will resurface.

white hair on a young person Regardless of what is happening in your life, make sure you get plenty of rest in order to avoid fatigue. You must also use whatever resources are available in order to bring your ideas to a tangible form. You are entering a cycle within seven days that will enable you to clearly develop plans that will bear fruit.

a person with white hair who does not have white hair in reality Both you and the person you dreamed about need to take precautions to avoid freak accidents. Be sure to alert this individual of this possibility.

tangled and disorderly hair Make sure, for the upcoming week, that you do not close doors and distance yourself from others because of your behavior. These people will later be a benefit to you.

wavy hair You will receive a gift from your special deity of greater mental inventiveness and intelligence. Use this time to take this gift for your personal benefit to bring your standard of living up to the level you desire.

if you do not recognize the person with wavy hair This person represents someone who will come into your life and relentlessly help you grasp your goals. They may not actually have wavy hair in reality, but the face will be the same. This will occur within the week. Good luck is with you.

to have your hair messed up by someone else Your lack of performance within the next two days will be important in someone else's eyes. This individual will feel let down by this. Take steps to prevent it from happening.

to mess up someone's hair You will be given solid advice about how to easily resolve a problem.

crew cut Compromise to reach agreements for old problems.

to have your hair pulled Be very aware of your behavior, especially for the next three days. You will appear very nervous when in the presence of a certain individual and this will leave you open for abuse. This person has determined you are an easy pushover. Take steps to alter this behavior.

to pull someone's hair Within seven days you will meet someone whom you will greatly desire in your life. When you first meet this person do not give the impression that you have a busy and cramped schedule. Tone this aspect of your life down because this person will not desire to seek your company.

to cut someone's hair Within seven days you will meet someone much younger than you. This person will rapidly become a significant part of your life and this will result in many important and positive changes in your life. This will be a very positive and satisfying cycle and you will experience many successes.

to see yourself getting a hair cut Within two days you will be pushed to the limit by someone else. You will be able to handle this correctly and with confidence.

hair cut at a salon You are procrastinating an agreement. Stop putting off decisions, the result will be successful.

to have your hair cut in a violent way or without your consent Because of a disagreement, a certain contract will suddenly be altered. This could escalate into verbal and physical violence between two people and is a very dangerous situation. Avoid this at the first sign of trouble. Remain calm and avoid all behavior that may escalate this. Make sure also that all agreements and contracts are put in writing.

to see yourself or someone else get a permanent Something will take place in your life that will be so unusual and extraordinary it will be impossible to explain its occurrence by any law of physics. Expect this to take place within three days. It will leave you with a sense of wonder and awe. You will have the feeling you have witnessed a miracle and have no way of explaining how it came about. After this transpires you will be able to present yourself to others in the best possible light and be able to handle yourself, other people and new situations in an appropriate manner. You are headed for a brilliant future and many blessings will come to you and your family.

to dye Pay attention to the color of the dye for a more detailed meaning to the dream. This dream may be suggesting a color to experiment with for a new look. You must also include a variety of new events in your life in order to add more spice and excitement to your daily routine, especially for the next seven weeks.

for those who dye hair in reality If the color of the dye is one that is totally unacceptable to you, be aware that certain chemicals used on the hair produce an unusual discoloration. Be very watchful of this for the next three days.

roots showing that need to be dyed For the next three days do what you can to remain calm and in control. A situation will occur during this time period that you will be tempted to involve yourself in. Do not compromise yourself and do not become entangled in the problems of another. This individual has a hidden agenda. Once you become involved it will be difficult to cut yourself loose and the situation will become progressively worse as time goes on. Stay uninvolved. Make sure also you do not leave your roots showing. You will not want to be caught off guard.

shampooed hair Do not allow another person's indifference to keep you from making positive changes in your life.

to dry your hair or to see someone else drying hair Someone who harbors a secret animosity toward you will attempt, within a five day period, to sabotage the plans you have to steer a situation in a certain direction that will benefit others. You are trying to work things out in such a way that everyone involved will enjoy future prosperity. Although this person knows you are right they will work against you, regardless of the destruction they will wreak on others. They are not aware of the degree of hardship they will bring to others. You have prior notice of this and can take steps to prevent this interference.

hair falling out Restrain your movements in order to keep from reinjuring an old injury. Avoid strains and any injuries due to physical activity.

to find hair in food You will be caught off guard when someone begins to show more interest in you. This person will provide you with private, intimate moments that will allow you to deepen the relationship. Be prepared for this to happen within three days.

to smell burned hair Within two days you will be surprised at a request to spend private moments with someone. This request will be unexpected and will come after repeatedly asking this person to spend time with you and after repeatedly being turned down. Curiosity will lead you to want to spend time with this person. The choice is up to you.

curly hair Good luck is with you. Make sure you follow your hunches; your intuitions are correct. Openness and the willingness to cooperate will win the favor of a special person, especially for the next three days.

hairy body You will be tempted to investigate a certain situation but you will be better off forgetting the whole incident.

to see hair grow on an unusual area of the body You are beginning to develop a close relationship with someone who will lead you to believe you can confide fully in them and can rely on their loyalty. Move forward with this person with extreme caution, especially for the next three days. This person will create an air of trust and allay any suspicions you have. They will also lead you to believe in future occurrences that will never take place. This person is a master of deception and illusion and has a hidden agenda that involves pursuing you for reasons known only to them. If they get wind that you may be becoming suspicious of their devious plans they will be able, because of their charm, to create a diversion to draw you away from your suspicions. Once you realize what is going on you will be suffering deep disappointments, a feeling of disillusionment and financial distress. It will take a long time to recover from this and get back to normalcy. You have prior notice of this and all the ammunition you need to make sure this does not take place. Practice common sense and you will successfully diffuse this. Do not become involved, do not compromise your feelings and do not let this person pry into your personal affairs. You are on the path toward a prosperous future. Many blessings will come to you and your family.

darker hair on someone you recognize or on yourself Listen carefully, someone in power is going to ask you for a favor within the week. This will be done very subtly and unless you pay close attention you may miss the opportunity to become involved in a situation that will benefit you both greatly. Notice the way you look with darker hair if the dream centered on you. This may be a color you would like to experiment with.

lighter hair on someone you recognize or on yourself For the next three days do not settle for less when making a choice. Check your options and do not set limits. Maintain a positive attitude. Good luck is with you. This may also be indicating a new hair color that would be very becoming or a color you want to avoid at all costs.

red hair Be very aware of something you are doing now that will cause financial damage later on. You will not be aware of the extent of the damage for a long time. Protect your expenditures now.

short hair Do not engage in guessing games with another person and do not drag someone in on this for the purpose of putting them through an emotional wringer. Back away from this behavior because it will backfire on you.

frizzy hair You will have the opportunity to meet someone you have long admired but have not had the courage to speak to. This will be a victorious seven day cycle and you will be able to successfully bring issues that are important to you to a satisfactory conclusion.

to set hair An assignment you have submitted will be turned down. Get special inside information in order to be successful.

combed hair Within two days someone will place so many demands on you that your life will become very stressful. Put your foot down and do not allow anyone to add this kind of stress to your life.

pin curl Anyone you see in this dream with a pin curl needs intervention and assistance for a particular problem. Within three days you will also referee two people who will find it impossible to reach an agreement about a specific problem. With your help they will find a solution.

pubic hair Within two days, a situation will take place that will be so extraordinary it will defy any law of physics. This strange event will leave you with a sense of awe and wonder and you will sense you have witnessed a miracle with no way to explain how it transpired. After this takes place, you will be able to present yourself at your best and be able to handle yourself, other people and situations in the best possible way. You will see greater improvements than you ever thought possible. Your sense of awareness will be heightened and you will be able to sense the knowledge you need to retrieve. You are definitely headed for a brilliant future and many blessings will come to you and your family.

wig For the next week a number of different opportunities will be presented to you that you can involve yourself in. Any of these could make you a very wealthy person. This is a time when conversations will be very productive in business and love relations. You will find various ways of promoting yourself for success and will meet many people with the wealth and resources to further your goals. You are in a very prosperous cycle and are headed for a brilliant future. From this point on you can expect an increase in finances and situations will take place one right after the other. Your life will change for the better in any way you desire.

hair gel This dream is alerting you that within three days you will be dealing with a certain person who is very knowledgeable about your likes and dislikes. This individual is also aware of the kind of lifestyle you do not approve of and the situations you are against. They will use methods of subtle persuasion and will formulate a plot to lead you into a lifestyle you would ordinarily reject. This person intends to lure you into doing something that goes against your principles. Many different tactics will be used in order to get you to do their bidding. This persuasion will be done in a very stylish way through the use of gifts, vacations, etc. It may take several gifts and a great deal of time to win you over but you will end up doing as this person wants. You have prior notice of this and can take the appropriate steps to handle this issue. Otherwise you are headed for a brilliant future.

hair rollers Make sure you are not caught off guard by someone who will unexpectedly drop in within the next two days. Place more importance on your personal appearance so you will be presented in your best light if someone does drop in without warning.

to feel or see hair rising on any part of the body due to an unexplained reason Within four days you will be entering an extremely lucky cycle and everyone involved in your life will share in this luck. You will also receive services that will enable you to complete your goals successfully and reach higher levels of achievement than you thought possible, especially with anything you feel is a priority for you. You can expect wonderful and amazing connections that will assist you in grasping and meeting your goals. You can also expect a mega merger and the energy generated between you and those you will be working with will bring you to a far higher level of success than you hoped for. Also you will benefit greatly by attending a festive event, participating in an educational experience or by attending a gathering in which one person will show an interest in you and your projects. You can look forward to a long period of tranquility following this experience and will enjoy a prosperous future. Anything negative witnessed in this dream may be avoided and you need to forewarn anyone you dreamed about to do the same.

hair accessories Do everything necessary to express the hidden desires you have for another. This will be possible within two days.

hair ball When attempting to solve a problem within the next two days, continue to reach out to others who may have the answers to resolve this issue.

hair bow In the next few days an extremely attractive and much younger person will verbally communicate that they are hopelessly in love with you. You are to follow your instincts on this and anything you choose to do will be correct. You are also going to have an abundance of health and many joyful events.

hairbrush When recovering from an illness be sure not to over medicate yourself out of a desire to get better faster. Proceed with caution.

haircut *to see someone get their hair cut* You will reach an agreement with another for sexual gratification. If you choose, this will lead to a long lasting relationship for as long as you desire.

if you recognize the person This individual has a very delicate situation to discuss with you that will bring you immense pleasure and satisfaction. Pay attention to the particular hairstyle. This may indicate a style you will wish to try out. If the hairstyle was unattractive, take steps to avoid it.

hairdo Anything or anybody foreign will be very lucky for you for the next seven days.

hairdresser Keep all behind the scenes work from a certain person. It would be better if this person is not aware of this until the work is completed.

hairline Develop greater detail with those ideas you plan to implement and you will get better results.

hairnet You do not have to choose between two areas in your life. You can deal very effectively with both. Just pace yourself differently.

hairpiece The next seven days will be very lucky for you. Be sure to handle a special request from another person with a great amount of care. You will be able to take care of this very successfully.

hairpin You will soon get a lucky break. This is also the time to take steps to bring a relationship to the highest level you can. Do your part in keeping the closeness going on between you. Love and affection will help you to focus on important issues instead of dealing with wasted energy. You are both headed for a brilliant future. You also need to make sure you do not forget any important upcoming events.

hair products *(gels, mousse, hair conditioners, etc.)* You are being alerted that within three days you will be dealing with someone who is very aware of your likes and dislikes. This person is also aware of the kind of lifestyle you are against and situations you refuse to enter. This individual will use methods of subtle persuasion and will devise a path that will lead you into the lifestyle you are against. This individual's intentions are to steer you into doing something that goes against your principles. Many different tactics will be used in order to get you to do their bidding. This persuasion will be done in a stylish manner such as gift giving, vacations, etc. It may take several offerings and much time to win you over but you will end up doing what they wish. You have prior notice of this so you can handle the situation appropriately and determine exactly what you will and will not do. Otherwise you are headed for a brilliant future.

hairspray Someone who is beginning to show an interest in you will be turned off by your continuing resentment of a former relationship. Become very aware of how you sound to another individual, especially for the next four days.

Haiti For the next four days be very receptive to your hunches in order to get a sense of what is required of you to handle a particular situation that will come up during this time frame. This dream may also be used as a reference point in time. If you dream of this country and see its name used in any context, the dream message will occur on this day.

Haley's Comet Avoid speculation about another individual. Within the week you will learn the facts concerning this person and the facts about their involvement in a certain situation.

half Within three days you will gain access to privileged information. You must also not allow a spat to come between you and a special person. For the next three days do not allow a disagreement to take place that could escalate.

halfback Within three days you will be relieved of a responsibility you have been wanting to free yourself from.

half blood Someone will express to you unusual and loving affection that will bring you joy.

half breed Many blessings are with you and your family and you are entering a very lucky seven day cycle.

half brother Many powerful friends will rally around you and help you out in a pinch within three days. This quick response will relieve a very stressful situation.

half dollar You will receive an unexpected gift within three days that will give you a special delight.

half moon Stay away from heavy lifting and heavy labor. Do not place so many demands on yourself for the next seven days. Get more rest, eat healthful foods and drink plenty of water.

halfpenny You will be inspired within the week, to develop a support system for yourself by seeking a variety of ways to have a steady flow of income. You will be successful and the thoughts you generate will come through for you.

half shell Within four days divorce yourself from a situation that has become very trying for you. This situation will only lead to a dead end.

half sister Pay attention to the events of this dream. Any negative event involving you or someone you recognize needs to be avoided in reality. You also have the chance to open communications with someone you are trying to attract. Once you have made this gesture, this person will show their interest in you. You will also be able to use your communication skills effectively in other areas of your life to bring relationships closer to you. Many blessings will come to you and your family and you are headed for a very prosperous cycle.

halftime You will be asked by someone to watch your behavior. Back off, stop nagging and make sure you control you actions. Many blessings are with you.

halfway house Do not display a wishy-washy manner in front of someone when dealing with a particular situation

this individual wants to involve you in. Deal with this in a direct manner and go on with your life.

halibut This dream is an extremely lucky omen. The success you achieve will only be as great as the energy you put into pursuing your goals. Your level of achievement is in your hands. This cycle will allow you to motivate yourself and move swiftly ahead. Do not procrastinate and proceed with confidence.

hall Do not allow feelings of depression to overcome you. This will only restrict you and keep you from moving ahead. Do not allow old hurt feelings and resentments to fester and keep you from completing your goals. This will prevent you from moving in the direction you desire.

town hall For the next three days you will be able to negotiate all business transactions successfully and bring closeness into those relationships you desire.

hallelujah Do not allow yourself to get so caught up in someone's stressful situation that it starts to spill over onto you. This is not a good time for you to become involved in someone else's issues. Use this cycle to involve yourself in personal issues that delight you. Keep to yourself for the time being.

hallmark Do everything you can to experience closeness with a certain individual within the week. You will not be disappointed.

Halloween Within four days you will be purposely asked to complete an assignment that will present a big danger to you. This is preventable.

hallucinate Someone will enact a well thought out plan to lure you into a situation that will deeply hurt your feelings. This person lacks the courage to tell you face to face that they want to end the relationship/friendship and will set up this incident to get the point across in a cruel manner. Do what you can to go on with your life without this person in it.

halo Find a way to further your education. Once you set yourself on this path, your life will change dramatically for the better for a long period of time.

to have a halo You will enjoy many tranquil, peaceful moments in life, but for the next two days make sure you do not put yourself in the position of imminent danger. Stay in a safe place and guard your life.

to see someone you recognize with a halo This person needs to be warned to stay in a safe place during this two day cycle and to make sure they do nothing that could cost their life. Within the week this person will also execute their plans and ideas. This will create an unusual situation that will dramatically improve their lifestyle and put this person on the path of a brilliant future.

halogen Do not give anyone the opportunity to insult you for no reason and do not place yourself in the position to be insulted by anyone for the next three days. Something lucky will also happen during this time period.

halter Someone you have a deep respect and love for will move out of your life. Otherwise, this dream implies good luck is with you.

ham Examine your future plans to determine whether they are realistically workable in order to save time and energy. Otherwise, you are headed for a brilliant future.

Hamburg Focus on stabilizing financial situations that need to be handled within three days. This dream may also be used as a reference point in time. If you dream of this city and see its name used in any context, the dream message will occur on this day.

hamburger Within three days you will develop a deep clarity of thought. This will allow you to gain the insight needed to make another person express their needs and desires. With this insight you will both be able to adopt plans for your future that will bring you mutual satisfaction and happiness. You will have the confidence to adopt big ideas and plans. Blessings are with you and your family.

hamburger bun You are dealing with a personal issue that is going to require special handling from an expert. Do not waste time. Seek help immediately from someone who is qualified to provide these services. You will find complete satisfaction.

hammer Ask yourself why you are unable to resolve certain problems. Once you have located the reason behind this you will develop personal empowerment and after two days you will be able to tackle these issues successfully. Good luck is with you.

jack hammer Within five days you will take strong steps in order to bring about the changes in lifestyle you desire. It will be difficult to introduce a new lifestyle but push yourself in this direction and you will be greatly rewarded. You will develop the strength to overcome difficult obstacles in order to bring this about. Go for it in spite of seemingly overwhelming difficulties. You must also take steps to alter the outcome or to avoid any negative event witnessed in this dream. Do everything you can to experience positive expressions in your life.

hammer and sickle Anything you undertake right now needs to be handled in a step by step process. Make sure anyone you put in charge has the proper qualifications, licenses and expertise to handle the job. Double check each service that is being provided and do not allow yourself to be taken. You will enjoy an abundance of health and are headed for a prosperous future.

hammerhead You are destined to meet someone within the week who is loving, generous and kind. This person will bring a great deal of joy into your life and this will be a dramatic improvement in your style of living, if you choose to pursue this.

hammerhead shark Within two days make absolutely sure a particular person knows how you feel about a certain situation in order to avoid a big misunderstanding later on. Take care of this as soon as possible.

hammock Within two days make sure everyone involved in your life knows exactly how you feel about a certain individual. This will clear up any misunderstandings and ensure that this person is treated with the proper respect. Relax and take more time out to pamper yourself, especially for the next three days.

hamper Someone is making a big issue of a small situation. Take an active personal role in handling this responsibly before it becomes too large to easily control. Take care of this within four days.

hamster You will soon acquire your greatest desire from life. This will be a very joyful time for you.

hamstring Certain situations in your life have evolved to the point of allowing others to take advantage of you. Do not allow this to get to the point of being intolerable and do not lose power over your own life. This will be especially important for the next two days.

hand/hands Within three days you will be entering a time of great wealth and prosperity. You can confidently expect this. You are deeply loved and will be given verification of this within this time period. Expect many wonderful moments. You have prior notice to prevent any negative situation regarding your hand from becoming a reality. Allow only positive situations to be expressed by you or anyone you recognize from the dream.

right hand Be very alert when someone speaks to you within three days. Pay attention to the negative remarks aimed at you and make sure you turn these statements around immediately while this person is still with you. Things will soon turn around and you will find yourself headed for a brilliant future.

something negative happening to your hand A situation will arise that will demand that you sacrifice yourself, your needs and wants, both emotionally and financially for another person. Think carefully about this before you make a decision on which way to go. Expect this to take place within the month.

sticky hands In spite of anything else that may be going on in your life, the thoughts and dreams you hold dear will become a reality on a much larger scale than you ever hoped for. You will successfully rid yourself of anything that will stand in your way and you will grasp your goals. The person you desire will also be irresistibly drawn to you for as long as you wish. This will be a very fortuitous cycle and you will accomplish anything you motivate yourself to do. Proceed with confidence.

deformed or unusually shaped Within five days you will meet someone who appears to have a beautiful, generous, cordial and polite personality. Do not allow yourself to be taken by this individual or to be deceived by their manner.

This person is very deceitful and has absolutely no fondness for children although they will lead you to believe otherwise. Be very leery of this person. Also be aware that although they portray a sweet demeanor, their entire agenda is to have you become responsible for each aspect of their life (i.e., financial, emotional well being, etc.). Once you begin to cater to this person and ensure their needs are met, they will become aggressive and verbally abusive. You will also have to be very aware of all of their actions because they tend to sneak around and do things on the sly, especially regarding your finances. Anything in this dream concerning your hands that could become a reality needs to be prevented. You must also be acutely aware of anyone you are beginning to become familiar with. This could easily lead to a situation where you will be absolutely tied in with this person and controlled. Otherwise, you are headed for a very healthy long life filled with greater prosperity.

to be holding hands This dream indicates that you will unexpectedly gain instant wealth. You will also be able to tackle any difficult task that will arise within the week. All doors that were formerly closed to you will now be open and other people will begin to view you in a different way. You will enjoy many new opportunities and achieve success.

to shake the hand of someone you do not recognize Within four days someone who is very interested in you will have the opportunity to get close to you and will reveal they want more than just friendship. If you choose to pursue this, the relationship will develop very rapidly and will provide a mutually dedicated union.

to shake the hand of someone you recognize Someone has an urgent need to reveal certain knowledge to you. Within the week, you will gain information about a particular situation from an unexpected source.

shaking hands You have a certain feeling about a person and want to involve them in your project. You are very independent and if you follow this instinct you will create a dynamic synergism. A fortunate and prosperous future is ahead of you. Good luck.

to wave at someone or have them wave at you You will have an urgent need to have something accomplished within the week that can only be taken care of by someone else. This could be anything in the way of a financial loan or a big favor, etc., that needs to be given to you immediately and hassle free. It will be such a large request it will be difficult for you to imagine it can be accomplished. Your intuition will lead you to the right person to approach. Proceed with confidence and explore all your options until you locate the right person to ask. As soon as a mutual agreement has been made you need to take immediate action so this matter can be concluded before this person has a change of heart. Many blessings are with you and you are headed for a prosperous future.

signal by moving hand Be very careful for the next three days and make sure you do not get more involved with someone you are beginning to grow close to unless you take extreme precautions. You will be led to believe you can give your full confidence to this individual and can rely on their loyalty. This person is very cunning and devious and is very skilled at creating illusions and deceptions. You will fully

believe certain events and situations will occur in the future that will never take place. An air of trust will develop that will leave you with no suspicions. This person has a hidden agenda that involves pursuing you for reasons known only to them and, because of their charm and charisma, they will easily be able to create diversions if they think you are becoming suspicious. By the time you realize what is going on you will have suffered disappointments, disillusionments, and financial setbacks. You will be able to get your life back in order but it will take some time. You have enough advance notice and all the ammunition you need to ensure that this does not take place. Practice common sense and you will be very successful in diffusing this. Refuse to become involved, do not compromise and do not allow this person to pry into your affairs. You will develop the confidence to put yourself on the path toward a prosperous future. Many blessings are with you and your family.

to see someone kissing a hand, to be kissed on the hand or to kiss someone on the hand This dream implies that one of two things will take place within two days. A very wealthy, nice, shy person will fall deeply in love with you. A joyful event will take place, you will receive a positive reply you have been eagerly waiting for, or you will have an electrical appliance you need to attend to before it falls into disrepair. Otherwise you are headed for a prosperous future.

to see a bruised hand Be wary of toxins around children in order to avoid accidental poisoning. Otherwise you will have a brilliant future. Take steps to prevent any negative event foretold in this dream. Experience only positive expressions in your life.

chapped hands By asking questions, being suspicious, and by developing a certain degree of objectivity, you will be so successful in diffusing a plot against you that it will be impossible for it to be successfully carried out. This plot will involve someone who wishes to create chaos and discomfort in your life. You will be able to use what authority you have in a responsible, efficient and effective way. You will also, within two days, experience many wins and victories and the generosity you have paid to others in the past will be repaid. Expect to receive many gifts and major wins. You are definitely headed for a brilliant future.

handbag Opportunities you have been waiting for will arrive within two days. You will enjoy a new start in life and all issues that have been dragging you down will come to an immediate halt. A new excitement and feeling of confidence will take over. Good luck is with you.

handball You will have a sense of urgency to commit to someone who has captured your interest. If you choose to take this route, you will enjoy a long term relationship filled with mutual happiness.

hand basket Think carefully and have all the facts at hand in order to effectively argue your point of view. Good luck is with you.

hand-blown glass Actively motivate another person to get things moving in the right direction in order to meet a specific deadline. This is especially important for the next three days.

handbook You will have the intuitive thoughts needed to overcome a difficulty. You will be able to deal with this in a confident manner. Remain balanced and you will block a major disappointment that is coming your way.

handcart Within three days someone will vigorously attempt to drag you into a debate. This could turn very ugly. Do everything necessary to remain involved.

handcuff You are very anxious about something you wish to communicate to someone else. Get beyond this and take the risk. You will be very glad you took the opportunity to deliver this message and that you did not take the coward's way out. The outcome will be far better than you envisioned. Many blessings are with you and this is a good three day cycle in which to accomplish this.

handcuffs You are entering a great cycle for accomplishing almost anything you desire, especially those things you originally felt were impossible.

if you recognize the person with the handcuffs This individual also needs to be alerted to avoid any situation that could result in an arrest.

if you recognize the person who is attempting to handcuff you This person has an urgent need to involve you in their life in some capacity. Make sure you keep any negative event you dreamed of from becoming a reality.

if you are attempting to handcuff someone This person is very eager to accept a lifestyle you are attempting to involve them in.

if you do not recognize the person you are handcuffing You will be given clear evidence of how much you are loved and appreciated

if someone you do not recognize is attempting to handcuff you Aggressively pursue your plans for the next three days. You will be successful with this as long as you are on the correct side of the law. Make sure you avoid any negative event in this dream in reality. Do everything you can to experience only positive expressions in your life.

handgun You can gain the advantage in certain situations as long as you set up meetings with those who are eager to accept your conditions. This will also bring joy to others who are waiting for you to make this move. You are headed for a brilliant future.

smoking hand gun Someone, without your knowledge, is feeling very abandoned by you lately because of your inability to express your feelings toward them. Do something special for this person to demonstrate the way you feel. Take steps to prevent any negative event you dreamed of from occurring and do everything you can to experience only positive expressions in your life.

in any other form This dream implies that one of two things will take place within two days. A very wealthy, nice, shy person will fall deeply in love with you. A joyful event will take place, you will receive a positive reply you have

been eagerly waiting for, or you will have an electrical appliance you need to attend to before it falls into disrepair. Otherwise you are headed for a prosperous future.

handicap This dream is an extremely lucky omen. You will be given the gift of mental inventiveness and this will allow you to deal with certain family situations. You will be able, within three days, to bring more balance and humor into the family in order to diffuse a nasty issue that seems to be escalating. You will also see progress being made in areas of your life you most desire to move ahead in.

handicap sign Do not allow a situation that will come up within three days to overwhelm you. You will be able to successfully handle this. Make sure you set mental limits with any situation that comes up during this time frame.

handicapped person Within the month any situation you become involved with, especially regarding love, will work to your favor. You will experience a rapid response to your needs and will be able to develop an extensive support system. You will also experience prosperity in ways you never imagined.

handicraft Within four days you will be able to effectively change certain situations to vastly improve your life. You will realize your goals in a very short period of time.

handkerchief Avoid the feeling of being rejected by someone who has promised to call. Within seven days someone will make this promise but because of an extremely busy schedule and many extraneous activities they will be unable to do so. At the time this individual makes this promise, make it clear that you expect it to be kept.

handle Someone you will be doing business with will quote high prices based entirely on the manner in which you are dressed. Make sure you do not pay more for something you can purchase for less.

handlebar Avoid any situation that will create anger and disagreements between yourself and another person. You will also be overwhelmed with excitement over some good news regarding love and money. You will receive this within three days.

handlebar mustache Do not allow your life to become so busy for the next week that you will ignore personal involvements that are very special to you. Your communication skills will be very refined. You are headed for a very productive and healthy life that will begin within two weeks. This is also the perfect cycle to find people to work with you who are loyal. Seek out those who have ideas similar to yours. This will help you develop the plans you are working on and to get your point across to those who will support your cause. Proceed with confidence. This is the best time to have things fall properly into place.

hand lotion You will have the opportunity to meet with

someone to clear up a long standing problem. Make sure that prior to meeting with this person you have an approach that will result in a satisfying conclusion.

handmaid Control your behavior and avoid any action that will result in a restraining order being placed on you. You should also avoid lending money to someone within three days who seems very desperate for financial assistance. This person does not need the money, has other ways of acquiring it and will not pay you back. Be very firm in your refusal to lend this money.

hand puppet You are working with someone whom you wish to become more involved with in some capacity. Be aware that this person has an explosive personality that they find very difficult to control. If you become more involved you will feel as though you are walking on eggs. You will find yourself saying what you think this person wants to hear rather than speaking your own mind. Do not involve yourself with anyone who angers this easily and get on with your life without this person in it.

handrail Within two days you will find yourself very dissatisfied with the services you are receiving from a certain agency, person, company, etc. Seek services from other agencies, etc., during this time frame and compare your level of satisfaction. This will save you a great deal of time. Having your needs met should be your priority for the next seven days.

handshake *to shake the hand of someone you do not recognize* Within four days someone who is very interested in you will have the opportunity to get close to you and will reveal they want more from you than just friendship. If you choose to pursue this, the relationship will develop very rapidly and will provide a mutually dedicated union.

to shake the hand of someone you recognize Someone has an urgent need to reveal certain knowledge. Within the week, you will gain information about a particular situation from an unexpected source.

handsome A light discussion with an unknown person will give you the boost you need to develop the potential to meet your goals. This will push you further toward a brilliant future.

handsome man Someone desperately needs you in a sexual way within three days. This person will go to great lengths to satisfy you emotionally and physically. You will find mutual satisfaction as a result. You are loved beyond your imagination, whether this is verbalized or not. An unknown person will also enter your life and help you realize your ideas, potentials, and ambitions. You will reach the goals you desire as a result of a light discussion you will have with this person.

handstand You will need a great deal of discipline and control in order to avoid physical and sexual contact with another. Be ready to change gears the moment this situation starts

to develop if this is something you choose not to happen. Otherwise you are headed for a very prosperous future.

handwriting Pay attention to the words written. They will foretell a future situation you will either want to avoid or to incorporate into your present life. This also implies someone you wish to have a deeper relationship with will begin to verbally express their love. Until now, this individual has only been able to express physical love. This will be a very lucky cycle for the next seven days and many blessings will come to you and your family.

hang *to hang* Be very cautious for the next two days to ensure you do not develop into a workaholic. This will be a temptation to you. Be sure to take time out for the special people in your life. You also need to pay special attention to the food you eat and the beverages you drink in order to avoid choking. Protect your life and don't put yourself in any situation that could result in strangulation. Otherwise you are headed for a very prosperous future and good luck is with you. Make sure you take all the necessary steps to avoid any negative event in this dream and alert anyone you recognize in this dream to do likewise. Do everything you can to ensure you experience only positive expressions in your life.

to see someone you do not recognize hang The plans you have made will not work out in the manner you hoped. Regroup and adopt an alternative plan in order to better achieve your goals.

to see someone you recognize hang Be sure to alert this person to avoid any situation that could result in strangulation. This is especially important for the next two days. This person also needs to be made aware that business negotiations need to be handled carefully in order for them to reach their goals. Make it a point to keep negative events in this dream from becoming a reality and alert anyone you recognize to do the same. Take steps to ensure you enjoy only positive experiences in your life.

hangar This dream is an extremely lucky omen. If you see an airplane in the hangar, you will achieve victory in any area you desire. You will also need to seek out the person or persons who have talents similar to yourself in order to offer assistance in developing your pet project. This is the best cycle to accomplish this and to bring your idea to fruition.

hanger Do not allow someone to harass you to the point of giving up something you cherish. Stand firm in putting an end to this kind of behavior. Do not compromise yourself. Deal with this in a way that will offer you safety.

hang glide Someone will promise undying love prior to engaging in a sexual liaison. After this, they will disappear and reappear from time to time for the express purpose of sexual gratification. If you desire a deeper commitment, do not become involved with this person. You will be very vulnerable to this for the next three days.

hangman It is very important for the next three days to seek a conversation with a very important person. It will be easier for you, during this time period, to make the proper request and connection before a situation begins to develop. Aggressively motivate yourself, regardless of what else is occurring in your life. Stay on top of this and make adjustments as you deem appropriate. You must also take steps to avoid or to alter any negative event portended in this dream and make sure all positive events come to pass.

hangnail Within three days you must evaluate whether someone who is working with you on a project will be able to keep up with your pace or whether this individual will hold you back. If you determine this person will be a ball and chain, take steps to stay uninvolved and get on with your life.

hansom Within the week you will have an urgent need to take care of a certain issue that can only be handled with the help of someone else. This could be on the line of a financial loan, a big favor, etc. You will need this help immediately and with no hassles. This will be such a large request that you will find it hard to imagine anyone would help you out. Follow your hunches and explore all your options. Your intuition will lead you to locate the one person who will be able to offer you this help. As soon as an agreement has been made you will need to act immediately so this person will not have a chance to change their mind. Many blessings are with you and you are on the path toward a brilliant future.

Hanukkah Develop an extra source of income as soon as you possibly can. You will need a greater cash flow within three weeks. Good luck is with you for this time period.

happy/happiness Within the week you will have an incredible need to accomplish something that can only be done with the help of someone else. This could be anything from needing money, a big favor, etc., that urgently needs to be taken care of immediately and with no hassles. You will find it difficult to believe someone will offer their help because this is such a big request. Follow your hunches and explore each option. You will be able to determine who the person is who will come through for you. As soon as an agreement is reached, move quickly so this matter can be concluded before this person has second thoughts. Many blessings are with you and you are headed for prosperity.

happy go lucky Someone will go to great lengths to involve you in a business arrangement. Once small problems and kinks are worked out through meetings and communication with this individual, you will find yourself to be the recipient of greater wealth than your partner. This opportunity will present itself within seven days.

happy hour You will receive victory and wealth in the direction you are going. You will achieve your goals and be surrounded by people who love and respect you.

harbor Do not play the referee between two angry people.

You will be physically and verbally abused by both parties. The moment you see this situation developing, leave the premises. This will occur within three days.

harbor seal Think carefully about an invitation you will be receiving within three days. The person issuing the invitation possesses a strange manner and a lifestyle you find offensive. Be prepared to tactfully decline the invitation.

hardball You will be asked by someone of importance to attend a specific outing but this person will not let on about the power and authority they possess. Because you know this ahead of time you will be able to behave appropriately. This person has many agreeable traits and is very eager to involve themselves with you. You are headed for a brilliant future.

hard boiled Pay close attention to the way your behavior changes when around someone who enjoys pushing your buttons to make you feel very anxious or angry. This individual does this for personal gratification and pleasure. Do not allow yourself to feed into this behavior and do not allow your personality to change as a result of this manipulation.

hardener An uncontrollable strange desire will overcome you. Take steps to control your behavior for the next two days. This desire could lead to a very regrettable action on your part.

hard disk Keep communication open.

hard drives Self-care, new self-image anyone?

hard hat Within three days you will be able to bring someone you have long desired close to you in a passionate way. This union will bring you a great deal of happiness if you choose to pursue this. You are headed for a brilliant future.

hard labor You will receive a thrilling gift within three days. You will also be able to pull yourself from a long term burdensome situation that has weighed on you for a long period of time. Good luck is with you.

hard shell Do everything necessary to bond yourself closer to a special person. Make this bond permanent by verbalizing your feelings and intentions. Good luck is with you.

hardware Someone will go to great lengths to discourage you from pursuing your intentions by giving you the run around and by making your goals hard to reach. Do not allow this to dissuade you from pursuing your ambitions.

hardwood floor An event is scheduled for the upcoming week that you must attend. You will be in the company of two admirers and will have the pleasure of watching them subtly attempt to win your affections. Although it is not now apparent to you, one of these individuals will possess a great deal of power and authority. Although you will find both of them charming and agreeable, one of them will be perfect as a lifetime partner. You can be confident you are on the path of a prosperous future.

in disrepair Make every effort you can for the next four days, to display the correct behavior toward someone you desire closeness from. This individual is not yet involved with you. At the beginning, you will feel this person has no interest in you but they will later come around. During this time period you will experience an abundance of health, a financial windfall will come your way, and you are headed for a prosperous future.

beautiful Think ahead and seek out a much needed conversation with others within three days. This will allow everyone to meet to consider ways to put a stop to something that will occur if everyone involved does not take aggressive steps now. This situation has the potential of hurting everyone involved. Alert each person and make a move now to prevent this. Otherwise, many blessings will come to you and your family.

hare All your plans will work out exactly as you have envisioned them. Use common sense and stick with your convictions, especially for the next three days.

Hare Krishna Treat your time as a special commodity and set limits. Budget your time wisely in order to accomplish as much as you can in a short period of time. This is especially important for the next week.

harelip Do not allow jealousy and envy to play a role in a special relationship. Control these emotions. You are headed for a brilliant future.

harem You will begin to realize someone's need for private time to take care of their needs. Do not become so demanding on another that you not only try to live their life but also become their warden. Back off and allow this person to have time on their own. This is especially important for the next three days.

harlequin Do not place yourself in the position to hear words of criticism from another person that you wish you had never heard, especially for the next three days.

harlot Do everything you can to promote group activities and to include special people in your life who feel as though they are being left out. It is important to do this within three days.

harmonica You will enjoy many wonderful days with a special person whom you have wanted to share activities with. This will be a wonderful three day cycle for you. Good luck is with you. For the next two days you must also make sure you do not allow someone else to handle your financial affairs. Tend to all personal affairs on your own.

harness Make sure you do not overlook an important matter that will occur within three days. Make out a schedule and be sure to include everything of importance. Within three days, you will also receive verification of the deep feelings

of love a special person has for you. This is an extremely lucky omen.

harness racing For the next three days when dealing with money situations, make it clear you need to know the precise time and the precise amount you will be receiving, otherwise this payment will not be received in time.

harp Someone is very eager to grant you a favor. Make your request within two days.

harpoon Focus on stagnated situations you have been unable to change. Within two days you will have the clarity of thought and motivation to tackle these situations.

harpsichord Someone of a different nationality will enter your life and present you with a variety of viewpoints you will find beneficial to use with your present plans. You will achieve success.

harrow Within three days you will have some doubts about certain plans, projects, etc., you are dealing with. You will have the feeling they are spiraling downhill, malfunctioning or failing in some way. You will develop the strength to get through this and the result will be the complete opposite of what you thought it would be. Move forward and everything will work out exactly as you had hoped. You are on the path for a brilliant future.

Harvard You will be making a public appearance within the year and this will allow you to demonstrate a special talent. Be prepared for an exciting time in your life. Good luck is with you and many blessings are coming to you and your family. This dream may also be used as a reference point in time. If you dream of this university and see its name used in any context, the dream message will occur on this day.

harvest You and a special person will realize you have underestimated your friendship. This friendship will develop into a romantic relationship based on mutual respect. You will have to develop a schedule that will allow you to see each other as often as possible. If you choose to pursue this relationship, it will bring immense joy into your life.

harvest moon You will be entering a wonderful romantic cycle within three days. You will enjoy many romantic evenings and exciting invitations to various functions. Good luck is with you and you are headed for a prosperous future.

harvest time Investigate the motives behind someone's desire to help you and to be close to you. This person is a hypocrite and is only interested in seeking information about your plans in order to undermine you. This can have a major effect on your future prosperity.

hash Ask someone within three days to put in a good word for you to a third person. This will result in a very fortuitous connection and will stir up a series of events that will help to promote your ideas during this time period.

hash browns For the next three days someone will, bit by bit, manipulate you out of small insignificant items. At first this will seem unimportant but after awhile it will add up to a significant amount. This will be done very subtly but you need to put an end to this opportunist early on. Otherwise, you are entering a very blessed and lucky seven day cycle.

hashish An unusual occurrence will take place and this will lead to feelings of inferiority when you are around another person because this individual is far more physically fit than you. You wish you had the same degree of stamina as this person. Refrain from putting yourself down and accept that each person has a different level of energy. Within the month you will also need to prepare for an additional drain on your budget. Set aside money now in order to meet this additional expense. Good luck is with you and prosperity is headed your way.

hash mark If you do not begin to demonstrate patience toward a certain person within a few days you will cause a permanent split in the relationship. This individual will not tolerate excessive demands on your part. If you choose to have this person out of your life, this is the best time to accomplish this. If you choose to maintain the relationship, change your behavior.

hasp Within two days you will be asked to handle a particular problem. Make sure you are emotionally equipped to take on additional responsibilities before you accept. You will also need to make sure you are aware of each aspect before you commit to this task.
broken hasp Be sure to take precautions to protect yourself when in unfamiliar places. Guard your life, especially for the next four days.

hassock Do not become involved in any unusual situations for the next two days because this will lead to embarrassment on your part. Make sure you are acutely aware of everything that occurs during this time frame in order to keep any unusual situation from developing.

hat *torn hat* Restrain yourself from expecting a certain person to behave in the manner you expect them to. This will not work to your advantage, especially for the next four days. Take steps to avoid or to alter the outcome of any negative event you witnessed in this dream and alert all those involved to do the same. Make it a point to experience only positive expressions in your life.
to pass the hat You are underestimating a situation that you will be involved in within five days. This situation promises to be a golden opportunity. Move on it before it slips through your fingers.
hat pin Someone will do everything in their power to undermine you and take something that rightly belongs to you. Be very watchful during this cycle and investigate to determine the source. Do everything you can to keep any negative situation in this dream from occurring in reality and alert anyone you recognize from doing the same. Do what you can to experience only positive expressions in your life.

Panama hat This is lucky omen. You will receive recognition and money for work well done.
in any other form You will receive the verification you need regarding a certain situation that involves the feelings of a very special person. You will soon hear the words of love you have been wanting to hear. This person is very kind, generous and tenacious about having you become a part of their life.

hatband Within three days you will be faced with a situation that will require you be true to yourself. Aggressively pursue what you want from someone else. Verbalize your needs and you will have these needs met.

hatbox Someone is developing a plan to deceive you in an unexpected way and at an unexpected time that will go unnoticed until it is too late. Be very aware of others during this time frame and avoid deception.

hatch Focus closely on your schedule for the next two weeks. Many things will be taking place but in particular, two people you are interested in will be vying for your attention. You will want to spend equal time with both of them. Make sure you keep yourself open so you will have time to fit everything into your schedule. Maintain a tight schedule in order to avoid conflicts and to allow time for yourself and your obligations.

hatchback Within three days determine the reasons why you refuse to face personal issues. Examine and explore the possibility of confronting your behavior. Take time off to regroup and you will be able to deal with your personal issues.

hatchery This is a perfect time to express your needs to a special person. You will be heard and your needs will be met within the week.

hatchet Within two days someone will be bent on pleasure seeking behaviors that involve you. Watch your behavior carefully and be sure you do not expose yourself to something you will later regret. You will have the integrity to protect yourself. You are also entering a very lucky two day cycle. Do everything you can to avoid any negative event foretold in this dream and alert anyone you recognize to do the same. Take steps to enjoy only positive expressions in your life.

hate *if you recognize anyone involved* This individual has a deep need to express their feelings to you. This is a good cycle to get things you feel have stagnated moving rapidly in the right direction.
in any other form Within three days you will enjoy much love and passion from the person you most desire. You will enjoy good luck and an abundance of health during this time frame. Do everything you can to keep any negative situation in this dream from becoming a reality and alert all those involved to do the same. Make sure you experience only positive expressions in your life.

hat pin Someone will do everything in their power to undermine you and take something that rightly belongs to you. Be very watchful during this cycle and investigate to determine the source. Do everything you can to keep any negative situation in this dream from occurring in reality and alert anyone you recognize to do the same. Do what you can to experience only positive expressions in your life.

hat rack Avoid crowded places for the next three days.

haunt Someone with a solid reputation will back you up on a business deal. Good luck is with you and you are headed in the right direction.

Hawaii Within five days a same sexed individual will lead you to a career you will find very satisfying. This career will provide you with a solid financial foundation for some time to come. Good luck is with you and you will enjoy an abundance of health. Blessings will come to you and your family. This dream may also be used as a reference point in time. If you dream of this island group and see its name used in any context, the dream message will occur on this day.

Hawaiian Shirt Be sure you do not put yourself in the position of being falsely accused of anything. An accusation of this kind could damage your reputation. Think ahead and take steps to prevent it.

hawk Become very aware of what you are communicating to others and of what you put into writing. Avoid making promises you cannot keep, especially for the next three days.

hay This dream symbolizes abundance. All of your speculations will successfully pay off.

hay fever Become concerned about toxic surroundings for yourself as well as for your children. Accidents are preventable.

hayloft Show affection toward someone who feels you have no interest in them.

hayrack You will be required to travel for business purposes within five days. Make sure you choose the wisest route, especially if there is a possibility of inclement weather. Rethink your current arrangements. Your present itinerary is not appropriate for your particular plans.

hayride This dream is a very good omen and you will achieve victory with your greatest ambition. You will also be able to resolve any conflict with the object of your affections. The person you are interested in will welcome you with open arms.

haystack This dream is a very lucky omen and you are headed in a prosperous direction. The information you seek will also be revealed to you within five days.

hazelnut Within three days a sexual desire you have for another will be realized and the desire will be reciprocal. You are well loved by others and are entering a very lucky cycle.

H-bomb Do everything necessary for the next three days to remain calm when a situation seems to be escalating to the point of a disagreement that will get out of control. You have prior notice of this and can completely avoid this situation. This could be a very violent and life threatening event. Move on with your life without this involvement. Take precautions to ensure any negative event you dreamed about does not occur to you or to anyone else you saw in your dream. Make sure you experience only positive experiences in your life.

head Be very realistic about a supposed friendship. This individual is pretending to be your friend but at the first opportunity will undermine your goals in some capacity. Remain cautious and go on with your life without this person in it. Do everything you can to alter any negative event witnessed in this dream either for yourself or anyone you dreamed about. Take steps to ensure you enjoy only positive expressions in your life.

two heads on one body You will soon be dealing with someone who leads a double life. This person may be concealing a very dangerous psychopathic character. Be very aware of the behavior of others for the next five days in order to pinpoint the person you need to take precautions against. Do not involve yourself with this individual in any capacity. Do what you can to see that this person is dealt with properly by the authorities.

to be beheaded An extraordinary situation will occur in your life within six months. This situation will bring a wealth of riches to your life. You are entering a cycle of health and tranquility. Many blessings are coming to you and your family. Do what you can to keep anything negative you dreamed of from becoming a reality. Enjoy only positive expressions in your life.

to see someone beheaded Victory is yours if you slow down and take the time to properly develop relations with another. Do what you can to get the other person actively involved in preserving the relationship. You will be able to accomplish this within five days. Take steps to avoid any negative event in this dream and keep it from becoming a reality. Forewarn anyone you dreamed of to do the same.

if you recognize the person This person will be eager to adopt your propositions. Do not allow anything negative in this dream to occur to yourself or to the person you recognize. Do everything you can to enjoy only good things in your life.

decapitated animal heads Within three days you will have the backing of someone who has the tenacity and energy to walk you through an important situation that will allow you to make the correct decision. This concerns someone who is abusive toward you. You will do everything in your power to put a stop to this mistreatment and will enjoy success.

human body with an animal head Make sure you do everything you can to prevent broken bones especially for the next three days.

anybody with the head of someone of a different nationality Be very aware of the whereabouts of young children in the family in order to avoid a kidnapping. You must also avoid any situation that gives a pedophile the opportunity to molest a young child.

body without a head A very young person will fall deeply in love with you and will remain loyal to you for a lifetime, if you choose to pursue this.

head without a body Take steps to prevent a fallout between you and a dear friend. A particular situation needs to be avoided for the next three days if you wish to preserve this relationship. If this is not prevented, both of you will be deeply hurt.

to be hit on the head Stop placing so much importance on someone who does not deserve this degree of loyalty and special handling. Back off and rethink your actions. You do not have to keep catering to someone in your life who does not deserve it. This will be especially important to remember for the next three days.

to see your head cut You will become very wealthy within six months. This dream also implies victory in achieving a goal. This will come about by working on this slowly but surely. Maintain a level of common sense after you achieve your success. Make sure you do not allow any negative occurrence you dreamed of to become a reality. Enjoy only positive expressions in your life.

big head You will be talking to a bewitching person. Be careful. You may find this person mesmerizing and go along with plans against your better judgment.

to recognize a man's head or a woman's body or vice versa You need to be acutely aware of this person because they will attempt to bring some emotional harm to you, either emotional or physical. Do everything you can to keep yourself safe from this individual. Get on with your life without this person in it because they are serious. Although they will present a very kind and nice demeanor, they are very evil and cunning. Within three days make sure you disassociate from this person, move on with your life and take steps to turn this situation around. Make sure you also take steps to turn any negative event you dreamed of around so you can experience only positive expressions in your life.

headache You are unaware of a very cunning and deceitful person who will take the first opportunity offered to them to put you in the worst possible scenario. This can be prevented by taking extra precautions when dealing with others for the next three days.

headcheese Someone whom you pay close attention to will tell you a certain story and, a few days later, you will hear a different version from a very respectable source. Do not be alarmed. Just be prepared to make your own private decisions about this.

head cold Handle each problem one at a time and step by step. You will be happy you did because within three days you will uncover certain situations that have not been dealt with properly in the past. You will also need to take precautions to avoid catching a cold during this time frame. Take steps to keep any negative event in this dream from becoming a reality and to ensure you experience only positive events in your life.

headdress Someone you care deeply about will change dramatically and you will be unable to determine the source of this person's irritability and irresponsible behavior. Do not become so deeply involved with this situation that it causes you stress. Back off and allow this individual to work out their issues on their own. Good luck is with you and you will enjoy many tranquil moments if you allow others to take care of things on their own.

headhunter Make sure, for the next three days, that you are very acutely aware of your surroundings and of who you are involving yourself with. Take care of yourself and develop a schedule during this time period that will enable you to spend most of your time alone. Someone will definitely attempt to do you harm.

headlamp Your intuitions about love are correct. Move quickly to accomplish what you need to take care of concerning love. The next three days will put you in the perfect cycle for this.

turn on head lamp You are loved beyond your imagination.

turn off head lamp Take care of your health.

headlight Take steps to pamper yourself and do things you enjoy as soon as you possibly can. Make sure any negative event you dreamed about does not become a reality. Do what you can to enjoy only positive expressions in your life.

headlight turned on Do not postpone any decision you will have to make within two days. Do not allow yourself or anyone to procrastinate on this situation. It is important that you move on this within two days.

headlight turned off People will begin avoiding you if you do not stop putting them off. Stop your critical, stubborn and complaining behavior. If you do not learn to compromise and share experiences with others, you will be headed for a lonely future. Get a grip on your behavior and take steps to put yourself on a new path.

headmaster You may unintentionally sabotage your own goals by talking too much to others. You are telling others too much of your business. Guard against this for the next three days.

headmistress Be very sensible when requesting that someone help you on something they are reluctant to involve themselves in. This individual lacks the courage to tell you this face to face and will instead talk behind your back. This will hurt your feelings if it gets back to you. Do not insist on trying to recruit someone who does not seem to be interested in helping you. Seek alternatives.

headphones What you hear over the headphones is a major clue to a future event. If it represents a negative event, take the necessary steps to either prevent it or turn it into a positive situation. If it is positive, take steps to include this in your life. This also implies someone has a problem they want to dump on you. They feel you should be the one responsible for resolving this. Do everything necessary to avoid involvement in this situation.

headpiece An abundance of health and wealth are coming to you, especially within seven days. This dream also implies a situation will occur within three days that will require aggressive behavior. You will act accordingly and the situation will be quickly resolved.

headrest Do not deny yourself moments of tremendous pleasure especially for the next two days. Do what you can to bring more tranquility and simplicity in your life.

headwaiter Do not allow inconsistencies to rule your personality, especially for the next three days.

heal Within the week you will receive prosperity in every level of your life, especially in those areas you most desire.

health You will achieve victory in those areas you most desire with the person you want to share this with. All of your hopes and plans will turn out as you have envisioned. You must also make sure any negative event you dreamed of does not become a reality. Take steps to ensure you experience only positive expressions in your life.

health club Pay close attention to any situation that develops within the next two days. This situation will throw you off course yet you will feel you are on the right path. Take the time to revise your plans in order to point yourself in the right direction. It is imperative that you attend to this within five days. You will also need to take steps to avoid or alter the outcome of any negative situation seen in this dream. Make sure you experience only positive events in your life.

health farm Avoid saying anything that will be damaging testimony if someone chooses to use it against you. Do everything necessary to keep yourself healthy.

health food Your present situation will change within two months and you will find it necessary to relocate. You have enough prior notice of this to make plans. Do not panic. You will enjoy your new environment far more than you realize.

health food store You will soon rejoice over the reconciliation of someone you know.

health spa Do not remain in an area where two people are fighting. Remove yourself from this environment immediately in order to avoid a shocking stressful scene.

hear *to hear the disembodied voice of someone you deeply respect* Follow the advice this person gives you to the letter. If the message foretells negative events, take steps to change the outcome. Whatever this person says about themselves

represents an accurate depiction of something that will become reality within two days. Take steps to alert this person to anything negative that is coming their way. This individual has enough prior notice to turn things around or to avoid the situation entirely. This dream also implies a physical pain that someone is experiencing will be concealed from you. Be alert to this for the next three days.

to hear the voice of a woman you do not recognize This dream is an extremely lucky omen. If the advice given is positive, do everything in your power to follow it. If it is negative advice, take steps to turn it around or avoid it altogether. You will also have the courage to withstand any hardships that are coming along for the next three days and will be able to successfully overcome any obstacle.

to hear the voice of a man you do not recognize If a positive message comes through, take steps to embrace it. If negative, take steps to alter the outcome or to avoid it completely. Within three days you will also experience a welcome financial change.

to hear demonic voices Step back and place yourself in a stress free environment. Seek more simplicity in your life and come to grips with certain behaviors that need to be stopped. Put an end to any addiction that has gotten out of control and place yourself on a path toward righteousness. Begin healing yourself. You will have the courage to do this within two weeks.

to hear the voice of a young child Whatever the child is requesting that is positive should be fulfilled. Any negative request should be avoided at all costs. This dream is also a warning that someone with a different opinion from you will attempt to impose their opinions on you. Do not allow this to block your creative way of thinking. Continue your present course of action.

in any other form Within two days a stranger with a shocking and strange lifestyle will attempt to win your friendship. Be alert to newcomers in the neighborhood who desire your friendship. Avoid all involvement. Anything negative connected to this dream must be avoided in reality and you need to make sure you experience only positive expressions in your life.

hearing aid Take steps to keep a precious and expensive item from being damaged for the next two days. You also need to take steps to protect your ears and take precautions to prevent permanent hearing damage. Take steps to keep any negative situation in this dream from becoming a reality. Do what you can to experience only positive events in your life. Forewarn anyone you recognize in the dream to do likewise.

hearse *to see someone you do not recognize driving a hearse* You will receive a gift of diamonds. You will also hear of an associate who has committed suicide in a violent way. This will occur during the week.

to see dead people in the hearse who have passed away You will be thrilled at the response you get in all financial matters. You will receive a large amount of money equal to the number of bodies you see. The larger number of bodies seen the larger the amount of money you will receive.

dead people in the hearse who are alive in reality Be

sure to alert these people to the possibility of becoming involved in a freak accident that could result in death, especially for the next three days.

if you see your body in the hearse Investigate the cause of your death in the dream. This will be a major clue of what you should avoid in order to prevent your own death. Be alert to the possibility of a vitamin or mineral deficiency caused by improper diet that will lead to system failure. Take precautions to avoid sudden stressful situations that will affect bodily functions. You must also be careful that you take all medications properly in order to avoid sudden death. You will also need to avoid all impulsive behavior, curb your sense of urgency for the next week and avoid becoming involved in something you have no business being involved with.

heart *hearts drawn on paper* Be very attentive and be sure that you do not ignore a very special person in your life. Make plans that both of you will enjoy within three days.

heart shaped anything This dream is very lucky and implies that within two days you will develop the inner strength and courage that comes from within. You will also develop a steel drive and the determination you need to motivate yourself to break through any barrier (physical or mental) and completely rid yourself of any aspect of your life that interferes with you moving forward. Once you rid yourself of this block, you will quickly bring into tangible form a new project that is much more to your liking and will be completed in the way you desire. You will also be greeted with open arms anywhere you go during this time period. You will be treated as though you have been placed on a pedestal by those you care about and this behavior will surprise you greatly. You are headed for a brilliant future and many new opportunities are headed your way.

to have someone injure you in the area of the heart Someone will plot to inflict emotional and physical harm on you from behind the scenes. This person wants to make sure they catch you off guard and unprotected. They have focused on you for no particular reason other than to gratify their own strange obsessions. This person has not given you any indication that anything is going on with them. Guard yourself completely to make sure you are absolutely safe and do not allow yourself to be in any area where this could take place. Remain on guard, especially for the next two weeks.

to stab someone in the area of the heart with any sharp object Your intuition will be sharper from now on than it ever before, especially for the next two days. Proceed with confidence. You will be victorious in getting what you want from a specific situation, agreement, person, etc., especially if you recognize the person you are stabbing. This dream also implies that someone is not treating you or someone else in the proper way. You will be very instrumental in getting this person to see the points of view of other people and they will become less angry, more easygoing, and more willing to work with. This will take time, work and patience on your part to make this a reality. Victory is coming your way and many blessings will come to you and your family.

open heart surgery You are in the perfect position to ensure that open heart surgery does not become necessary for you or for anyone in your family. Start now to turn around anything that could lead to this. Be sure to eat healing foods, drink plenty of water, and get enough exercise. Aggressively seek time off and relaxation time to prevent this from occurring to you or a loved one. Do what you can to educate those you care about to take care of themselves.

in any other form Within three days you will be invited to join a social group. This involvement will bring you a great deal of pleasure and will introduce many new surprise events to your life. All of your relationships will be very peaceful and tranquil for the next seven days.

heart attack/failure *if you dream of someone else having a heart attack* Forewarn this individual to take the necessary precautions to prevent a heart attack in reality. Someone who has taken a long time to involve you in their life will now make a move. Do not waste time. This is now the time to follow your heart's desire. You will be pleasantly surprised at the behavior and demeanor this person expresses toward you. You are now entering a lucky seven day cycle.

if you are the person suffering heart failure Take steps now to keep this from occurring in the future by changing your lifestyle now. Make it a priority to reconstruct your life in such a way that promotes health. Within three days you will also be able to demonstrate your love to someone you care about in the manner they desire. This will occur in a wild romantic setting. Good luck will be with you for the next seven days.

in any other form Do everything you can to keep yourself healthy and to avoid a lifestyle that promotes heart problems. Pay close attention to this dream and do everything in your power to keep any negative aspect from becoming a reality. This dream may also imply that someone is having difficulty expressing their true feelings for you. This is the best time to become aware that it is important to allow this person to be comfortable enough with you to open up and express their true feelings. Otherwise, you are headed for a prosperous future.

heartbeat You will have a better chance of reconciliation if you make your move within three days. Also you will gain a quick response to a specific request for information.

heartburn For the next three days, concentrate and attend closely to details when it comes to financial matters in order to head off trouble that can be prevented now.

hearth Do not lend money or anything of value to another person. You will not be repaid. This is especially important for the next three days.

hearthstone Do not allow yourself to be verbally chastised by someone who wants you to enter into an agreement you do not desire to become a part of. This will occur within three days and when this happens, cut the conversation short because it could escalate into a very violent argument.

heat Arrange your schedule in such a way that you are able to accomplish as much as you possibly can in a limited amount of time.

heater Within the week expect that someone will relate an important message to you. This message will contain knowledge that will enable you and your family to create a new and better lifestyle.

heat exhaustion All business transactions that involve travel will be immensely lucky for you and will bring you a lifestyle you never anticipated. Go for it. Good luck is with you.

heathen Pay close attention to your financial interests. Stocks will go up and all things related to finances will improve. This is a good time to think of investing. You are headed for a very prosperous future.

heather Within two days you will be placed in the position of having to settle for less. Don't allow yourself to be cornered. Rethink the situation in order to be better able to handle this matter when it comes up.

heat lighting Do not let down your guard. Remain alert for the next two days in order to prevent a hazardous accident. Scrutinize each new situation closely and you will be able to prevent this occurrence.

heat pump Pay close attention to what someone is attempting to communicate to you. It will be easy to agree with everything this person suggests but these words may be misunderstood at a later date. This could put you at a disadvantage later on. Make sure you have a perfect understanding of what you are agreeing to, especially for the next three days.

heat shield Take precautions and make sure you do not overextend yourself in your attempt to involve someone else in your life. This person is sending mixed messages by playing hard to get and at the same time leading you on. They will continue to do this for as long as you allow it. Get on with your life without this person in it. Someone else will better appreciate your affections.

heat wave Do everything necessary to get the best medical attention possible within five days in order to keep a minor ailment from escalating into a crisis situation. The moment you sense something is not quite right with your health, seek professional help. Make sure you avoid any negative situation portended in this dream and warn anyone you recognized to do the same. Make sure you experience only positive events in your life.

heaven You will enjoy tranquility with your family and a peaceful lifestyle for a long time to come. Also continue to reach out in special ways to others who are important to you. Do everything you can to avoid anything you dreamed about that had a negative connotation, and make sure anyone you recognize does the same. Take steps to ensure you experience only positive expressions in your life.

heavy Do not allow temptations to guide you. You will be tempted to enter into a conspiracy with someone to gain access to something you really want. Do nothing that will put you in a position you will regret for a lifetime.

to see someone who is heavy in weight Be aware that someone in your vicinity may be a sexual or child abuser. Protect young children from perverse behavior.

heavy metal Do not deprive yourself the privilege of doing something different simply because it seems outrageous or unusual. You will find enjoyment by adding different elements to your life in a healthy way.

heavyweight Someone will be overjoyed with your attitude toward them. As a result of your treatment, this person will create many festive occasions for your benefit. You will also have the strength, clarity, and tranquility to make definite changes in your life with those who are important to you. Make sure you do not involve yourself with anything that seems either mundane or too serious. Move on with your life and avoid all situations that make you feel uncomfortable. Do everything you can to avoid any negative event in this dream and ensure you only experience positive events in your life. Alert anyone you recognize to do the same.

Hebrew Within two days you will reach a wonderful decision when deciding on a new lifestyle. You will also enjoy the introduction of new people into your life and will be exposed to new and different experiences that are far better than you are used to. Peace and tranquility will be with you for a long time to come.

Hecate *(Greek mythology)* You will successfully diffuse a devious plot against you by asking questions and by being suspicious of the actions of others. Expect this within seven days. This plan will involve chaos and discomfort of some sort in your life. You will be able to utilize what authority you possess in a responsible, efficient and effective manner. You will experience many victories in the near future and the generosity you have paid others in the past will be rewarded in this cycle. You will receive many gifts and are headed for a brilliant and victorious cycle. Any negative event portended in the dream needs to be changed and you should experience only positive expressions in your life.

hedge If, within five days, someone waffles over an agreement you will be entering into, back off. This will create problems within two weeks and it will be difficult to get this situation back to normal. Otherwise, good luck is with you. You need to take steps to keep any negative situation from this dream for you or anyone you recognize. Take steps to experience only positive experiences in your life.

hedgehog Dig deeply and investigate the benefits that are due you. You will get a clear picture of what you are owed within five days.

heel Make sure, within three days, that you do not allow someone to make plans involving you that you do not want to be a part of. Do not give anyone the authority to speak for you or to make decisions for you during this time period. A situation could occur that makes you feel you are taken advantage of.

heifer Make sure you attend to someone who is attempting to attract your attention in a very subtle way. This person's feelings will be hurt if you are not attentive to certain things they have done for you. Many blessings will come to you and your family and you will be able to handle this very successfully.

height *any form* You have a friend who will become very wealthy in a short period of time. This person will go to great lengths to involve you in their new and exciting lifestyle.

heir A situation will work out so perfectly within two days that you will find it very easy to facilitate a new lifestyle.

heiress A particular hobby you have will result in a good source of income. Also a relationship you want to develop is possible within three days.

heirloom Nothing will take your place as far as your loved ones are concerned. You are loved more deeply than you can imagine. Within five days you will also experience an extremely creative train of thought. Use this gift to lay the foundation for a better life. You will be very surprised at how well your plans fall into place.

Helen of Troy Face up to changes in a relationship that you have not allowed yourself to deal with. It is imperative that you begin to handle this within three days. You will find the courage to allow situations to flow in a direction that has not been openly spoken about. Accept this in a calm manner and you will be able to resolve all issues in a way that is acceptable to both parties.

helicopter This is a time for celebration because you are bringing many of your goals to reality. This will be a victorious time for you. You will empower yourself and achieve victory within three days because you will have enough heightened clarity of thought to change direction when you need to and head in the direction you need to go. You are definitely headed for a brilliant future. Any negative event connected with this dream that involves you or anyone you know can be altered. You have three days in which to do this.

helium Do what you can to keep all livestock and/or pets healthy and accident free for the next three days.

hell Within seven days someone you know who does not appear to be a wicked person will do everything within their power to get you under their control. You will regret any involvement with this person. The moment you notice the things you do with this individual are ethically or morally wrong, stop all contact. They will attempt to encourage the beast within you to react and to adopt a lifestyle that will take years to get away from. Do everything necessary to rid yourself of this person. Get on with your life without this individual and relentlessly protect yourself from this person's companionship.

if you recognize someone in hell Forewarn this person that someone who does not appear to be wicked will go to great lengths to control them. If they succumb, they will regret this at a later time. They need to stop all contact with this person and go on with their lives without this person. Make sure any negative event depicted in this dream does not become a reality and be sure to forewarn the person you recognized to do the same. Take steps to ensure you experience only positive experiences in your life.

hellfire Someone will over dramatize the telling of a certain situation until you feel a great deal of stress. Calmly and tactfully put a stop to your involvement in this and do not allow yourself to get to the point of feeling panic over the contents of this conversation. Take steps to protect yourself from freak accidents for the next seven days, especially if you are planning any medical procedures.

hello You need to be verbally aggressive with someone who needs to be set straight. Remind this person of the facts, especially within the next four days. They need to be reminded of the original agreement they made with you and you need to make sure they do not sidestep their responsibilities. You are headed in the right direction. Your degree of determination will determine the level of success you will achieve. You are definitely headed for a prosperous future.

helmet Within three days someone will do everything within their power to steer you from doing what you know you should be doing. Seek the freedom to act as you should, in the best way you know, to correct a particular situation that is not quite to your liking. Everything will work out within five days if you take steps to change the situation.

help Take steps to eliminate any interference you may be getting from an authority figure. Come to grips with your feelings and get on with your life. You will find this much easier to do once you rid yourself of this intense emotional situation. Make it a point to change this within three days.

to cry out for help Do not allow yourself to stagnate to the point of being unable to enjoy the simple things in life. Make a list of easily enjoyable events that will not put a strain on your budget. Make it a point to get out and do these things to eliminate stress from your life. You are entering a very lucky cycle and will enjoy an abundance of health and tranquility if you take the time to rethink your decision and use common sense for the next three days. Do everything you can to keep anything negative in this dream from occurring in reality and take steps to only enjoy positive expressions in your life.

to ask for help and receive it Someone desires you in a sexual way. This person will go to great lengths to satisfy both of you. This will be a wonderful time for you if you choose to go this route. You will also find any request you expect a positive answer to will be granted. Good luck will be with you. Make it a point to avoid any negative situation you dreamed of and do everything you can to experience only positive expressions in your life.

to hear someone else call out for help Make it a point to grow as rapidly as those around you. Continue your personal growth and continue to learn in order to keep up with others. Within three days it will be very clear why this is important. Do not allow any negative event you dream of to take place in reality and make sure you forewarn anyone you recognize to do likewise. Make it a point to experience only positive expressions in your life.

to give help Focus on creating a more stable foundation for yourself. Within three days you will acquire the necessary resources to accomplish this. This foundation will stand for a lifetime.

to ask for assistance and fail to receive it Do everything necessary to grow at the same or a more rapid pace as those around you. Keep growing and learning in order to keep up with those who are important to you. Within three days it will become very clear why this is necessary. Make sure any negative event you dreamed about does not become a reality and make sure you only experience positive expressions in your life.

helper Take steps to resolve any internal issues you have with a particular authority figure. Come to grips with your feelings and move on with your life. You will find life much easier because you will no longer have to deal with extraneous emotional issues. You must also be very cautious around water and electrical equipment.

to have an assistant You need to be careful with water and electrical wires.

helpmate Someone new will enter your life with similar habits as someone you knew in the past. These habits were intolerable and you felt you were on an emotional roller coaster. You will also be unable to tolerate these habits now. The moment you notice these traits in a new person, take steps to avoid involvement in the same game playing behavior. Go on with your life without these problems.

helter skelter *any form* Do not indulge in anything you know is addictive. You know in advance this could put your personal life and integrity in jeopardy. Be prepared to refrain from indulging in anything that is detrimental to you, especially for the next three days. Have compassion for yourself and do nothing that is harmful.

hem Within three days you will feel a deep desire to commit to a relationship. If you choose to take this path, you will enjoy a very successful union and both of you will share much happiness.

hemlock Within three days you will hear two separate conflicting opinions about a particular issue. Step back and check out both options. In reality, both would be successful.

hemoglobin Offer a greater financial restitution to someone who deserves it. You will successfully arrive at the appropriate figure.

hemophilia You are deeply involved with someone in an emotional way but this person is nervous about the depth of the relationship. Extra demands from you will drive this person away, especially for the next three days. If you want this relationship, allow this person time to be comfortable enough to become more demonstrative and giving. If you choose to wait, this relationship will be very fruitful for both of you.

hemorrhage Money you need will be granted if you make the request. Remain calm and think carefully about how best to handle financial situations that will be coming up during this time period. You will be successful and good luck is with you.

hemp Back off and do not attempt to manipulate others.

hen You are a visionary and are able to clearly see the future. Take the lead and point others in the proper direction. Take advantage of this cycle of mental clarity and apply it to all areas of your life.

henbane Someone has already made up their mind that they are not interested in dealing with anything that involves you. Avoid disappointment by backing off and not pushing for any involvement. Otherwise, you are headed for a brilliant future.

Hendrix, Jimmy Within five days you will come to realize what heaven is when you recognize the creative and profound thoughts that are coming from within you. Motivate yourself to develop these thoughts with confidence, neither over nor under doing them. Execute these thoughts on a grand scale and do not allow yourself to develop tunnel vision. Become flexible but not overly so. Do not allow yourself to take today's moments for granted because these moments will be your future memories. Use common sense and get in sync with your health regarding food and beverages. You will victoriously achieve your goals through your journey in life and are headed for a brilliant future.

henhouse Do not use short cut methods to rush through a particular situation. Slow down and work carefully in order to do things properly and without error.

henna Maintain a cheerful demeanor when resolving a conflict within three days.

hepatitis Any negative event connected with this dream that involves you or another person needs to be avoided in reality. You have three days to prepare for this and to ensure you and this person experience only positive events in your lives. Be very aggressive when dealing with upcoming situations in order to resolve them completely before they reach crisis proportions.

Hera *(Greek mythology)* Within five days you will be granted by the gods an enormous capacity to achieve excellence in anything you apply yourself to. Anything negative portended in this dream should be altered and take steps to experience only positive expressions in your life.

herb A close friend will develop a romantic interest in you. This will surprise you but if you choose to go along with this, you will enjoy many moments of pleasure, new activities and a deep companionship, especially for the next three days. Everything will work out beautifully.

herbal Someone from very far away will send you a beautiful present that you will enjoy for a long time to come. Important decisions that will come up within three days will require a negative answer from you. You will be tempted to agree to anything but be firm on a no answer.

herbal foods You will enjoy greater fortune within three days and you will experience more blessings for you and your family for many years to come. Eat more healthful foods, drink plenty of water, and get more rest.

herbal medicine Do not postpone any pending projects. Eat healthy foods, drink plenty of water and get more rest.

Hercules Within three days you will experience a tremendous change in your financial status. You will have sufficient funds to cover all necessities as well as those luxury items you desire. This dream is a good luck omen. Make sure you get plenty of rest and be on the lookout for someone who likes to contradict you. Do not allow anyone to upset your equilibrium during this time period.

herd This dream is an extremely lucky omen. Keep your eyes open for a golden opportunity you will overlook if you are not paying attention. This opportunity will offer you financial security. It will be presented to you within three days.

heredity You will inherit the entire estate of a close relative. This will take you by surprise but no one will have the power or grounds to dispute it. Good luck is with you.

heresy Ask for special considerations for the next three days and they will be granted.

heretic Regardless of what is going on in your life, maintain confidence and proceed as if you were on a mission. You will see the light at the end of the tunnel as long as you do not give up hope. You are definitely headed for a prosperous and healthy long life.

heritage Do not allow old emotional problems to resurface by allowing someone to rehash old memories. Do what you can to keep yourself in the present and do not allow old wounds to fester. You are entering a lucky seven day cycle.

hermaphrodite Pay close attention to the physical and emotional state of a young child. Make sure this child's needs are being met, especially for the next three days.

hermit Don't allow yourself to get caught up in the glitter and glamour that someone else flaunts. This person has a tendency to be somewhat irresponsible. Within three days, someone will glamorize a particular situation that will not work out the way they make it sound. Back away and carefully make your own decisions. You will also experience an abundance of health.

hermit crab Do everything necessary to avoid a break up between you and someone special, especially for the next three days. During this time frame, you will want information from someone with extensive knowledge in the area you are interested in. This person will go to great lengths to keep this information from you. Do everything necessary to get this information either from this person or from an alternative source. Also within three days an opportunity will arise that will bring you a set of circumstances that will allow you to bring about a change in lifestyle that you desire. Your determination and drive will bring you greater rewards. You will be able to overcome any obstacle and walk swiftly through the changes you are eagerly waiting to embrace. You are headed for a brilliant future.

hernia For the next four days take steps to ensure any negative event seen in this dream does not occur. You also need to make sure you remain uninvolved in any request someone makes of you for the next three days. Although you may be tempted to offer assistance, it will be better for both of you to stay uninvolved in this upcoming situation. It will not work out.

hero Do not divulge your plans to anyone for the next two weeks. Keep your affairs to yourself. Trust your instincts and go for it.

Herod This dream is a very lucky omen. You will quickly recover from a financial difficulty. You will have the opportunity to do this within the week.

heroine Someone will be very visibly drawn to you and can barely contain their desire. It is up to you whether you choose to become involved. This person will go to great lengths to ensure you are comfortable in their presence and will do almost anything to ensure your interest in them. Anything you choose will benefit you. Be aware also that you have five days to change or alter any negative event that was foretold in this dream.

heron Do not allow yourself to be cheated in a business deal. You are asking for less than you should be receiving.

hero sandwich This dream is alerting you to the fact that someone will come to your house and accidentally break an expensive item. Be very watchful of your treasures in order to avoid the disappointment you would suffer if one were damaged. This is likely to occur within five days. Also an opportunity will come up within three days that will bring about a set of circumstances that will change your lifestyle in the way you most desire. Your drive and determination will bring you greater rewards and benefits than you ever imagined. You will be able to overcome any obstacle in order to swiftly go through those long awaited changes. You are headed for a brilliant future.

hero worship Within the next day or two you will undergo pressure from someone because you will stand up for your rights and will refuse to compromise your feelings. You have prior notice of this so take steps to remain calm throughout this time period.

herpes This is a warning to avoid any situation that could expose you to this disease or any contact that would spread the infection. Avoid any sexual contact for the next two days. Take steps to avoid any negative event witnessed in this dream and make sure you experience only positive expressions in your life. Also within three days an opportunity will occur that will bring about a set of circumstances that will change your lifestyle in the way you most desire. Because of your determination and drive, you will reap greater benefits and advantages than you ever imagined. You will be able to walk these changes through any obstacle in order to achieve your goals. You are on the path toward a brilliant future.

herring For the next three days negotiations will not bear fruit. Postpone all conferences during this time period in order to ensure a better outcome.

herring bone This dream is a very lucky omen. You will also overhear a conversation that will be very damaging to another person if it is repeated. Make sure you keep this information to yourself.

hex *to have a hex placed on you* Pay close attention to the person who placed the hex on you. This person is very immoral and wicked in reality. Also within three days a set of circumstances will occur that will bring about the changes in your lifestyle that you most desire. Because of your drive and determination, you will reap greater benefits than you ever thought possible. You will overcome any obstacle in order to quickly get through those long awaited changes. You are headed for a brilliant future.

if you do not recognize the person This represents someone who will shortly enter your life and will cause you a great deal of emotional harm. Avoid anyone you feel has the power to cause this stress.

to put a hex on someone Pay close attention to your behavior in this dream and put a stop to all negative actions depicted. If the dream reveals positive behavior on your part, promote this in reality. This dream is a very lucky omen and indicates you will quickly recover from any emotionally draining situation. It also implies that a series of circumstances will occur within three days that will bring about much desired changes in your lifestyle. You will reap great benefits and rewards because of your drive and deter-

mination. You will be able to overcome any barrier or obstacle in order to bring about the changes you have long waited to embrace. You are on the path toward a brilliant future.

hexagon Avoid any situation, for the next two days, that you feel will lead to an argument or debate. All debates should be avoided.

hi Do not allow yourself to be available to someone who once caused you a great deal of discomfort. At first this individual will appear different to you but, in reality, still harbors the same old hang ups. Get on with your life without this person in it. Also within three days, an opportunity will arise that will bring about a set of circumstances that will let you adopt a lifestyle change you desire. You will be able to overcome any obstacle and will walk swiftly through the changes you are eagerly waiting to embrace. You are headed for a brilliant future.

Hiawatha A situation will occur within three days that you can be assured you will get the assistance and support you need to handle properly. It will fall into place as you wish.

hibernate You will marry a wealthy, attractive, charming individual if you choose to seek this person out within seven days. You will be happy for a lifetime with this individual. Also you will experience an abundance of health and wealth during this time frame.

hibiscus You will achieve victory over certain situations that will come up within five days. Good luck is with you.

hiccup You or someone you know will conceive identical twins. Also you will receive a large inheritance in the near future from a close relative who adores you.

hickory Take precautions to protect yourself from an injury incurred in a dangerous fall. Pay close attention to all possible situations where this could occur and watch where you walk.

hide Play it safe for the next five days while visiting an unfamiliar place. The moment you feel uncomfortable or sense anything unusual, leave the premises immediately. Take steps to remain safe and do not expose yourself to any strange situations.

someone hiding from you This person you are confiding in is not sincere or loyal to you. Be very careful not to reveal any secrets for the next three days.

if you recognize the person hiding from you This individual lacks the courage to tell you they have no wish to be involved with you in any capacity. Take the initiative to avoid anyone who gives the slightest indication of displeasure while in your company.

you are hiding Pay close attention to who and what you are hiding from. This individual will cause you a great amount of disappointment in reality. Take steps to stop any situation that will lead to this feeling. Take steps to keep anything negative you dreamed of from becoming a reality.

Within three days you will have to offer emergency medical assistance to someone in need from an injury due to a fall. You must also do everything necessary to keep yourself healthy. Do everything you can to experience only positive expressions in your life.

to see someone hide themselves or something from others Open your eyes and be very aware of facts you wish to keep from others. This will keep someone with dangerous intentions from gaining the knowledge they need to do you harm. Expect this within three days. This could also be something in the nature of physical harm coming to you as a result of your emotional reaction to this person's possession of this knowledge (i.e., heart attack, stroke, etc.). Take extreme caution during this time period.

to hide something Pay attention to what you are hiding. This will provide a major clue to the meaning of this dream and tell you what you should keep hidden from others. Also you are about to take responsibility for an event that will take place within five days that should not be occurring. This responsibility will fall into your lap unless you make it very clear you will not accept this. If you do not stand firm you will be blamed when this situation turns out wrong. Take steps to stay ahead of this and avoid involvement.

animal You will experience a large victory within two days. This situation once appeared to be impossible to handle, but within this time frame you will achieve success in overcoming it. Good luck is with you.

hide and seek You will soon be involved with someone who does not have what it takes to enter into a firm relationship. This individual will disappear from your life on a consistent basis. They will keep promising commitment but it will become clear this will occur only when this person wants you and you do not have the option to be a part of their life unless you are invited. Within two days, if you choose, you will both come to some kind of agreement about how the relationship should develop.

hieroglyphics This dream is an extremely lucky omen. Your status will rapidly improve until you will be able to achieve the victory you have long desired. Your life will then take a tremendous turn for the better.

Hi Fi Make sure that children and young adults are being properly cared for. Ensure they have their needs met and you can account for their hours. This is especially important for the next three days. You will also hear good news and this will be the cause of much joy and celebration in the family. Good luck is with you and you and everyone involved are headed for a prosperous future.

high *any form* Your deepest fantasies will come to pass within three days. You will enjoy a wonderful, joyous, thrilling and pleasurable experience. Do not deprive yourself of this tremendous joy.

high beam Someone will approach you within three days for a romantic interlude. It would be very much to your advantage to pursue this. If you choose, this could be a very

happy union. You will also achieve victory in those areas you most desire. Good luck is with you.

high chair Your maid has good intentions and is trustworthy.

high heeled shoes *any form* Because of the unexpected declaration of someone's love for you, you will experience a feeling of exuberance and excitement. This can develop into a relationship of any capacity you choose and will lead to mutual fulfillment.

highland You will enjoy yourself immensely when in the company of others for the next two days. Do not keep yourself from enjoyable times although you will be tempted to do so. Good luck is with you.

high priest/priestess Be very aware of a situation that may be more advantageous to you than you originally thought. Go for it. This situation will present itself within five days. Make sure anything negative you dreamed about does not take place. Do everything you can to experience only positive events in your life.

high tech Someone you meet in the near future will give you a valuable tip. Use this to improve your situation in life.

highway Situations will begin to develop within three days and if you involve yourself in this you will later receive many positive benefits for work well done. Although you will not receive many financial rewards at the moment, as things develop your rewards will reach the level comparable with your work. Good luck is with you and you are headed for a brilliant future. Any positive event represented in this dream concerning yourself and another person needs to be brought to fruition within three days and any negative event needs to be prevented within three days. Take steps to enjoy only the positive aspects of life.

hijack Within three days you will sense an excited attitude from someone else. This person will be very verbal in their attempt to get their point across and put everything in the proper perspective. They will also attempt to involve you in a union that will result in marriage. If you choose to go in this direction, the marriage will be very emotionally fulfilling. Anything you ever wanted from a relationship is here so do what you can to bring this about. You are headed for a brilliant future. Any negative event portrayed in this dream needs to be prevented within three days. Do everything you can to experience only positive expressions in life.

hike Push yourself to express the feelings you have for someone. It is important to do this within three days.

hill For the next three days, demonstrate the gentlest and most positive side of your nature. Someone will be making a decision about you and it is important they see this part of you before they make this decision. You must also make sure anything negative you dreamed about does not become a reality. Make sure you warn anyone you recognized to do the same.

to go up a hill Nothing will keep you from successfully reaching your goals. Victory is yours.

to go down a hill Within three days you will have to deal with a very wicked individual. This person will do what they can to twist others' words to their advantage and will give you conflicting and unreliable information. Be aware of this and take steps to avoid this person. Otherwise, you will be entering a lucky cycle within the week as a result of a correct decision on your part.

hillbilly Be very aware of your involvement with family members for the next three days and do not become embroiled in a tough situation. Do not allow anyone to disturb your balance.

hilt Make sure, for the next three days you do not dissuade someone from becoming involved with you because of your obsessive behavior.

Himalayas Someone you care for will move to an area that will be costly to communicate via phone. You will experience a deep emotional loss as a result. This will occur within three days so be prepared to face this loss. This dream may also be used as a reference point in time. If you dream of this mountain chain and see its name used in any context, the dream message will occur on this day.

Hindu Carefully watch your words for the next three days. Anything spoken in haste may be resented and cannot be taken back. This may result in the severing of a close friendship.

hinge Someone will commit an act that will have severe repercussions and you will benefit from this person's downfall. This will occur within the week.

hinge joint Within three days you will find the perfect person to work with you. Proceed with confidence. This individual has wonderful organizational skills and creative ideas that will benefit you. Good luck is with you.

hip Proceed with confidence. You will achieve success with your plans and ideas and within five days you will be able to achieve your goals.

hipbone Remain in a safe environment for the next five days and take steps to avoid freak accidents. Make sure your home environment is safe during this time frame as well. Take steps to avoid any negative event witnessed in this dream and make sure you experience only positive expressions in your life.

hip huggers Develop a sympathetic manner when someone asks for your help. Be very compassionate with someone who is unable to go into detail about the depth of their problems and doesn't show distress. Don't take this matter lightly. Expect this to occur within three days.

hippie Refuse to participate in any situation that seems important for the next three days. This situation is not in sync with your lifestyle although it appears to be on the surface. You will be tempted to get involved but this will force you to change course and will be a bigger issue than you anticipated. This situation will affect your lifestyle in a long run.

hippopotamus Within the week someone will attempt to involve you in a relationship. At first you will have mixed feelings but your hesitation is unwarranted. You will have a delightful experience if you choose to pursue this. Involve yourself completely and enjoy yourself on every level you desire. You must also take steps to avoid any negative event seen in this dream and warn anyone you recognized to do the same.

hire Take it easy for the next three days and place yourself in a relaxed mode with no emotional stress.

to hire someone Pay close attention to the behavior of the person you hire in the dream. This will offer you a clue of how someone will act around you within three days. If it is negative, take steps to change it and if it is positive, promote it. This dream is also telling you not to be talked into assuming someone else's responsibilities, especially for the next five days.

to be hired Pay close attention to certain people who are personally involved in handling certain situations for you. Be more attentive to your own affairs for the next five days.

Hispanic A particular situation you desired in the past will be a possibility within five days. Anything you want to happen regarding this particular situation is possible now. Good luck is with you.

hiss *to hear any animal, yourself or person hiss* You will enjoy an abundance of health, spiritual healing and tranquility for the next three weeks and within the week you will enjoy a big celebration. Everyone involved will rejoice in a big way. For the last half of March and all of April you are also destined to bring an idea, project or event to tangible form. This will reach a higher level of perfection than you ever anticipated. This project will take on a life of its own and you will easily walk it through any channel necessary for its completion. This will be a blessing to you and will result in a celebration for you and everyone else involved in this process. You are on the path for a brilliant future. Make sure for the next six weeks you take steps to prevent any negative event you dreamed of and warn anyone involved to do the same. Pay close attention to what is being hissed at. This will offer you further clues to the meaning of this dream.

history Do everything you can to avoid betraying someone for the next three days. This will result in a heated argument that will escalate into violence. Avoid this by remaining loyal.

hit Within five days you will find the solution to a very difficult problem you are now involved with.

to be hit by someone Do not allow any stressful situation to come between you and a special person. The moment you see this situation begin to evolve, take steps to turn it around. Any event in this dream that is negative needs to be prevented and all positive events need to be promoted.

to hit someone All out of town business transactions will be tremendously successful. Victory is yours. Also the person you desire in your life will become more involved emotionally in each level of your life. Good luck is with you. All negative events in this dream must be avoided at all costs and all positive events need to be promoted.

to be accused of hitting someone Within two days you will receive the gift of greater healing and heightened psychic abilities by the Deities. As a result, you will develop greater organizational skills and be able to put these gifts and your talents to use in a dynamic way. Many blessings will be with you for a lifetime and you are headed for a brilliant future.

hit and run *to be the one who hits and runs* Do not treat someone you care about in such a way that will drive them away. You must also make sure for the next two days that you are not involved in a hit and run accident.

to be the victim of a hit and run Be very cautious with your involvement with others. You are in danger of contracting a sexually transmitted disease. Take precautions to avoid this and any other negative event seen in this dream. Make sure you only experience positive expressions in your life.

if you recognize the hit and run driver Alert this person so they can keep this incident from occurring within two days. Good luck is with you. You also need to make sure any negative incident you dreamed of does not become a reality. Take steps to enjoy only positive experiences in your life.

hitch Within three days you will definitely be making a mistake. Someone you are fond of does not like your impatient attitude. Take steps to avoid behaviors that will keep you from the involvements you want, especially for the next three days.

hive Someone much older than you will welcome you with open arms and be willing to help you in any capacity. You have prior notice of this and can act in the appropriate manner. Many blessings are with you and this person. You are definitely headed for a prosperous future.

hoard An unusual occurrence will leave you feeling inferior to someone. You will feel someone much older than you is in much better physical shape. For the next three days make sure you do not allow these feelings to overcome you. Do not be so hard on yourself but let this serve as a reminder to get more exercise. Do this in a limited fashion and recognize your capabilities.

hoarfrost You have to make your likes and dislikes known. This will create a stronger rapport between you and the person you will be communicating with. You will then be able to adopt a mutually satisfying relationship.

hoarse Prior to talking with someone for the purpose of getting something off your chest, develop a clear idea of what you really want to communicate. Talk in a way that will bring this individual close to you instead of creating a distance between you. You will enjoy good luck for the next seven days regarding all forms of communication.

hobby Dismiss all plans you have for exchanging property. This is not a good idea at the moment and will not be to your advantage.

hobbyhorse Do not allow anger to rule you. Take the time to regroup and back off from this emotion. Everything will fall into place as you expect.

hobo Within five days someone will want to visit you for a few days. This person is not living the lifestyle they choose and desires to visit you because they know they will be treated with respect. This individual will not verbalize the problems they are having at this time but it will be clear that something is wrong. Back off and leave it up to them to choose the proper time to open up, otherwise you will drive them away and will not be able to offer assistance in the manner you wish. Good luck is with you.

hock This dream is an extremely lucky omen. You will undergo a tremendous change in your life. Within two days you will go to someone for financial help and this individual will be very eager to help in every way.

to see someone hock something You will be asked to give financial backing to someone you do not know well. This proposal will be very lucky for you and you will be handsomely rewarded if you choose to become involved.

to hock something A very exciting surprise will come your way within three days. Someone will give you an unexpected, small but expensive gift.

hockey For the next two days do not allow anyone to sway you by using emotional ploys. Do not become involved with anything that is distasteful to you as a result of this individual's pleadings. Do not compromise your character now, you will later regret it.

hoe You will be asked, within five days, to come up with documents that will take time to locate. Do everything necessary to locate this paperwork and turn it over to the proper person in a timely fashion. This will allow everything to run smoothly and easily. Avoid the stress that will result by not meeting the deadline.

hog Be wary of someone you have just been introduced to. This individual is treacherous and many people suffer misfortunes after being in contact with them. Get on with your life without this person in it.

hold *any form* Someone you passionately desire will be eager to communicate their feelings for you. You will connect on a deep emotional level and be mutually fulfilled if you choose to go this route. Expect this to occur within three days. Make sure you promote anything positive you dreamed about and do everything you can to avoid or to prevent any negative event.

holdup Hold off on certain moves and developments you want to implement for at least the next few days. There are certain aspects of this project that are not accurate and you need to investigate further so you do not waste time, effort or money. Be sure to avoid any negative situation in this dream or take steps to alter the outcome. Take steps to ensure you only experience positive expressions in your life.

hole Within two days you will have a disagreement that will lead to a large quarrel with a member of the opposite sex. Keep your distance, take steps to avoid this situation entirely and make sure you keep anything negative in this dream from becoming a reality.

hole-in-one Do not allow yourself or anyone else to hinder your moves or to cause you to stagnate, especially for the next three days. Do not limit yourself and make sure you force yourself to be more verbally aggressive in order to point yourself in the right direction.

hole puncher Within three days you will have to deal with someone whom you know enjoys creating chaos and stressful situations. Prepare yourself. During this time frame this person will create a monster of a situation that will escalate to the point of extreme chaos. Make sure you take the necessary steps to avoid this person by making other plans for amusements during this time period.

holiday Within two days you will be moving to an unfamiliar area. Although this area will be unknown to you, you will find it to be a wonderful experience and you will meet many new people who will add excitement to your life.

Holland Keep going in the direction you are going. You are headed for a brilliant future. You will also hear the words of love you have been wanting to hear from the person you have been wanting to hear them from. This dream may also be used as a reference point in time. If you dream of this country and see its name used in any context, the dream message will occur on this day.

hollandaise sauce For the next seven days you will have an enormous amount of energy, ambition, and resourcefulness. These traits will get you exactly where you want to be going. This is the perfect cycle to move on those things you have to take care of. Doors of opportunity will open for you in ways you never knew were possible. Proceed with confidence.

hollow You will have to take major steps in order to bring about the changes you want. These changes will greatly benefit you and everyone you are associated with.

holly Face your commitments head on and do not allow

yourself to become wishy-washy. Social events that will soon be taking place will also be immensely enjoyed. Good luck is with you.

Hollywood You will be arriving at some well formed ideas within two days that, if implemented, will give you what you need to grasp your goals. Make sure you take all the proper steps to avoid any negative event you dreamed about and be sure to enjoy only positive expressions in your life. This dream may also be used as a reference point in time. If you dream of this city and see its name used in any context, the dream message will occur on this day.

holocaust A situation that has been tearing you down emotionally will quickly stabilize and you will see a dramatic improvement in your life within four days. Take the necessary time to recuperate from this situation and do not take on another burdensome problem. Enjoy life and keep yourself safe. Any negative event in this dream that could become a reality must be prevented. Make sure you only experience positive events in your life. Warn anyone you recognize in this dream to do the same.

hologram Within five days you will be selected for a leadership position whether you choose this position or not. You will have to dedicate much of your private time toward successfully organizing a particular event. You will do a wonderful job. Good luck is with you.

holster You will be dealing with someone who has a bad habit of wasting other people's time. This individual will commit themselves to performing a task that is due at a certain time but will drag this out. Do not waste your time and do not involve yourself with this person. You will then be able to avoid a stressful situation.

holy Within the week you will agree to a marriage that you greatly desire and you will have many long years of happiness with someone special.

Holy Bible Pay closer attention to your health and guard yourself from any health hazard, especially for the next three days. You also need to pay attention to your older loved ones. Older people often need love and attention more than younger people. Within three days you may have to do something for an older person to make their life easier. Good luck and an abundance of tranquility will come to you and your family for a long time to come. Do what you can to avoid any negative incident in this dream and make sure you only experience positive events in your life.

Holy Communion Pay close attention to the young people around you to make sure they are properly nourished and get the proper exercise. Take steps to correct those things in their life that need correcting to ensure these young people enjoy a healthy lifestyle.

to take Holy Communion You will learn of the birth of twins.

Holy Day You are headed in the right direction and you will be richly rewarded for a favor you will do for someone within three days. Many blessings will come to you and your family.

Holy Father You will realize your goals. You will also be dealing with two different situations concurrently that will bring you a great deal of luck and prosperity. Make sure you deal with both situations. You will be tempted to forego one in order to focus on the other. Do not lose your confidence and focus on both of these issues equally. You are headed for a brilliant future and a very tranquil time is headed your way. Be sure you promote any positive event in this dream to the fullest and do everything you can to prevent the negative.

Holy Ghost Be very aware of your surroundings and take steps to protect yourself from freak accidents. Be careful not to over or under medicate yourself or to eat any foods that may be tainted. It is also important to be very careful not to be led down the wrong path. You will get the impression that something is all right for you when in reality it is wrong. You will be faced with this within three days. Many blessings are with you and something special will happen that will create an excitement and joy that will last for at least three weeks. Anything negative in this dream needs to be avoided and all positive situations need to be brought to full bloom.

Holy Grail Slow down, regroup yourself and focus on enjoying life to the fullest. By taking this new attitude you will find more joy than you imagined was possible. Good luck is with you.

Holy Roman Empire Within three days you will meet a stylishly dressed individual with a flair for the dramatic. This person is very intelligent, a good conversationalist and wealthy. You can learn a great deal from them and will have a life long friend, if you choose to pursue this.

Holy Spirit You are entering a very lucky and fortuitous cycle and will achieve victory in almost everything you want to achieve for the next week. Make sure your health is guarded. Be sure to eat the right foods and maintain a healthy lifestyle and be especially careful of over medication, food poisoning and freak accidents. You and your family will enjoy much tranquility for a long time to come.

home You will be loved and cherished for a lifetime by those you care about. For a more in depth definition, look under house.

owning or living in more than one home Do everything necessary to put your love into action. Give those you care about evidence of your feelings for them. This will be very important, especially for the next three days. Any negative episode witnessed in this dream needs to be prevented or altered. Take steps to enjoy only positive expressions in your life.

a comfortable home Only associate with those people you find delightful for the next month. Make no allowances

for anyone else you feel you should see. Only associate with those you feel comfortable around. If you make allowances for others you will have a very distasteful time.

a home in chaos Make sure monies you have allocated to a certain place actually goes where it is intended. If you do not become personally involved and hold tight constraints on your money, you will find it will be used for purposes it was not intended for. Be on your guard, especially for the next five days.

rest home Encourage yourself to continue when you have doubts and things are not progressing in the way you feel they should. Maintain a high confidence level, everything will work out in the way you wish them to.

to lease a home Someone who has consistently turned you down will have a change of heart and will now be eager to involve themselves with you. Back off and do not become involved. This will not be to your advantage. Any event in this dream that is negative and can be applied to your life needs to be prevented.

in any other form Your life will dramatically improve because someone will restructure their own life and this will affect yours as well. This transition will occur within three days and will vastly improve your status. This will be a welcome and refreshing turn of events for everyone involved. Good luck is with you. You also have plenty of time to alter any negative aspect of this dream or to incorporate positive events into your life.

homeless You are not getting the most important and significant facts about a particular situation from someone who is important to you. This is a matter of great concern to you. Take every step to get the facts and resolve this issue completely. For the next five days you will also be very eager to set aside time for the person you have an interest in. This person will disappoint you by being bored in your presence. You have prior notice of this and can take steps to prevent its occurrence. You must also take steps to make sure anything witnessed in this dream does not become a reality and promote any positive event to the fullest.

homemade Make sure someone does not keep you from tackling a situation you need to take care of by steering you in the wrong direction. Stay balanced so you can clearly see what it is you are doing. It is important that you remain focused for the next three days.

homemaker Get more training and experience prior to becoming involved in a particular situation. Let others know you are interested in handling this as a learning experience. Do not allow your confidence to lag; you will be very victorious. This will come up within three days.

home plate Do not allow someone to verbalize their hatred for someone else to you. Keep yourself busy for the next few days so you do not have to listen to these words of hate and the desire for revenge. Let this person handle their own problems and get on with life.

home run You will enjoy an abundance of prosperity,

health and love. Many blessings are with you and your family. Make sure anything negative in this dream that could become a reality does not occur and promote any positive event to the fullest.

homesick Do not assume a persona that confuses others. Too much of a change will be too drastic for others to comprehend. Stop confusing others with your behavior. You will also need to be careful when traveling and take steps to avoid any hazardous situation for the next five days as well as any other negative situation you see in this dream. Be sure to forewarn anyone you recognize to do the same and take steps to ensure you only experience positive expressions in your life.

homespun You will fail the first time you attempt to deal with a particular situation. Regroup and try again later. You will be successful.

homestead For the next three days do not allow someone who is attempting to control you to get the upper hand. Immediately inform this individual you will not allow yourself to be controlled by them or by anyone else. If you allow this to continue, you will be miserable with this person. Make sure anything negative in this dream does not take place and do everything you can to promote the positive.

home video Be very attentive to someone who does not easily show emotions but implies through body language that something is not quite right. This individual is considering suicide and needs help in getting back on the right track. You will be successful in putting a stop to this situation and in giving help to someone who is emotionally vulnerable right now. This will occur within three days. Make sure you bring any positive message in this dream to fruition and avoid or alter the outcome of any negative message.

homework For the next three days you will be successful in tackling any situation that appears complicated. You will develop the confidence you originally lacked and will be able to handle any situation that seemed impossible. Good luck is with you. Be sure you bring any positive message in this dream to full bloom and make sure you prevent the occurrence of any negative event.

homing pigeon Do not allow yourself to be trapped in a ménageâtrois situation without your knowledge. Someone will approach you while denying any involvement with anyone else. Maintain your confidence and take steps to avoid this kind of arrangement. All negative messages portended in this dream need to be prevented and all positive messages need to be promoted.

hominy Because of situations that are out of your control, a planned celebration will not take place. Move the date up on your calendar and plan this celebration for an earlier time.

homosexual You will experience a new freedom within two days due to an unusual occurrence that will help you to get

beyond a particular situation that has limited your potential in some way. This issue has led you to feelings of discouragement and despair in the past. You will find the courage, develop the motivation and gain the energy needed to remove whatever is limiting you. Many blessings are with you and your family. You will also need to take steps to prevent the occurrence of any negative event witnessed in this dream and make sure you only experience positive expressions in your life.

honesty *to hear the word* You will learn of the unexpected death of a close relative and this will take everyone by surprise.
  in any other form Be consistently aggressive in your actions for the next three days.

honey Be prepared for a large victory that is coming your way within five days. Be consistent in your actions and make sure you behave appropriately in all areas of your life. Promote any positive event witnessed in this dream and prevent the occurrence of any negative event.

honey bear Do not allow an argument to break out between you and someone else because of a difference in opinion, especially for the next three days. Remain uninvolved in this kind of behavior. The result of this argument will depress you greatly. Make sure you accentuate any positive message in this dream and prevent any negative message from taking place in reality.

honeybee You will be very lucky in all negotiations dealing with business and matters of the heart. It is also important to make sure any negative event witnessed in this dream does not become a reality and take steps to experience only positive expressions in your life.

honeycomb Someone you do not spend much time with due to their busy schedule will make an unexpected visit. This individual will display higher spirits and a better sense of humor than usual. This will be a totally delightful visit. They will be very eager to grant you any wish you desire as long as it is within their capacity to grant. A surprise gift is also in store for you within this cycle.

honeydew Affirm the needs of those who are waiting for this within two days in order to lessen their stress. Be considerate and consistent. This will bring your life the balance you need within five days.

honeymoon All business and love negotiations will be very lucky for you now. Reenter any relationship you feel you want to reconcile. This cycle is perfect for bringing about those emotional changes you desire and all relationships will work out beautifully. You will also experience an increase in prosperity. Any portion of this dream that foretells a negative experience can be turned into a positive experience in reality. You have the ability to do this, especially for the next three days.

honeysuckle Within five days you will surrender your love and affection to someone and you will behave in such a way that others will adore you. You will enjoy a fantastic time during this time frame. Good luck is with you. Any part of this dream that portends a negative experience can be turned into a positive experience in reality. All positive aspects need to be accentuated.

Hong Kong Within seven days you will have the opportunity to cater to others from a different ethnic background. Because of your hard work, eagerness to please, and ability to handle each situation with diplomacy and tact, doors will be opened to you on a permanent basis. As a result, you will be offered many new opportunities and will experience an increase in wealth. Good luck is with you. This dream may also be used as a reference point in time. If you dream of this city and see its name used in any context, the dream message will occur on this day.

honk All negotiations that you are involved in will be extremely successful. Someone new will also enter your life and will, if you choose, become a lifelong friend. This person is very charming and will share many wonderful stories with you. They will also give you an important message that will offer you a different viewpoint of a certain project or concept you are presently working on. You will be able to use this knowledge to improve your lifestyle. Expect this to take place within three days. Something unusual will also occur within four days. You will find someone who is willing to help you and will relentlessly stick to their goals until your needs are met.

to honk at someone Be wary of someone who has led you to believe you can confide in them. Do not depend on this person's loyalty, they will let you down. Do not become involved with gossips.

to be honked at Don't allow yourself to get caught up in game playing. Someone will attempt to draw you on a path that will lead to discomfort and stress for you. Work to keep this from occurring, especially for the next three days. You must also make sure any negative aspect of this dream does not become a reality and take steps to enjoy only the positive aspects of life.

honky tonk You are loved beyond your imagination and you will have verification of this within two days. You will be surrounded by those who love you, respect you and are loyal to you.

Honolulu You will have the strength and inner courage for the next five days to make some unusual and extraordinary changes in your life. Many blessings will come to you and your family and you are entering a lucky five day cycle. Do what you can to keep any negative message in this dream from becoming a reality and take steps to promote the positive. This dream may also be used as a reference point in time. If you dream of this city and see its name used in any context, the dream message will occur on this day.

honor Do not overextend yourself regarding a particular situation that will come up within five days. This situation will require physical labor to the point of exhaustion. Take yourself away from the situation, regroup, eat healthful foods, drink plenty of water and get plenty of rest.

honor roll You are moving in the direction of prosperity and will be celebrating an unusual occurrence that will happen within the family. You will also have a conversation with someone who is much younger than you. You will tell this young person something very profound that will allow you to connect with them. This will also allow them to change their lives in a way they never thought possible. Many blessings will come to you and your family.

hood Within three days you will have the opportunity to accept a once in a lifetime situation that could lead to greater wealth and power. You will have the awareness, during this time period to recognize and accept this opportunity.

to look under the hood of a vehicle Face up to your personal problems regarding a particular relationship as soon as possible. Do everything you can to avoid any negative aspect of this dream that could become a reality. Forewarn anyone you recognize in this dream to do the same.

hooded coat Push yourself toward those goals you are eager to achieve. Your success will depend solely on your willingness to push yourself forward.

hooded sweatshirt You are going in the right direction. You will be provided access to vast amounts of information and tapping into this knowledge will give you the tools you need to accumulate enough wealth to live the lifestyle you desire. You will have a long and healthy life. Many blessings will come to you and your family.

hoodlum Someone you are interested in, in some capacity, will not be the person you need to rely on in any form. Do not allow yourself to be taken. Take the time to select and review much more carefully when it comes to the character of those you choose to associate with, especially for the next seven days.

hoof Do not become overly involved in anything that could be dangerous for you. Refrain from abusive tendencies and take steps to keep yourself safe. Discipline your actions for the next seven days.

hoofed feet Within five days, someone you feel very comfortable with will very subtly begin to detach themselves from you. Although this person is aware that you have done nothing wrong, they have a great deal of anger and resentment toward you. Allow this to happen gracefully and allow this person a way out. If this person stays in your life they will create many distasteful moments for you and will have difficulty refraining from blurting out hurtful statements. Get on with your life without this person in it and take every precaution to keep any negative situation in this dream from becoming a reality. Do everything you can to promote any positive situation.

hook *picture and planter hooks* Within three days, a situation will arise that will require you to determine whether someone you are working with is keeping up the pace. This person may not be working to their full potential and it will reach the point where you will be doing the work of two unless you are alert to this. Focus on solving this issue so you can get the help you need without taking on any extra responsibilities. Speak your mind and make it known that this person has to pull their own weight. Do everything you can to maintain a stress free life. Many blessings are with you and you are headed for a prosperous future. You will enjoy a financially secure retirement.

in any other form Be very alert to the fact that someone is devising a plan to take over property you own. Aggressively seek this person and do not allow yourself to be manipulated into letting this take place. Step back, regroup and prevent this cowardly act.

hook and eye Someone you know who is very charismatic, confident and has a wonderful sense of humor will do everything in their power to bring you closer to them. This individual will invite you to an enjoyable outing and is planning to ask you to be a part of their life. A variety of things will occur on this outing that will make it clear to you that you want to make major permanent changes in your life. You will rejoice in these changes. Someone will also request your affection within a three day period. You will be overjoyed at this and more than willing to surrender yourself to this person. Many blessings are with you and your family.

hooked nose Listen carefully and be very tolerant of someone who is anxious and upset. Remain calm, supportive and generous with your time. This will mean a great deal to this individual. Expect this to occur within three days. You must also make sure any negative event witnessed in this dream does not become a reality and take steps to accentuate the positive.

hooker This dream is a very lucky omen. Follow your instincts and your own counsel. Anything you set into motion will reach a successful conclusion. Victory is yours.

hookworm Be very disciplined with your behavior, especially around children. Do not allow yourself to be irresponsible or to act on impulse when in the company of young people. Control your emotions and do nothing inappropriate for the next three days.

hoop For the next three days you will achieve success in everything you set your mind to.

hoot owl Be alert to the fact that you will be abandoned without notice by someone you are emotionally attached to. This person has difficulty committing to a relationship to the degree you desire. You can prevent this future occurrence by restraining your emotions. Take steps now to avoid being hurt a month from now. This relationship is workable if you do not allow your emotions to gain the upper hand.

owl hooting Someone you have a great deal of respect and high regards for will die within seven days. This is out of your control. You will also need to make sure your pets are safe from disease and accident.

quiet owl Become acutely aware that an individual, whom you least expect to cause problems, will want to inflict emotional harm on you for personal reasons. This will be done in a very subtle and conniving way. Intensify your efforts to guard your reputation and make sure your words are understood and accurately reported. Protect everything that is emotionally precious to you from someone who merely seeks sick self gratification. This is likely to occur within three days.

hop *to hop with someone you recognize* Both of you need to avoid the situation in the dream that made you hop. Alert this other individual of any negative situation or danger you witnessed in the dream that could lead to injury. This is also the perfect time to use your communication skills to reconcile a particular situation in your life. This renewal will bring you greater benefits than you ever hoped. Good luck is with you.

to see someone hop whom you do not recognize Other people will be very eager to embrace your suggestions. This three day cycle will offer you the strength and clarity to formulate your next step.

to hop You will be able to successfully bring out the truth regarding certain situations that will occur over the next three days. You will be able to accomplish this task in a satisfactory manner with no stress.

in any other form Take steps to provide entertainment for yourself. Become more involved in social functions in order to add more spice to your life. Seek entertainments that are new to you and learn to enjoy life to the fullest.

hope *any form* Your clarity of thought will lead to the formulation of certain plans. Once you put these plans into action, you will be amazed at what you are able to accomplish within the week. Trust yourself and proceed with confidence.

hopscotch Within five days someone will make outrageous demands on you. Firmly refuse to comply. These requests will be way out of line and you need to make it clear this individual cannot get away with this behavior.

horizon *any form* You will receive the nurturing you have been longing for. You will also find spirited nourishment within three days in forms you never expected. Many blessings will come to you and your family.

hormone In order to meet your needs, you will have to specify exactly what you require, both verbally and in writing, within five days. This will serve to pinpoint your needs and motivate those who work for you to get what you require. Everything will fall into place perfectly. You have this five day time period to do this.

horn Practice common sense. This attribute will guide you from moment to moment. For the next five days you will also need to pay close attention when someone subtly attempts to pry into your personal affairs. This person will try to catch you off guard in order to glean private information from you.

hornbill Make sure you treat others in the manner you wish to be treated, especially young children. This is particularly important for the next five days.

hornet Pursue the things that will give you emotional satisfaction for the next five days.

hornet's nest No matter what a situation looks like that will lead you to feel discouraged, aggressively seek out what rightly belongs to you. Learn to tolerate a certain individual who is standing in your way. You will be able to clearly see your next move and successfully gain what is yours. You will benefit greatly from this.

horn rim glasses You will be asked to give financial assistance to a relative who is undergoing financial hardship. This cycle will give you the means and opportunity to help out those in financial distress. You are deeply loved, respected and appreciated by many people, even those who are unable to verbalize their feelings. You will be able to sense this by their behavior and mannerisms toward you.

horoscope Within two days you will be given the gift of greater mental inventiveness and clarity of thought by your higher power. Put this gift to good use and you will have an immediate improvement in your circumstances. Your sex life will improve and you will prosper in each area of your life for the next month. This is also the perfect time to get an astrological reading if this is something you desire. Do this within five days.

horror Do everything you can to remain stress free for the next five days. If someone gives you advice within three days, don't take it the wrong way. This person is offering advice only because they love you. Any horror from the dream that relates to a reality needs to be altered. Any situation that is within your power to change needs to be changed within the week.

hors d'oeuvre Take steps to expose yourself to a new set of friends and different social environments. Add stimulation to your life by attending various new functions and outings. You will find this very beneficial in more ways than one, especially for the next seven days.

horse *to see someone riding a horse* Within three days you will be overwhelmed by the manner in which someone treats you. This person will treat you in an extremely affectionate and generous manner and you will get the sense that these feelings are genuine. You will be deeply touched in an emotionally fulfilling way and you will be brought together with this person in mutual contentment. Proceed with confidence, you are headed in the right direction and will enjoy a very prosperous future.

to ride horse bareback or see someone ride bareback Within five days a situation will come up that will require professional attention. Get this help quickly and don't waste time deciding whether or not you need it. You must also do everything you can to keep any negative event in this dream from becoming a reality. Make sure you forewarn anyone you dreamed about to do the same.

blind horse Keep your thoughts detailed and structured when preparing to initiate any plan. This habit will bring you many future benefits. Within seven days you will start dealing with issues and people in a more straightforward and structured fashion and will be handling situations in a more scientific way. Any negative situation in this dream that could become a reality needs to be changed or prevented.

race horse Riches are in store for you if you keep doing what you are presently doing. Pay close attention to the events in this dream. If a positive message was revealed, take steps to promote it in reality. Also what you felt was out of reach is now within your grasp.

war horse Any big plans you have for the next three days will be executed successfully and brought to completion. During this time frame you will have the joy of grasping your ambitions.

white horse This dream is an exceptionally lucky omen for you and you will experience a rapid increase in wealth within three weeks due to an unusual occurrence. Success will abruptly come at a time you least expect.

wooden horse This dream is an extremely lucky omen. Within three days you will have a great opportunity to involve yourself in a very loving, romantic relationship. If you choose to go this route, you will enjoy a terrific wonderful life. Any negative event connected to this dream can be changed or avoided completely. Any positive event needs to be brought to fruition.

to ride a flying horse Within the week you will develop the strength to handle upcoming stressful situations. Use your sense of resourcefulness to look at the ins and outs of all of these issues. You must also take steps to prevent any negative event seen in this dream and do everything you can to only experience positive expressions in your life.

to see someone you recognize ride a flying horse Within three days you will find the reasons you need to inspire you to change your romantic outlook on life. You will now find a way to grasp a situation you felt was impossible.

to see someone you do not recognize ride a flying horse Pay close attention to the actions of the person on the horse. This will offer you a major clue to who you will be dealing with within three days. This may be either a positive or a negative situation. You will have the time to carefully plan how you will properly handle this upcoming situation. Also you are entering a cycle that will require you to set aside more time for tranquility and sexual fulfillment. Make sure you take the time to fulfill your needs. You are headed for a brilliant future.

saddle horse For the next few days, eat no unusual foods. Watch your stomach.

to fall off a horse You are just about to break ties with someone whom you should not be distancing yourself from. This person will play a major role in your life and you will regret they are no longer a part of your life. Keep close ties to your precious friends. Take additional steps to keep any negative event in this dream from becoming a reality. Do what you can to ensure you only experience positive events in your life.

to trim a horse's mane to make it bristle Be very wary of someone you have just met. This person is very treacherous and will cause many people to suffer misfortunes after coming into contact with them. Get on with your life without this person in it.

horse carriage Someone who demonstrates a small liking for you will suddenly develop a deep emotional love.

in any other form Pay close attention to what your heart is saying. Pursue what you want on an emotional level and play an active part in having your emotional needs fulfilled. Within three days you will receive exactly what you want. Blessings and good luck are coming your way.

horse and buggy For the next few days your presence will be requested at a variety of functions. You will enjoy yourself immensely and will be the center of attention at a number of these functions. You will receive the love and affection you desire from the person you want it from.

horse cart You will be surprised to receive a positive answer to a request you expected a negative answer to. Good luck is with you.

horsehair Within the week you will become very aware of someone's sexual desires for you. This person will go to great lengths to get you to surrender emotionally to them. It is your decision whether or not you want to pursue this. Good luck is with you.

horseradish Within three days someone will drop subtle hints about an area in their life they desire you to be responsible for. This person will expect you to take it upon yourself to change their outlook on life. This individual feels they are unable to make improvements in their life. You have the conviction and ability to help this person make the changes they need to make. You are headed for a brilliant future and you will be able to accomplish these changes much quicker than you realize.

horseshoe This dream is an extremely lucky omen. You will rejoice because you will have won the love and respect of someone you have long desired to have in your life. This lucky cycle will benefit anything dealing with business transactions. You will see a big improvement in your finances.

horseshoe crab Do not allow your imagination and suspicions to run wild, especially for the next three days.

horsetail You will want to force an issue to gain information about a particular topic. You will be able to gain the knowledge you need by using this tactic and will make the correct decision based on fact instead of guesswork.

horsewhip Guard everything that is emotionally precious to

you (i.e., reputation, private life, career, etc.) from those who demonstrate envy. Avoid friction.

hose Move quickly in those areas you desire in order to bring about needed changes in your life. A gift you are planning to give to someone will also, in turn, be given to someone else. Think ahead and change your plans to avoid being hurt because you feel as though this person was not appreciative of your efforts. Plan a different way in which to express your appreciation.

hospital Be consistently understanding when dealing with certain matters that will be coming up within the next five days. You will be able to display the proper attitude at all times. Do everything necessary to build up your resistance. Treat your health as a special commodity. This is an extremely lucky omen.

someone you know in a hospital Within three days a certain person will cause you to experience mixed emotions because what they say does not accurately reflect what they feel. Before making any kind of move, make sure you have the right feedback so you can make the right move. Be sure to alert the person you dreamed about to avoid illness or to seek help immediately if they are ill in any way. You have enough time to give ample warning.

you are in the hospital Because of an unusual occurrence, you will need to nourish others in a special way. You will also feel swamped within five days because of your need to nurture a large number of people in a short period of time. You will be able to get through this calmly. Offer the nurturing these people need. Take steps to avoid the illness you dreamed you were suffering from, especially for the next three weeks. Otherwise, this is a very good omen and luck will be with you.

if you see faces you do not recognize You will be asked for assistance by someone. Do what you can to help. This will be a very prosperous time and a time to bring in the benefits you want from life.

host Someone will request your company to visit someone who is ill within five days. You must also make sure you accurately understand what you are being told by someone else. Make sure the information is factual during this time frame.

hostage You will finally be able to get in touch with a very elusive person. Within a few days you will be given an attentive audience by this person and will be able to explain what is most important to you. Rehearse your conversation ahead of time so you can gain the most from this person's time. Much will come from this meeting.

hostess A lovely person will let you know you are a priority in their life. It will come as a surprise that this person wants a full commitment from you.

hot Within five days an unusual natural disaster will occur. This will cause you a great inconvenience and you will need to take steps now to keep yourself safe. You have time to take these precautions if you act now.

someone being visibly overheated Take the most profitable course of action and all of your plans will result in a more improved and greater level of success. Your enterprise will be appropriately respected by yourself and others. Do everything you can to keep any negative event in this dream from becoming a reality.

being overheated in some form or another You will enjoy a new growth in spirituality and will be able to take care of a burdensome responsibility in ways you have never done before. During this three day period you will make clear choices and will make better use of your resources than you have in the past. This will enable you to complete your tasks successfully. Do everything you can to keep any negative event in this dream from becoming a reality. Make sure you experience only positive expressions in your life.

hotbed Be prepared to determine what you really want from someone you are interested in. Once you reveal your true feelings, you will be able to specify the depth of the relationship. The other individual may want more from this union than you. Be prepared to make compromises for mutual satisfaction if you choose to go in this direction. The more time you spend nurturing this relationship, the greater the passion and the deeper the emotional feelings will be. Take steps to keep any negative event you witnessed in this dream from becoming a reality.

hotcakes Open up your communication and show your affection to the one you care about. Put your love into action and give this person your feeling because this person is feeling very neglected. It is important that you do this within three days. Take any negative situation in this dream and turn it into a positive. Make sure you experience only positive expressions in your life.

hotdog Many blessings will come to you and your family. Also you will be put in charge of a large group of people, corporation, etc. You will eventually be paid a large salary for your work and will benefit greatly from your involvement. You must also work to turn any negative message in this dream to a positive. Be sure to warn anyone you recognize in the dream to do the same.

hotdog bun You will be asked to perform a particular task within three days and you will find yourself better equipped to handle this than you originally thought. You will gain the inspiration you need to motivate yourself to complete this task successfully. Go for it.

hotel Someone you are very fond of will begin to behave in a very cruel manner toward you. Even after you speak to them about this matter they will continue, and over the next few weeks this will develop into a pattern of behavior that will escalate to the point of public displays of cruelty and verbal abuse. This will continue in spite of this person's declaration of love toward you. Refuse to live a lifestyle of continued abuse. Only a stress free environment will enable you to develop to your fullest potential. If it becomes neces-

sary, live your life without this person in it. Do everything you can to promote any positive message in this dream and take steps to prevent any negative message.

hot flash Within two days someone will demonstrate a very kind gesture toward you and you will be at a total loss of words. This will be an extremely lucky omen for the next seven days.

hot line You are about to make a mistake. You are very fond of someone who is also very fond of you but you are impatient because the relationship is not developing as fast as you would like. As a result, you will attempt to rush things and will become very demanding. This behavior will only drive this person away. Invest your time in developing your personality in order to project a more positive image. This individual will eventually grow into the relationship and you will both be able to reach a mutual understanding. Any negative message in this dream needs to be prevented and you need to take steps to enjoy only positive experiences in your life.

hot pants Someone will be intensely aroused by your physical appearance within two days. This individual will go to great lengths to involve you in a relationship. If you choose to pursue this you will find yourself surrounded by love and treated in the manner you wish to be treated. This involvement will last for a long period of time.

hot pepper Do not waste your time by deciding whether to become personally involved in someone else's issues. Your hesitation will create an unusual occurrence that will be beyond the control of both of you. Be very aware of this and make a point of becoming involved before the situation gets out of control.

hot plate Do everything you can to express yourself graphically in order to make yourself perfectly understood. This will enable you to turn your ideas into reality. This is especially important for the next three days.

hot potato Separate yourself from thoughts that have nothing to do with the present. Focus only on what is important now. Good luck is with you. Any negative event portrayed in this dream needs to be avoided or altered and any positive event needs to be promoted.

hot rod Be very secretive and do not allow others to know, for the next three days, the changes you are planning in your life. This will keep other people from interfering with your focus and determination. You need to concentrate entirely on your lifestyle changes, without outside negative interference, in order to be successful. You are going in the right direction. Good luck is with you. Protect yourself from any negative message foretold in this dream and do everything you can to promote the positive.

hot spring Be more sympathetic toward someone who will be undergoing a great deal of stress in their life. Become acutely aware of what others are going through so you can offer your support. This will be short lived so do what you can to help this person through this crisis and make sure any negative event seen in this dream does not become a reality. Forewarn anyone else in this dream to do the same.

hot tub Loosen up and schedule your life in such a way that, within a few days, you will be able to bring something very special into your life. Your involvement will bring you joy and tranquility. You must also be aware that your plans to help someone in a secretive way will not work out. Change your plans and move confidently in other areas of your life. Do everything you can to bring any positive event to full bloom and make sure any negative event does not become a reality.

hot wire Make sure any negative event portrayed in this dream that is remotely connected with reality does not occur to you or to anyone else. You have five days in which to do this. Take this opportunity to change your life around so you and anyone else you recognize in the dream experience nothing but prosperity. This is also a warning, for the next three days, to take steps to protect yourself from an unknown person who randomly chooses to bring harm to certain people. Do not make it easy for other people to prey on you. You have prior notice of this so you can keep yourself in a safe environment.

hound You have the perfect opportunity for the next three days to obtain the knowledge you desire from someone else. This knowledge gives you the opportunity to handle a particular situation correctly.

hour This dream is an extremely lucky omen. Pay attention to the particular hour specified in this dream. Schedule any important event, conference, etc., for this time for the next seven days. This hour will be the most fortuitous for you during this time period. All communication held at this time will bear the most fruit. Any negative event occurring in this dream at a specific hour needs to be attended to, avoided or altered. This applies also to anyone else you recognize from this dream.

hourglass Someone who carries a great deal of animosity toward you from the past will reenter your life within three days. In spite of friendly appearances, this person is still seeking revenge and is still a very cunning adversary. Protect yourself and get on with your life without this person in it and make sure you protect yourself from any negative aspect of this dream.

house You will be loved and cherished for a lifetime by those you care about. For a more in depth definition look under home.

house carried away by flood, destructive weather, etc., Make sure you do everything in your power to protect yourself from contagious disease. Be very aware that you will be a carrier and could pass this illness on to others who are susceptible to it. Be very aware of your environment for the

next three days and make sure you do not spread this illness. Be sure to keep yourself away from illnesses you may contract.

houses under construction Someone is focused on you for the sole purpose of sexual pleasure. This person is not interested in any kind of relationship but only in sexual gratification. Be very clear about both of your intentions so there will not be any misunderstandings. It is up to you to choose whether this is the kind of relationship you want to pursue. This is a good cycle for building a firm foundation for those who are interested in buying or building a home. All negotiations involving property will be lucky for you. Do everything you can to avoid any negative event in this dream from becoming a reality.

a particular house This may represent the house of someone you have not seen in awhile. Investigate the neighborhood and determine who the person is the dream is directing you to talk to. Any negative situation in this dream that could become a reality needs to be avoided. Prior notice of this will keep this from occurring. You must also not allow yourself to be so available to another person that may not be sharing the same feelings for you. Do not overextend your feelings so you will not be taken advantage of. You will be liked better if you restrain your feelings and do not make yourself so available, especially for the next five days. Make sure anything negative connected to this dream does not become a reality.

houses burned to the ground If you recognize the house, you have one week to alert the owners of the possibility of a fire. Also within five days someone will do everything in their power to deepen their relationship with you. This person will try to communicate to you their desire for involvement and will do what they can to deepen this involvement and push the relationship at a quicker pace.

home beautification or repair You may want to have this task performed in reality. Also someone you want to involve in a plan will support you fully in putting your ideas into tangible form.

to see a burning house You will reconcile with someone who is special to you. This will result in a loving, passionate relationship.

farmhouse Someone will be very eager to grant you what you wish. This will be especially true for the next three days.

gatehouse Do not waste your efforts on others who have asked for your time. These efforts will not be appreciated and you will feel you have been taken for granted.

glasshouse Do not place yourself in the position to have your vehicle hijacked. Be especially careful of this for the next two days and make sure all of your precious objects are not taken from you without your knowledge.

broken windows in glass house Be very careful and do not make extra demands on someone who is special to you. This individual feels overwhelmed due to certain situations that are occurring in their life right now and will come to you seeking a listening ear. If you choose to offer your time, this person will be forever grateful to you.

halfway house Do not display a wishy-washy manner in front of someone when dealing with a particular situation this individual wants to involve you in. Deal with this in a direct manner and go on with your life.

icehouse For the next three days, in order to achieve success, you must skillfully use the gift of diplomacy and tact when involved in all negotiations. Your feelings and the feelings of others could be easily hurt during this time period if you are not careful. Take it slowly and behave accordingly in order to avoid this. You must also do everything you can to keep any negative message in this dream from becoming a reality and take steps to only experience positive expressions in your life.

madhouse Good luck is with you. You will be able to purchase, at a very reasonable price, something you greatly desire if you move quickly.

open house Within seven days you need to make all of the correct decisions by using a team approach, otherwise a large number of people will be angry at you for making decisions without consulting them. Any negative event viewed in this dream must be avoided in reality and make sure you allow only positive expressions in your life.

packing house You will be in the position of handling money that belongs to other people. Your versatility and the way you diversify money into different accounts to generate a profit will be noticed by those in authority.

rooming house Within the week, someone will extend themselves in a very special way. This person will surprise you with a party or a special gift in appreciation.

row house Keep your ambitions to yourself and allow yourself the time to develop your plans before you tell anyone else.

safe house You or someone you know will be misled by other people to believe you should do something you feel differently about. Although those people who are misleading you fully believe this is the best option, they have no idea what the consequences of their choice will be. This will put you or this other person in a dangerous and troublesome situation. Any negative event seen in this dream needs to be prevented for you and anyone you recognize in this dream. Do everything you can to experience only positive expressions in your life.

schoolhouse You will enter a relationship that will require you be very tactful. You will feel as though you are walking on eggs because of the explosive personality of a special person. You may want to avoid entering into this relationship.

steak house Know when to apologize.

Victorian house Although you are around many powerful and influential people, because of their position of authority or the wealth they possess, there is one other person you are fated to become involved with. This will be an opposite sexed person and this involvement will reach any proportion you desire. Make it a point to leave yourself open to any situation that will expose you to situations where you can meet this person. This will take place within five days and conversations will flow easily between you. You will rapidly develop a sense of closeness and your feelings will grow. This person is well established and more financially secure than you ever expected. You are both destined for a wonderful and tranquil life and will both enjoy an abundance of health and a prosperous future.

warehouse Pay attention and concentrate for the next three days. Someone will attempt to interfere with your train of thought. This person will lead you to believe your thoughts are not that great or convince you, you are headed in the wrong direction and have you doubting your abilities. Otherwise this is an extremely lucky omen, especially for the next week. You will not only be able to turn this situation around but will also be able to express yourself fully to those who are important to you in a way that will bring them closer to you. Many blessings are with you.

whorehouse You will see clearly within five days, what you need to do because you will learn from an example set by another person. Keep your eyes and ears open for this so you can see and determine what you choose not to have going on in your life for the next two weeks. Do what you can now to stop this before it becomes an issue. Many blessings are with you.

to lease a house Someone who has consistently turned you down will have a change of heart and will now be eager to involve themselves with you. Back off and do not become involved. This will not be to your advantage. Any event in this dream that is negative and can be applied to your life needs to be prevented.

to have someone request to live with you on a permanent basis A certain situation will occur that will be so unusual and extraordinary that no law of physics can explain this. Expect this to take place within three days. It will leave you with a sense of awe and wonder and will be as though a miracle has occurred. You will have no way of explaining how this came about. After this transpires, you will be able to present yourself at your highest level and be able to handle situations, other people and yourself in an appropriate manner. You are headed for a brilliant future and many blessings are with you and your family.

owning or living in more than one house Do everything necessary to put your love into action. Give those you care about evidence of your feelings for them. This will be very important, especially for the next three days. Any negative episode witnessed in this dream needs to be prevented or altered and take steps to enjoy only positive expressions in your life.

in any other form Your life will dramatically improve because someone will restructure their own life and this will affect yours as well. This transition will occur within three days and will vastly improve your status. This will be a welcome and refreshing turn of events for everyone involved. Good luck is with you. You also have plenty of time to alter any negative aspect of this dream or to incorporate positive events into your life.

houseboat If this dream displays a positive event, you will want to incorporate this in your life. If negative, you have seven days to avoid this or to alter the outcome. A situation will also occur that may cause you to pass erroneous judgment on someone else. Guard against this for the next three days. You are on the path for a brilliant future.

housedress For the next three weeks you will be very successful with any real estate negotiations.

housefly This dream signifies victory. The number of flies seen indicate the size of achievement you will realize. This will occur within three months.

househusband Within three days you will come into some unusual information that will serve as a tool to lay a solid foundation for your future. Alter or prevent any negative event in this dream from becoming a reality and make sure you and anyone you recognize in this dream experiences only positive expressions in your lives.

housekeeper Be very diligent and tenacious when handling your affairs. Do not rely on someone less experienced than you to manage your personal business. Personally tackle your own tasks and you will be amazed at what you can accomplish. Promote any positive event you dreamed of and avoid any negative event. Alert anyone you recognize to do the same.

housewife Be very aggressive when dealing with a situation that will come up within three days in order to maintain control and handle it correctly. Avoid any negative event portrayed in this dream and promote any positive expressions in your life.

housework Become very aware of what you need to include in your life in order to become the person you want to be. This is especially important for the next three days.

housing project Do everything you can to ensure anything you dreamed of that was negative connected with you or someone you recognize does not occur. You have seven days to alter this event. You must also make sure when you offer assistance to someone that you are giving accurate information. Any referrals given should be checked first to ensure the accuracy of the statements so you do not send this person on a wild goose chase. You are headed for a brilliant future and will achieve victory in many levels of your life.

howl *to hear an animal howl* You will be placed in a situation that is very uncomfortable and will create mixed emotions on your part. You will feel a need to rescue someone at a tremendous emotional cost to you. Do not immediately volunteer your assistance. Take time to think this through in order to arrive at the correct decision. Many blessings will come to you and your family. For a more descriptive meaning, look up the particular animal that is howling. Any negative event connected to this dream needs to be prevented in reality and you need to forewarn anyone you recognize to do the same. Take steps to experience only positive expressions in your life.

hubcap Someone who acts indifferently toward you is not really this way. This person actually desires to be involved with you in some capacity and wants to share future plans with you if you choose to act on this. This person will feel gratitude toward you and will feel free to take the lead within

a five day period. You will be able to experience a full and satisfying life together.

huckleberry This dream is an extremely lucky omen and is alerting you that no matter what is going on in your life right now you will be able to withstand any hardship that may arise within the next two days. You will be able to proceed with confidence and handle anything you feel may be overwhelming. You are headed for a brilliant future.

huddle Embrace life to the fullest. You are also involved with a group of people who, as a general rule, look down on certain actions. One member of this group, in their desire to bend the rules, will twist the words of another individual to make it look as though this is acceptable. They will then attempt to recruit you in an attempt to step around these rules. Make sure you double check everything and stick by the rules.

hug The person you hug in this dream is someone who wants to hug you in reality. This dream will give you an indication as to what move you should make now. Expect this to evolve within three days. You must also keep any negative event from becoming a reality and alert anyone you recognize to do the same.

if you do not recognize the person You will be invited to dine at someone's house and will be served food that you will be unable to eat because of dietary restrictions, religious beliefs, or personal taste. Do not assume this person will be insulted if you explain the reasons behind your refusal. It would be even better if you notify this individual in advance about your dietary needs. They will be eager to prepare something you can eat so you can both enjoy your time together.

in any other form Be sure you play a very active role in ensuring your emotional desires are fulfilled. Within five days you will also be able to visualize the path you need to take to ensure a brilliant future. Good luck is with you.

hugging *to see others hugging* This dream represents good luck for the next five days. You will begin to experience an incredible energy and a need to make big changes in your life that will benefit you greatly. Because of a conversation you will have with another person, you will be shown other options for meeting your goals. As a result your enthusiasm for the path you were taking may be diminished somewhat. This dream is letting you know this may be a time to step back and carefully regard your options. It may be that another path will be more beneficial or you may choose not to make any changes in your life at this time. Either way, you will arrive at the right decision for your future. You may also decide to add more in the way of romance in your life and this addition will give you more zest. Proceed with confidence, you are headed for a prosperous future.

hula hoop Someone you have known for some time will call unexpectedly and ask subtle questions in order to pull certain information from you. After a short period of time this person will propose marriage to you. This individual will preface this question with statements that they have known you for a long time, have no one in their life and you would be a good couple. The person has a steady income and some property but is neither rich nor poor. If you choose this route, you will find it is the right thing to do. Within three days someone will also ask for your expertise and services. This person will pay you handsomely and will be so delighted with your work that you will be paid even more than you originally asked. Go for it, you will not be disappointed.

hull Be sure to conduct yourself appropriately and address others properly when attending a meeting with an important individual. First impressions are what count. Prepare yourself ahead of time in order to give a good impression.

hum This is an extremely lucky omen. Within five days you will find yourself experiencing a wealth of tranquility, health and harmony with all of your friends and family members. Good luck is with you.

human/human figure For the next five days you will possess a certain command and greater clarity of thought. You will be able to express yourself succinctly if you separate yourself from those you associate with daily. By doing this you will be able to make the right decisions that will ultimately lead to a comfortable lifestyle.

to see a human figure (yours or someone else's) Pay attention to all events connected with this figure. Each negative event may be altered and each positive event may be enhanced by taking action now. You will also be surprised and delighted to learn of another's deep hidden feelings for you. Finances and love matters will improve.

perfect human figure Within five days you will be placed in the position of vigorously caring for someone until they are able to improve their quality of life and physical state to the point of social and personal acceptance. Also for the next five days, you will be so swamped with social activities you will have to take extra pains to keep your appearance and attire in top condition. This cycle will be very successful for you.

horrifying human figure You are overextending yourself to the point of burnout. Take steps to maintain and improve your health. Eat healthful foods, drink plenty of water and set limits on what you are willing to do for others. All requests made of your special deity, within seven days, will also be granted, no matter how impossible this request seems to be.

melting human figure Someone will finally come to terms with their life and make a decision they know you have long waited for. This decision will have a major impact on your life. You will both make mutual plans for a brilliant future. Expect this decision within the week.

someone you know melting This person is very eager to fulfill your wishes, with no limitations.

golden figures Each positive event connected to this dream needs to be converted into a reality as quickly as possible. Each negative event may be altered. This dream is a lucky omen and you will magically possess the inner strength to handle forthcoming situations. You will enjoy prosperity, balance and tranquility in your life. You will also be blessed with the clarity of thought needed to develop a plan and to execute it successfully. This plan will bring about the changes you so desire to experience in your present life. Luck will be with you, especially for the next seven days.

hummingbird Move swiftly for the next five days to put your ideas into tangible form. Certain unusual situations will occur during this time period that will allow you to bring this about with ease. This is an extremely lucky omen filled with an abundance of health.

humor Be very sure, for the next three days, that whomever you are communicating a certain situation to fully understands what you are trying to say in order to avoid misunderstandings and later regrets.

hump You will be the recipient of a large financial windfall. The larger the hump, the larger the amount of money you will receive. This is an extremely lucky omen. Expect this within five weeks.

humpback whale For the next four days you need to be focused and very analytical about a move you are about to make. As a result you will become involved in new dimensions in your life that will open opportunities bringing you more prosperity than you thought possible.

humpty dumpty Do not put your ambitions on hold in spite of the chaos occurring in your life now. Continue to handle each situation as best you can while continuing to move ahead on your plans. Good luck is with you.

hunchback Regardless of the nature of this dream, you will be the recipient of a large financial windfall within five weeks. The larger the hump on the hunchback, the larger the amount of money you will receive. This is an extremely lucky omen. You must make sure any negative event does not become a reality and do everything you can to promote the positive.

hundred Follow your own counsel. Take steps to avoid quenching the eagerness someone feels for you. You will be very surprised at the behavior someone will demonstrate. This will bring a great deal of joy into your life. Good luck is with you and you are headed for a brilliant future. Anything negative connected with this dream needs to be altered in reality and all positive events may be made tangible.

hunger Allow the love and affection someone feels for you to flow freely. Do not deprive yourself of the feelings this person has for you. Enjoy life, especially for the next three days, but take steps to prevent or alter the outcome of any negative event and make sure you experience only positive events in your life.

to feel hunger You will truly be able to enjoy the company of someone you have desired for the next three days. You will enjoy an abundance of health.

to satisfy your hunger Do not allow yourself to place your hopes on someone who will be unable to come through for you. Be alert to this situation within three days.

to spill your meal You and another person will go down a path that will, unbeknownst to you, be very dangerous because of an unfortunate event that will take place. Speak with this other person in order to reschedule an event you are planning within the next few days. You can avoid this dangerous situation.

in any other form Get the expert advice you need to allow relationships to flow in the manner you desire. It is especially important that you ensure all relationships, in any capacity, function at the highest level for the time being.

hunt *to hunt* The attitude you perceive from someone is inaccurate. You may get the impression that someone likes you more than they actually do. Don't push yourself on someone who, in actuality, does not care for your company. For a greater meaning to this dream look up the particular animal that was hunted. This dream also implies you will be receiving a very expensive gift.

hunting knife Your indifferent attitude toward another will create a disagreement within a certain group. Watch your behavior, especially for the next three days.

hurdle Someone whom you would least expect will rush to your aid in a time of need. This particular situation will arise within three days and will require immediate attention. You will be surprised at the promptness in which you receive help.

hurricane Avoid all long distance travel for the next five days. This is a very dangerous cycle for long distance commuting.

hurricane lamp Pay close attention to children in the immediate family to ensure they do not fall prey to an evil person. Do not allow this person's hidden agenda to unfold. Do everything you can to alert all those who care for these children.

hurt feelings Someone will enter your life within a few days for the sole purpose of satisfying their own desires. This individual will stay in your life only for the time it takes to get what they are after. Make sure you do not allow anyone to use you for their own purposes.

to see someone express their hurt feelings Make sure you do not give up when dealing with a specific situation. Proceed with confidence. You will definitely get through this feeling of giving up. You will emerge victoriously.

husband *to dream of your husband* Pay attention to the events in the dream connected with your husband. You have seven days and will have the power to alter or avoid any negative event. Incorporate any positive event into your life within five days. Also you will be going through a lifestyle change and will be introduced to exotic and exciting experi-

ences. You will enjoy yourself immensely and will incorporate these experiences into your life.

someone else's husband Any event seen in this dream will accurately take place within four days whether positive or negative. Forewarn anyone you recognize from the dream to take steps to avoid any negative event and to embrace the positive. The person you dreamed about could represent someone you will be dealing with during this four day period with the same characteristics, mannerisms, etc. Think ahead. If this person has attributes that you find distasteful, they will be represented in the new person who will enter your life. If this person has attributes you find appealing, actively pursue a relationship in any capacity you desire. Also you will have the clear and brilliant thoughts you need to guide you successfully through certain situations. These issues will require you to take risks and to extend yourself. Demonstrate a bold and courageous demeanor so these thoughts can be brought to tangible form. As a result you will experience more prosperity in life, both financially and health wise. Focus on your goals and be tenacious. You are headed in the right direction.

to dream of a husband when you are single in reality Regardless of what is occurring in your life right now, you will fully connect with someone in every capacity. This will result in a long lasting, tranquil and happy union.

in any other form You are headed for a brilliant future filled with prosperity and joyful moments. Doors that were formerly closed to you will now be open. This is the time to rejuvenate stagnated projects. Good luck is with you. Any event depicted in this dream that portends a negative event is within your power to avoid or alter. All future positive events need to be embraced.

hush Someone you least expect will request your company. This individual is from another country and will extend to you the opportunity to take advantage of their vast stores of knowledge. This knowledge will enhance your life once you put it into practice.

hush puppy Now is the perfect time for you to promote and display your talents to others. Do this within five days and you will find yourself heading in the direction you desire. You will experience success and prosperity.

hut Within five days, all important relationships need your personal attention in order for others to avoid the feeling of neglect. Special people are yearning for your closeness. You need to let them know you have only feelings of love and affection for them. Do not allow any of your relations to stagnate because of your behavior.

hutch Let your interest be known to others and you will be taken under someone's wing for extensive training. You will progress at a rapid pace. You will use this knowledge in ways you least expect but will benefit you.

hyacinth You will receive a lifetime annuity that will be left to you by a relative. This will come within five days in a very surprising way.

hybrid Others will attempt to persuade you to neglect your interests. Do not allow this to occur, especially for the next three days.

hydraulic pump You will be in an extremely lucky cycle for the next two weeks. You are definitely headed for a brilliant future.

hyena You will be involved in a number of conversations over the next three days and you will be very distraught over the lack of feelings someone displays toward you. This will surprise you and lead you to a feeling of despair. Do not allow this to take over. Quickly regroup yourself and remain calm. This is beyond your control but you have prior notice and will be able to handle yourself properly.

hygiene Do not waste time trying to get someone to reach an agreement with you. This person will not give in to your wishes. Move on and seek an alternative plan. Avoid distasteful moments. Good luck is with you.

hymn Do not allow anyone to get into the habit of directing your behavior through the use of body language. You will get the feeling that you will be unable to make a move without first checking with this person. They will train you to respond to their every move. This cycle will allow you the courage to put a stop to this behavior and put both of you on the right track. You will also be able to use this cycle to direct your energies in the areas you are most likely to achieve victory.

hypnosis Do not allow anyone to bully you into handling something you do not wish to deal with. Be firm in your refusal to take this on. Do everything you can to avoid complying to someone else's wishes, especially for the next five days.

hypnotize You need to avoid disturbing thoughts that will randomly enter your mind and create distress. These thoughts keep you from moving on and tackling new and bigger projects. Do everything you can to motivate yourself to move on with your life in a positive fashion. Anything negative connected with this dream can be altered or avoided and anything positive needs to be incorporated into your life.

hypocrisy Do not place yourself in the position of having to deal with a hypocrite and make sure you avoid this kind of behavior in yourself. Be very wary of someone who will go to great lengths to have you comply with their wishes against your will. This is likely to come up within three days.

hypocrite Someone will push you into a situation until you begin to sound as though you lack confidence in what you are doing. Be alert to this for the next three days and do everything you can to maintain your level of confidence on this matter. Develop the manner you wish to have come across to others.

hypodermic This dream is a symbol of abundance and an increase in finances will come from unexpected sources. You are headed in the right direction.

hypodermic that is not operating correctly Be wary of someone who will create a situation that causes you to become suspicious of someone else. Regroup and do not allow this to unfold in this way. This dream is an omen of good luck and you will have many lucky events for the next two weeks. You can be assured you will receive a small present from someone who cares for you.

hypodermic needle This dream symbolizes an abundance of health. Pay attention to the scenario involving the needle. If this is a negative event, take steps to prevent its occurrence. You have two weeks to handle this. If you recognize anyone connected with this dream, alert them to do the same. You must also check your options and refuse to settle for less.

hysterectomy Take steps to prevent any negative situation connected with this dream from occurring within three days. Anyone else connected to this event needs to be warned to take steps to prevent it. Stay in a state of equilibrium for the next three days and treat each person and situation equally. A situation will arise within this time period that will require you to be in the company of many people. This is the mentality you will need in order to overcome and deal with this issue properly. You will enjoy a bright and brilliant future. Many blessings will come to you and your family.

hysteria *any form* Within three days you will become involved in a situation that will leave you feeling overwhelmed, depleted and as though you have overextended yourself. Take notice of what you are becoming involved with so you do not fall prey to these feelings. Stay focused and you can avoid this entire scenario.

I

I Become very focused on who you are and go after what you really want. Decide what you need to put into your life that will enhance your personality. Face challenges head on in order to incorporate into your life those things that will add completion to your identity. Build yourself up to be the quality person you want to be and do not deprive yourself of what you need emotionally, physically or mentally. Identify those aspects of your personality that require enhancement. Good luck is with you.

Icarus *(Greek mythology)* Be very alert to all incoming calls and mail. Schedule your life and handle all personal responsibilities yourself. Make sure you handle all of your duties in a timely fashion and do not overlook something that needs to be handled within a particular time frame. You must also take any negative message foretold in this dream and turn it into a positive situation.

ice Because of your loving behavior toward another, you will be able to draw out those aspects of this person's personality that demonstrate a behavior toward you that you desire. Be very aware for the next five days that behavior will determine the degree of success you will have. You will be treated exactly as you wish to be treated and you will receive the love you desire from those you care about. Avoid any negative event in this dream and take steps to experience only positive expressions in your life.

ice cube You are entering a very lucky seven day cycle for love, business and finance. Anything that involves conversation and the use of your communication skills will be very productive. This dream also implies you will meet someone who will be very supportive in a mutually agreed upon manner. This situation has the potential of many unusual and intense possibilities and will allow you to experience a sex life that will be loving and romantic. You will both be surprised at the tenacity you have to bring this relationship to the level you desire. This will be a cycle for a wealth of opportunities and good health.

block of ice with something in it Pay attention to what is in the block of ice. This will offer you a clue to something you need to research. If it is a person in the ice, pay attention to the gender and this will indicate the sex of the person whom you need to speak to within three days. This person will play a major role in helping you to accomplish your goals, either by offering assistance, providing knowledge, assisting in research, or by offering financial help. During the course of the conversation you have with this person you will find a different approach plan that you never thought of before. It will become very clear to you that if you examine a route you should take, doors of opportunities will open to you and you will be able to accomplish, in a short time, what would normally take a much longer time to complete. Without prior knowledge you will not be open to this connection and you will not pick up this new approach. It will bring you to a different place with stronger foundations. Also if it was a person in the block of ice, it indicates at one time this person was distancing themselves from you for no apparent reason. Within the week this person will unexpectedly be more receptive. It is destined you will have a conversation with this person that will eventually lead to a mutually loving, satisfying, emotionally fulfilling sex life. This person will be willing to support your plans and goals and will offer their suggestions and help to make this a workable situation. This will be a very lucky cycle. Any dream you have of ice implies you are entering a productive cycle, will experience good health, and an increase in finances.

ice clinking in any container You will be in the right place at the right time to grasp the opportunity of a lifetime. This will bring you the benefits you need in order to make positive lifestyle changes. Old burdens and issues that have been plaguing you will immediately disappear. You will get a quick response from those you require services from in order to facilitate a smooth and speedy transition. You are headed for a brilliant and exciting new life.

to see ice melt Someone will finally get a grip on them-selves and make a decision you have long awaited. This individual is aware you have been waiting eagerly for this decision to be made and it will have a big impact on your life. You will both make mutual plans that will lead to a brilliant future. Expect this within seven days.

ice age Develop a structured way of behavior in order to stick to your major goals. This dream is a very lucky omen and you will find you are able to resolve issues quickly and successfully.

ice bag Conduct yourself in the way you know you have to in order to enlist the response you want from another person for the next three days. Make sure you think clearly and handle upcoming situations properly in order to receive major benefits.

iceberg Your relationships will have a strong foundation and you will soon be making plans that will bring mutual satisfaction to all parties. All relationships, in any capacity, will be fortuitous because of the strong foundations developed during this cycle. A family member will also ask you for an extremely difficult favor. You will be able to successfully accomplish this task within five days. Because you have prior notice of this, you will be able to plan ahead and handle it accordingly. Any negative aspect of this dream needs to be prevented or altered in reality and any positive aspect needs to be enhanced.

iceboat You will come across privileged information that will change your opinion about a certain individual. Don't jump to conclusions and be sure to conduct yourself properly at all times and act as though you had never received this information. This will occur within five days. Do everything you can to avoid any negative situation witnessed in this dream and take steps to enjoy the best life has to offer.

icebox You will begin to change your point of view about certain matters as a result of someone else's influences. Make sure you stay focused on your goals and do not allow someone to steer you off course. Do not allow your ambitions to die and make sure any negative situation depicted in this dream does not become a reality. Forewarn anyone else you recognized in the dream to do the same.

ice cream You are headed for a financial windfall and riches will come your way within five days.

ice hockey Gossip will be the main factor in breaking down the family unit. Make sure you do not participate in this and do not allow this to continue to the point of a breakdown within the family unit, especially for the next three days.

icehouse For the next three days, in order to achieve success, you must skillfully use the gift of diplomacy and tact when involved in all negotiations. Your feelings and the feelings of others could be easily hurt during this time period if you are not careful. Take it slowly and behave accordingly in order to avoid this. You must also do everything you can to keep any negative message in this dream from becoming a reality and take steps to only experience positive expressions in your life.

Iceland Be keenly aware of your sense of intuition and discipline yourself to use this sense correctly. You will quickly benefit from this gift. This dream may also be used as a reference point in time. If you dream of this country and see its name used in any context, the dream message will occur on this day.

ice milk Have the confidence not to question anything that works to your favor for the next three days. Just accept this good fortune. You will achieve prosperity in every level of your life, whether physical, emotional, mental or perceptual. All proposals will be very fortuitous for you during this time period and it would be to your benefit to render a positive response. This is an extremely lucky cycle.

ice pack For the next two days make sure you do not allow the hasty actions and words of others to leave you feeling uncomfortable. Don't allow this to cause you to lose confidence in your forthcoming plans. Remain focused and in control of your decisions. Pay close attention to what the ice pack was being used for and keep any negative event from occurring for the next three days. If someone you recognize is using an ice pack, alert this individual to a possible negative event.

ice plane Be sure you allow special people in your life the time to take care of their personal needs without creating the feeling of guilt or stress because they feel they are neglecting you.

ice skate Within three days your abilities will be tested and challenged by someone at a time you least expect. Because you have prior notice of this, you will have the power to handle it correctly when it occurs.

I Ching Do everything you can to remain firm when it becomes necessary for you to say no. Stick to your decision in order to protect yourself, especially for the next five days.

icicle This dream is an extremely lucky omen. Within three days you will be victorious in those areas of your life that overwhelmed you. You will also hear pleasing words you have longed to hear within this time period.

icing Within five days you will be involved in relentlessly helping someone until they are able to improve their lifestyle in terms of emotional, physical and social normalcy. You have the choice of deciding whether or not you choose to involve yourself in this. You will have the emotional and physical stamina to handle this matter, if you so choose. Many blessings are with you and you will be able to make the correct decision in this.

icon Put aside all grudges and put your energy to better use. Release these negative feelings from your conscious for your own well being. It is important to do this within five days.

Idaho You can hold down expenses by making sure you properly insure all valuable property. Follow your intuition. All travel arrangements will be successful and you will enjoy a safe pleasurable trip. This dream may also be used as a reference point in time. If you dream of this state and see its name used in any context, the dream message will occur on this day.

idea You will, with another individual, develop a wonderful work plan while brainstorming. Both of you are headed for a brilliant and prosperous future.

identical twins This dream is an extremely lucky omen for you and is a reminder you have committed yourself to two concurrent events. One of these events is far more important and crucial. You need to correct this as soon as possible.

if the twins are dressed identically You are entering an extremely lucky seven day cycle and you will be hearing news about the birth of twins in one capacity or another.

identification/identify *to ask someone to identify themselves, whether you recognize this person or not* You will, within two days, place yourself in a horrifyingly dangerous situation. Become acutely aware of your surroundings and keep yourself safe and protected. Good luck is with you.

to identify someone whether you recognize this person or not This person is someone who will bring you enormous wealth and will provide you with a pool of resources that will give you the chance to dramatically change your life, especially in those areas that require a certain amount of expertise. Move quickly on this and place yourself in the position and environment that will encourage this to happen. Many blessings are with you and you are headed for a brilliant future.

to be asked for your identification You will innocently create a situation that will ultimately lead to your arrest. Once you have this dream, do anything and everything to avoid doing anything that will lead to this. You have prior notice and can keep this event from taking place, especially for the next three days. Otherwise, this is a very lucky omen.

to be identified by someone else You will be appointed to a position of power and will experience victory within two weeks. Also your timing is right for quick action regarding certain issues. You are headed for a brilliant future.

in any other form Pay attention to what you are really focusing on and what kind of thoughts are surfacing. You are having thoughts that would cause anyone else to shudder. Think carefully about what would really happen if you carried out your thoughts and carefully analyze the results. If they unfolded in the way you desire they would greatly affect your life and the lives of others. You are placing yourself in a very reckless position and this is alerting you to the need to seek professional help. Head this off immediately and you will be able to redirect your thought patterns and place yourself on a more positive path. Many blessings are with you and you will be successful in getting in touch with your thoughts and redirecting yourself.

identification card An event will take place that will be so extraordinary no law of physics can explain it. This unusual occurrence will take place within three days and will leave you with a sense of awe and wonder. You will feel as though you have seen a miracle with no way to explain how it happened. After this takes place you will be able to present yourself to others at your highest level of performance and handle yourself, other people and situations in a highly efficient manner. You will see improvements on a grander scale than you ever anticipated. You are headed for a brilliant future and many blessings are with you and your family.

identity crisis You will become deeply involved with someone you normally would never have considered. Deep affection will rapidly grow between both of you. If you choose to go in this direction, the outcome will be wonderful. This will be a very good cycle for you.

idiot Do not allow anyone to aim displaced anger toward you. Don't allow yourself to become sucked into a conversation that could escalate to a violent episode between you and another party and don't be lured into expressing anger in return. This should be your main focus for the next three days.

idol Make sure you do not assume an air of indifference with others. This will only lead to confusion and resentments, especially for the next five days.

igloo Motivate yourself to incorporate a number of events into your life. You will see big improvements within the next five days. These changes will continue for the next month. Many blessings are with you and your family.

ignition For the next five days remain alert in all aspects of your life. Take steps to avoid any hazardous situation for you and those you are close to.
   malfunctioning Within five days you will be dealing with someone who will lead you to believe they are respectable, professional, have career stability and financial security. This person is very eager to involve themselves in your life on some level and because of your belief in them and the comfortable feeling you get in their company, you will want to become involved with them. This individual will give you every indication you will have easy access to them any time you wish and give you several phone numbers, company addresses, etc., as proof of this. If you take the time to try and track this person down, you will find it impossible to reach them at their place of work or at any of their phone numbers and it will take days for them to return your call. You will begin to realize that this person has misled you and possesses a far lower station in life than they claim. If you become involved with this person you must develop a cunning manner in order to keep them from violating your feelings or insulting your intelligence. You will be able to handle this successfully. You are in a very lucky cycle and are headed for a prosperous future.

ignore *trying to get close to someone but they ignore you* Be very wary for the next five days. Someone you have asked to leave your life and who has promised to leave you alone will break this promise. Take the time to prepare yourself in some way to avoid being pinned down by this person and make it clear that you want nothing to do with them. You will need to be emotionally equipped to handle this delicate issue. Organize your thoughts and feelings and do not allow anyone to think you are willing to commit to something you are unwilling to. Make sure there are no misunderstandings. You will be successful in getting your point across in a way that will not be offensive. Proceed with caution and you will be able to handle this delicate situation.

iguana Look into anything that is an improvement of an old product when you consider investing. It is also important to set aside quality time for your relatives and children.

ill *to be ill* Pay close attention to the illness you dreamed of and take steps to avoid this illness in reality. This is likely to occur within five days. Do everything necessary to maintain your health. Drink plenty of water, eat healthful foods, exercise and get plenty of rest. Do what you can to build up your immune system. Alert all those you recognize in the dream to avoid illness. Within two weeks you will also need to take the time to clear out your schedule. An opportunity will be presented to you during this time period. You will recognize this opportunity as something that would be beneficial to be involved in and you will have the means to grasp this opportunity. You will experience no extra issues or burdens as a result of your involvement. You are headed for a brilliant future.
   to see others ill This dream is a warning to alert this other individual to avoid any illness seen in this dream.. Blessings will be with this person. Make sure also you do not allow anyone to impose themselves or their lifestyle on you by using trickery or deception. Be very careful you are not subtly manipulated into adopting a lifestyle or habits you find distasteful. This will be very important for the next five days. Stay disciplined.
   in any other form Someone will ask you for your assistance within five days.

illegal *any form* Within five days you will be dealing with someone who will go to great lengths to mislead you into believing they are very respected, professional and stable in their career as well as financially secure and credible. This person is very eager to become involved with you in some way. You will believe them and because you will feel comfortable and assured in their company, you will also desire involvement. You will be given phone numbers, company addresses, etc., as assurance you will be able to contact them at any time you wish, but if you take the time to try and track them down you will find it will be impossible to reach them. This person will take hours and sometimes days to return your calls and you will realize they possess a far less impressive lifestyle than they have led you to believe. If you allow yourself to become involved with this person in any capacity, you will set yourself up for a big let down. Do not allow this person to violate your emotions or to insult your intelligence. Be very disciplined and shrewd and you will be able to handle this successfully. Otherwise, you are in a lucky cycle and are on the path towards a prosperous future. It is also important not to engage, or allow anyone you know to engage, in activities that will result in breaking the law. Any negative situation viewed in this dream needs to be prevented and all positive events need to be brought to fruition. Do this within five days and take steps to ensure you only experience positive expressions in your life.

illegitimate Within five days you will be dealing with someone who enjoys creating chaos and stressful situations. This individual also enjoys reopening old wounds. It is best if you keep yourself from this person.

Illinois Someone will attempt to convince you something that righteously belongs to you is not yours. Practice common sense and don't allow yourself to be taken. This dream may also be used as a reference point in time. If you dream of this state and see its name used in any context, the dream message will occur on this day.

illumination A new opportunity will present itself to you. You will become very excited about this because you now have the means to grasp it. You will enjoy a new start in all areas of your life where you desire changes. All burdens and issues that have been plaguing you will come to an immediate halt. Drastic changes will occur and leave you with a new exciting zest for life. All negotiations that take place over the next seven days will also be highly successful. Everyone you are involved with will help to bring all your plans and ideas to a successful completion.

illustrate *to illustrate* You will be very surprised that within five days someone in a position of power will relentlessly work for your benefit. You are entering a lucky cycle and are headed for a brilliant future. Pay close attention to the illustrations. They will provide major clues to the meaning of this dream. If these illustrations foretell a negative situation, you will have time to change the outcome. If positive, take steps to incorporate them into your life.

image The image you see is a major clue to what this dream foretells.
   magical, dramatic images In spite of how grim your life appears now, dramatic improvements will take place shortly because of unusual circumstances. Many blessings are with you.

imagination Do not jump to conclusions and do not allow your imagination and your thoughts of another person to rule you. This is a cycle that will promote a very active imagination and you will be provided with very clear thoughts about how to bring these thoughts into tangible form. Good luck is with you.

imbecile Do everything you can to keep from degrading others and to refrain from name calling. Set limits on what

you are willing to do, especially for the next three days.

immaculate conception This dream implies you are entering a good cycle for strengthening family unity. Understanding and a deeper closeness will develop between you, your family members and a special person in you life. Communication will come from the heart and words will be filled with love. Many blessings and tranquility will come to you and your family.

immigrant Within the month you will finally reach your goals because you will be able to finally complete a major piece of work you have been struggling with. You are headed for a brilliant future.

immorality Someone will attempt to push you into a romantic situation. Do not waste time on this relationship no matter how tempted you might be. This union will not work out for you.

immortality Be very careful of what you say for the next three days. You may have a slip of the tongue and inadvertently hurt someone's feelings. Nothing you do will ever erase the words you have said. Carefully guard what you say during this time period.

immune Stop being so possessive. You are destroying yourself with this behavior and are encouraging others to avoid you.

immune system Do everything necessary to keep your immune system intact and take steps to build it up. You will be invited to a special event and everyone will be very happy to see you there. Be very choosy about who you want to take. Your partner's attitude will shock many people and will turn everyone off. The individual you plan to take does not fit in at this event and others will be very uncomfortable. Think carefully about this ahead of time.

immunity Many situations will be occurring over the next five days. You will have to be very determined in order to handle these situations and make the major changes you desire to make. Remain focused and develop a tenacious attitude.

impala It will take a great determination and team effort to handle a complicated situation that will be coming up within five days. Stay flexible and correct this situation immediately.

impale *to impale* Someone you have known for a long time will take the relationship to a different level. It will become more romantic and affectionate. If you choose to go in this direction, you will find this to be a wonderful cycle for love with this person. Good luck is with you.

impatience *in any form* You are headed in the wrong direction. Stop and refocus on what you are doing. Also someone has devised a plot to lure you into a secluded area for the sole purpose of committing bodily harm. Be very wary for the next three days and take steps to avoid this situation at all costs.

impeach It will be a major benefit if you take the time to research more about the character of someone you will be dealing with within the next five days. Gain this information as tactfully as you can and keep it to yourself. Good luck is with you.

impersonator For the next three days you will become overwhelmed by a feeling of suspiciousness. Do not allow anyone to convince you this is merely paranoia on your part or to try to water the situation down. This dream is sending you a sense of heightened awareness about something you need to be more attentive to. You will be able to handle everything in an appropriate manner and will not feel, at a later time, you could have done something different. Take the proper steps to deal with this issue now.

male or female Within a two week period you will uncover an unsuspected power in areas of your life you never suspected and you will soon be aware of the high level of authority that you possess. This will motivate you to investigate and experiment with new and different lifestyles as well as greater levels of social functioning. These experiences will open your eyes to new ways of living and you will experience gratification in areas you have never experienced, both mentally and emotionally. Doors will be open to different sources of income. You must also take steps to avoid any negative event connected to this dream. You are headed for a brilliant future.

import Within two days you will need to pay close attention to the point of view of someone you will be dealing with in order to decide on the correct steps you need to take for your own happiness.

impossible/impossibility You will discover an unexpected power within yourself that you never expected. Within the week you will become very aware of this power and of the high level of authority you possess. Because of this discovery you will be motivated to experiment with different lifestyles and experience new levels of social functioning. You will meet new people who will open your eyes to new experiences and you will be very eager to adopt new ways of living. As a result, you will enjoy gratification in areas of your life you have never experienced before, either mentally or emotionally. Doors will open to you and you will receive greater sources of income from many different avenues. Any negative situation connected to this dream may also be avoided or altered in reality and any positive event will be brought to full bloom. You are headed for a brilliant future.

impostor You will assume something will automatically happen in your favor because it has in the past. This time it will be different and you need to prepare for this within seven days.

impound Do not present yourself in such a way that confus-

es other people because of the inconsistencies in your behavior or mannerisms. Other people will be unable to tolerate this behavior and will become very distraught, especially for the next three days. Stop this behavior. Anything you saw in this dream that signifies a negative event needs to be prevented, especially for the next five days. Make sure you experience only positive expressions in your life.

impregnate Pay attention to any negative event in this dream and take steps to avoid this in reality. You must also make sure you do not allow the opinions of others to interfere in the decisions you have to make regarding an upcoming situation.

impress *to impress* Decide, ahead of time, what you really want to reform and take action on this immediately.

impression *an effect on the mind* For the next two weeks you will possess an overwhelming sense of being grounded, emotionally balanced and confident. As a result, you will be able to handle any situation that requires this aspect of your personality. Work on those areas of your life you desire changes in and you will be given the opportunity to bring prosperity into your life at any level you wish. You are headed for a prosperous future. This dream is telling you to go full speed ahead and you will achieve victory. Any negative event witnessed in this dream can be changed in reality.

imprint, physical pressure mark, etc. Within a five day period you will come to terms with your own identity. You will come to realize a part of yourself that you have never seen before and this will lead to a sense of pride. This aspect of your personality will see you through any unusual situation that will come up within the week and will lead to more self appreciation and self love. Any negative event connected to this dream may also be avoided or altered in reality and any positive event may be promoted.

impressionism You are in a wonderful cycle to demand what you want from your higher power. Be very specific and direct about your wants and needs. Develop a list of priorities for the next two weeks that will assist you in developing the way you want to live your life. You will be able to meet your goals in peace and tranquility. Many blessings will come to you and your family and good luck is with you. You must also take steps to keep any negative event you saw in this dream from becoming a reality.

impulse You will definitely get a lucky break. This is also the time to take steps to maintain a relationship at the highest level you can. Do your share to keep the closeness ongoing between you. You will find that love and affection will help you focus on important issues instead of dealing with wasted energy. You are both headed for a brilliant future.

impurity Do everything you can to arrive at a clever idea or solution so you can work independently on a situation that will develop within three days. This will enable you to work alone without having to depend on others. Clever thoughts and plans will come to you with great clarity. You will be able to resolve this situation successfully.

inaugurate *to inaugurate* You will be inspired by a new idea that will later bring you large profits. This will occur in a short while if you choose to pursue this. You will also hear of someone's engagement.

to be inaugurated This dream is a very lucky omen and love will come to you if you choose to have this in your life. It will come from someone you least expect.

Inauguration Day Make sure the information you have reaches the person it is intended for at the time you intend. If you don't take special steps to ensure this, the recipient will be waiting a long time for this information. You will also be invited to celebrate someone's wedding. It is important that within five days you take steps to ensure any negative message in this dream does not become a reality and all positive messages need to be incorporated in your life.

inbreed A very dangerous situation will come up within five days. You will be physically injured because of someone's unusual behavior. Be prepared to protect yourself at all costs. You have prior notice of this and can take steps to prevent it.

incandescent lamp You will finally receive a long awaited proposal for marriage. Happiness will come to everyone who hears of this. Good luck is with you. Riches and joy will fill your life.

incense You will be appointed to the position of power you have long desired. You will have a wonderful life and will enjoy yourself immensely.

incest Do everything you can to keep this from occurring in reality. You have prior notice and can prevent anything negative from happening in your life or in the lives of those you care about. You must also take steps to avoid contracting an infection, especially for the next days.

inch Be very alert. Within five days you will come across a very powerful and wealthy person who will do everything in their power to meet your needs in every capacity. Be very aggressive and go after what you want. This dream is a guarantee you will go through life with not only the necessities of life but also with the refinements you desire. Good luck is with you. Move quickly on this.

incognito *any form* Within five days a stressful situation will occur when you are with a particular group of people and angry words will be exchanged. Do whatever you can to avoid involvement in this situation. Find a peaceful activity to become involved with.

incubator For the next five days, many different people will give you their input and offer their assistance to help you get to the place you want to be in life. Because of this massive support, you will gain great benefits almost overnight.

indentation *any form* Do everything necessary to build a deep foundation in a relationship that you can build upon. You will finally find the solitude you have long desired.

indentured servant Pull yourself together and remain calm for the next three days. A situation will arise that will tempt you to get involved. Do not allow yourself to become so desperate over the problems of another person that you become entangled with this situation. Once you do, it will be difficult to pry yourself loose and this issue will become progressively worse as time goes by. Remain uninvolved.

Independence Day Do not deprive yourself of anything you feel you should be doing for the next five days. Go for what you want to experience. Good luck is with you.

India Make sure you confirm that no obstacles exist between you and someone else. Open communications will allow you to develop a relationship in the way both of you desire. This dream may also be used as a reference point in time. If you dream of this country and see its name used in any context, the dream message will occur on this day.

Indian Do not decide at this time to start revising plans. This is not the best cycle to do this. Otherwise, this will be a very enjoyable five day cycle. Trust your hunches and go with what you feel.

Indiana All of your romantic plans will work out exactly as you desire regarding a very special person. You will enjoy a surprising outcome. This dream may also be used as a reference point in time. If you dream of this state and see its name used in any context, the dream message will occur on this day.

Indian corn You will be very surprised because someone will turn out to be much more than you had originally thought. Your original assessment was wrong and you will be exuberant to discover this person's true character. This will come to light within two days.

Indian pipe All information you receive for the next four days will be unreliable. Recheck your sources and reject all faulty information.

Indian pudding You will be unbeatable because of the tenacity you display in reaching your goals. This will be your time to celebrate and rejoice.

Indian Summer Someone you have not seen in years will bring you unexpected good news. You are headed for a brilliant and prosperous future.

Indian wrestling The person you are interested in is not of the same sexual orientation as you. If you are romantically interested, make sure you carefully check out this person's interests. Make sure within five days you take steps to ensure that all negative events do not become a reality and take steps to ensure you only experience positive expressions in your life.

India paper Within three days you will be invited for an outing with someone you respect and admire. If you choose to go this route, you will enjoy yourself immensely.

indigo Within five days, if you choose, you will have an exciting enjoyable time while on a romantic outing.

Indochina You will possess a piece of property or special items that will be cherished by your loved ones long after you have passed away. You will begin to work toward this within the month. This dream may also be used as a reference point in time. If you dream of this country and see its name used in any context, the dream message will occur on this day.

industrial revolution Be prepared to protect yourself from any emotional chaos for the next five days. Avoid big changes that will bring about distasteful moments you don't feel you should deal with.

industry Follow the advice given to you very carefully. The information will come very quickly so make sure you pay close attention. You will need this advice to help you structure your plans in such a way to accomplish what you desire. If you are uncertain whether you are hearing everything correctly, take steps to have this information repeated slowly and in an easily understood manner.

inebriate *any form* Make sure you are not billed for something you do not receive. If you do not pay close attention you will pay for something you do not owe.

infant You have thoughts of revising and merging your business with a larger corporation. Your ideas are good. Go for this and you will achieve success. Anything negative in this dream that could become a reality needs to be prevented within five days and do everything you can to experience only positive events in your life.

infantryman Someone is feeling very abandoned by you. Within five days do everything you can by way of special plans, gift giving, special notes, etc., to show affection for those who are special to you.

infection Within five days a married person will be very attracted to you and will aggressively seek your affections. Put a stop to this early on and keep this situation from developing to the level this individual desires. This is a potentially dangerous situation. You must also take steps to prevent the development of any infection. You have enough time to avoid it and to forewarn anyone you recognize in the dream to do the same. Take steps to ensure any negative event you dreamed about does not become a reality. Good luck is with you.

infidel Do not allow anyone to gain knowledge of your plans for the next seven days. Once these plans are executed and working properly you can allow others in on them.

inflatable recreational items *(i.e., rafts, toys, etc.)* It is important you schedule time out for those who are important to you. Make sure no one interferes and situations do not infringe on this time. You will also need to put into motion any intelligent thought you have. This will be a very powerful move on your part. You are headed for a very brilliant future.

inflate *to inflate* You will dislike the extra responsibility that will be placed on your shoulders within the week. Do everything you can to move quickly on this in order to remove yourself from this duty. This three day cycle will give you the energy and astuteness to handle this successfully. Keep your stress level under control.

   to see an inflated item explode Do not allow your plans or feelings to be known to others. Pay close attention to the exploded item. This will give you additional clues to the meaning of this dream.

influenza An important matter will become a major issue if you do not become personally involved. Attend to this within five days. You will be able to take care of this successfully if you begin work on it now.

infrared You will be invited for a cozy, romantic evening by someone you least expect. This individual is very dangerous and you need to make sure you do not place your life in this person's hands. This is likely to occur within four days.

ingot Drop the suspicions you have of another. This individual is doing nothing wrong and means you no harm. They will do anything within their power to help you.

inhale A wonderful celebratory event will come up within three days. Make sure you mark this on your calendar and give yourself plenty of time to prepare for it. You are loved beyond your imagination and you will have verification of this within a three day period. You must also take steps to avoid or to change the outcome of any negative event portended in this dream. Make sure you and anyone you recognize in this dream experiences only positive experiences.

inhaler You are definitely headed in the wrong direction. Make sure you regroup and examine those things in your life that bring you comfort. Be wary of any ongoing activity that may become habit forming. Aggressively seek out ways to stabilize and normalize your life.

inherit The hopes you had in the past will now be rejuvenated. Any desire you have now will be granted. You are entering a tremendous cycle. All positive events connected to this cycle also need to be brought into reality. All negative events need to be prevented or reworked until the outcome is altered. A financial tip that you receive will be totally reliable. Good luck is with you.

inheritance tax Within five days you will have the opportunity to have a private conversation with someone who is very evasive and difficult to pin down. You will be able to successfully get your point across to this person and will receive a positive response if you carefully plan your approach ahead of time. Take steps to ensure all negative events witnessed in this dream do not become a reality.

injection You will have an urge to quickly gratify your emotional needs. You and this other person will quickly reach the level of developing a mutually satisfying relationship. Expect much love and affection and a stable financially rewarding union, if this is what you desire.

injury Make sure you avoid the scenario displayed in this dream and take steps to keep it from becoming a reality. Alert anyone you recognize in the dream to avoid an injury. Do not become involved in the problematic stressful situations of others. This will create unnecessary anxiety in your life. You can do without this situation.

involving detached flesh Within five days you will be pleasantly surprised on three separate occasions. These surprises will be as a result of an unexpected gift, hearing the words you have longed to hear, and learning of an unexpected financial windfall. You will also have the perfect opportunity to pursue what you once felt was impossible. All things are possible now. Ensure that any negative situation seen in this dream does not become a reality.

ink This dream is an extremely lucky omen. You will receive gifts from someone you least expect within five days.

India ink This dream is an extremely lucky omen for you. You will be able to quickly recover from and relieve yourself of any serious upcoming situation. Discipline yourself and stick to the rules.

red ink Do not alienate yourself because of your failure to respond to others or because of miscommunication due to your body language. Pay close attention to the manner in which you communicate with others. If you do not make changes, you will fail to enlist the good will of others.

to run out of ink or any other form Someone will come to you within a few days for the express purpose of satisfying their own desires. They will stay around only for the time it takes them to get what they are after. Make sure you do not allow anyone to use you for their own purposes.

inkblot Do everything you can to keep a young person from becoming involved in a very troublesome situation, especially for the next three days. Pay close attention to the design revealed by the ink blot. This will offer you a major clue to the meaning of this dream.

inkwell Make the proper inquiries to determine whether someone working with you on a project is up to completing the task in the same amount of time that others would be able to. Make sure you are hiring competent and responsible people and make sure they are pulling their own load.

in law Any negative event foretold in this dream that in-

volves you or another person can be changed. Keep a low profile and keep your mind on regular routine tasks. Be aware of any errors that could occur within three days. Make sure you attend to all mistakes immediately so everything will fall into place as it should. Many blessings are with you and your family and you will achieve an abundance of health.

inlay You are headed for a brilliant future. A small risk taken within three days will lead you to this path. You will be presented with various opportunities and any one of these will be fortuitous for you. This is a wonderful cycle for you to grasp new goals.

inmate You will receive information about someone that would be best kept to yourself. This will occur within five days. This dream is a good omen and you will enjoy an abundance of health.

inn You are seeking companionship with a certain individual. Once you allow this person to know your feelings you will find these feelings are reciprocal. Make sure all negative situations seen in this dream are prevented or altered.

inner tube Someone will go to great lengths to involve you in a relationship. Be aware, this person is lying about their marital status. You may choose not to become involved.

inning Do not allow your emotions to get out of hand and avoid going to extremes. Look at the whole picture and you will get a better idea of the depth of involvement you want with another person.

innkeeper Within three days an emotional pain from the past will be stirred up again by your family. Do what you can to prevent this occurrence. It could lead to a major disagreement between all involved parties. Make sure anything negative you dreamed of does not become a reality.

innocence Someone whose company you will keep within the week will lead you to believe there will be more affection and demonstrative behavior between you than you have now. Don't put your faith in this belief. This individual will sharply turn against you once you demonstrate a friendlier attitude. Resist this behavior. Good luck is with you.

inoculation Take the time to step back and determine what is keeping you from moving ahead. This is the perfect time to look over all aspects of your life and prioritize your goals. You will find this to be a major benefit. Do this within the week.

inquisition You will be facing a danger that is impossible to be aware of without this dream. You will be the victim of a random act of violence committed by a stranger. Be very wary for the next three days and avoid being anywhere where this could happen. Do whatever you can to protect your life.

inquisitor Do not procrastinate on any important issue you feel should have already been taken care of. This is a good cycle to correct major situations. Move on this now.

insane/insanity *any form* This dream implies genius and a brilliant future. Good luck is with you.

insect For the next five days take precautions to avoid contracting a serious infection or illness. Avoid exposure, this illness could be deadly.

insect eggs Be very cautious and wary about where you are being led emotionally. For reasons known only to them, someone will lead you to believe you are loved completely by them. Words of love may or may not be used at this time but all the romantic trappings will be there (i.e., flowers, gifts, romantic outings, etc.). Your feelings will grow stronger and deeper than this other person's feelings. If you allow this to develop into lovemaking, you will not be touched in any way that implies that love is present. You will feel very empty and cold as a result and will fail to connect with this person on any level that you felt was there. Rather than putting yourself through this emotional upheaval, you have enough notice to avoid this scenario completely. Go on with your life without this person in it, because they have a hidden agenda that involves you doing something for them. This situation will only bring you unhappiness so take steps to avoid it completely. Otherwise, you are headed for a prosperous future that will start to evolve within seven days.

insecticide Within five days someone will very tactfully declare their love for you. If you choose to go in this direction you will find this person to be the complete opposite of what they appear. Be very wary and do everything you can to avoid involvement with them.

inseminate Within four days you will experience love and affection from someone you least expect. This dream also implies that anything that was once impossible to achieve is now possible for you. Go for it.

insight For the next three days when someone comes to you with a problematic situation, take time in solitude to formulate a good plan to handle this issue prior to responding to this individual.

insomnia You will arrive at the correct choice when having to make a major decision within three days. Everything will work out beautifully.

inspector Be keenly aware of your investments. As these investments grow, be careful not to become careless, especially for the next five days. Make sure anything negative that is portended in this dream does not become a reality.

instep Within three days you will have the means to detail and calibrate your thoughts in such a way that you will allow someone to feel comfortable and at ease in your presence. Conversations will flow and you will develop a sense of closeness. This person will speak words they have been longing to tell you. You are headed for a prosperous future and will be able to touch others deeply with your communication skills. You and this other person will enjoy a wonderful and tranquil life together if you choose to go this route.

institution Someone will manipulate you into agreeing to let them stay with you. Be very aware of this and set limits on what you will or will not do. Don't be intimidated into doing something you do not wish to do. You must also pay close attention to the institution you dream of and of those people you dream about. If this was a negative dream, take steps to avoid this situation in reality and warn those who are involved to do the same. If the dream was positive, make sure you include all positive aspects in your life and in the lives of those who were involved in the dream. Good luck is with you.

instruction Within five days you will be charged for services you never received. Be wary of con artists.

instrument *to see a variety of instruments* You are headed for a financial windfall. Riches are coming your way within five days.

insulation For the next four days you will be making decisions based on mental clarity. Take advantage of this cycle in all areas of your life.

insulin Within seven days, someone with extensive knowledge and experience in your area of interest will take you under their wing in order to train you properly. This will work for the benefit of both of you. Any negative aspect of this dream may also be altered and any positive aspect should be included in your life. Alert anyone you recognize in the dream of either the negative or positive aspects.

insurance Someone whom you have admired greatly will turn out differently than you have envisioned. Avoid disappointment by not going overboard with someone you find interesting. Make it a point of insuring everything of value you own and make sure anything negative witnessed in this dream does not become a reality.

fire insurance An earthquake will occur within the month. Prepare yourself ahead of time for this and make sure all of your property is properly insured.

intelligence Demonstrate your interest to someone who may not be aware of your true feelings. Do not deprive yourself and make sure you bring enjoyment to your inner child.

intelligence test Do not settle for less than you deserve and do not place yourself in the position to have to. This is especially important for the next three days.

interest You will experience good luck and great success in all of your endeavors. It would also be wise to shop around for the lowest interest rates when purchasing any item on term rates.

interior decorating Within three days you will be asked to handle a particular problem. Make sure you are emotionally equipped to handle this situation before you agree to become involved. It would be better to bypass this altogether and focus on your own situations.

intermarriage Your life will turn around and you will enjoy a much improved lifestyle. You are headed for a brilliant future. Do not take life for granted and make sure you take the time to enjoy each moment. This dream is an extremely lucky omen. Within five days, someone will also come into your life and rush you into a friendly relationship. You will get mixed messages on this outing and will be led to believe this person desires romance. Once you respond, this individual will begin to back off and withdraw from the relationship. This is a warning to take the friendship for what it is and expect nothing more. You will also need to make sure anything negative you dreamed about does not become a reality.

intern Within three days you will be involved in a very embarrassing situation. Make sure you are keenly aware of your behavior during this time period in order to avoid this situation completely. Your thoughts will be very intuitive and your hunches will be right on target. You will also have the ability to diffuse negative thoughts and attitudes. You will be able to do this at the precise time you need to and will no longer have to deal with the mental blocks these faulty thoughts and attitudes place in your way. Proceed with confidence and remain balanced no matter what else is going on in your life right now. You are headed for a life full of enjoyment and filled with interesting and influential people.

internal medicine Within five days an opportunity will present itself that is well within your power to grasp. This will allow you, within a short period of time, to make positive changes in every area of your life. All old issues and burdens will miraculously disappear. This will leave you with a new zest for life.

internal revenue Make sure certain of your behaviors and mannerisms are not responsible for the break up of the relationship of someone you know. You have prior notice of this and can become aware of certain behaviors and can make the necessary changes to prevent this occurrence. This is likely to occur within five days. You must also make sure any negative event in this dream does not become a reality.

international dateline Keep your interests to yourself. Also, within three days you will be involved in a decision that will give you no escape hatch. Avoid having to make a decision that gives you no option to back out.

internet Express yourself in a romantic way.

internist You will be extremely lucky in receiving the services you require for the next four days. This assistance will come very quickly and you will successfully meet your needs.

interpreter Pay attention to the languages involved. These will offer you a major clue to the meaning of this dream. Within five days, you will receive news that will be difficult to comprehend. Do not involve yourself or volunteer your assistance until you have a very good idea of what is going on. Mixed messages need to be clarified.

interrogate Your efforts and motives will be questioned by those in authority whether or not you are doing the correct thing. Within three days all of your moves will be closely monitored. Remain calm and do what you can to remain stress free. You will have the courage to get through this. Many blessings are with you and good luck is with you.

interrogation Within five days be acutely aware you need to let someone know exactly what is going on in your life. Take pains to set the record straight. Sometimes it takes a while for others to fully comprehend all that is happening. Be patient and persistent until this person understands.

intestines Do not allow anyone to talk you into becoming involved in a conspiracy. This will backfire and will create turmoil in your life. It is also important to pay heed to anything in this dream that may be connected to reality. If it foretells a negative event, take steps to avoid the event or to change the outcome. If this involves another individual, make sure you forewarn them to take steps to avoid this negative occurrence.

intoxication Within two days you will become very aware of an emotional hang up you need to work on. You will have the strength and tranquility to successfully rid yourself of this burden and to develop a lifestyle free of this issue. Go for it.

intravenous/IV *in any form* You will be, within the next four days, given a gift of greater mental inventiveness by your higher power. Put this gift to practical use in order to change your present circumstances. You will experience instant wealth, a brilliant future and have the clarity of thought you need to correctly direct the fortune you will be coming into. Make sure that anything negative you dream of that could become a reality does not occur and take steps to ensure you experience only positive expressions in life.

introduction Be very wary of the motives behind an individual who appears very helpful. There are underlying reasons for this behavior you need to be aware of. Make sure you do not fall prey to something that could be very harmful to you. Be very attentive to any positive or negative message in this dream that you will either want to embrace in your life or avoid. Do everything you can to keep any negative occurrence you dreamed about from taking place in your life.

introvert For the next five days you will be very mentally alert and this will allow you to communicate to someone who is very shy, in such a way that will allow them to open up to you. This person has wanted to talk to you this way but has been too uncomfortable. You will be very surprised at the information you gain from this individual.

intuition Whatever you dream of that deals with your intuition or that of another will come to pass. You have enough time to either avoid a bad situation or to make a positive event become a reality. Be aware also that there is too much interference in your present life. Take steps to eliminate this outside interference so you can use this heightened awareness and intuition to your advantage. You will then be able to make the necessary changes to create the perfect lifestyle for yourself. Create a private space where you can get away from it all and reduce stress. Use this space just to experience tranquility and peace and allow nothing to interfere. You are definitely headed for a brilliant future.

invade *to invade* Be aware that a deep secret is being hidden from you. Do whatever you can to bring out the truth within five days. It is extremely important that you determine what is being hidden from you. It would be detrimental to your welfare if this secret remains hidden.

invalid You could easily become the victim of a pay per call service. Be aware that these numbers add up. At first the amounts will seem insignificant but will increase to outrageous proportions. Be alert to any fraud that appears legitimate on the surface.

invention A business enterprise that is capable of generating large amounts of money will be offered to you by someone you do not know well and whom you would never expect to extend this offer. If you choose to accept this partnership, this enterprise will be very profitable for both of you. All inventions seen in the dream would be very fruitful for you to process in reality, especially if it relates to something that is occurring in your life at the present time.

inventory An insincere person will agree to meet you at a set time and place but has no intention of actually meeting with you. Be prepared for this to take place within five days and avoid wasting your time on this matter.

invest Within five days an unknown individual will play the part of cupid. This person will try to get you to meet with someone they know because they feel you will enjoy a good time together. If you choose to pursue this, you will have a very delightful time. Any event depicted in this dream you feel is connected to something in reality needs to be pursued, if positive, and avoided, if negative.

investment company This dream is an extremely lucky omen. Anything you desire from a relationship in any capacity is now a possibility.

invisible For the next four days become very creative and determine what you need to do in order to achieve financial security. Carefully analyze your decisions and follow your hunches.

to view anything that becomes invisible A particular work situation you have developed will become tangible. You will soon be able to harvest the fruits and gain great wealth from the hard work you have done. Many blessings will come to you and your family.

invite *to be invited* You are entering an extremely lucky cycle for the next two weeks and are headed for a brilliant future.

inviting *any form* You will receive a lifetime annuity within five days that has been left by a relative. This will come to you in a very surprising way. Do everything you can to avoid any negative situation depicted in this dream and take steps to promote the positive. Do what you can to experience only positive expressions in your life.

invoice You will be offered an extraordinary invitation to a fabulous event you will not easily forget. You will enjoy long nostalgic conversations with other people about years past. This memory will last for a lifetime. Any negative event portended in this dream also needs to be prevented in reality. Make it a point to enjoy only positive expressions in your life.

iodine Do everything necessary to prevent the occurrence of any unusual situation. For the next five days, be keenly aware of any intruder who will attempt to take advantage of you.

IOU This dream is an extremely lucky omen for love and business. You will win the respect and love of the person you most admire. If you choose to pursue this, a long term relationship will be the result.

Iowa Someone who cares a great deal for you will come into greater power and authority. You will be invited to an exclusive place some distance from you and you will enjoy yourself immensely at this person's expense. You will have a very safe journey. This dream may also be used as a reference point in time. If you dream of this state and see its name used in any context, the dream message will occur on this day.

Iran Write down all of your plans in detail for the next five days to ensure that nothing interferes with your goals. This will allay any future argument. This dream may also be used as a reference point in time. If you dream of this country and see its name used in any context, the dream message will occur on this day.

Iraq Doors will be open to you and opportunities will be presented that normally would not be offered. Be aware of this so you do not allow opportunities to slip through your fingers. This is especially important for the next five days. This dream may also be used as a reference point in time. If you dream of this country and see its name used in any context, the dream message will occur on this day.

Ireland You are not fully using the power and authority you possess. Pull the necessary strings to benefit yourself. Within five days you will gain awareness of your power and be able to use it to your advantage. This dream may also be used as a reference point in time. If you dream of this country and see its name used in any context, the dream message will occur on this day.

Iris *(flower)* Within three days you will have a very romantic date that will remain in your memory for a lifetime. This will be due to the unusual nature of this outing. If you choose to attend, you will have a wonderful time.

iris *(eye)* Someone will challenge you for your position within five days. This person will attempt to grab what is righteously yours. Since you have prior notice of this, you will be able to handle this matter with greater success.

Irish For the next four days anything you risk involvement with will be completely safe. You will find great success with this endeavor.

Irish coffee Any request for services made by you will result in a quick response. A situation will come up and leave you feeling overwhelmed within four days. Help is on the way.

Irish Republican Army (IRA) Someone who appears very nice will attempt to con you in a particular situation that will give them the upper hand. Be acutely aware of this possibility within four days and take the appropriate steps to handle it.

Irish Setter For the next three days make sure you do not leave yourself open for the emotional pain someone will cause by lying to you.

Irish stew Make sure you are headed in the direction you need to be going and make sure you receive what you request regarding business transactions. You will be led to believe what you ask for will be what you will be receiving. This is not the case. Check everything out carefully.

iron Do not overextend yourself emotionally for the next four days. Take care of yourself and do what you can to remain in a tranquil environment.

Iron Age For the next five days give yourself enough time to successfully complete necessary tasks.

iron curtain Let others know the extent of involvement you desire regarding a particular situation. People around you are under the impression you only want to be involved in a minor way when you really seek a deeper involvement.

ironing board Within five days someone will place many demands on you and will focus on getting you to do exactly what they want you to do. If you feel as though you will be powerless to resist, put yourself in an environment where others have little, if no, accessibility to you.

iron lung Do not become involved in an angry verbal exchange for the next four days with someone you feel is in the wrong. This person will do everything in their power to convince you they are right. Get on with your life without this person in it and do everything you can to keep any negative occurrence in this dream from becoming a reality. Make sure you experience only positive events in your life.

iron worker A misinterpretation of someone else's actions will lead you to a huge embarrassment. Make sure what you read from someone is accurate and attempt to cut through mixed messages. This will prevent an embarrassing situation within five days. Do what you can to experience only positive events in your life and make sure all negative events witnessed in this dream do not become a reality.

Iroquois You have the knowledge and means to make those changes in your life you desire. This dream is an extremely lucky omen and you are encouraged to move ahead with your plans.

Isaac *(from the Bible)* Within five days you will be able to locate the means to raise your standard of living. Many blessings will come to you and your family.

Isaiah *(from the Bible)* Within seven days you will be motivated to bring more changes into your life. You will put more emphasis on the work you need to do in certain areas to bring you more prosperity. Many blessings are with you and your family.

Ishmael *(from the Bible)* Actively motivate others to rally to someone else's defense. This will give this individual a support system they would not otherwise have.

Ishtar *(mythology)* Motivation on your part will gain the attention of someone who can help to facilitate a transfer to an area you desire. This dream is an extremely lucky omen for you.

Isis *(Egyptian mythology)* Focus on the complete picture. Another individual has all of the details and is fully aware of everything that is going on. Enlist this person and open communications so you can also fully understand the situation. This is an extremely lucky omen and an abundance of health will be coming to you within five days. This healthy disposition will remain with you for a long time. This is also the perfect cycle for working toward healing any relationship. Expect improvements in many areas of your life.

Islam You will have very fruitful conversations that need to be taking place in this time frame in order to bring about changes for everyone concerned. These changes will bring more prosperity. Proceed with confidence.

island Within five days you will receive credible advice from someone you felt was not giving you totally reliable information. This dream is an extremely lucky omen, especially for those involved in romantic or financial negotiations.

isotope Be wary of someone you consider a good friend. This person is plotting to destroy the emotional ties you have with another person. Emotions of jealousy and envy will cause this person to do something they have no business doing. Protect yourself for the next four days.

Israel Within five days you will have to dig deeply to locate an organization with the expertise and support system for a family member. This individual has a specific need that will require your emotional and financial resources to resolve. You will find a satisfactory solution. This dream may also be used as a reference point in time. If you dream of this country and see its name used in any context, the dream message will occur on this day.

Italy Within five days you will achieve victory in those areas of your life you most desire. Stay with each situation until you start to see results. This will result in long term happiness. This dream may also be used as a reference point in time. If you dream of this country and see its name used in any context, the dream message will occur on this day.

itch Within five days you will meet someone you find irresistible and you will find it very difficult to control your urges. Allow this person to know your feelings and you will be well received. This will develop naturally into a fully satisfying love relationship. You will receive great riches and an abundance of health. You must also do everything you can to prevent the occurrence of any negative event witnessed in this dream and make sure you only experience positive expressions in your life.

IUD Anything negative connected with this dream that concerns you or another individual needs to be changed or altered in reality within four days. Make sure you experience only positive events in your life whenever possible. Do what you can to prevent someone from forcing their opinion or themselves on you. Be frank with this person from the start or this will escalate to an increasingly distasteful situation. This time frame will give you the means to put a stop to it easier than if you wait for a later date.

ivory Do not restrict yourself. Allow someone to connect emotionally with you. You will be the recipient of much love and affection and will also receive a gift of money you can leave as a legacy, but only after you have lived a long, healthy, productive life. Take it slowly and enjoy life.

Ivory Coast Do not overlook anything for the next five days that will cause stress if left unattended. Deal with this in a timely fashion. This dream may also be used as a reference point in time. If you dream of this place and see its name used in any context, the dream message will occur on this day.

ivory tower Be very attentive to those who are special to you. Be very sure your behavior, mannerisms and speech give off the message you want others to read. It is extremely important that you reveal yourself as an affectionate and caring person during this cycle.

ivy You will achieve a great victory within five days but it is important you not flaunt this victory in front of others. Increase your control over achievements in order to fully enjoy them. This dream is an extremely lucky omen and blessings will come to you and your family. Make it a point also to avoid or alter the outcome of any negative event witnessed in this dream. Do everything you can to bring any positive situation to full bloom.

Ivy League Carefully detail each of your travel arrangements and check carefully to ensure that nothing wastes your time. This refers particularly to traffic delays. Also you will be very attracted to someone, sexually and emotionally. This individual will also be very attracted to you. This will be a very fortuitous meeting for both of you.

Iwo Jima Be very specific about the plans you will make for the remainder of your life. Until now you have not carefully detailed any plans. Make sure you sort out your priorities. This dream is a very lucky omen for health and love. Be very possessive about the plans you have in life, especially for the next five days. You will also need to make a point of preventing any negative situation from taking place in reality. Do everything you can to promote the positive. This dream may also be used as a reference point in time. If you dream of this island group and see its name used in any context, the dream message will occur on this day.

J

J You are entering the perfect time to indulge in greater mental creativity. You will be delighted at the thoughts that become available to you that you can apply to your present endeavors. You will quickly be able to develop the lifestyle you have long waited for. Learn to express yourself openly and nourish yourself in a healthy manner. Many blessings will come to you and your family.

jack Within five days you will need an exceptional amount of money. You will ask someone for a loan whom you feel really doesn't have the resources to help but you will be very surprised not only that they come through for you but at how quickly they respond. You will be able to repay this individual much quicker than you expected. Your financial situation will improve within the month. You also need to realize you are a sacred vessel and should take steps to nurture yourself in the best possible way. You will be surprised at how quickly magical changes will occur in your life.

jackal Within five days someone will divulge the truth about a particular situation you have been uncertain about. This knowledge will lift an old burden off your shoulders.

jackass For the next five days take steps to avoid using the power you have over someone because of their affections for you. Do not use this power as a tool to seek revenge because of something they have done to you. This behavior will bring you trouble that will be difficult to unleash yourself from. Use a better method to clear up this issue without leaving negative feelings. You also need to make sure you do not allow any negative event in this dream to become a reality for you or for anyone you recognize. Make sure you experience only positive expressions in your life.

jack cheese Within five days someone will not accept a negative response to a request they make of you. You will be confronted by this individual and they will attempt to take what they want from you. Be prepared so you will be able to handle this properly and take steps to keep any negative event seen in this dream from becoming a reality. Forewarn anyone you recognize in this dream to do the same. Take steps to ensure you only experience positive events in your life.

jacket You will enjoy a seven day cycle filled with social activity. This is also the perfect cycle to demand what you desire from your divinity and to have these desires granted.

leather jacket For the next seven days you will be well accommodated by those who support you. This will come as a surprise because you felt you were not receiving approval from those who meant a great deal to you. Their support will be very refreshing. This will be a victorious time for you.

Jack Frost For the next five days you will do everything in your power to avoid interference from someone who wields a great deal of power and authority in your life by confronting mutual issues that need to be dealt with. This cycle will enable this to occur without stress or chaos.

jackhammer Within five days you will take strong steps in order to bring about the changes in lifestyle you desire. It will be difficult to introduce a new lifestyle, but push yourself in this direction and you will be greatly rewarded. You will develop the strength to overcome difficult obstacles in order to bring this about. Go for it in spite of seemingly overwhelming difficulties. You must also take steps to alter the outcome or to avoid any negative event witnessed in this dream. Do everything you can to experience positive expressions in your life.

jack-in-the-box Allow yourself to see someone for what they really are and face up to this person's behavior. This will allow you to experience a freer lifestyle without their interference. The freedom to express yourself should be a priority.

jack-in-the-pulpit Within five days you will see more motivation by family members to generate family activities and greater familial unity. You will enjoy this immensely and will help to organize the functions successfully.

jackknife Within two weeks you will receive a gift of greater mental inventiveness from the gods. Motivate yourself to apply this gift in the areas you desire. You will also make great changes and improvements in your sex life. This is an omen of health and tranquility. Drink plenty of water, eat healthy foods and make sure you avoid any negative situation witnessed in this dream. Warn anyone you recognize to do the same. Make sure you experience only positive events in your life.

jack mackerel You will be requested to appear at several different social functions and you will enjoy popularity and an open reception by others. During this social cycle, you will meet someone who will play a primary role in your life. Take steps to maintain a healthy cardiovascular system by eating healthy foods, exercising, and maintaining a stress free lifestyle.

jack-of-all-trades Confidently approach others to work on a solution to a stressful situation that will be mutually satisfying for everyone involved.

jack-o-lantern Find a place where you can meditate in peace in order to determine what you really want from a specific situation you are not satisfied with now.

jackrabbit Become aware, over the next five days, and determine what a young person is doing that may be physically and emotionally detrimental to their health. Encourage this person to create a more healthy environment for themselves. This young person will later be grateful you took the time to point this out to them.

Jackson, Jesse *(Politician, Activist, Minister)* A fantastic future is in store for you, especially for the next three weeks. You will enjoy discussions with others about certain situations and issues that need to be brought to light. Your comunication skills will have a powerful effect on others and will bring about profound and vastly improved changes that need to take place. This is the perfect cycle to bring light to any issue that needs to be handled that at any other time would be resistant to change. This is also the time when things can easily be overturned. Proceed with confidence. Many blessings are with you and you are on the path toward an abundance of prosperity.

Jackson, Michael Someone will send a message to you via a physical channel (i.e., flowers, gifts, etc.) that they are interested in you. Once you know this person is interested, romance will quickly blossom and you are being told to go full speed ahead. You will achieve success. Regard the power this person symbolizes as the power you will possess for the next five days. Pay close attention to what these people are telling you because this will be an accurate depiction of what will be occurring in reality. If this is a negative message, take steps to prevent it's occurrence in reality. Otherwise, you are headed for a prosperous future.

Jacob *(from the Bible)* This is an omen of health and wealth. Build a stronger foundation in a relationship that is important to you. This will motivate those involved to become more supportive of your needs and desires. Many blessings will be with you and your family, especially for the next seven days.

jade You will be surrounded by very loyal people who love you deeply and will show you much affection, especially for the next seven days. Extend yourself emotionally to those you care about. Look up the color for more definitions.

jade plant If you choose, the person who is special to you will remain with you for a lifetime. You will have many more moments of enjoyment together than stressful moments, and you will enjoy a life together that resembles a honeymoon filled with love and joy. Many blessings are with you. This is an omen of health.

jaguar Someone will fall irresistibly in love with you and will allow you to know their deep feelings for you. If you choose to go in this direction, you will not only enjoy the refinements of life but a deep abiding love as well. This dream is an extremely lucky omen and many blessings are with you and your family.

jai alai Within two days you will feel overwhelmed with excitement over a gift that you will receive. This is also the time to expect an abundance of health.

jail Do not be so quick to respond to a situation that will flare up within seven days. You will gain more information about the situation as time goes on. As you gain more insight into this issue, you will be able to make the proper decision. Within three days someone will come into your life eager to have a friendly relationship. After awhile you will begin to get mixed messages. This individual will begin to hint at a romantic involvement. Do not waste your time with this person because they are only playing games and are looking only for a short term relationship. Do not take this for anything more than it is. Have an enjoyable time, then get on with your life. You will enjoy future prosperity. Make sure any negative event seen in this dream does not become a reality and strive to experience only positive events in your life. Warn anyone you recognize in this dream to do the same.

jailbird You will somehow gain the strength and wisdom to determine a way to strengthen the bond between yourself and a loved one. You will enjoy a great deal of tranquility in this relationship.
to see someone else as a jail bird You will become involved with someone who will bring you a great deal of laughter and passion. This relationship will develop into a deep mutual love. Make sure you or the individual you recognize from the dream do nothing to put yourself in jail.

jailbreak Do not allow yourself to become desperate due to the problems of someone else. Do everything you can to tactfully avoid involvement in someone else's problems. Go on with your life.

jailer Do everything you can to avoid focusing on another individual to the point of forcing yourself on them. This behavior is not welcomed by this individual and you are making a spectacle of yourself. Back off and control your behavior.

jalapeño You will suddenly advance to a higher plateau in life than you had ever imagined. This will occur within two weeks. You will enjoy an abundance of productivity, an increased flow of income, productive conversations and more affection and loyalty from others. Other people will also express their desire to be a part of your plans and work force. You are headed for a brilliant future and will enjoy an abundance of health. All of this will occur in a shorter period of time than you expected.

jalopy Someone you will be dealing with directly within two days, needs to be checked out. This individual is an impostor. You must also not take for granted things that, in the past, have happened automatically because they will not fall into place the way you have been accustomed to. Develop a thrifty attitude with your money. For the next few weeks, pay as little as you possibly can for things you are interested in purchasing and do what you can to stash away money during this time period so you can meet your financial demands. Anything you believe you need to reform needs to be acted on during this time period. You will be successful in making these changes. You will also be attending a celebration due to some unusual news that will be arriving within three days.

jam *(fruit, the preserve)* Your intuition will lead you to a great future and your life will undergo a dramatic change in all matters of love and finances. You will also gain greater health, pizzazz and a zest for life and you will receive more love and affection from others.

Jamaica For the next few days make sure you worship yourself as you would a sacred deity. You are a sacred vessel that needs to be treated like a precious commodity. Once you start to appreciate yourself for who you are, you will find this will radiate to others and they will appreciate, love and respect you. Anything that involves travel will also be very lucky for you, especially for the next seven days. This dream may also be used as a reference point in time. If you dream of this island group and see its name used in any context, the dream message will occur on this day.

Jamaican rum You will enjoy yourself immensely when attending an event with a large crowd of people within five days. Make sure you arrive home safely.

jamb Within five days someone will purposefully create chaos in your life. This person will attempt to take something from you by applying pressure on someone with authority. Stand your ground and make plans ahead of time in order to take the necessary steps to prevent this.

James *(from the Bible)* This dream is an extremely lucky omen. A surprise is headed your way within three days and you will be experiencing an abundance of health. Many blessings will come to you and your family. Any plan you want to implement will also be realized within seven days. Move quickly on this.

jangle Whatever is being jangled represents something that is important to include in your life. If this represents something negative, take steps to prevent the occurrence of this event in reality. Someone who appears to be a real friend to you is being asked by others to glean information about your private life. Be very firm on just how close you want someone to become and how much you want others to know. This is especially important for the next seven days.

Janis Joplin Within seven days you will come to realize what heaven is when you recognize the creative and profound thoughts that are coming from within you. Motivate yourself to develop these thoughts with confidence, neither over nor under doing them. Execute these thoughts on a grand scale and do not allow yourself to develop tunnel vision. Become flexible but not overly so. Do not allow yourself to take today's moments for granted because these moments will be your future memories. Use common sense and get in sync with your health regarding food and beverages. You will victoriously achieve your goals through your journey in life and are headed for a brilliant future.

janitor Do not allow your life to stagnate to the point of being unable to enjoy the simple things in life. Make a list of events you can easily enjoy and take steps to do so. You will find you will develop a new lease on life. You will also be lucky for the next week and life will become sweeter, gentler, easier and more tranquil. You will also need to take steps to keep any negative event in this dream from becoming a reality to you or anyone else you recognize. Do everything you can to enjoy only the best that life has to offer.

janitorial equipment Within three days an unusual occurrence will result in physical injury. Be very aware of this and make sure nothing becomes a physical danger to you within this time frame. You must also make sure the unusual behavior of someone else does not put you in a dangerous position. You have prior notice of this and can take steps to prevent it. Otherwise, expect an abundance of health and this dream is a very lucky omen for you. Make sure any negative event witnessed in this dream does not become a reality and do everything you can to enjoy only positive expressions in life. Forewarn anyone you recognize in the dream to do likewise.

January This will be an exciting month for you. Many events will occur that will bring much excitement to your life. Someone will unexpectedly bequeath something to you because they owed one of your relatives. This will be due to the embarrassment of a long overdue debt and will be an attempt to make up for this. You will enjoy a wonderful new lifestyle as a result. Any negative event portended for this month needs to be prevented and anything positive you want to occur needs the proper work to ensure it does take place.

Janus *(Roman God)* A mysterious ailment will disappear as suddenly as it appeared and you will feel as though a miracle has occurred. You will enjoy an abundance of health and tranquility.

Japan All pending legal matters will work out to your advantage. This also implies that you will have a great deal of luck with miniatures in any form. All work that requires detail will result in greater satisfaction. Good luck is with you. This dream may also be used as a reference point in time. If you dream of this country and see its name used in any context, the dream message will occur on this day.

Japanese beetle Make absolutely sure that guarantees made now will hold up in the future.

jar Become more aware of the location and condition of your possessions. Become more possessive of your costly belongings to ensure they do not become damaged.

jasmine Within five days a promise you felt would not be fulfilled will come through for you. Do everything you can to ensure this occurs during this time frame.

jasper This dream is an extremely lucky omen. You will also find a way to bring structure and order to your life especially within the next five days.

jaundice Within five days an emotional issue that has been bringing you down will normalize. Structure and stability will enter your life. You will also need to protect your property and the lives of others from fire during this time period. Protect yourself from anything negative you see in this dream and take steps to ensure it does not become a reality in your life or to anyone in the dream that you recognize. Make sure you only experience positive expressions in life.

Java You will quickly find what you are looking for. Keep your own counsel.

javelin Do not deprive yourself of special privileges that are due you. You must also avoid others who will subtly convince you not to seek knowledge or privileges you need in order to develop and grow.

jaw Do not become disgusted and frustrated with a particular situation so quickly. Stay with this until it is resolved and make sure any negative issue in this dream does not become a reality. Take steps to enjoy only positive events in your life. Make sure you warn anyone you recognize from the dream to do the same.

jawbone Within five days someone will discover information about you that could open up a situation you would prefer to keep hidden. You have prior notice of this and can take steps to keep this from occurring. It is also important to take steps to ensure any negative issue in this dream does not become a reality. Make sure you experience only positive expressions in your life and warn anyone you recognize in the dream to do likewise.

jawbreaker Someone has led you to believe they will purchase a particular item for you. Take steps to acquire this item on your own instead of relying on someone else to get it for you. You will waste time and energy and may risk losing this item altogether if you do not make a move on your own.

jaw line Someone, within two days, will keep something from you so you won't become angry. Try to get this information from another individual because it is important you have it in order to live a more tranquil and fulfilling life. Add more amusements and incorporate activities that will make you happier. You are definitely headed for a prosperous future.

jaws of life Find a tranquil spot for yourself and bring more humor into your life. Introduce yourself to a variety of events and lifestyles and make an effort to add spice to your life. Do not allow anyone to place any undue responsibilities on you and refuse to accept anything other than peace and tranquility, especially for the next seven days.

jaybird Do not allow anyone to discourage you from pursuing a relationship with that special person in your life. This also implies you will receive a long awaited marriage proposal. If you feel hesitant and unprepared for this, try to talk yourself into accepting. You will enjoy many riches and much joy in this union.

Jaycee This dream is an extremely lucky omen. Focus on what needs to be said that is not being said, especially for the next five days.

jaywalk If you get an elusive, detached and evasive reaction from someone whom you request services from, take the necessary steps to receive the assistance you are paying for without having to deal with a bad attitude from those rendering help. Hire someone who is very attentive to your needs.

jazz Slow down, you are moving too fast with a particular relationship. Back off and allow this relationship to develop naturally. The other person feels pressured and overwhelmed. Otherwise, the relationship will work out beautifully for both of you.

jealousy One of your secrets will be revealed. If you desire to keep this hidden, take all the necessary steps to protect your privacy and take extra steps to ensure any negative event witnessed in this dream does not occur in reality. Warn anyone whom you recognized in the dream to do the same and make sure you only experience positive expressions in your life.

if you experience jealousy Someone will go to great lengths to take something from you that you are emotionally attached to. Protect yourself and your belongings to ensure this does not take place. This is likely to occur within seven days. Take steps, also, to prevent the occurrence of any event that will create jealousy within you.

to see someone else experience jealousy You will experience betrayal from someone who is related to you. This response to a situation is the opposite of what you expected. You have prior notice of this and can take steps to ensure this does not happen. You must also make sure any negative event you dreamed about does not occur in reality.

jeans You are headed in the right direction and will enjoy a brilliant and prosperous future. A wonderful individual will also come to you with soothing words at a time when it is important for you to see the other side of a troublesome situation. You will enjoy many loyal and faithful friends for the next seven days.

blue jeans You are headed in the right direction and will enjoy a brilliant future. This dream is also a promise of wealth in the near future.

jeep A secret love affair involving a certain individual you had no suspicions about will be revealed to you within seven days.

Jehovah This is a reminder to reaffirm your beliefs and faith. Brilliant changes will begin to occur very rapidly. Peace, tranquility, and harmony will come to you and your family.

Jehovah's Witness If you fail at something on the first attempt, make an effort to keep trying from a different perspective. Regroup and recenter yourself and you will be very surprised at what you will accomplish over the next seven days.

Jekyll and Hyde Within five days someone will create distress and chaos by having an outburst of anger. This individual will begin yelling and screaming uncontrollably while at a meeting and this episode will upset many people. Control your own emotions and remove yourself from this situation immediately.

jelly You are entering a very lucky cycle for at least a month. You will be able to reconcile those relationships you desire to bring unity to.

jelly bean Do not allow someone who newly enters your life to bring with them the same problems you experienced with someone else from your past. These issues brought you many very distasteful moments. Make sure undesirable patterns are not repeated in your present life. Move on with your life without participating in game playing.

jellyfish Do everything you can to avoid mishandling a personal problem you have with a special person in your life.

Treat this issue with respect and give it your highest priority. Communicate in such a way that will bring greater bonding instead of creating distance. By handling this correctly, you will be able to retain what you need from this relationship.

jelly roll You will be accidentally sent to the wrong address. It will take you awhile, after you have become comfortable, to realize you are at the wrong place and have no business being there. This also implies you will be entering a fun filled social cycle.

jeopardy Someone will behave in such a way that will leave you feeling as though you don't want to be with them. After acting as though they are eager to have you in their company, they will purposefully act in a disgusting manner. This will cause you to back off on your own. This will save this individual the trouble and discomfort of breaking away from you.

Jeremiah *(Hebrew Prophet)* This is the perfect time to make decisions that are out of the ordinary. You will enjoy luck and many blessings, especially for the next five days.

Jerico Within five days you will begin to receive the payoff for work well done in the past. This will be a time of plenty for you and your family. This dream may also be used as a reference point in time. If you dream of this city and see its name used in any context, the dream message will occur on this day.

jerky Become more considerate of children and young adults. Receive those who need you with open arms, especially for the next seven days.

Jerry Garcia Within one month you will come to realize what heaven is when you recognize the creative and profound thoughts that are coming from within you. Motivate yourself to develop these thoughts with confidence, neither over nor under doing them. Execute these thoughts on a grand scale and do not allow yourself to develop tunnel vision. Become flexible but not overly so. Do not allow yourself to take today's moments for granted because these will be your future memories. Use common sense and get in sync with your health regarding food and beverages. You will victoriously achieve your goals through your journey in life and are headed for a brilliant future.

jersey You will be loved, cherished and protected for a lifetime by the person you most desire.

Jersey City If you desire, it is now the time to purchase real estate at a low price especially from those who are in a hurry to sell. Good luck is with you. This dream may also be used as a reference point in time. If you dream of this city and see its name used in any context, the dream message will occur on this day.

Jerusalem You will have an extremely busy schedule for the next two weeks. During this time period you will receive a call from someone you have not seen in years who will immediately capture your interest. Do not allow yourself to be sidetracked from things you really need to take care of. Instead, carefully budget your time in such a way that you can include everything in your life without neglecting one aspect. You have plenty of time to easily arrange this. This dream may also be used as a reference point in time. If you dream of this city and see its name used in any context, the dream message will occur on this day.

Jerusalem artichoke Do not allow yourself to judge or criticize others and do not prod others to do the same. Control your emotions and do not allow this behavior to take place, especially for the next week.

Jerusalem Cherry Do not push someone away as a result of your behavior. Control your emotions.

Jesse *(from the Bible)* This is a perfect time to ask someone for their assistance on a project you want to work. This project will consume much of this individual's time but they will be willing to work steadily to complete this endeavor. This will be a mutually satisfying enterprise.

jester For the next week make sure you run your own errands and deliver your own messages. This will ensure you not waste time and that these errands are taken care of properly.

Jesuit Become very aware that a number of people will go to great lengths to control your time. Make sure you attend to this and have a firm say in how you run your life. Also you need to be cautious about a situation you will be involved with before the week is out involving another person. It would be a good idea to have this individual discuss in detail exactly what this issue entails prior to making a move.

Jesus Do not place yourself in the position for the next five days that will allow a special person to betray you in any capacity. Deep emotional feelings will be uprooted and cause deep pain because you will put yourself in the position to allow this to happen.

to hear the name in any form Someone will lead you to believe they care for you and are eager to see you. This individual will plan to meet with you for a wonderful romantic date. They will stand you up and you will feel a deep emotional let down. Once you decide to contact this person you will be coldly and crudely put off. Prepare yourself for this in order to avoid a deep hurt.

to see Jesus in the dream Your thoughts will be magically illuminated and you will be able to clearly express your thoughts in such a way that will lead to the enhancement of your life. You will feel solid and whole and will be able to handle any situation confidently and competently. Others will be able to see these changes in you and this blessing will stay with you for many years to come. The knowledge and wisdom you gain from this dream will always remain with you. Many blessings will come to you and your family. You are on the path toward a brilliant future.

Jesus carrying the cross, on the crucifix or being crucified Make sure you are not symbolically crucified by others who are plotting to do this. Someone you least expect will attempt to cause you extreme emotional harm in order to seriously damage your well being. You will be able, with this prior notice, to take the necessary steps to protect yourself in all capacities. Make sure all your bases are covered and you will be able to handle this situation victoriously. For the next two weeks the powers of your god will be with you.

in any other form There are several reasons why Jesus will appear in a dream. One of these is to warn you that a trap is being laid for you without your knowledge. Someone intends to inflict harm on you in either an emotional or physical way. This damage will affect your life deeply. Another reason is to alert you that you may be misdiagnosed for a particular illness, scheduled for an unnecessary operation, or be given a medication that is not needed. Be careful that you avoid overmedication in any form. You must motivate yourself to determine exactly what you need in your life. Jesus will also warn you to anticipate unexpected accidents and unforeseeable circumstances in your life. This could be anything that could cause you to be impaired in some way or cause your death. There is something you need to be acutely aware of so you can be alert enough to avoid it. You may also be in danger of becoming involved in something you have no business being involved with that could throw you completely off track. It would then be impossible to achieve your goals. Be aware you may also unwittingly do something that will steer someone else off track. You will need to be aware of this in order to bring this person back on track. You are being told to be the person who will inspire someone to go in the right direction. This cycle involves the three day period commencing on the morning you have this dream. You will experience an excitement for a long time to come as a result of this dream and you will be able to successfully tackle each major issue in your life. You are on the path toward a brilliant future.

jet You will encounter someone you have not seen in years while going about your everyday business. This individual will be delighted to see you and will invite you to a very enjoyable outing. Good luck is with you.

jet engine Inspire an older person to include more enjoyable activities and more excitement to their life.

jet lag You are entering a very lucky seven day cycle. Take advantage of this time period to achieve victory and to seek a resolution to all issues you have pending. You must also make sure you do not include people in your life who enjoy provoking arguments and creating chaos.

jetliner For the next five days do not postpone any pending projects.

jetsam Within three days you will be contacted by an old friend who will request special assistance from you. You will be able to satisfactorily give the help this person asks for.

jettison Within three days you will have a very successful private conversation with someone that will help to expedite a specific goal you have in mind.

jetty For the next five days you will gain the advantage in a certain situation by setting up meetings with those who are eager to concede to your wishes. This will also be a good cycle for those who are waiting for you to include them in this situation. This will be a very prosperous and lucky cycle for you. Many blessings will come to you.

Jew Within five days a dear friend will confide a close kept secret to you. This person only wants you to hear them. You can give comfort just by listening to this individual. You must also do everything necessary during this time cycle to allow any romantic situation to flow naturally. This will allow you to experience a closer union.

jewel You are deeply loved and will experience loyalty and many happy moments with someone who is special to you.

jeweler Anything you felt was impossible regarding a certain relationship will now be possible, within the week. Also you will receive a gift you will treasure.

jewelry Someone who is special to you will be more attentive to you, will show more affection, and will offer you more respect, love and loyalty than you ever felt possible. This will be a very delicate and tenuous cycle for both of you. Be very considerate of this person's open display of affection and be sure to show affection in return. This individual is seeking verification from you of your feelings. The following week will be a very lucky cycle for love. Any negative event witnessed in this dream needs to be changed to a positive expression in your life.

junk jewelry Someone, with an unusual, flamboyant personality, will enter your life at an unexpected time and place. If you choose, you and this person will have wonderful times together and this relationship will become as involved as you allow it to. Both of you will enjoy a wonderful future together if you desire.

jewelry box Be very alert for the next seven days. Someone will attempt by way of their mannerisms and body language, to communicate to you the deep feelings they feel for you. This person is very interested in involving themselves in your life in any capacity, especially romantically. This cycle will be very lucky for love and for all financial transactions.

Jewess You will need to maintain a calm composure during a very delicate situation that will arise within three days. This will buy time and will enable a compromise to be worked out between the parties involved.

Jewish *any form* Within three weeks you will be presented with an opportunity you need to pay attention to. Make sure this does not slip through your fingers. You will also experience a special excitement because of this opportunity that will last for a long time to come. Happiness will be yours during this time period.

Jewish calendar This dream is a very lucky omen for you. You will experience prosperity and an abundance of health for a long time to come.

Jew's harp Within the week you will notice someone who is very special to you will have a different manner and a different way of handling situations. Do not become concerned by this. This refreshing new behavior will bring you many benefits.

Jezebel *(from the Bible)* All of your plans will work out exactly as you have envisioned. Seek more relaxation time. Many blessings will come to you and your family.

jib Do not do business with the person you are considering doing business with and stay alert for the next seven days.

jib boom Within the week someone will approach you with something they think you should handle. Do not accept any new projects during this time frame.

jig For the next five days play the part of peacemaker.

jigger Within five days you will rid yourself of a tormenting situation. This problem will disappear completely, never to return.

jiggle You will not be able to have a normal relationship with someone who wants only to relate over the phone or by written correspondence. If this is not what you are looking for, move on with your life without dealing with this issue. This is a good time for you to purchase items you have long desired. The price is right at this time.

jigsaw puzzle Within five days you will need to become aware of your uncontrollable desires. These impulses will bring you ruin. Control your behavior.

jihad Within five days you will have a very distasteful experience. Most of your family members will turn against you because you are not willing to release something to them. This could lead to a violent situation. Become very aware of your safety and take steps to protect yourself.

Jim Crow Within four days you will be able to focus on those things you are not doing that keep positive situations from occurring. Once you are able to locate the specific behaviors you want to change, you will begin to experience more positivity in your life.

Jimmy Hendrix Within five days you will come to realize what heaven is when you recognize the creative and profound thoughts that are coming from within you. Motivate yourself to develop these thoughts with confidence, neither over nor under doing them. Execute these thoughts on a

grand scale and do not allow yourself to develop tunnel vision. Become flexible but not overly so. Do not allow yourself to take today's moments for granted because these will be your future memories. Use common sense and get in sync with your health regarding food and beverages. You will victoriously achieve your goals through your journey in life and are headed for a brilliant future.

jimsonweed Do everything you can to bond closer to a special person within the week so that, if you choose this path, the relationship will become permanent.

jinx Someone will seek to learn quite a bit about you. Do everything you can to keep details of your life from becoming common knowledge to another person. This person feels nothing but malice toward you. Be very protective of your personal life.

jitterbug Someone you know who usually has a bad temper and disposition will, for the next seven days, conduct themselves in a wonderful, delightful and charming way. Something you are unaware of has contributed to this change in mood. This individual will enlighten you about this at a later time.

Joab *(from the Bible)* You are being too flexible and tolerant of the inappropriate behavior of another. You need to put a stop to this within the week. Many blessings are with you and this will be a very prosperous time for you.

Joan of Arc Within five days you will become more concerned about your financial status. Take immediate steps to alleviate your financial situation.

Job *(from the Bible)* Within the month you will begin to experience many wonderful events and will begin to enjoy your life immensely. Do not allow anything to disturb the sense of peace that will be with you for a long time to come.

job For the next seven days treat your time as a special commodity. You will need to be very disciplined and will have to budget your time in order to get as much accomplished as you can within this short period of time. This also implies you are deeply loved by someone who is very loyal to you. Pay close attention to anything in this dream that you could incorporate into your life that would be beneficial to you. Take steps to either avoid any negative situation or to change the outcome.

to ask for a job Within three days make sure you set aside some time to clear your mind and to put yourself through some mental gymnastics in order to pinpoint certain suspicions you have about another person. This will allow you to devise a plan to determine whether these suspicions are valid and, if so, how to go about resolving them. You will deal with this issue successfully if you motivate yourself now. This is the perfect cycle to find the answers you are seeking. You are headed for a very prosperous future.

job corps Do everything necessary for the next seven days to keep yourself from a particular situation that will put your life in danger. Someone will attempt to murder you. You will meet someone, within this time period, who has nothing but malice and bad intentions toward you. Do what you can to remain uninvolved with this person and take steps to protect yourself.

jobless All plans you have made for the next seven days to improve your financial status will work to your advantage. This is a very lucky cycle for you to motivate yourself financially.

jock Within five days someone who has consistently turned down your request for assistance will have a change of heart and will be very eager to offer their help to assist you in completing a mission. This is a very lucky cycle for those in love.

jockey For the next few days a certain amount of risk will be connected to an agreement someone wants you to enter into. This will be a very fortuitous situation and you have very little to worry about. You can confidently proceed. You must also take any negative event foretold in this dream and turn it around to a positive. Make sure you forewarn anyone you recognize to do the same.

jockey shorts Take steps to motivate someone to behave in the romantic way you desire. This individual is seeking the go ahead to proceed in a sexual, romantic and erotic way and will then take full charge of this situation. Good luck is with you.

jockey strap Someone close to you will urge you into an extraordinary lifestyle. The changes they are proposing are very distasteful to you. This individual will approach you within seven days and will attempt to forcefully push this lifestyle on you. You have prior notice of this and need to be aware you have to put your foot down at the beginning and refuse to compromise. Otherwise, it would take years to get away from this situation. Good luck is with you.

jock itch Within ten days you will be the recipient of a windfall by way of a lottery, gambling returns, etc. This will be a substantial amount of money from an unusual source and will bring you wealth for a lifetime. Good luck is with you.

jodhpur You will not have sufficient funds to cover an event you are planning to attend. Plan ahead to avoid embarrassment.

Joel *(from the Bible)* Do not allow anyone to put you in a situation where you will have to cover them financially. This will occur in a very subtle form within the week. Make sure you are aware of this and aggressively handle it to a successful conclusion.

Joe Montana *(famous football player)* You will be able to rise to all unusual challenges for the next four days and be

able to instantaneously salvage any unusual situation that requires this trait. You will develop resiliency and enjoy a prosperous, healthy and tranquil life.

jogger Someone will finally come to grips with themselves and make a decision you have long waited for them to make. This person knows you have been eagerly waiting for this decision to be made and it will have a major impact on your life. You and this individual will make mutual plans for the future and you can anticipate it will be brilliant. Expect this within seven days.

John *(from the Bible)* You will be appointed to a powerful position with much authority. Expect this appointment to take place within the week. You will be making the right decisions and are definitely headed for a prosperous future. Many blessings are coming to you and your family.

John Lennon Within ten days you will come to realize what heaven is when you recognize the creative and profound thoughts that are coming from within you. Motivate yourself to develop these thoughts with confidence, neither over or under doing them. Execute these thoughts on a grand scale and do not allow yourself to develop tunnel vision. Become flexible but not overly so. Do not allow yourself to take today's moments for granted because these will be your future memories. Use common sense and get in sync with your health regarding food and beverages. You will victoriously achieve your goals through your journey in life and are headed for a brilliant future.

John Paul I You are headed for a brilliant future.

John Paul II An abundance of health and prosperity will come your way. Any scheduled surgery will also be successful during this cycle.

John the Baptist Think ahead. The person you care deeply for has led you to believe feelings are mutual. This person has no intention of developing a long term relationship and will deeply disappoint you. You will be let down at the worst possible time. Do not allow yourself to believe an untruth.

joint You will get everything you desire from a love relationship. You must also be very careful you do not selectively hear only what you want to hear. Make decisions based only on facts for the next seven days.

joint checking account Dig deeply before involving yourself in the plans of others. You have not been given all of the facts and you should focus on this incomplete information, especially for the next seven days. Make it a point to turn any negative message into a positive one and make sure you alert anyone you recognize to do the same.

joke Someone will enter your life who has a problem with displaying obsessive behavior toward those they are merely acquainted with. Take steps to ensure you do not become the focus of this person's life.

joker Someone in a position of power and wealth will promise to help you out with a specific situation. In reality, this individual will bail out and leave you disappointed. Make sure you do not fall prey to this over the next week and take steps to turn any negative event in this dream into a positive one. You must also alert anyone you recognize in the dream to do the same.

Jolly Roger Make sure you watch out for dangerous falls, especially for the next three days.

Jonah *(from the Bible)* Become aware that a youngster who is close to you is associating with another youngster who poses a danger to them. This young person has a cruel streak and is capable of performing violent acts against animals, etc. Take steps to keep this young child from the violent influence of this other child.

Joplin, Janis Within seven days you will come to realize what heaven is when you recognize the creative and profound thoughts that are coming from within you. Motivate yourself to develop these thoughts with confidence, neither over nor under doing them. Execute these thoughts on a grand scale and do not allow yourself to develop tunnel vision. Become flexible but not overly so. Do not allow yourself to take today's moments for granted because these will be your future memories. Use common sense and get in sync with your health regarding food and beverages. You will victoriously achieve your goals through your journey in life and are headed for a brilliant future.

Jordan For the next few days you will have doubts about someone you know. This dream is telling you to dispel these doubts because this individual is very loyal to you. You must also do what you can to avoid behaving in an overly authoritative way toward someone else. Watch your behavior. This dream may also be used as a reference point in time. If you dream of this country and see its name used in any context, the dream message will occur on this day.

Joseph *(from the Bible)* You will enjoy a tremendous amount of tranquility in your relationships. For the next month you will enjoy a variety of admirers, one of whom, if you desire, will become a permanent part of your life. This dream is an extremely lucky omen and an omen of prosperity.

Joseph Campbell You will find, for the next three months, you will be at the peak of experience and will be so together that you will instinctively know you will reach the finish line before the race has really begun. You will have the feeling of confidence that comes from knowing you will succeed. You will feel the strength that comes from your inner core. Follow your goals as if you were on a mission and this will bring you to a victorious completion of your goals. Within this time frame, your sense of ethics and judgment will be intact and you are headed for a fantastic future.

Joshua *(from the Bible)* Challenge yourself to grasp the opportunities and positions that await you. You feel, right now, as though you are unable to handle this position but you will gain the confidence and determination to win this position and excel at it. Good luck is with you.

Joshua Tree Within seven days you will be in the company of a very powerful person who has the authority and power to pull strings on your behalf. Make sure you motivate yourself in such a way that you do not miss out on this opportunity. You will enjoy an abundance of health during this cycle and many blessings will be with you and your family.

Josiah *(from the Bible)* Become aggressively verbal when requesting services for another person. This person depends solely on you to work on their behalf. This cycle will promote success in this endeavor. You must also become very focused, for the next seven days, on what is really going on with a particular family member so you can take aggressive steps to handle this matter correctly. Good luck is with you.

journal For the next week you will need to become aggressive and do the necessary legwork in order to grasp exactly what you want from a specific situation that would otherwise fall apart. Take steps to ensure your plans fall into place exactly as you wish.

journalism Within the week you will receive exactly what you expect in a business transaction.

journalist Do not overextend yourself for the next two weeks. Do everything you can to make private time for yourself.

journey Make it very clear to someone as soon as their intentions become obvious, that you are not interested in a relationship with them. Do not demonstrate a wishy-washy attitude toward this person.

journeyman Become interested in a collectible hobby. This hobby will bring you many wonderful moments and will, at the same time, bring you a supplemental income.

joust Make sure your involvements do not pose a risk for you.

jowl Do not become involved in any new ventures or investments. They will prove unlucky for you.

joy Within seven days a casual relationship will develop into a deeper commitment, if you desire. This relationship will develop into a mutually satisfying union.

joyride Within five days you will become involved in a group setting where opportunities will present themselves. These opportunities will involve great bargains and the sale of goods that you can take advantage of. You will locate a luxurious item someone wants to get rid of, not because they need the money but because they are tired of this item. Take steps to keep any negative event seen in this dream from occurring in reality and alert all those concerned to take the same precautions. You will enjoy an abundance of health and wealth and are headed for a prosperous future.

joystick Think carefully and detail each move before a special event takes place. This will occur within the week and it is important that you behave appropriately.

Jubal *(from the Bible)* Make sure the advice you receive comes from someone with experience and reliability in the particular area you require assistance in.

jubilee Within two weeks you will be invited to a distant city where you will attend a wonderful event. You will enjoy yourself immensely and will enjoy a safe journey.

Judah Within the month you will purchase, at a low price, what seems to be an insignificant item. In reality, this item is priceless. Good luck is with you and opportunities will abound for you this month. Motivate yourself to take advantage of them.

Judaism Act immediately on a situation you need to attend to that involves another individual. Act on this within two days, otherwise you will lose the chance to be successful. You will enjoy an abundance of prosperity, health and love. Many blessings will come to you and your family.

Judas *(from the Bible)* For the next seven days be consistent in your actions and manner in order to avoid confusing others. It is very important, during this time frame, not to put out mixed messages and to make sure others are not misled. Good luck is with you.

judge Do not allow yourself to place so much importance on another person that you overextend and abuse yourself emotionally and mentally, especially for the next five days. Take steps to change the outcome or to avoid any negative event connected to this dream.

Judges *(book of the Bible)* Follow your instincts for the next seven days. All of your hunches can be relied on fully. This will be a situation that will involve someone else in your personal life. This is not the correct thing for you to do. This individual is not the right person to involve in this situation.

judgment day For the next five days pay close attention to everything occurring in your life and take the time to regroup. Restrain all impulsive behavior and curb your sense of urgency. This will keep you from becoming involved in something you have no business being involved in. Many blessings are with you and your family.

judo For the next five days you will be very eager to set aside time for the person you are interested in. This person will disappoint you by acting bored for the entire time they are with you. You have prior notice of this and can keep this from taking place.

jug Within four days, because of your determination, certain plans will become a reality. This will lead you to a better lifestyle. You will be able to remove any mental block that is preventing you from moving in the direction you desire and you will develop confidence in your abilities during this cycle.

juggernaut Do everything you can to keep a special person from slipping out of your life because of your lack of involvement.

juggle *to juggle* Someone will unexpectedly call you within five days and will request your company for a day's outing. You will enjoy yourself at various events and amusements. You will not see this person again for a long time.

jugular vein For the next seven days you will need to restrain your behavior. You will also need to be attentive, demonstrative, and tolerant toward someone who is very special to you. This person has become very angry and upset over a situation that has taken place in their life. It will be days before this individual comes to grips with this shocking situation.

juice For the next seven days avoid focusing on someone else's problems. It would be a mistake to involve yourself in their life or to try to assist them in their situation. Slow down and reassess your thoughts so you can act appropriately. Do not allow your own assumptions to lead you to make an incorrect decision. Look up the specific juice you are drinking in order to gain a more detailed meaning to this dream. This dream is an extremely lucky omen.

jujitsu Make sure, for the next two days, you are emotionally equipped to assist someone who is desperately in need of your help. It would be better to seek the proper professional assistance for this person instead of offering your help.

jukebox You will have a fantastic and extraordinary invitation to a fabulous event that will not be easily forgotten. You will have long nostalgic conversations with others about years past. This memory will last a lifetime.

Juliet Do everything you can to rid yourself of emotional hang ups you have resisted ridding yourself of. This will allow you to feel emotional fulfillment. By allowing these hang ups to continue, you are depriving yourself of an emotional involvement with another person. Deal with this within two weeks because someone will enter your life who will not tolerate this behavior. You will feel much pain and regret if you allow this person to walk out of your life because you are unable to become deeply involved with anyone. Good luck is with you.

Julius Caesar A certain situation that is very much out of the ordinary will occur that will require you take a certain amount of risk to become involved. Move ahead with confidence. You will develop the determination to overcome any risk involved. Everything will work out exactly as you have envisioned.

July This dream is a very lucky symbol and a promise that you will receive health, wealth, love, spiritual strength and an abundance of blessings. Continue with confidence on the path you are taking.

jump *to jump over or to see someone jump over something* For the next five days you will be collecting money from a variety of sources. Various hobbies and odd jobs will give you pleasure and extra income. You must also take the time to do research before you purchase a certain item. You will save money this way.

to jump or skip or to see someone else jump or skip You are aggressively seeking to know someone you are not now acquainted with. Be the first to open up communication and you will be surprised at how easily this person reciprocates.

to jump or to see someone jump from a moving object It will be strongly requested that you curb a particular behavior or attitude toward someone who is close to you. Keep tight control over this behavior for the next two days and correct your attitude before someone remarks on it.

to jump or to see someone jump into open space (i.e., from an airplane) Your success depends solely on your determination to apply yourself when it comes to important situations.

to jump on For the next three days avoid settling for less. Someone will lead you to believe you will be better off leaving a certain situation. This is not the case. Regroup and rethink the situation. Put yourself on the right track and follow your hunches.

to jump off You will fail to take care of a particular situation because you will be using the wrong tool or the wrong information. Carefully think this situation through so you can do this properly the first time and avoid wasting precious time.

to jump in place Do everything you can to prevent problems and emotional upsets that are not of your making from spilling over on you. Keep yourself stress free and do not allow other people's problems to become yours.

to be jumped by an attacker Make very sure no one usurps the power and authority that belongs to you. Be acutely aware someone will also attempt to bring you emotional pain by spreading hearsay. Make sure anything emotionally precious to you is not disturbed in any way and turn any negative event in your life into a positive event.

to jump someone or to see an attacker jump another person Victory is in your future. For the next two days leave yourself open for any opportunity that will present itself to you. Go full speed ahead with this opportunity. This is a very fortuitous cycle for you. Make sure any negative situation that involves you or someone else does not become a reality and do not allow negativity to take over your life.

if you recognize the person who is jumped Warn this individual of the possibility of these negative events occurring in their life.

to be jumped by an attacker and get away You will develop the determination you need to turn each negative aspect of your life around within seven days. Good luck will be with you and blessings will come to you and your family.

computer jump Within three days a situation that requires the assistance of others will work out well and everything will fall into place. This cycle is perfect for choosing the correct person to work with you.

to see anything jump a track Do nothing for the next three days that will cast doubts on your love or fidelity.

to jump to conclusions You are loved beyond your imagination and you will have verification of this within three days. You are in a cycle of prosperity and happiness.

to jump off anything that is high A certain person will take steps to create a relationship between you and another individual. You are fated to enjoy a beautiful, full blown love relationship. This will blossom within a few days and will bring much joy into your life. This is the perfect cycle to connect to another person in an emotional way and this will be so successful they will respond in the exact manner you wish. This also implies you are headed in the right direction and will be able to fully express yourself regarding all personal issues. You will be very detailed and focused and, as a result, will be able to accomplish a great deal and enjoy many successes in life. You will magically develop the strength and courage you need to handle each issue in your life and will enjoy peace and tranquility. You will also be granted an unexpected favor but it is important that you put yourself in the position to talk with many powerful and influential people. State your needs clearly and succinctly and you will promptly be given the money you request from a particular individual. You will enjoy victory in those areas of your life you deem to be the most important now and you will also learn of some good news within the week. You are headed for a brilliant future. You must also pay very close attention to all conversations for the next three days and make sure all negative messages and events portended in this dream do not become a reality. Take steps to ensure all positive messages are brought to full bloom.

in any other form You will process a great variety of thoughts and will have an irresistible urge to include pleasure in your life. You will feel a need to run from one form of recreation to another. Expect this to occur for the next two weeks. Take steps to keep any negative event witnessed in this dream from becoming a reality and warn anyone you recognize to do the same.

jumper *distance jumper* Do everything you can to avoid taking risks with any new ventures, especially for the next seven days.

jumping bean Someone will be irresistibly drawn to you to the point of being visibly shaken. This individual will go to great lengths to make you feel appreciated and loved.

jumping mouse Loosen up your work schedule for your mental and physical well being.

"jump in with both feet" *to hear the phrase* This dream is an extremely lucky omen and you will receive much recognition for work well done as well as a large financial bonus.

jump rope Do not allow yourself to stagnate or to allow yourself to get to the point where you are going nowhere. For the next two days focus on what you need to do in order to put yourself on the right track. You will have the energy and a wealth of ideas that will enable you to turn this situation completely around and develop a better lifestyle. You are headed for a brilliant future.

jump seat Within five days you will be in the company of an extremely sensitive person. You will unintentionally say something that will deeply hurt this person and will cause them to break down in tears. Think ahead and do everything necessary to keep this situation from occurring.

jump start Someone will discuss their lifestyle with you in an attempt to get you involved. This lifestyle will be very distasteful to you. Let them know your feelings of disgust from the beginning so they will not get the impression you are interested in joining them in their recreational pursuits. Any event in this dream that may relate to a situation in reality (i.e., to need a jump start) also needs to be avoided. All other parties you dream of need to be alerted to this situation.

jumpsuit Think ahead. The items you require are limited to what the stores have in stock. Shop early for a good selection and to acquire what you need in time to meet your needs. This dream is an extremely lucky omen and you will enjoy an abundance of health and reasoning powers.

June You will definitely have a support system and a network of knowledge you can pull from that will help you to position yourself in a comfortable lifestyle. This month will bring you many opportunities for celebrations and joyful occurrences. Prepare yourself for unexpected joyful news that will come your way within three days. You are definitely headed for a brilliant future. This month will also leave you feeling as though everyone is on your side and are supporting your goals.

June bug You will be strongly motivated, for the next few weeks, to complete a task you feel is almost impossible to complete concerning a love relationship. You will be victorious in all matters involving love.

jungle You will be immersed in an idea that you will focus on completely. Your thought patterns will develop in such a way that you will be able to pinpoint exactly what you need to do to successfully execute your plans. This dream is an extremely lucky omen. You will also need to make sure you only experience positive expressions and do what you can to alter any negative event. Warn anyone else involved in this dream to do the same.

to find your way out of the jungle Many rejoiceful events are coming up for you within two weeks. Do not ignore a special person whom you can share these moments with. Share your joy with the person who is very special to

you. The synergism between you and another person will be an unbeatable force. The driving force working for you is love. The more hopelessly lost that you dream you are, the greater the love between you.

to walk through a green jungle You are definitely headed for a brilliant future. You will be making all of the right decisions for the next three days.

to walk through a dying jungle You have been keeping things pent up for too long. You will finally have the courage to communicate your needs to those who are important to you. Do not allow yourself to become so timid that you are unable to voice your needs. Once you speak up, you will be surprised at the quick response you receive.

to become lost in a jungle Within three days, you will have to be specific about the amount of time you are willing to devote to a particular situation. Create a stress free environment and allow yourself to be nourished in peace.

jungle fever Do not question the deep emotional feelings that are emerging from you. Allow the situation between you and a special person to flow naturally. You will be surprised at the amount of joy you feel.

jungle gym Do not allow feelings of resentments to become established within you, especially for the next three days.

junior Any unexpected travel you do for the next two weeks will be connected to a fantastic opportunity. This will bring you more prosperity than you envisioned. Good luck is with you.

junior college Make sure the energy you put out to others comes from a positive place so others will view you in a positive light. This will be extremely important for the next two days.

junior high school Be very careful when handling tools for the next three days and make sure a tool does not become a lethal weapon.

junior league Your determination and faith will prevail. You will bring into reality exactly what you need to make your life comfortable.

juniper A particular situation is very burdensome to you because you lack the knowledge to understand what is actually occurring. Within two days someone will fill you in on the particulars and this burden will be lifted. Tranquility will prevail and all burdens that drag you down will be immediately halted.

junk Do not exercise power and authority over another person by removing your affections when someone does not behave in the manner you wish. Simply allow this person to know your feelings and you will be surprised at the response you receive. You are wasting time when you use power plays.

junk car *to see a junked car* An unusual occurrence will make you feel inferior to someone else. You will feel as though someone who is much older than you is in much better physical shape. This person has a great deal of stamina and you will feel as though you are letting yourself down. Don't be so hard on yourself but take it as a reminder to begin exercising in small easy steps. Remember everyone has different levels of energy.

junk food Do not focus on what is taking place in your life. Focus, instead, on what is not taking place that has not been fully addressed by you.

junkie Do what you can to refrain from thoughts and behaviors that hinder a relationship from growing closer. Look at yourself in detail and determine those aspects of yourself that keep those you feel close to at arms length. This is the time to develop the courage to address those issues and to make a complete turn around in order to develop a personality that will draw others to you. This month will allow you to turn yourself around completely. Good luck is with you.

junk jewelry Someone, with an unusual, flamboyant personality, will enter your life at an unexpected time and place. If you choose, you and this person will have wonderful times together and this relationship will become as involved as you allow it to. Both of you will enjoy a wonderful future together if you desire.

junk mail For the next two weeks, allow yourself to become involved in the unusual. This will allow you to grow and develop in an extraordinary way. Enjoy new experiences. This is a very lucky omen for you.

junk man/woman *(dealer)* Reach out to someone special in a special way through your mannerisms and communication. It is very important for the next three days to put your love into action.

junkyard Take care of only one thing at a time to ensure each situation is brought to a satisfactory conclusion.

Juno *(from Roman mythology)* Any effort you put out for the next three days will be well worth it. This dream is an extremely lucky cycle so go for what you want now.

Jupiter This dream is an extremely lucky omen and fortunate in every way. An older person will, if you desire, provide you with the relief you are seeking in any capacity. Help will come in the nick of time. This person is very generous, demonstrative and giving of themselves and will stand by you relentlessly, if you so desire. For the next year you will achieve victory in anything you set out to accomplish. Good luck is with you.

juror For the next two days do not place yourself in the position to be talked about unkindly.

jury For the next three days, be very wary and do not let yourself fall prey to a very dangerous individual. Be very

focused on your surroundings and take all necessary steps to keep this from occurring. This is preventable.

just *any form* Within five days you will be able to muster up the energy and anything else it takes to follow your instincts regarding a situation you feel should be taking place in spite of what others say. This situation needs to occur. It will bring improved changes into your life and into the lives of others. Proceed with confidence. Everything will work out successfully.

"just because" *to hear this phrase* Be wary of someone who will, in spite of their pleasant demeanor, hold a secret hatred toward you. Make sure this individual does not gain an advantage over you in any situation you are involved in. You will receive an unexpected financial windfall.

justice Within two days you will have the verification of the love and respect others feel for you. You will be well loved for a lifetime.

justice of the peace You and a special person will enter into a relationship that will endure for a long time. The love you have for each other will be obvious to those around you and you will both be well respected by others.

"just in case" Within five days you will have to deal with someone who will attempt to keep someone you are close to from maintaining that closeness. This person will do everything they can to demolish this friendship. They will devise a distasteful scenario that will serve to split up this relationship. It will be done in such a subtle way it will be difficult to determine what instigated this split up. Be very alert to someone who has a secret hatred toward you. You will also experience a financial windfall.

"just kidding" Within three days you will be able to use profound communication skills to gain someone's absolute attention. You will be instrumental in opening this person's eyes in such a way that they can motivate themselves and raise their standard of living. You will then be able to glean the information you need from others by using these communication skills. This information will be extremely valuable and advantageous to both of you. Many blessings are with you and you are headed for a brilliant future.

jute Do everything you can to attend some of the local entertainments that will come up in a short period of time. This will provide you with a great deal of stimulation. This dream is a good luck omen and many blessings will come to you and your family.

juvenile Within three days a particular situation involving a young person will be of particular concern to you. Relentlessly seek the proper method to resolve this situation.

juvenile court Within three days a decision needs to be made quickly no matter how difficult it seems. Don't waste time with this. Make sure any negative event in this dream does not become a reality for you or for anyone else you recognize. You are on the path toward a prosperous future.

juvenile delinquent Take steps to refrain from the behaviors and thought patterns that keep a special person from getting closer to you. Look at your behavior in detail and determine those aspects that keep others at arms length. This is the time to courageously address those issues and develop a personality that will draw others close to you. Good luck is with you.

juvenile hall Make sure a disagreement does not escalate to the point where it cannot be resolved. It will be a waste of time to attempt to patch things up and there will be no way to continue this relationship. Take steps to avoid this, especially for the next three days. Do everything you can to keep anything negative in this dream from becoming a reality for you or anyone else you recognize in the dream. You are headed for a prosperous future.

K

K Motivate others to rally around you. You will be able to circulate widely and encourage a large group of people to support you. Start now and you will ensure a brilliant future for yourself. You will be victorious in grasping your highest ambitions.

Kaiser For the next three days, do not allow yourself to become overwhelmed with new responsibilities.

kale A certain individual has no interest in pursuing a relationship in any form with you. This person wants you to back off and wants to get on with their life without you in it.

kaleidoscope Become directly involved in the personal problems of another person, especially for the next three days. This individual will request your help and any assistance will be deeply appreciated and warmly received.

kamikaze You and a special person will work equally hard to ensure a relationship will endure and true love will blossom. Go for it.

kangaroo In order to receive the benefits that are righteously yours, you need to be more persuasive with those individuals you will have to deal with, especially for the next three days. This will be a very victorious cycle for the next week. Use this time frame to accomplish those things you need to take care of.

kangaroo court Unpleasant words exchanged between you and another will not be easily controlled. Do everything necessary to keep this from occurring.

kangaroo rat Someone who has been cruel to you will feel remorse and will render you an apology. This will occur within three days. Many blessings will come to you and your family.

Kansas Within three days you will quickly acquire the knowledge you are seeking by conducting your own thorough research. Also, make sure, for the next three days, that you dress appropriately for any unusual and unexpected weather. This dream may also be used as a reference point in time. If you dream of this state and see its name used in any context, the dream message will occur on this day.

karate You will now have the means to discuss important issues that have been dragging you down. This will be a non stressful and non threatening situation no matter what the context of the issue. Use this cycle to work on difficult and explosive situations.

karma Listen to your heart and do not pursue anything unless your heart is in it. You will achieve victory in important matters if you follow your hunches and listen to your own counsel, especially for the next three days.

katydid Someone does not have the courage to let you know they have no interest in a romantic relationship. Do not push yourself on anyone for the next two days who is not interested in you.

kava Seek the help and advice from someone within three days who has the skill and expertise to offer you assistance.

kayak Avoid coming across, by way of mannerisms and behavior, in a way that confuses someone else. This person will be unable to tolerate this behavior and will be very distraught, especially for the next three days. Avoid this behavior.

keel Do not become involved in problematic family issues at this time. It will take much longer to resolve than expected.

keelhaul Make it an issue to clarify a situation or behavior that someone else finds questionable. Do this within three days, or take steps to avoid all questionable behavior entirely.

keep *for others to keep something of yours* Do not take the law into your own hands. Handle each situation legally and properly for the next three days.
    in any other form A major shift will occur in your life that will be out of your control. Be prepared for this within three days and expect the unexpected.

keeper The distasteful feelings you have about someone are accurate. Follow your hunches.

keepsake You will be highly respected by others but someone you care about does not feel that way toward you. Otherwise, good luck is with you.

kelp Move quickly within two days in order to close an important business deal you have been trying to push through.

Kennedy, John F. A golden opportunity that comes only once in a lifetime will be offered to you within three days. You will be blessed with the clarity of greater mental inventiveness needed to develop a plan and execute it successfully. This plan will bring spectacular changes you so desire to experience with tranquility and good luck in your life.

Kennedy's The Within three weeks you will meet someone who finds it very important to foster a deep personal relationship. This person needs and wants a strong family unit. This is a great cycle for circulating and finding this individual if you desire this kind of union. This person will be very wealthy and will have a tremendous influence over your life. You are headed for a brilliant future and many blessings will come to you and your family.

kennel You are not getting the important, significant facts about a certain situation from someone who is important to you. This is of great concern to you. Do everything you can to get the facts and to resolve this completely.

Kentucky Become a team player. You and other co-workers need to understand the importance of working together. You will enjoy a successful outcome as a result. This dream may also be used as a reference point in time. If you dream of this state and see its name used in any context, the dream message will occur on this day.

Kentucky Derby If you desire love from someone, you must first learn to love yourself. The confidence and love you have for yourself will attract others very quickly.

kerchief Be sure to express yourself fully and let your opinions be known. This will be very important to you within three days.

kernel Within three days carefully focus on developing detailed, well articulated plans to execute in your life. Allow destiny to take its course and provide you with a more plentiful, successful future. All of your efforts will be well worth it and you will begin to see results in this time period.

ketchup Someone is leading you to believe they accept your point of view and that they are genuinely interested in becoming a part of your projected plans. This individual is wasting your time and leading you to believe falsely. Go on with your life without this person.

kettle Within three days you will experience deep emotional pain because someone has set up a situation that will lead you to feel betrayed. Avoid feelings of pain and fragility by refusing to become involved with someone who puts you on an emotional roller coaster. Free yourself from this abusive situation and keep negative situations from occurring.

kettledrum Someone is totally disinterested in you. Do not push yourself on anyone who is not interested in developing a relationship. Get busy with something else and move on with your life.

kettle of fish Within three days you will benefit greatly if you make yourself available for an upcoming trip. Do not hesitate. Pounce on this opportunity and you will achieve great prosperity in the future.

key Within three days you will become involved in some unusual circumstances that will definitely improve your standard of living. Good luck is with you and many blessings will come to you and your family.

to be given keys You will move ahead with speed and will be able to grasp your highest ambitions. This will be an extremely lucky cycle and you can expect this to come about in a short while.

to give keys You will surrender yourself in a sexual way within three days to someone you greatly desire. If this is not your choice you have enough notice to keep it from occurring.

to have your keys taken away Consistently and persistently make sure what you want to see come about will occur within three days. Involve yourself personally, otherwise it will fall apart.

ring/bunch of keys You will be invited to numerous functions and events over the next seven days. You can be very selective about the events you choose to attend. Any one of these will offer you a chance for greater prosperity and for ways of enriching your personal life. If you desire, you will have a number of quality people pursuing you that you can choose from. This is a wonderful cycle for prosperity and social events. Good luck is with you.

broken key A promise someone made to you will not be kept. You will learn of this within three days. Do everything within your power to make sure this does not occur.

to lose keys For the next three days, motivate yourself in order to put yourself on the right track. This is the best cycle to investigate what you need to do and to calmly arrive at a solution.

to put a key into a lock Each relationship that is important to you needs your personal attention in order to allow those you care about to know you have only the finest care and love for them. Do not allow any of your relationships to stagnate to the point where your loved ones feel deprived of your attention.

to use a key effectively It will be very important within a two day period to have a meeting with certain individuals and to make connections and the necessary requests before an important situation starts to develop. This will ensure it does not fall apart before it takes off. Stay on top of this and you will be able to make the correct adjustments in time. Pay attention to this now and everything will fall into place as you desire. Good luck is with you and your family. You are headed for a brilliant future.

to fail to unlock with a key You will be dealing with

someone who is very inconsiderate of the feelings of others. This individual is only interested in their own personal gratification. Do not involve yourself with this person and get on with your life without them in it.

to successfully lock You will be dealing with someone within two days who will refuse to take no for an answer. Prepare ahead of time how best to deal with this and don't become stressed out. You will reach your highest ambitions within three days. Many blessings are with you. You must also make sure you deal only in facts for the next week and not what you selectively choose to believe. Face facts and get on with your life.

a lock that falls apart when a key enters A family member is in grave danger of being killed. If you recognize someone from this dream, make sure you warn them their life is in danger. Otherwise, alert all family members to prevent this.

extra set of keys This is an alert to have an extra set of keys somewhere in order to be on the safe side in case you become locked out. You will enjoy extremely good luck, especially during this cycle.

master key Make sure you make your opinions known and that others are aware of your likes and dislikes. Be straightforward in your communication with others to ensure there is no confusion about what you will or will not accept.

keyboard Do not be too proud to accept a gift of money, especially for the next two days. This dream is an extremely lucky omen.

key club Make sure you are valued for who you are, not for what you have.

keyhole Keep your personal interests to yourself, especially from those who are overly curious. Explain tactfully to these people that your personal business is private in such a way to avoid hurt feelings.

to use a keyhole in an unusual way You will be dealing with someone who irritates you because of their bad habit of procrastinating. This individual finds it impossible to become involved in anything at the time they promised but will motivate themselves only when it suits their purpose. When you speak with this person, cleverly determine when to make your move. This will keep you from being disappointed.

to look through a keyhole Think carefully and regroup in order to determine what you need to do to put yourself on the right track. Do not let others manipulate you to the point of being led away from your goals. Pay close attention to what you saw through the keyhole. If it applies to your life and is a negative situation, take steps to avoid it or to alter the outcome. All positive events need to be incorporated in your life.

to look through a keyhole and see an eye looking back Within two weeks you will learn of a new addition to your family. Those who are not interested in extending the family need to take precautions to prevent this. This is an extremely lucky omen and you will enjoy much future prosperity.

skeleton key An event will occur within seven days that you must not miss. You will have the pleasure of watching

two admirers subtly attempt to win your favor. Although it is not apparent to you, one of them possesses a great deal of authority and power. Both of them will be very agreeable and charming and you will enjoy having one of them in your life. You can be confident you will make the right choice for a prosperous future.

Key Lime pie Take steps to prevent anything now that will have shocking repercussions in the far future. This situation revolves around a family member and you will feel deep remorse for not preventing it now. Many blessings are with you.

keypunch Within five days someone will attempt to involve you in a complicated plot to commit theft while withholding some of the facts. Do everything you can to avoid involvement in this situation. Remain wary and astute in order to detect this plot prior to becoming involved.

key ring In the not so distant future, life will improve and every day will seem like a holiday. You will be able to do exactly as you please and enjoy many facets of your life you have been unable to enjoy before.

keystone You will enjoy sensual sexual pleasures within the next five days if you so desire.

Key West Any reconciliation you want with another is possible now. Do what you can, within this four day cycle, to bring this about if this is what you desire. This dream may also be used as a reference point in time. If you dream of this city and see its name used in any context, the dream message will occur on this day.

khaki You have grossly underestimated a situation you will become involved in within five days. Move on this quickly before you let it slip away. This will be a wonderful opportunity for you.

kibitz Be watchful of the negative thoughts you are allowing to run through your mind. Do not become so immersed in these tapes that you become physically ill. Aggressively pursue a positive attitude.

kick You will be dealing with a false person who will appear enthusiastic about beginning a relationship. Once this person has gratified their desires, they will still be unable to build on a relationship. This individual lacks the ability to nurture a relationship and to allow it to grow. Be alert to this and do not allow yourself to be taken advantage of. Get on with your life without this person in it. You will also need to be very careful to not put yourself in the position to be blamed for the disappearance of a valuable item. Otherwise you are headed for a very prosperous future.

to kick someone Do not borrow money from anyone who will tell everyone about this loan, especially if you do not wish your private business to become public. This individual will be eager to lend you this money and will assure you this will not occur. Avoid this situation entirely.

to be kicked Do not place yourself in the position to have to care for someone for a long period of time. You will later feel you were tricked into accepting this physical, as well as financial, responsibility and you will regret this. Do what you can to prevent this.

kickball Within three days a decision you have made with someone will be interfered with by a third individual. This person will attempt to change the original agreement. Be aware of this situation and take firm steps to maintain the original agreement.

kick off Do everything you can to avoid bullying into someone else's decisions. Back off and leave things as they are. Allow others to conduct business their way.

kickstand Within two days find a way to specify your needs to an important individual. You will be successful and your needs will be met.

kid For the next three days make sure young children are not present when angry, aggressive altercations are likely to take place. You need to make sure they are not present when angry, foul language is being used. Take a firm stand on this and immediately remove children from this environment. You must also not allow a third person to bully their way into a decision you have made or force you to change an agreement you have made with another person. Stand firm on this.

kid gloves Within five days you will receive physical and verbal verification of a certain situation. You will then be able to decide whether or not you want this situation in your life. Many blessings are with you.

kid leather Any solid foundation you are seeking in your life in any capacity is your destiny to have. Within the week, you will be able to visualize the manner in which you can make this happen. Good luck is with you.

kidnap This signifies there is an extreme urgency pertaining to a certain situation that contains undertones of evil. Be acutely aware and cautious that you or someone you recognize in the dream does not fall prey to a situation where a kidnapping could occur. This is extremely important for the next three days. Do not take this warning lightly and make sure you and all those involved create a safe environment for yourself. You have prior notice of this and can take the necessary steps to protect yourself. Do not allow yourself to be so easily swayed into doing something out of the ordinary. Someone will also be very enthusiastic about starting a relationship that will not be anything you should desire to become involved in, especially for the next three days. Good luck and many blessings will come to you.

to dream of kidnapping someone You will soon be hearing from someone who is a fugitive from justice. This person will let you in on this secret within two weeks. Remain

uninvolved. If you are considering a kidnapping in reality, seek professional help and refrain from this act.

to dream of being kidnapped You will meet someone, within the next week, who possesses great wealth and will enter your life with the intention of involving themselves with you in some capacity. It will be up to you to determine the level of commitment you want. This person is very loyal and will stay with you for a lifetime. Take the proper steps to ensure you are not abducted in reality within two days. This is preventable.

if you recognize the person This dream implies that someone with similar traits as the person you dreamed of or the person themselves will enter your life and want to become involved in some capacity. This person is extremely wealthy and it is your choice whether you want to become involved or not. If there is some negative aspect to this person, you can take steps to remain uninvolved.

if you do not recognize this person Any clue you can pick up from this individual's behavior will offer you a premonition of something you will experience with someone within two days. If it is a negative situation, take steps to prevent its occurrence in reality. If it is a positive situation, make sure you bring it to its full potential.

knowledge of a kidnapping Don't fight someone else's battles. It is better to give moral support in private. This is especially important for the next two days. You must also take steps to keep this dream from becoming a reality and if you do have knowledge of a kidnapping, seek professional help.

to be kidnapped and held for ransom Within five days, you will meet someone who possesses great wealth and will come into your life with the intent of involving themselves with you in some way. This is not normally the kind of person you would involve yourself with but their financial status is a powerful lure. Once you become involved you will have to negotiate each expenditure. This individual will turn out to be miserly and very tight with their money. Take steps to avoid this situation. Make sure you do not place yourself in the position to be kidnapped and held for ransom.

kidney Pay close attention to the content of this dream and make sure you either avoid or alter any negative situation. Encourage all positive situations. You will also need to actively seek assistance, whether from government agencies, resource groups, etc., that will properly meet your needs. Within three days make it a point to seek out this group. Many blessings will come to you and your family. This cycle is very lucky for accomplishing almost anything you set your mind to.

kidney beans For the next three days avoid large crowds and large open spaces. Play it safe for this time period.

kidney stone Educate yourself now on health matters in order to prevent kidney stones in the future. Take steps to avoid or alter all negative aspects of this dream. Within three days someone will also undermine you in such a way that they will take something that is righteously yours. Be very watchful and determined to prevent this from occurring.

kill A powerful position and a financial advancement will be placed in your hands. This will be an appointed position. This will be a very victorious cycle for you and you will be able to accomplish everything you set out to do. If anything negative was depicted in this dream, take steps to change it or avoid it entirely.

to kill someone who is already dead in reality or to see someone do it Back off from someone who requires more private time to take care of personal matters and career goals. Stop being so demanding of others, especially for the next three days. Remain relentless in the pursuit of your own goals. You will be in an extremely lucky cycle for the week.

to kill a special person or a relative The person you are killing in the dream is, in reality, committing acts that cause their loved ones a great deal of pain. You will be instrumental in bringing assistance and harmony to this individual's family as well as to them. Your thoughts will be illuminated in very specific ways that will allow you to advise these people on how to handle this situation. This will enable them to bring more love and tranquility to their lives. This is especially important for the next three days. Anything negative witnessed in this dream needs to be avoided in reality. Forewarn anyone you recognize to do the same. Take steps to ensure you only experience positive events in your life.

to kill someone else What you once felt was impossible is now in your destiny to achieve. If anything negative was depicted in this dream, take steps to change it or avoid it entirely. Forewarn anyone you recognize to do the same. Take steps to ensure you only experience positive events in your life.

to be killed Take steps to protect yourself and to keep this dream from becoming a reality, especially for the next three days. Pay attention to any event in this dream you can apply to reality. This will allow you to gain additional clues to an event that will take place during this time frame. Play it safe. If anything negative was depicted in this dream, take steps to change it or avoid it entirely.

if you recognize the person who killed you Take steps to protect yourself from this individual and to keep this dream from becoming a reality. Relentlessly apply yourself in order to achieve a special goal you desire within three days. If you do not become personally involved, this goal will not be accomplished and you will suffer much disappointment. If anything negative was depicted in this dream, take steps to change it or avoid it entirely.

"lady killer" - slang term You will be offering assistance to someone who has a mental illness they are unaware of. You will find this person the proper help within the week.

to kill an animal Do not become alarmed. You will, within two days, hear a personal story from someone you have a great deal of confidence in. Within five days after that you will hear a different version of the same story repeated to you from another respectable person. Do not waste your time trying to determine the accuracy of either story. Conduct your own research to gain verification. This will put a stop to all gossip and save you many headaches. You will be able to successfully tackle a situation that will become overwhelming for everyone concerned within a three

day period. If anything negative was depicted in this dream, take steps to change it or avoid it entirely. Good luck is with you and many blessings will come to you and your family.

killer Be very aware you will be speaking to someone in a way they choose not to be spoken to. This individual is very temperamental and is likely to respond with anger. This could escalate to a dangerous situation. Do everything necessary to prevent this.

killer whale Be very aware and conscious of how you word your thoughts for the next three days. You will be dealing with someone who is likely to blurt out some very hurtful statements. Keep your conversation to a minimum in order to avoid this. You will also be able to tackle large problems during this time frame and bring them to a successful conclusion. Good luck is with you.

kiln Someone will be very eager to reconcile with you in any capacity within three days. Good luck is with you.

kilogram Be very aware of how you treat someone whom you have invited to a gathering. This individual will feel so left out because of the manner in which you behave that you will permanently drive them away. Make sure people feel welcome in your presence.

kilometer Do not take any nonsense from someone who behaves in a threatening manner toward you, especially for the next two days. You have prior notice of this and can take steps to prevent this occurrence.

kilowatt Avoid those areas you frequent for the next three days because they pose a danger to you. Find a safe haven during this time frame.

kilt Make sure you do not become involved in a manipulative situation that will involve two other people plotting against you. These people will attempt to gain the upper hand and an unfair advantage over you within three days. Remain mentally alert when dealing with others during this cycle.

kimchi Do everything you can to avoid becoming involved with someone who is unreliable. This individual is very lax and appears and disappears at will. In spite of their reassurances of promptness, this person will never show up when expected. Avoid dealing with any new person for the next three days.

kimono Within three days you will expose yourself to some extraordinary activities. These new experiences will bring prosperity to your life and will vastly raise your standard of living.

kin Make it a priority within two weeks to tie up all loose ends regarding financial issues. This will ensure future financial stability.

to dream of your relatives Pay close attention to what

your relatives are doing. This will give you a clue to what is needed in your life or what you need to keep out of your life for the next month. You will also begin working with someone on the development of an idea that will lead you to a brilliant future. Other people will depend on you to take the leadership role when making a big decision that will come up within two days. You will have the strength and the encouragement you need to make the right choices.

someone else's relatives Within two days you will need to make sure you realize you are under no obligation to act in the way anyone else wises you to and make it clear you are under no one else's control. You will be able to rid yourself permanently of someone who thinks they have the authority to control your behavior, manner or speech and thought patterns. You will be able to do this with very little anxiety because of the tact and diplomacy you use to handle this matter. You are headed in the right direction and are on the path toward a prosperous future.

a relative that you do not, in reality, have This could indicate you have a relative you are not aware of. This could also be guiding you to a certain message. For example, if you dream about a brother you do not have, you will need to look up the meaning for brother. Pay attention also, to the character and personality of the person in this dream. This may refer to someone you want to introduce into your life who will be instrumental in bringing prosperity. This is a lucky cycle and you are headed for a brilliant future.

marrying a relative This is an assurance that your life will turn around and you will enjoy a brilliant future. Enjoy life fully and do not take life for granted. This dream is an extremely lucky omen. Someone will come into your life within a few days. This person will come on eagerly and rush you into a friendly relationship. At first you will get mixed messages while on a date and you will feel this person desires romance as well. After you begin to respond to this aspect of their behavior this person will back off quickly and withdraw from the friendship. Take this as a forewarning to enjoy the friendship and take it no further.

to hear the word Practice a tolerant attitude for the next three days. Several situations will arise concurrently that will require controlled personal handling. Remain calm and you will arrive at a successful conclusion.

kindergarten This dream is a very lucky omen. Someone will offer you assistance very quickly with a situation you desire to resolve in a hurry. You are deeply loved and appreciated by those you care about.

to see yourself as a child in kindergarten Avoid all accidents and illnesses that are within your power to prevent, especially for the next three days.

kindle Do not commit yourself to see anything through to completion for the next three days. This would be a grave mistake. You will be unable to complete anything you start during this cycle.

kindling wood Someone you are very impressed with will invite you on an outing. The time is right and if you choose to do so, this will be a very exciting time for you. Good luck

is with you.

king Meditate in your favorite form and demand from your higher power what you specifically need. Eat healthy foods and drink plenty of fluids. You will experience a great deal of prosperity and many blessings will come to you and your family. You will also experience many pleasurable moments with the person you most desire.

king cobra Within two days a shift will occur regarding certain situations in your life and these issues will become unbearable to you. You will, because of your prior knowledge of this, be able to handle everything calmly and successfully. Take steps to eliminate stressful situations from your life. Keep in mind that you do not have to commit to anything you do not want to.

king crab Become very aware of the behavior of another person. This individual will begin to behave very strangely around you and will become increasingly more dangerous. You need to do whatever you can to protect yourself from someone who could cause you harm. Move on with your life as safely as you can.

kingfish Within three days you will attend an event and will experience an instant attraction for someone there. The feeling will be mutual. If you choose, you and this individual will enjoy many memorable future events.

King Lear Guard your privacy and do not compromise on what you need and want in your life.

King, Martin Luther *to dream of the person, the name or the birthday* Take big steps to raise your standard of living by focusing on your goals on a grand scale. Avoid tunnel vision. You will also involve yourself with a group of people who will give immediate support in dealing with a bleak situation. This group will be able to restore stability, give financial assistance and lend confidence where despair and despondency prevailed. Everyone involved will experience a beautiful expression of joy and tranquility. Many blessings will come to you and your family.

Kings *(from the Bible)* This dream is an extremely lucky omen and for the next two months you will experience prosperity. Many blessings will come to you and your family. If you choose, you and another person will also fall deeply in love and will be together for a lifetime.

king snake Make sure you are not channeling your energies into an unfruitful area. Do not overextend yourself for others. Back off and make sure you set limits.

king's ransom *to hear the phrase* Think carefully before signing an agreement to commit yourself to anything. You must also be very aware of your fluid, food and medicine intake. This is the cycle to be very aware of your health. Take steps to protect yourself.

kiosk Be forewarned. You are involved with someone who

is anxious about the depth of the relationship. Extra demands from you will push this person away. Decide whether you wish to pursue this. You must also be acutely aware of someone of the opposite sex who wants to do business with you within three days. Remain calm, put yourself in a stress free environment and enjoy some solitude. You will also receive an abundance of health during this time period.

kipper Within two days someone will communicate their passion for you and their eagerness to be with you. If you choose to pursue this, you will enjoy many mutually satisfying moments together.

kiss Be very aware of events that will be unfolding over the next five days. When making a major decision, take steps to ensure you do not compromise your own needs and desires. During this time period you will also need to take steps to love and pamper yourself. Take the responsibility to improve and maintain your physical appearance and health. This is a good cycle to have all dental and medical work done, as well as anything to improve your physical appearance. This is an extremely lucky cycle for you. Anything negative witnessed in this dream needs to be avoided in reality. Forewarn anyone you recognize to do the same. Take steps to ensure you only experience positive events in your life.

kissing someone of the same sex passionately and affectionately Within a two day period you will enter an extremely lucky cycle and each person involved in your life now will share in your luck. You will also receive services that will enable you to successfully reach your goals. You will reach a greater level of success than you thought possible, particularly with anything you deem to be important. Expect many connections that will help you to meet your goals. You can also anticipate a mega merger and the energy generated between you and those whom you will be working with will promote you to a greater level of success than you anticipated. This also implies you will derive major benefits by attending a festive event, participating is an educational experience, or by attending an event in which someone will take an active interest in promoting you and your plans. A long period of tranquility will follow this and you will enjoy a very prosperous future. Any negative event depicted in this dream can be prevented in reality. Forewarn anyone you dreamed about to do the same.

passionately kissing a same sexed person and finding this distasteful The person you dreamed about represents someone in your life with the same character traits, good or bad, as someone you will be dealing with within five days. You have prior notice of this and can take steps to avoid them if you dislike these aspects of their personality and can take steps to avoid repeating old hang ups and patterns. This person is not someone you will be kissing in reality but represents someone you will be dealing with in some manner. You will know who this person is because of the way they conduct themselves, their character traits, personality, etc. You have prior notice of this and can handle yourself appropriately. This is an extremely lucky cycle and you are headed in the right direction. All plans set into motion during this

time frame will be well received and all business negotiations will work to your benefit. This also implies you will be involved in a certain situation that will be very much to your liking because of tips you will gain through a conversation with someone else. These tips will trigger something that would be advantageous for you to aggressively seek during this time frame. This will be something that will come as a pleasant surprise and will be worth a lot of money. You are headed for a brilliant future. Look for propositions to occur out of the blue during this time frame.

to be kissed by someone you recognize You will either be dealing with this individual or with someone with similar traits. Make sure, for the next three days, you do not tolerate any negative situation from the person this dream represents. This dream may also be representative of someone whom you enjoy being with. You have prior notice of this and may either avoid this individual or take steps to be in their company. Also, take life easier and add more spice to your life. Involve yourself in a variety of situations that will give you enjoyment but play it safe.

to kiss a child Within a few days you will experience great happiness because you will be able to do what you want and gain a certain freedom. You will also be treated better by others. You will receive more affection, consideration and respect.

to kiss a bride Take your best performing co-worker with you on a business trip to expedite the job.

to kiss a bride groom You are depended on to make the correct decision. Proceed on this and you will be successful.

to see a groom kiss the bride Your financial intuition is correct.

to kiss or be kissed repeatedly in an affectionate and passionate way Within three days you will be overwhelmed by the manner in which someone treats you. This individual will treat you in an extremely affectionate manner and you will be verbally assured of their feelings for you. This could be in any capacity, i.e., gratitude or romantic feelings, etc. Their unexpected and genuine words will leave you feeling deeply touched. This will come either from the person you dreamed about or from someone with similar traits and mannerisms. This individual will be very tenacious in their efforts to bring you into their life. Good luck is with you.

kiss someone's body Do not allow yourself to reject an opportunity that, at the moment, is easy to become involved in. Do not take any opportunity for granted that is within your power to take advantage of for the next seven days. Do not assume you will have the same opportunity at a later time. Situations, opportunities and chances with other people will not come so easily at a later time.

to have someone kiss your body Someone will be seeking exactly what you are when it comes to emotional involvement and commitment. You will enjoy complete power when it comes to decision making in this relationship. All situations you felt were impossible are now possible.

kissing a hand, any form This implies one of two things will take place within two days. A very wealthy, nice, shy person will fall deeply in love with you. A joyful event will take place, you will receive a positive reply you have been eagerly waiting for, or you will have an electrical appliance you need to attend to before it falls into disrepair. Otherwise you are headed for a prosperous future.

to kiss an animal Do not behave overly demonstrative with someone you do not know well, especially for the next three days. This would be too overwhelming for this person to accept.

French kiss Stop wasting so much time analyzing the behavior of another. Don't allow this person to slip away. Use your time to focus on the positive aspects of their behavior instead of the negative. You are headed in the right direction both romantically and in business affairs.

if you recognize the person you are French kissing This person is very eager to satisfy your emotional needs. This is a lucky omen that will lead to improvements in matters of love and money.

peck someone's cheek Do not rely on others to run errands for you, especially for the next few days. Run your own errands.

someone pecks you on the cheek Stop imagining the worst. Stay calm and things will work out for the better.

to neck - slang term Make it a point to be available at certain events in order to meet someone who is much older than you. This person will be instrumental in helping you meet your goals. Exposure to social events will be the key ingredient in causing these changes in your life and will dictate how things will unfold within three weeks. The level of intensity will dictate the degree of success.

kissing *to see other people kissing* This dream is an extremely lucky omen and this cycle of luck will remain with you for the next seven days. You will begin to feel an incredible energy and desire to make great changes in your life that will benefit you greatly. Through a conversation with another person you will be shown other paths toward meeting your goals. This conversation may diminish the enthusiasm you had for your original path. This is letting you know that perhaps this is the time to step back and review your choices. It may be that another path will be more beneficial to you or you may decide not to make these changes at this time. Either way, you will make the right decision for your future. You may also find you are lacking romance and this dream may be a reminder to incorporate more of this into your lifestyle in order to add zest to your everyday life. You are definitely headed for a brilliant and prosperous future.

kissing cousins Within five days you will have the opportunity to speak with someone who has a great deal of power and authority. This individual will be very eager to join your team of associates. You will feel grateful you have this person on your side.

kiss of death Within five days you will be the recipient of an unusual and rare offer. Pounce on this offer and be grateful for the opportunity. You will also receive a gift or prize during this time frame.

kiss of life Someone will go to great lengths to impress you within five days. This person has a strong financial base and will be able to provide you with a more comfortable lifestyle

than you ever envisioned. Proceed with confidence, this person finds you refreshing and stimulating and enjoys your company.

kiss of peace You will be appreciated greatly by someone because of the manner in which you treat this person, your speech, and the way you carry yourself around them. Many blessings are with you and you are headed for a brilliant future.

kitchen Within the week, someone who feels a deep gratitude to you for responding to them in a time of need will use this cycle to express these feelings. This individual will also bring you a small gift of appreciation. You will feel overcome by emotion over this person's words of gratitude.

kitchen cabinet *any form* Within seven days someone will become very aware of you in a very special way. This person will pursue you romantically and will become determined to marry you. They will proceed slowly yet persistently in the direction of marriage. If you choose to pursue this, the relationship will be long lived and you will enjoy prosperity. Follow your instincts. Your hunches will be correct, especially for the next three days.

kitchenette Within a three day period someone will be very eager to grant your desires. Use this cycle to ask for what you need and this wish will be granted.

kitchen gadgets You are unaware that someone is completely infatuated with you. You will find out about this within three days and will be involved in a thrilling cycle for both of you. This will develop into mutual love and delightful physical contact. This is also a good omen for health and love.

kitchen garden Regardless of anything that is going on in your life right now you will, within five days, be able to overcome any long term burden. You are headed in the right direction and will be experiencing more pleasure and many more joyous social events in the future. You will focus on achieving a peaceful and stress free life.

Kitchen God *(Chinese God)* Any industry, business or company you choose to involve yourself in will be tremendously lucky and all mergers and cooperation between companies will be lucky. You will become very detailed, organized and structured in ways that will make successful moves with very little stress. You are headed for a very prosperous future and many blessings are coming to you and your family.

kitchen sink Become very organized when dealing with delicate situations that will arise within the week. Make sure you keep yourself emotionally intact and follow your own plans and rules. Do not allow anyone to assume you are willing to commit to a particular issue you have planned. Monitor your behavior carefully to ensure you are not misunderstood. This also implies an unpredictable situation will occur within two days that will bring you immense pleasure. Pay attention to the contents of the sink. They will offer you additional clues to the meaning of this dream.

kitchen tongs This is a good luck symbol for you. You will have the precise words you need to communicate with another person to resolve a long standing problem that has been plaguing both of you. This will happen within three days.

kitchenware Take steps to appreciate the efforts of your loved ones. Do something special to show your appreciation, especially for the next three days.

kite A mystery that has been plaguing you for some time will surface shortly. Everything that has been a puzzle to you will suddenly be made clear and you will fully understand the direction you need to take. This is an extremely lucky omen.

kitten A close friend or family member will ask you for assistance that you must refuse. Tactfully and diplomatically remain uninvolved.

Kitty Hawk For the next five days all legal matters will be settled in your favor.

kitty litter Do everything you can to make younger people feel more comfortable in your presence and make sure all their needs are met, especially for the next three days.

kiwi Concentrate on your finances and detail each move. Within two weeks you will need a greater cash flow than you have anticipated. Take steps now to ensure you have extra cash in order to avoid the extra stress a deficit would cause. You are headed for a very brilliant future.

klutz You have been led to believe you can fully trust a certain person to handle large responsibilities. Once you put your trust in this person, you will be let down in a big way. This individual fully believes they are capable of handling this kind of responsibility but their ego is larger than their abilities. Be aware of this and do not risk anything of importance.

knapsack Within the week all anguish will disappear. Do everything you can to uplift yourself and add enjoyment to your life, especially for the next three days.

knead *to knead bread* Carefully delegate specific chores to those you are dealing with. Some people are not equipped emotionally, mentally or physically to handle the tasks you have assigned to them. You will save time and energy if, at the start, you delegate tasks to those who can handle them.

knee Become very aggressive in the manner in which you conduct yourself around someone you want to involve in your life romantically. Because of your mannerisms, you will not be taken seriously.

kneecap You will need to use a variety of ways to meet your goals but they are reachable if you seek several alternative methods.

knee jerk Be careful associates do not take advantage of you, especially for the next two days.

kneel *to see others kneel* Someone you supported in the past will be eager to involve you in a venture you very much desire to become involved in. This will occur within two days. Good luck will be with you in this project.

to kneel Do not allow any negative situation to develop over the next five days. You have the ability to maintain yourself and all personal issues in a positive fashion.

to see people kneeling at an altar For the next five days anything you felt was impossible is now a possibility. Favors will be granted more readily in this time period. You are headed in the right direction and many blessings will come to you and your family.

to kneel at an altar Do not allow yourself to become entrapped in a situation that will leave you defenseless, especially for the next three days.

in any other form Do everything you can to avoid creating suspicions and do not allow jealousy to develop in others because of the way in which you carry yourself. This will backfire within two days.

kneepad Within three days you will be responsible for breaking an expensive piece of hardware or tool. Do everything necessary to avoid having to lay out any new expenses to replace what is broken.

knickers You will be traveling within the month. Start making your plans now for a safe and stress free journey. You will have many precious moments to remember.

knickknack Be aware chemicals you are handling may be harmful, especially for the next three days.

knife You will have the mental clarity to develop specific and structured plans that will pay rich rewards in the future. You are putting yourself on the path toward a brilliant and prosperous future.

to see a knife used in a violent way Be relentless and aggressive when pursuing your goals, especially for the next three days.

switch blade Before you volunteer for anything, make sure you know exactly what is required of you and do not allow your time to be misused. This is especially important for the next three days. Good luck is with you.

knife edge Do not borrow money for the next five days because you will be unable to repay this loan.

with blood You will receive an unexpected windfall within the month. You will enjoy a prosperous future and will put the money to good use to reap even greater rewards.

knight Become aware within three days that you need to assume responsibility for relationships that are precious to you. Make sure you do not become lax in those areas you need to apply yourself to. Use your creativity to spark passion, love, to instill mutual respect, and to keep relationships from becoming stale.

knit *to knit* This dream is a very lucky omen. Do not allow secret meetings, hidden issues or conspiracies to transpire that are within your power to prevent, particularly for the next three days.

knitting needle You will have the team effort you need to protest and fight for a cause. Good luck is with you.

knitwear You will make a financial decision within three days that will raise your standard of living and lead to a brilliant future.

knob Become more demonstrative toward someone who cares deeply about you and needs you to show your feelings toward them. For the next week this behavior will be greatly appreciated. Look up door knob for an added definition to this dream.

to see a doorknob that appears locked Insist on special privileges and considerations for the next five days and do not allow others to assume you can handle more than you can. Let others know you need special assistance and consideration during this time period. This is the perfect cycle to make these requests.

to see a doorknob that appears unlocked It will be very important within a two day period to have a meeting with certain individuals to make connections and the necessary requests before an important situation starts to develop. This will ensure it does not fall apart before it takes off. Stay on top of this and you will be able to make the correct adjustments in time. Pay attention to this now and everything will fall into place as you desire. Good luck is with you and your family. You are headed for a brilliant future.

knock *to hear a rap at the door* Be very alert for the next three days of anything that is unfolding in an unusual way. Stay on top of any out of the ordinary occurrence to ensure it does not develop into a negative situation. It is within your power to alter any situation and to maintain tranquility.

in any other form (i.e., to knock a hole in wall, floor, etc.) Within three days you will have to deal with someone whom you know for a fact likes to create chaos and stressful situations. Prepare yourself during this time period because this individual will create a monster of a situation that will escalate to the point of never returning back to normalcy. Make sure you take steps to avoid this situation by making other plans for amusement during this time frame.

to hear strange knocking from a machine, toy, etc. Do not lose your sense of alertness, especially for the next three days and do not let down your guard. Do not allow yourself to be persuaded into going someplace that could represent a hazard to you and remain alert in all aspects of your life. Be careful when involving yourself in new situations with another person that could lead to accidents. This individual could unwittingly cause something to occur that could hurt you. It is very important, during this time period, to choose wisely what you will or will not involve yourself in.

to hear knocking at the door, etc., and not answer Within seven days you will be invited out by someone you do not know very well. This individual will terrify you because of their strange manner and will, at some point, become very dangerous. This will be a horrifying experience and you will not be able to find the means to escape. Do everything you can to avoid anything to do with this situation. You have prior notice of this and can prevent this occurrence. You also must avoid going to any unfamiliar places or to someone else's house whom you do not know well. You will be held against your will in a life threatening situation.

knockout *to see someone else's defeat* For the next three days any negative event in this dream that relates to reality needs to be avoided or changed. During this time period you must also take steps to keep any unusual situation from developing without your knowledge. Remain alert in order to detect anything that may otherwise be overlooked.

to see something knocked out of the area You are definitely making all the correct moves and are motivating yourself to achieve success. You will also find a connection you have long wanted to make with a certain person but have been unable to pin down will be made within the week. Anything you felt was impossible in the past is now possible. Any get away place you have in mind will provide you with the mini vacation you need and will give you many pleasurable moments. You are headed for a brilliant future.

to be knocked out by anything Someone is plotting to violate your rights within five days for their own emotional gratification. They will attempt to persuade you to become involved in a situation that will become increasingly distasteful, sexually or in any other capacity. This involvement will go against your better judgment and will. Do not put yourself in the position where you will have to compromise yourself in order to get out safely. This is preventable. Good luck is with you.

knocked out *to see someone knocked out due to drunkenness* Within ten days you will be entering an extremely lucky cycle and each person involved in your life will share in this cycle. You will receive services that will allow you to complete your goals successfully and you will achieve a higher level of success than you anticipated regarding anything you place a high degree of importance on. You can expect, during this time period, to make many wonderful connections that will assist you in grasping and meeting your goals. You will merge successfully with other people and the synergism created will advance you to a greater level of success than you hoped for. This also implies you will gain benefits by attending a social event, through an educational experience, or by attending a gathering in which one person will demonstrate an interest in you and your plans and offer their assistance in helping you to complete them. A long period of tranquility will follow this and you can expect a brilliant future. Any negative event portended in this dream can be avoided in reality. Forewarn anyone you recognized in the dream to take the appropriate steps.

knock over Think ahead and within four days you will be able to prepare yourself for a conversation with someone who is involved in a certain situation. This will allow you the time to get everyone involved together to discuss how to put a lid on a particular issue to stop a negative event from occurring. Alert others now to the possibility of this taking place. Many blessings will come to you and your family.

knot Do not place yourself in a situation where a disagreement with a special person will escalate into a major argument.

to untie a knot Anything you felt was impossible is now possible. For the next five days you will successfully achieve what you desire.

know *"to know better"* Within five days someone who harbors a secret hatred against you will attempt to sabotage you in your attempt to steer a situation a certain way on someone else's behalf. Although this person knows you are right, they will go against you in spite of the destruction it may wreak on others. You are attempting to work everything out so everyone can enjoy a more prosperous future. You have prior notice of this and can take steps to prevent this interference. This person has no idea of the depth of hardship they will bring to others.

for you or anyone in the dream to know what to do or say Be alert to someone who, in spite of their pleasant behavior, harbors a deep animosity toward you. Make sure this person does not gain the upper hand in any situation that involves you. You will also receive an unexpected financial windfall.

know/knowing - to know Within five days you will deal with a person who will go to great lengths to keep someone you are close to from maintaining a close relationship and will do everything they can to destroy your close feelings with that special person. They will devise a distasteful scenario for the sole purpose of causing a split in your relationship and it will be done in such a subtle way that it will be difficult to determine what instigated this split up. Be very alert to anyone who harbors a secret hatred toward you. You will also experience a financial windfall.

"know how" You will be able to muster up the energy and anything else it takes, within five days, to follow your instincts regarding a particular situation you feel should be taking place. In spite of what others feel, this situation needs to occur. It will bring vast improved changes into your life and into the lives of others. Proceed with confidence. Everything will work out as it should.

"know it all" Take a firm stand, within three days, with someone who has developed a free and easy attitude with your money. Handle this in such a way that it will not occur in the future.

"know nothing" Play games of chance for the next five days. You stand a good chance of winning.

knuckle You have three days to keep any negative occur-

rence in this dream from becoming a reality. Within four days you will also need to make sure you are in the right physical condition to maintain a steady pace and handle the things you need to take care of. The moment you begin to feel overwhelmed, back off and relax.

knuckleball Someone is sending a nonverbal signal and is desiring your assistance. You have been unable to pinpoint the problem and need to be more alert for the next three days in order to offer the right help.

knucklebone This dream is offering you a clue of what you need to avoid for the next three days. You must also be very careful to avoid any facial injuries during this time period that are within your power to prevent. Good luck is with you.

knucklehead You will attend what you thought would be a very elegant event. It will turn out to be quite the contrary. Be prepared to casually take what comes, and you will find it very enjoyable. You are headed for a very prosperous future.

knuckle joint A group of people will request a meeting with you to discuss a certain situation that requires your input. You will be able to express yourself very succinctly. Good luck is with you.

knuckles *rapping* An upsetting episode will occur within five days and you are being made aware of this now so you can either take steps to avoid it or change the circumstances. You have enough advance notice of this and you will be able to handle this appropriately. Make sure anyone you dreamed about is also made aware of this situation and can act accordingly. Do what you can to ensure you and everyone involved experiences only positive expressions in your lives. This also implies someone will speak with you about a particular issue that is taking place in their life. This issue is something they are very dissatisfied with and they only need a listening ear. Do what you can to ease this person's stress. Remain personally uninvolved. You will also be able to determine, through a heightened awareness triggered by this dream, what you need to be taking care of regarding a particular issue that is taking place in your life. This will be very advantageous to you and will bring you a prosperous future.

koala Do not place limits on your expressions of feelings for someone special, especially for the next three days.

Kodak Within the month you will become a wealthy person due to some very unusual circumstances. You have prior notice of this and can increase your chances by remaining alert to new opportunities and by playing games of chance.

kohl Push yourself and do exactly as you wish. Do not deprive yourself of intimate moments you wish to enjoy with someone of the opposite sex. This is a very lucky omen and many beautiful events will come out of this relationship. You are headed in the right direction and prosperity will be yours.

kohlrabi Develop trust in someone with whom you can delegate certain responsibilities in order to free your time for more enjoyable pastimes.

Kokopelli This is an omen of victory in all levels of your life. This dream is also telling you that the person who interests you is not as attentive as you would like. This is a minor problem. Restrain yourself from complaining about unimportant issues. This person is on their way toward a brilliant future and wants you to be a part of it. You will also come into your own wealth and this process will begin within a month. You will enjoy financial stability and money will come to you from many different directions. You have no reason not to enjoy all of it. You will also receive the verification you need involving the feelings of a very special person. You will soon hear words of love that you have been longing to hear. This individual is generous, kind and very tenacious about having you become a part of their life. Good luck is with you and many blessings will come to you and your family.

Koran Within three days make sure you are not dealing with obstacles that have not been addressed that will keep you from developing the kind of relationship you desire. Address these invisible blocks as soon as you can.

Korea For the next five days take extra steps to protect your liquid investments. Set up an appointment with those who can offer you a safer way to protect your money. This dream may also be used as a reference point in time. If you dream of this country and see its name used in any context, the dream message will occur on this day.

kosher Do not allow anyone to bully you into doing something you find distasteful for the next two days.

K ration Make sure for the next five days you keep the lines of communication open and allow conversations to flow openly without any restraint. This is important because you will gain information that is important for you to have. You can use this information to change those people whom you wish to maintain a close relationship with.

kraut This dream is an extremely lucky omen. Make sure you follow all rules and instructions. This will save you time and money, especially regarding traffic situations. This is particularly important for the next two days.

Kremlin Be very alert to important information that will be coming in. This may also be used as a reference point in time. If you dream of this place and see its name used in any context, the dream message will occur on this day.

Krishna A new and mysterious acquaintance will enter your life within three days. This person will share many amusing anecdotes with you that will give you many moments of pleasure. You are headed for a brilliant future.

krona You will make connections with the right person for a particular project or event you have in mind. This person will be totally reliable.

krypton You will receive special knowledge, skills or ideas from an older person. This individual will take delight in helping you to develop skills they have expertise in. Within seven days, you will develop plans that will utilize these skills and ensure a wonderful future.

Kubla Khan Someone who has a difficult time controlling their jealousy will want to involve you in their life. Having prior notice of this you can decide how to limit your involvement with this person.

Ku Klux Klan Within three days you will have a successful and fruitful conversation with someone that will bring forth some important facts to enlighten you. This will allow you to pinpoint certain details you would otherwise overlook.

kumquat Within three days take time out to choose someone you can delegate certain tasks to and can rely on until you resolve a present situation.

kung fu Do everything you can, for the next four days, to encourage a special person to get closer to you. Put love into action and you will be successful in developing this closeness.

kurd Do whatever you can, within three days, to project the image you desire to a special person. Follow your instincts and you will achieve success.

Kuwait Set aside time within three days to determine the areas in your life you are most vulnerable in. Prepare yourself in such a way that these vulnerable areas are not open to attack by another and plan ahead of time the ways in which to correctly handle an upcoming situation. This dream may also be used as a reference point in time. If you dream of this country and see its name used in any context, the dream message will occur on this day.

L

L Prepare yourself now for the manner in which you must conduct yourself when you meet someone who absolutely overwhelms you. Something about someone you will meet within five days will attract you greatly. You will be at an event, etc., and be overwhelmed by the presence of a particular individual. Because you have prior notice of this, you can prepare a method in which to make yourself known to this person and a way in which to make yourself attractive to them. Good luck is with you and you are headed for a prosperous future.

lab Drive a hard bargain for the next three days when you are purchasing an item you desire. Others will respond to the price you quote. Good luck is with you.

label This dream is a very lucky omen and you will achieve victory in any area of your life you desire, especially for the next week. It is also important to pay close attention to what is printed on the label. This will provide an additional clue to the meaning of this dream. You are definitely headed for a brilliant future.

labor Someone you greatly admire will unexpectedly ask you to attend a social function with them. You will have a wonderful, enjoyable time and the evening will fall into place exactly as it should. This person will never contact you again simply because of their inability to commit.

labor *to see a woman in labor* You will hear of a birth of twins. Apply yourself and express your ideas graphically within a few weeks. This will give others the chance to really visualize your ideas and this will work to your advantage. A compromise on an agreement will end problems and you will be better off in the long run.

to be a woman in labor You will be, within the next five days, given a gift of greater mental inventiveness by your higher power. Put this gift to practical use in order to change your present circumstances. You will experience instant wealth, a brilliant future and have the clarity of thought you need to correctly direct the fortune you will be coming into. Make sure anything negative you dream of that could become a reality does not occur and take steps to ensure you experience only positive expressions in life.

laboratory Determine what you may be doing that will result in a loss of financial security. Pay close attention to your behavior and take steps to change the aspect that will cost you financially, especially for the next three days. Within three days you will also have the opportunity to get away for a very relaxing mini vacation. This will offer you a more wonderful time than you have ever imagined. An abundance of creative thoughts will come to you during this time period. Keep a record of these ideas and move on them for great benefits. Good luck is with you.

Labor Day Within five days someone who was previously cold to you will warm up and treat you with more respect. This will confuse you and lead you to be suspicious. Put these feelings behind you. This individual has simply had a change of heart.

labor party Motivate others to rally around you and to offer assistance with a task that you need help with. This is the perfect cycle to get that help you have been looking for.

labor room You will begin receiving money from a billed source, but because of circumstances over the next week, you will receive less than anticipated. Be patient, but relent-less. In time you will receive the full amount. You may also be required to perform physical labor without pay. You must also be very aware that someone you have put out of your life and has promised to leave you alone will break this promise within three days. Prepare yourself in such a way that it will be difficult for this person to pin you down. Make it very clear you want nothing to do with them. Prepare yourself emotionally to deal with this delicate situation. Organize your thoughts and feelings so you will not be misunderstood and make sure you are not willing to commit to something you are unwilling to. You will be able to get your point across in a tactful way without offending anyone. Proceed with caution and you will successfully handle this delicate situation.

to see a delivery You will hear of a birth of twins. Apply yourself and express your ideas graphically within a few weeks. This will give others the chance to really visualize your ideas and this will work to your advantage. A compromise on an agreement will end problems and you will be better off in the long run.

to be in a delivery You will be, within the next five days, given a gift of greater mental inventiveness by your higher power. Put this gift to practical use in order to change your present circumstances. You will experience instant wealth, a brilliant future and have the clarity of thought that you need to correctly direct the fortune you will be coming into. Make sure anything negative you dream of that could become a reality does not occur and take steps to ensure you experience only positive expressions in life.

Labrador Retriever Do not allow others to talk you into something that at first seems innocuous but later has an element of danger. For the next three days, do not become involved in anything, even if it appears safe.

labyrinth Be very aware that someone you will be very attracted to will, within five days, be emotionally disturbed and will be unable to help themselves. Avoid becoming involved in a situation that will make your life very unhappy.

lace Within two days assess your present situation so you can take the correct steps to move forward successfully.

lacquer Make every effort you can, for the next four days, to behave in such a way that will bring someone you desire close to you. This person is not yet involved with you and at first you will feel they are not interested in you in the way you desire. During this time period, you will also experience an abundance of health, a financial windfall will come your way, and you are headed for a prosperous future.

lacrosse Someone will furnish you information about someone you are romantically interested in. The information you receive will be reliable. Good luck is with you.

lactate Do not waste time by allowing a friend to handle certain tasks for you that they are unable to handle. This will lead to disappointment on your part. This individual will lead you to believe they can handle these jobs but will fail in their effort.

lactose Remember the mistakes you have made in the past. Do not dwell on these errors but use them as an experience to avoid making the same mistakes in the present.

lad You are loved beyond your imagination and can remove any doubts you may have about a special person in your life and their feelings toward you. This individual's feelings toward you are genuine and you will enjoy a positive and prosperous future with this person. You will experience much joy and this cycle will bring you an abundance of health and blessings.

ladder You will be taking all of the right steps to experience victory within the next three days. You are headed for a brilliant future. Move quickly and do not waste time.

fireman's ladder The connection you want to make with a special person that you have found difficult in the past will, within seven days, be a very distinct possibility. Use this cycle for any communications you desire to make.

to go up a ladder or to see anyone else go up a ladder The emotional feelings from another that you were deprived of in the past will be given to you within five days. This person has discovered a way to demonstrate their feelings. You will bask in feelings of appreciation and love.

to go under a ladder or to see someone else go under a ladder. Decide what needs to be reformed and act on it quickly so those who are involved can start enjoying a new lifestyle.

if the ladder is too short Make sure, for the next two weeks, you are not caught short financially. Begin now to find ways to increase your cash flow in order to eliminate unnecessary stress.

easily adjustable ladder Within five days you will be able to satisfy the romantic and sexual demands of another.

hard to adjust ladder You will receive news of the death of a male family member.

ladder back chair Begin acting in the proper manner in order to handle a situation that is occurring now. If not handled properly, this situation will escalate to the point of chaos. Get it under control within five days because it will be far more difficult once it has gotten out of hand.

ladies' room Be very careful you do not have clothing stolen from you. Within the week you will be missing some clothing items unless you take precautions to prevent a theft.

ladle For the next three days closely adhere to the law in order to avoid a citation.

lady This dream is an extremely lucky omen. You will successfully achieve a romantic goal you are after within five days.

First Lady For the next seven days you will experience a deep sense of confidence and balance. As a result, you will be able to take care of those issues that demand this aspect of your personality. Use this time period to work on those is-

sues in your life you want to make changes in. You will have the opportunity to bring prosperity into your life at the level you desire. You are on the path toward a brilliant future.

ladybug Within five days you will receive the proper medical treatment for a long standing problem and all medical advice will be totally reliable. You will rid yourself of all pre-existing problems and all problems that are developing at the present time. You will also need to take the proper measures to prevent fire on any of your properties.

ladyfinger You will have many passionate nights to remember with the person you most desire. This will begin to develop within three days. This is very much the cycle for lovers.

lady in waiting You will come to a decision with that special person in your life that will be mutually satisfying and will also meet all of your financial needs.

"lady killer" *slang term* You will be offering assistance to someone who has a mental illness they are unaware of. You will find this person the proper help within the week.

Lady of the Lake You will enjoy yourself immensely while on a vacation. This will be an unexpected invitation to a distant city and you will have a very safe journey.

lady slipper You will find someone who will provide you with the finer things in life as well as the expenses to cover your basic needs. You will meet this person within five days and both of you will fall head over heels in love. Go for it.

lager The plans you have made involving another person will not work out. Do not allow yourself to become too emotionally involved and do not become obsessed. Your feelings will be hurt if you do not remain detached. Do not set yourself up for a disappointment.

lagoon A friend of yours has come into some money and wants to share their pleasures with you. You will also enjoy a pleasurable surprise from someone you would least expect this from.

lair Do everything necessary to check out the person you are romantically involved with. This individual does not have the same sexual inclination as you and is under the impression you are aware of this. You will also be involved in some unusual occurrences that will bring you prosperity and an increase in your health status.

lake This dream is an extremely lucky omen. You will become aware of the emotions someone feels for you that, until now, were kept hidden. Because of this knowledge, you will want to surrender to this person. If you choose to pursue this, you will enjoy a lengthy relationship filled with love. Pay close attention to the events in this dream. You have the time to prevent or alter any negative event and all positive events should be included in reality. This is a perfect cycle for demonstrating the love you feel for another person. An event will also take place within the family that will be rejoiced by all. Many blessings will come to you and your family.

Lama You will see a definite improvement in your health and finances within five days because something unusual will occur that will stimulate your cash flow.

Lamaze For the next five days you will be surprised at the amount of support you get from the opposite sex. This will be a very good support system that will back you when you most need it.

lamb Within five days a close friend will strongly urge you to make lifestyle changes. This is a great cycle to experience many new events. Good luck is with you.

Lamb of God You will be extremely fortunate and will experience an abundance of prosperity. Many blessings will be with you and your family for a seven day cycle.

lamb quarters You are loved beyond your imagination.

lambskin For the next five days be very aware of your behavior and do not push someone to behave in a romantic fashion. This person is resisting this behavior because of their inability to behave in this manner. Accept this individual for who they are and for what they are willing to do. In time they will be able to express themselves in a more acceptable fashion.

lame Do everything necessary to avoid someone who slacks off, especially for the next three days. This behavior will make you very irritable and anxious. Avoid this person at all costs.

lame duck Do everything you can to avoid inadvertently violating the rights of others.

Lamentations *(Book of the Bible)* For the next five days avoid those people who enjoy provoking anger in others.

laminate *to laminate* Within five days a special friend will send you a small gift through the mail.

lamp Apply yourself, for the next five days, so you can present your ideas graphically to others. They will then be able to visualize your unusual plans. This will be of great benefit to you.

> *to turn on* Be very confident and determined in the manner you go about handling things over the next two days. Others need to see this from you.

> *to turn off* Avoid someone who enjoys keeping others at a distance. This person does this in order to avoid the closeness of a relationship and will destroy any effort you make to develop closeness. Go on with your life without this person in it.

lampblack For the next three days you will experience many temporary delays on a project you are trying to bring to a conclusion. Do everything you can to calmly accept this and to go about your business in a stress free manner.

lamplighter Within five days you will be able to resolve all conflicts you have with a special person.

lampoon Do not allow episodes from the past to ruin the present, especially for the next three days.

lamppost Allow a professional person to bring clarity to a confusing situation that will arise within three days. A specially trained person will quickly cut through all of the confusion.

lamprey eel For the next two days control your moods and do not allow them to destroy present situations that may not get a chance to develop if you continue your present behavior. Allow situations to develop in the manner they were intended.

lampshade Within three days you will get a call from someone who does not have the courage to express their desire to rekindle a relationship. If you wish to reconcile, just give this individual a little push and you will reunite in a more loving, stronger relationship. Good luck is with you.

> *glass* Someone is planning to violate your rights, within the next five days, for their own gratification. This person will try to manipulate you into becoming involved in a situation that will become increasingly distasteful to you sexually or in any other capacity. This involvement will go against your will and against your better judgment. Do not allow yourself to be placed in a position where you will have to compromise yourself in order to get out safely. This is preventable. Good luck is with you.

lance Within three days make a new request for assistance concerning a plan you wish to execute. You have previously been turned down by someone, but this person will have a change of heart. It will be easier for them to come around if you make the first move. Good luck is with you.

Lancelot This is a very lucky omen, especially for domestic unity and harmony. Do everything necessary to help bring about domestic harmony and to schedule special events together. Do everything you can to help another person to build up their sense of security within a romantic union. You will benefit by this renewed sense of security.

land *lush land* You will benefit from many prosperous changes in your life within the month. You will either inherit land or someone will bequeath a valuable item to you. You will also benefit from work well done in the past. This time period will be very good to seek new ways to turn a profit. The lusher the land, the greater the benefits you will receive. Good luck is with you and many blessings will come to you and your family.

arid land Do what you can to begin the process of developing a healthy attitude, a healthy environment and a healthier diet. It is important you do this in order to ensure that within two weeks your life will turn around because of changes you will make in your life. Good luck and many blessings are with you.

property Within three days you will need a tremendous amount of control. You will meet someone you find irresistibly attractive. The feeling is mutual. If you choose to pursue this, you will enjoy yourself immensely and will enjoy a very tight, solid relationship.

landfill Within two weeks an extraordinary, unusual situation will occur that will prompt you to relocate. This will be a very fortuitous change. Good luck is with you.

landholder For the next two days, display your most charismatic personality as well as your educational skills to others because you will then be able to influence and win over a very powerful and influential individual who will back you in your goals. Go for the impossible.

landing craft You are deeply missed and will soon hear of this.

inoperative landing craft For the next week carry yourself in such a way that you appear younger than you are in order to gain the confidence of those you want to support you. This will also lend a positive image of yourself to others.

landing gear Do not set yourself up to receive less than you deserve because of the way in which you will handle a particular situation. Do everything you can to get the positive response you need from others. You have prior notice of this and can do much to encourage a better outcome.

landing strip Any negative situation you dream of can either be altered or avoided in reality within three days. All positive events need to be encouraged. A request you make for assistance will also work out very successfully because you will choose the right person to join your team.

landlocked You will fail to handle a situation in the correct manner within three days. Do whatever you can now to avoid failure. Regroup and rethink this situation in order to handle this correctly the first time.

landlord Do not allow anyone into your life who has already revealed hang ups and bad habits that you choose not to put up with. Get on with your life without this person in it.

landlubber You will have a wonderful time in the company of someone you care about at a special retreat, park, etc. Good luck is with you.

landmark Pay close attention to the particular landmark that you dreamed about. This will point to a clue that will lead you to an event or opportunity that needs to be investi-

gated and explored. This opportunity will then lead to an advantage that will enhance your lifestyle or the ongoing projects you are now working on. Make sure any negative event you saw in this dream does not become a reality and take steps to ensure you experience only positive expressions in your life.

land mine Do not overindulge in alcohol, food or medications. This will not agree with you. Other people will support your desire not to become ill.

land of nod For the next three days, the manner in which you present yourself, your eagerness, your enthusiasm and desire to handle a personal problem for someone else will win over their confidence.

landowner A partnership you desire to enter into with another person will be extremely successful and prosperous. Good luck is with you. All negative events connected with this dream can be turned around to the positive.

landscape For the next three days, in order to make yourself clearly understood, put all your plans in writing and graphically plot out each of your ideas. This is an extremely lucky dream for lovers. The more beautiful the landscaping, the more fortuitous the union. Each improvement you desire will come to be.

landscape gardener For the next two days carefully watch your paperwork. Make sure you do not misplace any important papers in order to avoid a panic situation at the last moment.

landslide Anything you do with a partner, for the next two days, will be a complete disaster. Back off and regroup yourself in order to competently handle this situation.

lane You have two days to turn any negative situation connected with this dream into a positive situation. You have enough time to ensure this works to your favor.

language Pay attention to the language spoken in this dream. Someone who speaks this language will enter your life and will greatly influence you in such a way that your standard of living will improve. You will be able to put yourself in the position to achieve a brilliant future. Be on the lookout for people who speak this language or areas where it is spoken and you will find a way to connect with this particular situation. You can also prepare yourself for an unexpected pleasure trip. You will have a safe and enjoyable journey. All business trips will be successful if taken during this cycle.

lanolin You will be invited out for an intimate dinner and conversation by someone who has a great deal of wealth but doesn't look the part. You will have the opportunity now to deepen this relationship, if you choose this path. This dream is a very lucky omen and you are headed for a brilliant future. You must also take all the necessary steps to avoid or to change any negative situation this dream foretells. Make sure you experience only positive expressions in your life, especially for the next five days.

lantern Give an increase in salary to those who deserve it. This is the cycle to do this. Good luck is with you.

lantern fish Within two days tackle those big plans you feel are overwhelming. This is the time to move ahead on this. Do not allow others to stop you.

lantern jaw Make time for those things you feel you need to become more educated in. This is the perfect cycle to get that extra training you need. You will find it easy to grasp what you are after.

lap Within three days you will find yourself among a group of people who want more control over a situation you are dealing with. Take steps to determine what each person is capable of handling and delegate each task accordingly.
to sit in someone's lap If you recognize the person, this individual will be very affectionate and willing to help you in any way they can whether this is emotional or financial in nature.
if you do not recognize this person Someone will tell you the next step to take that will be instrumental in the decision you have to make within three days. This decision will bring you a more secure status whether this is in an emotional or financial way. Move with confidence and everything will fall into place exactly as you have envisioned. Use this cycle to your advantage to bring about changes in those aspects of your life you desire.
to have someone sit in your lap Be sure you set aside some time within three days to clear your thoughts and brainstorm in order to pinpoint the suspicions you have about a certain person. This will allow you the chance to devise a plan to determine if these suspicions are valid and, if so, how to resolve them. You will be successful in dealing with this issue if you motivate yourself to do so. This cycle will give you the best opportunity to find the answers you are looking for. You are headed for a brilliant future.

lapdog Avoid anything, for the next three days, that creates friction. This dream is an extremely lucky omen and good luck is with you.

lapel Be very gentle when dealing with someone who is very shy, especially for the next three days. If you do not handle this situation correctly the first time around, it will be difficult to involve this person in your life and impossible to reinvolve them. Do it right the first time.

Lapis *semiprecious stone* This dream is a lucky omen for you and for all those who are interested and involved in your immediate situation. You are in a powerful five day cycle for achievement and for accomplishing everything you attempt. You will also develop more integrity. People in your life will demonstrate greater love and affection toward you. Do nothing to slow down the momentum of those feelings. Every-thing in your life will flow more smoothly and you will be blessed with better health and more tranquility.

Lapland Within two days you and a particular group of people will reach a decision about resolving a situation that needs to be taken care of.

laptop You will not be rejected.

lapwing Any surgery scheduled within the month will be extremely successful.

larceny A certain person has designed an evil, conspiratorial plot that will involve you as a major player without your knowledge. You will be a pawn for this individual to use in order to reach a goal. This will conclude in a very dangerous situation and could cost your life. Be very aware of the roles you play in the lives of others. This episode will begin within the week. Take steps to protect yourself and since you have prior notice of this you can take the proper steps. Good luck is with you.

lard Take steps to prevent damage to those things you take an unusual pride in. Protect your belongings.

large Pay attention to anything that is represented in this dream in a large size. This will provide a major clue to something or someone who will be entering your life and will give you the means to expand your life. You will then be able to experience an increase in prosperity, especially for the next three days. Anything you see presented larger than life also indicates something you will need to focus on in reality. If it represents a negative event, take steps to keep this from becoming a reality. It if represents something positive, promote it to the fullest and take steps to incorporate it into your life. You will also gain the clarity of thought needed to assist someone who desires you greatly to express their feelings and plans for your future together. This cycle will give you the ability to bring your ideas together in tangible form. If you choose, this is the perfect cycle to easily tackle those big ideas and plans you felt were too overwhelming in the past. You are definitely headed for a brilliant future.
large opening A cluster of events will occur one after the other with each bringing you a tremendous amount of joy, wonder and awe because things are happening so quickly. You will also possess a powerful energy you are going to be able to direct and control. At the same time these events are taking place you will be able to bring other people under your complete control. Because you have prior notice of this you will be able, within five days, to direct this energy in such a way to successfully complete anything you wish in a superb way. You will be able to overcome any difficult obstacle and it will now be very simple to deal with it. Your intuition will be right on target. Follow your hunches about a new relationship. Many blessings are with you and your family.

large intestine Be very aware a certain individual will set you up in order to take advantage of you. Do not allow yourself to be jerked around or taken advantage of, especially for the next three days.

largemouth bass For the next three days take special care of the outer surface of your body. Make sure you avoid nicks, cuts and bruises. This dream is an extremely lucky omen and anything you felt was impossible is now possible.

lark Do whatever you can to involve yourself with something unusual and outrageous. This will point you in the direction of greater riches and prosperity. Your financial situation will vastly improve.

larva Do not allow another person to impose their beliefs and ideas on you. Take a strong stand for the next three days because someone will attempt to sway you into accepting what is unacceptable to you. If you do become involved, you will come to regret it tremendously.

larynx Any trouble that develops within the next two days will be easily resolved. Do not panic.

lasagna Within three days you will be involved with someone you greatly desire. This person will treat you in the manner you wish. Both of you will enjoy deep passionate moments, if you so desire. You will both make plans for the future you can adopt and live with. This will be a long term relationship. This dream is a good luck omen for those who are in love. You are headed for a brilliant future full of riches and health.

laser Use the next three days to renew your feelings for another so they can respond appropriately to your feelings. Let others know your true feelings.

laser disc Regroup in order to respond appropriately to a problem that will arise within three days. You will have the courage and determination to handle this correctly.

laser light Manipulative obstacles or ideas have mentally kept you from moving in the direction you desire. Within three days your path will become clear of those mental blocks that keep you from moving ahead. This cycle is also good for the successful conclusions of all negotiations, agreements, litigations, etc. Make any revisions in your plans that will facilitate a successful completion of your goals. You are headed for a brilliant future.

lash Within a few days you will be entering a cycle of peace and tranquility in your domestic life as well as your life with a special person. Set aside special time to spend with someone you care about.

lasso You will rise above your present problems within the week.

Last Judgment You will hear a confession of a past crime from another person. Although this will shock you, do not allow yourself to pass judgment or to repeat this conversation to anyone else.

last rites Within three days something unusual will occur and you will rush to the rescue of an unknown person. Prepare for this mentally and you will handle everything correctly. Good luck is with you.

Last Supper You and your family will enjoy an abundance of health. Many prosperous events will present themselves to you that will improve your standard of living in those areas you most desire. Expect this to take place within the month. Many blessings will come to you and your family. Be very aware of your environment and take steps to avoid any unnecessary discomforts.

Las Vegas A beautiful person will enter your life, relentlessly befriend you, and offer you financial assistance until you get on your feet. If you choose, you will also have many admirers to choose from within the month whom you can create a successful marriage with. This union will provide you with long-lasting love and financial security. Make it a point to provide more love and attention to those around you. This dream may also be used as a reference point in time. If you dream of this city and see its name used in any context, the dream message will occur on this day.

latch You are loved beyond your imagination and you will receive verification of this within three days.

latchkey You will receive a promotion in those areas of your life you desire. You will also receive a financial gain within three days.

later *any form* You are making the correct moves and are motivating yourself to achieve victory. You will also be able to make an important connection with a certain person you have been unable to connect with in the past. This will take place within the week and all things you felt were impossibilities are possible now. Schedule a short get away in order to clear your mind and you will enjoy many pleasurable moments. You are on the path for a brilliant future.

latex Take full responsibility for those things you want to successfully work out. You will gain respect for this. This is especially important for the next three days.

lather A big change due to unusual circumstances will take place in your life that will result in an increase in wealth. You will also retain your relationships with those who are very special to you.

Latin An invitation that you make to someone you desire will be accepted and this person will quickly fall in love with you. This will be the cycle to make a romantic move, if you choose. You will enjoy an abundance of health and prosperity. You are headed for a brilliant future.

Latin America Someone will immediately fall head over heels in love with you. This individual will do the necessary groundwork for you to know them better and to make it easier for them to involve you in their life. They will also be very attentive to you and will take steps to appease you in every way. You will have many wonderful moments together and if you choose to go this route, you will have a fantastic time with a fantastic person. This dream may also be used as a reference point in time. If you dream of this country and see its name used in any context, the dream message will occur on this day.

Latino Any business proposal you choose to become involved with for the next two days will be very advantageous to you. Whatever route you choose to take will provide you with a brighter future than you have ever envisioned. Good luck and many blessings are with you.

Latin Quarter You are in a very powerful cycle for the next seven days and you will be able to accomplish just about everything you set out to accomplish. Many blessings are with you and your family.

latitude Do everything you can to avoid the company of someone you know is acting suspiciously. Your feelings that this person is acting under a hidden agenda are correct. Follow your hunches. You will also receive unexpected word that someone wants total commitment from you in a relationship. If you choose to take this path, you will enjoy a successful and long lasting relationship. Good luck is with you.

latrine *to use* You and a special person are looking for changes to improve your relationship. You are now open to conversations and new ways to demonstrate love and a new closeness that will benefit the union. This will serve to improve the relationship in all aspects. If you choose to pursue this, the other person will be more than eager to go along with this process. Any other negotiations you need to attend to will work to your advantage during this time period because this is the best cycle for communications.
to flush the toilet after use The above changes will occur very rapidly. Good luck is with you and you are headed for a brilliant future.

Latter Day Saint's Demand from your god what you want. Call upon him or her for your needs, be specific in your demands and all of your burdens will disappear. Your god is with you and you are headed for a very prosperous life. Many blessings will come to you and your family.

lattice This dream implies someone in a high position and with a great deal of money and authority is interested in you. This individual has yet to verify this but your instincts are correct. You will receive verification of this within seven days. Good luck is with you.

latticework Do not enter into any conspiracies or secret plans of another. Get on with your life without involving yourself. This is especially important for the next three days.

laugh *to laugh* This dream is an extremely lucky omen and is a promise you will be able to gain a great deal for a small sum.
others laugh You will be asked to perform a favor in exchange for a large sum of money. This money will be the answer to a long standing debt. You and your family will enjoy an abundance of health, love and tranquility.
to see a demon laughing Time is running out for you. You are in danger from a very evil person. Although this person has not yet demonstrated any sign of their evil nature, they will remove their mask of normalcy once you grow closer to them. You will need to investigate to determine who this person is. This will take place within four days. Do not allow this person to get close to you and take steps to protect yourself.
in any other form It is safe to involve yourself in risky business negotiations. Proceed with confidence and everything will work to your advantage. You are headed in the right direction.

laughing gas Doors of opportunity that were formerly closed will now be open to you. Investigate the one you choose to become involved in. Any of these will offer you great benefits.

laughter *any form* Be very sure for the next three days that whomever you are communicating a certain situation to fully understands what you are trying to communicate. This will prevent misunderstandings and regrets later on.

launch *launch anything* An ex lover will seek you out to reconcile if this is what you desire. You will enjoy many tranquil conversations that will leave you feeling rejuvenated. This is something you seek and many benefits will come from this union. Good luck is with you.

launch pad Be prepared. For the next three days people will make strange demands of you and your time. Be firm about what you want to do and what you refuse to compromise on. You must also take steps to avoid food poisoning, especially for the next three days.

launder Do not discuss politics or religion for the next three days with anyone. This will definitely lead to trouble

Laundromat You will resolve problems that have been causing you a great deal of anxiety within three days. Everything will work out better than you have envisioned. Take care of business and everything will fall into place perfectly. You will have a very busy three day period ensuring everything falls into place as you desire.

laundry You will hear the words that will verify the deep feelings someone has for you. You are deeply loved by the person you most desire. You will enjoy many special moments within the next three days and will have the freedom to spend quality time together.

laundry list Someone will send a message verifying their deep feelings of love for you. A token of love will be sent that will make this very clear.

laundry woman You will experience a great deal of tranquility in your romantic union. If you desire, you will begin to achieve this within three days.

laurel In spite of anything that may be going on in your life, romance will bloom if you choose to take this path. Your special deity is with you and many blessings will come to you and your family.

lava Take steps to protect your estate against unfair practices. Do not allow anger to come into your life. Remain calm and collected, especially for the next three days and you will be able to handle everything very successfully.

lavatory Maximize your communication skills and learn to get your feelings across to someone else, especially authority figures. You are entering a three day cycle that will prepare you for successful communications.

lavender Within three days you will meet someone with a very charismatic and attractive nature. At the time you meet this person, you will have no interest in meeting anyone but will find they have a deep interest in other cultures and the lives of others. During the course of the conversation you will learn they are deeply attracted to you and will go to great lengths to ensure you become involved in their life. You can make of this relationship anything you choose. During this cycle you will also develop very clear and creative thoughts as well as the clarity to execute them and to put them into tangible form. Many blessings are with you. Eat properly, drink plenty of fluids and meditate in your favorite form.

law Within three days you will be contacted by someone who will become involved with you in some way. This individual will tenaciously approach you for friendship but will lack the courage to take this relationship to the level they desire. This will be very confusing and you will be unsure of the next step to take. This individual's personality is such that they will take the relationship up to a certain point, then it will be necessary for you to take over. Good luck is with you and you will be able to handle this successfully.

law abiding Do everything necessary to remove yourself from a stressful situation. The moment you see this start to develop, take yourself to an enjoyable environment until the situation works itself out. Expect this to occur within three days. Good luck is with you.

lawbreaker Make sure you keep all secrets and confidential information to yourself, especially for the next three days. You will be encountering a very nosy person.

lawmaker Someone who is very special to you will go through some very trying times for the next three days. Show consideration for this person's needs.

lawman Schedule a physical exam. There may be something that you are overlooking regarding your health. A specific ailment may need to be treated.

lawn *unkempt* Get a grip on your temper and do everything you can to control yourself. An unusual situation will occur that will cause suspicions and jealous feelings. If you do not take proper precautions, these feelings will develop into an uncontrollable rage and you will do something you will later regret. Do not feed into these suspicions and the moment you sense this anger beginning to escalate seek professional help.

beautifully kept lawn You are entering an extremely lucky cycle for the next seven days. You will meet someone who is fluent in several different languages. This individual will come into your life at a time when you need a support system. They are very charismatic, generous and prosperous and will be able to provide you with a support system. You will get the help you need in any capacity and this involvement has the potential for developing into a romantic situation if you choose. Motivate yourself to circulate in order to meet this person during this time frame. Many blessings are with you and your family.

lawn bowling Within three days you will have an easy opportunity to achieve the leadership position you are after. You will be well received by others. Many blessings are with you.

lawn mower Your success depends totally on the decisions you make within three days. You cannot depend on others for a support system during this time frame.

lawn tennis Do not deprive yourself of special moments with someone who is in a better position than you are. Make an effort to spend quality time with this person. You will benefit greatly from them in the long run.

Law of Moses This dream is an extremely lucky omen, especially in matters that deal with education. The knowledge you are seeking will be easily obtained in this cycle and a dramatic improvement will occur in your life. You are headed for a brilliant future. Many blessings will come to you and your family.

lawyer Put yourself in a position of rebirth in those areas you most desire. You will rise to great heights in areas you seek changes in. It is also very important that you carefully watch someone who is special to you who is, without their awareness, becoming deeply involved in addictive behavior. This will reach a point of being uncontrollable and they will be unable to regain control over their behavior. This will begin to develop within seven days. Do everything within your power to make this person aware of this problem before it escalates to this point. Anything negative in this dream that refers to a situation in reality needs to be avoided or altered in some way. If positive, bring it to full bloom. Otherwise, good luck is with you and many blessings will come to you and your family.

laxative Do not put yourself in the position of having to deal with any legal action taken against you.

lay *to be laid down gently by an unknown source* Develop a quiet conviction in the manner in which you handle a particular situation that will arise within three days. This will allow you to avoid stress and to rapidly handle situations in the correct manner. Proceed with confidence.

layer This dream is an extremely lucky omen and you are headed for a very prosperous future. You will be undefeatable because of the tenacity you will develop within a few days. This is exactly what you need to realize your ambitions. This dream also implies that someone from the past will drop in on you unexpectedly with joyful news.

Lazarus *(from the Bible)* Anything dealing with musical instruments will be very lucky for you. Many blessings are with you and you will soon be rid of a serious illness that has been plaguing you.

lazy Do not only imagine yourself as someone who can perform specific tasks and do not procrastinate any longer. Move forward in this time cycle because you will be victorious in anything you want to accomplish.

leach Do everything you can to avoid living beyond your means. Do not purchase anything that will lead to financial defeat later on.

lead Use common sense when making plans for the next few days. Make up a budget that will help you prepare for your financial needs over the next few months and set aside some money that can be used for emergency purposes.

leader You will find yourself unexpectedly helping someone in distress within three days. Be sure this does not leave you open to someone else's hidden agendas. Do what you can to help but do not become involved in this person's problems.

lead pencil You will experience a special pleasure when attending an event you have been invited to. You must also do what you can to improve your physical appearance before entering this new environment.

lead poisoning Take steps to avoid lead poisoning and to prevent this from occurring with any member of your family. Exercise extreme caution for the next three days. You will also unexpectedly find yourself in an unusual situation with a very dangerous person. Be acutely aware of your environment in order to avoid this situation completely. You have prior notice of this and can take steps to prevent it.

leaf You are entering a dynamic, prosperous cycle and are headed for a brilliant future. During this time period, you can make specific demands from your higher power and they will be manifested regardless of how impossible they seem.. This cycle will also give you the opportunity to reach mutual

agreements and understandings with a special person. These will involve big plans for the future that will come to pass if you choose.

leaf bud You will receive good news within five days and be very pleased with the outcome of a business affair you are concerned with. This is a lucky omen for you as well as it is lucky for love and finances.

leafhopper Do everything you can to complete your goals even if it involves risk taking. This is the best cycle for this and you will gain backing for this.

leaf spot You will have a deep desire, within three days, to investigate a certain situation that seems peculiar to you. Back off and leave things as they are without involving yourself in this issue.

leafstalk The advice you get from someone who cares deeply for you will be completely accurate. Follow this person's suggestions for your own well being.

leafy *anything* A special situation could occur between you and someone else that involves finances and love. If you choose to pursue this, you will not only benefit financially but will find deep permanent abiding love. Do not allow this to slip away. Good luck is with you.

league It would not be a good idea, for the next two days, to invest too heavily in the advice of others.

leak *to unsuccessfully stop a leak* Riches and power will come to you within seven days as a result of what you are now actively pursuing. Many blessings will come to you and your family.

in any other form Be aware of a financial drain that should be causing you concern now. Begin looking for ways to generate extra income because you will need this money within two weeks. Money you expect during this time period will not arrive in a timely fashion.

leak proof A close friend will contact you within five days with the news that they have come into some power and authority. This individual has also come into a great deal of money and wishes to have you join them in a joint venture that will benefit you greatly for a lifetime. Good luck is with you.

leap *any form* This dream is an extremely luck omen. For the next three days make sure you double check all information you receive to ensure its authenticity. You will also hear good news from a friend you have not heard from in some time.

leapfrog This is a very lucky, prosperous and productive cycle for you. You will be appointed to a position you have wanted for a long time that will include a salary increase.

leap year You can look forward to a delightful date within a three day period if this is what you choose to involve yourself in. Someone will, unbeknownst to you, play cupid and you will find yourself attracted to this person. You can take this relationship as far as you please.

lease Be very aware of where and how you spend your money. You could easily become involved in a scam that appears legitimate. Any situation involving leases also needs to be carefully scrutinized within three days. Any negative situation foretold in this dream can be prevented. Otherwise, to dream of a lease is very lucky.

to lease a house Someone who has consistently turned you down will have a change of heart and will now be eager to involve themselves with you. Back off and do not become involved. This will not be to your advantage. Any event in this dream that is negative and can be applied to your life needs to be prevented.

leash You will have the courage to make it clear to someone that you refuse to be put on an emotional roller coaster. Do not allow yourself to be manipulated into becoming involved in distasteful situations. You are making all the right moves and are motivating yourself to achieve success. You will also, within the week, finally connect with an individual you have been trying to pin down for some time. All things you felt were impossible in the past are now possible. Schedule a short get away to a remote and quiet area in order to gain tranquility. This mini-vacation will leave you with many pleasant moments. You are headed for a brilliant future.

leather Within three days you will receive enormous personal powers from the gods as well as health and strength. You will be able to accomplish a variety of things in this time frame. This dream is also alerting you that what you are pursuing and feel is not important will be a golden opportunity. You are entering a lucky three day cycle.

leather bag If you make it a point to be as creative as you can, you will find the means to possess the items you desire for a small price.

leather jacket For the next seven days you will be well accommodated by those who support you. This will come as a surprise because you felt you were not receiving approval from those who meant a great deal to you. Their support will be refreshing. This will be a very victorious time for you.

leatherneck Insist that others complete what you need to have done as scheduled. This is especially important for the next three days.

leather suit You will develop the confidence and strength to make great strides toward accomplishing your goals. Each step you take will increase your level of prosperity. You are headed for a brilliant future.

leave *to not want to take leave* Someone who harbors a secret animosity toward you will attempt, within five days, to sabotage your efforts to steer a situation in a certain direction

to benefit another person. Although this person knows you are right, they will go against you in spite of the destruction it will bring to others. You are trying to work things out so everyone will enjoy more prosperity. You have prior notice of this and can take steps to prevent interference. This person does not understand the depth of hardship they will bring to others.

to beg your leave Within three days you will have the valor and clarity of thought to handle certain tasks that need to be taken care of and the decisions that need to be made. You will then be able to implement changes and carry them out in the way you desire. You will enjoy an abundance of health in this time cycle.

to leave someone directions All negotiations will be extremely successful. A new person will also enter your life who will be a friend from the very beginning. This person will be very charming and will share many wonderful stories with you. This individual will tell you something that will be an important message to you. This message will give you a different way of looking at a certain project or concept that you will be working on. You will be able to use this knowledge to improve your life in many ways. This will occur within three days and, if you choose, this person will be a friend for life.

to take one's leave Be extremely cautious, very alert and acutely aware of someone you are affiliated with who will, within three days, attempt to pull the wool over your eyes. This person will devise a plan to get you to commit to something without you being suspicious of their motives. Make sure you are extremely aware because this plan, which is known only to them, will cause you a great deal of discomfort and irritation. You have prior notice of this person's intentions and can take steps to protect yourself. Otherwise, you will receive abundances in other areas of your life due to new opportunities that will present themselves to you at this time.

to see someone leaving your presence Within the next three days if you did not recognize the person who was leaving your presence, ask questions, become suspicious, and develop a certain degree of objectivity. You will then be so successful in diffusing a plot against you that it will be impossible for it to be successfully carried out. This plot will involve someone who wishes to create chaos and discomfort in your life. If you recognize the person, you can take the appropriate steps to bring about a positive result to a future event as well as preventing a negative situation from occurring in reality. You will be able to use what authority you have in a responsible, efficient and effective way. You will also, during this time period, experience many wins and victories and the generosity you have paid to others in the past will be repaid. Expect to receive many gifts and major wins. You are definitely headed for a brilliant future.

"leave me alone" *to use this phrase or to hear someone else us this phrase* You will stumble across a devious plot that someone has conspired with others against you. You have prior notice of this and can take the necessary steps to turn this into a positive experience. Do not fall prey to another person for reasons known only to them. Otherwise you are headed for a prosperous future.

leavening Insist that you have the flexibility you need to complete a certain task on time.

"leave something behind" *to use this phrase or to hear someone else use it* Someone you know will try to change someone else's behavior by using heavy handed and rough behavior. Think ahead. By using common sense, a clear head and skillful words, you will be able to settle everything down once it begins to flare up. You will be able to make others feel comfortable and agreeable enough to diffuse this issue. You will also hear some good news during this cycle.

lecher Your drive and determination will lead to a great future and your life will undergo a major change in all areas of love, money and health. You will enjoy more love and affection from others and will gain a new zest for life.

lectern Do not allow the negative attitudes of others to affect you. Continue going in the direction you are headed and if need be, change company. This is especially important for the next three days.

lecture Insist that all information given to you is backed up by proof. This is particularly important for the next week.

Leda *(Greek Mythology)* Explore ways of making a relationship more exciting to you and that special person in your life, especially for the next five days.

ledge Keep a watchful eye on verbal agreements you have made to ensure they are kept. Keep a written account to ensure these negotiations do not start dissipating. This is especially important for the next three days.

ledger Be very flexible for the next three days. It will be essential to your well being.

ledger board Start investigating the possibilities of a part time job in addition to your current job. You will be able to meet your obligations on time this way. After you have caught up, get back to your normal routine. This will eliminate unnecessary stress on yourself and others.

leek Practice foresight and determine realistic ways of meeting a budget before you get into financial trouble. This is especially important for the next two days. You will be able to generate greater wealth by budgeting properly.

left Within three days you will receive an enormous amount of enriched mental inventiveness from your higher power. You will then be able to take steps to show the world what you are capable of and will be able to bring into tangible form your thoughts and ideas. Begin this process now and within the month you will have a finished product. Many blessings are with you and your family.

left handed Within three days people from various back-

grounds will enter your life. Each individual will be very special and will have a variety of special events they will want to share with you. Schedule your time with these people during your most energetic hours so you can grasp as much as you possibly can and when you set out to achieve a goal, strive for excellency. You are also heading for a brilliant future and many blessings are with you.

leg/legs Make sure you have the necessary information to do the best you possibly can. Conduct research and get the necessary training to complete your tasks as skillfully as you can and on schedule. Do the necessary legwork in order to achieve the goal you are after.

beautiful legs Within seven days you will be granted, by the gods, an enormous capacity to achieve excellency in what you set out to apply yourself to.

skinny legs You will achieve great victory in the choices you make and this will lead you to a brilliant future. Good luck is with you and many blessings will come to you and your family.

to see others sit on the floor with legs crossed Within two days make sure you come to understand you are under no obligation to behave in any way someone else wants you to. Make sure you are under no one else's control and you will permanently rid yourself of someone who feels they have authority over your behavior, manner of speaking, thinking or reacting. You will be able to do this with very little anxiety because of the tactful and easy manner in which you handle this. You are headed in the right direction and are headed for a very prosperous future.

you or someone sitting with their legs crossed, Indian style Think ahead and seek out a necessary conversation with someone within three days. This will allow everyone to get together to discuss a way to put a stop to something that will occur if you and everyone involved do not take aggressive steps. This incident has the potential for hurting everyone. Take steps now to prevent this and alert all those involved. Otherwise, many blessings will come to you and your family.

to cross your legs or see others' legs crossed An event is scheduled for the coming week that would be to your advantage to attend. You will be in the company of two admirers who will subtly attempt to win you over. You will find both of these people to be very charming and agreeable, and although it does not show, one of them possesses a great deal of power and authority. You would be very happy choosing one of them as a lifetime partner. You are on the path toward a very prosperous future.

legs that appear unusual in any way Expand your knowledge and skills by taking additional course work. This will be the direction to take for a much needed change. Anything connected with travel over the next two weeks will also bring you more prosperity than you ever imagined. Pursue a variety of things you need to do. You will have the energy needed to tackle these changes. Good luck is with you and many blessings will come to you and your family.

broken leg Do everything necessary for the next four days to keep your temper under control. A distasteful situation will arise that will render you suspicious and jealous of the behavior of someone close to you. You will also be driven into a murderous rage over this. Take steps to keep this rage from developing and do not cater to this emotion. You are placing too much importance on another and not enough on yourself.

hairy legs Your friends will soon expect you to take the lead. Restrict your responsibilities and stay in the background.

legal holiday Keep your eyes open and listen carefully for the next two days to ensure there are no surprises to catch you off guard. Look for hidden agendas. If you practice diligence, you will be able to successfully ride through this cycle.

legal pad You will receive an unexpected windfall within three days.

legal tender For the next three days, actively motivate yourself to communicate with an individual who is difficult to pin down. This will bring you many benefits. This will be a very lucky cycle for you.

legend For the next three days you could physically accomplish so much more if you remain flexible, listen to the soothing music you enjoy, and do those things that make you feel good about yourself. Carefully plan activities that will bring joy into your life.

Legionnaire's disease Let go of your ego and allow those who are equipped to offer you assistance to render their help within three days.

legislature Avoid anyone who will purposely maneuver a situation to make you look as though you are making a nuisance of yourself. Watch out for these tactics for the next three days.

leg of mutton/lamb Do everything necessary to ensure your continued good health. Check your schedule for the next three days and avoid any activity that is a risk to your health. Drink plenty of water.

legume For the next four days, pay close attention to what is occurring in your environment. You will then be able to determine what you need to include or avoid in your life. Be very attentive to developing situations during this time frame.

leisure Within two weeks a situation will arise that will prove to be bigger than you can handle on your own. Don't panic. Help is on its way and you will be able to enlist a support system that will help to see you through.

leisure suit For the next three days your instincts will prove correct. If you feel as though the person you are dealing with is procrastinating and dragging you down, move on without this person.

lemming Do not display a personality to others that appears unpredictable. This behavior will be completely unacceptable to others whom you are trying to enlist for assistance in your life.

lemon For the next seven days you will be given enormous strength from your higher power. This will be an extremely lucky and victorious cycle for you. You will also be able to resolve all old hang ups you dislike because of the mental clarity you receive. You will also be blessed with the creative ideas you need to bring someone closer to you in the way you desire. Many blessings are with you and you are headed for a brilliant future.

lemonade You and another person will come to a decision that will bring both of you immense joy and tranquility. You will also experience an increase in wealth.

lemon butter You will enjoy a very leisurable, relaxing time as well as tranquility and harmony for the next seven days. This will be a very lucky cycle and you will be able to bring those things you felt were impossible to reality. Take advantage of this cycle.

lemon drop Any business you become involved in that involves a great deal of travel will be very beneficial to you. You are definitely headed for a brilliant future.

lemur Take steps to rid yourself of old emotional hang-ups you have resisted working on. This will allow you to feel deep emotional fulfillment. By allowing these problematic issues to continue, you are depriving yourself of an emotional involvement with another person. Deal with this within two weeks.

Lenin You will not receive the documents you are expecting and you will also receive bad news within two days. Do what you can now to ensure all documents reach the proper destination on time.

Lennon, John Within ten days you will come to realize what heaven is when you recognize the creative and profound thoughts that are coming from within you. Motivate yourself to develop these thoughts with confidence, neither over nor under doing them. Execute these thoughts on a grand scale and do not allow yourself to develop tunnel vision. Become flexible but not overly so. Do not allow yourself to take today's moments for granted because these will be your future memories. Use common sense and get in sync with your health regarding food and beverages. You will victoriously achieve your goals through your journey in life and you are headed for a brilliant future.

lens Do not overtly display emotions toward someone you do not know very well. This will be seen by others as socially unacceptable behavior. Pay close attention to the way you conduct yourself for the next three days. Behave appropriately at all social gatherings.

Lent Within three days make it a point to express your feelings to others who are unsure of the way you feel about them. You will feel deep appreciation and love from others for the next five days. Many blessings are with you and your family.

lentil Within five days you will win the love of another person. This individual will express deep passion for you. You will experience mutual affection and tranquility during this time period.

Leo You will hear delightful news within three days. Someone will let you know of another person who is romantically interested in you. If you choose to go this route, this person will be very involved in bringing happiness into your life in any capacity. You will also be invited to a very elegant function within the month. This will be a very prosperous cycle for you and many blessings are with you.

leopard Any negative event seen in this dream you feel could take place in reality needs to be changed or avoided. You also need to take a strong stand within five days in your refusal to go along with the plans of others. Do not compromise in your refusal to get involved.

leotard A stranger in distress will involve you in a situation that could be very dangerous. Make sure you get outside help instead of taking over the responsibility of another person. Expect this to take place within three days.

leper This dream is an extremely lucky omen and implies you will be in a lucky cycle for at least a month. It also implies that during this time period you will meet someone who appears, at first, to be very charming and easy going and acts as though they will do everything within their power to get close to you. Once you get close, this person's true personality will come out and you will be very repulsed by this. Otherwise, many blessings and good luck are with you.

leprosy Question the motives behind the sudden interest someone shows toward you. This person will eventually open up to you and request assistance from you. Think this through carefully before becoming involved because it will take a long time to get out from under this.

lesbian Because of your determination, within five days your plans will become a reality. This will result in a much better standard of living for you. You will be able to remove any mental block that keeps you from moving in the direction you desire. You will also develop a new confidence in your abilities during this time frame.

lesion Someone lacks the courage to let you know they are not interested in a romantic involvement with you. Do not push yourself on someone else for the next two days who is not interested in you.

lesson *any form* You will be able to gain the advantage in certain situations by scheduling meetings with those who are eager to concede to your wishes. This will give joy to those who are eager to hear from you. You will experience health, prosperity and an abundance of blessings. Good luck is yours for this seven day cycle.

lethal A very tricky situation will develop within two days involving someone you feel a deep attraction to. Do not allow this person to play games with you. Move on with your life and do everything you can to turn a negative situation into a positive one.

lethargy Seek out a good support system and decide what you need from this group. You will receive a quick response to your needs if you consistently work to receive it. Do this within two days and be specific about the particular services you require.

letter *call letter* You will soon be laid off from your job. Seek alternative employment.

in any other form Recall what was written. Anything negative that is connected with reality can be altered or avoided in reality. If positive, take extra steps to ensure it takes place. This dream is a prosperous omen and you are headed for a brilliant future. Expect some unexpected good news within five days.

letter bomb Within five days the plans you have been developing will reach fruition.

letter box Do not allow anyone to steer you from the path in which you are destined. You will enjoy a brilliant future.

letter carrier Do not, within five days, unintentionally sabotage the plans of others. Make sure you are aware of your actions toward others and don't allow your behavior to interfere with the hard work of another person.

letterhead Anything you visualize that is to your liking should be brought into your life. If you see anything negative in the dream, take steps to ensure this does not occur in reality. You will also enjoy an abundance of health, finances and emotional stability during this time period.

letter of credit Someone you care deeply about will return for a reconciliation. This will result in a permanent union, if you choose to become involved.

letter opener Keep your eye on secretaries or anyone who acts as a liaison who may be preventing important messages from getting through to someone else. If you encounter this within three days, do what you can to control yourself. This person enjoys pushing buttons.

lettuce For the next three days your intuitions about love and money will be correct. Attend to these hunches and they will lead to prosperity in a big way.

leukemia For the next month do whatever you can to encourage love and family closeness. Plan family events and let your imagination run wild to create rich, rewarding experiences for the family to enjoy. Many blessings are with you and your family.

levee A certain individual has led you to believe they can assist you far more than they are able to. Because they have misled you, they will do whatever they can over the next few days to back out because of either lack of skills, knowledge, or finances. Allow this person a graceful retreat and go on with your life. Because you have prior notice, you can avoid involvement. You and your family will enjoy an abundance of health, wealth and tranquility.

level Make sure you weigh the pros and cons prior to involving yourself in a certain plan. This is especially important for the next three days.

level *(instrument used to determine whether a surface is even)* Someone will go to great lengths to create a relationship between you and another person. Your destiny is to enjoy a beautiful, full blown love relationship that will bloom within a few days and will bring joy to your life. This is the perfect time to emotionally connect with this person and they will respond in the manner you most desire. This dream implies you are headed in the right direction in life and it is very important that you fully express yourself in all personal matters. You will be able to focus yourself in a detailed fashion and be able to achieve a great deal as a result. You will enjoy many successes and will magically possess the inner strength you need to handle any situation. You can expect much tranquility in your life. An unexpected favor will also be granted but you will need to put yourself in the position to speak with powerful and influential people. State your needs directly and clearly. As a result you will be granted the money you requested from someone in a prompt fashion. You will achieve victory in those areas of your life you deem to be most important. You can expect to hear some good news within the week and are headed for a brilliant future. Make sure you pay very close attention to all conversations over the next three days. All negative messages and events taking place in this dream can be altered and all positive messages can be promoted. This is a very lucky dream for you.

lever Do everything necessary for the next five days to develop positive spending habits. You will have deep regrets if you do not curb your spending.

Levi Many blessings are with you and your family and you are entering a very prosperous cycle. You also need to take a good look at a certain situation because there is a lot left to salvage and renew that you may be unaware of.

Levis You are headed in the right direction and will enjoy a brilliant future. You are also promised wealth in the near future.

Levi Strauss You are headed for a brilliant future. You must also look carefully at a certain situation before you de-cide to reject it. There is a lot more involved than you realize that you may be overlooking. Good luck is with you.

Leviticus *(from the Bible)* This is alerting you that you will be overcome by guilt about something you will do that you were against from the beginning. This situation will arise within two days and you will need to take action against it. Look carefully at everything you are tempted to involve yourself in, on any capacity. You will also enjoy an abundance of health during this cycle but make sure you take all the necessary steps to remain uninvolved in anything you should not become involved in.

Lhaso-Apso Something is occurring behind the scenes with another person for reasons known only to them. This individual enjoys creating distasteful moments and chaos in the lives of others. Be extremely aware of your surroundings, and of any unusual episodes in your life. Take steps to avoid this and work to bring stability and balance into your life.

liaison Within five days someone who has been sent from the gods will enter your life in order to offer you relentless assistance, inadvertently, and at random times for the upcoming year. This person will steer you in the direction that is more favorable and will shape a path that will allow you to reach levels of grand proportions. This will bring great prosperity to your life. Your divinity is with you.

liar/lie Within five days think of an alternate person to complete a task for you instead of the original one you had in mind. The first person will be a mistake. You will also find a way to say something that is very difficult in a way that does not offend yet still gets your point across with a minimum of duress and emotional distress.

to lie Anything negative in this dream that refers to a situation in reality needs to be avoided or altered in some way. If positive, make the effort to bring it to full bloom. Within three days an invisible block that has been holding you back will disappear. It will never return to burden you. You will also hear the words of love you have longed to hear within four days. This will provide you with the opportunity to change your entire lifestyle and to experience more prosperity, if you choose to involve this person in your life. You are headed for a brilliant future.

for someone else to lie Difficult words need to be said and let the chips fall where they may. This is a necessary step to take in order to stabilize a particular situation and to have everything return to normalcy.

to be called a liar or hear someone use that word Any plans you put into action that involve someone else will result in this person becoming very interested in you in a romantic way. Since you have prior notice of this you can choose to either prevent this situation from occurring or to allow this situation to flow. If you choose to allow this relationship to bloom, it promises to offer more than you ever anticipated.

to catch someone in a lie or to hear someone tell a lie Within four days someone will make an unexpected proposition to you. This proposal will be so good it will be difficult to accept because of its outrageousness. It seems it would be impossible to accomplish and because of its unbelievability you will want to pass on it. Take a few days to think this through. Do not close doors or burn bridges. Take the time to experiment with this to see if it is possible. While you are mulling this over you will still have the feeling this is not a possibility. Go for it. It will work out and this person will keep each commitment. Good luck is with you.

to be caught in a lie This implies that within three days someone will purposely use language in a way that is meant to corner you into agreeing to something they wish you to do. This person will do everything in their power to pin you down and surrender, behave in a manner they wish, or to make statements they wish you to make. Be very aware of this. This individual will be very forceful in getting their way. You have prior notice of this and can take the appropriate steps to avoid being put at a disadvantage.

libel Do whatever you can within five days to get the kinks out of the plans you have made in order to achieve a successful outcome. Remain optimistic about the situation you are working on.

liberal Remain wary for the next three days when a stranger enters your life in a very public setting. This will be a very stressful situation for everyone involved. Quarrels and disagreements will come out of this. Do what you can to remain uninvolved.

liberal arts You will have guests at your home and one of them will accidentally expose themselves while sleep walking. You have prior notice of this and can take steps to keep this incident from occurring. You will also be invited to an unusual gathering with people you find very interesting. You will have a very rewarding time. Good luck is with you.

liberty Within three days you and another individual will be very eager to surrender to each other. You will both share many deep passionate moments if you choose. You are loved beyond your imagination. Good luck is with you.

Liberty Bell Someone will place themselves in the situation where you can easily take advantage of them. For the next three days, take extra steps to control the beast within you. Be sure to do the right thing and be aware this person is very emotionally attached to you. This dream is an extremely lucky omen and this luck will remain with you for the coming month.

Libra You will become involved with someone who looks at life with a tremendous amount of optimism. This person will be instrumental in helping both of you forge a path that will lead to a brilliant future and has been chosen by the gods for this purpose. This path will ultimately lead to a path that will provide you an abundance of health and tranquility. Your special deity is with you. This cycle will lead to flexibility and you will be able to take a number of paths to

achieve the same goal.

librarian Within three days you will be overcome with excitement about something good that is headed your way. Step back before you become too excited about this in order to make sure this is exactly what you need.

library Go full speed ahead with a planned concept that seems overwhelming. You will successfully gather the necessary resources and tools to bring about your desired goal.

library card This dream is an extremely lucky omen. Anything you felt was impossible is now a possibility within the next seven days. Also, prepare yourself for an enormous surprise that will catch you off guard and fill you with enormous joy. Good luck is with you and you will enjoy yourself immensely during this time period.

Libya You will be asked to work with someone who seems very difficult to get along with. Don't allow this initial impression to fool you. This will turn out to be a beautiful experience if you choose to go this route. During this cycle you will be able to tenaciously apply yourself until you reach your goals. This dream may also be used as a reference point in time. If you dream of this country and see its name used in any context, the dream message will occur on this day.

lice Within three days someone you are interested in will begin making moves to get close to you. You will see a change toward more affection and tranquility.

license Someone will approach you in a romantic way within five days. This individual will pursue you relentlessly and will not allow you to say no to a relationship. They are interested in a permanent relationship and will apply themselves to make it a healthy working union.

license plate Within five days you will have what it takes to reach your highest ambitions and will receive grand improved changes in your life.

lick *any form* Someone in another area or in a far away place has a deep need to see you. This person misses you a great deal and will contact you soon to express their feelings toward you. They will also extend the means to travel to their locale so you can spend time together. If you choose to go in this direction, you will enjoy yourself immensely.

to be licked Someone will send you a material message (i.e., flowers, candy, a gift, etc.) to express their deep feelings for you. This person also desires that your involvement grow and bloom. Good luck is with you.

to lick someone Pay close attention to who you were licking. If you recognize the person, this individual will be instrumental in helping you to shape a brilliant future. If you did not recognize this person, you will be offered a large amount of money for services you can easily provide in a non stressful way. Good luck is with you.

licorice Keep your sources of information to yourself, particularly for the next five days and especially if money is involved. You are loved beyond your imagination and for the next three days you will be surrounded by people who care deeply for you.

lid Do whatever you can for the next five days to allow others to see your involvement in a particular situation. This will help motivate them to back you up.

lie detector Within five days someone will lead you to believe they possess a greater position of authority than they do. Do not request from this individual more than they are able to deliver in order to avoid disappointments.

lie down *to see someone or yourself lying down in an unusual position* You are beginning to feel close to someone who will lead you to believe you can fully trust them and can be sure of their loyalty and devotion to you. Make sure, for the next three days, you do not become any more involved with this person than you already are unless you take extreme caution. This person is very clever and is a master of deceptions and illusions, and will lead you to believe certain events will take place in the future that will never occur. A hidden agenda is at play here that involves pursuing you for reasons known only to this person. Because of the trusting atmosphere, you will suspect nothing, and if this person thinks you are developing suspicions they will easily create a diversion to steer you away. Once you comprehend what is going on you will have suffered emotional damage and financial set backs. It will take some time but you will recover from this. You have prior notice and will have everything you need to make sure this situation does not take place. Use common sense, do not compromise and do not let this person pry into your affairs. Do not get involved. Otherwise you are headed for a brilliant future and many blessings will be with you and your family.

to see yourself lie in a restful position Expect within the next three days that you will be celebrating a victory you have achieved. Proceed with confidence.

lieutenant Within three days you will be in the company of someone who treats you with a great deal of respect. If you are interested in pursuing this, behave in the appropriate manner and if you show interest, this person will pursue a permanent union. You will both remain loyal for life and you will be well provided for financially.

lieutenant colonel Within five days someone who is aware they should have been treating you more fairly will come to their senses. They will apologize for their past rudeness and will verbalize their desire for a change in behavior toward you.

lieutenant commander For the next three days be very attentive and listen to what is not being said. Do what you can to get to the bottom of the situation so you can conduct yourself appropriately.

lieutenant general Within the next five days you will cause someone a great deal of pain and a feeling of being left out and abandoned because of your lack of affection. Make it a priority to show your feelings to those you care about.

lieutenant governor Be very aggressive for the next five days and go for what you really want. You will be able to communicate to someone in such a way that another person will be willing to meet your needs and desires in the way that you wish. You will also experience better health and a new zest for life. You will begin to look at life from a more optimistic point of view. Good luck is with you.

life For the next five days make it a point to sit down and make a list of your most important priorities. This will help you to direct yourself to the path you should be seeking for greater future rewards.

to plead for your life Take every precaution necessary to make sure you are not leading yourself down a dead end path. This will create a very stressful future. You have prior notice of this and can take the necessary steps to steer yourself toward the correct path. Many blessings are with you and your family.

afterlife This indicates you are living too much in the past. You need to focus on the present and add enjoyable activities in order to enjoy yourself now.

life belt Commitments you have made in the past with another person need to be revised. This will allow you both to handle anything that comes up within the next two days and still maintain this commitment.

lifeboat Make sure you determine someone else's exact motives so you can make an accurate decision about how involved you want to get with this person. Good luck is with you.

life buoy Pay close attention, for the next three days, to your food and fluid intake to ensure against contamination.

lifeguard Pay close attention to the events in this dream. You will have the chance to avoid or change anything negative that is connected to a situation in reality. Promote any positive event. You must also be aware that a group of people have talked amongst themselves to conspire against you in a subtle way. It will be easy for you to be taken in by these people without being aware of their motives. Be acutely aware of your involvements and of the motives of others. This is especially important for the next five days.

life insurance Take steps to change anything negative in this dream that should be avoided in reality. Stressful situations that have been dragging you down will also dissipate. Do not involve yourself with any new stressful, time consuming situations for the next five days. Look at the month ahead as a time to relax and replenish yourself.

life jacket This dream is a warning to you and to those around you to be wary of any water accidents. Play it safe, purchase a life jacket and make sure those you are close to do likewise. Start making the moves now to ensure a financially secure future. This is the best cycle to begin making these moves. You are headed for a brilliant future.

lifeline Pay close attention to the events in this dream. Take steps to avoid all negative situations in reality and make it a point to promote any positive situation. This also implies that within three days, someone you meet in a crowded environment will approach you to set up a future meeting time. If you choose to know this person better, you will find you have many things in common and the opportunity is there to develop a permanent, loving union.

life preserver You will fall deeply in love within the week with someone who is deeply respected by you and others. This person will love you beyond your imagination and will appreciate all of your efforts.

life raft A small risk taken now will yield large profits, especially for the next five days.

lifesaver Take steps within three days to motivate yourself to pursue business dealings between yourself and people in power. These people desire closeness from you although they do not express this. Subtly and tactfully work yourself into a position of closeness with them. You will have the opportunity to accomplish this during this time cycle.

lift *to lift or see someone lift an enormous amount of weight* Whatever is occurring that keeps you from moving forward in the direction you need to go, needs to be dealt with. Within three days, a situation will occur that will enable this.

to be unable to lift or see someone unable to lift something Focus your energy on healthy pursuits and avoid angry and jealous emotions for the next five days. Keep a light rein on your emotions.

to see something lifted that is not ordinarily lifted You will soon be the recipient of a large amount of money. This will bring you a tremendous amount of joy and a stress free future.

to see yourself or someone being lifted by something into the air by one part or your whole body Make it your business to place yourself into the area it is necessary for you to be in, in order to save a situation in the nick of time. You have prior notice of this and will be able to figure out, just in time, what you need to be doing. This situation will fall into place just as you desire. Move quickly, confidently, and courageously, especially for the next five days.

in any other form You are entering an extremely lucky cycle.

light For the next seven days you will have your energy as well as the enthusiasm of others at your disposal. You will be able to channel this energy and contain it in such a way that you will be able to quickly realize your ambitions. You will be received well by others and doors of opportunities will be open to you. Good luck is with you.

red Something is occurring, behind the scenes, with another individual that is beyond your control. For reasons known only to this individual, an effort is being made to create chaos in your life and a distasteful episode. Make sure you become acutely aware of any unusual activity or behavior in order to maintain balance and stability in your life. You must also become very alert to all incoming calls, mail or scheduled conferences you are personally responsible for. Make sure you handle them in a timely fashion.

flashing red light Within five days you will assist someone who is in need of medical attention. This person will be grateful to you and will recover rapidly. Other situations will occur that you would be better off turning down. Do not procrastinate in asking for assistance when pursuing a goal. You will be given the help you need.

to go against a red light You will be successful in diffusing a devious plot against you by asking questions and by being suspicious of the actions of others. This plan involves bringing chaos and discomfort of some sort into your life. You will be able to utilize what authority you possess in a responsible, efficient and effective manner. You will experience many victories in the near future and the generosity you have paid others in the past will be rewarded in this cycle. You will receive many gifts and are headed for a brilliant future.

green light Take a giant step and view your goals on a grander scale. This will be a tremendously lucky cycle for you.

yellow light You will be subtly easing into a less stressful life cycle. Someone also desires to be with you but is being very cautious about expressing the depth of commitment they desire. Be patient. This person will take their time but will surrender in a very delightful way to you. Many blessings are with you and this will be a tremendous cycle for romance.

flashing-signal light You will be asked by someone special to you to demonstrate a deeper level of love. This person feels as though they are far more affectionate than you are. Do what you can to correct this situation. Good luck is with you.

malfunctioning Within five days you will be dealing with a certain individual who will mislead you in a big way. This person will have you believe they are well respected, professional, financially secure and enjoy a very credible lifestyle. They would very much like to become involved in your life in some capacity. This individual is very believable and you will be so comfortable and assured in their company that you will want to become involved with them also. You will be led to believe you can have easy access to this person at any given time and you will be given phone numbers, company addresses, etc., so you can reach them, but if you take the time to try and track them down it will take a long time for them to get back to you. It will dawn on you that you have been misled and this person has a less impressive status than you thought. If you allow yourself to become involved, you will be in for a let down. Become very shrewd and disciplined in order to keep anyone from violating your emotions or insulting your intelligence. Because of your prior notice of this, you will be able to handle this successfully. You are in a very lucky cycle and are headed for a prosperous future.

tail light Within three days someone will be very eager for you to sign some papers. Regardless of how wonderful you think this move would be, do not sign these papers. They will not offer you any advantage but you will not know of this until a later time when it is too late to change paths. Take all the necessary precautions and do not sign these papers.

light bulb Within three days you will be offered a special opportunity. Not only you, but everyone else, will benefit and profit from this. Your involvement and expertise are the ingredients needed to set plans into motion and to bring it to the highest potential. Go for it.

that does not give out light Take steps to prevent any negative event foretold in this dream from occurring in reality to you or to another person. Focus on regular routine tasks and maintain a low profile for the next three days. Be aware of any errors that could arise during this time period and be sure they are attended to immediately so everything will fall into place as it should. Many blessings are with you and your family and you will enjoy an abundance of good health.

three way Within three days you will enjoy the competence and confidence to squeeze everything you can from your talents as well as the intelligence to make your mark on the world. Riches will come to you and you will be treated kindly by others. Many blessings will come to you.

to turn on Be very confident and determined in the manner you go about handling things over the next two days. Others need to see this from you.

to turn off Avoid someone who enjoys keeping others at a distance. This person does this in order to avoid the closeness of a relationship and will destroy any effort you make to develop closeness. Go on with your life without this person in it.

lighter Prepare yourself carefully so when you meet with a certain individual in three days, you will be able to draw the truth from them with a minimal amount of stress. This will enable you to get to the bottom of a certain situation that you have a great deal of curiosity about.

lighthouse For the next three days take the easy way out when resolving certain situations you need to handle. This will be the correct way to handle this, although you will feel hesitant about this method. Good luck is with you.

lightning Pay attention to the events in this dream. They will offer you clues to future events in your life that you can work to bring to reality or to prevent, depending on the particular event. A project or situation you have been working on for some time will also be completed within seven days. You will rejoice during this cycle because you will have finally reached your goals.

to see anything struck by lightning Build up a greater bond between yourself and another person. At the first sign of a disagreement, become personally involved in ensuring this does not damage the closeness between you. Attempt to establish normality in your life as soon as possible in order to avoid stress. Expect this disagreement to occur within three days.

if you recognize someone who is struck by lightning This individual is very close to burning out emotionally with a certain situation. Become personally involved with this person in order to warn them of the danger of giving up. Suggest they take a five day mini vacation in order to become more centered and to replenish and reenergize themselves. This will help to prevent a complete burn out.

to see someone struck by lightning whom you do not recognize Remain flexible when dealing with a particular situation involving another person that seems very difficult to handle. This will occur within five days and you will be able to shed light on this issue and bring normality to the situation.

to be hit by lightning Take steps to avoid any preventable accidents for the next three days. Develop a deep love and respect for yourself. Work on ways you can make yourself feel good about yourself and to develop a love of life. You will be able to drastically raise your standard of living. You will enjoy prosperity and an abundance of health.

white lightning Be careful you do not allow yourself to be vulgarized by others who would take advantage of you financially, physically, and emotionally. Set limits and keep others from demanding you meet their needs. Make sure your needs take priority for the next five days. Take time out from the demands of others and make sure you do not overextend yourself. Especially, watch out for one person who is demanding of you. A very prosperous cycle is heading your way.

lightning bug Make sure you make the effort to display special behavior toward someone special you desire closeness with who is not yet involved with you. During this cycle you will do all of the right things to encourage this. You will be able to have this special person in your life if this is the way you choose to go. Many blessings are with you and your family. You will achieve an abundance of health and prosperity during this cycle.

lightning rod For the next three days most of your thoughts will be centered on someone you wish to make love to. You can easily make this a reality. This individual also has an interest in you. If you choose to take this path you will find once you make the first move, the other person will quickly respond to you. You will find this to be a mutually satisfying relationship.

light opera Within five days situations you are not yet focused on will take precedence and you will be able to do what is necessary to acquire the items you have long desired with no strings attached. You will also receive an inspiration that will give you an optimistic view of life. You will have an enormous amount of energy and will be able to turn situations around to your advantage. This cycle will be prosperous for you in many ways.

lightweight Within five days you will overcome a long term financial burden. You will find an easy way to overcome your troubles during this time cycle.

like You are definitely going to see a financial improvement within the next two days. Expect to be more focused on personal matters.

  dislike Make sure you don't repeat whatever you saw that was distasteful to you or someone you recognize in the dream in reality. This implies you be relentless in the next three days in those areas you feel you need to experience changes in. Put to use the heightened clarity of thought you experience in this time frame, thrust forward, move forward in the directions you feel you should be moving toward. Move rapidly in order to benefit from this lucky cycle.

lilac You will be invited to an event, within three days, that you do not want to miss. Make sure you mark this on your calendar because, during this time period, you will have so many other events occurring you may overlook this one. You will reap major benefits by being present at this event. Good luck is with you.

Lilliputian Do everything necessary not to put yourself in the position of being sexually violated.

lily Someone you know has the power and authority to pull strings on your behalf. Good luck is with you.

lily of the valley You will receive some unusual offers from someone you least expect within three days.

Lima You will enjoy victory in those areas of your life you most desire. This will lead to grand emotional changes and a greater stabilization of your life. This dream may also be used as a reference point in time. If you dream of this city and see its name used in any context, the dream message will occur on this day.

lima bean Have a camera ready for the next five days so when the opportunity presents itself, you will be able to capture precious moments. You must also make sure the equipment you are using is in adequate condition.

limb *(tree)* You will hear the news that a situation has been resolved in your favor within three days.

limbo Within five days bring a situation to the attention of others who lack the knowledge of this and insist that a resolution be reached at a mutually agreed upon time. You will be able to bring this about very successfully.

Limburger cheese You will be lied to by someone who will try to build up your hopes with false promises. Do not pay attention to this and you will avoid disappointments.

lime Seek the help and advice you need from someone who has the skill and expertise to help within three days. This dream is a very lucky omen for you.

limeade Do what you can to encourage a special person to grow closer to you. This will be a very important issue for you within five days. Good luck is with you.

limerick Certain issues will be developing within five days that you need to get to the bottom of. You will be able to put a halt to these issues if you become actively involved. This cycle will enable you to successfully deal with situations that need to be addressed.

limestone You will be able to effectively communicate with those you feel are too intimidating to approach. Good luck is with you.

lime sulfur Be very aware of someone who is very evil minded and conniving. This will be someone you least expect who will do everything within their power to cause you emotional harm. Do not place yourself in a situation where someone can take advantage of you. Be very overprotective of yourself and your belongings for the next five days.

limewater Do not openly display your emotions to someone who does not appreciate it. Be very careful for the next three days in order to avoid disappointment.

limey Take steps to prevent any negative event you dreamed of from occurring in reality. It is important, for the next five days, to let a special person know their presence in your life is of great value to you. Make sure they know nothing of material value will ever take their place.

limousine/limo An opportunity you are excited about will present itself and you will now have the means to grasp it. You will enjoy a new start in all areas of your life where you desire changes and all old burdens and issues that have been plaguing you will come to an immediate halt. Drastic improved changes will occur and leave you with a new exciting zest for life.

Lincoln Make sure you remain alert to the possibility of any conspiracy against you. This will come at an unexpected time and will involve a situation that will catch you off guard. Avoid putting yourself in the position to be conspired against in any capacity. You have prior notice of this and can avoid this situation entirely. You will also develop an irresistible impulse to travel to some exotic place. If you begin planning now you will be able to bring this to a reality. This trip will be very emotionally rewarding and you will have a safe journey.

Lincoln Continental Within five days you will develop a greater clarity of thought. Use this gift to develop a plan that will bring you greater prosperity. Trust your instincts and behave in such a way that will bring you more benefits.

line Within seven days you will be able to quickly rid yourself of troublesome situations. You will need to be on top of these issues to make sure they are resolved completely and successfully. You will have the calmness of manner and

flexibility during this cycle to handle this with ease. Go for prosperity in your life.
it.

hot line You are about to make a mistake. You are very fond of someone who is also very fond of you but you are impatient because the relationship is not developing as fast as you would like. As a result, you will attempt to rush things and will become very demanding. Invest your time in developing your personality to project a more positive image. This individual will eventually grow into the relationship and you will both be able to reach a mutual understanding.

to wait in line or see someone waiting in line Within three days you will be able to resolve pressing responsibilities with ease. You will be surprised at how quickly this will develop and at the ease with which burdens will be lifted.

linebacker Someone will become very interested in you within five days. As time goes by this person will become less able to handle their obsessive behavior. Do what you can to get on with your life without becoming involved with this person in any capacity.

line drive Make it a priority to return to basics and to practice more simplicity in your life, especially for the next five days. Do not become involved in any further situations and clear up all ongoing projects in order to have more leisure time.

linen You will soon have verification of love from someone. These deep feelings will become known to you within three days. You will experience deep physical passion in the way you most desire. This dream is an extremely lucky omen, especially in matters of love.

clean Within seven days you will be able to clearly analyze someone's behavior toward you so you can behave toward them in the proper fashion. You will have the confidence to behave in the way you are required. This will be an extremely lucky seven day cycle. Good luck is with you.

line of credit Do what you can now to build up a financial base so that within the month you will be able to handle all your financial matters. This will eliminate financial stress and you will be able to make ends meet.

line of fire Make sure that for the next five days you do not become involved in a particular situation due to a sense of obligation. You need to get more information on what you are becoming involved with before you make any decision. This involvement will not be to your advantage.

liner Within two weeks you will begin to reap the benefits from work well done in the past. These rewards will be greater than you have ever envisioned.

lingerie Within five days the opportunities you have been waiting for will be presented to you. This will give you the chance to make a new start in those areas of life you most desire. You will be able to develop and execute your plans in a very professional way and will be able to enjoy more

linguist Within five days you will receive, as an unexpected gift, an all expense paid vacation to a region you desire to travel to. This will be very rewarding to you.

link You will be paying too much attention to a total stranger and this person is someone you do not need to have any involvements with. This individual is evil minded. Otherwise, good luck is with you but get on with your life without this person in it.

linoleum Decide for yourself, ahead of time, what you need to change in your life and act on it immediately.

linseed Within the week a family member will take you into their confidence. Make sure the information is given to the right person so they can seek the best professional advice. Do everything you can to put yourself in touch with the right person. This advice will prove to be invaluable.

lint Maintain a friendly demeanor with someone who is responsible for handling your money. Be prepared to meet daily for financial updates. Start this process now and be diligent in your function as supervisor.

lion You will be easily taken by a conniving friend. This individual will become a very cunning enemy and will go to great lengths to secretly sabotage an important opportunity moments before you gain knowledge of it. Since you have prior notice of this you can determine who this individual is and address the situation properly. This will allow you to turn this issue around to your advantage.

lioness You will feel overwhelmed by a bad situation made worse by an alarmist. Make sure you understand that a small problem has been blown way out of proportion and do whatever you have to do to avoid stress. Schedule a time out in order to regain your sense of tranquility and make sure nothing disrupts your quiet time for the next four days.

lionfish Do what you can to ensure no obstacles exist between you and someone else. Open communication will allow you to develop a relationship that is mutually satisfying. Good luck is with you.

Lion's Club Take care of yourself, especially for the next five days. Avoid unhealthy relationships and keep yourself stress free.

lip A proposal that you make within three days will be warmly received by others.

lip gloss This dream is a lucky omen and you will enjoy a very stress free and tranquil cycle. Look up the color of the lip gloss for more meaning to this dream. This is also a good time to address those opportunities you once had an interest in. These opportunities will now be open to you.

lip read Someone who possesses the expertise you are interested in will be happy to take you under their wing and support your efforts to learn this specific skill.

lipstick This will be an extremely lucky cycle for you. If you see anything written in lipstick, you will also need to pay attention to the message, this will give you an extremely important clue to the meaning of this dream. If it foretells a negative event, take every step to prevent its occurrence. If positive, make it your business to bring it to reality. You are loved and appreciated by those around you. Many blessings are with you and your family. Involve yourself with something that appears to be a bit risky within two weeks. This will bring you major benefits.

to see someone you know wearing lipstick This person is very eager to talk with you and express to you what is emotionally important to them. This will give you greater clarity and you will be better able to understand specific situations that involve this individual. Look up the color for more meaning to this dream.

lipstick tube You will soon be dealing with someone associated with an agency who possesses a great deal of expertise and knowledge of certain resources. This person is in power because of their ability to procure grants that will lead you to resources that will meet your needs. This individual will decide to do something for you on the side and they will have you go through them instead of the agency so they can write themselves a job. They will be paid for the job from the agency as well as from you. Make sure you do not allow yourself to be diverted or to have your path compromised because you will miss your goal and lose out on the means to accomplish this. You will sense a feeling of strangeness from this transaction that will be a result of your heightened awareness. This feeling is letting you know you are not penetrating to the right path. Expect this to occur within three days and you will catch on to this just in time. You have prior notice of this so you can take steps not to be preyed upon. Otherwise, you are headed for a brilliant future and will accomplish what you are destined to accomplish.

liquid Be more resourceful for the next day regarding situations you are going to be involved in. Determine what you need and want out of a specific situation. The color of the liquid will also supply major clues to the meaning of this dream.

liquid diet You will receive a fantastic gift that you least expect at an unexpected time from someone who has deep gratitude for you.

liquid oxygen For the next five days avoid putting yourself in a situation where you feel a distasteful situation will arise. You can avoid this entire incident.

liquor Within seven days you will become involved in an entirely new way of living life. You will do this without great effort and without incurring many expenses. You will be introduced to many memorable moments.

lisp While attending an event within the next few days you will undergo some major upsets with another person. You can avoid this by either not attending this event or by being very alert and preventing its occurrence.

list Do everything necessary to motivate yourself to change your direction in life in order to provide yourself with more prosperity. Look at things on a grander scale and go for it, especially for the next five days. Pay attention to what is on the list. This will offer you a major clue to what you should be avoiding or bringing into your life.

listen Be more attentive to others. You are also destined to have a memorable time while on a romantic outing, if this is what you desire.

list price A fantastic glamorous person will request your company and, if you choose to attend this event with them, you will enjoy this evening immensely.

liter A friend of yours is very excited about an upcoming trip you are both planning. Do not get caught up in day dreaming about this and make it very clear to this person that you expect them to pay their share.

literature Within five days you will ensure a positive outcome to a particular situation because you will dig deeply to uncover important needed information.

lithograph The person you are interested in involving in a particular situation is unreliable and is not interested in your plans or goals, although you may be led to believe this. Get on with your plans and seek an alternative person to assist you.

litmus paper You will go from one extreme to another in order to accomplish a desire in life. This is a good cycle for making big changes in your life.

litter Do not divulge your plans to anyone. Keep all of your goals to yourself, especially for the next five days. This dream is an extremely lucky omen and you are headed for a brilliant future.

to litter Someone is mentally devising a plan to deceive you within three days. Become very aware of the behavior of others during this time frame. Avoid being deceived.

trash You will not be able to pay back money you will ask to borrow within five days. Do not put yourself in the embarrassing position of being unable to repay someone in a timely fashion.

litterbug Within five days you will accidentally stumble across some information about another person that will shock you. Keep this information strictly to yourself.

littermate Within the week you will hire someone to do some repair work for you. The estimate will be much higher than the job calls for. Look around for a better estimate.

little Within three days you will unexpectedly rise to a greater level of life than you ever envisioned. You will be more productive, see an increased income and have productive conversations with very loyal and affectionate people who want to be a part of your dreams and goals. You are headed for a brilliant future and will experience an abundance of health in a shorter period of time than you expected.

Little Big Horn You will be under a tremendous amount of pressure within five days for standing up for someone else's rights. Do not compromise but prepare yourself for this pressure and behave with dignity.

Little John You will find the solution, with medical assistance, to a recurring pain within three days. Relentlessly search for a solution until you find the proper help.

little people You will find, in three days, that someone you desire will support you financially, almost as though they wish to adopt you. If this is something you wish, make sure you actively seek this out. This will come with no strings attached and will make many of your dreams a reality.

liturgy Come to a decision quickly and do not waste time, especially for the next five days. You will be glad you did.

liver This is an extremely lucky omen. Make sure any negative event connected to this dream does not become a reality and make sure you incorporate each positive event into your life. Educate yourself on liver functioning and take steps to ensure your liver remains healthy. You will also have an unplanned opportunity to speak with someone in private within five days. Move quickly in order to communicate the words you have been wanting to say in order to conclude an important ongoing situation. You will be very effective in getting your point across to this important person.

livery stable Within five days you will begin to experience the release of mental barriers and obstacles in life. This is also the perfect cycle to rid yourself of unhealthy addictions.

livestock You will arrive at a way of handling something that will work for you although it will appear at first as though it never would. This will prove to be the solution to an important issue. You must also not allow yourself to be intimidated by others because of your point of view. Try new things and you will find they will make a big difference in your life.

live wire Within five days unusual events will begin to happen that will result in you going from rags to riches in a very short while. You will be able to accomplish a great deal in this cycle.

livid Someone is going to make a big issue out of a small incident. Become personally involved in any situation that resembles this kind of situation so you can control it before it leads to chaos.

living Within three days you will be introduced to a very exciting, exotic person who will quickly introduce you to a new way of life that you will enjoy immensely if you choose to involve yourself.

living room Continue to look for a solution to a particular issue. Within three days you will find the answer to the best way to handle and conclude this problem.

living room furniture Within two days you will be invited to a social function at the last minute. Get into the mood of the event and you will find you not only enjoy yourself but will also meet many distinguished people.

living will Any clues in this dream that pertain to reality may be used to avoid or encourage a future event, especially for the next three days. For this time period you will also need to practice preventive measures in all areas of your life and drive defensively.

lizard Practice an easy going manner when in the presence of someone who puts on airs because they possess more and have more money than you. Do not allow this person to intimidate you with their behavior and do not allow yourself to be overly impressed with this person's behavior. You will gain respect from this individual for a lifetime. Eventually they will want to involve you in their life in a romantic way. If you choose to become involved, you will share many beautiful moments together and the finest things that money can buy. Pay attention to the color of the lizard. The particular color will offer major clues to the meaning of this dream.

crawling lizards This is an extremely lucky omen. You will, however, need to stand up for your rights. Someone has promised they will come through for you at a future date. This was an agreement between both of you but the other person will attempt to get out of this pact. Bear down on this individual relentlessly at the first indication they will not come through for you. Don't waste time on this. Put the pressure on so everything will be taken care of in a timely fashion. This may involve a few uncomfortable moments. Control your anger in order to control the situation.

red lizard Someone of the opposite sex is willing to perform any task for you in exchange for sex. This individual will even offer to bypass being paid in lieu of sexual pleasures and will relentlessly pursue this goal. Be very aware of this situation and expect it to occur within three days. If you choose to go this route, this individual will provide the services you desire.

green lizard Someone will promise to pay you a certain amount of money at a certain time and will promise to deliver at a certain time. Bear down on this person without resorting to violent behavior or language. During this cycle, you will arrive at the appropriate behavior in order to coerce this person to deliver the money in a timely fashion.

brown lizard Do what you can to set aside time for solitude and quiet. Enjoy the peacefulness and quiet moments. Love yourself, get plenty of rest and find a stress free environment you can enjoy yourself in. Pamper yourself, eat healthy foods and drink plenty of water. You are headed for a brilliant future.

llama Within three days, you will find a lost object you have been searching for.

loaf Become a team player. You will need to understand the importance of working well with others and will enjoy a successful outcome as a result.

loafer Someone you know will evoke painful feelings from the past. This individual is not necessarily the type of person who caused the original feelings. Feel free to enjoy this relationship free from the anxiety that you will re-experience the same pain. Expect this to occur within four days.

loan Trust your heart and express your deepest emotions to another person, especially for the next ten days.

in any other form A certain unusual situation will take place within three days that will give you great joy. You will also enjoy health and tranquility during this time frame.

loan shark A mysterious plot is developing without your knowledge. Be very aware of any unusual situation that will occur over the next three days and play detective.

loathe Make sure you keep something unusual from occurring at an unreasonable hour.

lobby Take steps to focus on the character of those you work with. Keep what you learn to yourself and you will be glad you stored up this knowledge.

lobe You will enjoy an early settlement of someone's bequest to you.

lobster Make sure you do not put yourself in the position to suffer terror at the hands of a dangerous individual. This person will lead you to believe they either wish to view something of value you are trying to sell or will wish to show you something you are interested in buying. Be very cautious of this for the next three days.

lobsterman You will learn of an inheritance that will cause you a great deal of anxiety before you receive it. Don't waste time and do what you can to protect your interests.

lobster pirate You will receive some disagreeable news within the next three days. This will be out of your control. Remain calm and handle it as best you can.

lobster pot Do not place yourself in the position for the next three days of having to take an unpleasant journey that will lead to many distasteful moments. Do what you can to prevent this from occurring.

lobster tail This implies there is a conspiracy among those you love and trust. This will occur within three days. Do not allow yourself to be taken by those you feel are loyal during this time frame. Postpone all agreements.

lock Insist on special privileges and considerations for the next five days and do not allow others to assume you can handle more than you can. Let others know you need special assistance and consideration during this time period. This is the perfect cycle to make these requests.

to be locked up Someone is planning to violate your rights within a five day period simply to satisfy their own emotional needs. This person will try to persuade you to become involved in a situation you will find increasingly distasteful as time goes by, either sexually or in any other capacity. This involvement will go against your better judgment and ethics. Do not place yourself in any position that will require you to compromise yourself in order to get out safely. This is preventable. Good luck is with you.

to be locked out Within three days you will be dealing with someone whom you know enjoys creating chaos and stressful situations. Prepare yourself. During this time period, this person will create a chaotic situation that will escalate to the point of never returning to normality. Make sure you avoid this person by making other plans for yourself for the next three days.

to ensure things are locked Within the next two days make sure you do not push a certain person the wrong way. By using tact you will successfully handle any situation that arises. Anything negative portended in this dream needs to be changed or altered and make sure you experience only positive expressions in your life.

to put a key into a lock Each relationship that is important to you needs your personal attention in order to allow those you care about to know you have only the best care and love for them. Do not allow any of your relationships to stagnate to the point where your loved ones feel deprived of your attention.

to use a key effectively to lock It will be very important within a two day period to have a meeting with certain individuals and to make connections and the necessary requests before an important situation starts to develop. This will ensure it does not fall apart before it takes off. Stay on top of this and you will be able to make the correct adjustments in time. Pay attention to this now and everything will fall into place as you desire. Good luck is with you and your family. You are headed for a brilliant future.

to fail to lock with a key You will be dealing with someone who is very inconsiderate of the feelings of others. This individual is only interested in their own personal gratification. Do not involve yourself with this person and get on with your life without this person in it.

to successfully lock something or someone in or out You will be dealing with someone within two days who will refuse to take no for an answer. Prepare ahead of time how best to deal with this and don't become stressed out about it.

a lock that falls apart when a key enters A family member is in grave danger of being killed. If you recognize someone from this dream, make sure you warn them that their life is in danger. Otherwise, alert all family members to prevent this.

lockbox Make sure all guarantees and warranties agreed upon what will be honored in the future. This is especially important for the next three days.

locker When attempting to get something off your chest, speak with someone only after you have developed a solid plan to clear these problems. Be tactful when talking to anyone who may be contributing to the problem. You will benefit greatly from these conversations.

locker room Pay close attention to your behavior for the next three days. If you are not careful, you will behave in such a way that you will permanently drive away a very special person. You can prevent this and you can take steps to bring this person closer to you instead of driving them away.

locket Do not allow yourself to be taken by someone who either does shoddy work or tries to pass off a cheaper repair as one that is more expensive. It will be easy to allow this to occur because of your lack of expertise. Be very careful not to allow this to take place.

lockjaw Within five days take steps to avoid the emotional harm that will come when someone loans you money and then puts pressure on you to pay them sooner than you had originally agreed upon. Do not put yourself in the position to be harassed by anyone. Find an alternative solution to your financial problems.

lockup Within seven days you will be invited out by someone you do not know very well. This person will demonstrate a strange manner and at some point will become very dangerous. This will be a terrifying experience and you will not be able to find a means of escape. Do what you can to avoid this person and do not go to any unfamiliar place or to someone's house whom you do not know well. You will be held against your will in a life threatening situation.

locomotive Within three days you will learn how someone feels about you and of their intentions and plans. You will receive verbal verification of the depth of involvement this person desires. If you choose, you will find permanent financial, emotional and physical security. This dream is an extremely lucky omen and you are headed for a brilliant future.

locust You will have the drive, courage, strength, and valor to handle certain situations that will occur within two days. You will be able to quickly handle all stressful situations.

lodge Devote more time, for the next three days, to an emotional relationship.

lodge pole Within three days you will be witness to an unexpected occurrence that will shock you. Change your schedule for this time period in order to avoid this scene.

loft Do not waste time waiting for someone to come through for you on a particular business arrangement. This individu-

al will not live up to their agreement. Move on without them in order to resolve your business plans.

loft bed You will find amusement at a comedy club or a performance of some kind.

log Within three days someone will become very attracted to you and will actively pursue you. This person is married and will do what they can to involve you in their life. Avoid this situation and move on with your life.

logbook Avoid impulsive behavior that you know is socially unacceptable for the next five days. Others will be very hostile toward you because of your actions.

logjam Within the week you will be placing your reputation in jeopardy because of your involvement with an evil stranger. This could easily escalate into violence. Be careful.

logo Avoid all arguments for the next two days.

logrolling You will be witness to an event that will demonstrate the ability of another person to create chaos because of their behavior. You will be discussing a business arrangement with someone whom you have already made prior arrangements with. This will involve a job of some sort that this person has agreed to do for you. A third person will suddenly come on the scene and start making changes with your arrangements to suit their purposes. This will be an opposite sexed person who will bully themselves into the conversation in such a way that it will be very difficult for you to regain control. Do what you can to keep this person from bullying you into making compromises. You have prior notice of this and will be successful in keeping this from taking place.

loin Be very aware of the choice of words you use for the next three days. There is a danger you will injure another person's feelings and you will not be forgiven.

loincloth You will have to make a decision within three days about an individual who constantly interferes with the choices you make in life. Within this time period you will make a mutual agreement with a third person. The other person will then interfere with your agreement and attempt to change things. This will escalate into a very ugly situation for everyone involved. Make it very clear, during this time period, that you will not tolerate this kind of behavior.

London Someone is very eager to give you some information you need. This information is of extreme importance to you. Make sure you acquire this within two days. This will also be a good time for you to visit London if you so desire. This dream may also be used as a reference point in time. If you dream of this city and see its name used in any context, the dream message will occur on this day.

lonely This dream implies that for the next week it is important not to focus on another person's actions, decisions or choices to justify your need to make changes. When you find your thoughts drifting to these concerns about another person as well as a particular situation, take that energy to recreate and reinvent yourself. Not only will you benefit personally but you will also benefit your personal environment as well as others. By starting your motivation and manner you will never find yourself lonely.

loner Do what you can to avoid being alone for the next five days. This will prevent an intruder from taking advantage of you or from gaining the upper hand.

lone wolf Someone will be very eager to involve you in some distasteful business that you are unaware of. This individual will make it appear as though this is something you should be doing. The moment you are aware of anything that resembles this scenario, stay away from any involvement.

longbow You will be grateful to someone within three days because of a favor they will grant you with no strings attached.

longhorn Do not allow anything to occur, for the next three days, that will steer you away from your ambitions. This will be a temptation but you will have prior notice of this and can keep it from occurring.

longitude Do not allow the inconsistencies of another to disturb your own sense of well being. You have prior notice of this so you can actively keep yourself calm in spite of the behavior of others.

long jump Be very aware of any changes in your intake of food, medications, etc.

longshoreman You will receive the promotion you are seeking. Prepare yourself now so that once the position is open you can apply for it with confidence.

look Aggressively pursue what you feel you need in life. Do not procrastinate, especially on issues you feel you need to take care of now. You must also pay attention to the person you were looking at who is recognizable to you. This will be representative of someone who will enter your life within five days and has the same character, good or bad, as the person you dreamed about. Remember back to the time period when the person you dreamed about was a part of your life. This will give you a clue to the personality you will either want in your life or will choose to avoid.

to look down from a high place Your deepest fantasies will come to pass within three days. You will enjoy a wonderful, joyous, thrilling and pleasurable experience. Do not deprive yourself of this tremendous joy.

dirty look Someone will unexpectedly become more demonstrative and giving toward you both emotionally and financially. This will occur within three days.

to look or see someone else look for something Think

ahead to the next four days and prepare yourself for a conversation with a certain individual who is involved in a particular situation. This will allow you the time to get all those involved together to discuss how to put a lid on a particular issue and to put a stop to a potential negative event. Alert all those concerned to this possibility. Many blessings will come to you and your family.

to look for someone and be unable to find them Someone you know is desperate to get out of their present living arrangements. This person is unable to help themselves because of physical, emotional or financial reasons. Something is keeping this person from mobilizing themselves to get on with their lives. For some reason this individual is unable to get out of this situation. You will hear about this shortly and this person will come to you for assistance in helping them out of this rut. Within five days you will be able to locate the resources to ease this person's needs and to help them. You will, however, have several discussions with them prior to this. Enter these conversations with caution so you can avoid hurting anyone else's feelings that may be involved. All negotiations you will be involved in, whether they involve business, romance or productive conversation, will be very successful. You are headed for a brilliant future.

to look for something in particular and be unable to find it You will need advice within seven days. Follow this advice carefully. The information will come to you quickly and you will need to pay close attention. You will need this advice to help structure your plans in such a way to accomplish what you desire. If you are unsure of what you are hearing you will need to have it repeated until it is fully understood. You will accomplish what you desire and are headed for a prosperous future.

to look for something in particular and find it Within five days you will be very surprised because someone will turn out to be more together than you thought they were. Your original assessment of their character was wrong. You will be joyfully exuberant to discover their true character. You are headed for a brilliant future.

to look and find what you are looking for (anything, person, etc.) You can expect within the next four days an idea, project or event will be brought to fruition and will reach a higher level of perfection than you ever felt possible. This project will develop a life of its own and you will be able to easily take it through any channel necessary for completion. This will be a blessing to you and to everyone involved in this process. An abundance of health, spiritual healing and tranquility will come to you.

loom Make sure you give out accurate, detailed information so you do not waste your time or the time of others. Getting your message across accurately should be a priority.

loon Do not allow yourself to become so intimidated that you are unable to take a small risk in accepting a project you can handle very efficiently. This opportunity will be presented to you within two days.

loop Take the time to screen out important papers before you toss out anything you think you no longer want. Do this within three days.

loose *anything that is loosely attached* A certain situation will occur that will be so extraordinary it cannot be explained by any law of physics. This will take place within three days and this strange, unexplained event will leave you with a sense of awe and wonder. You will sense you have seen a miracle and will have no way of explaining how it came about. After this transpires, you will be able to present yourself to others at the highest possible level and will handle yourself, other people and situations in an appropriate manner. You are headed for a brilliant future and many blessings will come to you and your family.

"loose person" - *slang term* Take the time to see the whole picture regarding something that will come up within three days. This will allow you to clearly understand what is going on and enable you to make the way you live the single most important thing right now. Proceed with confidence. You are headed for a very prosperous future.

loot Make sure you are not taken advantage of by someone who is out to defraud you, especially for the next three days.

lord You will be able to accomplish a lot more for the next three days by handling things on your own. This is an extremely lucky omen for doing things by yourself. Many blessings are with you and your family. You are headed for a brilliant future.

Lord's Prayer Your determination will lead you to a greater future. Many blessings will come to you and your family.

Lord's Supper You and your family will enjoy an abundance of health, wealth and tranquility for many days to come.

Los Angeles Because of your sudden determination to reach your ambitions you will be able to realize them quickly within the month. You will be able to successfully complete a research project you have in mind and are headed for a brilliant future. This dream may also be used as a reference point in time. If you dream of this city and see its name used in any context, the dream message will occur on this day.

lose Within three days you will find love and respect with a person you least expect. If you choose to pursue this, you will enjoy a permanent union. You must also pay close attention to what you lost in this dream. If this was an object you recognize, make sure this loss does not become a reality for you.

lost *to be lost* Within three days you will experience an excitement with another person over a well thought out plan. This person will accept your ideas in the manner in which you desire and will react accordingly.

to see someone else lost Do not overlook a situation that needs immediate attention for the next three days. You are not taking something seriously that should be attended to.

lot *(piece of property)* Within three days you will need a tremendous amount of control. You will meet someone you find irresistibly attractive and the feeling will be mutual. If you choose to pursue this, you will enjoy yourself immensely and will enjoy a very tight, solid relationship.

Lot *(from the Bible)* Exercise extreme caution for the next three days in order to make the correct decision. Many blessings are with you and your family and you are entering a cycle for an abundance of health.

lot *(large quantity)* Allow yourself enough time to reach a particular destination that is important for you to get to at a specific time. Within three days a business opportunity will also be presented to you that would be very profitable to become involved with. Good luck will be yours.

lotion Do not allow anyone to physically, verbally or sexually abuse you. This will be passed off as playful activity when in reality it is abuse, especially in regards to sexual activity. It will become more serious as time goes on. Be firm and set limits so no one takes advantage of you in any form. Be acutely aware of this for the next three days.

lottery/lotto Someone will act toward you in ways that far exceed your expectations and they will express themselves beautifully. You can expect a proposal that will fill you with joy and will be impossible to refuse. You are definitely headed for a brilliant future. This coming month will be a very lucky cycle for you. You will win at a game of chance after investing a small amount of money. Anything connected to this dream will be extremely lucky for you, especially if you remember any numbers you can apply to various games of chance. Small risks will be very profitable for you in all manners of business negotiations for the next three days.

lotus For the next three days do everything necessary to ensure an agreement you make will be carried out to the letter.

lotus eater Set limits and make sure you are not abused in any way. Be very firm when someone makes negative comments to you and refuse to accept this behavior.

loudmouth Pay attention to what this person is saying. It will offer you a major clue to something you will either want to incorporate in your life or to avoid if negative. You will also be very surprised at the change in behavior someone demonstrates toward you. You will be shown a greater kindness and this person will demonstrate a greater appreciation of your efforts. There will be a permanent change in attitude because someone has come to grips with their behavior and is on the road to reforming.

to be a loudmouth Do what you can to demonstrate your true feelings toward someone who cares a great deal for you but is unsure of where they stand. You must also pay attention to what you were voicing. This will provide a clue to what you may be overlooking that you need to personally attend to.

loudspeaker What you hear over the loud speaker is a message you need to attend to. If it is a positive message, take steps to incorporate this into your life. If negative, take steps to avoid or alter it. Someone is also very interested in you but will back off because they feel you will not live up to their expectations. If you are interested in this individual, behave appropriately and take steps to retain this relationship. This person is picking up a false impression of who you are instead of your true personality.

Lou Gehrig's disease Do not become so caught up in outside events for the next two days that you will gradually shift to the wrong direction. This will be because the line between what you desire and the path you should not take is so thin. Make sure this does not occur during this time cycle. Avoid stubbornness. It not only makes you uncomfortable, but also affects others.

Louisiana An unexpected opportunity will be presented to you by an unexpected person whom you do not know. Jump at the chance to become involved. This will be a financially rewarding situation for you to take part in. Many blessings are with you and you family. This dream may also be used as a reference point in time. If you dream of this state and see its name used in any context, the dream message will occur on this day.

lounge Stay in control. Within three days you will become very angry with someone who likes to drag things out and this will make you feel as though you are wasting your time. Prepare for this and do not allow this person to evoke angry feelings in you at the expense of your health.

lounge car You will be in the company of the person of your choice within three days. Do not allow yourself to be caught off guard because you will want to look your best.

lounge lizard This dream is an extremely lucky omen. Take an assertive, no nonsense stance with someone who will want to get out of an agreement you have made at an earlier time. Make sure you do not accept only part of the agreement. Push for total fulfillment.

louse You are headed in the wrong direction regarding a romantic situation. This person would later be very instrumental to you and your future. Rethink your position.

louver For the next three days avoid anything that creates friction between yourself and others. This dream is an extremely lucky omen. Good luck is with you.

love For the next three days any love situation will be very lucky for you. This is the chance to make things work for you and to go for what you want. During this cycle, all relationships will renew themselves and friendships can become love relationships. Celebrate your love relationships on a grand scale and make the effort to love yourself by bringing things into your life that will bring you joy. You will also enjoy a love affair if this is something you desire. This is the perfect time to circulate and to make yourself available. You will have many admirers to choose from. Any person you pick will be a good choice. Good luck is with you. You will also gain many new assistants who will be very eager to support you with your work load. They will help you to complete your project and you will be very pleased with the results.

love apple Someone misses you a great deal but will do everything in their power to keep their emotions to themselves. Within five days you will be able to verify the identity of this individual. This dream is a very lucky cycle and you will enjoy an abundance of health for at least a month.

love beads Any creative project you are now developing will leave a mark on this world. At this time you will have no problem processing paperwork intended for someone in authority. Move on this project quickly.

lovebird It is a lucky omen to dream of a love bird. This dream represents an abundance of finances and love. Within five days you will meet someone whom you will admire physically. This person has reciprocal feelings for you. Any love felt will be more intense with your partner than with yourself. It is your option to pursue this if you choose. Be aware that all love relationships during this time period will be reciprocal.

love bug You will be involved within five days with someone who is not ready to commit. Be very patient with this person if you wish to develop a relationship with them. If you demand that this person become more demonstrative at this time you will drive them away. Back off for now and allow this person to proceed at their own pace.

love feast Within five days someone you are destined to meet will enter your life full of love and passion. This person will quickly move to have you involved with them in a sexual way. If you choose to go in this direction, this person will be loyal, will desire a permanent union, and will work for a healthy, solid relationship.

love games You will use your creative thoughts to create a fantasy evening with someone you care a great deal for. You will be able to draw the love and passion from the person you desire in a very romantic environment. Good luck is with you.

lovemaking You will rejoice over a great financial decision that someone you know will make. This will result in a great improvement in your financial status and lifestyle. You will also experience a new abundance of health.

to be rejected while love making You need to be acutely aware of someone who will, within five days, do what they can to trick you in some way. This individual is a monster in disguise. Be aware of this and guard yourself carefully.

love potion You will be pushed to the limit by someone who will tease you in a sexual way. You will be unable to handle this situation correctly. Prepare ahead for this so you can develop the means to handle this in the proper manner.

lover You will meet someone within the next few days with the qualities of a life long mate.

love seat Do what is necessary to stay uninvolved in situations you find distasteful, especially for the next week.

low *any form* Someone you do not know well will, within five days, request a private sexual encounter with you. This person is very intimate and will do what they can to involve you in their life. If you choose to take this route, this person will make sure you enjoy yourself and you will take delight in their company. This person is capable of offering great friendship and loyalty.

low life Get back to basics and simplify your life. Do not place any unnecessary demands on yourself, especially for the next five days.

low pressure Make sure you take precautions when you are out pleasure seeking. Do not allow peer pressure to involve you in something you find distasteful and that will later lead to regrets.

low profile Do not speak negatively of anyone, especially for the next seven days. You will regret this action.

low rider Within five days an unusual situation will occur among a group of people and they will discuss the need for your services in order to have their needs met. You will be approached with a proposal that you will easily be able to handle and will receive a handsome payment for your services. Go for it. Good luck is with you.

low tide For the next five days you need to do as much as possible to involve yourself with a special person in order to keep this person from feeling left out. Make sure your priorities are straight and you spend time with those who are important to you.

lox This dream is an extremely lucky omen and you are definitely headed for a brilliant future. You will also enjoy an abundance of health.

lozenge Take special steps to keep someone who is important to you from slipping out of your life because of your lack of involvement.

lubrication Make sure you watch the level of attention you are paying to a special person. This behavior may not be acceptable for the circumstances. Make sure you conduct yourself properly.
   using lubricants for sexual purposes with someone you recognize Someone will be very eager to respond to any

demand you make for the next five days. You will be welcomed with open arms. This cycle will be very advantageous to you.

luck Concentrate for the next three days and make a list of those things you feel would be lucky involvements for you. Actively pursue anything in your power and opportunities will begin to present themselves. You will then be able to choose the path you wish to explore. You are headed for a brilliant future and prosperity will come your way once you become motivated.
   to hear yourself wish someone good luck This dream is a powerful symbol and is a promise you will grasp the goals you are pursuing. You will be in a very victorious cycle for the next two weeks. Anything negative portended in the dream needs to be altered or changed. Make sure you experience only positive expressions in your life. Your special deity is with you.

lug Any involvement you have in a creative project will be very successful and will bring many benefits to all those involved.

lug wrench Make sure you have an extra set of keys where you can get to them. Within five days you will be locked out and it will be very costly to hire a locksmith.

luggage Recheck all of your major appliances within two days. You will find the equipment you use during this time period will not work properly unless you make an effort to repair and fine tune all your machinery. You must also make an effort to keep your promises.

luggage tag Make it your business to discuss your needs with a special person over the next two days. This person will be very willing to comply once they are aware of what you require. You must verbalize your needs in order to have them met.

Luke *(from the Bible)* Practice consistency when dealing with a particular issue you are developing until you reach perfection. Be patient and, although it will look as though you will never reach this point, you will.

lukewarm Make sure, for the next five days, that you treasure your possessions far more than you have in the past.

lullaby Make it a point to pay more attention to the older people and young children in your life whom you wish you could see more often. Time passes rapidly and you will find that it has been far too long between visits. Make sure you set aside special time to spend with these precious people especially for the next three days.

lumber Make sure you stay on top of situations and continuously follow through to ensure others are performing their tasks. Make sure everyone follows through with their work in a timely fashion. The job will not be completed on time unless you become actively involved.

lumberjack This dream is an extremely lucky omen. Many opportunities will be presented to you within the month and your lifestyle will dramatically improve. Anything connected to this dream that is significant will be important in helping you to pave a path for your children.

lumberyard Within five days someone will request that you perform a favor for them and will pay you generously for your time. You must also need to develop a support system that will allow you to live your life in a more unique fashion.

luminous You will enjoy a beautiful festive event within three days. Push yourself to become involved in order to glean the most enjoyment from this event.

lump Make sure you tell those who are special to you that you love them. People need to hear this from you. Within the week unusual situations will also occur that will bring you great prosperity.

lumpfish You will learn of a pregnancy within two months. Heed this omen if it is something you personally need to be aware of. You must also need to make sure you do not ingest any food, drink or medications that may cause an allergic reaction and be alert to food poisoning.

lunacy When on an outing with someone you will accidentally blurt out an insulting remark to someone else. Watch your behavior and make sure you do not make this mistake. You will not be asked out again by this individual if you do not. This is preventable.

lunar Although you feel as though your talents will get you nowhere, if you involve yourself in the appropriate way for the next month, you will get the exposure you need to bring you fame.

lunar eclipse Make sure you meditate in your favorite form. This is the time that, no matter how difficult it may seem, any demand you make from your deity will be granted. Many blessings will come to you and your family.

lunatic You are thinking about asking out someone you think is interesting. This person is not at all what they appear to be. Get on with your life without this person in it and quickly direct your interests toward someone else.

lunch Make sure the gift you are about to give someone else is well received. Think ahead about what you are planning to give and if you need to make changes, this is the time to do it. A situation will also start to develop within three days that will involve two people of equal power who will have to go up against each other to prove themselves to others. Emotions will be high because everyone will be interested in who comes out ahead. The older of the two will emerge the winner and this will satisfy everyone involved. You will also experience an unexpected windfall. You are definitely

headed for a brilliant future.

free lunch The head of the household will make an emotional appeal to someone in power. This will bring more abundance of wealth to the family. Move quickly, this cycle will last for seven days. This dream is also an omen of luck for this time period.

luncheon Make sure you do not blurt out an untruthful statement that should not be made. This will hurt a special person's feelings to the point that a separation will be the result. Make sure you word your thoughts carefully. This dream also implies that, within three days, you will be asked out on a date. If you choose to go, you will have a very entertaining evening. Go for it.

luncheonette This dream is a very lucky omen. Within three days you will begin to experience new abundances in life. Do what you can to keep your stress levels down by removing yourself from stressful situations. It will be especially important during this time frame. This is a fortuitous cycle for bringing you benefits once you become motivated.

luncheon meat Someone you are close to will inform you they are planning to move out simply because they do not have the funds to remain where they are. This will catch you off guard. Prepare yourself for this.

luncheon meeting You will overextend yourself to someone who will enslave you in some capacity. This does not necessarily mean this person does not care for you. This person, however, does not see you as an individual who needs time to take care of your own affairs.

with a large group of people You will receive many future benefits by taking time out for yourself in order to organize your own thoughts so you can decide what you wish to involve yourself in.

lunch room Focus on those situations that need to be handled properly concerning a young adult or child. Make sure their needs are handled properly and in a timely fashion. It is especially important that you involve yourself in this for the next two days.

lung Anything you see in this dream that is connected to reality can be changed or avoided. If it is positive, make sure you promote it; if negative, take steps to avoid the event or to alter the result. Within three days when having a conversation with someone else, the tone of the conversation will change into a flirtatious romantic exchange. Good things will come out of this if you so desire. For the remainder of the month you will enjoy yourself immensely in anything you undertake.

lungfish Process important ideas within three days that you have been considering developing. During this time period you will be able to determine whether these ideas will be workable for you. You are headed for a brilliant future.

lure Prepare yourself. For the next two days you will be around an irritable person. Ignore this behavior even though you have to be involved in some capacity. This mood will pass.

lust Make sure your priorities are set up in the proper order. You will also do wonderful, creative things with your outer appearance. Imagine the physical changes you would like to make. This will be the proper time to do so. Good luck is with you.

lute For the next five days be very aware and do not allow anyone to purposely steer you in the wrong direction by giving you the wrong address, phone number, directions, information, etc.

Lutheran Within a three day period you will be among a group of people who will want to gain control over a situation you are presently dealing with. Take steps to determine what each person is capable of handling and delegate tasks accordingly.

luxurious Do not take on any additional financial burdens simply because you want to be kind hearted. Within five days you will also somehow become involved with someone who has a touch of finesse, flair and glamour, and is also very wealthy. This person will go to great lengths to involve you in their life because of their loneliness. This individual needs that one special person to make their life complete. If you choose, this special person could be you. You are definitely headed for a brilliant future.

luxury car An unexpected business offer will be extended to you (i.e., mail centers, Laundromat, etc.) by an unexpected person. If you choose to involve yourself, this enterprise will be very fruitful.

lye Don't allow someone special to slip away from you because of inconsistency or an abusive manner. Especially for the next three days.

lyme disease Avoid possessive behavior for the next five days. Others will not appreciate this. Also, make sure you and your family members do not contract this disease.

lymph Do not place so much importance on another person. This person is not very appreciative and will take you for what they can, either emotionally or financially. You are headed for a disappointing experience unless you set limits immediately.

lymph node Push yourself harder for the next three days in order to accomplish your goals. Make sure you maintain your health and get plenty of rest. Stay out of stressful environments for at least a month.

lymphoma A wealthy individual will unexpectedly offer to buy a large amount of your product. Financial security will come your way if you practice common sense for the next five days. A professional person will give you the advice

you need.

lynch Do not make your home a prison to others, especially for the next three days. This will backfire if you do not correct your behavior.

lynch mob Be very careful that someone with an emotional hang up does not focus on you. This could result in many distasteful moments of terror within the week.

lynx Plans that you put into writing will be very difficult to put into practice. Be sure to recheck your plans and simplify them in order to avoid unnecessary work.

lyre Make sure you guard against accidents for the next three days. Keep yourself and your family safe for the next three days.

lyrebird Within the week, you will experience victory because of your valiant integrity when you are required to make a decision. You will not compromise your principles but will develop a quiet conviction and relentlessness in your pursuit of money, contracts, items and agreements as well as productive conversation. Do not give up until you succeed. This dream is offering large clues that will help you with a dramatic move you are planning to undertake. This move will bring immediate and positive changes to your life. Any negative event seen in this dream needs to be present in reality and you will need to take steps to experience only positive expressions in your life.

M

M Be very cautious for the next five days and do not be so eager to jump into the unknown. Analyze your feelings and do not allow others to change your opinion. This refers particularly to political, religious or cult groups. Involvement with certain groups will make your life a disaster. Find alternative ways to spend your time that will bring you greater joy and tranquility. Go on with your life without any unusual group involvement.

Macadamia nut You will arrive at a timely and satisfactory solution to a critical problem. Many blessings are with you and you are headed for a prosperous future.

macaroni Anyone you recognize in this dream will be the person who will come to your assistance and change your life in a very prosperous way. This dream is very lucky for romance and finances.

macaroni and cheese For the next two weeks you will be sharing many enjoyable times with new acquaintances. If you choose to do this, you will acquire new friendships you will cherish for a long time.

macaroon Within five days someone will do everything they can to involve you in detective work. If you choose to do this, you will experience many thrilling moments you will cherish for a lifetime.

macaw For the next three days none of your business negotiations will bear fruit. Postpone all transactions for this time period in order to ensure a better outcome at a later date. Think ahead. Within five days you will misinterpret an overheard conversation. As a result, tempers will flare up. For more clues look up the prominent colors of the macaw. Good luck is with you.

Macbeth You will have to speak up for someone within the week who would be punished for something they did not do.

Maccabees, the *(from the Canonical Bible)* Within a four day period you will be able to perfectly calibrate your thoughts and verbalize them so well that someone who desires you will become so secure and comfortable in your presence they will speak in an open and frank manner. This will spark the development of a relationship and a warm, open union. You will also be able to use your communication skills to bring anything you want into tangible form and you will be able to remove all barriers due to poor communication. This will be a magical cycle for you. Any positive event reviewed in this dream symbolizes and foretells an event you should foster in reality. All negative scenes must be avoided.

mace Make sure you take the correct action regarding another person's behavior. Make sure you deal properly with this individual because their behavior will have a strong impact on how they will be treated by others. This will weigh heavily on your conscience if this individual is not treated well by others.

machete The decisions you make about a certain person should not be interfered with by others. You will have the final word. Analyze your thoughts carefully and do not allow others to influence your selections and choices. Do not allow yourself to be manipulated by others and only write out those wishes you know will be respected and carried out by others.

machine/machinery Be very protective over your talents, skills and genius. This is the perfect cycle to put things in their proper order.

washing machine Aggressively investigate any situation at the beginning stages so you will know how it develops if left to develop naturally. This will give you a clear picture of those aspects you want to become involved in. Do not over or underestimate any situation. Proceed with confidence.

machine gun For the next three days you will be able to

arrange things in such a way that all situations will be enormously beneficial to you. An increase in finances will come your way during this time cycle. This dream is an extremely lucky omen. Anything negative witnessed in this dream needs to be avoided in reality. Forewarn anyone you recognize to do the same. Take steps to ensure you only experience positive events in your life.

to use the machine gun in a violent manner You are definitely headed for a brilliant future and success will rapidly come to you.

to recognize someone holding a machine gun This individual will be instrumental in one way or another in brightening your future.

if a machine gun is used against you Do not lean on another person whom you are truly not interested in, especially for the next two days.

macho Someone with an emotional problem will need assistance within two days. Lend your services so this person will be able to get assistance and stop suffering. Relentlessly seek help until they are able to get the help they need.

mackerel You will experience victory in those areas of your life you most desire. You will also receive a long desired gift from a relative. Victory and an abundance of health are yours.

mackintosh Protect your privacy and do not tolerate unacceptable behavior from others.

macramé You will be treated in a sexual way in just the manner you wish by someone who is special to you. You will also be emotionally touched by this individual. If you choose, you will both make long range plans together and the relationship will endure. This dream is a very lucky omen. You will also enjoy luck in finances and you are loved by many.

mad It is quite likely you will go on an ocean voyage for business purposes. This will be tremendously successful for you.

to be mad Protect yourself in every way you can for the next five days. There is a danger you are unaware of. Take every step to protect your health.

to see someone else mad You will acquire a new acquaintance who may suddenly become dangerous and seek to injure you in some way. Do not involve yourself for the next five days with someone you do not know very well. Pay attention and take precautions.

madam A partnership you desire to enter into with another person will be very successful and prosperous. Good luck is with you. Take steps to avoid or to alter any negative event connected with this dream.

madhouse Good luck is with you. You will be able to purchase, at a very reasonable price, something you greatly desire if you move quickly.

Madison Avenue An unusual, unexpected occurrence will arise that will allow you to do something uniquely different such as taking a spur of the moment trip. You will enjoy yourself a great deal. Good luck is with you.

madman Within five days someone will begin to plan how to create an unusual scenario that will allow them to violate your rights for the sole purpose of satisfying their own emotional gratification. Be acutely aware of this in order to avoid being caught off guard. This person will do everything they can to cause you to fall into their trap. You have prior notice of this and can take steps to guard against this distasteful situation. Proceed with confidence. Good luck is with you.

mad money A professional person will do everything within their power to involve you in a mutually satisfying relationship. This unity will last a lifetime if you so desire.

Madonna Within three days you will have an irresistible urge to do something unusual and outrageous. Go with this feeling and you will find emotional gratification at low risk to you, if any. You will treasure this memory for a long time.

madras Be very factual in all situations that you are dealing with for the next three days. Otherwise you will give someone the wrong impression who is attempting to involve you in a venture. Don't blow it.

Madrid This dream is a very lucky omen. Within three days you will describe a goal to a particular individual. This person will be so eager to become involved with your venture that they will offer financial backing. They have a brilliant business sense and will back you all the way. If you choose to go in this direction, you will receive profits in a short period of time. This dream may also be used as a reference point in time. If you dream of this city and see its name used in any context, the dream message will occur on this day.

Mafia A friend will call you with the news that their spouse has been unfaithful for the length of their marriage. This will be a shocking turn of events for them. Lend a listening ear for a few weeks until they can get a grip on themselves and gain new confidence. This is a lucky omen for you. Take small risks in games of chance and you will receive a handsome pay off.

magazine Whatever you were viewing in the magazine will offer you a large clue to the meaning of this dream. This will involve a future event you will either want to incorporate into your life or to avoid. You will also be exposed to a variety of amusements and will enjoy a hectic social life. Any event you choose to attend will bring you an enormous amount of joy and tranquility. This cycle promotes happiness.

Magdalene, Mary Your psychic abilities will be enhanced, you will be enlightened, gain a new clarity of thought and physical health in abundance. This will begin to manifest itself within two days. Use these abilities for the next month to express yourself to the fullest potential. Good luck is with you.

Magellan A deep inspiration will come to you and will serve as a great motivator. You will find out within two days that you are better prepared than you thought and you will be more motivated than ever before during this time period.

magenta You will request love from someone within three days and will be instantly gratified. You will enjoy physical and emotional pleasure to the fullest.

maggot You need to do everything necessary to avoid forcing yourself on another person. You will be tempted to do so within the next seven days but in spite of the appearance that this is acceptable behavior on your part toward this person, refrain from acting this way. The other individual will be repulsed by your actions and you will find it difficult to forgive yourself later. You must also make sure your environment is free of toxins.

Magi Follow your hunches and intuition, especially when dealing with other people for the next three days. All of your suspicions will be right on target.

magic/magical This dream is an extremely lucky omen. For the next month you will enjoy an abundance of health and financial security because unusual circumstances will take place that will allow this to occur. Do not limit yourself or deprive yourself of unique experiences and involvements that will come up within five days. Enjoy your life fully, eat healthy foods, drink plenty of water and get plenty of rest. Life will reward you handsomely not only in a financial sense but spiritually as well.

you are magical This dream implies you are entering a lucky cycle and within three days you will experience an inner courage and strength that comes from within you. Your steel drive and determination will drive you to break through any physical or mental barrier and will be able to rid yourself completely of any aspect of your life you disapprove of or that interferes with your forward movement. Once you have gotten rid of this block, you will quickly bring any new project to tangible form. Your plans will be completed in the way you desire. You will also be placed on a pedestal and will be greeted with open arms anywhere you go during this time frame. This will surprise you greatly. You are on the path toward a brilliant future and many new opportunities are headed your way.

magical, dramatic images In spite of how grim your life appears now, dramatic improvements will take place shortly because of unusual circumstances. Many blessings are with you.

to view anything that becomes invisible A particular work situation you have developed will become tangible. You will soon be able to harvest the fruits and gain great wealth from the hard work you have done. Many blessings will come to you and your family.

magician For the next five days you will need to be focused and very analytical about the moves you are about to take so you can be aware of those situations that require your immediate personal attention. As a result of this, an entirely new dimension will open up in your life and an unexpected prosperity will be yours.

if you recognize anyone performing magic This person possesses the necessary tools and skills to relentlessly push both of you forward to ensure you have a prosperous future. You are definitely headed for a brilliant future.

to perform magic In spite of anything else that is occurring in your life, your efforts to achieve will be accelerated toward achieving that special goal. Many blessings will come to you and your family and good luck is with you. You will find those things you felt were impossible are now possible.

to see someone you do not recognize practicing magic A new acquaintance whom you will speak with within three days will make certain you develop a stable, financially secure plan.

Magna Carta You will be in a very powerful cycle for the next week. You will be able to accomplish just about anything you attempt. Many blessings will come to you and your family.

magnesium For the next three days do everything you can to avoid involvement with someone who is lax and consistently slacks off. This behavior will only make you irritable and anxious. Avoid this person at all costs.

magnet You will realize your character and demeanor are the perfect tools to allow someone you desire to feel comfortable enough to express their deepest desires and plans involving both of you in the immediate future. Discuss these plans tactfully and gently and you will be able to tackle them together. This dream is a very lucky omen for both of you. You will be able to focus on the positive qualities you possess and will be very creative during this cycle.

magnetic field Someone whom you think is your friend will, within three days, egg you on to commit an act that will bring misery to you. Do not allow yourself to be manipulated.

magnetic force Do not allow anyone to involve you in anything before you are ready to become involved. Follow your own mind and don't be pushed into something you do not want to do. Do not compromise.

magnify *to magnify* Within three days you will become acutely aware of issues that need to be taken care of that you are now overlooking. It will be necessary to request immediate attention. This three day cycle will be the perfect time to play detective.

magnifying glass Pay attention to what is seen under the magnifying glass. This will offer a clue to a forthcoming event that will be either positive or negative. If it is negative, take steps to avoid it or to alter the outcome. If positive, make sure you take steps to include this in your life. This dream also implies that someone will magnify a situation to the point where it will seem far better than it is. In reality, this is not something you really need to get involved with, especially for the next two days.

magnolia Make sure you take big steps forward with any situation you will be handling within three days. Do everything in grand style and avoid tunnel vision when you are developing your creations. Think in terms of a grand scale.

magpie Protect your sense of hearing. At the first indication of hearing loss, seek help and avoid any situation that could result in hearing damage.

Maharaja Stop being so compromising and patient with everything and everybody. Face issues head on and do what is necessary to handle them.

mahogany You will meet someone within five days who will find you very attractive and will want to become instantly involved with you. If you choose, this person will stay with you in a permanent, loving relationship. This individual is capable of making an enormous amount of money but spends it just as quickly. This problem can be managed and changed until you establish a financially secure future.

maiden Do not cause disruption when the family elects to come together by insisting they do something other than what they originally planned to do. Back off and rethink your responses.

maiden of honor Become more diligent and consistent in order to allow your relationship to take the shape you desire. You will have to be the one who leads the way.

mail Make it a point to drop hints to a new admirer who will enter your life within two days. This person will ask you out and you will find they are exactly what you are looking for in your life. Make sure you are very attentive and affectionate toward this individual if this is the path you choose to take. Anything negative witnessed in this dream needs to be avoided in reality. Forewarn anyone you recognize to do the same. Take steps to ensure you only experience positive events in your life.

mailbag Within two days you will receive emotional fulfillment from a special person.

mailbox Take precautions to ensure all mail reaches its proper destination.

mail carrier For the next two days, no matter how defeated you feel about a particular situation, do not accept defeat. Boldness will lead to success.

mailgram Pay attention to the contents of the mailgram. If it is a negative message take steps to prevent it in reality If it is positive, make sure you incorporate it into your life. Someone special will also have a small gift for you that will bring you tremendous joy. Expect this within five days.

mailman/woman You will soon be getting a lucky break. Do your share to maintain a relationship and this will add to the closeness, love, and affection that develops. Within two days, no matter how discouraged and defeated you feel, you must also refuse to give in to these feelings. Assume a bold attitude. You are headed for a brilliant future.

maim Wait at least a month before making a commitment about a career or a relationship. This will lead to more success and better harmony. Take steps to change any negative event in reality and do everything you can to experience only positive expressions in your life.

main Give an increase in pay to those who deserve it. This is the correct cycle for this. Good luck is with you. Within three days someone you meet will also decide you are the one they want in their life on a permanent basis. This person will be very eager to fulfill all of your demands and will love every moment they have in your company. It is up to you whether you choose to have this person in your life.

Maine Do everything you can to reach an agreement with others regarding an emotional situation. This will successfully resolve a particular problem. Also within three days you will be dealing with a certain person who is acutely aware of your likes and dislikes and the kind of lifestyle and situations you are against. This person will use many different methods of subtle persuasion and will develop a plan that will lead you into a lifestyle you are against before you develop any awareness of what is going on. This person's intent is to lead you into doing something that goes against your ethics. They will use many different tactics and methods to accomplish this. This may be anything in the nature of gift giving, vacations, etc. It will take a long time and many different offerings to win you over but you will finally end up doing what this person wants you to do. You have prior notice of this and can take the appropriate steps to prevent it. Be sure you know exactly what you will or will not do. Otherwise you are headed for a brilliant future. This dream may also be used as a reference point in time. If you dream of this state and see its name used in any context, the dream message will occur on this day.

mainmast You will receive a call from someone in a distant place who will request that they move in with you for a short period of time until they can get on their feet. You will spend many rewarding moments with this person if you choose to accept this option.

mainsail You will find a large sum of money within a few days in an unexpected place. Make sure you keep your eyes open because there will be no claims on this money.

mainstream You will learn of a friend's engagement to be married and will be invited to join in on the festivities. Good luck is with you.

main street Stay away from anyone in a bad mood for the next two days. The moment you are in a situation with someone who is verbally abusive or says something to hurt your feelings remove yourself from the area.

maitre'd For the next few days tell only the truth. Everything will work out well for you if you do.

maize A special person in your life wants you to take the time out to make love to them. Surrender yourself to this demand as soon as you possibly can.

majesty Within two days you will surrender yourself to someone and express your love to this person in a passionate way if you choose to take this route.

major Someone who has a bad attitude about the way they handle life will take a personal interest in your well-being. This person is very wealthy and works in the same field in which you choose to make a career. Within three days, this person will make themselves available to you in any capacity you choose.

majorette Someone whom you choose not to be involved with will depend on you for transportation. You will need to make it known to this person you cannot taxi them around. Your time is precious.

make believe You have the chance to win money by playing your favorite games of chance within the week.

makeup *to make up after a spat* You will experience an abundance of health, spiritual healing and tranquility within three weeks and within the week a celebration will take place that will bring joy to everyone involved. This is also a promise to you that an idea, project or event will be brought into tangible form and will reach a higher level than you ever thought possible. This project will take on a life of its own and will easily pass through any channel it needs to go through. This will be a blessing to you and a cause for celebration for each person involved in this process. You are headed for a brilliant future and prosperity will come to you within the month.

makeup *to feel you need some make up* For the next two days make sure you do not settle for less than what you have coming to you. Take each situation one at a time and step by step and refuse to allow yourself to be taken. Make sure you are clear on each step you take in order to have a firm figure that you will settle for.

liquid make up This is an extremely lucky omen. You will experience an abundance of health and wealth in areas you do not expect and you will be able to achieve victory in those areas you most desire. You are entering a very lucky seven day cycle. This dream also implies that you need to become verbally aggressive with someone, within five days, in order to coerce them into interacting with you in the manner you desire. If you motivate yourself during this time frame, you will be successful. Proceed with confidence.

malamute Keep going in the direction you are headed. You will be exposed to many opportunities this week and will experience a brilliant future.

malaria For the next three days develop yourself in such a way that you are armed with knowledge. This is the tool you will need in order to avoid being taken by surprise this month. You will then be able to handle all situations appropriately.

Malaysia Within three days a situation will occur that will require that you act in such a way to protect your reputation. This dream may also be used as a reference point in time. If you dream of this country and see its name used in any context, the dream message will occur on this day.

male Within the month a male who is close to you will surprise you at how they were able to cleverly bring to tangible form an invention of theirs. This invention will be very simple but very necessary.

to dream you are male when in fact you are female Within five days you will be entering a very lucky cycle and everyone involved in your life will share your luck. You will be offered services that will enable you to successfully complete your goals and reach a higher level of achievement than you hoped for concerning anything you place a high level of importance. During this time period you can expect many wonderful connections that will assist you in meeting and surpassing your goals. You can also expect a mega merger and the energy created between you and those you will be working with will bring you to a far higher level of success than you hoped for. This dream also implies you will gain benefits through attending a festive event, an educational experience or a gathering you will attend in which one person will show an interest in you and your projects. You can look forward to a long period of tranquility following this and will enjoy a prosperous future. Any negative event associated with this dream may be avoided for you or anyone you dreamed about.

male chauvinist pig You will receive a generous loan that you can repay at your convenience and at your pace within five days.

malignancy You will have the opportunity within the week to get it right this time. This is the last chance you will have to correct any past mistakes. This is the perfect time to put everything in the proper perspective. You also have the power now to change any negative event that was foretold in this dream.

mall This is an extremely lucky omen. Anything you felt was impossible is now a possibility for you within the next seven days. Prepare yourself for an enormous surprise that will catch you off guard and fill you with enormous joy.

Good luck is with you and you will enjoy yourself immensely during this time period.

mallard Be intensely aware of someone who has the intent of hurting a special person. Take steps to keep this from occurring, especially for the next seven days.

mallet This dream is alerting you to the fact that someone who has had too much to drink will ruin a special occasion. You have prior notice of this and can take steps to ensure this does not take place.

malpractice Someone whom you consider wonderful and who has a great sense of humor will desire a conversation with you. This conversation will lead to a sense of emotional fulfillment. If you choose to take this further, this individual will be very eager to develop a relationship.

malt Within three days all those who dream about malt and are afflicted with an illness will make a rapid recovery. You will also become aware of an admirer who has lacked the courage to reveal their feelings. This person will let you know they have, for a long period of time, desired an involvement with you.

Malta Any person or event you recognize from this dream will be the instrument that will point you in the right direction toward a brilliant future. An admirer will also make it clear to you that they desire to become a mate for life. This individual possesses enormous wealth. If you choose to go in this direction, this will become a permanent relationship. This dream may also be used as a reference point in time. If you dream of this city and see its name used in any context, the dream message will occur on this day.

malted milk Within a few days you will find a number of ways to gain financial backing from various associates who are eager to come to your support. Think this over carefully and make the correct moves because this enterprise will set you up for life.

Maltese You are headed for a brilliant future and, if you desire, will marry someone within the year who possesses enormous wealth.

malt liquor You will be required to make a decision within three days that you must not postpone. Accept your responsibilities at the time and take care of them.

mamba Make sure you are not the one who blurts out something in front of a couple that will be the major cause of a separation in the future. Be very aware of your words for the next five days.

mambo Within five days if you desire, someone will touch you very sensually and make love to you in the manner you desire. You will be emotionally fulfilled in ways you never have before. If this is what you want, take steps to make sure this comes about. Good luck is with you.

mamma You will receive an unexpected surprise from someone who has treated you with much kindness.

mammal Give someone the benefit of the doubt regarding rumors and gossip that will come about within five days.

mammoth Someone will insist you become a part of their future plans. It is up to you whether you choose to go in this direction.

man Be sure you play a very active role in having your emotional needs met. Within five days you will be able to visualize the path you need to take for a brilliant future. Good luck is with you.

angry You are wanted sexually by someone but you are unaware of their desire. Should you choose to pursue this relationship, it will be financially advantageous to you.

black This dream implies victory, power and a pleasurable time with an older and powerful person. This will be financially advantageous to you and will be emotionally rewarding as well. You can develop this relationship to the degree you desire for as long as you choose. This person will pursue you tenaciously.

black-dressed Maintain your confidence when another person tries to make you feel desperate. You are headed for a brilliant future.

crying You will be charged for services never received. Be careful of con-artists and lawsuit chasers. This may occur within a few days.

cutting wires Be aware of the surroundings of small children. The child may be an innocent bystander and meet with foul play.

deranged Do not place so much importance on others and do not leave yourself open to a surprise attack in an unfamiliar place.

handsome Someone desperately needs you in a sexual way within three days. This person will go to great lengths to satisfy you emotionally and physically. You will find mutual satisfaction as a result. You are loved beyond your imagination, whether this is verbalized or not. An unknown person will also enter your life and help you to realize your ideas, potentials, and ambitions. You will reach the goals you desire as a result of a light discussion you will have with this person.

happy You will experience greater sexual satisfaction than you believed possible with someone you desire within a few days.

homeless Someone you know needs temporary lodging. Do not offer your home as this would be an unwise decision.

milk man Bargain hunting will be extremely lucky for you, especially while supplies last. You will also enjoy stronger emotional ties with someone who is special to you, especially for the next three days. Keep this closeness permanent.

murdered man Someone will attempt to force or coerce you into something distasteful. Avoid any confrontation at the first sign of this and leave the situation tactfully.

muscular Handle your affairs and duties promptly.

older You will find a timely, satisfactory solution to a crucial situation.

overweight You will hear reports of a sexually or physically abused child. If the one committing the act is yourself, stop abruptly and seek help, for you will be discovered shortly and prosecuted. If someone else is committing the act, advise them to stop and seek help, as they will shortly be discovered and prosecuted.

policeman Be patient with a loved one who is incapable of verbalizing love, because you are loved beyond your expectations.

to see a police officer in the background (sex unknown) Be acutely aware of the behavior of someone who desires familiarity. This person will be deceitful and conspiratorial.

professional(s) You will shortly grow rich through marriage only if you make your marriage desires publicly known. Prosperity, love and health belong to you.

red haired Be very aware of something you are doing now that will cause financial damage later on. You will not be aware of the extent of the damage for a long time to come. Protect your expenditures now.

sexually aroused Love yourself and give yourself a smart gift. Do things that will make you feel good about yourself. Within a few days you will enter into a long desired secret arrangement and you will be completely satisfied with the arrangement. Pay attention to the person in your dream who has their penis exposed. This person will represent the person who is interested in you in some capacity. This could be sexual in nature but could also be in another context. This representation is primarily symbolic (i.e., a child with an exposed penis may indicate an adult with a childlike nature or this adult will be younger than other male counterparts you know).

short This dream implies you will enjoy domestic happiness with much affection and deep emotional love. You will experience this within three days.

skinny Move quickly. You will achieve prosperity in every level of your life. Accept whatever comes your way as your good fortune. Be confident and do not question anything that works to your favor for the next five days. Any opportunity presented to you will be very fortuitous during this time period so render a positive response. Stocks will also go up. Go for it.

sleeping Guard yourself against automobile accidents and any preventable injury, especially for the next three days.

sloppy You will be in the company of an immoral and wicked person. Do not be deceived and be alert to this for the next two days.

strange You need to be more protective over your possessions for the next two days. Your finances are at stake.

suicidal Each man you see in your dream who commits suicide represents a financial gain of approximately one thousand dollars. This will occur within the week.

tall A new and affectionate admirer will become known to you. Should you pursue this, it will lead to a lasting commitment. Expect this within three days.

to hear a disembodied man's voice Pay attention to the message given. If negative, take steps to change the outcome. If positive, take steps to incorporate it into your life. This dream also implies someone who acts indifferent to you is, in reality, not this way. This person actually desires very much to be involved in your life. If you choose to become involved, make the first move and let it be known you would like more involvement. Your plans will also fall into place just as you have envisioned. Do not hold back on big projects. Tackle them immediately and you will experience prosperity.

horrifying male figure You are overexerting yourself to the point of physical exhaustion. For the next week, do everything you can to maintain and improve your health. Eat healthy foods, drink plenty of water and set limits on what you are willing to do for others. Each request you make of your god will also be granted during this time period, no matter how impossible the request may seem.

man of God You are headed for a new and prosperous lifestyle.

perfect male figure Within five days you will find yourself in the position of having to care for someone until they are able to get on their feet. This person will improve their quality of life and physical state to the point of social and personal acceptance. During this time period, you will be swamped with social engagements and will need to take extra pains to maintain your appearance and attire. This will be a very successful cycle for you.

youthful-faced Your plans of love will work out to your advantage in a surprising way.

well-dressed A yearning for a certain person will be realized.

working with wires (any) Someone is plotting your murder. Be aware of your surroundings and the people around you for the next seven days.

slang term Make sure, for the next three days, that you maintain your sense of alertness and caution. Do not allow yourself to be persuaded into going someplace that could be a danger to you. Remain alert in all aspects of your life. Be especially cautious when involving yourself in new situations with another individual who will inadvertently cause you injury. For this time period, choose wisely what you will or will not involve yourself in.

washer man This is a very lucky omen and you will be experiencing much prosperity in your life within two weeks. Things you thought were impossible to become a part of are now possible during this two week period. Doors will be open to you and you will be welcomed with open arms. Many blessings are with you and your family.

to see a man's head on another body You need to be acutely aware of this person because they will attempt to bring some emotional harm to you, either emotional or physical. Do everything you can to keep yourself safe. Get on with your life without this person in it because they are serious. Although this person will present a very kind and nice demeanor, they are very evil and cunning. Within three days make sure you disassociate from this person, move on with your life and take steps to turn this situation around. Make sure you experience only positive expressions in your life.

to hear the phrase "dirty old man" You will have the strength to regroup and to make a move toward someone you desire in order to push things along in the direction you want to go romantically. This person is not aware of your feelings as yet. Good luck is with you.

to hear phrase "man of the world" You will need to control your envy and jealousy for the next three days.

to hear the phrase "man of the house" Do not focus on specific negative aspects of an individual person. Focus instead on what this person represents to you and on their capabilities. You are wasting time on negativity.

manacle Make sure all of your conversations are concise and lead fully in the direction you wish them to go. Listen carefully to your words to ensure there are no confusions about your true feelings and be sure you get your point across.

manager Within three days you will sense that there is a big secret being hidden from you. You will have to subtly conduct an investigation to determine what will emerge. Do not allow anyone to know you are trying to get to the source because you'll never learn the facts this way.

manatee You will come to realize the importance of another person and their input into your life. This individual places a lot of importance on making sure you are comfortable.

mandarin Make sure children in the family are being looked after properly and that their whereabouts are known.

mandarin duck Avoid people who complain and who are constantly miserable. You will have to deal with this within five days. You have prior notice and can make yourself scarce in order to avoid ruining pleasurable moments.

mandarin orange All of your romantic plans will work out exactly as you envision with someone who is special to you. You will enjoy a surprising outcome.

mandolin Be a little outrageous and go overboard on a project you will become involved in. The grander and more outrageous the ideas, the more successful it will be. You will gain a lot of respect from this enterprise.

mandrake Become very possessive of your belongings and make sure you do not lose something due to irresponsibility. This is likely to occur within five days.

mane You will receive a marriage proposal within the week. If this is what you want, respond immediately. This person will not ask a second time.

man-eater Do not get involved in someone else's problems, especially for the next week. Be firm and discipline yourself to stay uninvolved.

mange Someone you know will be too sexually aggressive for you. Bring this issue to this individual's attention in such a way that their feelings are not hurt but you are able get your point across. This will lead to more respect and understanding from this person.

mango Team effort should be a priority. Share responsibilities with others. This is especially important for the next seven days.

mangrove Do not allow anyone to volunteer your services for the next two days regardless of how rewarding they make it sound.

manhandle A deep inspiration will come to you and serve as a great motivator. You will find out within five days you are better prepared than you thought and you will be more motivated than ever before during this time period. If you witnessed anything negative in this dream, take steps to prevent this in reality.

Manhattan An opportunity will present itself to you, within five days, that is well within your power to grasp. This will allow you to make positive changes in each area of your life that you desire in a very short period of time. All of your old issues and burdens will miraculously disappear and will leave you with a new zest for life. This dream may also be used as a reference point in time. If you dream of this city and see its name used in any context, the dream message will occur on this day.

manhole Make sure children who are under your care are protected and well taken care of.

mania Remain firm on your decisions once they have been made, especially for the next seven days.

manicure Do not waste your time trying to get someone to reach an agreement with you. This individual will not give in to your wishes. Seek an alternative plan and avoid distasteful moments. Good luck is with you.

Manila Regardless of what is going on in your present life, because of your determination, you will reach your ultimate ambition. This dream may also be used as a reference point in time. If you dream of this city and see its name used in any context, the dream message will occur on this day.

manila envelope You will make all the correct decisions and will choose the ultimate role to take within the week. You are headed for a brilliant future.

manna Within the week you will rejoice because of some unusual good fortune that will change your life. Prosperity and good luck is with you.

mannequin Keep your opinions to yourself for the next three days in front of family members, otherwise things will escalate to the point of no return.

man o'war Take steps to involve yourself with someone you feel will be important to you in the future. Start building

bonds now and strengthening this friendship. You will have an opportune time to accomplish this within five days.

mansion You will soon be liberated from a long-standing burden. What was not possible in the past is now a possibility. You have every opportunity now to bring your desires into reality.

manslaughter Make sure you do not go along with the plans of another and be very careful you do not go against your better judgment, especially for the next five days.

mantel Someone will go through the trouble of playing down the potential of a certain project so you will not be interested in becoming involved. Make sure you get all the facts. This information will come to you at the precise time you need it. Take the time to process it ahead of time.

mantra Someone whom you are very loyal to will lie to you. Be especially aware of this within the next three days. This will be out of your control and will be done for no particular reason.

manual On a whim someone you are not interested in will approach you romantically. Be firm in your refusal and get your point across.

manure Trust your decisions for the next two days. Your instincts are correct.

manuscript Your creative projects will be received with open arms throughout the world.

Manx cat Take steps to exclude people from your life who enjoy provoking arguments and creating chaos.

map You need to remove any mental block that is keeping you from moving ahead. You will clearly be able to pinpoint those areas that need to be changed. By erasing these blocks you will begin moving forward rapidly. Be especially attentive to what the map is revealing. This will indicate some place you should or should not be going, depending on dream message.

maple Someone will be unable to contain their excitement when they are around you. This person will expose their enthusiasm when in your company. Expect this to occur within three days.

maple leaf Take the leap into an emotional involvement even if you have doubts about it. This relationship will deepen. Go for it and rescue yourself from loneliness.

maple syrup Make sure you set limits on the amount of labor you will perform for another without pay. You will also receive an unexpected gift you will be very happy to get. You are headed for a prosperous future.

maraschino cherry This dream implies you will be surrounded by many powerful and influential people but there is one person you are destined to become involved with. This will be someone of the opposite sex and will be on any level you choose. Leave yourself open to situations that will expose you to other people you will meet that you can become involved with. You will soon have the chance to meet this person. Conversations will flow easily between you and a sense of closeness will rapidly develop. This individual is well established and more financially stable than you expected and you will both enjoy a wonderful, tranquil life, an abundance of health, and a prosperous future.

marathon If you want more understanding, a deeper involvement and a greater demonstration of feelings, you will need to verbalize this within five days. This person is anxious to hear this from you.

marble You will make a friend for life. This person is much older than you, is very nervous and has enormous wealth. Although you will never take advantage of this person's generosity, your life will be blessed with tokens of appreciation in the form of small gifts. This friendship will begin within three days and no one will ever be able to interfere with your friendship.

marble cake Make it a point to enjoy more of what nature has to offer. Get back to basics and enjoy what is around you. Love yourself, pamper yourself and treat yourself to marvelous events.

marbleize *to marbleize anything, any form* Something wonderful will happen that will catch you completely off guard within five days. Good luck is with you.

march Do not send mixed messages by using inappropriate body language. Make sure the message you give is one you can stand behind. This is likely to occur within three days.

March Be very straightforward and up front when participating in any discussion that involves a salary or any financial transaction. This will be a very important issue within three days.

Marco Polo Investigate the possibility of changing direction and seek alternatives to the path you are presently on.

Mardi Gras You will be the person who will inspire and steer large groups of people to work together for an important cause that will improve mankind. Work on this quickly and you will be able to resolve certain concerns. This group will relentlessly back your ideas.

mare You will have an important sexual encounter with someone whom you feel is special and important in your life. *if you see a painted mare* You are about to give birth to a new idea that you will market soon and will bring you financial prosperity. Find a way to act quickly on this.

mare's tail A negotiation that everyone has doubts about will result in success. Proceed with confidence.

margarine You will be received with more warmth at someone else's house than you ever thought possible. This will take you very much by surprise.

sweet margarine You will be introduced to an influential person who will, in turn, introduce you to a group of powerful friends. You will develop powerful allies from this group who will offer assistance to you in the future.

margarita Refuse to be hassled by any individual and shield yourself from any stressful situation for the next three days.

margin Push yourself to the limit when dealing with situations that will occur within the next three days. This dream is an extremely lucky omen.

marigold Many blessings will come to you and your family. You are in a very prosperous cycle. You will also be speaking with someone who owns a business. This person will offer to sell you some items and are unaware of their worth. At the time they are offered you will be able to purchase them at a reasonable price but if you wait, within two days this individual will discover their real value.

marijuana Prevent the permanent split up of a relationship that is important to you. Carefully review your behavior for the next month to determine what you are doing that may cause this. You have prior notice of this event and can keep it from taking place.

marimba Be very aware that someone you no longer want in your life and who has reassured you they will leave you alone will break this promise within five days. Do not allow yourself to be pinned down by this person and make it clear you want nothing more to do with them. You will need to be emotionally equipped to deal with this delicate issue. Organize your thoughts and feelings and give this person no indication you are willing to commit to something you are unwilling to commit to. Make sure there are no misunderstandings. You will be successful in getting your point across in a way that will not be offensive to anyone. Proceed with caution and you will successfully deal with this delicate issue.

marina Make sure you take advantage of the perfect moment to open up to someone and get your point across when dealing with your specific needs. This person can quickly meet your needs.

marinade Research your next move when making a decision about situations that will arise within the next three days so you will be able to deal with upcoming situations appropriately.

to marinade Change your everyday routine in order to confuse someone who has been stalking you for the purpose of doing bodily harm.

marine Make sure you do not go to the extremes regarding an issue that will arise within two days. Avoid crowded places during this time period.

marionette Someone will request you spend some private moments with them in order to talk about a deep secret this person wants to reveal to you.

marjoram Someone will promise undying love to you within three days. This person is serious and will remain loyal for a lifetime if you choose to go this route.

Mark *(from the Bible)* This dream implies you are entering a very lucky cycle and you will soon be making up for a lack of social activity with a group of wonderful people. You will share much laughter, cement your friendships and enjoy many mutual hobbies. A relative will also give you a beautiful gift that you will treasure for a lifetime.

mark You and another person are seeking ways to improve your relationship. You now feel open to conversation and new ways to demonstrate love and to bring in a new closeness that will benefit the union. This will work to improve the relationship in every aspect. If you choose to pursue this, the other person will be more than willing to go along with this process.
to see insignificant marks Do not undergo unnecessary surgery for the next seven days. Research this in more detail and get a second opinion.
burn marks on wood Within three days, someone will diplomatically drop subtle hints about a particular area of dissatisfaction in their life that they would like to see you become responsible for. This person wants you to take it upon yourself to make the necessary changes to improve their life and they feel they are stonewalled and cannot get through this situation. You will have the conviction and compassion to do this for them and it will lead them to a better lifestyle if you take the initiative. Many blessings are with you.
in any other form Make sure you do not allow someone to harass you out of something you value. Make sure you firmly put an end to this behavior and take steps to protect your valuables.

marker *to use a marker* You will be dealing with someone who will lead you to believe they are interested in you. Once you become involved, this person will give you excuse after excuse why they cannot see you. Get on with your life without dealing with this person.

market Move on with your plans, they will work out exactly as you have envisioned.

marketplace Be sure you do not overlook an event that will be attended by a special person you should meet.

market price Expect a wonderful, unexpected surprise that will be yours within three days.

marlin Something unusual will occur within four days. You will be able to locate someone who is willing to help

you and will stick with you until your needs are met.

marmalade Pay attention to the facts and refuse to accept anything unless it is backed up by proof. You will also experience a certain increase in wealth that will take you by surprise and will be for work well done. This will occur within three days.

marmoset Do everything necessary to ensure you will be traveling safely. Make sure your transportation is solid.

maroon Pay close attention to the news for the next two days. Something important you need very much will become available to you.

marquee Someone will have an enormous amount of feelings for you. You will receive verification of this within three days and will enjoy a tremendous amount of abundance and prosperity in areas you least expect. During this cycle you will be able to grasp something you have always wanted. Motivate yourself to make things happen during the next month and you will achieve what you most desire. This cycle will last for the next month.

marriage For the next month you will be in a cycle that will permit anything you want to happen to occur. Do not take anything for granted and apply yourself to those areas of your life that you want to achieve success in. Follow up your goals until they are completed in the manner you wish. You are definitely headed for a brilliant future. Within three days, someone will start talking to you in ways that will let you know they are obsessed with the idea that you both belong together as a unit. You have prior notice of this and can decide now how you want to handle this situation. If you decide to go in this direction, it will be a very affectionate and financially secure union.
civil marriage Two of your friends will be moving in together. This will be a good arrangement.
common law marriage Do whatever is necessary to avoid being jailed. You will be injured by another inmate.
if you recognize the person who is getting married This person you dreamed about very much desires this to happen and has the opportunity to make this occur with the person of their choice if they motivate themselves for the next three months.
someone getting married who is in actuality already married You and the person you recognize will experience new dimensions in your life that are open for exploration regardless of anything that may be going on in your life right now. You will not only have these opportunities but will also be able to align yourself with those people and situations that will enable everything to work out perfectly. Move quickly and pounce on any opportunity that will present itself within three days. You are definitely headed for a prosperous future.
marriage with someone you have never thought of marrying You will be involved with someone other than the one you dreamed of. This person is someone with enormous potential and great wealth. You will enjoy a tranquil, stable

and financially secure life.

marrying the spouse of a relative Do what you can to avoid someone who, until now, has not been violent but has that potential. An unusual situation will occur within three days that can escalate to the point of violence and this individual has the potential to inflict mortal injury. Make sure you find a safe haven that this person has no knowledge of. Do what you can to protect yourself and your environment. Good luck is with you.

to marry a step relation Be keenly aware of the way certain situations are developing in the family. Disagreements will start to develop within three days that will escalate to the point of being out of control. Back off and take steps to prevent this from occurring and do not allow others to participate in such behavior.

marrying someone you have no desire to marry Aggressively go after and grasp what is righteously yours. Relentlessly pursue this until you come out the winner. This is especially important for the next three days.

to see animals marry You will receive a large sum of money that has been owed to you for a long time. Expect this within three days. You are headed for a prosperous future.

marrying someone who is deceased This dream is an assurance that your life will turn around and you will have a brilliant future. Enjoy life fully; do not take life for granted. Someone will come into your life within a few days, will come on eagerly, and will rush you into a friendly relationship. At first you will get mixed messages while on a date and you will feel this person also desires romance. After you begin to respond to this aspect, they will back off quickly and withdraw from the friendship. Take this as a forewarning to enjoy the friendship and to take it no further. Otherwise, this dream is an extremely lucky omen.

to see an in-law marry another of your relatives Within five days, someone will plan an unusual scenario that will give them the opportunity to violate your rights for the sole purpose of their own emotional gratification. Be acutely aware of this in order to avoid becoming caught in their trap. You have prior notice of this and can take steps to guard against this distasteful situation. Proceed with confidence. Good luck is with you.

to see a step relative marry another of your relatives You will witness an event that demonstrates how another person can create chaos because of their behavior. You will be involved in a business discussion with someone you have made prior arrangements with. This will involve a job of some sort that someone has agreed to do for you. A third person will enter the scene and start changing your arrangements to suit their purpose. This will be an opposite sexed person who will bully their way into this conversation in such a way that it will be difficult for you to regain control. Do what you can to keep this person from forcing you into making a compromise. You will be successful.

to see an ex-relative marry another of your relatives Be sure you play an active part in satisfying your emotional desires. You will also, within five days, be able to visualize the path you need to take in order to ensure a brilliant future.

Good luck is with you.

marrying a relative This dream is an assurance that your life will turn around and you will enjoy a brilliant future. Enjoy life fully and do not take life for granted. This dream is an extremely lucky omen. Someone will come into your life within a few days and will eagerly rush you into a friendly relationship. At first you will get mixed messages while on a date and feel that this person desires romance also. After you begin to respond to this aspect of their behavior, this person will quickly back off and withdraw from the friendship. Take this as a forewarning to enjoy the friendship and take it no further. You must also make certain you or anyone else you recognize in the dream do not become involved in any romantic interplay with a close relative. Make sure any negative event witnessed in this dream does not become a reality for yourself or anyone you recognize in the dream. Take steps to ensure you experience only positive events in life.

your ex getting married Within the week several events will occur that you need to expose yourself to. Motivate yourself to take advantage of these issues because they will offer you once in a lifetime opportunities. Mobilize yourself in order to catch each opportunity. Otherwise, you are headed for a brilliant future.

intermarriage Your life will turn around and you will enjoy a much improved lifestyle. You are headed for a brilliant future. Do not take life for granted and make sure you take the time to enjoy each moment. This dream is an extremely lucky omen. Within five days, someone will also come into your life and will rush you into a friendly relationship. You will get mixed messages on this outing and will be led to believe that this person desires romance. Once you respond, this individual will begin to back off and will withdraw from the relationship. This is a warning to take the friendship for what it is and expect nothing more. You will also need to make sure anything negative you dreamed about does not become a reality.

marriage broker If you choose, take a big step now toward accepting a proposal. This three week cycle is perfect for bringing this about. Focus on this and work to make it a reality.

marrow Within three days a very optimistic person with a fantastic sense of humor will enter your life. This person will inspire you to view a certain situation from a different perspective and this will allow you to experience more joy in your life and to view everything from a more positive point of view. Good luck is with you.

marrowbone Put more spice into your life. Enjoy life more fully, pamper yourself, be good to yourself and do things that will add joy to your life. Take steps to improve your appearance as well. Above all, keep up your health by eating the proper foods, drinking plenty of water and getting plenty of rest. Good luck will come to you and your family.

Mars In order for you to evolve, grow and develop into the person you are capable of becoming, remove yourself from interference. You are experiencing a lot of stress and over involvement in personal issues. You need to remove yourself from this pressure. This will allow you to process a clarity of thought that will ultimately lead to a more prosperous future. This is the perfect cycle for lifting yourself from a stressful situation and grasping new opportunities.

marshal Be acutely alert for the next three days not to allow someone to enter your life who has a strong animosity toward someone else but is acting as though they do not. This is preventable and you have prior notice so you won't be caught off guard. This will keep physical or emotional harm from coming to you for the next two weeks.

marshmallow You will definitely experience sensual pleasure and will be emotionally fulfilled within three days. This is a prosperous cycle for love and finances. Many blessings are with you.

martial arts You will have a difficult time enlisting the affection you desire from a special person for the next three days.

Martian Be very wary and do not allow a total stranger to catch you off guard in an environment that will leave you open to experience an enormous amount of terror at the hands of a dangerous and evil individual. This is a life threatening situation and is preventable. You have prior notice of this and can take steps to keep this from occurring.
 if you recognize the person in the dream This is the individual who needs this protection.
 if you do not recognize the person in the dream This is the face of the person who will do you harm.

martini Do what you can to develop the foresight to keep yourself from developing a dangerous illness. You have prior notice of this and can take steps to avoid being in any environment where you can contract a contagious illness. If you are planning to visit a foreign land, prepare yourself appropriately in order to avoid any dangerous contamination.

Martin Luther King *to dream of the person, the name or the birthday* Take big steps to raise your standard of living by focusing on your goals on a grand scale. Avoid tunnel vision. You will also involve yourself with a group of people who will give immediate support in dealing with a bleak situation. This group will be able to restore stability, give financial assistance and lend confidence where despair and despondency prevailed. Everyone involved will experience a beautiful expression of joy and tranquility. Many blessings will come to you and your family. Refer to the definition "to dream about a deceased person" for a greater definition of this dream message. You will find this definition under the word "dead".

martyr For those who are pregnant, this is a warning to avoid anything that may trigger a premature birth. Take precautions for the next three days.

Marx You will be in a cycle where genius of thought will predominate. Write these thoughts down and quickly execute them for your benefit.

Marxism You will discover a side of a person you never knew before. You will notice angry, revengeful and envious feelings from this person within three days. Do what you can to spare yourself unpleasant moments. The moment you see any negative emotions develop, leave the premises.

Maryland Within five days you will be invited to an unusual event that will take place in very unglamorous settings. Do not deprive yourself of the delight you will experience by associating with these people in this setting. An abundance of health and prosperity will be yours for the next month. This dream may also be used as a reference point in time. If you dream of this state and see its name used in any context, the dream message will occur on this day.

Mary Queen of Scots You are placing too much importance on another person and you need to focus on other matters. You also need to place more importance on your small possessions. It is quite likely you will find these items missing weeks after they have been picked up by someone. Protect your small valuables for the next three days.

Mary, Virgin This dream is an omen of prosperity. You are also being asked to focus on treatments you need in your life to bring back a sense of normalcy and balance regarding your health. Move quickly and motivate yourself to perform the necessary tasks to move ahead in life. Victory is with you. You will retain a sense of excitement about your future for the next seven days.

marzipan Someone will quickly return to your life to reconcile and rekindle a relationship. This person will go to great lengths to reinvolve you in their life. If you desire this, you will be loved beyond your imagination.

mascara Within three days you will receive a wonderful small item if you are properly motivated to be at the right time and place to receive it. Keep your ears and eyes open to take advantage of this opportunity. You will enjoy an abundance of health, love, appreciation and affection during this time frame.

mascot Make sure you do everything you can to discourage laziness for the next three days.

masculine Someone will offer you a deep permanent commitment. This will start to develop within two days.

mash All legal proceedings will be settled in a timely fashion in your favor.

masher Avoid irritable people for the next two days.

mask Look at the facts and deal with situations head on. Avoid the habit of viewing everything through rose colored glasses. Find a solution to this issue by dealing with the facts.

to wear a mask You will be handling a certain situation with a lower level of seriousness than you should. Bear down on yourself, get serious and deal with your responsibilities in a serious manner. Handle all situations that will be coming up within three days.

to take off a mask You will be able to put things successfully back into order within three days.

to see others wear a mask Make sure you do everything necessary to protect those things that are most precious to you whether material, physical or emotional. Someone will, within three days, launch a campaign to cause you harm. This person wants to ruin you in one way or another. This can be prevented. Prepare yourself for this. You will be equipped with the emotional courage to go through this and to handle it with dignity. You will also be victorious over a vicious individual.

if you know the person wearing the mask This is the individual who will bring harm to you in one way or another. Be keenly aware of this person's intentions, especially for the next three days.

if you have no sense of who is wearing the mask Be keenly aware of your finances and where you are headed. A particular situation involving finances is at stake here and you need to attend to it and get it back into order.

masked ball Someone will attempt to persuade you to do something they know you do not like doing. This person will manipulate the conversation in such a way that you will end up doing what they wish you to do. This will begin to develop within three days. Do everything you can to resist involvement in a distasteful situation.

masking tape You will receive an inheritance that will be contested by another individual. Take the proper measures now to ensure that something that is given to you will not be taken from you. You will also need to keep a low profile and keep your mind on routine tasks. Be very aware of any errors that could occur in any capacity within a three day period and take care of any mistake immediately so everything can fall in place correctly. Many blessings are with you and because you have prior notice, you can avoid any unnecessary problem. You are headed for a brilliant future.

if masking tape is being used for any purpose that does not involve violence Become more possessive of your personal belongings. Their value will be far greater than you originally anticipated.

if masking tape is being used for violent purposes Do not offer your home for the purpose of any gathering. This will result in a brawl between two people. Be especially aware of this for the next three days and take subtle steps to avoid this issue.

masochism A new and affectionate admirer will become known to you within three days. If you choose to pursue this, it will be a lasting commitment. This relationship will flourish to the level you desire.

Mason Dixon Line For the next three days you will have to maintain a very cheerful demeanor because you will have to solve a conflict between two people.

mason jar Do everything necessary to fulfill your desires. The upcoming five days will be an important time for you to explore these feelings and to learn to express your desires in a satisfactory manner.

masonry Someone from a far off place will send you an unexpected beautiful gift that you will treasure for a lifetime.

masquerade You will have to deal with an extreme situation within three days. A small situation will be embellished in a big way by another individual and you will learn of these untruths during this time period. Remain calm in order to handle this in the proper way.

Massachusetts Someone with a beautiful and sunny disposition will enter your life and the more you involve yourself with this person, the more you will feel as though you have received a blessing in life. This individual will bring humor into your life and will teach you to look at things more optimistically. You will also receive a gift from a friend that will bring you a joy that you will want to reciprocate. This dream may also be used as a reference point in time. If you dream of this state and see its name used in any context, the dream message will occur on this day.

massacre *if much blood is involved* You will go from rags to riches and will be the recipient of a large amount of wealth within seven days.

massage You can ask for special consideration for the next five days and it will be granted.

to receive a massage Someone will do everything within their power to cheat you in a business deal. Investigate the situation further so you can handle yourself appropriately.

to give a massage to someone you recognize You will experience a large victory within seven days because you will tackle a situation that was once an impossibility. It is now possible to handle this issue during this time frame. Someone will also be very eager to become involved with you.

to give a massage to someone you do not recognize Someone will approach you within three days for the intention of involving you in a romantic interlude. If you pursue this you receive victory on a higher plane of life than you ever imagined.

masseur Be very wary of an involvement with someone who will always want a little something from you. After a time, all of these little favors will add up. If you handle this correctly, you will be able to maintain this involvement without having to perform endless small tasks.

mass media Do not allow yourself to be steered in the wrong direction for the next few days. Someone who shows an interest in you will not be sexually interested in you. The attraction they have is merely platonic. You are misreading body language and receiving mixed signals. You must also be careful not to put into writing anything you wish to keep a secret.

mast Shoot for the big ideas. You will have the confidence to explore plans on a big scale. This is the perfect time to do this and to have your plans flourish in a short period of time.

mastectomy Do not allow a situation to develop within two days with someone who really has no business involving themselves in your life. This will escalate to a very stressful situation if you do not take steps to normalize your life now. If you dream of any negative event that could occur in reality, you need to take all the necessary steps to ensure it does not take place. You have the time to handle this now. All positive events portrayed in this dream may be brought to reality.

master No matter who you are, you will receive many calls and requests from people who want advice from you. You will find a number of these kinds of requests for the next seven days. This can reach the point of becoming overwhelming. Choose to offer help in only those situations you want to give help in. Keep yourself stress free. It is not your duty to accept the responsibility of everyone else's problems.

master key Make sure you make your opinions known and that others are aware of your likes and dislikes. Be straight forward with others to ensure there is no confusion about what you will or will not accept.

Master of Arts Dissuade an individual who feels they have the power to speak for you. Limit your involvement with this person and take back the power to speak for yourself. You will have to deal with this within seven days.

master of ceremonies Pay close attention to what the M.C. was talking about. This will offer you major clues to what the future holds for you. You have the time to either keep this event from occurring or to promote it as best you can. You must also need to be very aware of an inconsistent person who will waste your time within the next three days.

Master of Science *(M.S.)* For the next four days you will need to be as efficient and effective as you can when dealing with important issues. Ask others to help you out financially because money will become an important issue within a two week period. You will have success in getting what you need from others during this time period. You will also receive a message from someone via a gift of some sort (flowers, candy, etc.). You will soon learn of this person's identity and of their interests in you and romance will quickly develop from this. You will also need to move quickly regarding an ongoing situation to achieve success.

masterpiece Within three days a beautiful and wonderful person will pass away and will be missed by many. This situation is out of your control. This is also the perfect time to refinish and refurbish a priceless possession of yours that needs a facelift. You will enjoy this project because you have not taken the time to bring this object's beauty to light.

master sergeant Prepare your days in such a way that you have the time to expose yourself to more opportunities and to more of the experiences you want from life. You will glean more benefits as a result of this new rescheduling. Begin this process within seven days.

masthead Do not allow anyone to weaken your confidence because of the way they speak to you. Keep your power intact and do not allow a defeatist attitude to take over.

mastiff Within three days you will gain the advantage in a certain situation by settling an agreement with someone in authority. Communicate with these people what you need and they will then be able to pull strings on your behalf. You will be very glad you motivated yourself in this direction.

mastodon You will be given the opportunity to speak to that one person you have long wanted to speak to within three days. You have prior notice of this and can plan what you want to say in a brief period of time.

masturbate The person indulging in this practice in your dream is someone who will be very eager to become involved with you in a sexual way. You will have the opportunity to develop a sensual and sexual relationship with this person within three days.

if you do not recognize this person This represents someone new who will come into your life who will be very pleased to be in your company and will go to great lengths to make you a permanent part of their life. This will be a very prosperous cycle for you and anything you once thought was impossible is now possible for you.

mat A very precious individual will be very taken by you when in your presence. This person will enter your life within three days and the conversation you have will be very interesting and free flowing. You will both come to a mutual agreement and reach greater horizons together. You must also not allow anyone to take advantage of your emotional and affectionate ways.

matador For the next three days focus on someone who carries themselves in a very quiet and simple fashion. Do not overlook this person's potential. Their intelligence borders on genius and they can help you in matters you lack the knowledge and skill to handle. This person will be able to offer you the assistance you need and will be able to steer you in the direction you wish to go. If you do not recognize the potential of this individual, you will miss out on this opportunity.

match Within two days you will hear the words you have wanted to hear that will verify a specific situation you are eager to get confirmation on.

to strike a match This is a confirmation that problems you are experiencing in your emotional love life will be resolved, and from this time forward you will experience only pleasurable moments. All negativity will disappear.

to be unable to locate a match Someone is very eager to see you but lacks the emotional courage to make it known to you. Within three days an opportunity will arise that will allow you to speak to this person in such a way that they will gain the confidence to speak openly about the feelings they have for you.

to recover a book of matches You are loved beyond your imagination and within seven days, you will have verification of that love. You will develop more flexibility about the things you want to expose yourself to and will experience more variety and spice in life. Good luck is with you.

matchboard Within three days someone will seek you out to introduce you to someone they know would make a good match for you. Be flexible, and if this is the route you choose to take, you will find a good permanent relationship with this individual.

matchbox Someone will express a beautiful act of love toward you and you will receive a wonderful gift that you will cherish for a long time.

matchmaker Someone who is much younger than you, very attractive, and has a great deal of money will seek a deep personal involvement with you. Do not be afraid. This person is very straight forward and honest about their feelings. If you desire, become involved and you will find this to be a very pleasurable experience. You can turn this into a permanent relationship, if you so desire.

mate Love yourself and take care of your needs first. Make sure you tell those who are special to you that you really do love them. Special people in your life need to hear these words.

material You are entering a cycle in your life that will expose you to many wonderful events. Go for it and enjoy your life fully.

maternity Pay attention to the person you saw in a family way. This individual has a wonderful idea that they want to develop and make tangible. This is also the perfect cycle for anyone you recognize to start a family, if this is their desire.

to dream of yourself in a family way This is the best cycle to take your creative ideas and put them into tangible form. Your ideas will be welcomed by others with open arms. If you choose not to start a family during this time period, take the necessary steps to prevent it.

mathematics Pay close attention to the numbers involved and the particular form of mathematics involved. If the numbers are high and the procedures involve an increase in numbers (i.e., addition, multiplication, etc.) the value of your personal items, investments, income, etc., will increase. Be aware also that any stressful situation you are involved in is

likely to increase as well. Good luck is with you.

matinee Be very careful you do not misinterpret other people's actions toward you. Do not jump to conclusions.

matrimony Be very aware that you do not have to choose between love and friendship. You can have both in the same person. You can begin to skillfully develop this within three days.

matron Any loan you make now will become very expensive. Be very careful of this for the next seven days.

Matterhorn You will have a fantastic time with someone at a particular event that will take place within two weeks. You will, however, never see this person again because they will move from the area. You have prior notice of this and can make the most of this time. Take steps to ensure you have the most joyous evening you can.

Matthew *(from the Bible)* You will be totally able and competent to handle a situation that will arise within seven days. Do not harbor doubts or develop a lack of confidence that will hinder completion of this situation. Go for it. Good luck and many blessings are with you and your family.

mattress You will successfully trump in all conversations related to love relationships and will be able to bring improvements in the manner you desire to a relationship with a special person. Although you feel you will not be able to accomplish much, you are guaranteed that anything regarding romantic matters will work out exactly as you desire. This will lead to a permanent union if you apply yourself for the next seven days.

matzo ball Make sure you do not give unfair leverage to another person by inadvertently supplying them with information that will later be used against you to damage your reputation. This is preventable and will begin to develop within two days.

maul *to maul* The next seven days will be an accident prone cycle. Take precautions to avoid all accidents.

mauve A financial settlement will bring you more wealth than you can envision.

May You will experience deep emotional love from another person. This will be verified by someone you had no suspicion of. You will enjoy a very lucky cycle that will enable you to take giant steps to do what you desire in grand style. Blessings are with you and your family.

Maya Angelou Within five days, you will have the strength and courage to face the challenges presented to you. You will not only successfully meet these challenges but will enjoy a long, healthy and prosperous life. You will also feel a tremendous relief once you have overcome these challenges. Proceed with confidence, you are headed for a brilliant future.

Mayan You will meet someone from an interesting ethnic background who speaks an interesting language. This person will be the answer to your financial problems. As you converse, you will discover you have something to offer that this person is willing to pay cash for. This will come as a surprise because you did not expect a buyer that day and did not expect to receive the amount offered. This will work out perfectly for both of you.

May day Be aware that within three days someone will push your buttons in such a way that it will take a great deal of energy to keep your temper under control. This will be done purposefully in order to provoke you to the point of a potential lawsuit that will take years to resolve. Take steps to avoid this scene. Many blessings will come to you and your family.

Mayflower Practice diplomacy and develop a soft manner when you inform someone of your interest in them. You will be received with open arms if you practice this within five days.

mayonnaise Someone is very eager to put in a good word for you so you can be placed in a position of authority. All you have to do is ask. This person will be more than generous in supporting this move and in being your mentor.

mayor The involvement you seek with another will take place within three days. This person will communicate their desire for an involvement with you. You have also desired this person for a long time. Good luck is with you.

maypole For the next three days you will be able to get a lot more for your money if you take the time to go bargain hunting.

mead Something will occur that will prevent someone from keeping a scheduled date with you. A rescheduled date will be much more rewarding. Do not let this disturb you. Reschedule for another time. Good luck is with you.

meadow Reward the person who has been emotionally supportive of you within three days. Now is the appropriate time to make this move. You will also meet someone whom you have been emotionally supportive of and this person will reward you.

meadowlark Do not interfere with the decisions of others, especially for the next three days.

meadow mouse Do not push yourself to the point of physical exhaustion and feelings of becoming overwhelmed. For the next four days do everything you can to regroup and build up your resistance. Make sure you schedule in some time for relaxation.

meal You will be dealing with two separate situations and it will become very clear that combining both of these will lead

to riches. You will be the one who will ultimately make this decision. Either choice you make will lead to your meeting your goals. One way is just better than the other.

to spill your meal You and another person will go down a path that will, unbeknownst to you, be very dangerous because of an unfortunate event that will take place. Speak with this other person in order to reschedule an event you are planning within the next few days. You can avoid this dangerous situation.

meal ticket Do not allow anyone to play emotional games with you. You will be very vulnerable to this for the next three days.

mealworm Do not allow your moods to control your behavior, especially for the next three days. You may scare someone away permanently whom you want very much in your life.

mealy bug Someone who has promised a position to you will purposefully withhold this position because of an emotional hang up of theirs. Seek an alternative position now.

mean Whatever you have scheduled for the next five days will result in a wonderful time.

"stop being so mean" - to say or to hear this phrase Be very cautious about where your feelings are taking you. Someone will, for reasons of their own, lead you to believe you are loved by them. The word "love" may or may not be used at this time but all of the romantic trappings will be there in the nature of gifts, flowers, romantic outings, etc. Your feelings will grow very deep and strong for this individual but if you allow lovemaking to occur, this person will not touch you in any way that gives you the impression they care deeply for you. As a result, you will feel very empty and cold. This person will be unable to connect with you, although they will put on a good act. Instead of putting yourself through this, you have enough notice to avoid this scenario entirely. Get on with your life without this person because they have a hidden agenda that involves you doing something for them that only they are aware of. This situation will only lead to unhappiness. Otherwise, you are headed for a prosperous future.

measles Do not overindulge in anything you are unfamiliar with and do not indulge in alcoholic beverages for the next three days. This is a recipe for disaster.

measure You will get a definite sense of the depth and capacity you can become involved concerning a particular project. You are also loved beyond your imagination and are respected deeply by others.

meat Within three days you will have to change your attitude toward someone you are involved with. This person has a feeling that you are not interested in them.

raw meat Be very aware of what is starting to unfold in your life. Within three days someone will enter your life and this will result in a subtle lifestyle change. Think very carefully and clearly about the direction you are headed. This change will seem to develop on its own with no control from you. Be very aware of this and do what you can to gain control over your life and to lessen the stress that others are placing on you.

red meat Slow down, you are moving too fast and coming on too strong. Everything will run smoother if you tactfully back off in areas you know you should in order to allow specific situations to work out on their own. This is a good luck omen and you are headed toward a healthy, wealthy life.

meatball Do not allow others to impose on your time or make demands on you that are totally inappropriate. You can expect this from someone within two days. Put a stop to it immediately.

meat hook Do everything necessary to get the extra training and knowledge you need to develop your skills. Within three days, you will be able to determine where you need this. It will be to your advantage to move on this now so you can be prepared ahead of time.

meat loaf Make sure, for the next three days, that you are appropriately dressed for the weather.

meatpacker Contracts that you sign within seven days will quickly bear fruit. Benefits will arrive quickly.

Mecca You will unexpectedly have to assist someone by doing something you strongly dislike. You will be richly rewarded if you decide to get involved with this situation. This dream may also be used as a reference point in time. If you dream of this city and see its name used in any context, the dream message will occur on this day.

mechanic If this dream portrays anything that should not be happening in reality it can easily be avoided. Within two days you will also discover that services you need to have done can be put on credit. This will make your life much easier.

medal You need to develop tenacity and stick to a project until it is completed.

medallion Someone is very eager to make a decision about your involvement with them romantically. This person is the type that scrutinizes everything and will be watching you very closely for the next three days prior to making their final decision. You have prior notice of this and can act appropriately. Good luck is with you and this is an extremely lucky omen. Many blessings will come to you and your family.

media Any negative event portrayed by the media can be avoided or altered in reality. Within two weeks you can also expect to receive a large salary you have worked very hard for. Someone in authority will decide you do not deserve the amount you anticipate. Take action now to ensure that you get what you deserve.

medical bag This dream implies that you will be surrounded by a number of powerful and wealthy people. There is, however, another person you are fated to become involved with. This person will be of the opposite sex and this involvement will grow to any level you wish. Leave yourself open for circulation and to issues that will give you the chance to meet this individual. You will enjoy easy conversation and gain a sense of closeness. This will allow a relationship to grow quickly. This person is well established career wise and is much wealthier than you ever expected. You are destined for a wonderful and tranquil life and you will both enjoy a prosperous future as well as an abundance of health. Make sure you alter the outcome or prevent any negative situation you witnessed in this dream and take steps to ensure you only experience positive expressions in your life.

medicine Pay attention to the events in the dream that concern medicine and take steps to prevent any negative occurrence. Any situation that does not appear to be going in the direction you desire also needs to be aggressively worked on until you are sure they will work out the way you wish.

medicine man Many times a particular situation may appear to be negative when, in reality, once you explore it in more detail you will find it is very beneficial to you. Do everything you can to explore your options prior to removing yourself from them.

medicine show Do not postpone any situation that requires a decision from you within three days.

medieval Watch what you eat and make sure you avoid food poisoning.

Mediterranean You will fall deeply in love with a very loving, intelligent individual. Although you feel as though you have few chances with this person, in reality, your chances are very high. Go for it.

Mediterranean Sea For the next five days you need to be aware someone will attempt to involve you in a situation that is very dangerous for you. Be sure you are not put on the path of unhealthy situations. Be very cautious of your surroundings and of who is prodding you to become involved in situations that appear, at first, to be good involvements. As time goes by you will find these situations are unhealthy and dangerous. Get on with your life without this person in it and continue on the path toward prosperity. This dream may also be used as a reference point in time. If you dream of this sea and see this its name used in any context, the dream message will occur on this day.

Medusa *(Greek Mythology)* For the next five days you will need to be aware that someone will attempt to involve you in a situation that is very dangerous for you. Be sure you are not put on the path of unhealthy situations. Be very cautious of your surroundings and of who is prodding you to become involved in situations that appear, at first, to be good involvements. As time develops you will determine this is unhealthy and dangerous for you. Get on with your life without this person in it and continue on the path toward prosperity.

meeting house Within five days you will become involved with people whom you do not know who want to involve themselves in your business. Do what you can to keep yourself balanced and be aware that no matter how much these people want to become involved, you ultimately call the shots. Do not allow yourself to become stressed out.

meetings *if the meeting is distasteful* Accept this as a clue to something you need to avoid in reality. You must also make it a point to visit, within two days, someone who is confined. This individual will appreciate your concern.

if the meeting is pleasant Look for this to happen in reality. You must also discuss each change of schedule you make with those who are interested in your welfare. This will keep another individual in touch with you and prevent a feeling of being left out. Do this for the next week.

in any other form You will be dealing with someone who habitually buys time by putting you off a few hours, days, or weeks at a time, until the time is right for them. This person will be unable to become involved in any capacity until the time suits them. Be clever when speaking to this individual in order to determine the exact time to make a move. This will prevent disappointments prior to that opportunity.

melba toast Think twice before taking a trip you have planned within two days. This will not work out in the way you have planned. This trip needs to be postponed indefinitely.

mellow Pay attention to that person in your dream who demonstrates a mellow temperament. This individual, in reality, has not given you all the information you need to be brought up to date. Investigate this situation in more detail.

melodrama *to dream of a melodramatic person* Within seven days, someone will over dramatize a situation you have revealed to them in a conversation. Prevent this by limiting the information you are willing to give while in conversation with others. Keep personal information to yourself.

melody You will definitely not take life for granted for the next five days. You will be involved in everything in order to bring more spice into your life. You will also do everything in your power to bring those you care about close to you. You will be able to verbalize your feelings in such a way that others will want to be with you.

melon It will become clear to you within three days that you are not, and will never be, the person someone wants you to be. Don't waste time and move on with your life.

melt If you see anything melting that should not be in reality, take steps to prevent this from occurring for the next two days.

if you dream of someone you know melting This person is very eager to fulfill your wishes with no limitations.

meltdown Do not overreact to someone else's stupidity for the next three days. Do not allow this person to influence you into becoming involved in something you have no experience in.

melting pot Do not expose the plans of another individual to a third person who has no business knowing about this. You will regret this immensely, especially if you do this within the next two days.

member Restrain yourself for the next two days from making demands on another person. Your behavior will be questioned by others.

membrane Do not allow another person to get into the habit of treating you in a hostile manner. Put a stop to this the moment it occurs or avoid anyone with this manner entirely. This is likely to occur within three days.

memento Although you may feel your actions and gifts of thoughtfulness toward another are insignificant, this individual will treasure these considerations for a lifetime.

memoir Pay attention to what is written in the memoir and you will find many clues to the meaning of this dream. If this represents an event that should not be happening, you have the time to take steps to avoid it. You must also make it a point to set aside some private time in your life so you can spend moments with a special person.

memorial Someone will behave in a cowardly fashion within two days. This will surprise you because they will not stand up for their own beliefs nor will they back you up when you need their support. Do not allow this to surprise you and since you have prior notice, you can behave appropriately and remove yourself from the situation with dignity.

Memorial Day Be very alert for the next few days. You will come across a very powerful and wealthy person who will go to great lengths to meet your needs in every capacity. Become aggressive and go after what you really want. This dream guarantees you will go through life with not only the necessities of life but also the refinements you desire. Move quickly on this. Good luck is with you.

memory Make sure you treat yourself with the highest level of respect and pamper yourself. Treat yourself to those exquisite moments and events you have long wanted to treat yourself to. Treat yourself to a physical make over as well.

Memphis You are in a cycle that promotes a high level of accomplishment. Anything you set as a goal to accomplish for the next seven days will be attainable. This dream may also be used as a reference point in time. If you dream of this city and see its name used in any context, the dream message will occur on this day.

ménageàtrois Be determined, for the next two days, to come to terms with a situation that involves another individual. Think ahead and determine the proper course to take when addressing this situation. Do not allow things to remain unresolved.

menagerie Do not invite anyone to spend a long time in your presence if you do not know them very well. This individual will bore you immensely at the very start and you will be at a loss about how to spend the remainder of your time together. Do not allow yourself to become involved in this situation.

Mendelssohn Face up to the priorities in your life that you are not attending to.

meningitis Some unbelievable news will come to you that will be quite shocking. This will involve a freak accident that will happen to a friend of yours. Do what you can now to warn those who are close to you. This is preventable and is likely to occur in an unusual environment.

menopause Within three days you will be able to convince others to collectively agree to show love toward a special person in the form of close communication and a small gift. This individual needs this kind of caring right now from this group of people.

menorah Take precautions to prevent any unusual occurrence in this dream from becoming a reality. You must also make sure you enlist the support you need for future negotiations. Take a close look at your plans and revise any errors so you will achieve success.

menstruation *to dream of having your period* It will soon be possible for you to acquire a large expensive item, such as a car or boat.
to dream of someone else having their period You will be sexually aroused by someone who seems completely inaccessible. Thoughts of this person will continue to arouse you and you will find this person will be more accessible than you realized. You will find a way to fulfill your desires.

mental illness Within five days you will be dealing with someone who will try to keep someone you care about from maintaining a close relationship. This person will go to great lengths to create a distasteful scenario that will result in a split-up. It will be done so subtly that it will be hard to determine who instigated this scene. Be alert to anyone who holds a secret animosity toward you. You will also experience a financial windfall and within this time period you need to determine what you need to say or do to change an issue that is not going in the right direction. This will involve the care of someone who is not under your direct su-

pervision. You are getting clues that this person is being cared for improperly and that nothing is being done to ensure they are leading a comfortable, fulfilling life. Find a way to tactfully discuss this individual's care in an inoffensive manner. You will arrive at a successful solution to this problem. During this five day period take all the necessary steps to keep any negative event in this dream from becoming a reality and forewarn anyone you recognize to do the same. Take the opportunity to bring any positive event to fruition.

mental retardation You should, for the next five days, show proper respect toward someone you feel close to and treat them in the manner you wish to be treated, regardless of what may be going on in other aspects of your life.

mental state *to dream that someone is discussing another's mental condition* Someone who is completely dependent on their care provider is being mistreated either unwittingly or on purpose. Do everything you can to become tactfully involved in order to help out this person. Many blessings are with you and your family and you will definitely experience a prosperous future.

mentor Do not give up until a particular problem is resolved, especially for the next three days. Be relentless.

Mephistopheles Someone will supply you with the means to acquire those fine items that you desire with no strings attached. Eat healing foods, drink plenty of water and get plenty of rest. Love yourself.

Mercedes Benz This dream implies you are headed for a brilliant future. Within the week you will be ready to make changes that will profoundly alter your life. You will develop and execute well thought out plans that will fall into place exactly as you desire. This cycle will also bring dynamic benefits to you regarding love and money. Good luck is with you.

mercenary Within five days you will have the chance to cater to others from a different ethnic background. Because of your hard work, eagerness to please, and your ability to handle situations with diplomacy and tact, doors will be opened to you on a permanent basis. As a result of this, you will experience an increase in income. Good luck is with you.

merchandise Do not overextend yourself to someone who does not care for you.

merchant Keep doing what you are doing now. You are headed for a brilliant future.

mercury Develop your talents and you will find in a few years you will have what it takes to be successful. You are headed for a brilliant future.

Mercury *(the planet)* You will receive a special invitation from someone and will find the need, within five days, to have someone close to you. You will be able to accomplish this within a three day period.

mercy killing You will receive a very shocking letter within three days. This letter will stun anyone who reads it. Take this seriously in order to get the protection you need.

Merlin Someone will enter your premises as an invited guest and a small item of yours will turn up missing. You will not suspect this person because you will not find it missing for a number of weeks.

mermaid Enjoy your freedom and your wishes will be fully granted within the month.
to see a mermaid change into human form and vice versa Be very aware that someone you have asked to leave your life and has promised to leave you alone will break this promise within five days. Do everything you can to avoid being pinned down by this person and make it very clear you wish to live your life without this person in it. You will need to be emotionally prepared to handle this delicate situation with tact and diplomacy in order not to offend this person. Organize your feelings and thoughts and you will be able to get your point across with no misunderstandings. Proceed with caution and you will be successful.

merry go round You will see a definite increase in demand for whatever you are marketing. Be prepared to meet this demand. A wonderful person will also soon enter your life who will provide you with an emotional fulfillment you have never felt before. You will also need to make sure you do not slave away to the point of exhaustion. For the next two days, set limits on what you are willing to do. Get the proper support system to help you meet the demands placed on you.

Mesopotamia You will receive the help you have been waiting for. When it arrives, you will be surprised at the timing. Pounce on this and move quickly in the direction you want. This dream may also be used as a reference point in time. If you dream of this place and see its name used in any context, the dream message will occur on this day.

mesquite Avoid all problems with special people in your life that could start to occur within three days.

message Pay close attention to the message relayed in this dream. This will either be something you want to bring into your life or something you choose to avoid. Play it very safe for the next two days because someone will give you something of value to hold for them. Make sure you do not accept this responsibility because something will happen to this item and you will be held responsible.

messenger Make sure you do not put yourself in the position where people will begin to speak unkindly about you because of your behavior.

mess hall *to be in a mess hall* A person you do not know very well will react to you in a very unreasonable manner and will demand you behave in a way that you find totally offensive. Expect this to occur within three days.
in any other form Someone who promises to come through for you on special issues will fail to come through. Find alternative methods to accomplish your goals.

Messiah Other people will attempt to persuade you to neglect your interests, especially for the next three days. Do not allow this to occur.

mestizo Within three days a relative will achieve domestic happiness after a long problematic time.

metabolism You will see a certain item that you want to purchase. You will be short on cash but someone will loan you the amount remaining toward the purchase. After you buy this item, this individual will decide they want it instead of the money you owe them. This scenario will take place within two days. If you find it distasteful, do everything necessary to prevent its occurrence.

metal *any form* You will have the support system and the network of knowledge you need to help you position yourself in a comfortable lifestyle. During this cycle you will enjoy many opportunities for celebration and joyful events. Prepare yourself for some unexpected joyful news that is coming your way within the week. You are definitely headed for a brilliant future. You will also be left with the feeling that everyone is on your side and is supporting your goals. Also make every effort you can, for the next four days, to behave in such a way that will bring someone you desire close to you. This person is not yet involved with you and at first you will feel they are not interested in you in the way you desire. During this time period, you will also experience an abundance of health, a financial windfall will come your way, and you are headed for a prosperous future.

metallic *anything with a metallic appearance* Do not allow yourself to become sidetracked or to ignore someone who is important to you, because before you know it time will have slipped away. Within seven days it is important to develop fun things you can do with a special person. Be sure to plan special outings, events and games you can enjoy together. Many blessings are with you and your family and you are headed for a brilliant future.

metallurgy Do not allow yourself to be pinned down or manipulated into doing something distasteful, especially for the next two days.

metalwork It is important that you get to the bottom of someone's suspicious behavior. It is imperative that you do this within two days.

metamorphosis Your wishes will be granted due to a financial windfall that will be coming your way within two weeks.

meteor Guard your cash, especially for the next five days.

meteor shower You are headed for a brilliant future and the professional advice you will be receiving will be accurate.

meter Be relentless and forceful when pursuing your goals, especially for the next three days. Within three weeks, riches will also start coming to you. This dream is a lucky omen. Whatever numbers you see displayed will be significant to you (i.e., dates, prices, times, lucky numbers in games of chance)

meter maid You will agree to do something within three days and realize at a later time you very much dislike what you are doing. Do everything necessary to avoid becoming involved in this situation.

methane You will know someone who acts as though they own you when in your presence, but once your back is turned they will act as though they want nothing to do with you. They will pretend you are the one who is pursuing them. Get on with your life without this person in it.

Methodist You are going through a splendid cycle and will be able to accomplish a great deal.

Methuselah *(from the Bible)* You will gain a clear idea of someone who is going to great lengths to undermine you in some way.

metronome Stay away from all toxins and do not allow anyone to introduce you to a prescription medication that they claim is good for you. This drug will only do you harm.

Mexican Within seven days you will receive an invitation to spend an evening with someone whom you will remember for a lifetime. If you choose, this person can be a mate for life. Good luck is with you.

Mexican American War Take the extra time needed to jot down those intelligent well formed thoughts that will come to you, before they are forgotten.

Mexico You will receive excellent advice from someone who is a professional in their field. Move quickly in order to avoid stressful situations. Apply this advice to the areas of your life where it is needed. This dream may also be used as a reference point in time. If you dream of this country and see its name used in any context, the dream message will occur on this day.

Mexico City Deal with a certain individual personally and avoid using the phone or mail services. This will allow you to accomplish what you need to take care of. This dream may also be used as a reference point in time. If you dream of this city and see its name used in any context, the dream message will occur on this day.

Miami Within two days you will develop a method that will allow you to achieve your goals. This will be a prosperous time for you and you are headed for a brilliant future. This dream may also be used as a reference point in time. If you dream of this city and see its name used in any context, the dream message will occur on this day.

Miami Beach Your mental abilities are very high now. Do not be shy about advising others on matters in which you are an expert. Good luck is with you. This dream may also be used as a reference point in time. If you dream of this city and see its name used in any context, the dream message will occur on this day.

mica For the next two days give it everything you have and apply yourself to those tasks you want to complete. You will receive a great deal of gratification from this because everything will work out exactly as you wish.

Micah *(from the Bible)* Do not betray your sources of information, especially for the next two days, regardless of the situation.

Michelangelo You will be offered a once in a lifetime golden opportunity and this will be presented to you within three days. You have prior notice of this and can motivate yourself to be there to accept this opportunity. Good luck is with you.

Michigan Be aware that several issues will come up within five days and you will need to motivate yourself to pursue one particular opportunity that will unexpectedly come to you. Think and act quickly because the person offering you this chance will be in a certain place at only one certain time and will be in the state of mind to offer this chance only once. If you act quickly you will not miss out on this. Expect this to occur in the near future and be sure to work out any aspects of this proposal you agree with in a tactful way so both of you can proceed successfully. In spite of any differences in lifestyles, this is a workable situation. This dream may also be used as a reference point in time. If you dream of this state and see its name used in any context, the dream message will occur on this day.

mickey Your intuition is accurate. Follow your hunches for the next three days.

Mickey Mouse You will enjoy peace of mind and tranquility for a long time to come and will enjoy many humorous moments with your family.

microfiche Watch out for someone who, when under the influence, will have a different personality and can be very embarrassing to you. This will occur within five days. Do whatever you can to avoid putting yourself through this.

microfilm Someone who is very eager for you to do something for them will get in touch with you within two days. It is your choice whether to get involved. Either way will work out well for you.

microphone Someone whom you are interested in becoming involved with and have set up a rapport with will lead you to believe they will contact you at a later date. This person will, however, never contact you again. Don't get your hopes up. No matter how much involvement you desire, it will not happen.

microscope Someone will be watching you very carefully as though you are under a microscope in order to gauge your actions to different situations. Although you will not be aware of this, your behavior around different people will be scrutinized as well as your character, ethics, etc. This person is seeking something specific. You have prior notice of this and can behave appropriately.

microwave Do whatever you can to tame the beast within you. Within two days you will lose your temper when under the influence and begin to shout at a particular individual in front of young children. Restrain yourself from behaving this way and seek help instead. Do everything you can to avoid verbal abuse toward others.

Midas *(Greek Mythology)* Anything you have been seeking for a long time, whether this is knowledge, a possession, etc., will be yours within two days. Many blessings are with you and your family.

middle Someone will pursue you, within five days, simply to gratify their own needs. The relationship will be based only on sexual gratification. You have this awareness now and can make your choices based on this.

Middle Ages Within two days you will want to go back to something that was an old hang up of yours. Do what you can to avoid falling prey to this. Get the help you need to avoid the desperation that results from getting caught up in these old habits.

Middle East Do not place yourself in a compromising position. This will develop within three days and you will find this very distasteful. This dream may also be used as a reference point in time. If you dream of this region and see its name used in any context, the dream message will occur on this day.

middle school *to dream of being in your middle school* This dream is a lucky omen. A hobby, learned in the past, can be used, in conjunction with something else, to create a second income. This idea will come to you within seven days.

to see yourself as a child in middle school For the next two days be alert to anything involving your health. All minor problems will have a tendency to escalate during this time period. Take care of all health problems now.

to see an adult you recognize as a child in middle school Warn this person to take care of all minor health problems now. It is important that these problems do not become life threatening.

in any other form This dream is a good omen.

midget *little people* You will find in three days that someone you desire will support you financially, almost as though they wish to adopt you. If this is something you wish, make sure you actively seek it out. This will come with no strings attached and will make many of your dreams a reality.

midnight Make sure that children and young adults seek the proper medical help for all ailments before they escalate to a life threatening situation.

midnight sun Do not demand so much from a young adult or child. You may be asking more than they are equipped to handle. Step back and make requests you are sure they can handle with ease.

midshipman Slow down when going after a situation you are very much interested involving yourself in. Investigate this thoroughly before you jump into this situation.

midsummer Within three weeks you will have to revise your plans. Aggressively attack all blocks, obstacles, people, etc., that stand in the way of your path toward prosperity. Once you have overcome this, you will be glad you have put yourself on the right track. Many blessings are with you and your family.

midwife It will be in your power to save someone else's life within three days. Do what you can to aggressively interfere in someone else's behavior in order to protect them. An unusual occurrence will lead you to investigate someone's whereabouts and their need for assistance. Good luck is with you and many blessings are with you and your family.

migraine For the next two days you will have to be politically correct in everything you do. If you do not, a violent argument will erupt due to the insensitive way you phrase things. This is preventable and you have prior notice to watch what you say. You must also subtly warn others around you to address other people with respect.

migrant You will have to extend yourself and give much more attention to others around you. This will be a cycle that will require you to give everyone a lot of attention. Remain calm and do not allow this to change your mood, especially for the next three days.

mildew Do not suggest that someone else put something into practice that you have not put into practice yourself. Make sure you are aware of all the effects prior to allowing someone else to attempt this.

mile Stop being so selfish especially for the next two days. Learn to share and you will not regret it. You will receive a great deal of gratification from this.

milepost You will ask for assistance from someone at a specific time but this person will not show up at the allotted time. Set up an alternative person to help you so you do not waste your time.

military This dream is an extremely lucky omen. You will need to devise a cleverly crafted compromise in order to prevent a violent episode from occurring between two groups of people who cannot see eye to eye. Both groups can have it their way if they compromise. Do not back off from your plan or violence is certain to erupt.

military police Someone will subtly convince you to do something without coming right out and asking. Do not make it easy for this individual and do not allow yourself to be used by this person. This is likely to occur within three days.

milk Regardless of anything else that is going on in your life now, the hopes and dreams you have will become a reality on a much grander scale than you ever anticipated. You will be successful in eliminating everything that is standing in your way. Someone you desire will also be irresistibly drawn to you.

acidophilus milk Make sure, for the next two days, you do not allow the hasty actions or words of other people to leave you feeling uncomfortable with yourself. Do not lose confidence in your ideas and plans. Remain focused and retain control over your decisions.

buttermilk For the next few weeks, you will be exposed to constant small problems and stresses. Take them a day at a time and they will be successfully handled.

ice milk Have the confidence not to question anything that works to your favor for the next three days. Just accept this good fortune. You will achieve prosperity in every level of your life, whether physical, emotional, mental or perceptual. All proposals will be very fortuitous for you during this time period and it would be to your benefit to render a positive response. This is an extremely lucky cycle.

sour milk Make sure any event you are planning to attend does not turn sour because of a shortage of refreshments. This will occur at an event you will be directly involved with within the week.

spilled milk You will be able to enlist the love of a special person and you will have verification of this within seven days.

to milk a cow You are destined to receive enormous wealth and you are headed for a brilliant future.

milk glass Anything connected to the medical field will be extremely lucky for you, especially for the next two weeks.

milkmaid Someone you are very attached to will move to a distant land for business purposes and will stay for a year. You have prior notice of this so you can handle future plans in the best way you see fit.

milkman Bargain hunting will be extremely lucky for you, especially while supplies last. You will also enjoy stronger emotional ties with someone who is special to you, especially for the next three days. Keep this closeness permanent.

milk shake You are about to make a mistake. You are very fond of someone and are becoming impatient because this person is not coming across in the manner you wish them to. You wish to rush this person into a commitment and will, over the next three days, become demanding and mistreat them. Back off and use your time to develop yourself into a warmer, more positive person. This individual will then mature and develop a more meaningful relationship.

milk snake Within three days spoiled goods, crop losses and an illness that threatens a child are all likely to occur. It is within your power to avoid exposing this child to any virus.

milk sugar This dream is a promise that from now on you will always have plenty of what you need. This will occur within three days because an unusual occurrence will allow it to happen.

milkweed This dream is an extremely lucky omen. You will definitely experience a reversal in your favor within three days. This will be a time where you will be able to accomplish those things that, for whatever reason, you were unable to accomplish before. Go for it.

Milky Way You are adored beyond your imagination and you will have verification of this within seven days from different sources. You will get a sense of how deeply others care and appreciate you. You will also be involved in a very enjoyable neighborhood party. Everyone involved will have a delightful time.

mill All legal negotiations will result in your favor. Someone who has just passed through some distasteful moments in their life will also choose you to be the first person they open up to. Display sympathy to this person for the next three days.

miller You will be dealing with a very kind hearted, educated individual who is, for some reason, unable to accept the responsibility of a deep emotional commitment. This will stand in the way of this person's pursuit of the relationship they desire but they are unaware they have this particular mental block to work around. You have prior notice of this so you can handle yourself appropriately when in this person's presence.

millet Structure a situation in such a way that you are aware of each small detail you may otherwise overlook, especially for the next three days.

milliner Within three days you will separate from someone who is very special to you. Control yourself and do not make a spectacle of yourself. Listen calmly and attentively to the reasons behind this separation and handle yourself appropriately and with civility.

million Although the person you are interested in is not as attentive as you would like, this is a minor problem. Do what you can to refrain from complaining about small issues. This individual is headed for a brilliant future and wants you to be a part of it. You will also develop your own wealth and this process will be starting within the month. You will have financial stability and money will come to you from many directions. There is no reason not to enjoy all of it. Many blessings will come to you and your family.

millionaire Make sure negotiations with other people will be agreeable to all parties involved. An unusual situation will occur that will result in a windfall for you. This dream is a very lucky omen and signifies that within a two day period your inner drive and courage will motivate you to break through any physical or mental barrier. You will be able to rid yourself of any part of your life that interferes with you moving forward. Once you rid yourself of this barrier you will be able to complete and bring into tangible form any new project in the way you desire. You will be greeted with open arms anywhere you go during this time period and will be put on a pedestal by everyone you care about. You are headed for a brilliant future and many new opportunities are headed your way.

millipede Do not allow yourself to be tied down to certain situations or individuals, especially for the next three days.

millstone Within the week, you will be invited to an unexpected fiesta that you should not miss. This is an extremely lucky omen.

mill wheel You are headed for a brilliant future. Your desires will be met and a special favor will be granted to you. Many blessings are with you and your family.

mime Be very cautious of situations that can lead to jealousy and to huge arguments within three days. This is a preventable situation.

mimeograph Do what you can to put yourself in a quiet environment so you can let your creative juices flow and bring your creativity to tangible form. This will make a real difference in your life. Many blessings are with you.

minaret Within three days, a member of your family will bring you into their confidence. This person needs your assistance and is counting on your help. Do what you can to offer your assistance and keep this information to yourself.

mince Time is running out and you are overlooking a situation that needs your attention. Investigate closely and dig deeply to determine the situation that needs to be quickly taken care of.

mincemeat Make sure you verify all overdue payments within three days and take steps to have them cleared up in order to avoid stressful situations.

mincemeat pie You are trusting the wrong person to make decisions for you especially for the next three days. Otherwise, it is a very lucky omen to dream of mince meat pie.

mind Become very aware of what you want and don't want from life and pursue only what you truly want, especially for the next three days. Eat only healing foods, get plenty of rest and drink plenty of water. Many blessings are with you and your family.

open minded If you involve yourself with the appropriate groups of people, you will find a once in a lifetime opportunity within the week. Allow these opportunities to come to you in such a way that you will be able to pick and choose the ones most suitable for you. You are entering a very lucky cycle that will bring you joy and you will be able to expand your horizons within this time frame.

"slipped my mind" You are beginning to feel a strong emotional pull that will take up much of your time because you will have no idea where this drive came from. This drive is causing you to focus on bringing something into solid form. If you determine that this urge you are feeling is inappropriate and/or socially unacceptable, you will have the time and enough notice to seek out the professional help you need to come to grips with your desires and to live at peace with yourself and these urges. The moment you sense this, get help. This is the perfect cycle to find the right person to handle this event. You will be able to take care of this and gain control over your emotions in a healthy way. Expect this to occur within five days. Otherwise, you are on the path toward a brilliant future.

mind reader Time is running out and you are in danger from an evil person. This person has not yet given any indication of their true character but once they get closer to you they will remove their mask of normalcy. Expect this to take place within a few days. Do not give this person a chance to get close to you and take every step to protect yourself.

mine Keep your mind on your investments and your speculations about stocks will be accurate. Trust your judgments, you are headed for a prosperous future.

mine detector You will be able to determine the person you should involve yourself with. This individual is very knowledgeable and will be able to offer their assistance in bringing a solution to a certain issue.

mine explosion Be relentless and dig deeply to find out the exact condition of a relative. You could be very instrumental in saving this person's life. Make sure this person finds the proper services they need and that their needs are being met.

mineral Within two days make sure you tackle those big plans you feel are overwhelming. This is the time to move ahead on these plans and do not allow others to slow you down.

Minerva *(Greek Mythology)* Within the week, regardless of difficulties that are arising from a number of different sources, you will find relief from old burdens and from any new situations. You will also hear good news about some options you have been wanting for a while. This cycle also promotes family harmony. Many blessings are with you and your family and you are headed for a prosperous future.

minestrone Do everything necessary to develop the support system a child or young adult needs to point themselves on the path toward less stress and greater prosperity. Many blessings will come to you and your family.

miniature *to see anything in miniature* Within three days you will be able to calibrate and detail your thoughts and put them into words so well that you will be able to help someone who desires, in every way, to get closer to you. You will be able to make this person feel very secure and comfortable in your presence. This will allow this individual to speak openly and frankly in a manner that will spur the development of a relationship and create a warm open union. You can also use these skills to bring anything you want into reality. This will allow you to remove all blocks due to poor communication. This will be a magical cycle. Any scene in a dream that you view in miniature symbolizes and prophesizes an activity you will foster. A negative scene can be avoided, in reality.

mini bike You have all the detailed information needed to properly assist someone when giving advice. When someone comes to you, open up and give them exactly what they need to carry on with their life more efficiently.

mini blind Within three days you will be overwhelmed with excitement about something good headed your way. Do not become overexcited about this. Step back in order to restrain yourself and to make sure this is exactly what you want.

minicomputer You will develop, within the next three days, a network of people who can support you, offer assistance and brainstorm with you to seek a solution to a situation that needs to be handled within the week. This will result in a successful conclusion.

minimum wage Within three days someone you know will be anxious to share their good news with you about an upcoming event. You will enjoy many days of harmony and tranquility.

miniskirt An event will occur within seven days that will be very memorable to you. This event will be very sensual and will stay with you for a lifetime.

minister You will be able to help a special person develop their potential and realize their goals. This person will be very grateful and you will be richly rewarded because of their enormous increase in wealth. Many blessings are with you and your family.

mink Within three days you will be asked to share in someone else's wealth. You must also remember that a relationship that is important to you will grow only as much as the other person allows it to. This is completely out of your control. You have prior notice of this and can handle yourself appropriately.

mink coat You will become attracted to someone whose

sexual appetite is a lot greater than yours. This individual will go to great lengths to involve you in their life in an excessive manner. Think carefully about this situation in order to act in the most appropriate manner so you do not miss out on this person's love and affection. But you must also get the message across clearly that their sexual appetite is much larger than yours. This individual will quickly take steps to accommodate you in order to keep the relationship mutually satisfying.

to have anything made of mink damaged Become bold and daring when attending to a specific task you need to take care of. This will inspire you to get the job done.

Minnesota Within the week you will be offered a much larger salary for a job than you anticipated. Many happy days are coming your way and many blessings are coming to you and your family. This dream may also be used as a reference point in time. If you dream of this state and see its name used in any context, the dream message will occur on this day.

minnow Organize yourself within the next two days in order to get what you want taken care of.

Minotaur You will definitely have the confidence to take the small risks needed to enter a particular situation that you know will make a difference in improving your standard of living. It is also important to make sure that you follow all rules and regulations. You have very strong feelings about something you feel must be accomplished now.

minstrel Within five days you will become caught up in a tug of war between two people as a result of your failure to take care of a certain situation. You will be expected to attend a function with two different people. Make sure you take care of this ahead of time and take steps to avoid all quarrelsome situations.

mint You will involve yourself in a conversation with a particular person within two days who will definitely offer you a fresh point of view on topics you have been discussing. This new point of view will give you the feeling that this is the correct way to go. Take notes, if necessary, to have at a later date for inspiration. Your intuition will be accurate. Go for it. Good luck is with you and many blessings will come to you and your family.

mint jelly Someone will want a full commitment from you and this will be verbalized within three days. You are headed for a brilliant future.

mint julep Be very aware of a person who scams others and slacks off on everything they promise. They will attempt to involve you in a scam within three days. This individual does not appear to be who they are so you must be careful not to become involved in any business transaction for this time period.

mint tea Carefully think over any sudden urges you get

within the next two days and make a point of writing them down. These thoughts will come in handy at a later date and will give you a fresh viewpoint of life. Many blessings will come to you and your family.

minute This dream implies that time is running out in certain situations you should be attending to. Make sure you do not overlook any situation that needs to be handled. If you find you have overlooked an important issue, make it a priority to take care of it now. This dream is a very lucky omen and many blessings will come to you and your family.

miracle Within seven days you will have the power given to you by the gods to turn impossible situations into any reality that you desire and you will be able to resolve any pending situation that creates stress. You will enjoy a peaceful tranquil life for some time to come.

miracle worker This dream implies that you are entering a lucky cycle and that within three days you will experience an inner courage and strength. Your steel drive and determination will drive you to break through any physical or mental barrier. You will completely rid yourself of any aspect of your life that you disapprove of or that interferes with your forward movement. Once you have gotten rid of this block, you will quickly bring any new project to tangible form. Your plans will be completed in the way you desire. You will also be placed on a pedestal and be greeted with open arms anywhere you go during this time frame. This will surprise you greatly. You are on the path toward a brilliant future and many new opportunities are headed your way.

mirage You will wish you had never been asked to become involved in a secret plan. This will be a stressful involvement and will occur within three days. You have prior notice of this and can make a point of staying uninvolved.

Miriam *(from the Bible)* An older, wiser person who is an expert in many different fields will help you find the solution to a very stressful problem that has been bothering you for awhile. Within three days you and this person will discuss this issue and you will be offered the help you need. Your intuition is accurate and you should rely on it, especially during this time cycle. This is also the perfect time to accomplish as much as you can for an improved lifestyle. Many blessings are with you and your family.

mirror By learning to cleverly use your communication skills you will be able to maximize your ability and wealth by communication and will be able to position yourself to speak openly with authority figures. This will result in grand benefits for you. This person will be more amenable to complying with your needs. Think and plan ahead in order to grasp other opportunities that will present themselves to you within three days.

to look in the mirror and see someone else in the mirror with you The person you see in the mirror is the one whom you will be able to get your point cross to in order to have your needs met at the time you desire. This person will be very eager to respond to your wishes.

to see anything distorted in a mirror Within two days you will have an offer that seems too good to refuse. Step away from this situation as fast as you can. This is something you should definitely not become involved in. Become acutely aware of your involvements for the next three days.

broken mirror Think ahead. You will be visited by a new acquaintance within three days and will be terrified of them. You will see no possible means of escape. Avoid this issue by having nothing to do with new acquaintances during this time period. Do not put yourself in the position of being held against your will. This is a life threatening situation that is preventable.

to look in the mirror and see someone looking back Your efforts will be questioned by those in authority whether or not you do the correct thing. You will have the courage to get through this. Someone will also attempt to have a conversation with you but hidden resentments from the past will not allow this to occur in a comfortable manner. These resentments will ruin the moment and the conversation will be cut short. You have prior notice of this and can take the proper steps to move on with your life in a stress free way. Otherwise, many blessings are with you and you are headed for a prosperous future.

if you recognize the person looking at you This individual will be very eager to discuss a particular delicate situation with you within five days. You will be able to reach a mutually satisfying agreement.

if the person frightens you The greater the fear, the greater the victory you will achieve. You will receive a positive response from someone in authority.

rear view You need to arrive at a clever idea that will allow you to work alone.

to see someone in your rear view Avoid mistakes by concentrating on all available alternative plans. You will then be able to choose the correct one.

to see someone look at you through a rear view mirror Someone will seek you out for the purpose of creating a very uncomfortable situation. Do everything necessary to avoid this person for the next two days. This person enjoys making others uncomfortable.

to look in the mirror and see someone else's face in the mirror instead of your own If you do not recognize the person you see in the mirror, this face will give you a description of someone you will become aware of within the next four days. You will need to be a good listener and use words that will uplift this person's spirit and motivate them to proceed with confidence. If you recognize the person you see in the mirror, they or someone this person represents will be very eager to respond to your wishes, adopt your propositions and be helpful to get your point of view across to others in order to have your needs met at the time you desire them. You will know who this person is by the character, dress, ethnic group, etc. Also conversation will provide you with tips that will trigger certain thoughts that will lead you to get in touch with someone who will follow through for you and bring many benefits into your life. You are on the path for a brilliant future and you will enjoy an abundance of health. You have the power to keep negative aspects of this dream from becoming a reality.

miscarriage Any negative event in this dream that relates to anything that may be occurring in reality needs to be prevented if at all possible. You must also alert those to whom this message may apply so they can take steps to prevent a negative event from taking place. This dream implies that it will seem too much to hope for that a situation will work out properly. You will also meet someone for a light conversation who still carries hidden resentments toward you for something that occurred in the past. As a result, this meeting will be ruined when this individual decides to rehash the past. Think ahead and decide how you want to handle this. You have prior notice and can handle this appropriately.

misdemeanor Within three days someone in authority will start to question your motives and actions. Prepare yourself so you can answer appropriately for yourself. Move quickly on this.

miser Make sure you pace yourself against others and are able to match the production rate of everyone else. Otherwise, it will be unfair for others to have to pull your weight. Take steps to rectify any unfair behavior.

misogynist You will be in the company of someone who has an extreme hatred for the human race. This person carries a chip on their shoulder about something that was done to them in the past and they feel everyone they come into contact with should pay for their misery. This will occur within three days. The moment you start to see this develop, remove yourself from the premises. This dream also implies that you have a talent you need to develop as much as you can for the next week. You will reach a peak of performance with this talent within a short period of time. Good luck is with you.

missing link Quickly wrap up everything you are involved in within three days and advance to the next step.

mission You will be very capable of handling situations that will occur within three days.

missionary Someone is interested in you sexually. The affection offered to you will escalate to the point where it will be very difficult for you to recover. Avoid this situation completely and stay away from all unwarranted attention.

Mississippi Think ahead and create the necessary atmosphere to facilitate the completion of a task. Do this within three days and you will be successful. This dream may also be used as a reference point in time. If you dream of this state and see its name used in any context, the dream message will occur on this day.

Missouri Explore inconsistencies and any unpredictable circumstances that will be present in a situation that will develop within three days. By doing this you will have the answers to any problems that may develop during this time

period. This dream may also be used as a reference point in time. If you dream of this state and see its name used in any context, the dream message will occur on this day.

mist Your patience will be tested within two days. Plan ahead for this.

mistake This dream is a very lucky omen for you. You will enjoy an abundance of health and will receive wealth in areas you never expected as a result of an unexpected income. You will be able to accomplish tasks that you felt at one time were impossible. This is a great cycle to tackle those big projects. Proceed with confidence. You will, within the next three days, enjoy a prosperous future.

mister Do not overlook a promise you have made to someone.

mistletoe You will enjoy physical pleasure within a few days by being repeatedly kissed. Make sure you are properly groomed and are not caught off guard.

mistress Begin organizing a specific plan to get what you want in the manner in which you desire. This is especially important for the next three days.

mite It will be very much to your benefit to honor the advice given to you by someone else.

mitt Look at both sides of an issue, especially for the next three days.

mitten For the next two days carefully watch your paperwork. Make sure you do not misplace anything of importance in order to avoid panic at the last moment.

mixer Make sure you only gravitate to people you know are loyal and have deep feelings for you, especially for the next three days. A situation will arise that will make it clear that you must associate only with these people.

Moab Become self reliant, especially for the next two days. Push yourself to complete what you know you must do. Many blessings will come to you and your family and you are headed for a brilliant future.

moat Keep a low profile and remain patient, especially for the next three days.

mob For the next two days take aggressive steps to control your thoughts for another person. Do not allow your days to become filled with obsessive thoughts about this individual. Concentrate on everyday matters and situations that are important to your life. You must also not allow the opinions of others to disturb your train of thought. Rely on your own counsel.

mobile home Take steps to avoid or to change anything connected in this dream that was negative so it does not become a reality. Within three days someone will also begin to look for reasons to doubt you. You have prior notice of this so you can begin to handle situations in an appropriate manner.

mobster Surround yourself with solitude and avoid placing yourself in situations that will lead to difficulty and troublesome situations, especially for the next seven days.

moccasin Determine those areas of your life that require more organization and structure. Do this within three days.

mocha Be very aware of errors that could be made within three days. Good luck is with you.

mockingbird What you have hoped for will come to pass within four days. This will be something very special that will bring you much joy and good news.

mock turtle soup Get as much work accomplished as you can for the next two days. You will need to clear up your schedule so you can enjoy upcoming events.

model You will enjoy special pleasures when attending an event you have an invitation to. Do everything you can to improve your physical appearance prior to attending this event.
to use as a plan or guide Within four days, someone will unexpectedly present to you an improbable and outrageous proposal that will seem too good to be true. Because of its outrageous nature, you will be tempted to pass on it. Take a few days to think it over and make sure you do not burn any bridges because you will want to explore it in more detail at a later time. You will continue to have the feeling that this proposal is not a possibility but you can be assured it will work out and that this person will keep each commitment. Good luck is with you.
to use as a standard for excellence You will quickly overcome any troublesome situation and will perform perfectly in any area of life you desire. You are headed for a very prosperous future.
in any other form Someone will treat you in ways that are far beyond your expectations and will verbally express their feelings to you in a beautiful way. You can expect to receive a proposal that will fill you with joy and will be impossible to refuse. You are definitely headed for a brilliant future.

model, nude Do not go out with someone purely for the sake of sexual pleasure, especially for the next two days. You will later decide that this individual is not attractive to you and this could lead to a dangerous situation because this person will feel used. Avoid this behavior.

model T Actions and deeds, not talk, are what will make a difference, especially for the next two days.

modesty Follow all necessary rules and regulations. You are headed for a brilliant future.

mohair A wonderful, generous, loving person will come into your life within three days. This individual will value you deeply.

Mohammed This dream is an extremely lucky omen. You will quickly recover from any serious upcoming situation and will be able to find relief. Discipline yourself and follow all the rules.

Mohammed Ali You will have to cultivate a daring attitude. You will need this for inspiration in order to make a real difference in those upcoming situations in your life.

Mohawk Do not become caught up in lingering doubts. Become clear about what is going on and stick to routine tasks.

Mohican This dream is alerting you to the fact that someone will visit your home and accidentally damage an expensive item. Be very watchful over your valuables in order to avoid disappointment. This is likely to occur within five days.

moisture You will be exposed to some unpredictable and unhealthy behavior within three days. Do what you can to avoid this situation.

molar That special person you choose to be in your life will always be the kind of person to comply with your desires. This individual will also become wealthy through unusual means within the month. You will finally be free of a burdensome situation that has been dragging you down for some time. You are headed for a very prosperous future.

molasses Weigh all the pros and cons regarding a certain situation for the next five days and proceed with caution.

mold Become very tolerant, especially for the next three days, about everything a specific person does or says. You will be very glad that you did. This will allow this person to open up and get to the bottom of what is bothering them.

mole Meet personal involvements head on for the next three days. This will allow you to put all necessary things in order.

molecule Do not waste time, especially for the next two days. Think ahead, regroup and make your move. You will be able to make the correct decision.

molehill Slow down, you are moving too fast. Within three days you will miss an important issue that needs to be dealt with.

molest Someone is having a difficult time reaching a decision they have to make concerning themselves. They will come to you to get some kind of direction regarding the way they feel they should be going. Listen carefully but do not offer any advice. This person will come back to haunt you again and again in the future if they make the wrong decision because they will need someone to blame for their mistakes. Be concerned but not involved. Any event in this dream that needs to be avoided in real life can be prevented.

mollusk Make sure, within three days, that you pay attention to situations you become involved in. Once a situation starts to unravel and begins to look as though it is not falling into place as it should, back off. Practice prudence, alertness and caution.

Molotov cocktail Someone you have not seen in a long time will unexpectedly drop by and take you on a pleasant outing. This person will seemingly be interested in you romantically and you will enjoy yourself immensely. They will promise to call but you will never hear from them again. This is not a result of anything you have done but is simply a result of this person's inability to surrender their feelings. Be patient and this person will come around. Within three days you must also make sure you are carefully budgeting your finances. Make sure all plans, time and money matters fall into place exactly as you have previously decided.

molt For the next three days, guard against any injury caused by a fall. This is preventable.

Mona Lisa Help someone who feels insecure when in your presence. Carry yourself in such a way that this person can relax and feel comfortable when they are around you. This is especially important for the next three days.

monarch Within five days you will meet a very imaginative person. This imagination needs to be tapped and developed by you and applied to your plans. These plans require a tremendous amount of creativity. If you both work together, your creative talents will make something happen quicker and on a much grander scale than you have envisioned. You will be surrounded, during this time period with people who will show you much love and affection. You are headed for a brilliant future.

monarch butterfly Within three days you will be able to detail your thoughts and put those thoughts into words in such a way that will enable someone who desires you to grow closer to you. This person will feel very secure and comfortable in your presence. This will enable them to speak openly and frankly with you and will spark the development of a warm open relationship. You can also be able to use these skills to bring anything you desire into reality and remove all blocks due to poor communication. This is a magical cycle for you.

monastery Within three days someone will come to you to resolve a stressful situation. Make sure you are aware of this so you can think ahead and be able to handle this appropriately with few problems. Move quickly on this so you can settle back and once more have some leisure time.

Monday Something unusual will happen on this day that

will be very much to your advantage. Regroup and rethink and make sure you are prepared for whatever comes your way. Do not allow this to slip through your fingers. Because you have prior notice of this, you will be alert and attentive and will be able to grasp this opportunity. Good luck is with you and you are headed for a brilliant future.

monetary Carefully watch the actions of another person for the next two days. This will give you a hint of the way you should handle yourself for the remainder of your involvement together. Be acutely aware of the attitude you should assume when you are around this person.

money Someone who played an important role in your life in the past will return within five days and, if you desire, will involve themselves deeper in your life. This individual has had a fortuitous life and will return with a fortune to share with you.

to collect or to see others collect money You are underestimating a situation you will be involved with within five days. Move on this before you let it slip through your fingers. This will be a golden opportunity.

to work with or count money Make sure you have your priorities straight and that you check both sides of an issue. Rethink your plans.

bag of money You will soon be filling a very powerful position. You will be very successful and will do everything necessary to hang on to it.

to steal money The safeguards you are using to protect yourself and certain situations will not work. These protective measures will be infiltrated. Take additional safety precautions.

to find money A healthy relationship will develop within five days with someone you feel very attracted to and this relationship will grow as quickly as you want it to. This individual is very willing to flow with the relationship in any direction you choose to take it. You are headed for a very prosperous future.

to lose money Develop a new approach for discussing a major concern. Anything negative witnessed in this dream needs to be avoided in reality. Forewarn anyone you recognize to do the same. Take steps to ensure you only experience positive events in your life.

counterfeit Your plans to secretly assist another will not work out. Prepare yourself, a large sum of money will come your way in the form of a windfall. Small risks will yield big dividends, especially for the next seven days.

to be paid in some capacity If this dream foretells a negative, take the appropriate steps to either alter the outcome or to avoid it entirely. If this foretells a positive event, make sure it is brought to reality. This dream also implies you have been trying to get at the truth concerning an important issue for a long time but each time you have run into a brick wall. Within the week you will be able to bring this matter to rest. An unusual situation will occur that will provide you with the necessary facts. Good luck is with you.

to pass counterfeit money Your determination will lead you to success in the area you desire, especially for the next three days.

to give away money This dream is alerting you of a very fortuitous proposal that will take place with three days. This proposal may be in any capacity. Accept it and move quickly on this.

to be given money You will be engaged in sexual pleasures that will bring you sensual tranquility within three days and this will continue for a long time to come if you so desire.

to handle other people's money You will be deeply involved with someone who has a tremendous amount of wealth and will eventually want to marry you. If this is the path you choose to take you will find it very fortuitous.

to see money fall from the sky An abundance of health and wealth will remain in your life for a long time to come. This cycle will begin to develop within three days. During this time of increased wealth, make sure you put away some money for a rainy day.

to see someone secretly hide money Within three days someone with loose morals will attempt desperately to influence you to take the wrong direction. Be very alert and aware of how easily things can turn around, especially during this cycle.

to throw away money or to see money thrown away You will take a vacation that will bring you good memories for a long time to come. You will enjoy a very prosperous future.

to win money If you desire, you will marry someone who will provide you with a great life. Do not linger on any decision. Take care of what you can now instead of procrastinating. You will enjoy a prosperous future. If you recall any numbers or denominations of bills, use this knowledge for games of chance. Small risks will yield large benefits.

to pay bills You will be involved in negotiations within five days. Although you have doubts, these negotiations will be very fruitful and will move along in a timely fashion.

to burn money Someone will desire more affection out of a platonic relationship. This will quickly grow into a wonderful romance and will rapidly lead to marriage if you so desire. You will win the heart of a very affectionate, sophisticated person who will care for you for a very long time.

to lend money Make sure you take steps to exclude any negative event from becoming reality and take steps to bring any positive event to fruition. You must also be aware that someone who pretends to be your friend is, in actuality, an enemy. This person is very cunning and will come into your life and attempt to involve themselves in your life in some way. Make sure you go to great lengths to keep this from occurring. Anything negative witnessed in this dream needs to be avoided in reality. Forewarn anyone you recognize to do the same. Take steps to ensure you only experience positive events in your life.

seed money Work within the system and take steps to complete a project. Make sure you get the best results possible.

to ask or be asked for money in exchange for sex Do not doubt the loyalty of your loved one. You will also be successful this year in meeting your goals. If anything negative was depicted in this dream, take steps to change it or to avoid it entirely.

to ask for a loan or to borrow money Give a raise in salary to the person who deserves it. You will also be taking huge steps to raise your standard of living. This will be accomplished by focusing on your goals in a grand way. Expect this to come about within ten days due to some unusual and joyful circumstance. Everyone involved in this will enjoy beautiful expressions of joy and tranquility. Many blessings will be with you and your family.

to ask for money and get it Help someone, within ten days, who feels insecure when in your presence. Carry yourself in such a way that this person can relax and feel comfortable when they are around you.

moneybags A wonderful change will occur in your personal life within three days. This will allow you to enjoy the better things in life. Also there will be many admirers you can choose from during this three day period whom you can become permanently involved with, if you so desire.

moneylender Watch the manner in which you behave in front of a certain person. This will lead this individual to believe that you will grant them something you are totally against. Do not give someone else the wrong impression with your body language.

money market Do not force your opinions on another. You must also take the necessary steps to prevent any event in this dream that you choose not to become a reality and do what you can to bring any positive situation to fruition.

money market fund Take every precaution to keep something negative in this dream from becoming a reality. You must also take extra steps to be more understanding of new people who will be entering your life within three days.

money order A certain unusual situation will take place within three days that will give you great joy. You will also enjoy health and tranquility during this time frame.

Mongol Practice a tolerant attitude toward your relatives, especially for the next three days.

Mongolian Someone you were kind to in the past will come into your life and schedule an unexpected meeting with you. This individual will let you know how well their life has turned out since they have last seen you.

mongoose Do not take chances with gambling in any capacity, especially for the next three days.

monk Protect yourself relentlessly from an act of violence for the next two days.

monkey An unusual situation will occur that will bring about disagreements and arguments among family members and friends. Make sure, for the next three days, you do everything you can to avoid any communication breakdown. Prepare yourself to avoid anything that could lead to disagreements.

monkey bars Be very structured and detailed for the next three days and be very careful with anything that involves finances.

monkey suit Be very reliable and consistent with someone who is special to you for the next three days. It will be very important that you demonstrate these attributes for this time period. Good luck is with you.

monkey wrench Someone whom you least expect will want to involve themselves, in some capacity, with your business plans. You will be very surprised and happy to get this reaction from this person. Expect this within five days.

monkfish Resist overspending because someone insists that you do. Good luck is with you. Eat healing foods and drink plenty of water.

monk's hood Anything is possible for the next three days. You are headed for a very prosperous future.

monogamy Take steps to turn any negative omen into a positive situation in real life. You must also make sure, for the next three days, you take time out to mull over an important decision so that when you make your final choice, you will be absolutely sure of the correctness of your decision.

monogram Someone you know has a very sweet disposition and is very eager to be on your side when you need assistance. This individual also has an unpredictable behavior that you need to be aware of before you become too involved. You are headed for a brilliant future.

monolith Behave in a manner for the next three days that demonstrates a sense of humor and tranquility. This atmosphere will allow the occurrence of unusual events that will be very advantageous to you.

monopoly You will have a meeting with someone, within three days, who has agreed that you do something together. A third person will step in and violently protest this agreement to the point where you will have to physically protect yourself from attack. Plan ahead and determine a way you can have this meeting without a violent episode taking place. You are headed for a brilliant future and many blessings will come to you and your family.

monorail Your success will come about within three days because of the actions of another person who cares a great deal for you. Good luck is with you.

Monroe, Marilyn For the next three days focus on getting as much as you can out of a creative talent. Put it in tangible form in order to be viewed by others. This will definitely make a difference in your life because of the height this talent can take you to. You will also, if you choose, have

someone in your life who will tenaciously work to raise your standard of living to a higher level than you ever envisioned. You are headed for a brilliant future. Refer to the definition "to dream about a deceased person" for a greater definition of this dream message. You will find this definition under the word "dead".

monsieur Simplify your life and surround your life with at least three days of solitude.

Montana You are headed for a brilliant career and healthy relationships. This dream may also be used as a reference point in time. If you dream of this state and see its name used in any context, the dream message will occur on this day.

Montana, Joe *(famous football player)* You will be able to rise to all unusual challenges for the next four days and will be able to instantaneously salvage any unusual situation that requires this trait from you at the moment it is required. You will develop resiliency and enjoy a prosperous, healthy and tranquil life.

Monterey Jack cheese You will involve yourself in a once in a lifetime experience and will cherish this memory for a very long time to come. This will unfold within three days. Eat healthy foods, drink plenty of water and get plenty of rest. Good luck is with you.

Montezuma A long standing debt will be unexpectedly repaid within three days.

Montreal The union you are planning to become involved with within three days will be a total disaster. Bypass this and go on with your life. This dream may also be used as a reference point in time. If you dream of this city and see its name used in any context, the dream message will occur on this day.

monument Think ahead and prepare so you will be ready to grasp an opportunity that you must not allow to slip through your fingers. This will regard a romantic involvement with another person. Good luck is with you.

mooch Research the best way to handle a health problem that will develop within three days. You will choose the correct way to handle this.

mood Make sure a relative does not involve you in a distasteful situation. As soon as you see this develop, remove yourself from the environment. Good luck is with you.

moon *to see the moon clearly* Take steps to ensure no member of your family is kidnapped. Alert everyone to take precautions because some very unusual circumstances could lead to their abduction. This is likely to occur within five days.

first quarter moon For the next week you will be in a cycle that will bring you a big victory and a wealth of opportunities. Be sure to put yourself in the position to push through an agreement in your favor by using whatever power and authority you have at your disposal. You have only a week from the time you have this dream to make this agreement a reality. This is the best time to make this happen and this agreement will be met with enthusiasm by all those involved. You are on a path for victory and many blessings will come to you and your family.

half last moon This dream is a very lucky dream and many blessings will come to you. This next three days is the perfect time to carefully evaluate the choices you need to make. You will be able to take the thoughts that are circulating in your mind to generate a larger amount of money than you ever anticipated. As a result, you will earn prestige and respect from your endeavors very quickly because of your motivation. You will be placed in charge of a large enterprise at a low salary but this will grow faster than you hoped and you will gain prestige and a larger salary as a result. Expect this to occur very rapidly.

full moon Within the week you will have a pressing need to accomplish something that depends on someone else's assistance. This could be something in the line of the loan of a large amount of money or a big favor that needs to be performed soon with no hassles. This request will be so large that it will be difficult for you to imagine it will be granted to you. Follow your hunches and you will be led to the person who will come through for you. Proceed with confidence and explore each option until you decide on the perfect one for you. As soon as an agreement has been made, take action immediately so this matter is concluded before this person has a change of heart. Many blessings are with you and you are headed for a prosperous future.

new Take the necessary time to review the whole picture regarding a particular situation that will come up within two days. You will come to a full understanding of what is actually going on and this will allow you to determine how you really feel and the manner in which you want to live the rest of your life. This will be the most important issue to you right now. Proceed with confidence. This dream also implies that any request you make will be granted, even if it is to someone who does not seem interested in you. Proceed with confidence and expect an abundance of health.

moonbeam You will be seen in a totally different light by someone who is special to you and someone whom you have a strong interest in. This will benefit your involvement with this person tremendously. Expect this to occur within three days. Many blessings are with you and your family.

moon child Do not deny yourself the intimate times you are depriving yourself of and do not waste time avoiding the person who is special to you, especially for the next three days.

moonfaced Prepare yourself for a very crowded schedule that will begin to occur within three days. Your social calendar will be full and you will enjoy yourself immensely. Go for it. Many blessings will be with you and your family and you are headed for a prosperous future.

moonflower For the next three days everything you set out to accomplish will be successful.

moon gate You will be enamored with your creative ideas and you will remain this way until these ideas are brought to tangible form. Many blessings will come to you and your family. Also, during this time frame someone will tell you they are deeply in love with you and has great admiration for you.

moonie Do everything necessary to avoid overextending yourself and becoming overly involved in any situation that you feel irresistibly drawn to. Protect yourself.

moonlight You will not be denied the affection you request from someone, especially for the next three days. You are deeply loved and appreciated by others.

moonlighting Face up to the reasons why you refuse to commit to a certain relationship. Deal with this so you can enjoy a more advantageous and less limited lifestyle.

moonshine Someone will, within three days, be alarmed at the deep feelings they have for you. This person will very quickly want to reveal their new found emotions and will be hoping the feelings are mutual. Good luck and many blessings will come to you.

moonstone Someone who is very precious to you in your life will, within three days, give you a very beautiful gift that you will cherish for a lifetime. This dream also implies that you will be treated with special consideration for the next three days. You are headed for a very prosperous future. Eat healing foods, drink plenty of water and get plenty of rest.

moonstruck Stop wasting so much time deciding whether you want to speak with the person of your choice. Your intent is to get this person involved in your life in some capacity and they will be very interested once you become openly communicative. Good luck is with you.

moor You will have to be sure of each step you take for the next three days to ensure that a particular situation will turn out the way you desire.

moose Do not prematurely expose your decisions to others. This will ensure that all of your plans will meet with success. This is especially important for the next three days.

mop Do not become involved in any policy decision that will be brought to your attention within three days involving a relative. State only what you choose to comply with.

morality Find a place of solitude and get down to business. Meditate in your favorite way in order to become very clear about what you need and want. This is especially important for the next three days. Good luck is with you.

morals An older person will seek you out for the purpose of involving you in a distasteful experience. Protect yourself, especially for the next three days, and do not allow this to occur. Make sure you are not manipulated into doing something you find immoral and distasteful.

moray eel Do not allow someone to start making strange demands of you. Be aware that this will begin to develop within two days.

morel Do not become too friendly with a specific person for the next two days. This person will respond to you in a very cold manner and this will cause you embarrassment.

Mormon Within three days make sure you structure and detail a specific situation in exactly the way you wish it to fall into place so others can act accordingly and there will be no room for confusion.

morning Pay close attention to all the clues offered in this dream so you can prevent or change any forthcoming negative event. It is also important that you do not rely on a friend who has repeatedly assured you they will come through for you. This individual is not reliable. Look for an alternative as soon as possible so you will not feel overwhelmed due to lack of support.

morning glory This dream is an extremely lucky omen and you will wallow in tranquility and peace for at least a month. You are definitely headed for a prosperous future. A very shy person will also open up lines of communication and will allow you to know where you stand within this relationship.

Morning Prayer Mediate in your favorite form and seek a peaceful tranquil area that you can remain in for at least seven days so you can release stress from your life. This is a perfect time to demand and specify exactly what you need from your higher power. In spite of how difficult a request you feel this is, it will be granted. Many blessings will come to you and your family.

morning sickness For the next five days, become verbally aggressive in order to allow a certain person to open up and request specifically what they desire emotionally from you. This assertive manner will be the correct one to assume.

Morpheus *(Greek Mythology)* This dream is an extremely lucky omen. What was not possible for you to achieve in the past is possible now. Eat healthy foods, drink plenty of water and get plenty of rest. Do not allow any opportunities to slip through your fingers for the next three days.

morphine Be very alert. Someone has tried numerous times, without success, to get in touch with you but a third party is purposefully preventing this communication. Make it a point to get through to this individual because they have an urgent matter to discuss with you and you need to make yourself available to receive this information. Good luck and many blessings are with you and your family. Any neg-

ative event connected to this dream need not become a reality. You have enough time to turn it around to a positive event.

Morse code Someone you least expect is an investigator in disguise. Make sure any behavior of yours that you do not want scrutinized or recorded is not seen by this individual. Since you do not know who this person is, be on your best behavior for the next seven days.

mortal You are entering a very exciting time. You will meet someone who will eagerly try to persuade you into a sexual encounter. You have had no idea this person felt this way but will become very excited at the prospects of looking at this individual in a different light. If this is something you desire, you will find it mutually satisfying. This cycle will bring you much promise for a successful relationship and you will be very prosperous in other areas of your life. Many blessings will come to you and your family.

mortar For the next three days you need to think carefully before you make statements to someone else. Once you make certain statements, you will have to stick with them. Make sure you do not say something you cannot take back.

mortgage Do everything necessary for the next two days to maintain your self confidence. Become very bold and aggressive and do not involve yourself with anything you know very little about. Any negative message given in this dream must be attended to so it does not become a reality. Good luck is with you.
   second mortgage Do not allow yourself to get tied up with certain situations or people, especially for the next three days.

mortician Take whatever steps are necessary for you to check out the person you are romantically interested in. This individual does not have the same sexual orientation as you and is under the impression you are aware of this. You will also be involved in some unusual situations that will bring you prosperity and will better your health status.

mortuary For the next five days apply yourself to presenting your ideas graphically so others will be able to visualize your unusual plans. This will be of great benefit to you.

mosaic For the next five days remain focused on the importance of certain relationships so you can handle everything appropriately. Make sure those relationships that are important remain close to you.

Moses For the next month you will experience brilliance and clarity of thought. This will guide you in situations where you may have to really extend yourself and take risks. Develop a bold and daring demeanor so the thoughts you have can be brought forth in tangible form. You will definitely experience more prosperity in your life. You are headed for a brilliant future. Many blessings will come to you and your family.

Moslem Within three days you will be able to successfully negotiate all old business transactions. You will also be able to bring closeness into those relationships that you desire. Many blessings are with you and your family.

mosquito Within three days you will encounter someone who has been plotting for a long time to back you into a corner in order to have you relinquish something they have been after. You have prior notice of this and can take the proper steps to avoid being manipulated.

mosquito hawk Someone who feels they have not been allotted the time for a long overdue conversation will aggressively seek this time from you. If you choose to make the time for this individual, you will find it will be very profitable for you.

mosquito net You will be asked for financial assistance from a relative who is in a very stressful situation. You will be able to provide this help and will be paid back in full, as promised.

moss Someone who has been trying to talk you into entering a business venture with them will pressure you to help them but lacks the seed money to get started. Carefully think out this plan because you would have to provide the capital.

mote Pay close attention to what you will be hearing over the next three days. What you will be told will be very instrumental in helping you to make a final decision about something you need to handle immediately. Make sure you get all of the information needed in order to make a wise decision.

motel If you dreamed of any negative event in this dream, take all the necessary steps to ensure it does not occur in reality. It is especially important that you take care of this within three days. Do what you can to experience only positive events in your life. Within five days you will also need to give yourself a break from outside interference and influences. Give yourself time within the next two days to quietly meditate in order to gain greater clarity in your thoughts.

moth This dream is an extremely lucky omen and is a promise that you will enjoy an abundance of health, wealth and finances as well as an improved standard of living. You will also experience a greater sense of protectiveness from a special person. This will create a sense of excitement because you will realize that someone cares for your well being. You are headed for a brilliant future.

mothball Make sure it is appropriate for you to make a romantic move toward someone you are interested in. This individual is interested in someone else and it may be embarrassing and inappropriate for you to make a move in this direction.

moth eaten Someone will aggressively and passionately pursue you and will clearly verbalize their desires in such a way that there is no mistaking this person's intent. If you choose to pursue this relationship, do not allow their aggressiveness to scare you away. Be sure you verbalize your concerns about this behavior. This will allow this person to accommodate you more and you will have a more pleasurable time with this individual, if you desire this involvement in your life.

mother Pay attention to the content of any discussion you had in this dream involving your mother. This will offer you a big clue to the meaning of this dream. If either of you reveal a negative message to each other, give it your full attention and take steps to attend to it appropriately within seven days. You must also be aware that you are the only person responsible for the successes you want to bring into your life. Do this by applying yourself and by being more aggressive in those areas you want to experience prosperity in. Anything else going on in your dream that involves your mother will be either a positive or negative representation of a future event that will occur within a seven day period. Take steps to handle this in the appropriate manner now. You will be able to keep this event from becoming a major problem now or years from now.

step mother Go out of your way to extend extra kindnesses to those much older than you. Within the next seven days, someone you have known for years will also be a support to you in an emotional crisis.

to dream of your mother angry Make your mother aware of the contents of this dream so she can take the necessary steps to turn this into a positive situation. This dream also implies that, within five days, a very conniving person will be able to bring you great emotional harm if you do not take steps to avoid it.

to dream of your mother being physically active in any form You need to stop a behavior you may not be aware of that will ultimately bring you harm. Look closely at your behavior for the next five days to determine the trait that will cause you physical harm and take whatever steps you deem necessary to change it.

to see your mother ill or behaving in an unusual manner Your mother is attempting to warn you that a small priceless item will be lost due to theft or carelessness on your part. Take aggressive actions to protect anything that is valuable to you.

to dream of a deceased mother You are headed toward a fortuitous future. Be courageous and explore several options in order to achieve your goals. You will be successful if you remain practical while taking calculated risks. You will see an immediate improvement in your life. Look under the definition of dead people for a greater explanation.

to dream of your mother dying Do not allow anyone to distract you from your ambitions. Do not let your dreams and goals die. Have faith and you will achieve success far quicker than you expected. You must also recall what she was dying of in the dream and take steps to warn her of this if it pertains to her.

mother figure Do everything you can to feel more at peace with yourself. Make it a point to do more for yourself and this will allow you to experience balance, tranquility and harmony. Above all, do not place yourself in any stressful situation for at least a month's time. Nourish yourself in such a way that you will feel fantastic just being alive. By doing this you will discover the path you need to take in a much easier fashion. You are headed for a brilliant future.

Mother Goose For the next three days do not waste time deciding on the move you want to make. Regroup yourself and rethink your options, but whatever you do, do it quickly. You will make the correct decision.

Mother Hubbard You will be relied upon to take the leadership position and will be able to handle everything with courage and confidence.

mother-in-law This dream is a good luck omen. For the next three days work to keep yourself abreast of all major occurrences. This will help you in decision making and in collaborating your ideas with others.

mother lode Someone is depending on you to come up with the correct answer for certain situations that need to be handled. Prepare yourself by getting the proper training and education to take the necessary steps, especially for the next seven days. You can also receive a financial windfall when you least expect it.

Mother Nature Meditate in your favorite form and your prayers will be answered no matter how impossible it seems at the time.

Mother of God This dream is an omen of prosperity. It is also asking you to focus on treatments you need in your life to bring back a sense of normalcy and balance regarding health. Move quickly and motivate yourself to perform the necessary tasks to move ahead in life. Victory is with you. You will retain a sense of excitement about your future for the next seven days.

mother of pearl You will enjoy a family get together that will unite you with all your loved ones and you will enjoy festivities at their best. You will also receive a gift from someone you least expect, within five days.

Mother's Day Anything connected with this dream that should be avoided because of negative contents must be attended to within the week. You are also loved beyond your imagination and you will be treated as a precious commodity by those who care about you. You are headed for a prosperous future.

Mother Superior Do not allow yourself to spend more than you should as a result of someone's manipulative tactics.

motion picture Make sure any romantic situation you are thinking of becoming involved in is not hindered by any feelings of discouragement and defeat. Do whatever you can to regain your feelings of aggressiveness and boldness in

order to carry yourself appropriately. This will allow you to gain the love and affection you are interested in having. This is especially important for the next five days. If you choose to take this route, you are heading for an emotionally fulfilling and prosperous future.

motion sickness Be very aware of your valuables, especially for the next three days and become very protective of your possessions. You must also not allow any negative event in this dream to become a reality. You have prior notice of this and can take steps to alter the outcome. This is especially important for the next three days.

motor Someone you desire passionately will want to communicate their eagerness for you. You will be mutually satisfied with this union. Expect this to occur within two days.

motorbike Be very aware of your needs, especially for the next two days, so you can get the professional services and help you need. Your needs will be met quickly during this cycle.

motorboat Focus on the specific desires you want met, especially during this cycle.

motorcycle Move forward at full speed in order to wrap up certain situations that need to be quickly attended to. During this process you will have to make sure no one tries to bully you or manipulate you into changing your plans or to compromise your wishes. This is especially important for the next five days.

motor home Someone you know has caused you a great deal of unhappiness in the past. This individual will contact you within two days with a new endeavor. Do not allow past differences to get in the way of a new project with this person.

motorist *to see someone drive your car* Either you or the company you work for has placed an advertisement. Be aware, if you are the interviewer, someone answering this ad will be a very dangerous individual. Take extra precautions for the next seven days against a deranged person.

in any other form You will be the target for romantic affection. This will appeal to you very much for the next two days, if you should pursue this. You will be happy for a lifetime.

motor scooter Push yourself to leave behind certain aspects of your life that you have outgrown and replace them with new involvements so you can grow in areas that will bring new and better changes to your life. You are headed for a brilliant future.

Motown Make sure you are listening to your intuition and do not be so quick to jump into the unknown. Analyze your feelings, especially for the next three days. Be sure you are bringing forth those experiences you need in your life. Any group activity will bring much joy into your life and will provide you with many activities that you will enjoy. Use this two week cycle to expose your talents in order to get the right response from others.

motto Encourage yourself to be more social for the next seven days. Any negotiation you are involved in during this time period should also be closely scrutinized to make sure you are making the correct decision.

mound Do not allow jealous anger displayed by another to manipulate you into doing something you have no business doing.

mountain Grand changes will occur within five days that will bring a wonderful experience into your life. Opportunities provide the chance for great riches to come your way. Any one of these you choose will bring you an abundance of prosperity.

mountain cat Someone has led you to believe you may become more familiar with them but they do not want you to behave in an overly friendly fashion in public. You will be made to look bad and this person will ignore you in front of others. This will occur within two weeks.

mountain dew Do everything in your power to keep someone from distancing themselves from you because of your manner, especially for the next five days.

mountain lion Be very aware of someone new who will be coming into your life within five days. It will be difficult to figure out this person's personality so don't waste your time concerning yourself with this. This individual will change their personality regularly and will run hot and cold. Go on with your life without getting caught up in this person's act.

mountain sheep Become very focused on what you do and do not want from life and go after what you really want for the next three days. Eat healthy foods, get plenty of rest and drink plenty of water. Many blessings are with you and your family.

mountie Do what you can to prevent the loss of any of your possessions for the next two days.

mourn All negative depictions in this dream may be prevented from becoming a reality. You have prior notice of this and have the time to keep anything negative from becoming a part of your life. Develop a more positive attitude and treat a situation more seriously than you have been treating it.

mourner Take all the necessary steps to keep any negative event from becoming a part of your life. You have the power now to keep this from becoming a reality. You must also take the time to focus more on what your intuition is telling you and go with what your instincts tell you, especially for the next three days. You will be greatly benefited by this.

mourning band Make sure you do not become attracted to

someone who is deeply involved in a project of theirs. Be kind to this individual but keep your distance.

mourning cloak Do everything necessary to keep chaos from erupting because of something you say without thinking about it first. This is especially important for the next three days.

mourning dove Someone you are considering asking for aid will immediately come to your assistance. This person will relentlessly help you until you come through this situation.

mouse Make sure before you set up rules and regulations, you are able to keep them yourself, especially for the next three days. Do not ignore an opportunity you will gain by paying attention to a valuable tip.

anything unusual that you see yourself or anyone else doing with a mouse Someone will take advantage of you and will use you without your knowledge. This person will use deception and dishonesty and will use you in this situation as an innocent unwilling participant. In the long run, you will be cheated. Pay close attention to your present situations and be acutely aware of the actions of others.

field mouse You may unintentionally sabotage the plans of another person. Be very aware of your actions for the next four days and make sure you do not inadvertently affect the lives of others because of your behavior.

mousetrap Within five days someone who secretly hates you will attempt to sabotage a situation you are trying to steer in a certain direction to benefit another. This individual knows you are right, yet will go against you in spite of the destruction it will bring to others. Your goal is to work things out so everyone can enjoy a more prosperous future. You have prior notice of this and can take steps to prevent interference. This person has no idea of the depth of hardship they will bring to others. Within five days a stressful situation will also occur as a result of angry words exchanged when you are with a particular group of people. Do whatever you can to avoid involvement in this situation. Find a peaceful activity to become involved with.

mousse You will be invited on an outing with a same sexed person to a very elaborate place. You will enjoy yourself immensely and will notice a novelty item that this person will buy for you that you will treasure as a memento.

mouth Pay attention to anything that is occurring with your mouth or someone else's mouth. If it is distasteful to you, take steps to ensure it does not occur in reality, especially for the next five days and make sure you alert anyone you recognize to take steps to avoid any negative event. You must also make sure you are not manipulated into doing something that goes against your nature or your better judgment, especially for the next five days.

to dream of yourself standing with your mouth wide open Someone will come into your life within three days eager to have a friendly relationship. As time passes you will begin to receive mixed messages. This person will begin to hint at a romantic involvement but is only playing games with you and wasting your time because they are seeking only a short term relationship. Do not expect more than this. Enjoy yourself and get on with your life. You will enjoy future prosperity. Do not compromise your own desires, especially during this time frame, and you will be able to grasp deep emotional fulfillment.

someone else's mouth agape Don't let business plans be known or you will be defeated. Quickly process these plans in order to bring them to reality.

blabber mouth For the next five days make sure you have a camera ready in order to capture precious moments and make sure the equipment you are using is in adequate condition.

cotton mouth Do not allow someone to escape punishment who may be a treacherous, dangerous person. Learn all you can about a person's character before you choose to ignore transgressions.

mouth organ You are definitely headed for a very bright future and you will experience an abundance of health and tranquility for the upcoming month.

mouthpiece Be careful that you do not become involved in something that, at first, appears to be innocent but will turn out to be very dangerous, especially for the next three days. Remain alert.

mouth to mouth resuscitation Within two weeks you will hear the words of love you have longed to hear. This will bring about major changes in your life that you are very prepared to involve yourself in.

mouthwash When speaking with someone whom you wish to be involved with in some capacity, make sure you speak in a straightforward fashion about what you are willing to do and what you find distasteful so this will become a healthy, emotional relationship.

move *to move over to make room for someone or something* You will have someone in your life within the week who will be very attentive to your every need. This dream also implies that you will receive a financial windfall.

to move Make sure you take steps to avoid anything in this dream that you do not wish to experience in reality. Start making the right moves now so events do not result in the negative circumstances you dreamed about. You will also be asked to join someone for some precious private moments. If you choose to go in this direction, you will find this to be very much to your liking and you will savor each moment.

to see others move This dream implies that you should take steps to prevent any negative occurrence in this dream from becoming a reality and to warn those you recognize to do the same. Make sure, for the next three days, that you watch things carefully in order to prevent something from occurring that could be a huge mistake.

to ask someone to move in with you or to be asked to move in with someone Take the most profitable course of

action and you will find your plans will be grander and will come from a much improved and higher level. Your enterprise will be respected by others.

to be asked to move out You will enjoy a mature growth of spirituality and will also be able to handle a pressing responsibility in a way you have been unable to do before. Within this three day period, you will be able to make clear choices and make good use of your resources like never before in order to complete your tasks.

the feeling of being unable to move when trying to awaken For the next seven days you will need to be very attentive and acutely aware of certain events that will begin to unfold and will have a serious and damaging affect on your future. These events will destine you to alter your life and point yourself in the wrong direction. You must become more assertive and muster up the courage and confidence to take the necessary steps to protect yourself from this situation, as well as watching the words you use when speaking to others, because your words may be used as leverage against you. Be observant of what is unfolding that will have a serious effect on your future. This will occur because of any of the following situations or a combination of the following situations:

- The influence that someone will have over you.
- Interference from someone who will steer you in the wrong direction.
- The control that someone in power will exert over you.
- The leverage that someone will gain by using your words to put you at a disadvantage.
- Someone who is in a position of authority who will make decisions for you.

Do not allow yourself to become vulnerable by not acting on your own behalf, because you will suffer emotional depletion as a result and will be guided in a direction you have no desire to go. Prod yourself to get your point across to those in authority. Make it a point to avoid everyday stresses caused by the decisions others make for you who have no business being involved. You are in danger of surrendering your control. Avoid unhealthy situations and circumstances and remain suspicious of all changes. Become confident and relentless in correcting those areas of your life that require corrections. You will then be able to put yourself on the right path. You have the power to change any negative aspect of this dream as well as changing your life to encourage positive expressions. Make sure all of your bases are safely covered. Practice common sense and your plans will be successfully carried out. You will place yourself on the path of prosperity.

to be aware that you are unable to move your body for a short time because of some unusual occurrence Your spirit wants you to see what is in front of you and to make sure you do not overlook anything. Take steps to ensure you are not being narrow-minded about something you are about to involve yourself in and make sure you get more than one perspective about this issue. Create several alternative ways to deal with this situation. Do not make excuses that will keep you from motivating yourself into moving forward. You will accomplish anything you need to at this particular time by being flexible and looking at things from a different angle. This attitude will offer you many alternatives to deal with this situation. Anything in this dream that was displayed to you is a major clue to what else you need to be doing in your life. If it was negative, take steps to prevent it in reality. If positive, make sure you take steps to promote it. You will be putting yourself in the position for a brilliant future.

movie Pay close attention to what you are watching. This will lead you to a clue that will portend a future event. If this event is negative, take the necessary steps to avoid it or to alter the outcome. If positive, make sure you take the steps to ensure a good outcome. This dream also implies that, within five days, you will find yourself working with someone who is surprisingly more sincere, selfless and eager to work with your suggestions than you had hoped. You will find your surroundings to be pleasing and the performance of tasks will be easier.

if you recognize someone in the dream This person represents a particular past event in your life. Recall what was happening in your life at this time. This may be an event you wish to take steps to avoid or something you will want to include in your present life.

moving walkway/sidewalk This dream is an extremely lucky omen and implies you will experience an inner strength and courage as well as the drive and determination you need to motivate yourself to push beyond any physical or mental barrier that interferes with your moving ahead. Within four days you will rid yourself completely of any aspect of your life that you disapprove of and once you do, you will successfully bring into tangible form a new project that you are excited about. You will also be greeted in a regal fashion and placed on a pedestal anywhere you go during this time period. You are headed for a brilliant future and many new opportunities are headed your way.

mow Do everything you can to spend more time with your loved ones. This should be a priority for the next three days. You will also need to attend to important issues you would otherwise overlook unless you make time for them and are at the right place at the right time.

Mozart, Wolfgang Amadeus This dream is a promise that your energies, talents, and/or creativity will result in life long riches. Within three days you will receive a declaration of adoration and a positive proposal of marriage that will soon become a reality. Proceed with confidence. You will be victorious in grasping all of your life's desires. Many blessings are with you and your family.

mozzarella Within a three day period the person you have been wishing would become more communicative with you will anxiously approach you to discuss intimate situations. Be sure to ask this person direct questions that involve you. This question will put both of you very much at ease. You will experience tranquility, good health and wealth during this cycle.

MSG Within three days someone will be genuine in the love they show for you and will be with you in a way you desire. Many blessings are with you. Make it a point to avoid anything you dreamed of that you wish not to experience in reality.

mucous This dream is a very lucky omen. You will accidentally overhear a conversation that will be very destructive to another person if it is repeated. Make sure you keep this information to yourself.

mud Make it a point to show more genuine affection and encouragement to those you care about. Develop a soothing manner toward those that need to be treated this way. It is very important that you do this for the next three days. You have time to alter anything negative in this dream that needs to be changed in reality.

to see an animal fall into mud You will have to replace old equipment with new equipment very soon. You have prior notice of this and can start putting money aside now so this will not be a burden to you.

to see someone walk through or standing in mud Within three days put some time aside to really clear your mind and do some brainstorming in order to pinpoint the suspicions you have about another person and how to go about resolving them. This will allow you to make a plan to determine whether your suspicions are valid, and if so, how to handle them. You will successfully deal with this issue within this time period if you motivate yourself now. This is the best cycle to find the answers you are seeking. You are headed for a very prosperous future.

to walk in mud You will have to decide whether to commit to a relationship. Someone else has become interested in the person you are involved with and if you do not commit, you will lose this relationship. If you do commit, this will be a very successful union. Move quickly and do not waste time and do not allow the opinions of others to hinder your decision. You will enjoy a prosperous future because you will be able to turn a negative situation into a positive one.

mud bath This dream is warning you that a very malicious person will come on to you and present a very trustful facade to you. This person will give you the impression that whatever they discuss with you will be kept between you. In reality, they are trying to glean as much as they can from you about another person. They will then go back to the person you were talking about with the information you gave them after they have assured you they will keep this information to themselves. Be alert to this situation so you can avoid this scenario altogether, because once the third party learns of this they will maliciously verbally attack you. This may escalate to violence. You have prior notice of this to ensure that it does not take place.

mud fish Within five days an emergency situation will arise that will definitely be out of your control. Prepare yourself for the fact that no matter what you do to prevent chaos, your plans will not work. Remain calm and do not panic. You will be able to resolve this successfully in the best way you can.

mudslide You will have to discuss a difficult situation with someone. This situation will rapidly develop into chaos and will continue to escalate beyond your control. You have prior notice of this and can avoid placing yourself in some distasteful situation. This issue will not be worked out because another party will not be willing to help you work it out. The harder you work at this, the harder they will resist.

mudslinging *any form* Within five days you will attempt to collect what is righteously yours. Unless you think ahead and devise a way to handle this in an appropriate manner, you will experience some horrifying moments. Avoid getting trapped in a distasteful situation.

muenster cheese You will feel that the time is right to move ahead on a particular project. Follow your hunches.

muff Carefully think through your plans and take the time to regroup in order to ensure that the next steps you take are the correct ones. Do this to avoid making a big mistake.

muffin Within three days you will be able to create a perfect romantic setting that will allow you to satisfy someone in the manner you desire. You will be able to create a healthy workable relationship out of this for both of you. Many blessings are with you and your family.

muffler Within three days someone with unrealistic ideas will persuade you to back up a certain situation. Make sure this person's extreme behavior does not result in you becoming involved in something you do not desire.

mug *full* You will gain headway in a present situation by setting up a meeting with those who are eager to hear what you have to say. This will yield a positive outcome.
empty Do not panic in times of distress. Things will work out for the better within a few days.
cracked You will lose a bet.
broken Lack of communication will result in a major set back. Think ahead in order to prevent this.

mugger You need to rush your work in order to meet certain deadlines. Focus on what you need to do and follow your own counsel.

mulatto You will find someone within the next three days who will bring you nothing but joy, prosperity and a healthy relationship. This individual has a rich educational background as well as an extensive network of friends. Should you choose to go into this relationship, you will be introduced to a new and varied lifestyle. This relationship will last a lifetime.

mulberry Do not allow yourself to be pushed into something that goes against your nature. You will also successfully respond to someone's request for emotional fulfillment.

mule For the next five days pay close attention to a person you will be associating with. This individual is very immor-

al and wicked. Do not allow yourself to become involved with them. You will regret this later on.

mule deer Keep a close eye on someone who means a lot to you for the next three days. This person may not be aware of some of their peculiar behaviors or a health problem that needs to be checked out by a physician.

mule skinner This dream is a lucky omen and is telling you that you will accomplish exactly what you set out to accomplish.

mulligan stew Be more independent in your approach to certain situations. Make sure you get your thoughts across to another individual, otherwise this situation will not work out.

Multiple Personality Disorder Someone you know will unexpectedly become very lax. As time goes by, this lazy trait will increase. Remove yourself from this person's surroundings before you become this way. You are headed for a prosperous future, keep doing what you are doing.

multiplication Someone you are very interested in will, within three days, bring a very healthy attitude into this relationship. Both of you together will be able to increase your prosperity and you will enjoy a wonderful life together.

mum Someone will treat you in such a way that you will be surprised and filled with joy by the kindness and courtesy shown to you. Many blessings will come to you and your family.

mumps You will be accused by someone of lying. This person will become known to you as a hypocrite and will commit slander against you. Go on with your life and do not allow this to bother you.

murder A powerful position and a financial advancement will be placed in your hands. This will be an appointed position. You are entering a very victorious cycle and will be able to accomplish everything you set out to do. If anything negative was depicted in this dream, take steps to change it or avoid it entirely.
to murder a special person or a relative The person you are killing in this dream is, in reality, committing acts that cause their loved ones a great deal of pain. You will be instrumental in bringing assistance and harmony to this individual's family as well as to them. Your thoughts will be illuminated in very specific ways that will allow you to advise these people on how to handle this situation. This will enable them to bring more love and tranquility to their lives. This is especially important for the next three days. Anything negative witnessed in this dream needs to be avoided in reality. Forewarn anyone you recognize to do the same. Take steps to ensure you only experience positive events in your life.
to murder someone other than a special person or a relative What you once felt was impossible is now in your des-

tiny to achieve. Anything negative witnessed in this dream needs to be avoided in reality. Forewarn anyone you recognize to do the same. Take steps to ensure that you only experience positive events in your life.

to be murdered Take steps to protect yourself and to keep this dream from becoming a reality, especially for the next three days. Pay attention to any event in this dream that you can apply to reality. This will allow you to gain additional clues to an event that will take place during this time frame. Play it safe.

if you recognize the person who murdered you Take steps to protect yourself from this individual and to keep this dream from becoming a reality in your life. Relentlessly apply yourself in order to achieve a special goal you desire within three days. If you do not become personally involved, this goal will not be accomplished and you will suffer much disappointment.

to murder an animal Do not become alarmed. You will, within two days, hear a personal story from someone you have a great deal of confidence in. Within five days after this incident, you will hear a different version of the same story repeated back to you from another respectable person. Do not waste your time trying to determine the accuracy of either story. Conduct your own research to gain verification. This will put a stop to all gossip and save you many headaches. You will be able to successfully tackle a situation that will become overwhelming for everyone concerned within a three day period. If anything negative was depicted in this dream, take steps to change it or avoid it entirely. Good luck is with you and many blessings will come to you and your family.

murmur A professional person who will be working with you in some capacity will give you accurate advice and will work with your best interests at heart. This individual will make all of the correct decisions for you.

heart murmur Help someone who is close to you to develop creativity. This help will be welcomed with open arms.

muscadine You are headed for a brilliant future and you are loved, without your knowledge, beyond your imagination.

muscatel Do not allow a threatening manner from another person keep you from organizing what you need to do professionally.

muscle Be very alert. You need to make sure the choices you make are the correct ones, especially for the next three days.

muscle man Handle all of your duties and affairs in a timely fashion.

Muscovite Make sure the conversations you have with someone you want to bring close to you will not work against you. You believe what you will be saying will come across to this person in a positive fashion when, in reality, this person will perceive it in an entirely different way. Be careful because this will create distance between you.

muscular dystrophy Make sure you voice your complaints to the right people, especially for the next three days, in order to avoid confusion.

muse Within five days you will be able to resolve all of the conflicts you have with someone who is special to you.

museum Make sure, for the next two days, you are emotionally capable of offering assistance to someone who is in desperate need of your help. It would be far better to seek the appropriate assistance for this person instead of becoming emotionally involved.

mushroom For the next five days you are going to have to push yourself in order to achieve success. You will be successful only to the degree that you push yourself.

music Within five days you will be able to grasp a once in a lifetime opportunity to meet that person who is perfect for you. You will be able to develop a beautiful relationship that will bring great wealth and power to both of you. It is your choice whether you want to pursue this or not.

familiar music Recall the time period of your life when you were most familiar with this music and what was going on in your life at this time. This will represent an event you will either wish to keep from reoccurring or one you will desire to reproduce. You are definitely headed for a brilliant future.

musical chairs Within two days make it a point to live your life to the fullest. Stop depriving yourself of the pleasures of life and take steps to add spice to your life by adding entertainment and amusements into your schedule. Good luck is with you.

music box An outstanding debt will unexpectedly be paid for you by someone else. You will hinder this if you investigate the source. Someone also wishes to give you a gift of money. Do not allow pride to get in the way.

musician Someone is very interested in you and is very eager for you to make the first move. Once you do this, you will be received with open arms. This also implies that you will be putting yourself on a new path toward an abundance of health and healthy relationships. You are headed for a prosperous future.

music video This dream is an extremely lucky omen. Within three days you will be undergoing a major transformation in your life. A friend will also point you in a new direction and will offer you much needed information that will help you to fulfill your desires.

musk Someone who has not treated you well in the past will feel remorse and will offer you an apology. Expect this within three days. Many blessings will come to you and your family.

musk deer A union you feel will be a disaster will be very pleasurable. You will experience wonderful things from this union for the next three days.

musket Within two days you will learn the intensity of another's involvement in your life. This will give you a great deal of joy.

musketeer You will be going through an extremely lucky omen for the next month. Your intuition will be accurate. Follow your own counsel. Everything you set into motion during this cycle will meet with success.

muskmelon Make sure you do not allow a persistent family member to involve you in something you find distasteful that involves the family. Take steps to bypass this situation.

musk oil You will acquire the knowledge you seek within three days by conducting your own thorough research. You must also make sure that during this time period you dress appropriately. Expect unusual weather.

musk ox You will become very clear within seven days about how to help someone help themselves and have their own needs met.

muskrat Learn to control yourself and learn patience with someone who is shy in order to allow them to gain confidence and the ability to open up enough to get close to you. This will occur within seven days.

muslin Do not deny yourself intimacy and quiet times with someone else, especially for the next three days.

mussel Protect yourself from any viruses, especially for the next three days. Treat any illness at the initial stage so it does not escalate into something more serious.

Mussolini An unusual situation will occur within the month with a person you do not know yet. This person will see an opportunity as far more fruitful than you do. This will cause you to attend to those areas of your life that will ultimately bring riches to you.

mustache Within two days you will become very aware of the deep feelings someone has for you. This person will quickly reveal their feelings toward you. Think carefully about whether you wish to be involved. You will want to surrender your feelings very quickly once you make your decision.

mustard This dream is a very lucky omen and represents prosperity and healthy relationships that will grow to the degree you wish. What you felt was impossible regarding relationships are now possible. Use this cycle to bring those you care about closer to you. You are loved beyond your

imagination and will be surrounded by those who will demonstrate this love, affection, and appreciation toward you within three days.

mustard gas Face up to your responsibilities and focus on how to handle them properly.

mustard plaster Someone will tell you an unrealistic story within three days. Follow your intuition. It is accurate.

mutant You cannot rely on the person you felt would come through for you. This person will let you down. Find an alternative.

mute Do not restrict yourself verbally to the point of being unable to state your feelings or to get your point across to the person who is special to you.

mutiny Make sure you watch your attitude for the next five days so you do not feel you have to apologize to anyone. Be aware you may be coming across rudely.

mutton Within three days you will rejoice, over some unexpected news. You will also receive words of love that you have long wanted to hear.

mutton chops Do not allow yourself to overindulge in alcohol, food, or medications. This will not agree with you. Others will support your desire to become physically fit.

mutual fund You and a special person will make an agreement to go into something together. The agreement you make within five days will be long remembered because of the unexpected abundances it will bring to you in the future.

muumuu Within five days do not overextend yourself by becoming involved in a particular situation. You will be required to perform physical labor to the point of exhaustion. Pull yourself away from this situation, regroup, eat healthy foods, drink plenty of water, and get plenty of rest.

Muzak Protect yourself from the elements, especially for the next three days. You will also be able to express your feelings to someone in the appropriate manner during this cycle.

myrrh You will hear news of a pregnancy. You will also experience future prosperity and many blessings will come to you and your family. You are on the right path to acquire many riches and are headed for a brilliant future.

mystery Within three days a situation will occur that will leave your enemies rejoicing over your failure. Pay close attention to your actions and be very alert during this time period in order to keep this from occurring.

mystic Your circumstances will rapidly improve and you will be able to permanently rid yourself of a long standing issue.

myth You will enjoy the freedom that has been made possible for the coming week because you will finally complete a long standing project.

mythical creature Within the month you will reach a solution regarding a family member, particularly a small child. This person will recover from a long standing illness. You can look forward to a prosperous future and will enjoy an abundance of health.

N

N Within the week, certain situations will occur because you have motivated yourself in areas of your life you need to attend to. Two people will also enter your life who do not know each other. Each of these people is capable of providing you with a new and different view of life. Both of them will be interested in you romantically and in other capacities as well. Each one is capable of loving you intensely and is educated in a way that could provide you with a wonderful lifestyle and financial security. Within the month both of these people will be eager to involve you in a permanent relationship. It will be very difficult for you to make up your mind and decide which of them you choose to have a relationship with. You will be able to make the right decision during this time period and you will receive exactly what you want and need from life. You are definitely headed for a brilliant future.

nab Do not waste time trying to decide on the exact words to express your feelings to another person. This individual is allowing the relationship to grow at the pace they desire. You will find this pace to be slow but once you express your feelings, you will be met with open arms.

nachos Within three days someone will demand unusual affections from you. The level of this relationship will then grow at a rapid pace. You had felt this was a platonic relationship but now understand that this person desires something deeper. This will delight you because you have long desired something deeper than friendship.

nag You definitely need to set limits with someone who, for the next three days, will have a difficult time making a decision. Tactfully set limits on how long you are willing to wait. Be careful you do not let time slip by when you could be doing something more important.

nail For the next three days focus on the best way to introduce someone to your family members whom you want to be accepted in any capacity. Everything will work out well during this time period.

nail file Within three days a situation that has been very

puzzling to you will become untwisted if you give it enough time. Do not become so stressed out about this. Remain calm and it will work itself out.

to file your nails Someone you know will appreciate your forthrightness. This will definitely clear up any faulty image they may have about you. You are seeking new experiences and will have many to choose from within the next seven days. You are definitely headed for a brilliant future.

nails Within two days you will hear delightful news that will capture your interest. This will involve someone who has just come into town.

painted You are beginning to feel a strong emotional urge that will take up a great deal of your time because you have no knowledge of the source of this drive. This urge is causing you to focus on bringing something into tangible form and will continue for a two week period. Within this time period you will be able to determine the reason and source of this feeling and you will begin to act on it. This overwhelming urge could be a result of a psychic ability and a heightened awareness that is pushing you in the direction you need to go. Although you have no real proof or verification, you will know on an instinctive level that if you act on this urge you will reap greater benefits than you ever felt possible. You will know this because of the excitement you feel. If you determine that this urge is inappropriate and socially unacceptable, you will have enough time and notice to seek out the professional help needed to come to grips with your desires and live at peace with yourself and these urges. The moment you sense this beginning to develop, seek help. This is the perfect cycle to find the person equipped to handle this event. It will be taken care of correctly and you will be able to gain control of your emotions in a healthy way. Otherwise you are on the path toward a brilliant future.

unclean and broken nails Do not overlook an upcoming important event that is to take place within three days. Recheck your schedule and be sure to include all important events.

long claw-like nails Someone who loves you misses you tremendously. You will learn more about this within three days. Through this relationship you will become empowered in a very beneficial way.

fingernails falling off fingers You will be let down because the hope you had for someone to pay you a certain amount of money by a particular date will not come to be. This person will change their mind about a particular arrangement you have made. Plan on agreements to be broken. Since you have prior notice of this, you will have the opportunity to cover yourself financially.

naked Within two days someone you find sexually attractive will make their interests known to you. This person will aggressively seek a sexual relationship and will offer you a permanent relationship. If you choose to go in this direction, you will be emotionally satisfied beyond your expectations.

name *to yell/scream out someone's name whom you recognize* This represents the person you need on your side when certain situations start to evolve. This situation could be very abusive and if you have this person with you, you will be saved just in time. Depending on the contents of this dream you can determine whether the significance of what was yelled needs to be attended to. If it was a negative message, take steps to ensure that all of your bases are covered.

to yell/scream out someone's name whom you do not recognize For the next three days make sure that you do not go anywhere without the company of someone else, especially if you are going out with someone or are meeting with someone you do not know well. This could be a potentially abusive situation. Having someone with you will save you from this. Depending on the contents of this dream you can determine whether the significance of what was yelled needs to be attended to. If it was a negative message, take steps to ensure that all of your bases are covered.

if you recognize the person yelling out a name You will need to alert this individual that certain situations will begin to evolve that could be very abusive. Warn this person that if they have someone with them they will be saved just in time. The person they need to have with them is the person whom they called out for.

to hear your own name This dream is an extremely lucky omen and is a reminder to focus on your surroundings for the next seven days. Some unusual circumstances will begin to unfold that will offer you a chance to grasp a once in a lifetime opportunity. This will be a very lucky chance to raise your standard of living in ways you never envisioned. Take the time to determine what you need to do. You are headed for a brilliant future surrounded by beautiful people who will love you beyond your imagination, back you up in your desires, and show you much appreciation.

to recall the name of a person This is the name of someone who will come into your life and open doors of opportunities that you never before knew existed. This will benefit you greatly if you choose to go in this direction. Good luck is with you for the coming month.

nickname For the next month you will be extremely lucky and successful and will receive many profitable benefits from various sources. Anyone you dream of who calls you by your nickname or someone with similar traits will be very eager to comply with your wishes for the next ten days. Proceed with confidence.

in any other form If you did not recognize the person or the name of the person you dreamed about, they will represent someone whom you will come into contact with in the near future. You will recognize them as the person in the dream because of the name, race, gender, age, character traits, etc. You will be dealing with this individual within four days and have prior notice if this is someone whom you choose not to associate with because of certain negative events you recall from the dream. Someone who will resemble the person you dreamed about will come into your life and will repeat distasteful patterns, share the same negative traits and whom you will need to avoid involvement with. If your recollection of this character is pleasing from the dream, you can take the necessary steps to welcome them into your life. If you recognize the person or the name of the person you dreamed about, you will be dealing either with that person or someone who resembles them because of the

name, face, gender, age, character traits, ethnic mannerisms, etc. You have prior notice to determine whether this person is someone you wish to involve or avoid in your life because of certain events you recalled from the dream or because of prior experiences that you wish not to repeat. Within four days someone will come into your life to repeat distasteful patterns or may share the same negative traits and/or share the same wonderful and fantastic attributes as the person you dreamed about. Then you will decide more appropriately whether this is someone you wish to bring into your life. Otherwise, this implies you will receive service from someone in this same time frame that will enable you to achieve a higher level of success than you ever imagined. You are headed for a brilliant future.

name brand Be sure your mode of transportation does not cause you problems, especially for the next three days. This is an extremely lucky omen and you are in a very prosperous cycle.

name calling Make sure you do not become involved with someone who has a very short fuse. You do not have the time to put up with this. Go on with your life without this person in it.

name dropping Within three days a particular individual who will become known to you will express an eagerness to become involved with you. If you accept this person into your life you will bring much enjoyment into your future. You will know who this person is by their nervous activity when in your presence. If you choose to pursue this, you will be surprised at the joy you will bring into this person's life. This person is very loyal and will always be there for you.

nap Become very aware of what will be developing in your life within the next seven days. Someone will intentionally drag you into a debate about a wrong they have done against you. This person is very angry because they know they are in the wrong and will argue until you give in without pushing them to make it right. Protect yourself from emotional or financial harm by not allowing yourself to be brought down to their level. Remain calm, take care of this issue quickly and avoid, at all costs, becoming involved in an angry, argumentative dispute. If you heed this message, you will be able to avoid an angry dispute. You are headed for a brilliant future.

napalm You will develop a way to discuss important issues that have been dragging you down. This will not be stressful or threatening no matter what the context of the issue. Use this cycle to work on difficult and explosive situations.

nape Anything unusual occurring in this area of the body implies that you will receive a financial windfall that will come at an unexpected time and when it is needed the most. This will alleviate some of the anxiety you are experiencing. You also have the power to rally powerful people around you that have good advice and good intentions toward you.

These people will come to you and offer their assistance when needed, especially during this seven day cycle.

napkin Be very aware of your surroundings and be cautious of freak accidents that may involve a sniper or a similar situation. For the next five days take precautions to ensure you do not become injured as an innocent bystander.

Napoleon You know someone whom you have doubts about and suspicions that they are keeping a secret from you. Your thoughts that you are being lied to are groundless. This individual is very loyal and truthful with you.

Narcissus *(Greek mythology)* Do everything you can to take advantage of this lucky cycle and to expose your talents. Push yourself in the direction you should be going in order to grasp fame. You are headed for a powerful and prosperous future.

narcolepsy Make sure you clearly understand your motives, feelings and behavior, especially for the next five days and make yourself aware that you could be your own worst enemy. This can be a fulfilling cycle that could bring you many benefits. Unless you look closely at your behavior, you will definitely miss out.

narcotic *any form* Be very aggressive with upcoming situations. Work to solve problems immediately before any of them reaches a crisis. Aggressive, relentless action is the only way to handle any personal crisis.

narrow *to look into something narrow* Someone you hire to perform services for you will continually come and go throughout the day. This individual has a problem with drugs. You will receive good results and this person will work hard but needs help for this problem. Most of this is out of your control but do keep this person as an employee.

to attempt to get through or to see someone else attempt to get through a narrow space Do not allow an overly responsible sense of duty overtake you. Within three days you will develop out of the blue, the feeling like you have to be responsible for everyone else's problems and issues. Do not allow yourself to fall into the pattern of having to ensure that everyone is comfortable. Once you become involved, it will be very difficult to get out of this pattern of behavior. Many blessings are with you but proceed with caution.

narrow minded Be consistent about what you say you are going to do and make sure you do not let down the person who relies on you. Do everything you promise to do in a timely fashion.

nasal Within two days be very alert to a questionable situation that will cause you a tremendous amount of embarrassment. Your reputation and character will be at stake.

Nashville Within two weeks you will hear from an old friend who wants to share good news with you. This individual has come into power and authority, will be a friend for life and will want you to share in their wealth. This dream may also be used as a reference point in time. If you dream of this city and see its name used in any context, the dream message will occur on this day.

Nassau Within three days you will experience the peace, tranquility and harmony that you have long desired and these feelings will be with you permanently. This dream is a good luck omen. This dream may also be used as a reference point in time. If you dream of this city and see its name used in any context, the dream message will occur on this day.

nasturtium For the next three days you will experience a greater sexual desire for someone. You will be surprised that you feel this way about this individual. If you choose to pursue this, you will definitely enjoy a fulfilling sex life with no repercussions.

nation Step back and make sure you do not cause someone to harbor bad feelings toward you because of a change you plan to make. Be very aware of cause and effect.

national guard Be very alert and carefully watch your passion when dealing with a certain aspect of your life over the next few days. This will ensure that you continue to head toward prosperity.

national park A trial examination is recommended so you do not lose sight of your assets. Focus on your weaknesses so you can make the necessary changes needed to pass this test.

national monument For the next two days do not allow power to go to your head, especially when supervising others.

Native American Use your communication skills more effectively and this will allow you to quickly achieve your goals. Expect this to occur within three days. You are definitely headed for a brilliant future.

nativity scene Within five days you will develop the inner strength and courage needed to make unusual and extraordinary moves. Many blessings will come to you and your family.

natural childbirth Keep your interests to yourself. Within three days you will also become involved in a discussion that will leave you with no way out. Avoid making a decision that entraps you.

nature You are entering a very lucky seven day cycle. Take advantage of this time period to achieve victory and to seek a resolution to all issues you have not concluded.

nature study For the next two days make sure you take every precaution to avoid contracting a serious illness. Take better care of yourself. This illness is preventable.

nature worship Someone will ask you to take a trip with

them that will not turn out well. Be alert to this and do not take this trip.

nausea Take steps to prevent whatever is causing nausea in your dream from occurring in reality.

Navajo Listen to your instincts and pursue nothing unless your heart is in it. You will achieve victory in important matters if you follow your hunches and listen to your own counsel, especially for the next three days.

navel This dream is alerting you to a danger that will occur within three days. Protect yourself and your health in every way possible from a life threatening situation from an unknown source. Make anyone else you recognize in the dream with a bare navel aware of this danger.

if you fail to recognize another person in this dream with a bare navel Within three days this individual represents someone who will go to great lengths to involve you in an unhealthy relationship. You will know who this person is by their desperation to involve you in something they desire. Eat healthy foods, drink plenty of water, rest and get plenty of exercise. Many blessings are with you and your family.

navigator A strange situation will occur. You will promise to call someone at a specific time but something will occur that will prevent this (i.e., phone out of order, etc.). Be more aggressive in your approach. If you cannot reach this person by phone, then use an alternative method. A failure to connect will result in this other person refusing to contact you in any form in the future because they will feel you stood them up. Avoid the break up of a healthy relationship due to a minor problem.

navy Within three days you will be involved with someone who will develop a relationship with you that will resemble a battleground. This will become a chronic state if you allow it. Once you see this situation start to develop, remove yourself from the relationship. This will become an ongoing situation that will become difficult to break out of.

navy bean Within three days you will find yourself unexpectedly helping someone whom you know is very deceitful. Rethink your next move. This will definitely backfire on you.

navy yard Life is too short. Be sure you tell those you feel strongly about that you love them. Become more open to your friends and family and make sure you openly and publicly verbalize your love for others. Do not hold your feelings inside. Your creative work will also be admired and you are headed in the right direction.

Nazarene/Nazareth Think ahead to the involvement you are in for the next three days. The person you are involved with will require a commitment from you. If this is something you want, make that commitment. If not, think twice about this involvement.

Nazi You will become involved with a very greedy person.

Protect yourself from this involvement. You will end up despising each other.

Neanderthal Make sure you do not challenge or tackle anyone else's ideas. This action will come down heavily and you will feel unable to get out of this situation. Prepare yourself to get on with your life without dealing with this issue.

Nebraska You will be warmly received by others in anything regarding business negotiations and will make an excellent impression on everyone involved. You are entering a victorious seven day cycle. This dream may also be used as a reference point in time. If you dream of this state and see its name used in any context, the dream message will occur on this day.

neck Anything unusual occurring on this area of the body implies that you will receive a financial windfall at an unexpected time when it is needed the most. This will alleviate some of the anxiety you are experiencing. You also have the power to rally powerful people around you who will offer good advice and have good intentions. These people will come to you and offer their assistance when needed, especially for the next seven days.

to dream of someone or yourself with a broken neck You will find you are living a lifestyle that goes against your basic principles. Make it a point to admit your feelings and face up to reality because you will quickly develop a completely different way of viewing your life. Although this may stir up deep and painful feelings you will be able to successfully handle this conflict in your life. It is better to make painful changes than to remain in an unbearable lifestyle. You will quickly recover and move rapidly toward a prosperous and more improved future. Anything negative witnessed in this dream needs to be avoided in reality. Forewarn anyone you recognize to do the same. Take steps to ensure you only experience positive events in your life.

to neck - slang term Make it a point to be available at certain events in order to meet someone who is much older than you. This person will be instrumental in helping you to meet your goals. Exposure to social events will be the key ingredient in causing these changes in your life and will dictate how things will unfold within three weeks. The level of intensity will dictate the degree of success.

red neck - slang term Make sure, in a romantic situation, you do not act in such a way that will drive the object of your affections away. You will also be introduced to new people in a new vicinity by someone who would like to involve you in their new lifestyle. This will give you the opportunity within three days.

neckerchief/neckband For the next two weeks pay close attention to all future involvements. Make sure that a once in a lifetime opportunity does not slip through your fingers. This opportunity will make a big financial difference in your life.

necklace Do not allow anyone to talk you out of a very substantial, stable opportunity by running down this opportunity and implying you would be unable to handle it. Do not allow yourself to feel incompetent and defeated or to allow this opportunity to slip away. Push yourself to take advantage of the opportunities offered to you during this cycle. The more precious the necklace, the greater the opportunity. You are headed for a brilliant future if you disassociate yourself from negative tapes.

necktie Within three days someone will surprise you with their flirtatious ways and will whet your sexual appetite with their relentless flirting. You will be delighted if you explore this new avenue. You are headed for a prosperous future and this aspect of your life will begin to unfold within two days.

necromancy Within three days any negative event connected to this dream needs to be avoided or altered in reality. Be acutely aware of the danger of fire and take steps to protect yourself and your valuables. Otherwise, many blessings will come to you and your family and you are definitely headed for a brilliant future.

nectar For the next three days focus carefully on developing detailed and carefully drawn plans to execute in your life. Allow destiny to take its course and to provide you with a plentiful successful future. All of your efforts will be worthwhile and you will begin to see results in this time period.

nectarine Within five days take steps to refrain from those thoughts and behaviors that keep a relationship from becoming close. Look at your behavior closely and determine those aspects that keep others at arm's length. This is the right time to develop the courage to address those issues and to turn yourself around. This will enable you to develop the kind of personality that will draw others closer to you. Good luck is with you.

needle For the next three days make it a point to keep feelings of suspicion and jealousy from running rampant in your imagination. Prevent this behavior.

needlefish Stop being so strict with yourself. Allow yourself to enjoy life to the fullest.

needlepoint Within seven days create an atmosphere of harmony and happiness for yourself.

needlewoman For the next week make sure you do not overlook an important matter. Attend to this issue before it gets out of hand.

needlework Be very aware of the way you handle yourself in public. You will be talked about because of the improper way you handle yourself.

negligee Stop behaving like a monster to your family and loved ones. You are responsible for your own happiness and need to handle your own responsibilities. Do not expect others to cater to you because they care for you and do not

start making unreasonable demands on others to fulfill your needs. Within the week, your loved ones will refuse to tolerate this behavior any longer. Seek professional help if needed and stop this behavior before it backfires.

Negro Maintain an upright lifestyle, carry yourself with confidence and be true to yourself. Follow your heart's desires and allow only beautiful expressions to emanate from you. For the next seven days show kindness to others as well as yourself. Pamper yourself and treat yourself with extra special care. Surround yourself with things of beauty that will inspire you. You are headed for a brilliant future.

Nehemiah *(from the Bible)* The person you wish to become closer to will start to demonstrate this behavior. An extraordinary change will take place in this relationship and you will show more affection and appreciation toward each other.

neighbor For the next five days do not perform any physical labor for someone else or volunteer your services to anyone. You will be overextending yourself.

neighborhood *run down* For the next three days be extremely cautious and move forward with someone only with extreme care. This person is someone you are starting to feel a sense of closeness to and will lead you to believe you can rely on their loyalty and can confide in them fully. This person is very crafty and skilled in creating deception and illusion. You will be led to believe that certain experiences and events will occur that will never take place. A hidden agenda is at play here that involves pursuing you for devious reasons known only to them. This person will go to great lengths to create an air of trust that will leave you free of all suspicions but should you start to develop suspicions they will be able, because of their charm and charisma, to divert you. By the time you fully comprehend what is going on, you will be suffering from deep emotional disappointments, disillusionments, and financial distress. It will take some time for you to recover from this and get your life back to a normal status. You have the ammunition you need and enough notice to make sure it does not take place. Do not become involved, do not compromise your feelings and do not allow this person to pry into your affairs. You will be very successful in diffusing this. You will develop the confidence needed to put yourself on the path toward a prosperous future. Anything negative witnessed in this dream needs to be avoided in reality. Forewarn anyone you recognize to do the same. Take steps to ensure that you only experience positive events in your life. Many blessings are with you and your family.

familiar neighborhood Any negative event in this dream that is connected to this neighborhood needs to be avoided in reality, especially for the next seven days. You must be careful not to listen to any gossip or involve yourself in any rumors that will have an adverse affect on you or your personality. Protect yourself from this type of involvement during this time period.

neon Pay attention to the words or symbols represented in neon. This will give you a clue to something you will experience within three days. Take all the necessary steps to avoid anything negative and make sure you bring all positive events to fruition. You will also accomplish as much as you want for the next three days regarding special situations that you are eager to move on.

neon fish/tetra Do not allow yourself to become overwrought because of someone else's situation. Apply yourself to remedying this situation with professional help or advise this individual to seek help. Move on with your life and do not allow this situation to act on you in such a way that you cater to this person and neglect your own well being.

neon lamp This dream is a very lucky cycle for you. Within seven days a luxury item that you have long desired will be yours. You are headed for a very prosperous future.

nephew Any negative association with the individual in this dream may be prevented or altered in reality and you need to make sure you alert this person to take necessary precautions. It is also important not to allow yourself to become overly friendly with a stranger. Something will occur that will cause this person to snap and they will, for no reason, become quarrelsome with you in public. Protect yourself from people with short fuses and do not go to unfamiliar places for the next three days.

Neptune Do everything necessary for the next two days to encourage a closer bonding with someone who is very special to you. Create moments where you can both enjoy humor and amicable conversations. You are headed for a brilliant future.

nerve You will hear news within two days that you will be given some property. The giver will take care of the transfer of this property once they know you are willing to accept it.

nerve cell Tie up all loose ends and uncover all the facts regarding any situation that seems mysterious and suspicious. Make it a point to stay uninvolved, especially for the next three days. Do what you can to maintain a healthy nervous system and a stress free lifestyle.

nerve center Do what you can to maintain a stress free environment, especially for the next seven days. Maintain a daily routine of quiet and tranquil moments. You are definitely headed for a brilliant future.

nerve gas You will be exposed to the actions of someone who will be barely able to contain themselves in your presence. This person will demonstrate love and kindness toward you. Make it a point to treat others with kindness and respect.

nervous *to see someone behave in a nervous fashion or anyone who is afflicted with a nervous condition* Someone is very eager to let you know how they feel about you sex-

ually. This person feels a deep passion for you that they are unable to verbalize. This cycle will allow this individual to open up and reveal their feelings to you.

to act nervously You will find yourself so attracted to someone within a three day period that you will find it difficult to contain yourself. You will find a way to get your feelings across to this person but it will take a two to three day period of pushing yourself to be able to do it. You are loved beyond your imagination by those around you and will be treated with deep regard and respect.

nervous breakdown Avoid the break up of a healthy, working relationship because your demanding and anxious behavior will push this person to treat you in the manner you wish to be treated. This will not occur anytime soon. Save your energy. This person will, in their time, start to express themselves in the manner you wish. If you choose to continue this relationship, be patient and get busy with projects of your own in order to avoid feelings of discontent.

nervous system Make sure you get plenty of rest, especially for the next three days. Get the sleep you need, eat healthy foods and get plenty of exercise.

nest Within three days you will need to develop a close bond between yourself and someone who is special to you. Set aside private moments for the both of you. It is important that you do this within this time frame. You are loved beyond your imagination.

nest egg Keep going in the direction you are going. You will enjoy various areas of opportunities within the week and will experience a brilliant future.

net Take steps to keep any unusual event in this dream from taking place in reality. Make sure you do not fail to enlist the support you need concerning any future negotiation. Take a careful look at your plans and revise any errors so you can ensure success.

Netherlands Within three days a new acquaintance will provide you with a new path in life and will introduce you to others who possess a high level of expertise and an influence in areas that will benefit you if you choose to take advantage of this. You have a prosperous future ahead of you. You must also make sure older people in your life are not being neglected and that their needs are being met. This dream may also be used as a reference point in time. If you dream of this country and see its name used in any context, the dream message will occur on this day.

nettle Make sure no one takes advantage of you for the next two days. Many blessings are with you and your family.

network For the next two days pay close attention to ensure that something unusual and out of the ordinary is not taking place regarding your business affairs. Be very aware of this to ensure that nothing goes wrong.

neurologist Be very wary of hidden agendas regarding an

individual's over helpfulness. Make sure you do not fall prey to something that could be harmful. You must also be very attentive to any message in this dream, negative or positive, that you will either want to avoid or to include in your life.

neurology Make sure your transportation is in proper working order, especially for the next three days in order to avoid delays.

neuron Within three days someone will go to great lengths to experience a sexual encounter with you. If you choose this option, it will lead to a permanent union.

neutron Someone will be very eager to reconcile within three days. Follow your heart and you will not make a mistake.

neutron bomb Avoid permanent separations in relationships that are important to you. Carefully check out your behavior for the next month to determine what you may be doing that could cause a permanent split. You have prior notice of this and can keep this painful event from taking place.

neutron star Make sure all conversations are concise and lead fully in the direction you desire. Listen to the words spoken and make sure there is no confusion about your true feelings. Be sure you get your point across.

Nevada Your hopes for travel will become a reality if you start pushing and planning for this now. This is the perfect cycle to develop these plans. You are loved beyond your imagination and you are encouraged to tell those you care about that you love them. Within the week you will have the financial means to do more enjoyable things in your life. Focus, during this time period, on ways to bring more entertainment into your life. If you dream of this state and see its name used in any context, the dream message will occur on this day.

never-never land Make sure you have your priorities in the right order and recheck your schedules to make sure you are handling them in the right order. Do not listen to anyone who will approach you within two days with a situation you should not be handling. Allow someone else to take care of it, it is not your concern.

new age Keep up your attire and pay more attention to your outer beauty. This will help build your self esteem and make you happier than you suspect.

newborn You will be offered an invitation for an intimate dinner and conversation by someone who does not look as though they have the wealth that they, in reality, possess. You have the opportunity now to deepen the relationship, if you choose. This is a very lucky omen and you are headed for a brilliant future. If this dream portends any negative event involving a newborn, you have the time to either alter the outcome or to avoid the situation altogether. Make sure the infant you know in reality has nothing but positive experiences in their life, especially for the next five days.

Newburg You will run into someone you have not seen in years while going about your everyday business. This person will be delighted to see you and will invite you to an enjoyable event. Good luck is with you.

New England Within three days you will find success and also attract the attention of a very wealthy person who will be seeking you out for some advice. If you choose to involve yourself with this person, the opportunity will be presented to you in this time frame. This person will be very attentive and attracted to you in several ways. This relationship will be very rewarding if you choose to take this path. You are headed for a very prosperous future. This dream may also be used as a reference point in time. If you dream of this region and see its name used in any context, the dream message will occur on this day.

New Hampshire Within three days you will confide in someone whom you have a great deal of confidence. This person will give you the appropriate advice to put you in the direction you should be headed. Live life to the fullest and find a variety of ways you can allow yourself to experience joy. Many blessings will come to you and your family. This dream may also be used as a reference point in time. If you dream of this state and see its name used in any context, the dream message will occur on this day.

New Jersey Within five days many unusual situations will occur that will arouse your interest and lead you to investigate further. Any of them that interest you will lead to joy if you involve yourself and experiment with different lifestyles. You are in a cycle where you can depend on your clarity of thought to make the correct decisions for yourself as well as others. Do not allow yourself to develop the attitude that you can take things for granted. This dream may also be used as a reference point in time. If you dream of this state and see its name used in any context, the dream message will occur on this day.

New Mexico You will be extended a fully paid invitation for a trip from someone who just wants you to have a good time with no strings attached. You can do as you please on this trip. If you choose to accept this invitation, you will learn more about yourself and be more open to the experiences that life can bring that you have not allowed yourself to become involved with in the past. You are headed for a very prosperous future. This dream may also be used as a reference point in time. If you dream of this state and see its name used in any context, the dream message will occur on this day.

New Orleans Within the next three days you will involve yourself with a group of people who, in spite of the doubts you may have, will be supportive of you and will fully embrace your goals. You must also need to pay closer attention to someone who is interested in becoming involved with you in a romantic way. All love and business affairs will be very fortuitous. It would also be a good time for you to get a reading. You are definitely headed for a brilliant future. This dream may also be used as a reference point in time. If you dream of this city and see its name used in any context, the dream message will occur on this day.

news Anything you feel is not going in the direction you desire needs to be worked on until it meets your standards of perfection. Once this is done, everything will fall perfectly into place. It is important that this is done within three days. Move on those things you want to see improved. This dream is an extremely lucky omen. Anything negative witnessed in this dream needs to be avoided in reality. Forewarn anyone you recognize to do the same. Take steps to ensure you only experience positive events in your life. Look under good news for a greater definition of this dream.

to hear bad news Within three days you will have to deal with someone who has a habit of creating chaos and stressful situations. During this time period, this individual will create a situation that will escalate to the point of never returning to normalcy. Make sure you plan other activities during this time period in order to avoid this individual. Anything negative witnessed in this dream needs to be avoided in reality. Forewarn anyone you recognize to do the same. Take steps to ensure you only experience positive events in your life.

to hear good news You are entering a very powerful growth cycle and can expect good news to arrive shortly. You will also receive a positive response to anything you hold as your highest priority, especially for the next seven days. Good luck is with you.

news agency Do not lose confidence with a difficult issue that will come up within two days. You will be able to resolve it fully and satisfactorily.

newscast Be wary of strangers. Within three days you will meet with a dangerous person who will try to inflict harm on you. Be keenly aware of this and do not involve yourself with any suspicious character during this time frame. You have prior notice of this and can make the right decisions to remain safe.

newsletter For the next five days make sure that you watch your valuables. Take steps to prevent the theft or loss of something that is important to you. You are definitely headed for a prosperous future. You must also take steps to keep any negative message from becoming a reality.

newsmagazine Within three days you will experience good health and victory in achieving important tasks that you find difficult in areas of your life you most desire.

newspaper You will receive mixed messages that will affect you emotionally and you will become unsure of the romantic feelings that someone has for you. Regardless of your feelings of insecurity, you can proceed with confidence.

This will be a great relationship. Be kind and affectionate, and you will be very surprised at what develops. This dream is an extremely lucky omen. You will also need to take steps to prevent any negative message you see in this dream from becoming a reality.

rolled up Someone will not be what they have projected themselves to be. You will be very disappointed by this.

newspaper boy Do not take life for granted, especially for the next three days. Take the time to determine what you really want and need during this particular time period in your life. The plans you desire to implement will also be successful.

newsperson For the next five days personally take over the handling of important paperwork to ensure it is processed properly and in a timely fashion. You will also receive a promotion in the area of your life you most desire.

newsprint Pay attention to any message you see in newsprint and take steps to keep anything negative from becoming a reality. Embrace any positive message and bring it to fruition. You are also taking a situation for granted that involves another person and they feel they should react to your cold attitude in the same manner. If you choose, you and this person can do much to achieve success if you decide not to treat this situation so loosely.

newsreel Within three days you will reach the conclusion that someone needs to do something for them self. You will have problems knowing how to break this to this person. Make sure when you present this request, you do it in an inoffensive way and make sure you have all the information you need to do a follow up and to make sure this person can handle this situation. This will be an extremely lucky week long cycle for accomplishing an almost impossible task.

newsroom Pay attention to what was discussed in the newsroom. This will supply a clue to a future event. Take steps to prevent any negative event from occurring in reality and make sure all positive events are brought to full bloom. Be very aware also of the stress levels in your life and pinpoint the environment that creates this stress. Make sure you become very aware of this and take the necessary steps to lower the stress levels and avoid this environment if possible. It is especially important that you do this within the next three days.

newsstand Encourage someone you know to seek enjoyment with something you have tried out in the past and found enjoyment in. Many blessings will come to you and your family.

newt Make sure you explore both sides of someone's aggravating behavior. For the next three days look at the source of this person's irritation and you will be able to respond correctly.

New Testament For the next five days make sure you do

everything in your power to follow all the rules and regulations. Stay organized during this cycle and you will receive exactly what you expect. Everything will work out as you envisioned. Many blessings will come to you and your family.

New Years Eve This dream is an extremely lucky omen. You will also successfully instigate a clean break in those situations you desire with no repercussions or stressful events to deal with. Anyone you recognize from this dream will be instrumental in adding joy to your life for the coming year. Anything negative witnessed in this dream needs to be avoided in reality. Forewarn anyone you recognize to do the same. Take steps to ensure you only experience positive events in your life. Many blessings will be with you and your family. You are headed for a very prosperous future.

New York *the state* Any dream involving this state is extremely lucky and any event you see will be an accurate depiction of something that will occur in reality. Make sure you do not allow a negative occurrence to take place. If this represents a positive event, make sure you promote it. What you hope will come to pass that is connected to a love interest or a business arrangement will take place within five days. This will alter your life tremendously. This dream may also be used as a reference point in time. If you dream of this state and see its name used in any context, the dream message will occur on this day.

New York City Within three days you will undergo some extraordinary and unusual changes in your life. These changes will occur with or without your help and will have a tremendous impact on your life. These improvements will occur with such rapidity that you will be surprised and enraptured with your improved lifestyle. You will enjoy a busy social life and many new people will want to meet you. Live it up. Many blessings will come to you and your family. This dream may also be used as a reference point in time. If you dream of this city and see its name used in any context, the dream message will occur on this day.

New Zealand Explore the unexpected and unpredictable. Make sure you become more self reliant and gravitate toward changes. Many blessings will come to you and your family. You are entering a lucky seven day cycle. This dream may also be used as a reference point in time. If you dream of this country and see its name used in any context, the dream message will occur on this day.

niacin Make sure you take steps to keep any negative event from taking place in reality. For the next three days do not allow yourself to get sucked into a debate someone wants to involve you in concerning a wrong they have committed. This could escalate to the point of violence. The moment you see this start to develop, remove yourself from this environment for your own safety. Proceed with confidence.

Niagara Falls You will experience long lasting joy and love from those you never really felt existed before and you will

enjoy a new spiritual awareness. You will undergo some extraordinary and unusual changes in your life that will not be prompted by any action on your part. These improvements will occur with great rapidity and will vastly improve your lifestyle. You will enjoy a busy social life and will meet many new people. Live it up. Many blessings will come to you and your family.

nick Face the world with confidence and optimism and anything you felt was once impossible is now a possibility. You can expect prosperity within five days.

nickel Within five days you will have to take a very daring approach when urging someone to do something for themself that can only be done by themself. If you choose, a wonderful person will also enter your life within three days and will provide you with an opportunity for romance at its fullest. Good luck will be with you for the coming week.

nickel and dime Within five days, make it a point to create the perfect environment to accomplish your goals and to enable you to better organize your life. This dream also implies that if you choose to allow it, someone will aggressively pursue you for a romantic interlude. You will be surrounded by people who are loyal to you and care a great deal for you.

nickelodeon For the next three days you will be able to competently deal with tough tasks. Because of your persistence and detail during this time period, you will be able to successfully eliminate all errors. You are headed for a very prosperous future.

nickname You will be extremely lucky and successful for the next month and will receive many profitable benefits from various sources. You will enjoy a prosperous month. For the next ten days anyone you dream of who calls you by your nickname or someone with similar traits will be very eager to comply with your wishes. Proceed with confidence.

niece Take steps to keep any negative event in this dream from becoming a reality. All lingering doubts you may be harboring will disappear because of certain situations that will occur within the week. You are on the path for a prosperous future.

night Be aware of your surroundings and play it safe. Someone will have doubts about you and will look for reasons to explain these feelings about you. You must also not allow old negative tapes to take over your way of thinking and do not look for quick fixes. You are headed for a brilliant future. Make sure you position yourself to reap benefits. Good luck is with you.

night blindness You are headed in the wrong direction. For the next three days step back, regroup, and decide how you want to position yourself in order to resolve a certain situation to your advantage. Listen to your own counsel and do not take anyone else's advice during this time frame.

nightcap For the next three days do what you can to avoid any accident that is avoidable. Be especially careful during the evening hours. This is likely to be a freak accident of some sort.

nightclub A situation will be revealed to you within three days that will clear something up that has been puzzling you and causing you stress. This will allow you to conduct yourself appropriately and go on with your life. You will also enjoy some festive events within the next five days that will bring you a great deal of joy. You are entering a very fortuitous cycle.

night crawler Within five days you will be pursued by someone who is developing an interest in involving you in a close friendship. A variety of things will develop as a result of this union and you will both receive many benefits from these developments. You will enjoy this relationship for a lifetime.

nightgown Be very watchful because a very fragile and delicate situation will develop within five days. Since you have prior notice of this you can behave in a soothing manner until this issue has time to blow over. Everything will then fall into place and compromises will easily be made. Good luck is with you and many blessings will come to you and your family.

nighthawk Do not take someone's gestures of kindness for granted. Do not allow this person to go on with their life without you in it and take steps to keep this person from feeling unappreciated. You are headed for a prosperous future.

nightingale Someone will come to you within three days with a plan that needs to be developed that is way ahead of its time. This individual wants to involve you in this venture. This journey will bring you both large profits and a prosperous future.

night light Within three days make sure you take care of anything that looks as though it is not going in the direction you choose. Take steps to review it in such a way that it falls into place exactly as you choose. You must also make sure you do not allow another person to manipulate you for the next three days.

nightmares *nightmares accompanied by sleep paralysis - the feeling of desperately struggling to move* Nightmares are simply a bad piece of theatre developed by the spirit to dramatize an impression by presenting a shocking scenario in an attempt to get a message across to the personality. There is a sense of urgency in the spirit's need to communicate and to ensure that you do not forget this message once you are awake. Most of the time this is a good message and indicates you will be presented with opportunities and benefits you should not miss. This dream may also represent something that you or someone you recognize has no business getting involved with. And may be a warning that you

or someone you recognize may be in danger of becoming trapped in unhealthy relationships that will profoundly affect your lives. Do not allow any interference from others to determine the course of your relationship, either by encouraging you to enter into an unhealthy relationship or by steering you from a healthy relationship. You have prior notice of this and can diffuse this situation and take steps to allow only positive expressions in your life. Make sure you alert anyone you recognize to do the same. Nightmares represent a clear sense of urgency and implies that you must attend to some issue. We should be honored and thankful that we have prior notice and can attend to either a positive or a negative message. For the next seven days do not allow your decisions to become clouded by any of the following situations or a combination of any of the following situations:

- The influence that someone will have over you.
- Interference from someone else who will steer you in the wrong direction.
- The control that someone in power will have over you.
- The leverage that someone will gain by using your words to put you at a disadvantage.
- Someone who is in a position of authority who will make decisions for you.

You will not know the extent of damage this person can cause because of their control. This dream is asking you to muster the courage and confidence needed to make sure you take the right steps to prevent a situation from developing that could seriously affect your future. Do not leave yourself vulnerable to this because you will be left with no recourse except to abide by the rules that others place on you. This will leave you with the unbearable feeling of emotional depletion and the feeling that you are caught up in a seemingly inescapable web. This dream is a sneak preview of how you will feel if you do not take steps to turn this around and to ensure that you experience only positive expressions in your life. This scenario is preventable. Do not allow yourself to become stuck by permitting yourself to become vulnerable. If you do not start acting on your behalf, you will suffer emotional depletion and your life will be steered in a direction you do not wish to go. Push yourself to get your point across to those in authority. Make it a point to avoid stress over everyday decisions that others have no business making for you. You are in danger of surrendering yourself to the decisions of others who have no business involving themselves in your life. Take steps to avoid unhealthy situations and circumstances and be suspicious of all changes. Develop confidence and be relentless in making corrections in those areas of your life that need correcting and you will be able to point yourself in the right direction. You have the power to change any negative aspect of your life. Make sure all of your bases are covered, play it safe, and use common sense. You will be able to carry out your plans successfully and put yourself on the path of prosperity.

night owl Be alert to the fact that you will be abandoned without notice by someone you are emotionally attached to. This person has difficulty committing in a relationship to the degree you desire. You can prevent this future occurrence by restraining your emotions. Take steps now to avoid this hurt a month from now. This relationship is workable if you do not allow your emotions to gain the upper hand.

owl hooting Someone you have a great deal of respect and high regards for will die within seven days. You must make sure your pets are safe from disease and accident.

quiet owl Become acutely aware that an individual, whom you least expect to cause problems, will want to inflict emotional harm on you for personal reasons. This will be done in a very subtle and conniving way. Intensify your efforts to guard your reputation and make sure your words are understood and reported accurately. Protect anything that is emotionally precious to you from this individual who merely seeks a sick self gratification. This is likely to occur within three days.

night school This dream is a lucky omen. Put your plans and ideas in order and set priorities so you do not waste time.

nightshade Rudeness and an abrasive attitude will be the proper attitude to take so you will not compromise yourself. Someone will attempt to coerce you into doing something you do not want to do. Be very aware of any negative event in this dream and take steps to avoid it in reality.

nightshirt This dream is very much a symbol of victory.

nightstand Take a firm stand and do not allow yourself to be cheated in any way. Something will come up that you should not allow yourself to become involved in. This will backfire. This dream is also a clue that you should not allow any negative event to occur in reality. Pay attention to what was on top of the night stand. This will offer a clue to an event you should take steps to avoid.

nightwalker You will be very excited because someone will request sex from you. You had no idea this person felt an attraction to you and you will become excited about the prospect of sex with this individual. This will be a very satisfying cycle for you and both parties will be mutually satisfied. This dream is also a promise of success with any product you are attempting to promote. A brilliant future is ahead of you.

to be one Be sure to take extra precautions when transferring money to an individual from one area to another. If precautions are not taken the money will be lost in transit. It would be a good idea to insure all mail containing money. Romance is in the air and you will have many memorable moments of passion.

to hire a prostitute This dream implies victory. You will take all the proper steps and meet all the right people to properly handle a project.

to be asked for money in return for sex Do not doubt the loyalty of your loved one. You will also be successful this year in meeting your goals.

night watch You will have a conversation with someone who analyzes every move and takes notes on every nuance of your behavior and speech. This individual does this in order to learn a great deal about the person they are speaking to by gleaning bits and pieces of information through casual conversations. Make sure you do not inadvertently give out information that can be used against you at a later date. Watch out for this over the next three days.

night watchman/person Within three days some unusual circumstances will take place that will cause you to rejoice at the good news you hear. Blessings are with you and your family and you are headed for a prosperous future.

Nile You will experience long lasting joy and love from those you never really noticed before and will experience a new spiritual awareness. This will lead to extraordinary changes in your life that will take place with no encouragement from you. These changes will occur rapidly and will vastly improve your lifestyle. You will enjoy a very busy social life and will meet many new people. Many blessings are with you and your family.

nine You can give someone a great deal of joy because of the affection you bestow on them. You will definitely be received with open arms. This individual will publicly show their appreciation for your affections. You are loved beyond your imagination and you will be surrounded by those who are loyal and appreciative of you. For the next nine weeks, you will be very lucky and this is the time to successfully tackle major issues with ease. You may also use this number to schedule important times and days for greater success. Use this number for games of chance. You will win big with a small investment. Many blessings will come to you and your family.

nineteen Be very aggressive in your quest for love. Anyone you are interested in who gives you the slightest indication they are also interested should be enough of a motivator for you to pursue this further. You will find this to be a very rewarding relationship. Many unusual events will occur over the next nineteen days that will give you a fresh approach to life. This new way of thinking will allow your inner child to emerge and give you a youthful view of life. You should behave in such a way that will make it easy for others to open up and feel comfortable in your presence. This is the time for you to develop yourself in those areas you most desire. You are headed for a stable, financially secure and long life. This is also a very lucky number for you to use in games of chance.

ninety You will see a big immediate improvement in your life within two weeks. An older person will be very eager to come to your help financially and emotionally in ways you desire. If you choose, this is one option you can take advantage of. Any carefully thought out calculated risk will result in a brilliant future for you.

nip Do not be surprised if, within three days, someone demonstrates a new attitude toward you. This person will be so involved and busy with other aspects of their life that it will be impossible for them to stay in touch with you. Relax and busy yourself with something you enjoy. This person will get their life under control, will contact you much sooner than you anticipated and will be delighted to have you in their life. Good luck is with you.

nipple Within five days you will have a variety of options to choose from that will allow you to meet your goals. As you go through this process, make sure you remain very practical. You will also be given verbal verification of the depth of someone's love for you. You are headed for a brilliant future.

Nirvana You will contact someone who will be a stepping stone toward your goals. This person will offer you a tremendous amount of support and will help you to reach the completion of a project.

nitrogen Do not allow yourself to become overwhelmed by negative thoughts that keep you from moving forward. Avoid this and you will find a very stable path. This is a very prosperous cycle for you.

nitrous oxide Do not allow yourself to plot out revengeful tactics against someone else. You are wasting your time on negativity that you will regret later. Get on with your life and do nothing that will make you feel remorse later on.

no Unusual circumstances will come up within three days that you need to remain uninvolved in. Do not allow yourself to be manipulated otherwise. Because of your firm attitude, you will set yourself up for a positive change that will take place during this time period. Take special notice of anything important that you must stand firm on your refusal to participate in, especially if it requires a no answer.

Noah *(from the Bible)* You will soon begin to feel a strong emotional urge that will take up a great deal of your time because you will be completely unaware of where the source is coming from. This drive is urging you to focus on bringing something into tangible form and will continue for the week period. You will be able to determine the reason and source of this feeling during this time period. This overwhelming drive may well be the result of a psychic ability and a heightened awareness that is pushing you in the direction you need to go. You will somehow know this on an instinctive level because of the excitement you will feel, although you have no real proof or verification.

Nobel Prize Do not allow the negative experience of another person to keep you from becoming involved in a certain situation. You will not have the same experience as this other person but will reap many benefits and will prosper. Good luck is with you.

nobleman Within three days you will meet a very attractive, courageous and generous person. Although this person is definitely interested in a relationship of a sexual nature, they will take a long time to act on their desires. You cannot rush this because this individual needs this time. If you have the patience to allow this person to get to this point you will enjoy a mutually satisfying relationship.

nod For the next three days be very careful while traveling. Remain alert during this time period to make sure nothing slips through your fingers. Quickly respond to any unusual situation personally to make sure it is handled properly.

noise For the next four days work to develop your creativity and decide what you need to do to achieve financial security. Carefully analyze your decisions and follow your hunches. You are also about to make a mistake and are headed in the wrong direction. Stop what you are doing immediately and rethink your position. Simplify your life, follow your instincts and intuition and you will avoid a chaotic situation that you do not need to be involved in. You are headed for a prosperous future and a life filled with tranquility and health.

to investigate unusual noises Someone you feel a special closeness to is undergoing a tremendous amount of stress that is being placed on them by another person. This person will come to you within a three day period in an attempt to explain this but will be unable to verbalize exactly what they are feeling. This individual is in great danger of having their spirit broken because the other party is being irresponsible and abusive in many areas of this person's life. This person feels very controlled and is suspicious about the methods being used. Although there is no particular method or motive, control is being implemented in a very abusive manner and yet they are continuing to remain in this situation. Now is the perfect time for this person to develop a more suspicious manner and to confront their own inability to get away from this situation. They need to be made aware that the moment they have this conversation with you, they must motivate themselves to move on. It takes a long time to break the spirit and this person needs to take steps now to make the necessary changes to reenergize the spirit. What does it take to mend a broken spirit? It takes a long time to get back a balanced sense of consciousness and much abuse to destroy it. Now is the time for this person to use your words of motivation to make the moves they have to make to get away from this abuse without making their motives known because this could easily turn into a distressful situation. The amount of abuse this person is under will only be realized when it is too late unless they start making a move now. Within three days you will also be able to use profound communication skills to gain someone's absolute attention and to get them under your complete control. You will be able to open this person's eyes in such a way that they can motivate themselves into raising their standard of living in a way that suits them. You will be able to flush out certain information that you need from others by using your communication skills. This information will be very beneficial and advantageous for both of you. Many blessings are with you and you are on the path for a brilliant future.

noisemaker Make it a point, within five days, to encourage closeness between members of your family and for the next three days make sure they are not creating distance between themselves. Encourage love and play the role of peace maker.

nomad Behave in an aggressive manner toward a certain

individual who requires this kind of behavior. This behavior will cause this person to back off and not interfere in a situation that is important to you. Good luck is with you.

nom de plume For the next five days make sure you always tell the truth and all assistants are obeying the rules and regulations. In order to avoid any chaotic situation, make sure you also obey the rules and regulations and stick to the right side of the law. Good luck will be with you for the next week.

noodle Within three days you will be invited on a short trip. You will feel very excited about getting away for a few hours but, in reality, this trip will take far longer than you ever anticipated. Prepare yourself appropriately for this trip and you will enjoy yourself immensely. You will also be able to make very clear decisions during this time period. As a result you will be rewarded later because of the profits you receive from your decisions.

noon This dream is an extremely lucky omen. Within three days, at noon, something unusual will occur that will bring you joy. You will be very clear about your next move.

noose A loyal and close ally will be jeopardized by a remark made by someone close to you. Take steps to prevent this within two days.

north Within two weeks, you will uncover an unsuspected power in unexpected areas of your life and you will soon become aware of the high level of authority that you possess. You will then be motivated to experiment with new and different lifestyles and newer levels of social functioning. These experiences will open your eyes and you will find yourself very eager to adopt new ways of living. You will experience emotional and mental gratification and doors will be open to new sources of income. Take steps to prevent any negative event from occurring and embrace the positive. You are headed for a brilliant future.

North Carolina You will meet the individual who will open doors of opportunity for you and offer their assistance in correcting any personal issue that needs to be taken care of. You will enjoy many days of tranquility and are headed for a brilliant future. This dream may also be used as a reference point in time. If you dream of this state and see its name used in any context, the dream message will occur on this day.

North Dakota Prepare yourself, the best is yet to come. Within the week you will experience a true wealth of harmony. You must also make sure all agreements are fully understood and binding prior to making your next move. This dream may also be used as a reference point in time. If you dream of this state and see its name used in any context, the dream message will occur on this day.

northeastern Focus on benefits that are due you that you have not yet received and that you may not be aware of.

Within three days investigate this thoroughly to ensure that you receive the benefits that will help you during this time period. You will definitely point yourself in the right direction.

northeast passage Surround yourself with those who demonstrate true loyalty and genuine love and caring for you. Gravitate towards these people and avoid those who do not seem interested in being around you. You will feel an urge to be with those who care for you within the week.

Northern Cross Do not do anything to someone else that you would not want done to you. Do not force others to do chores and jobs that you do not want to do yourself and focus on hiring someone who specializes in doing this work.

Northern Ireland Any request you make for a loan regarding a big ticket item will be granted, especially for the next five days. Many blessings are with you and your family and you are definitely headed for a brilliant future. This dream may also be used as a reference point in time. If you dream of this region and see its name used in any context, the dream message will occur on this day.

northern lights You will find that something you thought would be a disappointment to another will instead fill them with joy. You will be very surprised at their reaction. Proceed with confidence.

Northern Territory Set aside the time to get the rest you need. Do this within three days because your social calendar will fill up and you will definitely need the rest. You will experience joy and many tranquil moments. This dream may also be used as a reference point in time. If you dream of this region and see its name used in any context, the dream message will occur on this day.

North Pole This dream is an extremely lucky omen for you. You will experience a number of special events and will be surrounded by many special people. If you choose, you will find that special person for the rest of your life. Take steps to keep any negative event connected to this dream from becoming a reality. You will enjoy many years of tranquility. This dream may also be used as a reference point in time. If you dream of this region and see its name used in any context, the dream message will occur on this day.

Norway A particular enterprise that you have developed will become tangible and you will soon be able to harvest the fruits of your labor and gain great wealth. Many blessings are with you and your family. This dream may also be used as a reference point in time. If you dream of this country and see its name used in any context, the dream message will occur on this day.

nose Mobilize yourself in order to make the contacts and connections you need to achieve your goals. Begin working on this now. You will find it much easier to make those contacts within three days. This dream is an extremely lucky omen. Take steps to prevent anything unusual you dreamed of from happening to you or those you recognize.

hooked nose Listen carefully and be very tolerant of someone who is anxious and upset. Remain calm and supportive. This will mean a great deal to this individual. Be generous with your time. Expect this to occur within three days.

runny nose Take steps to prevent exposure to any illness that could lead to a runny nose, especially for the next five days. You will experience an enormous amount of tranquility within the month.

to see someone touch noses or touch your nose to someone else For purposes of their own, someone will lead you to believe that they are completely in love with you. Words of love may or may not be used but all of the trappings will be present (i.e., flowers, gifts, romantic trysts, etc.). Your feelings will grow very strong for this individual but if you allow this person to make love to you, you will not connect on the level you felt existed for you. You will not be touched, kissed or loved in any special way, although this person will put on a good act. As a result, you will feel very cold and empty. Rather than putting yourself through this, get on with your life without this person. You have enough notice to avoid this scenario entirely. This person has a hidden agenda for you to do something for them that only they are aware of and this will only lead to unhappiness on your part. Otherwise you are headed for a prosperous future that will start to evolve within the week.

nosebleed Within the month you will receive an inheritance that will allow you to achieve enormous wealth and tranquility for a lifetime.

nose cone A special person will create an argument with you within three days. Do what you can to prevent this because it will escalate out of control.

nosedive Within five days someone will come into your life and request money from you. This individual will bear down on you and will attempt to manipulate this loan out of you. Do what you can to avoid this encounter completely.

nose drops Make sure you handle your affairs personally and make sure any situation that needs your personal touch gets it. Do not allow any unpleasant situation to slip up on you because you do not take care of your business personally.

nosegay Limit the time that you allow others to take from you. Make sure that you budget your time for the next three days because you will find yourself running late for other important matters.

nose guard For the next three days check first before you volunteer to do someone else's chores. If you do not, you will find this to be a very distasteful experience that will overwhelm you.

nose job If you feel this is something you want done in real

life, make the necessary plans to have this surgery performed. If you dream of a nose job with a negative outcome, make sure you do not experience it in reality. A friendship that you have pinned your hopes on needs both parties to nourish it in order for it to grow. This friendship will be very precious to you and will last a lifetime.

nose ring You will surrender to a marriage with happy, lasting results. This marriage will be one that both of you will be in general agreement on and will be a solid, loving relationship for a lifetime. You are headed for a brilliant future.

Nostradamus This dream is a lucky omen. You will meet someone who is fluent in several difficult languages. This person will come into your life at a time when you can utilize these language skills to meet a goal. This person will later desire a romantic union. Both of you will live to be old together. Find someone to give you a reading. You are in a very lucky cycle.

nostril Someone will lead you to believe they accept your point of view and are sincerely interested in becoming a part of your developing plans. This person is wasting your time and misleading you. Get on with your life without this person.

not *to hear the phrase "do not do this"* Within five days you will be involved with someone who will lead you to believe they are a very respected, professional, financially secure person with a stable career and credible lifestyle. This person is very eager to involve you in their life and because of their believability and the comfort you feel in their presence, you will want to become involved with them. You will be given every indication that you can easily contact them at any time but after checking various phone numbers, company addresses and after leaving messages with a secretary, you will find this person to be very difficult to track down. It will take hours and sometimes days for you to get a return call. It will dawn on you that this person has inflated their status and if you do become involved you will be disappointed. Develop a shrewd and disciplined attitude in order to keep this person from violating your emotions or insulting your intelligence. Because you have prior notice of this you will be able to handle this with success. You are entering a prosperous cycle and are headed for a brilliant future.

to hear the phrase "not much fun" For the next three days you will have a deep suspicion that something is going on. Do not allow anyone to persuade you into believing that you are being paranoid or try to water your suspicions down. Your spirit is sending you a heightened awareness about something you need to attend to. You will be able to handle everything in an appropriate manner and will not feel as though something could have been handled differently at a later time. You will be able to deal with this issue in an appropriate manner now.

notary public You are frequently paying visits to a couple who fights just prior to your visit and immediately following your departure. One member of this couple dislikes you and does not want you to visit but is unable to communicate this to you. Be very aware of what is occurring and make sure you do not go anywhere you are not wanted, especially for the next two days. Otherwise, this is a lucky cycle for you.

note You will enjoy many pleasures because someone from the past will reenter your life and you will take up where you left off. You have much to share together and will find many common interests that you will want to enjoy. You also find that you both have talents that the other is interested in and you will both exchange and swap ideas. This friendship will last a long time. Many blessings will come to you and the family. You will also enjoy an abundance of tranquility and health in your life.

notebook Do not overextend yourself by becoming involved in a situation that will come up within five days. You will be required to perform exhaustive physical labor. Remove yourself from this situation, regroup yourself, eat healthful foods, drink plenty of water and get plenty of rest.

notepads A wonderful celebratory event will be coming up within three days. Make it a point to mark this on your calendar so you will not forget and so you will have plenty of time to prepare yourself. You must also pay close attention to the words written on the memo pad for big clues to future events. If it is a positive message, take steps to promote it. If it is a negative message, take steps to alter the outcome or avoid it completely. You will also need to be prepared within the next two days. You will hear the words of love you have longed to hear in a letter. This relationship will move swiftly ahead.

notepaper For the next three days think ahead. You need to be very careful and have all your facts at hand in order to argue your point of view in an effective way. Do everything in a timely fashion.

notice Pay attention to what was presented on the notice. If it portended a negative event, take steps to prevent it, especially for the next three days. An unusually powerful and important person will offer you assistance in a personal situation that will bring a tremendous amount of relief, especially for the next three days.

noun Do not jump on the bandwagon and attack anyone else in any manner. Do what you can to be a peacemaker.

nova Within three days someone will constantly and subtly come up with certain issues that will keep you from accomplishing what you need to do. Be very aware of this and continue to stick to your schedule.

novel A grand event will occur within three weeks that will bring a tremendous amount of joy to all those involved. Prepare for this ahead of time so your physical appearance and attire are intact. Many blessings are with you and your family.

November You are definitely moving in the direction you should be going. Doors will be open to you that were formerly closed. You will also conclude and resolve all situations that you seek a closure to and this will bring about an enormous improvement in your standard of living. You will be surrounded by those who love and respect you. Good luck is with you and you are headed for a prosperous future.

novocain For the next week you will need to put some restraints on your behavior. You need also to be attentive, demonstrative and tolerant toward someone who is important to you. This person has become upset and angry over an issue that has taken place in their life. Give this person a few days to come to grips with this shocking situation.

now Do what you feel will bring joy into your life. Remove yourself from stressful situations and find a place where you can wallow in peace, especially for the next seven days. You will experience more kindness from others.

nozzle Within three days you will definitely have to set a new direction for yourself. Your original plan will not work out because there have been changes that you are not aware of. Revise your plans and make sure what you are doing is adequate.

nuclear bomb Do not suffer in silence any longer. Get the help you need so you can have your needs met properly. You will then be able to live your life more fully.

nuclear energy A certain situation is taking place that you have not yet touched upon and needs to be investigated and looked into promptly. Reach out to a variety of people who have the knowledge you do not have. Unless you take this course of action, things will not work out as they should.

nudity Within three days you will surrender to someone who has long desired that you do just that. You have prior notice of this and can carefully consider whether you choose to do this or not. You will be able to handle this situation properly.

your nude body - if it appears healthy You can expect good health for a long time. You will immediately gain a financial improvement in areas where you have been experiencing anxiety. You will also experience an unexpected surprise gift of some sort and the person you least expect will unexpectedly call or visit. This individual will encourage intimacy and quiet moments. If you decide to go along with this, you will enjoy yourself immensely with no strings attached.

your nude body - if something appears wrong or unusual Take steps to prevent any negative aspect you witnessed in this dream. Correct and prevent bad health habits. Eat healthful foods, and maintain good health. You will have the strength to correct any problem. Many blessings will be with you for a long time.

nude bodies You will enjoy a romantic liaison, if you choose. This is a good cycle for romance. You will also learn of an acquaintance's surgery. A good rapport will be developed regarding business affairs.

nude body - old An unexpected surprise gift will arrive.

nude body - young Think ahead in order to avoid a serious problem with a special person. For the next few days discuss changes you are making that involve your loved ones. Seek a mutual decision.

nude baby Do what you can to feel happier about your life. Appreciate life and consistently and persistently do what you can to enjoy it.

nude model Do not go out with someone purely for the sake of sexual pleasure, especially for the next two days. You will later decide that this individual is not attractive to you and this could lead to a dangerous situation because this person will feel used. Avoid this behavior.

to be reluctant to take off clothes This dream is a warning that you will be stricken with guilt about something you will do that you were opposed to before you did it. This will come up within two days and you need to take a stand against it. Look more carefully at what you are willing to involve yourself in. Also, you will enjoy an abundance of health during this cycle, but you do need to take steps to avoid becoming involved in something you should not become involved with. Also, make sure that anything negative connected to this dream does not become a reality.

nugget Within five days you will receive a benefit of some sort (i.e., job order, etc.) that will be more financially beneficial than you anticipated. Do not turn this opportunity down. Many blessings will come to you and your family.

nuisance Make sure you do not unwittingly become a nuisance to someone else. Be very aware of subtle changes in your relationships with others to ensure that you do not make yourself a pest without meaning to. This will be especially important for the next three days. Good luck is with you.

number Someone who has not yet told you of their interest will have a major victory in their life that will bring them a tremendous amount of wealth. This individual will then tell you of their interest in you. This relationship would bring you a tremendous amount of benefits and a wonderful life of sharing that you never envisioned if you choose to pursue this. Good luck is with you. Many blessings will come to you and your family. You must also pay attention to the numbers seen in this dream. They will bring you a tremendous amount of luck in games of chance. Use these numbers also for scheduling conferences, dates, meetings, etc.

Numbers *(book of the Bible)* You will enjoy a prosperous future, an enormous amount of health and many blessings will come to you and your family. Meditate in your favorite fashion and any request that you make of your deity will be granted. You are also in the perfect cycle now to carry out any plan that you have been contemplating. You will be able to develop these plans with ease. Within three weeks a reading will give you knowledge that will help you with certain tasks. Good luck is with you and many blessings are with you and your family.

nun You will have the intuitive thoughts that you need to overcome difficult situations and will be able to diffuse negative thoughts and attitudes during this time period. You will therefore not have to deal with this situation again in your life. Remain balanced and calm in spite of outside influences. Many blessings are with you and your family.

nurse Take extra precautions to keep any negative event seen in this dream from becoming a reality and make sure you experience only positive expressions in your life. You will also meet someone within three days who will take a while to warm up to. Once you have, you will find this person is not at all like you thought they were and you will enjoy their company tremendously. You are headed for a brilliant future.

wet nurse You can proceed with confidence with what you have in mind to develop within five days. Everything will work out exactly as you have envisioned.

nursemaid Push yourself to pursue the big ideas. Do not allow yourself to fall behind and make sure you complete your tasks.

nursery *(children's nursery)* Within three days, you will receive much needed information that has been very difficult to come by. This information will help you to expand your horizons.

nursery *(plant)* *any form* You will suddenly advance to a higher plateau of life than you ever anticipated and will enjoy an abundance of affection and productive conversations with others as a result of this success. People who were impossible to get along with will now demonstrate a refreshing attitude toward you. Health, wealth and good luck will be with you.

nursery rhyme Within three days you will find it very difficult to accept someone's information as being authentic. This individual is being very truthful with you and you should avoid wasting your time on doubts and suspicions.

nursery school Make sure you are taking every precaution to ensure the safety of young ones, especially for the next three days. By doing this, you can eliminate any dangerous situation that may arise.

nut For the next two days behave in such a way that will make a special person in your life feel special. This will also keep this person from seeking emotional satisfaction elsewhere.

nutcracker For the next three days make sure you stay relentlessly on track and do not allow yourself to be manipulated into getting off the right track. Go for the big ideas. This is the perfect cycle to accomplish big goals.

nuthatch Make sure you are coaching someone who is close to you in a loving way to get them through a certain situation until it is completely resolved. It will be deeply appreciated, especially for the next three days.

nutmeg Within the month you and another person will travel to a delightful place. You will have a wonderful time and will return home safely. You will also introduce new activities into your life that you will find enjoyment with. You are headed for a very prosperous future.

nutshell You will soon receive a proposal for marriage and will faithfully commit to this relationship. This relationship will last a lifetime and you and your partner will have a prosperous future.

nymph Do not allow anyone to talk you into becoming involved in a conspiracy. This will backfire on you and create turmoil in your life. You must also pay close attention to anything in this dream that may be connected to reality. Take all the necessary steps to prevent a negative occurrence and forewarn anyone you recognize to do the same.

nympho/nymphomaniac Love yourself and do everything necessary to bring more joy into your life. Incorporate a variety of new experiences into your routine. Be kind to yourself and do things that are soothing. Drink plenty of water and eat healthy, healing foods. You will also be very happy with the performance of someone from whom you have requested assistance. This person has the ability to make clear decisions and to execute them efficiently. You will work well together and will experience many joyful moments until the task has been completed.

O

O Think carefully of ways you can appreciate life better. Once you have done this you will enjoy many private moments with someone you care about. You will be able to find the appropriate things to do that will deepen the bond you have with this person and you will learn to appreciate others better. You will be financially and emotionally fulfilled for the coming month.

oak This dream is a very lucky omen. Someone you want to have surrender to you emotionally will do so and the sky will be the limit. Both of you will have a pool of resources to pull from to make life easier. Many blessings are with you and your family.

oak leaf Make a list of priorities and stick with them. You will successfully complete your tasks in a short period of time.

oar You are suffering from either a vitamin or mineral deficiency. It would be a good idea to get a check up and determine what is lacking within three days. Good luck is with you.

oat Within three days someone will purposely strike up a conversation with you. This person will carefully scrutinize you and every word you use. They will then formulate an opinion of your character. Be alert to this and handle this in the best way you see fit. You will also receive some very good news during this time frame.

oatcake Within three days someone will come to you with some confidential information. Do what you can to discourage this person from divulging this information to you. If you do not, you will feel as though a burden has been placed on you.

oat grass Do not allow anyone to become pushy and bossy toward you. The moment you see this start to develop, cut it off immediately because this person will push this behavior to the point of embarrassment.

oath Over the next three days devote your time and energy to those who need your input to resolve certain issues. Otherwise, these issues will quickly fall apart and you will regret not offering your assistance.

oatmeal Someone will ask you to help them to get a quick response from another individual. You will be able to get others to respond to this person's needs appropriately and promptly. This person will be very thankful that you were there at a time when they needed you. You will have an abundance of health and tranquility in your life for a long period of time. Many blessings will come to you and your family and you are headed for a brilliant future.

Obadiah *(from the Bible)* For the next five days do not allow your lack of determination and self confidence block you from bringing a certain situation to completion and do not create extra barriers that will hinder your progress. Proceed with confidence and push yourself to take care of what you need to. You will then feel a real sense of accomplishment and well being. You will also invest wisely and this will result in prosperity.

obey Make sure you are acutely aware of your surroundings. Within three days you and a companion will go somewhere that will represent a danger to both of you. Do not accidentally wander into an unfamiliar area that could be a hazard to you. Be sure you follow all the rules and regulations and stay on the right side of the law in order to avoid distasteful situations.

ob/gyn Become personally involved in those situations you want to fall into place perfectly, especially for the next week. You will be successful. Make sure you take steps to keep any negative event in this dream from becoming a reality and make sure you alert anyone you dreamed of to do the same. Do everything you can to ensure you experience only positive expressions in your life. For more depth of the meaning look up the definition of woman's clinic.

obituary Release yourself from an obligation that will become a bigger challenge for you than anticipated. This would be a wise move for you.

object Get rid of those suspicions and jealous feelings. These tapes serve no purpose except to make your life uncomfortable for yourself and others. Make sure you come to grips with this and start living your life in a more peaceful and tranquil manner.

oboe When communicating with someone of importance who possesses a great deal of authority, express your concerns openly and you will get a quick response in an appropriate manner.

obscenity Do not respond to a situation in the hopes that it will be handled with a quick fix. Give yourself time to sort things out so you can handle this situation correctly. It is especially important to do this within three days.

observatory Your actions will be carefully scrutinized for the next three days as though you were being viewed under a magnifying glass. Someone will attempt to find fault with you in some way. You have prior notice of this and can watch your actions and handle yourself in an appropriate manner.

obsession Within three days, someone will create chaos, stress and despair in the manner they communicate with you. The moment you see this start to develop, maintain your control and remove yourself from the situation.

obsidian Within five days someone special to you will send you a gift through the mail.

obstacle Become more assertive in certain areas of your life and become more aggressive and less timid, especially for the next three days. Someone will see your leadership abilities. Proceed with confidence.

obstetrician Make your own opportunities, especially for the next two days. A variety of vocations will present themselves that you can choose from. Your life will become more rewarding in areas you desire.

occult Do not allow curiosity to take control and do not venture into the unknown. There is a thin line between curious inquiry and active involvement and you are approaching this line. Step back, what you are being told is misleading. You need to regroup and come to grips with a situation that needs to be understood immediately in order to avoid danger. This needs to be accomplished within three days. Get plenty of rest and avoid all stressful situations. Take all negative messages and relentlessly work to change the outcome.

occupant Make sure you are acutely aware of someone's shortcomings so you can take steps to provide this person with what they need. This will enable them to work at their full capacity in areas you expect a high level of efficiency.

ocean Expect someone to enter your life within three days

who has a great deal of passion for life as well as the ability to fulfill your emotional and romantic needs. You are headed for a prosperous future.

with rough waters You are headed in the wrong direction. Take the time to regroup and investigate what you need to do in order to put yourself on the right track. Do not allow anyone to manipulate you in such a way that you are led off the correct path.

ocean wave This dream is telling you of a situation that will come up within the week. Someone will say that they will do one thing but will then turn this around and claim their intentions were otherwise. This person will wait until the last moment to make you aware of this. Be very alert so you can plan ahead of time how to handle yourself appropriately.

oceanography In order to keep a special person from demanding attention, volunteer your services prior to having this individual make this request. This person is seeking assurance from you. Be very clear with them about how you feel and put this matter to rest.

Oceanus (*Greek Mythology*) You will receive verbal verification from someone you care about who has a special place in their heart for you. You are loved beyond your imagination. You will experience more tranquility and an abundance of health.

ocelot For the next five days you will exhibit greater mental alertness and good communication skills. This will allow you to reach out to someone who is very shy.

ocher This dream is a very lucky omen. Within three days you will receive a gift from someone and this will leave you with a lasting impression of excitement. This dream also implies that for the next three days you must become very aggressive in order to ensure other people do not violate your life. You will also receive good news within five days.

octagon For the next three days put all your plans into writing in order to be understood with clarity. Make sure you graphically plot out each idea. This dream is extremely lucky for lovers and each improvement you seek in your life will come to be.

octane Within three days be aware that you will unintentionally encourage someone to do something that will only bring them misery and they will then blame you for the results. Avoid this distasteful situation.

October For the entire year you will have the power and relentless behavior to handle a particular situation in spite of anything else you feel may prevent you from grasping your goals. You will achieve what you have set out to accomplish within this time frame. Proceed with confidence until you reach your destined goal. Your intuition will be especially clear regarding matters of the heart and business associations. Within three days you will find that all things you felt were impossible regarding love matters are now possible. In the past you and another person were once interested in each other but this failed to develop into a relationship because of differences in your lifestyle. It is destined, within this time period, that you and this person come together once more and enjoy a mutually fulfilling and long lasting relationship. Other people will also be interested in you during this time period. Many blessings are with you and you are headed for a brilliant future.

October Revolution *(Russian)* Someone will describe a particular situation that happened to them involving something that another individual did to them. You will get the sense they have done this to themselves because they have a hidden agenda of their own. This will make you feel differently about them and their character. Do not allow this person to know how you feel and get on with your life. The story told by this individual is completely unreliable. This will occur within three days.

octopus Within three days someone will become very demanding of your time and your financial resources. This person has many outstanding debts and will entangle themselves in your life in such a way that you will feel guilty and compelled to give money to them. Before you know it you will be giving out money on a regular basis until this person is able to get out of debt. You have prior notice of this and if you choose not to allow this to develop, put a stop to it early on. This person will not create a healthy relationship.

oddity Within three days you will be able to permanently resolve a financially draining situation.

odds makers You will marry the person you most desire, if this is your choice. You are loved beyond your imagination and will receive more love, affection and appreciation than ever before.

odds, the *any form* This dream implies that the odds are in your favor, especially for the next three days. Someone will also give you a tip that will greatly benefit you.

ode For the next few days think ahead and do not impulsively indulge in any activity you find distasteful.

odyssey *(Greek literature)* You will have an awesome time for the next three days and will have memories you will cherish for a lifetime.

Oedipus *(Greek literature)* Make sure that within the week your body is maintained properly, especially regarding your food intake and rest. Good luck is with you.

Oedipus complex Within three days, do not unintentionally lead someone to believe you can handle certain tasks. This person is under the impression you are able to do so. Do them a favor and do not waste their time. Give this person the chance to find someone with the proper experience and expertise.

off *any form* Do not allow yourself to get caught up in the

behavior someone demonstrates toward you. This individual will lead you to believe they are romantically interested in you but will, out of the blue, decide they will get on with their life without you. Regardless of how it may seem at the beginning, there is no chance this will become a serious involvement. Do not jump to conclusions, you are being misled. Anything that seems too good to be true regarding any negotiation probably is. Do not allow yourself to be pulled in. Good luck is with you.

offbeat You will not be able to win over someone you desire in a passionate way but will want to attempt this within three days. Make sure you let romance develop slowly in the appropriate surroundings and atmosphere. You will have more success this way instead of being in a rush to make things happen. Go slowly and take it a step at a time to make sure everything falls into place the way you want. Good luck is with you.

off Broadway Within the week you will be entering a wonderfully exciting social cycle that will bring you many new interests as well as introduce you to a variety of new people with whom you can interact intelligently. If you choose, you will also have the opportunity to enjoy romance. You will enjoy many unforgettable moments that you will treasure for a long time to come. You are headed for a brilliant future.

off-color Within three days, someone you do not know well will overtly demonstrate a display of emotions toward you that will make you feel uncomfortable. Otherwise, many blessings will come to you and your family.

offense You will be offered a rare opportunity that you should pounce on. This opportunity will make a difference in your life in those areas you desire. You are headed for a prosperous future.

offer For the remainder of your life you will experience nothing but tranquility and will feel at peace in your surroundings. You will experience a great deal of joy in your life and many blessings will come to you and your family.

offering Make sure you do not go to extremes for the next three days. Do not allow yourself to become overextended in any area of your life, especially regarding emotions. Many blessings are with you and you are headed for a brilliant future.

office Anything connected to this dream that could be a negative event needs to be avoided or altered in reality. Do what you can to experience only positive events in your life. For the next three days you must also do everything within your power to avoid the break up of relationships that are important to you because of the manner in which you treat others. You are respected and loved beyond your imagination. Good luck is with you.

officeholder For the next three days monitor your time carefully to ensure that precious moments and hours are not wasted. Budget your time.

office hours Make sure you do not misplace, because of your busy schedule, money or items that are important to you. Proceed with caution for the next three days.

office personnel Do whatever is necessary to turn any negative situation into a positive situation. You have prior notice of this and can alter it or change it completely and make sure you only experience positive events in your life. Someone will also seek what you are after in a very secretive and underhanded way. You have the time to take steps to prevent this. Good luck is with you.

officer Make sure you take steps to keep anything that was negative in this dream from taking place in reality. Within three days you must also make sure you have all the information you need before you visit an unfamiliar place in order to avoid wasting time looking for this place. Proceed with confidence during this time period.

    warrant officer Someone who is married will be very attracted to you and will do everything in their power to lure you into a relationship with them. Do everything you can to protect yourself from this situation. It will definitely backfire on you.

official You will split apart from a relationship permanently. Expect this to occur within three days.

off ramp Take the time to step back and determine what you need to stop doing and become uninvolved in. You are also definitely overlooking something that requires your prompt attention in order for it to fall into place perfectly. It is important to attend to details for the next three days.

off season For the next three days, it would be to your advantage to strengthen the bonds of those relationships that are important to you. Increase your personal involvement in order to ensure peace and tranquility.

off shore For the next three weeks everything will fall into place exactly as you wish. You are definitely headed for a prosperous future.

off sides You can vastly improve your situations over the next three days if you are determined. Good luck is with you.

off white Your intuition will be right on target when it applies to financial matters and business negotiations. You will be tremendously successful if you follow your own counsel, especially for the next three days.

ogre Do everything you can to avoid the inadvertent violation of someone's rights.

Ohio Within three days you will meet a wonderful person whom you will spend hours speaking with. This person is gentle and generous and you will find that you have many

similarities in life. You will also find that you have many interests in common. You will enjoy your time together so much that you will decide to meet again. If you choose to take this relationship to a deeper emotional level, you have that option. You will spend many wonderful moments together for the next seven days, and are headed for a prosperous future. This dream may also be used as a reference point in time. If you dream of this state and see its name used in any context, the dream message will occur on this day.

oil Be alert, you are about to make a mistake. You are fond of someone in a special way and this person is also fond of you. Do not take any relationship for granted and learn to be more open and communicative with those who are special to you. Make sure you make special time to spend with those you care about.

oilcan Within three days someone will borrow something from you and will promise to return it to you. If you do not stay on top of this situation, you will never get it back. Make it a point to keep reminding yourself to get this item back or refuse to lend it out. You are entering a very tranquil cycle and blessings will come to you and your family.

oilcloth Do not give up any of your private personal time in the belief that something else is more important. Guard this time and guard the time you spend for restful activities. Others will soon get the idea that you have no private time for them or yourself.

oil color For the next three days you will be channeling your energies in the right direction. Keep going in the direction you are going. For greater definition, look up the individual colors you saw in this dream.

oiler Within the next three days you will find yourself in an unplanned but romantic situation. If you choose, this will evolve rapidly into a permanent relationship.

oil painting For the next four days take steps to keep any negative event that was depicted in this painting from becoming a reality and make sure you promote any positive event. You must also do what you can to display your talents and showcase your skills. Within this four day period you will connect with someone who has all the right resources to put you on the path of success.

oil paper For the next four days pay close attention to the emotions you will be experiencing. If there is something you feel is distasteful to you, remove yourself from this stressful situation. Perform soothing activities and make sure you provide yourself with a stress free environment. It is important that you are good to yourself during this time period.

oilskin For the next five days you will experience an abundance of love and will appreciate the verification of the feelings others have for you. You are deeply loved by a special person. Do not deprive yourself of this ecstasy.

ointment Within three days, be very aware of someone who will start taking steps to involve themselves with you. This person will take special pains to ensure that this involvement lasts at least a week and will use this time to maneuver a way to get under your skin so you will constantly be giving them special attention. After some time this individual will arrange this in such a way that your attentions will be expected and will become a duty. If you do not continue this behavior, this individual will leave. If you do not choose to go through this, cut this relationship off at the first sign of this behavior.

O. J. Simpson Within three days you will need to think carefully about the direction you are being led. Because of some unusual circumstances that will occur, you will feel compelled to negate absence of malice. By using extraordinary calculated motivation and by thinking ahead, you will be able to avoid being set up for this situation. You will also avoid being depleted of your resources and people who would vulturize you. You will be able to successfully sidestep this issue because of your prior notice. Otherwise, you are headed for a prosperous, healthy and tranquil life.

OK If you agreed to something in your dream and you feel you shouldn't do it, avoid it in reality. Someone will also request your affections and you will be very eager to grant this request. If you choose, you will experience wonderful passionate moments together. If you decide not to pursue this, you can handle this situation appropriately.

Okeechobee Lake This dream is an extremely lucky omen and this luck will stay with you for the next three months. This dream also implies that you will have a long and healthy life with your family. You are headed for a brilliant future.

Okefenokee swamp You need to incorporate healthy activities into your lifestyle. Drink plenty of water, get plenty of rest, eat healthy foods and make sure you avoid unhealthy relationships. You must also make sure you are not misdiagnosed and treated for the wrong illness.

Oklahoma Make it a point to experience different ethnic foods and introduce yourself to different lifestyles. This will add spice to your life and a new excitement that will come from mingling with people of different cultures. You will have the opportunity to do this within two weeks. Good luck is with you. This dream may also be used as a reference point in time. If you dream of this state and see its name used in any context, the dream message will occur on this day.

okra Within three days you will be contacted by an old friend who will request special help from you. You will be able to give the assistance this person is after.

Oktoberfest You will find a solution to a problem that will arise within three days. This will be taken care of very quickly. Good luck is with you.

old *any form* Someone will come into your life within three days who will help you develop a positive approach to life. This will help motivate you to bring romance into your life as well as a chance to enjoy life in ways you have never allowed yourself. Many blessings are with you and your family and wonderful days are ahead of you.

old age Do not settle for less. Live life to the fullest and do not allow anyone to compromise your beliefs or desires by allowing someone to persuade you to do something you should not be doing, especially for the next three days. Many blessings are with you and your family and you are headed for a brilliant future.

Old English Sheepdog Do not allow anyone to persuade you into making plans you are not interested in. Be very aggressive in doing what you feel is best at this time regarding your plans for the future. It is important that you do this within three days.

Old Faithful Focus on your family's needs and make sure that you alert them to take care of themselves, especially for the next three days.

old maid Decide what you really want from someone you are interested in before your feelings are revealed. Specify the depth you are willing to commit yourself to. The other person may want more from this relationship than you are willing to give.

Old Testament Someone you have not seen in years will bring you good news that is totally unexpected. You are on the path toward a brilliant, prosperous future.

old wives tale For the upcoming four days any information you receive will be completely unreliable. Recheck your sources and reject all faulty information.

olfactory You are loved beyond your imagination and will see visual proof of this soon (i.e., an unexpected gift). You will experience a greater demonstration of love and more joy with a wonderful person. Many blessings are with you and your family.

olive Within three days go back to square one and start over with a certain situation. Educate yourself and plan ahead to make sure it is done correctly this time and make sure everyone involved will feel satisfied with the new developments. Good luck is with you and many blessings will come to you and your family. You are headed for a brilliant future.

olive branch Within five days motivate yourself to activate an opportunity to open up for you. You will be able to create opportunities for yourself that will not only excite you but will change your life tremendously. Eat healing foods, and do something special for yourself. Many blessings are with you and you are in a very lucky cycle. You must also rely on your intuition because it will quickly point you toward the path you should be headed. You are loved beyond your imagination.

olive leaves Do not take so long to make a move toward the person you desire. This cycle is perfect for bringing about romance and pursuing that special someone. You will enjoy an abundance of health and all negotiations that involve finance and business will work to your advantage. Many blessings will come to you and your family and you are headed for a very prosperous future.

Olympic Games Detail and investigate the options that are being made available to you. Make sure nothing new will be brought in later that you are unaware of. Exercise, eat healing foods, drink plenty of water and get the rest you need. Allow your body to function at its highest level. You have a wonderful life ahead of you.

Olympus *(Greek Mythology)* Make sure any pleasure seeking activity you are engaged in does not become an expensive habit. This will keep you from going in the direction you should be going. Many blessings will come to you and your family.

omelet Within a few days you will become involved in organizing an event for a young person that will be very memorable for this individual because you will go to the trouble to make sure each detail falls into place exactly as you have envisioned. You will experience much joy and many festivities. Victory is yours. This dream also implies that if you choose, you will enjoy emotional fulfillment with the person who means a lot to you. You will say the right things to each other to ensure closeness. Proceed with confidence.

omen Take every precaution to avoid or alter any negative omen you were given in this dream in order to prevent any chaos in your life Certain situations will arise within three days that will require you stay true to yourself. Relentlessly pursue what you really want from someone else. Strongly verbalize your wants and you will receive them. Many blessings will come to you and your family, and you can expect an abundance of good health.

omnivore You will experience prosperity in your life due to a very unusual and extraordinary situation you will be able to capitalize on to your benefit. Many blessings are with you and your family.

Onassis, Aristotle Within three days you will be introduced to a lifestyle that is totally different from your own. You will experience new impressions and wealth that will bring you much pleasure for a lifetime.

Onassis Kennedy, Jackie Within five days you will hear word of an unexpected inheritance.

one This is a very powerful number and symbolizes victory. You will grasp the goals you are pursuing. Your special

deity is with you in anything you choose to grasp and you will be able to raise your standard of living. You are loved by many people, will be surrounded by them and will have verification of how much you are appreciated and loved within the month. You are entering a very lucky cycle and many blessings are with you. Use this number to schedule special meetings, conferences and dates, etc., and for use in small risks at games of chance.

one track mind Someone will lead you to believe they will take care of a certain situation for you at a specific time. Look for an alternative because this person will not come through for you in a timely fashion. Avoid the irritation that will result from this situation by seeking other avenues in which to handle this issue.

one two punch Within three days, you will be dealing with someone who will do anything that anyone wants of them in order to make other people happy. This individual, however, is only going through the motions and finds these tasks to be distasteful. Make sure other people really enjoy performing certain tasks. You are entering a cycle that will give you an abundance of health. This will be a very lucky time period for you.

onion Within four days any joint venture you are interested in being a part of will yield wonderful results. This venture will also bring prosperity for everyone else involved.

onion rings Although you feel something is impossible, all things are now possible, especially for the next seven days. You are entering a very lucky and prosperous cycle.

onionskin This dream is a very good omen and symbolizes luck. You will be able to turn a very negative situation into a positive situation and will be able to take a distant relationship and turn it into a very loving and tranquil one.

onionskin paper Someone will go to great lengths to give you the money you need within five days. You are also headed for a prosperous and loving future.

onside kick Avoid domestic friction with someone you care about. Set aside some private time out of your busy and rewarding life to spend with your mate.

onyx You are in the position to demand what you need and want from your higher power. Specify what you need and your desires will be met no matter how impossible they may seem. This stone is a very powerful symbol and a promise that you will have a brilliant future. Look up the color for additional definitions. Many blessings are with you and your family.

ooze Within three days you will definitely achieve success with the help of another person who will relentlessly support you. Proceed with confidence.

opal Within three days, someone will contact you and will go to great lengths to involve you in their life. This was once someone you were interested in but never pursued. This time you will be highly interested in this person and you will receive everything you ever wanted from a relationship. Everyone you know will also be very excited about this new development. This is a very powerful symbol for negotiations and conversations. You are loved beyond your imagination and many blessings will come to you and your family. You are entering a very lucky seven day cycle.

fire opal Within three days someone will enter your life who harbors a great deal of bitterness towards themself. This person has never been loved in the way they desire. Make sure you do not become a target of revenge for this person. Make it very clear that you wish to continue a friendship but will not be a scapegoat for their misery. This dream also implies that this is a good luck omen for those in love, especially if the opal is fiery.

open Within ten days a great event will occur that will be celebrated and talked about for weeks. A joyous occasion will take place to everyone's delight. Many blessings will come to you and your family and you will be entering a very lucky cycle.

small opening You will be taking huge steps to raise your standard of living. This will be accomplished by focusing on your goals in a grand way. Expect this to come about within five days due to some unusual and joyful circumstance. Everyone involved in this will enjoy beautiful expressions of joy and tranquility. Many blessings will be with you and your family.

large opening A cluster of events will occur one after the other with each bringing you a tremendous amount of joy, wonder and awe because things are happening so quickly. You will also possess a powerful energy that you are going to be able to direct and control. At the same time that these events are taking place you will be able to bring other people under your complete control. Because you have prior notice of this you will be able, within five days, to direct this energy in such a way to successfully complete anything you wish in a superb way. You will be able to overcome any difficult obstacle and it will now be very simple to deal with it. Your intuition will be right on target. Follow your hunches about a new relationship. Many blessings are with you and your family.

open-eyed Make sure other people keep their hands off your money and that you keep unusual circumstances from taking place regarding finances. Many blessings are with you.

open fire A promise will be broken to you within three days. You can prevent this.

openhanded Be acutely aware that an accident can occur that will cause harm to someone else as a result of a fall. Make sure unusual accidents do not occur in your presence. Be on the lookout for this. Many blessings will come to you and your family and you are headed for a prosperous future.

open heart surgery You are in the perfect position to en-

sure that open heart surgery does not become necessary for you or for anyone in your family. Start now to turn around anything that could lead to this. Be sure to eat healing foods, drink plenty of water, and get enough exercise. Aggressively seek time off and relaxation time to prevent this from occurring to you or a loved one. Do what you can to educate those you care about to take care of themselves.

open house Within seven days you need to make all of the correct decisions by using a team approach, otherwise a large number of people will be angry at you for making decisions without consulting them. Any negative event viewed in this dream must be avoided in reality and make sure you allow only positive expressions in your life.

open market Because of the tenacity you display toward reaching your goals, you will be unbeatable. It will be your time to celebrate and rejoice.

open minded If you involve yourself with the appropriate groups of people, you will find a once in a lifetime opportunity within the week. Allow these opportunities to come to you in such a way that you will be able to pick and choose the ones most suitable for you. You are entering a very lucky cycle that will bring you joy and you will be able to expand your horizons.

open sesame Make the time to have an overdue conversation with someone who is special to you. This will definitely make a difference in the approach that both of you will take regarding certain situations you will be involved with in the future. You are headed for a brilliant future. Proceed with confidence.

opera Someone is highly attracted to you and is contemplating making a move toward you within three days in order to bring you closer together. If you allow this to proceed, you will be surprised at how quickly this will develop into a permanent union. This will be a very productive cycle and implies you will be very lucky in love.

opera glasses Make sure you do not take those relationships that are important to you for granted. Make it a point to take relationships seriously in order to keep those you care about close to you. Demonstrate your feelings verbally and with action, especially for the next seven days.

opera house You are definitely headed in the right direction You are entering a very lucky cycle and this is the time to tackle those hard to handle issues. You will be successful in handling these in the proper fashion.

operation Anything you dreamed of that had negative connotations must be altered or avoided in reality. Any positive event needs to be promoted. It will also be requested that you offer your assistance in the care of a sick person. This individual will quickly recover with tender loving care. This is also a very lucky cycle for you.

operator For the next three days do what you can to put

your love into action. Show kindness and generosity toward the children in your family as well as toward young adults. Make sure you eliminate all hostile behavior and provide a peaceful, stable environment.

Ophelia *(Shakespearean Drama)* For the next three days avoid any negative game playing. Do not get caught up in any exchange of words. Maintain a positive frame of mind regarding certain situations that will develop during this cycle.

opiate Do not allow yourself to add fuel to the fire of any chaotic situation, especially for the next three days. This will be a waste of time for you and others. Be acutely aware of any abusive situation that may be occurring with children or young adults that you must not allow yourself to have a hand in. Do not allow this to take place with your knowledge and make sure any behavior of this sort is stopped. Make sure young children have their needs met. Your input will make a difference in the lives of these children.

opinion For the next three days, make sure you do not overlook the opinion of someone who is very quiet and shy and has difficulties making their opinions known. Handle this appropriately and encourage this person to be more open. This individual has a wealth of information if you seek this opportunity out. Many blessings are with you.

opium For the next five days avoid doing any investigative work you feel is necessary to clarify a certain situation. Another person is more skilled and is in a better position to do this. You are entering a very tranquil cycle. Make sure any negative event you may have dreamed of does not become a reality.

opossum Do not unwittingly place yourself in an unusual freaky situation. Make sure any extraordinary occurrence does not lead to your involvement in something you have no business being involved in. Good luck will be with you for the next two days.

opportunity Within three days a kind and beautiful person will enter your life and relentlessly support you financially until you get on your feet. You will also find that doors that were once closed to you are now open and what you once felt was impossible is now possible. Many blessings are with you and your family.

opposites Do not associate with the wrong person. Someone who has a history you are unaware of will injure your status in the long run. For your own sake, retract your involvement with this person.

oppression Create a stress free environment for yourself. Get more rest and relaxation, simplify your life and find some amusements for yourself. Be good to yourself, eat well and drink plenty of water.

Oprah Winfrey *famous talk show host* This dream is a powerful symbol for you and implies you need to associate with those who have the education and knowledge to enlighten you in such a way that you can evolve and grow. Positive attitudes will rub off on you and you can be assured that loved ones do not outgrow you. Try to make yourself available to as many self help experiences as possible so you can develop your personality into what you desire. Allow closeness to grow within family circles. The opportunity and time are ideal now to bring about the changes you so desire to accomplish in this area of your life. Your God is with you. Within three days you will experience many blessings, an abundance of health, and are headed for a brilliant future.

optic fiber For the next two days be very confident and determined in the manner in which you handle things. Others need to see this trait in you.

optic nerve Do not listen to gossip, especially for the next two days. Even if you do not say anything, others will comment on your presence. This will get back to the individual talked about and an ugly situation will erupt because of it. Prevent this occurrence.

optimism Within seven days you will clearly be able to analyze someone else's behavior toward you so you will be able to behave in the appropriate manner. You will have the courage and foresight to determine the correct way to conduct yourself and to follow through with this. You will enjoy a lucky seven day cycle. Good luck is with you.

oracle Take every precaution to keep any negative event from taking place that was foretold in this dream. You must also, within five days, take a very strong stand in your refusal to take part in someone else's plans. Make it very clear how you feel and do not compromise.

oral Question the motives behind someone's sudden interest in you. This person is planning to ask something of you and it will take a long time to get out from under this obligation. Unless this is something you are willing to do for a long time, do not involve yourself with this person. Many blessings are with you and your family.

oral sex Someone will go to great lengths to ensure your success in the business world. You are also loved and appreciated, especially by those who fail to demonstrate their feelings.

oral surgery Watch out for secretaries or anyone who works in a similar capacity who will keep your calls and messages from getting through to someone you are trying to reach. For the next three days do everything you can to control your emotions. This individual enjoys game playing. You must also take steps to avoid any negative event portrayed in this dream that could occur in reality. You are entering into a very lucky cycle and many blessings will come to you and your family.

orange *the fruit* Within this next seven day cycle you will experience a big victory that will bring you a wealth of opportunities. Put yourself in the position to bring about the completion of an agreement in your favor by using whatever authority you have. You have seven days from the time you have this dream to accomplish this. You can be certain this is the best cycle to handle this and the contract will be greeted with enthusiasm by all those involved. You are on a very victorious path in life and many blessings will come to you and your family.

    the color This dream is a very victorious omen and implies that within ten days, no matter what is occurring in your life you will be able to focus on what you need to be doing in order to reach your goals. You will also be able to use your abilities to pull strings on your behalf. You will develop the confidence you need and will maintain this level of confidence until you succeed. Many blessings will come to you and your family. You are definitely headed for a brilliant future.

orangeade Your intuition about love and money are right on target. Follow your hunches and you will move quickly in this cycle to gain prosperity in a big way.

orange pekoe tea This dream is a lucky omen for love. Within three days you will be able to clearly detail your thoughts and put them into words in such a way that you will enable someone else to open up to you and express their deep desire for you. Your actions will allow this person to feel comfortable and sure of themselves in your presence. Because of this, a relationship will develop into a warm and loving unity. This cycle will also allow you to bring anything that has been blocked because of a lack of communication out into the open.

orangewood This dream implies that any enterprise you become involved in will be a success and will improve your life immensely.

orangutan For the next three days you will be walking a very thin line and it will be very easy for someone to steer you in the wrong direction. Do what you can to maintain clarity of thought in order to avoid this situation and put yourself on the right track. Make sure you remain alert during this three day period.

oratory You will find success in areas you felt were impossible, especially for the next three days.

orchard You will be entering a three day cycle that will require you to give special attention to someone you care a great deal for. You will also need to demonstrate a great deal of patience.

orchestra You will experience a great deal of excitement after someone expresses their true feelings for you. You will have all the evidence you need to know this person is totally in love with you.

orchid You will achieve victory in those areas in which you felt you were not equipped to attain success. This dream also implies that someone will seek refuge in your company. This person will feel safe in your presence because your influence will steer them in the right direction. They will not impose themselves on you and will be unaware of the reason why. Once they feel secure about themselves they will get on with their lives and you will not experience any stress over this. You will be surrounded by those who respect and love you and many blessings will come to you and your family.

ordain Someone will lead you to believe they can assist you a great deal more than they can. Now that this person has blown their abilities out of proportion, they will, within five days, want to back out of this commitment. This will happen, not because of their lack of willingness to help, but because they lack the resources, finances, or skills to live up to their promise. Give this person a graceful way out. You have prior notice and can take steps to avoid this situation at the onset. Many blessings will come to you and your family.

ore Within the week you will be able to put yourself in the proper frame of mind and have the clarity of thought to bring order into your life. You will also rid yourself of anything you no longer need to take care of and will experience more tranquility in your life. Within two days, you will need to weigh each side of each situation in order to make the correct decisions regarding love and money. You are headed in the right direction.

oregano For the next five days many people will offer you their assistance and will give you advice to help you reach the place you want to be in life. Because of this support system, you will be granted many benefits almost immediately.

Oregon Anything that appears unusual for the next three days will be something you should become involved with because it will bring you tremendous luck and prosperity. Anything that was impossible in the past is something you can now achieve with ease. Many blessings are with you and you will experience an abundance of health and a long life. This dream may also be used as a reference point in time. If you dream of this state and see its name used in any context, the dream message will occur on this day.

Oregon Trail Within three days you will have an unusual opportunity to have your goals within your grasp.

organ Within three days make sure you weigh all the pros and cons before you become involved in a certain interest of yours. You are headed for a prosperous future.

organ grinder Over the next five days do everything you can to curb your impulsive spending. If you do not control this behavior you will have many regrets in the future. Many blessings are with you and your family.

organizer *(the person)* Many blessings are with you and your family and you are entering a very prosperous cycle. Make it a point to look closely at old situations, there is much to salvage and renew. Focus on each situation and scrutinize it carefully before you reject it. You are headed for a prosperous future.

organizer *(office equipment)* Within three days you will be able to accomplish as much as you desire regarding a project you want to push ahead on. You must also motivate yourself to bring more enjoyment to your life. Many blessings will come to you and your family.

orgasm Someone will enter your life within three days who has been selected by your deity to relentlessly offer you assistance at random times over the next year. This person will constantly steer you in the direction that is most favorable to you and will, with your input, shape a path for you to achieve great things. You will achieve much prosperity in your life. Think along grander scales. Your special deity is with you.

orgy Within three days you will have, within your grasp, an unusual opportunity. This dream is an extremely lucky omen and implies that something you have secretly wished for will be manifested in your life. Expect grand changes in matters of business and love in those ways you most desire. Pay close attention to your actions to ensure you continue to go in the direction you should be going.

Orient, the This dream is a very lucky omen. You will be able to purchase a luxury item you have long desired. Anything connected with travel during this cycle will be very lucky for you also. This dream may also be used as a reference point in time. If you dream of this region and see its name used in any context, the dream message will occur on this day.

Oriental rug You will find a way to say something very difficult to another person in a way that does not offend yet will get the point across with a minimal amount of discomfort and distress. Do everything you can to keep yourself stress free. You are headed for a very bright and prosperous future.

original sin Make sure you alter or avoid any negative event you foresaw in this dream for your own sake. Determine what is really behind a certain family situation and investigate to determine the facts in order to prevent something from taking place that should not be occurring during the coming week.

oriole You have a pretty good idea of what is going on but you do need to clear up mixed messages. You will also need to budget your time carefully so you have plenty of time for those who are important to you, for yourself, and for all of your future obligations. Be sure you write everything down so you do not have conflicting schedules.

Orion *(Greek Mythology)* Within three days an invisible

block you have that hinders your progress will no longer be there and will not return. Anything negative in this dream that is connected with reality must be taken care of. Take steps to promote any positive event that could become a reality.

ornament *(personal)* Within the week, someone will enter your life who has been selected by your higher power to relentlessly assist you in any capacity over the next year and at random times to steer you in directions that are more favorable. This person will work with you to plot a path of grand proportions that will lead to prosperity in your life. Think on a large scale. You are headed for a prosperous future.

ornament *(Christmas, etc.)* Within seven days someone will enter your life to offer assistance in any area you desire for the upcoming year. This person has been chosen by your divinity and will work with you at random times to help you plan a path that will lead to great prosperity. Think in terms of grandness. You are headed for a prosperous future.

orphan You will be able to communicate directly with someone whom you have been trying to pin down for some time. You will get your point across and will have your needs met within this seven day cycle. Utilize your communication skills wisely and proceed with confidence. You will be extremely successful.

Orpheus *(Greek Mythology)* For the next three days dig deeply for the reasons you are reluctant to confront personal issues. Explore ways you can confront your behavior and you will be able to resolve all issues within this time frame.

orthodontist Behave in a more affectionate manner toward those who need your affection. Make it a point to fulfill their emotional needs. Any negative omen in this dream can be changed or avoided in reality. Make it a point to experience only positive events in your life. Many blessings are with you and your family.

Oscar Focus on your goals and push yourself to conclude a situation that will have dynamic results.

Osiris *(Egyptian God)* Within four days, you will have the opportunity to express your hidden desires to another. This will bring instant gratification and your feelings will be reciprocated. At the same time make sure everyone in your family is comfortable with your behavior. Do everything necessary to encourage bonding within the family. You are definitely headed for a brilliant future.

osprey Within two days someone will attempt to involve you in their pleasure seeking activities. Watch yourself closely and do not allow yourself to be persuaded into becoming involved in an activity that you will later regret. You will have the confidence to protect yourself appropriately. You will be entering a lucky cycle within five days.

osteomyelitis Do everything you can to spruce up your attire and do not allow yourself to get caught up in an every-day rut. Take your time doing things so everything will work out in your best interest, especially for the next two days. You must also make sure you will be physically equipped to handle what will be coming your way within this time frame. Proceed with confidence. You will be able to accomplish what is in your destiny to grasp.

osteoporosis Someone will be very excited to be in your presence and you will savor these moments. This will begin to develop within five days. You will also be entering a cycle where you will be able to quickly conclude all those things you wish to take care of. Many blessings will come to you and your family.

ostrich Within two weeks you will discover an unsuspected power in areas of your life. This will come as a surprise to you and you will soon gain awareness of the high level of authority that you possess. You will then be motivated to experiment with new and different lifestyles and different levels of social functioning. This will open your eyes and you will find yourself eager to adopt new ways of living and will experience mental and emotional gratification in your life. This power will open doors to new sources of income. Pay close attention to any negative event portrayed in this dream and take all necessary steps to avoid it.

otter Try to offer more assistance to someone who needs it in order to help them to motivate themselves and to be more willing to go forward in the direction they need to go. This will be more beneficial for both of you. Many blessings will come to you and your family.

ottoman For the next five days you will gain the advantage in certain situations by setting up conferences with those who are willing to go along with your wishes. This is also a good cycle for all of those people who are waiting for you to include them in this situation. This is a very lucky and prosperous cycle for you. Many blessings are with you.

Ottoman Empire Be alert for the next two weeks. You will have to make drastic changes if you become involved in a stressful situation. No matter how much others seek to involve you, remain detached from this issue. Seek peace, tranquility and a stress free lifestyle. Proceed with confidence.

ouch Within three days you will be treated with much love and passion from the person you desire this behavior from. You will enjoy an abundance of luck and health within this time frame. If you recognize someone from this dream, this person has a need to express their feelings to you. This is also the cycle to get things moving that you feel have stagnated. You will experience a great deal of respect, love and appreciation from others during this time period.

Ouija board This dream refers to the occult. Do not allow curiosity to take control and do not venture into the unknown. There is a thin line between curious inquiry and

active involvement and you are approaching this line. Step back; what you are being told is misleading. You need to regroup and come to grips with a situation that needs to be understood immediately in order to avoid danger. This needs to be accomplished within three days. Get plenty of rest and avoid all stressful situations. Take all negative messages and relentlessly work to change the outcome.

ounce Someone will do everything in their power to undermine you and take from you something that is righteously yours. Be very watchful during this time period but investigate closely to determine the source. This will be a very lucky cycle for you and you will be able to accomplish many things you felt were impossible before.

Our Father This dream is a reminder to reaffirm your beliefs and faith. Brilliant events will begin to happen suddenly and surely. Whatever was revealed to you in this dream must not be revealed to another person until it has been manifested in reality. Any message revealed about another person should be given to this individual so they will have the time to change any forthcoming negative event or work to enhance any future positive event. This applies to the dreamer as well. You will also receive a sense of optimism and confidence that will allow you to turn your life around. You are headed for a brilliant future. This feeling of excitement will stay with you for a long period of time and will assist you in the task of turning your life around more rapidly. Blessings will be with you and your family.

Our Father's Prayer Within seven days you will be victorious over a major illness and will recover rapidly and miraculously. You are definitely headed for a brilliant future.

Our Lady This dream is an omen of prosperity. It is also asking you to focus on treatments you need in your life to bring back a sense of normalcy and balance regarding health. Move quickly and motivate yourself to perform the necessary tasks to move ahead in life. Victory is with you. For the next seven days you will retain a sense of excitement about your future.

out *any form* For the next two weeks be very attentive to your environment. A stranger who will come into your life will seem very nice and decent but is a very dangerous individual who will seek to cause your death. They have a hidden agenda that involves a very violent sexual violation against you. You have prior notice of this and have the time to prevent it.

outboard motor Someone will come into your life within three days and surprise you because they will try in every way possible to get your attention. You will enjoy every moment of this but you must determine ahead of time whether this is something you wish to encourage. If you choose to pursue this, watch your behavior because any abruptness on your part will discourage this individual. You will have mutually enjoyable times together and close loving moments.

outbuilding Someone with a dynamic reputation will back

you up in a business deal. Good luck is with you and you are headed in the right direction.

outer space Within five days a same sexed person will lead you into a career that you will find very satisfying and will give you a solid long lasting financial base. Good luck is with you and you will enjoy an abundance of health and a long life. Any unusual event in this dream that could be connected with reality must be avoided. Make sure you only experience positive events and work to bring them to full bloom. This dream also implies that within two days someone will do everything they can to take advantage of your generosity and good intentions. Be alert to this and take steps to avoid it.

outfielder Your biggest wish will be granted within two days. Expect big changes that will change your life dramatically. Wonderful things to come into your life within the month.

outhouse Someone with a great reputation and a great deal of power will back you up in a business deal. Good luck is with you and you are headed in the right direction.

outlaw This dream implies there is a situation that needs to be put back into order and that you need to gain control of. Do this within five days, otherwise it will escalate to the point of a total loss of control over the issue. Be very alert to those situations that demand your careful personal attention. Don't allow yourself to be caught off guard.

outnumbered *to be outnumbered* Within two days make sure you begin lobbying for a connection with those people you want to steer in your direction. Relentlessly seek these people out and clearly get your point across until they are swayed to your position regarding an important upcoming situation. This will ensure everything falls into place to your advantage and for everyone else involved. Many blessings will come to you and your family and you are headed for a brilliant future.

outpost Avoid anyone who enjoys keeping others at arm's length. This person does this in order to avoid the closeness of a relationship and will destroy any attempt you make to create closeness. Go on with your life without this person.

outrage This dream refers to the occult. Do not allow curiosity to take control and do not venture into the unknown. There is a thin line between curious inquiry and active involvement and you are approaching this line. Step back, what you are being told is misleading. You need to regroup and come to grips with a situation that needs to be understood immediately in order to avoid danger. This needs to be accomplished within three days. Get plenty of rest and avoid all stressful situations. Take all negative messages and relentlessly work to change the outcome.

outrigger Make sure you do not put yourself in the position to be falsely accused of anything. Any accusation of this sort will bring a strike against your reputation. Think ahead to prevent this.

outstare *if you are the one doing this* Within seven days motivate yourself to accomplish what needs to be taken care of. You will be very successful if you choose to take advantage of this lucky cycle.

to see someone try to outstare you or someone else Someone is pursuing you simply for sexual pleasure. You know this ahead of time and can decide whether you desire this kind of relationship. You will become aware of this within three days.

oval *any form* Do not continue to run disturbing tapes that interfere with your ability to tackle big projects. You have no evidence this will not work out. Go for the big ideas and everything will work out great. You have no reason to hold yourself back. Eat well, protect your personal environment and drink plenty of water.

ovary Within three days you will need to verbalize your needs to someone you know is willing to come to your assistance. Your needs will be met immediately. You are headed for a brilliant future.

oven For the next five days become acutely aware of the need to let someone else know exactly what is going on with your life. Make a special effort to set the record straight. Sometimes it takes a while for others to fully comprehend all that is happening. Be patient and persistent until this person understands.

overalls This dream implies that someone will do everything in their power to undermine you in such a way that they can grasp what is righteously yours. Be very watchful and determine who this person is. Proceed with confidence.

overbite You will gain a position in the public eye, win many honors and be well liked by others. You will be able to accomplish what you want with those hard to tackle issues. This is a very lucky cycle for you.

overboard You will receive a surprising proposal for marriage within five days. You will accept and form a loving union in a short while. You will also need to take steps to avoid or alter any negative event foretold in this dream. Alert anyone else involved so they will be able to take the proper precautions. This is also the time you can bond more closely with those who are important to you. You will enjoy more tranquility in your life.

overcast Someone with a dynamic personality will back you up in a business plan. Good luck is with you and you are headed in the right direction.

overcoat Be very aware of what you are communicating and putting into writing. This dream also implies that all of your speculations will pay off very successfully.

overdose For the next three days make sure anything connected with this dream that could become a reality is either turned around or prevented entirely. Do everything you can to experience only positive experiences and prosperity in your life. This dream also implies that a same sexed person will extend a once in a lifetime opportunity to you. In spite of your doubts, you will be able to handle this and will be able to raise your standard of living. Anyone you recognize should also be alerted to avoid any negative event. Many blessings are with you and your family.

overeat Make it your business to add some excitement to those relationships that are important to you. An extra effort on your part will put back the excitement that has been missing for some time. You will also experience definite improvements in your business relations.

overexpose Within three days someone will try to contact you in order to work out some special business arrangements. This is a warning not to become involved because any arrangements made will not work out regardless of how things look. Otherwise, good luck is with you and you will enjoy an abundance of health. Many blessings will come to you and your family.

overflow Be aware that you are not being as affectionate and loving as you should be with a certain person. Be especially careful of this behavior for the next three days and treat those you care about in a special way.

overhand knot Within four days you will receive some news that will be difficult for you to comprehend. Don't even try, most of it is untrue. Get on with your life and do what you can to avoid getting upset over this.

overhaul You will find a way to say something to someone that is very difficult for you to say. You will be able to get your point across with a minimal amount of stress and emotional disturbance.

overhead Be aware that actions and deeds mean far more than words, especially for the next two days.

overhead projector Someone will be so much happier with your attitude toward them that they will keep the knowledge of this change to themselves in order to keep it the same. Proceed with confidence and things will work out exactly as you have envisioned.

overnight Within four days any professional service you seek will result in a successful outcome. Good luck is with you for the next seven days.

overpower This dream is a very lucky symbol. A long standing problem will be resolved within three days. You are headed for a very prosperous future.

to be overpowered Make sure that whatever you want to accomplish within three days is accomplished even if you have to take aggressive measures. This may involve late nights, deep investigative work and good communication

skills to ensure success.

to overpower someone Within three days any situation that requires detailed negotiations will have a successful result.

overpriced Show affection to someone who doubts your feelings for them.

overprotective Within five days, do everything necessary to get all the kinks out of the plans you are involved in. You will enjoy a successful outcome.

overseas You will be traveling for business purposes within five days. Make sure you take the wisest route especially if the weather is bad. Carefully think over your travel arrangements to ensure a safe and comfortable trip.

overseer Within two days verbalize your needs to someone else. This individual will be able to direct you to the proper places to get what you need.

oversexed Love yourself and do everything necessary to bring more joy into your life. Incorporate a variety of new experiences into your routine. Be kind to yourself and do things that are soothing. Drink plenty of water and eat healthy healing foods. You will also be very happy with the performance of someone from whom you have requested assistance. This person has the ability to make clear decisions and to execute them efficiently. You will work well together and experience many joyful moments until the task has been completed.

oversleep Do not allow violence to erupt within the next four days. You will be discussing a situation with someone who is too stubborn to bend. You have prior notice of this and can avoid becoming involved with a stubborn person. Don't waste your time over this.

overspend You will enjoy an abundance of health and many blessings will come to you and your family. You are also completely unaware of someone's infatuation with you but you will become aware of this within three days. This will become a thrilling cycle for you if you so desire. It will also develop into a mutually loving, sensual union. If this is something you desire, move quickly.

overtime Your urge for a sexual encounter with a certain person will be realized within a three day period. Move quickly on this and set up the perfect romantic environment.

overture You will receive a positive answer to what you felt would be a negative response. Good luck is with you and you are headed for a brilliant future.

overweight You need to be keenly aware of what you eat and drink in order to avoid allergies, toxic reactions and food poisonings.

overwork Within two days you will find assistance with an ongoing situation that you feel at the moment is almost impossible to turn around. This dream also implies that within four days someone you have been wanting to see will surrender to you and grant you your wishes.

ovulate Be realistic about a particular friendship. Someone is pretending to be your friend but at the first opportunity they will do everything they can to undermine you in some capacity. Be cautious and go on with your life without this person in it. Otherwise, this is a very lucky seven day cycle and you will be triumphant in those hard to tackle situations.

owe *to owe* You can be very optimistic about a particular situation you are working with, for the next three days. This will involve money that is owed to you. You are well loved and are in a very lucky cycle. Be very realistic about a friendship. Someone is feigning friendship but will, at the first opportunity, undermine you in some way. Take precautions and go on with your life without this person. You are headed for a bright future.

owl Be alert to the fact that you will be abandoned without notice by someone you are emotionally attached to. This person has difficulty committing to a relationship on the level you desire. You can prevent this future occurrence by restraining your emotions. Take steps now to avoid this hurt a month from now. This relationship is workable if you do not allow your emotions to gain the upper hand.

owl hooting Within seven days someone you have a great deal of respect and high regards for will die. You must also make sure your pets are safe from disease and accident.

quiet owl Become acutely aware that an individual, whom you least expect to cause problems, will want to inflict emotional harm on you for personal reasons. This will be done in a very subtle and conniving way. Intensify your efforts to guard your reputation and make sure your words are understood and reported accurately. Protect anything that is emotionally precious to you from this individual who merely seeks a sick self gratification. This is likely to occur within three days.

ox You need to be determined for the next three days to help someone, especially an elderly person, to have their needs met. Take steps to brighten this person's life by bringing to them some kind of entertainment. Let this individual know they are well loved and appreciated. This will mean more to them than you can ever imagine. Many blessings will come to you and your family.

oxford *(shoe)* Within three days you will rejoice over the development of a romantic relationship. Good luck is with you and you are headed for a prosperous future.

Oxford University Within three days you will find someone who will be able to successfully assist you with a situation you feel is almost impossible to turn around. Proceed with confidence. This dream also implies that all your projects will be met with success.

oxtail Within three days you will find that the person you

want to join you as a co-worker in a joint venture will be very eager to do so. This will be a very successful union. Take steps to ensure this turns out exactly as you have envisioned. Good luck is with you.

oxygen Good luck is with you and you should do everything you can to prevent any negative occurrence you see in this dream from becoming a reality, especially for the next three days. Take steps to warn anyone you recognize in this dream to take all the necessary precautions as well. Do not place yourself in the position within this time period to allow someone to treat you in an uncivil and indecent manner. Many blessings are with you and your family.

oyster Proceed with confidence. Your ideas, plans and projects will all be met with success. Others will relentlessly help you achieve the goal you are after.

oyster bed You are unaware of the cunning and deceitful manner of a certain individual. This individual is relentlessly pursuing a path to put you in the worst possible scenario. Take precautions when dealing with other people, especially for the next three days. Do what you can to keep this person out of your life. This dream also implies that within seven days an opportunity will be presented to you through someone else. Because of this person, you will be able to put yourself on the path of prosperity. Look for unusual and outrageous situations. These are the ones that will lead to success. Many blessings will come to you and your family.

oyster cracker You will be dealing with a person who leads a double life. This individual is concealing a very dangerous character trait. For the next five days be very aware of the behavior of other people in order to pinpoint something the law may need to know about. Do not become involved directly with this person but do what you can to make sure they are dealt with by the proper authorities. Many blessings are with you and your family.

Oysters Rockefeller Someone will take you into their confidence regarding a distasteful situation to see if your advice will ease their concerns. You will be able to offer fresh ideas so this person can see a different perspective. This approach will enable them to get on with their life as a fully functional person and it will benefit you in the long run. This dream also implies you will come into a financial windfall within three days. Play games of chance at low risk with heavy benefits.

oyster stew This dream is a very lucky omen for you. Be very aware for the next three days when a stranger unexpectedly enters your life in a public setting. This person will create a very stressful situation for everyone involved. This will lead to quarrels and disagreements. Be very cautious and remain uninvolved.

oyster white This dream is an omen of health and tranquility. You will also receive an exciting gift within three days.

Ozark Mountains You will enjoy abundance and plenty in those areas of your life you desire. Anything connected with travel will also bring you luck. Many blessings are with you and your family. This dream may also be used as a reference point in time. If you dream of this mountain range and see its name used in any context, the dream message will occur on this day.

ozone Someone is eager to know you better on a friendly basis. You can also expect an increase in wealth.

P

P A group of people in authority will meet within a few days to nominate you to a high position. This will change your life for the better and you will enjoy a fabulous lifestyle.

pablum Within five days, you will communicate with someone who needs to know quite a bit about you. It is up to you whether you wish to divulge your personal affairs.

pacemaker It may be suggested to you that you need a certain product that will be introduced to you. Get a second opinion. You must also make an effort to keep the decisions you make about a particular person free from the interference of others. Carefully analyze your thoughts and do not allow others to dictate your choices and selections or manipulate you. Only put those wishes you know will be respected and carried out by others in written form. You will appoint someone you fully trust to carry out your wishes in a respectful manner. You will get a quick response to this and are headed for a brilliant future.

Pacific Any project involving silk screen printing and the printing of any fabric may be a profitable enterprise for you.

Pacific Islands Within three days you will become aware of someone's deep feelings for you. This person will verbalize these feelings in the perfect setting, at the perfect time. You will be very excited when you hear these words spoken. This dream may also be used as a reference point in time. If you dream of this island group and see its name used in any context, the dream message will occur on this day.

Pacific standard time Concern yourself deeply about money that someone is requesting from you. This will allow you to avoid grief at a later time.

pacifier You will meet someone you are romantically interested in. This person will attempt to pacify you by corresponding over the phone or through the mail. This is the closest this person will come to you. Move on with your life.

pacifist Within three days it is very likely that goods will spoil, there will be crop losses, and an illness will threaten the health of a child. It is within your power to keep those events from taking place.

pack Make sure the buck stops with you in matters involving children. Do not pass responsibility on to someone else.
pack of cans (six-pack) Do not overextend yourself. Budget your time and be considerate to yourself.
backpack Take care of yourself and do not ignore your health. At the first sign of trouble, take the necessary steps to avoid loss of time at work.
pack of cigarettes An opportunity you are excited about and have been long awaiting will present itself. You now have the means to grasp it. You will have a new start in all areas of your life where you desire changes and all old burdens and issues that have been plaguing you will come to an immediate halt. Drastic changes will occur that will leave you with a new exciting zest for life.

package An unexpected surprise event will occur. You will also receive many gifts.

packages *frozen that starts to thaw* You will be entering a cycle for the next two days that will find you having difficulty receiving services in a fully satisfactory manner. Specify, in writing, exactly what your needs are. This will ensure satisfaction on your part. If anything negative was depicted in this dream, take steps to change it or avoid it entirely.

package store You will want to purchase a particular item. Ask a friend who works at a store that sells this item to buy it for you at a bargain price.

packer A strange occurrence will happen to someone you are close to. Warn this person about this in advance. If you don't, this event will be discussed in negative terms by others for several days.

packinghouse You will be in the position of handling money that belongs to other people. Your versatility and the way you diversify money into different accounts to generate a profit will be noticed by those in authority.

pack rat Do not be so jealous of others. This behavior will backfire.

packsaddle You will be asked to arbitrate between two people because your opinion is highly respected. This will result in a successful outcome.

pact You will quickly respond to a tip from a reliable source and will shortly acquire property.

paddie Children expect kindness. Show your best side.

padding You will be selected to be the beneficiary of a settlement.

paddle Someone who normally has a good disposition will be irritable and nasty for a few days. At the first hint of this, avoid this person until their former pleasant demeanor is restored.

paddlefish Within a three day period you will develop a network of people who will support you, offer you their assistance, and brainstorm with you in order to seek a solution to a particular situation and issue that needs to be taken care of within the week. This will result in a successful conclusion.

paddle wheel New plans require careful and special handling.

padlock You will purchase a long desired item with someone else's money.

padlock falling apart Someone is attempting to murder you. Do everything necessary to prevent this occurrence. You will also face financial devastation if you do not take steps to prevent it.

padré All out of town shows held for the purpose of displaying goods will have a favorable outcome. They will be successful almost to the point of contagion.

pads Within three days you will work out a plan that will enable you to put aside money for a wonderful vacation if this is something you desire. You will enjoy yourself immensely.

pagan You will overcome physical pain and mental anguish. These problems will disappear overnight.

page Someone who has consistently turned down your request for help will have a change of heart and offer assistance to ensure the accomplishment of your project. Listen to others and give subtle encouragement where needed. Within two days, someone will also call you in an effort to rekindle closeness. Because of your busy schedules, you have both ignored this effort in the past.

torn page Control your temper around those who are important to you, especially for the next five days.

soiled page Do not assume a certain situation will automatically turn to your advantage. Make an effort to assure this will take place, especially for the next three days.

ripped page Do not confuse love with financial interests.

balled up page Travel will be financially lucrative.

folded page Promptly ask for help to correct a wrong committed against you.

pageant Be willing to take a few risks in order to enter into new relationship agreements. This will ensure emotional satisfaction for both of you as well as greater simplicity and happiness for the future.

page boy Control yourself for the next two days and don't allow your moodiness to control you behavior. Avoid all impulsiveness.

pager Any message heard over a pager will come to pass within two days. Pay attention, you are being alerted. If the voice is recognizable, this implies that the owner of the voice misses you and has been losing sleep in their desire to communicate with you. You will also be invited to a daytime outing that will bring you a great deal of pleasure within three days.

pagoda Be careful when handling finances and drawing up a budget. A mistake will take years to correct.

paid *to be paid* For the next seven days it is essential that you devote your time to positioning yourself in such a way that you can create excitement and generate a greater interest regarding a new situation. You will be able to segment more success about a new product, plan, idea or conversation. You will gain excellent feedback that will bring about more productivity and more fun. You will also create a non stressful outcome to what is a priority to you now. You will be able to bring everyone involved together in building a common understanding. You will determine what, where, and how to effectively achieve a chief victory on a grander scale than you anticipated. Your goal is to make the world aware of these exciting ideas, etc., and will find they are well received by others.

pail *empty* A domestic problem will create stress. Prior knowledge of this will give you the chance to stay calm and create a favorable outcome.

to carry a full pail with sloshing liquid Do not rely on someone who has repeatedly promised help. This person is insincere and will disappoint you. Make alternative plans.

full pail You will meet someone special through a third party.

filled with milk Someone will declare deep love for you and will commit to a relationship.

pain *to see others in pain* You are preparing to tell something to someone in confidence. Postpone this. You will later regret this action.

to be in pain Spend money only on yourself.

painkiller Help someone special to develop a sense of security. It will be reciprocal.

paint/painter Others will receive you with open arms. They feel you have a dynamite reputation and you will get the backing and support you are seeking. You will find that others are eager to work with you on your current enterprise. Greater success will be yours. You will also profit in a variety of ways and see the payoff for work performed in the past. This is a fortunate omen.

to paint You will relocate to a new residence. Pay close attention to what is being painted and look up the meaning of the object or color painted for more clarity to the message. You are headed for a brilliant future. Within five days you will also be granted the gift of greater healing and heightened psychic powers by your higher power. You will be able to develop greater organizational skills and will be able to use this talent in a dynamic way. This gift will be wisely used by you and many blessings will follow you for the rest of your life. You are headed for a brilliant future.

to see paint mixed You will be asked to join a desirable club and will enjoy yourself immensely.

to see a painter at work You and someone special to you will enjoy a long and healthy sex life. You will go through changes with this person and will adopt new ways of relating that will result in an improvement in your sex life. You must also make a point of looking up what was being painted for a more detailed description of this dream.

to hire a painter A friend who lives in a distant place will offer you an all expense paid vacation. You will have a fantastic time and enjoy a safe return.

war paint Someone interested in you will go to great pains to make sure all your needs are taken care of, as well as the finer things in life, with no strings attached. If you choose, this relationship will develop as you wish, especially for the next two weeks. Many blessings are with you and you are headed for a prosperous future.

paintbrush Do everything you can to bring more fun and amusement to your life and take steps to create a stress free environment. Do not overload yourself with the problems of others. Remain free of the demands and responsibilities of other people and do not create any extra burdens and responsibilities for yourself. Take a small restful vacation. Read, listen to music, eat healthful foods and be good to yourself.

painting *oil painting* For the next four days take steps to keep any negative event that was depicted in this painting from becoming a reality. Make sure you promote any positive event. You must also do what you can to display your talents and showcase your skills. Within this four day period you will connect with someone who has all the right resources to put you on the path of success.

watercolor painting Pay attention to what was depicted in this painting. You will be given a clue to something you will either need to pursue or an event or opportunity that needs to be investigated. You will find this will enhance your life and give you a distinct advantage in the direction you are going. You must also make sure anything negative you saw in this dream that could become a reality is avoided or altered and take steps to ensure you only experience positive expressions in your life. This dream also implies that this is the perfect three day cycle to carefully evaluate the choices you will have to make. You will be able to take the thoughts you have been developing and devise ways to generate more income than you ever anticipated. As a result, you will gain respect and prestige from your endeavors. Your motivation will rapidly bring this about and you will be placed in a large scale position of authority at a low salary. This position will grow in importance and prestige along with a large salary as the result. Expect this to occur soon.

pair *of anything* This dream is a lucky omen. You will hear about the reconciliation of a couple you are friends with.

paisley When you see difficulties start to escalate between two men, leave the scene. Expect this to occur within a few days.

pajamas You will save money by researching the item you plan to purchase. You will have a memorable time at an outing with someone you care a great deal about.

Pakistan Within three days a situation that requires assistance from another will work out well. You will choose the right person to work with. This dream may also be used as a reference point in time. If you dream of this country and see its name used in any context, the dream message will occur on this day.

palace This dream is a promise of grand and wonderful changes in your life.

burning palace This dream indicates a pending divorce.

palette In a few weeks, you will go through a period of greater popularity and financial well being, as well as better able to enjoy life. This time period will be calm and you will feel very fortunate. Look up the colors on the palette for additional clues. Do not let a mechanical problem tie you up unnecessarily.

paleontology Someone who has been cold and distant in the past will unexpectedly welcome you with open arms. Do not allow yourself to be resentful of past actions against you. This person is serious in their attempt to reconcile.

palette knife Within a few days, you will plan an all-expense paid vacation. This trip will be short but you will gain a feeling of happiness and warmth. Luck is with you.

pallbearer You will be required to curb your attitudes and behaviors for the next two days. Watch for this.

palm *clean palms* Success in your career will depend on consistency and research.

dirty palms If you promise to call someone, make sure that you do.

to hurt Your home may be dangerous for children. Install safety devices.

abnormality on another's palm Someone has done everything they could to pay a debt back to you in a timely fashion. Because of unexpected circumstances, this will be impossible and this person will ask for your patience. Grant this request and everything will work out well for you.

an unusual touch on the palms by you or another person You will be spending a great deal of time devising a way to communicate the deep feelings you have for someone special. It seems impossible to reach this person in the manner you wish. This person also has difficulty verbalizing their feelings. Express your feelings in written form and you will receive a prompt and positive response.

dark marking on inside of palm This dream implies that

someone who is very dear to you will pass away. This death will be as a result of suicide. This will occur within five days unless you actively motivate yourself to seek a way to prevent this process. This individual will not give any indication they are planning this but by careful investigation you will get a sense of who they are and can take steps to prevent this tragedy. Anything negative connected with your own palm or with the palm of someone else you recognize can be prevented in reality.

in any other form You will enjoy victory within seven days in spite of present appearances. This dream also implies that you will spend time analyzing the transition of a friendship with someone special to something much deeper. You will enjoy this development and both of you will delight in extra time spent together.

palm *(tree)* You and your family will experience abundances in life. An ill relative will also recover.

palmetto For the next few days do not allow anyone else's problems to upset you or another person's mood to spill over on you.

palmistry *to have your palm read* Pay close attention to the words spoken to you. Each negative message may be altered and each positive message may be embraced. Certain aspects of your life must also be regarded in the most private way. Guard your privacy, especially for the next five days.

to read someone's palm Seek a reading in real life. You will also need to focus on the issues that have priority now and be sure to lend your personal touch in order to avoid anything that will create an imbalance in your life. Do this within five days.

in any other form Within five days, you will have an irresponsible impulse to prod someone to open up and communicate with you. Don't lose courage. Force yourself to move ahead on this. You will be successful.

palm leaves An abundance of health, spiritual healing, and tranquility will come your way within a three week period. A celebration will occur within the week that will cause everyone involved to rejoice. During the last two weeks of March and for the entire month of April, a particular idea, project or event you have been working on is destined for a successful completion and will rise to a grander scale than you ever thought possible. It will take on a life of its own and you will be able to easily take this through any channel in order to get through this process. This will be a blessing to you and everyone involved in this process and will be cause for a great celebration. You are headed for a brilliant future.

Palm Sunday Be more open to business proposals and converse more with those of different ethnic groups. Your willingness to help will be much appreciated.

palomino Aim for higher goals. You will accomplish more and have more success.

pampas grass Be sensitive to the health problems of someone who is special to you.

pamphlet Display your charisma, proper upbringing and education. You will be admired by influential people within five days. Do not allow timidity to hold you back.

pan Do not pick up the tab or be talked into spending more than you intend.

hot pan You will have the perfect opportunity to get a second chance at a certain situation. Go for it and you will find that things will turn out exactly as you had envisioned. Good luck is with you. Make sure you bring any positive message in this dream to full bloom and make sure you keep any negative message from becoming a reality.

frying For the next three days, avoid settling for less. You are thinking of leaving a situation. Rethink this decision, you will not be better off and will be heading in the wrong direction.

Pan *(Greek mythology)* Do not allow yourself to stagnate to the point of allowing those who are close to you to outgrow you.

Panama Ocean cruises will be fortunate for you now. It would also be a good idea to take dance lessons at this time. You are well on your way toward developing plans for your independence. This cycle offers you the chance to build confidence, heal physically, and make improvements in your financial situations. You are making all the right moves to ensure a bright future. This is a prosperous cycle for you and you will be able to turn those situations around that require improvements. Many blessings are with you and your family and all requests made to your god will be granted. This dream may also be used as a reference point in time. If you dream of this country and see its name used in any context, the dream message will occur on this day.

Panama Canal Communicate your desire for another person, to that person. You will be happy that you did. This dream may also be used as a reference point in time. If you dream of this place and see its name used in any context, the dream message will occur on this day.

Panama hat This is lucky omen. You will receive recognition and money for work well done.

pancakes You will feel a deep mutual love for another person.

flipped pancake You will enjoy passionate physical love for another. If you choose to pursue this, it will occur very quickly.

pancreas Do not take risks regarding any new venture.

panda Do not give others the false impression that you are interested in them.

Pandora *(Greek mythology)* Carry yourself in such a way that you appear younger than you feel. This will give others a positive impression of you. Anything negative portended in this dream needs to be altered and make sure you experience only positive expressions in your life.

pane *to see a reflection of another's face in a window pane instead of your own* Look ahead, someone will write a check to you and there will be insufficient funds to cover it.

to see your reflection in a window pane Within a two week period you will rapidly advance to a higher plane in life than you ever imagined. You will enjoy an increase in productivity, income, productive conversations, and more affection and loyalty from others. Other people will express their desire to be a part of your plans. You are headed for a brilliant future and will enjoy an abundance of health. All of this will occur in a shorter period of time than you ever anticipated.

cracked pane A close relative will become unemployed.

broken pane Empower yourself ahead of time by putting everything important into writing.

window pane/shield You are on the right path and are headed for a brilliant future. You are also promised wealth in the near future.

panel Prepare yourself. For two days you will be around someone who is in an irritable mood. Ignore this, you will have to be involved with this person but do not have to become emotionally involved with their behavior.

paneling Someone new will enter your life with the same bad habits as someone you knew previously. These habits caused you great emotional pain. At the first hint of trouble, back off. This person will involve you in the same kind of game playing.

panel truck Within a three day period, someone you know will be very eager to share good news about an upcoming event. You will enjoy many days of harmony and tranquility.

panhandle You will fail at the first attempt to deal with a particular situation. Regroup, try again and you will succeed.

panic attack *acute* For the next two weeks be extremely aware of what will be unfolding in your life. Think very carefully and clearly about the way you are stepping into a subtle lifestyle change that is being created by someone else or by yourself. This lifestyle seems to be developing on its own with no control from you. Be very alert to this and take steps to gain control over your life and eliminate the stresses that will be placed on you. You have to be more aware of what is developing and remain alert, especially for the next month. Steer yourself around disguised demands that will feel, at the time they are being made, not as demanding as they will be. The responsibility you assume will put a tremendous amount of strain and pressure on you. You will find it a very tedious chore to meet everyone's demands and needs. At the time this is going on you will have no concept

of the pressure you are under and will be doing this as a matter of routine because you want everything to run smoothly and easily. You will not have the time to think about any of this while it is going on. You will finally reach a point of being overextended and become emotionally and physically fragile but will continue to proceed in the same fashion. The more you give of yourself, the more others will take. You will reach the point of not having anyone to talk to about this pressure, and will not have anyone to turn to for help to relieve this stress. You will begin to find this subtly destructive lifestyle intolerable. You need to take steps to stop what you are doing before it becomes a problem so you do not find yourself in this situation eight months from now. This lifestyle may lead to illness and it will take you a long time to recover from it. Seclude yourself from these demands at this time in order to refocus, have time to think, develop a creative idea, and bring it to tangible form. This idea will leave a mark on the world and you are destined to bring it about. Do not allow anyone to pry into your affairs or to question your reasons for this sabbatical. Steer yourself away from the subtle demands of others and their projects for at least eight months. Make sure you limit all stress and keep your life simple. If you allow yourself to get to this point, use all the support systems (i.e., crises lines, support groups, self help groups, hot lines, self help books, etc.) you have at your disposal as well as any professional help you may need. Make sure you eat properly and get plenty of rest. Think defensively (i.e., comedy club, comedy videos, etc.) in order to create the perfect lifestyle for yourself. Do not be so restrictive with your inner child. Let your creative thoughts flow and support your ideas. You will put yourself on the perfect path for a brilliant future.

pansy In a few days, you and your loved one will have a fantastic time together.

panther Do not allow others to emotionally devour you. You will be fraudulently taken in by someone in an everyday situation (i.e., phone fraud).

panties This is a good time to make any decision that is out of the ordinary.

silk panties Aim for higher education.

cotton Do not sell yourself short and you will achieve what is important to you.

soiled panties Pay attention to what is not being said. This will be your clue to success.

pantomime You will be asked to attend a reunion with several friends. You will attend a comedy event and enjoy shared laughter and good times.

pantry You will find success by working with foods.

pants *wool* Use your creativity to give and receive more love. Look up the color of the pants for greater meaning to this dream.

cotton denim (Levis) You are heading in the right direction and will have a brilliant future. This dream implies grandness. The particular color of the Levis will provide more information to the meaning of this dream.

all other pants The position you have long desired will go to another person. This person will, however, move out of state and the position will then be yours. Do not despair.

to soil Do not overindulge in alcohol, you will regret it for the next two days.

pantsuit *beautiful pantsuit* Think ahead to your next move. Have an overdue conversation with a potential colleague to gather different approaches to a problem. This conversation will single out those people who should be working with you based on how they respond to new ideas. Do this within seven days.

pantyhose Your initiative in handling personal matters will win the trust of someone you are eager to win over.

papa *to hear this phrase* You are loved beyond your imagination.

papal cross *any form* This dream is giving you a warning that you need to pay close attention to for the next three days. A certain situation will begin to spiral downhill if it is not taken care of. Do everything you can to head off a negative event that will put you on the wrong path. Listen to your hunches and they will alert you to certain people that you do not need to associate with. Be aware that other people may attempt to do you harm in a subtle and conniving way at any time that you leave yourself unguarded. Take steps to protect yourself and everything that is precious to you. You have prior notice of this and will be able to handle this situation appropriately.

papaya You will receive a romantic tip from a friend that will lead to many successful romantic days.

paper You will hire an assistant to help complete a project. This person will be eager to help and the project will be successful.

balled up papers Listen carefully to friends in order to avoid misunderstandings for the next three days.

folded papers or neatly stacked papers For the next three weeks use your creativity to head off problems caused by another's irresponsibility and mishandling of a situation.

burned paper Keep a healthy state of mind and avoid unpleasant conversation. Shield yourself from an emotional breakdown that will be a result of this, especially for the next four days.

balled up newspaper Someone will not be what they have projected themselves to be. You will be very disappointed by this.

slip of paper Take the necessary time to look at the whole picture when an issue arises within three days. This will give you the time to understand clearly what is going on and allow you to make the way you live your life the single most important issue right now. Proceed with confidence.

You are on the path toward a very prosperous future.

to serve someone with papers You will feel very insecure about your relations with others. Within two days you will gain the evidence you need to validate the feelings of love others have for you.

to be served with papers The papers you are being served will provide a major clue to something you may want to avoid in the future. If it is a positive legal writ, such as a deed or will, promote this action in reality. This time period is also a good cycle for you romantically. Things will quickly move forward for you.

writing paper It is very important that you attend a specific function because it will be very glamorous and exciting for you. Be sure to prepare for this ahead of time because it will require formal attire and you will want to look your best. You will meet many influential people who will become friends for life and you will enjoy yourself tremendously. You will also become very aware that the person you most desire feels the same way about you during this time period. You will both develop many affectionate feelings toward each other and you will be very excited about this new development. You are on the path for a prosperous and brilliant future.

paperback In a short time, your desire to become committed in a relationship will deepen. This desire will be realized and the relationship will last a lifetime.

paper bag This dream is a very lucky omen. You should also take steps to improve your appearance.

paperboy Put your thoughts into writing so they will be clearly understood by others.

paperclip For the next few days, do nothing questionable regarding money.

paperhanger Within five days, motivate yourself to force an opportunity to open up for you. You will create opportunities that will change your life tremendously and add excitement to your life. Be sure to eat healing foods and treat yourself to something special. Many blessings will come to you and you are entering a very lucky cycle. You will also need to rely on your intuition because this will lead you to the path you need to take. You are loved beyond your imagination. You will also learn of missing paperwork that is imperative for you to sign. Do not panic, this paperwork will turn up.

paper tiger Within three days a member of your family will open up to you and bring you into their confidence. This person needs your support, patience and a listening ear. Everything will work out well for this individual.

paperweight A direct approach concerning an impending deadline will relieve anxiety and you will be glad you gave the project your personal touch.

paperwork A partnership formulated with the person you have in mind will spell disaster. Find an alternative.

Papier-mâché You have many different, conflicting opinions and are unsure which one to act on. In reality, each one will work successfully.

papoose Within a few days a financial emergency will occur. Be alert for this and do what you can to resolve it.

paprika Take a nice bubble bath, treat yourself and make every effort to be kind to yourself. Drink plenty of water and maintain your health.

pap test Be prepared. Someone you plan to meet will be in a terrible mood. As a result of their particular mood, you will suffer. This person will do something inconsiderate or will be insensitive to your needs and you will pay the price, either financially, physically or emotionally. Expect this to occur within three days. Anything in this dream that portrays a negative event and could become a reality needs to be avoided at all costs. Make sure you experience only positive expressions in your life.

papyrus Prepare yourself for a trip you will have to make for personal business reasons. It will be very successful.

parachute You will be mesmerized by an eccentric and this will lead to a very successful relationship.

parade Give a raise in salary to the person who deserves it. You will also be taking huge steps to raise your standard of living. This will be accomplished by focusing on your goals in a grand way. Expect this to come about within three days due to some unusual and joyful circumstance. Everyone involved in this will enjoy beautiful expressions of joy and tranquility. Many blessings will be with you and your family.

paradise Cosmetic surgery will be very successful for you. You will look wonderful.

paraffin This is a fortunate dream for games of chance.

parakeet Let the love you feel for someone be seen by others.

parallel Go for the big ideas and do not allow others to stop you.

parallel bars Within three days make sure you do not overlook something of importance. You will also receive verification of the deep feelings a certain person has for you during this time period. This dream is an extremely lucky omen for you.

paralysis Get the medical help you need to regain your health. Do everything you can to prevent any accidental injury.

paralysis, sleep *the feeling of being unable to move when trying to awaken* For the next seven days you need to be very attentive and acutely aware of certain events that will begin to unfold and will have a serious and damaging affect on your future. These events will destine you to alter your life and point yourself in the wrong direction. You must become more assertive and muster up the courage and confidence to take the necessary steps to protect yourself from this situation. Watch the words you use when speaking to others because your words may be used as leverage against you. Be observant of what is unfolding that will have a serious effect on your future. This will occur because of any of the following situations or a combination of the following situations:

- The influence that someone will have over you.
- Interference from someone who will steer you in the wrong direction.
- The control that someone in power will exert over you.
- The leverage that someone will gain by using your words to put you at a disadvantage.
- Someone who is in a position of authority will make decisions for you.

Do not allow yourself to become vulnerable by not acting on your own behalf. You will suffer emotional depletion as a result and will be guided in a direction you have no desire to go. Prod yourself to get your point across to those in authority and make it a point to avoid everyday stresses caused by the decisions others make for you who have no business being involved. You are in danger of surrendering your control. Avoid unhealthy situations and circumstances and remain suspicious of all changes. Become confident and relentless in correcting those areas of your life that require corrections. You will then be able to put yourself on the right path. You have the power to change any negative aspect of this dream as well as changing your life to encourage positive expressions. Make sure that all of your bases are safely covered. Practice common sense and your plans will be successfully carried out. You will place yourself on the path of prosperity.

to be unable to move your body for a short time because of some unusual occurrence Your spirit wants you to see what is in front of you and make sure you do not overlook anything. Take steps to ensure you are not being narrow-minded about something you are about to involve yourself in. Make sure you get more than one perspective about this issue. Create several alternative ways to deal with this situation. Do not make excuses that will keep you from motivating yourself into moving forward. You will accomplish anything you need to at this particular time by being flexible and looking at things from a different angle. This attitude will offer you many alternatives to deal with this situation. Anything in this dream that was displayed while you were in this particular stage is a major clue to what else you need to be doing in your life. If it was negative, take steps to prevent it in reality. If positive, make sure you take steps to promote it. You will be putting yourself in the position for a brilliant future.

paramedic Do not allow yourself to become caught up in the glitter and excitement of romance without carefully thinking this through. Allow love to grow at a slow pace and you will enjoy greater success. Do not chase someone away by moving too quickly, especially for the next three days.

paranoia Take classes in sensitivity training in order to change impolite, rude behavior.

paraplegic *if you are a paraplegic* Stop being so strict with yourself. Loosen up your rigid schedule for your own health.

to help Within a few days you will learn that a relative in a distant place has left you a large inheritance. You will be shocked and surprised that you even had this relative.

parapsychologist Be very cautious. You are beginning to adopt a destructive pattern of thinking that could lead to physical ailments that have no organic basis. In spite of the number of physicians you consult, you will be told nothing is wrong. Become disciplined and diligent now and take steps to keep this from occurring. Act quickly to change your thought patterns and mental attitude. Start treating your body with the respect it deserves. Increase your exercise to a comfortable level that is enjoyable and soothing to you. Make necessary lifestyle changes, alter your diet and eat healthful foods. Reschedule your life in such a way that will lessen the physical demands on your body and add soothing enjoyment to your life. You must also remove yourself from anyone whom you feel uncomfortable around that adds extra stress to your life. You will enjoy a healthier lifestyle by practicing this regimen. Take precautions to avoid or to change the outcome of any negative event in this dream and keep it from becoming a reality. Do everything you can to enjoy only pleasant experiences in your life. You are headed for a prosperous future and many blessings will come to you and your family.

parasite You will be working with a group of people who want control over the project you are handling. One person will want to take credit for work you have done. Do not panic, put everything in writing in order to keep everything straight.

parasol Surprisingly, an influential person will eagerly do paperwork for you to ensure your success in a business purchasing deal.

paratrooper Avoid domestic friction with a loved one. Set aside some time from your busy and rewarding life for some private time with your mate.

parcel You will be in the company of a very sensitive person who embarrasses easily. Remain aware of this person's needs.

parcel post Prepare ahead to avoid the embarrassment of running short of cash while making a purchase.

Parcheesi Take steps to prevent damage to the garments you are planning to wear, especially for the next three days.

parchment You and your staff will seek and reach a mutual agreement.

parent Within a few days you will receive long hoped for news. This news will regard an increase in income that will free you from financial problems and allow you to indulge in the finer things in life. Your relatives will also be lucky for the next few days.

pariah For the next two days, carefully think over any sudden urges you may get and make it a point to write them down. At a later time, these thoughts will be of a great benefit to you and will offer you a different viewpoint of life. Many blessings will come to you and your family.

Paris This is a fortunate time for all investments and speculations. This dream may also be used as a reference point in time. If you dream of this city and see its name used in any context, the dream message will occur on this day.

parish For the next two days don't believe everything someone tells you. Be aware that when you are hearing an outrageous story you are being lied to. You must also think ahead. For a long period of time someone has made demands on you and your time. This person will leave for a trip and you will get the impression that they are returning but this is not the case. You will have no way of locating them. After a few weeks you will miss this person deeply. Before this individual leaves, let your true feelings be known. This person has always felt like a burden to you and you need to change this.

park In order to go far, project an interesting image and carry yourself well. An influential person will notice you and make a decision that will help you reach your goals. This will be an interesting time for you.

with beautiful lawns For the next few days you will be immersed in feelings of love. You will have a glow in your eyes, prompted by an unplanned, spur of the moment, sexual encounter with a certain person. This satisfactory sensual feeling will create an aura of passion that will last a long time for both of you. You are headed toward a brilliant future of sexual pleasure with this person.

in seasonal transition For the next seven days leave yourself open for a destined golden opportunity that will be coming your way. It is important that you are in the right place at the right time to receive this fortunate chance. This cycle will prepare you to receive great wealth.

amusement park Find a quiet spot to allow yourself to release stress. You will also receive a wonderful invitation from someone you have always admired and you will have an awesome time.

park *to see a luxurious car parked* You will achieve a long desired goal within three days because of the willingness of another person to help. Be alert to this opportunity. You are also in a very good position to demand from your higher power what you want. Be specific and direct about your needs. For a three week period you will be developing a list of priorities that will serve as an aid to supervising the manner in which you live your life. Take some time to reflect in peace and tranquility. Your project will be moving ahead rapidly and will bring profitable results.

to have difficulty parking a car An unexpected distasteful event will occur to you and your beloved. You have prior warning of this and have the time to prevent any strange event from taking place.

to have an easy time parking a car Victory is yours. A target group will support you on a specific endeavor.

to see your car parked You can accomplish much by projecting an interesting image of yourself around an influential person. This person will be connected to a project you are presently working on and will also influence your life. You will enjoy working on this project. Maintain an interesting demeanor to ensure continued interest from this person.

parka The person you are interested in will show you a great deal of affection once you make the first move.

parking attendant You are entering a cycle of peace and tranquility and you will do only what you want to do. Good luck is with you.

parking garage Do not allow yourself to be jerked around or others to take advantage of your generosity. Conserve your energy for the next two days and make sure it is channeled in the right direction.

parking lot Within a few days, you will be dealing with someone who enjoys twisting around facts to make it appear as though they are in a stressful situation. This person enjoys having you run to them to offer assistance. Do everything necessary to avoid this extra stress. Do not become entangled in this person's affairs.

parking meter This dream is a warning to you. Someone will show you a different way of life and this lifestyle will appear alarming and disturbing to you. The impression of this style of living will stay with you for some time. Firmly decide early on that this is something you are not interested in being a part of. You may decide to keep this experience private. For the next four days, you must also avoid getting a ticket for failure to put money in the meter. Someone who has been disagreeable in the past will become agreeable to something you propose now.

Parkinson's disease Do not travel overseas for a few weeks. To do so puts you at the risk of contracting contagious diseases. Wait awhile or get someone who is not as vulnerable to take this trip.

parkway Think ahead. For the next few days you will be involved in a risky situation. Make sure you get some guarantee of safety.

parliament This dream will give you a clue to a forthcoming event you will either want to encourage or discourage. For the next week, treat yourself as a special commodity and schedule your time carefully so precious moments are not wasted.

parlor You will enjoy harmony in your love union.

Parmesan cheese Be forewarned. You are involved with someone who is nervous about the depth of the relationship. Extra demands from you will drive this person from you. Decide whether you want to pursue this.

parochial school For the next two days, make sure you are emotionally able to assist someone who desperately needs your help. It would be better to seek professional aid instead.

parole officer Someone will do everything in their power to involve you in a relationship. Be forewarned, this person is lying about their marital status and you may choose not to be involved.

parquet Avoid malnourishment. Take better care of your body.

parrot Within a few days you will misinterpret an overheard conversation. As a result, tempers will flare up. Think ahead. For more clues, look up the prominent colors of the parrot.

parrot fish You will enjoy an abundance of blessings. You will also receive the flexibility and ability you need to become more spiritual. This feeling will be especially strong for the next five days.

parsley You are eager to attend a joyous occasion and you will meet someone whom you admire and respect. This will result in a joyous union. Eat more cooked parsley, nutritious foods and drink plenty of water.

parson Someone you know who lives far away desires an extended invitation from you. If you give one, you will have a marvelous time for a short while but this person will need to return home earlier than expected.

parsonage You will enjoy yourself at a long anticipated event.

Parthenon Within a few days you will be making a decision for a young child. Be careful, this may not be the correct decision at this time. This dream may also be used as a reference point in time. If you dream of this historical site and see its name used in any context, the dream message will occur on this day.

partner Extra training and education will enable you to establish the perfect partnership. It will make you a more desirable business partner, as well.

partridge A doubtful investment will become lucrative in the future.

party Within three days your fantasies and desires will be played out. If you do not deprive yourself of this, you will have the experience of a life filled with joyful, thrilling, and pleasurable moments. Go for it because you will enjoy yourself immensely. If anything negative was depicted in this dream, take steps to change or avoid it entirely.

to prepare a party You will soon celebrate your own wedding. If anything negative was depicted in this dream, take steps to change it or avoid it entirely.

to be invited Because of the success of work performed now, you will have a secure and happy retirement. If anything negative was depicted in this dream, take steps to change or avoid it entirely.

to enjoy a party You will attend a small party. You must also make sure you meet your personal involvements involving others with the confidence that they will lead toward a mutually satisfying conclusion. If anything negative was depicted in this dream, take steps to change it or avoid it entirely.

cocktail party Within three days you will be very clear about the changes you want in your life, the behaviors you wish to put a stop to, and anything new you wish to introduce into your life. Any negative event seen in this dream may be altered or avoided in reality.

formal party You will fall deeply in love and will be very eager to make a commitment in a short period of time. If anything negative was depicted in this dream, take steps to change or avoid it entirely.

party line For the next three days be very careful not to involve yourself with outrageous and unusual behavior. This will be dangerous and your part in this will change your life. You will come to regret this later.

party pooper You will be asked by someone to do something that seems to be an impossibility. Work on this in a methodical and relentless way until you are able to mold and shape it in the manner you wish. You will be successful.

party popper A number of unexpected functions will be taking place one after the other. You will be flooded with invitations that you will be able to take your pick from. Make sure you do not turn down one particular function because this will be more glamorous and exciting than any other and will require that you dress formally. Make sure you prepare yourself for this in plenty of time so you will be in top form. Do not deprive yourself of this enjoyable event. You will have a wonderful time and will meet a number of influential people who will be friends for a lifetime. You will win a door prize at this function and the larger the party popper you dream about, the larger the event will be. You may also receive an unexpected gift from someone you least

expect. You will also become aware, during this cycle, that the person you have deep feelings for feels the same about you. You will have very affectionate feelings for each other and both of you will be very excited about this new development. You are on the path for a very prosperous and brilliant future.

pass *to get a pass or to see others get a pass* Someone will develop a great deal of trust in you and will give you the honor of placing a tremendous amount of responsibility on your shoulders. You will be looked upon by others as having a great amount of authority. This will occur within three weeks. Many blessings are with you and you will be surrounded by loyal people.

to be unable to get a pass or to see others unable to get a pass In spite of your efforts to push a situation to come out the way you want, you will fail in this attempt. Since you have prior notice of this you can save the time and effort you would waste on this and apply it to a more fruitful enterprise. You must also make sure you remain safe and avoid unfamiliar surroundings for the next three days. Do not become involved in any unusual situation for this time period.

to pass the hat Do not underestimate a situation you will be involved with for the next five days. This will be your golden opportunity. Move on it before it slips through your fingers.

to pass a driver's test A cluster of unexpected events will occur one right after the other. You will also receive a flood of invitations that you can pick and choose from. One special invitation is one you should not miss. This one is more glamorous and exciting than any of the others and will require formal attire. Make sure you prepare yourself ahead of time for this so you look your best. Do not deprive yourself of this enjoyable event. You will not only have a fantastic time but will meet a number of influential people who will become good friends for a lifetime. You will win a door prize or receive some gifts at this event. During this cycle you will also become aware that the person you most desire feels the same way about you. You will have very affectionate feelings toward each other and be very excited about this new development. You are headed for a very prosperous and brilliant future.

to pass a written exam Within three days you will suddenly be free of a long standing burden. You will not have to go through a difficult and lengthy process to achieve this.

passage Be forewarned, in a few days you will have unexpected people in your company and they may have a horrifying agenda planned for you. Do everything you can to avoid them.

passageway A professional friend will handle paperwork for you, free of charge. This will allow you to obtain a valuable item and you will be grateful for a lifetime. Expect this to take place soon.

passbook Do not be such a mystery to others for the next five days. An associate will also lie to you.

pass by This dream implies luck. Troubles will be easily resolved in a few weeks.

passenger *to be in a plane* You will reconcile with someone you have not seen in a long time. Feelings will be deeper than ever before. This union will be short lived because of this person's other commitments. It is your choice whether to enjoy the two years you will have together or to seek counseling. It is unsure whether this relationship will develop further because growth depends on both parties.

to be a passenger in anything else Someone who cares deeply for you wishes to tell you. This person will be unable to because of their career interests, lack of time and their inability to commit.

passion You will receive great critical acclaim and awards for work well done. This will create a fantastic feeling.

passion fruit Within three days take steps to help a young person leave a destructive situation and enter a healthy constructive environment. You will also receive great critical acclaim and awards for work well done. This will leave you with a fantastic feeling. You will also be treated, sexually, in just the manner you wish by someone special and you will also be touched emotionally by this person. If you desire, you will make long range plans with this individual and will be together for a long time. This is a lucky omen for you. You will enjoy luck in financial affairs and will come to see that you are loved by many people.

pass out *to dream of someone passing out due to drunkenness* Within five days you will be entering an extremely lucky cycle and each person involved in your life will share in this cycle. You will receive services that will allow you to complete your goals successfully. You will achieve a higher level of success than you anticipated regarding anything you place a high degree of importance on. You can expect, during this time period, to make many wonderful connections that will assist you in grasping and meeting your goals. You will merge successfully with other people and the synergism created will advance you to a greater level of success than you hoped for. This dream also implies that you will gain benefits by attending a social event, through an educational experience, or by attending a gathering in which one person will demonstrate an interest in you and your plans and offer their assistance in helping you to complete them. A long period of tranquility will follow this and you can expect a brilliant future. Any negative event portended in this dream can be avoided in reality. Forewarn anyone you recognized in the dream to take the appropriate steps.

Passover Find a place to meditate deeply and decide what you really want from life. Many blessings will be with you and your family.

passport Proceed with confidence. You are presently unsure where you stand in the life of another person. This person is extremely powerful. Remain calm and do not blurt out statements and requests that will shift what power you

have over to this individual. Within three days, without being asked, this person will clarify their feelings with a simple sure statement. You must also pay attention to the photo in the dream and determine the particular age bracket you are in. Then remember what was occurring during this time period in your life. If this was a distasteful time, take steps, within the week, to ensure that this cycle does not repeat itself. If this was a positive time determine within three days the element that is now missing from your life that made this a positive time period. Work to regain that missing part to ensure greater happiness and success.

passport picture The people you see in this picture only offer unhealthy relationships and will want to disable your ability to meet your goals. Guard everything that is emotionally precious to you such as reputation, private life, career, etc., from those who demonstrate envy, etc. Avoid friction but make sure all of your bases are safely covered. Any negative event represented in this dream can be avoided in reality.

to see yourself in a passport picture Love, have patience with and take care of yourself. Pay close attention to your attitude and behavior. Make sure you do nothing that will make life more complicated and do not become your own worst enemy, especially for the next three days. You may choose to make alterations in your life based on imperfections you notice in the picture or improvements you choose to enhance. Examples of this are body adornments, hair color, style, clothing, etc. Make sure you change or avoid any negative message foretold in this dream and that you forewarn anyone you recognize in the dream to do the same. Take steps to experience only positive expressions in your life.

to see yourself in a passport picture as a child Regard your health as a precious commodity in order to avoid a serious illness. This can be prevented by taking the proper steps now.

to see the passport picture of a famous person Regard the power this person symbolizes as the power you will possess for the next five days.

to see someone you recognize Pay attention to the qualities you like or dislike about this person. This will represent a quality found in someone else whom you will be dealing with within four days. Take steps to alter or avoid any negative event portended in this dream and alert those you dreamed about to do the same. Make sure you experience only positive expressions in your life.

passport in any other form Pay attention to each detail of the passport. The details will offer you clues to an occurrence that will take place in the near future. Any negative event seen in this dream is preventable.

password Do not abandon someone who is depending on you and is unable to care for themselves.

past Do not dwell on the past, look ahead to the future.

pasta Look ahead and meet with someone for a deep conversation to find the answers you need for handling a crisis situation. This meeting will lead to an answer with the help of a third person.

paste Reveal yourself to another so they will know your true feelings.

pasteboard There are other dimensions available to you in your life. Do not limit yourself. Motivate yourself and avoid indolence in order to discover new options.

pastel Within a few days you will experience the peace and tranquility you have yearned for.

pastor This dream implies good luck.

pastrami Use more clarity when communicating with others. Someone feels you are still interested in them romantically because of your failure to communicate clearly and thinks you are merely being rude. Make a point to communicate the truth with more clarity.

pastry Someone will be full of flattery and will flirt pleasantly with you. This will take place for two days until you both decide to go out together. This flirtation can develop into whatever you choose.

    Danish pastry Think twice about lending money to people who have always paid you in the past. This time this person will be unable to repay you.

pasture Think ahead; problems will arise. Take on fewer responsibilities in order to have the time to handle these problems promptly and quickly. You will be successful.

patch You will receive an abundance of affection from those you care about.

patchwork Someone will whine and complain because of your failure to show affection. Promptly show your feelings in order to avoid an emotional crisis.

pâté Respond quickly to all correspondence regarding important papers.

patent A new position and opportunity will open up for you within a few days. Be prepared to move quickly on this.

patent leather Wear the proper clothes for your climate. Do not become overheated, under heated or suffer due to improper attire.

path Be careful not to break an expensive irreplaceable item. Pay attention to the type of path depicted in the dream for a more detailed meaning.

    blocked For the next week you will have to manipulate obstacles, objects, terms, contracts or agreements with others that stand in the way of your success. Do this, even if it involves a revision of plans in order to provide a clear path to your goals.

    to cross a path Within two days you will rise above administration problems. Have a conference in order to re-

group and brainstorm with others. Good ideas will be generated and energy will be renewed to ensure success.

    war path Something is taking place behind the scenes involving another person for reasons only known to them. This individual enjoys creating chaos and disturbing events in the lives of others purely for their own pleasure. Be very aware of your surroundings and of any unusual episodes in your life. Take steps to bring balance and stability into your life.

patience You will be in a cycle for the next few weeks that demands you give extra attention and affection to others. Be patient and congenial. This cycle will end.

patient Pay close attention to your investments, speculations, stocks, bonds, etc. Your instincts are correct and you can safely trust your judgments. You are headed for a prosperous future.

patina Stick to facts and you cannot fail.

patio You will rise above your overburdening problems within the week.

patois You will see something within a few days that will disgust you.

Patron Saint This dream implies good luck.

patriot Benefits will arrive quickly after signing a contract.

patrolman Stay with your goals until you achieve success.

patrol wagon You will hear a friend's confession about a past crime and this will shock you. Do *not* take any action or repeat this confession to anyone.

pattern Exercise caution. You will unexpectedly find yourself in a cozy situation with a very evil person. Be aware of your surroundings or take steps to avoid this situation completely.

patty Look for honesty and sincerity in hired help to avoid being cheated.

Paul *(from the Bible)* In a few days your assistance in the form of time and money will be required for a family in need. This family will bounce back soon. You are in a powerful position to offer help right now. Connections you have with referral services will also be helpful.

Paul Bunyan You will be unexpectedly required to help an unknown child in an unknown area. You may also have to file a police report on this.

pauper Sex and affection will be an important primary feature in your life. Take steps to make the best decisions regarding this matter and practice safe sex. Referral services will also point you in the right direction for a wonderful future.

pave Do not tolerate the petty behavior of another.

pavement Get the counseling necessary to improve your behavior.

pavilion You will get help from influential people this week in order to make changes in your living arrangements.

paw The person you are interested in will lead you to believe they will contact you for a romantic interlude. You will be very disappointed because this person will let you down.

pawn In three days, you will receive a positive answer to a request you expected a negative response to. If you choose to pursue it for the next month a situation centering around romance will work to your favor. You will be able to actively work to quickly bring this about. Your actions will enable the person you are interested in to respond appropriately. You will then be able to develop a strong support system. You are headed for a brilliant future and many blessings will come to you and you family.
    to pawn You will need to break out of your daily rut in an effort to bring positive changes to your life. If this is quickly done, you will be surprised by a social invitation.

pawnbroker You will be listened to attentively this week. This is your chance to communicate openly in an effort to have your needs met. Think ahead and use this time wisely.

pawnshop A beautiful older person will come to your rescue and will relentlessly defend you financially until you get on your feet.

pay *to dream of your desire for unremitted pay* Take steps to prevent this in reality. It is certain to happen within three days with the person you recognize from the dream. If you do not recognize the person, you will be asked out by someone and will be under the impression that this will be their treat. You will, however, be embarrassed when asked to pay your share. Make sure you address this beforehand so you understand fully what to expect. You will enjoy your life fully for the next seven days because you will attend a variety of preplanned events. Everything will fall into place as you have envisioned. Many blessings are with you. Proceed with confidence.
    to see someone else pay your bills You will get successful results from a new assistant. If you see someone you recognized paying your bills, expect this to become a reality within three days.
    to be paid Someone will desperately attempt to introduce you to someone this week for a date. This will become a wonderful event and you will enjoy yourself immensely.
    to pay someone A conversation with a romantic partner will result in future plans for living arrangements and you will both agree to live together.
    paying bills To dream of paying bills signifies luck. You

will also receive a fantastic invitation.
    to receive a bill The amount you see on the bill represents a particular monetary amount that you will be overcharged. This dream is alerting you to become actively involved in comparing prices when shopping. This extra effort you make will result in a surprising and pleasing difference in the amount you will pay for certain items. It would be to your advantage to shop around. Within three days someone will also try to trick you in order to gain a financial advantage over you without suspicions on your part. You have enough notice of this and can take steps to avoid this situation. At the same time that these other two events are taking place you will receive an unexpected gift. Although you will wonder why this is being given to you, it will simply be that someone wants to demonstrate their affection toward you. You are headed for a prosperous future and will receive an abundance of health and financial security. If anything negative was depicted in this dream, take steps to change it or avoid it entirely. Any negative event foretold in this dream needs to be avoided in reality.

paycheck You will enter a cycle that will require you give extra attention to everyone. Be patient.

payday Pay your bills promptly.

payment *to dream of your desire for payment* Take steps to keep this from occurring in reality. This is certain to happen within three days with the person you recognize from the dream. If you do not recognize the person, you will be asked out by someone and will be under the impression that this will be their treat. You will, however, be embarrassed when asked to pay your portion. Make sure you address this beforehand so you understand fully what to expect. You will enjoy your life fully for the next seven days because you will enjoy a variety of arranged events. Everything will fall into place as you have envisioned. Many blessings are with you. Proceed with confidence.
    someone made a payment for you You will gain the knowledge and means to put yourself on the right path to make changes and new beginnings in those areas of your life that you desire them in. This dream is an extremely lucky omen.
    to meet a payment Within three days, arrange your lifestyle in such a way that will also accommodate someone who is very special to you. During this cycle you will have to make these changes in order to have someone feel welcome in your life.
    to fail to meet a payment All business guarantees made to you will hold up in the future.
    to receive pay or to hear the phrase "pay me later" It is essential for the next four days that you devote your time to positioning yourself in such a way that you can create excitement. Generate a greater interest regarding a new situation. You will be able to segment more success about a new product, plan, idea or conversation. You will gain excellent feedback that will bring about more productivity, more fun and will create a non stressful outcome to what is a priority to you now. You will be able to bring everyone involved to-

gether in building a common understanding. You will determine what, where, and how to effectively achieve a chief victory on a grander scale than you anticipated. Your goal is to make the world aware of these exciting ideas, etc., and you will find that they are well received by others.

in any other form This dream is a very lucky omen and implies that within three days someone will be very eager to grant you a favor. This person is also in the position to pull strings on your behalf. Use this cycle to encourage this situation to take place. You are headed in the right direction.

payola Clarify your thoughts in such a way that you will be able to steer yourself through certain situations that will be coming up within the week. Step back and carefully review your actions each time you need to think things through and you will be able to handle everything with ease. Free yourself from stress by bringing more joy and entertainment into your life and treat your body like a sacred vessel. Eat properly and get plenty of rest. Drive defensively and make sure your transportation is in good repair.

pay phone Do not become involved in the squabbles of unfamiliar people for the next two weeks

P.C. Reward someone with a pleasant surprise.

pea Think ahead. Unexpected changes will occur within a few days. These changes are not serious although they will seem to be at the time. Exercise, eat healthful foods and drink plenty of water.

sweet peas Tenderness will grow between you and someone special to you especially within the next five days. Allow special moments to flow naturally, especially for the next seven days.

peace *to feel peace in your dream* You will enter a new dimension in life that will bring you a passion for all things and a pizzazz for living that you have never experienced before.

peace corps Do everything within your power to keep stress from becoming a major part of your life and do not allow it to affect your life for the next three days. It will soon appear as though everything will start happening at once. Remain calm and handle each issue as it comes.

peacemaker Be attentive to legal papers.

peace officer You will soon get a promotion with an unusually large financial gain.

peace pipe You will soon experience dynamic work relations with co-workers.

peace sign You will be able to offer help to a special person that will enable them to develop their potential and realize their goals. This person will be very grateful and you will be richly rewarded because you will see their enormous increase in wealth. Many blessings will come to you and your family.

peach You will invite someone you have long desired on a date and soon find that this person has been deeply in love with you. You must also do whatever is necessary to stay healthy. Drink plenty of water.

peach cobbler It is important for you to plan ahead for you and your family's well being. Additional expenses will arise in the future.

peacock Do not allow someone to take advantage of your friendship.

peacock plumage *used decoratively or for any other purpose* A number of unexpected events will occur one after the other. You will receive a flood of invitations that you will be able to pick and choose from. One of these invitations is one you should not miss because it will be more glamorous and exciting than any of the others. Make sure you prepare yourself for this ahead of time because it will require formal attire and you will want to look your best. Do not deprive yourself of this festive affair. You will not only have a good time but will also meet a number of influential people who will become lifetime friends. You will also win a special door prize at this event. During this cycle, you will be made aware that the person you desire feels the same way about you. You will both feel great affection toward each other and excitement about this new development. You are headed for a prosperous and brilliant future.

peacock plumage spread out Partners are very cooperative now and both of you will make up for what you have not done in the past. You will be more romantic and enjoy more fun time together. The colors of the peacock's plumage will lead to more clues.

pea jacket Do not promise a delivery if you are not able to get it there in time. Over the next few days someone will also manipulate you little by little out of small insignificant items. At first this will seem insignificant but will add up to quite a bit after a while. This will be done in a very subtle fashion but you need to put an end to this before it becomes a major issue.

peak Take full responsibility for things that do not work out over the next week. You will be respected for this.

peanut Do not push away a loved one because of your method of communication.

peanut butter You will soon find a new group of friends and share many jokes and much laughter.

pear You will be emotionally satisfied because you realize your ambition. This will occur within a seven day period.

pearl Someone who is interested in your success will be instrumental in promoting your talents and creative materials. Because of this person's involvement, you will profit rapidly and events will accelerate quickly.

Pearl Harbor This is a lucky omen and your wishes will be granted. Stop being so selfish. Run for public office, circulate and share your personality. Fulfill the dream you have for a job in the public eye. You have an incredible cycle coming up for improvements that will last for a long time to come. This dream may also be used as a reference point in time. If you dream of this naval base and see its name used in any context, the dream message will occur on this day.

peasant Resist complaining to others about something that you feel is unfair. Stay with this situation and you will be rewarded for your perseverance in handling this situation.

peashooter Someone you have developed an interest in and have had a good rapport with will lead you to believe they will contact you at a later date. This person will, however, never contact you again. Do not allow yourself to build up hopes. No matter how much you want to become involved it will never occur.

pea soup A business proposal that you will become involved with in two days will be very lucky. If you choose to take this route, this project will bear fruit. This dream also implies that someone you have been wanting to hear from will contact you soon.

peat moss Do not pull out of a project you are working on with another person. This co-worker will resent you. Remain until the project is completed and you will be rewarded.

pebble Put into writing, each service you will be paying for. You will receive a bid for a job but after a few weeks, you will realize the primary portion of the job was not included in the bid and you will be asked to pay more.

pecan This dream implies luck with low risk games of chance. Eat properly and drink plenty of water.

pecan pie This dream refers to the occult. Do not allow curiosity to take control and do not venture into the unknown. There is a thin line between curious inquiry and active involvement and you are approaching this line. Step back, what you are being told is misleading. You need to regroup and come to grips with a situation that needs to be understood immediately in order to avoid danger. This needs to be accomplished within three days. Get plenty of rest and avoid all stressful situations. Take all negative messages and relentlessly work to change the outcome.

peck *(a kiss)* *someone's cheek* For the next few days do not rely on others to run errands for you. Run your own errands.
    someone pecks you on the cheek Stop imagining the worst. Stay calm and things will work out for the better.
    any bird peck Do not prolong the finalization of a small business venture.
    to be pecked at You will become clearly aware of the

feelings that someone has for you. This person is completely in love with you. This feeling will overcome this individual very rapidly and they will have difficulty containing themselves. Also you will finally rid yourself of the problem of not focusing on your relationships. You will become very consistent in not only giving more time and attention to important relationships but also on anything else that demands this kind of behavior. This new behavior will stay with you for a lifetime. You are headed for a brilliant future.

pectin Be very focused for the next five days and pay attention to what is really going on with a certain family member. Take aggressive steps to handle this matter in the appropriate way.

pedal Find help quickly for your paranoid tendencies.

peddler Do not leave yourself open to someone who may have a hidden agenda. This could result in an unusual and perverse experience and will bring you many uncomfortable and distasteful moments. Take steps to avoid this for the next three days. The person involved in this is someone you feel comfortable with but will turn on you the moment you allow yourself to be vulnerable. Keep yourself safe.

pedestrian *any form* You are waiting to hear news from afar. You will receive this news soon and will be very happy about it.

pediatrician Assist a young child by helping out with their education. You may also find that a small child has a physical impairment due to a food allergy.

pedigree Do not allow your feelings to be known right now.

peek *to sneak a peek on tiptoes* Within three days someone you feel a special closeness to will come to you to explain what is going on in their life. This person is under a tremendous strain being placed on them by someone else but will be unable to explain exactly what they are feeling. This person is in danger of having their spirit broken because the other party is behaving in an irresponsible and abusive manner in many areas of this person's life. They are being controlled and are becoming very suspicious about the methods being used. There are no specific motives or methods, but they are, for some reason, remaining in this situation. This is the perfect time for them to develop more suspicions and to confront their inability to move beyond this controlling situation. It is important that you make this person aware that the moment they have this conversation with you, they must motivate themselves to move on. It takes a long time to break the spirit and this person needs to make changes in order to reenergize themselves. How does someone mend a broken spirit? It takes a long time to get back a balanced sense of consciousness and a lot of abuse to destroy it. This is the perfect time for this person to be able to hear your words of motivation and to make the necessary moves to get away from this abusive person without making their motives apparent. This could turn into a situation that will cause this person, as well as yourself, a great deal of duress. You will be able to use profound communication skills during this time period to gain someone's absolute attention. You will be instrumental in opening their eyes in some way so they can motivate themselves to create the lifestyle they desire. You will also be able to flush out the information you need from others by using your communication skills. This information will be very beneficial and advantageous for both of you. Many blessings are with you and you are headed for a brilliant future.

to peek at something or someone This is one time in your life that you will be able to show others the very best you have to offer and demonstrate your best character when it comes to nurturing someone else. Within three days, this will come as very much of a surprise to you when you have a calming and soothing affect on someone, even those who have treated you badly. You will also, during this three day time period, have a number of admirers vying for your attention at different times and without any awareness of each other. You are being forewarned about this so you will not be caught off guard by the demands these admirers place on you. You will successfully handle and treat each one equally and be able to fulfill each one's emotional needs. Share yourself with as many people as you desire because you will be able to handle yourself appropriately, treat yourself with respect, and you will be surrounded by people who love and respect you. This dream is also warning you that a very malicious person will come on to you and will present a very trustful facade to you. They will give you the impression that whatever they discuss with you will remain confidential. In reality, this person is trying to pump you for information about a third party and will then take everything you say back to this person. Be very aware of this situation so this scenario can be avoided altogether because you will be confronted with this and it could escalate to a violent episode. You have prior notice of this and can take steps to ensure that it does not take place. Pay close attention to the details in this dream. They will offer you a clue to an event or something else that needs to be investigated and taken advantage of. This will enhance your life and benefit you greatly in the direction you are headed. You will also need to make sure anything negative that you dreamed of is avoided or prevented in reality and that you experience only positive expressions in your life.

peek-a-boo You will ask someone for help at a certain time but this person will not show up. Seek an alternative person so you do not waste your time.

peel Complete and finalize an overdue project before the price goes up for materials or services.

to peel something or to see someone peel something For the next three days, do not allow anyone to force drugs or drink on you and do not become involved in any other situation that you should not be involved in. Firmly discourage this behavior and others from egging on this behavior. Stay away from unhealthy lifestyles and vigorously protect yourself.

peeled objects *(fruits, vegetables, etc.)* You will experience a big victory during this time period that will offer you an abundance of new opportunities to choose from. Put yourself in the situation by using whatever authority you have to bring a particular agreement to completion in your favor. This is especially important for the upcoming week. During this seven day period you will motivate yourself to push this agreement through and it will be welcomed by all those involved. This is the best time cycle to bring this about. You are headed for victory and many blessings will come to you and your family.

peeler *(vegetable)* Within four days, you will ask for some assistance. It will be difficult to ask for this help because you know it involves a great deal of time for the person giving aid. This is the perfect time to move on this. You will be successful.

peephole A roommate may suddenly become hostile or violent in their interaction with you. This will be due to a physical or mental disorder. Prepare yourself for this and you will be able to make the correct decision for handling this.

peeping tom Neighbors will talk to you about their dissatisfaction with your pet project. Discuss all projects beforehand.

to see a peeping tom looking in Someone has a hidden agenda they want to involve you in. This will be a very distasteful situation. Make sure you do not allow yourself to be taken advantage of.

if the person poses no threat Someone you do not yet know will want to involve you in their life in order to share pleasurable moments with you in some capacity. You will meet this person soon and this individual will bring a great deal of joy to your life. You are headed for a very prosperous future and many blessings are coming to you and your family. Make sure any negative event connected to this dream does not become a reality.

if you do not recognize the peeping tom This person represents someone who will come into your life and relentlessly help you to grasp your goals. This will occur within the week. Good luck is with you.

if you recognize the peeping tom For the next three days, do what you can to remain calm and in control. A situation will develop during this time period that you will be tempted to become involved in. Do not compromise or become entangled in the problems of another. Be acutely aware that this person has a hidden agenda. Once you become involved, it will be very difficult to pry yourself loose and the situation will become progressively worse as time goes on. Remain uninvolved.

peep show Do everything you can to rid yourself of some unusual responsibilities that will be coming your way. If these are not delegated to others, you will become solely responsible for these issues. Do not leave yourself open for any extra burdens or responsibilities.

peg Be wary of someone you have just been introduced to.

This person is lecherous and many people have suffered misfortune after being in contact with them. Stay away from this individual.

Pegasus You will enjoy victory in all areas of your life. Blessings will come to you and your special deity will be with you.

peignoir Within three days you will achieve emotional fulfillment in the manner you wish. You will be in a lucky cycle for the next seven days.

Pekinese Someone you know has a problem that they expect you to resolve. This person feels you are responsible for this problem in some way. For the upcoming week, avoid this person so problems do not come up that you will have to deal with.

pelican You and your family will receive many blessings and a small project you are working on will bring profits.

pellet Refuse to do anything you find distasteful.

pelt You will be distressed over the accident and injury of a friend.

pelvic examination You or someone you know will be led to believe that you should do something you feel differently about. This person fully believes this is the best option for you although they have no idea of the damage that could be done. This would put you or someone you know into a dangerous and troublesome area of life. Any negative event depicted in this dream needs to be avoided. Do everything you can to experience only positive expressions in your life. Otherwise, you are headed for a prosperous future.

pelvis Something will take place within the week that will be very memorable to you. This will be a very sensual experience and the memories will stay with you for a lifetime. Make sure you take steps to prevent any negative occurrence in this dream from becoming a reality and ensure that you experience only positive expressions in your life.

pen This dream is a lucky omen. You are in a powerful cycle for achievement and will accomplish everything you attempt.

felt tip pen Someone you have known for a long time will call unexpectedly and ask subtle questions to draw information from you. After a short period of time, this person will bluntly ask you to marry. This will be prefaced by the statements that they have known you for a long time, have no one in their life and you would be a good couple. It is your choice whether to pursue this or not. This person has an income and property but is neither rich nor poor. If you choose this route, you will find it is the right and proper path for you.

pencil Do everything necessary to avoid arguments and the company of someone whom you know is wicked. You must also make sure your drinking water is pure and contains the proper minerals.

pendant Determine what you really want from someone you are interested in so after your feelings are revealed, you can specify the depth you are willing to commit to a relationship. The other person may want more from this relationship than you are able to give.

pendulum A lovely person will let you know you are a priority. It will come as a surprise that this person wants full commitment from you. This will occur in a short period of time.

penguin Be suspicious of everything over the next few days and be especially suspicious of a nosy person.

penicillin Demand from your deity what you want and call upon him for your needs. Your burdens will grow lighter. Your special deity is with you.

peninsula Someone in a position of power is romantically interested in you. Victory is with you in all phases of your life.

penis Within a few days you will enter into a long desired secret arrangement and will be completely satisfied. Pay attention to the person in your dream who has their penis exposed. This person will represent the person who is interested in you in some capacity. This interest could be sexual in nature but could also be in a different context. This representation is primarily symbolic (i.e., a child with an exposed penis may indicate an adult with a childlike nature or may indicate this adult will be younger than other male counterparts you know).

sexually aroused penis Be good to yourself and reward yourself with a small gift. You will enjoy many blessings.

to see a penis becoming erect You will be able to communicate your thoughts in such a way that will enable someone who feels passionately about you to get close to you in the manner you desire. This person, in return, will enjoy this closeness and will treat you with a high regard and respect.

penitentiary Do not remain in the company of a constant complainer.

penknife As hard as it will be to accept, what you hear will be the truth for the next two days.

pen name Within two days you will become involved in a conversation with a certain person who will offer you a fresh viewpoint on topics you have been discussing. You will get the feeling this new point of view is the way to go. If necessary, take notes on this for future inspiration. Your intuition is on target; go for it. Good luck is with you and many blessings are with you and your family.

pennant Do not make any financial loans to a neighbor for the next two weeks. This person is not in the position to repay you.

Pennsylvania This is an extremely lucky omen for you. Within five days you will come into a financial windfall that will allow you to clear up all your debts within the month. This is also alerting you to eat healthy foods, drink plenty of water and take supplements that will add more calcium to your body. Many blessings are with you and you are headed for a brilliant future. This dream may also be used as a reference point in time. If you dream of this state and see its name used in any context, the dream message will occur on this day.

penny A dream of pennies is very lucky and many blessings will come to you. This is the perfect time for you to evaluate any choices you will have to make. Do this within a three day period. You will somehow take the thoughts that are circulating in your mind to devise ways to generate a larger amount of money than you ever imagined. You will gain a certain amount of prestige and respect from your endeavors. This will occur rapidly because of your motivation. You will be put in charge of a large scale situation at a lower pay rate than you expected. By making compromises at the time this is offered to you, it will soon convert into a larger position than you ever imagined and you will gain prestige and a large salary as a result. This will occur very rapidly.

penny arcade Use prudence when dealing with a senior citizen.

pen pal You will become a very successful celebrity and will be esteemed by the public. This will occur very rapidly.

pension You will have to take the initiative with a particular group of people in order to revise plans and avoid future problems.

pentagon You will wish you were never let in on a secret because you will feel burdened as a result.

pentagram Make sure you handle another person's property with care. Within three days you will be entrusted with something of value that belongs to someone else. Treat this item as though it were your belonging or you will risk your position of trust.

Pentecost Think ahead, make the time you spend with children or grandchildren a priority.

penthouse Do not discuss politics. This will cause you trouble.

peony You will experience love and tranquility within a love relationship.

people *many busy people (not a crowd)* Keep copies of all papers submitted to you for your permanent records.
large crowd You will receive an unspoken verification that your current hunches about love are accurate. This will

lead to romance.
group You will receive a surprise gift as a prize. Lucky you.
famous people Someone will send a message to you, via a physical channel (i.e., flowers, gifts, etc.) that they are interested in becoming a part of your life. Once you know this person is interested, romance will quickly blossom. You are being told to go full speed ahead and you will enjoy success.
to talk with a famous person Go full speed ahead with your present enterprise.
loitering You will have to protest and strike out against an injustice. This can be done without anger.

pepper You will react quickly in an emergency and will rescue someone in a life-threatening situation. You will be honored for this action.
red pepper For the next five days you will be entertained and amused by someone with a flair for passion. This person will go to great lengths to show the passion they feel for you. You will enjoy this immensely. You are entering a very lustful cycle.
sweet pepper Do not forget the plans you have made to attend an event with a special person.

peppermill You will be asked to become involved in a strange situation that appears to be a conspiracy. Be very firm in your refusal to become involved and do not allow others to believe you will be a part of it.

peppermint Within two weeks you will finalize a real estate deal and this will yield higher profits than expected. Romantic relationships will also go from bad to wonderful. This will take you by surprise. Go with this feeling.

pepperoni Within two weeks you will be involved in a strange occurrence. Think ahead and be forewarned, you may want to prevent it, or at least lessen its impact.

pepper shaker Within a week, your reputation will be at stake because of your involvement with an evil stranger. This could escalate into violence. Be forewarned.

peppertree Make a list of goals you wish to accomplish. Visualize this list and it will make goals easier to accomplish.

pep rally You will only grow and progress as much in a relationship as the other person allows you to. This is completely out of your control but you have prior notice of this and can handle yourself appropriately.

pep talk Within three days certain situations will take place and it is important you not make matters worse by dwelling on the events that are taking place. Motivate yourself to get busy on new projects that you need to focus on.

perch Someone will lie to you within three days.

percolate Do not become involved in risky situations for the next few days.

percussion instrument Do not enter a romantic situation with the friend of a friend. This will not work out.

peregrine falcon For the next two days, do not allow the opinions of others to interfere with your thoughts and plans. Follow your own counsel when it concerns someone who is important to you. Take the time to regroup and add some enjoyment to your life.

performance *to perform* Do not buy what you cannot afford right now.
to see another perform Avoid all gambling for the next two weeks.

perfume You will be asked a favor in exchange for a large sum of money. This money will be the answer to a large outstanding debt. This dream is also a lucky omen and you will receive a large abundance of love and affection.

peridot Doors that were formerly closed to you are now open. Others will see you in a different light and you will have more opportunities and success. You will have an abundance of prosperity and health for a long time to come.

period *if you dream of having your period* It will soon be possible for you to acquire a large expensive item, such as a car or boat.
if you dream someone else is having a period You will be sexually aroused by someone who seems completely inaccessible. Thoughts of this person will continue to arouse you. You will soon find this person to be more accessible than you realized.

periodical Someone will distance themselves from you. Do not take this personally; this is their problem.

periodic table Within five days someone who is close to you will undergo a strange incident. Forewarn this person because they may want to keep this from taking place.

periscope An old lover will seek you out. A reconciliation will occur and this will result in tranquility and physical rejuvenation for you. The body, spirit and mind will heal and you will experience tremendous personal growth. Keep those doors open. Eat properly and drink plenty of water.

periwinkle You will receive a large sum of money for the product you are marketing.

perlite Within two days, an offer will be made to you that will seem too good to refuse. Do not accept this because it will not be what it appears to be.

permanent For the next two days, a romantic situation you felt was impossible is now a possibility. This situation concerns someone who has a very aloof manner. Good luck is with you in all phases of this situation.

to have someone request that you be with them on a permanent basis Within three days a situation will occur that is so unusual and extraordinary that no law of physics can explain it. It will leave you with a sense of awe and wonder and be as though a miracle has occurred. You will have no way of explaining how this came about. After this transpires, you will be able to present yourself at your highest level and be able to handle situations, other people and yourself in an appropriate manner. You are headed for a brilliant future and many blessings will come to you and your family.

peroxide Put more color and spice in your life. This will give you a different viewpoint of life.

persecute Someone you meet within the next few days will develop an on again off again relationship with you. Be sure you do not get caught up in this crazy cycle.

Persephone *(Greek mythology)* Within seven days your life will dramatically improve because someone will restructure their own life which will affect yours as well. This will vastly improve your status. This will be a welcome and refreshing turn of events for everyone involved. Good luck is with you. You also have plenty of time to alter any negative aspect of this dream or to incorporate positive events into your life.

Persia A long awaited endorsement will suddenly come to you. This dream may also be used as a reference point in time. If you dream of this country and see its name used in any context, the dream message will occur on this day.

Persian cat You will see someone you are acquainted with in a different setting than normal. Although this person knows you, you will be snubbed. Do not take this personally. Wait until this person speaks first.
cat jumps off A special person in your life will suddenly become jealous. Answer questions, be calm, and let it go. This person needs to satisfy suspicions.

Persian rug You will thoroughly enjoy a wonderful night in front of a fireplace after a wonderful dinner.

persimmon For the next two days, people will make strange demands on you and your time. Be firm in your refusal to become involved.

Persius *(Roman)* You will soon receive the specific aid you need for a specific situation. This assistance will come at a very unexpected time and will allow you to feel immediate relief.

person *to see a person hiss* An abundance of health, tranquility and spiritual healing will be with you for the next three weeks. Within the week you will enjoy a celebration that will result in rejoicing for everyone involved. For the last half of March and for the month of April, you are destined to complete an idea, project or event. This project will reach a high level of perfection and will take on a life entirely of its own. You will be able to easily carry this through any channel it has to go through for the process to take place. This blessing will result in a big celebration for you and each person involved. You are headed for a brilliant future. You must, for the next six weeks, make sure anything negative seen in this dream does not become a reality for you or anyone you dreamed of. Pay close attention to what is being hissed at. This will offer you a clue to further meanings of this dream.

to search for someone and not find them where you would expect them to be Someone you know is desperate to escape from their present lifestyle. This person will find them self incapable of helping them self because of physical, emotional or financial reasons. Something is keeping them from changing their life. For some reason they are unable to escape this situation. You will learn about this in a short while and this person will come to you for some kind of assistance to help them change their life. Within three days you will be able to locate the resources to meet their needs and help them out. You will, however, have several conversations with this individual prior to this. Handle each conversation with caution to avoid hurting the feelings of anyone else involved. Each negotiation will be a success, whether this involves business, romance or productive conversation. You are on the path toward a brilliant future. Look up foreign person for a deeper definition to this dream.

"loose person" - slang term Take the time to see the whole picture regarding something that will come up within three days. This will allow you to clearly understand what is going on. It will also enable you to make the way you live your life the single most important thing right now. Proceed with confidence. You are headed for a very prosperous future.

in any other form If you did not recognize the person or the name of the person, they will represent someone you will come into contact with in the near future. You will recognize them as the person in the dream because of the name, race, gender, age, character traits, etc. You will be dealing with this individual within four days and have prior notice if this is someone you choose not to associate with. Someone who resembles the person you recognize in your dream will come into your life to repeat distasteful patterns or may share the same negative traits. Or share the same wonderful and fantastic attributes as the person you dreamed about. If your recollection of this character is pleasing, you can take the necessary steps to welcome them into your life. You have prior notice to determine whether this person is someone you wish to involve or avoid in your life, because of certain events you recalled from the dream or prior experiences that you wish not to repeat. Otherwise, this implies you will receive service from someone in this same time frame that will enable you to achieve a higher level of success than you ever imagined and a long period of tranquility. You are headed for a brilliant future. Anything negative portended in this dream needs to be altered. Make sure you experience only positive expressions in your life.

personality *Multiple Personality Disorder* A close relative will contract a strange and rare illness. It will take a long time but this relative will recover. Proper nutrition will hasten recovery. Proper meditation will also put you on the right track.

famous personality You are being told to go full speed ahead and you will enjoy success. You must also pay attention to what this person was doing. Look this up for a clearer meaning to this dream.

personnel You will enjoy yourself at a last minute unexpected invitation and will share much light-hearted laughter.

perspiration Within a few days you will have a conversation with someone you know who will begin to show envy toward you. You will feel uncomfortable and not as secure as you should and feel you should take out more insurance on your car or yourself. You will somehow feel as though you are doing something wrong. Do everything necessary to make yourself feel secure.

Peru You will meet a very gentle, dynamic person. You will be loved and protected for a lifetime and will have a peaceful, tranquil life. This dream may also be used as a reference point in time. If you dream of this country and see its name used in any context, the dream message will occur on this day.

perversion You will resolve all legal matters.

pervert A friend of yours will become a very cunning enemy. They will, unbeknownst to you, attempt to sabotage a terrific opportunity just moments before you acquire it.

peso Within a few days you will start to feel uncomfortable about small expensive items (jewelry, etc.). Take steps to protect these items.

pest A certain person has caused much discomfort to you in the past. They will recontact you within two days with a new endeavor. Do not allow the past to get in the way of a new situation with this person.

pest controller Within two days either you or someone you hold dear and precious will be ill treated in a very subtle, yet painful manner. This treatment will come from someone you least expect and you will quickly develop hurt feelings and harbor resentments toward this individual. You have prior notice and can be prepared for this incident or take steps to avoid it completely. You are also headed for a big victory during this time period that is completely unconnected with this scenario.

pestle Become acutely aware of what you want and do not want from life. Go after only what you truly want for the next three days. Eat healthy foods, get plenty of rest and drink plenty of water. Many blessings will come to you and your family.

pet You will be busy for a few days but you will receive a call that is important for you to pay attention to. Make time to take all incoming calls.

lost Within the week you will be invited out by someone you know only slightly. This person will behave in a strange manner and will, at some point, become very dangerous. You will not be able to escape this horrifying experience. Do whatever you can to avoid this situation. You have prior notice of this and can prevent this occurrence. You must also avoid unfamiliar places and not go to anyone's home you do not know well because you will be held against your will in a life threatening situation.

to dream of a deceased pet This is a lucky omen for you and for all those who are interested and involved in your immediate situation. You are in a powerful seven day cycle for achievement and for accomplishing everything you attempt. You will also develop more integrity. People in your life will demonstrate greater love and affection toward you. Do nothing to slow down the momentum of those feelings. Everything in your life will flow more smoothly and you will be blessed with better health and more tranquility.

petal Maximize your strengths by learning to communicate with authority figures.

Peter *(from the Bible)* You and your family will be blessed with an abundance of health and good luck for a long time.

petite Within three days you will be able to verbalize your calibrated thoughts and put them into words so well that you will be able to help someone who wishes to get closer to you. You will be able to make this person feel very secure and comfortable in your presence. Your actions will allow this individual to speak openly and frankly in a manner that will spark the development of a relationship and create a warm, open union. You can also use these skills to bring anything you want into reality. This will allow you to remove all blocks due to poor communication. This is a magical cycle. Any scene, in a dream, that you view in miniature symbolizes and prophesizes an activity you will foster. A negative scene can be avoided in reality.

petit four For the next two days, make sure you are communicating with a special person in a way that is understood by both of you. Choose your words carefully when speaking to this person.

petri dish Take care of yourself and take yourself away from stressful situations. Eat properly and get plenty of rest.

petroleum Get a physical examination.

petroleum jelly Within five days, someone will enter your life and lead you to believe they are interested in you sexually. This individual, however, has no interest in you, sexual or otherwise. You will be uncertain of the reasons this person has entered your life. Don't waste your time. This person will offer you very little and is unsure of what they want from you.

petticoat Keep all secrets and information confidential.

petty cash Think ahead and think of your family and business associates before deciding to change jobs.

petty officer You will enjoy tranquility and good fortune.

petunia You will have better success with a hard to reach person if you act quickly, because this person will be in a good mood for the next few days. After this, the person will leave town for a while.

pew Someone close to you will go through a very stressful time for the next few days. Be more cautious.

pewter Go for the big ideas and do not allow them to frighten or intimidate you. Go for it.

peyote Make sure your drinking supply is safe for the next seven days.

phantom Someone you hire to perform services will continually disappear throughout the day. This person has a drug problem. You will receive satisfactory results and this person is a good worker but needs help for this problem. Most of this is out of your control but do keep this person on as an employee.

pharmacist You will have a job offer but this job is too demanding on your time and health. Seek alternative means of support.

pharmacy You are placing too much importance on a stranger. Your freedom may be jeopardized.

Pharaoh For the next few days you will doubt a friend's words. Believe your friends; you are being told the truth.

pheasant You will soon come to see your vanities and will take steps to change. You will regain a new sense of modesty and wisdom.

Phi Beta Kappa Practice consistency, especially for the next three days. This trait will allow you to successfully achieve your goals. Follow your instincts because your hunches are correct. You will also develop a new clarity of thought. You are entering a lucky week long cycle and many blessings are coming your way.

Philadelphia You will be very successful in the performing arts and will become a very well known figure. This may also be used as a reference point in time. If you dream of this city and see its name used in any context, the dream message will occur on this day.

philanthropist Do not deprive yourself of special moments with someone you feel a great deal for. Do not make excuses and deny yourself the company of this person. This will become an issue within two days. Change your behavior in order to avoid future hurt.

Philemon *(from the Bible)* You will be able to decide on the person you should become involved with. This person is very knowledgeable and will be able to help you resolve a certain issue.

philharmonic For the next three days practice consistency if you want to reach your goals successfully. Follow your intuitions. You will develop a new clarity of thought and this will facilitate your success. Many blessings are with you and you are entering a lucky week long cycle.

Philippines You will purchase real estate at a low price from a friend who is in a hurry to sell. This may also be used as a reference point in time. If you dream of this country and see its name used in any context, the dream message will occur on this day.

philodendron You will have a beautiful companion for life.

philosopher This is a lucky omen. You will meet someone who is fluent in several difficult languages. This person will come into your life at a time when you can utilize these language skills to meet a goal. Later on this individual will desire a romantic union and both of you will live to be old together. Find someone to give you a psychic reading. This will be lucky for you now.

phlegm Avoid contracting a disease from another person. Meditate in your favorite way in order to balance your system.

phobia Confront your fears and do not allow them to control you. A necessary confrontation will lead to rapid healing.

Phoenix Whatever you and your family does as a unit will be successful. You will enjoy an upward spiral of great moments. This may also be used as a reference point in time. If you dream of this city and see its name used in any context, the dream message will occur on this day.

phoenix *a legendary bird* Put yourself in the position of being able to experience a rebirth in whatever area you desire. You will achieve and accomplish everything you attempt. You are in a powerful cycle.

phone *to pick up and someone has picked up on the other line without speaking* You will be dealing with someone on an everyday level who is in need of mental health services. Be patient and kind yet cautious. Try to help this person but go on with your life.

to call for help and be unable to get through You will unexpectedly be fired from a job because you will leak information to another person. This individual will then carelessly take the information to the wrong person. You must not give the impression that the shock of losing this position can be prevented or that you no longer desire an important position. This event is preventable. You must also make sure

you do not set yourself up in any situation where you will be unable to get help via the phone, especially for the next three days.

to dial for help and receive it Pay a bill immediately to avoid legal action. Do this now.

to enjoy a phone conversation You are entering a good cycle. You and someone special will mutually agree on joyous, big plans for the future. This will end in success.

to ask for someone to phone and not be available in reality The person you are asking for is unavailable. Don't lose patience. Try again within five days. This person will be very happy to hear from you.

to not understand the other person on the phone Develop your plans and focus on what should be in order. Smooth out and tighten up all facets of the plan in order to avoid interference on the way to success.

to hear the phone ring Someone in your life very much wants to speak to you but lacks the courage to call. If you know who this person is, make the first move. This person is emotionally unable to pick up the phone and lives with this anxiety each day.

cellular phone During a time of total chaos, someone will rescue you. This person is like an angel in disguise.

pay phone Do not become involved in the squabbles of unfamiliar people for the next two days.

head phones What you hear over the headphones is a major clue to a future event. If it represents a negative event, take the necessary steps to either prevent it or turn it into a positive situation. If it is positive, take steps to include this in your life. This also implies that someone has a problem they want to dump on you. They feel you should be the one responsible for resolving this. Do everything necessary to avoid involvement in this situation.

phone booth You have been desiring a special item for a long time. You are now able to find the exact item you need at a bargain price and you finally have the money to pay for it. This will make you ecstatic.

to attempt to call out on a non-working phone A special person in your life will try to pass false judgments on you. Try to put more love into action and express it in a romantic way. A gentle approach will put confusion to rest.

to wait for a pay phone or phone booth Do not depend on another for your success. The responsibility lies with you and will depend on your own merit. Do not waste time waiting for others to rescue you. Explore new options, especially for the next two days. Focus intently on ways to remove yourself from this rut and do not waste time feeling sorry for yourself. Success will rapidly come to you.

push button Within five days, someone will plan to violate your rights for their own emotional gratification. This person will attempt to manipulate you into becoming involved in something you find increasingly distasteful and disgusting. This involvement will go against your better judgment and against your will. Do not place yourself in any situation where you will have to compromise your principles to get out safely. This is preventable. Good luck is with you.

in any other form Embrace and love yourself. Take time out to tie up loose ends. You must also take steps to begin building your liquid assets and property assets. You will find the means to do this with the help of someone else. This person will reach a complete agreement with you and will begin the process within two days.

phone number *a phone number is requested and not given* Within three days, while casually conversing with a group of people, an impromptu mini-conference will develop. From this, you will be exposed to various points of view and this will lead to a more structured method of handling a particular person or situation.

in any other form Someone is very eager to hear from you but lacks the courage to make the call. You need to make the first move. This person cares a great deal about you and would enjoy a lengthy conversation with you. These numbers are also lucky for you and may be used in games of chance. This dream is also providing you with the number of someone you have lost contact with. Treat relationships more seriously for the next seven days. If you recognize anyone in the dream, this is the individual who desires to speak with you. You will also assume the leadership role whether you chose this position or not. This will allow you to motivate others to make a group decision regarding the care or lifestyle of another person.

phone tap This is alerting you that someone with their own opinions will try to impose them on you. Do not allow this to block your original creative way of thinking and make sure you continue on your present course.

phonograph Take time out from your daily routine to really enjoy life. Pay close attention also to the words heard on the phonograph. If this is a negative message, take the time to alter the outcome. Any positive message needs to be embraced and promoted. You will experience more joy and tranquility in this cycle.

photo All negotiations will be very lucky for you.

photocopy Anything concerning electrical music instruments will be lucky. Even a photograph of one will be fortuitous for you.

photo finish Any work that involves paper will bring you luck. A burst of creative energy will lead you to the correct path. This is also a good luck omen and you have the promise of a brilliant future. If you are a writer, you will have creative bursts of energy. In matters of love a joyous occasion will unexpectedly arise.

photograph Be patient with someone who enjoys making others angry even though this problem is not yours. This person needs help with their attitude. The people seen in others angry even though this problem is not yours. This person needs help with their attitude. The people seen in photographs in this dream offer only unhealthy relationships. They will want to disable your ability to meet your goals. Guard everything that is emotionally precious to you, such as reputation, private life, career, etc., from those who demonstrate envy. Avoid friction.

physical Be diligent and efficient with your responsibilities.

physical education Someone you know is just getting over the death of a family member and you will be the first person contacted. Subtly suggest an alternate lifestyle that will generate more health.

physical examination You are loved beyond your imagination. Do not deprive yourself of the pleasures this person's deep feelings for you could bring. You will experience appreciation and love from those you care about within the week.

physical fitness You will act as an interpreter for someone who does not speak your language well and is unable to stand up for themself.

physical therapy Humor someone who is expressing anger at another. Deflect this anger without appearing patronizing because it will spill over to you.

physician Do not simply imagine yourself as a famous person. Place yourself in the company of those who can steer you onto the correct path to achieve fame. You will achieve victory if you move quickly and connect with the right people.

to be examined by a physician Pay close attention to the reason you are at the physician's office and take preventive measures to ensure this does not occur in reality. You must also make sure you personally handle all of your own affairs so you can get a clear idea of what needs to be taken care of.

to be examined by a physician and find something wrong Take preventive measures to avoid developing the illness depicted in the dream. Take steps to avoid any preventable accidents to yourself or to others in your care. You must also take steps not to leave yourself open to emotional pain as a result of someone's lack of consideration.

to witness or hear of someone else being examined and finding something wrong If you recognize the person, alert this individual to use preventive measures to ensure this illness does not occur in reality. Make it a priority to determine your needs and work to fulfill those needs. Take steps also to avoid becoming involved in a group that creates chaos in the lives of others. This group is well known for this behavior and it will be to your advantage to avoid them. You will experience good luck for the next seven days and you and your family will experience many blessings.

physics Someone you disliked from the past will reappear and attempt to be a part of your life. Do not include this person in your life. Move on.

piano You will attend a social event and find that someone you know is romantically interested in a mutual friend. These two will have a wonderful life if you choose to help bring them together.

Picasso You will create some beautiful designs that will popularize your line of merchandise. You must also make sure that a friend who is leaving the country has the appropriate funds to return.

piccolo Someone new in your life who wants to become special to you will become very melodramatic and will stage many theatrical episodes once you refuse their advances. This person will go to great lengths to demonstrate their desire for you. This will take place within three days. Be prepared so you do not compromise yourself or grant them their desires if this is not something you want at this time. Otherwise this is a very prosperous cycle and you are headed in the right direction. Think ahead. Within three days someone will say stupid, insensitive, inconsiderate things to you in front of others. Take this person aside, beforehand, to express your feelings on this behavior and you will be able to prevent this.

pick Think ahead. Do what you can to keep others from being dissatisfied with your services. Get more information in order to ensure you provide adequate service.

pickax Proceed step by step on a project in order to attend to all important details.

picket Arrange your lifestyle in such a way that it complements your loved ones.

picket fences Within seven days you will be dealing with a vain and deceitful person. This person has consistently been in trouble with the law and wishes to involve you. Avoid this.

picket line A friend will ask you out and will take you places where it is certain you will be seen together. This person is trying to give the impression there is more to the relationship than there is. If this is not the impression you wish to give, decide whether you want to continue going out.

pickle You will acquire a great deal of knowledge and wisdom in one field. People throughout the world and throughout your life will request information about this topic from you. This will be a blessing for you.
dill pickle Someone will be very interested in you sexually. This person is also interested in a relationship and is possessive in a pleasant way. Pursue this for the next five days and it will develop into a strong union if this is what you choose.

pickpocket For the next two to three weeks you will be dealing with someone who is very rude, ill-mannered, and critical. Avoid this person in order to keep from being insulted.

pickup *if you are being picked up* All things you hold dear will become closer and dearer and you will feel more love in all your relationships.
if you are picking up Redesign your thoughts to allow your mind to be more receptive.

pickup truck A relaxing getaway will produce wonders for your imagination. You will enjoy an abundance of creative thought.

picnic Arrange your schedule in order to accomplish as much as you can for the next week. You will be meeting with someone who has valuable information and you will need to make the time to meet with this person. Become creative with your time so you can fit this person in. This information will be valuable for your career.

picture *to see people in the picture* The people you see in this picture represent people who will only offer unhealthy relationships and want to disable your ability to meet your goals. Guard everything that is emotionally precious to you such as reputation, private life, career, etc., from those who demonstrate envy. Avoid friction. You must also be patient with someone who enjoys making other people angry. This problem is not yours. This person needs help with their attitude. For greater definition of this word, see photograph.
to see yourself in a picture Love yourself, have patience with and take care of yourself. Pay close attention to your attitude and behavior. Make sure you do nothing that will make life more complicated and do not become your own worst enemy, especially for the next three days. You must also pay attention to what is happening in the picture. This will provide a major clue to a forthcoming event. You may choose to make alterations in your life based on imperfections you notice in the picture or improvements you choose to enhance. Examples of this are body adornments, hair color, style, clothing, etc.
to see yourself as a child in the picture Regard your health as a precious commodity in order to avoid a serious illness. This can be prevented by taking the proper steps now.
to see someone you recognize Pay close attention to the qualities you like or dislike about this person. They will represent characteristics found in someone else whom you will be dealing with within four days.
group picture Pay close attention to those who are close to you. Within five days, this dream implies you will be dealing with someone who shares similar traits with the individual in the pictures. These traits may be negative (i.e., deceitful, envious, etc.) or positive (i.e., humorous, giving, etc.) You have the opportunity to alter old patterns or to enjoy the positive aspect of this forthcoming event. Also within a few days, a known person or persons with the tendency to be conniving will lead you into uncomfortable situations.
to see a famous person's picture Regard the power this person symbolizes as the power you will possess for the next five days.
if someone is taking your picture Take the pains to look your best for the next two weeks. You will meet someone you will need to impress at the first meeting.

to take pictures of someone The person you rely on will jeopardize your reputation by spreading falsehoods.

picture negatives Stay in touch with those worthy of your friendship.

to draw a picture Pay close attention to what is being drawn. This will provide a major clue to what will be forthcoming in your life within two days. You may either take steps to avoid this event or to promote it to the fullest. The picture in the dream may also represent an object you wish to possess. You will also find you will work successfully with someone from a different ethnic background and you will both experience an abundance of prosperity. Take steps to improve your appearance. Any negative event seen in this dream can be prevented in reality. Be sure to forewarn anyone you recognized in the dream to do the same.

picture, drawing Be acutely aware of what is being drawn. This is forewarning you of a future negative situation that needs to be turned around or avoided. Alert anyone you dreamed about to do the same. During this cycle you will also be surrounded by people who love and are loyal to you.

drawing of a person This person is someone who will enter your life and appear to be a very pleasant and charismatic person to be around. Do whatever is necessary to avoid involvement with this individual. This person will be the cause of you losing something that you value greatly. They will also do what they can to encourage you to indulge in the bad habits they indulge in and will attempt to encourage you to indulge further in the bad habits you already have.

picture album For the next three days, protect yourself in every way possible. A danger will be directed at you from an unknown source. Protect yourself and your health and insist on playing it safe on every level of your life. People depicted in the album only offer unhealthy relationships. They will do everything in their power to keep you from meeting your goals. Take steps to protect everything that is emotionally precious to you (i.e., reputation, privacy, career, etc.) from those who appear kind but possess a great deal of envy.

picture and planter hooks Within a three day period, a situation will come up that will require you to determine whether someone you are working with on a particular project is keeping up with the pace. This person may be slacking off to the point where you are doing the work of two people if you do not remain alert to this. Focus on solving this problem so you can get the assistance you need without accepting extra responsibilities. Speak up and let this person know they have to pull their own weight. Maintain a stress free life. Many blessings are with you and you are headed for a very prosperous future. You will also enjoy a financially secure old age.

picture window Keep a copy of all important papers in two different locations.

pie A new love will quickly blossom for you.

apple Make sure your children and parents are priorities.

peach You will receive a long hoped for demonstration of love from someone you have longed for.

banana cream You will receive a one of a kind luxury gift. Happiness will be yours.

Boston cream pie Within a three day period you will meet a kind, generous person with a wonderful sense of humor. This person is free to pursue romantically. In a short while they will grow to like you a great deal. Enjoy yourself.

custard pie You will meet new people with pizzazz and a great deal of information that you need.

meat pie Do not commit yourself socially to people you do not know well.

cobbler (any kind except peach) You have the ability to transfer real estate into a real profit. This is the right time for you to do this.

cobbler (peach) It is important to make plans ahead for your family's future because new events will arise that will need to be attended to.

pecan pie This refers to the occult. Do not allow curiosity to take control and do not venture into the unknown. There is a thin line between curious inquiry and active involvement and you are approaching this line. Step back, what you are being told is misleading. You need to regroup and come to grips with a situation that needs to be understood immediately in order to avoid danger. This needs to be accomplished within three days. Get plenty of rest and avoid all stressful situations. Take all negative messages and relentlessly work to change the outcome.

piece For the next two weeks make sure you do not overextend yourself. Do everything you can to set aside private time for yourself.

piece of cake You will receive good news concerning romance. This cycle will bring you luck in love.

piecrust Use the discount privileges of a friend to purchase something you desire. Your friend will be very eager to work with you on this, especially for the next two days.

pied piper For the next three days be very aware of situations that could lead to jealousy and arguments. Take steps to keep this from taking place.

"pie in the sky" This is an extremely lucky omen for you. You will be able to develop the steel drive and the courage you need to get beyond any barriers and boundaries, whether mental or physical, that are holding you back from accomplishing what you need to do. You will be able to rid yourself of these entirely in the manner you wish. You will also go somewhere and be greeted with a warmth and appreciation you never expected. You will be very surprised at the royal treatment you receive.

pier You will have many memories of the next few nights. You will enjoy passionate love and affection.

Pieta Within the week, you will get exactly what you desire in a business transaction.

pig *large pig* This implies luck in all directions of your life. Health is yours.

several pigs Do not live beyond your means or purchase items you cannot afford. This will spell financial defeat.

to hear the phrase "you pig" Be wary of someone you have just been introduced to. This individual is treacherous and many people suffer misfortunes after being in contact with this person. Go on with your life without this person in it.

pigskin Think ahead. You are included in a relationship with someone who wants a marriage commitment. You will have doubts about this union. Follow your instincts. This person, after marriage, will become very verbally abusive and you will go to couples therapy. Nothing will change this person.

in any other form For the next three days, take a responsible and reasonable approach when handling a difficult issue involving someone who is close to you. Your involvement will make a big difference in this person's life. Develop more understanding in order to keep this situation from getting out of control. Unless you approach this logically, it will become chaotic. You will have the strength you need to handle this. You must also pay close attention to the details in this dream. They will offer you a clue to an event and/or something else that needs to be investigated and taken advantage of. This will enhance your life and benefit you greatly in the direction you are headed. You will also need to make sure that anything negative you dreamed of is avoided or prevented in reality. Make sure you experience only positive expressions in your life. You will enjoy an abundance of health and are headed toward a victorious future. Many blessings are with you and your family.

pigeon You will be able to accomplish a variety of things during this time period. What you are pursuing that you do not feel is very important is worthwhile for you to go after. This may be something you have overlooked or not fully concentrated on. This is also the perfect time to use your communication skills to convince someone to pay you the money they have agreed to pay. Start thinking about your retirement so you can be financially secure in your senior years. Expect an abundance of health during this time frame.

pigeon toed You are going in the wrong direction and need to focus on what needs to be changed. This will allow you to change direction and enjoy a successful outcome.

to see someone pigeon toed You will be able to lessen and ease health problems by reading and gaining information about better ways to beat this problem.

piggyback Do not allow yourself to become ill over the next week. It will take a long time to recover. Take in proper nourishment to build up your resistance.

piggybank This is a good luck symbol especially in matters of love and education. The knowledge you gain by furthering your education will dramatically change your life for the better.

pig latin Back off and slow down your pursuit of a situation you are very interested in. Investigate carefully before you jump into this situation.

pigmy Someone you meet soon will attempt to have you relate to them on a more personal basis. You will not like this person. Be tactful because you will come to like this person later on and if you behave rudely, this person will behave vengefully. It will then be difficult for them to trust your motives.

pigpen The person you dearly love will come back to you and wish to reconcile.

pigtail Think ahead. You will meet a heartless individual who will set you up for a lawsuit. Be careful.

pike For the next three days do everything necessary to avoid putting yourself in the position of sustaining physical injury .

Pilate (Pontius) *(from the Bible)* Do not marry a greedy person because this person will attempt to bring out your own greed. This person lives only for money and you would grow to despise this individual. Learn to live without this person in your life.

pile A neighbor's pet will run loose and damage your property. Think ahead and talk with your neighbor in order to prevent this.

of anything In a short time, you will be moving into new unknown dimensions. Be sure you do not take any unnecessary risks.

small pile of anything Be aware that your finances are starting to dwindle and take steps now to prevent this.

pile driver You will unexpectedly find yourself helping someone in distress. Be aware of hidden agendas and remain alert.

pileup Be careful not to engage in slander. This will backfire.

pilgrim You will witness a gruesome scene while in an unknown area but no one will know you were there. You can either tell the police and take risks or keep silent and seek counseling.

pill Mental inventiveness and manual talents, along with imagination and confidence will lead to a satisfying income. Go for the big ideas.

birth control pills Within five days you will be entering into an extremely lucky cycle. Everyone involved in your life will share in your luck. You will also be offered services that will allow you to successfully complete your goals and reach a grander level of achievement than you thought possible, especially with anything you feel is a high priority. You can expect many wonderful and amazing connections that will assist you in meeting your goals. You can also anticipate a mega merger and the energy generated between you and those you will be working with will promote you to a far higher level of success than you expected. This dream also implies that you will gain benefits by attending a festive event, participating in an educational experience, or by attending a gathering in which one person will show an interest in you and your projects. A long period of tranquility will follow this experience and you will enjoy a prosperous future. Any negative event witnessed in this dream can be prevented and anyone you recognized in the dream needs to be forewarned to do likewise.

sleeping pills You are denying your feelings by isolating yourself from the person you are destined to surrender to. This life is not a rehearsal, get out and live it.

pillar Follow your intuition and stabilize your life.

pillbox Do not rely on the friends of other people to come through for you. They do not know you. You must also make sure you do not take medications needlessly.

pillow You will make an excellent impression on a new business associate and will be asked to join in with a person or persons of influence in their endeavors. You will be warmly received. This dream is an omen of victory.

pillowcase Within three days you will enjoy a pleasurable change of circumstances . Be sure to take advantage of this.

pillow sham You will have the confidence to take the small risks you need in order to enter a particular situation that will improve your standard of living. Make sure you stick to all rules and regulations. You will also have strong feelings about something you feel must be taken care of promptly.

pilot Decisions made in the past will resurface. Some of these decisions no longer apply. Revisions made now will turn situations into advantages for you.

pilot light A pet will recover from a long illness and this will lead you to feel joy.

pimento Do not put yourself in the position to be disgraced.

pimp Be very cautious for the next three days and move forward with someone only with extreme caution. You are beginning to develop a sense of closeness toward this charming and charismatic person and they will lead you to believe you can fully confide in them and depend on their loyalty. This person is a master of deception and will lead you to believe that certain events and situations will take place in the future that will never occur. Instead, this individual has a hidden agenda that involves pursuing you for some evil intent that is known only to them. They will go to great lengths to create an atmosphere devoid of all suspicion that will lead to your absolute trust. If they do sense any suspicions they will create a crisis to divert you from these feel-

ings. Once you begin to understand what is going on you will have suffered disillusionment, disappointments, and may suffer financially. It will take a long time for you to recover from this and get your life back on track. You have prior notice of this as well as everything you need to make sure this does not take place. Practice common sense and you will successfully diffuse this issue. Do not compromise your feelings, do not allow this person to interfere in your private affairs and do not become involved. You are on the path toward a prosperous future. Many blessings are with you and your family.

pimple You will hear that your family has gotten a pleasant surprise and this will lead to happiness on your part.

pin Build a foundation in a relationship before building up hopes. Learn more about this person.

surgical pins Someone will attempt to lure you into some unpleasurable moments and distasteful conversations. For the next three days do not allow yourself to be pinned down or manipulated by anyone.

campaign/political or pins that make a statement of some kind Within three days you will develop a sense of urgency to attract the attention of someone you desire. Follow your hunches. You will find, in this person, a similar lifestyle and ideas. If you choose to pursue this, it will be possible to establish a relationship in this cycle. You will find this person to be very demonstrative and affectionate and you will both have a great deal of love to share with each other. You must also pay close attention to the message on the button. This will offer a clue signifying something you will want to embrace in your life or something you will want to take steps to avoid or alter. This dream is also asking you to face facts and to stop looking at everything through rose colored glasses. You are making it easy for someone to lie to you because you give the impression that you prefer not to deal with cold hard facts. Change this behavior and face situations head on.

to have someone remove a button from you or someone else Play it safe and do not allow an opportunity to slip through your fingers. Pay close attention to all future involvements to ensure you do not allow an opportunity to slip by.

safety pin Pay attention to everything you are told instead of selectively listening only to what you want to hear. This will allow you to see the whole picture and will ensure you react appropriately. You will then be able to successfully and confidently complete your tasks.

straight pin Do not allow yourself to become tied down. Circulate and become actively involved with those who are special to you. Do not compromise your feelings.

clothes pin A distasteful and uncomfortable situation is rapidly coming your way. Within three days, you will need to take steps to avoid this. Begin acting on this the moment you see the situation start to develop because it will be very hard to correct once it has gotten out of hand. This situation will escalate very quickly out of control unless you are alerted to it.

bowling pins Someone with an uncontrollable urge to spend time with you will go to great lengths to convince you to see them. If you choose to go in this direction, you will enjoy yourself immensely and will experience many unusual and delightful moments. Many blessings are with you and you will experience much luck during this seven day cycle.

diaper pin Take extra precautions when transferring money from one location to another. Insure all money against loss for the next seven days. Good luck is with you during this cycle.

bobby pin Watch for an upcoming event and take steps to enter it on your calendar. You must also make sure you do not present a demeanor that discourages others from being open with you. Someone will wish to speak with you but will find it difficult because of your manner.

push pin For the next few days you will be pursued by someone who is far better off than they appear. This person will quickly become a close friend and will, in turn, offer financial help. Do not take this for granted.

piña colada You will attend an unexpected festive situation and someone will make several attempts to speak with you. Pursue this and this person will become one of the best friends you'll ever have. Remember, a friendship will grow only as much as you desire it to. You will share some of the best years of your life with this person.

piñata You are talking yourself out of many great ideas by replaying negative tapes. Alter those tapes and you will be surprised at how quickly you will be able to gain the tools needed to launch great plans. This is the perfect cycle for this. Good luck is with you.

pinball machine Avoid any body language that promotes suspicion.

pincers You will do whatever is necessary now to improve your physical appearance.

pin curl Anyone you see in this dream with a pin curl needs intervention and assistance for a particular problem. Within three days you will also referee two people who will find it impossible to reach an agreement about a specific problem. With your help they will find a solution.

pincushion Do not lead others to believe you have a lack of respect for yourself.

pine You will have a quickly developing union with someone you deeply desire.

pineapple Keep your deepest ambitions to yourself.

ping pong At the first hint of disagreement with your mate, collect yourself and calm them down. If you don't, this will escalate and both of you will be on an emotional roller coaster for weeks.

pink You will have higher power's protection and the help you need to develop an emotional and financial balance. This will be a lucky and tranquil time for you. You have many admirers, but the one you desire most will return your love and affection.

pink elephant Within four days you will receive a very unexpected proposal. This proposition will seem too good to be true and you will be tempted to turn it down because it will seem impossible to accomplish. Take a few days to mull this over and do not close doors or burn bridges. You will want to experiment with this idea at a later time to see if it is a possibility. It will take place as planned and the person who presented this to you will keep each commitment. Good luck is with you.

pinking shears You will receive wonderful unexpected tidings from a business associate. You will also come to realize that you have a close bond with this associate.

pink slip Make sure for the next few days you hold your feelings and emotions in check. You will become emotionally caught up in a situation where you feel you have been left out of a particular group. Do not make matters worse by feeding into this. Focus on other issues that are more important for you to attend to.

pinky This dream is a very lucky omen. You will win a prize and your sense of receptivity will be very strong.

pinprick Be cautious of jealousy that will lead to a big argument.

pinstripe You will go out with a beautiful person. This will be a glamorous occasion and you will enjoy it immensely.

pint A situation will arise within two days that will give you a sense of lost self-confidence. You will be able to resolve difficult situations immediately by regrouping yourself.

pinto Let your creative juices flow and develop a zest for life. You will find the real estate you want and will be very happy about this.

pinto bean You will hear of a death that will disturb you for several days.

pinup Your desires will be met and a special favor will be granted. Blessings are with you.

pinwheel Someone will attempt to push you into their beliefs. Be firm. Otherwise this dream is a lucky omen.

pioneer You will be in the company of a very kind hearted, educated person who is unable to commit to a relationship for reasons known only to them. This problem stands in the way of this person's pursuit of a relationship they desire. They are not aware of this mental block but you have prior notice of this and can take the appropriate action.

pipe A family member will take you into their confidence and ask for your assistance. Advise this person in ways that will improve their life.

pipe bomb Be careful while traveling for the next two days. Take all precautions to remain safe and to avoid accidents.

pipe cleaner For the next few days you will feel more assured about family relations that appear to be falling apart. This cycle promotes healing and closeness.

pipe cutter Mental pain and anguish will disappear within two days due to an unexpected situation.

pipeline You will shortly hear of the death of a close family friend.

pipe organ Agree only to what you want to do. When offered a package deal suggest the job be broken into two parts so you handle what interests you and make sure someone else handles the other portion.

pipes Get a body massage within a few days. This will allow you to accept and love yourself more.

pipe wrench The people you care about may not understand your personal point of view and until your beliefs are actualized, no one will be able to visualize their workability. Within the week you will also be offered a much larger salary than you anticipated for a particular job. Many joyous days are coming your way and many blessings are with you and your family.

piranha Be relentless and aggressive when going after what belongs to you. Your aggressive attitude will bring results. Passivity will only allow others to overlook you and you will never retrieve your belongings.

pirate Be careful of electrical wires around water. Do everything necessary to prevent injury or death by accidental electrocution.

Pisces You will soon find an old item that has been overlooked in the family for half a century. This is a priceless commodity and will be given to you to do as you choose. Old hang-ups that limit you will also suddenly disappear over the next few weeks. This dream is a lucky omen. Keep an eye on your investments and do not become careless.

pistachio Do everything necessary to hasten marriage plans. This will be a blessed union.

pistol This signifies danger. If you have been trusting another to make your payments, be careful. You may lose property due to missed payments because of this person's carelessness. You have a full month to rectify this.

pita Great riches will soon come to you.

pitcher You will have an advantageous marriage in every way.

pitchfork A very young person will fall deeply in love with you and will make great demands on your time and affection. Choose whether you want this from a relationship.

pitch pipe Do not allow yourself to run on empty. Do everything necessary to maintain your emotional health.

Pittsburg Watch your health. You are overextending yourself and this may lead to health problems. This dream may also be used as a reference point in time. If you dream of this city and see its name used in any context, the dream message will occur on this day.

pituitary gland A certain person is convinced you will be able to handle a particular situation that they are required to handle. Make sure you do not become involved because this will not work out for either of you. Otherwise you are in a lucky seven day cycle.

pit viper Stop being so selfish with others for the next two days. Learn to share with others and you will receive much gratification as a result.

pixie For the next two days be wary of false friends. You have two friends who associate with each other and are untrue to you.

pizza You are unsure about a reunion with some close friends. These friends are very loyal to you and you will have a wonderful time.

pizza cutter For the next month, it will be a good idea to promote group activities. This may be something in the nature of card games, parlor games, etc. Something lucky will also occur within a group situation and you will gain information that will enhance your life.

pizzeria You will achieve great success in the cycle you are now in.

place *to talk of a place* You will finally rid yourself of a dishonest friend.

placebo This is an unfavorable time for your plants. Take steps to protect them.

place kicker You will have to be in the company of a certain person who enjoys creating chaos and stressful events. Prepare yourself. Within three days this person will create a monstrous situation that will escalate out of control. Make plans now to busy yourself with various entertainments for this time period in order to avoid this person and this particular situation.

placemat Some small precious items will be stolen. Take steps to protect them.

placenta Take steps to keep your scalp healthy and prevent hair loss. Keep your skin healthy. Drink plenty of water and eat healing foods. Visit a dermatologist at the first sign of trouble.

plaid Someone you will be dealing with appears to be very healthy but is not.

plainclothes policeman You will be questioned about some unusual illegal behavior that is out of your control. An associate has committed an act and you will be questioned. You are forewarned and will be able to alter the outcome.

plan Whatever you are working on will work out the way you envision. If the outcome is negative, you have the chance to change it.

plane *to ride* An anticipated upcoming event will bring a joyful reunion.

to see one A lucky event will happen to you today.

to see someone else in one Guard your emotions. Someone you are attracted to is leading a busy life. This person wants to be with you but cannot. Keep busy and this person will come around.

to see an explosion You will hear of a freak accident that will result in the death of a friend. Warn anyone this may apply to.

to fall out Be careful, your relationship is in jeopardy. You have prior notice of this and can take steps to rectify this.

"planet Earth" Play a very active part in satisfying those emotional feelings you have. Make sure you provide yourself with what you want on an emotional level. You will also, within five days, be able to visualize the path you need to take to ensure a brilliant future. Good luck is with you.

"planet Hollywood" You are making all the right moves and are motivating yourself in such a way to achieve success. You will also finally be able to pin down an elusive person you have long desired to make contact with. All things you once felt were impossible to achieve are now possible. Schedule a mini vacation to a remote get away spot and you will enjoy many pleasurable moments. You are on the path toward a brilliant future.

planets/planetary You have the skill, creativity and flair to become a great comic book illustrator, etc. Get the education needed to meet these goals.

plank Try to be kind and affectionate to a former lover. Make this person a friend instead of an enemy. This relationship can still be salvaged.

plant You will quickly rise above any bothersome situation and will be able to perform perfectly in any area you desire. You are headed for a very prosperous future. A simple favor granted to another will also be appreciated for life. At a later time you will be rewarded with a nice gift.

to give a plant as a gift Within a few days you will be giving moral support to a young adult. You may need professional assistance from various agencies but will receive personal satisfaction from this work sooner than you think.

to receive a plant as a gift You will soon be invited out by someone you deeply desire and will find that this person also has deep feelings for you. You will enjoy yourself with this person for the next five days.

to clean a plant For the next five days develop a network of people who will support and assist you for a two year period in order to promote and market your product. Work quickly and consistently and you will have success with this project.

to water a plant A long time dream of a relationship will come true. Make an effort to communicate and you will receive all you wanted from this union. This will be a very lucky cycle.

plant food You have all of the information you need to give to a certain person who is seeking advice. When this person comes to you, open up and give them exactly what they need to run their life more efficiently.

rubber plant Meditate in your favorite form and encourage personal growth. You will enjoy much tranquility in your life. Do whatever you can to include romance in your life and live life to the very fullest. You will enjoy many blessings and good luck will be with you.

a budding plant You will be granted your deepest desires.

to transplant, propagate or graft, etc. Anything you plan to start that will create changes must be detailed. Leave nothing for the last minute. You will really see grand changes in your life.

to plant anything Make sure, when you offer assistance to another, that you have all the details and information necessary to give proper advice. All referrals given should be checked first to ensure accuracy. The plans you have set in motion should be reviewed in detail to ensure this is being properly handled.

in any other form You will be presented with an exciting opportunity that you have long awaited for. You will now have the ability and means to take control of and handle anything you need to. You will enjoy changes in those areas of your life you most desire. All old burdens and issues that you have been dealing with will be resolved. Drastic changes will occur that will leave you with an exciting outlook on life.

plantain Within a four day period certain plans will become a reality due to your determination. This will lead you to a better lifestyle. You will be able to rid yourself of any mental blocks that keep you from moving in the direction you choose. You will acquire confidence in your abilities during this time period.

plantation Do not allow resentments to get in the way of your future goals. A better attitude will yield a better way of life.

plaque You will suffer misery, misfortune and troubles because of circumstances that will arise within a few days. Take steps to assure that situations that are externally calm, but in discord internally, do not explode.

plasma You will enjoy a job position that will take you to virtually every city in the world on a per diem basis.

plaster Watch out for explosions caused by electrical motors.

plasterboard An older, well respected person will converse with you concerning an impending decision. You will be guided to the correct decision by this person.

plaster cast For the next five days allow yourself time to contemplate and reflect on your ideas and feelings. This will allow you to connect with those aspects of your life that you want to improve. You will be able to do this better if you give yourself the time to mull over the decisions you will be making.

plaster of Paris Watch out for pickpockets and loss of belongings while traveling.

plastic You will enjoy a stress free life for a long time to come.

plastic bag A cluster of events will occur one after the other and will bring you a tremendous amount of wonder, joy and awe. You will also possess a powerful energy that you will be able to direct and control at the precise time these other events are rapidly developing. As a result, you will be able to bring others under your control. You have prior notice of this and will be able, within the week, to successfully direct this energy to complete anything you wish. You will be able to rise above any obstacle and it will now be a simple matter to deal with any overriding problem. Follow your intuition. Many blessings will come to you and your family.

plastic basket Do not put off talking with someone about your special needs. After discussing important matters with this person, you will find they will be more than happy to assist you. This is a lucky omen for you. You are much loved and esteemed.

plastic explosive You are being asked not to put on a persona that confuses others. Too much of a change is too drastic for others to comprehend. Step back and stop confusing others with your behavior. You must also be careful while traveling and avoid any situation that may be hazardous for the next five days.

plastic flowers You will be with that special person for a lifetime and you will enjoy each moment. Also an unusual event will take place within the next few days. This will bring you much joy and happiness.

plastic food containers For a two day period, do everything

you can to lobby for a connection with those you want to steer in your direction. Relentlessly seek out these people and get your point across to them until you are able to sway them to your position. Your actions will ensure everything falls into place to your advantage and for everyone else involved. Many blessings will come to you and your family and you are headed for a brilliant future.

plastic surgery Someone will approach you romantically. This person has a very jealous mate who will learn personal information about you in order to stalk you. Take precautions and stop this behavior early on. Anything negative in this dream that could become a reality needs to be prevented. Otherwise, you are headed for a brilliant future.

plate Someone is eager to hear from you and to share some good news with you.

plateau You will receive abundances in every area of your life.

plate glass Rely only on yourself to resolve the problems at hand. Do not give up until it is completely resolved.
  cracked A close relative will become unemployed.
  broken Empower yourself ahead of time by putting everything important in writing.

platform Let others take the lead and assume some of the responsibilities for a while.

platform shoes Develop the motivation to make something happen. You will be able to ask the key questions to determine what it is you need to do. Wonderful events will occur that will permit what is destined to happen.

platinum You are treating a very serious matter lightly. You will need to become more serious about it and take care of this matter promptly. You will also be given a gift by an older person that will be worth a great deal in the future.

platinum blonde All legal negotiations will result in your favor. Someone who has gone through some rough moments in their life will also choose you to be the person they open up to. Be sympathetic to this individual, especially for the next three days.

Plato Stand up for your convictions and develop a determined nature. Your actions will shift things in the direction you desire.

platoon You will be offered a salary for a single short term project. This will take care of all of your spending needs for those items you have long desired.

platter Do not waste time on someone else's business. You are headed in the right direction. This dream is a very lucky omen. Keep a journal and concentrate on your goals. You will be glad you did because you will be held accountable for your actions.

platypus Someone you have known for a long time and have a lot of respect for will call you for advice. Help this person but do not become involved.

play You will be lucky in all low risk games of chance for the next three weeks.

player piano An older, wise person will help you reach the crux of a problem very quickly. Follow this person's advice for the next two days and you will find you will be able to solve complicated issues very quickly.

playful *to be playful to someone or have someone act playful toward you.* An abundance of health, spiritual healing and tranquility will come to you within three weeks. A celebration will also occur within a week that will spark a sense of rejoicing for everyone involved. For the last two weeks of March and the entire month of April you are being promised that an idea, project, or event will be brought into tangible form. This project, etc., will reach a level of perfection, take on a life of its own and will easily pass through each channel you have to take it through. This project will be a blessing and a cause for celebration for you and for everyone involved in this process. You are headed for a brilliant future.

playground Within the week, you will spoil an event because of your demands on others. Think ahead and take steps to avoid this behavior.

playhouse The romantic moments you enjoy over the next few days will brighten your life.

playing cards Follow your intuition. If you are playing solitaire in this dream you will be married and will have many wonderful years together.

playmate Someone you have known for many years will take a long trip and you will never hear from this person again. To avoid this, get all the information necessary to track this person down.

playpen The entire family will rejoice over the resolution of a long term problem.

playwright You will receive financial help from a family member eager to finance your project. You will not have to repay this loan because your relative is only interested in your success. You will achieve your goals.

plaza Anything connected with music will be lucky for you.

plea Develop a support system of loyal friends who will stick with you and affirm your ideas over the years.

plead *to plead for your life* Take every precaution necessary to make sure you are not leading yourself down a dead end path. This will create a very stressful future. You have prior notice of this and can take the necessary steps to steer yourself toward the correct path. Many blessings are with you and your family.

please *to please* Someone you are very fond of needs to spend more time with you. Within the week, this person will need extra closeness but you will not be conscious of it. This individual is very sensitive and knowledge of this will protect this person's feelings.

to hear someone use this word For a three day period, take charge of your thoughts and do not allow yourself to react to old thoughts and memories. These thoughts are not productive and only waste the time and energy that could be used for something far more productive. Do not bring this behavior to another person.

if you recognize the person using this phrase This implies that someone needs a favor from you and will make this request. Make it your priority to handle this to the best of your ability at the time this favor is asked of you.

to use this word Make sure you show special consideration to another person regardless of what else is going on in your life. This person has developed strong feelings for you and needs to feel confident about the foundation of this relationship. Make it a priority to show more consideration for the next three days.

pleat Be sure to keep all disputes and desires in the open in order to avoid emotional stress in the future. Keep the lines of communication open before committing to a reconciliation.

pledge *to pledge money unexpectedly* You will be given a large sum of money.

to pledge the flag Meditation will center and balance you.

pleurisy You will have memorable days and enjoy many pleasures over the next few months.

Plexiglas You will unexpectedly need to render financial help and will be quickly repaid.

pliers Meet someone head on who is avoiding repayment of a debt to you. Do this in a nice and tactful way and repayment will quickly come after this confrontation.

plod Make sure your blood circulation is normal and watch your cholesterol levels. Exercise by walking, eat a balanced diet and drink plenty of water.

plot Watch out for a secretary who enjoys plotting to keep your calls from the person you are interested in. Be persistent in other methods of approach. Avoid going through this person or anyone else who works in this capacity.

plow You will receive a gift of orchids.

plug For the next seven days you will be unbearable because of your tenacity and relentlessness in pursuing your goals. You are in a very lucky position. You will be celebrating a joyful victory.

electric plug You will have a conversation with a wealthy, older person. You will be unaware of this person's wealth and will converse about your skills, creativity and ideas. This older person will then, after a three day period, offer to finance your ideas and will put you in touch with those who will assist in launching your plans.

electric wall socket You and someone you recognize in this dream will motivate yourselves in an unusual way that will enable you to get in touch with an, as yet, unknown person. You and the person in this dream will both have this experience although they will be totally unconnected. Conversations will flow easily between you and the person you have yet to meet, in a delightful way. You will both have the feeling you have not experienced this in a long time, if ever. The person you will meet possesses an artful sense of timing as well as the unusual ability to sense the feelings of other people. They are capable of bringing pleasure to others and fully committing themselves. They are also able to put themselves in a subservient role, tastefully and within limits, as well as having the capability of pampering others to the extreme, but not overly so. You will find this to be very delightful and will never have a distasteful moment. If you choose to have a relationship, it will grow as much as you want and will be a mutually satisfying and nurturing union. Expect this to occur within three days and alert the person you dreamed about to expect this as well. You are headed for a brilliant future.

plum This is a lucky omen and you will enjoy many abundances in life. Someone will extend themselves to you in order to make you comfortable during a visit.

plumage You will be in a romantic mood now and will enjoy yourself more with that special person. Look at the color definition for a more detailed meaning of this dream.

plumber You will take a wonderful trip, see many beautiful sights, enjoy yourself immensely, and enjoy a safe return. You will remember this trip for the rest of your life.

plumb line Within three days make sure you clear up all overdue bills in order to avoid stressful situations.

plume Look up the colors of the plume to receive extra clues to the meaning of this dream. This is a lucky omen for love. You will be invited to a large formal elegant party. Start looking for the proper attire now because you will not find anything at the last minute. Make sure to check what others will be wearing in order to dress appropriately.

plum pudding Be relentless and investigate deeply to determine the exact condition of a relative. Your actions could be the main factor in saving this person's life. Make sure this person receives the services they need and that all their needs are met.

plump Take the lead in pursuing new challenges and contracts. You will be very successful.

plunder You will be hospitalized for several days due to an infection if you do not take steps to prevent this. Drink plenty of water and stay healthy.

plunger Stop taking unnecessary risks regarding plans to investigate the unknown. Become more informed before taking any more steps in this direction.

Pluto For the next few days avoid anyone who angers easily. This person wants everything to go their way.

Plymouth Be loyal to that special person and involve yourself more in the relationship. This dream may also be used as a reference point in time. If you dream of this city and see its name used in any context, the dream message will occur on this day.

plywood Do everything necessary to feel more comfortable and confident about how you look to others.

P.M. You have become too involved in too many things at one time. Focus on each situation separately and work on it until it is resolved.

pneumonia For three days, watch that the limbs of small children are protected and out of danger. Take precautions to ensure these children do not injure or lose any parts.

poach Do not take responsibility for someone else's valuables for the next few days.

pock Prior to making a financial decision, explain why you want to take the situation in a new direction. This will prevent confrontations later on.

pocket Practice meditation through prayer in order to encourage personal growth. Your inner spirit will be tranquil and you will regain a new sense of joy.

to look for something in a pocket that is not there Maintain a sense of alertness for the next three days and do not let your guard down. Someone will attempt to persuade you into going somewhere that could be a danger to you. Remain wary in all aspects of your life and be very cautious when involving yourself in new situations with another person who will unwittingly cause you injury. For these next three days, it is very important for you to wisely choose what you will and will not allow yourself to become involved in.

empty Within three days, you will have to deal with someone who enjoys creating chaos and stressful situations. Prepare yourself. Within this three day time span, this person will create a monster of a situation that will escalate to a point of being impossible to control. Make other plans that will offer you enjoyment and an excuse to avoid this person's company.

to find what you are looking for in a pocket An event will occur within seven days that you must attend. You will be in the company of two admirers and you will have the pleasure of watching both of them subtly try to win over your affections. Although it doesn't show, one of them possesses a great deal of authority and power and you will find both of these people to be very agreeable and charming. You would enjoy having one of them as a lifetime partner. You can be confident that you will put yourself on the path of a prosperous future.

pocket billiards You will receive the approval you have been long seeking. You and someone you care a great deal about will be surrounded by wonderful people and will enjoy many beautiful days together, romantically, emotionally and in terms of health.

pocketbook Do not allow the presence of a recently estranged person to keep you from attending a social function. An event is also scheduled for the coming week that is important for you to attend. You will find yourself in the company of two admirers who will attempt to win over your affections. Although it is not apparent, one of them possesses a great deal of power and authority. Both of these admirers are very agreeable and charming and you would enjoy having one as a partner for life. You can be confident that you are on the path toward a prosperous future.

pocket handkerchief Within three days you will have the power to save someone's life. Do everything you can to aggressively intervene into someone else's behavior in order to save their life. An unusual event will lead you to investigate this person's whereabouts and their need for assistance. Good luck is with you and many blessings will come to you and your family.

pocketknife Your plans will work brilliantly, move quickly.

pocket money Do not become jealous of the behavior of someone who is special to you. You must also avoid doing anything that will create envy in others. Otherwise, this dream is a good luck omen.

pockmark This cycle demands you give a lot of attention to others. Remain calm and do not allow this to change your attitude, especially for the next three days.

pod You are talking too much at the wrong time.

podiatrist Do not waste your life by carrying a chip on your shoulder. Rid yourself of negativity.

podium Do not allow an opinionated person to impose themselves on your way of life. Do not allow anyone to block your path.

Poe, Edgar Allen Do not overextend yourself with credit. Watch your finances.

poem For the next few days think ahead and do not impulsively indulge in any activity you find distasteful.

poet Within two days, a close loyal ally to your company will be jeopardized by a remark from a special person you

favor. Prevent this occurrence.

poetry You will receive a very large inheritance. It would be to your advantage to make mutually agreeable plans to tap into this before the benefactor passes away.

pog Within three days your fantasies and desires will become yours. You will enjoy the experience of your life filled with joyous, thrilling and pleasurable moments if you do not deprive yourself of this experience. Go for it because you will enjoy yourself tremendously.

poi Be very cautious. Someone is secretly trying to gather information about you for their own purposes. This is likely to occur within two days. Keep all personal information from falling into someone else's hands.

point Within three days, it is important that each proposal you make quickly reaches a certain point in negotiations. Include all new pertinent information. Present this concisely in order to gain a quick approval.

pointer *with pinpoint light* This is alerting you that within five days someone who was once a part of your life will make a verbal plea to reenter your life in a way that will appeal to you greatly. This person treated you in an insensitive, harsh and abusive manner in the past to the point of going on with your life without them. This individual will bring to you a new proposition about sharing your life together and will have plans that will offer you a solid foundation. You will be bothered with flashbacks about what your life with this person was in the past. This dream is letting you know you do not need to experience any sleepless nights and you can enjoy a good life together. This person is now a very responsible and reasonable person and you can proceed with confidence in a new relationship that will be solid and permanent for as long as you want. You are definitely headed for a brilliant future and all those involved will benefit from this union.

poison This is the time to try out new styles. Your intelligence along with a new style will now open doors that were formerly closed.

poison gas Do not expose yourself to a deadly disease for the next two days. Do everything you can to prevent this now.

poison hemlock You will demand a high level of efficiency from others and this will help you gain the financial security you need. Avoid being overly disagreeable while making your demands.

poison ivy Be positive and push yourself to include romance in your life while you still have time to enjoy a long time of togetherness.

poison oak You would rather live in a style that goes against your principles than admit your feelings of disillusionment. Make it a point to become certain of your feelings and face up to reality. You will find you have completely different feelings about someone or something in your life than you thought. Although this may stir up deep painful feelings, you will be able to prepare yourself and face up to this dichotomy in your life. You will heal very quickly and move quickly toward a more dynamic way of life. You are headed for a prosperous future. It is better to make painful changes than to remain in an unbearable lifestyle.

poker For the next three days do not overextend yourself by helping a close friend. This could lead to resentments. Play any numbers you see in this dream in games of chance. You must also take steps to prevent or alter any negative event foretold in this dream and make sure you only experience positive expressions in your life.

Poland You will receive a great favor from a powerful person. This favor will change you and make you wealthy. You also need to make sure you do not allow anyone to prevent you from handling your responsibilities. This dream may also be used as a reference point in time. If you dream of this country and see its name used in any context, the dream message will occur on this day.

polar This is a lucky omen. Everything you see in this dream will come to pass within three months.

polar bear Do not allow anyone to intimidate you into not asking for what is yours financially. Go in and demand what is yours rather than avoiding the issue.

Polaroid You will confide a secret about your plans to leave. This secret will leak out and your plans will become known to others. Avoid any confidences for at least three days.

pole Calm down. You have done everything you can to rid yourself of an irritating problem. Within three days, this problem will work itself out.

pole bean Do everything you can to develop the support system that a child or young adult needs to guide themselves to a path of less stress and greater prosperity. Many blessings will come to you and your family.

polecat Something you have relied upon will fall apart. Develop an alternative plan.

pole vault Do not delay last minute decisions concerning anticipated events. You cannot fail. This is a lucky omen.

police Someone is developing a plot to violate your rights for the purpose of their own emotional gratification. This person will attempt to manipulate you into becoming involved in a situation that will become increasingly disgusting and distasteful for you. This involvement goes against your will and against your better judgment. Do not put yourself in any position where you will have to compromise your princi-

ples in order to leave safely. This is preventable. Good luck is with you.

to be confronted Do not make any decision about love for the next three days. This decision will be wrong for you.

to ask for help from a police officer Someone who is interested in you will be very fragile due to a broken relationship that has left them stressed. You must handle this person carefully. The wrong word may drive them away. Watch out for this for the next four days. Things could work out and a dynamic union will be the result.

to see police in the background Be wise and adhere to all legal rules. Be wary of who you are talking to, this person is a conniving friend.

to be followed by the police You will get a cold reception at a friend's house. Remain calm. This friend will later apologize for this treatment.

to hear "call the police" Do not lose your sense of alertness, especially for the next three days. Do not let your guard down and do not allow yourself to be persuaded into going someplace that could represent a danger to you. Remain alert in all aspects of your life and be very cautious when involving yourself in new situations with another individual who could inadvertently cause you injury. It is extremely important, for this time period, to choose carefully what you will or will not involve yourself in. Take special steps to prevent any negative event foreseen in this dream from becoming a reality.

police car You have overlooked an urgent matter that needs to be taken care of. This matter is of acute importance and needs to be attended to now. If you see another person connected with this dream, this person has an urgent need to discuss an important matter with you. It is important that you meet with them to find out what they have in mind. Do this in such a way to avoid being subtly manipulated.

to see someone in the police car you recognize This dream implies immediate danger from the person you see in the squad car. This will be something in the nature of a sexual assault and you will contract a sexually transmitted disease. Take extra precautions against this person.

to see someone in the police car you do not recognize You will be stopped for a minor traffic infraction. For two weeks, take extra precautions while driving to avoid a ticket.

if you are driving the police car You are unknowingly allowing a troublesome situation to develop that needs to be aggressively attended to. Discipline and structure yourself in order to grasp each situation before it disperses to the point of chaos because once it reaches this point you will lose the ability to begin again. Push yourself now to resolve each issue and do not allow yourself to get bogged down with extraneous matters that are out of your control. Stay focused. You need to make sure you do not become the major cause of problems. Focus on the aspect of your behavior that leads to this and do nothing that will cause problems with the law.

police dog Stand firm and do not allow others to belittle and manipulate you. Do not compromise your feelings or allow this behavior to continue out of fear of losing a friendship.

This person will stand by you.

policeman Be patient with a loved one who is incapable of verbalizing love. You are loved beyond your expectations.

policewoman Remain free for a while. Someone else will come into your life.

policy Be suspicious. Ask questions and dig deeply for the truth of the matter.

polio Within a day or two objections will arise due to words said in a conversation. Stop and listen to the objections. They will subtly relate to a future situation. Step back, you may be able to repair these inequities.

Polish Do not allow an authority figure who has, up to now, manipulated your life and blocked your ambitions to stop you from achieving success.

polish *car* Maintain a low profile and keep your mind on routine tasks. Maintain a constant vigilance against any errors that could occur in any capacity for the next three days. Handle any mistake immediately so everything can fall into place correctly. Because you have prior notice of this you can take steps to avoid unnecessary problems. Many blessings are with you and you are headed for a brilliant future.

politician Be more serious about a matter you are treating too frivolously.

polka Experience, imagination and skill will spell wealth. You are dynamically heading in the right direction.

polka dot You will travel during this next year for educational purposes. This will include foreign travel and you will enjoy a brilliant life.

pollen You will win a law suit.

pollution You will suffer financial loss if you are not watchful of your circumstances.

pollywog Within three weeks you will have to change your plans. Take aggressive steps to remove all blocks, obstacles, people, etc., that stand in the way of your future prosperity. Once you have overcome this you will be glad you have put yourself on the right path. Many blessings are with you and your family.

polo Practice tolerance for at least a week. This dream is also an omen of luck.

polo shirt You will soon be able to decide on the person you should involve yourself with. This person is very knowledgeable and will be able to offer their help in finding a solution to a particular issue.

poltergeist *if you are a poltergeist* This is a promise that

you will be able to convince the listener of any creative idea, project, etc., in order to back you.
  to see a friendly poltergeist All of your ambitions will be successful and lead to wealth. Love matters will be lucky.
  to see a frightening poltergeist Pay more attention to your stress level and make sure this stress does not handicap you. Otherwise, this dream is a lucky omen for you.

polyester You are moving too fast for the plans you have submitted. Slow down your pace for a couple of weeks, then resume this fast pace and you will not lose out on any future opportunities.

polygraph You will achieve success because of the creation of a new, much needed substance. Your invention will be an everyday substance that will be used worldwide.

polygraph test For the next two weeks it is essential that you devote your time to positioning yourself in such a way that you can create excitement and generate a greater interest regarding a new situation. You will be able to segment more success about a new product, plan, idea or conversation. You will gain excellent feedback that will bring about more productivity, more fun and will create a non stressful outcome to what is a priority now. You will be able to bring everyone involved together in building a common understanding. You will determine what, where, and how to effectively achieve a chief victory on a grander scale than you anticipated. Your goal is to make the world aware of these exciting ideas, etc.. You will find that they are well received by others.

Polynesia This dream promises you a more loving relationship in the future. It may also be used as a reference point in time. If you dream of this island group and see its name used in any context, the dream message will occur on this day.

polyp Be sure you take extra precautions to protect yourself when in unfamiliar places. Guard yourself carefully for the next four days.

pomade Do not travel for the next few days unless you are the one driving.

pomegranate You will be offered a professional opportunity that will heighten your career. Everyone involved in a certain project will be more than eager to cooperate. Each person will experience success within two weeks and each facet will fall into place exactly as you desire. Move ahead on your plans and ideas. Many blessings will come to you and your family. This is a lucky omen.

Pomeranian Within two days someone will request that you handle a particular problem. Make sure you are emotionally able to take on added responsibilities before you agree to help. Make sure you are aware of each aspect of this problem before you commit yourself.

pompadour Within three days someone will want to show you how deeply they care for you and how involved they want to get. This person will perform a series of chores and favors for you and will be at your beck and call. Show your affection openly and be considerate of this person's generosity and efforts. Be very cautious, do not hurt this person's feelings, and do not become suspicious of this person's motives.

pom pom Set aside more time for sex and for much needed recreational functions in order to put aside complaints from a special person.

poncho Use the mass media to promote your product.

pond Someone will be very interested in you and eager to please. This dream also implies that people in authority will nominate you to a position of leadership. If you choose this path, it will affect your life on a permanent basis and will ensure a prosperous future.

dirty and stagnated Be very cautious of the way you speak to someone over the next three days. Someone will overreact to your words and it will be difficult to calm this person down. Take steps to avoid this situation. Set your goals high in other areas of your life and these goals will be met within three days.

with stagnated water Be very aware that someone you have asked to leave your life and who has promised to comply with your wishes will break this promise within five days. Take steps to prepare yourself in some way to avoid being pinned down by this person and make it very clear that you wish to have nothing to do with them. You will need to be emotionally equipped to deal with this delicate situation. Organize yourself emotionally and do not allow anyone to believe you are willing to commit to something you are not. Make sure you are not misunderstood. You will be able to get your point across in a way that will not be offensive. Proceed with caution and you will be able to handle this issue successfully.

fish pond Someone will demand a great deal of your time and attention, to the point of overwhelming you. This will continue for a few days, then the situation will ease as this person begins to feel more secure with you. Be patient and accommodating until this levels off.

pond in any other form This is an extremely lucky omen. It is also important you do not venture so quickly into the unknown with someone you have just met. Otherwise, this is a good cycle for romance and love.

pond scum Situations will occur within three days. Do not make these matters worse by dwelling on them. Focus on those new projects that need attending to now.

pontiff Focus on getting in touch with your inner self. Meditate and develop your spirituality in order to understand what you need to do in life.

pontoon Structure an event in such a way that you are aware of each tiny detail you may otherwise overlook. Be wary of this for the next three days.

pony This is an appeal for you to notice something that should not escape your attention.

pony express Within the week you will be able to relieve yourself of all old burdens as well as any new issues. You will also hear good news about different options you have been wanting to hear about for some time. This cycle promotes family harmony. Many blessings are with your family and you are headed for a prosperous future.

ponytail You will receive a quick profit after signing a contract.

poodle You will receive good news from a close relative.

pool You will receive the approval you have been long seeking. You and a loved one will be surrounded by fantastic people and will enjoy many wonderful days, romantically, emotionally and health wise.

poolroom Be very careful when out pleasure seeking. This could lead to some very serious complications in your life. Play it safe and let others know of your whereabouts at all times.

pool scum Situations will occur within three days that you will only make worse if you dwell on them. Focus on those new projects that need attending to now.

pool table Do everything necessary to promote closeness between yourself and family members. Do not distance yourself or assume an air of coldness. Communicate in a way that will bring others together. Do this within three days.

poor Sex and affection will be an important primary feature in your life. Take steps to make the best decisions regarding these matters. Do not waste time and be sure to practice safe sex. Referral services will point you in the right direction for a wonderful future.

poorhouse Be wise and face problems now so you can enjoy wealth and power later on.

popcorn You will experience a very magical cycle. Almost overnight you will meet someone and quickly marry. You will enjoy a good life, good health, financial security, and loyal friends.

Pope Concentrate on getting in touch with your inner self. You will be entering a phase in your life where you will want to meditate and become more spiritual in your own way. Also understand and center yourself enough to determine what you need to do in life. Pay close attention to anything you discussed with the Pope. If it was a negative concept, you will have to move quickly within the next three days to resolve and conclude this issue. You will need to bring this around to a positive situation. If this was a positive concept, do everything you can to bring this to full bloom for yourself or for anyone else involved. You will enjoy a life of tranquility and will have an abundance of health during this cycle.

popgun Your attitude will lead to a heated passionate argument with friends. Take steps to change your outlook on life.

poplar tree You will soon enjoy a family reunion.

poplin Develop a better attitude toward family members. Do not overextend yourself financially and control your impulse to spend when attending an outing. This may jeopardize the family's income.

poppy seeds Do whatever you can to understand the motives of a loved one. Remember this is a very special person. Show compassion.

porcelain You will receive an appeal for a personal loan from a person you have started to care about. This person will repay the loan. Make sure you do not speak negatively of anyone for the next few days.

porch For the next few days, do not speak negatively of anyone.

porcupine Think ahead so you can avoid getting stuck in a rut; otherwise, you will have to take on two jobs to survive. Within six weeks, a good and kind friend will force you out of this rut with an offer of a second job and an offer of emotional support. This is a good luck omen.

porcupine quill For the next three days, remain aware of a stranger who will come into your life in a very public setting. This person will create chaos for everyone by starting quarrels and disagreements. Do what you can to remain uninvolved in this situation.

pores This is a good luck omen.
goose bumps Someone you consider a friend will become a very cunning enemy. This individual will attempt, without your knowledge, to sabotage a very important opportunity just moments before you receive knowledge of it. You will be able to successfully turn things around to your satisfaction. You have prior notice of this and can make sure that you receive the information you need without interruption.
in any other form A special person has asked you to attend several functions and you have turned them down. Two things will occur if you make a point of attending a function. You will meet someone who will work successfully with you at a later time and you will make that special person happy.

pork To see a large pig is lucky in all aspects of your life. Health is yours.

several pigs Do not live beyond your means or purchase items you cannot afford. This will spell financial defeat.

pork chop *to eat* The potential exists for immediate danger to you and a friend and you will be treated for an injury. Think ahead to prevent this.
in any other form Someone will apologize to you for a past hurt.

pornography Watch your attitude for the next few days because you will have to apologize for hurting someone's feelings. Within two days you will be lied to. Be sure not to rely on anyone's information for this time period.

porpoise Travel expenses with a buddy should be shared. Do not be convinced otherwise.

porridge Do not let your imagination rule you.

porter Do not allow yourself to be a pushover with other peoples' problems.

porterhouse steak This is a lucky omen and you have a brilliant future ahead of you.

portrait For the next three days, keep all references of a personal problem out of conversations with someone who is, without your knowledge, interested in you. Do not appear negative.

Portugal You will receive unexpected love and appreciation from your family. This dream may also be used as a reference point in time. If you dream of this country and see its name used in any context, the dream message will occur on this day.

Portuguese man-of-war For the next three days you will have to demonstrate a certain degree of patience. This cycle will put you in the position of having too much to do and you will find yourself going from one thing to another in your attempt to handle many issues simultaneously. This will be a big waste of time for you. Prepare for this now and practice patience, otherwise you will become emotionally and physically depleted. Remain calm and you will be able to take care of everything you need.

pose You will enjoy power and riches because of a windfall inheritance.

Poseidon (*Greek mythology*) You will receive an unusual gift. This gift will be a conversation piece and will make you popular and happy.

posse In three days, other people will be angry at you because you will stick with your convictions and will refuse to go along with everyone else. This will be short lived. Stick with your convictions.

possessions To dream of possessiveness over certain personal items will lead you to treasure these items more. This is the correct response. Do not take your treasures for granted.

possum Problems with a neighbor's pets needs to be ignored. Any attempt to solve this will lead to a dispute. Given time, the problem will solve itself.

post *any form* For three weeks, remind yourself of important events that may be forgotten due to a busy schedule. You feel now that these events do not have the same priority as certain ongoing projects but you will soon find out that if you miss one of these events it will prove to be just as important.

postage *any form* Within seven days you will be working with someone you feel an attraction for. This person is not someone you should become involved with. Keep everything strictly business.

postage stamp This is a good luck omen. For the next two days, work to keep yourself currently up to date on all major happenings. This will aid in decision making and in collaborating your ideas with others.

postal employee Within three days the person you wish were more communicative with you will anxiously approach you to discuss intimate situations that involve both of you. Be sure to ask this person questions that concern you. This conversation will put you very much at ease. You will experience tranquility, good health and wealth during this cycle.

postcard This dream is a reminder not to ignore or forget the older people in your life who have been significant to you. Do small things for them in order to show your appreciation.

poster Become very centered on what you want and don't want from life. Pursue only what you really want for the next three days. Eat healthy foods, get plenty of rest and drink plenty of water. Many blessings will come to you and your family.

postmark Watch out for an animal scratch. This is preventable.

post office Take precautions to ensure that all mail reaches its proper destination.

Post Office Box Within five days, you will receive wonderful news. You will receive a large settlement that will come sooner and will be larger than you expected.

post person *(letter carrier)* You will have a lucky break. Do what you can to maintain a relationship by promoting closeness, love and affection. Within two days, no matter how discouraged or defeated you feel you must refuse to give in to these feelings. Assume a bold attitude. You are definitely headed for a brilliant future.

posture Practice consistency until you reach perfection. You will be happy that you did after you achieve financial success.

posy You will enjoy a fantastic sex life.

pot *cooking* You will gain the promotion you are seeking involving a certain special person.

to win the pot You will receive a great deal of money. A carefully worded plea will bring you a reconciliation with someone who is important to you.

flower pot Protect yourself, and do not allow yourself to be taken in by a scam that requires you give a small amount of money on a regular basis over a period of time. After this amount is tallied, it will add up to a substantial amount of money.

potassium Take care of your vital organs and make sure your heart is healthy. Eat healthily and exercise. A friend will also invest a great deal of money into a long time dream. This will not be successful. This person needs to rethink their goals. Attempt to talk to them about this.

potato Be sure you check out different marketing techniques and work toward choosing the correct one before putting out your product. Someone will also, within three days, communicate their deep feelings and their desire for a commitment to you. This individual will do everything within their power to appease you. This will include favors, chores and planned activities. Show your appreciation to this person and openly demonstrate your affection. Be very careful not to hurt this person's feelings and dispel all suspicions of their motives.

sweet potato You will be interested in someone whose sexual appetite is much greater than your own. This person will go to great lengths to involve you in their life. Carefully think over this situation in order to make your feelings clear yet not miss out on the love and affection this person has to offer. This person will take steps to accommodate you in order to keep the relationship mutually satisfying.

potato bug Take a very close look at your investments over the next four days. Pay close attention as well to someone who is making romantic overtures towards you. It will not be suitable to have a sexual encounter with this person because of the real possibility of contracting an unrevealed contagious disease. Take precautions to protect yourself sexually and financially.

potato chip Build up a support system in order to maintain a healthy lifestyle.

potato salad All negotiations will be very successful for you. A new person will also enter your life who will become a lifelong friend. This individual will be very charming and will share many wonderful stories with you. They will also give you an important message that will open your eyes to a different perspective on how to view a certain project or con-

Potbelly 500 Power

cept that you will be working on. You will be able to use this knowledge to make drastic improvements in your life. This will take place within three days.

potbelly You will work with someone who will pay you generously for domestic duties and you will enjoy a satisfying life. Actively seek this job.

pot holder Push yourself to have a good time at a family outing that will take place within a few days.

pothole Take time out to promptly handle important paperwork. This will ensure you receive what is due you in a timely fashion.

pothook Make sure you tell people you are in love with the person you are involved with.

potion You will be paid a special compliment that you will treasure for a long time.

potluck This is a good luck omen and a promise of abundance in all levels of your life. This dream also implies that you will be introduced to something exotic and provocative within days. You will also fall deeply in love and this relationship will last a life time. You will be in a very lucky cycle during this time period. Take advantage of this.

potpie Your children will rally around you and offer their assistance when you explain your situation and needs. You are deeply loved.

potpourri Make up for what you are lacking socially. Take someone special with you to add to the fun.

pot roast You will enjoy a happy family reunion with much food and festivities.

potter Think ahead, failure to keep a promise will only add more stress to an already stressful situation.

potters field This is an extremely lucky omen and a surprise is headed your way within three days. You will experience an abundance of health and many blessings will come to you and your family. Any plan you wish to put into tangible form will also be realized within the week. Move quickly on this and show respect for others.

potters' wheel You will be immersed in feelings of love for the next two days. You will have a sparkle in your eye prompted by unexpected sexual activity with a certain person. This will fill you with sensual pleasure and will be a passionate cycle for you. You are headed for a brilliant future filled with sexual pleasures and riches.

pottery Make sure you tell that special person that you love them. People need to hear this.
broken pottery You can avoid many depressing and dis-

tressful moments by not going on that trip you planned. Something will go tragically wrong and no one will be there to help you. Take steps to really take care of yourself.

pouch Surrender to the needs and feelings of another special person. You will be glad you did.

poultice This is a very lucky omen. You will experience a beneficial reversal of fortune within three days. This will be a good time to accomplish those things that for some reason you were unable to tackle before. Go for it.

poultry You will get a sudden pay raise and someone with a beautiful singing voice will also fall deeply in love with you. If you choose to pursue this, you will share a wonderful union for years to come.

pound You will be hearing of a pregnancy. Any negative event in this dream that could become a reality needs to be prevented and you need to take steps to ensure you experience only pleasant expressions in your life. You will also receive a financial windfall comparable with the amount of pounds you dreamed about.

pound cake You will shortly be celebrating your own wedding.

pour *to pour* Someone will attempt to trick you into spending more than you are able at this time.

poverty Become aggressive with your decisions. Everything will work out beautifully.

P.O.W. Do not allow yourself to fall back into a bad habit that you have broken. Be cautious of your behavior for the next few days.

powder Within three weeks, news of your talent and creativity will reach a future partner. You will reach a satisfactory agreement.

powder keg You will soon receive a very rewarding telephone call. This will result in a luncheon date.

powder puff You will ask for help from someone but this person will not come through at the appointed time. Line up an alternative person so you will not waste your time.

powder room You will fall in love with a musician.

power Someone you elevated socially will grant you your secret wish.
will power Do not make excuses for those aspects of your life in which you know you are not conducting yourself properly. Face facts and discipline yourself in such a way that you become the person you want to be. This cycle will permit you to make these changes with ease if you act quickly. During this three day cycle, you will want to demonstrate

that special personality that you want others to see and you will leave a positive impression. Prioritize your desires in other areas of your life. This cycle will allow you to accomplish this. Take steps to keep any negative event in this dream from becoming a reality and make sure you alert anyone you recognize to do likewise.

power plant This is an extremely lucky omen. You are headed for a brilliant future. You will receive a proposal that will be very hard to turn down. If you choose to involve yourself in this, you will enjoy a better lifestyle than you ever envisioned. Proceed with confidence.

pox Make sure to protect children in all swimming areas.

practical nurse You will be asked out and while on the date, you will accidentally blurt out an insulting remark. This person will never ask you out again. This is preventable so think ahead in order to avoid this.

prairie Avoid strangers for awhile. Someone may prove to be dangerous to you.

prairie chicken Within three days you will receive an unusual gift that you do not really like. Exchange this for something more to your liking.

prairie dog This is a good luck symbol. Your co-workers and you are looking at ways to complete a project quickly without stress. This will be successful.

prairie oyster Within three days you must avoid blurting something out that should remain confidential. This will lead to the separation of a couple you are acquainted with. Be careful to keep secrets hidden.

prairie schooner You will have a desire to move to a new location within a three week period. During this cycle, you have the option to choose this alternative or to stay put. If you choose, this is the best time for relocating.

praline Follow up all decisions with action.

prank You will feel insulted within three days by a casual remark meant as a joke. With warning, you can decide not to take everything so seriously.

prawn Watch your temper. You will publicly display your anger and will regret this at a later time.

pray *to pray* A past emotional crisis left you with a skill you will need within three days. Because of your past experience, you will be better able to deal with this now with less stress.

to see others pray A close relative will have a need to reach out to you for help. Your advice and listening skills will help them over this crisis. This problem will be short lived.

prayer For a three week period, make it a point to meditate in your favorite way.

prayer beads This is a very lucky omen. Take the time to meditate and to do special things for yourself. Enjoy the solitude you desperately need. Be aware that neglecting to pay attention to some facet of your life will result in your death. Become relentless in your attentiveness.

prayer book This is a good luck omen. You will experience more abundance in all areas of your life. Become more aware of the stress levels around you and create a stress free environment for yourself. This is especially important for the next ten days. Be relentless in taking care of all new situations in a prompt and timely manner.

Prayer of Manasseh *(book of the Canonical Bible)* Do not allow yourself to feel inferior to someone else because of the occurrence of unusual situations. Do not permit someone in authority to bring about these feelings. This is very important for the next two days. Stay balanced, focused and allow yourself time to regroup.

praying mantis Do not place yourself in a situation that will expose you to a deadly virus. An infected person will keep the knowledge of their disease from you for the intent of purposely infecting you. This will occur within a ten day period.

preach *to hear preaching* A teenager will have a personal crisis and will come to you for help. Remember your feelings as a youth and you will be able to offer good advice. Your words will stay with this person for a lifetime and will change the course of this young person's life.

to preach Pay your taxes early. A financial need will arise later and you will need money to handle this.

predator Beware. A young child will show fear and disgust toward another person. Pay attention to the discomfort this child feels. Do not push them to be friendly or to be in the same area as this other person. This could lead to a great deal of discomfort and many sleepless nights for this young person.

predestination *to ask for your destiny without hearing the results implies luck* Within two weeks a special person will come into your life. You will experience romance and generosity from this person. You are also being asked to get a reading. Any negative event connected to this dream must be avoided in reality.

to dream that you get results This implies luck. Follow what you are told to do. If you receive a warning, heed this and take precautions to prevent bad occurrences and take steps to ensure that any negative event foretold does not become a reality.

pregnancy *to be pregnant* Quickly determine your immediate needs and take steps to have these needs met.

to see yourself pregnant in a dream while not pregnant in reality You will hear news of someone's freedom after a long legal struggle or incarceration.

to touch yourself and seem pregnant but not visually appear pregnant Follow your urges for the next seven days. These are extremely lucky for you. All of the plans and ideas you put into motion will reach fruition and you will prosper on a much larger scale than you ever imagined. Good luck is with you.

false in any form The person you are thinking of asking for assistance will not be able to help. Think of an alternative person within four days.

in any other form Do everything necessary to realize your goal even if it involves small risk taking. Make more connections in order to make your ideas flourish. You should also take the opportunity to openly flirt with anyone you are attracted to. If you ask this person out, they will accept. Any negative event foretold in this dream that could become a reality needs to be prevented for yourself or for anyone you recognized in the dream. Otherwise, you are headed for a healthy, prosperous future that will begin to evolve within five days.

pregnant pause You will view an episode that will show you how another person can create chaos because of their behavior. You will discuss a business arrangement with someone you have made prior arrangements with. This will involve a task of some sort that this person has agreed to do. A third person will enter the arena and start making changes in your arrangements to suit their feelings on how things should be handled. This person will be of the opposite sex and will bully themselves into the conversation in such a way that it will be difficult for you to take control. Do whatever you can to keep this person from bullying you into making compromises. You have prior notice of this and can successfully keep this from taking place.

prep school Someone will shortly come into your life who is in constant need of a small handout. Be sure to keep a little something on hand for this person. Should you choose not to be involved, you have prior warning and can take precautions to keep this from taking place. At the first indication of problems, put a stop to your involvement.

Presbyterian You will soon rise above your current difficulties.

preschool Crying over small matters will not help your attitude and will stand in the way of success. Focus more on ways to be happy instead of depressed. Force happiness on yourself and stay with it.

prescription Escape as quickly as possible from the torch you are carrying. This torch is a depressing burden and is keeping you from enjoying life. You will also need to be ready for a new person who will enter your life within two months.

present *to receive a present* You will be shocked by the animosity shown to you by another person. After they have

seen you for awhile from a distance, and have seen your true character, they will demonstrate greater warmth and friendliness and you will develop a nice relationship.

to give a present You will enjoy many days of fun and dancing. This will be a very social cycle for you.

in any other form You will spice up your life by giving a social function for people from all walks of life, nationalities and religions. Your life will be enriched and you will gain a variety of new opportunities. This will occur within two weeks.

preserve For the next two days you need to do whatever you can to avoid disagreement. It is better to have a conversation to patch things up.

President or former President *(of the USA)* This indicates grandness, power and victory in every level of your life. It also implies you will enjoy exhilarating changes in your way of living. You will also soon meet with someone you do not know yet who has a flair for visual affects. Add drama and style to your appearance if this is something you choose. This will lead to a pleasurable meeting and a larger income flow within five days.

President's wife or former President's wife Within seven days, you will have an overwhelming feeling of being solidly grounded, balanced and confident. As a result, you will be able to handle situations that require this aspect of your personality. Use this cycle to work on those areas of your life that you want to make changes in. You will have the opportunity to bring prosperity into your life at the level you desire. You are placing yourself on the path toward a brilliant future.

Presley, Elvis Someone will send a message to you via a physical channel (i.e., flowers, gifts, etc.) that they are interested in you. Once you know this person is interested, romance will quickly blossom and you are being told to go full speed ahead. You will achieve success. Regard the power this person symbolizes as the power you will possess for the next five days. Pay close attention to what these people are telling you because this will be an accurate depiction of what will be occurring in reality. If it is negative, take steps to prevent its occurrence in reality. Otherwise, you are headed for a prosperous future. Refer to the definition "to dream about a deceased person" for a greater definition of this dream message. You will find this definition under the word "dead".

press *(to iron)* Define what is urgent for you to handle. Do not tackle those difficult situations that can be delegated to others. You will find that some things were not that important for you to handle.

press *(mass media)* Do not allow yourself to be emotionally steered in the wrong direction for the next few days. Someone who shows interest in you will not be interested sexually. The attraction is merely platonic and you are misinterpreting body language and mixing signals.

press conference Do not put into writing what you wish to keep secret.

pressure cooker A certain person will go to great lengths to pull you away from a certain group of people or a plan so that you are no longer associated with them on any level. This individual will work relentlessly to ensure this takes place. Investigate this in detail so you can protect your interests.

pretend Do not become involved in anything out of the ordinary for the next two weeks.

pretty Complete transactions quickly in order to meet deadlines.

pretzel You will be interrogated about the actions of another.

prey *to be the prey* Within two weeks, someone will make a romantic gesture toward you, then later snub you. Be forewarned so you can avoid bad feelings over this.

price *to see price* Within five days someone you converse with will reveal a sincerity and selflessness that will allow you to feel very comfortable around them. You have never seen this aspect of this individual's personality before and it will seem almost like a breath of fresh air. You must also work with the numbers you saw when engaged in negotiations and for games of chance. You will be in a cycle of luck for the next seven days.

price tag Be alert to situations that will throw you off the correct course. This is an extremely lucky omen. Remember the dollar value and use these numbers in small risk games of chance for a high return.

prick Someone you did a favor for in the past will return the favor when you are in need.

prickly heat You will come out ahead in this cycle if you do not jump to any conclusions.

prickly pear Make it a point to eat more fresh vegetables and fruits to ensure your health is maintained properly. Drink plenty of water and create a stress free environment.

pride Do not allow yourself to be hurt by another's lack of appreciation.

priest In the next few days do not allow any personal information about yourself to be known.

prima donna Think before you volunteer your time. This time could be better spent with your family.

primal Family problems can be avoided if you heed certain warning signs.

primate Be very selfish when giving of yourself.

prime minister You are relying on the help of a certain family member but this assistance will not come because of a new situation in their life. Look for alternative help.

primitive *any form* Get back to the basics and simplify your life. Do not needlessly use chemicals.

primrose Do not treat special people in your life cruelly. Get help to change your attitude.

prince You are entering the perfect cycle to explore ways to generate extra income to ensure your future. For the next five days, you will also be seen in a very favorable light by someone who is special to you. This person will offer you affection and loyalty and will display a very giving attitude toward you. You will share many precious moments together. You will also experience a special power in those areas of your life you had no idea you had this kind of power in. Many blessings are with you.

Prince Charming You will have to extend yourself more and give more to others for the time being. Be patient and this time will pass. Your efforts will be greatly appreciated.

princess Find out the intentions of someone you have been seeing romantically.
Princess Diana (Princess of Wales) You will come to a decision with that special person in your life that will be loving, mutually satisfying and will also meet all of your financial needs.

principal Stand by your convictions and stand up for someone special who feels you do not want to back them up.

print *to print* Do not slave for someone's love. You are already well loved and do not need to do this.
in any other form This is a lucky omen. Let others know that your time cannot be manipulated. Get back to your priorities.

printing press This is a lucky omen. You will have, as a mate, someone who will relentlessly try to keep you close and keep the union together.

prism For the next four days, anything that appears unusual or out of the ordinary is not a good situation to become involved in.

prison This implies you will be given a blessing. You will learn of a pregnancy and a new addition to the family. You must also take steps to prevent anything in this dream with a negative connotation from becoming a reality. Do everything you can to experience only positive expressions in your life.

prisoner This is an omen of blessing. You will need to strive to make adjustments with people who are important to you.

to be Uncertainties you feel about another are accurate. Follow your hunches. You must also make a point of preventing any negative event foreseen in this dream from becoming a reality and take steps to experience only positive events in your life.

privacy *any form* Find time to meditate and determine what is really important.

private eye You will soon need new equipment or appliances. Begin putting money aside now so you can meet this expense.

"private moment" *to hear the phrase to ask for a private moment, or to have someone ask you for a private moment* Within ten days you will be entering an extremely lucky cycle and everyone involved in your life will share in this luck. You will also receive services that will enable you to complete your goals successfully and reach higher levels of achievement than you thought possible, especially with anything you feel is a priority. You can expect wonderful and amazing connections that will assist you in grasping and meeting your goals. You can also expect a mega merger. The energy generated between you and those you will be working with will bring you to a far higher level of success than you hoped for. This dream also indicates you will benefit greatly by attending a festive event, participating in an educational experience, or by attending a gathering in which one person will show an interest in you and your projects. You can look forward to a long period of tranquility following this experience and will enjoy a prosperous future. Anything negative witnessed in this dream may be avoided and you need to forewarn anyone you dreamed about to do the same.

private school You are loved beyond your imagination. Do not deprive yourself of the deep emotions and pleasures that are being made available to you. You will enjoy appreciation and love from others within the week.

prize *to dream of winning a prize* You will earn extra money by running errands for someone in need. Do not let sympathy stand in the way of getting paid.

prizefight Take a walk and go over your thoughts. You will attain clarity and make the right choices in life.

prize money A friendly verbal exchange will quickly develop into a romantic overture. Good things will come from this and good luck is with you. You must also pay attention to the location depicted in the dream. This indicates that you will receive a cash prize there. Go for it. Any numbers seen in this dream may be used for games of chance.

prize winner Within four days someone's new rules and

regulations will have a strong impact on your life. Take everything slowly and calmly and do not allow this to be a source of stress in your life. Everything will turn out much better than you expected.

probate Two years from now, you will receive inherited property. You will be taken to court by a close relative of the deceased and this person will win. Take steps now to ensure that the will is in proper order. You must also, within five days, do everything you can to keep any negative event foretold in this dream from taking place. Work to enjoy only positive experiences in your life.

probation *if you are on probation in a dream* Things can get out of hand with people who do not know how to take no for an answer. Take steps now to prevent this. If anything negative was depicted in this dream, take steps to change it or avoid it entirely.

someone else is Do not promise romance to someone while you are still on the rebound. If anything negative was depicted in this dream, take steps to change it or avoid it entirely.

probation officer Work with people who want to work with you to put your plans together in an organized fashion.

processed cheese Carefully scrutinize the differences between the plans you wish to implement within the next three days. This will allow you to correctly choose between them.

processed food Do not develop an overdependence on a certain person, especially for the next three days. Stop yourself and strive to be versatile with the resources you have available. Develop a support system and do not place undue strain on one person. You will also attend an event within two weeks and hear a performance by someone with a wonderfully magical voice. This will fill you with awe and wonder. You are headed for a prosperous future and many blessings are with you. Any message with a negative connotation needs to be altered or prevented in reality. Make sure you only experience positive expressions in your life.

procession *funeral* Within three days you will involve yourself with unusual situations that will vastly improve your standard of living. Also the larger the funeral procession and the larger the attendance, the greater the prominence and importance of someone who will pass away within the week. Otherwise, good luck is with you and many blessings will come to you and your family.

civil procession You will be taking huge steps to raise your standard of living. This will be accomplished by focusing on your goals in a grand way. Expect this to occur within three days due to some unusual and joyful circumstance. Everyone involved in this will enjoy beautiful expressions of joy and tranquility. Many blessings will be with you and your family.

hostile procession in any form You will receive a verbal threat that will affect you tremendously. Either this person is sure of who they are talking to or is mistaking you for someone else. In either case, this is an extremely dangerous situation to be involved in for the next three days. You need to increase your awareness in order to stay safe and clear of anyone's focus who has an evil intent. Because of your prior notice of this you will be able to avoid harm. Use any person you have at your disposal to make sure you remain safe.

processor Quickly process important ideas you have been considering. Do this within two days and you will be successful. It is also important for the next two days to not cancel anything that needs to be attended to. Anything regarding processors that have negative connotations needs to be prevented in reality. Take steps to ensure you only experience positive expressions in life.

prodigal son Tell your family that you love them.

produce Regarding children, make a point of learning their needs, whether this concerns clothing, food or emotional support.

produce market You will be appointed to a position of power and will achieve victory within two weeks. This is also alerting you that the timing is perfect for you to act quickly regarding certain issues. You are headed for a brilliant future.

profanity Focus on what needs immediate attention. Within two days you will be able to make the correct decision regarding an important matter.

profession Someone will resent your honest opinion after making a request for candidness. Avoid this, especially for the next three days.

professional You are entering a very lucky cycle and this implies that you will have the inner strength and courage that comes from within. Your drive and determination will serve to motivate you in such a way that you will be able to break through any barriers, whether mental or physical, and rid yourself of any aspect of your life that stands in the way of success. Once you have accomplished this, you will easily bring any new project to fruition and complete it in the way you most desire. You will also be welcomed with open arms anywhere you go during this time period. You will be put on a pedestal and greeted like royalty. You are headed for a brilliant future and many new opportunities are headed your way.

professor Speak up in order to improve your sex life.

profile *to see yours* Stop being so short tempered. You may have a food allergy that causes this. Get a doctor's advice.

to see another's profile Be more selective about what you will and won't do for another.

profit Do not overextend yourself when trying to win someone over. This person is not interested.

progeny Make a list of your priorities and make sure they are in the right order.

program Do not give too much of your efforts to others.

prohibition Someone will depend on you for answers to pass an exam. Prepare for your own education instead and suggest a tutor.

project Teach small children to be self reliant.

projection booth Start working now on a way to increase your cash flow. You will need the extra money within three weeks in order to make ends meet because certain situations will come up that will require extra cash. You have prior notice of this and can take steps now to ensure this will be taken care of.

projector Watch that you don't destroy your credit. You will be very fragile for a few weeks.

prom You are becoming too focused on someone and will make this person a victim of your cruelty. Get help for your behavior.

Prometheus *(Greek Mythology)* Stay focused because you will have your hands full dealing with an over dramatic person. This person is very arrogant and egotistical. Remain calm and stable. Empower yourself by really thinking ahead to what you want from this person.

promise Think ahead. If you do not have enough money, put aside some for emergencies. Make sure you do not take on other people's financial problems as your own.

Promised Land For the next three weeks meditate and you will gain clarity about the steps you need to take in your life. This may also be used as a reference point in time. If you dream of this Biblical site and see its name used in any context, the dream message will occur on this day.

proof *to not have proof of something* You will definitely experience a big victory within the week that will bring you a wealth of opportunities to choose from. Place yourself in the position to expose yourself to these opportunities by using any power you may have to bring a conclusion to an agreement in your favor. You have a one week period from the time you have this dream to push this agreement through and it will be well received by everyone involved. You are headed for a victorious future and many blessings are with you and your family.

in any other form Do not allow yourself to stagnate.

proofread Control you obsessive behavior and stop doing everything you can to get attention.

propane gas Watch your behavior. You are placing too much importance on another person and are emotionally overextending yourself with this individual. Take care of yourself in order to avoid later disappointments, especially for the next three days.

propeller Examine your motives for associating with someone you do not know well. Do this prior to making any further decisions. This person is very selfish and is only out for themselves.

property Push yourself harder for the next few days in order to accomplish your aims.

property tax Do not allow yourself to become passive and satisfied with your present circumstances. Take the time to make changes in the way your enterprise is going and you will see a rapid improvement with this new direction. This is also a good omen for love and health.

prophecy If you hear a prophecy, follow it exactly for this is very lucky. If you are giving a prophecy, follow this for it is also very lucky. Do not allow yourself to be caught off guard. Develop knowledge about everything you are committing yourself to. For the next four days you must make sure any negative message in this dream does not become a reality.

prophet Prior to criticizing their behavior do not forget the extra chores your mate has to accomplish.

Prophets *(from the Bible)* You will be entering a very intuitive cycle for the next two days. Your hunches will lead you in the right direction.

proposal You are entering a lucky cycle. You will soon have the opportunity to purchase a priceless, one of a kind item. Go for it. Any positive proposal you dreamed of will also become a reality and all proposals that have a negative connotation must be avoided in reality. This is the perfect time to accomplish anything you felt was an impossibility. You are headed for a brilliant future.

prosecute Within a few weeks, you will be meeting with a certain group of people. None of them will be right for your project. Wait a few weeks and you will find the perfect co-workers.

prosecutor You and someone close to you will realize you have underestimated the depth of your friendship. It will quickly develop into a romantic relationship based on mutual respect, if this is what you desire. You will enjoy many wonderful years together.

prospect This dream indicates that someone is reaching out for your help and is unable to verbalize this need. This will take only a few days of your time and you will enjoy successful results.

prospector Examine steps that may be taken to ensure your health. For the next two weeks, small stresses will tax your

well-being.

prosperity You will enjoy many blessings and will experience unusual abundances in each area of your life.

prostitute You will be very excited because someone will request sex from you. You had no idea this person felt an attraction to you and you will become excited about this prospect. This will be a very mutually sexually satisfying cycle for both of you. This dream is also a promise of success with any product you are attempting to promote. A brilliant future is ahead of you. Any negative message regarding prostitutes needs to be avoided in reality. Do everything you can to experience pleasant events in your life. If anything negative was depicted in this dream, take steps to change it or avoid it entirely.

to be one Make sure to take extra precautions when transferring money from one area to another. If precautions are not taken the money will be lost in transit. It would be a good idea to insure all mail containing money. Romance is also in the air and you will have many memorable moments of passion. If anything negative was depicted in this dream, take steps to change it or avoid it entirely.

to hire a prostitute This implies victory. You will take all the proper steps and meet all the right people to properly handle a project. If anything negative was depicted in this dream, take steps to change it or avoid it entirely.

to be asked for money in return for sex Do not doubt the loyalty of your loved one. You will also be successful this year in meeting your goals. If anything negative was depicted in this dream, take steps to change it or avoid it entirely.

call girl You will become quickly involved with someone you have just met. This person is demonstrative and loving and this will be a happy union.

protein Avoid disillusionment with a venture because you overextend yourself. You are asking too much of yourself and talking yourself out of pursuing what you want because of self doubt. Push yourself. You will succeed.

protest The same misfortunes are being brought to you by different people with the same problems. Avoid these people completely in order to prevent emotional distress. This will occur within the next two months. At the first indication of this take steps to avoid getting sucked in.

Protestant A professional person will unexpectedly offer to purchase a large number of your products. This will lead to a large profit.

prove Do not allow yourself to stagnate.

to be unable to prove something to someone During this coming week you will experience a big victory that will bring you a wealth of opportunities. Be sure to position yourself with whatever power and authority you may have at your disposal to bring about the completion of an agreement in your favor. You have only this one week period from the time you have this dream to push through this agreement. You can be assured this is the best time to make this happen and your agreement will be greeted with enthusiasm by everyone involved. You are on a victorious path in life and many blessings will come to you and your family.

to have someone prove something to you or to prove something to someone else You will have an incredible need to have something taken care of that can only be done with the help of someone else. This could be along the line of a financial loan or a big favor. It will appear to be such a big request that it will be hard for you to believe it will be given to you. Follow your intuition and this will give you a clue to the person who will be able to help you out. Proceed with confidence and explore all of your options until you locate the right person. As soon as an agreement has been made, move quickly so this person does not have the chance to change their mind. Many blessings are with you and you are headed for a prosperous future.

proverb Simplify you life and get back to basics. Keep your projects simple and you will achieve success.

Proverbs (*Book of Bible*) Be very analytical when presenting ideas to another. This will open new doors for you. Create interest in others and you will receive an abundance of health and financial success.

province Do not make your home a prison. Others who live with you will feel they have no freedom. This will eventually backfire on you.

provoke You will be helping a relative who is unable to help themselves due to illness. The person you will need to contact for help in providing services is miserable and will enjoy making life miserable for others. Because of the position held, this person will make life hard for you. This person also enjoys watching others become angry. Do not put yourself in the position to be affected. Because of your calm manner, you will achieve your goal but this person will do what they can to sidetrack you.

prow Do not go overboard on anything now and do not make any moves for three weeks.

prowl Responsibilities you have delegated to others will turn out well only if you baby-sit the project.

prune You will be ordered around by someone with emotional hang ups. This will anger you. Avoid this situation.

Psalms (*Book of Bible*) Within a few days you will choose the right physician for your health problems. After following the advice given and after taking the correct medications you will feel immediate relief. For the next few years you and your family will enjoy abundances in life, good health and tranquility.

psyche You will observe a new inner power and will be able to execute plans in the right direction, see every move with clarity and remove any block on the path to success. You will be able to diffuse all negative situations. Your instincts

are correct, follow them. You will enjoy many blessings.

psychiatry Do not hesitate to back off from situations that do not meet your expectations.

psychic *if you are the psychic or if you receive a reading* Follow the advice given. This will also be a good time to get a psychic reading. This dream is a lucky omen and you will be going through a lucky cycle for the next few days. You will need to also make up for lost social events with those who are close to you. Follow your instincts.

blue sight (paranormal sight that allows psychics to track down murderers) Be very careful. You are beginning to adopt a dangerous pattern of thinking that will lead to health problems that have no physical or organic cause. You will consult many physicians who will tell you they find nothing wrong with you. Be diligent and take steps now to prevent this from occurring. Act quickly to change your pattern of thinking and your mental attitude. Begin treating your body with respect, increase your exercise level, make lifestyle changes, alter your diet, and reschedule your life in such a way to lessen physical demands on your body. Divorce yourself from anyone who may be making you feel uncomfortable. You can easily avoid this situation by redirecting the way in which you live your life and can avoid a loss of health by practicing this regimen. Take steps to avoid or alter any negative event in this dream that could become a reality. Do everything you can to experience only positive expressions in your life. You are headed for a prosperous future and many blessings are with you and your family.

in any other form This is a lucky omen. You will experience a new freedom within two days due to an unexpected and unusual circumstance. Take steps to prevent any negative event in this dream from occurring in reality and make sure you only experience positive expressions in your life. You are definitely headed for a brilliant future.

psycho Within a few weeks, someone with a mental illness will focus on you. At the first indication of this, take yourself to a protected area and stay away from this person. Take extra precautions whenever you leave this sanctuary. You have prior notice of any negative event involving a psycho and can take the appropriate steps to prevent it in reality.

to use this word in a dream Be acutely aware of what will be taking place in your life for the next two weeks. Think clearly about the way you are gradually and subtly adopting lifestyle changes. These changes appear to be developing on their own with no influence from you. You need to be keenly aware of what is evolving and you need to remain alert for the next month to the hidden demands of others. You will not feel as though they are placing much stress on you at the time they are being made but as time goes by these responsibilities will place a tremendous amount of strain and pressure on you. You will find it a tedious chore to meet everyone's demands and needs but you will have no concept of the pressure you are under. You will continue to meet these demands as a matter of routine because you want everything to go smoothly and easily. You will not have the time to think about any of this at the time it is occurring but you will finally reach the point of being overwhelmed and overextended. This will leave you emotionally and physically fragile yet you will continue to go on in the same manner. The more you give to others, the more others will demand of you and you will have no one to turn to for help once you begin to find this destructive lifestyle intolerable. Take steps now to put a stop to it before it becomes such a big problem that you are unable to get away from it. Within eight months you will become ill as a result of your lifestyle and it will take you a long time to recover. Seclude your time so you will have the opportunity to develop a creative idea and bring it to tangible form. Your idea will leave a mark on the world and it is in your destiny to complete this task. Do not allow anyone to pry into your business or to question you while you are in this self imposed seclusion. Steer yourself away from the demands of others and their projects for an eight month period and make sure you eliminate stress and maintain a simple lifestyle. Use any professional help and support system you may have at your disposal. Think defensively in order to create the lifestyle you desire. Let your creativity flow and support yourself emotionally. Eat healthful foods and drink plenty of fluids. You are on the path toward a brilliant future. You also need to take steps to keep any negative event you witnessed in this dream from becoming a reality. Forewarn anyone you know whom you dreamed of to do the same and take steps to ensure you experience only positive events in your life.

psychopath For the next three weeks, be aware of your surroundings. Do not put yourself in danger by being in dark areas. Follow your instincts while at home. You may want to rent a watch dog or use an alternative method of protection.

psychosis *any form* You will enjoy victory and profound life changes. Your circumstances will improve dramatically.

psychotherapy Do not be so quick to jump into the unknown. Analyze your feelings and do not allow others to change your opinions. At this time, groups, especially communal religious groups, are not for you.

pterodactyl Within three days you will separate from someone who is very close and special to you. Control your emotions and do not make a scene. Listen calmly and carefully to the reasons behind this separation and handle yourself with dignity.

ptomaine poisoning A friend will reveal a secret of yours to someone who is important to you. This will result in an explosive argument. Avoid this in the future by keeping your personal life to yourself.

pub You will be invited to an unexpected festive event within the week. This is something you should not miss. This dream is an extremely lucky omen for you.

puberty Follow your heart; you cannot go wrong. The direction you are taking in life will also change.

pubic hair Within two days, a situation will take place that will be so extraordinary it will defy any law of physics. Within three days, this strange event will leave you with a sense of awe and wonder and you will sense you have witnessed a miracle with no way to explain how it transpired. After this takes place, you will be able to present yourself at your best and be able to handle yourself, other people and situations in the best possible way. You will see greater improvements than you ever thought possible. Your sense of awareness will be heightened and you will be able to sense out the knowledge you need to retrieve. You are definitely headed for a brilliant future and many blessings will come to you and your family.

pubic region *to see someone with no visible sexual organs, only hair* Within five days someone will enter your life and give you the impression they will function sexually as a total person. This individual, however, has no interest in you, sexual or otherwise. You will be unsure of the reason why this person has entered your life. Don't waste your time. This person will offer very little and is unsure of what they want.

public phone Do not become involved in the squabbles of unfamiliar people for the next two weeks.

public relations For the next few months, gather names and phone numbers for future networking regarding anything you are writing. Find reliable friends who will help you out for the next two years in marketing your product.

public sale Keep all new interests to yourself. When you do express your interests to others, explain it in such a way that no one will mistake what you are talking about.

public school A tutor should be a priority for children with a learning disorder.

public servant Guard against accidents for the next three days.

public utility Research a neighborhood before you move in. A fabulous residence will prove to be a dissatisfaction because of the neighborhood. You will see this place within a week.

publish If you see someone in a dream who is about to publish, remember this person's face. You will meet them at a later time and will gain assistance in altering your lifestyle.

to be a publisher You know someone who is a genius. Stop by to visit this person and state your goals for enlightened feedback. You will be able to empower yourself with this person's help.

pucker For the next two days you will have to behave in a politically correct manner in everything you do. If you do not, a violent disagreement will break out due to the insensitive way you phrase things. This is preventable and you need to carefully watch what you say to others. You must also subtly warn others around you to address other people with respect.

pudding You will be going all out to host a family reunion. Be sure to include a special person on the guest list that you will otherwise overlook unless you make the list ahead of time and double check to ensure everyone is included.

puddle You will be mistaken for someone else within the week and this will cause you embarrassment. Prevent this by avoiding places you do not frequent.

pueblo A plan worked out on paper will be different when put into practice. The manual labor will be more tedious than expected. Revise your plans quickly in order to save time.

Puerto Rico Being around water will be good for you. Your thoughts will be clear and you will enjoy tranquility. Fresh ideas will come to you and you will feel a new zest for life. All unseen barriers will be lifted. This may also be used as a reference point in time. If you dream of this country and see its name used in any context, the dream message will occur on this day.

puff Provide comfort to someone in mourning.

puffball Someone wants to involve you in playing detective. If you choose to become involved, you will safely achieve results and some thrilling times. Years from now you will have pleasant memories to savor.

puffer fish Within two days get the professional help you need in order to handle those things that require immediate attention.

pug Do not let jealousy and envy play a part in a special relationship. Control yourself. Otherwise, you are headed for a brilliant future.

pug nose Within a few days, you will have to diffuse angry emotions in your home in order to avoid a heated argument. Do this by creating a calm climate.

Pulitzer Prize Do not make any investments for the next three days.

pull You will be very happy that you have pulled the person you desire closer to you in a permanent relationship.
to see anything pulled up This is an extremely lucky omen. You may also make it a point to pursue the resolution of a particular situation in a variety of ways. Commit yourself to this and you will find an easy solution to something you felt would be problematic. Many blessings are with you. Proceed with confidence.
to see anything pulled down Do not experiment with any

risky situation on any level, especially for the next three days. Stay clear of any potentially dangerous situation that does not appear dangerous on the surface. Do this by refusing to become involved in any unusual occurrence. Keep yourself safe.
to pull someone's coat (slang: to get someone's attention) For the next four days, think ahead and carefully plan for a conversation you will have with someone who is involved in a particular situation. This will allow you the time to gather together all those involved in order to put a stop to a potentially negative event. Alert everyone involved. Many blessings will come to you and your family.
to pull someone to you or to be pulled toward someone Become very assertive when it comes to drawing a certain individual closer to you. This cycle is perfect for behaving in a way that will allow this individual to feel comfortable in your presence. This will then allow them to express the words you have long wanted to hear. Many blessings are with you and your family. You are headed for a very prosperous future.
to pull an animal down or to see an animal pulled down You will be involved with a certain person within five days who will be very eager to become a part of your life. This individual will have you believe that they are well respected, professionally stable, financially secure and lead a very credible lifestyle. Because you believe this individual and feel so comfortable in their presence, you will want to become a part of their life. You will be given the impression that you will have easy access to them at any time you wish, but if you try to reach them through the various phone numbers and company addresses you have been given, you will find it almost impossible. It will sometimes take days for this person to return any calls. It will dawn on you that this person has led you to believe they have a far more impressive status than they do. If you allow yourself to become involved with this person in any capacity, you will be deeply disappointed. You must be shrewd and disciplined in order to keep anyone from violating your emotions or from insulting your intelligence. You have prior notice of this and will be able to handle this very successfully. Otherwise, you are in a very lucky cycle and are headed for a prosperous future.
if you recognize this animal Do everything you can to keep any negative event you dreamed of from occurring to this particular animal.

pullet Do not put yourself in the position to hear criticisms from another person, especially for the next three days. These will be words you wish you had never heard.

pulley Do not allow anyone to bully you around.

Pullman Do not allow yourself to get tied down to certain situations or people, especially for the next three days.

pullover Do not allow someone to manipulate you into spending more than you can afford.

pulp The face you see in this dream will belong to the person who will open new doors and steer you into new areas of life that will brighten your future.

pulpit Protect your valuables from vandals.

pulse For the next few weeks you will share laughter with many new people and you will cement new friendships with others who share your hobbies.

puma Show off your talents to your friends. They will then spread word of your skills and you will be flooded by calls from people who want to utilize your talents.

pump Within a few weeks riches will start coming to you.

pump in action You will be given the authority to develop something that needs to be completed in an entirely different way. Practice leniency with others because those who are working with you need to be allowed the freedom to develop creative ideas. These ideas will assist you in completing your projects.

to see anything pumped up You will dislike the extra responsibility that will be dumped in your lap this week. Do whatever you can to move quickly on this in order to get out from under this duty. This next three day cycle will give you the energy and astuteness needed to handle this successfully. Keep your stress level under control.

to see something pumped up, explode Do not allow your feelings or plans to be known to others. Pay attention to what exploded in the dream. This will give you additional clues to the meaning of this dream.

to pump someone up to do something For the next three days, make sure you do not stand in the way of someone's accomplishments by behaving in a bullying or disapproving way. Refrain from this behavior.

to pump anything down Drop any project that has not yielded results. Move on to a new project which will give you a greater feeling of achievement and bring you more financial rewards.

pumper Hire someone for a few hours to help you clear out your desk/personal habitat so you can move on with what you should be doing instead of getting bogged down with everything else. You are headed for a brilliant future.

pumpernickel bread Take care of your skin and, if necessary, visit a dermatologist.

"pumping iron" *any form* Do not ask others to perform what seems to be an impossible task. Many blessings are with you and you will enjoy a lucky seven day cycle.

pumpkin Someone you know will be punished for an act they did not commit. Speak up for this person or you will suffer emotionally to the point of insomnia.

pumpkin seed Do not pass the buck when it concerns family responsibilities. Do everything you can to ensure that all your obligations are met. If you lack the necessary education to meet these demands, take steps to correctly gain the training you need.

pun Think before you speak. Your words could injure another person for a very long time and you will later have to apologize.

punch Make children your priority and make life comfortable for them.

punch bowl You are being encouraged to accept a new group of people into your life. This will lead to the opening of new doors and opportunities. Express your desires to this new group of people and you will quickly meet your goals. Look up the definition for the contents of this punch bowl for a more detailed meaning to this dream.

punching bag For the next few days be sure to keep your feelings and emotions under tight reign. You will find you have been excluded from a certain situation that you feel you should have been included in. As a result you will become so focused on this issue that you will become emotionally caught up in it. Do not feed into this and make matters worse. Focus, instead, on those issues that are much more important for you to attend to.

puncture Whatever you see punctured needs to be repaired or kept safe in reality. Keep all mechanical devices in good working order. Do everything you can to keep the occurrence of any negative event witnessed in this dream from becoming a reality. Ensure you only experience positive events in your life.

punish Be wary of an evil stranger because your reputation will be at stake. You do not know who this person is but others do. This person is constantly seeking someone to prey on. You must also ensure that any negative situation foretold in this dream does not become a reality.

punishment Be careful when using herbs while cooking. You may over-spice something and ruin dishes that you are preparing for a guest.

punk Be very careful of accidental injuries, especially those that involve painful blows to the body that are caused by your own actions. This is especially important for the next three days.

punk rock Do not limit yourself. Go see musicians in concert whom you are unfamiliar with. You are in a cycle that encourages you to be more social.

punt *sports term* You do not need permission to accomplish those things that need to be taken care of. Your success will be determined by how willing you are to move forward in the direction you choose.

to punt Take inventory of your schedule to make sure you are not overextending yourself socially.

boat Avoid any change that will turn things around in a bad way. Keep a watchful eye on work projects to ensure situations do not turn sour.

pupil All arrangements made by you will fall nicely into place and will work out the way you want.

puppet Do not allow yourself to be bullied or manipulated out of something that is rightfully yours.

puppeteer The face in the dream belongs to someone you should never do business with. If you are unable to recall the face, protect yourself in all business transactions for the next four days.

puppy Someone you meet within a few days will fall deeply in love with you. This person is much older than you and will request much of your attention and time. Let this person know early on the degree of your involvement in order to avoid hurt feelings.

purchase *any form* You will be the only one with the opportunity to buy a certain stock. This will rapidly grow in value and a certain status will be attached to this purchase.

puree Stop second guessing and jumping to conclusions. Stay with the facts.

purgatory Pay attention to all little issues that are falling apart so that by the fourth day they will not reach crisis proportions. Attend to them now.

purify You will be introduced to another person through a friend but your friend does not know this person well. Do not be taken in because this new person has many strange hang-ups and has been involved in many strange occurrences. You do not need this in your life.

puritan Stop being so nasty to others. Allow kindness to rule unless you want to be treated badly in return.

purl You will experience domestic tranquility and gain riches within a few years that will last a lifetime.

purple Within two days you will feel an extraordinarily powerful inner strength that you have never felt before and will experience a metamorphosis. You will enjoy many blessings and will be in tune physically. Meditate and your prayers will be answered. You will feel a new power, will be able to govern the direction of this power, will be able to make the correct decisions and will have the confidence to carry them out. Your foresight will become stronger and you will be able to see situations with clarity. These feelings will remain for a lifetime. Drink plenty of water and eat healthful foods.

royal purple For the next three days you will be surrounded by love and will be accepted with open arms. Follow your intuition. Luck and many blessings are with you, and you will achieve victory in all of your goals. Go after what you want.

purr Within two weeks someone will make it appear that you are interested in them romantically. This will be done to strengthen their own ego.

purse You will quickly rise above any bothersome situation and you will also handle all areas of your life perfectly. Expect a prosperous future.

full Focus only on your desires for the next two weeks.

empty Do not confess personal secrets to anyone else.

to lose Someone will want to be sexually close to you, then will want to move on with their life.

pocketbook Do not allow the presence of a recently estranged person keep you from attending a social function. An event is also scheduled for the coming week that is important for you to attend. You will find yourself in the company of two admirers who will attempt to win over your affections. Although it is not apparent, one of them possesses a great deal of power and authority. Both of these admirers are very agreeable and charming and you would enjoy having one as a partner for life. You can be confident that you are on the path toward a prosperous future.

in any other form This implies blessings, tranquility and peace of mind.

pus You will become a victim of a phone fraud. You will need to pay each time you dial a number (for prize information, etc.) but this number will be faulty in some way (static, low volume) and will need to keep redialing at an extra charge. Guard against this fraud.

push Push yourself to leave a situation you no longer need or have outgrown.

to push someone or to see people push each other Make sure you play a very active part in getting what you want on an emotional level. Within a five day period, you will be able to focus on and visualize the path you need to take to ensure a brilliant future. Good luck is with you.

if you are physically pushed You will become involved in a situation with the opposite sex that will later cause you shame. Think things through first.

to be able to push something open This implies that within the week you will have an urgent need to accomplish something that requires someone else's help either financially or as a big favor. This needs to be taken care of immediately and with no hassles. At the time you will find it difficult to believe that such a large request could be granted. Follow your hunches, carefully explore your options and you will be led to the right person to help you out. Once an agreement is struck, take immediate action before this person has a change of heart. Many blessings are with you and you are headed for a prosperous future.

push button You will need medical attention for the next few weeks. If you visit a doctor at the first sign of illness, you may cut the healing process in half. You will enjoy a successful outcome.

to dream of pushing buttons and successfully open something Someone you know will attempt to reform the behavior of someone else by using their bad temper. Think ahead so you will have a way of counteracting this by using skillful communication to settle everything once it starts to flare up. You will be able to make others feel more comfortable and more agreeable. Clear thinking and a skillful use of words will diffuse this issue. You will also receive good news during this time period.

to push buttons and be unable to open Be very cautious about where you are allowing someone to take you emotionally. Someone, for reasons only they are aware of, will lead you to believe you are loved completely by them. Words of love may or may not be used but this person will present a scenario of love (i.e., gifts, flowers, romantic outings, etc.). You will quickly develop strong feelings for this person but if you allow lovemaking to occur, you will not be touched, loved or kissed in any special way that implies you are loved by them. This individual will try to put on a good act but you will feel cold and empty as a result. Do not put yourself through this emotional upheaval. You have enough prior notice to avoid it entirely. This person has a hidden agenda in mind that involves you doing something for them that only they are aware of. This will only lead to unhappiness. Otherwise, you are headed for a prosperous future that will begin within the week.

pushcart You will receive money within five days by playing games of chance.

pusher Do everything necessary to avoid communicating in a way that will hurt another person. Words, once spoken, can never be retracted. Each aspect of this dream that is negative may be altered in reality and each positive aspect may be embraced.

push up An unusual yearning you have for a sexual encounter with another person will be realized within a few days. This other person will go to great lengths to ensure happiness.

pussy willow A phone message will force you to focus on an individual you never thought about romantically. This person wants you more deeply than you know. This will be a fun, giddy relationship.

putt Make planning ahead a priority for the next few days. Make lists, plan events and plan your finances. Prioritize your life.

putter A partnership you are considering will be dynamic. You will receive what you want from it and will accomplish your goals.

putty You will pin down an elusive person and a conversation will lead to a mutual agreement. You will enjoy a good association with this person.

putty knife This is a very lucky omen for you and implies that within two days your inner courage and drive will motivate you to break through any physical or mental barrier you

may have that prevents you from moving forward. Once you have rid yourself of this barrier you will be able to bring any new project you have into tangible form in the manner you wish. You will be placed on a pedestal by all those you care about. You are on the path for a brilliant future and many new opportunities are headed your way. You can also expect a financial windfall to come to you.

puzzle Someone will attempt to create a mysterious aura for the purpose of keeping you more interested in them. Treat this person with respect and kindness.

pygmy You are thinking of buying a pet. Your first choice now will cost a great deal due to health problems. Wait awhile for a better choice.

pyramid You are promised a great relationship with someone and this person will go to great lengths to ensure happiness. You will enjoy yourself with this person and will have a fantastic life together if you choose this path.

Pyrenees For the next seven days all plans that require negotiations will work out beautifully for you. Use this cycle for negotiations. Good luck is with you. Love yourself, get plenty of rest and eat healthful foods. This may also be used as a reference point in time. If you dream of this mountain range and see its name used in any context, the dream message will occur on this day.

python Someone will breed jealousy in order to make you feel unsure about a relationship. This person's intent is to take a special person from you and create suspicions. Avoid this person and ignore this situation if at all possible.

Q

Q Although it looks as though things will not work out because of snags, confusion and set backs, it does not mean you are headed in the wrong direction. Within seven days because of your consistent work patterns, you will also see a clear path free from interruptions and you will not have to work so hard to get things to fall in the manner you desire. Continue what you are doing and you will accidentally stumble over a way to get things moving at a faster pace. You will gain greater financial security than you ever envisioned as a result of this. Your senior years will be financially secure. Many blessings are with you and you are headed for a brilliant future.

Q-tip This implies that within five days someone will want you to move in with them. It is your choice. Either way you decide will be right for you. If you choose not to make this move, be sure to take a rain check so the doors will remain open. You must also be sure you help others in need during this cycle.

Quaalude You will be given an invitation to an intimate dinner and conversation by someone who is far wealthier than they appear. You have the chance now to deepen the relationship if this is what you wish. This is a very lucky omen and you are headed for a brilliant future. If this dream foretells any negative event, you have the time to either change the outcome or to avoid the situation altogether. Make sure you experience nothing but positive experiences in your life, especially for the next five days.

quack Within three days you and another person will want to surrender to each other your deepest emotional feelings and the passion you feel for each other. Good luck is with you and you are loved beyond your imagination.

quack (*fake doctor*) All financial negotiations you will be dealing with for the next seven days will have a fantastic result. This is the best cycle for you to deal with financial affairs. You must also make it a point to avoid any dealings with quackery in any form and warn anyone you recognize in the dream to do the same.

quadrangle While having guests in your home, one of them will accidentally expose themselves while sleep walking. You have prior notice of this and can take steps to keep this from occurring. You will also be invited to a very unusual gathering, meet people you find to be very interesting, and have a rewarding time.

quadratic equation Within two days you will receive some very encouraging news regarding finances. You will proceed very rapidly toward a brilliant future.

quadriplegic Someone is becoming very inconsistent and will begin to cause a problematic situation with the plans you need to get moving on. Avoid delays on those issues that have a set deadline.

quadroon You are entering a very lucky cycle and many blessings are with you.

quadruplet Move quickly, give your prompt attention to important matters and behave responsibly when taking care of important papers. This will ensure you receive what is due you in a timely fashion.

quagmire Someone will inadvertently place themselves in the position to be easily taken advantage of by you. Make sure, for the next three days, you take steps to control the beast within you. Do the correct thing and do only what you can live with. This person is attached to you in many ways. This is an extremely lucky omen and will be for the next month.

quail Think ahead and be alert. This dream implies you need to go to great lengths to let someone know you are interested in them. It is not that this person does not feel the same toward you, it is simply that it takes this individual some time to realize what is going on with themselves and others. Do everything necessary to attract this person's attention. Sometimes it takes something unusual to get your feelings across to another person.

Quaker This implies that victory is yours if you take steps to slow down and develop your relations with others in the proper way. Do what you can to get another person actively involved in preserving the relationship. This will work for you within five days. If you recognize the person in the dream, this is the person you need to work with in cementing the relationship.

quaking aspen Your faith will deepen and develop in the direction you choose if you become more faithful to yourself and develop more self confidence. Be consistent and refuse to compromise your feelings, especially for the next three days.

quantum leap Within two days you need to become more informed by reading, asking questions and educating yourself on health matters. Take a preventive approach when dealing with health issues in order to maintain your health.

quarantine Go full speed ahead. The concept you have developed now seems overwhelming but will be successful because you will be able to develop the resources and gather the tools needed to bring about your desired plans.

quarrel Take all the necessary steps to prevent any negative situation in this dream from becoming a reality. Also a precious collection of yours will be damaged if you do not take steps to ensure its safety for the next ten days. Take preventive measures.

quarry Within three days you will receive the backing you need from someone who has the tenacity to relentlessly walk you through an important situation. You will be able to make the right decisions to turn things around in your favor. This involves someone who is pursuing you for the reason of causing you physical harm. You are headed for a brilliant future.

quart A deeper bond will occur between you and another person. This feeling will remain for a long time and will begin within three days. You will also be focusing on your responsibilities. Deal with them with enthusiasm.

quarter Within three days some much needed information will come to you from an unexpected source. This also implies that you will be included in secret organizational plans that you have been wanting to be a part of. Look for this to happen within seven days. Many blessings are with you and your family.

quarterback Take steps to prevent any broken bones, especially for the next three days.

quarterdeck Avoid, at all costs, a fallout between you and a close friend over a situation that will occur within the next three days. Instead, bring about more closeness and bonding.

quarter horse Stay focused on personal issues that you want no interference with. Once someone or something starts to interfere, cut this behavior off quickly. You will be able to maximize your tranquility and will achieve what you want to achieve regarding this situation.

quartet You will be required to work with someone who seems, at first, to be very difficult. Don't let this fool you. It will turn out to be a beautiful experience if you choose to work with this person. During this cycle, you will be able to meet your goals by successfully applying yourself.

quartz This is an extremely lucky omen and this month long cycle will be filled with prosperity for you. Anything you set out to accomplish will be successful and what you felt was impossible in the past is now very possible. You must also pay attention to the color of the quartz for a more detailed description of this dream. Many blessings are with you and you are headed for a very prosperous future.

quartz lamp/heater Within five days you will acquire greater clarity of thought. Use this to develop a plan that will bring you greater prosperity. Trust your instincts and behave appropriately in order to put yourself at an advantage.

quasar There will be a dramatic change in your life due to someone else's irritating behavior. You are being made aware of this ahead of time so you can take steps to avoid this. Stay clear of this situation until this person returns to normal so you will not put yourself through any major hassles. Good luck is with you and you will enjoy tranquility if you allow others to take care of their own behavior.

Quebec You are being alerted that, when assisting someone who is trying to get needed services, you will be asked for help in processing the information they need within three days. Step back and cleverly assess what you need to do first to avoid wasting your time, energy and efforts. This will enable this person to get what they need in a timely fashion. You are entering a prosperous cycle for the next seven days and many blessings will come to you and your family.

queen Peace, harmony and blessings are yours for a long time to come. Within seven days you will grasp your highest ambitions and are definitely headed for a brilliant future.

lady in waiting You will come to a decision with that special person in your life that will be mutually satisfying and will also meet all of your financial needs.

Queen Anne's lace *(plant)* You will receive some very private information about a particular situation you are working on. For the next three days be sure you do not allow someone to blurt something out that you have told them.

Make sure you tell this person to keep this information to themselves.

Queen Mother Within three days you will finally rid yourself completely of a certain situation. You will have the calmness and flexibility during this time period to handle this situation. Go for it. You are headed for a prosperous future. Within the week you will also be able to rid yourself of troublesome situations so you can work at your top level.

queer You will definitely develop a support system and a network of knowledge you can draw from that will help you to secure a comfortable lifestyle. During this time period you will have many opportunities in which to celebrate joyful occurrences. Prepare yourself for some unexpected joyful news that will come your way within the week. You are headed for a brilliant future and this cycle will leave you feeling as though everyone supports your goals and is on your side.

quesadilla Avoid a permanent separation in any relationship that is important. For the next month carefully monitor your behavior to determine what you may be doing that could cause a permanent break-up. Since you have prior notice of this you can take steps to avoid this painful event.

quest This is alerting you that within two days you will be anxious to change your day to day living habits. You will be able to turn things around very rapidly and will experience a much improved lifestyle. Maintain discipline and use common sense. You are definitely headed for a prosperous future.

question *if you see yourself evading questions in a dream* This implies that this is exactly what you should be doing in reality. Give as little information as you can about what you are involved in at the present time. Maintain this attitude for the next seven days. Do not allow yourself to be caught off guard in those areas you do not wish to divulge to others. Recall the responses you gave to various questions and this will lead you to a major clue of what you should or should not be doing in reality. If it foretells a negative event, make sure you take the proper steps to change it. Also you need to prepare yourself for questions that will be asked of you within seven days. This will allow you to answer these questions appropriately so everything will fall exactly as you have envisioned. You are headed for a brilliant future and others will respond to you in such a way that will make life easier and bring you tranquility.

to see others being questioned For the next three days be more considerate. A special person will be going through a very special time. Show more sympathy and patience toward this person until they get through this situation. This will occur within three days.

if you recognize the person being questioned or doing the questioning Someone is very eager to get a message through to you. This is of the highest priority to this individual and within three days you will be contacted. If you recall that a negative event took place in this dream, take steps to avoid it and to warn anyone else involved to do the same.

if you are questioning someone and are not getting the response you need This implies that within three days something you need to get the correct response to will not come through for you. You have prior notice of this so you can do what you have to do to turn this verdict around to get the response you need. The questions asked in this dream and the responses you get will offer you major clues to the meaning of this dream and will give you the answers to what you should or should not be doing in order to raise your standard of living.

in any other form Be aware that someone will become very interested in you within five days. As time goes by this person will find it more and more difficult to control their obsessive behavior and possessiveness toward you. Since you have prior notice of this, you will be able to have a quiet conversation with this person in order to prevent this behavior. This will result in a more tranquil attitude toward you and a mutually satisfying lifestyle. You are definitely headed for a brilliant future.

question mark Do not allow yourself to stagnate to the point of not being able to accomplish the things you need to. Make it a point to break out of old patterns that keep you from moving ahead. Bring more joy into your life, simplify your life, and get plenty of rest. Many blessings will come to you and your family.

questionnaire Pay close attention to what was printed on the questionnaire. This will give you a clue to what you will either want to avoid in reality or to embrace. Make sure you experience only positive expressions in your life. Your intuitions about love are accurate. Move quickly to accomplish what you need regarding this issue. This is a perfect three day cycle for this.

Quetzalcoatl *(Aztec God)* Within five days you will develop the strength and inner courage to make unusual and extraordinary changes. Many blessings are coming your way.

queue Do not become involved in anything that you are considering investing in at this time. This would be an unwise decision.

quiche lorraine Take steps to build up your finances now so next month you will be able to wisely handle your expenditures without the stress of being unable to make ends meet.

quick freeze Within five days do everything you can to refrain from having thoughts or displaying behavior that will hinder a relationship from becoming closer. Carefully study your behavior and determine those aspects of your personality that will keep those you care about from getting close to you. This is the time to develop the courage to address these issues in order to develop your personality in such a way that others will be drawn to you. You will be able to turn yourself around this month. Good luck is with you.

quickie Your intuition will broaden and will be accurate. For the next seven days follow your hunches and judgments. Meditate in your favorite form, drink plenty of water, and eat healthy foods.

quicksand For the next seven days be very careful not to get caught up in a dangerous situation or to become involved in a freak accident. Alert anyone else involved to do the same. For this time period, find a safe haven to protect yourself from harm. Many blessings are with you and your family. You are loved beyond your imagination, especially by those you least expect. Proceed with confidence.

quicksilver Within five days you will have the opportunity to cater to other people from different ethnic backgrounds. Because of your hard work, eagerness to please and your ability to handle each situation with tact and diplomacy, doors will be permanently open to you. You will enjoy many new opportunities and will experience an increase in wealth. Good luck is with you. You must also do whatever is within your power to cater to yourself and do things that make you feel good. Do this as quickly as you can. Many blessings are with you and your family.

quiet *any form* Do not postpone any decision that has to be made within two days. Do not allow yourself or anyone else to procrastinate on this issue. It is important that you move quickly during this time period.

quill For the next three days be careful of dangers you may not be fully aware of. Watch your surroundings and do not depend on your judgments. Otherwise, you will be entering a prosperous cycle for the next month. You will enjoy an abundance of health and many blessings are with you and your family.

quilt You and your family will be given many blessings and you will enjoy an abundance of health and a good financial standing. Also information you need and have been deprived of will come to you from an unexpected source within three days. You will receive verification of love from someone who is very special to you. You will be surrounded by love, admiration and appreciation by those you care about. Many prosperous situations will come your way.

quilting bee For the next two days make sure you carefully watch out for a newcomer in your life. This person has the same problems and hang ups as someone else who was previously a part of your life. You have no wish to tolerate this behavior again. The first moment you notice any game playing in your life, either stop this person in their tracks or get on with your life without this person in it. Many blessings are with you and your family.

quince Blessings will be with you and your family for the next three days. Reaffirm your beliefs and faith. Wonderful things will begin to happen slowly but surely. Whatever is revealed to you in this dream should not be repeated to anyone until these events start to happen unless the message is directed to someone else. Take steps and alert anyone else involved to take steps to avoid any negative event. You will have the confidence and optimism to drastically alter your life for the better.

quinine Be wary of someone who has led you to believe you can confide in them. You cannot depend on this person's loyalty. Do not involve yourself with gossips. You must also do what you can to prepare yourself financially now so next month you will be able to handle yourself in a financially secure way without the stress of being unable to meet your bills. Many blessings are with you and your family.

quintet Your wishes will be granted within the month. Dramatic changes will occur and your lifestyle will dramatically improve. All of your travel plans will work out perfectly. Expect beautiful things in your life within this time period. Your ideas, plans and projects will all be met with success. Other people will persistently and relentlessly help you to reach the path you are after. You are headed for a brilliant future.

quintuplet Within three days someone is very eager to reconcile with you. Follow your heart and you will make the correct decisions. You will also have a wide variety of options and opportunities to choose from within the month. You will be able to grasp as many of these options as you wish and will enjoy dramatic improvements that will raise your standard of living, especially in ways you most desire. Your sexual drive will be at a peak and you will exude a great deal of charisma and be well received by others. Many blessings will be with you and your family and you are headed for a prosperous future.

quit Do not overextend yourself by taking on a situation that will come up within five days. This will result in your performing physical labor to the point of exhaustion. Remove yourself from the situation, regroup, eat healthy foods, drink plenty of water and get plenty of rest.

quiver Push yourself toward those goals that you are eager to reach. Your success will depend solely on your ability to push yourself to reach these goals. Analyze what is going on in this dream that relates to what is occurring in your life now and make any necessary changes. You are also wasting too much time analyzing someone else. That energy really needs to be devoted to other things in your life that have more priority. Do this within the week.

Quixote, Don This dream is a warning to you to avoid any situation that could result in your exposure to any disease or situation that will result in the spread of an infection. Avoid all sexual contact for the next two days. People will also avoid you and not want to be in your company if you do not stop putting people down. Stop finding fault with everyone else's suggestions. Learn to compromise and stop your stubborn behavior. Unless you learn to experience things with other people, you are headed for a lonely future. Get a grip

on your behavior and set a new path for yourself in life. This is especially important to do within five days.

quiz For the next three days your negotiations will not bear fruit. Postpone all negotiations for this time period in order to ensure future success. You will also meet a very attractive, charismatic, and generous person. Proceed with confidence with this individual in any capacity you choose. You will be extended a special privilege just by being around this person. Take advantage of what this person has to offer that will make a big difference in your life. Many blessings are with you and your family and you are entering a lucky seven day cycle.

quiz show Within five days you will get caught up in a tug of war between two people. This is because you will fail to take care of a situation in which you were expected to accompany two different people to the same function. Take care of this now and take steps to avoid situations that will cause quarreling.

Quonset Within two days you will be put under pressure from someone because you will stand up for your rights and refuse to compromise your feelings. You have prior notice of this and can take steps to remain calm throughout this situation.

quotation This is a good time to make any decision that is out of the ordinary, especially for the next three days. Good luck is with you.

quote Do not allow yourself to be cheated out of a business deal. Make sure you ask for what you deserve.

R

R You are promised grand changes in your life and will receive a large inheritance within three months. Weigh the pros and cons very carefully in order to gain clues to the direction you need to take with your new found fortune. This will allow you to enjoy a stress free life, free from old hang ups. You will then be able to have a brilliant future.

Rabbi You are ignoring an individual who has the resources to help point you in the right direction. Seek out the opportunity to converse with this person. Do this within four days.

rabbit Love will flourish when you least expect it. Romance is in the air.

to eat Keep the relationships that are important to you stress free and work to keep the union together. Do not seek out ways to put distance into a relationship. This union is now stronger than it has ever been and will only improve as time goes by. Don't repeat old patterns of behavior.

snow shoe rabbit Do everything you can to protect children and young adults who require closer supervision, especially for the next three days. Make sure they do not come to any physical harm. Many blessings are with you and your family. You have prior notice of this and can keep any negative event from taking place.

rabbit ears Business dealings will not work out as you anticipate. This will be a major concern to you for weeks to come. Find a way to deal with this loss or find an alternative enterprise. Your instincts are right on target and will serve to steer you in the right direction.

rabbit punch Guard your possessions and do not put yourself in the position of being robbed. You will also be invited to a wonderful outing and will enjoy many wonderful exotic foods.

rabbit's foot You will be in a very lucky cycle for the next seven days concerning all phases of finance. Seek professional help with your financial matters in order to improve your status. You are definitely headed in the right direction.

rabble rouser For the next three days use every excuse you can to stay at home. Unusual circumstances will occur that will make you wish you had. You must also be more receptive to the new ideas presented by someone who is close to you. Wonderful opportunities will arise from these ideas.

rabies *any form* You will be successful in handling the dishonest dealings of relatives.

raccoon Do not loan anything of value. You will also enjoy yourself immensely for the next seven days because a new, attractive person will enter your life and you will have private moments together.

race *to hear the word* Someone you are interested in seeing owns a pet that you are allergic to. Notify this person of the problem prior to making a visit. Your social life may suffer with this person unless you make a point of seeking solutions to this problem.

lose a race A deadly trap has been laid out for you by someone who gains pleasure in injuring others. Be careful.

win a race Circumstances that will be coming up within a few days will create a great deal of stress. Prior notice of this will give you the opportunity to develop a calm demeanor and will lessen the impact.

to see a race in any form Watch out for a person with a mission. This person will put you through many moments you find distasteful. Heed this warning and do not allow this person to take up your valuable time, especially for the next three days.

to race anything or to race somewhere without competition You will achieve a big victory during this cycle that will offer you an abundance of new opportunities. Using any power you may have at your disposal to conclude an agreement to your benefit within the week. You have seven days from the time you dreamed this to motivate yourself to push this agreement through. This is the best time period to accomplish this and the agreement will be well received by all those involved. You are on a path toward victory and many blessings will come to you and your family.

if you are actively involved in a race and lose Become consistently aggressive for the next seven days in all phases of achievement in order to grasp your goals before this opportunity slips through your fingers. You must also take steps to ensure you are not usurped by another who will attempt to force a compromise. This would result in a loss to you in some capacity.

if you are actively involved in a race and win You will enjoy victory in those areas of your life you most desire. All negotiations will bring success to you within seven days.

racehorse Riches are in store for you if you keep doing what you are presently doing. Pay close attention to the events in this dream. If a positive message was revealed, take steps to promote it in reality. This dream also implies that what you felt was out of reach is now within your grasp.

racetrack Do everything necessary to avoid accidents for the next three days. This is a very accident prone cycle. Get plenty of rest and stay alert. Find the tranquility you need to bring more balance into your life.

Rachel *(from the Bible)* Joy is yours. A short journey will bring you much happiness and all business trips will be very advantageous to you. You are headed for a prosperous future.

racing form Seek safety for yourself in all of your enterprises. You will succeed by practicing adventurousness.

rack Practice more freedom with your actions and enjoy yourself more, especially for the next seven days.

racket Within five days something will occur that will completely throw you off balance. Focus on removing yourself from this situation completely and do not allow this to fester. Get on with your life as though it never occurred. This will help everything in your life get back to normal as quickly as possible. If you become involved, you will never accomplish anything and you will linger on this for a number of days.

racquet ball Take steps to make someone aware of the deep feelings you have for them. You are now entering a cycle that will make this an easier process and you will find other people more receptive. This also implies that unexpected wealth is coming your way.

radar Make sure you are paid in full before you allow anyone to take a valuable you are selling. Do not accept a check as payment because it will bounce.

radar beacon A calm demeanor and fewer demands will allow a special person to blossom into a great lover.

radarscope Show more concern for older people. Make sure their needs are met and you will find yourself having a wonderful time with interesting people.

radial tires You will have difficulties due to your indifferent behavior.

radiance An opportunity you are excited about and have been long awaiting will present itself to you. You now have the means to grasp it. You will have a new start in all areas of your life where you desire changes. All old burdens and issues that have been plaguing you will come to an immediate halt. Drastic changes will occur and leave you with a new lease on life.

radiation sickness Enjoy yourself in a grand and elegant manner.

radiator Make sure all guarantees received within seven days will hold up in the future.

leaky radiator Take a close look at everything you are doing in order to avoid costly errors. Make phone calls to gather necessary information to ensure everything is being handled the proper way.

radio Avoid peer pressure and do what you want in order to enjoy a better future. Also, it is important to pay attention to the message given over the radio. This message will indicate a forthcoming event that you will either want to change or promote. This also implies the person you will soon be dealing with will give you a sneak preview of what you will be having to deal with. You are in a very prosperous and lucky cycle and you and your family will receive many blessings.

radioactive You will soon be enjoying life to the fullest. You will receive long awaited news indicating good results. Everything will take on a new emotional twist to your advantage. Stay flexible with all those new changes and accept all love that is given to you. Your family will demonstrate a new warmth and a special gift is in store for you.

radio frequency You will soon go on a short journey and return home safely.

radiology Pay close attention to all of your personal dealings for the next seven days. Greatness will follow.

radio wave Do not allow anything to keep you from moving forward in the direction you desire. You are going in the right direction.

radium You will have the gift to communicate exactly what you need and want. You will be able to successfully get your message across and receive a good reception from others.

radium therapy Become very concerned about the behavior of young children and adults. Do not make any thought-

less remarks.

raffle You will be introduced to a new opportunity that will stabilize your finances. This will vastly improve your life. Good luck is with you.

if you recall any numbers Use these numbers in any way you find advantageous. These numbers may also be used in games of chance for five consecutive times for big winnings.

raft Use careful strategy when choosing the correct words needed to steer a group of corporations to your favor. You will be able to gain large donations from these companies and also have success when dealing with small groups. Take advantage of this cycle.

rag Within two weeks you will be invited to attend a large celebration. At the time you receive this, you will feel as though this would be too hectic for you. It is a good idea to go anyway and stay for half the time. You will enjoy yourself tremendously.

rage Become aware now of the state of your financial affairs a month from now. You can avoid financial stress by saving some money. Be very wise concerning spending matters at this time. You must also avoid doing anything for the next few days that will result in a restraining order being taken out on you. Control your behavior.

raggedy *to see yourself raggedy* This is a very lucky omen and implies that, within a three day period, you will develop the inner strength and courage you need that comes from within. Your steel drive and determination will motivate you to overcome all hidden physical and mental obstacles you need to rid yourself of. You will also be able to change any aspect of your life you disapprove of that keeps you from thrusting yourself forward. Once you do this, you will quickly see a clear path to gain the knowledge you need to develop those aspects of your life you most desire, as well as the lifestyle you desire. You will accomplish this quickly during this time cycle. You will also be placed on a pedestal and be treated like royalty wherever you go. This will come as a big surprise to you. You are on the path toward a brilliant future and many new opportunities will be presented to you.

in any other form It is important you are alerted to a situation that will, because of a freak accident, leave you trapped in an enclosed area that you will find impossible to get out of. Expect this to occur within two days. Otherwise, you are headed for a prosperous future.

Raggedy Ann You are loved beyond your imagination. For the next seven days you will be surrounded by those who will demonstrate love and affection toward you in unusual ways. A wonderful cycle is coming your way and you are headed for a brilliant future.

raglan For the next three days actively motivate others so things can move in the direction they need to. This cycle will allow you to achieve this task easier.

ragout Within three days seek needed services from an agency. You will be able to have your needs satisfied.

ragtime Within three days someone will enter your life for the sole purpose of requesting a large sum of money. Avoid this person by using any means you have at your disposal. This person is not in need and will not pay your money back.

ragweed This is a very lucky omen and you will enjoy an abundance of health. Bring together friends for advice and help when you need them. They will be there for you.

raid Someone will enter your life within a few days who marries people purely for financial gain. Move on with your life without this person in it.

to be raided by bandits A married person will attempt to involve you in an unhealthy relationship. Place no confidence in the words of any individual who is married, and do not allow yourself to be amused by anything out of the ordinary, especially for the next three days. This will backfire.

military raid Avoid any action that will result in a restraining order against you, especially for the next seven days.

police/drug raid Someone will do everything in their power to lead you in the direction of emotional or physical harm. This will catch you off guard at a very unexpected moment. Carefully scrutinize all situations and take steps to protect your environment. Avoid any situation that allows someone to gain the upper hand, especially for the upcoming week.

business raid Your business will take a turn for the worse for all who are involved in the stock market. Play it safe during this time period. This also implies that someone will overcharge you for services you will not need. Make sure, for the next seven days, this does not occur.

rail Be kind and do not make thoughtless remarks to a newcomer who feels insecure enough as it is. Don't be cruel to others.

railbird For the next few weeks avoid heavy labor, heavy lifting and an excess of demands on your time.

railroad Develop a compassion for yourself. You will be undergoing an emotional crisis. Treat yourself gently and take in some pleasurable moments while going through this. This will occur within four days and you need to be aware that this situation is out of your control.

rain *to see others in the rain* Simplify your life and trust your instincts, especially for the next three days. You will want to reach out to someone you desire to be closer to. You will find that you are loved very deeply by this individual. Blessings will come to you and your family.

rain water Do not allow silly misunderstandings to arise. Keep everything running smoothly for the next two days. Remain alert to ensure that a spat does not occur.

in any other form You will be able to rid yourself of all past hang ups and be able to alter your life for the better. Others will be more receptive to your ideas and more loving to you in this cycle. Change your attitude and behavior in such a way to make others more willing to support your plans and ideas.

rainbow Others will be acutely aware of your needs and will work to form a strong support system until you are on your feet. You are headed toward a brilliant future and good luck is with you. This cycle will last for seven days. Move quickly in order to accomplish as much as you can during this time period.

rainbow fish You have been involved in various groups that offered many joyful activities. You have now reached a level where you feel you have outgrown this group. Move on with your life. Don't feel guilty but don't burn any bridges either.

rainbow trout For the next three days you will be able to successfully negotiate all business meetings. These meetings will result in prosperity for yourself. You will also be able to arrange events after these meetings to increase your financial status.

rain check Tell others to become acutely aware of their surroundings, to take care of themselves, and to protect themselves from harm. You need to be very aware of the food you eat and what you drink in order to avoid food poisoning, allergies or toxic reactions. Feel free to accept or give a rain check.

raincoat Do everything necessary to focus on the character of those you work with. Keep this information to yourself. You will be glad you stored up this knowledge.

raindrop Be very aware of all natural disasters and take steps to keep yourself, your family, and your property safe.

rainfall Be careful you are not struck by any moving vehicle while traveling on foot.

dirty While participating in a debate, you will be taken by surprise when someone accuses you of having a hidden motive. This will occur within the week. Remain calm and avoid getting sucked into a debate. Simply put your complaints down in written form and turn it over to this individual.

rain forest Within five days you will win the love of someone you desire. The product you develop will also be popular for more than a decade. You are headed in the right direction.

rain gauge Within three days you will have to deal with a very desperate person who will go to great lengths to entangle you in their problems. Avoid this situation in any way possible.

rainmaker Practice diplomacy and develop a soft manner in order to win the promotion you seek in any capacity; personal or career wise. Do not allow anyone to place an excess of extra responsibilities on you.

rainproof Plan your days ahead of time and you will find exposure to more opportunities and will be better able to handle the demands that others place on you. Utilize your talents. Do this now so you will not deplete your energy and you will be able to better juggle your responsibilities.

rainstorm Within seven days a family member will create confusion within their household. After other family members become involved, everyone will get together to arrive at a decision about how to handle this situation. Remain in the background and do not become actively involved.

raise *(pay)* You can gain the advantage in certain situations by setting up meetings with those in authority. These people are willing to pull strings to help you. You will be glad you made this move.

raisin Be very careful. Your vehicle will be stolen if precautions are not taken within seven days. Otherwise, this is a very lucky cycle and will bring you an abundance of health, tranquility and prosperity. Many blessings will come to you and your family.

Rajah Someone has a very serious and important question to ask you. You will be contacted by this person within three days.

rally You are in a one of a kind cycle and will experience many different pleasurable events. Each one will be very different and will be attended by a variety of individuals. You also have a variety of different people attracted to you in a romantic way. This is such a good cycle that any choice you make of a romantic partner would turn out well. Since you have prior notice of this, make sure you take advantage of this cycle to add more spice to your life.

ram For the next three days do whatever you can to prevent someone from falling and becoming seriously injured while in your presence. This could result in a severe injury. Be alert. Good luck is with you and your family. During this cycle you will also be able to handle anything with a clear head.

ramp You will enjoy an event that will be celebrated and talked about for weeks. Expect something joyful to occur within the near future.

rampage Within two days you will be cornered by someone you have been trying to avoid. Take steps to avoid accidentally bumping into this person. Any negative event depicted in this dream needs to be prevented in reality.

ranch Do not push away someone who loves you deeply. Express your love by actions instead of words. Bring this person close to you and work on changing your behavior for

the entire month.

ranch house Keep your hands off other people's money. For the next three days, avoid any unusual situations involving the finances of others.

rancher Schedule an overdue conversation with those you need to talk to in order to determine your next move. These talks will offer you different approaches to a difficult issue. Within seven days you will be able to decide who will work better with you depending on their response to your ideas.

ranchero A partnership you are thinking about forming will result in disaster. Within three days search for an alternative partner.

rancid Other people will be angry at the unilateral decisions you make concerning them. Be sure to include others in your decision making processes, especially for the next two days. Be sure to carry out the responsibilities you have agreed to undertake. If you cannot keep your promises, don't make them. Anything negative connected to this dream that could become a reality needs to be changed.

random Do not push yourself on another person. This person is not interested in this type of behavior. This is likely to occur within three days. You will also be able to unexpectedly attain a long desired goal.

range *stove top* This is a good luck omen. Someone is highly attracted to you in a sexual way. You will be eager to surrender yourself sexually once you know who this person is. If you choose to take this path, you will have a fantastic time.

ranger Within three days someone will ask for extra affection from you. As a result, the relationship will develop to a deeper level than you ever expected. This was a platonic relationship but you are now aware that this person desires romance. All relationships in any capacity will develop to a deeper level and you will enjoy greater love, bonding and encouragement, if you choose. The quality of your life will definitely improve and many blessings will come to you and your family. Pay attention to your attitude for the next two days and make changes where needed. A friend of yours will also set you up on a blind date. This individual has never met your future date but will describe them to you in a positive manner because their love interest has described them in this fashion. Be aware that you may be shocked by this blind date. If you are in the mood for an adventure, accept this date. If not, decline the offer.

rank Take steps to start developing new associates. Begin disassociating from the old crowd and the same old places. Develop new interests and social activities while you are disengaging from the old group.

rank and file Do not pay attention to the words of an alarmist. You will avoid much stress by remembering they enjoy blowing issues out of proportion. This is likely to occur within two days.

ransack You are entering a seven day cycle that will give you the advantage you need to gain victory and a powerful position in areas you are presently working on. A very lucky event will also occur to you during this time frame.

ransom You will be asked to offer financial assistance to a relative who is in a crisis. You will be paid back soon.

to hold something or someone for a ransom For the next three days remain very alert and do not allow anyone to talk you into going someplace that could represent a hazard for you. Stay alert in all areas of your life. Be careful when involving yourself with new situations with another person who could, without meaning to, cause you harm. It is very important to choose carefully what you will or will not involve yourself in. You must also take all the necessary precautions to prevent any negative event you dreamed of from becoming a reality.

to be held for ransom Within five days, you will meet someone who possesses great wealth and will come into your life with the intent of involving themself with you in some way. This is not normally the kind of person you would involve yourself with but their financial status is a powerful lure. Once you become involved you will have to negotiate each expenditure. This individual will turn out to be miserly and very tight with their money. Take steps to avoid this situation. You must also make sure you do not place yourself in the position to be kidnapped and held for ransom.

rant Prepare several alternatives for meeting your goals. Do not rely on others to come to your rescue.

rape *to be involved in a rape* When you explain your interest to others, word it in such a way that there can be no misunderstandings. Be very clear about your desires for the next month. Take steps to avoid any involvement in a rape in reality.

to recognize someone involved in a rape The person you dreamed about will go to great lengths to violate your rights. Take steps now to avoid this distasteful situation.

to see a rape Within two days you will have to take a stand to clear up a long standing problem with another person. Be prepared to offer alternative solutions.

in any other form Someone you are deeply in love with will have a child with someone else. This does not imply, however, that you and this person cannot make this relationship work. You have the choice whether to pursue this or not. You will hear of this in the near future. Any negative event foretold in this dream needs to be prevented or avoided in reality.

Raphael You will come to the realization that you need to do things on your own rather than demand time from others. These people need this time to take care of their own business. Step back and allow others more time.

rapid transit Clear your mind and unclutter your environment in order to develop clarity in your thinking. This will allow you to rapidly decide which path you need to take for those times that require instant decision making over the next few days.

rapist Become very protective over yourself and take extra precautions when you transport money from one location to another. The person who is to receive the money will claim they never received it. Be aware of this possibility for the next three days.

Rap music Pay close attention to the message given through this music. You may either turn a negative message into a positive event or enhance a positive message. You will also be very excited about news you will be receiving within three days by mail. Make sure, also, that you have money to cover your expenses for the next three days.

rapper You will hear words of love you have long waited to hear. This will happen within five days. Remember the words of the rapper. If this dream implies a positive message, be sure to bring this into your life. If it is negative, take steps to change the outcome.

rap sheet For the next three days don't take anything for granted, especially regarding business.

rapture For the next three days you will need much discipline and control in order to refrain from sexual contact. Be ready to rapidly switch gears when needed. You would regret any sexual contact at this time.

rare Avoid doing anything that will cause angry feelings between you and someone else. This situation will escalate to the point of physical violence. Do everything necessary to prevent this.

rarebit Once you have made arrangements, plans or deals with another person, be sure you do not allow a third person, especially someone of the opposite sex, to bully their way into the situation and attempt to take control. Expect this within five days.

rascal Be very careful of the negative thoughts you are running through your mind. Do not allow these messages to take over to the point of causing you to become physically ill. Aggressively pursue a positive attitude.

rash *to see a rash on someone else* You are loved beyond your imagination. You will have strong verification of this within three days. Do everything necessary to maintain a closeness in your relationships.

to see a rash on your skin Get to the bottom of a crucial situation. Think carefully in order to determine your next move. Good luck will be with you for a long period of time. Take steps to avoid anything that will cause your skin to break out.

on face An unusual circumstance will occur that will provide you with more wealth. A very wealthy, shy person will fall deeply in love with you. Be sure to keep your eyes open for anyone who fits this description if you choose to move in this direction. Do nothing that causes a rash to break out on your face.

rasher Keep problems from resurfacing for the next two days. By taking steps now you will be able to resolve these problems permanently.

raspberry You will make the correct decision concerning someone who wants to be close to you. Take this opportunity to allow yourself emotional gratification.

rasp Do not deny yourself the company of someone who wants to be close to you. Take this opportunity to allow yourself emotional gratification.

rat Someone who is interested in you will attempt to disassociate themself from another person because they have lost interest in them. This individual will develop an elaborate plot to keep you in their life in ways you have no desire for. They will not be truthful to you until they are able to get the other person out of their life or will find a way to be with both of you without your knowledge. Take steps to avoid involvement.
anything unusual that you see yourself or anyone else doing with a rat Someone will take advantage of you and use you without your knowledge. This person will use deception and dishonestly and will use you in this situation as an innocent unwilling participant. In the long run you will be cheated. Pay close attention to your present situations and be acutely aware of the actions of others.
white rat Someone who is conniving but very subtle in their attitude will become a financial and emotional drain to you. This person is someone you respect and like a great deal. Back off and become aware of how this relationship is evolving and take steps to protect yourself and your interests.

ratchet You are headed in the wrong direction. You need to stop and rethink your plans within the week.

ration Other people consistently count on you to make sound decisions. You are the first person many people call on in times of need. People think well of you and you are deeply loved. This dream also indicates you will accomplish a great deal with very little leg work.

rat kangaroo Be wary of someone who is playing on your sympathies for the express purpose of having you handle one of their problems. Do not allow anyone to take advantage of your kindness.

rat poison Make sure you do not become involved in something that seems innocent but turns out to be a horrible ordeal. Do not become involved in the conspiracies of others.

rat race This three day cycle is one that will allow you to accomplish what you formerly felt would be impossible. Take advantage of this productive time period.

rat snake Be careful who you interview for the next three days. Do not give out more information than you intend.

rat tail A great event will be celebrated within a few weeks. This will be a surprise to you and a great joy for everyone involved.

rattan You will be asked to join in a partnership with someone.

rattler An older same sexed person will manipulate you out of money that rightfully belongs to you. It will be difficult to collect due to the nature of the manipulation and it will appear to others that you have been repaid when you have not. Put detailed transactions on paper and make sure you get signatures from all parties to ensure this does not occur.

rattlesnake You have consistently requested that another person refrain from doing something that irritates you yet this person will continue the same behavior. This will result in an argument that may escalate into physical violence. Use tact and diplomacy to ensure this does not occur. You must also make sure any negative event involving a rattlesnake does not occur to you or to anyone you recognize.

rattrap Someone of the opposite sex will do everything in their power to make you feel comfortable while in their presence. This individual will also lead you to believe you have more power and authority than they have. This will be done nonverbally for the intent of triggering a reaction from you when a certain situation arises within three days. This person will then swiftly turn against you and chastise you for displaying the same behavior they encouraged. You are dealing with someone who receives gratification in the humiliation and chastisement of others, especially members of the opposite sex. Do not allow yourself to get sucked into this.

ravel Offer more praise toward your family for the next five days.

raven Do everything necessary to keep a persistent, nasty person from dropping in on you whenever they feel like it. These visits ruin precious moments in your life. This individual's behavior will only get worse as time goes by.

ravenous Within three days someone will be generous with you in the ways you most desire. Luck is with you.

ravine Act on your intuition. This will be a powerful cycle for signing agreements.

ravioli Within three days, a situation will occur that deserves a positive answer from you. You must also make a point of demonstrating love to others by making small gestures of appreciation. You will be going through a two day cycle where others will also be showing love toward you.

raw Be aware that you could be embarrassed while on an outing with another person. This individual will run out of funds, not be able to cover expenses and will look to you to pick up the tab.

rawhide For the next two days make sure the person you are explaining important matters to grasps exactly what you mean in order to avoid making a huge mistake.

raw silk Be gentler, more encouraging and more of a soother to someone you care about. Make a point of showing more affection and this will become a very rewarding cycle for both of you.

ray A situation will arise within two days that you should say no to for your own protection. This refusal to get involved will add balance and tranquility to your life. Be aware of people you will have to deal with who have no conscience and are only interested in instant gratification.

bright ray that begins to dim The hopes you have that someone or something will come through for you will not occur. Get busy with your plans so this let down does not become a hardship for you.

ray *(electric)* For the next three days use your best strategy for getting what you desire. What you once felt was impossible will now be possible during this time period. You are entering a very lucky seven day cycle.

ray fish Use your power, authority and leverage to persuade a particular group to come through for you to meet the needs of another person. Do not allow others to talk you out of doing what you know is right.

ray flower Within three days you will be relieved of a heavy burden you have been dealing with for a long time. You will also receive respect, affection and consideration for a long time to come from the person you most desire. Tranquility, joy and blessings will be yours and you are entering a lucky seven day cycle.

rayon Spend more time with your family and less time with those who are less important to you. Begin this process within two days. This dream is a good luck omen.

razor Think ahead and regroup. Do not assume an attitude of defeat when forced to undergo a difficult task. Before tackling this task, get inside information that will allow you to move ahead with confidence.

razorback You are moving too quickly. Slow down for the next two days and plan a strategy that will point you in the direction you want to move.

reactor Someone with an active imagination is developing plans that involve you. Answers to questions this person asks of you will point them in the right direction to promote prosperity for both of you.

read You will need to pull strings in order to motivate activity in a distant city. This will make a big difference in the

outcome of certain events and will bring you greater rewards.

to read Do not disturb the plans of anyone else.

if you remember what you read This is an omen of a forthcoming event. You have the time to diffuse any negative outcome or to promote any positive event. This is likely to occur within seven days.

to see someone else read Do not allow another person to waste your time by dwelling on past mistakes. This is the time to focus on and plan your future. You will also be speaking with someone who will reveal a great deal of valuable information. Expect other people to be very generous with you for the next three days.

in any other form A conversation you will be having within five days will be carefully scrutinized by another person. Your speech patterns and the manner in which you word sentences will be analyzed so this individual will be able to make a final decision on whether they choose to have you in their life, as well as whether they can learn something from you. You have prior notice of this and can conduct yourself accordingly. Many blessings are with you and you are headed for a brilliant future.

reading *to have or request a psychic reading* Within a few days it is important that you have a reading done. You are losing a major portion of your dreams and are unable to grasp certain substantial details. A reading will fill in these important details and offer you the correct meaning. You will be spurred toward important revelations that will allow you to make major changes in your life. Attend to this immediately in order to preserve tranquility in your life. This dream also implies that you need to carefully scrutinize situations that are presently unfolding in order to ensure they are moving in the direction you choose. This is an extremely lucky time cycle. Follow your instincts; your intuition is right on target and you are definitely headed for a prosperous future.

to see someone have or request a psychic reading This doubly implies that it is important for you to seek a reading. Something very important is occurring that you need to be aware of. The only way you will become aware of this is through a reading because you are losing details of the dream in the transition between sleep and wakefulness.

to give a reading Pay close attention to the events and messages given at the time of the reading. If they are positive, take steps to include them in your life. If they are negative, you have three days to avoid all negative events or to alter the outcome. Whatever you were hoping for will also come to pass within two days. You are headed for a brilliant future. Make sure you seek a reading for additional major clues to the meaning of this dream.

reading desk Take the experience you have gained from past mistakes and apply them to similar situations that will arise within three days.

reading room Reduce your expenditures for soft goods. Seek out bargains for the next three days. This is a good cycle for sales.

real estate Before you make a statement to someone else, make sure you mean it and will be able to stand by it. Within two days, you will be tempted to make promises you will be unable to keep.

real estate broker Pay attention to what you are being told. If this dream portends a negative event, take steps to turn it around or prevent it. If the message is positive, take steps to promote it. Do not place yourself in the position to be accountable for the life and behavior of another person. Move on with your life without this additional stress.

realism For the next three days make sure romance does not fade away. Always place romanticism first in your relationships and encourage someone special to contribute in the same way. This will ensure mutual love and satisfaction.

reality Remain focused on the importance of your relationships. Within three days there is the danger of ties being severed with someone who is important to you. Take the necessary steps to ensure this does not happen.

ream You are considering having a medical procedure performed. This is not a good time for this. Postpone this until another time.

reamer Do what you can to add more spice and excitement to your life. Avoid being upset by the inconsistencies of others.

reap Within three days refuse a request you know you should be saying no to. Keep tranquility in your life.

rear For the next three days, avoid being led by someone into a disagreement with a third person. This will backfire on you. Be very aware and don't allow yourself to be led down this path.

rear admiral For the next two days be tenacious about holding on to your money. You will be tempted to spend money you will later need.

rear end Be very alert. Within three days someone will enter your life and create absolute chaos. You will find this very distasteful. Make sure you cut this relationship short to avoid going through this.

rearguard Take steps to ensure others do not overextend themselves emotionally or physically to make sure you are comfortable. Make sure this person knows you appreciate this but that you would be more comfortable if they relax. Good luck is with you.

rearview mirror You need to arrive at a clever idea that will allow you to work alone.

to see someone in your rear view mirror Avoid mistakes by concentrating on all available alternative plans. You will then be able to choose the correct path.

to see someone look at you through a rear view mirror Someone will seek you out for the purpose of creating a very uncomfortable situation. Do whatever is necessary to avoid this person for the next two days because this person enjoys making others uncomfortable.

to look in a rear view mirror and see someone looking back Your motives will be questioned by those in authority. You will develop the courage to see this through. Someone also desires to have a conversation with you but hidden resentments from the past will stand in the way. These past feelings will ruin the moment and the conversation will end early. You have prior notice of this and can make the proper moves to get on with your life with a minimum of stress. Otherwise, many blessings are with you and you are headed for a prosperous future.

if you recognize the person looking at you This individual is very eager to discuss a particular delicate situation with you. Within five days you will be able to reach a mutually satisfying decision.

if the person frightens you The greater the fear, the greater the victory you will achieve. This dream implies you will receive a positive response from someone in authority.

reason *"what is the reason?" - to hear this phrase* Within a five day period, someone who harbors a secret animosity against you will try to sabotage a situation you are trying to steer in a certain direction on someone else's behalf. Although this individual is aware that your actions are right, they will go against you in spite of the destruction they will bring to others. You are trying to work things out so everyone involved will enjoy more prosperity in the future. You have prior knowledge of this and can take steps to put a stop to this interference. This person is not aware of the hardships this will bring to others.

rebate Within three days do not involve yourself with anything you know very little about. Someone will attempt to involve you in something they know a great deal about. If you are not sure of this, say no. Be sure to keep your life simple.

Rebecca *(from the Bible)* Maintain your self-confidence and keep an open communication with authority figures. You will have the courage, clarity and confidence to make the correct move with an authority figure within three days.

rebel A same sexed person will reach out for help. Make sure time is not wasted due to miscommunication. You will give the wrong information for their needs. Make sure you are clear about what is being asked of you in order to avoid a mistake.

rebirth Take lessons from a professional in order to devise a clever plan of opportunity. Do not ignore your needs in favor of the object of your affections. You also have to transform your needs into tangible acquisitions. You will then head toward a more prosperous future. This cycle will last for the next seven days.

reborn You will have the ability and capabilities to handle top level responsibilities. You will be able to clearly redefine your position in a way that will lead to greater prosperity.

rebound An emergency situation will arise within three days that will be out of your control. You will be able to respond quickly and properly to all crises. This will be resolved to your satisfaction as well as others. Don't panic.

recall *to be unable to recall something in a dream* Take the necessary time to properly view the entire picture when a particular issue comes up within a two day period. You will then have a full understanding of what is happening and this will give you the opportunity to determine how you really feel and how you want to live your life. This should be the single most important issue to you right now. This also implies that any request you make, even if it is to someone you feel is uninterested, will be granted. Proceed with confidence. You will succeed on a far grander scale than you ever anticipated. You will enjoy an abundance of health and are headed for a brilliant future.

receipt *to receive a receipt* The amount shown on the receipt represents a figure you will be overcharged. This dream is alerting you that within ten days you must actively involve yourself in comparing prices when making purchases. Because of the extra effort you make, you will be surprised and pleased at the price you will pay for certain items. You will see a substantial difference in the amount you thought you would pay and the amount you will actually pay. It would be to your advantage to shop around. Within three days someone will also attempt to pull the wool over your eyes in order to gain a financial advantage over you. You now have prior notice of this and can take steps to avoid this situation. At the time these two events are taking place, someone will give you an unexpected gift. You will wonder why you are receiving this but it will simply be because this person wants to show you some sort of affection. You are headed for a prosperous future, an abundance of health, and financial security. Move quickly and touch base with all old friends, business acquaintances, etc., in order to build up a support system to meet your needs. This can only be done with the input of others. Pay close attention to the numerical figures. Use these figures in any way you deem important. Keep these figures in mind when planning a purchase. You have the time to allow them to work to your advantage.

receive Be sure to double check all joint funds and make sure you set up a separate account for your own nest egg. You may need extra money of your own.

receiving blanket Before you take steps to bring order into a situation, make sure you know whether this plan will work out in such a way to add stability to your life.

receiving line Do everything necessary to bring more comfort, ease and free time into your life without causing a disturbance in the lives of others.

receptacle You are headed for a brilliant future and all of your hunches are on target.

reception You will get the approval you seek in order to back up your plans. Your ideas will be very well received. Follow your hunches. You are entering a lucky seven day cycle.

to be invited to a reception The best of your abilities will be expected of you within two days. You will be very successful.

to host a reception You will win someone's affections and will receive much love and affection in return. This will occur within two days if you choose to do so.

to be honored at a reception Someone else's rules and regulations will strongly effect your life within two days. Remain tranquil and do not allow this to cause you undue stress.

reception room You will hear very good news within two days and the resulting joy will remain with you for a long time to come. You must also set up a less demanding schedule for the next week. Be very wary for the next three days and move forward with a particular individual with extreme caution. The person you will be dealing with will lead you to believe you can fully confide in them and can rely on their loyalty. This person is cunning and is skilled in creating deception and illusion. This person will lead you to believe in future events that will never take place and has a hidden agenda that concerns pursuing you for devious reasons known only to them. This individual will go to great lengths to create an atmosphere free of any suspicious undertones and you will trust them completely. You will find this person to be very charismatic and charming and will skillfully create diversions if they feel you are becoming suspicious. By the time you realize what is going on you will suffer deep emotional disappointment, disillusionments and financial distress and it will take a long time to recover from this. You have prior notice of this situation and if you practice common sense you will be very successful in diffusing this issue. Refuse to become involved, do not compromise yourself and do not allow this person to pry into your affairs. You will develop the confidence to put yourself on the path toward a prosperous future. Many blessings will come to you and your family.

recess Remain alert. Within three days you will attend a gathering that will result in disaster if you do not ignore one guest who becomes verbally abusive to the other members of the group. Do whatever you can to avoid becoming entangled in this situation and leave the gathering as soon as you are able.

recession You will have to carefully diffuse a situation that will rapidly develop into a crisis. Handle this now and you will avoid being thrown off the course you need to take.

recipe The person you rely on is focused on gaining control of their life and cannot be depended on for additional responsibilities. Find alternative help.

recital Gather people together for the purpose of raising money for an important issue. You will be able to get the support you need from others to raise these funds within the week.

reckless For the next three days keep a tight rein on your emotions. Someone will attempt to put you on an emotional roller coaster. Do not allow yourself to be put through this because of another person's insensitivities. Remain calm and collected.

recliner Within three days you will converse with someone who is an authority on certain information you need and this person will be able to point you toward the right direction. Do not ignore the opportunity to gain invaluable tips.

recluse Within three days, weigh the pros and cons concerning a certain situation to ensure the pieces will fall together as you have anticipated.

recommendation Consider all alternatives prior to making a decision or taking another step. Within three days someone will also talk with you in such a way that will allow you to gain additional confidence regarding a particular situation.

reconciliation Within three days you will encounter someone who is very obnoxious and rude to everyone at a group gathering. Remain calm and make no attempt to control this person's behavior until you can get away. Control your temper and enjoy this time with others as best you can. Good luck is with you.

reconstruction For the next three days be very careful. Someone will ask you questions in an attempt to draw certain information from you. This person will then twist your words around and use this information against you. Watch your conversation.

record Become focused on someone who carries themselves in a very simple and quiet manner. Do not overlook the importance of this individual. They possess a great deal of power and influence over others. Within three days you will be dealing with an issue that this person has expertise in. Do not bypass the opportunity to tap into this individual's knowledge and power. This issue will quickly be resolved with help. Actively seek this person out during this three day period. Also, pay close attention to the message you hear on the record. This foretells a future event. You will have the opportunity to alter any negative message and embrace the positive.

recording/recorder Within five days you will realize you are wasting time on someone you desire. You have been taking too long to make a move. The cycle is perfect now for making a romantic overture and this person will respond in a very positive fashion. You must also pay close attention to the message you hear in the recording. This foretells ei-

ther a positive or negative event. You can either avoid the negative event, or take steps to change it. You can then embrace the positive.

record player You will be able to perform to another's satisfaction regarding a romantic situation. Within a three day period you will have the courage and desire to fulfill another in an emotional way and in the manner they wish to be fulfilled. Good luck is with you.

records *to dream of finding and going through records* This is a good luck omen. You will finally be permanently free of a troublesome situation that has been dragging you down for a long period of time. You are headed for a prosperous future.

to see others go through records For the next three days, carefully guard a priceless object to ensure it is not damaged. You are also entering a very lucky cycle.

recovery room Remain cautious and stay alert to what your body is telling you. If you do not feel well, don't push yourself to the point of feeling worse. Slow down until you feel better in order to avoid a serious fall resulting from unsteadiness. Return to normal activities only after you get back to normal. Remain very alert for the next three days.

recreation For the next three days become very tolerant of everything a specific person does or says. This behavior will allow this individual to feel more confident. Make sure this person does not feel deprived and ensure they feel comfortable enough to get close to you if you choose to grow closer to this person.

recreational vehicle Carefully check all comments made by others prior to agreeing to anything. Focus on the stability you feel you will need for the upcoming two weeks.

recreation room Make sure you do not set up impossible to reach goals for others. Don't push so hard. Instill confidence in others and offer compassion in order to enable them to be successful in life.

recruit Meet personal involvements head on if you desire mutual satisfaction. The next three days will offer you the perfect cycle to take advantage of this.

rectangle For the next three days remove yourself from the influence of others. You will then be able to give yourself a break from outside interference. Attend to your own counsel and you will discover a new clarity of thought. This cycle is dynamically lucky for you. You will begin to possess a new command of your life and will be able to sort out what has been going on and the direction you choose to take now. You will be able to confidently make the correct decisions and are headed toward a brilliant future. Many blessings will come with you and your family.

rector You are planning to start a costly project without the appropriate funding. Start networking and you will be able to locate funding through a government project. You will also be able to work closely with someone who complements you and both of your talents will bring in profits from this project. Start this process within the week. This is the perfect cycle for success

rectory Do not put your plans on hold at the first indication of problems. You will be tempted to do this within three days. Continue to go in the direction you had originally considered.

rectum *any form* Within two weeks you will discover an unsuspected power and you will soon be aware of the high level of authority you possess. This will motivate you to experiment with new and different lifestyles as well as new levels of social functioning. These new experiences will open your eyes and you will find yourself eager to adopt new ways of living. You will experience gratification in areas you have never experienced, both mentally and emotionally. This will also open doors to different sources of income. For the next three days do whatever is necessary to meet certain deadlines. This will allow you to reach your goals sooner. Any negative event connected to this dream may be avoided or altered in reality and any positive event may be promoted. You are headed for a brilliant future.

recuperate Do not allow the unrealistic convictions of another to sway you from backing certain issues. Follow your own counsel.

recycle Within three days stabilize a tricky situation and do not allow yourself to develop a habit of complaining. This habit will only confuse the issue. Avoid this and you will clearly be able to see what needs to be done next. You must also pay attention to what you are recycling. This will give you a major clue to what you may want to focus your energies on in real life.

red You will feel rejuvenated, experience more passion and better health. You will also develop a greater sense of integrity. Eat healthy foods, drink plenty of water, and promote the regeneration of your body. Other people in your life will become more selfless and demonstrate greater love and affection toward you. Within three days, a greater passion will be shown toward you by someone you care about. You will follow your heart's desire during this time period. This also implies you should not slow down the momentum of love and affection shown to you by others. Allow things to flow smoothly and do not deprive yourself of affection.

red alert Someone will turn on their passion toward you. You will experience more affection and passion from others for the next three days.

red ant You will soon come to grips with an important career matter. Carefully scrutinize the plans you hope to execute in order to determine their workability and whether you choose to put them into action. This is a very lucky omen and each plan will work out exactly as you wish once you

have taken the time to review them. Expect a pleasant surprise. You will also realize your ambitions about writing a book.

to see you or anyone else bitten by a red ant This is an omen of victory. You will enjoy great clarity of thought and this will lead you to riches. You will also enjoy a romantic interlude if this is something you choose.

red blood cells Get an up to date blood analysis within seven days. You may have a deficiency that needs to be treated in some way. You must also develop a concise plan that will allow you to meet your goals in the shortest possible time with the least amount of hassle. You are headed toward a peaceful and restful cycle.

Red Cross You will have to deal with someone, within three days, who is coming across with an aggressive attitude and bullying tactics in order to demonstrate power over you. This person will attempt to manipulate you into doing what they want you to do. You can take steps now to avoid being under someone else's control.

red dye Within three days you will have to explain a particular situation. Avoid sounding as though you lack confidence and are hiding something. Do not behave in a way that creates suspicion because someone will take delight in seeing you in this position. Regroup and carefully rethink your tactics.

redemption Domestic conflicts will arise within two days. You can deal with these situations easily by being honest and by using a great deal of patience. Discuss these issues until they are resolved to everyone's satisfaction.

redemption center Do not push yourself to the point of feeling overwhelmed and physically depleted. For the next two days do everything in your power to regroup and build up your resistance.

red eye Keep a close eye on someone else's health. Continually watch this person to ensure there are no serious health problems. Push this person to get the proper care they need in order to recover.

redeye gravy Do not waste time deciding to make a move toward someone you desire. Do not deprive yourself of emotional fulfillment by hesitating. Good luck is with you during this cycle. Make sure you take steps to handle this situation.

red fox You are the only person responsible for your success. Make sure you do not allow others to waste your energy on their causes.

redhead Someone is focusing on you for the purpose of engaging in an underhanded power play. This will be done so subtly that you can easily be taken advantage of. Keep your eyes open and take steps to prevent this.

red herring Avoid stringing someone along. This will backfire on you. This is particularly important for the next two days.

red ink Do not alienate yourself because of your failure to respond to others or because of miscommunication due to your body language. Pay close attention to the manner in which you communicate with others. If you do not make changes, you will fail to enlist the good will of others.

red light Something is occurring behind the scenes with another individual which is beyond your control. For reasons known only to them, an effort is being made to create chaos and a distasteful episode in your life. Make sure you become acutely aware of any unusual activity or behavior in order to maintain balance and stability in your life. You will also become very alert to all incoming calls, mail, or scheduled conferences that you are personally responsible for. Make sure you handle these in a timely fashion.

red light district Within two days you will receive privileged information about an associate. This information will have an effect on how you view certain situations concerning this individual.

red meat Slow down, you are moving too fast and coming on too strong. Everything will run smoother if you tactfully back off in areas you know you should to allow specific situations to work out on their own. This is a good luck omen and you are headed toward a healthy, wealthy life.

redneck Make sure, in a romantic situation, you do not act in such a way that will drive the object of your affections away. You will also be introduced to new people in a new vicinity by someone who would like to involve you in their new lifestyle. This will give you the opportunity to enjoy yourself with people you otherwise would never have met. This will occur within three days.

red oak Develop a more independent attitude and listen to your own ideas and counsel. You are right on target. Good luck is with you for the next seven days.

red pepper For the next five days you will be entertained and amused by someone with a flair for passion. This person will go to great lengths to show the passion they feel for you. You will enjoy this immensely. You are entering a very lustful cycle.

Red Sea You are entering a very tranquil time and an abundance of good luck, health, and prosperity will come to you and your family. Great changes will take place in this cycle. This may also be used as a reference point in time. If you dream of this sea and see its name used in any context, the dream message will occur on this day.

red snapper For the next five days develop a calm and sympathetic demeanor when communicating with another person. Although it doesn't seem so, this individual is going through a great emotional crisis. Maintain your calm manner and eventually this person will open up to you.

red squirrel This is a good luck omen. You will accomplish exactly what you set out to accomplish and will get exactly what you want most in spite of how difficult it may seem.

red tape You should not allow just anyone to be responsible for another's welfare. You may choose someone who does not have the knowledge and expertise to handle this job. Be very insistent on the quality of care you want for this person.

red tide Don't allow the beliefs and ways of another to impose on your life. Someone will be tempted to do this to you within two days. Be alert to this. Major changes will take place in your life if you allow this person this kind of authority.

red wine When someone consistently uses negative statements to belittle you, make it a point to turn them into positive statements while still in the presence of the other person. Good luck is with you. You are deeply loved by others.

redwing Someone is having difficulty reaching out for help in a time of need. This will be brought to your attention within two days. Pay close attention to the behavior of others in order to determine the problem and be able to offer the proper assistance. You will enjoy a successful outcome.

redwood Within seven days someone from a completely different ethnic background will work very successfully with you. You are headed for a very prosperous future.

reed You will become very excited by an invitation you will receive. You will quickly surrender to this person and will be mutually satisfied. You will both work together to establish your future life plans.

reed instrument Within three weeks you will plan and eventually take a much needed pleasurable vacation. You will enjoy yourself and have a safe return.

reed organ Guard against injuries caused by falls, especially for the next two days. You are in a lucky cycle and will be receiving an abundance of blessings and good health.

reed pipe Do not walk out on someone for any reason. This person will not tolerate it and will cause a very distasteful moment for you. Even if you do this in jest, it will be taken seriously and will result in chaos.

reef *rock, coral or sand* Gather together a group of individuals to get their explanation about a certain problem in order to tackle this situation. This will be coming up in the near future. Develop clarity and confidence in what you are doing.

to reef a sail Someone who harbors a secret animosity against you will attempt to wreck the plans you have made to benefit another person. Although this person is aware that you are right, they will go against you within five days in spite of the destruction it will wreak on others. You are trying to work everything out so everyone can enjoy a more prosperous future. You have prior notice of this and can take steps to prevent this interference. This person is not aware of the depth of hardship they will bring to others.

reefer Do not display jealousy and envy toward others. Another person will not want to put up with this behavior and you will be unable to develop a relationship with this individual in any capacity. Be very careful of this for the next seven days.

reef knot Accomplish what you have set out to do. Be tenacious and relentless in your quest. You will not regret this because as soon as it is completed, you will find yourself in a very successful cycle.

reel Pay close attention to situations you have become involved in. Once a situation starts to unravel and looks as though it will not fall into place as expected, back off. Other participants will drop out as well. This particular project was not meant to be at the present time. Remain calm and try again when conditions are better. Above all, remain calm.

referee You will see great improvements in your life within two weeks because of someone else's misfortune. Someone else's mistake will allow you to achieve victory in your life.

reflection Be very cautious. Someone is trying to catch you off guard at an unexpected time and place for the express purpose of gratifying their immediate emotional needs. You will be dealing with someone who lacks a conscience. Take steps to prevent all violent acts against you.

to see your reflection or someone else's reflection in a window pane Within a two week period you will rapidly advance to a higher plane in life than you had ever imagined. You will enjoy an increase in productivity, income, productive conversations, and affection and loyalty from others. Other people will express their desire to be a part of your plans. You are headed for a brilliant future and will enjoy an abundance of health. All of this will occur in a shorter period of time than you ever anticipated.

to see a reflection of another's face in a window pane instead of yours Look ahead, someone will write a check to you and there will be insufficient funds to cover it.

to see your own reflection on anything else This is a major clue to what you need to avoid or add to your life as well as an indication of something you may want to add or detract from your appearance in reality. Someone will also ask to meet you at a set time and place within a few days but this person will not keep the date. Do whatever is necessary to avoid disappointment.

to see the reflection of someone you know on anything else This individual is very interested in you and is very anxious and eager to have time alone with you in order to verbalize their need to involve you in their life.

reflector Within seven days you will put yourself in the position to commit a crime that will result in you being heavily sought after by the law. Do everything necessary to enlist another person's help in the prevention of this event. Get professional help in order to turn your life around instead of wasting your time paying for a crime that you commit. Good luck is with you.

reform *to reform* Someone you least expect will come to your aid at the last moment. Good luck is with you and your family. You will enjoy an abundance of blessings.

reformation Pay close attention when making financial plans and drawing up a budget. There is the potential for making an error that could take years to clear up.

reform school Make sure you take steps to avoid committing an unspeakable action that you will later regret. For the next three days use the highest degree of control to avoid this action. It will only result in a degrading and regrettable lifestyle.

refried beans Become willing to accept small risks in order to enter into a new kind of relationship. This relationship will expose you to a new dimension in life with all the comforts you desire in a relationship. You will enter into agreements that will benefit both of you for life.

refrigerate Make sure you do not place yourself in the position to experience severe, frigid weather. Be sure to control your environment, especially for the next three days.

refrigerator You will discover that you possess an unexpected level of power in areas you did not suspect. You will become acutely aware of this within five days. This will bring you a new set of friends, new social events and you will be able to visualize a new life style that you will be eager to adopt as your own. This new way of living life will agree with you and cause you to flourish. This will also result in a new source of income. All negative events connected with this dream may be changed or avoided. Make sure anything seen in the refrigerator that does not belong there does not signify something that will occur in reality.

to repair Carefully investigate what you sense is a peculiar family situation. A relative is behaving in a suspicious and mysterious fashion. Carefully discern whether this relative is purposely being kept from developing and maturing at the proper rate. If this is the case, make sure you intervene and seek help to ensure this individual has their needs met. This person desperately needs help and is unable to break away from abusive circumstances. Remain calm and be prepared to take a professional approach in order to reach a successful conclusion to this problem.

refrigerator car Be very cautious. Within two days you will be a witness to an altercation between two men that will result in a physical fight. Do not become involved. Leave the premises.

refuel You are preparing to confide something to someone in privacy. Rethink this move. This person will twist your words and make your life very uncomfortable. Restrain yourself from talking about this, especially for the next three days.

refugee Help someone who is special to you to develop a sense of comfort and security when in your presence.

refund Pay careful attention to certain rules and regulations that are in the process of being changed. These changes will occur slowly and subtly but once they take full effect you will find them difficult to tolerate. Pay close attention to this gradual unfolding of events. You have the opportunity to speak up now and change the course of events before they become intolerable. You will be able to work toward a mutual agreement about what you will and will not be able to tolerate.

refuse *to be refused* Within three days you will see an excited reaction from others about a well thought out plan that you are thinking of instigating. You will be eager to have this plan accepted by them.
 to refuse When someone is explaining something, do not allow someone else to interfere and refute the testimony of the first person. This will result in the deprivation of certain knowledge that you require. Watch out for this, especially for the next two days.
 in any other form You have been attempting to get at the truth concerning a personal matter for a long time but each path you have taken had led you to a brick wall. You do know one person from your past who has all the facts. Do not dwell on this matter. This individual will go to the grave with this secret. Focus on bringing joy into your life and let this matter go.

refuse *(garbage)* For the next two days be cautious and careful of the choices you make. Make no decisions that will restrict you from moving forward. Remain alert and carefully think through all alternatives.

reggae Do not allow the theatrical mannerisms of another person to prevent you from recognizing their professionalism.

regiment A lack of communication will result in a major setback. Take a few days to consider what you want to communicate to someone who will contribute a wealth of information.

register *to register* Within three days you will meet a very imaginative person. This person will go to great lengths to include you in a plan that will enhance your life.

registered mail You will meet someone who is not on the same economic footing as you. This person is very wealthy and will do everything in their power to include you in their life. They will provide you with love, affection and generosity as well as a wonderful lifestyle. The opportunity is there if you choose to become involved. Be aware of the name on the mail delivered in the dream. This individual has an urgency to contact you and will ask assistance in some capacity within three days. You are entering a lucky cycle and will experience an abundance of health and tranquility.

registered nurse Within two days you will have a conversation with someone and will be asked by a third person to explain the contents of this conversation. Be aware that you will have to explain to a large group of people why you divulged information to another person that was to be kept in confidence. Take steps to keep all conversations to yourself.

regulate *to regulate* Someone will come to you and expect you to be their rescuer and crusader. Do what you can to help this person handle their problems on their own.

regurgitate Within two days you will be entering into certain negotiations. Go ahead, even if you are doubtful about proceeding. The outcome will be much better than you ever anticipated.

rehabilitate Do not behave in a manner that will lead someone to believe you are willing to settle for less. Otherwise you will be taken for granted and will receive far less than anticipated.

rehearse *to rehearse* Make sure a young family member is having their needs met, especially for the next two days. Make sure this child is being properly cared for and is not undergoing physical or verbal abuse.

rehearsal Do not force your opinions on another person. Although this person may not let you know that they find your manner distasteful, make sure you do not cross that line for the next two days.

Reich Before entering into a personal venture with someone else, demand loyalty prior to discussing details of the project. Otherwise, this person will want to back out once they have all of the information. Stress loyalty and you will find the right person to be your partner.

reign Someone will avoid you after having a conversation in which you prove to be very stubborn. This person will want nothing more to do with you after this discussion. If you choose to maintain your friendships, allow room for compromise. A good healthy relationship should be your priority.

reimbursement *to be reimbursed* For the next ten days it is essential that you devote your time to positioning yourself to create excitement and generate a greater interest regarding a new situation. You will be able to segment more success about a new product, plan, idea or conversation. You will gain excellent feedback that will bring about more productivity, more fun and will create a non stressful outcome to what is a priority to you now. You will be able to bring everyone involved together in building a common understanding. You will determine what, where, and how to effectively achieve a chief victory on a grander scale than you anticipated. Your goal is to make the world aware of these exciting ideas, etc., and will find they are well received by others.

rein Become more loyal with the person who is the object of your affections. Make a point of affirming your loyalty for the next two days. This person needs to feel comfortable and secure with you when undergoing a situation that will shortly arise.

reincarnation This is very dynamic and symbolizes a victorious growth cycle. You will be relentless and determined and will develop a pursuing quality that arises from within. These qualities will bring your desired goal to you and will bring grand changes into your life, no matter how impossible it seems. You will achieve anything you desire. Pay close attention to the words and events depicted in this dream because this will be an accurate depiction of what will occur within eight weeks. Pay special attention to any colors depicted in this dream and look them up for a more detailed description of the meaning. Take steps to prevent any negative message foretold in this dream and make sure you experience only positive expressions in life.

reindeer For the next two days pay close attention to your emotions and feelings to determine whether you want to continue putting yourself through a particular situation. Whether you choose to or not, make it clear to others where you stand.

reinforced concrete Do not take gambles with people who do not have the experience to implement your plans. Within two days make sure you are very clear about how your plans are being handled.

reject Make sure you do not panic over a situation that will arise within two days. Make certain it does not reach the point where you are unable to make a clear decision. Handle each problem calmly and steadily and you will find that they turn out better than you anticipated.

to reject someone or something in any form Within three days you will receive an excited reaction from others for a well thought out plan you are thinking of instigating. You are very eager to have this plan accepted by others.

rejection *to be rejected by someone* Within four days make every effort to display the correct behavior toward someone who is special to you. You desire closeness from this person but are not yet involved. At the beginning you will feel this person is not interested in you in the way you desire. During this time period you will experience an abundance of health, a financial windfall will come your way, and you will be on the path toward a prosperous future.

rejection slip Make sure, especially for the next two days, that you are more understanding of a new acquaintance. This person lacks the confidence and social skills to open a conversation but once they are comfortable you will find

they are a joy to be around.

rejoice A situation will take place within a few days that will cause you deep joy. The excitement caused by this will last for a long time. Tranquility and health will be yours.

rejuvenation Within the week you will experience a total rejuvenation in those areas you most desire. Focus on those things you want to transform and work to give them a new appearance. This is a dynamite cycle for you.

relations Be aware that the assistance you are asking for from an agency, etc., will be hampered by the rude behavior of the person assigned to you. Do not allow anyone to cause your temper to flare or throw you off balance. Calmly and tactfully request that your needs be met by asking assistance from someone higher up. Do this within two days and you will successfully attain your goal.

relative Within two weeks make it a priority to tie up all loose ends regarding financial issues. This will ensure future financial stability.

to dream of your relatives Pay close attention to what your relatives are doing. This will give you a clue to what is needed in your life or what to keep out of your life for the next month. You will also begin working with someone on the development of an idea that will lead you to a brilliant future. Other people depend on you to take the leadership role when making a big decision that will come up within two days. You will have the strength and the encouragement you need to make the right choices.

to dream of someone else's relatives Within two days make sure you realize that you are under no obligation to act in the way anyone else wishes you to. Make it clear you are under no one else's control. You will be able to rid yourself permanently of someone who thinks they have the authority to control your behavior, manner, speech or thought patterns. You will be able to do this with very little anxiety because of the tact and diplomacy you use to handle this matter. You are headed in the right direction and are on the path toward a prosperous future.

to dream that you have a relative that you do not, in reality, have This could indicate you have a relative that you are not aware of. This could also be guiding you to a certain message. For example, if you dream about a brother you do not have, you will need to look up the meaning for brother. You also need to pay attention to the character and personality of the person in this dream. This may refer to someone you want to introduce into your life who will be instrumental in bringing you prosperity. This is a lucky cycle for you and you are headed for a brilliant future.

to dream of marrying a relative This is an assurance that your life will turn around and you will enjoy a brilliant future. Enjoy life fully and do not take life for granted. This is an extremely lucky omen. Someone will come into your life within a few days. This person will come on eagerly and rush you into a friendly relationship. At first you will get mixed messages while on a date and you will feel this person desires romance. After you begin to respond to this aspect of their behavior, this person will back off quickly and withdraw from the friendship. Take this as a forewarning to enjoy the friendship and take it no further. You must also make certain you or anyone else you recognize in the dream do not become involved in any romantic interplay with a close relative. Make sure any negative event witnessed in this dream does not become a reality for you or for anyone you recognize in the dream. Take steps to ensure you experience only positive events in life.

to hear the word Practice a tolerant attitude for the next three days. Several situations will arise concurrently that require controlled personal handling. Remain calm and you will arrive at a successful conclusion.

to dream of a relative you do not have but may under certain circumstances acquire Within three days you will be placed in a potentially dangerous situation. This person will relentlessly try to sell you on an idea they truly believe in. You would be acting in an irresponsible manner if you allow yourself to be placed in this position. You are in danger of inadvertently putting yourself or this other person in a potentially fatal position. You have prior notice of this and have the choice of not becoming involved. Any negative event portrayed in this dream that concerns you or anyone you recognize needs to be avoided or altered. Forewarn this person to do likewise. Do everything you can to experience only positive expressions in your life.

relax *to relax* Someone you were kind to and bestowed a favor on in the past will remember you and unexpectedly offer you a financial gift or a relationship position.

relay *race* This is a very lucky omen, especially if you are the winner. You will achieve victory with a position you desire, whether this relates to a financial or a relationship issue.

relegate *to relegate* Someone will invite you to an outing and will then attempt to lure you into a secluded area for the purpose of inflicting emotional and verbal abuse. This person has a chip on their shoulder and wants to take it out on you in a private place. Do not allow yourself to be placed in this position.

relic Work steadily and detail your plans in order to successfully meet your goals.

relief map Someone will volunteer money for something you greatly desire to purchase. Do not hesitate. Accept this offer. You will be able to repay this in a timely fashion.

religion Within three days someone will purposely create an argument with you in order to avoid keeping a promise they have made to you. Remain calm and do not allow this person to provoke an argument. If you remain calm, the outcome will be to your advantage.

relish Get a medical check-up to determine whether you are anemic. Be sure to get the proper foods to build up your blood. You are loved beyond your imagination by family members and will see evidence of this within the week.

remedy Do not become overly friendly with someone you have doubts about who appears to want only friendship from you. This individual will ultimately become overly possessive and begin to stalk you. Take steps to protect yourself in the manner you feel is best for you.

remember *to dream of being able to remember* Take the time you need to review the whole picture when a particular issue comes up within two days. This will allow you to fully understand what is happening and will give you the chance to determine how you really feel and how you want to live your life. This should be the single most important issue in your life right now. This also implies that any request you make, even if it is to someone you feel is not interested in you, will be granted. You will succeed on a grander scale than you ever imagined. You can proceed with confidence, expect an abundance of health, and are headed for a brilliant future.

to be unable to remember something in a dream Take the necessary time to review the complete picture when a certain situation comes up within two days. You will then be able to comprehend what is happening and this awareness will give you the chance to determine how you really feel and how you wish to live your life. This should be a priority to you now. Proceed with confidence. Also any request you make will be granted even if it is to someone you feel is not interested in you. You can anticipate an abundance of health.

reminder Do not deny yourself to someone who depends on you for their emotional needs. Do not purposely set someone up for disappointment if you are not prepared to meet their needs. Watch your behavior and make sure you do not communicate the wrong message.

remnant For the next three days you will be more focused on improving your physical appearance. As a result of this, you will experience big changes.

remorse Within three days, you will receive the necessary information and assistance to complete a particular task.

remote control You will soon be clearly aware of the deep feelings someone has for you. This person is hopelessly in love with you. This emotion has developed very rapidly and this individual will be unable to contain themselves. This dream also implies you will change your behavior and start focusing on not only those relationships that are important to you but also on anything else that demands this trait. This change will stay with you for a lifetime. You are definitely headed for a brilliant future.

remove Immediately face up to personal problems in a relationship.

to dream of yourself or anyone else removing something that will make something else operational or inoperative A cluster of events will occur one after the other with each bringing a tremendous amount of joy, wonder and awe because things are happening so quickly. You will also possess a powerful energy that you are going to be able to direct and control. At the same time these other events are taking place you will be able to bring other people under your complete control. Because you have prior notice of this you will be able, within the week, to direct this energy in such a way to successfully complete anything you wish in a superb way. You will be able to overcome any difficult obstacle and it will now be very simple to deal with. Your intuition will be right on target and follow your hunches about a new relationship. Many blessings are with you and your family.

Remus Within seven days do what you can to assist yourself in those areas in which you feel you are losing control. This will involve personal communications (verbal or written). This is the best time to take advantage of productive conversations and negotiations. You will enjoy a prosperous outcome. Proceed with confidence.

renaissance Within the week you will be invited to an outing by a very kind and generous person and will be very excited at the prospect of this date. Make this a pleasurable event. For some unknown reason you may never see this person again but will have pleasurable memories for a lifetime. This situation is beyond your control.

rendezvous Be alert. Someone will give you the impression they are very eager to see you. Don't allow yourself to be taken. This is just an act. Once you take the offer to meet, this individual will back off and act as though they never wanted to be with you. This will occur within seven days. Take steps to avoid this embarrassing situation and remain unmoved.

renegade Do not compromise on your goals in life.

renewal You will undergo dramatic changes that will improve your life. You are headed in the right direction for prosperity.

rent A same sexed person will lead you to a vocation you can develop on your own. You will then experience independence and satisfaction and will eventually reap greater profits than you would by working for someone else. Good luck is with you. Be aware that any negative message you receive from this dream may be altered. All positive messages may be promoted. Many blessings and good health are connected with this dream.

rental unit Make sure for the next three days that in spite of how much a person promises to come through for you, you will be let down. Do not enter into any agreements you do not feel sure about with people you are not sure you can trust. You will later regret this.

renter Someone with a dynamite personality and reputation will want to enter into a business plan with you. This is a lucky omen for you. Go for it.

if you recognize the renter Take steps to alter the out-

come of any negative message and promote any positive ones.

repair For the next three days you will be treated with love, affection, appreciation and passion. Do not deprive yourself of this treatment. You are entering a cycle that will give you an abundance of health.

to repair something Be ready for an unusual and remarkable event to occur within three days. At the time this is taking place, you will be able to think clearly enough to go through each step you need to take in order to get through this cycle comfortably. Your curiosity will be very strong during this cycle and you will need to be very firm and disciplined in order to keep it under control. You will enjoy an abundance of health during this time period.

repairman For the next three days refrain from all heavy labor and strenuous athletic pursuits. Even if you are in top physical condition, you are in a cycle that will require pampering.

repay *to repay* Everything is possible for the next three days. Prepare for the best and line yourself up for what you really want. You will be successful in reaching your goals.

repayment *to be repaid* For the next eight days it is essential that you devote your time in such a way that you can create excitement and generate a greater interest regarding a new situation. You will be able to segment more success about a new product, plan, idea or conversation. You will gain excellent feedback that will bring about more productivity, more fun and will create a non stressful outcome to what is a priority. You will be able to bring everyone involved together in building a common understanding. You will determine what, where, and how to effectively achieve a chief victory on a grander scale than you anticipated. Your goal is to make the world aware of these exciting ideas, etc., and find they are well received by others.

repellent Certain pleasure seeking behaviors and entertainments will become habit forming and very expensive to maintain. Control your behavior and do not abuse your finances.

reply *to reply* Make sure you respond to others in a manner that conveys a sense of humor and tranquility so they will feel comfortable when working with you on your project. You will be very pleased with the results.

report Refuse to comply to a negotiation or request that will come up within two days. Refuse to become involved in any manner.

report card Make sure you do not unintentionally walk into a seemingly safe procedure that will result in a freak accident. Postpone all procedures for the next three days that could have disastrous results.

repress *to repress* Learn to express yourself fully in life and take the time to enjoy all aspects that interest you. Do this without overextending yourself financially or physically. Open yourself to others who want to include you in their life for wonderful enjoyable moments. This is the perfect cycle for this.

reprimand Pay very close attention, for the next four days, to someone who wants to control you with a gesture or a move of some sort. This will be done by using a manner of communication that suggests suppressed anger. Do not allow yourself to be manipulated by this and do whatever is necessary to live your life without this control over your behavior and without this person. Within three days the opportunity will be right for you to rid yourself of this intimidation.

reproduce Offer extra praise and love to family members and loved ones. Allow them to feel how important they are to you. This is especially important for the next three days. You are deeply loved.

reptile Be very aware of someone who is so isolated in life that they reach the point of doing something outrageous. Do everything necessary to help anyone who fits this description within the next three days.

Republican Within three days make sure you have absolute clarity of thought. Make sure you have mulled over your decisions prior to making any choices. You will find the correct one.

Republican party Within two days someone will over dramatize a certain situation that you have revealed to them in a conversation. Avoid this by limiting the amount of information you are willing to give to others, otherwise you will regret everything you said to this person.

request Within five days you will capitalize on the mistake of another. Someone else's misfortune will indirectly give you the opportunity to move ahead. Blessings will come to you and your family.

requiem Within two weeks you will become very successful through the efforts of someone else. The friend of a friend will pull strings for you in ways never imagined. Good luck is with you.

rerun An inheritance you will receive in the future will be less than was promised. Handle this situation in the proper way now to ensure you receive what is rightfully yours and is what the donor desires.

to see a rerun in any form Pay close attention to the contents of the rerun for clues to a forthcoming event. This will point to a situation that occurred in the past and is likely to repeat itself. If it was distasteful, you can take steps to change the outcome. If it was a pleasant event, you will want to take steps to ensure that it is repeated. Someone will also begin to demonstrate an unusual amount of affection towards you. For the next three days, stop being so analytical and just enjoy this wonderful cycle.

rescue *to rescue someone* Watch young children around alcohol. Make sure they do not accidentally ingest any beverage containing alcohol. A group of people you have been working with to reach an agreement will make a decision within five days that will favor you.

research Pay attention. Relationships will grow only as much as both parties are willing to let them. Communicate with the person you desire to continue a loving relationship with. Determine through this conversation what both of you need to do to make love work. This will have a tremendous affect in bringing this relationship to a deeper level.

resemblance Anything you see that bears a resemblance to an event in the past indicates that this event will reoccur within three days. If this was a negative event you have the time and knowledge to alter the consequences or to avoid it altogether. If it was a positive event, you can take additional steps to promote this event to the fullest. You must also try to avoid anxiety over a business relationship that is moving far more rapidly than you anticipated. When you begin to feel uncomfortable with this situation, slow down and re-group until you feel more confidence. Talk with others about this and work to remove the stress that accompanies this. Everything will work out well.

reservation Your presence will be requested at several different functions during the same time frame. To avoid hurt feelings, let each person know your schedule and alert them that you will attend but not at a specified time. You will be making the rounds to each function. This will be a stress free, tranquil and joyous cycle for you.

reserve You have promised someone a certain item but it will not be as easy as you thought to obtain. As soon as possible, start tracking it down so you will have time to acquire and deliver it during the time frame you had anticipated. If you wait until the last moment, you will not have the time you need and this will lead to disappointment.

residence Within three days a very special person will make sexual demands on you. This person has also developed a completely new attitude that is very refreshing to you. This will be a surprising transformation and you will find it a delightful experience if you choose to become sexually involved. You will experience a deeper level of lovemaking than you ever thought possible with more of a sense of commitment and emotional connections. Good luck is with you.

resident You are in a cycle of great change. You will have a strong desire to change your behavior, attitude and appearance. Others will notice this deep personal growth. You will obtain a sense of freedom and a release of old hang ups that you feel have kept you from going in a new direction. Expect this to take place rapidly.

residential home Respect your health, simplify your life, and at the same time add more spice to your life. This will also be pointing out an area where you will soon be living. You must also make sure that, if you dream of an area that does not feel quite comfortable to you, it will be an area that is dangerous for you to be in, in any context. Play it safe and avoid all residential areas that feel unsafe. Keep in mind that this area will represent a locale where someone you are searching for can also be located. This dream implies that you also have no reason to doubt the person who is showing love and affection toward you. You will enjoy a steady, stable and mutually nourishing lifestyle for a long period of time.

resin Do not allow haunting memories of past careers to stand in the way of success in a new career and future opportunities. You will experience a great change for the better if you move in the direction you desire.

resort You will travel extensively and will enjoy yourself immensely while experiencing different cultures and lifestyles. Do not forget those who are important to you when you get caught up in the excitement of a new environment and lifestyle. Avoid hurt feelings and focus on special relationships that need to be nurtured. Do not allow yourself to become an insensitive and uncaring person, especially for the next seven days.

respirator Do everything necessary to keep your lungs in a healthy condition. If you develop a mild illness, do not ignore it to the point where it becomes a major crisis. Play it safe.

if you recognize anyone connected to the respirator Take the time to warn this person against allowing a minor illness to escalate into a major problem. Remind this individual to play it safe and remain healthy.

respiration Live life to the fullest and nurture those aspects of your personality that crave nurturing. Pay close attention to your behavior. You may be overcrowding your schedule to avoid commitment. Face your commitments head on and don't deprive yourself of a loving, workable relationship. Do what it takes to enjoy life and leave yourself open to new experiences.

respiratory system For the next two days be very cautious about giving any information about someone to another person.

if you dream of your respiratory problems Take steps to turn any negative situation into a positive situation or make sure you avoid it altogether.

respond Pay close attention to an individual who is isolating themselves to the point of it being unhealthy. Within three days this person is destined to succumb to suicide unless intervention is provided. Do what you can to prevent this tragedy.

rest *to rest or to see others resting* You are destined for a once in a lifetime opportunity. Take advantage of this opportunity for greater wealth and power. Many blessings are

with you and you will soon enjoy a cycle that promises much wealth.

to see yourself lie in a restful position Expect within the next three days that you will be celebrating a victory you have achieved. Proceed with confidence.

restaurant Anyone you recognize at the restaurant in this dream represents someone you will dine with, within five days, at a restaurant. You will also need to be straightforward when making a request or seeking information when conversing with someone for the next week. This will be a far more successful approach than attempting to manipulate the conversation in order to subtly pin this individual down. Do everything necessary to avoid causing discomfort to an individual you are negotiating with.

greasy spoon Be very careful of your pleasure seeking activities. Make sure these do not develop into serious complications. You also need to let others know your whereabouts at all times in order to play it safe.

to be at a restaurant alone Within seven days, a scheduled appointment will be broken by the other individual. Make sure you have alternative plans and reschedule the appointment in order to keep things moving in the direction you want it to go.

rest home Encourage yourself to continue when you have doubts and when things are not progressing in the way you feel they should. Maintain a high confidence level, everything will work out in the way you wish them to.

résumé Your success will depend solely on how willing you are to push yourself toward your goals. You need to work independently in order to reach your aims. You also need to pay close attention to the résumé itself. This will give you major clues to a forthcoming event that you may wish to avoid completely or to work to bring about.

restrict *to restrict someone from doing something* For the next three days be very careful of putting restrictions on someone you would not want placed on yourself. This also implies that within three days you are destined to meet someone of the opposite sex who will come into your life. If you involve yourself with this person in any capacity, you will find they have many restrictions before they reach any kind of agreement.

resurrection You will enjoy a long and healthy life and many blessings. You will also be able to accumulate enough wealth to provide the essentials of life as well as the refinements you desire. You will enjoy stability throughout your long life. Many blessings will come to you and your family.

retard *any form* Any medical procedure scheduled during this cycle will result in success. With tender loving care, your recovery will be rapid and you will quickly return to your normal state of health. Many blessings are with you.

retardation *mild* Someone has led you to believe they are fully able to handle large responsibilities but once you entrust them with these tasks, you will be let down in a big way. This person fully believes they are capable of assuming big jobs but their ego is larger than their abilities. Be acutely aware of this and do not risk anything of importance.

retread tires Meetings, conferences and all personal communications will be very fortuitous for you, especially for the next seven days. You will be able to use your communication skills very successfully.

return This is a very lucky omen for you and implies that a very unusual situation will take place resulting in a financial windfall for you. Within five days your inner drive and courage will also give you the motivation to break through any physical or mental barrier that interferes with you moving ahead in life. Once you rid yourself of those aspects of your life that are holding you back you will be able to bring any new project into tangible form. You will be welcomed with open arms by everyone you care about. You are on the path toward a brilliant future and many new opportunities are headed your way.

to see yourself or someone else refuse to return something Within four days you will be more thrilled and overjoyed than you ever felt before because of several unconnected events that will occur almost simultaneously and will be more successful than you ever thought possible with very little effort on your part. This will be a result of your motivation, being in the right place at the right time, by following your hunches and by paying attention to your perceptions. You will experience much more of this within the month. Any negative event portrayed in this dream needs to be altered or avoided in some way.

return ticket A reunion you feel will be a disaster will turn out to be a very pleasing and wonderful experience. Victory is with you.

Reuben sandwich You will have a fantastic invitation within the week that you must not turn down. This will open doors for meeting a very special person who will help you to improve a particular situation in your life. You are headed in the right direction.

reunion *any form* For the next two days make sure you understand that you are under no obligation to behave in any manner that someone else wishes you to. Make sure you are under no one else's control and within this time period you will be able to permanently rid yourself of a certain person who thinks they have control over your behavior, manner of speaking, thinking or reacting. You will be able to accomplish this with very little anxiety because of your easy manner and tactful attitude. You are going in the right direction and are headed for a prosperous future. All negative events depicted in this dream need to be avoided and make sure you promote each positive event.

Revelations *(from the Bible)* Be relentless in bringing a special project to completion. Push yourself to tie up all loose ends. This will bring great benefits to you, especially

for the next seven days. Anything you view in this dream that portends a future event needs to be avoided if the results are negative, or promoted if a positive event is foretold.

revenge Someone you are interested in, in some capacity, is waiting for you to make the first move. You will have more success if you make this move within three days.

Revere, Paul Someone will enter your life within seven days, and if you choose to pursue this, they will be the one you will spend your life with. This will be a very stress free, fruitful and happy union.

Reverend Trust your hunches. Your intuition is right on target. You will also be able to effectively debate an issue and get your point across successfully.

reverse *to see yourself doing anything in reverse* Have an intimate conversation with someone in order to encourage big changes. You will be very successful.

in any other form You will experience new dimensions and meet new challenges with a newly hired assistant. At the first indication this new assistant is having trouble, schedule a meeting to avoid any disruption in the work schedule.

revise *any form* A long standing debt will be unexpectedly repaid to you. Actively pursue money that is owed to you and you will receive this money promptly if you act within seven days.

revival Demonstrate more respect and regard towards children and young adults. Watch your behavior.

revolt Be very cautious for the next seven days. Someone will purposely attempt to steer you in the wrong direction. This will be done in an attempt to keep you from reaching your goals.

revolution This is a good luck symbol. You will be undergoing some major transformations. A new friend will also point you in a new direction and will provide you with the necessary information to successfully fulfill your desires. Make sure any negative occurrence in this dream does not become a reality.

revolve You have constantly informed someone of a behavior that irritates you. Within three days this person will purposefully repeat this behavior for the purpose of provoking an argument that will escalate into physical violence. Tactfully remove yourself from this environment to avoid being under this person's influence. Do not allow someone to throw you off balance.

revolver Be alert. Within the week, you will be abandoned without notice by someone you are emotionally attached to. This will be due to unwarranted jealousy and you will experience many distasteful moments if you allow yourself to be sucked into this type of behavior and mistreatment. Think ahead. This person needs to keep their emotional problems out of the relationship in order to maintain a stable environment. Do not allow this to become your problem and get on with your life without putting yourself through this scenario. Anything negative in this dream relating to a revolver needs to be prevented or altered in reality. Good luck is with you.

revolving door You know someone who has a habit of treating you very harshly and of creating stressful situations for others. If you know you will be around this person within four days, do everything you can to remain calm and stress free. Do not allow yourself to get caught up in this person's games.

reward For the next four days you will be extremely lucky doing things on your own. Follow your own counsel and anything you set into motion will reach a successful completion. Victory is with you.

rewrite Within seven days someone who has led you to believe in their loyalty will let you down. Do everything you can now to keep this disloyalty from causing a shameful or embarrassing situation. Do not divulge any information to this person that can be used against you.

rhapsody Someone has already planned on how to spend the money that is coming to you. Be sure to set limits on what you will allow someone to do with your money.

rhesus monkey A family member will go to great lengths to involve you in a distasteful discussion that will later lead to a big argument with other relatives. Do what you can now to prevent this from occurring.

rheumatic fever Refrain from demanding that someone behave in the manner you expect them to. This person has led you to believe they would be more demonstrative than they are. If you push this person to be the way you want, you will be emotionally hurt by the backlash. Accept this person on their own terms. You must also take steps to protect your health and the health of your family.

rheumatoid arthritis Someone is devising a plan to subtly move into your home. This will result in a very chaotic situation if you decide to ask this person to stay with you. Do not allow yourself to be manipulated into this stressful situation.

rhinestone You will become very clear about how you can help someone who desires you greatly. Your thinking ability will be enhanced and you will gain the ability to allow this person to feel comfortable enough with you to express their needs and desires. You will then work toward a mutually satisfying relationship. You will also have enough clarity of thought to bring ideas into reality. This will be a good luck omen for the next seven days.

rhine wine Make sure you do not overindulge in anything that will bring harm to you. Refrain from abuse and keep yourself safe.

rhinoceros Take the time to investigate events as they begin unfolding this week. Prepare for the unexpected in order to reduce stress. You will be successful in handling big issues.

rhinoceros beetle You will achieve success with anything you set up to do for the next seven days.

rhinoplasty Within the week you will be asked to handle certain emotional problems. Be sure you are emotionally equipped to take these on prior to committing yourself. Do not overextend yourself and make sure you have all the details before becoming involved.

rhino virus Protect yourself from any virus that, if not treated aggressively during the initial stages, will escalate into something far more serious. Take care of yourself, stay warm, eat healthy foods and drink plenty of water.

Rhode Island Within two days someone will unexpectedly ask you to spend private moments with them. If you choose to go on this outing, you will share many memorable moments. This may also be used as a reference point in time. If you dream of this state and see its name used in any context, the dream message will occur on this day.

Rhodesia Do everything necessary to make someone aware of the deep passion you feel for them. This person is uncertain about your feelings. Put your love into action and be consistent about this for the next seven days. Don't let your love die. This may also be used as a reference point in time. If you dream of this country and see its name used in any context, the dream message will occur on this day.

rhododendron Luck will follow you and will be with you for a very long time. Within five days begin preparing for the advent of a new and wonderful relationship you have long desired.

rhubarb Think ahead and regroup. You are headed in the wrong direction.

rhyme Do not settle for less because you deserve the best. Make the time and effort to go for what you really want. You will be successful in completing your goals.

rhythm Something very interesting will occur within the week. You will meet someone irresistible and will have a strong urge to have this person in a sexual way. This person feels the same way but will fail to demonstrate it. Subtly make the first move and things will evolve from there. You will enjoy victory in all of your goals during this time period.

rib Do not deny intimate time with another person by wasting time on less important matters. Do not allow this behavior to continue or it will become a major issue between you and that special person.

ribbon Within three days you will make an independent move toward a specific individual who is very difficult to talk to because of their intimidating personality. You will be able to break through this intimidation and get this person to behave toward you in the manner you desire. Everything will work out exactly as you had envisioned. You are headed for a brilliant future. Pay attention to the color of the ribbon for a clearer understanding of this dream.

blue ribbon Within the week, someone will become aware of you in a very special way. This person will pursue you and become very determined to marry you. This individual will proceed very slowly yet persistently in the direction of marriage. If you choose to pursue this, the relationship will be long lived and you will enjoy prosperity. Follow your intuition. Your hunches will be on target especially for the next three days.

rib eye You will do something to encourage someone else to grow closer to you within five days.

rice Be prepared for a very crowded social calendar. You will be invited to numerous social functions and be very popular with both sexes. You will achieve victory with each goal you set within this time period.

wild rice This is an extremely lucky omen and you will be surprised when you receive a very luxurious and unexpected gift.

rice paper This is a symbol of prosperity and also implies that a friend will surrender to your sexual desires, if you choose to pursue this. The union will be very solid, happy and last for a long time.

rich An unusual situation will occur with another person. This individual will be drawn to you in a sexual way, is much younger than you, is very attractive, kind and generous. You will have a hard time understanding their behavior because they will go to great lengths to become involved with you. Follow your instincts, they are right on target. For additional information see wealth.

rickets Think carefully about whether you desire to be placed in a situation where you will share close quarters with another individual. If so, do what you can to make your surroundings comfortable without appearing overly obvious.

rickrack Make a point of staying out of someone else's business, especially for the next three days.

rickshaw Within the week you will fall deeply in love with someone at a social function. Although you feel this is an impossible relationship, all things are possible now. You are headed toward a very prosperous future.

ricotta Become determined to come to terms with a certain situation where you will share close quarters with another individual. Do what you can to make your surroundings comfortable without appearing overly obvious.

riddle Deal with your refusal to commit to a certain relationship. This will be a great relationship for you. Do what you can to avoid destroying it forever.

ride All of your plans will meet with success. You will enjoy popularity with both sexes. All information coming to you for the next seven days will also prove valuable. You are headed for a brilliant future.

uncomfortable ride Make sure you are not being steered in the wrong direction.

ridge Concern yourself deeply about money that someone will request from you within three days. You will be able to avoid regrets later on by refusing to extend a loan.

ridicule You will have to give out a great deal of information about yourself to another person. Make sure you comply fully so this person will have the necessary information to make an important decision in your favor.

riding school Within three days you will be invited to a daytime outing that will take place out of doors. Do everything you can to participate in this event.

riffraff For the next three days, do everything you can to control your moodiness. Avoid hostile behavior.

rifle Someone will become very aware of the deep feelings they have for you. Within three days this person will reveal these feelings in the perfect setting, at the perfect time. As a result, you will be overwhelmed with happiness.

rifle fire Become open when communicating your desires to another person. You will also hear from a relative who lives in a distant place and is anxious to tell you about something they would like you to have as an inheritance.

rifleman/woman You are wasting too much time deciding to talk with someone about your desires. Make this move quickly because this is the perfect cycle to make your desires known. You will be greeted with open arms by this individual. You are also presently involved with someone who is very nervous about the depth of a relationship in any capacity. Demands from you will drive this person away within three days. It is your choice whether to pursue this behavior or to avoid losing this person.

rig Within three days someone will try to manipulate you because of your kindness and generosity. Avoid becoming involved in the temper tantrums of others. The moment a conversation starts to get out of hand, depart from the scene. Protect yourself from others.

right angle Find a place where you can concentrate and meditate about your deepest desires so you can come up with a focused plan detailing the steps you need to take next.

right field A training discipline and more education will enable you to establish the perfect business partnership you desire.

right hand Be very alert when someone speaks to you within three days. Pay attention to the negative remarks aimed at you and make sure you turn these statements around immediately while this person is still with you. Things will soon turn around and you will find yourself headed for a brilliant future.

right of way Within three days someone will begin to complain because of something left undone by you. Avoid distasteful moments by taking care of your responsibilities now.

rigor mortis Make sure you do not get involved with outrageous and unusual behavior. Pay close attention in order to avoid getting into trouble. Rethink and refocus in order to put yourself on the right path.

rime You will rise above your overburdening troubles within seven days. Be aware that someone will expect you to immediately take on new and separate responsibilities. Remain uninvolved.

rind You will finally receive the information you have been waiting for. Be sure to check the accuracy of this information with a third person. There may be more information that has been omitted.

ring The assistance you will be needing in terms of money and time from another person will be granted to you. This backup will come at the exact moment you need it and relief will come to you promptly. Develop the confidence to ask for this kind of assistance and it will be granted to you.

to see a ring worn on the hand For the next five days you will be in a favorable position with someone very special. The more rings seen in this dream, the more favorably you will be treated by this person. This individual will display much affection, loyalty and a giving attitude toward you. You will both share many exciting moments together. You will experience a power you are just now beginning to become aware of in areas you had no idea of. Many blessings are with you.

to be given a ring You will experience a new tranquility in your life within three days. You will also meet a dynamic person with a lot of passion for life and will be invited by this person for an outing that, although short, will be very enjoyable and will create lasting memories.

to see a ring that you recognize Recall what was happening in your life in which you experienced negative events, take steps to keep these events from reoccurring. If this represents a pleasant time in your life, work to incorporate those things in your present life that will bring you joy and prosperity. You will also be making big changes to raise your standard of living by focusing on your goals in a grander scale than you ever have before. This will be as a result of an unusual, joyful, circumstance that will occur within two days. Everyone involved will enjoy beautiful expressions of joy and tranquility. Many blessings will be with you and your family.

broken ring The person you are interested in will lead you to believe they will contact you at a later time for a romantic interlude. Do not set yourself up for disappointment, this person will not contact you.

to lose a ring and be unable to find it Exercise extreme caution for the next three days. Someone will unexpectedly trap you in an unusual situation. You will then get caught up in some very strange occurrences. Be very aware of your surroundings and pay close attention to situations that will be coming up during this three day cycle so you can avoid this completely.

to have a ring taken from you Think ahead. Make sure you calmly handle all changes that will be arising within three days in a step by step fashion. These changes will not be serious but will be stressful. Exercise good eating habits, get plenty of rest and drink plenty of water. This cycle will end very shortly.

to recover a lost ring Whatever is needed for you to make big changes in your life will occur within three days. Focus on the changes you need to make and personally detail each step necessary to make these changes. You will take extraordinary measures to ensure they come about. Good luck is with you and many blessings are headed your way.

to give a ring as a gift Consider whether this is something you would like to do in reality. If this dream represents a negative event, take steps to avoid this in reality. If the dream represents a positive event, make sure you incorporate this in your life. Someone who is very interested in your success will go to great lengths to ensure you achieve your goals. Good luck is with you.

to dream of a ring in the exact duplicate of one you were given in the past Someone will enter your life possessing traits similar to the person who originally gave you the ring. Make sure you treat this person with greater kindness and understanding than you treated the original giver of the ring. This person will have either hang ups or delightful traits similar to that of the first giver. Look at the total picture and decide whether you want to pursue this relationship. If you do, take steps to avoid repeating old patterns of behavior. You will be deeply loved in spite of any hang ups.

ringer All business negotiations you undertake within the next three days will be extremely lucky for you. If you choose to go in this direction, these negotiations will quickly bear fruit.

ring finger You will soon find yourself in the position to have to ask for assistance. It will be difficult to ask for help because you know that it will involve a great deal of time from the person giving assistance. This cycle is perfect for getting the help you need without annoying someone else.

ringing *to hear continuous ringing* Be aware that someone is attempting to catch you off guard at an unexpected moment for the express purpose of gratifying their emotional needs. This could lead to a violent sexual assault. Play it safe and take steps to prevent others from taking advantage of you, especially for the next five days.

ringleader Do everything necessary to avoid arguments for the next three days, especially in front of a large group of people.

ringlet Do not become involved in a political discussion. This will only cause distress and trouble, especially for the next three days.

ringmaster For the next five days be very determined to reveal the interest you have for another person. Once you reveal your feelings, you will be able to specify the extent you are willing to commit to a relationship. You will also be able to openly discuss your future plans together. Proceed with confidence, you will be received with open arms.

ringworm Be very alert. Within seven days, your reputation will be at stake due to your involvement with a stranger who has a very evil background of which you are unaware. Be sure, during this time frame, not to involve yourself with any new acquaintance and guard yourself very carefully.

rink Do not put yourself in the position of buying something you will later not be able to afford.

rinse Only say what you do not mind having repeated and what you don't mind hearing again from others.

Rio de Janeiro An old lover will seek you out and, if you choose, a reconciliation will take place. This will result in dramatic transformations in your life as well as physical and emotional satisfaction. Tranquility will come to you as a result of this unity. This also implies that good luck is with you and many blessings will come to you and your family. This may also be used as a reference point in time. If you dream of this city and see its name used in any context, the dream message will occur on this day.

riot Within four days you will need to face up to your priorities. Take the time now to list your needs in order of importance.

riot gun Within four days doors that were formerly closed to you will be open. You will be able to grasp new opportunities that will make your life more prosperous.

rip Within three days someone will make some very strange demands of you. Be very firm about the amount of time you are willing to extend to others.

rip cord You will have a great deal of success resolving a trivial but lengthy legal matter.

rip current You will not enjoy yourself if you accept a last minute invitation regardless of how much you try. Avoid disappointment and a waste of time.

ripe Be very attentive to all incoming calls. Although you

will be experiencing a very busy cycle, there is one call you do not want to miss. This will be coming in within three days.

ripple Do not rely on a friend to come through for you. This friend will let you down.

rip tide Watch your pet closely for the next three days. Make sure it does not become ill due to improper supervision.

Rip Van Winkle Within two days expect grand changes to occur as a result of some extraordinary and unusual circumstances. Take small risks with games of chance for a large return in finances. Take the time to schedule some personal time for yourself to demonstrate your skills to others. This will open doors for greater benefits.

rise *to rise* Within three days you will receive an unbelievable offer that seems too good to refuse. This will be the opportunity you have been waiting for. Go for it. You will also experience victory with any goal you set out to accomplish within seven days.

to see anything rise You will be able to communicate your thoughts in such a way that will enable someone who feels passionately about you to get close in the manner you desire. This person, in return, will enjoy this closeness and will treat you with a high regard and respect.

risk *anything that seems risky* Within four days you will get the assistance you need for a particular situation. Because of this, you will experience immediate relief from your burdens.

rites Make sure you specify each situation very clearly and ensure that others understand exactly what you mean in order to avoid miscommunications and mistakes. Keep away from secretive situations and work to promote confidence in others.

ritual Pay attention to the events in this dream. Anything that suggests a negative event should be avoided in reality and anything positive needs to be promoted. This also implies that someone who is helping you in a work related situation will keep appearing and disappearing throughout the day. This person is not responsible for this because they are dealing with an addiction problem. They will, however, work hard to satisfy you. Good luck is with you and your family will receive many blessings.

rival Within three days a friend will come to you and tell you something that you will find unbelievable. This individual is telling you the truth.

river Do not put yourself in the position to be verbally abused. For the next three days do everything you can to avoid being insulted.

riverbank You are now in a good position to demand what

you want and need from your deity and your needs will be met. You will also reassess your priorities for the next few weeks. You will be able to develop a list of plans that will be superior to the way you live life now and you will undergo dramatic changes in your life. You must also make it a point to find a peaceful spot to do nothing but relax and enjoy tranquility.

riverbed Strongly voice your opinions about situations that will come up within three days. This is the proper way to handle this issue.

riverboat Expect unexpected people to drop in on you to request that you accompany them on an outing. You have prior notice of this so you can choose whether you want to go or not. If you choose to go, you will enjoy wonderful companionship and will be surrounded by very loyal people.

rivet Become very verbally aggressive for the next five days because someone will give out subtle messages indicating you have said something you did not say but is similar to what was said. Stay alert.

Riviera You will experience love and affection from someone you have long desired. This will come in such a way that it will take you completely by surprise. Explore ways to reach the deepest emotional fulfillment you can, especially for the next seven days. This may also be used as a reference point in time. If you dream of this city and see its name used in any context, the dream message will occur on this day.

roach Be very aggressive in pursuing what is righteously yours. Do not compromise and make sure you take the initiative to grasp what belongs to you. This is especially important for the next three days.

roach clip Make sure you are not taken by someone who is in power and authority. Do not compromise and grasp what is righteously yours.

road *clear open road* This is a good luck symbol and represents future tranquility that will last for a long time. This also implies that you have many admirers but the one you desire most will return your love. Expect this within seven days.

rough road Be very careful of jealous moments that will lead to arguments with someone special to you. For the next week do not fall into any situation that can lead to disagreements.

roadblock You will be insistent about eliminating any mental blocks that keep you from moving in the direction you choose. Make time for solitude so you can focus on the ideas that come clearly to you for the next seven days.

road hog Persist in pursuing what you want from a particular situation, especially for the next seven days. This will ensure that everything unfolds exactly as you wish.

roadhouse Make sure you are physically equipped to handle any excessive demands you place on yourself and are able to handle what comes your way within the week. Pay attention to the events that occurred in this dream and take steps to prevent all negative events from reoccurring.

roadie Someone will come to you because they have faith that you will be able to handle a particular situation that they will require you handle within three days. Back off because you will not be equipped to handle this issue.

road racing You will be very surprised because you will unexpectedly receive a very luxurious gift.

roadrunner Take steps to personally handle all your own errands and responsibilities. Do your own footwork.

roadster You will enjoy definite changes that will occur within the week involving you and another person as a result of the plans you both develop. These plans will enable you to live a far more sophisticated and luxurious lifestyle and you will be able to afford extensive travel. Many blessings are with you and your family and this will be a prosperous and lucky cycle for you.

road test Do not overtly display your affections toward someone else, especially for the next three days.

roadwork/road worker Do not make any major decisions for the next three days. Give yourself time to think about this very carefully.

roam Do everything necessary to promote closeness between yourself and those you will be dealing with on a long term basis. You will be glad you took these steps.

roan Make sure you are alert to someone else's behavior for the next three days. This will give you a clue to the direction you should take.

roar Make sure that, while shopping, you are not taken for your money. Don't forget to collect your change.

roast Within two days make sure you fully prepare yourself prior to inviting someone to visit you and spend time at your house. Make sure you have everything you need to make a guest feel comfortable.

roaster You must gain control over your temper. Someone will purposely do what they can to provoke you into a disagreement. Remove yourself from this situation immediately and do what you can to restrain your emotions.

robber Within three days, someone you desire greatly will communicate their desire for you and will comply with all of your wishes. This union will be very successful if you choose to take this route.

robe Make sure you drive a hard bargain, especially for the next three days. Stick to the amount you have already decided to spend and you will be successful. You will be well rewarded for work well done in the past and the pay off for this work will come now. For the next five days you will enjoy the mobility that this extra money will give you. You will also bond closer to someone you desire and this will lead to a permanent relationship. You are headed for a brilliant future.

robin Someone will be very happy to grant you a favor and is in the position to pull strings on your behalf. Do not allow your feelings of timidity to keep you from making a request. Once you are granted this favor, an event will occur that is destined to take place.

Robin Hood Within three days someone will involve you in some very adventuresome outings. This will be very unexpected and will leave you with a wonderful outlook on life. You must also make sure you do not compromise your belongings and do not allow yourself to be taken by a manipulative person.

Robinson Crusoe Within two days put yourself in the frame of mind to imagine what can be accomplished in areas you are interested in exploring. You will arrive at a plan that will be very advantageous to you.

robot Within three days you will become embroiled in a very embarrassing situation. Make sure you are very aware of your behavior during this time period in order to avoid this situation entirely. You will also make the final move on an important issue within five days.

robotic toys Become verbally assertive with someone within two days in order to prod this person to interact with you verbally and emotionally in the manner you expect and deserve. You will be successful in your request. There is a sense of urgency to this. Proceed with confidence.

rock Do not waste your energy on the issues of another person who wants to involve you in their concerns. Your efforts will be wasted and your energy will be better spent elsewhere. Get on with your life without this involvement. Also a situation that has been very difficult for you to become involved in is now open to you. You will be treated with much favor. Plans will also be discussed with another individual until you are mutually satisfied. These plans will lay down a solid foundation for the future. Look forward to the beginning of this process within seven days. You are headed for a brilliant future.

rock and roll Someone will come to your assistance just in the nick of time. Help is on the way.

rock candy Do not give up your private time and intimate moments with a special person, especially for the next three days.

Rock Cornish Get more rest and do what you can to pro-

vide a tranquil environment for yourself. Eat healthy foods and drink plenty of water. Many blessings are with you.

rock crystal Your intuition regarding matters of the heart is very clear now. You will be able to communicate in such a way that will bring people closer to you.

rocker You will be touched in a very sensual and romantic way and this will leave you feeling emotionally fulfilled. If you desire, you will have the opportunity to be with someone you are very attracted to within three days.

rocket Avoid any group activity that could result in injury and in you not being able to live your life fully. Within three days, something is likely to occur that will also immobilize you. Sexual favors will be requested of you and it will be up to you whether you choose to go this route.

rocket ship You will receive a gift of mental inventiveness within seven days. If you jot these thoughts down to develop at a later time, you will be amazed at the benefits you receive. You will enjoy a very stress free and tranquil cycle. Good luck is with you.

rock garden You will receive verification of love from someone within five days. You are loved beyond your imagination and are headed for a brilliant future. The person you recognize from this dream is the person who will be very eager to fulfill your wishes.

rocking *any rocking motion* Make sure you reveal your best behavior and character to others. This will ensure others will be comfortable and nourished in your presence and/or will include you in their future plans whether financial, romantically or in any other form. During this three day cycle others will feel a need and/or nourishment, attention and affection from you. You may also be dealing with a disabled person who will come to you to offer benefits in some capacity.

rocking chair Within three days you will become aware of someone's open affection toward you. In the past this person has displayed a cold manner toward you. You will also be welcomed with open arms in those arenas you desire.

rocking horse Expect to receive an abundance of everything you need as well as many moments of rejoicing. Within five days a particular issue will also start to evolve that will be completely out of your control. You will experience a wave of beautiful emotions as a result of this unexpected joyous occasion. Many blessings will come to you and your family and you are headed for a brilliant future. You must also take steps to avoid any negative event portrayed in this dream. Within seven days you will enjoy an unexpected reconciliation with someone you thought was lost to you.

rock lobster Control your sexual urges toward someone you will be around for the next three days.

rocks *rocky seaweed covered coastline* Take the aggressive stance in bringing the individual you desire in your life closer to you. This cycle will allow you to behave in such a way that will result in this individual feeling comfortable enough in your presence to say those words you have long wanted to hear. Many blessings will come to you and your family. You are headed for a very prosperous future.

rock salt You will enjoy a long and happy life.

Rocky Mountains You will come into instant wealth within the week. This may also be used as a reference point in time. If you dream of this mountain range and see its name used in any context, the dream message will occur on this day.

rocky mountain sheep Your assertive behavior will put an end to a potential problem that will occur within seven days.

rocky mountain spotted fever Do not allow yourself to be put on an emotional roller coaster. As soon as you see this situation start to develop, get busy with something else for the sake of your health. You must also make sure you do not put yourself in the position to contract this illness.

rod Be prepared. Within five days a number of situations will enter your life. You will have the opportunity to choose from many options and any involvement you choose will offer you a tremendous opportunity for a more prosperous way of life. You are headed for a brilliant future. Within this cycle you will also receive a positive response to a request that you expected a negative answer to. Good luck is with you.

gold rod You will have the chance to grasp a golden opportunity to bring someone closer to you in an unusual involvement. This cycle will offer you the best chance for this to occur. Take full advantage of this time period to bring a special person close to you in the manner you desire. You will be able to discuss plans that both of you can quickly put into action.

rodent Someone who is interested in you will attempt to disassociate themselves from another person because they have lost interest in them. This individual will develop an elaborate plot to keep you in their life in ways you have no desire for. They will not be truthful to you until they are able to get the other person out of their life or to find a way to be with both of you without your knowledge. Take steps to avoid involvement.

anything unusual that you see yourself or anyone doing with a rodent Someone will take advantage of you and use you without your knowledge. This person will use deception and dishonesty and use you in this situation as an innocent unwilling participant. In the long run you will be cheated. Pay close attention to your present situation and be acutely aware of the actions of others.

roe You will have to deal with someone who will be emotionally uncontrollable because of shocking news they have heard. You will be able to give this person the support system they need for a short amount of time.

roe deer Do what you can to seek help for someone in need once you are aware of their problem. You will find the means to have this person's needs met.

rogue Do not underestimate your abilities and do not allow yourself to become your own worst enemy. Stop shortchanging yourself. You will be able to accomplish anything you wish that will enhance your life. You are entering an exciting, fulfilling cycle.

role model Keep a close eye on your time for the next five days. You must also be very aware of the behavior of others for the next week and handle yourself appropriately.

roll Situations that were going badly will turn around and yield a positive result. You must also pull yourself together and remain calm for the next three days. An issue will come up during this time period that will tempt you to become involved. Make sure the problems of other people do not cause you to become so desperate that you involve yourself with their issues. Make sure you do not compromise yourself. Once you do, it will be difficult to pry yourself loose and this issue will become worse as time passes. You are only seeing the tip of the iceberg. Remain uninvolved.

to roll over in a car Situations that were going badly will turn around and yield a more positive result.

roll bar When in the presence of small children, make sure that you watch your language and do not allow angry, aggressive, bullying tactics or foul language to take place. This child will be unable to understand this behavior and will become frightened. Expect this within two days.

roll call This is an extremely lucky omen. Expect an amazing and wonderful situation to occur within five days.

roller Place importance on your personal appearance and budget your time so others do not waste it.

roller coaster Do not become involved in a particular group that is determined to fight a certain cause. You will be given the wrong information and will regret joining at a later time.

to ride Make sure you do not allow someone to take you on an emotional roller coaster ride, especially for the next three days. Get control of your life to avoid becoming sucked into this type of abuse. If this dream portends a negative event, take extra steps to prevent its occurrence in reality or make sure you prevent it altogether.

roller derby Make sure someone you are with does not verbally abuse you in public. You have prior notice of this and can avoid any situation where this could happen.

rollers *(hair)* Make sure you are not caught off guard by someone who will unexpectedly drop in within the next two days. Place more importance on your personal appearance so you will be presented in your best light if someone does drop in without warning.

roller skates You will have a terrific opportunity to enjoy life to the fullest for the next three days. You will enjoy much harmony and tranquility. Blessings are with you and your family.

to roller skate Within three days the choice you make to include someone in your life will be the correct choice. You will receive many benefits in any area of your life you choose.

to see others roller skate You will receive an unexpected call or message from someone you should not allow in your life, especially within the next three days. This person will create chaos in your life. Do everything you can to avoid this individual.

if you recognize the person roller skating Someone you know has a problem dealing with you for whatever personal reasons they have. For some reason this person does not want to work with you on certain issues. Do not force this issue, you will be treated better by someone else.

rolling pin Someone has intentionally planned to bring emotional or bodily harm to you. Be cautious and acutely aware of your involvements with others, especially for the next three days. Take control over what you will and will not allow to happen in your life.

rolltop desk Do everything necessary to gain the upper hand in a particular situation that will be introduced to you by another person. Do not compromise yourself.

Roman You are well on your way toward developing plans that will give you the independence you need. This cycle promotes confidence, physical healing and improvements in all financial matters. You are on the path toward a bright future. This is a prosperous cycle and you will be able to make changes in those areas of your life that need to be improved. Many blessings will come to you and your family. All requests made to your special deity will be granted. Pay attention to the events occurring in this dream. If they were positive, expect a positive manifestation in reality. If they were negative, do everything necessary to alter the outcome. Someone will also go to great lengths to assist you in everyday matters to make sure you grasp your goals.

Roman candle Take steps to leave yourself open so others can approach you regarding certain situations that will be very advantageous to you. You are headed for a brilliant future.

Roman Catholic Expect a long standing burden to be lifted from your shoulders. All difficulties will quickly end.

romance Do everything within your power to bring more love and romance into your life. Look for a special someone who can bring you emotional fulfillment. Make your moves now and you will experience this within the week. This is the perfect cycle for this if you choose to go in this direction. Make yourself more accessible to those who are eager to be

in your company. Many blessings are with you and your family.

if you recognize the person involved This individual is very eager to offer their support in areas you most desire.

Roman holiday Remain focused for the next three days in order to keep emotional situations from escalating to the point where it will be very difficult to return to normality.

Roman numeral Within five days take steps to list your priorities in their order of importance in order to experience greater benefits and opportunities that will present themselves to you during this time frame.

Romans *(Book of the Bible)* It will be asked of you to render financial assistance to a relative in need. This cycle will give you the means and the opportunity to help out several relatives in financial distress. You are loved deeply, respected and appreciated by many people, even those who are unable to verbalize these feelings. You will know this by their behavior and by their mannerisms.

Romano cheese Move ahead with confidence on those plans that need to be implemented.

Romeo A professional staff that you seek out for help will stick with you until a problem is resolved. Someone is eager to see you but is hesitant about revealing their true emotions. This individual will ask to see you within the week but in reality you both know that you will meet within two days. Do not allow yourself to be caught off guard. This person's enthusiasm will lead them to call you and ask to drop in at a moment's notice. Be sure your physical appearance is up to par. This will be a very lucky cycle for you.

Romulus Remain focused for the next seven days in order to pinpoint those issues you want to rid yourself of, then work to make the proper moves to accomplish them. These moves will raise your standard of living and will give you the lifestyle you desire. You are headed for a prosperous future. This is a cycle that will require you demonstrate eagerness to work on those issues you want to change.

roof *leaking* Do what you can now to generate extra income as a preventive measure. You will need this extra money within three weeks. Motivate yourself in some way to accomplish this. This is the perfect time for this.

to unsuccessfully stop a leak Riches and power will come to you within seven days as a result of what you are now actively pursuing. Many blessings will come to you and your family.

in good repair You need to involve yourself more with an important relationship to ensure that it doesn't develop problems. By making this special effort, you will be able to add a special loving element to those relationships you care about. Do this within seven days.

in any other form Be aware of a financial drain that should be causing you concern now. Begin looking for ways to generate extra income because you will need this money within two weeks. Money that you expect during this time period will not arrive in a timely fashion.

rooftop Do not give others the impression you are limiting your feelings, especially for the next two days. Accurately reveal your feelings to those you care about.

rook Make sure someone you meet within three days does not become too quickly involved in your life. This person will initially appear very generous and kind but will rapidly want to become involved in every aspect of your life to the point of emotional suffocation. You will find it distasteful and will have difficulty getting rid of this individual. If this is something you do not want in your life, do what you can to prevent this intrusion on your privacy at the beginning.

rookie Make sure you protect your own values and that others respect you, especially for the next seven days.

room Make certain that prior to committing your time to being in the presence of someone else, you carefully think this through. At first you will feel excited about being in their company but as time goes by you will feel uncomfortable and want to leave. Set aside only a small amount of time to ensure you will enjoy yourself before committing a large block of your time.

club room You will go from rags to riches within a few years and this will be as a result of much help from others.

state room Within a few days, you will become a bore to another person by continually discussing a topic this person has no interest in. This person will listen quietly to avoid hurting your feelings. Listen to yourself and try to prevent this behavior.

stockroom You are entrusting the wrong person to make decisions for you. Be very watchful of this for the next three days. Otherwise, it is a very lucky omen.

waiting room Take steps to prevent any negative event in this dream from becoming a reality. You have prior notice of this so you can experience only positive expressions in your life. This also implies the opportunities offered to you that you expect to not work out, will fall into place exactly as you desire.

to make room You will have someone in your life within the week who will be very attentive to your every need. This also implies you will receive a financial windfall.

room and board Within three days an unusual situation will occur. The behavior or appearance of a certain person will not be in sync with the impression you have of this individual. Once you are in this person's presence you will find them far more charming and delightful than you ever anticipated. Seek more time with them. Good luck is with you.

rooming house Within the week, someone will extend themselves to you in a very special way. This person will surprise you with a party or a special gift in appreciation.

roommate Pay attention to the behavior of the roommate, this will be an accurate description of what will occur in real-

ity within seven days. You have enough time to make any necessary changes to alter or avoid a negative event. If this is a positive event, do what you can to promote it in reality. You will also have every opportunity during this time period to ensure you experience your deepest desires. If you choose to pursue a love relationship, this is the perfect cycle to do so. You will have the opportunity to choose from several people who will make their desires known to you. This opportunity will also bring you prosperity and many benefits. Blessings are with you and your family.

room service Within five days a mysterious situation will develop. As time goes by, this situation will become even more intriguing. Do not try to become involved or attempt to get to the bottom of it. Back off and the mystery will become known to you. This will spare you the trouble of your involvement. Anything connected with business, love or finances will also be extremely fortuitous for you for the next three days.

rooster This is a very lucky symbol. If the rooster is crowing you will be victorious in those areas of your life you feel you will not succeed in. Within five days you will develop the confidence to handle those things. Within seven days you will gain power over those areas you felt you have no power or say so in .

root You will get to the bottom of a certain situation within three days and will be able to determine what the truth is. This will keep you from drawing the wrong conclusions and being misled. Give yourself several alternative ways to handle a plan you will be involving yourself in within the week. This way you will have many paths to choose from and will have the opportunity to bring prosperity into your life from many different channels. Many blessings are with you and your family. You are headed for a prosperous future.

dried up and wilted Quickly motivate yourself to ensure that your finances do not become depleted. You cannot depend on tightening your budget by using your present method of securing money. Find ways to increase you finances. Prepare yourself for what may be coming up within three weeks. This is the cycle for doing what is necessary to make ends meet.

root beer Within three days you will receive terrific news that you have long waited to hear. This unexpected news will leave you ecstatic. For a long time you have been wanting someone to commit to you in some capacity and within three days this individual will come around. Many blessings are with you and you family.

root canal You will receive accurate advice from someone who will steer you in the direction you should be going. Professional help that you seek, in any capacity, will work out very well for you, especially for the next seven days. Any negative event seen in this dream can be avoided or altered in reality. Make sure you allow any positive event to reach full bloom in reality. Also, within the week you will have to present your feelings accurately to someone else in order to keep them from doing something they would otherwise do without your input. This will keep this individual from doing something that would be harmful to the relationship. Good luck is with you.

root cellar Prepare yourself for a change that will be occurring in your life. This will involve an unexpected transfer that requires a relocation. Handle this calmly and you will find this to be a very positive and prosperous change for you.

rope Within seven days you will develop an instant interest in someone during a casual conversation and you will both expose certain feelings and facts about yourself during the course of this conversation. This will spark a meeting of the minds and will expose you to a path of life you would never have known had you not had this meeting. You are headed for a brilliant future. Anything negative foretold in this dream needs to be altered or avoided in reality and you need to make sure you encourage only positive events in your life.

to tie together It is important that you focus on what needs to be immediately attended to. This will enable you to reach a very important decision about an important issue. For the next five days a variety of equally important and troublesome situations will also come up. Work at your highest level on each of these situations to ensure they are resolved successfully. Remain flexible, calm and relaxed throughout this ordeal. Your life will once more reach a balanced state.

to see anything being tied up Within three days someone will present themselves as having a much higher level of authority than they actually have. Because you are aware of this, make sure you do not demand from this person more than they can deliver in order to avoid disappointments, misunderstandings and many distasteful moments. You have prior notice of this and can behave appropriately.

to walk or dance on a rope Do not allow any of your emotions to take control. Meet each issue head on and do what you can to resolve them. Make it a point to keep any negative issue you dreamed about from becoming a reality.

rope used in a violent manner You are letting your loved ones outgrow you because you continue to hang on to old patterns of behavior. Focus on changing your behavior, especially for the next two months.

to be knocked or see someone else knocked against the ropes in a boxing ring Do not allow yourself to be intimidated into giving up something you cherish. Regard your time and energy as the precious commodity it is. You are easily taken advantage of due to your kindness and willingness to give up your time, labor and energy for others. Look carefully at situations that are taking too much from you because you will become overwhelmed without your awareness. Any negative situation seen in this dream must be avoided in reality and make sure you alert others to do the same.

Roquefort Cheese Within three days you will be in the possession of some hard to get information. You will be very surprised that you were able to get this information and it will give you a better way of handling present situations.

rosary Make sure you do everything in your power to protect yourself from any unusual situation that may occur within the week. You will also have the courage and confidence to deal correctly with a situation that will occur during this time period. Do not expose yourself to any serious, contagious illness. Seek tranquility, harmony and joyous events for the next week. This dream is a promise of great abundance in those areas of your life you most desire.

rose Someone will verify the love and passionate feelings they have for you. This will catch you off guard and will come from someone you deeply desire. From here on out both of you will take all of the right steps to ensure a lengthy and fulfilled relationship. These new and wonderful changes will fill you with joy for a lifetime.

rosebud You will enjoy a very prosperous future. Certain situations will occur that dramatically improve your love life and it will reach a higher level than you ever envisioned. This relationship, if you choose to take this path, is headed for a wonderful and prosperous future.

rosebush You will be able to communicate in a profound and direct way to another person in order to get your feelings across. You will be received with open arms and are definitely headed for a brilliant future. You will also receive verification of the love and passion that someone you desire feels for you. You will both work very hard to develop a full and prosperous relationship. Good luck is with you.

rosemary Within seven days you will acquire a long desired possession and will rejoice over your ability to achieve this.

rose thorn You are entering a very lucky cycle that will last for the next four days. Your thoughts and intuitive senses are very clear and you will be able to use this gift to your advantage in order to resolve a very difficult situation. You will also be able to say something to someone in such a way that will get your point cross with very little chaos. Many blessings are with you.

Rosetta stone Within two days you will receive the gift of greater mental inventiveness and clarity by the deities. Put this gift to good use and you will see an immediate improvement in your life. Your sexual drive will improve and you will prosper in each area of your life for the next month.

rosewater The relationships that are important to you will grow only as much as you nurture them. Do everything necessary to bring closeness into a relationship that you desire to promote. You must also carefully watch out for young children who may be in need of more supervision. Many blessings are with you and your family.

Rosh Hashanah Within seven days you will be very excited about an opportunity that will present itself to you. You will also have the ability and means to grasp and retain this extraordinary opportunity. This will give you a new start in those areas of your life that you most desire. A difficult situation will also be resolved during this time period if you make the effort to expedite it. You will be entering a future that will offer you a tremendous amount of prosperity.

rosin You will experience anxiety over the next few days because of various decisions that will be taking place. Put these feelings aside. All changes that occur will bring tranquility and prosperity into your life.

roster Over the next ten days make yourself available when an unusual invitation unexpectedly comes your way. Take advantage of this invitation and you will bring into your life a wonderful situation that is difficult for you to even imagine. Go for it.

rot An event will take place within the week that is imperative for you to attend. You will enjoy the company of two admirers and find pleasure in watching both of them subtly attempt to win your affections. Although it doesn't show, one of them possesses a great deal of authority and power. You will find that both of these people are very charming and agreeable and you would enjoy having one of them as a lifetime partner. You are on the path toward a brilliant future.

rotor Someone with a mysterious lifestyle will attract your interest. As a result, you will be exposed to other cultures by someone from another country. This will brighten your life and you will enjoy many pleasurable moments. You will also be extended a permanent invitation to this person's country of origin.

rottweiler Over the next three days someone you will be in contact with will be sending you mixed messages due to a confusion in words and behavior. Do not involve yourself with trying to sort all of this out. Go on with your life without attempting to interpret this person's behavior.

rough Do not allow your imagination to run wild and do not develop unwarranted suspicions about a special person. Back off, regroup and gain firm control of your mental processes. Nothing is going on. You are headed for a brilliant future and you and your family will receive many blessings.

roughage Treat yourself in a way you have never before so you can express yourself with wonderful joyous events and be able to experiment with different lifestyles. Remove yourself from stress and eat healthful, healing foods, drink plenty of water and do things that make you feel very relaxed and soothed.

roughhouse For the next three days do what you can to prevent festering painful memories from surfacing. The moment you see this begin to develop, replace this preoccupation with an activity that makes you feel very good about yourself. Experience joyful events in your life instead of immersing yourself in pain.

roulette Within three days you will have the chance to involve yourself in a very loving wonderful relationship. If you choose to go this route, you will enjoy events that make you feel terrific about being alive. Any negative event portended in this dream can be altered or avoided. If positive, take steps to make this a reality.

round Within five days you will be able to promote yourself and rally others around you who will support you financially for a special idea you are developing. This will be a very promising development and the alternatives that also come up will bring you many benefits. Move quickly on this.

roundhouse Do everything you can to avoid overextending yourself because you are trying to keep up with someone else's demands and wishes, especially for the next five days. Many blessings are with you and your family.

round steak An unusual situation will occur that will lead to mental clarity on your part. This will enable you to make a wise business investment that will rapidly lead to wealth. You are headed for a prosperous future.

round table You will have many more guests attending a function than you had originally planned. Be prepared for this and make sure you stock extra food and refreshments for this eventuality.

roust The person you care deeply about will make it easier for you to become involved in their life. You will experience a great deal of joy and laughter as a result. This also implies that within three days you will find yourself helping someone you know in distress. This will all work out well for you. Good luck is with you.

route Do what you can to develop a clever idea or solution that will allow you to work independently on a particular issue that will come up within three days. You will then be able to work without outside interference. Your thoughts will come to you with great clarity and you will soon resolve this issue.

rover You are unaware that someone has attempted to get in touch with you several times in order to have a conversation, because their message has not been given to you. Pay close attention to who may be trying to get an important message across to you.

row *to row* Friendships will only grow as much as you allow them to. Do everything you can to keep a relationship alive and flourishing.

rowboat In a few days you will be working in close quarters with a very attractive person. Make sure nothing happens. This would not be a wise involvement. Keep everything strictly business.

row house Keep your ambitions to yourself and allow time to develop your plans before you tell anyone else.

royal Your intuition is right on target and you will enjoy a very lucky seven day cycle. An older, wiser person will help you reach a solution to a problem very quickly. Within three days this person will offer you the advice needed to quickly resolve a problematic situation.

royal blue If you choose, you can spend a lifetime with a special person and many special moments together. This also implies that an unusual set of events will occur within four days that will help to bring this union about. Good luck is with you.

royal flush Someone who wants to be involved in your life has a very jealous manner. This person will later become very possessive of your time and suspicious of who you spend your time with. If you choose to have this person in your life, do everything you can to correct this flaw now.

royal jelly Do not ignore a situation you are treating very lightly. This is a very serious situation and you should focus on resolving it as soon as possible. It is especially important to do this within two days.

royal purple For the next three days you will be surrounded by love and accepted with open arms. Follow your intuition. Luck and many blessings are with you, and you will achieve victory in all of your goals. Go after what you want.

royalty You will be offered a salary for a short term project that will supply most of your spending needs as well as the means to acquire a few luxury items.

rub For the next two days rely solely on your own decisions when solving a problem. Do not give up until this problem is resolved. You will be successful when relying on your own counsel. This also implies you need to get more rest, take better care of yourself, eat properly, drink plenty of water and pamper yourself.

rubber The entire family will rejoice over an unexpected upcoming event. Be more flexible when dealing with everyday situations. Simplify your life.

rubber band Watch out for a secretary who takes joy in not delivering your messages to the person you want to speak to. Within three days make sure you are able to speak to the person you want to about an important matter.

rubber cement Take the lead when dealing with new challenges. Other people expect this from you and you will be very victorious when handling new situations.

rubber check Be very careful not to say something at the wrong time. You may blurt out something you have no business saying out loud.

rubber gloves You will have a desire to expose yourself to new experiences and new horizons. You will no longer be able to take anything for granted that you may have in the past. You will be emotionally gratified when a golden opportunity presents itself to you within five days. You will grasp victory because you recognize this opportunity for what it is. You will then be able to pursue your destined future.

rubberneck Make sure the limbs of small children are protected and out of danger. For the next five days alert others to be very protective of small children.

rubber plant Meditate in your favorite form and encourage personal growth. You will enjoy much tranquility in your life. Do whatever you can to include romance in your life and to live life to the very fullest. You will enjoy many blessings and good luck will be with you.

rubber stamp Someone you have known for a while and have a great deal of respect for will leave and you will never hear from them again. Take steps to ensure you find a way to keep in touch with this person if you desire to maintain the friendship. This is an extremely lucky omen and many blessings are with you.

rubbing alcohol A wonderful person will enter your life for a while and this will be a great time for you. Enjoy it while it lasts because this person will soon move away.

rubbish Do not accept the responsibility of someone else's valuable possessions, especially for the next two days.

rubble Do not overextend yourself when helping a close friend. Do not become resentful, just avoid putting yourself in this position.

rubella Within three days you will be praised for work done by someone else. Make sure you quickly give credit to the proper person, otherwise following events will cause you a great deal of embarrassment.

Rubens, Paul Make sure you inform those who will be working with you that you demand a high level of efficiency. This will allow you to get the task done quickly and with less effort.

ruby You are entering a very lucky romantic cycle. You will experience hot, dynamic passion with another person within five days and they will verbalize exactly what they want and need from a relationship. If you choose, you will enjoy a healthy, passionate relationship that will be permanent. You will also receive the support you need within a short period of time. You will experience new health and vigor. Your intuition is right on target and you will enjoy victory in any area you desire within the week.

rudder Stand firm and do not allow anyone to belittle or manipulate you in any way. Do not compromise your feelings or allow this to continue out of fear of losing a friend. You would be better off going through life without this person in it.

rude Within seven days you will be able to persuade someone to accept your wishes and opinions. This is a lucky omen and good luck is with you.

ruffle You will meet someone special almost overnight and this will lead to marriage much quicker than you ever expected. This will be a very healthy, financially secure union and you will be good friends for as long as you desire.

rug *to clean, shampoo* Treat an important issue you are now working on in the same manner in which you would treat a pleasurable event. Move quickly for the next three days in any area that enables you to promote growth. You will be pleased with the results.

in any other form This is a very lucky omen and implies that a very unusual situation will take place resulting in a financial windfall. Within two days your inner drive and courage will also give you the motivation to break through any physical or mental barrier that interferes with you moving ahead in life. Once you rid yourself of those aspects you will be able to bring any new project into tangible form. You will be welcomed with open arms by everyone you care about. You are on the path toward a brilliant future and many new opportunities are headed your way.

rugby Do everything you can to understand the motives of someone who is special to you. Listen carefully so you can determine the best way to promote tranquility. Show compassion and appreciation. This person will remain loyal to you.

rugby shirt Do not speak negatively of anyone for the next two days, especially if you will be overheard. Your words will be repeated to this person and will cause major problems.

ruins Within two months there will be a major scandal in the executive high offices. This will be very shocking to you but will be very beneficial. This scandal will give you the opportunity to position yourself beneficially for life. This is a once in a lifetime chance that you never dreamed was possible. Good luck is with you and you are entering a very dynamic, victorious cycle. Pay close attention to the location of the ruins. If you recognize the area, be sure to stay away from this location for the next three days. You must also quickly process important ideas that you have been considering during this time period. You will be able to accomplish any goal you are after.

to see someone in ruins This is a warning to someone you know that they should be very careful not to have an accident that will tragically affect their life. Warn this person so they can be more aware of their surroundings.

rule Be very careful when engaging in pleasure seeking behaviors. This could lead to serious consequences in your life. Guard your life and precious possessions for the next three days.

to rule Be sure to watch your attitude so you won't have to apologize for hurt feelings, especially for the next two days.

ruler Avoid water accidents in any capacity for the next three days.

rum Within seven days you will receive an unusual and unexpected gift. You are entering a very lucky cycle and others will be very eager to surround you with love and affection.

rummage sale Do not ignore an older person who has played a significant part in your life. Take time out to show the love and affection you still feel for this person.

rummy The person you have been wishing would be more communicative with you will finally open up. Reward this person by being very kind, friendly and flexible. You are entering a cycle that promotes communication and health.

rump You will rejoice over unexpected good news that you receive regarding love.

Rumplestiltskin Make sure all children and young adults are being cared for properly and that all their needs are being met. You must also make sure everyone knows where their children are for the next three days in order to prevent one from becoming lost from you. You are entering a blessed cycle for you and your children.

run *to run* You will be immersed in the feelings of love that someone has for you. You are headed for a brilliant future.

to run and be caught by someone or something You must be very careful not to contract a virus or a sexually transmitted disease.

to run away Be sure to tell special people in your life how much you love them. Other people need to hear this, especially for the next three days.

if you recognize the person running away All negative events depicted in this dream need to be avoided and you will need to encourage the person you dreamed about to promote each positive event.

to run into someone or have someone run into you by accident or to see someone run into someone else by accident Pay very close attention to your behavior. Within five days you will do something with another person that will affect this individual deeply. This person will develop a mental distortion of something you do innocently, and they will over-react to the extreme. Their mind will lead them to believe they must do something to lessen their anguish. Be very aware that a very minor situation will cause extreme emotional harm because this person will build up this episode and inflict great damage on you. This will leave you feeling very bewildered and depleted. Your spirit is alerting you to this situation through this dream so you can avoid deep pain and can stay away from unhealthy relationships completely. Otherwise, you will always be walking on eggs around this individual because they will only bring negativity and chaos to your life. Take steps to prevent any negative event in this dream from taking place in reality and make sure you experience only positive expressions in your life. You are definitely headed for a brilliant future. Pay attention to the face of the person who ran into you. This is the person most likely to inflict this pain. You can avoid this by having prior notice of this situation.

to run into someone you have not seen in a long time Think back to the time in your life when you were familiar with this person. Any good and positive behavior you were practicing at the time should be repeated and all negative aspects of your life need to be avoided during this cycle. This also implies that this person is someone you will want to see, will run into accidentally within five days, or you will run into friends of this person who will talk about this person to you. You will be made aware that this person wants to contact you. There may be a reason you and this person need to connect at this point in your life. Alert this individual to any negative event viewed in this dream so they can take steps to prevent it in reality. You will also run into many other people, whom you have not seen in some time. You will have an enjoyable time during this cycle because you will receive many invitations to a number of events from people you have not seen in a while. You will experience a tremendous amount of joy and will broaden your horizons. This will lead to extra advantages and opportunities. Take steps to prevent any negative event in this dream from occurring in reality and make sure you only experience positive expressions in your life. You are definitely headed for a brilliant future.

to see something run into someone or something else by accident Focus on what is going on in your life. Several things will need your immediate attention within five days. One particularly troublesome issue could very well arise that will need extra attention. You will need to pounce on these issues before they become a big problem. Work diligently on each of them so they will be taken care of in time to prevent them from escalating. Your intuition and receptivity will heighten. Remain calm and flexible and before you know it your life will be back in balance. You will experience times of peace and prosperity. Any negative event viewed in this dream can be prevented in reality. Make sure you experience only positive events in your life. Alert anyone you recognize to do likewise.

to run from someone attempting to run you over with anything and escape A certain individual will go to great lengths to create a relationship between you and another person. It is your destiny to enjoy a beautiful, full blown love relationship that will blossom within a few days and bring joy into your life. This is the perfect cycle to emotionally connect with another person. You will be so successful that this individual will respond to you in the exact manner you desire. This also implies you are headed in the right direction in life and you will be able to express yourself fully regarding all matters of personal interest. You will be able to focus yourself in a very detailed manner. As a result you will be able to achieve a great deal and enjoy many successes in life. You will magically possess the strength and courage you need to handle each issue in your life and be able to enjoy peace and tranquility. An unexpected favor will also be

granted but you will need to put yourself in the position to talk with powerful and influential people. State your needs clearly and directly and you will immediately be given the money you request from a particular individual. You will achieve victory in those areas of your life that you consider to be the most important now and you will also hear some good news within the week. You are on the path toward a brilliant future. Pay very close attention to all conversations for the next three days and make sure all negative events and messages foretold in this dream do not become a reality. Take steps to ensure that all positive messages are fulfilled.

to be told by someone to run Be sure that within three days you put aside some time to clear your head and do some mental brainstorming so you can pinpoint the suspicions you have about another person. This will give you the chance to devise a plan to determine whether these suspicions are valid and if so, how to go about resolving them. You will enjoy success with this issue if you motivate yourself now. This is the perfect cycle to find the answers you are looking for. You are on the path toward a prosperous future.

to tell someone else to run This is warning you that a devious individual will come and present a very trustful facade. They will give you the impression everything you say will be kept between you. In reality, this person will be pumping you for information about a third party and will then take your words back to them. Be aware of this so you can avoid this scenario entirely because once it takes place you will be confronted with what you have said. This could escalate to a violent situation. You have prior notice of this and can take steps to ensure this does not take place.

to see someone run and get caught Within three days you will be asked out by someone who is a fairly new acquaintance. This person will behave in a strange manner and terrify you because they will become very dangerous and you will have no means of escape. Do whatever you can to avoid this situation. Do not go to any unfamiliar place or to anyone's home you do not know well because you will be held against your will in a life threatening situation. This is preventable.

to run after something or someone you are unable to catch An unexpected cluster of events will occur one right after the other and you will receive a number of invitations that you will be able to pick and choose from. It would be wise to make sure you attend one specific event. This one will be more glamorous and exciting than the others and will require you dress in formal attire. Make sure you prepare yourself for this event so you can look your best. You will have a very enjoyable time and meet a number of powerful and influential people who will become friends for a lifetime. You will win a door prize at this function. During this cycle you will also be made aware that the person you desire feels the same as you. You will share many affectionate moments and will both be very excited about this new development. You are headed for a prosperous and brilliant future.

to run from someone or something and not get caught You are definitely making all of the correct moves and motivating yourself to achieve victory. Also, a connection you have wanted to make with a certain type and kind of person but have been unable to make in the past will be successfully made within the week. Any get away place you have in mind will give you the mini vacation you need and will leave you with many pleasurable memories. Anything you felt was impossible in the past is now possible. You are definitely headed for a brilliant future.

to see someone you do not recognize run away from you You are entering a terrific cycle for the next seven days. Take each plan, goal, idea, project, etc., that needs to be opened up, elaborated on and viewed on a grander scale. This is the perfect time for this. Proceed with confidence.

to run after someone or something and catch up For the next four days make your best effort to demonstrate the behavior needed to bring someone you desire close to you. At first, this person will not seem interested but you will find that your first impression was false. During this period, you will experience an abundance of health and a financial windfall. You are headed for a prosperous future.

to run out of anything Make sure you do not develop a defeatist attitude when working on a specific situation. Proceed with confidence and you will definitely get over this feeling and emerge victorious. All negative messages and events occurring in this dream need to be altered and all positive messages should be promoted. This is a very lucky dream.

to see something run over Within the week you will be asked out by someone you know only slightly. This person will terrify you because of their strange behavior and will, at some point, become very dangerous. You will not be able to find a means of escape. Do whatever you can to avoid this situation. You must also avoid all unfamiliar places and make sure you do not go to someone's home you do not know well. You will be held against your will in a life threatening situation.

in any other form A number of events are scheduled to take place within seven days that would be to your advantage to attend. You will enjoy the company of two admirers who will subtly attempt to win you over. This may occur at the same or different functions. Although it doesn't show, one of these people possesses a great deal of authority and power and you will find both of them to be very agreeable and charming. You would enjoy having one of these admirers for a life long partner. You can be confident you are on the path toward a prosperous future.

runaway Within three days you will be overcome with the feeling that something suspicious is going on. Do not allow anyone to convince you that you are being paranoid or attempt to water these suspicions down. This implies that your spirit is sending you a sense of heightened awareness about something you need to be more attentive to. You will then be able to handle everything in an appropriate manner and not feel you could have done something different. You have prior notice of this and can take the appropriate steps to deal with this issue now.

rune You will soon hear of someone's pregnancy.

rung You will unexpectedly experience an increase in income within the month.

runner Become very assertive with your desires and wishes. Do this tactfully and gently and everything will work out beautifully for you, especially for the next three days.

runt This is the perfect time to promote your talents. Challenge yourself to do so. This will impress others within a few weeks. Good luck is with you.

rural Avoid strangers for the next two days. It will prove to be dangerous to mingle with people you do not know during this time period.

rush *to dream of you or someone else rushing* This is a lucky omen and a promise of health and wealth. You will achieve victory in those areas of your life you most desire. You are entering a very lucky seven day cycle.

rush hour Within three days you will be involved in a car accident while attending an outing. Take steps to avoid this.

Russia Make sure you handle all necessary paperwork promptly and direct the paperwork to the proper people. A long awaited promise will also be granted within the week. This may also be used as a reference point in time. If you dream of this country and see its name used in any context, the dream message will occur on this day.

Russian blue Within three days you will overwhelm someone with an unusual gift they do not expect. You will feel joy that you were able to grant someone's desire. You will also have a strong desire to relocate. This cycle is perfect to find an alternative place to live. Good luck is with you and many blessings will come to you and your family.

Russian dressing You have greatly underestimated a situation that you will become involved in within five days. Move quickly and do not let it slip away. This will be your golden opportunity.

Russian leather Within five days you will be exposed to an exquisite lifestyle and will experience a high level of culture. You will be exposed to new events and festivities that you never thought you would experience. These events will bring you a lot of joy. Good luck is with you.

Russian Orthodox Church You will enjoy yourself for many days with friends. You will be dancing, dining and enjoying many festivities. This is a good cycle for you. You and your family will receive many blessings and you are entering a seven day cycle of health and wealth.

Russian Roulette Someone you did a favor for in the past will return with a wonderful surprise for you. This person will invite you to share in their wealth. You will also be very lucky with games of chance by taking small risks that will yield large dividends within seven days. You must also take steps to ensure that any negative event in this dream does not become a reality.

rust Be aware of the lack of sensitivity and appreciation someone feels for you. This will come up within three days. Do not allow this to hurt you in any way. Anything you see with rust in the dream needs to be protected from the elements in reality.

the color Get back to the basics and simplify your life. Be compassionate with yourself and stand by your convictions. For the next seven days you will experience many moments of tranquility because of the love shown to you by another person.

rustproof Be aware that someone will ask you for your honest opinion and will then resent your honesty. Avoid being put into this position for the next seven days.

rutabaga Before you offer advice to someone else about their future, take the time to look at what is wrong with this picture. Take things a step at a time, and write down each detail to make sure this advice will be accurate.

Ruth *(from the Bible)* Carefully screen your list of priorities and determine the ones that need to be handled immediately. This will lead to a very prosperous life. Show your family, by your actions, that you love them.

RX Do not give too much of your time to others. You must also make sure you are not using too many medications, either over the counter or prescribed and make sure your medications agree with you.

Ryan, Briceida *(this book's author)* You will find that for the next ten days you will be at the peak of experience and will be so together that you will instinctively know you will reach the finish line before the race has really begun. You will have feelings of confidence that come from knowing you will succeed. You will feel the strength that comes from your inner core. Follow your goals as if you were on a mission and this will bring you to a victorious completion of your goals. Within this time frame, your sense of ethics and judgment will be intact and you are headed for a fantastic future.

rye Stop your obsessive behavior and stop being so controlling and possessive. You will also have an abundance of love in your life. Allow others to express their appreciation without limits. Good luck is with you and many blessings are with you and your family.

rye bread Make sure you protect yourself from the weather. Keep warm and do not allow yourself to be caught out in the elements without proper attire. Many blessings are with you and your family.

rye grass You will be able to accomplish a very difficult

task that you will have to handle within five days. You will have the courage and clarity of thought to calmly and tactfully accomplish what you are after. Victory is with you.

S

S Some time ago, you and a friend toyed with the idea of creating molds for silver jewelry. This friend is now deceased. Think about pursuing this project again. This creative project will bring you riches and a brilliant future. These molds may also be used to create gold jewelry.

Sabbath A young child will need help throughout their young life. You will need to offer constant encouragement, motivation and the means in which this child will be able to empower themselves. Do not lose patience. This child will grow up to be successful and wealthy.

saber You have enemies waiting to rejoice at your failure. You will enjoy victory against all odds.

saber-toothed tiger You are expected to be somewhere important at a certain time. Your plans will fail if you are late. Make sure you get there on time.

sable You are trusting someone who is unworthy of your trust. This person is also irresponsible and you will soon get a sense of their character. Use alternatives.

sabotage Tell the truth to avoid the embarrassment of being caught in a lie. Spare yourself by speaking truthfully to begin with.

saboteur You are taking too much time thinking about contracts that need to be signed. Move quickly; these papers will arrive within a week or two.

saccharin A very dear older person who deeply loves you needs your help for the next week. Be there for them.

sachet Do not listen to gossip or allow jealousy into your life.

sack *empty* Trust only what you see and only half of what you hear. Be very careful during this cycle.

full You will be able to successfully get your point across regarding your dissatisfactions.

sackcloth Your wishes will be fulfilled.

sack race You will be able to help someone special to you develop their potential and achieve their goals. This person will be very grateful to you and you will share in their increase in wealth. Many blessings will come to you and your family.

sacrament Your circumstances will rapidly improve.

sacred This is a very lucky omen and implies that you will develop, within four days, an inner courage and strength that arises from within. Your steel drive and determination will motivate you to break through all hidden obstacles, physical or mental. And to rid yourself of any aspect of your life that you disapprove of that keeps you from being thrust ahead. Once you have removed this hindrance, you will quickly see a clear path, acquire the knowledge needed to develop those areas in your life you most desire and develop the perfect lifestyle for yourself. This will be the perfect time cycle to easily accomplish this. You will also be placed on a pedestal and greeted like royalty anywhere you choose to go. This will come as a big surprise to you. You are headed for a brilliant future and many new opportunities will present themselves to you.

sacred cow Someone you are interested in becoming involved with will lead you to believe they will contact you at a later time. This person will never contact you again. Do not get your hopes up in spite of how much you desire this involvement. It will not work out.

sacrifice Be very strict regarding your business affairs, finances, and accounts.

sacrilege You will develop a great talent and within the year successfully use this talent for profit. Someone will also come into your home and take a small item that will not be missed for some time. Expect this within the week and take precautions.

sacrilegious Do not slave yourself over a worthy cause. Protect yourself and do not overextend yourself physically for the next two weeks.

sacroiliac A close male family member from a distant town needs your help but this person finds it difficult to ask for help. Make an effort to reach out and find what you can do to help.

sad *any form* This is an announcement of an impending engagement. You must also make a point of not being so demanding of someone who loves you dearly. This will happen within the week.

saddle You will soon move into a new position with more authority. The long burdened problems will also be dealt with soon and will not return.

saddlebag Do not give the cold shoulder to someone who has trusted you and has been kind to you. This will cause hurt feelings. Be very aware of your attitude.

saddle block You will receive a letter that will shock you

with horrible frightening statements. You must report this to the police. You are forewarned that this will happen, so remain calm. Do everything necessary to ensure your safety.

saddle horse For the next few days, eat no unusual foods. Watch your stomach.

saddle seat Do not put yourself in the position to be criticized.

saddle shoes Keep your opinions to yourself and play it safe.

saddle soap Be careful when engaged in pleasure seeking activities. Someone will attempt to involve you in negotiations that will have serious implications.

saddle sore You are enjoying your freedom but you will soon feel a need to marry. You will be more sure of yourself this time.

sadism A special gift for someone will get you in trouble with someone who is special to you. Jealousy will arise. Take steps to avoid this. Any negative event in this dream must be prevented in reality.

sadomasochism Protect your career and make a list of do's and don'ts. Make sure you do not become unwittingly involved in a sadomasochistic situation unless this is something you desire.

safari Someone has been trying to talk you into a business venture but lacks the seed money to get it started. Rethink this plan, because you will have to provide the capital.

safari jacket Within a two week period you will be involved in an unusual circumstance that will bring you great wealth. You will travel extensively for the next few months and enjoy every minute.

safe You are headed in the wrong direction regarding a romantic situation. This person would later be very critical of you. Rethink your position.

safecracker Give a small gift to a special person just to share your love and express your pleasure.

safe deposit box You will unexpectedly receive a gift of flowers from someone you least expect. This will be the start of something very special.

safe house You or someone you know will be misled to believe you should do something that you feel differently about. Although those people who are misleading you fully believe this is the best option for you, they have no idea what the consequences of their choice will be. This will put you or this other person in a dangerous and troublesome situation. You have prior notice of this and can take steps to ensure this does not occur.

safety belt Be consistent and persistent in the attitude of love you show toward someone who is special to you. You will be surprised in their change of attitude.

safety glass Someone will give you a container of items to hold for them. When this person returns to pick the items up, you will be accused of going through the container and taking some. Be cautious of this and do not allow it to occur.

safety net The direction in which you are heading will be unfulfilling. Take the time to rethink and look for alternative directions.

safety pin Pay attention to everything you are told instead of selectively listening only to what you want to hear. This will allow you to see the whole picture and ensure you will react appropriately. You will then be able to successfully complete your tasks.

safety razor Do not allow yourself to be driven anywhere for the next few days. The driver is careless and you will be involved in an accident.

safety rules You will be introduced to lifestyle changes by another. These changes will turn your life around in a positive way and you will blossom into a more joyous and happy person.

safflower You have been waiting for a long time for help. This week, someone will come through for you.

safflower oil Within the week you will be offered a bigger salary than you ever anticipated. Many happy days are coming your way and many blessings are with you and your family.

saffron Use strength of character and be relentless when getting the job done.

sag *anything* Watch your intake of all fatty foods and watch your cholesterol. Eat healthful foods, drink plenty of water and exercise.

saga Domestic problems will come to an end very quickly.

sage *(wise man)* You will soon come to terms with your sexual problems and resolve a very important issue.

sage *(spice)* Protect your health.

sage brush You will join a group that will teach you more about yourself. This will bring much joy.

Sagittarius You will be able to make your point known with an influential group of people. You will then feel a greater sense of independence. Aim for the big ideas. Victory is

yours.

saguaro cactus You will receive the verification you need concerning a certain situation regarding the feelings of someone special to you. The words of love you have been waiting to hear will be spoken to you. This person is very kind, generous, and serious about having you become a part of their life.

Sahara You will be put in a situation where you feel anger because of jealousy or envy. You have been purposely set up to feel these emotions. You have prior notice of this and can alter your reactions. This dream may also be used as a reference point in time. If you dream of this desert and see its name used in any context, the dream message will occur on this day.

sail You will finally be able to turn down a persistent request for a loan. This will occur within the week.

sailboat *to sail in calm waters* You will be sought out to spend a special evening with a special person. This person is someone you least expect.

to sail in rough waters Your special talents have gone to your head. You have placed yourself above everyone else to the point that it is difficult for anyone to communicate with you. Change your attitude.

sailcloth Get in touch with an attorney about an upcoming situation. This issue will occur within three weeks so start interviewing now.

sailfish A close relative will finally achieve domestic happiness after a long stormy relationship.

sail maker Find out what someone is up to and quickly get to the bottom of an important incident.

sailor Within two days you will come to the realization that you are not obligated to behave in any manner that someone else wishes you to. Make sure no one else has any control over you and work to rid yourself of someone who expects you to behave, speak and think in the way they want you to. You will be able to do this with tact and diplomacy and with very little stress. You are headed in the right direction and are headed for a prosperous future.

working sailors For the next three nights, avoid going out in order to avoid any close contact with the criminal element.

sailors congregating calmly Choose a business partner you feel comfortable working with. Finding this partner should be a priority to you now.

sailplane You will undergo an important change within the next five days that will finally allow you to achieve domestic happiness. This is a change you have long desired.

Saint *if you do not recognize the saint* All Saints are affiliated with major positive changes in life. Pay attention to any words spoken to you and follow all advice to the letter. You will also experience a quick healing of any affliction. Focus on any ailment you may have and begin treatment immediately to avoid escalation of this problem. Simplify your life in order to allow yourself to be open to these new changes. These changes will be subtle and will arrive slowly. Be patient. There are several reasons a saint will appear in a dream. One of these is to warn you that a trap is being laid for you, without your knowledge. Someone intends to inflict harm on you in either an emotional or physical way. This damage will affect your life deeply. Another reason a saint may appear is to alert you that you may be misdiagnosed for a particular illness, scheduled for an unnecessary operation, or will be given a medication that is not needed. You must also be careful that you avoid overmedication in any form. You must motivate yourself to determine exactly what you need in your life. Saints also warn you to anticipate unexpected accidents and unforeseeable circumstances in your life. This could be anything that could cause you to be impaired in some way or cause your death. There is something you need to be acutely aware of so you can be alert enough to avoid it. You may also be in danger of becoming involved in something you have no business being involved with that could throw you completely off track. It would then be impossible to achieve your goals. Be aware also that you may be unwittingly doing something that will steer someone else off track. You will need to be aware of this in order to bring this person back on track. You are being told to be the person who will inspire someone to head in the right direction. This cycle involves the three day period commencing at the time you have this dream. You will be provided with a miracle, wonderful resolution regarding any issues in your life, and you will experience as a result of it a successful recovery in all areas of your life. You will experience an excitement for a long time to come as a result of this dream and you will be able to successfully tackle each major issue in your life. You are on the path toward a brilliant future.

Saint Andrew You will rejoice upon coming out of a depressing cycle. Upon awakening, you will feel lighter and a burden will be lifted from you. Negative thought patterns will disappear and you will feel the excitement of a new beginning. This will last a long time. Blessings will be yours.

Saint Augustine Be sure to turn off all electrical appliances and make sure all candles and fires are extinguished. Take all precautions to protect yourself and your property from fire.

Saint Bernard Try to understand what is happening regarding a special person. You are being left large clues by them implying they need more time with you. Make adjustments in your time to make this possible. It is also important to bring tranquility and harmony to the place you will be spending most of your time. Do not create chaos and do not become your own worst enemy.

Saint Jude - Thaddeus If this Saint visits you in this dream, it implies he is very eager and excited about being a team player regarding a situation you feel is absolutely impossible for you to find a fair resolution to. You will be pro-

vided with a miracle because he is the Saint for desperate and impossible cases. This miracle will provide you with a just and fair resolution for everyone involved and will lessen any hurt or stress that may go into this. Light will be brought in where there was only darkness as well as depressing situations. You will feel the excitement and will be thankful and honored that St. Jude wants to be a part of your team. He is only waiting for you to ask for his help. St. Jude will launch a campaign and everyone involved will feel a difference in their lives as well as being uplifted because of his involvement in your life. Another reason this Saint may appear to you is you are in the process of bringing some positive change into the world. Your efforts will be appreciated by others because your thoughts, ideas and plans will be brought to fruition and will benefit humankind. This Saint is letting you know they will do everything they can to bring your work to its highest level so it will be readily available to anyone who needs it and will offer a healthier environment for those who are seeking what you are offering. St. Jude will come to your aid with anything you need assistance and you may ask for anything from this Saint once he has appeared. This Saint is also available to you at any time you wish to call him in but will be especially available during any particular time in your life involving something specific you need his help in. Many blessings will be with you. You will enjoy tranquility and health for a long time to come.

Saint Michael *(the Archangel)* This implies that any number of things could be occurring in your life at this time and you are very honored that St. Michael appeared in a dream to you. You may be, at this time, dealing with some stressful situations that require immediate attention concerning high level administrative red tape or injustices that someone in authority has aimed at you. They will have a major negative impact on your life or in a crisis situation that you will unexpectedly find yourself in. At this point, St. Michael will rush to your aid and will be very eager to be a participant in either one of these issues. He will take you under his wing, so to speak. Although it will not actually be something you can see, you will sense a dramatic change in your life due to your clarity, determination and courage. This will come at a time when you feel there is no way to win a just decision in your favor from a big agency or administration that overwhelms you with their power. You need to begin covering your bases now so you will be able to meet that challenge. Prepare yourself by logging your moves and keeping notes on all of your activities. Use your common sense and you will find yourself safely covered. You will enjoy enormous strength and victory in those areas you most desire. You are being alerted to grasp whatever power you can align yourself with and to develop the motivation, courage and determination you will need to handle this on your own. You will have the backing, support and help from St. Michael to deal with this. You are also being told there is a tremendous excitement coming from St. Michael because you may be working in some specialized field. This may be something that deals with education, health, careers, mass media, or self help programs. This has to do with anything that concerns being well balanced and bringing more balance to others in those areas they desire. The archangel is very excited and eager to be a part of your team in bringing this project to its highest possible level and to make your offerings of help accessible to as many people as possible. Anything you have written, have begun writing, are thinking of writing, or are putting in verbal form that will help others and give balance and tranquility to the lives of others will be greeted with enthusiasm. If you are in a transition, you can move confidently ahead with St. Michael's help as well as with the help of other angels who will be asked to align with him in a team effort. The energy you gain will help you to develop your ideas and put them into tangible form to allow others to help themselves. St. Michael will eagerly give his assistance in any area you need help. You may ask anything of this Saint and he will be available at anytime you wish to call upon him with your needs. Look up the definition for angel for additional information. You will enjoy a long and healthy life and you are headed for a brilliant future.

Saint Veronica This is an extremely lucky omen and the appearance of this Saint implies you will have definite verification of an immediate recovery in areas of your life in which you are feeling stressful and anxious. The excitement you feel over this recovery will last you a lifetime. This will be an immediate response to something you feel an urgent need for. You and anyone you dreamed about will have an immediate recovery from an illness or any situation that deals with blood, if this is the issue you are concerned about. Otherwise you will see an immediate resolution to a particular issue that you are feeling stressed about. You will enjoy an abundance of health and prosperity for a long time to come. This dream is even more remarkable if you see St. Veronica with a veil.

Saint Andrew's cross Examine your emotional well-being to ensure you have rid yourself of negative thoughts. Release these thoughts. Give yourself the chance to have a rebirth of attitude and concepts.

the sign of the cross - any form The more you practice optimism, the more you will be able to achieve this attitude. You will also strongly feel the love and affection that a variety of people have for you and you will receive praise and honor. You and your family will also receive an abundance of blessings for a long period of time.

Saint Anthony's fire Take the time to examine all of your achievements and talents. All of them have been successful but there is one that can be redeveloped. Revitalize this talent for great rewards.

Saint Elmo's fire A planned vacation will turn out to be a financial drain. Make alternative plans.

Sainthood You need to be more nurturing to your loved ones.

Saint Patrick's Day You will reach your goals and realize your ambitions if you allow your business partner to share and brainstorm with you. Together, you will devise a suc-

cessful plan for a rise to the top.

Saint Valentine's Day An important document needs to be signed but only after it has been checked over thoroughly by an attorney.

sake This is the best time to express your needs to someone important to you. You will be heard and within the week your needs will be met.

salad Treat yourself well; take a nice bubble bath or do everything you can to be kind to yourself. Drink plenty of water and maintain your health.

salad bar You will slowly and subtly gain extensive knowledge about an unusual topic. It would serve you well to write a book and earn a profit. You are already being asked to share your knowledge.

salad dressing Unless you get help now you will be unable to make the grade you are after.

salad oil Do everything you can to release some unusual responsibilities that are headed your way. If you do not delegate some of these tasks to others, you will be overwhelmed. Do not leave yourself open for any additional burdens or responsibilities.

salamander An event you are anticipating will be a disappointment.

salami A close relative will shortly meet with a crisis and need help from you. This relative will need to control their behavior or the crisis will be prolonged. Do what you can to make this easier.

salary Admit that your actions are wrong and take the necessary steps to make positive changes.

to pay a salary You will benefit because a particular project will be undermined by another person.

to dream of a salary cut Do nothing that will bring you shame.

sale Within a few days, a same sexed acquaintance will speak unkindly about you in order to ruin your reputation. Do not become involved in this pettiness and get on with your life.

public sale Keep all of your new interests to yourself. When you do express your interests to others, explain it in such a way that no one will mistake what you are talking about.

sidewalk sale Victory depends solely on you and your personal involvement in order to ensure that your project will reach maturity.

yard sale A tremendous opportunity will open up for you if you place yourself in the right place at the right time. You will grasp exactly what you are after and will see an increase in those benefits you are seeking. Many blessings are with you and your family.

to rush to a sale You are entering a lucky cycle and it would be to your advantage to do everything you can to maintain a relationship at the highest possible level. You will find that by doing your share in keeping a relationship close you will save a lot of wasted energy. This will allow you to focus on important issues. You are both headed for a brilliant future.

Salem Do not eat crabs and salty foods for the next two months. These foods will not agree with you. You will also learn of a secret enemy. Do not make this person aware that you know about them. This may also be used as a reference point in time. If you dream of this city and see its name used in any context, the dream message will occur on this day.

sales advertisement Certain situations will arise that will incur unusual thought processes. You will then have an irresistible impulse to go in that direction. Once this is done, it will generate additional funds and wipe out all old debts. Set aside time for brainstorming.

salesclerk For the next three days you need to be very cautious in the manner in which you address someone. Someone will overreact to your words to the point of irrationality and it will be very difficult to calm this individual down. Avoid this situation at all costs. Set your goals high in other areas of your life. These goals will be met within three days.

salesperson Be prudent and practical while informing an older person of their living status. You must also make it your business to specify your needs to an important person in your life. You will have success with this if you act immediately.

sales representative You will receive a gift of sapphire jewelry.

sales slip You will receive something you have been expecting that will bring you joy.

sales tax Your companions are very honest and truthful with you.

Salisbury steak This is an extremely lucky omen. Within three days you will experience a reversal of fortune in your favor. You will then be able to accomplish those things that, for some reason, you were unable to take care of before. Go for it.

saliva *any form* Your wishes will be granted and you will also soon receive a financial windfall.

salmon Be very cautious. A theft will occur that you need to be alerted to. You will be in contact with this person within five days. Take precautions. In spite of any difficulties that may be coming from a number of different sources, you will also find relief from all old burdens and any new issues with-

in the week. You will also hear good news about options you have long wanted to come your way. This cycle promotes family harmony and many blessings will come to you and your family. You are headed for a prosperous future.

salmonella Make sure you eat no suspicious foods that could cause food poisoning.

Salome Do not try to keep up with those who are better off than you. Avoid false pride. This will create unnecessary stress.

salon Someone is persistently pursuing you for marriage. Should you pursue this, the person will later state that they were not in the correct state of mind and seek an annulment.

saloon This is a lucky omen and family problems will stabilize. A close friend will also relieve you financially just when you need it the most. Guard your cash.

saloon keeper Someone you have known for some time will become the love of your life.

salsa For the next week you will need to become assertive and perform the necessary legwork in order to get what you desire from a particular situation that will otherwise fall apart. Take steps to ensure that your plans will fall into place exactly as you wish them to.

salt Someone is very interested in marrying you. Be aware that this person's children are spoiled and will purposely nag you and destroy your private time with this special person for the purpose of breaking apart the union. You may choose to avoid this misery.

salt and pepper You have left someone in charge of making your property payments. After two months you will realize they have not been made and foreclosure procedures have begun. This is a dangerous situation. For the next two months, handle everything personally.

salt beef An assistant you hire within three days will be untrustworthy and will not keep secret projects a secret. This can be prevented. Carefully check out those you hire.

saltcellar Be forewarned, you will be interviewing for new roomers. One person will strike you as ideal but after this person moves in, you will find they are very territorial and have a problem relating to others. This person is the same sex as you and will make constant demands on your time and energy. This will become very distasteful to you. Do extra research before renting out a room.

saltine Within a few days, you will get a clear picture of the identity of the person who is undermining your accomplishments.

Salt Lake City You will enjoy yourself immensely with someone who is very physically attractive. You are also interested in becoming involved in the movie industry and will surround yourself with people who are already involved. You will be offered a role, even if it is a minor one. Take care of yourself and do not allow your appearance to slide. This may also be used as a reference point in time. If you dream of this city and see its name used in any context, the dream message will occur on this day.

salt lick You will work hard for very little pay. Do not give away your efforts.

saltpeter Make sure you do not inadvertently allow toxins to enter your bloodstream.

salt pork Be very suspicious of a nosy person. Change your behavior and do not act so conceited.

saltshaker Do not put all your efforts into one project. Be versatile and scan your environment for other alternatives.

saltwater An ocean voyage will bring you much joy and you will begin to experience more passion in life.

salty Move quickly to make sure anything being built for you is weather proofed.

salute Get more education in your field in order to advance in life.

salvation You will receive gifts of diamonds.

Salvation Army You will hear of a close relative who will need care for the rest of their life. This is out of your control. There is no cure for this and you will need to demonstrate patience for a long time.

salve You will become friends with a group of very powerful people who will remain your friends for a lifetime.

Samaritan You will be despondent over the marital problems of a close relative. This relative will go through a lot of pain and will continue to do so until they come to grips with this issue.

Samoa A desirable out of the way vacation spot will be made available to you by a professional friend. They will offer this to you with no strings attached. Take advantage of this and you will have a wonderful time. This may also be used as a reference point in time. If you dream of this island group and see its name used in any context, the dream message will occur on this day.

sample Prepare to have an unexpected nose bleed sometime in the next week while in the presence of a large group of people.

sampler The product you will be marketing will be immensely successful.

Samson *(from the Bible)* Over the next two weeks you will have to deal with many small irritations, but this will be followed by a relatively calm period that will last a long time. This will be as a result of your ability to handle these small issues now.

Samuel *(from the bible)* When requesting services from another person you will need to become verbally aggressive. This person depends on you alone to work on their behalf. You will achieve success in this endeavor. Good luck is with you.

Samurai Within a day or two you will be able to understand clearly where a relative is coming from. You will understand the conniving nature of this relative and will be able to react appropriately.

San Antonio You will travel to a far place and will experience a wonderful unusual visual performance. This memory will stay with you many years. This may also be used as a reference point in time. If you dream of this city and see its name used in any context, the dream message will occur on this day.

sanctify A puzzling secret has finally been deciphered and the result will bring joy.

sanctuary A close friend is contemplating suicide. If you have any idea who this person is, reach out before this is acted upon and help this person get on the right track. You will be successful.

sand You will receive a gift. You will also find a way to express the pain you feel concerning someone who is close to you. This person needs assistance due to a poor physical condition. You will be able to resolve this major issue by discussing with others the best way to help the individual. This will occur within seven days.

sandal You will have a night of dancing and uplifting inspiration and will develop more passion for life.

sandalwood Do not pass judgments on others. This dream is very lucky and indicates you will enjoy success.

sandbag Be watchful to avoid water damage.

sandbar Be more sensitive to the feelings of others.

sandblast You will marry someone and will have many children of the same sex. You will lead a comfortable, though not rich life and you will experience many ups and downs. The children will grow up to be generous and very successful. You will enjoy good health, many grandchildren and a long life. This will occur unless you actively choose an alternative lifestyle.

sandbox Protect children from injury caused by pets and deep lacerations. This will occur suddenly within three days and can be prevented by being more watchful.

sand dollar You will hire a highly intelligent, skilled, same sexed person to help market your idea. This person's skill and advertising methods will bring success.

sand flea A co-worker desires your input on a project. This will give you a chance to rectify a commitment that you made in error in the past.

sand flies You will receive riches and will be able to vanquish all bills.

San Diego You will be offered two alternative paths regarding lifestyle and residence. Both are very good choices. Research will provide the better of the two choices. Someone in San Diego will also be capable of giving your life a bigger boost in order to facilitate change. This may be used as a reference point in time. If you dream of this city and see its name used in any context, the dream message will occur on this day.

sandlot Domestic issues will demand more attention and time from you.

sandman Focus on an unexpected crisis. Resolve it and your life will become easier.

sandpaper Small changes will work wonders with a loved one. A small outing and more time with this person will change the nature of the relationship.

sandstone This is a very lucky omen. Listen to your partner and try doing things a little differently. You will enjoy a little experimentation.

sandstorm Your mental energy is very high. Do not be shy about sharing information with others so they may utilize your services more efficiently.

sand trap This week let someone else carry the stress and responsibilities.

sandwich Deal with people on a personal basis in order to improve the outcome of your life and bring greater profits.

sandwich box Within four days you will achieve your goals. Other people will be eager to cooperate with you on this. This also implies that you will enjoy an abundance of health.

sane Money shortages are not to be taken lightly. Gain more control of all money coming in and going out. Important accounts could be endangered.

San Francisco Be the first to make a move and you will gain more success. You will benefit by the purchase of

property. Keep communication open in order to allow easy approach by others. You will also be invited to a wonderful, elaborate yacht party. Following as a result of this you will be invited to a series of unique events. Each will be different and wonderful and will be accompanied by a romantic aura. This may also be used as a reference point in time. If you dream of this city and see its name used in any context, the dream message will occur on this day.

Sanhedrin You will become involved in a tug of war with another person in an attempt to keep them from doing something. Expect this within three days.

San Helena Your intuition is correct and whatever you see projected will be accurate. Go for what you believe is right. Your judgment is on target. This may also be used as a reference point in time. If you dream of this city and see its name used in any context, the dream message will occur on this day.

sanitarium You are a very caring intelligent, and loving person but you have limited yourself. You do not give yourself permission to express self confidence and to break out of the mold of humility and from an environment that you have outgrown. Give it all you have for the next two days and those you are working with will gain more confidence in your abilities.

sanitary You will be approached with an unusual once in a lifetime offer. You and this person can go a long way with this opportunity. This is very lucky and the returns will be very profitable.

sanitary napkin Do not betray your sources. You will also be asked to help a person who has some naughty problems. Suggest a counselor.

San Jose You will be invited to a graduation. This will require that you dress in glamorous attire for the gathering afterwards. This may also be used as a reference point in time. If you dream of this city and see its name used in any context, the dream message will occur on this day.

Sanskrit Someone will try to create a disturbance with you. You have the chance to avoid this situation entirely if you take steps now. Protect yourself. This also implies that you should not allow anyone to waste your time on nonsense. During this cycle you have to accomplish things that need to be immediately taken care of.

Santa Claus A wonderful older person will do everything they can to ensure your happiness. Through a conversation you will work out a comfortable agreement. You can then work out a stress free solution that will provide financial stability and a stable living arrangement.

Santana, Carlos A fantastic future is in store for you, especially for the next two weeks. You will be thrust forward into a life filled with an abundance of prosperity. This will seem to be almost magical and you will experience special qualities and abilities.

sap Place yourself in the position to better your life. Eliminate self perpetuated interferences that create chaos and destruction.

sapling Someone will come to you with a get rich quick scheme. Turn your back on this completely.

sapphire There will be a time in your life that allows you to travel extensively and visit most of the wonders of the world, exotic cities, and breathtaking scenery. You will experience most of the beauty offered and have wonderful memories of this. You will receive strength in body, mind, soul and in your vital organs. Eat appropriately and drink plenty of water. Your psychic abilities will be heightened for a long time to come. Expect this to unfold within seven days.

sapsucker You will be asked to work for someone who is very hard to get along with. Before taking a job, make sure you work out acceptable arrangements so you can get along.

Sarah *(from the Bible)* You will come up with a treasure of an idea. You will be preoccupied with ways to make this idea work and ways to market it. It will be tremendously successful.

saran wrap You will become closer to that important person in your life.

sardine You will be in unbearable emotional pain because of your inability to convey your side of an issue. Do not get caught up in this because you can take steps to remove yourself from this situation. Life is too short. Do whatever you can to find contentment.

sari Do not allow one of your ideas to be undermined because this idea would have brought you extra money. The result will be this person stealing a desired position. This knowledge will allow you to proceed with caution and confidence.

sarsaparilla Seek professional advice and services. This will give you the skills and knowledge needed to complete an ongoing venture.

sash Skills learned in the past will become handy in the future. Investigate past talents that will bring future benefits.

sash *(cord)* Someone you know will betray you. You know who this person is so do what you can to protect yourself and avoid betrayal.

sasquatch Peace of mind is dependent on self respect. You will also fall in love with a much older person. This could be a fantastic relationship.

Satan Anything negative that occurs in this dream will be fulfilled accurately in real life if you do not take steps quickly to avoid it. Make sure you only experience positive expressions in your life. You will also need to take the necessary steps to avoid a problematic situation that is unfolding. You must assert yourself and make sure all of your bases are safely covered. You can protect everything that is emotionally precious. You can do this by making sure you do not put yourself in the path of destruction. During this time period, someone will enter your life who is very immoral and wicked. This person will cause you great emotional harm. You have prior notice of this and will need to take every step you can to avoid them completely. You will have the ability and strength to endure anything you are required to handle. Make corrections in those areas of your life that require changes. Do everything within your power to make sure problematic areas are rerouted to ensure that you set yourself on the righteous path. Dramatic positive changes will be easier to accomplish at this time. Search for tools that will allow personal growth and do not allow loved ones to outgrow you. Find ways to shed outmoded ways of thinking and behaving in order to keep your loved ones around you. Stop being so verbally abusive to others in public and in private. The necessary help will arise from private counseling, group therapy and self help. These groups will help with a myriad of problems such as drug, alcohol, sexual, and gambling abuse. Attend to what is going on around you and be compassionate to yourself while you are making changes. If you pay attention to the warning the dream is delivering and make the necessary changes, you will find your life will change dramatically and you will face a brilliant future. Because this serves as a warning, you have prior notice to turn your life around in a dramatic way, filled with tranquility, peace, and joy.

to dream of Satan laughing at you Time is running out for you. You are in danger from a very evil person. Although this person has not yet demonstrated any sign of their evil nature, they will remove their mask of normalcy once you grow closer to them. You will need to investigate to determine who this person is. This will take place within four days. Do not allow this person to get close to you and take steps to protect yourself.

satanic Avoid self-hatred. Love yourself more and be more compassionate toward yourself. Meditate in your favorite form in order to gain clarity.

Satanism Do not betray yourself. Maintain your upright living style and have confidence in the way you carry yourself. Be true to yourself.

satchel Play new and fun games with a group of friends. Enjoy yourself and enjoy new and different foods.

satellite Someone will take every step they can to undermine you and take something from you. During this cycle you must be very watchful and investigate this matter to determine the source.

satellite dish For the next three days aggressively take control of the thoughts you are having for another. Do not allow your days to be filled with obsessive thoughts of this person. Concentrate on your daily routine and/or other issues that are important to your life. Do not allow the opinions of others to disturb your train of thought. Rely on your own counsel.

satin Blessings are yours. A buddy of yours will become a great business partner. It would also be a good idea to look up an old lover.

satisfy You will be the object of another's attraction. This person loves you deeply.

saturate Do not sell your blood.

Saturday Someone will respond to a special emotional request you have been craving. This will happen on Saturday and will bring you a great deal of joy. This joy stems from both the granting of the request and from the giver's recognition of your wants. Pursue your goals and you will accomplish your dream and achieve tranquility.

Saturday night special Think ahead, keep your life together and avoid any activity, acquaintance, or behavior that will have negative repercussions in the future. Monitor your lifestyle carefully to ensure that nothing will be held against you at a later time. This could prevent you from elevating your life and career.

Saturn Take care of all necessities quickly. Do not procrastinate.

satyr You will be able to attract people who can accomplish a great deal in a very short period of time. Use this opportunity to your advantage.

sauce Do not be taken in by someone's insistence for sex. This person has no regard for your feelings but is merely trying to satisfy their urges.

saucepan Your ability to recognize that your family is headed for a crisis situation will allow you to handle this successfully by using tactful persuasion.

saucer Within the next week you will suddenly be threatened emotionally and physically after going to another person's house. If you feel this will happen, do not go. Your instincts are correct. You will also need to stop being so evasive and get to the heart of a situation in order to avoid friction with someone else.

sauerbraten Avoid unnecessary strain to the body and do not lift heavy items.

sauerkraut You will be delegated to complete a difficult assignment. A satisfying completion and detailed reports

will advance your career.

Saul *(from the Bible)* You will receive a letter and package from a distant land. You will not know the sender but it will come from a secret admirer who has a professional career.

sauna You will unexpectedly find a very old collectible in a pouch. After advertising this find, no one will claim it. You will enjoy the collection and it will be worth a great deal. This will be found in an unexpected place. Keep your eyes open and make a conscious effort to locate this treasure.

sausage *to cook* You will fulfill your deepest desires.

to eat You will win the trust of the one you love most.

to make or see them made You will enjoy the company of someone you respect and have a deep love for.

blood sausage Within three days, you will receive a very thrilling gift. You will also be able to rid yourself of a long term burdensome situation that has dragged you down for a long time. Good luck is with you and a brilliant future is yours.

in any other form Someone will unexpectedly declare their love for you. As a result, you will experience a feeling of exuberance and excitement. If you choose, this can develop into a relationship in any capacity you choose and will lead to mutual fulfillment.

sauté Watch out for someone who is unable to control their alcohol intake, who will cause embarrassment at a special outing.

savage Do not put yourself in a situation to be taken advantage of sexually. Make it clear that you are not interested.

savings account A trap has been set for you by a violent enemy. Avoid this at all costs.

Savings and Loan There is much turbulence ahead in your life but you will have the inner strength to get through this. This will be happening throughout this next week. Remain calm.

savings bond Do not involve yourself in any unusual situations for the next two days because this will embarrass you at a later time. Make sure you are acutely aware of everything during this time period and do what you can to prevent any unusual situation from occurring.

savior You are in a good position to demand what you want and need from your god and this wish will be granted. For the next few weeks you will be in the process of reassessing your priorities. You will make a list of plans that will be far superior to the way you live life now and this will lead to dramatic changes. You must also find a peaceful spot and do nothing but relax and enjoy tranquility.

saw *to see anything being sawed that should not be (i.e.,* *padlock)* This implies that certain situations will occur within four days that spell danger. These situations will catch you off guard so take steps to protect yourself. Remain safe and do not expose yourself to unusual situations or environments that will place you in a vulnerable position for the next three days.

in any other form You can accomplish more alone. You will be in a very lucky cycle for the next seven days. Blessings are with you and your family.

sawbuck Discussions will be very productive and successful.

sawdust Within four days a troublemaker will become aggressive in an unexpected, isolated setting. Take precautions and do not allow yourself to be caught off guard. Rely on your judgment. You will also receive a gift of jewelry.

sawfish You will be invited to an unexpected fiesta within the week that you should not miss. This is an extremely lucky omen for you.

sawmill Someone has plotted to lure you into a place for the intention of murder. This will occur within five days. Be cautious, monitor your activities and schedule. This can be prevented.

Saxon Within three days someone you know will be eager to share some good news about an upcoming event. You will enjoy days of tranquility and harmony.

saxophone Refuse to become upset by someone who subtly denigrates you in front of others. Avoid this person and the places this person is likely to frequent. Think ahead, you will cross paths with them within two days.

say *to hear the phrase* It is too risky to lend money now.

scab A close relative needs help in breaking a dependence on their parents. This person feels desperate but is getting older and feels confused about the direction they should take. You will be able to help by offering gentle guidance. Stay until this task is fully accomplished.

scabbard If you are not patient with a certain person for the next few days you will bring on a permanent split in the relationship. This individual will not tolerate excessive demands from you. If you want this person out of your life, this is the perfect time for it but if you want to maintain the relationship, change your behavior.

scabies Local travel will not be very productive. Be very wary of other drivers in order to avoid accidents.

scaffold Help someone who needs assistance with their appearance because of the result of an illness. This may be as simple as hair care, make up and skin ointment. Be gentle.

scald You will soon find yourself involved in a beautiful, unplanned, romantic setting. If you choose, this situation could easily and quickly develop into a passionate evening.

scale Someone is anxious to see you but is hesitant to let you see their true emotions. This person will request to see you within a week. In reality, both of you know you will see each other within two days. Do not allow yourself to be caught off guard. This person's enthusiasm will lead to a phone call and a request to drop in at a moment's notice. Be sure your physical appearance is up to par. You are also entering a lucky cycle.

scallion Someone is very eager to grant you a favor and is in the position to pull strings on your behalf. Do not allow timidity to keep you from asking for this. The granting of this favor will lead to a destined occurrence.

scallop Use more compassion and greater communication skills with your loved ones.

scalp You will receive a piece of property as a gift. This property is located at a distance from you.

scalpel You are appreciated and loved more than you can imagine because of your sincerity.

scampi Trickery is associated with a new attraction. Do not dwell on this and move on with your life.

scandal Someone in your neighborhood will commit suicide by hanging. If you have a sense of who this person is do what you can to prevent it.

Scandinavian Do not rush into a relationship that seems to be just what you want. Look before you rush in.

scapegoat Within a four day period a casual visitor accompanied by another person will start a quarrel with you. Be alert to this and if you can, avoid it.

scar You will always be surrounded by members of the opposite sex. You will find this to be more comfortable and the correct action for you.

scarab This is a lucky symbol and a promise of health, wealth, love, spiritual strength and many blessings. Continue what you are doing with confidence.

scare You will hear word of an unexpected inheritance within three days.

someone else is scared Your mate will not approve of a luxury item that you seek. Avoid arguments.

to be scared You will receive what you are pursuing within a very short time.

to be scared by someone you do not recognize You will receive a proposal of marriage within five days from someone you care deeply for. This union will last a lifetime.

to run from someone you do not recognize who scares

you Make sure this dream does not become a reality. Play it safe and do not place yourself in any situation where this could occur. Within three days someone will attempt to force you to comply with something you find distasteful. Although you will be afraid to refuse this demand, you will find the means to do so.

to be scared by someone you do recognize This person will make a sexual request and you will want to fulfill it but feel a tremendous amount of stress associated with it. Do not compromise and do only what you want to. Find ways to release stress and create a tranquil environment, especially for the next five days. If this person is depicted negatively in the dream, take steps to prevent any negative event from taking place.

to scare someone else Don't place so much importance on someone who is only trying to confuse you emotionally. Stop catering to this individual and sever your emotional ties. Treat yourself well and you will notice a big change in this person's behavior within five days.

to scare someone you recognize This individual will be eager to offer relentless assistance to help you attain your highest goals.

to be scared of a shadow A depraved person will attempt to force you into a distasteful sexual act. This act may be filmed or watched by another person. Take steps to prevent any behavior you find immoral or despicable.

scarecrow Get plenty of rest, be compassionate with yourself and do not allow yourself to become physically overtaxed by another's demands.

scarf Do not be a monster to your family. Treat your family with love and compassion and never talk down to your special person or to children.

scarlet Your cardiovascular system and kidneys are strong and you have a healthy sex drive. All negative emotions will be driven away. This is a good luck color for love and you are doing well in life. Continue to maintain your lifestyle.

scarlet fever Your sexual drive will be satisfied.

scarlet letter You will feel sorrow for the death of the spouse of a newly married friend due to a freak accident. Do everything you can to alert this couple of danger. This will occur within a week unless someone takes steps to prevent it.

scarlet tanager Do not discuss your financial status with someone you do not know well.

scar tissue Be aware ahead of time that the person you are fascinated with will eventually murder you for insurance money if you marry them. Avoid this.

scatter Avoid any infections that will result in hospitalization. Take precautions.

scatter brain *to hear this phrase* Do not demand too much

from a child. Become more supportive of children. Do not speak to a child in such a way that will cause emotional problems that will destroy this child's self esteem and ambition.

scatter shot Be wary of shark bites.

scavenge Be more generous with your talents.

scavenger Do not pay any attention to a mysterious situation. It will work out to your advantage. Stay calm.

scenery Someone you have entrusted to sell your products will get into the habit of not paying you in time. It cannot be helped. This person has a problem with drugs. Change the situation and move on with your life.

beautiful For the next four days think ahead and carefully plan for a conversation you will be having with someone who is involved in a certain issue. This will give you the opportunity to get together all those involved in order to determine how to keep a negative event from taking place. Many blessings will come to you and your family.

scenic A good friend will introduce you to one of their friends and this person will seek involvement. Your friend will later go through a lot of trouble to break up this relationship.

scent Someone you desire passionately will want to communicate how they feel about you. You will be mutually satisfied with this union. Expect this to take place within two days.

scepter Stop being deceitful and do not rely on trickery to succeed. You will be caught.

schedule Do everything you can to keep the promises you make to others.

scheming Someone is pursuing you simply for the pleasures of sex. You know this ahead of time and can decide if you want a relationship based solely on sex.

schizoid At the first hint of mental illness get immediate help. It will take work, time and self-determination, but you will be cured.

schizophrenia Someone you have known well for many years will suddenly start behaving inconsistently about the friendship and their emotions will run hot and cold. This person will soon approach you for the loan of a large sum of money. You have time to prepare a way to avoid this person and get on with your life.

schnapps Someone will take extreme steps to discourage you from pursuing your intentions. This person will give you the run around and make your goals difficult to reach. Do not allow this person to dissuade you from pursuing your ambitions.

schnauzer You will gain a position in the public eye. Do not forget those old friends who may not seem to fit into your new life.

scholar The health of a very young child will suffer greatly if you do not seek medical help at the first sign of illness.

scholarship Strengthen your love life and speed up your efforts to bond closely with someone who is special to you. Open up communications.

school Do not become sidetracked and take care not to ignore a loved one. Make new plans that will include both of you.

   public school A tutor should be a priority for children with a learning disorder.

school board A fight will occur that will involve someone special to you over nonpayment of a loan made to you. This will lead to a separation. You may choose not to make the loan.

schoolbook A phone conversation will result in a quarrel. You can prevent this by remaining calm.

schoolboys Do not display outbursts of temper in public places.

school bus Stop being so gullible and stay on top of all situations.

school crossing Do not expose yourself to the illness of others. Play it safe.

school days A close friendship will be destroyed because of your attitude. This can be prevented.

schoolgirl Within two days your life will become more social and you will have few dull moments.

schoolhouse You will enter a relationship that will require you be very tactful. You will feel as though you are walking on eggs because of the explosive personality of a special person. You may want to avoid entering into this relationship.

schoolmarm Do not waste time and energy trying to analyze another person's behavior. This energy can be better applied elsewhere.

schoolmaster You will need to slow down the progress of an ongoing project in order to review it in more detail. This will ensure that it is in the proper order and is being handled correctly. This will save you costly delays.

school project This is an extremely lucky omen and you will enjoy an abundance of health and riches in areas you

least expect. This wealth will be as a result of an unexpected income. You will also accomplish tasks you once believed were impossible. Now is the perfect time to tackle those big projects. Proceed with confidence. You are headed for a prosperous future.

schoolroom While having a group of friends over, a roommate of the opposite sex will suddenly appear half dressed from another room and will give others a bad impression. This occurrence is preventable.

schoolteacher You are being too possessive. Be careful not to destroy a relationship with someone who cares deeply for you because of this behavior.

schoolwork Be calm when talking to someone who harbors different opinions than you. This person angers easily.

schoolyard You will enjoy intimate companionship at its fullest.

schooner Take your time with paperwork and carefully review everything you are involved with. You must also take extra time to check all safety devices in your home.

science Your equipment and machinery will start to break down. Prevent this by making sure that all parts are in good working order.

science fiction Do not allow a habitual liar to build up false hopes. You will also experience an improvement in finances.

scissors You and a special person have created something tangible together. This person wants to share this with their family. Try to be more open to this and do everything necessary to establish friendly relations with this person's family members.

scissors hold Within a few days, someone who has animosity toward you because of jealousy will seek revenge. Be aware of this and try to prevent it.

scissors kick Within a day or two, a luxury item of yours may break. Keep this in mind and take steps to prevent it. You will otherwise have to pay for repairs.

scissors tail A new group of people will open doors of opportunity. This will allow you to better express your desires. You will also enjoy a new social life and attend many exciting functions.

scold *to scold* Change the route you take for the next few days. You are being stalked by a robber.

sconce *with candles* Do not misinterpret another's actions toward you. You will think this person is romantically interested in you but they are not, and you will later be embarrassed if you continue to believe this is the case.

scone Open a line of verbal communication with someone whom you feel uncomfortable with. At the moment, you are being confused by nonverbal cues.

scoop Be careful around machinery in order to avoid accidents.

scooter You will lend an expensive piece of machinery to someone (i.e., engine, motor, etc.). This will become lost and the borrower will be unable to pay you back. Do not lend out property for the next two weeks.

scope Put out feelers to determine the identity of the person who is attempting to cause you emotional injury. You can avoid this hurt.

scorch You do not have to choose between friendship and love. You can have both in the same person.

score *to score* Do not allow yourself to be so self centered.

scoreboard When selling a valuable possession, make sure you are paid in full or you will never see your valuables, the buyer, or your money again.

scorecard You will receive a strange message. After this, be suspicious about everything and everybody around you because there is danger. You can avoid this.

scorekeeper Indifference on your part will cause someone special to quarrel with you. Making up will be fantastic.

Scorpio You will enjoy a romantic evening of candlelight, music, and soft spoken words. Your sex life and romantic life will be exactly as you choose. This is an extremely lucky cycle and you are headed for a prosperous future. Things that you felt were impossible in the past are now possible. Make it a point to motivate yourself during this time period to grasp each opportunity that presents itself.

scorpion Someone will enter your life who is a conniving and evil con-artist and lives off other people's money even to the point of murder. This person also schemes to marry for money and has focused on you. They will do everything in their power to get what they want. You have prior notice of this and can handle this situation in such a way to protect yourself and keep this person from your life. Expect this person to enter your life within five days. The person in love with this individual could also harm you because they have no idea what is going on. You must also make sure you do everything in your power to protect yourself from contagious disease.

Scot Take control of your temper and take every step to control yourself. An unusual situation will occur that will create feelings of suspicion and jealousy. If you are not

careful, these feelings will escalate into an uncontrollable rage that will drive you to do something you will later regret. Do not feed into these suspicions. The moment you sense these feelings starting to develop, seek professional help.

scotch Do not underestimate yourself and don't allow yourself to be your own worst enemy. Stop shortchanging yourself. You will be entering an exciting, fulfilling cycle that will provide you the choice to do anything you choose to enhance your life.

scotch tape You will receive information you have been long awaiting. Check with a third party to determine the accuracy of this information. There may be newer information that is lacking in the original.

scoundrel Treat an important situation you are now involved with in the same manner that you would treat a pleasurable event. Wherever you can promote growth make a move to achieve prosperity and you will be pleased with the results at a later time. Do this within three days.

scout This is the time to take advantage of your talents. Challenge yourself to do so and you will impress others within a few weeks. Good luck is with you.

scoutmaster Someone with a mysterious lifestyle will attract your interest. You will be exposed to other cultures by someone from another country and this will brighten your life. This person will give you pleasurable moments and you will be extended a permanent invitation to this person's country of origin.

scrap Do not make thoughtless, unkind remarks to any child or young adult.

scrapbook Do not invest at this time. The losses will be big.

scrape Someone will demand that you give more in the way of finances and emotions than you are able to at this time. Do what you must to change this. Budget your time and money.

scrap iron Within three weeks someone will attempt to lure you to a different vicinity in order to do whatever they wish in this vacated area (i.e., robbery, etc.). Follow your instincts.

scratch You will have to deal with a very desperate person who will go to great lengths to get their way. Avoid this person for the next four days.

scratch pad You will develop a plan within three days to start putting away money for a wonderful vacation. If you choose to pursue this, you will enjoy yourself immensely.

scrawl Be very aware for the next three days and go forward with someone only with extreme caution. The person you will be dealing with and are starting to get close to will lead you to believe you can confide in them totally and can rely on their loyalty. This person is cunning and very skilled at creating illusion and deception and will have you believe that future events will occur that will never take place. This individual will go to great lengths to create an atmosphere that will lend trust to all their motives yet they have a hidden agenda against you that involves pursuing you for devious reasons known only to them. This person is very charming and charismatic and will, if they feel you are becoming suspicious, create a diversion to distract you from these suspicions. By the time you realize what is happening you will suffer deep emotional disappointments, disillusionments and financial loss. It will take you a long time to fully recover from this episode and get your life back to normal. You have prior notice of this and all the ammunition you need to ensure this does not take place. Practice common sense and you will successfully diffuse this situation. You will develop the confidence you need to put yourself on the path toward a prosperous future. Many blessings will come to you and your family.

scream Watch out for a sniper in your area. You could be injured as an innocent bystander.

to scream out someone's name whom you recognize This person is someone you should have on your side when a certain situation starts to develop that could get out of control. This could be a very abusive situation and by having this person next to you, you will be saved right in the nick of time.

to scream out someone's name whom you do not recognize For the next three days make sure you do not go anywhere without the company of someone else, especially if you are going out with someone or are meeting with someone you do not know well. This could be a potentially abusive situation. Having someone with you will save you from this.

if you recognize the person screaming out a name You will need to alert this individual that certain situations will begin to evolve that could be very abusive. Warn this person that if they have someone with them they will be saved just in time. The person they need to have with them is the person whom they called out for. Make sure you alert this person not to go out alone because it is a potentially dangerous situation.

screaming *any form* Be very cautious and do not become involved any deeper with anyone for the next three days unless you use extreme caution. The person you will be dealing with will lead you to believe you can fully confide in them and rely on their loyalty. As a result, you will start to grow closer. This individual is very cunning and skilled at creating deception and illusion and will have you believing in future occurrences and events that will never take place. This person has a hidden agenda that is known only to them and will go to great lengths to create a setting that will leave you trusting them completely. This individual is also very

charismatic and charming and will, if they believe you are developing suspicions, create a diversion to allay those suspicions. Once you understand what is going on, you will have suffered disappointments, disillusions and financial distress. It will take a long time for you to recover from this and get your life back to a normal status. You have prior notice of this and everything you need to ensure that this does not take place. Use common sense and you will be successful in diffusing this. Refuse to get involved, do not compromise your feelings and do not allow this person to pry into your personal affairs. You will have the confidence to put yourself on the path toward a prosperous future. Many blessings are with you and your family.

screech Someone will come to you, within four days, with an unlikely and unexpected proposition that seems too good to be true. Because of this you will be tempted to turn the proposal down. Take a few days to think it over and do not close doors on this in spite of its unbelievability. You will later want to explore ways of seeing if it is possible to accomplish this. Even when you are mulling this over you will still have the feeling that this plan is an impossible task but you can be confident that it will take place and that this person will keep each commitment. Good luck is with you.

screen *(Oriental, room divider)* Prepare for your future. This is an extremely lucky omen, within the next five days, for you as well as for anyone who is involved in your life at this particular time. Expect amazing and wonderful connections that will enable you to reach and achieve your goals. You can expect a mega merger and the synergism working between you and those who will be working with you will bring you to a far higher scale than you ever imagined.

screen door/window Do not give gifts to those you do not know well. You will regret this at a later time.

screen test Be very attentive because an unusual occurrence will develop regarding a person, project or position that will lead to a financial windfall. You may marry someone who will leave you with a monthly pension, develop a project that will deliver you monthly royalties, or secure a position that will offer you monthly provisions for a lifetime. You are in a sound position to receive this in the near future. For the ten days develop your curiosity to ensure you do not miss out on these benefits. You will receive an abundance of health, many blessings and are headed for a brilliant future.

screen writer You will achieve power and find a new source of income. Look for this position to come to you soon.

screw Be wary of freak accidents and make sure your body is well-protected. This could occur anywhere but most accidents happen at home.

screwball You will have a wonderful time at a comedy club.

screwdriver You will win a small prize.

scribble pad This implies that within two days you will become aware of an issue you have completely overlooked. This issue will require immediate attention. Focus, in detail, on what needs to be done now in order to avoid a crisis. Make a conscious effort to remember the message written on the pad. If the message is positive, take steps to promote it. If not, take steps to alter the outcome.

scribe Let others know how you feel about a certain situation. Keep conversations open.

scrimmage A questionable situation will cause you embarrassment. Be sure you protect your character and reputation.

scrimshaw You are headed in the wrong direction.

script A long time friend will come into some money and call you to share in this good fortune. This is a very lucky omen for you. Many powerful friends will also rally around you with good advice and help you out in a pinch.

scripture You will come out of a major stress by using your own abilities and strengths and be able to handle any pressure while undergoing these changes. Blessings are yours.

scriptwriter Your dreams and ideas will come to fruition and you will be very successful. You will also be asked to provide more input to others.

scroll You have a friend who will come into power and authority and this person will be a friend for life. After this friend has passed away, you will retain many treasured memories.

scrooge Stay away from heavy labor, heavy lifting and from placing too many demands on yourself for the next week.

scrotum You will have to choose between two people. The one rejected will be understanding.

scrub Displays of physical affection to another person will get you into trouble. Control your behavior.

scrub brush Someone will request that you do something that seems impossible to accomplish. Work on this relentlessly and methodically until you are able to shape and mold this situation into what you want. You will be successful.

scrub person You will learn a secret about a friend. Keep this knowledge to yourself.

scuba diving Understanding will improve between you and your mate and this will last for a long time.

sculptor Gain greater knowledge of the medication and diet

needed by someone you are caring for.

sculpture Make it a point to gain more education in your field.

scum Someone is feeling very abandoned by you. Act quickly to make sure this person knows how special they are to you. Do everything you can to give them an adequate description of your true feelings. You will then be able to bring this person a great deal of pleasure and it will be deeply appreciated. Put your love into action and anything you want to develop on a permanent basis with another person will occur within five days. This also implies that a gift of any kind will enhance this development. You are loved beyond your imagination.

scurvy Face up to your responsibilities and obligations.

scythe Do not allow another person's stress to disturb your emotional equilibrium.

sea *rough* Group activity will become very stressful. Be aware of the pressures you are undergoing. You may decide to lessen your involvement in order to cut back on stress levels.
glassy calm This indicates that tranquility and peace will enter your life.
to swim in You will go on a romantic outing and will enjoy yourself immensely.

sea anchor This is a lucky omen. You will find that in times of financial stress, many people will be able to lend you the money you need in order to get your feet on the ground.

sea bass You will meet someone within a few days and find this person is worth your trust.

Seabee Slow down your pace and take the time to thoroughly investigate a particular situation before you rush in. It may not be wise to involve yourself.

seabird Do not injure anyone's feelings and keep your opinions to yourself.

Sea Biscuit Don't let your imagination run wild and learn to control your behavior.

sea breeze Accept the life you have created until you are financially able to make it into what you desire. Remain practical and work at this, step by step. Changes will be subtle but will take place.

sea captain For the next three weeks, do not release personal information about a project you are working on to people who are curious. Be very private and careful.

seacoast You are wasting too much time analyzing the behavior of another. As a result, an opportunity may slip away. Make sure you grasp every opportunity that comes your way.

sea cow Volunteer your time for a cause that is very important. You will receive emotional rewards and an improved status for your commitment.

sea duck This indicates that someone feels a great sexual desire for you. You will also enjoy a fulfilling sex life for the next two days.

sea eagle Check your blood pressure and get a physical check-up to ensure that you maintain your good health.

sea elephant Any investment you become involved in will be fortuitous.

seafarer You will meet someone within a few days and receive what you expect out of love. You will also receive important information that you have wanted for a long time.

sea green This implies that you will be entering a wonderful three day cycle. For the next two days you must also make sure you do not let anyone else handle your financial affairs. Personally take care of your own business.

seagull Guard against depression.

sea horse You will soon receive an unusual expression of love from a special person.

sea island You will be in a delightful cycle for the next few days.

sea kale Beware of danger. Your perceptions are off and your judgment is faulty. Take care of yourself and your surroundings.

sea lamprey You are socializing too much. Take care of your physical health.

sealing wax Guard your eyesight.

sea lion You will unexpectedly receive a gift of rubies.

sealskin Someone you will show a friendly affection for will misinterpret these feelings and you will find yourself in a bizarre quarrel.

seam Someone you assume is a friend dislikes you and only pretends friendship in order to hurt you in some way. Protect yourself.

seaman The person you feel is your adversary and nemesis will be moving out of your life within two days.

seamanship Work steadily and thoughtfully in order to reach your goal.

seamstress Within a few weeks, someone will begin showing affection toward someone who is special to you because you are not openly demonstrating your feelings. Do everything necessary to head off this situation. If you do not, this person may be taken away and you will be deeply hurt. This is preventable.

séance Riches and power are promised to you in the near future. You also need to get a psychic reading.

sea otter If you fail to be on time at an important event, you will lose out in a big way.

seaplane Learn to control your sexual urges.

search Do not let power go to your head.
to search for someone and not find them where you would expect Someone will come to you because they are feeling desperate to leave their current living arrangements. This individual will find themself unable to make a move because of physical, emotional or financial reason. Something is keeping this person from mobilizing to change their life. For some reason they find it difficult to escape their present circumstances and are very eager and desperate to escape. You will learn of this soon and this person will come to you to ask for assistance of some kind to help them out of this situation. Within five days you will be able to locate resources that will meet their needs and help them out. You will, however, have several conversations with this individual prior to this occurrence. Be very cautious when engaged in these conversations to avoid hurting the feelings of anyone else involved. All negotiations involving finance and romance will be a success for you. You are on the path toward a brilliant future.
to dream of searching for a boyfriend/girlfriend and being unable to find one This implies that there is a situation you need to divorce yourself from. This issue is something that will soon no longer matter. You must move on with your life. You are trying now to get someone to react to this situation in a certain way but in a few weeks it will no longer make a difference in your life. Some people need to learn to handle certain issues on their own and have their own experiences so they can evolve and grow. Situations constantly change and need to be handled in different ways. Do not interfere with someone to the point that they become unable to handle issues on their own.

sea serpent Beware of medications that will affect your thyroid. Eat healthy foods. Drink plenty of water and do nothing that will affect the balance of your system.

seashore Develop the determination to stick with what you know is right and this will ensure that you reach your goals.

seasickness This is a good time to exchange property.

season Within two weeks you will find someone who will

love you for all seasons and for a lifetime.

off season It would be to your advantage, for the next three days, to strengthen the bonds of those relationships that are important to you. Increase your personal involvement in order to ensure peace and tranquility.

seasonings A serious illness can be prevented if you protect yourself better.

season ticket Someone in a position of power and who is very wealthy will offer their assistance regarding a certain issue. This person will back out of this promise and disappoint you. Make sure you do not fall prey to this over the next week.

seat You will have many wonderful days ahead. You will meet more people and attend more social events and functions.

to see many people seated A surprising reconciliation will occur. You had given up hope that this person would ever return but they will come back just as you were forgetting the relationship. It is your choice whether you choose to pursue this. If you make this choice, the relationship will move quickly into a mutually satisfying and meaningful union.

to sit down You will have an unexpected phone call and a pleasant surprise.

saddle seat Do not put yourself in the position to be criticized.

seat belt Communicate to others in order to achieve your goals.

seat cover For the next three days be very patient with a special person who is unable to verbalize their true feelings. You are loved beyond your imagination. This cycle will bring you much love and appreciation from others.

car seat cover Do not allow yourself to be doubted after telling a true, but unbelievable, story.

Seattle You will receive a telephone call from a distant friend. The information given, plus your contacts, will lead to riches and success. This will be a highly exciting time. This may also be used as a reference point in time. If you dream of this city and see its name used in any context, the dream message will occur on this day.

sea turtle Make sure you are not overlooking a potentially abusive situation that involves a much younger person. Do not allow another person to be mistreated once you become aware of this issue.

sea urchin Within a three day period you and someone who is very special to you will separate. Control your emotions and do not create a scene. Listen carefully and calmly to the reasons behind this separation and handle yourself in a civil and dignified manner.

seaweed You will receive a pleasing unexpected declaration of love. You must also take care of yourself and eat more greens.

second Take time out to praise your divinity. Meditate and attend church. You will enjoy a greater fulfillment than you have ever experienced before.

second base Treat your time as a special commodity and set limits on the time you are willing to spend on unnecessary distractions. Budget your time wisely in order to accomplish as much as possible in a short period of time. This is especially important for the upcoming week.

Second Coming You will receive an unexpected inheritance.

second level or floor The opportunity you have been waiting for will arise within two days and you will make a new start in all areas of your life. All old burdens and issues that have been dragging you down will come to a halt. Major changes will add a new excitement and a new dimension to life and you will develop and execute plans in all phases of your life.

Second Lieutenant Take precautions to avoid any injury to the head.

second mate Be very frank about your wants and needs for the future, especially to those who feel it does not fit into the scope of their lives.

second mortgage Do not allow yourself to get tied up with certain situations or people, especially for the next three days.

secret You will receive much affection and tranquility from a new acquaintance.

top secret You will easily be taken by a conniving friend. This person will become a very cunning enemy and will purposely go to great lengths to sabotage an important opportunity just before you gain knowledge of this. Since you have been forewarned, you will be able to determine who this person is and address the situation. You will then be able to turn this around to your advantage.

secret agent You will soon be receiving some benefits and it would be better to keep this your secret.

secretary You will be asked to join a group of people who seem secretive and mysterious. Make sure you do not become involved in any group you know little about.

secret ballot Make sure you keep your feelings and emotions in check for the next few days. You will find you have been excluded from a situation or a group of people. As a result, you will become focused on this issue to the point where you get emotionally caught up in it. Do not make matters worse by feeding on this. Focus on other matters that are much more important.

secret police A close friend of the family will become a sexual partner for life.

secret service Watch out for muscle strain on the arms, legs or hands. Do not overextend yourself physically and do not allow yourself to be manipulated into performing physical tasks for others for the next two weeks.

sect Within a few days you will notice you have misplaced important papers. This will cause you a great deal of anxiety. Do not panic and take steps to prevent this by safeguarding all important paperwork.

section Do not spend any extra money for things that are unusual or out of the ordinary.

security You will help a relative leave an emotionally painful relationship. Do what you can to promote emotional healing in order to live a normal life.

security blanket Rejoice, you are deeply loved.

security guard At one point in your life you were associated with someone who treated you harshly and in such an abusive and inconsiderate way that you decided to get on with your life without this person in it. This dream is telling you that within five days this person will make a verbal appeal to reenter your life in a very appealing way and will offer you a new proposition about your life together. This person will present plans that will offer you a solid foundation for a relationship. You will, however, be plagued with flashbacks of what was. This is letting you know that you do not need to waste any sleepless nights because you can have a good life together. This individual is now responsible and reasonable and you can confidently enter a new relationship that will be solid and permanent for as long as you want. Everyone involved will benefit from this union and you are headed for a brilliant future. This dream is also letting you know that any negotiation you enter into with this person or with any other person in this five day period must be handled in such a way to safeguard your life as the precious commodity that it is. Make sure any negative event you witnessed in this dream that could become a reality is either avoided or prevented and take steps to make sure you experience only positive expressions in your life.

sedan Take extra steps to increase closeness and show love to those who are important to you.

sedative You will feel left out due to rapid changes in your life. Be very attentive to the needs of young children.

Seder You will receive shocking but exciting good news that will fill you with joy for a long time. This will occur within three days.

seduce Seek help for an old emotional problem that keeps

arising. At the first sign of this, begin work to resolve it.

see To dream about your vision implies luck in all aspects of your life.

seed/seeds Before you give advice to someone about their future, take a good look at what is wrong with this picture. Take things step by step, and write down each detail to ensure that the advice given will be accurate. Information gained ahead of time in this case will be helpful in regards to referrals and information kept on hand but all referrals given should be checked first to ensure accuracy. This person will be very financially secure in the future. Always encourage stabilization of emotional relationships.

to plant Make sure when you offer assistance to another that you have all the details and the information necessary to give proper advice. The plans that you have set in motion should be reviewed in detail to ensure that they are being handled properly.

seedbed Do not push your in-laws around. Be cautious in the manner in which you communicate. Treat them properly.

seedcake Do everything necessary to prevent a premature birth. Warn others if it is appropriate.

seedling You will receive the professional help you have been seeking for a long time. Your health will respond well to this treatment.

seed money Work within the system and take steps to complete a project. Make sure you get the best results possible.

seed oysters You will enjoy a very prosperous life.

seedpod Your accomplishments will be received with honor.

seer A small risk will yield big profits. Do everything necessary to get a psychic reading. This will be to your advantage.

seersucker Do not give out your opinion in spite of how hard another person tries to pull it out. Two things can occur. Refusal to give out information will later be held against you and should you give out this information, you will be betrayed by the person receiving it. Do everything necessary to keep either one from occurring.

seesaw You are in danger of dealing with an explosive situation caused by someone who enjoys creating chaos. Do not react to this.

segregation Strong urges to travel will come over you. If you decide to travel you will have a wonderful time and will return safely.

seismograph Be very practical when making the final decision regarding the purchase of a major appliance, especially for the next three days. Good luck is with you.

seizure You are being forewarned that someone very close to you will be caught in a lie. Take care that you do not suffer emotional pain.

Selene *(Greek mythology)* You will victoriously grasp your highest ambitions.

self abuse Do whatever you have to in order to develop your potential. You will receive assistance at the last moment from someone you will probably never see again. This is also a warning to reform an ongoing behavior that is causing you emotional distress. Stay as stress free as possible.

self analysis Your coldness and aloofness toward a loved one will drive this person away, never to return.

self assurance Stop being so stubborn.

self competence Do not allow others to make demands on your time.

self confidence You will be sexually active with someone who will always need you.

self defense Be wary of hypnosis. Allow no one to hypnotize you for any reason.

self employed Do not overextend yourself physically. You are running on emotional energy. Do not become too involved with a close relative.

self examination Meditate in your favorite way and examine your innermost thoughts and goals and determine what you need in life.

self fulfillment Take a quick analysis of your life. Determine what is missing, what you need, and ways in which to fill these needs.

self hate You are facing serious problems. Look at ways to handle these problems within a few days before they become a crisis.

self hypnosis Do not delude yourself. Face reality and deal with things as they occur.

self image Choose your friends wisely.

self improvement You will be going through a stage of self improvement for the next few months. You will also change your physical appearance for the better.

self indulgence Someone will want to give you a pet. Decide for yourself whether you want this or not.

selfish You will become involved with a selfish stubborn

person within two days. If this is not what you want to deal with for the rest of your life, do not become involved.

self portrait Do not allow yourself to get back into a difficult situation that you left in the past. You may have forgotten the pain. This will remind you of these past feelings.

sell Everyone will be pleased with the partner you have chosen to spend your life with. You will also need to do everything necessary to become more independent.

seltzer Doors that were formerly closed to you will suddenly be open. You will be seen by others in a different light and new opportunities will be presented to you. Good luck is with you.

selvage You will receive good news through the mail within three days.

semen This implies that, if you choose this path, someone you are interested in will be eager to become a part of your life. Let your desires be known. You will enjoy many wonderful moments, sexual satisfaction and a mutually satisfying exchange within seven days. Aggressively pursue this. A little encouragement will allow this person to make the first move. If the person allows you to see their face, this implies that this person desires you to make the first move. Good luck is with you and your family.

semester For the next two days try to tolerate anything that comes up regarding other people and do not deprive those you care about of your affections. You will also have a very lucky experience within five days that will create an overwhelming feeling of excitement within you and this feeling will stay with you for a long period of time. Happiness and health will be yours.

semi-automatic A powerful revelation will occur within three days and will bring you a great sense of excitement because it will come directly to you from someone else's heart. Many blessings will come to you and your family. Any event in this dream that signifies a negative event can also be altered or avoided in reality. All positive messages need to be encouraged. Otherwise, this is an extremely lucky omen. Within three days, certain events will begin to occur at a very rapid pace. Take steps to put a lid on each situation you do not want to develop any further and do not wish to deal with. Many blessings are with you and you are headed for a brilliant future.

semi-circle You will hear of a very problematic situation. This will affect you only if you allow it. Relax, this problem will work itself out.

seminar Keep close track of your time.

seminary You will be involved in a very poor legal transaction. Keep records of everything. Read everything over carefully and keep track of each important piece of paper. Do not sign anything until you are sure this transaction is to your advantage.

Seminole Someone you know will suddenly become very lazy. As time passes, this laziness will increase. Remove yourself from this environment before you become this way. You are headed toward a prosperous future. Keep doing what you are doing.

semi-sweet Make it very clear to a certain person that you are not interested in a relationship the moment their intentions become obvious. Do not act in an undecided way around this person.

semitism You will have difficulty with children because of the company they are keeping. Protect your children from negative peer pressure and closely monitor friends for a six month period.

semi-trailer The answers to mysteries that have been bothering you will surface in a short while.

senate Do not arrange things behind the scenes. This will backfire on you.

senator Do not physically or sexually harass anyone. Be very conscious of your attitudes toward others.

send You will have to deal with a roommate who suddenly behaves in a psychotic manner. You will go through a few hours of terror but it turns out all right.

senile Do not trust children with anything of value.

senior citizen You will take a new approach to a complex problem and will find the solution you seek. You will also become very active in a very positive way and will find delight in attending new festivities. People will attend who will make it their business to ensure your financial security.

senor/senora You will encounter a very strange attitude from a superior. Do not place any importance on this behavior.

senorita You will receive an unusual and unexpected declaration of love from someone you hardly know.

sensitivity You will receive very shocking and alarming news over the phone within a few days. You are forewarned and can prepare yourself for the best way to handle this when it occurs.

sensor Avoid any argument that will involve the entire family.

sensual Keep up your appearance. Show off and have a great time.

sentence Do not allow your children to have so much con-

trol over your money.

sentimental You will enjoy a very social life.

sentinel Someone will accuse you of flirting with a stranger. Be very cautious of your behavior for the next week to protect yourself from all accusations.

sentry You will enjoy a very quiet and beautiful romance.

sentry box Better times and good news are coming. Anticipate this soon.

separation You are loved beyond your imagination.

sepia By carefully coaching another, you will gain fame through the popularity of the person you coach.

September You will experience a rush of greater mental intuitive energy. As a result, you will be quick to make changes which will grant major benefits to you and someone who is special to you. Mark your calendar because the days between September 23 and October 22 will bring you strange activities, gifts, and major benefits that you will need to take advantage of. You also need to ensure that your pulmonary system functions properly. This is a reminder to incorporate preventive medicine and/or a healthy lifestyle into your life in order to promote greater health. You are headed for a brilliant future. You will be very lucky for a long time.

septic You are unsure about the reputation of a friend. Do not become anxious over this because this friend is true to you.

septic tank You will unexpectedly come into a large sum of money within a few days and will also be taking on heavy responsibilities that may be more than you can handle. Think carefully before you accept this extra responsibility.

sepulcher Within three days a very delicate situation that appears to be spiraling downhill will take a turn for the better. Remain calm. Everyone involved will have the mental acuity to proceed in the correct fashion.

sequins The more expensive and elaborate your plans, the better the results. Be fanciful with your building plans and you will find more success through this refinement.

Sequoia Your opinions will gain a strong backing from others.

Sequoia Park Any committee you start will be very successful. Give each step your personal touch. This may also be used as a reference point in time. If you dream of this national park and see its name used in any context, the dream message will occur on this day.

serape Someone you meet under strange circumstances will play an increasingly larger role in your personal interests. This will please you.

seraph You will have an increasing amount of satisfaction and tranquility for a very long time.

serenade Do not allow the criticisms of other people keep you from discussing financial discrepancies.

serenity Keep doing what you are doing, you are headed in the right direction.

sergeant Take yourself away from an emotional situation and you will soon find the correct solution to this issue.

sergeant major Do not allow yourself to be sweet talked into manipulating someone else. You will deeply regret this involvement.

series Let someone know exactly how much time you are willing to commit to a project beforehand so there will be no disagreements.

serious *to be* Get some rest and relaxation. Create a stress free environment and nourish yourself.
others Do not deprive yourself emotionally.
to hear the phrase Be willing to discuss your emotional wants and needs. Follow your heart.

sermon You will be verbally threatened with violence. Take this threat seriously and get the appropriate help. This person is serious.

Sermon on the Mount You will become ill within two days. Do not take this lightly, it will develop into something more serious.

serpent Stop being so demanding of a special person. This will cause an argument that will last until a separation occurs.
sea serpent Beware of medications that will affect your thyroid. Eat healthy foods. Drink plenty of water and do nothing that will affect the balance of your system.
to stop a serpent from capturing anything You will enjoy victory in reaching your goals. Put more emphasis on creating positives out of negatives. Practice this immediately after the dream to ensure there are no disappointments or failures in meeting your goals.
to chase a serpent You will be able to turn a dangerous situation into a very triumphant one within a few weeks.
aggressive serpent A secretary will play petty games to promote jealousy for their own gratification. Do not concern yourself, nothing is really happening between this person and someone who is special to you.

serum Someone will unexpectedly drop in on you at a very strange time. This visit will bring you much satisfaction.
servant A blessed event will be celebrated by all.

to be a servant Strange events will occur rapidly over the next few days. You will also need to find ways of securing your income for the future.
to fire servants Protest loudly and use your influence to benefit people who do not have the clout that you do.

serve *to serve* You will plan an excursion within the next four days. Take precautions by consulting an expert on the locale and by researching the area.
to be served Ongoing group plans will be more beneficial to you than to your co-worker. If you are having second thoughts about becoming involved, don't. This will be a lucky cycle for teamwork.
to serve someone with papers You will feel very insecure about your relations with others. Within two days you will gain the evidence you need to validate the feelings of love others have for you.
to be served with papers The papers you are being served will provide a major clue to something you may want to avoid in the future. If it is a positive legal writ, such as a deed or will, promote this action in reality. This time period is also a good cycle for you romantically. Things will quickly move forward for you.

service Avoid dark and shadowy places. You will be frightened by something unexpected.

service station You will be renting a reception hall for a special event. Be sure you check to ensure it has not been double-booked for the evening of your event.

serving tray Someone you know will unexpectedly request a private sexual encounter. This will be a surprise and a shock to you. If you choose to pursue this, this person will let the world know of your intimacy and you will find this to be very delightful. It is your choice whether to pursue this or not. This time period will be very lucky for you.

sesame You will have to be politically correct in everything you do for the next two days. If you do not, a violent argument will break out because of your lack of sensitivity. This is preventable and you have enough notice of this to watch what you say. You must also tactfully remind others to address everyone with respect.
open sesame Make the time to have an overdue conversation with someone who is special. This will definitely make a difference in the approach that both of you make toward certain situations you will be involved with in the future. You are headed for a brilliant future. Proceed with confidence.

set *to be set to do anything in any form* High energy, legwork and attentiveness will be needed from you for the next few days in order to achieve success with an ongoing situation.
to set hair An assignment you have submitted will be turned down. Get special inside information in order to be successful.

to set back Show appreciation toward others and demonstrate your strong feelings for them.

to be set straight Stick to the truth of the matter.

to be set up Do not change any new arrangements you will be making this week.

to set someone straight Stay calm and collected for the next three days. A situation will come up during this time period that you will be tempted to become involved with. Do not allow yourself to become so upset with the problems of others that you attempt to take on their problems. Once you become involved it will be very difficult to become disentangled. You are only seeing the tip of the iceberg. Stay uninvolved.

settee Request special attention and help when you need it and do not allow yourself to be intimidated. Take care of and protect yourself.

settlement Do everything you can to introduce more amusements into your life and create a stress free environment. This will allow you to remain mentally healthy and maintain mental clarity. Remain free of the demands and responsibilities of other people and do not create extra burdens and responsibilities for yourself. Take a mini vacation. Rest, read, listen to good music, eat well and be good to yourself.

settler You are on the path toward a brilliant future. Your desires will be fulfilled and a special favor will be given to you. Many blessings are with you and your family.

seven This is a very lucky omen. Do not tell anyone your dreams for the next seven days. Allow only energetic, highly motivated people to work with you on assignments. You are in a wonderful cycle. Use this number when playing games of chance for the next seven days. Play the game for seven consecutive times. Mark your calendar and be acutely receptive on these particular days in order to receive benefits that will facilitate prosperity.

seventeen This is a lucky number to use in games of chance. Any unusual circumstance and occurrence during the next seventeen days needs to be included into your plans because greater success will be yours. This is a lucky cycle for you. Mark your calendar for these days and be acutely receptive on these particular days in order to receive benefits that will facilitate prosperity.

Seventh Day Adventists You will have an extraordinary invitation to a fabulous event that you will not easily forget. You will enjoy long nostalgic conversations about years past and this memory will last a lifetime.

seventy This is a lucky omen and indicates that you will go to extremes in your generosity to families who are in a time of need.

Seven Wonders of the World This is a lucky omen and you will be in a lucky cycle for months to come. Do not,

however, attempt do-it-yourself shortcut projects. Hire a professional. The job will be completed in half the time and for less money.

several You will be severely challenged by someone within the next few days. Rise to meet the challenge.

severance pay Someone will unexpectedly offer help to you.

severe It will be necessary to consult a professional. Make sure you are seeing the right consultant.

sew Someone who is running a successful scam will want to involve you. This will not work. Remain uninvolved.

sewer Do not, under any circumstance, shout angry words at another. You will never be able to take these words back and this will lead to permanent painful feelings.

sewing machine Use your power of authority to help others benefit from your position.

sex ***to be paid for sex*** You will be victorious while working with an associate toward a successful completion of a project.

to pay for sex Do not doubt yourself. Follow your own counsel when dealing with a situation that will arise within three days. You are going in the right direction.

to see others pay for sex Think ahead, someone owes you money and will be unable to repay you. Be creative and cleverly work out a situation that will enable this person to compensate by performing needed labor or contributing a needed skill. This will ensure you are repaid in another form. Arrangements need to be made within three days.

to ask or be asked for money in exchange for sex Do not doubt the loyalty of your loved one. You will also be successful this year in meeting your goals. If anything negative was depicted in this dream, take steps to change it or to avoid it entirely.

if you recognize the person you are sexually involved with This dream indicates that you will enjoy a marvelous short-term event within two days that will give you short-term pleasure. You will also be presented an opportunity within three days that will enable you to make extra cash. Watch for this opportunity. This dream also implies that you are using this dream to express a desire to have a pleasant emotional and sexual encounter, because you or this person you dreamed about want to take the safe approach via the dream without dealing with the consequences. Any negative aspect of this dream may be prevented in reality.

using lubricants for sexual purposes with someone you recognize Someone is very eager to respond to any demand you make from them for the next five days. You will be welcomed with open arms. This cycle will be very advantageous.

oral sex Someone will go to great lengths to ensure your success in the business world. You are also loved and appreciated, especially by those who fail to demonstrate their feelings.

you are a member of the opposite sex Within five days you will be entering a very lucky cycle and everyone involved in your life will share your luck. During this time period you can expect many wonderful connections that will assist you in meeting and surpassing your goals. You can also expect a mega merger and the energy created between you and those you will be working with bring you to a far higher level of success than you hoped for. This also implies that you will gain benefits through attending a festive event, through an educational experience or through a gathering you attend in which one person will show an interest in you and your projects. You can look forward to a long period of tranquility following this and enjoy a prosperous future. Any negative event associated with this dream may be avoided.

crotch Someone you cared deeply about will return from a sudden departure overseas. This person went away in order to test your feelings for them. As a result, you have become resentful and have stopped caring. Be very honest about how you feel in order to move on with your life.

anything unusual occurring in the crotch area with either sex This implies that you make sure there are no miscommunications, mixed messages or misconceptions. Make sure others are hearing exactly what you are saying and what you think you are hearing is exactly what you are hearing. For the next three days do not allow yourself to be sucked into any disagreements or volatile situations. Remember you have the power to change any negative situation foretold in this dream concerning either yourself or someone else. Many blessings are with you and you are headed in the correct direction.

in any other form Any dream you have involving sex indicates that you must not become lost in the exuberance and excitement that follows a pleasant sexual dream to the point of not practicing caution in everyday affairs. This could lead to a freak accident. You must also make sure you practice safe sex. Be extra good to yourself and reward yourself with a small gift. You will enjoy many blessings. Any goal you set out to accomplish will be completed successfully. You will also receive the proper advice from a qualified professional and things will work out to your advantage. Any negative event depicted in this dream needs to be prevented in reality.

sex appeal It is important that you have people in your life who really understand you and believe in what you stand for so they can have a better grasp of your circumstances. It is important that you specify your needs clearly so they will become more supportive.

sex chromosome You will come to an understanding between yourself and a special committee. This will be very enjoyable.

sex symbol You will have an unusual opportunity to reach your goals within the next two days.

sextant Within three days you will enjoy love and passion from the person you desire the most. You will enjoy good luck and an abundance of health during this time period. This person has a deep need to express their feelings to you. This is a good time to get the things you feel have stagnated moving rapidly in the right direction.

sexual harassment *any form* Within a five day period someone is planning to violate your rights simply for their own emotional pleasure. This person will try to manipulate you into becoming involved in something you find highly distasteful, sexually or in any other capacity. This involvement will go directly counter to your better judgment and will be against your will. Do not place yourself in a position that will require you to compromise yourself in order to get out safely. You have prior notice of this and can prevent this occurrence. Good luck is with you.

sexual intercourse *to enjoy* Someone you are close to will make a great financial decision that will result in large financial improvements in your life.

to find sexual intercourse distasteful You will meet someone with a great deal of wealth who is obsessed with owning and controlling you. Once this individual is secure in the knowledge that they have you, they will leave. This may take a year and until this happens you will be given anything you desire. In reality, although this person may be sexually attractive to you, you will be hesitant about complying because of the feeling that something is not quite right. Your instincts are correct, this person will break your heart.

to hear the phrase Within three days, you will find the encouragement you need to meet you goals.

entering into a fresh and new relationship If you choose, a new relationship will grow into a very stable union.

to recognize the person you are engaged in intercourse with Someone desires you deeply in a sexual way and you will gain knowledge of this within two days. The option is open to you whether to act on this or not. If you choose this option, you will find the encounter very satisfying.

violent sexual encounter Within two days take steps to prevent a violent sexual encounter from occurring.

sexually aroused penis Be good to yourself and reward yourself with a small gift. You will have many blessings.

sexual organs *to see someone with no visible sexual organs, only hair* Someone will enter your life within five days and will give you the impression they function sexually as a total person. This individual, however, has no interest in you, sexual or otherwise. You will be unsure of the reason why this person has entered your life. Don't waste your time. This person will offer very little and is unsure of what they want.

pubic hair Within two days, a situation will take place that will be so extraordinary it will defy any law of physics. Within three days, this strange event will leave you with a sense of awe and wonder and you will sense you have witnessed a miracle with no way to explain how it transpired.

After this takes place, you will be able to present yourself at your best and will be able to handle yourself, other people and situations in the best possible way. You will see greater improvements than you ever thought possible. Your sense of awareness will be heightened and you will be able to sense the knowledge you need to retrieve. You are definitely headed for a brilliant future and many blessings will come to you and your family.

shack Do not misinterpret another's body language to mean they have a sexual interest in you. You will be mistaken.

shackles You will be easily tricked by someone within a few days. This person is a monster in disguise. Be wary and guard against this event.

shade It would be a good idea to change your schedule and route for the next few days. You will be robbed of some luxury items if you do not.

shades *(window)* *to pull one down* Within a three day period you will experience an interesting display of attention from a member of the opposite sex and you will be thrilled to receive this attention.

to put the shades up When you have a romantic episode, include all of the right touches, create the perfect atmosphere and take time to experience the full range of romantic foreplay. This is likely to occur within four days.

shadow *to see your shadow* You will be pushed to the limit by someone within two days. You will be able to handle this situation correctly and with confidence.

to see another's shadow Don't involve yourself in situations that you find distasteful.

a pleasing shadow Your wishes will be granted in business and love matters. You are entering a good luck cycle for the next seven days. Take advantage of this time period for business and love matters.

to be afraid of a shadow A depraved person with a strong sexual appetite will attempt to coerce you into performing a sexually immoral and distasteful act. This act will be watched first hand and will be recorded on film for later viewing. You have the power to avoid this. Do not involve yourself with this person or allow yourself to be taken for granted. Do not engage in any activity you feel is immoral and do not gamble. Any negative event foretold in this dream may be avoided or altered in reality. Take steps to alert anyone you dreamed about to do the same. Make sure you only experience positive expressions in your life.

perfect human shadow Within five days, you will be placed in the position of vigorously caring for another individual until they are able to stand on their own feet. This person will be able to improve their quality of life and physical state to the point of personal and social acceptance. You will also be swamped with social activities for this time period. Make an effort to keep up your appearance and attire. This will be a successful cycle for you.

horrifying human shadow You are overextending your-

self to the point of physical exhaustion. For the next week, work to improve your health by eating properly, drinking plenty of water and setting limits on what you are willing to do for others. In spite of how impossible it may seem, all requests made of your higher power will now be granted.

to see an unidentifiable person in the shadows Within five days you will be dealing with someone who will lead you to believe they are very respected, professional, stable in their career, financially secure, and have a very credible lifestyle. You will find this person to be very eager to involve you in their life in some capacity. They will be very believable and you will be so comfortable and assured in their company that you will want to become involved with them. This person will give you every indication that you have easy access to them at any given time and you will be given several phone numbers, company addresses, etc. to track them down. If you take the time to try to get in touch with them you will find it is impossible to reach them. It will take hours or days for this person to return any calls. You will come to the realization this person has led you to believe they have a more impressive status than they do. If you allow yourself to become involved in any capacity you will be let down. Be very shrewd and disciplined in order to prevent anyone from violating your emotions or insulting your intelligence. Because you have prior notice of this you will be able to deal with this issue very successfully. You will be very lucky and are headed for a prosperous future.

shadowbox Take it slowly for the next seven days in order to avoid accidents of any kind.

shaft Do not talk so much about your job on your days off. People will think you are not interested in them.

shag carpet You will have wonderful luck with a new business associate.

shake *to grab someone by the shoulders and shake them* You are growing very tired of something that is occurring in reality and you will be very anxious to communicate to someone else what you are tired of. This will be obvious by the way you shake this person in the dream. Pay close attention to who you were shaking and the reasons why. The person you dreamed about will either be the person you need to encourage to make changes in their life or will represent someone (by way of personality, mannerisms, etc.) whom you wish would make changes. You will then be able to make it clear to this individual and to yourself what you want them to change, or anything new that you want to introduce into your life.

to be taken by the shoulders and/or shaken, etc. Someone will take advantage of you without your awareness. This individual will be deceptive and dishonest and will use you in a situation as an innocent, unwitting participant. You will be cheated in the long run. Pay close attention to your ongoing situations and be acutely aware of the behavior of others in order to prevent this.

shaker Plead with a relative to act on your behalf for what you need help with.

Shakespeare You will now have the long awaited opportunity to join a certain desirable group. Motivate yourself to act on this so this opportunity will not be passed on to someone else. You will also find this group to be very social and will enjoy high living. This will bring you great joy.

shaking *to see another person shaking* Someone desires you very much. Within four days this person will not be able to control themselves. You will know a bit more about them after a short time and will have more information about what they will be able to offer in a relationship.

to see yourself shaking Someone you hold very dear to you will be ill treated in a subtle but painful way by someone you least expect within two days. As a result of this, you will experience hurt feelings and quickly develop feelings of resentment toward this individual. Do everything you can to avoid this scenario and if you must go through it, take steps to be emotionally prepared. This also implies you will enjoy a big victory that is not connected in any way with the aforementioned situation but will occur within the same time period.

shaking hands You have a certain feeling about a person and want to involve them in your project. You are very independent and if you follow this instinct you will create a dynamic synergism. A fortunate and prosperous future is ahead of you. Good luck.

to be shaking hands You will be falling deeply in love and will be eager to make a commitment soon.

shale Let someone know in a very caring way that you are not ready to become involved just yet. You will be pleased about their desire for involvement and will be ready to commit within a two week period. Assure this person you will contact them when you are feeling more secure.

shallot Stick to your plans. Be fruitful.

sham Do not allow yourself to be taken in by con artists for the next two days.

shame You will suffer grief over the loss of a close relative.

shamefaced You will enjoy life and will always be surrounded by people you enjoy as well as their families. These people will all be the opposite sex. This will be a close knit, caring group.

shameful You will attend a funeral in the near future.

shampoo Someone who holds you in high regard will fall deeper in love with you as time goes by. You will need to continue showing a deep commitment.

shanghai Within two days a new turn of events will immediately affect your romantic life. Make sure you do exactly

what you want to.

shank For the next few days, try to limit your spending when in the company of others. Handle this subtly and with tact.

shanty Be very careful of situations that can lead to jealousy and arguments, especially for the next three days. This situation is preventable.

shape Someone who has the power and ability to help you will be unwilling to. Do not rely on your first choice.

perfect human shape Within five days you will find yourself caring for someone until they are able to care for themself. This person will improve their physical well being and quality of life until they reach social and personal acceptance. You will also be swamped with social engagements and must make an effort to maintain your best appearance and wear your best attire during this time period. You will enjoy a very successful cycle.

horrifying human shape You are overexerting yourself to the point of physical burn out. For the next seven days do what you can to maintain and improve your health. Eat healthful foods, drink plenty of water and put limits on what you are willing to do for others. For the next week, all requests you make of your god will also be granted no matter how improbable they may seem.

shapeless Someone you are involved with in some capacity will have last minute troubles. It is better to delay any decisions for a few days.

share Someone you are involved with wants to minimize their involvement with you. Be patient. After a few months, this person will seek a deeper relationship and will become very generous and kind. Take it easy now and back off.

shareholder Be very cautious for the next two weeks.

shark You will have the courage to become less timid and more assertive. Once this process begins, you will feel relieved and confident. You are also putting too much importance on someone who is only trying to confuse you emotionally by giving mixed messages. Do not become too involved and stop catering to this person.

to kill a shark Do not point fingers at others. Work on resolving your own problems.

to eat Someone who has caused you emotional pain in the past will return to see if you will be as vulnerable as before. This time this person will pursue you. It is your decision whether you want to go along with this. You will also overcome all of your obstacles.

shark swimming away from you Place less importance on others and more on yourself. You will also be relieved of a long standing burden.

to be bitten Focus on what is really behind a family situation. Be suspicious and wary of everything for the next seven days to ensure that all of your bases are covered. Remain alert; this will keep you from being taken by surprise by anything unusual. Do not permit anything to threaten your family status. Jealousy and game playing can easily lead to arguments that will disrupt family tranquility. Any negative event occurring in this dream needs to be prevented in reality. You have enough prior notice to protect yourself.

the shark is biting someone else Take the time to warn the person you dreamed about and recognize to be acutely aware of their surroundings and protect themselves from danger for the next four days. Do everything necessary to assist this person and ensure that they are safe while in your presence. Make sure, also, that you check all facts given to you and ensure that information you receive is not the product of someone else's imagination.

aggressive shark Take every necessary step to prevent incarceration because of your aggressive behavior. Learn to control this behavior. Do not jeopardize your freedom.

sharkskin Do not leave yourself open to someone who has a hidden agenda. This could lead to a very unusual and perverted experience that will bring you many unpleasant and distasteful moments. Take steps, for the next three days, to avoid this. This person is someone you will feel very comfortable with. You will be surprised that this person will turn on you the moment you become vulnerable. Keep yourself safe.

sharp *the slang term* Within the week you will be asked out by someone you do not know well. This person has a strange manner and will become a danger to you. You will be unable to escape from this horrifying experience. Do everything you can to avoid having anything to do with this situation. This is preventable. Avoid all unfamiliar places and do not go to anyone's house whom you do not know well. You will be held against your will in a life threatening situation.

sharp *quick-acute* Someone will commit an act they have no business doing and will be caught. You will benefit greatly by this person's downfall.

sharp *cutting or piercing* Seek out someone with clout and influence to help you in a particular situation.

sharpen Take the time to see the benefits before pulling out of a situation. Things you originally felt were distasteful will turn out not to be. Be more flexible in order to gain greater benefits.

sharp shooter Someone will pull out of a project at the wrong time. Be prepared for this and begin searching for a replacement ahead of time.

shatter *to see glass shatter* You will need to be aware of another person's irresponsibility. This will catch you off guard. Be prepared and do not allow yourself to be taken.

shatterproof Prevent loss of property or valuables due to excess moisture.

shave *to shave* You will be tempted by an attractive offer. Go for it. It is in your destiny to accept this offer.

in any other form This indicates that it is important for the next five days not to focus on another person's actions, decisions or choices to justify the need to make changes in your life. The moment you find your thoughts drifting to concerns about what another person is doing or how a situation is evolving, take that energy to reinvent and recreate yourself. You will then be able to improve your personal environment and benefit yourself and others.

shawl For the next three days do everything necessary to protect yourself and a friend from harm after six p.m. You will be harassed by a group of dangerous people.

Shawnee Be very careful and take steps to avoid injuries, especially accidental self-inflicted blows to the body. This will be very important for the next three days.

sheaf Circumstances will change within a few days and you will not be so willing to adopt another person's way of life. You will be irritated because of this. This situation is out of your control so do whatever is necessary to maintain your peace of mind.

shears You will live a long life. Eat healthful foods so you can enjoy this life illness free. You will also be blessed with the ability to form detailed and clear thoughts. This will help you to successfully deal with an upcoming issue. Expect this to take place within a few days.

sheath Someone's state of mind you are focused on now is not that healthy. Be cautious when making joint decisions.

shed You will receive a prize through the mail; lucky you.

sheep Start compiling information ahead of time before resuming responsibility for the work of those you supervise. Someone will be interested in reviewing your methods.

sheepdog The person you will be seeking financial help from will want to speak to you in private. This person wants this transaction to remain a secret. Be sure to keep this private if you want the loan.

sheepherder Your agenda will be filled with time consuming problems for the next few days. Do not allow the problems of others to take up your time because it is better spent attending to necessary things.

sheep, mountain Stay focused on what you really want from life and go after it for the next three days. Eat healthy foods, get plenty of rest and drink plenty of water. Many blessings will come to you and your family.

sheep shearing Negative thoughts about that special person are unfounded.

sheepskin You will enjoy matrimonial harmony.

sheers You will receive what you want out of a relationship.

sheet Be firm and consistent while maintaining a positive way of life.

sheet cake A special person in your life will plan an unusual pleasurable evening. This will please both of you.

sheet lightning Plan your next move carefully.

sheet metal Something very important and dynamic will happen in your life. Be patient. You are destined for this event.

sheet music Business contacts will be eager to help you out in a venture you are now putting into action. It only takes a phone call.

sheik You will become aggressive in the pursuit of something you want. Be patient and take it a step at a time over the next few days.

shelf Someone will demonstrate affection toward you. Take this seriously because this person loves you deeply.

shell For the next few days apply yourself fully in your pursuit of something you really need to do. You will reap big dividends.

shellac Do not allow yourself to be talked into a ménage à trois. This will be a disaster and all those involved will be hurt.

shellfish Become very bold and daring while taking care of a certain task. You will then be inspired to complete the job. Within three days, you will also have to divulge a great deal of information about yourself. This will give someone a chance to understand you better and they will then be able to pull strings and make decisions in your favor. You are headed for a brilliant future. Go ahead with the big changes you want to make in our life.

shell game You need to think carefully about plans to pull out of a situation. Do not make any sudden changes now.

shell shock Avoid the creation of any personal problems.

shelter For the next few days you will begin to develop doubts about someone you know. This is letting you know that you can put aside these doubts because this person is loyal to you. You must also do what you can to limit your business with someone else. Watch your behavior.

sheltie A special person will suddenly rush you into a sexual

relationship. This will be a once in a lifetime event.

shepherd Be more sympathetic to someone who is dealing with an issue that is truly out of their control. This person really has a feeling of helplessness.

Shepherd's pie Make sure people respect and appreciate your abilities to produce.

sherbet You will have a wonderful time with a group of young children. You will also need to make sure that people who request your paid services receive it. Make yourself available to those who are in need of your services.

sheriff Get plenty of rest in order to keep your mental energy going.

Sherlock Holmes Put your affairs in order within a few days.

sherry In a short time, someone will ease their way into your heart. Before you know it, you will be totally in love. This person will care deeply for you.

Sherwood Forest Someone will attempt to sway you to their side. This person has a bad disposition and a bad reputation. Do everything necessary to avoid involvement. This may also be used as a reference point in time. If you dream of this place and see its name used in any context, the dream message will occur on this day.

Shetland pony You will always be the center of someone's life for the remainder of their life.

Shetland wool Do not dwell on decisions that are made by others and are out of your control.

shield You will enjoy a spending spree with someone else's money at their encouragement.

shilling Avoid nosy people who are seeking private information from you. Get on with your life without them.

shimmer Watch the chemicals you work with. Some are odorless and seem harmless but still pose a risk. You and a special person will also be in perfect agreement over a major decision. You will experience deep and kind feelings toward them.

shin You will be dealing with a workaholic of the same gender. Remind this person we have only one life and that they need to slow down and enjoy it.

shine Make sure any event you are planning to attend is not ruined because food or refreshments, etc., run short. This will take place at an event you will be involved with within the week.

shingle A much younger person will offer assistance in the most timely fashion.

shin splint This implies that within three days you will be in the presence of a certain individual who will verbally coerce you to agree to something they want you to do. They will do everything in their power to corner you and coerce you into behaving in a manner they wish as well as having you verbalize statements they wish you to make. Be very careful of this because this individual can be very forceful in trying to get their way. You have prior notice of this and can take the appropriate steps to avoid it.

ship You need to be focused and analytical about each move you make. This will allow you to achieve prosperity.

to see yourself on board Someone will suddenly seem more attentive toward you.

to see a shipwreck Do not give your new address to anyone if you do not want to be found. It is better to get a P.O. Box. Any negative event seen in this dream needs to be prevented in reality.

to see a ship on fire Emphasize more romance and foreplay in your sexual encounters. Any negative event seen in this dream needs to be prevented in reality.

to see a ship sink Do not allow prying family members to alter your decisions. Sometimes advice is good, but not during this cycle. Any negative event seen in this dream needs to be prevented in reality.

to be on a ship in rough seas You are headed in the wrong direction. Take the time to regroup and investigate what you need to do in order to put yourself on the right track. Do not allow anyone to manipulate you in such a way that you are led off the correct path. Any negative event seen in this dream needs to be prevented in reality.

shipbuilder Sharpen your skills and put them to use in a different way to provide financial security.

shipmates You will receive a beautiful, expensive gift from afar.

shipment A favor will be granted to you.

shipping clerk A younger person will fall deeply in love with you.

shipping room Life's greatest rewards will be yours in the near future.

shipyard Life is too short. Be sure you tell those you feel strongly about that you love them. Become more open to your friends and family and make sure you openly and publicly verbalize your love for others. Do not hold your feelings inside. Your creative work will also be admired. You are headed in the right direction.

shirt Think ahead. Your future will blossom in any field that involves travel. This cycle will be very fortunate for you. Within two days you will begin the process of placing

yourself in the position to experience greater wealth and you can expect a brilliant future.

soiled Be more affectionate with those you care about.

torn Keep a close eye on all expected mail. An important piece will be intercepted by someone else and you will not receive it. Keep an eye on this for the next two weeks.

polo shirt You will soon be able to decide on the person you should involve yourself with. This person is very knowledgeable and will be able to offer their help in finding a solution to a particular issue.

shirttail Use your inventive talents for greater profit. This is a great cycle for displaying these talents and you will be a brilliant success. Someone will also be eager to get you involved in a project that will be presented to you within two days but you will not be excited by the idea. Realize that the benefits are far greater than you ever anticipated. Good luck is with you.

shirtwaist A very unusual event will take place and this will lead you to feel inferior when in the company of another person. This feeling will be there because this person is far more physically fit than you are and you will wish that you had the same level of stamina they do. Do not belittle yourself and accept the fact that each person has a different energy level. Within the month you can also expect an extra drain on your finances. Start putting aside extra money now so that you will be able to meet this additional expense. Good luck is with you and you are headed for a prosperous future.

shish kebob Within a few days you will have to make a public appearance. Allow yourself time to get there, otherwise you will run late. You will receive applause and many accolades after your appearance.

shiver Within three days you will receive a powerful revelation that will be particularly exciting because it will come directly to you from someone's innermost feelings. Many blessings will come to you and your family.

shock Use protective measures against con artists.

shock absorber If you are not willing to go along with something, state your mind clearly.

shocking For the next few days, someone in authority will be nicer to you than anyone ever has. Do not allow this niceness to precede a work overload.

shock therapy Make sure that all the people who will be attending a reunion show up without overt problems or emotional stress. Make sure there are no lingering animosities or unresolved problems before you allow the reunion to proceed.

shock wave You will not be supported in your decisions by that special person in your life.

shoe bag This is an omen for health, prosperity, and ongoing financial success. A roommate will also hold small trivial things against you that you do not expect. Prevent any small issue from turning into a resentment and do not allow anyone to take advantage of you. Be very aware of this over the next two days.

shoe rack Move quickly. For the next three days you will be in a very lucky cycle. You are working on several things that require immediate attention. Utilize this cycle to improve these situations.

shoes *new* Someone will enter your life full of kindness. This will develop into the deep love you have always wanted. At first this will seem to be an impossibility but now all things are possible.

used Stick to your work schedule and go all out for entertainment in your spare time.

high heeled Because of the unexpected declaration of someone's love for you, you will experience a feeling of exuberance and excitement. If you choose, this can develop into a relationship on any level you choose and will lead to mutual fulfillment.

platform Develop the motivation to make something happen. You will be able to ask the key questions needed to determine what it is that you need to do. Wonderful events will occur that permit what is destined to happen to take place.

raggedy This is a very lucky omen for you. It implies that you will develop the strength and courage from within that you need within a two day period. This drive will motivate you to overcome all hidden mental and physical barriers and rid yourself of any negative aspect of your life. You will quickly see a clear path and acquire the knowledge you need to develop those aspects of your personality you wish to improve on. You will also be able to develop the perfect lifestyle for yourself. This is the perfect cycle to accomplish this. You will be placed on a pedestal and greeted like royalty anywhere you choose to go. This will come as a big surprise to you. You are headed for a brilliant future and many new opportunities will be presented to you.

saddle shoes Keep your opinions to yourself and play it safe.

tennis shoes You will hear news of a pregnancy. You will also enjoy prosperity and many blessings will come to you and your family. You are definitely on the path toward a brilliant future. If you see the exact shoes you dreamed of being worn, your dream will become a reality within three days. Any negative event depicted in this dream needs to be turned into a positive.

tight Do not panic at events that are out of the norm. These are temporary situations.

many pairs This is a lucky omen. You will hear about the reconciliation of a couple you are friends with.

in any other form You are entering a wonderful cycle to win over someone you are interested in romantically. Take

aggressive action on this in order to prod this person to communicate openly with you in the manner you desire. You will suffer no repercussions for being the one who makes the first move if you do this with kindness and open, friendly conversation. Both of you are headed toward a brilliant future. If you see the exact shoes you dreamed of or worn by someone else, expect your dream to come true within three days.

shoeshine You will enjoy victory in all phases of your life.

shoestring Remove that chip from your shoulder and enjoy life on its own terms.

shoe tree You will enjoy a bounty from anything you grow.

Shogun Your relationships will be filled with tranquility and peace. For the upcoming month you will be pursued by a variety of admirers. One of them will become a permanent part of your life if this is something you desire. This is an extremely lucky omen and you are on the path for future prosperity.

shoot *to see someone shoot someone else* Within the week you will be invited to an outing by someone you know only slightly. You will become terrified by this person's strange behavior and this person will, at some point, become dangerous. You will not be able to find a means of escape. Do what you can to avoid this situation. You have prior notice and can prevent its occurrence. Do not go to any unfamiliar places or someone else's house whom you do not know well. You will be held against your will in a life threatening situation. Any negative event in this dream that could occur in reality needs to be changed into a positive expression. You have prior notice and can take steps to handle this.

to shoot Express your feelings to those you care about and take steps to become involved sexually with someone you are currently interested in. Invite this person, within five days, to a planned romantic setting. Any negative event in this dream that could occur in reality needs to be changed into a positive expression. You have prior notice and can take steps to handle this.

to be shot at You are waiting to receive important papers. Do not allow yourself to feel so complacent about the arrival of this paperwork. Another person is eager to intercept the papers before you receive them in order to gain the advantage. Take steps to prevent this occurrence. Any negative event in this dream that could occur in reality needs to be changed into a positive expression. You have prior notice and can take steps to handle this.

shootout For the next four days, do not allow others to waste time when dealing with important paperwork. Time is valuable and someone will intentionally delay filling out papers that are important to you. Tactfully demand that the work gets done in order to avoid missing deadlines. You will then benefit from a prompt response.

in any other form You will gain headway with an elusive person if you act within two days because this person will be leaving for a vacation and will be in a good mood. You must also get a grip on your temper and take steps to learn to control yourself. You will find yourself becoming suspicious and jealous because of a strange situation that will develop and drive you into uncontrollable rage. This rage will cause you to do something you will later regret. Once you notice these feelings starting to develop, seek professional help in order to avoid committing a regrettable act. Any negative event in this dream that could occur in reality needs to be changed into a positive expression. You have prior notice and can take steps to handle this.

shooting gallery Remove all invisible barriers by utilizing good communication skills and by dealing with situations head on.

shooting star Your wishes will come true. You will also be invited to an elegant aristocratic event and will enjoy yourself immensely.

shop Develop a more romantic attitude and go all out for a romantic evening.

consignment shop You will come into riches from an area that is presently unknown to you. Move ahead on this with confidence.

shoplifter Divorce yourself from the actions of others.

shopping bag This is a very lucky omen. Choose an advocate to handle an ongoing situation so you can get on with your life.

shopping center Allow yourself to have fun for the next few days. Be outrageous and do the forbidden in a fun way. Go all out for a good time. This is a wonderful and lucky cycle for you.

shore Within four days someone will present an unexpected and unlikely proposal to you. This proposal will seem so good that it will be difficult to accept because of its outrageous nature. It will seem impossible to accomplish and you will want to pass on it. Take a few days to mull this over and make sure you do not burn any bridges. At a later time you will want to explore this in more detail to determine whether this can be brought to fruition. Although you will have the feeling that this proposal is an impossibility, it will happen and this person will keep each commitment. Good luck is with you.

beautiful You will experience a wonderful love that you have been long awaiting.

offshore For the next three weeks everything will fall into place exactly as you wish. You are definitely headed for a prosperous future.

polluted You have been waiting for a particular love for a long time. Do not ruin this by not being romantic enough. Separate romantic moments from time meant for physical activity. Do not combine these activities and love will blos-

som to maturity.

rocky seaweed covered Become assertive in your approach to bring a particular individual closer to you. This is a perfect cycle for behaving in such a way that will cause this individual to feel comfortable enough in your presence to say those words you have longed to hear. Many blessings will come to you and your family and you are headed for a prosperous cycle.

shorebird A casual relationship will develop to a deeper level. The other partner will leave the relationship because you will be unable to express your feelings. You will feel that by expressing your deep feelings, you would drive them away. This is clearly a case of misunderstanding. Get together with this person to clarify the status of the relationship.

shortage Within two days either you or someone precious to you will be mistreated by someone else in a subtle but very painful way. This will be someone you least expect and you will soon begin harboring hurt feelings and deep resentments toward this person. Do everything you can to avoid this situation altogether or, if you cannot avoid it, take steps to prepare yourself emotionally. This also implies that you will enjoy a big victory that is completely unconnected with this issue but will take place during this time period.

shortbread Do everything possible to introduce more fun and amusement into your life and work to create a stress free environment. This will allow you to remain mentally healthy as well as maintaining your mental clarity. Do not overload yourself with the problems of other people and free yourself of responsibilities and burdens that do not belong to you. Do not add any extra burdens and responsibilities of your own creation. Take a short vacation, rest, read, listen to good music, eat healthful foods and treat yourself well.

shortcake Special knowledge that you have acquired and recorded needs to be protected until it is copy written. This will be a special gold mine for you. Hasten the copywriting process.

shortchanged This implies you will be short changed within a few days.

short circuit You will be asked by someone to do something so difficult that it will seem impossible to accomplish. Methodically and relentlessly work on this until you shape and mold this project into what you want. You will find success.

shortcut Do not take shortcuts on a project. Carefully go through each detail to ensure it is done correctly. Also you will receive a verbal threat that will affect you tremendously. Either this person is not sure of who they are talking to or is mistaking you for someone else. In either case, this will be an extremely dangerous situation to be involved in and is likely to occur within three days. You need to increase your awareness in order to stay safe and clear of anyone's focus who has an evil intent. Because of your prior notice you will be able to avoid harm. Use any power you have at your disposal to make sure you remain safe.

shorten You will develop the confidence to take the small risks that are necessary to handle a particular situation that will vastly improve your standard of living. Make sure you follow all the necessary rules and regulations. You also have some very strong feelings about something you feel should be accomplished soon.

shortening You will receive advice from someone who has prior experience with your problem. It is wise that you follow this person's advice.

shorthand Someone in your immediate vicinity will be afflicted with a mental illness. This person will become overly aggressive and behave oddly around you. You have been forewarned and will be able to avoid this within three days.

shortstop For the next few days you will need to keep your feelings and emotions in check. A situation will take place that will leave you feeling as though you have been left out of something. As a result, you will become very focused on this to the point of obsession. Do not make matters worse by feeding into it emotionally. Focus on other matters that are far more important for you to take care of.

shortwave Do not involve yourself in petty games that involve withholding love from someone you care about. It will not last and you will regret it.

shot Within two days, you will reach out emotionally to someone in a time of need. This person will be unable to respond to the extent you desire and this will leave you bewildered. Regroup, remain calm and go on with your life. You cannot depend on others to fulfill all of your emotional needs. Learn to rely on yourself. Any negative event in this dream that could occur in reality needs to be changed into a positive expression. You have prior notice and can take steps to handle this.

to see someone else shot Someone has a deep desire to speak with you but has not yet found a way to get across some important information. This information will ease your mind and allow you both to freely exchange information about a particular situation. This also implies that you will come into an unexpected windfall just in the nick of time. Make sure any negative event portended in this dream does not become a reality. Alert everyone involved that you recognize to take steps to avoid injury. Many blessings will come to you and your family for the next seven days. Any negative event in this dream that could occur in reality needs to be changed into a positive expression. You have prior notice and can take steps to handle this.

to be shot Within the week, you will have an overwhelming feeling of balance, confidence and the sense of being solidly grounded. As a result of this, you will easily handle those situations that require this aspect of your personality. Use this cycle to work on those areas of your life that you desire to change. You will have the chance to bring prosperity into your life on any level you desire. You are on your way toward a brilliant future. You must also take steps to prevent any negative event in this dream from becoming a reality. You have prior notice and can take steps to handle it.

shotgun Understand and recognize that you are very important in another person's life. Nothing in the way of personal possessions could take your place. Your love will deepen. Any negative event in this dream that could occur in reality needs to be changed into a positive expression. You have prior notice and can take steps to handle this.

to hear a shot gun blast You are your own worst enemy. Attempt to visualize what you are doing because you could get yourself into serious legal trouble. Devise a plan that will require you to be supervised in order to keep from breaking the law. Any negative event in this dream that could occur in reality needs to be changed into a positive expression. You have prior notice of this and can take steps to handle it.

in any other form Situations will occur within three days and you must make it a point of not making them worse by dwelling on the issues that are taking place. Motivate yourself to get busy on new ideas that you need to work on.

shotgun wedding An angry enemy will be seeking revenge against you. This could lead to a physical public attack. Take precautions to avoid this.

shot put Within a few days you will become increasingly involved in a situation that becomes more mysterious as each day goes by. Do not give up your attempt at solving this. The answer will soon come.

shoulder Any endeavor you become involved in will be more fulfilling than you originally anticipated. It is important that you develop your venture as soon as possible.

to be tapped on your shoulder or any other form Someone will send you a material message (i.e., flowers, candy, a gift, etc.) to express their deep feelings for you. This person also desires that your involvement grow and bloom. Good luck is with you.

to tap someone on the shoulder or any other form Pay close attention to who you were tapping. If you recognize the person, this individual will be instrumental in helping you to shape a brilliant future. If you did not recognize this person, you will be offered a large amount of money for services you can easily provide in a non-stressful way. Good luck is with you.

to grab someone by the shoulders and shake them You are growing very tired of something that is occurring in reality and you are very anxious to communicate this to someone else. This will be obvious by the way you shake this person in the dream. Pay close attention to who you were shaking and the reasons why. The person you dreamed about will either be the person you need to encourage to make changes in their life or will represent someone (by way of personality, mannerisms, etc.) whom you wish would make changes. You will then be able to make it clear to this individual what you want them to change, the behavior you want them to stop or start, or anything new that you want to introduce into your life.

to be taken by the shoulders and/or shaken, etc. Someone will take advantage of you without your awareness. This individual will be deceptive and dishonest and will use you in a situation as an innocent, unwitting participant. You will be cheated in the long run. Pay close attention to your ongoing situations and be acutely aware of the behavior of others in order to prevent this.

to hear the phrase and to get the cold shoulder Someone has plotted ways to get what they want and need from you and you will be drained by this person's constant requests for favors that they can do themselves. You must also become aware that you will be spending money on them, a little bit at a time. This money will add up over time. This person is also insincere and unable to be open and upfront with you. This individual is one thing to you and something else to others, and will tell people only what they think people want to hear. You would be better off without them in your life.

shoulder bag Someone will ask for a loan from you. Think carefully about this before making a decision because this loan could lead to later regrets and resentments.

shoulder blade You will be undergoing changes and will experience a new way of living.

shoulder harness You will shortly be transferred to a new location.

shoulder holster Be prepared for surprises for the next few days. Do not allow yourself to be caught off guard. Remain calm.

shout *to shout* Do not become involved in an angry, petty verbal exchange with a cunning individual who is aching for a fight.

shove *to shove* A new responsibility will be a showcase for your actions. Be very conscious of what you are doing.

"shove it" *to use this phrase or hear it used* This is a warning that within three days you will be associating with someone who is very aware of your likes and dislikes. This person also knows about the kind of lifestyle and issues that go against your principles. By using methods of subtle persuasion, this person will be able to devise a plan that will slowly lead you into the lifestyle you are against. Many different tactics will be used in order to get you to do their bidding such as gift giving, vacations, etc. It may take several offerings and a great deal of time to win you over but you will end up doing exactly what they want. You have enough notice of this to plan how to appropriately take care of this

situation and decide exactly what you will or will not do. Otherwise, you are headed for a brilliant future.

shovel A close friend will attempt to break up your love relationship because of their jealous feelings.

show Conserve your energy and do not overextend yourself.

showboat Your special plan will be dismantled within three days. Do what you can to prevent this. By moving quickly and tying up loose ends, you will find success. Maintain your wittiness and optimism.

show business Explore the differences between several plans. Do this carefully and thoroughly in order to make the right choice. You can relax after the decision is made.

showcase You will achieve great things and be admired and esteemed by the public at large.

showcase of your property You own something of far greater value than you are aware. Take steps to protect your valuables. Within three days, someone will attempt to purchase an item at a far lower cost than it is worth.

broken down showcase Be careful not to sustain bodily injuries for the next four days. Be very protective of yourself.

any other form Have faith in yourself and show faith in anyone who is performing work for you. This also implies that you are loved, admired and respected by other people.

shower The process of making travel arrangements will leave you ecstatic. If you choose to go you will enjoy yourself immensely and have a safe return.

shredded paper A number of unexpected functions will be scheduled to take place concurrently and you will be flooded with invitations you can choose from. One particular event will be far more exciting and glamorous than the rest and you need to make an extra effort to attend this one. It will require formal wear and you need to take extra time to prepare yourself so that you look your best. Do not deprive yourself of this event because you will enjoy yourself immensely and will be introduced to a number of influential people who will be friends for life. You will win a door prize at this function. You will also become aware during this time period that a certain person you desire feels the same about you. You will both enjoy many affectionate moments together and will both be overcome by this new development. You are headed for a bright and brilliant future.

in any other form You will experience a very tranquil period in your life, especially for the next three days. During this time period, you will experience situations that result in a lessening of your financial burdens. All burdensome situations will disappear and you experience more harmony, peace and tranquility in your life. Make sure you do not lend any money to anyone, in spite of the confidence you feel that you will be paid back.

shrimp The person you want to approach romantically will become very offended. Adjust your behavior, this person is not interested in you and you must move on with your life. Watch out for this for the next three days.

shroud Be careful around water and avoid accidents. This will be a very accident prone cycle for the next three days.

shuffleboard Keep yourself open to new ideas presented by a special person who cares about you a great deal.

shunt A particular situation has been tearing you down emotionally. This issue will soon revert to a more stable and normal status. You will be relieved of a burden and all mysteries concerning this issue will be revealed. Good luck will be with you for a long time.

shush *to shush someone or to be shushed* This is an extremely lucky omen and implies that you will soon be entering a very lucky cycle. It is also making you aware that there is something you need to keep to yourself. If you do not, it will result in someone blurting out something that should never be said. Someone is also keeping something from you that you need to know about and is waiting for just the right time to spring it on you to catch you off guard. This will be done for the sole purpose of watching your surprised reaction. You will need to do everything you can to flush out this information beforehand.

shut *to shut* You will be loved like you have never been loved before.

shutter A conversation with a very physically attractive person will lead to great private moments.

shuttle Someone you are interested in owns pets that you are allergic to. Alert this person to the problem before you plan a visit. Attempt to make alternative plans.

Shylock Do not expect a certain person to behave in the way you expect them to. This will not work out to your advantage, especially for the next four days.

shyness You are unaware of a trap that has been laid by a heartless person. This person seeks only their own pleasure. This serves as a warning to avoid entrapment for the next four days.

shyster You need to make sure there are no miscommunications, mixed messages or misconceptions. Make sure others understand exactly what you are saying and that what you think you are hearing is exactly what is being conveyed. For the next three days, you must also not allow yourself to become carried away with disagreements and volatile situations.

Siamese A flurry of miscellaneous problems will arise over the next few days. You have prior notice of this and can work to remain calm until this cycle passes.

Siamese twins You will shortly take on a new project. You will have a splendid time and this project will bear monetary fruit. You will, however, make only half of what you expect for the time being, but in time, your labors will bring you the full value of your worth. Do not become discouraged, it will pay off. It is your choice whether you want to involve yourself in this or not. This is a lucky cycle for you and any other area you choose to explore will be equally lucky.

Siberia You will have a lot of festive fun and activities with friends. Any personal information you hear about another person needs to be kept private. This may also be used as a reference point in time. If you dream of this country and see its name used in any context, the dream message will occur on this day.

sick *to recover from an illness* Within two weeks, take the time to clear out your schedule. An opportunity will be presented during this time period that you will recognize as something you would benefit from. You now have the means to grasp this opportunity and will experience no extra issues or burdens as a result of your involvement. You are headed for a prosperous future. You will also be asked by someone to assist them in suicide. Do not even think of it. Offer assistance and help to enable this person to overcome these thoughts. The person will eventually heal themselves with help.

to see yourself sick when in reality you were not Whatever illness you see yourself afflicted with in this dream is the illness you will be succumbing to in a short while. This is serving as a warning to avoid this illness. You must also make sure you do not lose any money for the next two days. Regardless of the discouragement and the feelings of defeat you have developed regarding a particular situation, refuse to allow these feelings to take hold. Proceed with boldness for the next three days and you will find success in meeting your goals.

sick daughter Within two days you will be making the wrong decision. In order to avoid a mistake, rethink all of your decisions during this time period. If you dream of any unfortunate situation or illness occurring with your daughter, you must also alert her to this occurrence so she can take steps to prevent it.

to see a lot of other people sick Blessings will be with you. Do not allow the issues of another to affect you in such a way that you want to take responsibility for their problems. Step back and allow others to handle their own lives. Otherwise, you are headed for a brilliant future.

to see others sick whom you do not recognize This will be a very prosperous time for you and a time to bring in the benefits you want from life. You will also be asked by someone for assistance.

to be sick and in reality you are sick Within two weeks, take the time to clear out your schedule. An opportunity will be presented to you during this time period that you recognize as something that would be beneficial to become involved in. You now have the means to grasp this opportunity and will also experience no extra issues or burdens as a result of your involvement. You are headed for a prosperous future. You will, in a short while, take steps to prevent any illness you see yourself afflicted with and will recover completely. You must also make sure you do not lose any money for the next two days.

to see another person sick you recognize This is a message to warn the other person to avoid the illness you dreamed of. It also implies that you need to examine very carefully any sudden changes that you will be going through. Blessings are with you.

person who refuses to admit illness This person stands to lose a great deal of money. If you recognize the person, alert them immediately so they can take steps to protect their valuables.

in any other form This implies that you will be asked by someone for assistance. Within five days you will also speak with someone who will verbalize their plans for the future and will choose those they desire to include in their life as beneficiaries. This individual will openly discuss with you the details of including you as a beneficiary. This is the time to speak openly. Many blessings will come to you and your family.

sick bay For the next few days make sure you keep your feelings and emotions in check. You will find you have been left out of a situation you feel you should have been included in. You will become very focused on this issue to the point where you will get emotionally caught up in it. Do not feed into this because it was not meant to be and do not make matters worse by getting emotionally involved. Focus on other things that are far more important for you to take care of.

sickle Be very careful that you do not become injured or cause another person serious injury because of negligence and neglect. Be very cautious. This will occur within three days. Look carefully at your lifestyle in order to make major permanent changes.

sick leave You are ignoring a situation that demands your attention and time is rapidly running out. Dig deeply to determine the issue that needs your attention. Take care of this immediately.

Sickle Cell Anemia This cycle requires that you give others a lot of attention. Remain calm and do not let this change your mood, especially for the next three days.

side You will be very distressed over the death of a close relative.

sidearm You will suffer a loss due to a dishonest relative.

sideboard The outcome of a meeting will yield unpleasant news within five days.

sideburns Great riches are in store for you. Continue in the same direction you are now taking.

sideline Take the time to detail your thoughts in such a way that you will be able to steer yourself around certain situations that will come up within the week. Step back each time you become confused to think things over and you will be able to easily guide yourself through these issues. Eliminate stress by adding more joy and entertainment to your life. Treat your body with respect by eating correctly and getting plenty of rest. Drive defensively and make sure your transportation is in good repair.

sideswipe You will receive extremely bad news within five days. You also need to do everything you can to avoid accidents for the next three days.

sidewalk A short journey will promise great happiness.

moving sidewalk This is an extremely lucky omen and implies that you will experience an inner strength and courage as well as the drive and determination you need to motivate yourself to push beyond any physical or mental barrier that interferes with your moving ahead. Within four days you will rid yourself completely of any aspect of your life that you disapprove. You will successfully bring into tangible form a new project that you are excited about. You will also be greeted in a regal fashion and placed on a pedestal anywhere you go during this time period. You are headed for a brilliant future and many new opportunities.

siege You will enjoy blessings and safety in all of your dealings.

sienna Within four days you will get an unexpected call from someone who will request your presence at a days outing. You will enjoy yourself at different events and amusements but will not see this person again for a long time.

Sierra You will reach your ambitions because of your adventurous nature. This may also be used as a reference point in time. If you dream of this mountain range and see its name used in any context, the dream message will occur on this day.

sieve Do not develop a suspicious manner toward others. You will, however, enjoy yourself immensely at a performance. You will be very popular and party invitations will run rampant. Good luck is with you. It is important to watch the preparation of the foods you eat very carefully to ensure no one tampers with the preparation. Otherwise, you will be surrounded by people who care a great deal about you and within three days you will receive verification of this.

sift Avoid money quarrels.

sigh You will be freer to indulge now because your lifestyle is less crowded. Take advantage of this cycle.

sight You will unexpectedly experience a pleasurable adventure.

double vision - to see double (blurry) Within three days with the proper medical help, you will find the solution to a recurring pain. Search relentlessly for a solution until you get the proper help. Any negative event in this dream needs to be altered or avoided and take steps to experience only positive expressions in your life.

sightless Avoid negative people and their advice.

sight seeing Make sure you are paid in full with cash before you allow someone to purchase a valuable of yours.

sign *for sale sign, etc.* Within three days you will make the right choice when faced with a major decision. Everything will work out beautifully. Take steps to avoid any negative event connected with this dream. This situation can be altered in reality, and all positive thoughts can be brought to tangible form.

flashing sale sign You will be asked by someone special to demonstrate a deeper level of love. This person feels they are far more affectionate than you are. Do what you can to correct this situation. Good luck is with you.

V-shaped sign A big victory will come to you within five days. Be consistent and make sure you behave appropriately in all areas of your life.

in any other form You are loved beyond your imagination and you will have this verified within the week from several different sources. You will gain a sense of the depth of love and appreciation others have for you. You will also enjoy a neighborhood party and everyone involved will have a delightful time. People who care about you may also have a difficult time understanding your viewpoint and until your beliefs are actualized no one will be able to visualize how they would work out.

signal Remain calm and make fewer demands. As a result, someone who is special to you will blossom into a wonderful lover.

signature *someone else's* Show more concern for older people.

your own You will enjoy pleasurable times and wonderful companionships. This is an extremely lucky omen and for the next five days you will be in a lucky cycle. You have also had a deep longing for a particular lifestyle. During this time period, doors will be opened to you that will put this lifestyle within your grasp. Be observant and become acutely aware of what is occurring because you will be thrust forward rapidly if you grasp the opportunity. This time period is also perfect for gaining the favors you ask for, as well as the chance to manipulate the event to your favor. Pay close attention to what your signature was on. This will offer a large clue to a more detailed meaning to this dream. For example, if you see your signature on a loan, a deed, traffic tickets, etc., look up the meanings of these items. This will give you the chance to either avoid or pursue the message

given in this dream. You are headed for a prosperous and healthy long life.

to ask to sign something You will have difficulties with a loved one. Do what you can to avoid this.

scrawled Be very aware for the next three days and do not become more deeply involved with a certain person unless you practice extreme caution. The person you will be dealing with and are growing closer to will lead you to believe you can depend on their loyalty and confide in them fully. This individual is very crafty and very skilled in creating deceptions and illusions and will lead you to believe that certain events will take place in the future that will never occur. This individual has a hidden agenda that involves pursuing you for devious reasons known only to them and will create an atmosphere that will have you trusting them totally. They will be able to, because of their charm and charisma, create a crisis to divert you from any suspicions you may develop. By the time you fully comprehend what is occurring, you will have suffered deep disappointments, disillusionments, and financial loss. It will take a long time for you to recover from this and get back to normalcy but you have prior notice and all the ammunition you need to ensure this does not take place. Use common sense to diffuse this, refuse to become involved, and take steps to avoid any compromise. Do not allow this person to pry into your affairs. Otherwise, you are on the path toward a prosperous future and many blessings will come to you and your family.

signboard Avoid anything you know will cause emotional distress and make you unhappy.

signing *unusual hand movements* Whatever you become involved in over the next five days will be far more time consuming than you imagined. Budget your time and take care of those things you need to do as quickly as possible, otherwise it will consume more of your personal time than you want. This is an extremely lucky omen and many blessings are coming to you and your family.

sign language Think carefully prior to signing an agreement committing yourself to anything. Be very aware of your fluid, food and medicine intake. Be very aware of your health and take steps to protect yourself during this cycle. You will also regret overindulging at a celebration. Be aware of this within three days.

silence Do not underestimate your authority and power. Go all out to make changes.

silhouette Be more of a participant than a bystander.

perfect human silhouette Within five days, you will find yourself caring for another person until they are able to improve their physical well-being and quality of life to the point of personal and social acceptance. You will also be overwhelmed with social engagements and it is important that you keep your physical appearance up and maintain your attire in top condition. This will be a very successful cycle.

horrifying human silhouette You are overextending

yourself to the point of burn out. For the next week, make sure you maintain and improve your physical health as well as set limits on what you will or will not do for others. Eat healthful foods and drink plenty of water. During this time period, all requests you make of your god will be granted, in spite of how improbable this request may seem.

silk *soiled* You are heading in the wrong direction. You are taking too many risks and, in spite of guarantees, your present situation will not work out.

in any other form You will experience a new freedom due to an unusual occurrence that will help you get beyond a particular issue that has limited your potential in some respects. This issue has led you to feelings of discouragement and despair in the past but you will now develop the courage, motivation and energy to remove whatever is limiting you. A platonic relationship will also change into a loving, romantic relationship if this is something you choose. You will find yourself very involved in encouraging this. After this person makes the first move, you will be even more encouraging. Cancel all social functions for a few days in order to bring this to fruition. Many blessings will come to you and your family.

silk hat Take the time to develop yourself into what you want to be in life.

silk panties Aim for higher education.

silk screen Take a close look at everything you are doing in order to avoid mistakes. Phone calls will help you gather the information you need to avoid mistakes and to point you in the direction you need to be going.

silk screen printing You will be mesmerized with feelings of love for the next two days. You will have a glow in your eye prompted by a premature sexual encounter with a certain person you desire. This will be a very sensual and lucky cycle for you for several weeks.

silk stocking Enjoy yourself and treat yourself to grand elegance. Make sure you avoid any negative event in this dream. This is the perfect time to bring any positive event to full bloom.

silkworm Avoid peer pressure and do what you want in order to enjoy life more.

sill You will be hearing good news. You must also avoid any conniving, tricky moves against you for the next two days.

silly Remind others of the affection you feel towards them.

silly putty Avoid situations where strange occurrences may occur. Do not allow yourself to become involved in distasteful affairs.

silo You are scheming to get money from someone else. Forget it. This person knows your game. Otherwise, this will be a very fortunate cycle for you.

silt Within a four day period you will unexpectedly become the target of someone's romantic interest. You don't know this person and find their behavior very distasteful. Let this person know tactfully that you want this overt flirtatiousness to stop. You do, however, find this person attractive enough to go out with and you will have a very enjoyable time.

silver You are entering a cycle where life will be enjoyable. You will also receive pleasant results from long anticipated news. Life will take an unexpected, pleasant emotional twist. Accept love and leave yourself open for all new changes that will be occurring. Your family will be more loving and you will receive a delightful present.

silver *color* Within five days you will be very surprised because someone will turn out to be more together than you thought they were. Your original assessment of their character was wrong and you will be joyfully exuberant to discover their true character. You are headed for a brilliant future.

silver beads For the next seven days you will be unbeatable because of your tenacity and relentlessness in pursuing your goals. You are in a very lucky position and you will be celebrating a joyful victory.

silver bells You will soon receive great news.

silver brooch You will enjoy a short trip and will return home safely.

silver certificate You will receive the gift of being able to communicate your needs and wants to those who are important to you. Your communication will be well received.

silver dollars This implies that although you are surrounded by many powerful and influential people, there is one other person you are destined to become involved with. This will be an opposite sexed person and this involvement will be in any capacity you desire. Leave yourself open to circulate and expose yourself to situations where you will have the opportunity to meet with this person. Conversations will flow easily between you and a sense of closeness will quickly emerge. This will allow a relationship to develop if this is something you choose to do. This person is well established in their career and more financially secure than you expected. You are both destined for a wonderful and tranquil life and will enjoy an abundance of health and a prosperous future. Take steps to avoid or to change the outcome of any negative situation in this dream and forewarn anyone you recognize in the dream to do the same.

silverfish Enjoy your new found love.

silver fox Be very concerned about the behavior of children and young adults and do not make any thoughtless remarks.

silver medal You will enjoy a new inheritance.

silver plate You will enjoy an abundance of health and love.

silversmith Be tactful in order to avoid a quarrel. It is also important not to neglect repairs that need to be immediately handled.

silverware Do not allow yourself to become manipulated by friends or family members into doing something that goes against your ethics. Demonstrate discipline and do not abuse yourself by over partying and overdrinking. These people will encourage you to do this. You are entering a very healthy cycle.

simmer Someone will purposely push your buttons in an effort to anger you. At the first indication of this, leave the vicinity.

Simon *(from the Bible)* Within three days you will be entering a wonderful romantic cycle and enjoying many exciting invitations and romantic evenings at a number of different functions. Good luck is with you and you are headed for a prosperous future.

Simpson, O.J. *(famous football player)* This implies that, within three days, you will need to think carefully about the direction you are being led. Because of some unusual circumstances that occur, you will feel compelled to negate absence of malice. By using extraordinary calculated motivation and thinking ahead, you will be able to avoid being set up for this situation. You will avoid being depleted of your resources and avoid people who would vulturize you. You will be able to successfully sidestep this issue because of this prior notice. Otherwise, you are headed for a prosperous, healthy and tranquil life.

sin You will be given a gift by the deities within five days in the way of healing and psychic powers. You will also sense the development of high organizational skills and will be able to execute this talent in a dynamic and positive way. Many blessings will follow you all of your life.

Sinai *Mount* Avoid taking unnecessary prescription drugs. Double check to ensure you are taking the correct medication. Mistakes are sometimes made. This may also be used as a reference point in time. If you dream of this mountain and see its name used in any context, the dream message will occur on this day.

Sinatra, Frank *(Entertainer)* You will finally be able to acquire long desired possessions. You will be given these by a very kind and generous person.

sincerity Do everything you can to avoid suspicions within a relationship. This change in your behavior will add to your happiness.

Sinbad Each of your plans will work out just as you have visualized them. Use common sense and stay with your convictions, especially for the next three days.

sinew Do not take any unnecessary prescription drugs and double check to make sure you are taking the proper kind and dosage. Mistakes are sometimes made.

sing *to hear one person you recognize sing* This person represents the character of someone you will be dealing with within five days. Be aware and open to the possibility that those could be negative or positive qualities and prepare ahead how best to deal with this person. During this time period the concerns you have will be properly addressed and will lead in the correct direction. You are headed for a brilliant future.

to hear one person you do not recognize sing Someone will attempt to manipulate you within five days into believing you are being overpaid by them. This individual will complain and attempt to get you to agree to accept less for work already done. Do not fall for this, you have earned the amount due you. Be very aware of the person's attitude toward you in the dream. If it is positive, encourage this behavior from someone in reality. If negative, take steps to discourage it. Otherwise, this will be a prosperous cycle for you.

singer *if you are* You will win the heart of an affectionate, kind, and consistent sweetheart. This person will be very tenacious in keeping this relationship.

if you hear a famous singer You will be very proud of your accomplishments and of the success you will achieve.

to hear a group of singers Keep your money to yourself and do not make loans for now. A conniving person wants a share of your money.

single You will have a great deal of nervous tension because of a shaky relationship. You will reconcile a love relationship and will gain what you want out of it. This is a lucky cycle and you can expect this to occur within four days.

single breasted suit Do not pressure others into complying with your wishes. Someone truly, deeply loves you but is emotionally unable to state this. Be patient, this person is simply unable to verbally declare love for now.

single file You will be sent notes and flowers from a secret admirer. You will enjoy this and will learn the identity of the sender within two weeks. You will be unusually delighted and both of you will now aggressively pursue a relationship.

single's bar You will be introduced to a new venture within two days. This will result in prosperity.

sinister Get a new attorney.

sink *to sink* You do not have the knowledge or means to start pursuing a particular goal. Do not allow yourself to be led down a path that will only result in disappointment due to lack of resources. Prior to beginning anything new, be sure you have everything you require.

to see yourself or anything else sink in grain Guarantees that you are given will not be genuine. Investigate closely in order to avoid disappointments. This let down will not be apparent for a long period of time.

to sink in quicksand or to see someone or something sinking Do everything necessary to protect yourself on all levels and areas of your life. Make sure all your bases are safely covered financially, physically, and emotionally. Take precautions now to ensure that everything flows in the manner you desire.

if you recognize the person sinking in quicksand This person needs to become aware that within the month a financial situation will not work out in the way they have planned. With prior notice, they will be able to make plans to stabilize their financial situations. Expect this to occur within two days.

sink *(kitchen)* Become very watchful and take extra precautions. Play your cards very close to your vest and do not allow others to know what your next move is. You must also become very organized when dealing with delicate situations that will arise within the week. Make sure you keep yourself together and closely follow your own plans and rules. Do not allow anyone to assume you are willing to commit yourself more to a particular issue than you are. Carefully monitor your behavior to make sure that you are not mistakenly misunderstood. This also implies that an unpredictable situation will occur within two days that will bring you immense pleasure and joy. You must also pay attention to the contents of the sink in the dream. This will offer you additional clues to the meaning of this dream.

sinker Be very cautious with your health. Make it a point to take care of all illnesses before they reach dangerous proportions. This could result in death. During this cycle, you will have the luck and strength to correct what needs to be and get back on the right track, especially regarding your health.

sinkhole You will have a long and healthy life and the valuables you own will suddenly increase in value. Be very careful when engaged in pleasure seeking activities; this could pose a danger to you. Within this time frame you must also not allow anyone to give your power to anyone else. This individual wants to gain control of something of yours and will attempt to manipulate you in order to gain power over you and a certain situation you are now dealing with. Make sure you do not fall prey to this person. Prepare yourself in such a way to avoid this occurrence.

sinus The way you are greeted by someone will influence the flow of the rest of the conversation. Continue to talk with this person in order to get your point across. Organize your thoughts before speaking.

Sioux You will receive a tip that will result in lucky investments.

sip This is a lucky omen especially if you hear yourself sip. All your doubts will be put to rest.

siphon You will soon be engaged to marry.

siphon bottle You will be involved in a dangerous fall. Watch closely to avoid this.

sir Quickly get to the meat of a situation in order to resolve it correctly. An older, wiser person will play an important role in your life. You will also get the chance to regroup and start over on stronger footing in a new cycle.

Sirach *(from the Canonical Bible)* Be sure you put aside some time within three days to clear your head and put yourself through some mental brainstorming. This will allow you to focus on the suspicions you may have about another individual and determine whether these suspicions are valid. You will then be able to come to an understanding about how to resolve this issue. If you motivate yourself now, you will be successful. This is the perfect cycle for you to locate the answers you are looking for and put yourself on the path toward a prosperous future.

siren You are headed in the wrong direction. You are taking too many risks, and in spite of guarantees, any ongoing issue you are involved in will not work out.

siren song It will be within your power to save the life of someone else within three days. Do whatever you can to correct this person's behavior and save their life. An unusual event will occur that will lead you to investigate someone's whereabouts and their need for assistance. Good luck is with you and many blessings will come to you and your family.

sirloin You are entering a very lucky cycle. Opportunities will come easily to you and provide you with a comfortable way of life.

sissy You have a real flair for drama. This artistic talent needs to be exposed. Relentlessly and consistently develop a network of people for the purpose of promoting this talent. Each day, for the next five days, add new names to this list.

sister *title for nun* You will have the intuitive thoughts needed to overcome difficult situations. You will be able to diffuse negative thoughts and attitudes during this time. You will therefore not have to deal with this situation again in your life. Remain balanced and calm in spite of outside influences. Many blessings are with you and your family.

step sister Get out in public and socialize and you will find the perfect person for a romantic involvement. Social gatherings will give you exposure and you will have a chance to meet the one who is perfect for you within the next week.

your sister in any form Pay close attention to the condition or situation your sister is in. If this is a negative situation, take steps to change it and make your sister aware of the contents of the dream so she can take additional steps to either avoid or alter the situation. If this is a dream that foretells a joyous event, make her aware of this so she can take steps to bring it to fruition. You will also be invited to a very elegant function as someone's guest. This person has a flair for glamour. Dress appropriately. For a two week period you will be very socially active and will enjoy yourself immensely.

your sister angry Make your sister aware of the contents of this dream so that she can take the necessary steps to turn this into a positive situation. This dream also implies that, within five days, a very conniving person will be able to bring you great emotional harm if you do not take steps to investigate and to motivate yourself to avoid this occurrence.

your sister being physically active in any form You need to stop a behavior you may not be aware of that will ultimately bring you harm. Look closely at your actions, for the next five days, to determine the behavior that will cause you physical harm and take whatever steps you deem necessary to change your actions.

sisterhood A close, sympathetic group with good conversational skills will benefit you emotionally. You will enjoy a successful outcome with all your affairs.

sister-in-law Do everything necessary to promote closeness with your in-laws. Do nothing that will create problems that result in distancing yourself from them. Look for situations that will bring closeness such as family outings, games, etc.

your sister-in-law angry Make your sister-in-law aware of the contents of this dream so she can take the necessary steps to turn this into a positive situation. This also implies that within five days a very conniving person will be able to bring you great emotional harm if you do not take steps to avoid this.

your sister-in-law being physically active in any form You need to stop a behavior you may not be aware of that will ultimately bring you harm. Look closely at your actions for the next five days, to determine the behavior that will cause you physical harm and take whatever steps you deem necessary to alter your attitude.

Sistine Chapel See a physician in order to facilitate a speedy recovery. This may also be used as a reference point in time. If you dream of this Cathedral and see its name used in any context, the dream message will occur on this day.

Sisyphus *(Greek mythology)* You will enjoy many intuitive thoughts and your hunches will be accurate in every way. You will also develop the skills you need to let go of negative thoughts and attitudes at the precise time you need these skills. You will no longer have negative thoughts that will hold you back. Proceed with confidence and remain calm in spite of what is going on in your life right now. You are on the path for a life filled with enjoyment and interesting and

influential people.

sit *to sit* You will receive a good surprise connected with your career.

to stand up and sit back down (anyone) Someone has erected unnecessary emotional barriers against you. Self realization will lead this person to tear down defenses. This person's behavior will indicate more openness and willingness to communicate. Be patient until their person comes around.

sitar You will be invited to visit someone in a far away place. If you choose to go, you will enjoy yourself and have a safe return.

sit in Do not allow anyone to belittle you. Speak up for yourself and do not put yourself in the position to be denigrated.

sitter You will gain financial security by temporarily taking on a second job.

Sitting Bull Take the time to explore your inner self.

situation comedy You are too loyal to a situation that does not deserve your loyalty.

sit up You need to do everything necessary to ensure that when you are working with fluid measurements, you do it with accuracy and as efficiently as you can. This is a time when you can set yourself up for a chaotic situation by not following all rules and instructions to the letter. Pay close attention to what you are doing, especially for the next three days.

sitz bath Make sure you structure a situation so you are acutely aware of each small detail that you may otherwise overlook. This is particularly important for the next three days.

six Within six days you will have to choose between two paths. Both are good but one is better. Meditate in order to choose the better one. The clue to making the correct choice is that one path will seem overwhelming. This will be the proper choice and will lead to riches and health. Use the number six for games of chance for ten consecutive times.

six pack Do not overextend yourself. Budget your time carefully and be considerate to yourself.

six pin Be careful not to fall from a horse while riding.

six shooter A very devoted person who is interested in your success will grant you a favor.

sixteen An older person will be very instrumental in your success and progress. You do not know this person yet but their influence and your determination to accomplish your goals will yield success. You will also be lucky at games of chance by using this number.

sixty Ridding yourself of old hang ups will change the way you operate your life. This change will influence another person into entering agreements with you, on your terms. This is a lucky omen. Use this number at games of chance for five consecutive times. One time will be a winner.

size *in any context* Within five days, you will overcome all long term situations that you have been working on for a long time. Relentlessly work on any issue that has become a burden. You are headed in the right direction, will soon experience many social events, and will sense a new freedom that comes from ridding yourself of this issue. Proceed with confidence. Good luck is with you.

skate Reprioritize in order to stimulate yourself to complete an ongoing project.

skateboard There is no reason to go to unusual lengths to achieve. A relaxing trip will stimulate creativity and allow you to retain the facts necessary for success.

skeet You will enjoy an intimate dinner date and have enjoyable memories of this evening.

skein You will have to restrict a friendship because you feel very much taken for granted and taken advantage of. This will start within a three day period. Be careful not to allow your friendship to be abused.

skeleton Be careful of being implicated in a fraud both directly and indirectly. It will be a combination of the two and if you are caught, you will be incarcerated for many years.

skeleton key All issues regarding antiques will be very lucky for you during this cycle. You will also receive great personal advice.

skeptic Do not allow new events to become a challenge. Allow changes to occur without exploring each detail. Handle matters calmly for your own peace of mind.

sketch Someone will suddenly demonstrate an unusual affection toward you within a few days. You will be very surprised and puzzled. Enjoy this and stop being so analytical.

to see sketches A transition needs to be made. You are moving too slowly. Tie up all loose ends. You will be handling new things over the next few weeks and cannot afford to fall behind.

sketch book Do everything you can to develop a support system so a child or young adult will have what they need to point themselves toward a path of fewer stresses and greater prosperity. Many blessings are with you and your family.

skewer Watch young children around alcohol. Ensure they do not accidentally partake of it. A relative will also have dental problems. Do whatever you can to offer assistance.

ski *to ski* You will enjoy a breakthrough and be able to handle events attentively and recover lost time. Keep your eyes open for new opportunities over the next few days.

skid *to skid* The relationship that is important to you will only grow as much as the other person allows. You will not have a meeting of minds.

to skid with a car Do not stay in a situation long enough to encounter an uncontrollable, abusive individual. At the first indication of this, leave.

skid row Someone in a group you are dealing with will never reach an agreement with you. This person will only waste your time and throw you off for at least two months. Seek alternatives.

skier Revenge will not bring satisfaction. It will only lead to regrets over a wrong doing. Let these feelings go.

ski instructor A priceless collection will be damaged and this will be very unsettling for you. Be aware of what is going on.

ski jump Join forces with others in order to break through a major obstacle. Shocking good news will also raise your spirits for a long time. Expect this to happen soon.

skillet Find someone who is very detailed instead of careless and messy, to do work for you. This person will need to factually record each move for you.

ski mask You are guaranteed all the luxuries and miscellaneous items you want in life. Expect this for the next three days. This will be a very dynamic time for you.

skim milk You will receive a surprising proposal for marriage. You will accept this proposal and enjoy a happy union.

skin You will solve a mystery that has puzzled you for years. With the help of family members you will get to the bottom of this secret. This will happen within three days. You will be happy with what you have learned and will feel richer for it.

to see your skin peel Within a three day period, someone will have a great urge to communicate their deep feelings for you and express the depth of involvement they feel for you. This individual will automatically perform a number of favors, chores and activities on your behalf. Your every desire will be realized. Make it a point to demonstrate your affection and consideration toward this person, take pains not to hurt this person's feelings, and dispel any suspicions you may have of this individual's motives.

face with a skin rash An unusual circumstance will occur that will provide you with more wealth and a very wealthy, shy person will fall deeply in love with you. Be sure to keep your eyes open for anyone who fits this description if you choose to move in this direction. Take steps to ensure you do nothing that will cause your face to break out and make sure you forewarn anyone you recognize to do the same.

goose bumps A special person has asked you to attend several functions and you have turned them down. Two things will occur if you make a point of attending a function. You will meet someone who will work successfully with you at a later time and you will make that special person in your life happy.

pig skin Think ahead. You are included in a relationship with someone who wants a marriage commitment. You will have doubts about this union. Follow your instincts. This person, after marriage, will become very verbally abusive and you will go to couples therapy. Nothing will change this person.

sheepskin You will enjoy matrimonial harmony.

skin cream You will experience many very intuitive thoughts that will be right on target. You will also develop the ability to rid yourself of negative thoughts and attitudes at the precise time you need to. You will no longer have to deal with the negativity that holds you back. Proceed with confidence and remain centered in spite of anything else that occurs in your life. You are headed for a life filled with enjoyment and many interesting and influential people.

face skin cream In a short while you will be dealing with a certain person who is associated with an agency that can lead you to resources that will meet your needs. This individual has a great deal of expertise and knowledge of these resources and is in power because of their ability to procure grants that will meet the needs of those who seek their help. They will decide on their own to do something for you on the side and will have you go through them instead of the agency. This will ensure they will be paid through the agency as well as through you. Make sure you are not steered from your path and do not compromise your goals because you will miss out on accomplishing what needs to be taken care of. You will become aware of this because of the sense of strangeness that will surround this transaction. This feeling will arise from your heightened sense of awareness and is letting you know that you are on the wrong path. Expect this to occur within three days. You will be able to catch this in the nick of time but since you have prior notice of this you can take steps now to avoid falling prey to this. Otherwise you are headed for a brilliant future and are destined to accomplish what you set out to accomplish.

skin diving An announcement you receive will be very difficult to comprehend. Remain calm. Things will work out.

skin flick Do not prolong an introduction to in-laws. Do everything necessary to ensure closeness in this relationship.

skinhead Someone will go to great lengths to involve you in a sexual relationship. This person is interested only in satis-

fying their sexual appetite.

skinless Someone will act very stubborn over a particular issue. This could lead to violence. You have prior notice not to become involved and take steps not to allow it to develop to this point.

skinny *to be skinny* You will be able to promote yourself into being appointed to handle an important task.

skinny baby Do not behave in a way that will lead others to become suspicious of you. You will never be able to erase doubts if you do. Be cautious of your behavior now.

any other form You will be able to sell anything to anyone for the next three weeks.

skinny dip You will feel overwhelmed by the closeness you feel toward a loved one. Be free and openly demonstrate this love. This person will treat you royally in return and will openly demonstrate love to you. You will feel very secure and loved in return. This will happen within a few days.

skinny man/woman Move quickly. You will achieve prosperity in every level of your life. Accept whatever comes your way as your good fortune. Be confident and do not question anything that works to your favor for the next five days. Any opportunity presented to you will be very fortuitous during this time period so render a positive response. Stocks will also go up. Go for it.

skin rash *any kind* Within a week, unusual circumstances will occur that will make you very wealthy.

someone else with a skin rash A very wealthy, but very shy person, will fall deeply in love with you. Keep a lookout for a very shy and sharp looking individual.

to see a skin rash on someone else's face You are loved beyond your imagination. You will see strong evidence of this within three days.

to see skin rash on yourself Get to the bottom of a certain situation now to keep it from escalating into chaos. Regroup in order to determine what your next move should be. Good luck will be with you for a long while.

skip You need to be focused and analytical about each move you make. This will allow you to achieve prosperity.

to skip or to see someone else skip Use extreme caution for the next three days and move ahead with a certain person only with extreme caution. The person you will be involved with and with whom you are beginning to feel some closeness to will mislead you into believing you can give them your complete confidence and can rely on their loyalty. This person is very cunning, very skilled in deceptions and creating illusions and will have you believing that certain events and situations will occur that will never take place. This person also has a secret plot that involves pursuing you for evil intentions known only to them. An atmosphere of complete trust will be created and you will suspect nothing at the time. Because they have a very charming and charismatic personality, you will easily be diverted from any suspicions you may develop and once you do comprehend what is going on, you will have suffered financially and emotionally. It will take a long time for you to recover from this and get your life back to normal. You have prior notice and all the ammunition you need to ensure it does not take place. Use common sense. Do not compromise your feelings, do not allow this person to pry into your personal affairs and above all do not become involved. You are on the path toward a brilliant future and many blessings will be with you and your family.

ski pants Keep anticipation and expectations of the near future at a low point now. Your expectations will come through, it will just take longer than expected. Keep jealous thoughts at bay.

ski plane Do not allow your temper to get out of hand for the next few days because someone else loses your valuables. Practice patience. All of this can be prevented by using caution with your belongings.

ski pole Because of what you have been told, your perceptions of a certain person is high. Upon meeting this person, you will find them to be rude and without manners. This person will later meet your original expectations and become a beneficial person to know. You will meet this person within three days.

skipper You will experience nervousness over a relationship that is moving far faster than you anticipated. You are not sure whether you want to slow this down or continue in the same manner. Remain calm and keep going in the same direction.

skirt Be very alert and remain calm when someone attempts to drag you into a debate about a wrong they did. Do not allow this person to bring you down to their level. Stay with the facts and handle it alone. Do not become involved in angry arguments. You will experience a successful outcome.

ski run Within three days you will have a light conversation with someone. This person will take something you said about another out of context, change it around, then take it back to the person you were talking about. This will result in a violent argument. Avoid this by not talking about anyone.

skull Be careful of being implicated in a fraud, either directly or indirectly. It will be a combination of the two and if you are caught, you will be incarcerated for many years.

smiling skull You are in danger of being involved in a fraud (i.e., phone fraud, solicitations, contests, etc.). You are very good hearted and too trusting. This will cost you financially, so beware.

skull with a crown You will enjoy fertility in all phases of your life. Stop being so timid. Timidity results in lost chances.

dagger going through the skull This will be a dangerous cycle for you. You will be injured by someone experiencing a psychotic episode. Prior warning of this will allow you to prevent it by being very aware of your surroundings and by avoiding outside activities for a week.

skull and crossbones Be careful of accidental poisoning. This will affect vital organs such as your liver and will result in death. Be very careful of *anything* that may result in toxicity and be very wary of environmental toxins. Be careful for a seven day period.

skunk You will rely on someone within the next few days to provide you with certain information. You need this information but this person will not deliver. Find reliable alternatives.

sky You will find the resources of a support group invaluable. This group will be there just when you need it.

dark sky Watch the actions of someone who is special to you. Standoffishness indicates the need for more attention and affection.

skydiving You will be in a great cycle for the next few months. Hard work completed in the past will now pay off and ensure your retirement.

skylight Your presence will be requested at many social functions. You are entering a cycle of popularity. You will also feel healthy and have a general sense of well-being during this cycle. Expect this to begin within a few days.

skyscraper Within a few weeks, you will feel the urge to marry. Follow this urge. You will find happiness and this person will perfectly complement your life. This individual will be very charming and agreeable.

skywriter You will be blessed with perfectly illuminated thoughts and have the courage to put these thoughts into action. This is an especially lucky dream for anyone who works with paper. You will be inspired to write. Go for the big ideas.

slacks Within a few days, a very special person will make sexual demands of you. This will be surprising but you will be amused. You will enjoy yourself immensely if you decide to participate.

slalom You will want to be included in a secret group plan. This will be a pilot for other plans. Let people know that you are interested. You will later be accepted and will be glad you pursued this.

slander Within a few days, you will begin making changes in your behavior and personality. You will later see real personal growth that will be noticed by others. This will also create a feeling of freedom after releasing personal burdens.

slap *to see someone slapped* Mental pain and anguish will disappear overnight.

to slap someone You will enjoy victory in all areas of your life.

to be slapped You will experience good luck for the next three days. You will begin to feel an incredible energy and need to make big changes in your lifestyle that will bring you major benefits. As the result of a communication you will have with another person you will sense a diminished enthusiasm for the path you were taking. This dream is alerting you that it may be the time to step back and review your options. You may find that another path is more beneficial to you or you may find that you do not need to make any changes at this time. Either way, you will come to the right decision for your future. Any negative event witnessed in this dream needs to be avoided in reality. Proceed with confidence. Riches will come to you.

slapstick You will find someone to be irresistible and very sexually attractive. Within two days, you will find this person has the same feelings about you. You will be the one to decide whether you want to become involved. Many joyous days are ahead of you and you are headed for a brilliant future.

slash ***to see something slashed*** Someone will back out of a prior promise they have made to offer you assistance. Find alternative help.

in any other form Rally a group together for financial support concerning a franchise. This will be successful.

slash and burn Treat your health with respect. Avoid contagion from viruses for the next three days.

slat Stop criticizing yourself.

slate Have sympathy for yourself when going through emotional pain. Treat yourself to fun times.

slaughter Someone with a charismatic and charming personality will ask you out. This person has a mental sickness and the primary reason for wanting to see you is to have a sexual experience, then murder you. This person seeks sex only for the purpose of murder yet appears surprisingly normal. This will be a nightmare unless you take precautions to keep it from occurring.

slaughterhouse Think ahead, someone who is special to you and a friend of yours will engage in a heated argument within three days. Prevent this in any way you can.

slave You will travel extensively and enjoy many different cultures and lifestyles. You will also speak with and get to know a variety of people from many walks of life. In particular, you will befriend a much older person of the same gender. You will learn of things never imagined from this person and gain a new and strange knowledge of life. This knowledge will later assist you in gaining prosperity and making lifestyle choices. Be grateful because this will lead to a grand life.

slave ship You will suffer sadness over the failure of a regrettable involvement that will occur within three days. Avoid involvement in order to escape sadness and regret.

slaw You will develop strength of character and a strong backbone. As a result you will achieve success.

sled Do not allow haunting memories of a past career stand in the way of success in a new career. You are being promised fantastic changes by your special deities.

sled dog Do not suggest that someone adopt a practice that you have not added to your life. Make sure you are aware of all the consequences of this action prior to asking or allowing someone else to practice this.

sledgehammer Do not purposely busy yourself with trivial matters to avoid commitment to another. Live your life to its fullest.

sleep It will take many fires to rekindle an old romance. This person will no longer have the same feelings for you if you continue to allow old arguments to flare up. This old argument will arise again within a week. Use caution and prudence or this person will leave your life forever.

to see others sleep Be aware of problems that involve travel for the next few days. Try to resolve these ahead of time.

sleeping baby You will enjoy happiness, peace and many blessings.

sleeping bag Do not give out personal information about another person for the next few days.

sleeping beauty Your intuition is accurate and you are on the path for a brilliant future. You will enjoy good luck regarding all business and love negotiations. You must also make it a point to meet your personal involvements concerning all meetings and discussions in a frank and candid manner. You will achieve mutually satisfying results in all situations that require your close personal attention.

sleeping car You will be very excited about the opportunity to purchase land at a low price. This property will quickly increase in value.

sleeping man/woman Guard yourself against automobile accidents and any preventable injury, especially for the next three days.

sleeping pills You are denying your feelings by isolating yourself from the person you are destined to surrender to. This life is not a rehearsal, get out and live it.

sleeping sickness You are destined to help someone who is unable to help them self due to poor health. This will not be as stressful as you anticipate and will bring you much joy. Blessings are yours.

sleep paralysis *the feeling of being unable to move when trying to awaken* For the next seven days you will need to be very attentive and acutely aware of certain events that begin to unfold and will have a serious and damaging affect on your future. These events will destine you to alter your life and point yourself in the wrong direction. You must become more assertive and muster up the courage and confidence to take the necessary steps to protect yourself from this situation. Also watch the words you use when speaking to others because your words may be used as leverage against you. Be observant of what is unfolding that will have a serious effect on your future. This will occur because of any of the following situations or a combination of the following situations:

- The influence that someone will have over you.
- Interference from someone else who will steer you in the wrong direction.
- The control that someone in power will exert over you.
- The leverage that someone will gain by using your words to put you at a disadvantage.
- Someone who is in a position of authority who will make decisions for you.

Do not allow yourself to become vulnerable by not acting on your own behalf because you will suffer emotional depletion as a result and will be guided in a direction you do not desire. Prod yourself to get your point across to those in authority and make it a point to avoid everyday stresses caused by the decisions others make for you who have no business being involved. You are in danger of surrendering your control. Avoid unhealthy situations and circumstances and remain suspicious of all changes. Become confident and relentless in correcting those areas of your life that require corrections. You will then be able to put yourself on the right path. You have the power to change any negative aspect of this dream as well as changing your life to encourage positive expressions. Make sure all of your bases are safely covered. Practice common sense and your plans will be successfully carried out. You will place yourself on the path of prosperity.

to be unable and aware that you are unable to move your body for a short time because of some unusual occurrence Your spirit wants you to see what is in front of you and to make sure you do not overlook anything. Take steps to ensure you are not being narrow-minded about something you are about to involve yourself in. Make sure you get more than one perspective about this issue. Create several alternative ways to deal with this situation. Do not make excuses that will keep you from motivating yourself into moving forward. You will accomplish anything you need to at this particular time by being flexible and by looking at things from a different angle. Anything in this dream that was displayed while you were in this particular stage is a major clue to what else you need to be doing in your life. If it was negative, take steps to prevent it in reality. If positive, make sure you take steps to promote it. You will be putting yourself in the position for a brilliant future.

sleepwalker You or someone you know will be misled by other people into believing you ought to do something that you have entirely different feelings about. These people fully believe that their ideas present the best options for you although they have no idea of the detrimental results this option will yield. This situation will put you or someone else in a dangerous and troublesome area.

sleepwalking When are you going to put a stop to a certain behavior, bad habit or ongoing negative situation?

sleepwear Work quickly to find someone willing to share your vision. Put your ideas into contract form. Work quickly. Good things are waiting for you.

sleepy For a few days, you will have to read everything very carefully.

sleet Within seven days, you will be open for a destined opportunity to come your way. This will be a wonderful opportunity that will bring you greater wealth. Anything positive that you possess will only increase in value and worth, and you will be on a much higher plane than before. You will receive from the Gods a gift of riches, both financial and spiritual.

sleeve Love couldn't come at a better time. You will have no reason to doubt the person entering your life within the next three days. This person is thoroughly committed and will offer a steady, stable lifestyle.

sleeveless Find out what your demands on yourself are. Make sure you do not overextend yourself by doing needless chores.

sleigh Find out what others have been saying about you lately. This will determine whether you are on the right path.

sleigh bell Someone you know will come to you within three days very eager to share their good news about an upcoming event. You will enjoy many days of peace and harmony.

slice *any form* Within a few days you will want to avoid attending an outing that will be held close to your home. Think about this carefully. If you go, you will enjoy yourself tremendously and will have a memorable visit.

slicker The situations you will be handling over the next few days will amaze you because of the speed in which you receive a successful outcome. Each negotiation you handle will result in your favor.

slide rule Do everything necessary to guard yourself from accidents.

slide trombone Rid yourself of anything that brings you discomfort. Change your lifestyle and include only those things that give you peace and comfort.

slime Do not allow the words of another person to affect you emotionally. This will occur within a few days. Ignore these words and go on with your life.

sling You will prepare to give a party for a large group of people. Only half of the people you invite will attend. You will plan to prepare food for this large number. It would be wise to purchase food that can be prepared quickly, prepare only half and if more people attend it will be simple to feed everyone.

slingshot You will be invited to attend a reunion in a few days. This will be a disaster. It is your choice to attend or to stay home.

slip All surgery performed during this cycle will have wonderful results and you will heal quickly with TLC. Most surgeries are successful, and you can hasten recovery by having a positive attitude and by following doctor's orders.

woman's undergarment You will achieve victory concerning a business partnership. You will also discover some beautiful leather goods at a bargain price. Someone who possesses great physical beauty and is financially secure will also fall in love with you. You must also be very careful of any injury that could be the result of an accident around boiling water.

half slip You will develop a clarity of thought and a certain command that comes from within and this will allow you to express yourself succinctly. This will come about if you separate yourself from those whom you associate with daily. You will then be able to make all the right decisions to lead you to a comfortable lifestyle.

cricket term Do not overextend yourself by overdoing physical exercise.

to slip quietly away without notice Do not allow yourself to be disloyal to anyone. You are deeply loved. You will also finally hear the apology you have been waiting for.

to see someone slip away quietly Within three days an argument will be purposely started and you will be blamed for it. The other party has certain plans and wants to argue with you in order to distract you from questioning them. You have prior notice of this and can prevent pettiness from escalating into a fight.

to slip and say something or hear someone else say something they should not have said Someone will purposely give you the wrong address, directions or phone number. Be aware of this and take steps to avoid it.

to slip and say something by mistake For the next two weeks your priority should be to improve your physical appearance.

to slip and get loose or free Within three days some tricky undertakings will take place from an unexpected source.

to slip or to see someone slip out of place by sliding You need to make a decision about a sexual situation with someone of the opposite sex. A discussion will lead to a satisfactory solution. Act on this as quickly as you can. Take steps to keep any negative event you dreamed of from becoming a reality and be sure to alert anyone else you recognize to do the same.

to slip or move with a smooth gliding motion You will be making a very personal decision within three days and will move ahead rapidly because of the success of this decision. Take all the necessary steps to keep a negative situation in this dream from becoming a reality and make sure that anyone else you recognize in this dream is aware of this so they can take the steps they need to avoid it. You will be in a lucky cycle for the next five days.

to slip because you wanted to Keep all your plans a secret. You will enjoy good luck with all of your speculations.

slip - a space between piers or wharves A close acquaintance will soon be tried for murder.

slip - a space between pier or platform that slopes into water You and certain members of your family will become involved in a joint venture. This is not a wise decision and you stand to lose your investment. Revise your plans and decide on a workable project, regardless of any family pressures.

slip - consistency of cream - word used for casting or cement You will enjoy a lucky cycle for the next four days.

slip - word used for planting or cutting This is a very lucky omen.

to hear "you mustn't allow to slip" You will have to deal with someone who is very emotional by nature. This person will, however, find emotional strength within a few days. This dream also implies that water is a soothing and healing substance for you. Do everything you can to surround yourself with water. You will also receive the positive answer you have been seeking for some time. Do all you can to ensure that you change the outcome of any negative event witnessed in this dream or make sure you avoid it altogether. Make sure you warn anyone you recognize in the dream to do the same. You are entering a lucky five day cycle.

to slip on a bar of soap For the next five days do everything you can to protect yourself and your surroundings because something will occur that could pose a great danger to you. This may be something in the nature of an undetectable toxic fume that may lead to sickness or death or you could become the victim of a random murder. Since you have prior notice of this you can take steps to secure your environment and protect yourself. Do everything you can to ensure that you experience only positive expressions in your life.

"it slipped my mind" You are beginning to feel a strong emotional pull that will take up much of your time because you will have no idea where this drive came from. It is causing you to focus on bringing something into solid form. If you determine that the urge you are feeling is inappropriate and/or socially unacceptable, you will have the time and enough notice to seek out the professional help you need to come to grips with your desires and to live at peace with yourself and these urges. The moment you sense this, get help. This is the perfect cycle to find the right person to handle this event. You will be able to take care of this and gain control over your emotions in a healthy way. Expect this to occur within five days. Otherwise, you are on the path toward a brilliant future.

slipcover Do not immediately reveal your feelings about a particular situation that you are not involved in.

slip knot Victory will be yours in those areas of your life you most desire.

slip noose What you believe to be a negative situation is incorrectly assumed.

slip off *as in market terms* Watch your behavior around small children, especially for the next month. A small child needs more care and protection. Do everything you can to avoid or change any negative situation you dreamed of and take steps to keep it from becoming a reality. Forewarn anyone you recognize in this dream to do the same. You are on the path for a prosperous and abundant future.

"slip one over on another" Do not allow anyone to take advantage of you financially, especially for the next month.

slipover Talk about your interest in moving to an area with someone whom you know lives there. You will receive information from this person that will create an enthusiasm to move. Once you move to that area, this person will have more information for you that will verify that you made the correct choice.

to be slipped over Be very candid and direct about your needs.

slipped disk Avoid all friction between yourself and a special person for the next few days. Put yourself out a little more and plan to attend a special event such as a concert to add some spice to your daily rut and add loving feelings to a relationship.

slipper Be relentless in accomplishing a special project you are working on, a project for someone else that is being performed for you, or a project you are doing for someone else. This will only reflect positively on your abilities. Do this for the next few weeks. Do everything you can to ensure you avoid any negative event and take steps to only experience positive expressions in your life. Be sure to forewarn anyone you recognize to do the same. You are on the path toward a prosperous and abundant future.

slippery *to dream of you or someone else sliding by accident* Do not allow old hurts to resurface and fester to the point of keeping you from completing your goals. The moment you sense this taking place, make sure you busy yourself with a different task to keep you moving in a healthier direction. You are headed for a healthy and prosperous life. There is also a danger, during this cycle, that your actions will be wrongly interpreted. Be very careful that your actions do not give the wrong impression, especially for the next week. Anything you dreamed of that represents a negative event needs to be avoided or changed in reality and you need to alert anyone you recognized in the dream to do the same. This will be a very lucky five day cycle for you.

"slip up" *to slip up* Make sure you do not overindulge with your needs. You must also take steps to alter or avoid any negative situation in this dream and forewarn anyone you recognized to take these same steps. You are definitely headed for a prosperous and abundant future.

slither *to slither* Push yourself to complete projects and to tie up loose ends. This will be a great benefit to you.

sliver *on someone else* Within two days take steps to keep others from ill treating someone who is precious to you. This mistreatment will be done in a subtle but painful way by someone you least expect. This will quickly develop into deeply hurt feelings and resentments toward this person. Do what you can to avoid this scenario or if you do go through this you will be prepared ahead of time. This dream also implies that you will enjoy a tremendous victory that is completely unconnected with this scenario but will occur in the same time frame.

slob Be wary. A risky situation will be coming your way in two days. Stay clear of this.

slobber Within the next few days you will quickly become involved with a very eager person who has a different lifestyle than you. You will wish you had been involved with this person sooner.

sloe gin Think twice about an invitation you have extended to someone to visit you. You will regret this visit.

slogan Be kind to children.

sloop Someone you are interested in is waiting for you to make the first move. Go for it.

slop Immediately face up to all personal problems regarding a relationship.

slop jar For the next five days you will be very eager to share time with someone you are interested in. This person will act bored the whole time you are with them and this will disappoint you a great deal. You have prior notice of this and can take steps to keep this from taking place.

sloppy *any form* Take the time you need now to investigate the overall picture regarding a certain issue that will come up within two days. You will come to understand what is really taking place and this will allow you to determine how you feel and how you want to live your life. This will be a priority to you now. Proceed with confidence. This dream also implies that any request you make will be granted even if it is to someone who has no interest in helping you. You can proceed with confidence and can expect an abundance of health.

sloppy joe Someone you meet in the future and become involved with will leave you at the altar. This person will never be seen again.

slot Move quickly toward whatever you are after.

sloth Think ahead. You are planning a small party but this party will expand and you will have more guests than you anticipated. This will be a very joyous occasion. Prepare ahead by stocking extra food and drink.

slot machine Do not make an investment in anything that looks promising at the moment. It will not work out.

slouch Do not let memories from the past interfere with something wonderful that will be coming up within a few days.

slow motion You will be very anxious about a decision that has to be made involving children. You will make the correct decisions. Someone has led you to believe they are capable of handling big responsibilities but once you entrust them with a big job, you will be let down. This person believes they are able to handle this large responsibility but their ego is larger than their abilities. Be acutely aware of this and do not risk anything of importance.

slug Someone will attempt to involve you romantically with a married person within a few days. Do everything necessary to avoid this.

sluice Within two days you will notice a certain element is missing from a conversation you have with another person. Because of this you will have a hard time reaching a decision that has to be made.

slum You will be able to effectively debate an important issue and will get your point across.

slur You will meet a very imaginative person and be included in a plan that will enhance your life.

slush Focus on situations that have stagnated and you have been unable to change. Within two days you will be able to develop the clarity of thought and the motivation needed to tackle these issues.

slut *to hear this word in any form* Within a few days, it will be necessary to hire someone who has more expertise than you for a particular subject. This person will assist in getting your project completed quickly and correctly. This dream is a lucky omen.

sly *any form* Take care of all legal papers.
small *to see anything in miniature* Within three days you will be able to calibrate and detail your thoughts and put them into words so well that someone who desires you will become very secure and comfortable in your presence. This will then allow this individual to speak openly and frankly in a manner that will spur the development of a relationship and

create a warm open union. You can also use these skills to bring anything you want into reality. You will be able to remove all blocks due to poor communication. You are entering a magical cycle. Any scene in a dream, that you view in miniature, symbolizes and prophesizes an activity you will foster. A negative scene can be avoided.
to see things in dreams on a smaller scale This is a good luck omen.
small opening You will be taking huge steps to raise your standard of living. This will be accomplished by focusing on your goals in a grand way. Expect this to come about within five days due to some unusual and joyful circumstance. Everyone involved in this will enjoy beautiful expressions of joy and tranquility. Many blessings will be with you and your family.
in any other form Watch yourself for the next few days. Temptation is running very high to be lazy in performing certain tasks.

small claims court You will become attracted to someone whose sexual drive is far greater than your own. This person will take steps to involve you in their life and will be relentless in their approach. Think carefully about this situation. You will need to decide how to act so you will not miss out on this person's love and affection yet be able to clearly get the message across that you do not have the sexual appetite they do. This person will then take steps to accommodate you in order to keep the relationship mutually satisfying.

smallpox Do not deny yourself a once in a lifetime love affair. Go for it.

smart You are being alerted that you will start to have doubts within three days about certain plans, projects, etc., that you are now dealing with. You will have the feeling that these plans are spiraling downward and failing in some way. You will have the strength to get through this and your plans will not fail. The result will be far better than you anticipated. Move forward with confidence. You are on the path for a brilliant future.

smart aleck Be very cautious, alert, and acutely aware of someone you are affiliated with who will, within three days, try to pull the wool over you eyes. This person will develop a plan to manipulate you into committing to something without any suspicion on your part about their motives. Make sure you are extremely aware of this because it will cause you discomfort and many distasteful moments. You have prior notice of this person's intentions and can take steps to protect yourself. Otherwise, you will receive many abundances in other areas of your life as a result of new opportunities that will be presented to you.

smart money You need to avoid procrastination and anyone who encourages laziness. Move quickly forward in the direction you know you should be going in order to be successful, especially for the next three days.

smart set You will achieve great success and whatever is making you feel anxious (your problems, dissatisfactions, etc.) will be easily explained to someone who is in power and who will be able to pull strings on your behalf. You will get a quick response and the assistance you need. You will then be able to get on with your life. Expect this to occur within three days.

smartweed You need to take all the necessary steps to avoid a particular illness that is easily contracted from someone else. This illness is not of a serious nature but it could escalate into something far more serious if not taken care of. Be very careful of this for the next three days and do everything you can to protect yourself from any unusual complications. Otherwise, this is a very lucky cycle and you need to move quickly on all your plans.

smash Take care of your health. It is a very precious commodity.

smell *to smell burning odors* Within two days, you will be surprised at the request of another to spend private moments with them. This request is unexpected and comes after repeatedly asking this person to spend time with you and after repeatedly being turned down. Curiosity will lead you to want to spend time with this person. The choice is up to you.

to smell a pleasing odor Practicality will bring you greater success. Get down to basics and practice common sense.

to smell a displeasing odor Do not allow inconsistency to rule your personal life.

smelling salts This is a warning not to be betrayed by someone you have deep feelings for. This person will tell you one thing and then tell other people conflicting stories that will anger you greatly. Avoid this emotional distress for the next few days. Make sure any negative event in this dream does not become a reality.

smelt Within three days make it a point to uncover the reasons you refuse to face personal issues. Explore and examine ways in which you can confront your behavior. Take time off to regroup and you will successfully deal with this matter.

smile You will receive some very encouraging news regarding your financial status. This will spell good fortune. You will also progress rapidly toward a more prosperous future. Expect this within two months.

smirk Do not involve yourself with another person in any illicit behavior when in unusual places. This will create a reputation you will be unable to erase. This will arise within a week. Remind yourself not to become involved.

Smithsonian Institute Within three days someone will come to you with a request for assistance. It would be an error to become involved or to try to help them out. Slow down and reassess your thoughts so you can act in the appro-

priate manner. Do not allow your own assumptions to lead you to make a decision in error. Otherwise this dream is an extremely lucky omen. It may also be used as a reference point in time. If you dream of this museum and see its name used in any context, the dream message will occur on this day.

smock Do not put extra pressure on another person. This will result in the break down of an otherwise good working relationship. Apologies will never be accepted and this person will never come back.

smog Be careful of the choices you make. Do not allow a decision to be made that will pin you down and keep you from moving ahead. This will happen within three days. Prevent this confinement.

smoke *to see clear smoke* A combination of methods will work better in giving your artistic talents exposure.

to see dark smoke You are in the position to resolve ongoing problems. Take steps to accomplish this within seven days.

to smoke Do not allow a lack of confidence and determination to keep you from bringing a situation, that will arise within five days, to completion. Do not create invisible barriers for yourself. Proceed with confidence and push yourself through this. This will result in a feeling of accomplishment and well being. You will also make a wise investment that will lead to prosperity.

to see others smoke You need to carefully consider the path you need to take that will lead you in the direction you want to go. This will allow you to reach your desired goals. The trust you have in a friend will also result in a big loss. Recheck your judgment.

if you recognize the person smoking This person represents someone in your present life with the same attributes as the person you recognize in the dream. You will be required to deal with this person within three days. You have prior notice of this and can react appropriately to either the negative or the positive character traits. You will also, within two days, move ahead rapidly with anything you desire. You can expect to find success with this.

in any other form The plans you have set into motion will not work out accordingly due to sabotage. Make sure you stay on top of this in order to prevent this occurrence. Move quickly on this. It is important to act within two days.

smoke alarm Take extra precautions against robbery. Any negative event witnessed in this dream needs to be turned around to a positive expression in reality.

smoke bomb Use discretion and recheck each angle before making a major decision. Any negative event witnessed in this dream needs to be turned around to a positive expression in reality.

smoke damage Within three days, a close relative will diplomatically drop subtle hints about a particular area of dissatisfaction in their life that they would like to see you become responsible for. This person wants you to take it upon yourself to make the necessary changes to improve their life. They feel they are stonewalled and cannot get through this situation. You will have the conviction and compassion to do this for them and it will lead them to a far better lifestyle if you take the initiative. Many blessings are with you. Any negative event witnessed in this dream needs to be turned around to a positive expression in reality.

smokehouse Do not allow someone into your life with the same behavior patterns that took so long for you to break. This will happen within a few days and will give you the feeling of ruin. Do not allow this to happen.

smokestack Within five days, give yourself some time to think and reflect on your feelings and ideas. This will allow you to touch on those aspects of your life that you wish to improve. You will be better able to do this if you give yourself time to mull over those decisions you have to make.

"smoking" *(slang term)* Within five days, you will resolve a long standing burden and will experience the freedom that comes from ridding yourself of this troublesome situation. Relentlessly work on any issue that needs to be taken care of. You will also enjoy a busy social life in the near future. Proceed with confidence. Good luck is with you.

Smokey the Bear Be friendly and outgoing to others. Do not take too long to introduce yourself to associates and neighbors. Take steps to make the first move.

smoking jacket A dynamic and charismatic person will unexpectedly call and insist that you spend the weekend with them. This will be on very short notice. Be sure to explain the reason why you won't go and take a rain check in order to avoid hurt feelings. Be sure to plan a definite date for the future. This union will be lucky.

smooth Be prepared to save extra money over the next few days. You will need this extra cash because of your association with another person.

smooth faced You will take steps to complement major changes in your life. These changes will also extend to every phase of your life.

smorgasbord You are headed in the wrong direction. Stop immediately and change course.

smother Do not allow yourself to be taken in by quackery. Over the next few days, select your physician carefully.

smuggle *to smuggle* Watch your behavior. Over the next few days, you will be rejected by the object of your affections and you will gain disapproval because of the way you handle a particular situation.

other people smuggling Within a few days, you will be setting yourself up for accusations. This can be prevented by carefully watching your behavior.

snack bar Within the week, you will need to encourage a young person to become more confident, resourceful and self reliant. Do it kindly and tactfully and give soft and gentle encouragement. This person will always remember this and make big changes in their life. From time to time you will need to give small encouragements so this person can blossom into a wonderful adult. You must also remain calm and non-argumentative for the next seven days when discussing a delicate family matter that will come up during this time period. Take steps to limit your involvement.

snaggletooth Show more regard for children and teenagers.

snail You will be selected to represent an older person. This person is no longer able to care for themselves for health reasons. Processes will be lengthy because you have to deal with public social services agencies. Be relentless and patient and do the right thing.

snake *baby snake* You will be with someone you must be aware of in order not to be taken advantage of. This will be someone you would never suspect of being a conniver or sneaky in any way. You will have no idea that this person's personality will twist in the manner that it will. Expect this to occur in two days. You have prior notice of this situation so you can be emotionally equipped to handle it and not leave yourself open to be prey to this person. This person is someone who has a hidden agenda you would never suspect and you could be easily taken. Otherwise, you are in a very tranquil cycle and are on the path toward prosperity.

black snake This implies infidelity. Within two weeks someone you are associated with, who has led you to believe in their loyalty, will be disloyal to you. This will result in shame, embarrassment and hurt feelings. Avoid this by not surrendering to another person for at least two weeks. To see someone you know who is associated with a black snake, implies that this person will be disloyal to someone, or someone will be disloyal to them within three days. Take steps to inform this individual of this situation so they can avoid chaos in their lives. Do not become personally involved.

rattlesnake You have continually requested that another person not do something that irritates you yet this person will continue the same behavior. This will result in an argument and may escalate into a physical fight. Attempt to be tactful and aware of the repercussions of an argument, especially for the next three days.

snake bite Within two weeks you will be abandoned without notice by someone you are emotionally attached to. This will be because of unwarranted jealousy on the other person's part. This person is heartless and has many emotional hang ups. You cannot keep this relationship and it is not your problem. Get on with your life.

snake about to strike Someone will lead you to believe you have a strong friendship but within three days you will meet this person in public and be cruelly snubbed. This seems to be a game this person plays when they are with other people. Do not set yourself up to be fodder for another person's ego trip. Avoid this embarrassment.

green snake You will have money coming in within two days but this money will already be spent in someone else's mind. Do not allow anyone to spend your money without including you in their plans. Good luck is with you.

to kill a snake You will enjoy victory over all of your emotional hang ups. You will be able to liberate yourself sexually and rid yourself of jealousy, envy, hypocrisy and aggression. These problems have long been obstacles to a loving relationship. This process will occur over the next three days and after two weeks someone will come into your life. You will be able to enjoy a fulfilling, mature relationship.

to drive a snake away Place less importance on others and more on yourself.

dead snake For the next two days, make sure you do not mistake the behavior and body language of another person and do not be so quick to suspect this person of wrongdoing. Allow this person to explain themself and you will be pleasantly surprised.

to run from a snake For the next four days someone will go to great lengths to steer you in the wrong direction. Be alert to this and do not allow yourself to be lured onto the wrong path.

with unusual colors Your family needs to be acutely aware of a grave danger that will arise within a few days concerning the whereabouts of children. A child is in danger of being kidnapped. Great pain can be avoided by knowing where children are at all times.

a snake hiss An abundance of health, spiritual healing and tranquility will come to you within three weeks. Within the week a celebration will take place that will cause everyone involved to rejoice. For the last two weeks of March and for the entire month of April, you are also being promised that an idea, project or event will be brought into tangible form and will reach a greater level of perfection than you ever expected. This plan of yours will take on a life of its own and will easily go through each channel necessary for completion. This will be a blessing to you and a cause for celebration for everyone involved. You are headed for a brilliant future. Make sure also that for the next six weeks any negative event you witnessed in this dream does not become a reality and warn anyone you dreamed about to do the same. Pay close attention to what the snake is hissing at for a more detailed meaning to this dream.

to stop a snake from capturing anything You will enjoy victory in reaching your goals. Put more emphasis on creating positives out of negatives. Practice this immediately after the dream to ensure there are no disappointments or failures in meeting your goals.

many snakes For the next two days make sure you do not mistake the behavior and body language of another person. Do not be so quick to suspect this person of wrongdoing. Allow this person to explain. You will be surprised. Several events will also occur within the week that you can expose yourself to. Motivate yourself to take advantage of these

opportunities because these will be offered to you only once in your lifetime. Do not put this off. Take steps now to grasp these opportunities. Mobilize yourself and seek exposure so you will not miss out on them. Otherwise, you are headed for a brilliant future.

dancing snake Within three days, you will be dealing with someone with a hidden agenda. This person will attempt to steer you in a direction that will offer them instant gratification. Avoid being taken in any capacity during this time frame. Proceed with caution and be wary of the motives of others.

in any other form Someone will attempt to violate your rights by swaying your judgment and willpower. Do not betray your principles and do not allow yourself to be placed in a dangerous position.

snake charmer All long standing debts will unexpectedly be paid to you.

snake dancer Someone you are close to will purposely steer you in the wrong direction regarding the pursuit of your goals. Be aware of this and avoid it. This could damage your future security.

snake doctor You are being asked to engage in introspection and meditation. Reach for your inner spirit for help in forming clear ideas and making better decisions. These ideas will come through your spirit. Don't allow yourself to become you own worst enemy. Meditate.

snake eggs Be extremely aware and cautious about where you are allowing someone to lead you emotionally. Someone will, for reasons of their own, lead you to believe you are completely loved by them. The word love may or may not be used at this time but all of the trappings will be there (i.e., flowers, gifts, romantic outings, etc.). Your feelings will grow deeper and stronger than this other person's feelings. If you allow the possibility of lovemaking, this person will not touch you in a way that implies they love you. You will feel very empty and cold as a result. You will fail to connect with this person on the level they have led you to believe was there. Rather than putting yourself through this, you have prior notice and can avoid this scenario completely. Get on with your life without them and the emotional upheaval they will cause. This person has a hidden agenda that will involve you doing something for them that only they are aware of. Avoid this situation entirely; it will only lead to unhappiness. Otherwise you are headed for a prosperous future that will begin to evolve within the week.

snake eyes This dream is a good luck omen. You will be undergoing a major transition. An old friend will also introduce you to someone you are interested in and will provide you with the right information to launch a romance.

"snake in the grass" *(slang term)* Do not allow anyone to breed jealousy. This person is a hypocrite and will give fake information in order to create jealousy. Ignore this and get on with your life.

snake meat Be keenly aware of your actions and stop playing games with another person's welfare. This person needs to live comfortably and you are preventing this because of your ego and by delaying the help that needs to go to someone in need. This behavior will backfire. Take steps to change this. You will not be there to see the suffering you will cause by abusing the power you have over another person. Remove this evil game playing from your life or someone will arrange for your murder.

to eat snake meat or to see someone else eat snake meat By asking questions, being suspicious, and by developing a certain degree of objectivity, you will be so successful in diffusing a plot against you that it will be impossible for it to be successfully carried out. This plot will involve someone who wishes to create chaos and discomfort in your life. You will be able to use what authority you have in a responsible, efficient and effective way. You will also, during this time period, experience many wins and victories and the generosity you have paid to others in the past will be repaid. Expect to receive many gifts and major wins. You are definitely headed for a brilliant future.

snake oil A former lover will attempt a reconciliation. Go on with your life without this person. This individual does not deserve a second chance.

snake pit Someone you have been giving assistance to will need more frequent attention in the future. Their pain will become greater and requests will come more often. You will slowly begin to be overwhelmed. Do everything necessary to prepare for this and seek outside assistance in order to lighten the load and help them resume their life.

snake venom You will soon meet a very charming, unusually wealthy person. You are very much attracted to each other. At first the relationship will work beautifully. For a long time you will be very spoiled and have everything you wish for. After a while, without warning, this person will drop out of your life explaining they were after only short term pleasure. Beware of anyone fitting this description. This person also demonstrates obsessive behavior patterns.

snap The next few months promise to be the best you have experienced so far. These few months will spoil you and you will take steps to maintain this delightful lifestyle.

snapdragon You will marry someone who is very well off and socially sound within a few months.

snapper An old friend will soon begin to behave very differently. This person is out to harm you and will behave very inconsistently. You will need to go on with life without this person.

snapping turtle An unusual situation will occur that will bring you a financial windfall. Many blessings are with you

and your family.

snare drum Do not take advantage of someone who has been very generous and kind to you.

snarl You will be overlooking a great business opportunity. Check out all options and check yourself out before making any decisions.

sneak *to sneak a peek on tiptoes* Within three days someone you feel a special closeness to will come to you to try to explain what is going on in their life. This person is under a tremendous strain being placed on them by someone else but will be unable to explain exactly what they are feeling. This person is in danger of having their spirit broken because the other party is behaving in an irresponsible and abusive manner in many areas of this person's life. This individual is being controlled and is becoming very suspicious about the methods being used. There is no specific motive or method but this person is being controlled in a very abusive way and they are, for some reason, remaining in this situation. It is important you make this person aware that the moment they have this conversation with you, they must motivate themself to move on. It takes a long time to break the spirit and this person needs to make changes in order to reenergize themself. This is the time when this person will be able to hear your words of motivation and make the necessary moves to get away from this abusive person without making their motives apparent. This could turn into a situation that will cause this person, as well as yourself, a great deal of duress. You will be instrumental in opening their eyes in some way so they can motivate themself to create the lifestyle they desire. You will be able to flush out the information you need from others by using your communication skills. This information will be very beneficial and advantageous for both of you. Many blessings are with you and you are headed for a brilliant future.

sneak away - in any form Give a raise in salary to the person who deserves it. You will also be taking huge steps to raise your standard of living. This will be accomplished by focusing on your goals in a grand way. Expect this to come about within seven days due to some unusual and joyful circumstance. Everyone involved in this will enjoy beautiful expressions of joy and tranquility. Many blessings will be with you and your family.

sneaker Help a small child add more recreation and amusement to their life.

sneak preview Within three days you will develop a network of people who will offer you support, assistance, and will brainstorm with you in order to find a solution to a particular issue that needs to be dealt with before the week is out. A successful conclusion will be reached.

sneeze You will receive good news in the morning and bad news in the afternoon. This mixture of emotions will be worked out in a stress free fashion.

to see someone sneeze and spray or turn anything foggy with a sneeze Within the week you will be entering an extremely lucky cycle and anyone involved in your life will share this luck. You will also be offered services that will help you to successfully accomplish your goals and you will reach a higher level of success than you thought possible, particularly with anything you deem important and of high priority. You can expect to make many amazing and wonderful connections that will assist you in grasping and meeting your goals. You can also expect a mega merger and the synergism working between you and those you will be working with will bring you to a higher level of success than you ever anticipated. This dream also implies that you will receive many benefits by attending a festive event, by participating in an educational event or attending an event in which one person will take an interest in promoting you and your plans. Following this you will enjoy a long period of tranquility and a prosperous future. Anything negative witnessed in this dream may be changed in reality and you must make it a point to forewarn anyone you dreamed about to do the same.

snicker Do not put yourself in an embarrassing situation.

sniffle You will need to become very aggressive when dealing with an emotional issue. This issue is adding chaos to your life. You will actively seek a solution within two weeks.

snifter Someone will subtly manipulate you into doing something without asking you outright. Do not make it easy for this person to use you. This is likely to occur within three days.

sniper Stop being so selfish with others, especially for the next two days. Learn to share and you will never regret this change of behavior. You will receive a great deal of satisfaction from this.

snob You will have to decide now what is best for you so you will have the answer in a few days when it is required.

snoop *someone else is* Be very aware of the actions of a close loved one in order to avoid confusion.
you are the snoop Within a few days you will have a sneak preview of an upcoming event.

snore Do not give up so easily when faced with a difficult situation, especially for the next few days. Take time out to explore the solutions to this issue before it becomes a crisis. You will regret it if you do not.
to be accused of snoring Make it a habit to include people who are important to you in major decisions.

snorkel For the next week, you need to restrain your behavior. You will also need to be more attentive, demonstrative and tolerant toward someone who is important to you. This person has become very angry and upset because of a certain

situation that has taken place in their life. It will be days before this person comes to grips with this issue.

snot Someone appears to have a deep anger and resentment toward you. Clear the air so this person knows where you are coming from. Someone will also put on airs around you and will attempt to impress you with their financial status. This will be done subtly for the purpose of creating envy. Ignore this behavior and get on with your life. This will be a very lucky cycle for the next five days.

snout You will need to make it a necessity to ask questions for the next few weeks. This will put you in charge and others will be happy that you are interested in them. Everything will run smoothly for you.

snow Within seven days you will be invited to attend two separate events that you must not miss. At each one you will have the company of an admirer and will have the pleasure of watching both of them subtly attempt to win your favor. Although it is not apparent, one of these admirers has a great deal of authority and power. Both of them have an agreeable and charming nature but you will enjoy having one of them as a lifetime partner. You can be confident that you will place yourself on the path of prosperity.
melted snow Someone will finally come to terms with their life and will make a decision you have long awaited. This person knows you have been waiting for this and it will have a major impact on your life. You will both make mutual plans for the future and you can be sure it will be a brilliant future. Expect this decision within the week.
for you or someone else to eat snow Don't deny intimacy to another by intentionally avoiding time that could be spent together. Do not allow this behavior to continue. Within a few days this issue will need to be confronted.

snowball This indicates prosperity in all areas of your life. An old friend will also surrender to your sexual desires and this union will last longer than you ever anticipated.

snow bank Prepare yourself emotionally for the beginning of a new relationship that you have desired for a long time. This will occur within a few days.

snowbird Do not settle for second best.

snow blower Within three days you will develop a sudden interest in the occult. Educate yourself and read about this before you dash into the unknown.

snowcap Evaluate what is needed in a love relationship. Allow your partner to freely express their needs.

snow cone Do not allow little negative remarks from friends about a project deter you from completing it.

snowdrift Think things over carefully. You have no guarantee you are headed in the right direction.

snowflake Your social calendar will be very crowded. You will be entering a cycle of popularity and your presence will be requested at many social events. Lucky you.

snow leopard Develop a bold and daring attitude when attending to a specific task that needs to be taken care of. This will inspire you to get the job done.

snowman An abnormal situation will occur between you and another person. This person will become abnormally aggressive in a sexual way. This will be a much younger, attractive person and you will not understand the reason behind this behavior. They will go to great lengths to seduce you. Follow your intuition on this.

snowmobile A secret admirer will reveal themself to you within a few days. This person will become more desirable to you because you will now see them in a different light.

snowplow Within a week or two you will need to see a dentist. Everything will work out fine and you will be happy you got it over with.

snowshoe Be very clear about whether you desire a romantic involvement with a certain individual or whether you simply want sexual involvement. Clear up all mixed feelings and make a decision.

snowshoe rabbit Do everything you can to protect children and young adults who require closer supervision, especially for the next three days. Make sure they do not come to any physical harm. Many blessings are with you and your family. You have prior notice of this and can keep any negative event from taking place.

snowstorm You will develop a strong sense of freedom and situations will work out just as you wanted them to.

snowsuit Avoid becoming a party to a gossip session. For the next few days, gossip will be flying and one person will attempt to drag you into a session to elaborate. Refuse the temptation to become involved.

snow tire Beware of sharp instruments and avoid all injuries.

snuff Someone will attempt to involve you in a conspiracy involving blackmail. Be cautious and avoid all involvement.

snuffbox This is a good omen. You will receive many blessings and verification of love from another person.

soak Guard yourself against anger and jealousy from another person for the next few days. These unseen emotions will be revealed to you and this person will attempt to injure you. Protect yourself.

soap *to use* You will enjoy an unexpected financial victory.

to see others use Allow yourself private, intimate moments with another person. Special moments are yours for the next few days.

to slip on a bar of soap Take steps to protect your environment and surroundings. Within five days something will occur that will pose a threat to you. This may be something in the line of an undetectable toxic fume that could lead to sickness or death, or you could become the victim of a random murder. You have prior notice of this and can take steps to avoid any danger, secure your environment and make sure you experience only positive expressions in your life.

saddle soap Be careful when engaged in pleasure seeking activities. Someone will attempt to involve you in negotiations that have serious implications.

soap opera You will have a long life, a large family, health and many blessings.

soapsuds Keep your eye on your goals and be determined to meet those goals. You will see a real change in your life over the next few days.

soapy water Make sure you get to the meat of a particular issue. Once you decide what the missing element is, you will be able to conduct yourself in such a way to resolve this in an appropriate manner.

sob *to see yourself sobbing* Because of an extraordinary set of circumstances that occur within three days, you will find yourself going on a spending spree at someone else's expense and with their encouragement.

to see many people sobbing Take the necessary steps to prevent an untimely death due to unusual circumstances. Take extra precautions for the next seven days.

in any other form Someone has led you to believe they are very easy going and rational. Be careful. You will find yourself confined with this person within three days and find only irrational, difficult and antagonistic behavior. Do not place yourself in the position to have to deal with a person like this. Do everything necessary to live a full life and do not allow others to control you. You must also make it a point not to push yourself too hard to help another person. This person does not desire help and doesn't have the courage to say so. This will happen this week.

sober *any form* Deal directly with your refusal to settle down in a relationship and make a commitment. You have a great relationship now. Don't destroy it.

sociable Be committed to finding what will work in your life. Act quickly by asking someone who makes a career of offering their services to others. This person will connect you with the right person to give you assistance at a later time.

social disease Be careful of odorless toxic chemicals in your immediate surroundings for a three day period.

few days.

Social Security This is a promise that from this time on you will have everything you need. This will begin within a three day period because an unusual event will take place that allows it to occur. You or someone you know will also be led by others to believe that you should do something you have different feelings about. This individual fully believes that this is the best choice for you but lacks the foresight to fully understand how detrimental this choice would be. By accepting this option one of you will be putting yourselves in danger. As time goes by, keep this decision from being pushed on you or this other person. Follow your own counsel and your own hunches and you will keep yourself out of danger, especially regarding health issues.

social welfare Make sure all your plans meet with success by being certain that all paperwork is completed and you have all the information you need on hand to have everything promptly processed.

social worker You are destined for a brilliant future. Maintain your determination.

socket Ask someone to put in a good word for you with someone they know, in order to get situations moving in the right direction. This will result in success. Do not be intimidated.

socket wrench Someone will attempt to intentionally steer you in the wrong direction. Think things through clearly. Do not allow yourself to be persuaded into taking someone else's advice instead of your own.

sock hop Reach a decision quickly to end a certain partnership that could risk your health.

socks Ask questions in order to decide on the correct solution to certain problems and to avoid disrespect from others.
    socks with holes For the next three days proceed with caution. A violent, emotional eruption will occur and this could escalate to violence. Take precautions to protect yourself. Leave the vicinity the moment you sense this incident is starting.

Socrates This is a cycle that will not allow you to withdraw your feelings. Speak the words you know that someone is longing to hear. You will have the confidence of steel you need during this time period to enable you to accomplish this. Go for it.

soda Someone you have not seen for a while will suddenly appear with a small gift and will apologize for staying away for so long.
    club soda You will be invited to a social function and from there will meet new friends who will invite you to more events. You will enjoy a full social life.

soda cracker You will receive your deepest desires within a

soda fountain Do not allow resentments to keep you from enjoying a good situation. You also need to review different options in order to free your mind and avoid staying fixed in a particular situation. Your way of handling this issue needs to be changed.

soda pop Organize and detail your thoughts. This will allow you to successfully navigate yourself through certain situations that come up within the week. Step back each time you need to think things over and you will be able to guide yourself through each issue with ease. Free yourself of stress by bringing more joy and entertainment into your life. Treat your body with respect. Eat healthy foods and get plenty of rest.

soda water In spite of anything else that may be going on in your life right now, all of your hopes and dreams will become tangible in a far grander way than you ever anticipated. You will be successful in eliminating everything that is standing in your way. Within two days someone you are attracted to will also be irresistibly drawn to you.

sodomy Someone will put you into a position of potential danger within three days. This person will relentlessly attempt to sell you on an idea they truly believe in. It would be an irresponsible act on your part if you allow yourself to be put into this position. You could be inadvertently placing yourself or this other person in a potentially fatal situation. You have prior notice of this and have the choice of not becoming involved.

sofa Make sure others value you for who you are instead of what you have or the authority you possess. You will also be going on an exotic vacation within two weeks. This will bring you a great deal of joy and you will have a safe journey.

soft The manner in which you are gazing at someone and the seductive use of your eyes will get you in trouble. Be aware of your facial expressions for the next few days.

softball Pay attention to the reasons why someone will freely offer their assistance to you for the next few days. You will be surprised to learn that this person is attracted to you. This dream is also a very lucky omen.

soft boil Push yourself to invest a large amount of time into cleaning up difficulties. Next month, you will be very happy that you did.

soft drink You have too much interference in your home, and too many people coming in and out. You need to add more balance to your life. You will be happy you did because within a month you will be dealing with a situation that will require more privacy.

softie Within the week, you will be in the presence of a very powerful person who has the power and authority to pull strings on your behalf. Do not fail to grasp this opportunity. You will enjoy an abundance of health during this cycle and many blessings will come to you and your family.

softener Avoid being out in unusual weather. Be wise and stay inside.

soft spoken Beware of mail fraud.

software Put all written material that needs to be protected under the copyright laws. You must also put extra money aside for a pet project you would like to market. This will ensure a quick response. This dream is a lucky omen and you will have luck for the next few months.

soggy Any enterprise you will be pursuing for the next few months needs to be rechecked. Make sure what needs to be done is done. After revising your project you will have much more luck and will successfully complete this project.

soil An old friend will suddenly develop an off again and on again relationship with you. This will puzzle you. Do not allow yourself to become too hung up on this situation. Get on with your life without this person.
top soil Regardless of anything else that may be going on in your life right now, within five days you will overcome any long term burden you wish to rid yourself of. You are headed in the right direction and will be experiencing more pleasure and more social events in the future. Focus on achieving a peaceful and stress free life.
to work with soil Focus and make sure that what you want to happen will happen.

solar Do not allow jealousy to stagnate you and interfere with your clarity.

solar battery You will receive a confidential confession from someone you least expect. This person has focused on you for some time. This will occur within a few days.

solar system Do not take advantage of your neighbor.

soldering iron Someone will be agreeable to cosigning on any venture you are interested in for the next few days. You will gain much support from this person. Use it.

soldier You are going in the right direction to bring about major changes in your life.

sole *to injure your sole* Someone will stick closely to you and boast about their financial status in order to persuade you to become interested in them romantically. This person lacks the courage to approach you first. If you make the first move, the relationship will move quickly into a sexual arrangement. This person is, however not as generous as they pretend to be. Avoid this person and move on with your life unless you want to engage in game playing with very few

rewards.
sole of foot This is an extremely lucky omen. Anything you felt was impossible is now a possibility for you within the next two days. Also, prepare yourself for an enormous surprise that will catch you off guard and fill you with enormous joy. Good luck is with you and you will enjoy yourself immensely during this time period.

sole *(fillet of)* Someone will go to great lengths to win your confidence. Be cautious, this person only desires privy to your current venture.

solicitor You are not giving yourself enough credit. You are well equipped mentally, emotionally and physically to handle most situations. Do not talk yourself out of taking on larger problems for the next few days.

solidarity Put yourself in the position to be acknowledged by that person you need recognition from.

soliloquy Be imaginative and delegate responsibility in order to avoid handling a major undertaking alone.

solitaire Follow your intuition. You will be married and have many wonderful years together.

solitary Know for sure what your plans are before you take action. Do this within a few weeks.

solitary confinement You will empower yourself if you are really aware of your assets, particularly concerning situations that you will be handling over the next few days. Become very aware of your worth.

solitude Time is running out. You are in danger from an evil person. This person has not yet given any sign of their evilness but upon getting closer to you they will remove the mask of normalcy. Expect this to occur within a few days. Do not give this person a chance to get close and take steps to protect yourself.

solo Problems will arise at a place that you frequent. Tread carefully around this problem and avoid any personal involvement. Remain clear of this place for the next few days because tempers will flare and emotional fireworks will take place.

Solomon *(from the Bible)* Define clearly what you can do to help another person. You will be granted a favor and will also make a spontaneous decision over the next few days that will bring you great pleasure.

solstice Within three days you will be dealing with a situation that will require that you remain true to yourself. Aggressively pursue what you want from someone else. Verbalize your needs and they will be met.

solution *(chemical)* Someone who is behaving irritably is only seeking affection from you. Do not lead this person on if you do not feel this way toward them and do not become involved with this individual. This situation will reveal itself to you over the next few days.

sombrero You will be falsely accused of involvement in an undesirable situation within a few weeks. Make sure you have a solid alibi during this time period.

somersault Politely ask others to respect your privacy.

son Well calibrated thoughts will bring many nights of romance and passion and you will be fulfilled both passionately and emotionally. All of your plans will work out well. Take steps to warn anyone you recognize of any negative event foretold in this dream so they can have the opportunity to avoid it. Any positive event needs to be promoted and you have the chance now to make this individual aware of the possibilities. This is an extremely lucky omen for you and for the other person you dreamed about for the next seven days.
   stepson Stop depriving yourself of situations in your life that would be very special to you. Bring more social change into your life. Peace and tranquility are yours.

sonata A fantasy of yours will be fulfilled and maintained for as long as you want. This will begin within a few days.

song Juggle your schedule in order to seize an opportunity you would otherwise miss. Make sure you motivate yourself to circulate in order to expose yourself to this opportunity and take steps to take advantage of it. Luck is with you.

songbird Someone will go to great lengths to help you out in a crisis.

songbook All legal negotiations will result in your favor. Someone who has undergone some distasteful moments in their life will also come to you as the first person they will open up to. Display sympathy and understanding toward this person for the next three days.

Song of Solomon *(from the Bible)* Future accomplishments will bring you many compliments. These accomplishments will also diffuse pressures that will be coming up soon.

Song of the Three Young Men *(from the Canonical Bible)* You will soon receive a gift of richer intelligence and greater mental inventiveness from the gods. Use this time to accept this gift and use it to your best advantage. This will allow you to raise your standard of living to the level you desire. You can expect this to occur within four days. You are headed for a prosperous future.

song sparrow Make sure your finances will cover merchandise you intend to purchase. Avoid embarrassment. Good luck is with you.

song thrush Do not allow yourself to be in an intimate set-

ting with someone you have no desire to be intimate with.

songwriter Anything you put into writing now will be very lucky for you. Someone will also help you become involved in a very satisfying union.

sonic boom You will be more appealing than ever to others and your social calendar will be full. Be sure you take proper care of yourself and eat properly. Enjoy yourself.

son-in-law This is an assurance that you will rejoice because you will acquire what you most want out of life.

sonnet Things will work out in exactly the manner you desire.

Son of God You are loved beyond your imagination and within the week you will have verification of these feelings toward you from several different sources. You will understand how deeply loved and appreciated you are by others. You will also be involved in an enjoyable neighborhood party and everyone will have a wonderful time. You are on the path toward a brilliant future. Your desires will be fulfilled and a special favor will be granted. Many blessings are with you and your family.

sonogram Disillusions will disappear and you make giant steps toward self improvement. You will develop your talents and abilities. Maintain this new zest for life. Things will work out well for everyone involved in your life. Do not stagnate due to your lack of confidence.

soot You will receive a positive response to something you thought would be negative.

soothsayer Treat yourself to a face to face conversation with someone who speaks straight from the heart. You can be certain this person speaks the truth.

sooty You will come to realize the person you are seeing romantically is your true love. This relationship will develop to a deeper level and meet with satisfaction for both of you.

sophistication Someone will fulfill a long standing promise and you will be very happy about this.

sophomore Make sure you have calibrated each action you plan to execute. You will be pleased you have removed all kinks before your plans are put into action.

soprano Make sure you are not sucked into any unexpected quarrels that occur in your presence within a seven day period.

sorcerer You will spawn a creative idea for a product that will become immensely popular and in demand. Do not allow anyone to dissuade you from reaching your goal.

sorcery Patience and perseverance will help for the next few days. Make sure you use all of your talents and inner strengths to meet you goals.

sore Do not allow any situation to threaten your career status. Become assertive and express your dynamic personality. Sift through your thoughts and focus *only* on the facts. This will direct you toward the path you need to take.

sorghum Do not allow anyone to break you of the habit of being consistent and on time.

sorority A former love has everything you need to make everything fall into place in your life. You can work together toward a goal without the emotional involvement. At first it will be all business, then romance will again enter the picture and both aspects will work out.

sorrow Out of sorrow, joy will soon arrive. Out of all difficulties will come a favorable result. Expect only joy now. Sadness will be diffused. You will also have a favorable return on an item you are selling and can expect financial success. This will be an unexpected surprise to you.

sorry *to hear the word* Between now and the next seven days a very significant situation will occur that will spur a series of upwardly, spiraling events for the next six months. This will dramatically alter your life for the better but the real significance of this will not be felt until the seventh month.
to be felt sorry for Immediately become more personally involved in a situation you feel is not going right.
to feel sorry for someone All unresolved situations from the past need to be taken care of within the next three days. Resolution of these problems will prevent interference with present day situations.

soufflé Do not become involved in any uncomfortable and difficult situations for the next few days.

soul Meditate in your favorite manner and your prayers will be answered. Expect a long, healthy and prosperous life.
"you got soul" - slang term, any usage Within five days you will be given the gift of greater healing and heightened psychic abilities by your higher power. You will gain higher organizational skills and be able to use this talent in dynamic ways. Many blessings will follow you all of your life. You are headed for a brilliant future.

soul food Within five days you will be given the gift of greater healing and heightened psychic powers by the Gods. You will develop greater organizational skills and be able to put this talent to use in a dynamic way. You will be able to use this gift wisely and many blessings will follow you for a lifetime. You are headed for a brilliant future.

soul mate Do everything necessary to develop more spirituality. You will be able to conduct yourself with more confidence than ever before. Take care of and treat yourself to

something unusual you have been wanting to do.

soul music Do something out of the ordinary. You will receive a declaration of adoration.

sound *loud* You will need more privacy in order to accomplish what needs to be done.
sound of children's voices You will enjoy victory regarding a very confidential matter in a few days.

sound effect Someone will come to your assistance in a time of crisis.

sound effects Within three days you will get the sense that your feelings for someone are deepening and you will go to great lengths to create a closer bond. Your efforts will be reciprocated and you will be welcomed with open arms by this individual. For the next two days you must also make sure you are emotionally able to handle a request for assistance that you will receive from another person. You may be overextending yourself and need to be aware of your present circumstances before committing yourself to anything.

sounding board Be determined to stand up for your rights and defend yourself.

soundproof Within two days you will need to do everything necessary to protect yourself and a friend. You will be traveling through a neighborhood in which there is an angry mob of people and you will be harassed by them. Avoid this by not going anywhere out of the ordinary for the next two days.

sounds *unusual to the ear* Do everything you can to avoid any action that will discredit you or anyone else, especially for the next three days.

sound track You are placing too much importance on someone who is only interested in mind games. This person plots ahead of time the games they want to play. Protect yourself from this person.

sound waves Take time out to ensure you are not missing out on any benefits before you leave a particular situation. There may be advantages you have overlooked and it may be wise to stay in the situation for a few more days.

soup You are going to hear of someone moving. This person will also be giving you many beautiful items that will be difficult for them to move to a smaller residence. You will be called by this person to verify that you will accept the offer. You will be very happy you did.
bowl of soup Take steps to develop a clear plan that will enable you to work independently on a particular situation that will develop within three days. This will allow you to avoid having to ask others for assistance. These thoughts and ideas will come to you with great clarity and you will be able to resolve this situation with success.

to carry soup - canned or otherwise You will begin to flourish and find a new source of unexpected income. Activate the thoughts that will bring this about quicker. This is the perfect cycle to do this. Good luck is with you.

to make soup Do not allow an issue to overwhelm you. You will be able to successfully handle a situation that will be coming up within five days. Good luck is with you. Take steps to maintain your balance.

duck soup You will meet someone who will soon be working closely with you. Do not put yourself in the position for anything unorthodox to develop. This is not the right environment for improper behavior.

soup kitchen Discuss all plans in detail with another person. Make sure there are no last minute corrections. These plans need to be completely free of error.

soupspoon Change your schedule around for the next few days in order to throw off a potential robber. This person has been watching you in order to determine your daily schedule.

sour Someone will attempt to change some prearranged decisions in a way that will not be to your benefit. Take a firm stand to stick with the first agreement.

sourball Someone will ask to see you within a week but, in reality, this person is eager to see you sooner. Their eagerness will drive them to drop in unexpectedly within a two day period.

source Pace yourself and proceed calmly, you are headed in the right direction.

sour cherry You will live a long and healthy life. Maintain healthy eating habits and drink plenty of water. Blessings are with you.

sour cream It would be a good idea to be very concerned and find out what is really happening with a special person. Spend more time with them and determine what is really going on.

sourdough Think carefully about any sudden urges you may get within the next two days and be sure to write them down. These thoughts will come in handy at a later time and will offer you a fresh point of view about life. Many blessings will come to you and your family.

sour grapes Think more of yourself and less of others for the next few weeks. You are giving too much of yourself to others.

sousaphone Be very cautious and make no extra demands on a special person right now. This person is overwhelmed by certain issues that are coming up in their life right now and will come to you for a listening ear. If you offer your time, this person will be forever grateful to you.

south *any form* This will be a lucky cycle for you. You will be able, within seven days, to use all of the right words to put another person at ease. This person will then be comfortable enough to share the deep feelings they have for you. This person finds it difficult to verbalize emotions and your ability to put others at ease enables them to find the courage to speak up. This is also a good luck symbol and blessings are with you.

South Carolina Someone will be more than willing to grant you a favor. Make this request within two days. This may also be used as a reference point in time. If you dream of this state and see its name used in any context, the dream message will occur on this day.

South Dakota You will be able to cleverly make a claim on a certain person's affections. You will be successful in gaining what you want and will experience intense love and passion from this individual. If you choose to do this, the option is available to you during this cycle. This may also be used as a reference point in time. If you dream of this state and see its name used in any context, the dream message will occur on this day.

souvenirs You have been mentally developing a love plan. This plan has been placed on hold for some time because of your hectic lifestyle. Within the next few days the person you are feeling affection toward will provide you with many pleasurable emotional moments. Do not miss out. A brilliant future is yours.

Soviet You will attend an unexpected reunion and this will result in a number of reconciliations. Expect this to take place within two days.

sow Do not allow anyone to run you around and take advantage of your generosity. For the next few days conserve your energy.

sow bug Have an intimate conversation with someone in order to expedite a change in your present circumstances. This will bring you a tremendous amount of relief.

soy Get through your present circumstances. Once you do this you will feel much more secure and anchored.

soybeans You will be surprised at who will make a romantic overture toward you. Watch and listen attentively for the next few days and you can expect a wonderful future ahead.

soy sauce You have been handling a situation very loosely. Once you bring this situation to its conclusion, you will find great relief.

space Determine what your plans are for the near future. Be very specific on your priorities right now and act on them.

spacecraft Someone will go out of their way over the next few days to change your plans. Do not allow this to occur.

space heater Someone will do anything to get out of a lease agreement. Do not lease property for the next two days or you will be asking for problems.

spaceman Within a few days someone who has purposely avoided you will apologize for their behavior. This person will go to great lengths to repair this relationship. Should you choose to reconcile, this relationship will be better than it ever was before.

spaceship You will decide to enter into a sexual agreement with someone who will keep you emotionally and sexually satisfied for as long as both of you desire to maintain this relationship.

space shuttle This is an extremely lucky omen for you and you are definitely headed for a brilliant future. You will also be offered a proposal that will be very difficult for you to refuse. If you decide to become involved in this you will find that you will enjoy a far better lifestyle than you ever anticipated. Proceed with confidence.

space station Someone will accuse you of failing to live up to your responsibilities within this month. Try to avoid this by living up to your responsibilities.

space suit Do not lean so heavily on someone else or demonstrate demanding behavior. Be fair to others and back off.

spade You will suddenly receive more love than you ever expected. Enjoy it.

spaghetti Do not underestimate your mental abilities. You have a certain genius and your ideas have great promise.

spaghetti and meatballs For the next three days, actively motivate others in order to get things moving in the right direction. Once this is accomplished you will be more financially secure.

spaghetti sauce A jealous but very wealthy professional person is seeking a relationship that will lead, if you choose, to marriage. This could be a very financially secure proposition and promises much happiness in the future.

spaghetti squash Well chosen words of love will bring you royal rewards.

spaghetti strap Take steps to get past your present circumstances without breaking any rules. You will be better able to get on with your life without dealing with this issue.

spaghetti western Watch out for damage due to mold and mildew.

Spain Proceed with confidence and your desire for fame will be realized. You are headed in the right direction. This may also be used as a reference point in time. If you dream of this country and see its name used in any context, the dream message will occur on this day.

Spam You rely too much on other people. Give them a break. You will be entering a cycle that will allow you to develop more independence.

span Postpone action until you have more information available to you.

spandex You will make the correct decision just in time.

spangle Watch out for impulsive spending. Keep yourself financially stable for the next few weeks.

Spaniard Clarify all questions you have and get solid answers before you decide on a secret rendezvous.

spaniel This is a good luck symbol. You have been deeply and intensely attracted to someone. When you are finally in the position to be with this person, you will hold back emotionally and physically because you will not be sure you can feel as deeply as anticipated once you have been with this person. After several days of mulling it over, you will decide that you are emotionally ready.

Spanish moss A variety of situations will occur within the week. These issues will take place consecutively and unexpectedly. Each one will bring you joy. Good luck is with you.

Spanish omelet Compare the pros and cons when trying to make a major decision. Weigh each one and you will reach the right decision.

Spanish rice Get professional help to enable you to break out of the habit of emotional self deprivation. Learn to break free, treat yourself well, and stop depriving yourself.

spank *to spank someone else* You will be victorious in grasping your highest ambitions.

to be spanked You will be verbally threatened. Take this threat seriously. Take yourself to a safe place because this person is focused on performing a violent act against you.

spanking Within five days someone who was once a part of your life and mistreated you to the point of your leaving the relationship will reenter your life with verbal verification that they want to become reinvolved. This will be very appealing to you and you will be offered a new proposal for a life together with solid plans for a good relationship. You will then have flashbacks of what your life was once like together. This dream is letting you know that you do not need to waste any time worrying about this because you can have a good life together. This person is now very responsible and reasonable and you can confidently reenter this relationship. It will be a solid and permanent union for as long as you desire and everyone involved will benefit. You are headed for a brilliant future.

spar Make it clear to another person that you will tolerate no nonsense. This will make things easier for you in the future.

spare You will request a large important favor from someone who will offer it free of charge. This service will change your life around significantly. Take advantage of this. The opportunity for this free service will never come again and you will save a great deal of money if you act now.

spareribs You will be given a special party by others to thank you to offer appreciation for work well done. This will take you by surprise. Make sure also that all of your mechanical devices have enough fluid to perform properly. Do everything necessary to ensure that all appliances work correctly in order to avoid stress in the near future.

spark Be aware of someone who, although they don't show it, fizzles with emotion whenever you are around. Once you find out who this person is, you will feel gratified. This person will be a valuable and important person in your life.

sparkler Within a few days you will encounter someone you have not seen in awhile but have always been attracted to. Stop being so passive and request that this person join you for brunch. Make it your business to bring them closer. This person also holds affectionate feelings for you.

spark plug One of your friends will make a large profit on the sale of a particular item. This sale will be prompted and arranged by you and concluded when you speak to another friend who desires to purchase this item. You will not make a profit but the sale will be mutually satisfying.

sparrow You will receive a gift of a beautiful caged bird. This is a lucky omen.

sparrow hawk A situation has evolved in your life that has been tearing you down emotionally. This issue will revert to a more normal and stable situation in a short period of time. You will feel relief from a burden and all mysteries surrounding this situation will be revealed. Good luck will be with you for some time.

Sparta Take care of any senior citizen who needs help. Friends will also reconcile over a past dispute. This will bring you happiness. This may also be used as a reference point in time. If you dream of this city and see its name used in any context, the dream message will occur on this day.

Spartacus There will be a new addition to the family.

spasm A friend will bring you a gift from a far off place where they have been vacationing. You will also need to discuss with someone the mixed emotions created by the manner in which they communicate. By bringing this out in the open, you will gain ground with this person.

spatter Within the week, you will be experiencing a series of many unexpected and unusual situations. These will occur one after the other. Prepare yourself mentally to cope with these situations and resolve them successfully.

spatula A complex situation will arise. It would be better to keep this matter confidential.

spawn Be forewarned. You are planning to marry someone you are very fond of. You will settle down and have a few years of marital bliss and beautiful children. You will, however, be deserted by this individual. They will no longer desire this relationship and will be unable to openly express it. You will never see this individual again. You have the choice to alter this path if you choose.

spay Follow your urges for the next week or so.

SPCA Be cautious while in unfamiliar areas. You will need to physically protect yourself from someone who attacks by surprise. Be extremely careful this week.

SPCC Allow yourself to enjoy something you have secretly deprived yourself of.

speak *to speak to someone who is not there* This is a very lucky omen. You need to develop a quiet conviction when going after needed services that you feel you are being denied. Tactfully repeat your requests until you are clearly heard. This applies to both professional services and emotional situations. Pay close attention to what the voice is telling you. You may be overlooking a positive situation that needs to be included in your life and embraced or a negative situation that is developing that needs to be attended to. This message will enhance your life in some capacity.

to speak with a disembodied woman's voice Follow the advice given in the dream to the letter. If you did not clearly hear the message, this implies that this is an extremely lucky omen. You will be able to withstand any hardship that will arise within the next three days.

to speak with a disembodied man's voice Pay attention to the message given. If negative, take steps to change the outcome. If positive, take steps to incorporate it into your life. This dream also implies that someone who acts indifferently to you is, in reality, not this way. This person actually desires very much to be involved in your life. If you choose to become involved, make the first move and let it be known that you would like more involvement. Your plans will also fall into place just as you have envisioned. Do not hold back on big projects. Tackle these projects and you will experience prosperity.

to speak with a deceased person's voice only You will experience victory due to the valiant integrity you use when making decisions. You will not compromise your principles.

Develop a quiet conviction and be relentless in your pursuit of something that righteously belongs to you. This may be in the form of money, contracts, items and agreements as well as productive conversation. Do not give up until you succeed.

in any other form You will soon become involved with someone who is not fully committed to a work relationship. This person will play games, create a hot and cold environment and you will seldom see eye to eye. You will need to develop a no nonsense approach because you will both be co-workers on a project within a few weeks. Once this attitude is adopted, you will accomplish much. Stick to business.

speaking in tongues You will be much happier in a different occupation.

spear Make sure you express precisely the ways you want your plans to be carried out. Do not be timid and do not hold back.

spearfish Do not allow past memories to affect your present life. These memories will crop up again over the next few weeks. Refuse to dwell on them and avoid the agony they will create.

spearmint Someone you are attracted to acts very indifferently toward you. In reality, this person desires you very much. Make the first move, and this relationship will reach fruition.

special You will soon be receiving exceptionally good news.

special delivery Within three days someone you know will ask you to share in their wealth. You must also keep in mind that a relationship that is important to you will grow only as much as the other person allows it to and that this is something that is completely out of your control. You have prior notice of this and can handle yourself appropriately.

special education This is an extremely lucky omen for love. Within three days you will be able to express your thoughts clearly and convince someone to open up to you about their true feelings. This person will feel comfortable around you because of your actions and this will result in a warm and loving relationship. This cycle will allow all communication to flow easily and openly.

special effects For the next few nights you will have dreams that are sneak previews of your future and they will offer you ways to improve your personal situations. The clues will be very specific in pointing out what you need for success.

specialty You will have many wonderful days with your closest loved ones.

species You will finally be free of your arrogant ways and free to live a fuller, richer, more emotionally fulfilled life.

specimen You need to be alerted to poor negotiations in the future. You will, however, have a great sex life.

speck You will patch up an old disagreement over the next few days. This will occur rapidly and everything will remain happy and peaceful from this point on.

spectacles After a pleasant, quiet dinner, while taking a pleasant stroll, a special person will choose inappropriate words to express their feelings. If you choose to let this bother you, the situation will escalate into hours of arguments. Ignore these words, they will be spoken unintentionally.

spectator *to be* A variety of very different events will arise. Each will be an all day event and will occur one after the other. You will be very busy but pleasantly entertained.

to see spectators Someone will perform a special favor for you that will give you much pleasure.

specter Avoid mixing medications. You will have a violent reaction to this. Be very cautious of this over the next few days.

speech Your lack of confidence will prevent you from accurately stating your feelings and opinions to others. This barrier will ultimately keep you from fulfilling your potential and create physical problems. Work on carrying yourself with assurance and confidence in order to break through this block. Within three days, your attempt will be successful.

speech disorder You will hear of a neighbor committing suicide by hanging within a few days.

speechless Someone will accuse you of lying. This person will become known to you as a hypocrite because they have lied and are now committing slander against you. Go on with your life and do not allow this to bother you.

speedboat After many years of having another person not speak to you, you will be contacted for a reconciliation. You will quickly recover a lost friendship.

speed bump You and a special person will reconcile after a bad lover's quarrel. The relationship will be better than it was prior to the argument. Blessings are with you.

speed freak Someone will go to great lengths to pull you out of a certain group or plan so you no longer have anything to do with it. This person will relentlessly work to disassociate you from this situation. Investigate this more thoroughly so you can protect your interests. You will also, for a three day period have to develop a certain amount of patience. You will find yourself in a cycle that will leave you with too much to do and you will be running from one thing to the other trying to handle each issue. This will be a big waste of time. Prepare for this cycle ahead of time and learn the art of patience, otherwise you will become emotionally depleted and on the verge of tears. Remain calm and you will be able to handle what you need to take care of.

speedometer Remain in a safe environment and avoid all accidents that will cost you your life. Be very cautious of your surroundings and situations, this is a very dangerous cycle for you.

speed *to speed* Protect your sense of hearing. At the first sign of any problems, seek help and avoid all situations that will cause you damage.

speed trap A close relative will have an accident and you will be required to spend several hours in the emergency room with them. Be sure to warn close relatives to remain in a safe environment for a few days.

spell Should you see someone placing a spell on you in your dreams, become very aware of who they are. This person is very immoral and wicked. If you do not recognize the face, it will represent someone who will soon come into your life. This person will cause you great emotional harm. Avoid this individual at all costs. You will have the ability and strength to endure anything you need to handle. Victory is with you.
to put a spell on someone Watch your actions. If they are negative, stop the behavior. If positive, continue. This dream is a very lucky omen for you. You will also recover quickly from an emotionally draining situation.
to see someone have a spell cast on them The person you see will come to emotional harm within three days. If you recognize this person, take steps to alert them to this potential damage.
in any other form Be very careful when engaged in pleasure seeking activities. You must also be sure you do not allow anyone to usurp your power and authority. This individual wants to gain control of something and will attempt to manipulate you in order to gain power over you and a certain situation you are dealing with. Make sure you do not fall prey to this person. Prepare yourself in such a way to avoid this occurrence. You will have the strength and ability to handle this situation. Good luck will be with you.

spell *to spell a word* You will be elected to a high government position.
to spell a word incorrectly The person you are confiding in is not being sincere with you.

spelling bee *to be in* You will receive a large inheritance from a relative.

spelunker Focus clearly on plans you expect to put into action in the near future. Decide what you really want from life and determine whether these plans are workable. You have the time to make changes in your plans to ensure their success.

spend *to spend* You have made arrangements with some-

one to pay you off in one lump sum but it will not work out this way. Work with this person to set up a payment schedule. Be flexible.

spendthrift An older person will soon move away and leave you their small pet as a gift. Take care of this animal as long as you are able.

sperm If you choose to take this route, you will enter into a union with an intelligent, physically attractive, wealthy, charming person with a dynamic career. You will be happy with this person for the remainder of your life.

spermicide Avoid suffering and sorrow caused by the carelessness of a friend. This will lead to your injury. Prevent this by remaining in a safe environment and do not put yourself in a situation where injury will occur.

sperm whale You will have large victories over the next few days. You also need to be aware of the possibility of injury and must make sure you remain in a safe environment.

sphagnum mass You will enjoy good health and a quick recovery from illness. This dream also implies joyful times are ahead.

sphere Avoid any situation, for the next few days, that will lead to a debate or argument with someone else.

sphinx You will be invited to a place that appears very unusual and gloomy. Follow your instincts, leave immediately and go home. Play it safe for the next few days, especially in strange environments.

spice You will attend a gathering with people of different cultures, walks of life, religions and races. You will enjoy yourself and sample many different foods.

spice islands A special talent will be given to you by the deities. A brilliant future is ahead for you.

spicy Someone you have not seen in a long time will drop by unexpectedly and take you on a pleasant outing. They will come on to you in such a way that will suggest a strong romantic interest. You will have a wonderful time. This person will promise to call but you will never hear from them again. You have done nothing wrong, this person is simply unable to surrender their feelings. Be patient, give this person time and you will be contacted.

spider Someone has already plotted what they need and want from you. You are being drained because this person continually asks you to do favors they can do themselves. Be aware, also, that you are spending money on this person, a little bit at a time and this money will add up. This person is insincere, unable to open up to you and is one thing to you and something else to other people. They will say what they think others want to hear. You would be better off removing this person from your life. Don't set yourself up for this dangerous cycle.

many spiders crawling around Anxieties experienced in a relationship are the result of possessiveness and jealousy by both partners. Let this anxiety go in order to enjoy a fulfilled union.

spider crab Do not enter into a verbally abusive argument with your loved ones. This will lead to a permanent break up within a few days. This is a dangerous situation.

spider mite The person who is approaching you romantically is dishonest about their feelings and is insincere about commitment. Be very wary of this individual. This situation is emotionally dangerous to you because you will fall deeply for someone who does not care for you.

spider monkey A very dangerous situation will arise among family members. A dispute will break out and abusive language can rapidly escalate into a physical fight that will result in injury. Use whatever means you have to prevent this.

spider plant A situation will arise within a few days involving a past love who left unexpectedly, with no warning, and no subsequent communication. This person will return with the hope of reconciliation. The reason for leaving will be explained and it will have had little to do with you. Future dreams will offer the answers for the behavior you need to assume concerning this reunion. Blessings and much love are with you now.

spider web Be alert. Do not allow someone to intentionally send you on a wild goose chase. You will have to have certain tasks performed by others in order to have your needs met but will be told it will be impossible to accomplish. Do not compromise and seek help from a higher chain of command. This is especially important for the next three days.

on you For the next two days, carefully screen all people answering any ad you have placed in the newspaper. It would be wise to avoid dealing with one of these people. Follow your instincts.

Spielberg, Steven It is essential for the next two weeks that you position yourself in such a way that you can create excitement and generate a greater interest regarding a new situation. You will be able to segment more success about a new product, plan, idea or conversation. You will gain excellent feedback that will bring about more productivity, fun and create a non stressful outcome to what is a priority. You will be able to bring everyone involved together in building a common understanding. You will determine what, where, and how to effectively achieve a chief victory on a grander scale than you anticipated. Your goal is to make the world aware of these exciting ideas, etc., and you will find they are well received by others.

spigot *to turn one on* You will soon meet someone with a wonderful sense of humor. You will care for each other and

this person will be free to date. Many days of laughter are ahead but this person will have a problem verbalizing their deep feelings for you. Be patient, they care deeply for you.

spike You will hear delightful news from a close friend who lives far away.

spill Circulate within your work environment so you will be noticed when a desirable position opens up.

spillway Someone who is disappointed in themselves will commit to attend a social function with you and will try to drop out at the last minute. This person is very unhappy. It would be a good idea to try and find an alternate until this friend feels more secure.

spinach Nothing will keep you from reaching your goals. You must also not assume that having sex with someone will win them over. This person simply wants a moment's pleasure and will then go on with their life.

spinal anesthesia Within a few days you will meet a very cheerful, responsible person. You will, at first glance, desire a relationship with this individual but within two weeks you will meet someone else who is far more suited to you. You will have to choose between the two.

spinal column What looks like silver is really gold in regards to an ongoing situation. Go for it.

spinal cord You will have to come up with better, more creative plans for your recreational time.

spindle Someone you have just met will whisper sweet nothings in your ear while you are slow dancing. This will happen within four days and will be very enjoyable.

spine Make your grandchildren a priority in your life. You will also have the courage, within three days, to stand firm about a certain decision no matter how others feel. This decision will be based on a gut reaction and you will feel there should be no compromise no matter how hard others push you to change your mind. You will be required to push for drastic changes in another person's lifestyle. This will ultimately lead to a change in your own lifestyle. Make sure they take place so all those concerned will benefit. You will have the courage and determination to execute these plans within three days.

of fish fin, porcupine, cactus, etc. Do whatever you can to eat those foods that help to build up your immune system and make sure you are getting adequate rest, especially for the next three days. Maintaining your health should be a priority to you during this time frame.

to see yourself or someone get punctured by a fish fin, porcupine spine, cactus spine, etc. Within two days, someone will relentlessly attempt to involve you in pleasure seeking activities that are not in your best interest. Carefully watch your behavior and don't be so willing to venture into the unknown. Take steps to protect yourself. You will otherwise be entering into a very lucky cycle and many blessings will come to you and your family. Remain very aware, for the next three days, of a stranger who will enter your life in a very public setting and create chaos by way of quarrels and disagreements. Do what you can to remain uninvolved.

spinet Express a more gentle positive side of yourself. A small child you are in constant contact with needs to be exposed to your gentle, humorous side. Stop being so strict with this child.

spinning wheel This indicates good luck, health and wealth. You will travel for business purposes and have a safe return.

spinster Push yourself to express the love you feel for another person.

spin the bottle You are loved more than you can imagine. Do not deprive yourself of the emotions and deep feelings that others are offering you. You will experience appreciation and love from others within the week.

spiral Within a few days, you will have to deal with a very evil person. This person distorts facts and twists words to their advantage. This will not only set you back but will also create a certain amount of damage. Be aware of this and take steps to avoid this person. Otherwise, this is a lucky omen.

spire Facts will be distorted and your words twisted to another's advantage. This person will attempt to gain credit for work done by you. Be wary of this for the next seven days. Tread lightly and this can be prevented.

spirit You will have victory in all phases of your life. You will share many blessings with your family and your ambitions will be realized. You must also supervise yourself more closely. Anything you do that will directly affect another person needs to be rethought in order to avoid chaos. Do everything necessary to maintain tranquility in your life, particularly for the next two weeks. You will also be able to tap into your rare and magical qualities to resolve upcoming important situations with those who are important to you. You will handle this well but it is important this be done immediately. For the next three days keep yourself healthy and try to live in a healthy way. Drink plenty of water and watch your intake of prescription drugs. Take steps to prevent anything negative from occurring that your spirit has warned you of in your dream and go all out to promote any positive message.

a living person's spirit This person needs to be aware that for the next three days, they need to live a more healthful, tranquil life. Supervise and encourage this person's activities carefully to ensure they drink plenty of water, eat properly and watch their intake of prescription drugs. Warn this person of any negative message. All positive messages need to be promoted. You will also encounter a former lover within a few days.

if you do not recognize the spirit Pay close attention to any message this spirit gives you. If you are warned of an impending situation, take immediate steps to avoid it. If you are being told of future positive situations, take steps to magnify the benefits. This is a lucky cycle for you and you will be able to use your abilities to handle anything that is important to you. All new transactions will be lucky.

dead person's spirit This is a lucky omen and signifies victory in all of your future plans. Anything you are presently working on will be successful as long as it is consistently and relentlessly pursued. Each message given will be accurate. Take steps to ensure that anything negative will not occur. Any positive message needs to be promoted. You must also take steps to alert anyone else of a message directed toward them. This is an immediate situation and requires aggressive action.

Holy Spirit You are entering a very lucky and fortuitous cycle and will achieve victory in almost everything you want for the next week. Make sure your health is guarded. Be sure to eat the right foods and maintain a healthy lifestyle and be especially careful of over medication, food poisoning and freak accidents. You and your family will enjoy much tranquility for a long time to come.

evil spirit Pay attention to the specific thing the spirit is doing. This will give you a clue to the area of your life that needs to be worked on. You are clearly stressed out from everyday situations and need to back off some. Do things for yourself and be good to yourself. Stress will cause major physical damage if you do not relax. Eat well, get plenty of rest and sleep. Drink plenty of water and stay out of other people's problems.

spiritual Meditate in your favorite form and be good to yourself. You will also be making stern decisions within five days and you do not have to explain this move to another person. Make this decision and go on with your life. You will have the confidence and willpower to make these strong choices. Many blessings are with you.

spit Be aware that certain young children may be suffering from the cruelty of other children. Give these children the guidance they need.

spitball The proper and immediate handling of an urgent situation will halt any last minute breakdowns.

spit curl You will need to establish a liaison with key people in order to gain clarity about several ongoing situations. One person will make you acutely aware of the most important facet of these issues.

spite The loan you are seeking will not be authorized.

spitfire Do not allow yourself to become a referee between two people. A verbal disagreement may escalate into physical violence. If you become involved, you will be injured.

spittle Do not force yourself on someone who is not interested in you.

spittoon Do not be careless. Other people are stalking you. Be alert to your surroundings and do not allow yourself to fall prey to anyone, especially for the next two weeks.

splash You will be in a state of panic over something told to you over the phone. This person will state a desire to commit suicide. Take steps to ensure this does not occur.

splashdown Someone desires to become close to you but lacks the courage and ability to communicate this. If you desire this person, arrange circumstances to bring you into an intimate situation. If you do not pursue this, you will lose interest. Years later, after it is too late, you will feel regret over this. Do not allow this chance to slip by. The opportunity is open for you to aggressively take steps to bring this situation to fruition, especially for the next three days.

splatter You will receive a beautiful bird as a gift.

spleen Take control over your environment and do not allow a family situation to put you in a tough spot. Do not allow anything to disrupt your balance.

splendor Do not sign any papers of importance until you get a professional person to carefully read over these documents.

splice Watch your words. Someone will deeply resent words spoken in haste and this will cause a deep separation in the friendship.

splint Make sure you behave in the appropriate way toward someone who has a conniving nature. You will become more aware of this person's character as time progresses.

splinter Someone will be caught committing an act they have no business doing. You will benefit from this person's downfall. Within two days you will also find yourself in a situation where someone you consider precious and hold close to you will be mistreated by someone you least expect. This will be done in a very subtle but painful way and you will quickly develop feelings of resentment toward this individual as well as a deep hurt. Do what you can to avoid this scenario completely or, if you must go through this, you will be prepared ahead of time. This also implies that you will achieve a great victory that is not connected with this scenario but will occur within the same time frame.

split Someone you care for will move to an area that is too far away to commute to and will be too costly for phone calls. You will feel this separation on a deep level for months to come.

split level Be very acutely aware of your fatigue level, especially while operating machinery. Find out the reason for this chronic fatigue and take steps to keep it from recurring.

split pea Keep the children you are associated with from becoming accidentally intoxicated by any substance. This will lead to accidents and injury.

split personality Two people who are closely related to each other will fall in love with you at the same time. Whatever you choose to do will cause resentments with the one left out. Be very careful with this situation because your choice may cause the breakup of a close friendship between these two admirers. A three way conversation will help alleviate negative emotions.

spoil Voice the sense of unfairness you feel to others and put your requests in writing.

sponge Someone will unexpectedly repay a long standing debt.

sponge bath Avoid becoming involved in anything indecent. You will be approached with an offer by a very heartless and immoral person. Do not accept.

sponge cake For a two day period, stay within the boundaries of your neighborhood. You will be in danger otherwise.

sponsor Do not allow yourself to be talked into being a sponsor and cosigning for anyone. You will be asked to do so within two weeks and the outcome will definitely be to your disadvantage. Refuse to participate. Within a three day period you will also develop a network of people who can offer you support and assistance and will brainstorm with you to find the answer to a situation that needs to be attended to within the week. You will reach a very successful conclusion.

spook Refuse to participate in any important situation that may arise within a few days and do not agree to any contracts and decisions during this time period. Use the newspaper and advertise in order to reach your goals.

spool Within three days you will find someone to work with you. This person will be filled with genius and has very well organized, success oriented ideas.

spoon You will come very close to murdering someone who has committed a violent act against a close relative. Seek help, warn this relative, and take precautions within a few days to prevent the initial violent act. Make sure also that you get to the heart of a particular matter. Once you determine the missing element, you will be appropriately able to conduct yourself in such a way to resolve this issue.

spoon fed Take it easy and do nothing for awhile.

spoor Be aware of the needs of the young people you are dealing with now.

sport fishing All written proposals, contracts, plans, etc., will be very lucky for you right now.

sports Take off all important jewelry while cleaning and performing heavy chores. This will protect the jewelry from loss and damage.

sports car Proceed with confidence, your ideas and projects will meet with success and you are headed in the right direction. Relentlessly and consistently pursue this goal. Within three days, a very successful person will go to great lengths to change their life around in order to be with you. Work together in order to synchronize your plans and make things run smoothly. It is your choice to pursue this relationship or not.

sportscaster Take precautions to protect all of your valuables and do not become too friendly with strangers.

sportsman A friend will be in a very argumentative mood and disagree with each one of your ideas. To avoid feeling harassed, find alternative activities that will take you away from this person.

sports medicine You have a special talent that sets you apart from others. Your skills are so esteemed it will become difficult for others to get close to you. Check your attitude.

sports wardrobe Develop another steady source of income as soon as possible. This will ensure financial stability.

sportswriter Respect other people's points of view as well as their ideas.

spot You will gain a friend for a lifetime and will share activities and good fortune. Both of you will be loyal and true to each other.

spotless Keep a very accurate account of what you are told by others. This will be important to keep for your own records. Avoid heated debates with anyone.

spotlight You will be able to offer help to someone you care about to assist them in developing their potential and realizing their goals. Because of their gratitude, you will be richly rewarded in the future due to an increase in their wealth. Many blessings are with you and your family.

spotted fever Agree to any decisions that will be made over the next few days. You will also receive a positive answer to anything you request.

spout Do not become stagnant by refusing to evolve and grow mentally and emotionally. It is important to mature and not let your loved ones outgrow you. This could be a serious situation. Allow yourself to reach higher levels of maturity.

sprain Decide what to do with all of the empty spaces in your life. Push yourself and you will be surprised at the creativity you develop for filling in these empty times. Luck is with you.

sprawl out Within a few days, allow someone else to run light errands for you in order to better budget your time.

spray You will have many questions and mixed feelings about a relationship you will soon enter with a very sexually attractive person. This person has a sexual appetite you will be unable to keep up with. Move on with your life in order to avoid hurt feelings at a later time.

spray can You will have misunderstandings and an inability to relate with someone you can easily avoid. Make the effort to avoid this stress.

spray gun Avoid the temptation to loosen your morals.

spread You will be involved in a court proceeding. This matter will not be resolved soon and will be very distasteful to you. Do everything necessary to avoid any behavior that will lead to court actions against you.

spread eagle You will be asked by someone to do something that should be a private matter. In reality, someone else will be watching without your consent. This will be a sexual episode and you will be spied upon. Avoid participating in any immoral and illicit acts.

spreadsheet You will unexpectedly run into a former love. The first time you were not ready for a deep commitment. Both of you are now ready to commit and the relationship will blossom. This person has also recently come into wealth.

spring Someone of a different nationality will enter your life and present you with a variety of viewpoints that benefit you and your ongoing plans. You will achieve success.

springboard Avoid arguments for the next two days.

spring cleaning Do not remain in a situation that continues to bring resentments and do everything necessary to leave. Good luck will be with you for the next two weeks. This is a lucky cycle for change.

Springer spaniel Your supervisor is becoming aware that you do not care for your job. Become aware of what is going on around you and take steps to make the appropriate changes.

spring fever When attempting to get something off your chest, speak to someone only when you have a solid plan that will clear these problems up. Be tactful when talking to those close to you who may be contributing to the problem. Many rewards will come from these conversations.

sprinkle For the next three days you will be able to verbalize your detailed thoughts in such an appealing way that you will put someone at ease and create an atmosphere of comfort when they are in your presence. Conversations will flow easily and you will develop a new sense of closeness. This person will tell you what you have long wanted to hear. You are on the path toward a prosperous future and will be able to communicate in a way that will successfully reach others. You and this other person will enjoy a tranquil and wonderful life together if this is your choice.

sprint In the near future, someone will put you in touch with people of a different culture and way of life. Normally, you would never visit this particular locale or meet these people, but as a result of this exposure you will enjoy an exciting cycle.

sprouts Avoid becoming involved in a ménage à trois. Investigate further, the person making advances toward you is married.

spruce All out of town business transactions will turn out perfectly.

spun glass Do not plan any new transactions for a few days and postpone all transactions that have already been planned.

spur *cowboy* Do not betray anyone to another person this week. A heated argument will begin and escalate beyond your imagination and this could become a very dangerous situation. Remain loyal.

to spur Take all precautions to prevent a sexually transmitted disease for the next two weeks.

spurn Do not divulge confidential information to anyone.

Sputnik Be very aware of your limits. Make sure you are not overextending yourself in any situation.

spy Do not allow a domestic situation to create anxiety. Take a long walk that will provide visual stimulation in order to clear your mind and restore mental tranquility. Before you know it, everything will fall neatly into place with just a little effort from you. This is a promise that you will find the solution to a difficult situation you are now involved in. Drink plenty of water to prevent dehydration.

spyglass Make certain your environment is safe.

squab Do everything necessary to speak with someone you have been wanting to talk to. This person is thinking of moving and once you give them your opinion, they will change their mind. Luck is with you.

squad You will have a one time opportunity to make a great deal of money in a short time with a small investment. Go for it. This is a lucky cycle for this.

squad car This implies immediate danger from the person you see in the squad car. The danger will be in the nature of a sexual assault and you will contract a sexually transmitted disease. Take extra precautions against this person.

if you recognize the person in the car You will be stopped for a minor traffic infraction. For two weeks, take extra precautions while driving in order to prevent this.

squadron You are in danger of being placed in a very dangerous situation by another person. For the next three days avoid anyone who will become very threatening to you in their efforts to force you to do something. You have prior notice of this so you can prepare yourself to handle this situation in an appropriate manner. You will also need to start paying close attention to a certain situation to ensure it does not spiral downhill. Do everything you can to head off any potentially negative event. Listen to your instincts and you will be alerted to avoid certain people you have no business associating with. Others will try to bring you harm in a subtle and conniving way at a time when you are most unguarded. Protect yourself and everything you hold emotionally precious to you. You have prior notice of this and will be able to act appropriately.

squall Do not treat the person you love in such a way that they will be permanently driven away. Your behavior will cause this person much suffering.

square Do everything necessary to vacate the area you are spending too much time in. Find an alternative area and reach for greater horizons.

square dance Someone is very eager for a reconciliation.

square deal Do not tell lies. This behavior will rapidly backfire.

square knot Do not make threats. The person you threaten is in a no nonsense mood and will come after you in a few days.

squash Do not allow another person's last minute plans to throw you off. Stay with your own plans and do not become discouraged. You will also receive a small gift.

squat You will feel relief after talking with someone who has had recent domestic problems because these problems have since cleared up.

squatter Do not exchange property. This is not a good idea.

squaw You will endure sexual harassment at the hands of someone you find irritating. It will not last long once you have confronted this person.

Squaw Valley You will be invited to a beautiful vacation spot within two weeks. You will have a wonderful time and return home safely. This may also be used as a reference point in time. If you dream of this ski resort and see its name used in any context, the dream message will occur on this day.

squeal A person you have recently left will come back desiring a reconciliation. This is a very dangerous situation. This person feels a great deal of animosity toward you and could do you a great deal of harm. Avoid this person.

squeamish In a few weeks you will have some free time. Become involved in clubs that focus on your favorite hobbies. You will enjoy this and it may offer you a chance to gain a second income.

squeegee Do not allow anger to rule you. Take a long walk during times of irrational anger to clear your head and calm down. Everything will fall into place better than expected.

squeeze *to squeeze someone* Make a point of being hospitable to a close relative who will visit you to escape family problems and relax. A few hours of stress free time will feel like days of leisure to this person.

to be squeezed Help a senior citizen become more active and meet more people. This will really brighten this person's life.

to see others squeezing each other There will be a new baby in the family.

in any other form Do not leave yourself open to anybody who may have a hidden agenda. This could result in an unusual or perverted experience that will bring you many moments of distaste and disgust. Take steps to prevent this, especially for the next three days. This person will be someone you feel very comfortable with but will turn on you the moment they sense you are vulnerable. Do everything you can to remain safe.

squeeze bottle For the next three days make sure you do not put yourself in the position that will allow someone to hold something over you. This person will, at a later time, use this to get you to do something you do not want to do. You have prior notice of this and can monitor your behavior carefully so this person has nothing on you. You must also give yourself some time for the next five days to mull over and reflect on your ideas and feelings. You will then be able to connect with those aspects of your life that you wish to improve. You will be more successful if you give yourself the time to carefully go over those decisions you will be making.

squid Within two days you will visit a beautiful crafts display and fall in love with a couple of exquisitely made pieces. You will be told by someone that they made the crafts and will make some specifically for you. You will give this person your phone number and address but never hear from them again because they are not the one who created these crafts and will only be playing with you. Do not allow yourself to be taken.

squint Whatever you wish others to do must first be put into practice by you. Others will follow your example.

squirrel You will receive an unusual request from someone you do not know well in the form of assistance and money. Fulfill this request and you will soon be handsomely rewarded.

squirrel eating An exciting surprise will come your way. You will receive a small gift.

dead squirrel Do not belittle someone who is unable to keep up with you financially.

grey squirrel This is an extremely lucky omen for you and you will enjoy an abundance of health, and wealth in areas of your life you least expected. This will be as a result of an unexpected income. You will now be able to accomplish those tasks you once felt were impossible. Use this cycle to tackle those big projects. Proceed with confidence, you are headed for a very prosperous future. For the next two days you must also make sure you are safe and will need to take steps to avoid all accidents.

ground squirrel Situations are going to change within three days unless you are willing to adopt other people's ways of living. Because of this you will become very irritated. Do everything necessary to maintain happiness. These situations are beyond your control. Otherwise, you are headed for a prosperous future.

red squirrel This is a good luck omen. You will accomplish exactly what you set out to do and get exactly what you want most in spite of how difficult it may seem.

tree squirrel Do not allow your time to be wasted by the nonsense of others. Develop a no nonsense approach with life and create a stress free environment for yourself.

squirrel cage You will be able to pin down a very evasive person. Within a few days, you will be able to gain an attentive audience from this person and explain what is most important to you. Rehearse your conversation so you can get the most from this person's time. Much will come from this meeting.

squirt Someone will ask to visit you for a few days. This person will want to visit you because they know you will not treat them in any ill manner. It will not be verbalized but they are now living in a destitute way. Do not bring this up until the other person mentions it first. If you do, this person will leave and you will not hear from them again.

Sri Lanka Whatever you ask for will come with no strings attached. A favorable outcome will be the result if you choose to act on it. This may also be used as a reference point in time. If you dream of this country and see its name used in any context, the dream message will occur on this day.

S.S. Do not place yourself in a position to have your vehicle hijacked. Be extremely cautious for the next two days.

stab *to stab someone* Do not become swayed by emotional pleas or become involved in anything distasteful. Do not compromise your character. Do everything you can to avoid any negative event witnessed in this dream and alert anyone you dreamed about to do the same. Take steps to ensure you only experience positive expressions in your life.

to witness a stabbing You will have a brilliant future once you bring your creativity to fruition. Take steps to avoid any negative event in this dream and forewarn anyone concerned in this dream to do the same.

to be stabbed in the back or to stab someone in the back by any sharp object Your intuition will be sharper from now on than ever before, especially for the next two days. Proceed with confidence. You will be victorious in getting what you want from a specific situation, agreement, person, etc., especially if you recognize the person you are stabbing. This also implies that someone is not treating you or someone else in the proper way. You will be very instrumental in getting this person to see other people's points of view. This person will become less angry and more willing to work with other people and will be far more easy going. This will take time, work and patience on your part to make this a reality. Victory is coming your way and many blessings will come to you and your family. Do what you can to avoid any negative event in this dream and forewarn anyone you dreamed about to do likewise. Take steps to ensure you experience only positive expressions in life.

to be stabbed in any other form This implies that someone will plot to inflict emotional and physical harm on you from behind the scenes and unbeknownst to you. This person wants to make sure they catch you off guard and unprotected. They have focused on you for no particular reason in order to gratify their own strange obsessions. This person has not given you any indication that anything is going on with them. Guard yourself completely to make sure you are absolutely safe and do not allow yourself to be in any area where this could take place. Remain on guard, especially for the next two weeks. Any negative event connected with this dream must be prevented and alert anyone connected to this dream to do the same. Make sure you only experience positive expressions in your life.

stable You will be asked to provide shelter for a family with children until they are able to become more financially secure. This will be short term and you will be richly rewarded once they have moved.

stack *(of anything)* In a short while you will be moving into new, unknown directions. Be careful not to take any unnecessary risks.

stadium *any form* You will be immersed in feelings of love for the next two days. You will have a sparkle in your eye prompted by unexpected premature sexual activity with a certain person. This will fill you with sensual pleasure and be a passionate cycle for you. You are headed for a brilliant future filled with sexual pleasures and riches.

staff *(work)* If you feel as though you are being undermined, follow your instincts. You are being taken.

staff You will have a disagreement that will lead to a big quarrel with a member of the opposite sex. You know who this person is. Keep your distance for the next few days and avoid arguments.

staff sergeant Someone you are very attracted to will insist the reason they cannot see you is due to a busy schedule. Go on with your life, this person is not interested in you.

stag Be acutely aware of competitors who do not easily give up. Work steadily and conscientiously until you accomplish your goals.

stage You will wish for an agreement from someone. This person will be very amenable to your wishes and you will receive what you require.

to see someone on stage Someone will wish to make an agreement with you. You feel very amenable right now. Step back and study your options before you agree to anything because right now the plans are too unstable. Make sure they are more precise before you become involved.

stagecoach *to ride in one* You are headed for a brilliant future.

to see one You will hear words you have been longing to hear for a long time.

stagecoach harness You will be exploring new territory and meeting people from all walks of life and cultures. You will enjoy yourself immensely.

stage door You will have to take serious action to bring about a major change. This will benefit everyone involved.

stage effects Someone will subtly begin to show affection toward you. Once you understand what is happening, there will be a wonderful mutual attraction. This will be happening soon.

stage fright Face your commitments head on. Do not allow friends, family, or social events to take your focus from what you should be doing.

stagehand Do not enter into business with the people you are thinking of doing business with. This will not work out well. Think of alternatives.

stage whisper Someone will make a request of you. Turn this person down. You are undecided but a positive answer will yield negative results.

stag horn This is a lucky omen. Think very carefully about backing out of a situation you had made plans to start. It would be to your advantage to drop this project and refuse to take on any new projects for the time being.

stagnate You will request something be done for you on credit. You have every intention of paying this person but something will happen to prevent this. As a result, a lien will be placed on your valuables. Try to prevent this. Although your intentions to pay are honorable, situations will arise to prevent it. Do not take on any credit.

stain Do not take on any athletic recreations unless you are in the proper physical shape to do well.

stained glass Within a few days you will visit unusual sites and marvel at the beauty of the landscape. This will bring you emotional satisfaction. This is a lucky omen and you will be going through a joyous cycle.

stainless steel You will have well-formed, organized thoughts that transform into greater ideas. You will develop these ideas into plans that help you achieve your goals. You will also have an enormous strength of will to carry these plans out.

stainless steel pipe A slightly older person will become your mentor. You will also gain a skill and knowledge from this person that will lead to a lifetime career and benefits, and financial security from this livelihood that will last a lifetime.

stairs You will receive much love and passion for the next seven days from those you desire. You enjoy luck in money and love. Use this luck to your advantage for the next seven day cycle. You will also rapidly pull yourself above any troublesome situation and perform perfectly in any area of your life that you desire. You are on the path toward a very prosperous future.

to go down Do not put yourself into a position that will later lead to an investigation and interrogation. Stay clear of all activities that will lead to this for the next four days.

stairs that go down (trapdoor) Be aware of a well thought out plot to commit a robbery at a party within seven days. All guests will be robbed of valuables and money. Do everything necessary to avoid this party and warn the other guests.

to go up You will enjoy your life fully through a variety of arranged events and amusements over the next few days. Several different people will also let you know how much they care for you and appreciate you. You will have peace and tranquility for a long period of time.

to go upstairs to an attic You will be romantically attracted to someone and will mention this to someone else. Do not allow this person to dissuade you from pursuing this interest for the next seven days. You must also make sure you tie up all loose ends before you run into a dead end.

to trip on Remain uninvolved concerning a certain family situation, no matter how difficult it may seem, especially for the next three days.

to fall down Within three days, you will seriously contemplate involvement with another person. Reassess and analyze this involvement. This person is selfish, has very rough manners and will never change. It is your choice whether you wish to enter this relationship but be aware that you will soon be very unhappy in this situation.

in disrepair Something is taking place behind the scenes with another individual for reasons known only to them. This person enjoys creating chaos and distasteful episodes in the lives of others. Become very aware of your surroundings and any unusual episodes in your life. Take steps to avoid this and bring balance and stability into your life.

stairway You will be romantically attracted to someone and will mention this to someone else. Do not allow this person to dissuade you from pursuing this interest, especially for the next seven days.

stairwell Investing in a jointly owned fund would be a wise decision now. Concentrate on privacy and set priorities. Glorious days are ahead.

stake A special person is ready to separate from the relationship. This person feels as though you don't care as much as they do. Change your attitude and show more affection in order to prevent a permanent split. You are deeply loved and your coldness hurts this individual. Work on reviving this relationship if this is the option you choose to take.

stale Expensive pleasure seeking may become a bad habit. Watch your behavior carefully and keep an eye on your spending habits.

stalemate Any project you fund for family and friends will become a huge success.

Stalin For the next few days keep yourself free from hazards in order to avoid accidents. A potential home accident is preventable.

stalk *to stalk* Pay close attention to this dream. You are being warned not to engage in this type of activity or you could risk prosecution.

to be stalked The person stalking you in a dream will be the one who will cause danger to you in real life if you do not recognize the person. If you do recognize the person from the dream, this individual will soon be the cause of mental anguish. This person's irresponsibility and inconsiderate behavior toward you may evoke such negative feelings that you become their stalker. Charges will be brought against you. Do not allow yourself to become manipulated into any negative behavior.

stalk *(plant stalk)* Dig deeply and discover the reasons behind your refusal to deal with a personal issue. Once you are able to tackle this issue, you will feel released from a burden.

stall *to be stalled* Put emphasis on a personal issue that requires special interest and care from a professional. Demand this attention and it will be handled correctly.

stall *empty* Require that hired help speed up production. Business will flourish as a result.

full Allow others to go their way while you go yours.

Make certain you set up a specific time for everyone to get together and bring each other up to date on issues.

stallion You will soon meet someone and be instantly attracted to this person both physically and emotionally. The feeling is mutual. This person will be wearing a wedding band only to ensure freedom and dissuade gold diggers. Go after this person after you hear their reasons for the wedding band. Be very friendly and cool and you will find this person has a different agenda for you. Good luck is with you.

stamina Do whatever you can to avoid becoming a pest. Others will begin to mistreat you because of this. Eat, sleep, rest well and drink plenty of water.

stamp This is a good luck omen. For the next two days, work to keep yourself currently up to date on all major happenings. This will aid in decision making and collaborating your ideas with others.

to stamp something Someone wants you to share their life in a very special way. This person will receive you with open arms and everything they own will be at your disposal. This individual will ensure you are respected as much as they and that your word carries as much respect. Their authority will carry over to you and you will carry on your life together as well as having the authority to conduct this person's affairs when they are unavailable. You will also receive a very exciting gift within three days. Many blessings are with you and this is a very lucky cycle for you.

stamp collection Make it clear to others that you have no desire to disclose details about your private affairs. Privacy will be a priority for you. This is an extremely lucky cycle for the next two weeks.

stampede Take care to know, ahead of time, certain financial details in order to head off a disagreement with others. Make sure you perfectly understand all discussions with others relating to financial affairs. A rumble will also break out at a social gathering within the next few days. This may result in injury if you are not careful to avoid this.

stand Think big and take on a major project. This will be quickly completed and you will achieve great success with it.

stanza Put yourself in another person's shoes in order to determine the correct way to handle a situation involving this individual.

staple If you ask for a large financial donation you will receive it within two months. Apply for this now so it will come through within this time period.

stapler Seek a support system and determine what you need from this group. You will get a quick response to your needs if you consistently work on it. Begin searching for this support group within two days and be specific about the particular services you require.

stapler gun You will be in an accident prone cycle for the next three days. Take special precautions to avoid any freak accident to yourself or others.

star Let a particular person make the first move. After this, both of you will receive what you want and need for mutual satisfaction. This will occur within two days.

evening star Become very aware of children and their surroundings to ensure that no danger comes to them. You also need to guard your valuables.

falling star You will feel much more sorrow over the illness and impending death of someone you have known for years and have grown close to. Within the week, you will also meet someone who will be very loyal and loving toward you and will be true to your interests. If you choose to add this person to your life take steps now to pursue this. Good luck is with you.

shooting star You will, within two days, receive an answer you have long wanted to hear. You will also have a long desired wish come true.

starch Recheck all major equipment within two days. You will find that any equipment you use during this time will not work properly unless you make an effort to repair and fine tune your machinery. This also implies you need to keep your promises.

stardust Your passion for a certain concept or viewpoint will be contagious to others. Your behavior will be flawless and anything you apply yourself to will be a success for the next three days. You are headed for a brilliant future.

stare *to stare* Pay attention to the mass media for the next two days. Important information that you badly need will become available to you.

someone else stare Someone wants to get to know you better in a friendly way. You can also expect an increase in wealth.

if you are the one staring Motivate yourself to accomplish what needs to be taken care of within seven days. You will be very successful if you choose to take advantage of this lucky cycle.

to see someone try to out stare someone else Someone is pursuing you simply for sexual pleasure. You know this ahead of time and can decide whether you desire this kind of relationship. You will become aware of this within three days.

starfish Someone is suffering emotional turmoil because of their inability to express hidden deep feelings for you. Develop a softer demeanor in order to allow this person to gain the courage to express these feelings. Create a safe, comfortable environment for this person for the next four days.

stargazer All written plans, proposals, contracts, etc., will result in your favor right now.

starlet Do not develop a superior attitude toward another.

Be especially careful of your attitude for the next three days.

starlight Within the week, an event will take place that will be very memorable for you. It will be of a sensual nature and will stay with you for a lifetime.

starling Make a quick decision and you will be able to keep out of a dispute between two other people.

Star of Bethlehem This is an extremely lucky omen. Within five days you will receive a financial windfall and this will allow you to clear up all debts within the month. You must also make sure you eat properly and drink plenty of water. Many blessings are with you, and you are headed for a brilliant future.

Star of David This is the perfect three day cycle for you to pull strings to get the financial backing you need to go after what you really desire in life. You are definitely headed for a brilliant future.

stars and stripes Help another person develop a new image by subtle persuasion and influence. Rapid changes will occur and this person will be grateful for the subtlety.

star sapphire You will be lucky in romance and love during this cycle and will receive some good news regarding romance. Regardless of anything else that may be taking place in your life right now, all of your hopes and dreams will become a reality on a far grander scale than you ever imagined. You will successfully eliminate anything that is standing in your way. You are definitely headed for a brilliant future.

star spangled banner You will be offered a small opportunity. You will find, after completing research, that this will become a golden opportunity for you. Luck is with you.

startle *to startle someone* Do not demonstrate a smart attitude. A colleague you are attempting to win over will be put off by this. For the next two days do what you can to develop a friendlier, less arrogant manner.
to be startled Do not surrender to someone, for the next few days, who is trying to win you over. You will find this situation is not what you thought it would be.

starve *to be starved* Do not give the go ahead for someone to handle a situation unless you are very sure of this person. This person's character is questionable. Be careful of who you choose for the next four days.
to hear this phrase Be acutely aware of someone around you who is a pedophile. This person takes children and abuses them during photo sessions. This person may be someone you least expect and will make pornographic albums.
others starving Someone who has come to your aid in the past will not be able to come through for you in your present personal circumstances. Look for alternatives.

state *(territory)* Determine in what way the particular state

fits into your present life. If it is in a positive way, embrace it. If negative, work on changing it. This will play itself out within the month. Within three days, you will also experience a deep feeling toward a new person in your life. Deep love will follow in a short time and the union will be successful. For extra clues, look up the particular state.
to be the recipient of a state check Be very attentive because an unusual occurrence will develop regarding a person, project or position that will lead to a financial windfall. You may marry someone who will leave you with a monthly pension, develop a project that will deliver you monthly royalties, or secure a position that will offer you monthly provisions for a lifetime. You are in a sound position to receive this in the near future. Develop your curiosity, especially for the next week, to ensure you do not miss out on these benefits. You will receive an abundance of health, many blessings and are headed for a brilliant future.

state *(of mind)* Do not jump to conclusions. You must also pay attention to the emotional state you were in while dreaming for the next four days. If this state was negative, make an effort to change it to a positive. If it was positive work to promote it.

statehouse Next month your entertaining costs will skyrocket. You will spend lavishly with great results and many compliments. It will be possible to produce the same results at a lower cost. Good luck.

statement Deal only with the facts. Do not rely on the statements of other people unless you know they are factual. Stay on top of current events.

stateroom Within a few days, you will become a bore to another person by continually discussing a topic this person has no interest in. They will listen quietly to avoid hurting your feelings. Listen to yourself and try to prevent this behavior.

station Do everything necessary to include romance in your life. Once you develop a romance, go out of your way to keep it flowing. You are in a good cycle for this for the next two months. Begin this process immediately.

stationary You will be able to clearly get your point across effectively to another individual who has greater mental acuity than you. You will reach a mutual agreement within four days.

station break Do everything you can to tie up all loose ends regarding certain negotiations that must be handled within five days.

station, service *for gas* Make others aware of the passion you have for your pet project. Make sure your work is not taken for granted in order to avoid future hurts. Do this within two days.
to pump gasoline You will be given the authority to de-

velop something that needs to be completed in an entirely different way. Practice leniency with others because those who are working with you need to be allowed the freedom to develop creative ideas. These ideas will assist you in completing your projects.

to be at a service station for any other reason Make sure the inheritance you are to receive is guaranteed for you alone. Have this put into writing immediately, otherwise, you will be fighting in court for your rightful share. Do this immediately.

station wagon You frequently visit a couple who fights prior to your visit and immediately following your departure. One member of this couple does not like you and does not want your company but is unable to communicate this to you. Be very aware of what is occurring and make sure you do not go where you are not wanted. This is especially important for the next two days. Otherwise, this is a lucky cycle for you.

statue Within a few days, you will find yourself in a situation that will require a quick response. Someone will immediately come to your assistance and remain with you until the situation is resolved to your satisfaction.

marble statue Someone you will be associating with for the next few days will be very aggressive in handling business affairs. Express your feelings of discomfort to this individual and mutual compromises will be made.

broken statue The person you feel will be deceitful will be dishonest with you. Follow your instincts for the next two days.

torso only You will feel a sense of urgency to consummate a relationship with someone who has captured your interest. If you choose to pursue this, you will soon enter into a long term mutually satisfying relationship. Happiness and good luck will be with you.

statutory rape Within two days, your intuition will give you the sense that there is a hidden danger developing in the mind of a same sexed person. This person's evil and dangerous thoughts are being focused on you. This person is plotting to catch you off guard at an unexpected time. Do whatever is necessary to protect yourself and to take all the necessary precautions.

stay You will be caught in a juggling act between love and career. Look at this situation carefully because you must not ignore either aspect of your life. Within two weeks, your schedule will become even more hectic. Learn to set priorities and schedule your life to include both love and career.

in any other form Within the week, someone will come into your life who will be attentive to all of your needs. You will also receive a financial windfall.

steak Praise the fact that you are alive and enjoy life fully without overextending yourself financially. Enjoy the simple pleasures.

steak house Know when to apologize.

steak knife Become mentally creative for the next seven days and determine what it would be like to change what you are doing now. Imagine the accomplishments you could achieve if you would make small changes. These small changes will yield big results.

steal *to be stolen from* If you are not happy with the person you are sharing your life with, make changes. Do not allow your life to be robbed of time and happiness.

to consider theft but resist the impulse You will be captivated by someone and will shortly enter into a meaningful relationship. You will enjoy each moment.

to steal Someone will go to great lengths to fake an injury in your presence for the purpose of collecting insurance. This will occur within seven days.

steam Two situations will come together beautifully and you will achieve a long desired goal.

steam bath Keep in mind each thing you dislike about a person you are trying to avoid in order to have the courage to go on with your life without this person.

steamboat Remain optimistic about your future because you are headed in the right direction.

steam engine Do everything you can to tuck away extra money. Practice setting aside petty cash for later emergencies.

steam iron Within the week you will rejoice over some good fortune that will vastly change your life. Prosperity and good luck are with you.

steamroller Do not allow yourself to be abused and harassed to the point of giving up something you consider valuable. Put a firm stop to this behavior, especially for the next five days.

steamship Revise your vacation plans and this will bring about a strong backing from others.

steam table Do not allow yourself to be persuaded into performing physical labor for others without pay. Do not overtax your energy for the next four days.

steel Create a method that will ensure a flow of communication between yourself and those you need to stay in constant contact with.

steel band Someone will go to great lengths to develop a sexual relationship with you. This person will promise undying love and you will remain together for a long period of time. You will gain knowledge of this within seven days.

steel blue You will be captivated by another person's mysterious lifestyle. This person will eventually become a lifelong mate.

steel drum Be wary and avoid fires for the next four days.

steel gray You will enjoy more tranquility and this feeling will remain with you for a long period of time.

steel guitar Within two days do everything necessary to create the quiet environment you need. You also need to watch children, as well as young adults, around alcoholic beverages.

steel wool Do not leave anything outside that will rust due to the inclement weather.

steelworker Be careful. You will become sleepy and drowsy in a hazardous situation. Make sure when you become this way, you are in a safe environment and do not operate heavy machinery at this time. Be especially careful for the next four days.

steeple You will enter group counseling. This method and the advice given is not correct for you. Seek alternatives.

steeplechase Do not allow other people to take up too much of your precious time. Learn to use and value your time as a precious commodity.

steer *someone steering* The person you see steering will be creating valuable changes in their life. This person will also need assistance from you so they will be able to confidently go on with their own life. You will be instrumental in helping this person make changes by instilling confidence.

to see yourself steering You are ready to make some direct changes in your life. You will have very well organized, well thought out plans that fall into place exactly as you want, especially within the next four days.

steer *(cattle)* Make sure your work time and recreation time balance out. You must also ensure work time does not overshadow your private time, especially for the next three days.

steering wheel You are putting into practice optimism and practicality. Your present situation will have a fortunate outcome.

stegosaur You are focusing on the wrong family member and are committing a grave error. Slow down and rethink your feelings because your assumptions will be incorrect.

stem Do not allow yourself to become overly suspicious about the behavior of others. Remain calm and relax. Things will become clear to you in the near future.

stencil Check first with someone before volunteering their efforts to a cause.

stenographer Someone who, in the past, wanted to be with

you will come back into your life. In the past, you were not interested. The situation is now different and you will be eager to be with this person. The relationship will work out for both of you now.

stepbrother You will enjoy success when bargain hunting.

stepchild You will be directly involved with a lazy person who, on the surface, appears energetic. Be wary of this; it will affect your life greatly.

stepdaughter Do not allow your indecisiveness to interfere with your determination and slow down your goals.

stepfather You will soon receive a proposal of marriage from a serious minded and intelligent person who is a fancy dresser, enjoys the finer things in life, and will always be a romantic. If you decide to marry, you will always enjoy romance.

Stephen *(from the Bible)* Put aside extra money now for emergency situations. This will come in handy next month.

stepladder You are dangerously close to burn out. For the sake of your health, do not continue overextending yourself. Otherwise, this is a lucky cycle for you.

stepmother Go out of your way to extend extra kindnesses to those much older than you. Within seven days, someone you have known for years will also be a support to you in an emotional crisis.

stepping stone You will marry someone with charisma and a great profession. This also indicates you need to look carefully at your present situation to ensure things run smoothly for the next two days.

steps Do not use short cuts to expedite a project. Do everything necessary to complete this properly. Otherwise, this is a lucky cycle for you.

stepsister Get out in public and socialize and you will find the perfect person for a romantic involvement. Social gatherings will give you exposure and you will have a chance to meet the one who is perfect for you within the next week.

stepson Stop depriving yourself of situations in your life that would be very special. Bring more social change into your life. Peace and tranquility are yours.

stereo Whatever you hear on the stereo is a direct message to you. If the message is positive, place extra importance on it. If the message is negative, do everything necessary to change it. If you recognize the voices, these people will be instrumental in bringing forth major changes. These are all clues that may be altered by what you choose to happen.

sterile Protect yourself and do not put yourself in a situation that will allow you to be indirectly cruel to another because of your supervisory powers. Your superior may request you lean heavily on another person and this will affect you emotionally. This will happen within seven days.

sterilize Take precautions around others and make sure you do not indirectly inflict injury by causing a large object to fall on someone within the week.

stern Take care that you do not eat anything that disagrees with you for the next few days.

steroids You will get a quick response from an agency regarding all crisis situations for the next two days. An individual worker will come to your assistance.

stethoscope Within two days you will request and receive wonderful physical and emotional pleasures from someone who deeply desires you.

stew Within three days someone will offer assistance to you. Once this person realizes they have become too deeply involved in a situation, they will make an impossible demand on you in order to gracefully back out of the involvement. Let this person know, ahead of time, everything the situation entails and allow them to choose the manner of assistance they give. You may not receive all the help you need but partial assistance is better than none and you will avoid angry feelings.

stewardess Stop doing and saying things that will prevent another person from securing a good job because of your jealousy and envy. You will regret this behavior.

stick *large* Someone will go to great lengths to murder you. Take every precaution to secure your safety and suspect everyone and everything for the next three weeks.

sticker price You will be putting out all of the proper signals to someone that will enable them to make the correct romantic move towards you.

stickers Do not expose yourself to anything contagious for the next three days. Someone will purposely expose you to illness.

stickpin Someone will lie to you within three days. Be watchful for this so you can better control your situation.

stick shift *you are using a stick shift* A dramatic change will take place in a platonic relationship. There will be more closeness and a greater affection between both of you. If this is what you want, this will be a wonderfully happy cycle. If you do not choose this, politely and tactfully discourage this person in order to avoid hurt feelings.
someone else is using a stick shift If you recognize the person, this individual will be going through dramatic life changes and will call on you for assistance. If you do not

recognize this person, someone will ask for a loan within four days but they will be unable to repay you because of their present circumstances. It is better to avoid lending money at this time.

sticky Review and evaluate your career choices over the next three days. The decisions you arrive at will be very successful. You must also take the time to relax in a manner that brings you happiness.

stiff Do all you can to clean up your image. Aim for improvement over the next three weeks.

still If you feel uncomfortable around another person, there is a valid reason for feeling this way. Follow your instincts for the next two days.

still *(whiskey)* Do not offer unsolicited advice. If you do, make sure all information is accurate.

stillbirth Demand assistance from your higher power to handle a difficult situation you are presently undergoing. Do this by way of your favorite form of meditation. You will be able to resolve this satisfactorily within three days. You will have a great deal of power within this cycle for handling difficult situations.

still life Do not overestimate a situation and make sure you understand all implications prior to claiming victory. Make any needed corrections in order to ensure victory.

stilt For the next three days make sure you are personally involved in each situation that requires your personal touch. Do this to ensure everything runs smoothly.

stimulate For the next two days, certain mannerisms and behaviors will be demonstrated by someone special to you. Do not jump to conclusions. Give this person a chance to explain them self. Keep your emotions in check.

sting Some things are meant to be just as they are. Make sure you do not overdo anything, especially for the next two days.
to see someone stung This is not the time to let someone know your feelings about another person. Keep your true feelings to yourself for the next three days in order to avoid any disturbance from a third party. Things will work out more to your satisfaction.
to be stung Within two days make sure the feelings and ideas you carry inside are brought to reality. This is a strong cycle for actualizing thought processes and bringing them to form.

stinger Stick to what you are doing until the difficult part is smoothed over. Stick with your behavior and persevere until you receive what you want because this is the best cycle to gain the advantage in any situation.

stingray Within three days, start paying close attention to the way you act in order to avoid forming certain patterns of behavior that others will find distasteful. These behaviors will force others to outgrow you. You have prior notice of this and can discipline yourself to behave in the proper manner. You are also overlooking a situation that needs to be handled. Investigate your life closely in order to determine the situation that needs to be taken care of.

stink Someone will go to great lengths to steer you in the wrong direction. Stay alert and refuse, for the next two days, to be lured in the wrong direction in matters that are important to you.

stir For the next two days do everything necessary to guard against spending your money. Hang on to your finances until this cycle is over.

stir fry For the next two days, make romance a priority. Allow situations to flow naturally. This will be a wonderful cycle.

stirrup Focus on your weak points over the next four days. These weaknesses are handicapping you and keeping you from achieving your goals. Work with these areas in order to prevent them from holding you back.

stitch Within two days, expect someone to deliver an apology in order to patch up a recent disagreement. This will leave you with a nice feeling.

stock Opinions from others will give you many great ideas and you will pinpoint one particular idea within the next two days. Move on anything positive you saw in this dream and correct the negatives. Good luck is with you.

stockade For the next two days, do not listen to the words of someone about another person who is important to them. This couple simply needs to stick it out and work out their own problems. You do not need to get involved except to encourage this couple to work on their personal issues.

stockbroker The next two days will be the start of something wonderful regarding financial deals and trade negotiations. This will turn out to be very lucrative and rewarding. Go for it.

stock exchange Government paperwork you are presently working on will not work out over the next month. Do everything necessary to ensure success. You must also look at similar situations that are working within the system. Approach this from a different angle with awareness and calmness.

stocking Bargains will be fantastic for the next two days.
hole in stocking The person you are looking forward to being with in the next two days will be cranky and a nuisance. Make alternative plans.
stocking cap For the next three days, the success of your

plans in the future will depend on your abilities and perseverance in handling certain situations. Take care of problem areas now and you will see great improvements.

stock market Make the first move to promote what you want in a decision making process. This will give you an edge over another person who is seeking a decision in their favor. Do this within a few days.

stockpile Make sure you clear up all overdue payments within three days in order to relieve stressful situations.

stockroom You are entrusting the wrong person to make decisions for you. Be very watchful of this for the next three days. Otherwise, it is a very lucky omen to dream of a stockroom.

stockyard A speedy reconciliation of a long friendship will occur after many years of not speaking. Make contact with this person and you will have many wonderful moments ahead.

stolen *to suspect a theft that turns out not to be* Within three days you will attract a person who can accomplish a great deal in a very short period of time. Use this cycle to connect with the person who can make this cycle very fruitful for you. You are definitely headed in the right direction. Proceed with confidence.

stomach *your stomach* You will be performing unpaid physical labor for someone else. Be sure this is what you want before you make promises.
someone else's Allow others to express their point of view. Mutual happiness and understanding will then be yours within two days.

stomachache Be wary for the next few days because a deranged person will stalk you. Guard your life and possessions.
pain in someone else's stomach Set up time for mutual creativity and time to express ideas that will yield great rewards.

stone Resist going to extremes. Look closely at all the aspects of a particular situation and this will determine how involved you want to become with someone during this cycle. You also need to look up the particular stone for a more detailed meaning of this dream. In spite of everything else, you are headed for a brilliant future.
in any other form A conclusion will be finally reached concerning a long anticipated negotiation you have worked hard on. Everyone involved will benefit from this mutually satisfying agreement. Expect this exciting event to take place within five days.

Stone Age For the next two days be nice to someone who will irrationally lose their temper if you do not watch yourself. Do everything you can to enjoy life with this person and to maintain peace.

stone china Keep a close eye on your investments. Your speculations will be on target. Trust your judgments. You are headed for a prosperous future.

stone crab Look carefully at existing patterns of behavior that you and others have long outgrown. Look at those aspects of your personality you need to develop. Accept new ways of behaving and get rid of the old.

stonecutter For the next three days you will be focused on those areas that concern you. This intense focus is not allowing you to get beyond your concerns and you are depriving yourself of something that could bring you tremendous joy. You are also unable to see what is happening to you and cannot visualize anything bringing you enjoyment. This also implies you are loved beyond your imagination.

stonewall You will soon be able to decide on the person you want to involve yourself with. This person is very knowledgeable and will be able to offer you their help in finding a solution to a certain issue.

stooge Make it a point to clear up all overdue bills within three days in order to avoid stressful situations.

stool *(bar)* For the next two days someone will behave toward you in an entirely different manner. This person will be kinder, more punctual and, overall, an improved being. Do not make any comments on this, just enjoy this change.

stool *(feces)* For the next four days, you will need determination to point your life toward a great future. You will be undergoing great changes in all areas revolving around love and money and you will develop a new zest for life and a greater love from others. Good health and good luck are yours.

stool *(bathroom seat)* Watch out for destructive behavior for the next two days. Work on ridding yourself of bad habits. You have the strength to do this now.

stoop over You will be in a business meeting in two days and find the other person very pleasant. This meeting will result in a very positive outcome.

stoop *(porch)* You are thinking about meeting with someone within two days who is a very difficult person to reach any agreements with. Wait out this cycle and try again in a week. It will be more successful then.

stop Take stock of what you are doing in your life and become aware of the things you need to change in order to move ahead. Stop all behavior that is damaging and out of the ordinary.

    asking someone to stop a certain behavior Within five days you will need to really take a stand in order to put a

stop to someone's disagreeable behavior and limit your involvement with someone or something that you are becoming more deeply involved with. Use any available means to stop this. You will be showered with gifts to keep you involved but you will need to be firm in your refusal to commit because you will later regret it. You will also experience an abundance of health and a clarity of thought that will allow you to handle this appropriately and with as little stress as possible.

    "stop being so mean" *to say or to hear this phrase* Be very cautious about where your feelings are taking you. Someone will, for reasons of their own, lead you to believe you are loved by them. The word 'love' may or may not be used at this time but all of the romantic trappings will be there in the nature of gifts, flowers, romantic outings, etc. Your feelings will grow very deep and strong for this individual but if you allow lovemaking to occur, this person will not touch you in any way that gives you the impression they care deeply for you. As a result, you will feel very empty and cold. This person will be unable to connect with you, although they will put on a good act. Instead of putting yourself through this, you have enough notice to avoid this scenario entirely. Get on with your life without this person because they have a hidden agenda that involves you doing something for them that only they are aware of. This situation will only lead to unhappiness. Otherwise, you are headed for a prosperous future.

    "stop following me" Within five days you will really need to put your foot down in order to stop someone's disagreeable behavior or to limit your involvement with someone or something you are becoming more involved in. This will be someone you wish you had not become so quickly involved with. In spite of the fact you will be showered with gifts to entice you, you need to back off and stay uninvolved. You will regret any involvement in the future. You will, during this time period, experience an abundance of health and a clarity of thought that will allow you to handle this appropriately and with as little stress as possible.

stoplight You will soon be making a decision that will put you on the wrong path. Rethink your decisions and reaffirm your goals.

stopwatch Stop being so strict with yourself and stop depriving yourself of those things you really want from life. You are doing this because you do not want to put forth the effort to achieve what you want. Stop being lazy; decide what you want and go for it.

store Take time with your present undertaking and go through everything in detail. Once you do this, you can proceed with confidence and know that everything is being done correctly.

    discount store You will have a better chance of reconciliation if you make a move within three days. This also implies you will receive a quick response to a request you have made for specific information.

department store For the next seven days, develop more affectionate, loving feelings toward someone special. Treat this person with extra kindness. Your disinterested behavior will destroy the love someone feels for you if it is not changed immediately. The upcoming cycle is perfect for correcting all past mistakes.

convenience store Keep your life simple and basic.

consignment store You will come into riches from an area that is presently unknown to you. Move ahead on this with confidence.

storekeeper Make sure everything you need to assemble comes with all the parts needed for this chore. An injury could occur because of improper assembly. Be especially careful for the next four days.

storeroom Trust your hunches and dig deeply for any information you need about a certain individual. Do this within two days.

stork You will be satisfied about good news you will be hearing within a few days.

storm You are creating chaos because of your spoiled nature. Use your energy for something constructive.

tropical storm You will have a better chance of reconciling with someone special if you act within three days. This also implies you will enjoy a quick response to your request for specific information.

storm center Make sure something that is to remain a secret stays a secret.

storm door Do not give the impression you are selfish.

storm trooper Do not postpone plans that will affect you deeply later on. Go ahead with your plans.

storm window Do not become involved with a deceitful hypocritical person who plays petty games with other people's emotions. Remain detached and uninvolved.

story *if someone is telling a story* The person in your dream bringing you a story would very much like to play a more active role in your life.

if you are telling a story Do not allow anyone to pry into your private life or to allow anyone to prey on your physical energies for the next two days.

to be told an untrue story If you do not recognize the person, a fantastic opportunity will be presented to you by a new acquaintance who has a special way of communicating. This character trait makes others feel important.

to tell an untrue story You are steering yourself in the wrong direction. Make the effort to determine the cause of this and decide on the direction you want to take. You have been led to believe, by yourself or by someone else, that something is correct, when in actuality it isn't. Dig deeply

and make absolutely sure you are not being misled about an important situation. This dream also implies certain plans made regarding a crucial situation will work to your advantage. Focus on your health as well as an everyday situation that you take for granted.

in any other form You will receive many blessings throughout life. Begin to develop a network of associates who will be able to interchange ideas and introduce to you a variety of circumstances that will spice up your life. You must also pay close attention to the contents of the story. This may represent something you desire to include in your life or in someone else's life or will represent something you want to take steps to avoid or change in reality. You will achieve great status in your life.

storybook For the next few days, be very diplomatic when digging for the information you are after.

storyteller Do not do anything until you have more information about an ongoing situation.

stout A member of your family will come to you for help and will bring you into their confidence within three days. Do what you can to offer assistance and everything will work out well for this individual.

stove Within five days you and one other person will arrive at a sure and rapid method to make more money. Go for it.

stovepipe Changes that will be taking place over the next few weeks will not be to your advantage. Investigate these changes and alter them until they work to your benefit.

stowaway For the next two days, do everything necessary to avoid becoming a nuisance to anyone.

STP Many of your secrets will be revealed to others within three days. If you have something in your life you choose to keep private, take steps to ensure it remains so. You will also hear from an old friend soon and will share many fun filled moments.

straight Communicate with someone who is planning to leave the area. Speak now and you will convince this person to stay.

straight chair Someone you have asked a favor of will feign agreement but in reality will leave you hanging. Find alternative help.

straightedge Do not allow yourself to be taken in by an emotional plea for money. This person is a con artist.

straight flush Someone you know has a deep emotional passion for you. You are presently unaware of this but it will soon be revealed. This person is very charismatic and enjoys life. You will have a great deal of fun with them.

straight jacket Keep yourself safe from drowning.

straight pin Do not allow yourself to be tied down. Circulate and become actively involved with those who are special. Do not compromise your feelings.

straight razor Do not leave your mate for a younger person. You will be making a terrible mistake.

strain Someone will cause you a great deal of personal strain. At first, this person will be very kind but later will become someone who requires a great deal of personal attention. Be cautious about where this situation is leading in order to avoid a very stormy argument at a later date.

strained food Do not allow yourself to become overly dependent on one specific person, especially for the next three days. Stop this behavior and attempt to be versatile with your available resources. Develop a support system and do not place excess strain on one person. You will also attend a musical event within two weeks and be in awe and wonder of being in the presence of someone with such a magical voice. You are headed for a brilliant future and many blessings are with you.

strange Any situation that appears strange to you, in a dream, is alerting you to a situation that will occur within the week. Take steps to prevent this if you choose not to allow it to happen. If it is a desirable situation, go for it.

stranger Take charge of any uncontrollable desire or urge you may have. This will lead to disagreements.

strangle *if you do the strangling* You will be able to stop someone who has been tormenting you and within three days you will be able to rid yourself of this person for life.
someone is strangling you You will lose a position within the month and this will affect your life in a major way. Do everything necessary to prevent this. You have the time to change any behavior that may cause this to occur.

strap *to be strapped down* Within four days you will reluctantly surrender to someone who loves you. You can avoid this by relentlessly monitoring your behavior. Do nothing to compromise your feelings. You must also avoid any situation that could lead to you being strapped down against your will.
to strap someone else down Someone will surrender to you within three days in the manner you most desire.

strapless You will be mourning the loss of a close friend within a few days.

straw You will pull someone you desire closer to you. This person has been very hard to get close to but will now be more amenable to your needs. This will occur shortly. Never take this situation for granted and make sure the relationship continues to grow.
if someone else is using a straw Someone will go out of their way to draw you closer to them. This will result in

warmer, closer feelings on your part. Blessings are with you. This is a good luck symbol.

strawberry A great event will be celebrated within a few weeks. This will be a big surprise to you and will bring you much joy. It will take a great deal of preparation on your part regarding gifts and attire so start planning now.

strawberry blonde You will be appointed to a higher position and will receive many honors and a great increase in financial status. This is the golden opportunity you have been waiting for.

straw boss Watch out for animal bites.

straw hat Do not spend other people's money, and be sure to keep your personal life to yourself.

straw man A group of people will become angry at the decisions you make. Take the opinions of these people into account when you make decisions that affect them.

straw vote You will be cornered by someone you have been trying to avoid. For the next week take extra steps to avoid this person.

stray *to stray* Do not push away a loved one because of the way you act. Your attitude implies you want your mate to leave. Do everything possible, in word and deed, to show your true feelings of love in order to hold your loved ones close to you.
others stray Someone will openly communicate their love and affection to you in order to bond you closer.

stream Within three days you will achieve a special long desired goal because of another person's willingness to help. Be alert to this opportunity. You are also in a very good position to demand what you want from your special deity. Be direct and specific about your wants and needs. For the next three weeks you will be developing a list of priorities that serve as an aid to supervising the way you live your life. Take the time to reflect in peace and tranquility.

streamer Within two days someone you know will be the subject of an investigation. This person's troubles will bring you down. Do not become involved in this situation.

street In matters of love and business, play your cards right. This dream spells victory in those areas of your life you most desire, but play your cards close to your vest. This will be an immediate occurrence. Stay alert. If you choose to pursue this, you will definitely experience prosperity.
to cross a street or see others cross a street An interesting situation will occur within two days. You will meet two different people at two different outings at separate times. You will be attracted to both of them without realizing they both share living quarters. Both are single and both will give you their phone number. Although they live in the same

place, they will have different phone numbers. You will call both of them, have delightful conversations and make plans for a date with both of them not knowing they live together. Prior to the first date, you will call one of them and the other will answer the phone. This will lead to a major confusion that you will keep to yourself. Then you will call the second person and the first will answer the phone. You will hang up because of confusion both times. Both of these people are unaware of what is happening and think you are interested only in them. Be very careful because if they learn you are interested in both of them you will lose both. Decide on only one person for your own good. This will be a very exciting time for you and you will have many admirers to choose from. You are entering a very prosperous time period.

two way street You are well on your way toward developing the plans you need for your own independence. This cycle stresses confidence, physical healing and financial improvements. You are on the path toward a brilliant future. This is a very prosperous cycle and you will be able to turn around those situations that require improvements. Many blessings are with you and your family and all requests made to your higher power will be granted to you.

streetcar This is a very lucky omen. You will receive many blessings throughout life and be influenced by a very wealthy and powerful person. This connection will enrich all phases of your life.

streetlight Within two days you will become involved with a certain person who will offer you a fresh viewpoint on particular topics you have been discussing. You will then gain a new feeling that you now know the right way to go. Take notes on the conversation for inspiration at a later time. Your intuition is right on target. Go for it. Good luck is with you and many blessings will come to you and your family.

street people You will be granted the help you requested for another person and the services you asked for will come immediately. You will receive a great deal of emotional satisfaction from this.

streetwalker Take extra precautions when transporting money from one location to another. Insure all money against loss for the next seven days.

strength Begin to develop a new network of associates for support in day to day situations. You will be able to count on these people in the future when you need assistance.

strep throat Take every precaution to avoid contracting a virus. Although this virus may be short term, it could result in a long and complicated illness.

streptococcus Someone you know has been a great support in times of need. You will want to give them a special treat within three days. You can also expect great wealth within a year.

stress You will be overwhelmed by a bad situation that will

be made worse by an alarmist. Make sure you understand that a small situation has been blown out of proportion. Do whatever you must to avoid stress and schedule time out for a retreat in order to regain tranquility. Assure that nothing disrupts your quiet time for the next four days.

stretch For the next few days, tell only the truth. Everything will work out well for you.

stretcher Move out of a situation that will become a bigger challenge than you anticipated. This will be a good move for you.

streusel You feel the time is right to move ahead on a project. Follow this hunch.

strike Maintain a friendly demeanor with someone who is responsible for handling your funds. Be willing to meet daily for financial updates. Begin this process immediately and become diligent in your supervisory functions.

strikeout Take a close look at attitudes and existing behaviors that you have outgrown. Look at new attitudes and behaviors you need to develop and let go of the old. This dream is also an extremely unlucky omen. You will need to offer a compromise in a clever way to prevent a violent episode from taking place between two groups of people who find it impossible to see eye to eye. Both groups can have it their way if they compromise. Stick with your plans to compromise or violence is certain to break out.

string *to pull a string towards you* Someone will kindly ask that you forget the past. This friendship was interrupted by a misunderstanding. You are willing to forget the past but be sure to set limits within yourself to avoid misunderstandings.

broken string An important meeting will be called off and will create a setback. Make sure the meeting is rescheduled prior to the cancellation. This will ensure an alternative time is available. Do this within seven days.

any other form Challenge yourself to make new friends who will provide you with exposure to different lifestyles.

string bean Be relentless and investigate to determine the exact physical or mental condition of a relative. Your intervention may be instrumental in saving this person's life. Make sure they find the services they need and that their needs are being properly taken care of.

string bikini Perform in the best way you can after launching a new career.

stringent Avoid all confrontations with anyone.

stringer Avoid all altercations that involve someone of importance to you in business. Use tact and firm communication skills to avoid unnecessary clashes before they begin.

string instrument You will juggle your schedule in order to include some romantic time for an exciting interesting person. You will be able to win this person over and have a wonderful time.

string quartet Kindness and warmth will create a good environment for you and your family.

strip A major personal decision you are in the process of making will work out.

to strip anything (i.e., paint, wall paper, auto, etc.) It is important that you have a meeting with certain people within a two day period in order to make the right connections regarding certain requests of yours. This will ensure an important upcoming situation does not fall apart before it has a chance to get started. Stay on top of this and you will be able to make the necessary adjustments in a timely fashion. Focus on this now and everything will fall into place as you have envisioned. Good luck will come to you and your family. You are headed for a brilliant future.

to be reluctant to strip This is a warning that you will be stricken with guilt about something you were opposed to before you did it. This will come up within two days and you need to take a stand against it. Look more carefully at what you are willing to involve yourself in. You will also enjoy an abundance of health during this cycle but you do need to take steps to avoid becoming involved in something. Also, make sure anything negative connected to this dream does not become a reality.

strip mining You will not be able to increase your income over the next few weeks by using your present method. Change your direction.

stripper Reassess your restrictions and demands on others, especially for the next three days. By preventing this behavior you will create a wonderful cycle for yourself.

strip poker Those you care about will fail to see your point of view and until your beliefs are actualized, no one will be able to see their workability.

striptease Do not become involved in any group that participates in random criminal activity against others, especially for the next four days. Hoodlum behavior will backfire and you will deeply regret this once you are behind bars.

strobe light Think carefully over the next three days. You will accidentally blurt out information about another person that a third person has no business knowing. This person may be hurt badly by this third person. Avoid this by watching what you say and by keeping all information secret.

stroganoff You will be the target of romantic affection and this will be very appealing to you. You will pursue this within four days.

stroke *in any form* Prepare to take time off to care for a sick individual. The quiet time spent doing this will inspire a

brilliant and creative idea. You will be grateful for this for a lifetime. Blessings are with you. Respect your health and take steps to maintain it.

stroll *to stroll with someone* Within four days, someone will take the liberty of appointing you to volunteer work without consulting you. This will turn to your advantage and you will receive unexpected financial and emotional benefits.

stroller Someone will ask you to read a joint agreement concerning a project you will both be involved with. When you are first approached on this, you will not show much interest. Be aware that you will benefit more than the originator of the project. Go for it. Within five days you will also go through many experiences that will bring grand and prosperous changes to your life. Your circumstances will vastly improve.

strong Have faith and confidence in yourself and put out signals that you have faith in those who work with you. Things will work better for you if you demonstrate this faith.

strongman Within four days, what seems to be a way to make quick and easy money will become a nightmare. You will regret your involvement in this situation if you do not take steps to avoid this decision.

strong will You are headed in the wrong direction career wise. Back off and start from a different direction.

structure *beautiful* You need to talk to a special person about your needs. This person will be more than willing to accommodate you. Don't suffer in silence.

strudel Do not pay attention to what others think you should have in the way of money. Make it clear that you deserve what you are requesting.

struggle You will have a deep desire to investigate a certain situation. You would be better off leaving this alone.

strum You will love and enjoy the same person for a lifetime.

strut *to strut* Do not close all doors on friendships. This will occur because of the manner in which you treat others. Be especially careful of this over the next few days.

strychnine For the next two days, be very cautious while eating out in order to avoid food poisoning.

stubborn Do not create a large incident out of a small issue.

stucco Do not put yourself down in front of others. Other people see a beauty you are unable to recognize.

stud Someone will pull you aside to reveal a shocking intimate situation. You will be surprised but it is better to keep this situation to yourself.

student A great event will be celebrated within a few weeks. This will be a surprise to you and will bring you much joy.

studhorse Be careful of injuries to the face. Avoid a black eye for the next two days.

studio The person you fall deeply in love with will never have the same feelings as you. Beware of pushing yourself on someone because these feelings will not be reciprocated. You will be tempted to do this within two days.

study A long desired vacation will be realized and this will be a dream come true. Your long time savings plan will finally allow you to take this trip within the week.

study hall You will be in the company of someone who is very kind, generous and well educated who, for some reason, is unable to accept the responsibility of a deep emotional commitment. This will stand in their way of developing the relationship they desire. This person is not aware they have this particular emotional block to work around. You have prior notice of this and can act in the appropriate way.

stuffing You will ask for and receive the assistance you are requesting from someone. They will offer more assistance than you expected and will lift a burden from you.

stumble Be careful you do not blurt out anything to injure the feelings of another. Your words could offend a number of people. Watch out for this for the next four days.

stump You will be able to build on the love feelings you have for another and your relationship will reach a higher level. Both of you will develop greater feelings for each other.

stun Make sure all equipment you will be working with has the proper amounts of lubrication. Ensure that you provide proper maintenance for your machines because you will need them in the future.

stun gun Within a few days, hard to attain information will come to you easily. Someone else will be able to acquire this information for you.

stuntman Be careful who you hire to perform repairs. Make sure these people come highly recommended and have the proper qualifications.

stupid Be watchful of the negative tapes you are running through your mind and do not allow yourself to become immersed in these tapes to the point of becoming physically ill. Assertively pursue a positive attitude.

sturdy Do not overextend yourself physically. Approach situations calmly and proceed in slow steady steps, especially for the next five days.

sturgeon When investing, look into anything that is old and improved. You must also set aside quality time for your relatives and children.

stutter The birth of twins will occur. Blessings are with you.

sty *to see on someone else* Within the week, you will be seeking professional advice. Once you get there, an attractive professional person will approach you sexually while rendering services. You will be surprised and shocked by this but will control yourself. You will, however, be drawn to this person. You will communicate at a later time and this person will reveal that they are married. Although they will continue to pursue you and you will feel an attraction, you will be able to resist urges.

to have a sty For the next few days, you will spend precious moments with the person you most desire. You have been discouraged because you felt these moments would never come. Now that they have, you will treasure them for a lifetime.

styptic pencil Within four days, you will demonstrate loyalty for the wrong cause. Take the time to reevaluate what you are doing.

Styrofoam Within three days you will have the opportunity to make improvements in the way young children think and in their attitudes about themselves. You will be giving them a treasure they will cherish for the remainder of their lives.

subcompact The thrills you have encountered in your life should be recorded on paper for family posterity.

subcontract Be very conservative with your finances this week. Before making any purchases, wait to see if you have the money to cover all necessary expenditures.

subjugate Within three days a situation will occur that will make it necessary to determine whether someone who is working with you on a particular project is keeping up with the pace. This individual may be having you do the work of two people if you are not alert to this. Focus on this so you can get the assistance you need without taking over any extra responsibilities. Speak up and let this person know they have to pull their own load. Remain stress free. Many blessings are with you and you are headed for a very prosperous future. You will enjoy a financially secure retirement.

submachine gun Discuss a recurring problem with your physician within a few days and put all your worries to rest. You will be glad you did.

submarine This will be an important time to connect emotionally with other people. Take some time to be alone in order to sort out your feelings instead of attempting to randomly connect. Sort out your true feelings within two days.

submerge Tie up all loose financial matters and look closely at your investments within two days.

subpoena *any form* Start taking steps to reduce your financial burden by unloading unnecessary bills. Strive to keep yourself in good health physically and emotionally. Maintain a healthy outlook on life.

to receive For the next month, do nothing that will cause you to receive a subpoena.

subscribe For a few days, record each new idea to ensure you will come back to it at a later time. One of these ideas will lead to a brilliant future.

subsidy You will have to work closely with a very attractive person in a few days. Make sure you do not put yourself in the position of allowing things to happen. This is not a wise involvement. While working with this person, keep it strictly business.

substance *any form that is not ordinary* Other people count on you to make good decisions. You are the first on many people's list to call on in times of need. You are well thought of and deeply loved. This also indicates that you will be able to accomplish a great deal with only a little legwork.

substitute You are planning to begin a costly project but will lack the funds to get started. By networking, you will be able to locate funding through an ongoing government project and will work closely with another person who complements your talents. You will both bring in a profit from this project. Begin to move in this direction within the week. This is the perfect cycle for success.

subtract Others think of you with such high regard that nothing can take your place in their mind. Stop being so negative.

subtropical You have decided to take a job for very little pay. Within a few days, your employer will decide you are worth more and unexpectedly boost your salary.

suburb When working on certain plans, do everything you can to avoid confusion. This will allow you to avoid financial loss.

subway You will be dealing with someone within a few days who seems to be very nice. This person is very much the opposite in reality. Guard yourself and take steps to avoid being alone with them because they will ultimately attempt to ruin your life.

subway station Take steps to guard your life and your personal belongings for the next three days.
success You will gain success within three days.

succotash If you want to be paid for your ideas, do not exchange these ideas with another person before you are paid.

suck Within three days someone will desperately need you in a sexual way. This person will go to great lengths to satisfy both of you emotionally and you will be mutually fulfilled.

sucker A young adult will make the wrong choices and will enter into a miserable marriage. Do everything you can to dissuade this person from making this decision.

sucker fish You will enjoy peace and tranquility in all of your family decisions.

sucker punch Make personal adjustments in your life to ensure the personal and emotional security of a young person.

suckling *(baby)* Love for others will solve many situations. Demonstrate love for family members.

suction Keep your eyes and ears open for an upcoming opportunity that will be presented to you within three days. This will be a way of making an extra income and will come at an unexpected time and when you will most appreciate it.

suction cup Do not allow your finances to become depleted by unnecessary spending.

Sudden Infant Death Syndrome (SIDS) Do everything you can to prevent any negative event in this dream from becoming a reality with you or anyone else you recognize, especially for the next two days. Also someone will hide behind their influence, resources and power after committing a horrendous crime. This will occur within three days and have a tremendous impact on your life. Investigate this situation and position yourself so you are totally protected from this. Any negative event you witness in this dream may also be avoided in reality. Otherwise, this dream is an extremely lucky omen. Within three days several events will begin to develop very rapidly. Do everything you can to put a lid on those situations you do not want to worsen or deal with. Blessings are with you and you are headed for a brilliant future.

suds Do everything necessary to keep others from outgrowing you. Keep growing and learning in order to keep up with those who are important to you.

formed by any beverage (champagne, beer, etc.) For the next ten days you will be unbeatable because of your tenacity and relentlessness in pursuing your goals. You are in a very lucky position and will be celebrating a joyful victory.

suede Be sure to keep an important person in your life informed of your schedule and events in your life to avoid suspicion and misunderstandings. This is especially important for the next seven days.

suffering *any form* You will become wealthy in a very short period of time. Although it is ultimately expected, success will come sooner than expected. Blessings are with you.

suffocate Avoid all stressful situations and shield yourself from stress in all areas of your life. You will also hear of someone losing a job.

sugar A relationship will grow into a marriage and you will have many tranquil moments in this union.

sugar beet Information you gain from research over the next few days will give you an important edge over others.

sugarcane You will be very eager to commit to someone for the next seven days. This is a very vulnerable time and if this is not your desire become very protective of yourself.

sugarcoat Look to someone who has the power to pull you through situations you are unable to handle alone.

sugar daddy Someone will come into your life and spoil you in any way you wish. This will occur soon and this person will be someone you have known for some time. Both of you will be mutually satisfied.

sugar diabetes Someone who has been married many times will want to become involved with you. If you choose to become involved; you will marry this person but the relationship will be short lived. Your partner will request an annulment after leaving you.

sugar maple Be sure you are emotionally equipped to handle a situation you will become involved with over the next few days and do not overextend yourself. Before you commit, make sure you have the emotional reserves to handle this.

sugarplum Someone is going to great lengths to determine what motivates you. This evaluation is occurring without your knowledge. Within three days, you will learn of this person's desire for you. Be sure that during this time period you take special pains with your appearance and your behavior.

suggestion You will find great success in the field in which you are headed. Move with determination.

suicide The person you dream about is under a great deal of stress and will come to you in a short time for help. Be willing to offer assistance, listen, and help this person through this crisis. If anything negative was depicted in this dream, take steps to change it or avoid it entirely.

to see a suicide committed This is a sign that you will gain approximately one thousand dollars for each person you see commit suicide in your dream. This is money you will earn through a new venture. This dream also implies that any money owed to you will be paid in full within a few days. If anything negative was depicted in this dream, take steps to change it or avoid it entirely.

suit *man's suit* Be prepared. Many situations will arise shortly that will require you make correct decisions. Be sure to take the time to think out and research each situation prior to making a decision.

woman's suit Someone wants to get close to you emotionally but, because of circumstances, will not allow themselves. Within a short time this person will have the time to spend with you and will be eager to promote this relationship.

wet suit You are overextending yourself to the point of exhaustion. For the next week, do everything you can to maintain and improve your health. Eat healthy foods, drink plenty of water and set limits on what you are willing to do for others. For this coming week, all requests you make will also be granted, no matter how impossible they may seem.

suitcase You will soon buy a special gift for someone who is special to you and this will demonstrate to this individual your loving feelings for them. This is the correct action for you. It also implies that you need to guard all precious possessions you do not want to lose.

suite Someone in the medical field will soon grant you a big opportunity that will be treasured for a lifetime.

suitor Let someone know how much they mean to you.

sukiyaki Be very kind and generous to someone who expects kindness but hasn't received it lately. This person dearly loves you.

sulfur You need to be very cautious in your involvements over the next three weeks. Make sure you do not become involved in anything evil or anything that will bring harm to anyone else. This will backfire and you will be the one hurt.

sultan This indicates an unwanted pregnancy will occur to you or someone you know unless proper precautions are taken.

sum Do not allow yourself to be caught in an uncompromising position for the next few days. Be cautious or you will be caught in an undesirable situation.

sumac Someone is seeking revenge against you for an action you are unaware you have committed. You will be set up by this heartless person and will suffer bodily injury. Be aware of your surroundings.

summer You will realize a long time desire. You will also obtain an ambition that will provide you with a golden opportunity. Expect this to happen soon.

summerhouse You have long desired to move ahead on a pet project and the materials needed to begin this will soon be obtainable.

summer sausage You will achieve victory in the most important area of your life.

summer school Be sure the people you hire to work on your property have the proper credentials and licenses. Get everything in writing ahead of time.

summer solstice Someone will attempt to claim injury while working on your property. Be very wary of this occurrence for the next two days.

summer squash Do not allow yourself to become so busy that you have no time to spend with special people.

summer theater While dealing with financial situations, be sure to gain a clear understanding of each detail.

summon *to summon* Do not place yourself in the position to receive a summons because of behavior that may be avoided. Be careful of this for a two week period.

summons Keep your eye on all your precious belongings and guard against theft.

summa wrestling The stock market will be dropping within a few days.

sun You will receive the inner strength, tranquility and peace of mind necessary to handle a situation that will occur within three weeks. This also implies you will enjoy a brilliant future and handle your ongoing situations successfully.

sunbathe Someone with a very different lifestyle will interest you. You will attempt to pursue this person repeatedly but this individual is too shy to express their disinterest.

sunbeam This indicates a brilliant future and much luck.

sunbonnet This is a good luck omen. Make the move toward someone you are interested in and this person will eagerly respond. A relationship will then develop rapidly.

sunburn You will be very interested in having someone who calls from a distant place come for a visit. This individual will come and take from you as much as they can. Be very cautious and make no invitations for the next few days.

sunburst Someone will evoke hurt feelings from the past. This person is not necessarily the same kind of person who caused these original hurt feelings and you are free to enjoy this relationship free from the anxiety that you will experience the same hurts. Be watchful of this for the next four days.

Sunday Something unusual and unexpected will happen on a Sunday. Be prepared because you will receive some unexpected, shocking, yet exciting and positive news. Good luck will be with you for the following month.

Palm Sunday Be more open to business proposals and converse more with those of different ethnic groups. Your willingness to help will be much appreciated.

Sunday school Do not permit yourself to put excess strain and pressure on others. This will result in a breakdown in communication.

sundeck A conversation that you will initiate with someone not involved in your personal life will bring up points you may have overlooked and will increase your ability to handle situations successfully.

sundial Do not allow the criticism of someone you are interested in to keep you from having a relationship with this person. This will occur within four days.

sundown A committee you are eager to begin will not be what you expect. You will be wasting your energy.

sundress Pay close attention to your schedule for the next two weeks. Several things will be taking place at the same time but most importantly, two different people will be vying for your attention at the same time. Your desire is to spend equal time with both of these people. Make sure you keep your schedule open so you can fit everything in. Maintain a tight schedule in order to avoid conflicts and allow time for yourself and your obligations.

sundry Someone you place importance on will disappoint you in their reaction to your kindness. Do not involve yourself with this person.

sunfish Within a few weeks you will be able to bank extra money and watch your assets increase.

sunflower Someone will surprise you with their request to spend private moments with you. This will occur within a few days. Curiosity will lead you to have this meeting and you will be pleasantly surprised at the outcome.

sunglasses For the next three days you will be overwhelmed by a certain feeling that something suspicious is going on. Do not allow anyone to tell you this is paranoia on your part or attempt to water it down. This dream implies that your spirit is sending you a sense of heightened awareness to something you need to be more attentive to. This will allow you to handle everything in an appropriate manner and you will not feel later on you could have done something different. You have prior notice of this and can take the appropriate steps to deal with this issue now.

Sun God For a very long period of time you will be able to receive and enjoy the finest things the world has to offer. You will enjoy yourself to your heart's content. The gods are with you and you will enjoy good luck.

sunlamp Someone close to you needs to take care of their skin. This person needs to seriously take steps against infections. Be tactful and suggest they see a professional.

sunlight Love and give yourself a small gift that you will treasure and enjoy. Do this within a few days.

sunny day You are well on your way toward developing plans for the independence you need. This cycle will promote confidence, physical healing, and improvements in financial situations. You will take the right steps to ensure a bright future. This is a prosperous cycle and you will be able to turn those situations around that require improvements. Many blessings are with you and your family, and all requests made to your divinity will be granted to you.

sunny side up The person you most desire will soon surrender to you in body, mind and soul. The person will love you deeply and this will quickly turn into an engagement and a marriage. The union will last a lifetime and bring you much happiness.

sun porch Do not sell your valuables for less than they are worth. Take the time to get the proper appraisals and the right price. Be especially aware of this for the next five days.

sunrise You will be emotionally fulfilled by the person you love.

sunroof You will find something of value that was lost and you will be able to keep this item.

sunscreen Whatever you hear from another person will be the truth. Put away all your doubts.

sunset Push yourself to do something outrageous and out of the ordinary. Have fun as long as you do not hurt yourself or others. Do what makes you happy.

sunshine What you felt was impossible is now very possible. Go for it.

sunspot Do not fall back into bad habits that took you so long to break.

sunstroke You will fall in love with a very materialistic person who is also very wealthy. This person will love you deeply. Keep yourself open to meet new people for the next two weeks.

sun suit You will be invited soon to participate in a sex orgy. It will be your choice whether or not to attend.

suntan Make two plans for dealing with an issue you will be encountering soon. The first plan will work out but you will need another plan for a situation that will arise immediately afterward. Be sure both of these plans are in place before the need for them arises.

super conductor All electronic devices will be beneficial to you right now.

superior Whatever you have in mind to put into action and promote will not work out. Make sure you do not feign superiority to anyone else.

Superman/Superwoman You will come to someone's rescue in a life and death situation and will be recognized as a hero afterwards. This will occur within a few days.

supermarket Within three days you will have the means to detail and calibrate your thoughts in such a way that will enable someone to feel comfortable and at ease in your presence. Conversation will flow, you will become closer, and this individual will tell you what they have been longing to say to you. You are on the path toward a prosperous future and will be able to reach others with your communication skills. You and this person will enjoy a wonderful and tranquil life together if you choose to go this route.

supernatural The events occurring in this dream will indicate the negative and positive directions in which you are headed. Make sure you take the time to turn the negative aspects into positives. This is a good luck omen. You need, also, to attend a reading to gain more insight and detail into this dream.

supernova You have all the detailed information you need to give someone the right advice and proper assistance. When someone comes to you, give them all the information they need to carry on with their life in a more efficient manner.

superstitious Do not focus on anyone in an attempt to make them a victim. Be aware of what you are doing with another person's feelings.

supervisor Develop more loyalty to someone who is important to you. Involve them in your day to day routine.

supper Someone wonderful will offer you a wonderful life with them with no strings attached.

supper club You can find great bargains now. Keep your eyes open for the items you have long wanted to acquire and take steps to maintain your health.

supply *to supply* A team effort will yield more results than working alone.

support Make sure, for the next two days, that you develop the support system you need for an ongoing project. You will need this system for successful completion of this project.

supporter You will receive news of the death of a distant relative.

suppository A long time friend will become wealthy and forget all about you.

supreme Be careful you do not overdose on medications. Be cautious, also, that you do not take drugs to the point of abuse and addiction.

Supreme Being You will have blessings in all phases of your life. Your higher power will always be with you and each member of your family. All of your ambitions will be realized.

Supreme Court Other people will tell you about their needs but without much clarity. Be sure you have a real understanding of what they want.

surcharge Someone you contact within two days will be very rude and will make it clear they are displeased to hear from you. This is someone you least expect to hear this from. Make sure you either avoid this or have a firm grip on your emotions prior to this occurrence.

sure This is a very lucky omen. You will enjoy an abundance of health and receive wealth in areas you never expected as a result of an unexpected income. You will be able to accomplish tasks that you felt at one time were impossible. This is a great cycle to tackle those big projects. Proceed with confidence. Within the next four days you will enjoy a prosperous future.

surefooted Within a few days, a close relative will be scrutinizing each detail of your life. You will be uncomfortable as a result of this. Do everything you can to remain calm.

surf Do not allow anyone else to use your credit accounts for the next few days.

surface Someone who unexpectedly appears in your life has everything to offer in a relationship. Your hopes will be high but this person is not interested in a relationship with you.

surfboard Avoid accidents of any kind due to carelessness.

surfboat Someone will go to extremes to stick with their principles and will be unable to compromise with you in any manner. Get on with your life.

surf cast Do not falsely accuse someone of wrongdoing. Even if you know something, do not judge this person. This situation will arise within five days.

surf fishing Do not pick up people you feel compelled to help. This is not a wise thing to do.

surfing You will be falsely accused of wrong doing within five days. Make sure you have a tight alibi and a firm grip on your emotional status.

surgeon Any surgery you will be undergoing in a few months will be a complete success. You will enjoy a prompt recovery and good health for life.

surgeons' knot You will have a sexual encounter with a business acquaintance. This will not work out well and you will be disillusioned.

surgery Avoid all cuts to the body. You will also, within five days, finally be able to rid yourself of a long time enemy. This person will disappear from your life and will never appear again.

open heart surgery You are in the perfect position to ensure open heart surgery does not become necessary for you or anyone in your family. Start now to turn around anything that could lead to this. Be sure to eat healing foods, drink plenty of water, and get enough exercise. Aggressively seek time off and relaxation time to prevent this from occurring to you or a loved one. Do what you can to educate those you care about to take care of themselves.

oral surgery Watch out for secretaries or anyone who works in a similar capacity who will keep your calls and messages from getting through to someone you are trying to reach. For the next three days do everything you can to control your emotions. This individual enjoys game playing. You must also take steps to avoid any negative event portrayed in this dream that could occur in reality. You are entering a very lucky cycle and many blessings will come to you and your family.

plastic surgery Someone will approach you romantically. This person has a very jealous mate who will learn personal information about you in order to stalk you. Take precautions and stop this behavior early on. Anything negative in this dream that could become a reality needs to be prevented. Otherwise, you are headed for a brilliant future.

surgical pins Someone will attempt to lure you into some unpleasurable moments and distasteful conversations. For the next three days do not allow yourself to be pinned down or manipulated by someone else.

surprise You will have success in diffusing a plot that someone has devised against you. It will be impossible for this person to execute their plan for bringing some sort of discomfort and chaos into your life. You will be able to use whatever authority you possess to efficiently and effectively deal with this in a responsible manner. You will experience many wins and victories during this time period and the generosity you paid to someone in the past will be repaid now. You can expect many gifts and major wins. You are definitely headed for a brilliant future. Also, take every step to keep any negative event in this dream from becoming a reality.

to be taken by surprise or to take someone by surprise For the next three days be prepared for something remarkable and peculiar to occur. At the same time you will have the clarity of thought needed to take you through the next step to get through this cycle comfortably. Your curiosity will be very keen during this time period. Be very firm and disciplined and do not allow your curiosity to control you. You will enjoy an abundance of health during this cycle.

surrender *to surrender* You will be very displeased by an associate who is unable to go along with your ideas. This will occur within a few days. Be sure you are very aware of what you are surrendering to in the dream. If it is distasteful, take steps to avoid it.

someone else surrenders You will have an enjoyable time with someone who will surrender to you in an unplanned sexual encounter.

in any other form Within three days you will be with someone who will purposely use words in a certain way that will coerce you into agreeing to something they wish you to do and will do everything in their power to force you to surrender to them, behave in the way they desire, or speak in the manner they wish. Be very aware of this. You have prior notice and can take the appropriate steps now to avoid it.

surrey Do not allow your loved one to slip away as a result of your abusive behavior and inability to communicate.

surrogate *any form* You now have the ability to communicate to your loved ones something that has bothered you for a long time. Feel free to express those things you find distasteful about your surroundings. This is the appropriate time to do this and you will find the support and love you need.

surround *to surround* Do not place bets on any sporting events. You will suffer great losses.

to be surrounded You will loan money to a relative who is temporarily short on cash but you will be repaid shortly. This will occur within a few weeks.

surveillance Someone is conducting a surveillance and is stalking you. Keep a close eye on your surroundings. This could result in bodily harm.

to conduct a surveillance Quickly locate needed information to complete an ongoing project.

surveillance camera Be very attentive because an unusual occurrence will develop regarding a person, project or position that will lead to a financial windfall. You may marry someone who will leave you with a monthly pension, develop a project that will deliver you monthly royalties, or secure a position that will offer you monthly provisions for a lifetime. You are in a sound position to receive this in the near future. Develop your curiosity, especially for the next three days, to ensure you do not miss out on these benefits. You will receive an abundance of health, many blessings will come to you, and you are headed for a brilliant future. Make

sure you do not put yourself in the position to be viewed by a surveillance camera doing something you don't want to be seen. Make sure any negative event witnessed in this dream is prevented in reality.

surveyor Make sure you do not put yourself in a position that will result in losing control over a dangerous situation and do not leave yourself open to an ambush that could lead to bodily injury.

survive *to survive* Be very cautious that you do not choke while eating for the next few days. Watch your food intake and be sure you have enough to drink. Blessings are with you and this is a very lucky omen.

to use this phrase You will have an abundance of energy and health.

Susanna *(from the Canonical Bible)* Although the person you are interested in is not as attentive as you like, this is a minor problem. Do not complain about small issues. This person is on the path toward a brilliant future and wishes you to be a part of it. You will also accumulate your own wealth and this process will start to evolve within the month. You will have financial stability and you will enjoy all of it. Many blessings are with you and your family.

sushi Be careful not to overindulge in food or alcohol. Monitor your intake.

suspect The person you have a passion for will soon leave the area on a permanent basis. You will hear of this within three days.

suspenders An anticipated long business trip will be shorter than predicted. The trip will be successful and you will have a safe return.

suspense You will visit a city loved the world over and will have an enormously enjoyable time. You will sample a variety of delightful foods, music and culture. Expect this to occur within two months.

suspicions You need to be aware and suspicious of everyone and everything for the next three days. Expect the unexpected.

suture Take precautions to prevent any blood disease and infections such as hepatitis and jaundice.

Svengali Someone will attempt to involve you in a ménage à trois. Avoid this in order to avoid future guilt. You will also be wasting your time because this person will not leave the one they are living with.

swab For the next two days, remember that people are giving you advice only because they love you. These people are concerned for your welfare, do not be so hard on them.

swabs A powerful individual who has had an influence in

your life will be instrumental in helping you reach your life long goal.

swaddling clothes You will gain full employment with a great salary.

swallow *(to swallow)* It is necessary to take steps against drowning for the next three days. Be aware that this could take place in a small amount of water.

swallow *(bird)* Do not lead another person on by giving out false signals of interest. Be respectful of other people's feelings and watch your body language.

swamp Efforts to bring about changes in your goals will meet with disappointment for the next three days unless you take steps to prevent it.

swan Something has been weighing heavily on your mind but you will finally be able to find peace and have tranquility from now on. You will find clarity of thought and love within three days.

swan dive Whatever you do for the next few days will be extremely lucky.

swan song Protect yourself from the occurrence of an embarrassing situation for the next three days. This event will not easily be erased from the minds of others.

swarm Someone is pushing you around just to see what they can get from you. They have no business doing this. At the first indication this is occurring, put your foot down and stop this behavior.

swashbuckler Within three days, someone will make a big issue over an unexpected trivial issue. Watch out for this and control it immediately.

swastika Guard your freedom, privacy and everything you hold dear for the next five days.

swatch Make sure you are at the right place at the right time in order to speak with an individual who will help assure your success.

swayback You will be accused of being fickle and unfaithful within three days. Be careful.

swear Focus on what requires immediate attention. Within three days you will be able to determine what is an important matter. Refer to dirty words for a greater definition of the dream.

sweat Do not allow another person's opinion to confuse you. This person will become angry because you do not follow their advice. So be prepared, within three days, to handle this anger.

sweatband You will be victorious in each phase of your life. Go for it.

sweatbox Expect only good surprises but be aware of impulsive behavior.

sweater Someone adores and loves you and is eager for a loving sexual encounter. Once you surrender to this person, you will enjoy every moment. You need to love yourself and avoid taking any health risks. Enjoy life.

sweatpants Within three days, a sexual encounter will be requested of you. Surrender and you will enjoy yourself immensely.

sweatshirt You have faith that your creative thoughts and abilities will work for you. Others lack this faith. Follow your instincts, you will be successful.

sweatshop Do not allow anyone to exploit your energy and physical efforts by underpaying you. This person will agree to pay you a fee to perform a certain job and will refuse to come through upon completion. Be aware of this for the next week.

Swede You will receive cards and flowers from a secret admirer for one week. This person will then express their love for you after this time period. You will be pleasantly surprised when you discover their identity. The relationship will move ahead rapidly and provide mutual happiness.

sweep *to sweep* A variety of different events will occur back to back and will provide enjoyment to you for some time. You will be very popular.

to see someone else sweep You will soon find your destined mate and you will be happy with this person for a lifetime.

sweeper You will find your soul mate and enjoy mutual love for a lifetime.

sweepstakes *to win* Someone you desire will fall in love with you. This will lead to a very successful marriage.

someone else wins You will soon win a prize. Luck is with you.

sweet You will be invited to an extravagant dinner and will enjoy yourself immensely among very sophisticated people. Your date will go to great lengths to make you fall in love with them. This person is also very wealthy but will hide this from you in order to avoid spending money. Do not deprive yourself of the best. This will occur within five days.

sweet and sour Two events will occur during a one day period. You will hear both good and bad news. The bad news will not be very serious and you will handle it with ease. Blessings are with you and your family.

sweet basil This will be an extremely lucky time for you in all phases of your life for a long time to come.

sweetbreads You will enjoy immense wealth and financial security for a long time to come.

sweet cherry Someone desperately wants to see you in order to demonstrate their affection for you. This individual will contact you very soon.

sweet clover You will have a very happy and mutually satisfying sex life.

sweet corn You will enjoy a very romantic, beautiful sex life with music, candlelight, dancing and all of the romantic trappings.

sweetening Your desires for love will be fulfilled.

sweetheart *to dream of your sweetheart* Each event you dream of will occur in actuality within two days. If it is a negative message, take steps to prevent it. Anything you see concerning your sweetheart will be a lucky omen and you can expect something special between both of you to occur within two days.

to dream of being called sweetheart Within two days someone you have special feelings for will eagerly ask you out. The time and place will be set and definite but unforeseen circumstances will prevent this person from appearing or calling. After several hours, this person will be able to reach you and apologize. You will be praised for your patience and cordiality.

sweet margarine You will be introduced to an influential person who will, in turn, introduce you to a group of powerful friends. You will develop powerful allies from this group who will offer assistance to you in the future.

sweet peas Tenderness will grow between you and someone special especially within five days. Allow special moments to flow naturally, especially for the next week.

sweet pepper Do not forget the plans you have made to attend an event with a special person.

sweet potato You will be interested in someone whose sexual appetite is much greater than your own. This person will go to great lengths to involve you in their life. Carefully think over this situation in order to make your feelings clear yet not miss out on the love and affection this person has to offer. They will take steps to accommodate you in order to keep the relationship mutually satisfying.

sweet talk You will persuade someone to let you spoil them for a lifetime. This person will accept, based solely on their love for you.

sweet tomato You will thoroughly enjoy a theater event with a special person and you will be emotionally satisfied.

sweet tooth You will soon surrender and marry your sweetheart. This will be a happy union that will last a lifetime.

sweet william Do everything you can to place yourself in a quiet environment so you can let your creativity blossom and come to tangible form. This will make a real difference in your life. Many blessings are with you.

swell *to swell* Someone special to you will make some unexpected demands of you. This will catch you off guard because you will be surprised at the new confidence and assertiveness demonstrated by this person. This will be a welcome sign to you.

swim *to swim* The person you are emotionally involved with will unexpectedly take on greater responsibilities. This will surprise you. This person will grant you more respect, love and sincerity while taking on more responsibility within the union. There is a feeling of greater unity and sharing. Accept this calmly and enjoy it.

to see others swim You will gain total acceptance from another person for your ideas and plans regarding a mutual undertaking. Everything will fall into place perfectly.

to swim with others If you desire to solidify a union with a special person, take steps to act on this now. This cycle is lucky for bringing unity to relationships and business affairs. You will also experience an abundance of health and finances for the next two weeks.

to swim in rough waters Do not allow a dangerous situation to unfold because you become over confident about what an individual has led you to believe they can do. For the next five days handle situations promptly and correctly in order to prevent a chaotic situation from developing.

in any other form Within four days an unexpected and outrageous proposition will be presented to you. This proposal seems far too good to be true and you will be tempted to turn it down because it seems too impossible to accomplish. Let this person know you want a few days to mull this over. Do not close any doors or burn any bridges because you will want to experiment with the proposal to see if it is a possibility at a later time. You will definitely maintain the feelings that this is not something that can be accomplished. Be assured it will happen and this person will keep each commitment they make to you. Good luck is with you.

swimming hole *dark, muddy* Do not allow negative tapes to guide your way of thinking. Avoid all negative thoughts.

in any other form You will be treated in the exact manner you wish to be treated. Good luck is with you.

swimming pool You will be asked to demonstrate your feelings toward another person because this person feels you do not care as much as you do. Set the record straight. You are very much adored by this individual.

swimsuit Do whatever you can to enjoy the very essence of life and avoid negative thinking.

swindler Someone has focused on you in an attempt to con you out of an item you have owned for some time. For three days, this person will aggressively attempt to purchase this item at a cheap price. Be wary and guard against this.

swine *any form* Take a pragmatic and responsible approach when dealing with a difficult issue that will come up within five days that involves someone you care about. Your involvement will have a major impact on this person's life. Strive for better understanding in order to keep this situation from reaching a level of chaos. This will occur if you do not handle this in a logical fashion. You will develop the strength to take care of this.

swine flu Someone will purposely involve you in an illegal activity within five days. You are unaware this is illegal so watch out for any potential scams within this time period.

swing *any form* You are in the process of making a decision that will directly affect you and another person. This person will depend on you to make the correct decision because of the profound impact it will make on their life. You will need strength and courage to make the proper move but the decision will be made correctly. Move quickly and do not waste time.

swinger *any form* You will be flitting from place to place and city to city while having a great time for the next few months. Discipline yourself and avoid going overboard.

swinging door Every opportunity will be presented to you within a few weeks to make a real difference in your life. Take a chance and pioneer new ideas. One of these ideas will make a profound difference in your life for a long time to come.

Swiss You are headed for a brilliant future. Within two days you will meet a very creative person who will work with you on a new project. This will grow into an important part of your life.

Swiss chard You will feel sorrow and pain over the misfortune of a good friend.

Swiss cheese Your production level will grow due to the discovery of important information you gain through personal research.

Swiss steak You will be financially secure due to an increase in funds for a long period of time.

switch *to turn on* A powerful well formed idea will grant you a new way of life. You will also become very detailed and precise in the manner in which you grasp your goals. As a result, you will become very successful.

to turn off You have a close relative who will drain you emotionally and financially. Guard against this for two days.

malfunctioning Within five days you will be with someone who will lead you to believe they are financially secure, have a credible lifestyle and are respected, professional and have a stable career. In addition, this person will give you every reason to believe you have easy access any time you choose. Because this person is believable and you feel comfortable in their presence you will be as eager to become involved with them as they are with you. After you attempt to contact them through the numerous phone numbers you have been given through company addresses and through their secretary you will find it impossible to reach them directly and it will take hours and days for this individual to return your calls. You will come to realize this person has misled you about their lifestyle and status. If you become involved with this person on any level you will be let down. Be very shrewd and disciplined in order to keep this person from violating your emotions or insulting your intelligence. You have prior notice of this and will be successful in taking care of this issue. You are in a lucky cycle and are headed for a prosperous future.

in any other form Think ahead very carefully and have all your facts at hand in order to argue your point of view in an effective way. Good luck is with you.

switchblade Take care of your teeth and do not bite into anything that could injure your teeth for the next five days. You will also arrive at an idea that will enhance the productivity of an ongoing project. Blessings and good luck are with you.

switchboard Attempt to give confidence and a positive outlook on life to a relative who is going through a painful crisis. The crisis will end shortly.

switch hitter A relative of the opposite sex will become involved in a dangerous situation. Warn this person that within five days they will be engaged in a dangerous confrontation unless steps are taken to avoid it.

Switzerland A very attractive, dynamic and kind person from a different country and of a different nationality will give you a gift you will treasure for a lifetime.

swivel chair There will be a new unexpected member of the family.

swizzle stick You will reach a fantastic agreement with the object of your affection.

sword Your thoughts, judgments and communications will be clear and you will make quick and correct decisions. Your strength and power will increase. Others will learn quickly from your ideas and decisions. Someone you felt had forgotten you will also return within three days and communicate to you that you are well remembered.

foil - fencing sword A close male member of your family who lives in a distant city desperately needs your help but has difficulty expressing their needs. Make it your job to reach out to this person and offer your assistance, especially for the next two days.

sword belt You will have no success in reaching an elusive person. All of your efforts will be futile.

sword dance You will not be successful in the performing arts for the next week.

swordfish Make sure you do not sour communications with another because you will be apologizing for a long time to come.

swordsman Do not make financial loans to a relative, you will not be repaid.

swordplay Do not attempt to strike against anyone within the week. It will backfire.

swordtail You will have no sex life for the next week due to unforeseen circumstances.

sycamore Your travel cycle is lucky. Enjoy yourself for the next two weeks.

symbol Watch the symbol carefully and gain clues from the representations of the symbols. You will enjoy good luck and a loving family for a long time to come.

symbolism This is very lucky omen for you and your family. You will enjoy an abundance of wealth and health.

sympathy You will receive very good news from a very good friend in a short period of time.

symphony Congratulations, you will be a big winner soon in games of chance. You will also receive congratulations for an event that will occur within a few weeks.

symptom Do not allow your emotions to get the best of you. Control your feelings and get on with your life.

synapse Decisions made in the past will resurface. These decisions will need to be reassessed and those that have been outgrown need to be discarded and new decisions need to be made.

syndicate Make sure you protect all property from fire. You will also receive a quick response to all requests for help for the next three days regarding papers that require you to seek help in preparing.

synthesizer Prepare for last minute changes that need careful handling in order to avoid chaos if not handled immediately.

synthetic Confront someone who is indebted to you and you will promptly regain every penny owed.

syphilis Be very aware of any blood infection and take extra precautions for the next five days. Do not expose yourself to any contagious blood disorder.

syringe Luck is with you for a very long time. A child or young person will also communicate to you something that is bothering them. This young person wants to be assured they are making the right decision. This person will also have a great deal of luck in life and will have good news to tell you.

syrup Within three days a disagreement will occur. You will need to do whatever is necessary to immediately patch up this relationship. It will be successfully resolved. A wedding will occur in the near future and you will win the person you most desire. This union will last a lifetime.

system Whatever is going on in your dream will occur in reality. If there is a problem, do whatever is necessary to rectify the problem. Take steps to maintain your health and safety. This is a lucky omen.

T

T Within the month, you will have the opportunity to meet a wonderful individual who is very open and eager to have someone in their life for a very meaningful and deep relationship. This person has many surprises in store and is fun loving, generous, caring and interested in traveling with someone who enjoys exotic places, romantic settings, and exclusive restaurants. This person has a huge appetite for the finer things in life as well as a large sexual appetite. You have the opportunity to involve yourself with this person but you must be prepared to give a lot of love and affection. If you choose to go in this direction, use your communication skills effectively in order to interest this person. You are headed for a healthy, long life filled with excitement. Do what you can to socialize and keep your eyes open for this incredible person. Good luck is with you.

tab You will divulge some personal information to another person about a certain situation you are working on. For the next three days, make sure someone does not blurt something out you have told them that they should be keeping to themselves. Talk to this person ahead of time so they know they should keep things to themselves.

Tabasco sauce You will unintentionally sabotage your own plans by talking too much and letting people know too much about your business, especially for the next two days.

tabby cat Do everything necessary to keep your health up to par. Check your vital signs, eat healthy foods and drink plenty of water.

tabernacle For the next three days you must be more considerate to someone special to you. This person will go through some very special times and you will need to show more empathy and patience toward them until they get through this. It will end within three days.

table You will feel as though you have to be relentless in convincing someone to work on something they are reluctant to do. This individual does not have the courage to tell you and will instead talk about you behind your back. This can be prevented by not pushing this person to work with you. Seek an alternative person. Otherwise, you are headed for a prosperous future and any negative thoughts you had about achieving your ambitions will dissipate. Anything you thought was impossible is now possible within the week. You will have the luck needed to grasp your goals. Many blessings are with you and your family.

work table You are definitely headed for a prosperous future and you will have a lucky month long period to take care of what you need. You also need to provide yourself with the solitude you need in order to clear your thoughts, especially for the next seven days. Proceed with confidence, you are headed for a brilliant future.

tablecloth You can keep yourself from mishandling a certain situation that will be crucial to you. Be very aware of your behavior or you will lose big. Within the week, try to change any behavior that could result in negative events. You are entering a very lucky cycle if you are cautious and are in tune to what you are doing.

table linen Make sure within the next five days you do not involve yourself in a situation you feel obligated to. Find out more of what is involved before you commit yourself. It will not be to your advantage.

table saw Do not become involved in anything you are considering investing in. This is not a good time to become involved in unusual situations.

tablespoon If someone seems hesitant and uncertain over an agreement you will be entering into within five days, back off. This will create problems within a two week period and it will be difficult to get this situation back to normal. Otherwise, good luck is with you.

tablet Do not pass false judgments or criticize anyone. Take steps to change this trait. Try to be more sensitive and practical in your ways.

table tennis Within two weeks you will begin to harvest work well done in the past. The rewards will be much greater than you ever envisioned. An abundance of health and wealth will be yours within seven days. This also implies that a situation will occur within seven days that will require aggressive behavior on your part. You will enjoy a successful outcome.

tabletop Within two days you will arrive at some well formed ideas that, if put into action, will give you what you need to grasp your goals.

tableware All legal matters will be settled in your favor within five days.

table wine A financial agreement will be reached within three days and will be in the exact form and structure that you desire. Everything you envision from this will come to be. Do everything necessary to bring more joy and happiness into your life. Regardless of whatever is going on now, focus on your own happiness. You will also get an invitation to an exotic event. Enjoy yourself.

tabloid Make sure your money actually gets to the place it is intended to go. If you do not remain involved personally and do not put tight constraints on your money, it will go for purposes for which it was never intended. Be on your guard, especially for the next five days.

taboo Meditate in your favorite form. This will be a delightful cycle for you, filled with happiness and joy. You will enjoy good luck for the next seven days. Trust your intuition. Many blessings will be with you and your family.

tack Within five days the opportunities you have been waiting for will present themselves to you. You will have the opportunity to have a new start in those areas of your life you desire them in. You will be able to develop and execute those plans very professionally and experience more prosperity in your life.

tackle Good times will start coming in and you will experience joy and happiness.

tachycardia Within three days an exciting surprise will come your way and you will be given an unexpected, small, but expensive gift.

taco Do not deny yourself moments that could bring you a tremendous amount of pleasure, especially for the next two days. Do everything necessary to bring more tranquility and simplicity in your life.

tadpole Someone has relentlessly promised that they will come through for you. Within two days this person will attempt to wriggle out of this commitment. This will make you feel someone is trying to pull the rug out from under you. You have prior notice of this and can turn this around by bearing down and insisting for the next two days, that this person keep their word. This will result in their handling exactly what they have promised. Otherwise, this person will manage to weasel their way out of it. Don't allow this to happen. You are entering a very lucky cycle. Proceed with confidence.

taffeta A greater mental inventiveness and clarity of thought will be gifts from the deities to you during this cycle. You will be able to create a very uncomplicated and stress free environment for yourself as well as being able to achieve exactly what you are after during this time period. Many blessings are with you and your family.

taffy Make sure you put your thoughts into writing so you will find it much easier to communicate something you have difficulty verbalizing. This is a good cycle for this type of communication with no stressful repercussions. Many blessings are with you.

tag Do not allow inconsistent behavior to rule your personality, especially for the next three days. You will achieve victory in those areas of your life you desire. Many blessings are with you and your family.

Tagalong Be prepared for a big victory that will be coming your way within five days. Be consistent in your actions and behave appropriately in all areas of your life.

Tahiti Someone with a greater sexual drive and appetite than you will be very eager to involve you in a relationship. This union will last a lifetime if you desire. Remember, however, the differences in your sexual drives and make sure you choose the path you most desire. Many blessings will be with you and your family and you are headed for a prosperous future. This dream may also be used as a reference point in time. If you dream of this island and see its name used in any context, the dream message will occur on this day.

Tahoe Any method you develop to communicate to another will be highly successful and well received, especially when used for negotiations. You are headed for a prosperous future and will be in a lucky cycle for the upcoming month. This may also be used as a reference point in time. If you dream of this lake and see its name used in any context, the dream message will occur on this day.

Tai Chi Be alert to any situation that will throw you off course, especially for the next three days. This will cause you to take the wrong path. Double check to make sure you are not headed in the wrong direction, especially if the course you are taking feels especially nice. Remain calm and think through all of your decisions very carefully. Be practical and use common sense. Otherwise, you are headed for a very prosperous future.

tail All of your hopes and plans will turn out exactly as you have envisioned, especially for the next seven days. You will be entering a lucky cycle. This is also the time to take steps to maintain a relationship at the highest possible level you can. Make sure you do your part in keeping this person

close to you. Love and affection will help you focus on those important issues instead of dealing with wasted energy. You are both on the path toward a brilliant future.

tailback Make sure you guard your reputation, especially for the next three days. Something will occur that will threaten this unless you are very cautious about how you conduct yourself.

tailbone Take steps to avoid or turn around any negative event connected with this dream and make sure you forewarn anyone you recognize in the dream to do the same, especially for the next three days. You will also be surrounded with love and receive verification of this within the week. You are loved, respected and appreciated beyond your imagination.

tailcoat Make sure you do not put yourself in the position to have to give damaging testimony against another person. Do not allow anyone to know how much you know in order to avoid this. Keep all knowledge about someone else private, especially for the next three days.

tailgate An extraordinary occurrence will take place within two months that will force you to relocate. You will need to start making plans now so you will be able to accomplish this with ease. If this is something you do not choose to do, you can start making plans now to avoid it.

taillight Within three days someone will be very eager for you to sign some papers. Regardless of how wonderful you think this move would be, do not sign these papers. They will not offer you any advantage but you will not know of this until a later time when it is too late for you to change paths. Take all the necessary precautions and do not sign these papers.

tailor For the next month you will enjoy yourself immensely with young members of your family. The younger the person, the more enjoyment, laughter and beautiful moments you will have. Also a wonderful person will enter your life and will play an important role in your present involvements. Positive events will take place in those areas of your life you most desire. You are loved beyond your imagination.

tailpipe You will learn of the reconciliation of someone. You will rejoice over this.

tailspin Make sure you do not stay in the same area with two people who are fighting. Remove yourself from the premises in order to avoid an emotionally shocking experience.

Taipei Be very tolerant and listen carefully to someone who is feeling anxious and upset. Be very calm, supportive and generous with your time. Your concern will mean a great deal to this individual. Expect this to occur within three days. This may also be used as a reference point in time. If you dream of this city and see its name used in any context, the dream message will occur on this day.

Taiwan You will meet a same sexed person who will relentlessly help you in areas of your life that you need assistance. This person will listen carefully to everything you say and will show you a great deal of consideration. This individual also has a good sense of humor and demonstrates patience. You are definitely headed for a prosperous future and you will be in a very lucky cycle for the next seven days. This may also be used as a reference point in time. If you dream of this country and see its name used in any context, the dream message will occur on this day.

Taj Majal You will be married to someone who is very kind, generous, affectionate and will remain with you for a lifetime. This will begin to evolve within the month. Good luck is with you. This may also be used as a reference point in time. If you dream of this historical site and see its name used in any context, the dream message will occur on this day.

take *any form* Be acutely aware that within seven days someone will purposely try to create problems between you and a special person. Make sure you do everything you can to discourage this situation and prevent its occurrence. This may take place at a time that you least expect and will take you by surprise. By the time you come to grips with this issue, the situation may already be occurring.

take apart *to take apart anything* Within two days it will be important to have a conversation with specific people in order to make the proper requests and connections before a certain situation begins to develop. This will keep everything from falling apart before it takes off. Stay ahead of yourself and you will be able to make the proper adjustments in time. Focus on this now and everything will fall into place successfully. Good luck is with you and your family. You are headed for a brilliant future.

"take it or leave it" *to hear or use the phrase* This is promising you that everything will work out for you if you just try, give it some time and take calculated risks. Good luck and many blessings will come to you, especially for the next three days.

take off *to fly* Do not push yourself on someone who is totally disinterested in you. This person is not interested in developing a relationship. Get busy with something else and move on with your life.

in any other form For the next five days refuse to become involved with anyone who puts you on an emotional roller coaster. Free yourself from this abusive situation and do everything you can to allow only positive events to take place in your life.

takeout Dig deeply and determine what benefits are due you. You will get a clear picture within five days of what you are owed.

take out food You will accomplish a great deal if you present a more interesting demeanor around influential people. You will encourage closeness with these people so prepare yourself to present an interesting image.

talc Within three weeks, news of your talent and creativity will reach a future partner. You will reach a satisfactory agreement to promote your talents.

tale *to tell an untrue story* You are steering yourself in the wrong direction. Make the effort to determine the cause of this and decide on the direction you want to take. You have been led to believe, by yourself or by someone else, that something is correct, when in actuality it isn't. Dig deeply and make absolutely sure you are not being misled about an important situation. This also implies that certain plans made regarding a crucial situation will work to your advantage. Focus on your health as well as on everyday situations that you take for granted.

talent Do everything necessary to stick with what you know is the correct and right thing to do. Do not let anyone else persuade you otherwise, especially for the next four days. Pay attention to the particular talent demonstrated in this dream that may be connected to reality. Any positive abilities this dream demonstrates in you or someone you know needs to be embraced in reality. You will be in a very lucky cycle for the next month. Tackle those big tasks with confidence.

talent scout For the next five days you will possess a commanding personality and clarity of thought. You will be able to express yourself succinctly if you take steps to divorce yourself from those you associate with daily. After you do this, you will be able to make the right decisions that will lead you to a comfortable lifestyle.

talent show Keep going in the direction you are headed. You are on the path toward a brilliant future. You will also hear the words of love you have been waiting to hear from the person you most desire.

talisman Someone you know with a charismatic, confident and humorous personality will do everything in their power to bring you closer to them. This person will invite you to an enjoyable outing and will ask you to be a part of their life. A number of things will occur on this outing that will make it clear that you wish to make major changes in your life on a permanent basis. These changes will bring you joy.

talk You will soon become involved with someone who is not fully committed to a work relationship. This person will play games, create a hot and cold environment and you will seldom see eye to eye. You will need to develop a no nonsense approach because you will both be co-workers on a project within a few weeks. Once this attitude is adopted, you will accomplish much. Stick to business.

sweet talk You will persuade someone to let you spoil them for a lifetime. This person will accept, based solely on their love for you.

talk show host This is a powerful symbol for you and implies that you need to associate with those who have the education and knowledge to enlighten you in such a way that you can evolve and grow. Positive attitudes will rub off on you and you can be assured that loved ones do not outgrow you. Allow closeness to grow within family circles. Your higher power is with you. Within three days you will experience an abundance of health and you are headed for a very prosperous future.

tallow For the next month you will experience tranquility, clarity of thought and an abundance of health. Many blessings will come to you and your family.

talon Watch out for dangerous falls. Take extra precautions to protect yourself for the next two weeks.

tamale Within five days you will receive an all expense paid trip, as a gift, to an area you really want to visit. This will come as a surprise to you and will be very rewarding.

tamarind Be very careful when making overseas travel arrangements for the next few weeks. Be cautious of contracting a contagious disease that you would otherwise not be exposed to. If you take the proper precautions, you will enjoy a successful trip.

tambourine Within three days you will meet a new acquaintance. This will lead to many affectionate and passionate moments with many other moments of harmony and tranquility. This will provide a tremendous change in your life that you will welcome.

tame *to tame* Within three days you will experience someone acting very much out of the ordinary and out of character in a sexual way. This person will present a more sexual and passionate demeanor. Enjoy this side of this person because this transformation will not last very long. You will enjoy many passionate moments with this individual. This dream is very lucky for you.

Tam O'Shanter An issue that has been pulling you down emotionally will stabilize within four days and you will see dramatic improvements in your life. Take the time you need to recuperate from this situation and do not take on another burdensome problem. Enjoy life and keep yourself safe.

tampon For the next week make sure you do not use a medication that is not right for you for a particular illness that you will come down with. This is not a serious illness but you could develop serious complications if you use the wrong medication without consulting a physician.

soiled tampon You will experience instant wealth

through a financial windfall of some sort. An extraordinary occurrence will give this opportunity to you. Many blessings are with you and you will experience an abundance of health and a prosperous future.

tan Your affections will be requested by someone within three days. You will be overjoyed by this and will be more than willing to give yourself to this individual. Many blessings will come to you and your family. You must also make two plans for a situation you will be dealing with. The first plan will work out but you will need another plan for a situation that will arise immediately afterward. Be sure both of these plans are in place prior to when the need for them arises.

to get a tan Do not get involved in a family situation in spite of how desperate it may seem to you. The temptation to get involved may be overwhelming. Step back, regroup and remain uninvolved. You will enjoy an abundance of health for a long period of time and are definitely headed for a prosperous future.

tanager Do not overextend yourself with a certain issue that will arise within five days. This situation will require that you perform physical labor to the point of exhaustion. Remove yourself from this situation, regroup yourself, eat healthful foods, drink plenty of water and get the proper amount of rest.

tandem bicycle This is a very lucky omen for you. Follow your instincts and your own counsel. Anything you decide to execute will be successful. Victory is yours.

tangelo Within three days you will be given the chance to accept a once in a lifetime situation that will lead to greater wealth and power. You will be aware enough, during this time period, to recognize this opportunity and will have the courage to take it.

tangerine Someone you do not know well will ask you for financial backing. This proposal will be very fortuitous for you and you will be handsomely rewarded if you choose to become involved.

tangle Someone you are interested in is not the person you need to rely on in any form. Take the time to select and review carefully the character of those you choose to associate with and do not allow yourself to be taken, especially for the next seven days. You will also need to place yourself in a stress free environment, seek more simplicity and come to grips with a behavior pattern that should be stopped. Put aside any addictions that may have gotten out of control. This is a great cycle for getting everything back in the proper order. This dream is a good omen for health and luck. You are headed for a brilliant future.

tango You are paying far too much attention to a total stranger. This person is not someone you should have any involvements with because they have an evil nature. Go on with your life without this person in it. Expect this to occur within seven days and do not involve yourself with an evil stranger who is charismatic and seems easy to get along with.

tank Do not involve yourself in a risky situation that seems to be a sure thing.

tankard Someone will want to associate with you who needs help with their angry attitude and constantly makes themselves and others around them miserable. Pay close attention to this and remove yourself from this unhealthy environment. Get on with your life, especially for the next three days.

tanker Put yourself on the path of righteousness and begin healing yourself from wickedness. You will develop the courage to do this within two weeks. You will also begin to normalize your life and heal yourself.

tanker truck For the next three days any negotiation you enter into will be enormously successful. Be very diligent and effectively handle your responsibilities. Do not rely on someone else who is less experienced than you to handle your responsibilities.

tank top Within three days you will meet a new acquaintance. This will lead to many passionate and affectionate moments. The remainder of the time will be very tranquil and harmonious for both of you. There will be a tremendous change in your life that you will welcome.

tanner You will be easily taken by a conniving friend. This person will go to great lengths to sabotage any opportunity just moments prior to your receiving knowledge of it. You can prevent this occurrence by making yourself aware of who this person is so you can handle this situation appropriately and turn it around so it can benefit you. You have the time and knowledge to prevent this.

tannery This is an extremely lucky omen for you. You will soon go through a tremendous change in your life. Within a two day period, you will also go to someone for financial assistance and this person will eagerly offer you this help.

tannic acid You are entering a very lucky cycle for at least six months. Within the week you will also learn of an unexpected inheritance. You are headed for a very prosperous future.

tansy The opportunity is there for you to do something spectacular that will allow you to move things in the direction you desire. This is the perfect cycle to accomplish those goals you are interested in accomplishing. Many blessings are with you and your family.

tantrum You are headed in the right direction and will gain access to vast amounts of information. Tap into this

knowledge and you will receive the tools you need to accumulate in order to live the lifestyle you desire. You will enjoy a long and healthy life. Many blessings will come to you and your family.

tap This is alerting you that someone with their own opinions will try to impose them on you. Do not allow this to block your original creative way of thinking and make sure you continue on your present course.

to be tapped on your shoulder or any other form Someone will send you a material message (i.e., flowers, candy, a gift, etc.) to express their deep feelings. This person also desires that your involvement grow and bloom. Good luck is with you.

to tap someone on the shoulder or any other form Pay close attention to who you were tapping. If you recognize the person, this individual will be instrumental in helping you to shape a brilliant future. If you did not recognize this person, you will be offered a large amount of money for services you can easily provide in a non stressful way. Good luck is with you.

if the tapping feeling is unpleasant to you Someone in another state or in a far away place has a deep need to see you. This person misses you a great deal and will contact you soon to express their feelings. This person will also extend the means to travel to their locale so you can spend time together. If you choose to go in this direction, you will enjoy yourself immensely.

if you enjoy the tapping feeling You will be entering a very lucky cycle for at least a month. You will also be blessed with a tremendous amount of health and wealth. This will ensure you will be able to keep up with your financial demands. Many blessings will come to you and your family.

tap dance Be alert to a deficit in another person's character. This individual will be unable to provide the emotional closeness you need and lead you to believe they will go the whole nine yards with you emotionally. This will be an impossibility because of an emotional hang up they have. This is beyond anyone's control. Otherwise, you will be overjoyed at the material abundance you will receive. Your business and financial affairs will improve vastly over the next five days.

tape *adhesive* Take good care of yourself, especially for the next five days. Avoid unhealthy relationships and keep yourself stress free. You are definitely headed for a brilliant future.

tape deck *(car tape deck)* The next three days will be an important time to connect emotionally with another person. Be very clear about the message you want to communicate before you speak. You will be able to make this connection so successfully that they will respond in the manner you most desire. If this message is negative you have enough time to ensure you only experience positive events.

tape *masking* Keep a low profile and focus on routine tasks. Be aware of any errors, in any capacity, that could occur within three days. You have prior notice of this and can take care of any mistake immediately in order to avoid unnecessary problems. Many blessings are with you and you are headed for a brilliant future.

tape measure Within three days you will be able to offer your love to someone you care about in the manner they desire. This will take place in a wild and romantic setting. Good luck will be with you for the next seven days.

tape player/recorder Within five days you will acquire a commanding personality and clarity of thought. You will be able to express yourself in the best possible way if you divorce yourself from those you associate with daily. You will then be able to make the right decisions that will ultimately lead to a comfortable lifestyle.

taper Within three days you will be profoundly aggressive in trying to determine the proper conclusion to a problem situation that keeps reoccurring. Good luck is with you. You must also take steps to avoid involvement with anything that poses a danger to you. Refrain from self abusive behavior and take steps to keep yourself safe. Practice discipline for the next seven days.

tapestry You will soon be able to develop a clear idea about what needs to be taking place concerning a special person. Be very clear about the steps you want to take on an emotional level. Victory will be yours and you will successfully accomplish what you set out to do. Any negative event you dreamed about needs to be avoided or prevented in reality.

tapeworm This is a warning to avoid all exposure to disease and any contact that would spread an infection. Avoid all sexual contact for the next two days. You will also need to do everything necessary to avoid forcing yourself on another person. You will be tempted to do so within seven days but in spite of the appearance that this is acceptable behavior on your part toward this person, refrain from acting this way. The other individual will be repulsed by your actions and you will find it difficult to forgive yourself later. You will also need to make sure that your environment is free of toxins.

tapioca Someone will request your expertise and services within three days and will pay you handsomely for this. They will be so delighted with your work that you will be paid more than you originally asked for. Go for it. You will not be disappointed.

taproom Be very careful and prevent a very precious item from being lost or damaged for the next two days.

taps This is a very lucky omen for you. Make sure you follow your own instincts and counsel. Anything you choose to implement will be a success. Victory will be yours.

tar Be careful how you address others and how you present yourself for the next week. Be very careful not to be prejudiced or do anything politically incorrect. Otherwise, many blessings to you and your family and you are headed for a brilliant future.

tar and feather You can avoid many depressing and distressing moments by canceling a trip you have planned. Something will go tragically wrong when there is no one to help you out. Do what you can to take care of yourself.

tarantula Be very aware that within the week you will be involved with someone, in some capacity, who will have you behaving in an impulsive way with your finances. This person could be very much a financial drain on you. Step back and be very conscious about every step you are about to make before you make it. You are walking a very thin line for the next seven days. Do nothing you will later regret. Proceed cautiously and slowly.

tardy Be sympathetic towards someone who asks for your help and be very compassionate with someone who is unable to express the depth of their problems but doesn't show any overt distress. Do not take this matter lightly. Expect this to occur within three days.

target Someone has a tremendous amount of expertise in an area you are interested in. This person will be very happy to take you under their wing and relentlessly teach you this skill until you have it mastered.

to miss a target or to see someone else miss the target Within two days someone will come to you and point you in the direction you should be headed. You will receive excellent advice during this time period and you are headed for a brilliant future.

to hit a target or to see someone else hit the target A wealthy person will seek you out for a special friendship. Proceed with confidence; you will have a fabulous time.

in any other form Within five days you will be able to gather your resources and the energy you need to follow your hunches regarding a certain issue you feel should be taking place. In spite of anything that others may say or do, this situation needs to occur. It will bring vast changes into your life and the lives of others. Proceed with confidence because everything will work out as it should.

tar heel Make sure you allow no one to involve you in plans that you want no part of, especially for the next three days. Give no one the authority to speak on your behalf or make decisions for you during this time period. A situation will occur that will make you feel you are being taken advantage of.

tariff Be wary of anyone you have just been introduced to. This person is very treacherous and many people suffer misfortunes after being with this person. Go on with your life without this person in it.

tarnish   You will receive some shocking news that will take you by surprise. This refers to the actions of one family member to another. This individual will physically abuse another person in order to possess their belongings. Spread the word among your family members to keep this from occurring.

taro root   Within three days you will be invited to join a social group. This involvement will bring a tremendous amount of pleasure into your life as well as many surprise events. This also implies that all of your relationships will be very tranquil and peaceful for the next seven days in spite of anything else that would indicate the contrary.

tarot card   Within three days you will be able to detail and calibrate your thoughts in such a way that will allow you to use the right words to enable someone to feel at ease and comfortable in your presence. Conversation will flow easily and you will both grow closer. This person will tell you everything they have been longing to. You are headed toward a brilliant future and will be able to reach others with your communication skills. Both of you will enjoy a wonderfully tranquil life together if you choose. Whatever was read will be an accurate depiction of a future occurrence. If it was negative, take steps to avoid it in reality.

tar paper   A friend of yours will become very wealthy in a short period of time. This person will do everything they can to involve you in their new, exciting lifestyle.

tarpaulin   You will be very eager to join a mysterious and secretive group within the week. Once you become involved, you will find this group to be very refreshing and enjoyable to be around. There will, however, be many secrets.

tarragon   Be very careful not to be thrown off track and ignore a very special person in your life. Make enjoyable plans that will include both of you within three days.

tartan   Be very wise for the next three days and very protective of yourself. Make sure your surroundings are very safe, especially during late hours. Proceed with caution and keep yourself safe. Many blessings are with you and your family.

tartar sauce   Think ahead. You will be invited to visit a new acquaintance within three days. This will be a dangerous person who will terrorize you and you will find no way of escaping this horrifying experience. Prevent this by having nothing to do with any new acquaintances during this time period and by not going to this person's house. Do not place yourself in the position of being held against your will. This will be a life threatening situation.

Tarzan   Do not be afraid to let the truth come out. This cycle is working very much in your favor to get your point across and to get the response you need from certain individuals. It is also important not to take on any abrupt physical recreations. You may be out of shape and you need to be in proper physical condition to take up any new activity. Stay healthy and take steps to avoid any health problems that would occur because you overstrain yourself. This is especially important for the next week.

task   Someone you meet will want to know you on a first name basis and relate to you on a more personal basis than you desire. Be pleasant and nice to this individual from the beginning because you will grow to like them and first impressions count. Be very aware of your behavior so things will fall in the direction you choose.

taskmaster   Become more resourceful for the next day especially with situations you are going to be involved in. Specify what you need and want from a particular situation. You will also receive a fantastic gift at an unexpected time from someone who feels a deep gratitude to you.

Tasmanian Devil   Whatever you do, curb your behavior. Do not become involved in stalking anyone. Do not harass anyone or constantly check on what they are doing. Stop being jealous and focus on constructive behavior, otherwise you will get into trouble with the law within three days. Do everything you can to come to grips with yourself before you end up in jail.

tassel   There is a greater chance of reconciliation with another person if you make your move within three days. This also implies you will get a quick response to your needs.

taste   Someone who has taken a long time to involve you in their life will now desire involvement. This is now the time to follow your heart. You will be very surprised by the behavior and demeanor of this person toward you and they will soon verify their deep feelings for you. You are entering a lucky seven day cycle. Many blessings will come to you and your family. Pay attention to what you are tasting and look this up for greater meaning to this dream. You are definitely headed for a brilliant future.

taste bud   This is a lucky omen and implies an abundance of health and tranquility. You must also make sure you do not tell anyone of your plans. For the next two weeks, keep everything to yourself and do not give out any details of your ideas. You will also be going through a very enjoyable cycle for the next week. You really should trust your hunches and go with what you feel.

taster   Someone will ask for your affections within three days. This will give you joy and you will be more than willing to surrender to this person. Many blessings are with you and your family.

tatting   For the next five days avoid placing yourself in any situation where you already feel a stressful situation will occur. You have prior notice of this and can take steps to avoid it completely.

tattler You will need to conduct a great deal of research prior to making a certain trip. Make phone calls and check out the area and current situations before traveling. You may want to cancel this trip and go at a later time.

tattletale Do not travel by plane for the next three days in order to avoid an air disaster. This dream also serves as a warning to friends and relatives who have scheduled a flight during this time period. Take steps to prevent accidents and injuries of any kind during this time frame.

tattoo Try to recall the particular tattoo you dreamed about and look up the words or design for a more detailed meaning. Take steps to prevent any negative message from becoming a reality and try to experience only positive expressions in your life, especially for the next week. Do not involve yourself with someone who has an unusual and outrageous idea. This person will tempt you to become involved and you will feel pinned down and trapped. Get on with your life without this person. You will be able to resolve a situation completely within the week. This will be a lucky cycle for you and you will enjoy good health.

taupe Within four days you will meet someone of a different nationality. You will both enjoy each other's company and share a variety of interests. This dream is an omen of happiness. You will also receive the help and encouragement you need to finish any project you desire.

Taurus This is an extremely lucky omen for you and you will experience an abundance of health and wealth in unexpected areas as a result of an unexpected source of income. You will also be able to accomplish tasks you felt at one time were impossible. Proceed with confidence. This is the perfect time to take on these big projects. You are headed for a brilliant future. It will also soon become clear to you that someone harbors deep feelings for you. This emotion will rapidly develop and this individual will be unable to contain themselves. You will, in addition, rid yourself of the personality trait of not focusing enough on your relationships. You will become consistent in your efforts to give your time to relationships that are important to you as well as anything that requires this focus. Expect this change to last a lifetime. You are headed for a brilliant future.

tavern Within three days someone will unexpectedly meet you in a crowded place. They will be very attracted to you. This person will introduce themself and ask you out to tea. If you desire this relationship, be sure to give this person a way to contact you. There is a potential here for a lifetime partner, if you choose.

tax Take every step to prevent or avoid a negative event in this dream from becoming a reality. You have plenty of time to do this. Make sure you experience nothing but tranquility and positive expressions in your life. Use good common

sense to plan a comfortable retirement for yourself. You will have the information you need within three days to steer you in the right direction and within this time period you will be rejoicing over a deep reciprocal love. You are headed for a brilliant future.

tax assistant Someone will become very interested in becoming involved with you romantically. This person does not speak your language and is unable to make them self understood. If you choose to pursue this, be more patient and attentive with this individual. You will have a fabulous life with this person if you choose to go in this direction.

taxicab This is a good omen and you are entering a lucky two week cycle. Assess your present situation within two days to ensure you are headed in the right direction.

taxidermy Within seven days you will be involving yourself in a completely new way of living life. You will be able to do this easily with very little financial output. You will be introduced to many moments you will cherish for a lifetime.

taxi driver *to be one* someone will attempt to bring an injury suit against you for insurance purposes. Be wary of this for the next three days.

to have one You are headed in the wrong direction. Rethink your goals and regroup. You must also maintain your optimism. You will be able to handle everything properly.

taxi stand For the next five days remain in a secure environment and take steps to avoid freak accidents. Take steps to ensure your home environment is safe during this time period.

Taylor, Elizabeth *(Movie Star)* You will be resilient and determined due to a powerful quality that will arise from within. Unusual circumstances will come up and you will be able to tap into this resource. You will be able to brilliantly see yourself through this situation. Anything you felt was impossible is now possible. Expect this within four days. After you overcome this you will enjoy tranquility for a long time to come. You are headed for a brilliant future.

T-bar lift Do everything you can to control your temper. A distasteful situation will take place that will create suspicions and jealousy in some capacity. If you do not take care, you will develop an uncontrollable rage that will drive you to do something you regret. Do not allow this emotion to continue to develop and do not feed into your suspicions. The moment you sense this rage developing, seek out a professional who can help you to overcome this. Take steps to avoid a situation you will have deep regrets about later in your life.

T-bill This is an extremely lucky omen. You will enjoy an abundance of health and an increase in income as a result of unexpected income. You will also be able to take care of certain tasks you have felt were impossible to deal with. This is the perfect time to handle anything you felt was impossible. Proceed with confidence. You are headed for a very prosperous future.

T-bone You will soon receive what you desire most from life and this will be a very joyous time for you. You will also experience an abundance of health and wealth in unexpected areas of your life as well as an improvement in your sexual drive. You will be able to accomplish big jobs that at one time seemed impossible. Proceed with confidence. You are headed for a very prosperous future.

T cell Do not compromise yourself to those who refuse to see your point of view. An aggressive sales approach will also expose your product to a greater number of people. Move quickly on this.

tea Within three days you will be able to perform in the manner someone you care about desires. You are entering a lucky seven day cycle.

tea bag The person you are thinking of involving yourself with will work out wonderfully. This situation will bear fruit for both of you. You are headed in the right direction, especially for the next three days.

tea biscuit Be more attentive and you will have a memorable time on a date if you so desire.

tea cake Someone will try to involve you in a relationship within the week. At first you will have mixed feelings about this but your uncertainty is unwarranted. You will have a delightful experience if you choose to pursue it. Involve yourself completely and you will enjoy yourself on any level you desire.

tea cart Someone will definitely appreciate your forwardness and this will clear up the false images this person has developed about you. You are seeking new experiences and will have many to choose from for the next seven days.

teach *to teach* For the next couple of days a situation involving a family member will develop into a disagreement and will reach a point you are not prepared for. You can avoid this by making it very clear what you will or will not be doing. Good luck is with you.

teacher Make sure all of your transportation is reliable so you will not suffer delays as a result of a mechanical breakdown. This also implies another person needs time to do things on their own. Try to understand this and do not be so demanding. Give this person time to take care of their own issues, especially for the next three days. Also, pay attention to what this teacher was telling you and take steps to keep any negative event from occurring in reality.

teacup Make sure you do not create friction between yourself and a special person. The head of the household needs to make sure all their bases are covered, especially when it comes to financial situations. Proceed with caution for the next three days to ensure arguments do not begin. Otherwise, this is an extremely lucky omen. You will enjoy an abundance of health and many blessings will come to you and your family.

tea dance You will receive good news because you will receive a positive response to what you expected a negative response. Everything you felt was impossible before will all be possible now. You are going through a prosperous cycle and are headed in the right direction.

tea garden You will develop a support system and a network of knowledge you can draw from. This will enable you to position yourself in a comfortable lifestyle. You will have many opportunities for celebrating and will enjoy many joyful events. Prepare yourself for some unexpected good news that will come your way within the week. You are on the path toward a brilliant future and will feel as though everyone is on your side and supporting your goals.

teahouse Make sure you do not become involved with someone who will snap at the slightest stress. This person has a short fuse and will become angry at the slightest provocation. You do not have time for this in your life. Become busy with something else so you do not have to deal with this.

teak Within five days you will see the positive end of a certain issue because you have dug deeply to uncover important information about this issue.

teakettle Do not take life for granted and really decide what you want and need and go for it. You will also have a variety of people enter your life who will offer joy and pleasure to your existence. You are headed for an awesome future.

teal Make sure you do not take life for granted and pay attention to people in your life you now feel are being neglected. This is the time to make corrections in those areas of your life that need correcting and make sure everything is headed in the direction it should go. Many blessings will come to you and your family.

teal blue This is the time to seek out opportunities you can review and grasp those you decide you want to pursue. During this cycle you will be able to spice up your life in more ways than one. Many blessings are with you and your family. This is also the time to experience an abundance of health.

team You will see someone socially whom you are very interested in and who has a strong interest in you. You will be seen in a totally different light and this interest will benefit your relationship greatly. Expect this to evolve within two days. Many blessings will come to you and your family.

teammate Within two months someone will start to make demands on you. You will have to produce papers and documents to account for things you are doing now. Make sure you start keeping an account of money and paperwork you will have to account for in the future so when it does come up, it will not be a stressful situation.

teamster Within two days become personally involved with those situations you want to fall perfectly into place. Everything will work out exactly as you desire.

teamwork Someone will intentionally try to drag you into a debate about a wrong they have committed against you. Remain calm and acutely aware of what is occurring. This person is very angry, knows they are wrong and have no intention of making it right. They will attempt to push the argument until you let it go without retribution. Protect yourself from any damages this person may cause, either verbally or financially, and do not allow this person to bring you down to their level. Stick to the facts and remain calm. Avoid, at all costs, becoming involved in any angry dispute. If you heed this message, a successful outcome will result.

tea party You will go from one extreme lifestyle to another in order to accomplish a lifelong dream. This will leave you feeling emotionally fulfilled. Proceed with confidence in any new endeavors.

teapot Do not take life for granted, decide what you want and need from life, and go for it. You will also have a variety of people enter your life and offer joy and pleasure to your existence. You are headed for an awesome future.

teardrop A certain individual has chosen to communicate to you a particular situation that will bring you joy. Involve yourself with this situation and you will find you will have many pleasurable moments.

tear gas Do not divulge your plans to anyone. Keep all plans (business, personal or otherwise) to yourself for the next five days.

tearoom Within five days you will accidentally stumble across some information while attending a particular event. This overheard information will be shocking to you. Make sure you keep this information to yourself.

tea rose You will receive an unexpected gift from someone you deeply respect and love. Do not deprive yourself of intimacy with someone you care deeply about. Indulge others and bring love to those you care about. You are headed for a brilliant future.

tears *crying* Within two days someone who has led you to believe in their loyalty will let you down. Regroup yourself and think ahead so you can handle this in the best way you can, once it becomes apparent to you. You are definitely headed for a brilliant future.

to cry This implies victory. All things you once felt were impossible are now possible. You will also receive, within

five days, the verification of love that someone has for you. This will result in a feeling of emotional fulfillment.

tease Be prepared for a big victory that will come your way within five days. Be consistent and act appropriately in each area of your life.

tea set If you take the steps to make yourself available and meet someone who is much older than you, you will find this person to be instrumental in helping you reach your goals. Exposure to social events will be the one ingredient that will determine how your future unfolds for the next three weeks.

teaspoon You will be under a tremendous amount of pressure within the next five days for standing up for someone else's rights. Do not compromise and remain calm.

teats Be prepared for a very crowded schedule that will develop suddenly within three days. Make sure you do not overlook something of importance within the week because of this schedule. Be sure to remind yourself of anything you should be attending to.

technician Within three days someone will develop a great deal of foresight about what both of you should be doing together in the near future. This individual will be very helpful because of their foresight and will help both of you to avoid a big mistake in the near future.

teddy bear Within five days express your true feelings to those who are unsure of how you feel toward them. You are deeply appreciated and loved and will experience this more in this time frame. Many blessings are with you and your family. Anything you want to achieve will be accomplished very successfully by you.

teen Within a day or two you will be undergoing a lot of emotional pressure because you will stand up for your rights and refuse to compromise your feelings. Remain calm throughout this time period and everything will work out.

teenybopper This is a warning that someone will visit your home and break an expensive item. Be very protective of your treasures in order to avoid disappointment. This is likely to occur within five days.

Teeterboard/teeter-totter Someone you are interested in, will not be the person you can rely on. Take the time to select and review the character of those you choose to associate with and do not allow yourself to be taken, especially for the next week.

teeth You have time to take care of anything you dreamed of that represented a negative event concerning your teeth. Do this within seven days. You must also not assume a certain situation will turn out exactly as you wish. Make sure you work on it so it will turn out like you want. Don't assume anything, especially for the next three days.

to brush your teeth or to see someone else brush their teeth You will be received with open arms due to your dynamic reputation. Others will be very amenable to a certain situation you will be introducing within three days.

broken teeth Do not overextend or over-involve yourself in any situation you feel irresistibly compelled to become involved in. For the next five days protect yourself emotionally and avoid getting involved in something you have no business being involved in. Proceed with caution.

beautiful teeth You are definitely headed for a brilliant future. Anything you felt was impossible is now possible for you to achieve. This is the cycle to tackle those tough issues. You will be successful.

your teeth falling out You are beginning to feel closer to a certain person who will lead you to believe you can trust them fully and can be sure of their loyalty to you. For the next three days make sure you do not become any more involved than you already are unless you take extreme precautions. This person is very clever and is masterful in creating deception and illusions. You will begin to believe certain events and situations will occur in the future that will never take place. A hidden agenda is at play here that involves pursuing you for devious reasons known only to this particular individual. And because an atmosphere of complete trust has been developed, you will suspect nothing. Because of this person's charm, if you do become suspicious, they will easily create a diversion to lure you away from these feelings. Once you understand what is going on, you will have suffered financial setbacks, and deep emotional distress. You will be able to get your life back on track but it will take a long time. You have prior notice of this and all the ammunition you need to ensure this situation does not take place. Practice common sense, do not compromise, do not allow this person to pry into your affairs and do not get involved. Otherwise, you are headed for a prosperous future and many blessings are with you and your family.

to have false teeth Do everything you can to keep your teeth and gums healthy. This two week period is the best cycle to have any necessary dental work taken care of.

to see someone else with false teeth For the next three days, do not entice someone sexually if you are not interested. This person will be very offended at being rejected.

false teeth in any other form Affection coming from another person within the next four days will be false.

teething ring You will feel someone is either keeping secrets or lying to you. This is definitely a figment of your imagination. This person is very loyal and truthful to you.

Teflon Within five days you will be able to win over someone else's love. This person will express a passionate affection toward you. Mutual affection and tranquility will be with both of you during this time period.

telecast For the next three days ask for special considerations and they will be granted.

telecommunications Within two days an acquaintance will provide you with a new path in life and introduce you to other people who have a high level of expertise. These people have an influence in areas that will benefit you if you choose to take advantage of this situation. You are headed for a prosperous future. You must also make sure the older people in your life are not being neglected and take steps to ensure their needs are being attended to.

telegram A certain issue you will need someone to work out for you will work out well because you will choose the right person. This is particularly important for the next three days.

telephone *to pick up and someone has picked up on the other line without speaking* You will be dealing with someone in need of mental health services. Be patient and kind yet cautious. Try to help this person but go on with your life.

to call for help and be unable to get through You will unexpectedly be fired from a job because you will leak information to someone. They will then carelessly take this information to the wrong person. Do not give the impression that the shock of losing this position can be prevented or that you no longer desire an important position.

to dial, etc., for help and receive it Pay a bill immediately to avoid legal action. Do this now.

to enjoy a phone conversation This will be a good cycle. You and someone special will mutually agree on joyous, big plans for the future. This will end in success.

to ask for someone who does not come to the phone The person you are asking for is unavailable. Don't lose patience. Try again within five days. This person will be very happy to hear from you.

to not understand the other person on the phone Develop your plans and focus on what should be in order. Smooth out and tighten up all facets of this plan in order to avoid interference on the way to success.

to hear the phone ring Someone in your life very much wants to speak to you but lacks the courage to call. If you know who this person is, make the first move. They are emotionally unable to pick up the phone, and live with this anxiety each day.

cellular phone During a time of total chaos, someone will rescue you. This person will be almost an angel in disguise.

pay phone Do not become involved in the squabbles of unfamiliar people for the next two days.

to attempt to call out on a non working phone A special person in your life will try to pass false judgments on you. Try to put more love into action and express your love in a romantic way. A gentle approach will put confusion to rest.

push button Within five days, someone will plan to violate your rights for their own emotional gratification. This person will attempt to manipulate you into becoming involved in something you will find increasingly distasteful and disgusting, whether in a sexual context or some other capacity. This involvement will go against your better judgment and against your will. Do not place yourself in any situation where you will have to compromise your principles to get out safely. This is preventable. Good luck is with you.

in any other form Embrace and love yourself and take time out to tie up loose ends. You must also take steps to begin building your liquid assets as well as property assets. You will find the means to do this with the help of someone else. This person will reach a complete agreement with you and this process will begin within two days.

telephone book Someone you are interested in will not deny you the affections you request from them, especially for the next three days. You are loved beyond your imagination. Pay attention to any of the contents you remember. They will accurately depict an important address or location you must be aware of. Any negative message you get from this dream can be changed or avoided. It is extremely important you jot down any address that is given to you in this dream. It will be important to you in some way within the next three days. Many blessings will come to you and your family.

telephone booth You have been desiring a special item for a long time. You are now able to find the exact item you need, at a bargain, and you will finally have the money to pay for it. This will make you ecstatic.

to wait for/by pay phone or phone booth Do not depend on another person for your success. The responsibility lies with you and will depend on your own merit. Do not waste time waiting for others to rescue you and explore new options, especially for the next two days. Focus intently on ways to remove yourself from this rut and do not waste time feeling sorry for yourself. Success will rapidly come to you.

telephone receiver Pay attention to anything that is told to you through a telephone receiver in a dream. This is an accurate message. Give this message every consideration because it will occur within the week. If the message is negative, take every step to ensure it does not take place. If positive, take steps to incorporate it into your life. Also someone who is feeling abandoned by you will start to complain about your lack of affection. Make it a point to show affection to this person in order to avert an emotional crisis.

telescope Whatever is seen through the telescope implies something you either want to embrace or avoid. This dream also implies you need to be more meticulous and detailed in anything you involve yourself in that concerns another person who is working with you. Make sure you express yourself in the best way you can and be as detailed as you are able. Many blessings are with you and you are headed for a very prosperous future.

television Any event depicted on the television in your dream is sure to take place within the week. This will also give you a strong clue to when a situation will occur that you need to be alerted to. Take the necessary steps to avoid any negative situation. This dream also implies that within three days someone will let you know of someone's interest in you. If you choose to pursue this, this person will bring happiness into your life in any capacity you desire whether this is emotional, financial or involves your career. You will also

be invited to a very elegant event within this three day time period. This will be a very prosperous cycle for you and many blessings will come to you and your family.

T.V. dinner Do not allow yourself to be abused or insulted in public because you will be unable to forgive yourself for allowing this to take place. Avoid any situation where this could occur for the next three days.

temper *if you recognize the person displaying the bad temper* This is the person who is trying to find the right words to ask you to assist them in a distasteful situation. Go on with your life without involving yourself in this issue. Excuse yourself with tact and diplomacy.

to have a bad temper Focus for the next two days on not overextending yourself. Someone will attempt to vulturize your time and energy to the point of exhaustion. Otherwise this is an extremely lucky omen. Proceed with confidence.

in any other form Do not allow yourself to become stagnated to the point you do not allow yourself to enjoy the beautiful things in life. Make a list of enjoyable activities you can do almost immediately for very little money. If you push yourself to do this, you will see a positive result in the way you feel about yourself. You will feel younger and have more zest for life. This is the perfect cycle for getting things moving in the direction you choose.

temperature Face up to the reasons you refuse to commit to a certain relationship. Get to the bottom of this so you can enjoy a less restrictive, limited lifestyle and enjoy greater emotional fulfillment. Aggressively seek to find your hidden motives. You are definitely headed for a brilliant future.

tempest Make sure you have a full understanding of your motives, feelings and behavior, especially for the next five days. Focus on this so you can avoid being your own worst enemy. Make any necessary corrections so you can point yourself in the direction you choose to go.

temple You will be treated sexually by someone special in just the way you desire. You will also be emotionally touched by this individual if this is what you want. You and this person will make long range travel plans and plans to add spice to your life. You will also enjoy many passionate nights together. You will enjoy a great deal of luck in financial affairs and you will both see you are well loved by many people and will enjoy an active social life. If you choose to take this path, this opportunity will present itself to you within five days. Proceed with confidence. Many blessings are with you and your family.

tempt You are headed for a prosperous future. Take a strong stand, for the next five days, in your refusal to go along with someone else's plans. Do not compromise and make it very clear that you do not want to be involved.

temptress Be consistent about what you say you are going to do. Make sure someone who relies on you is not let down. Do everything you promise in a timely fashion.

you with unexpected joyful news.

tempura Stop wasting so much time deciding whether you want to speak with the person of your choice. Your intention is to get this person involved in your life in some capacity. Once you express your desires, this person will be very open about their wish to become involved. Good luck is with you.

ten Victory is with you because of the team effort put forth by those who will come through for you. You will receive a dynamic response from others you will be dealing with. You will receive great feedback with situations that benefit others as well as yourself within this three day time frame. Use this number for games of chance with small risks and big pay-offs. Many blessings are with you and your family.

tenant Question the motives behind someone's sudden interest in you. This person will attempt to get close to you and assist you in every way they can and will eventually open up to you and request your assistance in having their needs met. Think this over very carefully because it will take a long time to get out from under this obligation. You will have to invest more time, energy and finances than you ever envisioned. Focus on putting yourself on the right track.

Ten Commandments You are headed for a brilliant future and this dream implies you are going to have an awesome exciting time for the next two days in a variety of things you will be doing. It is also important to make sure someone who seeks your advice is steered to the right counselor. Make sure you do not take on any unwanted responsibilities. For the next few days, your assistance, in terms of time, energy, and finances, will be asked from a needy family member who is away from home. Act quickly to ensure a successful turnaround. You are headed for a brilliant future.

tender Life will get gentler and sweeter within the week. You will enjoy greater tranquility, and more comfort in your life. Many blessings are with you and your family.

tenderfoot Someone who is very precious to you will, within three days, give you a very beautiful gift that you will cherish for a lifetime.

tenderloin Within five days a plan you have been working on will work out exactly as you had envisioned.

tendon Eat healing foods, drink plenty of water and take care of your physical well being in a more tenacious way for the next three days. Be alert to a very questionable situation that will occur within two days that will cause you a great deal of embarrassment and will damage your reputation.

tenement This is an extremely lucky omen and you are on the path toward a prosperous future. You will develop the tenacity you need to be undefeatable for the next few days. This is the trait you need in order to realize your ambitions. Also within five days, someone from the past will drop in on

Tennessee Within three days you will be given the opportunity to accept a once in a lifetime proposal that could lead to wealth and power. You will develop the awareness, during this time period to recognize and accept this chance. This may also be used as a reference point in time. If you dream of this state and see its name used in any context, the dream message will occur on this day.

Tennessee Walking horse Set aside private moments for you and a special person. It is important you do this soon. You are loved beyond your imagination.

tennis Doors that were formerly closed to you will suddenly reopen and you will be seen by others from a different perspective. New opportunities will be there for you to choose from. Good luck is with you.

tennis elbow Do not allow anyone to steer you from the path in which you are headed. You will enjoy a brilliant future.

tennis shoes You will hear news of a pregnancy. You will also enjoy prosperity and many blessings will come to you and your family. You are definitely on the path toward a brilliant future. If you see the exact shoes you dreamed of being worn, your dream will become a reality within three days. Any negative event depicted in this dream needs to be turned into a positive.

tenor You will hear from a friend who wants to share the news that they have come into some power and authority. This person will be a friend for life and will want you to share in their good fortune.

ten penny nail You are going in the wrong direction and will only run into a dead end. Regroup yourself and calmly scrutinize the choices you have available to you in order to come up with an alternative direction.

ten speed bike Within a five day period make sure you do not unwittingly sabotage the plans of another. Be very aware of your actions so you can avoid interfering with another person's efforts. Otherwise this is an extremely lucky omen and you are headed for a brilliant future.

tent Within three days a certain situation will occur that will leave your enemies rejoicing at your failure. Heed this message and take steps to avoid failure. Proceed with caution. Regroup and carefully review your status.

tentacle Something will occur that will cause you a tremendous amount of embarrassment. Your reputation and character may be at stake. Watch your behavior for the next two days so you can avoid this situation and emotional distress.

tepee Any project or situation you are working on now and neglect, will come back at a later time when you least expect and will have to be dealt with. It will then cause you a big irritation. Complete all of your projects now to avoid this hassle. You will definitely be able to pinpoint what you need to be doing now to avoid this problem.

tequila This is a very lucky omen. You will quickly overcome a financial difficulty within the week.

teriyaki Someone you care deeply about will return for a reconciliation. If you choose to get reinvolved, it will be on a permanent basis. In spite of anything else that may be going on in your life do not lose your confidence, you are definitely headed for a brilliant future.

terminal Your circumstances will improve rapidly and you will be able to rid yourself permanently of a difficult issue that has been plaguing you for some time.

term insurance You will experience a greater sexual desire for someone and it will surprise you that you feel this way. If you choose to go in this direction, you will enjoy sexual fulfillment. Pay attention to anything you need to have insured and make sure the insurance you have is adequate within five days.

termite Do not associate with the wrong person. This individual has a history you are not fully aware of and your status will be injured in the long run. For your own sake, disassociate from this individual.

term paper Make sure you watch out for a person who serves as a secretary or has a similar role. This individual will keep your calls and plans from reaching the person they are intended for. When you encounter this, within three days, maintain your composure. This person enjoys pushing other people's buttons.

terrace You will enjoy the freedom that will be possible within the week because you will finally successfully complete a long project. Good luck is with you.

terra cotta Step back and do not allow a change you are planning to make within two days to have serious repercussions on someone else. Be very aware of cause and effect.

terrapin You will become involved in a number of conversations over the next three days that will leave you very distraught over the lack of feelings someone displays toward you. This will be a surprise to you and you will feel despair over this. Do not allow this feeling to overcome you. Quickly regroup yourself and remain calm. This situation is beyond your control but you will be able to handle yourself properly.

terrarium You will meet someone with brilliant ideas who will help you put your plans into tangible form. This person will go to great lengths to make it a reality because of their

enthusiasm. A dynamic improvement will take place in your life that you never before felt was possible.

terrier Your intuition about love and money are right on target. Follow your hunches and you will move quickly toward prosperity in a big way.

territorial Within the next five days someone will be intensely, sexually aroused by your appearance. This person will go to great lengths to become sexually involved with you. If you choose to go in this direction, you will experience a maximum amount of love for a long time to come.

territory Do not allow power to go to your head, especially when supervising others. This is likely to occur within three days.

terrorist For the next month, do what you can to encourage love and a closer unity within the family. Do whatever you can to create more family outings that everyone can enjoy. Let your imagination run wild and create unusual events that will bring the family closer. Many blessings are with you and your family. You must also remove yourself from any stressful situation during this cycle so you can experience nothing but harmony and tranquility.

terry cloth Within the month you will find the solution that will result in the physical recovery of a family member, particularly that of a small child. You will enjoy a prosperous, healthy and brilliant future.

test *to fail a test* Be very aware of the company that young children keep. Monitor their friends and protect them from a negative peer group until you feel this child can make clear and confident decisions on their own. If you dream of any negative event that could become a reality, take steps to turn this around to a positive situation. You have prior notice and can do this for yourself or for anyone you recognize in the dream. Make sure you experience only positive events in your life. Do not underestimate your power and strength. These attributes will come through for you when you need them. You are headed for a prosperous future. Many blessings are with you and your family.

to pass a test A cluster of events will unexpectedly start to occur concurrently and you will be swamped with invitations to specific functions that you will be able to pick and choose from. One specific invitation is one you must not turn down. This particular function will be far more glamorous and exciting than any of the others and will require formal attire. Prepare yourself ahead of time so you will look your best. You will meet many influential people who will become life long friends and you will have a fantastic time. You will win a door prize at this event as well. You will also become aware, during this time period that the person you desire the most feels the same way about you. You will share many affectionate moments and both of you will be very excited about this new development. You are both headed for a very prosperous and brilliant future.

in any other form Within three days you will need to seclude yourself in order to clear your head so you can pinpoint the suspicions you have about a specific person and decide how to go about resolving them. This will give you the opportunity to make plans to determine whether your suspicions are valid and decide how best to resolve them. If you motivate yourself now you will be able to deal with this situation successfully. This is the perfect time period for finding the answers you seek and you are headed for a prosperous future.

testament Many blessings are with you and your family. Within three days you will receive a positive answer to a request you felt you would receive a negative answer to. You are headed for a prosperous future. Anything you recall from this dream that implies a forthcoming negative event must be changed or avoided in reality. Make sure you only experience positive expressions in your life.

test drive Within five days you will become caught up in a tug of war between two people. This will be the result of your failure to take care of a situation in which you promised to attend a function with two different people. Make sure you take care of this immediately and avoid all situations that will result in quarrels.

testicle You will develop the support system and a network of knowledge you can pull from to help you position yourself in a comfortable lifestyle. This cycle will bring you many opportunities for joyful celebrations. Prepare yourself for some unexpected joyful news that will come your way within the week. You are headed for a brilliant future. You will also feel everyone is on your side and is supporting your goals.

testimony Victory is yours and many blessings will be with you and your family. If you can recall the testimony, make sure you take steps to turn around anything negative. If positive, make sure you bring it to full bloom in reality. Someone has also led you to believe they can assist you a great deal more than they are able. Because they have given you this impression, they will do everything they can for the next five days to back out of this commitment, not because they do not want to help but because they lack the resources, finances or skills. Give this person a graceful way to back out. You have prior notice of this and can avoid becoming emotionally involved when it becomes apparent this person will be unable to live up to this commitment.

testosterone You need to demand a higher level of efficiency from others. This will lead to your future financial security.

test pilot Within the week certain things will start to occur because you have motivated yourself in certain areas of your life that you need to move ahead on. Regroup and rethink your plans and you will determine exactly what you need to do in this cycle. Proceed with confidence. You will be able to point yourself in the direction you need to be going.

test tube Do not waste time in deciding on the exact words you want to use to express your feelings to another. This person is only allowing this relationship to grow at the pace they desire but you will want this relationship to develop at a greater pace. Once you express these thoughts, you will be met with open arms. The other individual feels as though you will be driven away if they move too fast and will be delighted this is not the case.

tetanus If you use your communication skills more effectively, you will be able to achieve your goals within three days.

tether For the next three days make sure you weigh all the pros and cons before you become involved in a certain interest of yours.

tetherball Prevent a permanent split in a relationship that is important to you. Watch your behavior carefully for the next month in order to determine what you are doing that will result in a break-up. You have prior notice of this and will be able to keep this painful event from taking place.

tetrazzine Pay close attention to the physical and emotional state of a young child and make sure the needs of this child are being met. This is especially important for the next three days.

Texas Someone you least expect who has accumulated a great deal will leave you an inheritance. This will come from a distant place. Do not be surprised when this occurs within the month. You must also take steps to keep any negative occurrence in this dream from becoming a reality. All positive events need to be embraced and made into a reality. You will also acquire a large sum of material wealth. Many blessings are with you and your family and you are headed for a prosperous future. This may also be used as a reference point in time. If you dream of this state and see its name used in any context, the dream message will occur on this day.

Texas Ranger Within three days someone will demand an increase in affection. This will result in the relationship developing to a deeper level than you have ever anticipated. This was a platonic relationship and you now know this person desires romance. All relationships in your life will develop to a deeper level with greater bonding and love. Encourage this. The quality of your life will definitely improve. Many blessings will come to you and your family.

textile You will need to take big steps to bring about the changes you want to take place. These changes will benefit you and everyone you are associated with. Face your commitments head on and do not allow yourself to become uncertain. Social events will also soon be taking place that will give you much joy. Good luck is with you.

texture Pay attention to the events in this dream. Within seven days you will either want to avoid certain events you saw in the dream or take steps to make them a reality. Otherwise, this cycle will be very lucky for you. During this time period, you will be able to take small risks that will yield big benefits for you.

Thailand You need to know where to draw the line. You will enter a discussion with someone within seven days who will be unable to reach an agreement. Set limits on how long you will discuss this before you tactfully part company. Time will slip away that you could be using for more productive purposes. This may also be used as a reference point in time. If you dream of this country and see its name used in any context, the dream message will occur on this day.

thalidomide Do everything necessary for the next two days to prevent a serious illness. Protect yourself in the best way you can. You have prior notice of this and can avoid exposure to contagious illnesses.

Thames River Make sure you make the correct choice between two decisions. Gather all the necessary information prior to making a decision. The right decision will put you on the path to prosperity. This may also be used as a reference point in time. If you dream of this river and see its name used in any context, the dream message will occur on this day.

Thanksgiving Day Do what you can for the next five days to curb your impulsive spending habits. You will regret this behavior at a later time. Many blessings are with you and your family.

Thanksgiving Dinner You will enjoy an abundance of everything you need and many times of rejoicing. Also a certain situation will begin to occur within five days that will be completely out of your control. This situation will bring you a wave of wonderful emotions as a result of this unexpected joyous occasion. Many blessings are with you and you are headed for a brilliant future. Any negative occurrence in this dream can be prevented.

thank you Someone you are interested in and who has an interest in you will suddenly see you in a different light that will benefit your involvement with them tremendously. Expect this to evolve within three days. Many blessings are with you and your family. You must also make sure any negative event portrayed in this dream does not become a reality for the next seven days. Do what you can to experience only positive events in your life.

thatch You are going in the wrong direction and will only run into a dead end. Regroup yourself and calmly scrutinize the choices you have. This will allow you to come up with an alternative direction.

thaw Do not deprive yourself of the intimate times you could be sharing with another. Don't waste the time you could be spending with the one who loves you, especially for the next three days.

theatre You are headed toward a brilliant future. Look very carefully at a particular situation before you reject it. There is more involved to this that has either gone unnoticed or has not been considered that will benefit you greatly. Good luck is with you.

theft Protect yourself by not becoming overly involved in a particular issue or overextending yourself emotionally, financially, or physically because you feel drawn to this issue. You are also headed for a very prosperous future and many blessings will come to you and your family.

theme song You will finally be able to purchase a luxury item you have had your eye on. You are entering a very prosperous cycle and many blessings are with you and your family.

Themis *(Greek mythology)* Within seven days a situation will take place that will be so extraordinary it will defy any law of physics. This strange event will leave you with a sense of awe and wonder and you will sense you have witnessed a miracle with no way to explain how it transpired. After this takes place you will be able to present yourself at your best and handle yourself, other people and situations in the best possible way. You will see greater improvements than you ever thought possible. Your sense of awareness will be heightened and you will be able to sense the knowledge you need to retrieve. You are definitely headed for a brilliant future and many blessings will come to you and your family. You must also be especially careful to avoid any negative event for the next seven days.

theologian Within three days you will be involved with someone who will develop a precarious relationship with you. Everything between you will seem to be a battle. Once this begins to develop it will become chronic if you allow it to. Once you sense this situation starting to evolve, avoid it at all costs, otherwise it will become ongoing and hard to break out of. Be acutely aware of this for the next three days.

theology Be very aware of a danger that could occur within three days. Protect yourself in every way possible from a life threatening situation from an unexpected source. Protect your health and safety in every capacity.

theory Within seven days someone will enter your life who has been selected by the gods and will offer their assistance relentlessly and at random times to tackle difficult tasks. You will be overwhelmed by the help this person will give you by being there for you tenaciously and at all the right times. You are headed for a very prosperous future. Proceed with confidence.

therapy *to hear the word* Someone will make a big issue out of a small situation. Be sure you take an active role in a situation that resembles this for the next few days so you can control it before it reaches chaotic proportions.

in any other form Someone will not deny you the affections you seek, especially for the next three days. You are more appreciated by others than you ever imagined and are headed for a prosperous future.

thermal You will receive some sort of property as a gift. This will be something you do not expect but will be greatly appreciated. You are also headed for a brilliant future.

thermal blanket This is a very lucky omen but you will accidentally overhear a conversation that could be very harmful to another person if it is repeated. Keep all information about another individual to yourself.

thermal underwear Do not insist on turning down something someone wants to give you. Do not allow pride to stand in the way of receiving a gift in any capacity. Accept this gift. Many blessings are with you and you are definitely headed in the right direction.

thermometer You will be associating with an individual who has many skills and attributes that could benefit you greatly. This person will be very eager to assist you in some way. You will be in the perfect cycle, for the next seven days, for this assistance to come your way. You will be able to use this knowledge to your benefit within this time period. Because of this, you will be able to improve your lifestyle for the better.

thermonuclear war You will find a way to say something that is very difficult for you to say to another person. This will be in such a way that will not offend yet will get the point across with minimal stress and emotional disturbance for both of you.

thermos Face up to the reasons you find it difficult to commit to a relationship. Get to the bottom of this so you can have a better and less limited lifestyle. For the next seven days investigate other areas of your life that you may be limiting yourself.

thesaurus Someone you do not know will purposefully attempt to start a fight with you in public. Do what you can to protect yourself when in a public setting you are unfamiliar with.

thesis You will be introduced within three days to a very exciting, exotic person who will quickly introduce you to a new way of life that you will find very enjoyable if you choose to involve yourself. You are also headed for a brilliant future. Proceed with confidence.

Thessalonians *(from the Bible)* Someone you spend very little time with will make an unexpected visit. This person will be in good spirits and have a better sense of humor than usual. This will be a very delightful visit. This person will also be very eager to grant you anything you wish as long as it is within their capacity to do so. A surprise gift will also come your way within this cycle. This is also the perfect cycle to promote and display your talents to others. Do this within five days in order to put yourself on the path you desire. This will result in success and prosperity.

thick A situation will occur that involves a promise you made to call a certain individual at a particular time and this person will eagerly await this call. Something will occur that will prevent this call from going through (i.e., broken phone, crossed lines, etc.). Be very aggressive and find alternative methods to reach this individual.

thick and thin This is letting you know ahead of time that an unusual circumstance will take place that will keep you from getting in touch with a certain person at a specified time. Do everything you can to reach this person.

thickening Difficult statements need to be said and let the chips fall where they may. This will allow situations to stabilize and return to normalcy.

thief Make sure each step you take for the next three days is secure in order to ensure certain circumstances occur as they should. Do not expose your decisions and plans too early. This is especially important for the next three days. Pay close attention to the events of this dream to ensure you protect yourself from this in reality and make sure you experience only positive expressions in your life. Many blessings will come to you and your family.

thigh Take the time to spruce up your attire and do not allow yourself to get caught up in a day to day rut. Take your time doing things so they can all work out to your best advantage, especially for the next two days. You must also make sure any event in this dream that implies injury to your thigh or anyone's thigh does not become a reality. Many blessings are with you and your family.

thighbone Within two days you will be invited to a social function at the last minute. Get involved and get into the mood of things. You will find this to be very enjoyable and will meet many people who will influence you in many ways. Go for it.

thimble Do not become involved in a policy making decision that will be brought to your attention within three days that involves relatives.

think Do everything you can to refrain from thoughts and behaviors that keep a relationship from growing closer. Within five days carefully look at your behavior to determine those aspects that keep those you care about at arms length. This is the perfect cycle to develop the courage you need to address the issues and a personality that will draw others closer to you. You will be able to turn yourself completely around during this month. Good luck is with you.

think pad This is only the beginning of the marvelous and exciting time of your creativity.

thinner Someone desires your company simply for sexual pleasure. Since you know this ahead of time, you can decide whether this is the type of relationship you want.

third base You will finally be able to pin down a very elusive person and get the answers you need to certain questions. This will be possible within five days. Within three days you will also unexpectedly find yourself giving assistance to someone who is very deceitful. Step back and rethink this involvement. This will definitely backfire on you.

third class Any event that resembles a situation in reality should be promoted, if positive, or avoided at all costs, if negative. This is especially important for the next three days. Within this cycle you will also need to practice preventive medicine and drive defensively in order to avoid any accident that could be your fault.

third degree For the next five days do everything necessary to get all the kinks out of the plans you are developing. You will achieve a successful outcome. Remain optimistic about the plans you are working on.

third dimension/3D You will regain a position in the public eye, attract many honors and be well liked by everyone. Continue going in the direction you are going. You are headed for a brilliant future and will be surrounded by people who care about you, respect you deeply, and are loyal to you. Many blessings are with you and your family.

thirst Practice optimism in front of someone who puts on airs and pretends they have so much more than others. Do not allow this person to intimidate you. If you do not appear impressed, you will gain respect from this person for a lifetime. Hold your head up, be sure of yourself and proceed with confidence. Many blessings are with you and your family. You will also need to take steps to prevent any negative event from occurring in reality either to yourself or others. Move quickly on this so you can experience only positive expressions in your life.

thirteen Think ahead. Any involvement you will get into within three days will need a commitment from you. Use this number for the next month as a lucky token either in games of chance or as a date to schedule important events, conferences, etc. Many blessings are with you and your family.

thirty A deep plot is developing without your knowledge. Be aware of any unusual situation that will occur within the next three days and make sure you investigate closely. You will also find that, for the next month, you will be dealing with a variety of situations. Each one will be exciting and will provide you with precious moments you will want to savor for a long time. Use this number for games of chance and you will receive small rewards you least expect. You are definitely headed for a prosperous future.

thistle You will definitely become involved with a greedy individual. Protect yourself from this situation because you will end up despising each other.

thong Allow others to know your interests and someone will take you under their wing for extensive training. You will progress at a rapid pace and will be able to use this knowledge in a way you least expect but will benefit you greatly.

Thor (*Nordic Mythology*) You are headed in the right direction and will be provided access to vast amounts of information. If you tap into this information, you will be able to gain the tools you require to take the best course of action and accumulate the wealth you need in order to live a desired lifestyle. You will enjoy a long and healthy life. Many blessings are with you and your family.

thorazine This is a warning to avoid any situation that will expose you to illness and avoid any contact that will spread an infection. Avoid all sexual contact for the next two days.

thorn For the next three days remain very aware of a stranger who will enter your life in a public setting and create a very stressful situation for everyone involved. Quarrels and disagreements will come out of this. Do what you can to remain uninvolved in this issue. Do not allow yourself to become caught up in the glitter and glamour that someone else flaunts. This individual is very irresponsible and will, within three days, embellish a particular situation that will not work out in the way they portray. Back off and make your own decisions. During this cycle, you will experience an abundance of health.

thoroughbred Someone will seek you out for the purpose of involving you in a distasteful situation. Be sure to protect yourself, especially for the next three days. This will be something that goes against your morals. Do not compromise your principles.

thousand Within three days you will have the chance to accept a once in a lifetime opportunity that will lead to greater wealth and power. During this time period you will be aware enough to recognize and accept this opportunity.

Thousand Island dressing Stop demanding so much of yourself, especially in those areas you have no proper training in. Be especially aware of this behavior for the next three days.

thread An agreement will come through for you earlier than expected and everything will work out better than you envisioned.

threat Do not put yourself in the position to experience terror at the hands of a dangerous individual. This will come about when someone insists you show them something of value that you are selling or a situation concerning your interest in purchasing something they are selling. Be very cautious for the next three days. This is a very dangerous situation.

three Find a place of solitude and meditate in your favorite form to become very clear about what you need and want from life. This is especially important for the next three days. Use this number for games of chance, or as a reference time to schedule important meetings, conferences, dates, etc. You are loved beyond your imagination and are headed for a brilliant future.

three ring circus Do not allow yourself to get sucked up into game playing. Someone will attempt to draw you into a life that will lead to discomfort and stress. Work to keep this from occurring, especially for the next three days.

three wheeler Make sure you do not challenge the ideas of another. Everything will come down heavily on you and it will seem impossible to get out of this situation. Get on with your life without this involvement. You are headed for a prosperous, fortunate future. For the next three days you will find everything will work to your advantage.

thresher Someone will take advantage of you without your knowledge. This person will use deception and dishonesty regarding a certain situation and will use you as an innocent participant. Pay close attention to your present situations and be acutely aware of the actions of others in order to avoid being cheated. You must also make sure your transportation is in proper working order, especially for the next three days. This will allow you to avoid unnecessary delays.

thrift shop Someone will go to great lengths within three days to involve themselves with you sexually. If you choose, this encounter will lead to a permanent union.

thriller Be very aware for the next three days of an unusual occurrence that will result in you being exposed in a state of undress against your wishes. You have prior notice of this and can prevent its occurrence. Otherwise you will enjoy a very prosperous future and can proceed with confidence.

throat Someone will unexpectedly start making demands of you. Be aware of this so you can refuse to put up with this behavior. Do not compromise. You are headed for many riches and good luck is with you. Your life will become richer in terms of material wealth as well as spiritual wealth. You will have everything you desire. You are headed for a brilliant future due to the development of some unusual circumstances. Expect this to occur within two weeks.

throb Do not allow yourself to become side tracked or to ignore someone who is important to you. Before you know it, precious time has slipped away. Make sure you tend to all of your relationships so you are able to retain the closeness that was there. Many blessings are with you and your family.

to see anything throbbing Any business enterprise you have planned will be received with open arms and you will make an excellent impression on anyone involved. You will be very victorious for the next seven days.

throne A lovely phone conversation will result in a quarrel. Remain calm for the next two days in order to avoid disappointment. This also implies that in matters of love you will definitely get the verification you need from someone you are very interested in. Many blessings are with you and your family.

throttle Do not talk yourself out of accepting a reliable, substantial and stable opportunity by thinking negative thoughts that lead you to believe you are unable to handle it. Do not allow yourself to feel defeated to the point of not moving ahead in a fresh new direction. Many blessings are with you.

throw Someone will inadvertently place themselves in the position to be easily taken advantage of sexually by you. For the next three days make sure you control the beast within you. Only do what you feel you can live with in the future. This person is also emotionally attached to you. Otherwise, this is an extremely lucky omen and will remain so for the next month.

to be thrown down by an unknown source Avoid the feeling of discomfort that comes from being depleted and lacking confidence. Learn to get your feelings across to someone else, especially an authority figure. Push yourself beyond the point of being able to do this and you will see very positive results. This cycle will allow you to develop the confidence to successfully carry out your plans. This will be a very lucky cycle.

to have anything thrown at you except eggs You are in a very good position to demand what you want from your higher power. Be direct and specific about your wants and needs. For the next five days you will develop a list of priorities that will serve as an aid in supervising the way you live your life and you will be able to meet your goals with peace and tranquility. Many blessings will be with you and your family. Good luck is with you.

to have eggs thrown at you To dream of fresh eggs being thrown at you is a warning that someone new who desires friendship is, in fact, a serial killer. Be aware and stay away from strangers.

in any other form This is a promise that the situation you are presently working on will work out to your satisfaction within five days. It also implies you need to move rapidly in order to benefit from this lucky cycle.

throw rug Do not become too friendly with a specific person for the next three days. This person will respond to you in a very cold manner. You can spare yourself this embarrassment by behaving in an appropriate manner with others.

thrush Push yourself in the direction of those goals you are eager to achieve. Your success will depend solely on your willingness to motivate yourself toward reaching those goals.

thrust/thrusting You are being pursued simply for sexual favors. You will know of this within two days and because you have prior knowledge that this will occur, you may decide whether you choose to go along or whether to dissuade this behavior.

thug For the next three days make sure no one takes advantage of you. Many blessings will come to you and your family.

thumb Avoid the split-up of a special relationship because this person will fail to pay back a loan. Within two days this individual will ask for a loan and you can avoid the end of a friendship by not lending this money in the first place.

deformed or unusually shaped Within five days you will meet a certain individual who seems to possess a beautiful, generous, and cordial personality. Do not allow yourself to be fooled by them because they are very devious and despise children. Although they portray a very sweet manner, be aware they have a hidden agenda that involves you becoming responsible for all aspects of their life, especially those involving finances and emotional well being. If you start catering to this person and ensuring their needs are being met, they will become aggressive and verbally abusive. You will also need to be very aware of all their actions because this person will be very sneaky and will do things on the sly, especially in matters concerning your finances. Be very aware of anyone you may be developing a familiarity with because this could easily lead to a situation that ties you in with this person in a very controlling way. Anything in this dream that relates to your thumb in a negative way needs to be prevented in reality. Otherwise, you are headed for a healthy long life filled with greater prosperity.

thumbtack Within two days you will receive some disagreeable news. This is totally out of your control. Remain calm in order to handle this the best way you can.

thunder Someone will develop the habit of spending your money without asking. Firmly put a stop to this the moment you see this start to develop. This person will put you in debt in no time at all. Compose yourself and remain calm. Handle this appropriately and maintain the friendship. For the next three days you must also protect yourself from any negative event in this dream and keep it from becoming a reality. Many blessings are with you.

thunderbolt Within three days someone you are very interested in will begin to move closer to you. Your relationship will take a turn and become more romantic and affectionate.

You will be very surprised at this turn of events. Feel confident you can be happy and be sure you behave appropriately.

thundercloud Within three days someone will surprise you with their flirtatious behavior. This person will attempt to provoke your sexual appetite by relentlessly flirting with you. You will be very excited by this new potential avenue to explore. Make sure, however, you do not get yourself into trouble because someone else does not approve of this behavior.

thunderhead For the next three days make sure you detail and structure each situation so it will fall into place exactly as you desire. Do this in such a way that will leave no room for confusion on the part of others. Do not slack off, there is no excuse for this.

thundershower Someone will do everything in their power to involve you in a romantic relationship. This individual is very possessive. Prior notice of this will allow you to decide what you need to do to handle a relationship of this type or whether you are even interested in becoming involved.

thunderstorm Do not put yourself in the position to go on an unpleasant journey over the next three days that will cause you many distasteful moments. Do what you can to avoid this completely.

Thursday A very unusual circumstance will take place that will lead to a financial windfall. This is also a very lucky omen and within a two day period your inner drive and courage will give you the motivation you need to break through any physical or mental block that hinders your forward progress. Once you are rid of those aspects of your life that hold you back, you will be able to bring any new project to tangible form. You will be welcomed by those you care about with open arms and placed on a pedestal. You are headed for a brilliant future and many new opportunities are headed your way. Any negative event connected with this dream needs to be altered or avoided for the next three days and alert anyone else involved so they can take steps to better themselves. Be sure to jot down any positive event you witnessed in this dream occurring on a Thursday so you can take the necessary steps to bring it to reality. You will also need to be aware of someone who will pursue you relentlessly and not allow you to say no to a relationship. This individual is interested in a permanent relationship and will work to make it a stable, fully developed unit for both of you.

thyme You will enjoy an abundance of health, are headed for a prosperous future, and anyone in your family who is experiencing ill health will quickly recover. Anything in the past you felt was impossible to accomplish is now possible.

thyroid Do not allow past events to linger with you and fester to the point that they interfere with your present life. This will, if you allow it to, keep you from moving ahead to a new and improved lifestyle. Take steps, if you view anything negative in this dream, to schedule an appointment with a doctor for a check up. Use your own judgment about the need to have your thyroid checked for any abnormality and make sure you alert anyone connected to this dream to do the same. Many blessings are with you and your family.

tiara For the next three days your negotiations will fail to bear fruit. Postpone all transactions for this time period in order to ensure success at a later date.

Tibet Within five days you will have what it takes to reach your highest ambitions and this will lead to grand improved changes in your life. This is also alerting you that someone who lives at a distance misses you a great deal and you will unexpectedly hear from them within two days. This is also a good time to visit Tibet if this is your inclination. This may also be used as a reference point in time. If you dream of this country and see its name used in any context, the dream message will occur on this day.

tick You have been led by someone to believe you can trust them fully to handle large responsibilities. Once you entrust them you will be let down in a big way. This individual fully believes they are capable of assuming heavy responsibilities but their ego is larger than their ability. Be aware of this and do not risk anything of importance.

tick (*the parasite*) Someone will be very eager to reconcile with you within three days. You will find it difficult to fulfill this request. If you follow your heart and feelings, you may be making a mistake. Think things through carefully. You must also make sure you do not inadvertently expose yourself to a contagious illness. Be very aware of your surroundings so you do not experience a tick bite or an insect bite of any kind. Forewarn anyone you recognize in this dream to do the same. Many blessings are with you and your family.

ticket *traffic ticket* For the next three days make sure you do not put yourself in the position to receive a traffic violation. This is also making you aware you will experience a number of broken engagements within seven days that you have been looking forward to attending with the person you desire. Aggressively ask for a rain check or these opportunities will pass you by because of busy schedules. It will be worth it to you to aggressively and charmingly seek the company of the person you desire.

ticket issued for any other violation or infraction Do what you can to change the outcome of this dream. You have prior notice of this and have many options on how to do this. Within three days, a verbal exchange with someone will also very rapidly develop romantic undertones. Good things will come out of this if you so desire. For the next few months, you will enjoy yourself immensely in whatever you choose to become involved in.

tickets for entertainment Do not restrict yourself so much that you are unable to verbally get your point across to the person who is special to you. It is important you use your communication skills to get your position across in any relationship that is important to you. Pay attention to tickets in your dream for specific events and take steps to attend these events. Any negative occurrence you dream of referring to events you have purchased tickets for or have planned to purchase must be avoided. Alert anyone else in the dream whom you recognize to do the same. You are headed for a prosperous future and you can proceed with confidence.

return ticket A reunion you feel will be a disaster will turn out to be a very pleasing and wonderful experience. Victory is with you.

in any other form The financial assistance you are seeking will come through for you if you stay in constant contact with the person you seek this from. Personally stay on top of this, otherwise this individual will put your request aside and forget about it. It is completely up to you and how motivated you are to achieve financial success in the future and to what degree. If you use this cycle to motivate yourself, you will be surprised at the level of success you will achieve.

tickle Protect the private time you need to spend with someone who is special to you, especially for the next three days. Otherwise, you are headed for a brilliant future.

to tickle someone The product you are marketing will be very successful.

to be tickled Make sure you have your priorities in the correct order. Be sure to check this out carefully. This dream is also letting you know you will be doing wonderful things with your outer appearance and you will look better than you ever envisioned. Picture the way you wish to look and you will find this new look compliments you.

tick tack toe *also tic tac toe* This is a very lucky omen and implies you are entering a lucky cycle. It also implies that once you make your needs known someone will be very motivated to help you achieve your goals.

tidal wave Avoid a permanent separation with those relationships that are important to you, especially for the next month. Check out your behavior and determine what you may be doing that would lead to this. You have prior notice and can keep this painful occurrence from taking place.

Tiddledywinks/tiddlywinks Do not allow negative thoughts to control your imagination for the next seven days. Don't allow yourself to treat someone in an inappropriate and disrespectful manner. Watch your behavior and treat others in the way you wish to be treated.

tide Watch your attitude for the next five days to ensure you will not have to apologize to anyone. You may not even be aware that your behavior is offensive to others. Otherwise, you are headed for a brilliant future. Proceed with confidence.

outgoing tide An event will be celebrated within a few weeks that will surprise you and bring you a great deal of joy. This event will take a lot of preparation but you will find you enjoy it immensely.

incoming tide A very wealthy person will fall in love with you. This union will be very successful and will eventually lead to a marriage, if you choose this route. This also implies you are surrounded by people who love you and are very loyal to you. Many blessings are with you and your family.

tie *(man's)* The design of the tie will lead you to one of the meanings of this dream. This is something you should either take steps to avoid or to incorporate into your life within seven days. Take steps to experience only positive events in your life. This also implies someone will ask you to demonstrate your feelings toward them. This person suspects you don't feel as strongly about them as they feel about you. They adore you completely.

tie *to see anything or anyone being tied up* Within three days someone will present themself as having a much higher level of authority than they actually have. Because you are aware of this, make sure you do not demand from this person more than they can deliver in order to avoid disappointments, misunderstandings and many distasteful moments. You have prior notice of this and can behave appropriately. See "rope" for more definition.

tiebreaker For the next five days be acutely aware that someone will try to steer you in the wrong direction by giving you the wrong address, directions, phone number, information, etc. Be keenly aware of what you are doing so you are not put on the wrong track.

tie dye Any figure you see in the pattern will determine whether this implies something you wish to avoid or promote in the future. This also implies someone's hidden feelings run very deep toward you. This will come as a delightful surprise. All things connected with finances and love will improve drastically.

tier For the next two weeks do not divulge your plans to anyone. Keep your affairs to yourself. Trust your instincts and go for it. The opportunity you have been waiting for will also arise within two days and you will make a new start in all areas of your life. All old burdens and issues that have been dragging you down will come to a halt. Major changes will add a new excitement and a new dimension to life and you will develop and execute positive plans in all phases of your life.

tie rod Someone will send you messages via a physical channel (i.e., candles, flowers, jewelry, etc.) to let you know the depth of their feelings. This person also intends that your involvement with them bloom and grow. Good luck is with you.

tiffany Make sure you have your priorities in the correct order. Recheck your schedule to ensure you have everything set up the way you desire. Do not listen to someone who will approach you within two days with a situation you should not be handling. Do not become involved, this is not your problem. You are loved beyond your imagination and you are encouraged to express your love to others.

tiffany glass Find some solitude and meditate in your favorite way in order to become very clear about what you need and want, especially for the next three days. Make sure, during this time period, that you detail and structure each situation exactly as you wish it to fall into place so others can act accordingly and so there will be no excuse for confusion or miscommunication.

Tiffany's *(the store)* Within the week you will have the financial means to do more with your life. Make sure you bring more enjoyable things into your daily routine.

tiger Do not underestimate yourself, do not allow yourself to become your worst enemy and stop short changing yourself emotionally. Push yourself to become emotionally involved. Within three days you will be entering a very exciting, fulfilling cycle. This cycle will give you the chance to involve yourself so you can enhance your life emotionally. You will be happy you did. Love is waiting for you. You must also be aware of someone's unusual behavior for the next three days to ensure they do not pull a power play on you. This person is very conniving and will deal with you in a very underhanded way. This will result in this person having the advantage over you. Otherwise, you are definitely headed for a brilliant future. Use common sense and proceed with confidence.

tiger eye This is the perfect cycle to open up and unleash yourself in order to live life to the fullest. Rid yourself of any burden that keeps you from moving in the direction you want to move. You will be able to focus on and pinpoint the reason you are unable to be the person you have the potential of being. This is the perfect time to rid yourself of all hang ups that keep you from experiencing life to the fullest. You will have the courage to move ahead. You are headed for a brilliant future and will be able to indulge in those things that will bring you more joy and emotional fulfillment.

tiger lily Do everything necessary to enjoy the marrow of life. This life is not a rehearsal, take the time to enjoy each moment. Enjoy, pamper and love yourself.

tiger moth Do not take on any additional financial burdens you should not be responsible for just because you want to be kind hearted. Within five days you will also somehow be involved with someone who has a touch of finesse, flair and glamour. This person is wealthy and will want to do everything they can to involve themselves in your life because of their loneliness. This individual has many friends and can buy many amusements, but lacks that special person to make their emotional self more complete. You can be that special person if you choose to go this route. You are headed for a brilliant future.

tightrope Keep all your sources of information to yourself for the next five days, especially if money is involved. You are also loved beyond your imagination and will be surrounded by people who love and appreciate you.

tightrope walker Within three days you will be very successful and will also attract the attention of a very wealthy person. You will be treated in the manner you wish to be treated.

Tijuana You are entering into a very lucky and prosperous cycle. Bargain shopping will be the way to go during this time period. You will be able to buy a surprising number of things at an inexpensive price. Also someone you find very attractive, interesting and charming has reciprocal feelings for you. Make sure this individual does not have another love interest because this could lead to a very dangerous situation for you. Play it safe because this person hides secrets very well and a third party could go into a violent rage if they learn about you. Otherwise, this will be a very prosperous cycle and you will be able to have a successful relationship once the person you are interested in clears up all old past relationships. Many blessings are with you and your family. This may also be used as a reference point in time. If you dream of this city and see its name used in any context, the dream message will occur on this day.

tile Do not push away the person who truly loves you. You truly care about this individual but are giving out signals that you want them to stray from you. Do everything necessary to patch up your differences. Make it a point to bond those you care about closer to you. Pay attention to the design and color of the tile you dreamed about. This will give you further clues to the meaning of this dream.

tiller You and a special person will be working for ways to improve your relationship. You will be open to communications and different ways to demonstrate your love. This will bring a new closeness to the relationship and many new benefits to the union. If you choose to pursue this, the other person will agree to go along with this process.

timber You will be able to achieve a very special goal you have been wanting to meet because of one person who shows an interest in helping you. This person will be able to pull strings on your behalf. Involve yourself in those areas of your life you know you must motivate yourself in to bring this goal about. It is particularly important to do this within seven days.

timber wolf Pay close attention to a certain person you know for the next five days. This person is very immoral and wicked. Do not allow yourself to be pressured by this person into any kind of involvement. You will regret this later on.

time You know someone of the same sex who has a hang up about dealing with other people and is very territorial. This individual will make demands on you and your time and this will become very distasteful to you. You need to make sure that for the next seven days you are budgeting your time wisely and make sure someone is not using up your time incorrectly. Your time is precious and should be spent in the manner you wish. You are headed for a brilliant future. Any specific time you dreamed of is to be used within this seven day period to schedule events, conferences, etc., that will put you at an advantage and yield greater benefits. Many blessings are with you and your family.

overtime Your urge for a sexual encounter with a certain person will be realized within a three day period. Move quickly on this and set up the perfect romantic environment.

time bomb Do everything you can to prevent a split between you and someone special, especially for the next three days. During this time, you will also desire information from someone with extensive knowledge in the area you have an interest in. This person will do everything they can to keep this information from you. Do what you can to get this information either from this person or from an alternative source. Someone is also attempting to con you out of something you own that they have had their eyes on for some time. Be prepared for the next three days to deal with this individual because they will aggressively try to convince you to sell them something at a cheaper rate.

time capsule Avoid acting in a possessive manner for the next five days. This will not go over well with others. Be very watchful and make sure you do not overextend yourself emotionally with someone else during this time period.

time card You are walking on a thin line that would be easy to cross and will be steered by someone to do so. Keep your thoughts clear and you will be able to point yourself in the right direction. Make sure you remain alert during this time period in order to avoid anything like this from occurring.

time clock This is a lucky omen for love. Within three days you will clearly calibrate your thoughts and be able to put them into words so well you will enable someone else to open up to you and express their desire for you. Your actions will enable this person to feel confident and very sure of themselves when in your presence and they will then speak up in such a way that will spark up a romance that will lead to a very warm union. This cycle will also allow you to remove any block that hinders communication.

timekeeper This is an extremely lucky omen. You will enjoy peace and tranquility for at least a month. You are definitely headed for a prosperous future. Someone who is very shy will also open up lines of communication with you and this will give you a tremendous amount of joy. You will understand where you stand in this relationship.

time machine You will enjoy an abundance of everything you need and will have many moments of rejoicing. Within five days a certain situation will also begin to evolve that will be completely out of your control. As a result, you will experience a wave of wonderful emotions because of this unexpected joyous occasion. Many blessings will come to you and your family and you are on the path for a brilliant future. Take steps to avoid any negative event portended in this dream.

timer Take steps to keep anything negative in this dream from becoming a reality. Any positive event should be brought to full bloom. You will also hear the words of love you have long waited to hear within four days. If you choose to involve yourself with this person, you will have the opportunity to change your life drastically for the better and bring prosperity into your life. You are definitely headed for a brilliant future.

Timothy *(from the Bible)* You will learn of an investigation conducted on someone you know. You will feel down because of the trouble this person has gotten himself into. You have a month of prior notice to alert this person of this dream and they can take steps to prevent this occurrence. You will then experience more tranquility and joy in your life. Many blessings will come to you and your family and you will experience an abundance of health.

tin Within three days you will reach a financial agreement with someone that will be in the exact form and structure you had envisioned. This also implies that you need to do what you can to bring more joy and happiness into your life regardless of what else may be occurring. You will also receive an invitation to an exotic event. Enjoy yourself.

tinderbox You will confide in someone you feel a great deal of confidence in. Within three days this person will advise you in the appropriate way to steer you in the direction you should be headed. Live life to the fullest and find a variety of ways in which you can allow yourself to experience the most you can out of life. You must also pay attention to any situation regarding someone else taking charge of making payments on your property. For the next two months, these payments will be missed without your knowledge. In order to avoid foreclosure procedures, do everything you can to keep tabs on what is happening with this person for the next two months.

tinfoil For the next two days make sure you understand you are under no obligation to behave in any way someone else feels you should and ensure you are not under anyone else's control. You will, once and for all, rid yourself of someone who feels they have authority over your behavior, the way you speak, think or react to things. You will not undergo any anxiety over this issue because it will be handled in a very tactful and easy manner. You are headed in the right direction for a very prosperous future.

Tinker toy You need to look at things from a variety of perspectives so resentments do not get in the way of you having fun with a variety of people. Do not keep yourself from enjoying different ways of living your life.

tin man Meditate in your favorite form, seek a very tranquil and peaceful place to enjoy for at least a week and release stress from your life. This is the perfect cycle for you to demand and specify exactly what you need from your deity. Regardless of how difficult your requests may appear, they will be granted. Many blessings will come to you and your family.

tin pail For the next two days make sure you understand you are under no obligation to behave in any way someone else feels you should. Ensure you are not under anyone else's control. You will, once and for all, rid yourself from someone who feels they have authority over your behavior, the way you speak, think or react to things. You will not undergo any anxiety over this issue because it will be handled in a very tactful and easy manner. You are headed in the right direction for a very prosperous future.

tinsel Any plans and negotiations that involve you and someone else could lead to feelings of interest on the part of this other person and they will have a desire to become involved with you. You have prior notice of this and can put a stop to this development at the onset or let it flow naturally. If you choose to pursue this, you will find this person very much to your liking. If you allow this romance to come to full bloom, there is much more there than you can anticipate.

tinsmith For the next three days you will be overcome by the feeling that something suspicious is going on. Don't let anyone convince you this is paranoia on your part or try and water it down. You are being sent a heightened sense of awareness about something you need to attend to. As a result, you will be able to handle everything in an appropriate manner and will not feel you could have done something different at a later time. Take the appropriate steps to deal with this issue now.

tint Pay attention to the colors of the tint for a greater definition of this dream. A request you make for help in assisting someone else will also be granted. These services will come in a timely fashion. You are headed for a healthy and prosperous future.

tin ware Within five days many unusual situations will occur. These situations will arouse your interest to the point you will want to investigate further. Any of these you choose to become involved with will bring you immense joy and expose you to different lifestyles. You are in a cycle that will bring clarity of thought for yourself and others.

tip Within three days someone you disliked in the past will attempt to reenter and want to play a big part in your life. Do everything you can to avoid involvement with this person without friction. Go on with your life without this person in it. Be aware also that someone you hire within the next three days cannot be trusted. Focus on looking for alternatives if you choose not to go through this distasteful situation.

tiptoe Someone you find attractive and who also finds you immensely attractive will keep someone special to them a secret. Be very cautious and step back from this situation because it could become very distasteful if the third person learns of your interests. You will also need to be very attentive to the person doing the tip toeing in the dream because this person knows something underhanded is going on that will hurt them deeply within the week. This is very preventable. Take steps to ensure everyone enjoys fruitful relationships and pleasant lives.

anything done on tiptoes Someone you feel a special closeness to will, within three days, come to you to try to explain what is going on in their life. This person is under a tremendous strain that is being placed on them by someone else but will be unable to explain exactly what they are feeling. This person is in danger of having their spirit broken because the other party is behaving in an irresponsible and abusive manner in many areas of their life. This individual is being controlled and is becoming very suspicious about the methods being used. There are no specific motives or methods but this person is being controlled in a very abusive way and they are, for some reason, remaining in this situation. It is important you make this person aware that the moment they have this conversation with you they must motivate themselves to move on. It takes a long time to get back a balanced sense of consciousness and a lot of abuse to destroy it. This is the perfect time for this person to be able to hear your words of motivation and make the necessary moves to get away from this abusive person without making their motives apparent. This could turn into a situation that will cause this person, as well as yourself, a great deal of duress. This individual will only discover the amount of abuse they are under when it is too late unless they make their move now. You will be able to use profound communication skills during this time period to gain someone's absolute attention. You will also be able to flush out the information you need from others by using your communication skills. This information will be very beneficial and advantageous for both of you. Many blessings are with you and you are headed for a brilliant future.

tire Within a few days you will get a clear picture in a dream of the person who is undermining your accomplishments. Take steps to avoid any negative events witnessed in this dream for the next five days. Take steps to make sure you only experience positive events in life.

tire marks Someone is trying to decide how to put a difficult situation into words so they can go on with their life without your association in the future. This will occur within three days. Think about this ahead of time so you can handle this appropriately and with dignity. Many blessings are with you and your family.

flat You will be easily taken in by a conniving friend. This person will become a very cunning enemy and will secretly sabotage an important opportunity just prior to you gaining knowledge of it. Since you have prior notice of this, you can take steps to determine who this person is and take care of this issue properly. You will be able to turn this around to your advantage. It is also important to do everything you can to arrive at a clever plan or solution that will enable you to work independently and without assistance on a situation that will arise within three days. These thoughts and plans will come to you with great clarity and you will be able to resolve this issue successfully. Any negative event seen in this dream can be avoided or the outcome changed in reality.

radial tires You will have difficulties due to your indifferent behavior.

whitewall tires Within five days you will find yourself caring for someone who is unable to care for themself. This person will improve physically and achieve the quality of life they need in order to reach social personal acceptance. You will also be swamped with many social engagements and must make an effort to maintain your appearance and keep your attire in the best possible condition during this time period. This will be a very successful cycle.

tire chain Do not allow yourself to force an issue on another person that they find distasteful. Lighten up, get off someone's back, and allow them to get on with their life if this is their choice. Allow other people to have their space and live their life as they wish. This situation will come up within three days. Handle yourself with dignity and get on with your life accordingly.

tire marks *to see tire marks on something that has been run over* Do not lose your sense of alertness for the next three days and do not let down your guard. This will leave you open for being persuaded into going somewhere that will put you in danger. Stay alert in all aspects of your life and be cautious when involving yourself in new situations with another person who may unwittingly cause you injury. It is very important to choose wisely what you are willing to become involved in, especially for the next three days. Take steps to prevent any negative occurrence you dreamed of from becoming a reality.

tissue Someone will go to great lengths to involve you in their life. You will learn of this within three days. This person is presently having difficulty with an ongoing relationship and will, within the week, be separated from this person and free to do as they wish. They will be very careful with their relationship with you due to their difficulties with the one they are leaving. This individual is very vulnerable and will welcome a kind and soft behavior from you without any unnecessary demands. You are on this person's mind and will be able to enjoy a good relationship without any interference. You are headed for a very prosperous future.

tissue paper Put all of your efforts into one specific area. Be versatile and make sure you include things that are important to you.

Titanic, the There is clearly too much interference in your life. Become very clear about what your family needs. Provide some private moments for yourself so you can focus on what you truly want.

tithe For the next five days, do what you can to become verbally aggressive in order to allow someone else to open up and request what they need from you.

title You will be overwhelmed because someone will present you with a problem that has been embellished and exaggerated. Be prepared to have a tight grip on your emotions so you can clearly see that this is a small issue that has been blown out of proportion.

Titus *(from the Bible)* Someone will demonstrate deep affection toward you and will be more than eager to help you in any way they can, either emotionally or financially. You will also be told by someone the next step you need to take to make a decision that has to be made within three days. This decision will bring more emotional and financial security. Be confident and everything will work out exactly as you have envisioned. Take advantage of this cycle to make changes in other areas of your life that you wish to improve.

TNT Within three days you will find a particular group you have had doubts about will be very eager to support you. Also, pay more attention to someone who is eager to involve you in a romantic situation. Anything having to do with love and business negotiations will be very lucky for you to follow up on.

toad Someone will purposefully involve you unwittingly in an illegal activity. They will try to persuade you to become involved in a get rich quick scam within three days. Otherwise, this is an extremely lucky omen. You will receive the emotional and financial support you need. Within five days, plans will fall exactly as you have envisioned.

toadstool You have three days in which to accomplish your goals. Make sure you take care of your health properly, make sure you get the rest you need and stay out of stressful environments for at least a month. You will have the clarity of thought to focus on what you need to accomplish during this time period.

toast Someone will enter your life within three days who will help you develop a more positive approach and attitude toward bringing romance into your life in ways you have not allowed in the past. This will allow you to do things from a different approach. Many blessings are with you and your family.

burned Do not put yourself in the position of being falsely accused of anything. Think ahead and take steps to prevent this. You will be able to acquire what you need most from life. You are entering a very joyous cycle.

toaster This is an extremely lucky omen and what seemed impossible in the past is now possible. Eat healthy foods, drink plenty of water and get plenty of rest. Do not allow any opportunities to slip through your fingers for the next three days.

tobacco You will be with a person who treats you with a high level of interest. If you are interested in a relationship, behave in a manner that encourages this. This person is interested in pursuing a permanent union. You will both be loyal for life and you will be well provided for, for a lifetime, if you choose to pursue this.

Tobit *(from the Canonical Bible)* Be prepared for the occurrence of an unusual and remarkable event. At the same time this is going on you will have the clarity of thought needed to take the steps to get through this cycle in an easy and comfortable way. You will have to be very firm and disciplined in order to control your curiosity. Expect an abundance of health during this time period.

today *any form* For the next two days make sure you tell only the truth and have the faith that everything will work out perfectly and will fall into place exactly as you have envisioned. This dream also implies that today will be a very lucky day and you will be able to tackle those tasks you find difficult. Take steps to avoid any negative event connected to this dream. You have prior notice of this and can make sure you experience only positive expressions in your life. Many blessings are with you and your family.

toddler This is a promise that the situation you are presently working on will work out to your satisfaction within seven days. This also implies you need to move rapidly in order to benefit from this lucky cycle.

toddy This is alerting you that anything you feel is not going in the direction you desire needs to be worked on. This is especially important for the next three days. Work on this issue until it meets your standards. Once you are able to do this, everything will fall perfectly into place.

toe You will feel despondent over the news of a close relative who is having domestic problems. This relative is going through a lot of pain and will continue to go through a lot of discomfort. Do what you can to support them until they get through this short term crisis. Many blessings will come to you and your family. This is an extremely lucky omen and you are definitely headed for a prosperous future. Take all the necessary steps to prevent any negative event foretold in this dream from becoming a reality. You have prior notice of this and can turn it around to a very favorable outcome within three days.

toe, broken Do not waste time to determine whether or not a particular romance will work and do not talk yourself out of going out with or having more to do with this individual. Everything will work out perfectly for you. You will have a wonderful time if you choose to pursue this.

toe dance Someone will go to great lengths to be flirtatious with you in a tasteful, enjoyable way. You will also enjoy a great deal of luck that will last for seven days. Take advantage of this lucky cycle to help you with your love relationships.

toenails *painted* You are starting to sense a strong emotional wave that will take up a big portion of your time because you will be unable to determine the source of this drive. Your urges are causing you to focus on bringing something to reality. This will continue for two weeks and you will constantly feel this deep emotional craving. Within this time period you will somehow arrive at the reason and source of this feeling and will then start acting on what you feel you should be doing. This powerful urge is the result of a psychic ability and a heightened awareness that is pushing you in the direction you should take. Although you will have no proof or tangible verification, you will instinctively know, because of the intense excitement you feel, that by acting on this urge you will gain more benefits than you ever imagined. If you deem this urge to be improper or socially unacceptable, you have the time and enough prior notice to seek out professional help and come to grips with your desires. This will allow you to live at peace with yourself and your urges. This is the right cycle for you to seek out just the right person who is equipped to take care of this issue. It will be correctly addressed and you will be able to gain control of your desires in a healthy way. You are headed for a brilliant future.

broken toenails or toenails falling off toes Someone will let you down because the money they have promised to pay you at a particular time will not come through. This individual will have a change of heart about arrangements you have both made. Plan on agreements to be broken. Since you have prior notice of this, you will have the opportunity to cover yourself financially.

toffee Be alert. Someone has tried numerous times, without success, to get in contact with you. This person is purposely preventing this contact from taking place. No matter what the motives are, you need to get it across that this person has an urgent need to contact you. Make yourself available to receive this information. Many blessings are with you and your family.

toga Within five days someone who knows they should have been treating you more fairly will come to their senses, apologize for their past rude behavior and verbalize a need to change their ways in the future.

toilet *to use in any form* You and a special person are looking for changes to improve your relationship. You are now open to conversations and new ways to demonstrate love and bring in a new closeness that will benefit the union. This will serve to improve the relationship on all levels. If you choose to pursue this, the other person will be more than eager to go along with this process. Any other negotiations you need to attend to will work to your advantage during this time period because this is the best cycle for communicating.

to flush the toilet after use The above changes will occur

very rapidly. Good luck is with you and you are headed for a brilliant future.

unusual things floating that have no business being there Make sure this does not take place in reality. Also, someone will be so satisfied and happy with your attitude toward them that they will want to demonstrate their feelings toward you but will keep this a secret until you are in a position of privacy and it can easily be revealed to you. You are loved beyond your imagination by people you least expect.

toilet bowl deodorizer A major personal decision you are in the process of making will work out beautifully.

toilet brush Your relationship with another needs to have some excitement added. With some effort on your part, you can replace what is missing. You will also have the enthusiastic support of a special person once the process has begun and you will experience a greater closeness than ever before. Begin this rebuilding within three days.

toilet tissue You are given a green light to move ahead on something. Follow your hunches and go for it. For the next ten days, everything you thought was impossible in the past is now possible.

toilet training You will decide to move away from a certain situation because you will find it is a bigger challenge than you first anticipated. You will be doing the correct thing.

toilet water You will be asked a favor in exchange for a large sum of money. This money will be the answer to a large outstanding debt. This is also a lucky omen and you will receive a large abundance of love and affection.

token Be very pragmatic when you request that someone give you assistance on something they are hesitant about becoming involved with. This person does not have the courage to tell you this to your face but will talk behind your back. Do not keep trying to enlist someone's help who is not interested in helping you unless you want to have your feelings hurt. Seek alternatives.

Tokyo This is an extremely lucky omen for those things in your life that you wish to see improved. Do not lose confidence with a difficult issue that will come up within the next two days. You will be able to resolve it fully and in such a way that will meet your standards. Do not lose confidence. This may also be used as a reference point in time. If you dream of this city and see its name used in any context, the dream message will occur on this day.

toll The head of the household will make an emotional appeal to the hierarchy of an establishment that will bring a greater abundance to this person and their family's lives. Move quickly because this cycle will last only a week. You will receive more if you act now.

tollbooth You are about to make a decision that will directly affect you and another person. This other person is really depending on you to make the correct decision because it will affect their whole life. You will need strength and courage to make the decision you have to make. Once you proceed, you will be glad you did because it will be the correct choice. Everything will fall into place perfectly and you will be free from the burden of making the wrong decisions. Good luck is with you. Move quickly on this and don't waste time.

toll bridge Stop making your home seem like a prison to others, especially for the next three days. This will eventually backfire if you do not take steps to correct your behavior.

tollgate You need to be acutely aware that someone who has an emotional hang up will focus on you. This would result in many moments of terror for you within the week. Take steps to avoid this.

Toll House cookies You need to develop a plan that will create a greater income because you will be needing more money within three weeks.

toll keeper Someone you least expect is a detective in disguise. Make sure any behavior you wish to keep private is not noticed by this individual. Be on your best behavior for the next seven days.

tomahawk Within five days you will cause pain to someone else. This person will feel left out and abandoned because you fail to show love and affection. Get a grip on your behavior and learn to show your love appropriately.

tomato Someone will come to you with a plea to forget the past. You had a friendship that was interrupted because of a misunderstanding. Be willing to forget the past but make sure this time you know what your limits are so this hurt does not occur again.

sweet tomato You will thoroughly enjoy a theater event with a special person and you will be emotionally satisfied.

tomb Do not deprive yourself of special moments with someone who is special to you by making excuses and not allowing yourself the time to spend with this person. This will become an issue within three days. Take steps to avoid this problem. You are also going in the wrong direction. Focus on what needs to be done now to set yourself on the right track. Make sure any negative event witnessed in this dream does not become a reality and alert anyone else involved to do likewise. Take steps to experience only positive expressions in your life.

tomboy Do not take life for granted, especially for the next three days. Take the time to determine what you really want and need in this time frame. A plan you want to implement will also be successful. Many blessings are with you and your family.

tombstone Do not constantly replay negative tapes. You are talking yourself out of some great ideas. Go for the impossible and you will be surprised at how quickly you can gather the tools and knowledge to launch the impossible. This is the perfect cycle for this. Good luck is with you. Make sure you do not allow any negative event seen in this dream to become a reality. Make sure you only experience positive events in your life.

tomcat The information you will be receiving within three days needs to be checked to determine authenticity. Any missing information will definitely make a difference in your success.

Tom Collins You will be traveling from place to place and enjoying yourself in each city you visit. You will visit many clubs and social outings and continue to enjoy yourself for a few months. Just be disciplined in how you spend your free time. Budget your time in order to bring as much pleasure into your life as you can. Many blessings are with you and your family.

tommy gun Plans that are put on paper will not be as easy to put into practice as you thought. The labor involved is far more intense than you had anticipated. Make sure you check this over carefully and devise an easier plan that will save time. You will be able to come up with a better idea.

Tom Thumb Within four days you will be able to calibrate and detail your thoughts and put them into words so well that you will be able to help someone who desires you, in every way, to get closer to you. You will be able to make this person feel very secure and comfortable in your presence. This will allow this individual to speak openly and frankly in a manner that will spur the development of a relationship and create a warm open union. You can also use these skills to bring anything you want into reality. This will allow you to remove all blocks due to poor communication. This is a magical cycle. Any scene in a dream that you view in miniature, symbolizes and prophesizes an activity you will foster. A negative scene can be avoided, in reality.

tom tom Within three days you will notice that someone will constantly interfere with your plans. This person does not mean to cause this problem but is so interested in what you are doing that this interference will continue. It would be better for you if you budget your time around them so you can use your other time to focus on what you need to be focusing on. You are headed for a prosperous future and many blessings will come to you and your family.

ton This will be a very exciting time. Someone will be very eager to persuade you into a sexual encounter and you will have no idea that this person felt this way about you. You will be left with excitement because of this new way of looking at this person. If you desire to pursue this, you will find it mutually satisfying. This cycle will bring much promise for the relationship and you will prosper in other areas of your life.

tone *if the tone is turned down* Unpleasant words will be exchanged between you and another person and this will not be easy to control Do everything you can to keep this from taking place.

tone deaf You will become very weary of something that is taking place in your life and you are growing anxious to communicate to someone exactly what it is you are growing tired of. Be very clear about what you wish for this particular person and yourself to change, the behavior you want to put a stop to, new behavior you wish for this person or yourself to add to your lives and anything new you want to introduce into your lifestyle.

tongs You will be dealing with someone who will give you far more than you request. Make sure you explain to this person that when you make a request, they must give you exactly what you want and make it clear what you are willing to put out. Otherwise, everything will be done to the extreme. Many blessings are with you and your family. Take steps to prevent any negative occurrence connected with this dream from becoming a reality. You have enough time to ensure you experience only positive expressions in your life. Many blessings are with you and your family.

tongue You need to be very aggressive for the next five days. Go for what you want. You will be able to communicate the appropriate words to another person so they can meet your demands and desires in the manner you wish. You will also enjoy greater health and a new pizzazz in life. Continue to look at life from an optimistic view. Good luck is with you.

unusual tongue behavior You will be dealing with someone who habitually buys time by putting you off a few hours, days or weeks until the time is right for them. This person will be unable to become involved in any capacity until the time suits them. Be clever when speaking to this individual in order to determine the exact time. This will prevent disappointment prior to that opportunity.

gesture of two fingers over the mouth with the tongue sticking out Within the week you will experience a new confidence, sense of balance and feeling of being solidly grounded. As a result of these feelings you will be able to tackle those situations that require this aspect of your personality. Use this time period to work on those areas of your life that you want to make changes. You will have the opportunity to bring prosperity into your life at the level you desire. You are headed for a brilliant future.

tongue depressor Within two days you will reach a decision about a career matter. Carefully investigate the plans you hope to execute in order to determine their workability and to decide whether you wish to put them into action. This is a lucky omen and each plan will work out exactly as you wish once you have taken the time to review them.

tongue twister Motivate and encourage yourself to go out and make new friends so you can provide yourself with a variety of lifestyles. You are also headed for a very prosperous future. Proceed with confidence.

tonic Within three days you will have the opportunity to provide yourself with some amusements that you remember from the past. You will recreate these amusements with others and this will bring you many joyful moments and memories from long ago. Allow yourself enjoyment without limitations during this time cycle.

tonight Anything this phrase was used for in a dream that implies a negative connotation is a warning for you to take steps to prevent this event from taking place. Make sure you only allow positive expressions to take place in your life. This also implies that within four days, someone will go to great lengths to have you believe an absolutely unbelievable story. Go with your instincts on this. This is also forewarning you that you may be overlooking something this evening. Focus on this so you will enjoy a positive result. This is a lucky cycle for you to tackle an issue you felt was impossible. You will be successful in accomplishing your goals.

tonsillitis For the next three days watch your health and make sure you do not come into contact with anyone who has an infection you do not wish to be exposed to. Make sure you maintain a healthy lifestyle. You will also need to make sure you have an accurate description of someone's opinion of you so you can make an accurate assessment of how involved you want to get with this person. Good luck is with you.

tonsils For the next three days you really need to think ahead clearly before you make a statement to someone else. Once you have done so you will have to stick with it, so make sure you do not say something you cannot back up. You have prior notice of this and will be able to handle it wisely. You will also need to take every precaution to prevent any negative event in this dream from becoming a reality. Many blessings are with you.

Tony Award Within five days you will be appointed to a leadership position whether this is something you wish or not. You will be required to dedicate much of your private time toward successfully organizing a certain event. You will do a beautiful job. Good luck is with you.

tool Someone who will prove to be dangerous will try to inflict harm on you within three days. Be keenly aware of any suspicious character who enters your life during this time frame. You have prior notice of this so you can make the appropriate decisions and remain safe. Pay close attention to the particular tool you dreamed about. This will give you an added clue to the meaning of this dream. Good luck is with you and many blessings will come to you and your family.

toolmaker You will be entertained with an added touch of romance and you will welcome this refreshing addition to your life. Go for it, full speed ahead.

tool shed For the next two weeks every opportunity will be offered to you to make big changes in your life. Take a chance and be a pioneer in new areas to see if you can handle them. One of the opportunities you grasp will make a big difference in your life for a long time to come.

tooth You have time to take care of anything you dreamed of that represented a negative event concerning your teeth. Do this within seven days. You must also not assume a certain situation will turn out exactly as you wish it to. Make sure you work on it so it will turn out like you want. Don't assume anything, especially for the next three days.

sweet tooth You will soon surrender and marry your sweetheart. This will be a happy union that will last a lifetime.

broken teeth Do not overextend or over involve yourself in any situation you feel irresistibly compelled to become involved in. For the next five days protect yourself emotionally and avoid getting involved in something you have no business being involved in. Proceed with caution.

beautiful teeth You are definitely headed for a brilliant future. Anything you felt was impossible is now possible for you to achieve. This is the cycle to tackle those tough issues. You will be successful.

your teeth falling out You are beginning to feel closer to a certain person who will lead you to believe you can trust them fully and can be sure of their loyalty to you. For the next three days make sure you do not become any more involved than you already are unless you take extreme precautions. This person is very clever and masterful in creating deception and illusions. You will begin to believe that certain events and situations will occur in the future that will never take place. A hidden agenda is at play here that involves pursuing you for devious reasons known only to this particular individual. And because an atmosphere of complete trust has developed, you will suspect nothing. Because of this person's charm, if you do become suspicious, they will easily create a diversion to lure you away from these feelings. Once you understand what is going on, you will have suffered financial setbacks, and deep emotional distress. You will be able to get your life back on track but it will take a long time. You have prior notice of this and all the ammunition you need to ensure this situation does not take place. Practice common sense, do not compromise or allow this person to pry into your affairs. Do not get involved. Otherwise, you are headed for a prosperous future and many blessings are with you and your family.

wisdom tooth Within five days you will have an urgent need to have something taken care of that requires assistance from someone else, whether this is in the nature of a large loan or a big favor that you need immediately with no hassles. This request will be so big it will be difficult to imagine that it will be granted to you. Follow your intuition and it will lead you to the right person who will come through for

you. Act with confidence and explore all of your options until you find the perfect one. As soon as you reach an agreement, be sure to take immediate action so the situation will be concluded before this person has a chance to change their mind. Many blessings will come to you and you are on the path toward a prosperous future.

toothache For the next five days be sure to watch your valuables and make sure they are not misplaced by someone else. You will also need to make sure you do not do anything careless that could result in damage to your teeth for the next three days. Take every precaution to keep your teeth healthy and be sure to have any necessary dental work performed during this cycle in order to avoid the pain of a toothache. You are headed for a brilliant future and many blessings will come to you and your family.

toothbrush Go full speed ahead with a concept you are developing that seems, at first, overwhelming. You will be able to gather the tools and resources to skillfully bring this to fruition.

to brush your teeth or to see someone else brush their teeth You will be received with open arms due to your dynamic reputation. Others will be very amenable to a certain situation you will be introducing within the next three days.

tooth fairy Motivate yourself to get through a mental block. Rebel against all attitudes that make you feel stuck in a rut. You will also hear news of someone passing away. This will be a dear friend whom you will miss terribly. This will occur within three days, is out of your control, and there is nothing you can do. Prepare yourself so you can handle this situation.

toothpaste You will feel deep sorrow and pain over the anguish of a friend who has had some misfortune. Do what you can over the next three days to provide comfort to this individual. This will not last very long. This person will bounce back quickly and everything will get back to normal soon after this. Many blessings are with you and your family.

toothpick Do not allow anyone to verbally chastise you because you do not wish to enter into an agreement. This will take place within three days. When it starts, take the initiative to cut the conversation short because it could easily escalate into a violent argument. You will also come to the conclusion, within three days, that you want someone to do something for themselves. This will be a problem for you because you will not know how to break the news to this person. Make sure you do this with kindness and tact but make sure you have all the information you need so this person can do the footwork. This also implies you will be going through a lucky cycle for the next week. You will enjoy more joy and tranquility in your life and receive a gift. Many blessings will come to you and your family.

toothpick holder Within three days be very strict with another person and demand that a certain behavior stop. Use this cycle to successfully accomplish this task.

topaz Brace yourself, you will receive delightful and joyous news within two days. You are also headed for a brilliant future and many blessings will come to you and your family. You are in the perfect cycle to demand from your god exactly what you need and want in your life and have your needs met. Proceed with confidence and meditate in your favorite form. You will receive mental and spiritual richness.

top banana Someone will finally come to grips with themself and will reach a decision you have long awaited. This decision will have a major impact on your life. You will both make mutual plans that will lead to a brilliant future. This will occur within the week.

top billing You will soon realize your goals. You will also be dealing with two concurrent issues that will bring you prosperity and good luck. Make sure you focus on both situations. You will be tempted to forego one and focus on the other. Maintain confidence and focus on both of these situations equally. You are headed for a brilliant future and tranquility is headed your way.

topcoat Make sure you are self reliant for the next two days and be sure you take the time to look at both sides of an issue. Explore the possibilities of what could unexpectedly take place before you make any major decisions. You are loved beyond your imagination, are deeply respected and will be surrounded by those who care a great deal about you. Other people will show their appreciation for you within the week.

top forty This is an extremely lucky omen. Within five days you will experience a wealth of tranquility, health and harmony with family and friends. Good luck is with you.

top hat The opportunities you have been waiting for will come to you within two days. You will have a new start in life and all issues that have been a burden to you will come to an immediate halt. A new excitement and feeling of confidence will take over. Good luck is with you.

topknot Something is occurring behind the scenes with another person for reasons known only to them. This person has a habit of creating chaos and distasteful moments in the lives of other people. Be aware of your surroundings and of any unusual situations. This will add balance and stability to your life.

topless Riches will come to you through an unusual and unexpected circumstance within two weeks. You will need to immediately address any negative event connected with this dream and make an effort to change this to a positive situation. You are definitely headed for a brilliant future.

topmast You will soon be able to grasp your goals. You will also encounter handling two different situations at the

same time and both will bring you luck and prosperity. Make sure you take care of both issues. You will be tempted to overlook one in lieu of the other. Do not lose your confidence and make sure you focus on both of them equally. You are headed for a brilliant future and tranquil times are headed your way.

topographer Within three days someone will want to show you how much they care for you and how involved they want to be. This person will perform a variety of activities, chores, and favors for you and will behave in almost a puppy like manner. Each desire you have will be fulfilled. Show your affection and demonstrate consideration for this person's generosity and efforts. Be very cautious and do not bruise this person's feelings or become suspicious of this person's motives.

topping Do everything necessary within three days to maintain your self confidence. Become very bold and aggressive and do not involve yourself in anything you know very little about.

top round You will soon realize your goals. You will be dealing with two different situations at the same time that will bring you a great deal of luck and prosperity. Make sure you handle them both. You will be tempted to let one go in lieu of the other. Do not lose your confidence and focus on both of them equally. You are headed for a brilliant future and a very tranquil time is coming your way.

top secret You will easily be taken by a conniving friend. This person will become a very cunning enemy and purposely go to great lengths to sabotage an important opportunity just before you gain knowledge of this. Since you have been forewarned, you will be able to determine who this person is and address the situation. You will then be able to turn this around to your advantage.

topsoil Regardless of anything else that may be going on in your life right now, within five days you will overcome any long term burden you wish to rid yourself of. You are headed in the right direction and will be experiencing more pleasure and social events in the future. Focus on achieving a peaceful and stress free life.

topstitch Within two days you will move to an unfamiliar area. Although you will know nothing about this region, you will find that it will be a wonderful experience and you will meet many wonderful new people who will add more excitement to your life.

Torah You are entering an extremely blessed cycle. You will also be involved with someone you feel is not being altogether truthful. Don't lose heart, this person is giving you accurate information. Anything someone has promised to you, although you may not receive it immediately, will come through.

torch For the next three days make sure any food or liquids you ingest are not tainted. This will keep you from developing food poisoning.

torchbearer You are headed for a prosperous future and will experience, for the next three days, an abundance of health and will achieve victory with those tasks you find difficult in those areas of your life you most desire. This dream also implies someone you have not noticed has been doing everything in their power to draw your attention to them. This person is interested in involving themselves in your life in some capacity. Many blessings are with you and your family.

torchlight You will need to protect your business reputation, especially for the next two days. Keep your personal life to yourself.

torch song Your production will greatly increase because of some valuable information you will uncover by conducting your own research. Good luck is with you.

toreador Put forth your best efforts in a new career, especially for the next week. Do the best you can with anything you choose to apply yourself to.

tormentor You may be eating something you think is good for you but, in reality, is not. This particular food may be counter productive to your health. Investigate your dietary needs and develop better eating habits. Investigate the ingredients of the foods to determine what may be causing you harm. Good luck is with you.

tornado Do everything necessary for the next three days to be sure you are adequately protected from the elements or from natural disasters. This will be an unexpected event so take extra precautions now. Otherwise, this is a very lucky omen. For the next five days you must also remain focused on important relationships. Behave in the appropriate way to ensure these relationships remain intact and close to you.

torpedo For the next two days make sure you keep other people who are making unwarranted demands on you from interfering with what you have going for you now. Save your energy for things you enjoy.

torpedo boat Be aware that someone will attempt to push a romantic situation on you. Do not waste time on this relationship in spite of the temptation you may feel. It will not work out.

torrent You will need to juggle your time in order to include some romance in your life. Reschedule your life now and you will be able to captivate the person of your choice and will enjoy wonderful times. You will feel very romantic toward this person and will be very physically attracted to them. Go for it.

torso You will receive disagreeable news within two days. This situation is out of your control. Remain calm and you will be able to handle this appropriately. Because you have prior notice of this you will be able to handle anything that comes up within the week with a minimum of stress and a confident attitude.

tortilla Express your deep feelings toward someone who is not quite sure of your feelings toward them. Make it clear to this person where they stand. You will also receive some joyful news that will delight you because you will hear exactly what you want to hear. Expect this within three days.

tortoise Be very aware of what you will be saying to others for the next three days. You may accidentally blurt out something you didn't mean to say and hurt someone's feelings very deeply. No matter what you do to make this situation better, you will never completely erase what you have said and the hurt feelings that went with it. Within three days you will also witness a strange occurrence. You will be shocked and wish you had never seen this. Do whatever you can to avoid this by rescheduling all planned events in this time period. You will also be very successful when bargain hunting. Barter with others and you will quickly accumulate many items you wish to purchase. You will experience good health, tranquility and harmony for a long time to come.

tortoiseshell Someone who loves you misses you tremendously. You will learn more about this within three days. This relationship will empower you in ways you find beneficial.

torture Commitments you have made in the past with another person need to be revised so you will be able to handle the changes that will come up within three days. You must also stay committed to present situations.

tostada Within three days you will experience a deep emotional pain because someone will set you up for betrayal. Avoid these feelings of pain and fragility by following your hunches.

tote bag Personally handle all of your important paperwork for the next four days to ensure it is properly processed. You will also receive a promotion in the area you most desire.

totem pole The spiritual fulfillment you are seeking will be given to you within three days. This is an extremely lucky omen and you are definitely headed in the right directions.

toucan You will receive a financial boost due to an unexpected increase in income for a long time to come. This will take care of many of your financial problems.

touch *to be touched* Someone will send you a material message (i.e., flowers, candy, a gift, etc.) to express their deep feelings for you. This person also desires that your involvement grow and bloom. Good luck is with you.

to touch someone Pay close attention to who you were touching. If you recognize them, this will be the individual who will be instrumental in helping you shape a brilliant future. If you did not recognize this person, you will be offered a large amount of money for services you can easily provide in a non stressful way. Good luck is with you.

in any other form Someone in another state or in a far away place has a deep need to see you. This person misses you a great deal and will contact you soon to express their feelings. They will also extend to you the means to travel to their locale so you can spend time together. If you choose to go in this direction, you will enjoy yourself immensely.

touchdown Take steps to keep yourself and your family safe for the next three days. Be very cautious and don't be so eager to jump into the unknown for the next five days. Analyze your feelings and goals carefully so you can ensure you are headed in the right direction.

touch football Avoid any clashes with anyone important who is involved in your business dealings right now. This restraint will allow your business to become very lucrative.

touch tone You are entering a very lucky cycle for at least a month. You will also be blessed with a tremendous amount of health and wealth. This will ensure you will be able to keep up with your financial demands. Many blessings will come to you and your family.

toupee Someone wants to touch you passionately and romantically in the exact manner you wish to be touched. Expect this to occur within three days. This also implies that riches will come to you.

tourist You will have to extend yourself, take risks and be bold. The thoughts you have can be brought forward in a tangible form. You will definitely experience more prosperous times in your life and you are headed toward a brilliant future.

tourist trap You will be given a terrific opportunity to get it right this time. You will have the chance to set certain situations right that were impossible in the past. This is an extremely lucky omen.

tournament You are taking a situation for granted that involves someone else. This other person will react in the same manner because of your demeanor. Do what you can to inspire both of you to become more involved in this situation. If you desire, both of you can experience success.

tourniquet Stay out of the lives and business of other peo-

ple and do everything necessary to keep others from interfering with your life. This is especially important for the next seven days.

tow A very powerful and creative idea will enter your mind and you will be able to put this to use immediately. This will allow you to live your life in a completely different way. Be very precise in each move you make in order to grasp your goals.

tow away zone This implies you will gain instant wealth at a time when you least expect it. You will be able to handle any difficult task that will be coming up within the week and all doors that were closed to you will now be open. You will be seen by others in a different light and able to grasp new opportunities and achieve success.

towboat For the next three days none of the negotiations you are involved in will bear fruit. Cancel all meetings during this time period and reschedule for a different time in order to ensure a better outcome.

towel For the next five days do not become so eager to leap into the unknown. Analyze your feelings and do not allow anyone else to change your opinions. This applies especially to groups with political agendas, some religious groups, and groups that delve into the occult. Any involvement will make your life a disaster. You have prior notice of this so you can set limits to remain safe. Get on with your life without unhealthy involvements.

tower You will experience a new wealth that will come to you through an unusual and unexpected circumstance that will take place within two weeks. Immediately attend to any negative event connected to this dream and take steps to turn it around to a positive situation. You are definitely headed for a brilliant future.

in disrepair Make sure you do not create friction between yourself and someone who is important to you. The head of the household needs to be sure that all bases are covered both financially and romantically, especially for the next two days. All negative issues need to be attended to now in order to avert a crisis.

tower control You must come to the realization that other people need the time to do things on their own. Do not demand so much of others who need time to take care of their own personal business, especially for the next three days.

Tower of Babel Within the week someone will become aware of you in a very special way. This person will pursue you in a romantic way and will proceed in a slow and determined way to marry you. If you choose this option, this relationship will be long lived and bring you prosperity. Follow your hunches for the next three days.

Tower of London Make sure that any negative event connected to this structure does not occur in reality. For the next three days do everything you can to ensure you experience only positive expressions in your life. Also, do whatever is necessary to keep your immune system intact and take steps to build it up. Keep yourself healthy. This may also be used as a reference point in time. If you dream of this historical site or see its name used in any context, the dream message will occur on this day.

tow head In the past you turned down a request from another person. Within three days this individual will make the same request but with the hidden agenda of creating an argument. Remain calm or this could cause you to become very angry.

town Within four days you will meet someone of a totally different nationality who is completely different from you who speaks several different languages. This person will offer you a gift of creativity that will bring you a tremendous amount of joy.

town car Do not allow pride to stand in your way of accepting a gift of money, especially for the next two days. This dream is an extremely lucky omen.

town crier Take steps to prevent any negative messages you heard from becoming a reality and make sure you only experience positive expressions in your life. Also someone will feel very passionate toward you and you will want to cater to someone emotionally, especially for the next three days. Good luck is with you.

town hall For the next three days you will be able to negotiate all business transactions successfully and bring closeness into those relationships you desire.

town meeting Take all the necessary steps to prevent any negative event you dreamed about from becoming a part of your life and to bring all positive events to full bloom. This is also a warning that a group of people have decided to conspire against you in a subtle way. Be acutely aware of all involvements and make sure you are fully aware of the motives of other people. This is important for the next five days.

toxemia/toxins Within three days you will come to the realization that someone needs to do things for themself. You will have difficulty with this because you don't know how to break this news to this person. Make sure you relate this to this individual in an inoffensive way and make sure you have all of the information needed so this person can do the necessary footwork. Do everything you can to maintain a toxic free environment for the next three days. You may not even be aware of any toxins and should not take anything for granted. Keep yourself safe.

toxic shock syndrome Take steps to avoid any negative event portrayed in this dream. Do this within three days and make every effort to deal only with what is positive in life.

This also implies that you speak your mind especially for the next two days. Develop your determination and aggressiveness. This is the way to go in order to put an end to a certain situation that is not working in your favor.

toy Pay close attention to the young people around you to ensure they receive proper nourishment and get enough exercise. Take steps to correct those things in their life that need correcting to ensure they enjoy a healthy lifestyle. Within five days you will also give your love and affection to someone and behave in a manner that will allow others to adore you. You will enjoy a wonderful time during this cycle. Good luck is with you.

electronic and robotic toys For the next two days, become verbally assertive with a certain individual in order to prod this person to interact with you verbally and emotionally in the manner you expect and deserve. You will be successful in your request. There is a sense of urgency to this. Proceed with confidence.

toy poodle Someone you know is very eager to involve themself with you in any capacity. In reality, this person is, without your knowledge, interested in you in a deep passionate way. Do what you can to bring this person closer to you or take steps to prevent the development of a relationship as you see fit. You are headed for a very prosperous future and many blessings are coming to you and your family.

toy store You will enjoy many blessings and a variety of opportunities that will come to you within the week. These opportunities will greatly improve your life. You will also experience tranquility on all levels of your life, especially if you allow yourself to experience a variety of amusements.

trace *to search for a trace of something* It was acceptable, at one time, for you to behave and handle yourself in a particular way when in the presence of another person. Within three days this will all change. There is no longer any reason for you to put on this purposeful act in front of this person. Also, take steps to make use of a certain resource you have not focused on because you are used to taking it for granted.

to leave a trace indentation of writing or to see someone leave a trace or indentation of writing on a piece of paper, etc. Within three days you will become thrilled and overjoyed in a way you have never been before because of several unconnected occurrences that will take place almost simultaneously. You will enjoy greater success than you ever had in the past with very little effort. This will be a result of your motivation and of being in the right place at the right time. Follow your hunches and listen to your intuition. Expect to experience this for at least a month.

to search for a trace of anything Within three days you will begin to change your viewpoint about a certain matter that, at one time, was influenced by another person's way of thinking. Stay focused on your own desires and goals and do not allow another person's interfering comments to stand in your way. This will be a very productive cycle for you if you avoid outside interference.

to trace anything Opportunities you have long awaited will arrive within two days. You will be given a new start in life and all old issues that have been burdening you will be resolved. A new excitement and feeling of confidence will take over. Good luck is with you.

"without a trace" You will be overwhelmed with a sense of urgency to commit to someone who attracted your interests. If you choose to pursue this, you will enjoy a long term relationship filled with mutual joy.

tracheotomy Make sure you take your complaints to the right people, especially for the next three days. You may be under the impression that you are taking your dissatisfactions to the right place and will waste time by not being properly heard. Good luck is with you.

tracing paper Make sure you do not gravitate toward someone with a hidden past who does not reveal this to others, especially for the next three days. Do not become involved with this person and do not involve yourself with any unusual situation that may occur within the week.

track You are taking a situation that involves you and someone else for granted. This person is also assuming your casual, cool manner. Handle this in such a way that both of you can increase your involvement in this situation. If you choose, you can achieve success by not treating this issue so loosely.

to have someone track you down You will start to have a change of view within three days about a certain issue. You have, in the past, held this viewpoint because of the influence of another person's thinking. Remain focused on your own goals and desires and do not allow anyone else's interfering comments to stand in your way. This will be a very productive cycle for you if you stay away from outside interferences.

to see anything jump a track Do nothing for the next three days that will cast doubts on your love or fidelity.

one track mind Someone will lead you to believe they will take care of a certain situation for you at a specific time. Look for an alternative because this person will not come through for you in a timely fashion. Avoid the irritation that will result from this situation by seeking other avenues in which to handle this issue.

race track Do everything necessary to avoid accidents for the next three days. This is a very accident prone cycle. Get plenty of rest and stay alert. Find the tranquility you need to bring more balance into your life.

track and field Someone you know is in a certain place in their life where they feel burned out with a particular situation and at the point of wanting to give up. Meet with this person and suggest they take a small five day vacation. Encourage this person to take the time to replenish themselves, and to become more centered in order to avoid a complete burnout. Take an active role in this and you will benefit by not having to care for this individual. Many blessings will come to you and your family and you are headed for a prosperous future.

track lighting For the next four days you will enjoy a brilliant mentality and charm and will relentlessly apply yourself to achieve and grasp a golden opportunity. This will dramatically improve your life. This is also the perfect time to investigate new areas of opportunity and add new dimensions to your life. Good luck is with you. All negotiations regarding love and business will be very lucky for you right now. Make it a point to reconcile any relationship you want in your life. This cycle is perfect for bringing about the changes you desire and all relationships will work out as you wish. You will also experience an increase in prosperity. Any portion of this dream that portends a negative event needs to be attended to immediately. You will have the ability to do this within three days.

track record Make sure you take steps to avoid any involvements in family reunions that will take place in five days. You will find yourself involved in messy arguments and disagreements that will bring you emotional pain for some time. Avoid this completely. You are headed for a prosperous future.

tract house You will be the recipient of an unusual and rare offer within five days. Accept this offer and be grateful for this opportunity. You will also be the recipient of a gift or prize during this time period.

traction Remain flexible when dealing with situations that are difficult for another person. You will be able to offer light to this person when they are only seeing darkness and you will be able to bring normalcy to this situation.

if you are in traction Make sure you do everything necessary to keep this from occurring in reality, especially for the next three days. You have prior notice of this and can avoid any negative event. This dream also implies that confusion may arise when working on certain plans. Take the time to ensure these plans are being executed properly to avoid monetary loss. Be acutely aware of this and take steps to ensure any job situation does not cost you.

tractor Conversations you plan to have with someone you desire to bring close to you will not work to your advantage. Your imagination has led you to believe that what you say will be right but this person will take it the wrong way and distance will be created between you. Make sure, ahead of time, that what you are planning to say will come across the way you intended.

trade For the next three days all of your thoughts and imagination will be centered on someone you wish to make love to. You can, if you try, make this a reality because they also have an interest in you. Once you make the first move, this person will quickly become involved with you. You will find this to be a mutually exciting experience.

trade book Anyone you recognize from this dream is the

person who will bring assistance to you in order to meet a certain demand that will be very prosperous for you and change your lifestyle for the better. You will be lucky in love and finances.

trademark You need to be very aware of your stress levels. You will be spending a lot of time in certain areas of your life that will generate more stress than you are used to. Become very aware of this and take steps to protect yourself. This will be especially important for the next three days. Make sure nothing makes you desperate to the point of illness. Many blessings will come to you and your family.

trade name This is alerting you that you need to display a certain amount of special behavior toward someone you want to be close to. This will be someone you wish to be involved with. Do what you can to make this flow easily and you will quickly have this person involved in your life. You will also experience an abundance of health and well-being in this time frame.

trader Within three days someone will do what they can to involve you in some detective work. If you choose to do this you will find yourself enjoying many thrilling moments and cherish this time for life. Everything will turn out well and you will be paid a large amount of money for this type of work. This situation will be positive in all respects.

trading stamp For the next five days you will definitely have to push yourself to be successful. You will achieve success only to the degree you are focusing and pushing yourself. During this time period, do everything you can to follow the rules and regulations and stay very organized. You will receive exactly what you anticipate receiving. Everything will work out if you push yourself.

traffic Within five days, situations you are not focusing on will command your attention and you will be able to focus on acquiring items you desire and gain the knowledge of how to possess these things with no strings attached. You will be inspired during this cycle and will look at things optimistically. You will have an enormous amount of energy and be able to quickly turn situations around to your advantage. This cycle will be very prosperous in many ways.

traffic court For the next two weeks you will be sharing a great deal of time, filled with laughter and joy, with many new people. If this is what you choose to do, make sure you involve yourself appropriately so you can allow this to happen in your life. This will bring you new friendships that you can cherish for a long time to come. Any legal situation will also turn out to your advantage. Avoid doing anything that will result in a court appearance, especially for the next three days, otherwise you are headed for a prosperous future.

traffic island Make sure you do not overlook an urgent matter for the next two days.

traffic light Look up the color of the traffic light for a clearer meaning to this dream. Within five days you will also be able to grasp a once in a lifetime opportunity to meet the one person who is perfect for you and you will be able to develop a beautiful healthy relationship. You will both be able to gain great wealth and power, if you choose to take this path.

tragedy For a three day period, demonstrate the gentlest most positive side of your nature. Someone will be making a decision about you and it is important they see this part of you before they make up their mind.

trail Within four days you will need to examine both sides of a particular issue that is irritating someone. By doing this you will be able to successfully resolve this issue.

trailer You will assist someone who needs medical attention. This person will be grateful that you were there when they needed you and will quickly recover. This will occur within three days. This is also asking you to take steps to avoid or alter the outcome of any negative event you saw in this dream. For the next three days make sure you experience only positive expressions in your life. You will also have to speak up for someone within three weeks to ensure this person is not punished for something they did not do.

trailer park Begin, within two days, living your life to the fullest. Stop limiting and depriving yourself of life's pleasures. Fill your life with activities and make it a point to become more social for the next week.

train You need to think ahead and carefully regroup your thoughts before making a statement to someone. Statements and promises you make now will have to be kept so make sure you do not say anything you cannot stick with. Since you have prior notice of this, you will be able to handle yourself appropriately. You are headed for a prosperous future and many blessings will come to you and your family.

train wreck You will become very interested in someone who will not allow themselves to be with you because of your social or educational background. This is alerting you not to build up your hopes because this individual will be interested in you up to the point when they realize you do not have the background they expect from you. They will accept you as a friend but nothing more. You will also need to keep yourself safe and take steps to avoid any injury or accident during this time frame. Otherwise, you have a very brilliant future in front of you.

to be hit by a train/see someone hit by a train Take time to look at the complete picture and explore all the facts regarding an issue that will come up within three days. This will enable you to fully understand what is occurring and allow you to make the way you live your life the single most important issue to you right now. Proceed with confidence. You are on the path toward a brilliant future.

to see a train jump a track Do nothing for the next three days that will cast doubts on your love or fidelity.

wagon train Someone is very interested in you and very

eager for you to make the first move. You will be very surprised that when you do you will be welcomed with open arms. This also implies you are putting yourself on a new path that will bring you an abundance of health and healthy relationships. You are definitely headed for a prosperous future.

trainee Do not procrastinate in asking for the assistance you need to pursue a particular goal. Do not allow yourself to be intimidated.

trainer Take steps to prevent anything negative in this dream from becoming a reality and make sure positive experiences are allowed to develop fully. You will also enjoy a clean break in those areas of your life that you desire. As a result, within three days you will be going through some unusual and extraordinary events. These events are out of your control and will bring improved changes to your life. Move quickly and you will be pleased with the effects these changes will have on your life. You will enjoy enormous wealth and an improved standard of living.

training school Make sure you behave appropriately in reaction to someone else's behavior. This is extremely important because you will have a tremendous effect on how others receive this person. Be very careful of the image you project of this individual. Your opinions could set this person up for life. You are headed for a lucky seven day cycle.

tram You will have to work with someone who is very hard to get along with. Before you make a move, make sure you know exactly what you have to do to make sure you are not overloaded. This is especially important for the next three days.

tramp Do everything necessary for the next three days to maintain your self confidence. Become very bold and aggressive and do not involve yourself in anything you have very little knowledge of. You must also take steps to prevent any negative event in this dream from becoming a reality in your own life. Do everything in your power to ensure you have only positive experiences.

trampoline Explore the unpredictable and unexpected. Make sure you are self reliant and able to gravitate to new changes that will occur in your life. Many blessings are with you and your family.

tranquility Do not deny yourself moments of great pleasure for the next two days and do everything you can to bring more simplicity and tranquility into your life.

transaction You are entering a very disturbing life cycle. It will soon become more tranquil for you. Someone is also very interested in you but is very cautious about the level of commitment they want to involve themselves in. Give this person some time and you will find they will soon be eager to surrender to you. Good luck is with you and this will be a

tremendous cycle for love. Any negative transaction you dream of needs to be prevented in reality. For the next three days, do everything you can to experience only positive expressions in your life.

transcendental meditation Pay closer attention to your health and protect yourself from any health hazards, especially for the next three days. Pay attention, also, to your loved ones. Older people often need love and attention more than younger people. Within three days you may have to do something for an older person to make their life easier. Good luck is with you and an abundance of tranquility will be with you and your family for a long time to come. All business and love negotiations will also be very lucky for you now. Make it a point to reconcile with anyone you wish to renew a relationship with. This is the perfect cycle for this and for bringing an increase in prosperity to your life. Take steps to avoid or alter any negative experience foretold in this dream. You will have the ability to do this for the next three days.

transcript Remain very focused, for the next five days, on important relationships so you can behave in the appropriate manner to ensure those relationships that are important to you remain close and healthy. This is also alerting you to change any negative event foretold in this dream within this five day cycle.

transfer Anything connected to this dream that represents a negative event needs to be turned around in reality. Take every precaution to allow only positive expressions to take place in your life. For the next three days make sure those who come to you to debate about a wrong they have committed do not suck you into an argument. This will start out being a casual conversation but will escalate to the point of becoming a danger to you. Be acutely aware of this situation in order to avoid verbal and physical abuse. The moment you see this start to evolve, remove yourself from the situation. Play it safe and protect yourself. Proceed with extreme caution.

transform This will offer you a clue of what needs to be transformed in your own life and you must take steps to bring these changes to full bloom. Within five days you will also overcome a long term financial burden. You will find an easy way to free yourself from this.

to transform yourself into something different This is offering you an important revelation because your spirit is alerting you that this is the character or personality that you will take on and project to others within four days. You will take on the positive power and respect of this particular animal, etc., or an attitude that may or may not be to your liking. Pay attention to any word spoken at the time of transformation that may lead to a clue to something you wish to pursue or to divorce yourself from. You have the time to prevent anything negative you dreamed about and turn it into a positive event or bring any positive event to full bloom. Anyone else you dream of should be alerted to do the same.

Do not stray from your priorities or goals until they are completely resolved. You will enjoy tranquility within the family structure and live a long and healthy life.

someone else transforming themself into something else This is alerting you that this person has transformed themselves to find out if their hidden plans are workable and whether they will come through to their advantage. Do not take this for granted because this could be a painful and humiliating experience. You have prior notice of this and can take steps to avoid it. This could also be referring to an event you do not want to miss because it could bring you many advantages. Make sure you seek out the clues that have been left behind so for the next five days you can avoid anyone who could bring about a stressful time in your life. Your spirit will leave behind clues to who this person is because the disguised person will always leave a trace of their identity through their character, clothing, speech, mannerisms, jewelry, etc. Your spirit will heighten your sense of intuition. The spirit could also have disguised itself to alert you to something you may or may not want in your life. Eliminate any negative expression and allow only positive expressions in your life.

to see yourself, someone or something transforming into something magical Look up the particular object for more profound clues to the meaning of this dream. This is an extremely lucky omen. For the next month you will enjoy an abundance of health and financial security because unusual circumstances will take place that will allow this to occur. Do not limit yourself or deprive yourself of unique experiences and involvements that will come up within five days. Enjoy your life fully, eat healthy foods, drink plenty of water and get plenty of rest. Life will reward you handsomely not only in a financial sense but spiritually as well.

if this transformation was into something that was not magical Look up the animal, whoever, or whatever this person was transformed into for further clues. If this person turned into something distasteful to you, they will take on the power and character of what they transformed themselves into. You have the time to make a decision ahead of time about whether you wish to involve yourself with this individual. You will have the strength and courage to deal with this for the next three days and will be able to maintain a stress free environment during this time. You will also be able to handle anything you felt was an impossibility and will be able to bring this to a successful conclusion. You are headed for a prosperous future and your intuition is right on target.

transformer Within three days you will be introduced to an exciting, exotic person who will show you a new way of life. You will find this new lifestyle very enjoyable if you choose to involve yourself.

transistor You will be witness to an episode that will reveal how another person can create chaos in the lives of others because of their behavior. This will occur when discussing a business arrangement you have made with a certain individual involving a task of some kind they have agreed to do for you. Another opposite sexed person will enter the scene and start making changes in your plans to suit their purposes. This person will bully themselves into the conversation in such a way that it will be difficult for you to take control. Do everything you can to avoid making compromises. You have prior notice of this and can successfully avoid it.

translation Within three days you will find yourself involved in a situation with someone who speaks the language you heard translated in this dream. This may also be alerting you to a place you may wish to go or need to avoid depending on the contents of this dream. In addition, this will give you a message of something you will either need to avoid in your life or bring to full bloom. This implies as well that the person you wish to get close to will suddenly come around and show you more love and appreciation. You will see a big change in this person's behavior within three days.

translator Pay attention to what is being translated. This will offer you a major clue to the meaning of this dream. You will be involved with someone who speaks this language and you are being alerted to an area you may wish to visit or avoid, depending on the contents of the dream. This will provide you with a message of something you either will wish to avoid or bring to fruition and implies that for the upcoming month you will have the clarity of thought needed to guide you through situations that will require you to take risks and extend yourself. Display boldness so the thoughts you have can be brought to tangible form. You will experience more prosperous times in your life. Focus on your goals and be tenacious. You are headed in the right direction.

transmission A strange uncontrollable desire will overcome you. Take steps to control your behavior for the next two days. This desire could lead to a very regrettable action on your part.

transmitter What you hear over the transmitter represents a major clue to a future event. If it is negative, take all the necessary steps to either prevent its occurrence or turn it into a positive situation. If positive, make sure you include it into your life. This also implies that someone has a problem they want to place on your shoulders. They feel like you should be responsible for resolving this problem for them. Do everything you can to avoid becoming involved in this situation.

transparency Regardless of anything else that is going on in your life, this is a promise that unusual circumstances will take place that will vastly improve your life. Within two weeks you will see this situation start to develop. It will have a major impact on your life and will bring you prosperity. Motivate yourself so this can become a part of your life more quickly.

transplant You will enjoy long lasting joy and find love with those you never noticed existed. You will also experience a new spiritual awareness. From this point on, you will become more optimistic and experience a new joy from unusual occurrences you have never experienced before. You are definitely going in the right direction. Whatever you were transplanting will offer you a clue to something you will either wish to include in your life or avoid.

transport Make sure you change any negative event you saw in this dream or avoid its occurrence. You will also be invited to an event within three days that you should attend. Make sure you mark this on your calendar because by the time this event takes place, you will have so much going on in your life you may want to overlook it. If you attend, you will reap many major benefits.

transportation *to be left with no transportation* This is alerting your personality that any rejection you experience with your relationships that causes you pain implies you are going in the wrong direction. Your spirit is letting you know you are placing too much importance and focus on a person instead of what you should be placing it on. The rage and disappointments you feel about not having your demands met or the non-involvement you feel from other people or one individual needs to be rechanneled into areas of your life that will allow you to grow and evolve (i.e., education, hobbies, etc.). Allow this person the privacy they need to evolve and they will come to you. Remember that just because this individual is not with you constantly or is not responding to your requests does not imply they do not care for you. Stop setting yourself for disappointment and pain. Lighten up, stop clinging so much and motivate yourself to add more joyous events to your life. Any negative event seen in this dream can also be turned around to a positive situation. You are the only person who is responsible for motivating yourself to achieve success.

to have your transportation broken down For the next three days do everything you can to avoid becoming seriously ill due to travel to an unfamiliar area where you are not properly prepared for the weather conditions. You must also make sure you are very aware of the threat of food poisoning and take steps to prevent it. Make sure you avoid any situation that will leave you without transportation.

trap Take steps to keep any negative event in this dream from becoming a reality. Make sure you only experience prosperity and positive experiences in your life. For the next three days practice preventive medicine and drive defensively to avoid causing any accident.

trap door Be aware of a well thought out plot to commit a robbery at a party within seven days. All guests will be robbed of valuables and money. Do everything necessary to avoid this party and warn the other guests.

trap door spider The person you will flirt with, within two days, will find this behavior very offensive. Step back and adjust your behavior so you do not suffer rejection. This person is not interested in you.

trapeze For the next three days you will be able to success-

fully negotiate all business transactions and will be able to bring closeness into those relationships you desire. You will also need to take steps to alter any negative message in this dream and change it into a positive experience. This is especially important for the next three days.

trapper Learn to change your manner in such a way that you can face the world with confidence and optimism. Everything you once felt was impossible is now possible. You can expect a prosperous life to start developing within five days.

trappist monk Do everything you can to make younger people feel more comfortable in your presence and make sure all their needs are met, especially for the next three days.

trapshooting Carefully watch the way your behavior changes when you are around someone who enjoys pushing your buttons. This person enjoys making you feel anxious or angry for their own personal gratification and pleasure. Do not allow yourself to feed on this behavior and do not allow your personality to change as a result of this manipulation.

trash Do not put yourself in the position to feel your rights are violated in any manner, especially for the next three days. Remain focused and stay alert during this time period.

trash can Within three days someone will enter your life eager to have a friendly relationship. As time goes by you will begin to receive mixed messages and this person will begin to hint at a romantic involvement. You will be wasting your time because this person is only playing games with you and seeks only a short term involvement. Enjoy yourself and get on with your life. Do not compromise your own desires during this time period and you will be able to grasp deep emotional fulfillment.

wastepaper basket Within three days you will become aware of the deep emotional feelings you have for another. Because of this enlightenment you will quickly want to surrender yourself to this person. Expect nothing but the best from this relationship. You will be emotionally fulfilled in this union. Tranquility and mutual understanding will be yours if you choose to go this route. Pay attention to the contents of the wastepaper basket and if it portends a negative event, take steps to alter the outcome or avoid the event altogether. Proceed with confidence. Many blessings are with you and your family.

trauma Practice optimism, especially in front of someone who acts as though they are better than you because they have more. Do not allow this person to intimidate you. If you do not fawn over this person, you will gain their respect for a lifetime. They will desire romantic involvement and ultimately desire a union. This involvement will be up to you but if you choose this path, you will both enjoy many beautiful moments together as well as the finest things money can buy. Many blessings are with you and your family.

travel Take the necessary precautions to prevent any negative event from becoming a reality. You have the time to change this and to experience only positive expressions in your life. This also implies you will achieve your highest ambitions in life. This will start to evolve within three days. You will develop an upright style of living and enjoy a confident attitude toward life. Be true and kind to yourself, especially for the next three days.

travel agency For some time someone has been plotting a way to get something from you they desire. You have prior notice of this and can take steps to avoid manipulation. Expect this to occur within three days.

traveler's check You will be dealing with someone within three days who will be conducting a business transaction with you. This individual will make an agreement to pay you a certain amount per month. For the first three or four months this person will pay you in a timely fashion but as time goes on they will have problems meeting their payments. You have prior notice and can decide whether you want to deal with this. Take steps to prevent any negative event in this dream from becoming a reality. Otherwise, you are headed for a very prosperous future.

traveling salesman Someone you know who lives in a distant place has an urgent need to see you simply because they want to see you. Someone else also feels a conversation with you is overdue and they have not had the time they need with you. This person will aggressively seek out time with you. If you take the time to talk with this person you will find the conversation will lead to something that will bring you prosperity.

travelogue For the next five days you will have to use a very daring approach to urge someone to do something for themself that can only be done by them. This also implies that, if you choose, someone wonderful will enter your life within three days who will provide you with an opportunity for romance and glamorous evenings. This person has a fantastic approach to life. You will also develop strong reasoning powers and be very focused on what you need from life, especially for the next five days. You are headed for a prosperous and healthy future.

travois For the next three days make sure that when you communicate a particular situation to someone they fully understand what you are trying to say. This will prevent misunderstandings at a later time.

tray Within two days be sure you affirm the needs of those who are waiting for this in order to lessen their stress levels. Be considerate to those who are important to you and be consistent in your behavior. This will bring your life the balance you need within five days.

treacle Within five days someone will want to visit you for a few days but they are not living the lifestyle they choose.

They will want to stay with you because they know you will treat them with respect. The problems this person is having at the moment will not be verbalized but it will be clear that something is wrong. Back off and allow them to choose the right time to open up, otherwise you will drive them away and be unable to offer the assistance they need. Good luck is with you.

tread Someone you know possesses great power and authority and is in the position to pull strings on your behalf. Do not act timid and do everything necessary within three days to ask this person for their help. This is a very lucky cycle and you are on the right path.

treadmill A professional person you seek services from will come on to you sexually and attempt to intimidate you into becoming involved with them. This will occur within three days. It is up to you to decide whether you want to have a sexual encounter and never see this person again or whether you want to avoid this altogether. This person will not follow through in contacting you later. You have prior notice of this and can handle yourself in an appropriate manner. Many blessings are with you and your family.

treason Within three days you will receive unusual offers from someone you least expect and achieve victory in those areas of your life you least expect. This will result in great changes and an improved lifestyle.

treasurer A very unusual and extraordinary event will occur that will bring you unexpected wealth. This will take place within three days and will come from a very stable source.

treasury For the next three days you need to think ahead so you will not be placed in a position that requires excessive physical labor. Take good care of yourself. This is an extremely lucky omen and you will enjoy improved health and an improved lifestyle. You will also meet someone who will be very protective of you and your well being. This will come at a time when you will be most appreciative of it. You are headed for a very prosperous future.

treasury bond Within five days you need to create the perfect atmosphere for success. Decide on those areas of your life that need more organization. If you desire, you will also be aggressively pursued for romance and affection and will be surrounded by those who are loyal and affectionate to you.

treat For the next five days have a camera ready to capture a pleasurable moment when it arises. You must also make sure your equipment is in perfect working order so you will not be disappointed when the opportunity arises. This will be a very lucky cycle for you and your family, especially for the next seven days.

treaty Pay close attention to what you will be hearing within three days. What you are not being told will be instrumental in determining your decisions and will bring your attention to what you need to be handling in your life. This is the time to aggressively seek out this missing information so you will be able to make the correct decisions.

treble You need to stand up for your rights. Someone has made a promise that they will come through for you at a certain date. This person will try to back out of this at a later time. Make sure you bear down on this person relentlessly the moment it looks as though they will not come through for you. Do not waste time. Push them to come through in a timely fashion. Since you have prior notice of this, you can choose an alternative person in order to avoid unnecessary stress.

tree For the next three days you will be able to competently handle rough tasks. Because of your relentless dedication, you will be rewarded with error free work.

to plant Make sure that when you offer assistance to another person you have all the details and information necessary to give proper advice. All referrals given should be checked first to ensure accuracy. The plans you have set in motion should be reviewed in detail to ensure this is being properly handled.

tree in bloom The person you desire will show more affection and love toward you than ever before, especially in public. This will result in the enjoyment of the beauty of life.

tree farm Give yourself a break from outside interference and from the influences of others. Give yourself some solitude and free time in order to develop clarity of thought. Do this within five days and you will be able to make all the correct decisions.

tree frog Someone will openly flirt with you at an unexpected place and time. If you decide to pursue this, romance will flourish and you will get exactly what you want from a romantic situation. You will be very lucky in all negotiations regarding business and love.

tree house Within five days bring a situation to the attention of others along with specific facts. Insist that a resolution be brought about at a specific time that is agreed upon by everyone involved. You will be able to bring this about very successfully.

tree of knowledge Certain situations will occur within five days that you will need to immediately get to the bottom of to put a stop to before they develop to their full potential. This cycle will allow you to uncover all of those things that need to be addressed.

tree of life You will be the object of another person's affection and this person will focus on you for the next three days. You will enjoy every moment of it and whatever happens next will be up to you. The cards are in your hand and you can push this in any direction you choose to go. This also

implies you need to focus on those areas of life you want to see changes in. This is the perfect cycle for this and opportunities will come to you in abundance. Make sure you take advantage of them and turn your life around in those areas you most desire. Proceed with confidence. You will experience good health and many blessings will come to you and your family.

tree shrew You need to bear down on a certain individual the moment you suspect they will not come through with their part of an agreement. Do not waste time on this and make sure this person will come through for you in the time period they said they would. This may involve a few uncomfortable moments and anger that you will have to control. You will be successful if you control your emotions.

tree squirrel Do not allow your time to be wasted by the nonsense of others. Develop a no nonsense approach to life and create a stress free environment for yourself.

tree surgeon The opportunities you have been waiting for will come to you within five days. You will then be given a chance to make a new start in those areas of life you most desire. You will have the chance to develop and implement your plans in a professional way and enjoy more prosperity in your life.

treetop Make sure it is correct to make a romantic move toward another person. This person is interested in someone else and it may be inappropriate and embarrassing to make a move in this direction. Protect yourself.

trellis You will be able to effectively communicate with those you feel are intimidating for you to approach. You will have the confidence to go through this and will effectively communicate what you desire. Take all the necessary steps to prevent any negative event you saw in this dream from becoming a reality. Do what you can to allow only positive experiences to occur in your life. This also implies that any lingering doubts that have been plaguing you will disappear within the week. You are headed for a prosperous future.

tremor Push yourself to achieve the goals you have been pursuing. Your success will depend on your willingness to motivate yourself to reach these goals. You must also make it a point to associate only with people you find delightful to be around for the upcoming month. Make no allowances for anyone you feel you have a duty to see and associate only with people you feel comfortable being around. If you do not, you will have many distasteful moments.

trench You will be delighted when someone shows their true feelings toward you. You will have all the evidence you need to know that this person is in love with you and this will leave you with a feeling of excitement. This is destined to occur and if you choose to go along with it, do everything necessary to allow this to develop naturally, otherwise take steps to avoid this completely. Pay close attention to what was taking place that you need to change in reality. Allow only positive experiences in your life.

trench coat For the next two days do everything you can to become very self reliant and make the effort to look at both sides of an issue. Explore every possibility of what could take place before you make any major decisions. You are loved beyond your imagination, are deeply respected by others and will be surrounded by those who care about you. Expect those you care about to show their appreciation within the week.

trench mouth Be very aware of your surroundings and play it safe. Someone will start to doubt you and look for reasons why they feel this way about you. Do not allow any negative attitudes and thoughts to eat away at your confidence and control your imagination. Do not look for a quick fix that will allow you to ignore the facts of what is really going on. Work on releasing these negative thoughts and do not allow your imagination to run rampant.

trespass Someone will aggressively pursue you in a romantic way and will verbalize this in such a way that there is no mistaking their intentions. If you choose to become involved, do not allow this person's aggressiveness to scare you to the point that you do not want to continue a relationship. It is better to verbalize what is making you uncomfortable so this person can better accommodate you. You will then be able to enjoy yourself fully with this person.

trestle Someone will promise to pay you a certain amount of money by a certain time and will agree to come across with a certain amount of money as scheduled. After this agreement has been made, this person will want to go back on this promise. Bear down on them in a nonviolent way. During this cycle you will determine the appropriate way to handle this person so they will deliver this money in a timely fashion.

trial Do not openly display your emotions to someone who does not appreciate it, especially for the next three days. Be acutely aware of this to avoid disappointment and embarrassment.

triangle This is an extremely lucky omen. You are definitely headed for a brilliant future and will enjoy more prosperity for the next month. You will accomplish as much as you desire for the next two days regarding a situation you want to get moving on.

tribe Do whatever you have to do to set aside time to experience solitude and quiet. Experience the tranquil peace of that particular moment. Love yourself deeply, get plenty of rest and find a quiet out of the way place where you can just enjoy yourself. Pamper yourself, eat healthier foods, and drink plenty of water. You are headed for a brilliant future.

triceps Be acutely aware of someone who is very conniving and evil minded. This will be someone you least expect and they will do everything in their power to do you emotional harm. Do not allow yourself to be placed in a situation where someone can take advantage of you, especially for the next five days. Be very protective of yourself and of your belongings.

triceratops Carefully analyze your life and decide what you need to stop doing or being involved with. You are also overlooking something that needs prompt attention in order for everything to fall into place as you desire. It is important that you do this within three days. You will be successful and are headed for a brilliant future.

trichinosis Within five days someone you feel comfortable with will very slowly and subtly begin to detach themselves from you. Although you have done nothing wrong, this person harbors a great deal of anger and resentment towards you. Allow this to take place gracefully and give this individual an easy way out. If you do not, they will stay in your life, create many distasteful moments, and be unable to avoid blurting out hurtful words. Get on with your life without this person in it.

trick You will take a leadership position within three days and everyone will rely fully on you. You will be able to handle everything with courage and confidence. Any negative message that comes through in this dream needs to be turned around and altered so you will enjoy only positive expressions in your life. If you recognize anyone in this dream, it is a lucky omen. You will be able to purchase a luxury item you have had your eye on. This person will be very instrumental in your ability to acquire this item.

trickle Within three days you will locate an object you have been hoping to acquire. This is a good cycle to look in different locales for this particular item. You will be lucky in finding it. During this cycle you will also enjoy a good sense of humor.

trick or treat Take every precaution to prevent anything in this dream that you choose not to occur in reality from occurring. It is also very important, for the next three days, to let someone who is important in your life know they are more important than any material item and nothing will ever take their place.

tricycle Within five days you will have the chance to cater to someone of a different ethnic background. Because of your hard work, ability to handle certain issues with tact and diplomacy, and your eagerness to please, doors will be open to you on a permanent basis. Opportunities will come your way and you will experience an increase in income. Good luck is with you.

trident It would be to your advantage for the next three days to strengthen the bonds in your relationships. Become more involved in order to experience harmony and tranquility.

trifle Guard your property and become very territorial. Take care of your health and make sure you drink plenty of water.

trigger Treat yourself in special ways that will make you feel fantastic on an emotional level. This will make you enjoy being alive. Experience the marrow of life. This will allow the path you need to take to come to you faster and easier. You are headed for a brilliant future.

trigger finger Someone will feel great excitement when in your presence and you will savor these moments. Expect this to occur within five days. Proceed with confidence. This person is prepared to enjoy a new lift in life with a special person in their life. Many blessings are with you and you can experience many days of good health.

trigonometry Express your deepest emotions to another within ten days. Proceed with confidence and expect wonderful and fantastic things to occur.

trillion For the next three weeks you will have nothing to complain about. Everything will fall into place exactly as you wish. You will find stability in anything you choose to become involved with and all negotiations will fall into place exactly as you have envisioned. You are definitely headed for a brilliant future.

trim Someone is depending on you to come up with the correct answers to certain situations that need to be taken care of. Motivate yourself, for the next week, to take the leadership role in certain situations. Other people expect this and you will be able to handle everything successfully.

Trinidad You will, within two weeks, have an irresistible urge to visit an exotic locale. You will be able to fulfill this urge and enjoy yourself immensely. You will have a safe trip, have memories you will savor for a lifetime, and will spend very little. This may also be used as a reference point in time. If you dream of this island and see its name used in any context, the dream message will occur on this day.

trinity You will soon be able to grasp your goals. You will also be dealing with two different situations concurrently that will bring you much luck and prosperity. Make sure you handle both issues. You will want to overlook one of them in order to focus on the other but it is important to focus on both of these issues equally. Do not lose your confidence. You are headed for a brilliant future and a very tranquil time.

trinket Within five days you will acquire greater clarity of thought and will be able to develop a plan that will bring you greater prosperity. Prepare yourself carefully regarding a certain situation, trust your instincts and behave appropriately in order to put yourself at an advantage.

to lose a trinket Someone you do not know will purposely attempt to provoke a fight with you in public. Do everything you can to protect yourself when in public places, especially for the next five days.

to be given a trinket Trust your heart and let others know your true feelings, especially for the next ten days.

to give a trinket Within the week you will be able to rid yourself of troublesome situations. You will be able to work at your highest level to ensure everything will be resolved successfully. You will have the calmness and flexibility to work in this manner. Go for it.

trip You will vastly improve your situation within three days if you are determined to do so. Good luck is with you.

tripe For the next three days do not waste time deciding which way you want to go. Regroup and rethink, but whatever you decide, do it quickly.

triplane Meditate in your favorite form and your prayers will be answered, regardless of how impossible your requests are.

triple sec Someone is pursuing you simply for sexual pleasures. You are being made aware of this ahead of time and can decide if this is the type of relationship you want. You will become aware of this within three days.

triplets Someone is seeking exactly what you seek in an emotional involvement. You will enjoy complete power in decision making when it comes to this relationship. Everything you felt was impossible in the past is now possible. You are headed for a brilliant future.

triskelion This implies real forward progress on any path you take.

trivia Be very conscious of your environment and take steps to protect yourself from freak accidents. You must also be very careful not to over medicate yourself.

troglodyte For the next weeks make sure you deal only with facts and not just with what you choose to believe. Face facts and get on with your life.

Trojan horse Your intuition will be right on target regarding financial matters and with anything that deals with business negotiations. You will be tremendously successful by following your own counsel, especially for the next three days. Proceed with confidence, you are headed for a brilliant future.

Trojan war You will enjoy a big family feast and everyone will be united for this occasion. Close friends and loved ones will be attending. This will occur unexpectedly within three weeks and will be a grand occasion. Harmony and joy will be prevalent at this festive event. Many blessings are with you and your family.

troll You will gain a position in the public eye, attract many honors, and be well liked by everyone. You will be able to motivate yourself in such a way that you will be able to achieve a great deal in a short period of time. This is also a magical time for you to demonstrate your talents to the fullest. You will go through a thorough and relentless process to have the right people view your talents and to get the support system and backing you need. You will gain success, especially during this time cycle. This is an extremely lucky omen and will be for some time to come. Many blessings are with you and you are headed for a brilliant future.

to see a troll behaving in a devious or an evil manner Closely attend to certain matters that will begin to develop within the week. These issues will ultimately have a profound effect on your life and you will be destined to alter your life as a result of these situations. You are in danger of being steered in the wrong direction. The control someone exerts over the decisions you make will be the cause of this misdirection. You will get the feeling you are immobilized and incapable of moving forward in life. You will also get the feeling you have no control over the decisions other people will make in your life. You must also be very careful of what you say to others because your words will be used against you as a further means of control. Since you have prior notice of this, you can take steps to steer your life in a more positive direction. Do not allow yourself to become vulnerable by not acting on your own behalf. This will result in emotional depletion and you will be steered in a direction you have no wish to go. Get your point across to those who are in positions of power and authority. Make sure you do not become involved in everyday stresses that will result from the decisions others make for you who have no business being involved in your life. You are in danger of surrendering control of your decision making. Do everything you can to avoid unhealthy relationships and unusual circumstances. Be very suspicious of all changes. Develop confidence, muster up the courage you need, and be relentless in making changes in your life that will put you on the correct path. You have the power to change any negative aspect of your life and make the necessary changes to ensure you experience only positive events. Play it safe, make sure all of your bases are covered and practice common sense. You will be able to successfully carry out all of your plans successfully and will put yourself on the path of prosperity.

trolley/trolley car Someone will become very interested in you within five days. As time goes by, this person will find it difficult to control their obsessive and possessive behavior around you. Do everything necessary to go on with your life without dealing with this behavior. You will also meet a wonderful person within three days you will spend hours talking to. This person is gentle and generous and you will find you have much in common. You will also find you have had similar events occur in your life at approximately the same time and you share common hobbies and amusements. You will have a strong desire to continue this conversation at a later time and if you choose, you have the op-

tion to make this relationship far more lasting and meaningful. You will enjoy many delightful social moments for the next seven days. Any negative event connected with this dream needs to be altered or avoided altogether. You have plenty of time to make sure you only experience positive events in your life. This is an extremely lucky omen and this luck will remain with you for the next week.

trollop Take steps to keep any negative event foretold in this dream from becoming a reality, especially for the next seven days. Use this advance knowledge to experience only positive expressions in your life. You are loved beyond your imagination and will be treated in a very special way with an open show of affection. You are headed for a prosperous future.

trombone Do not pay attention to any mystery situations. Play it cool and everything will work out to your advantage. Do not allow your imagination to run wild. You will also enjoy good health and wealth for the next month. Many blessings will come to you and your family.

troop/trooper A deep plot is developing without your knowledge. Be aware of any unusual situation for the next three days and play detective to determine the nature of this plot. You will become aware of what is going on during this cycle.

troopship Return to basics and practice simplicity in your life, especially for the next five days. Regardless of what else is going on around you, do not become more involved than you already are and do what you can to clear up what you are now involved in so you can have more leisure time.

trophy Be very alert, you are about to make a mistake. You are very fond of someone who likes you in a special way. Do not take any relationship for granted. For this particular time period you need to be more communicative and more open to those who are special to you. Make sure you make special time for those you care about.

tropical fish Within the week an abundance of health and wealth will come your way. This also implies that a certain situation will take place that will require you to use aggressive behavior. You will act accordingly and this issue will quickly be resolved.

tropical rain forest You will enjoy great clarity regarding the new dimension you are pointing yourself toward. This will bring you tranquility and pleasures beyond your belief. In the past, you have felt it was beyond your ability to move in the direction you desired but now you have a renewed confidence in your abilities. You will move quickly and achieve what you are after. Within the week, you will have the feeling of being solidly grounded and will develop a sense of balance and confidence. As a result, you will be able to tackle certain situations that require these traits. Use this cycle to change those areas of your life you want to alter.

You will have the chance to bring prosperity into your life at the level you desire. You are headed for a brilliant future.

tropical storm You will have a better chance of reconciling with someone special if you act within three days. This also implies you will enjoy a quick response to your request for specific information.

tropics Do not allow yourself to spend more than you should, particularly because of the manipulative behavior of another. Do what you can to keep this from happening, especially for the next week.

troubadour Make sure you keep something from happening that should not occur at an unreasonable hour. Remain alert and play it safe, especially for the next three days.

troublemaker Make sure you do not put yourself in the position to be terrorized at the hands of another. This person will insist that you come to show them something of value you are selling or will insist that you come see something of value that you wish to purchase. Be very careful, this is a situation that could be life threatening. Be acutely aware of your surroundings and of the situations you will be putting yourself into, especially for the next three days.

troubleshooter Take steps now to defend yourself financially so that for the next month you will be able to handle yourself very well. This will enable you to avoid the stress of not being able to make ends meet.

trousers Someone will borrow something from you within three days with the promise that they will return it in a timely fashion. If you don't stay on top of this you will never get it back. You have the choice to either consistently remind this person to bring it back or opt not to lend it out in the first place. Be very protective of your belongings, especially for the next three days. Many blessings are with you and your family.

trousseau This is an extremely lucky omen. Within five days you will experience an abundance of tranquility, health, and harmony with family members and friends. Good luck is with you.

trout This is an extremely lucky omen and this luck will stay with you for the month. It also implies you will have a long and healthy life with your family. It is also important to avoid feeling discouraged over a relationship you are interested in becoming involved in. Let yourself feel free to pursue this. Do whatever it takes to regain your aggressiveness and boldness in order to handle yourself in the appropriate manner. You will then be able to acquire the affection and love you desire. This is very important for the next five days. Do not deflate your ego by replaying old negative tapes.

trowel Do not demand so much of yourself and do not discuss your financial status with someone you do not know

very well. Meditate in your favorite form and do what you can to bring more laughter and joy into your life. You will experience more amusements and light hearted times for the next week. You are doing the correct things for yourself.

Troy You will learn of an inheritance that will bring you a great deal of anxiety before you receive it. Aggressively and relentlessly go after what is righteously yours because you are destined to receive this bequest. You are headed for a long and prosperous future. You will enjoy good health and many blessings will come to you and your family. This may also be used as a reference point in time. If you dream of this ancient city and see its name used in any context, the dream message will occur on this day.

truancy For the next five days make sure you do not involve yourself in a situation because you feel you are obligated to. Gain more information about what you will be involved with before you proceed. Any involvement would be your disadvantage.

truant officer Concentrate on your finances and detail each move you make. You will need a greater cash flow within two weeks than you have anticipated. Take steps now to make sure you have the extra cash needed to reduce the stress that a deficit would cause. Otherwise, you are headed for a brilliant future.

truck Exciting revelations will take place within three days. Each difficult and mundane situation will turn around and you will get the sense that everything is healing and you will be satisfied with the outcome. Agreements will also be made among people who once could not reach an understanding with each other.

filled You will hear word that someone you know will definitely be moving away. An abundance of opportunities will also come your way within five days that you can choose from to bring more perfection to your life. Many blessings will come to you and your family.

empty Someone who, at one time, decided on their own and without your knowledge that they were not interested in becoming a part of your life in any capacity has had a change of heart. This person now wants to explore the possibility of opening up a relationship on some level. You have the opportunity and the choice now to decide whether this is something you want to become involved in. You will also hear some good news and receive a small gift. You will experience much pleasure at this time.

tanker truck For the next three days any negotiation you enter into will be enormously successful. Be very diligent and effectively handle your responsibilities. Do not rely on someone else who is less experienced than you to handle your responsibilities.

truck driver You will be the target for romantic affection. This will appeal to you for the next two days. If you should pursue this, you will be happy for a lifetime.

pick-up truck A relaxing getaway will produce wonders for your imagination. You will enjoy an abundance of creative thought.

in any other form This is a good cycle to tackle any big issue you need to take care of. The outcome will be more favorable to you at this time. Someone also has a great need to discuss with you the details of an ongoing situation they are involved in. It is important you put aside time for this within three days.

Truckee Someone who has a tremendous amount of expertise in an area you are interested in will be happy to take you under their wing and relentlessly teach you a specific skill until you have it down perfectly. You are headed for a prosperous future. This may also be used as a reference point in time. If you dream of this city and see its name used in any context, the dream message will occur on this day.

trucker Do not give up any private intimate time for the next three days thinking that something else is more important. Guard this as well as the private time you spend for yourself. Others will soon get the impression that you are not available emotionally for anyone. Focus yourself, regroup and rethink in order to aggressively protect this area of your life.

truck farmer Focus on your specific desires so you can have them met during this cycle.

truck stop Take aggressive steps to leave behind certain aspects of your life that you have outgrown and replace them with new involvements so you can develop and grow in areas that will bring new and improved changes to your life. You are headed for a prosperous future.

true-false test Do not demand so much of yourself, especially in those areas where you lack certain knowledge and skills. Be acutely aware of this behavior for the next two days.

truffle For the next five days make sure you do not involve yourself in certain situations just because you feel an obligation. Gain more information about what you will be involved with before you take the next step. It would be better if you do not get involved; it would not be to your advantage.

trump card You will unexpectedly rise to a higher level in life than you ever envisioned within a two week period. You will experience an abundance of productivity, an increased income and productive conversations. You will be surrounded by very loyal and affectionate people and others will express a desire to be a part of your plans and goals. These people will wish to assist you and impart the wisdom they have acquired as well as anything else you wish to learn. This will be of special importance to you for the next five days. You are headed for a brilliant future and will enjoy an abundance of health in a shorter period of time than you expected.

Trump, Donald This will give you a clue to something you will either wish to avoid or bring to fruition, and also implies

that, for the next month, you will have the clear and brilliant thoughts you need to guide yourself successfully through certain situations. These issues will require you to take risks and extend yourself. Demonstrate a bold and courageous demeanor so these thoughts can be brought to tangible form. As a result you will experience more prosperity in life, both financially and health wise. Focus on your goals and be tenacious. You are headed in the right direction.

trumpet You are channeling your energies in the wrong direction and this will be especially apparent for the next three days. Listen to your intuition before you make the next move and do not be so quick to jump into the unknown. Analyze your feelings for the next week to ensure you are experiencing what you feel you should. All group activities will also bring more joy into your life and bring you a wealth of new activities you will enjoy immensely.

trumpet flower Do not allow yourself to become sidetracked or to ignore someone who is important to you because before you know it, time will have slipped away. Within seven days, it is important to develop fun things you can do with a special person. Be sure to plan special outings, events and games you can enjoy together. Many blessings are with you and your family and you are headed for a brilliant future.

trundle bed Take it easy for the next three days and put yourself in a relaxed mode with no emotional stress. This is also warning you not to be talked into assuming someone else's responsibilities, especially for the next three days.

trunk You will receive disagreeable news within two days. This situation is out of your control. Remain calm and you will be able to handle this appropriately. Because you have prior notice of this you will be able to handle anything that comes up within the week with a minimum of stress and a confident attitude.

trunk (*elephant*) This is an extremely lucky omen and you will enjoy an abundance of health. You will also receive an unexpected income and as a result will receive riches in areas you never expected. You will also be able to handle certain situations you once felt were impossible. This is the perfect time to tackle those big tasks. Proceed with confidence. You are headed for a very prosperous future.

trust *distrust from yourself or someone else* You will find yourself in an unplanned, yet very romantic situation within three days. If you choose, this will rapidly evolve and bloom into a permanent relationship.

in any other form Within two weeks you will begin to harvest work well done in the past. You will be paid handsomely and this will be a joyous time for you and your family.

trust fund Carefully scrutinize all the facts to make sure you are making the correct decisions. Do not allow another person's jealousy or display of temper to keep you from doing what you think you should be doing, especially for the next week.

truth Someone you feel is very trustworthy and loyal is, in fact, deceitful. You will learn of this within three days. Do not allow yourself to be taken by someone you feel you can trust with a certain situation that will come up during this time period.

truth serum Certain issues in your life have developed to the point of you allowing others to take advantage of you. Do not let this get to the point of being intolerable. Do not lose control and power over your own life. This will be especially important for the next two days.

tryst Keep going in the direction you are now heading. You are on the path toward a brilliant future. You will also soon hear the words of love you have been long wanting to hear from the person you most desire.

tsar Someone who will unexpectedly enter your life has all the qualities you want from a relationship. Do not push yourself on this person; they are not interested in a relationship. Do not set yourself up for disappointment.

tsetse fly For the next two days do not allow anyone to use emotional games to sway you into becoming involved with anything you find distasteful. Do not compromise your character. You will regret it at a later time.

T-Shirt Within five days you will develop the strength and inner courage to make some unusual and extraordinary moves that will benefit you. Many blessings will come to you and your family.

T-square The opportunities you have been waiting for will present themselves and you will enjoy a new start in those areas of your life you wish. You will be able to execute and carry out all of your plans very successfully and enjoy a very prosperous life. For the next three days do not allow anyone to stand in your way and keep you from moving forward.

tub *to use* You and a special person are looking for changes to improve your relationship. You are now open to conversations and new ways to demonstrate love and to bring in a new closeness that will benefit the union. This will serve to improve the relationship in all aspects. If you choose to pursue this, the other person will be more than eager to go along with this process. Any other negotiations you need to attend to will work to your advantage during this time period because this is the best cycle for communicating.

full of clean water or with bubble bath Within five days you will receive an all expense paid trip to an area you wish to visit. This will be very rewarding and will come as a surprise. Motivate yourself to put yourself in situations that will allow this to occur quickly. Many blessings will come to you and your family.

with dirty ring Avoid any entanglements with someone

who is trying to set you up for a lawsuit. This person will attempt to ruin you financially and will try to destroy your reputation. Make sure you avoid this for the next three days.

to be in a tub with someone else or with a group of people After you have people over to your house, a few guests will remain. A guest of the opposite sex will accidentally expose themself. If you wish to avoid this scene, avoid having guests over for the next five days. You will also have the opportunity to bring someone you desire close to you. If you wish, the time is right to move this relationship toward romance within the week. You are headed for a very prosperous future.

to spray yourself, something or someone with clear water in the tub You will achieve a big victory during this upcoming cycle that will offer you an abundance of new opportunities. Position yourself in such a way, by using whatever power of authority you may possess to work the completion of an agreement to your favor. This will be especially important for the next week. You have a seven day period from the time you have this dream to push this agreement through and it will be well received by everyone involved. This is the perfect cycle to take care of this task. You are on a victorious path in life and many blessings will come to you and your family.

washtub Seek an alternative answer to a situation that will begin to develop within seven days. Start preparing yourself now for different options you can take the moment you feel they are needed. This is particularly important when you begin to sense things developing along a line you do not desire. Proceed with confidence, you are headed for a prosperous future.

tuba You will be paying far too much attention to a total stranger. This is not someone you should have any involvements with. This person is evil. Good luck is with you and you need to get on with your life without this person in it.

tube Take steps to keep any negative event connected to this dream from becoming a reality. Make it a point to experience only positive events in your life, especially for the next seven days. You also need to do whatever you can to display your talents by showcasing your skills. You will connect with someone who has the resources to point you in the right direction for a prosperous and wonderful future. Motivate yourself in such a way that you will interest those who will pull strings on your behalf. Many blessings are with you.

tuber Within five days you will be asked to come up with certain documents that will take you some time to locate. Take every step to locate this paperwork and turn it over to the right person in a timely fashion. This will allow everything to run smoothly and with ease. Avoid any stress that will result from not meeting a deadline.

tuberculosis Do everything you can to protect yourself from any infectious disease, especially for the next three days. Remain alert and do not expose yourself to contagious illnesses. You must also do everything in your power to stop someone from creating distance between you because of the way you behave, especially for the next five days.

tuck *to tuck* Insist, for the next five days, on special considerations and privileges. Do not allow others to believe you can take on more than you can handle. Open up and tell people you know that you need support and assistance, consideration and some leniency. This is the cycle to make these requests in order to receive major benefits.

Tuesday Be aware of any negative event in your dream that occurred on a Tuesday. If so, take the necessary precautions to keep this from happening in reality. This also implies that this day is an extremely lucky time for you. You can expect something very unusual and wonderful to occur on this day. You will also receive good news or a gift. You are headed for a brilliant future.

tug Within a couple of days you will be under a great deal of pressure because you will stand up for your rights and refuse to compromise your feelings. Because you have prior notice of this you can take steps to remain calm throughout this time period.

tugboat Make it a point to motivate someone to get things moving in the right direction. This will enable you to meet a specific deadline that is particularly important for the next three days.

tug of war You will receive an invitation within three days. Think carefully about this. The person issuing the invitation possesses a strange manner and has a lifestyle that you find offensive. Prepare yourself to tactfully decline this invitation.

tuition Someone will do everything in their power to involve you in a romantic relationship. This person is very possessive. This advance knowledge will enable you to be able to handle this relationship in the manner you desire if you are interested in becoming involved.

tulip Pay close attention to the emotions you will experience for the next two days. If you are involved in anything distasteful, take steps to remove yourself from the situation. Stay away from stressful environments, do things that are soothing for you and make you feel good in your surroundings. It is important to be good to yourself. During this cycle you will be surrounded by those who feel affectionate toward you and you will receive more love, respect and appreciation than ever before. You will feel more alive and rejuvenated during this time period than ever before and are promised a brilliant future.

tumble You will be easily taken advantage of by a friend who will become a very conniving enemy. This person will go to great lengths, without your knowledge, to sabotage all of your goals. Be very alert to this for the next five days and make sure you do not have any negative interference.

tumbler You will enjoy an abundance of love from someone and will deeply appreciate this time period when the love and appreciation others feel for you is verified by a very special person. Do not deprive yourself of this pleasure, especially for the next five days.

tumbleweed Take steps to keep any negative event depicted in this dream from occurring in real life. You have prior notice of this and can ensure you only experience positive expressions in your life. Develop a more positive attitude and treat a particular situation more seriously than you have in the past. Remain alert to this, especially for the next seven days.

tumor Make sure you have guarantees that will hold up in the future. Ensure for the next three days that each guarantee is solidly backed up. You are headed for a prosperous future.

tuna Any scene depicted that you do not wish to become a reality must be avoided or altered so you can experience only positive expressions in your life. Make sure also that you and someone special to you do everything you can to bring a closer bonding to your relationship. You will find that you both come up with a creative idea within three days that will assist in creating this bond. You will enjoy good luck, enjoy many blessings and have a prosperous future.

tune You and someone who is close to you will mutually work on ensuring that a relationship will last and that love will blossom. Go for it.

tuner Within five days someone will go to great lengths to impress you. This person has a strong financial base and will be able to provide you with a very comfortable lifestyle. Proceed with confidence. This person finds you very refreshing and stimulating and enjoys your company.

tunic You will be taken in by someone who will provide a service for you and because you have little knowledge of the service provided, this person will charge you for a more expensive part, supplies or technique than was actually used. Be extremely careful that this does not happen to you.

tuning fork Within three days any request you make will be warmly received. You are very popular and are loved beyond your imagination.

tuning pipes You have grossly underestimated a situation that you will be involved with in five days. Move quickly on this before it slips away because this will be your golden opportunity.

tunnel You must be careful of someone who will cleverly and skillfully attempt to involve you in their life for at least three weeks. This person will use this time period to make sure they do everything they can to get under your skin. This will ensure that you constantly give them attention, special treatment and cater to their wishes. After a while this person will not even have to ask or demand these things from you; it will be assumed that you will automatically do them. If you do not cater to this individual, they will quickly drop you and never speak to you again. If you choose not to go through this, get away from this person the moment you see this start to evolve.

tunnel vision Take steps to prevent any negative event depicted from becoming a reality. Focus more on what your insights and inner thoughts are telling you. Follow your intuition, especially for the next three days. You will be greatly benefited by this.

tupelo Make sure you do not become involved with someone who is very involved with a project you are working closely on. Be kind and friendly but do keep your distance, especially for the next three days. You will do the correct thing.

turban For the next five days you can avoid causing emotional harm to another person. This will be as a result of someone lending you money and putting the pressure on you to pay them sooner than agreed upon. Do not put yourself in the situation to be hassled for money. Either find an alternative source or start saving now to avert any financial crisis in the future.

turbine For the next two days be extremely careful. You will be talking to someone who will lead you to build up false hopes about them. Be very protective of yourself so you can avoid disappointments.

turbojet This is a good time to attend to those opportunities that were close to you at one time. These opportunities will now be yours to grasp. Motivate yourself in such a way that you can leave yourself open to new opportunities. Many blessings are with you and your family.

turbulence Do everything you can to experience nothing but positive expressions in your life. Make sure you take steps to ensure that any negative event witnessed in this dream does not become a reality. Someone will request you surrender emotionally and physically to them and will be very eager to fulfill this request. Since you have prior notice of this, you can give yourself fully and enthusiastically and you will, if you choose, enjoy many passionate and fulfilling moments together. If this is not something you choose, you can handle yourself appropriately.

turd Do everything you can to keep chaos from erupting because of something you do without thinking, especially for the next two days.

tureen Pay attention to your behavior for the next three days. If you do not, you will permanently drive a special person away. You can prevent this and can take steps to

bring this person closer to you. You will be able to do the correct thing for the next seven days.

Turk You will learn, within three days, of someone's intentions, plans and feelings for you. You will come to understand how deeply this person wants to be involved in your life. If you choose to pursue this, you will be financially, emotionally and physically secure for a lifetime.

turkey This implies that you need to do whatever you can to create a healthy lifestyle. Make sure you eat healthy foods, drink plenty of water and get plenty of rest. This also implies that any assistance you ask for within seven days will come through for you. You are entering a lucky cycle that will bring you an abundance of health and wealth. Make sure you write down each important event so you will not accidentally overlook an important commitment you may have within two weeks.

turkey shoot Do not become involved in any situation that seems to be very important for the next three days. This situation is not in sync with your lifestyle, although on the surface it appears to be. You will be tempted to involve yourself but this will put you off course and will become a bigger issue than you had anticipated. Your life will be affected in the long run.

Turkish bath This is an extremely lucky omen and is letting you know you are headed for a brilliant future. You will have the courage, strength and valor to handle any situation that will come up within two days. Although they may be stressful, they will be quickly resolved.

Turkish coffee Make it a point to appreciate the efforts of your loved ones and do something to show your appreciation for them, especially for the next three days.

turmeric Be very aware that someone is developing a plot to take over property that you own. Seek this person out and take aggressive steps to keep this manipulation from taking place. Step back, regroup and prevent this cowardly act.

turn *to turn or to see others turning* You will enjoy success with what you are working on now and will have many enjoyable times in a variety of ways for the next two weeks.

to not have a turn at something or to see someone else not get a turn You will learn of the death of a loved one and this will shock and surprise everyone involved. Within five days you will also have a disagreement with someone of the opposite sex that will lead to a major quarrel. Keep your distance and take steps to avoid this situation entirely.

to do things in turn Be prepared; a big victory will come your way within five days. Be consistent and behave appropriately in all areas of your life.

to dream of anything that will not turn on or off Within five days you will be dealing with someone who will mislead you into believing they are well respected, professional and stable in their career. This person would also have you believe they are financially secure and enjoy a very credible lifestyle. This person is very believable and because of your feelings of comfort and assurance in their company you will want to become as involved in their life as they wish to be involved in yours. You will be given every indication that you will be able to track them down at any given time. You will be given several phone numbers, company addresses, etc, but if you try these numbers or leave a message with the secretary, it will take hours and sometimes days for this person to return your calls. You will realize you have been led to believe they have a more impressive lifestyle than they actually do. If you allow yourself to become involved on any level, you will be in for a big disappointment. Become disciplined and shrewd in order to keep this person from violating your emotions or insulting your intelligence. Because you have prior notice of this, you will be able to handle this successfully. You are in a very lucky cycle and are headed for a prosperous future.

to wait your turn or for someone else to wait for a turn Within three days you will be able to resolve pressing responsibilities with ease. You will be surprised at how quickly this will develop and at the ease with which burdens will be lifted.

in any other form For the next three days be consistently aggressive in your actions.

turncoat Involve yourself with something that seems to be a bit risky because this will bring you major benefits within two weeks.

turnip You will find a successful solution to a problem that will arise within two days. You will wrap this up very quickly. Good luck is with you.

turnpike A close friend or family member will ask you for assistance that you will have to turn down. Remain uninvolved in a tactful and diplomatic way.

turnstile For the next three days make sure you become directly involved in the personal problems of another person. This person will ask for your help and any assistance given will be deeply appreciated and warmly received.

turntable You will gain information by accidentally eavesdropping on a group of powerful people. This information can be implemented to your benefit. You will also need to make sure, prior to establishing rules and regulations for others, you are able to keep them yourself, especially for the next three days. Become acutely aware of what others are saying and, more particularly, what they are leaving out. Devote more time to this for the next three days and you will find out what you need to be alerting yourself to. You will handle this successfully.

turpentine Do not endanger your reputation by assisting a minor in what could be a very dangerous endeavor. Be very careful that a kind gesture on your part does not put you in jeopardy.

turquoise *stone or color* Someone who is interested in you is the type of person who will ensure your needs are met as well as providing you with the finer things in life. This person is very attentive. You will enjoy greater wealth than you ever imagined whether you allow this person in your life or not because something new will come along within two weeks that will enable you to gain great wealth. You will also experience a long period of health and healthy relationships. Many blessings are with you and your family and you are headed for a brilliant future.

turtle Within three days you will witness a strange occurrence. You will be shocked and wish you had never seen this. Do whatever you can to avoid this by rescheduling all planned events during this time period. You will also be very successful when bargain hunting. Barter with others and you will quickly accumulate many items you wish to purchase. You will experience good health, tranquility and harmony for a long time to come.

turtledove Within three days you will experience sexual satisfaction with someone you have desired for a long time. This will continue for as long as you wish. You will enjoy a great sex life and tranquil living arrangements on a permanent basis.

turtleneck Someone is very eager to talk to you about something that is emotionally important to them. This individual will bring more clarity to a specific situation that involves them. They want more attention from you and are also committed to give you attention. You are entering a lucky seven day cycle.

tusk Discipline your behavior, especially when around small children. Do not become irresponsible and act on your impulses, especially when in their company. Control your emotions and do nothing inappropriate for the next three days.

tutor Make sure you do not volunteer any more information in an interview than is necessary. Make sure this does not happen for the next three days.

tutu Become more resourceful regarding certain situations you will be involved in. Specify to yourself what you need and want from this particular situation, especially for the next five days.

tuxedo Do not settle for less. Do everything you can to live life to the fullest and do not compromise your feelings for anyone or allow anyone to sway you from doing what you should be doing, especially for the next three days. Many blessings are with you and you are headed for a brilliant future.

T.V. dinner Do not allow yourself to be abused or insulted in public because you will be unable to forgive yourself for allowing this to take place. Avoid any situation where this could occur for the next three days.

twang You will be invited out within three days by a same sexed person to a very elaborate locale and you will enjoy yourself immensely. In this outing you will notice a novel item that this person will purchase for you. You will treasure this memento for a life time.

tweak You will find great amusement at a comedy club or a live performance of some sort. Do not be bashful. Go all out and enjoy yourself as much as you can.

tweezers A new and wonderful person will enter your life who has a stronger sex drive than you will ever have. You will never be able to satisfy this person's sexual appetite but you will be able to talk with this person and describe your problem in detail. Arrangements can be made that will be mutually satisfying. This will develop into a permanent relationship if you choose.

twelfth night You will visit an area within five days filled with evil and wickedness. Be sure to research your plans before you travel and take steps to keep this from taking place.

twelve This is an extremely lucky number. You can use this number for games of chance for a small risk with a heavy return. Use this number to schedule important events, meetings, etc., on this day or time for greater success and benefits. Twelve days from the day you had this dream, something unusual and lucky will occur in your life and within the time frame you will receive wonderful news that will offer you support where you need it. Many blessings are with you and you are headed for a very prosperous future.

twelve apostles This is the time to request from your higher power what you feel is impossible. This will be granted you. You will gain the spiritual knowledge and nourishment you seek within seven days. You will also experience an abundance of health and many blessings will come to you and your family.

twenty This number is extremely lucky for games of chance. You can invest little money for large gains. Use this number as a date to schedule important meetings, events, etc., for greater benefits. Within twenty days after the dream you will receive wonderful news that will bring you the support system you seek and twenty days after you have this dream, something very unusual and lucky will occur in your life. Many blessings are with you and you are headed for a prosperous future.

twig A planned celebration will not take place because of situations that are out of your control. Reschedule and plan this celebration at an earlier time.

twilight Make sure your vehicle is in good working condition. Take care of your transportation in order to avoid frus-

tration and delays. Do this within three days.

twilight zone You will receive a fantastic gift that you least expect at a time you least expect it from someone who feels a deep gratitude toward you. Also do everything you can to make sure you are not going in the wrong direction, especially for the next three days. Carefully investigate the situation to ensure you are on the right path.

twill Someone you are interested in has no interest in pursuing a relationship with you. This person wants you to back off and to get on with their life without you in it.

twin This dream is an extremely lucky omen and you will experience an abundance of health. Something very lucky will also occur within two days and within two months your life will be completely turned around. You will experience a much higher standard of living and enjoy improvements in each area of your life. Do not allow anyone to talk you into making plans you have no interest in, especially for the next two days. Become very aggressive in making the plans you want for the future. You will need to do this to avoid all outside interference. Use your own judgment and go with what you feel is right for you. You are headed for a brilliant future.

twine Focus on your family's needs and make sure you issue a strong warning to them to take precautions to remain safe, especially for the next three days. An old issue will also resurface during this time period. Go back to square one and treat this as though it is a brand new situation. Many blessings are with you and your family.

twinkle *any form* Do not allow thoughts of discouragement to take over and dissuade you from pursing a romantic interest. Do everything necessary to regain your assertiveness and boldness in order to carry yourself in such a way that will allow romance to enter your life. This is especially important for the next five days. If you choose to pursue this, you are headed for emotional fulfillment and a very prosperous future.

twister For the next five days do not put yourself in any situation where you know there will be chaos and many distasteful moments.

two Use this number in games of chance for small risks and high returns. Use this date or time to schedule special meetings, conferences and events, etc., and you will receive major benefits. This dream also implies that two different individuals will be vying for your attention and will seek involvement with you in some capacity. Expect this within seven days. You will enjoy this immensely but you must make sure that, within two days, you do not mishandle the situation. One of these people could be hurt deeply by your mismanagement. Handle this with prudence, delicacy and grace. Many blessings are with you and this is a lucky seven day cycle. Within two days a much desired improvement will also take place because certain unusual circumstances will occur that will help to bring these improvements about. Your imagination will be very active and you will have the clarity of thought needed to develop and promote these improvements and you will be able to bring your plans into reality. During this two day period you can also look forward to two very lucky events that will unexpectedly occur to you. This is a very lucky omen and many blessings will come to you and your family.

two bits You are currently working on two different projects. You will be more successful by merging two into one.

two faced Within five days you will visit a place filled with depravity and wickedness. Carefully research your plans before traveling in order to keep this from occurring.

two step You will receive a wonderful invitation from someone you least expect. Pursue this and you will have a wonderful time.

two way street You are well on your way toward developing the plans you need for your own independence. This cycle stresses confidence, physical healing and financial improvements. You are on the path toward a brilliant future. This is a very prosperous cycle for you and you will be able to turn around those situations that require improvements. Many blessings are with you and your family and all requests made to your special deity will be granted.

two wheeler You are making all the correct moves and are motivating yourself to achieve victory. You will also finally connect within the week, with a certain person whom you have been unable to contact in the past. It would also be a good idea to take steps to schedule a small vacation to a quiet get away spot. This will leave you with many pleasurable memories. All things that were impossible in the past are now possible and you are headed for a brilliant future.

tycoon This dream is an extremely lucky omen for family unity. Understanding and a deep closeness will develop between you and your relatives and with a special person. All communication will seem to come from the heart. Many blessings, tranquility and harmony will come to you and your family.

tyke For the next few days close relatives will be scrutinizing every aspect of your life. Ignore this situation, although it will cause you some uncomfortable moments. You have prior notice of this and can take steps to make this as stress free as possible. You can also expect some great news within two days.

Tyler, Richard You can expect a number of unexpected functions to occur one after the other and you will be flooded with invitations that you can take your pick from. One of these events will be far more exciting and glamorous than the others and you need to make sure you do not miss it.

This function will require formal attire and you will need to make sure you prepare yourself in plenty of time so you will look your best. You will win a door prize at this function, will enjoy yourself tremendously, and will meet many influential people who will become lifelong friends. You will also become aware, during this time period, that someone you desire deeply feels the same about you. You will enjoy many mutually affectionate moments and will both be very excited about this new development. You are on the path toward a prosperous and brilliant future.

type You will become involved in something that seems to be very innocent on the surface. It will turn out to be a horrifying experience within the next three days. Be very alert and carefully rethink all your moves.

typewriter Within two weeks you will hear the words of love you have longed to hear. This will bring about some huge changes in your life that you are very eager to involve yourself in.

to hear this word You will find that, for the next seven days, you will be at the peak of experience and will be so together that you will instinctively know you will reach the finish line before the race has really begun. You will have the feeling of confidence that comes from knowing you will succeed. You will feel the strength that comes from your inner core. Follow your goals as if you were on a mission and this will bring you to a victorious completion of your goals. Within this time frame, your sense of ethics and judgment will be intact and you are headed for a fantastic future.

typecast You will be involving yourself, for the next seven days, with a completely new way of living life. You will be able to do this very easily with very little financial output. You will have many moments of extreme joy.

typeset Within three days negotiations you will have with someone in power will be very successful. Everything will work out exactly as you have envisioned. You are setting yourself up for a very prosperous future.

typewriter Within two weeks you will hear the words of love you have longed to hear. This will bring about some huge changes in your life that you are very eager to involve yourself in.

typhoid/typhus Within five days motivate yourself in such a way that will enable an opportunity to open up for you. You will be able to create opportunities that will not only excite you but will vastly improve your life. Rely on your intuition and you will be guided to the path you should be taking. Eat healing foods and do special things for yourself. You are in a very lucky cycle and many blessings are with you.

Typhoid Mary Someone will try to push a romantic situation on you. Do not waste time on this situation no matter how tempting it may seem. It will not work out.

tyrant Do not involve yourself in something that seems to be innocent to you. This will turn out to be a horrifying experience, especially for the next three days. Be very alert and take steps to avoid this experience.

U

U A very powerful, well formed idea will cross your mind that you will develop and put to use immediately. This will give you an entirely new way of living life. You will also be very detailed and precise with each move you make toward grasping this new goal and you will be very successful. Be very aggressive and detailed in your pursuit. You are headed for a brilliant future.

U-boat Pay very close attention to what your heart is telling you. Take a responsive approach and welcome this challenge. Allow things to become serious between you and another person. The mood is right for this to happen. It is also important not to allow yourself to over or underestimate a particular situation during this cycle. Let your intuition guide you.

udder Do not take so long in making a move toward the person you desire. This cycle is perfect for bringing romance into your life and for pursuing that special person. You will also enjoy an abundance of health and all negotiations dealing with business and romance will be successful. Many blessings are with you and your family and you are headed for a prosperous future.

UFO Take major steps, for the next three days, to avoid the deep depression and bitter loss that would result from a child's kidnapping. Be acutely aware of the child's whereabouts at all times. It would be a good idea to practice child safety until your child becomes an adult.

abductee to a UFO or any other form Regardless of how many physicians you consult to determine what is taking place with you physically, you will be told that nothing is organically wrong with you. This dream is letting you know that in spite of your feelings that something is wrong, nothing is, and you need to be happy with this fact. Healing will quickly come to you if you start treating your physical complaints from a different perspective. Redirect your thinking patterns and work to change your attitude. Stop treating your body in an unreasonable way. Do what you can to schedule in more physical exercise, change your diet, and make alterations in the way you think in order to remove any form of stress. Reschedule your life to lessen physical demands on your body and remove yourself from anyone who makes you feel uncomfortable and adds extra stress. You can easily turn this into a positive situation by redirecting the way in which you live your life. It will take time but you will re-

cover and be healthier than you were before you began this new regimen. It is also for you to take steps to change any negative event in this dream that could become a reality and make sure you experience only positive expressions in your life. You are headed for a prosperous future and many blessings will come to you and your family.

ugly Be very alert to what you will be saying in the next three days. You may have a slip of the tongue and say something you did not mean and hurt someone very deeply. Once you say these words, you will never be able to take them back.

ugly American For the next two days take no risks due to your bad temper. This behavior will result in a permanent split between you and someone who is important to you. Openly communicate with this person in order to maintain growth in this union.

ugly duckling This serves as a warning that someone will come to your house and accidentally break an expensive item. For the next five days be very watchful of your precious items to avoid the disappointment you will suffer if one were damaged.

Ukraine Someone will try to stick to their principles to the point of irrationality. This person will refuse to compromise with you at all. Go on with your life without this person in it. This dream may also be used as a reference point in time. If you dream of this region and see its name used in any context, the dream message will occur on this day.

ukulele Make yourself available for an upcoming trip within three days and you will benefit greatly from this. Pounce on this opportunity immediately and you will enjoy a very prosperous future.

ulcer Within the week all of your anguish and depression will disappear. Do everything you can to uplift your mood and to add enjoyment to your life. It is important that you start this process within three days.

ultrasound Take steps to avoid a difficult financial situation within the family. A family member will bear down on you for emotional and financial assistance and this will be a drain to you. Be alert to this so you can avoid all entanglements for the next two days. Do not put yourself in a situation where this could happen to you.

Ulysses Think ahead. Get expert advice and this will keep you from getting into a tight spot within two days. You have prior notice of this and can take steps to prevent it. Otherwise, everything during this time frame will be very prosperous for you.

umber Investigate the options that are available to you and make sure that no actions will be taken against you in future situations. Eat healthy foods, exercise, drink plenty of water and get the rest you need to allow your body to function at its highest level. You have a wonderful, prosperous life ahead of you.

umbilical cord Within three days you will become involved in an unusual situation that will improve your standard of living. You will move ahead rapidly and be able to reach your highest goals. This is a very lucky cycle for you. Consistently and persistently make sure that what you most desire will come about during this time period. Become personally involved in your pursuit. Someone will also be seeking exactly what you desire in an emotional commitment and involvement. You will have absolute power in your decision making policies and all things you felt were impossible are now possible. You are headed for a brilliant future. You will also, within the week, be invited to a number of functions and events and can be very selective about those you choose to attend. Any one of them will offer you the opportunity for greater prosperity and ways of enriching your personal life. If you choose, you will have many admirers of quality to choose from. Many blessings will come to you and your family.

umbrella You need to put a stop to your overly possessive attitude in personal affairs. Do not destroy yourself with this behavior. You are encouraging others to stay away from you. Do not lean so hard on someone who is close to you. Make it a team effort when dealing with corporations, negotiations, proposals, etc. Take an aggressive approach and work closely with others. This is an extremely lucky time for you to work in cooperation with others and you are headed for a prosperous future. Eat healing foods and drink plenty of water.

umbrella plant You will win your heart's desire within two days.

umbrella tree Do everything necessary to motivate yourself to change the direction you are going in life. This will enable you to achieve more prosperity. Look at things on a grander scale and go for it, especially for the next five days.

umpire Someone you know is very eager to reconcile with you but is unable to put this into words. You will work out a way to reconcile and will work toward mutual understanding and a satisfactory life together for a long time to come.

uncle Someone will do something unusual and extraordinary on behalf of a family member. This person will do favors for a special person that will raise their standard of living and bring them more prosperity. You will feel gratitude and joy over what they have done. You can expect this within five days. Many blessings are with you and your family and you can expect many happy days ahead of you. If you recognize anyone in this dream connected with a negative event, take steps to alert this individual as well as to encourage them to promote any positive event. You also have prior notice and can avoid any negative event from occurring in your life.

Uncle Sam Be more attentive to someone special and you will have a very memorable time on a romantic outing if this is what you desire. Take steps to avoid any negative event foretold in this dream and make sure you promote any positive message.

Uncle Tom Make sure for the next three days that any pleasure seeking activities you become involved in do not become habit forming and expensive. This habit will keep you from going in the direction you should. Many blessings are with you and your family.

uncomfortable *something is making you feel uncomfortable* You are beginning to feel a strong emotional wave that will take up a great deal of your time because you will have no awareness of where this is coming from. This drive will cause you to focus on bringing something to reality. This will continue for a two week period and during this time frame you will somehow arrive at the reason and source of this drive and start acting on it. You have prior notice of this situation and if you determine it to be socially unacceptable you have the time to seek professional help to come to grips with your desires. The moment you sense this starting to occur, seek help. It is in your destiny during this cycle to find that one person who will be able to handle this problem. It will be properly addressed and you will feel you are in control of your emotions in a healthy way.

under Proceed with confidence. This dream signifies riches. You will also receive valuable information within two days.

underarms You will soon be attending a special event. Everyone is looking forward to seeing you but think carefully about who you will be taking. This person's attitude will be very offensive to many people and will cause eyebrows to be raised. Do not try to fit someone into surroundings where they do not belong. Think about this ahead of time so you can handle this properly.

underclothes You will be speaking with someone you are interested in becoming involved with in some capacity. Make sure you handle yourself in a straight-forward manner. Let this person know what is distasteful to you and what you are willing to do so you can work together for a mutually fulfilling relationship.

underdog Someone will try to interest you in a joint financial venture. Do not become involved. This will not work out for you. Any joint financial involvement will be a disadvantage to you for the next five days.

underdressed Someone has plotted ways to get what they want and need from you and you will be drained by this person's constant requests for favors that they can do themselves. You must also become aware that you will be spending money on them, a little bit at a time. This money will add up over time. This person is also insincere and unable to be open and up front with you. This individual is one thing to you and something else to others, and will tell people only what they think people want to hear. You would be better off without them in your life. Make sure, in the next three days, you do not over or under dress for any event you will be attending. Anything negative portended in this dream needs to be altered or changed. Make sure only positive expressions occur in your life.

underground *any form* Take steps to change or avoid any negative event connected with this dream. You have enough prior notice of this to turn it around in such a way to experience only positive events in your life. Certain situations that will also arise within the next three days will require that you remain true to yourself. You must also relentlessly and aggressively pursue what you really want from someone else. Verbalize your desires and all your needs will be met. Many blessings are with you and your family and you can expect an abundance of health.

Underground Railroad Several things will occur within five days. You must display determination to make sure the changes you desire in your life take place. Remain focused and tenacious in spite of anything else that is going on in your life.

undersea Delegate specific chores very carefully to those you are dealing with. Some people are not emotionally, mentally or physically able to handle the tasks assigned them. You will save time and energy if you give the tasks to those who can handle them.

undershirt Those in authority will respond quickly to your needs.

understanding For the next three days carefully avoid saying something that could be a big mistake. Make it a point to spend more time with your loved ones. This should be a priority for you during this time period because important issues will come up that you will not be aware of unless you spend time with your loved ones. Many blessings are with you and your family.

undertow Do not openly display your affections to someone you do not know very well. This will be too overwhelming for this person to accept, especially for the next three days.

underwater Someone will greatly appreciate the way you treat them, the way you speak to them and the way in which you carry yourself. Many blessings will come to you and you are headed for a brilliant future.

underwear The object of your affection will offer you a pleasant and unexpected surprise. Any idea or plan set into motion over the next two days will be dynamically successful and will have a wonderful outcome.

children's For the next four days, think carefully and plan what you will say to someone who is involved in a certain situation. This will buy you the necessary time to gather together everyone involved and to determine how to put a lid on a particular issue and how to stop a negative event from occurring. Many blessings will come to you and your family.

underworld Pay close attention to any negative message in this dream. You have prior notice of this and can take steps to avoid any event or to alter the outcome. This dream also implies victory and you will be able to grasp your goals. Your higher power is with you and anything that promises to raise your standard of living is within your reach. You will achieve this by being acutely aware of those people who are potential enemies who are pretending to be very friendly and concerned for your well being. Your instincts will guide you on this. Do not allow yourself to be taken. Protect yourself for the next five days and make sure no one brings physical or emotional harm to you.

underwrite You will feel compelled to help a homeless person. This is not a very wise thing to do. Remain uninvolved no matter how desperate this person's situation seems to be or how tempted you are to get involved, especially for the next five days.

undressed You will be led to believe by someone you will be dealing with that they will take care of a certain situation for you by a specific time. Look for an alternative person to do this or do it yourself. This individual will do what they promised to do but not in the time period specified. Avoid irritation and disappointment by seeking another way to handle this situation.

to see someone you recognize in a state of undress This person is very eager to become involved with you in any capacity and will be very instrumental in bringing prosperity and new opportunities into your life, especially for the next three days. This is also the perfect time to ask a favor from another person and have it granted.

to see someone you do not recognize in a state of undress Within five days you will successfully resolve a situation because you will dig deeply to uncover vital information about this issue.

unearthly Think ahead. You will be invited to visit a new acquaintance within three days. This person is extremely dangerous and will put you through a terrifying experience that will leave you with no means of escape. Have nothing to do with any new acquaintances for this time period and do not put yourself in the position to be held against your will. This is a life threatening situation.

unemployment claim *to put in a claim or see someone else put in a claim* You will definitely experience a big victory during this cycle that will bring you a wealth of opportunities. Position yourself, using whatever power you possess, to bring about an agreement to your favor, especially for the next seven days. You have a one week period from the occurrence of this dream to motivate yourself to push this agreement through and you will find it will be well received by all those involved. Have no doubt that this is the best time to bring this agreement about and it will be greeted with enthusiasm by all those involved. You are headed for a victorious future and many blessings will come to you and your family.

unfaithful Within three days you will have to deal with someone who will go to great lengths to make others happy. This person is only going through the motions and finds these actions very distasteful. Make sure people who are performing certain tasks really enjoy them, otherwise it would be better to get an alternative for everyone's sake. You are entering a cycle that will provide you with an abundance of health. This will be a very lucky time for you.

unfold Become very assertive when you are around someone you want to become involved with in a romantic way. Because of this behavior, you will be taken more seriously.

unfurl Within five days someone you feel very comfortable with will start to detach themselves from you in a very subtle way. Although you have done nothing wrong, this person harbors a great deal of anger and resentment toward you. Allow this person to back out gracefully because if they remain in your life they will not refrain from saying hurtful things and will cause you many distasteful moments. Get on with your life without this person in it.

unhitch Be relentless in the pursuit of your goals.

unicorn You are in the position now to demand what you need and want from your deity. Specify your needs and your requests will be answered, no matter how impossible your requests may seem. This is a very powerful symbol and a promise that you will enjoy a brilliant future. For the next four days, any joint venture you are interested in becoming involved with will have fantastic results. This will be prosperous for everyone involved. You will also be able to turn anything you feel is a negative situation into a positive and prosperous one, particularly if it involves love and business. You are definitely headed in the right direction.

unicycle It will take a team effort to correct a certain situation that will be coming up within five days. Be flexible in order to correct these issues immediately.

uniform A new acquaintance will come into your life within three days who will share personal moments of their life that you will find amusing and stimulating. You are headed for a brilliant future.

union *to hear the word in reference to a relationship* You will set aside a weekend to spend with a very special person. This individual will spend less time with you than you anticipated. Although they will be in your presence you will not feel they are with you because they will be busy making calls or tending to paperwork. Do not allow yourself to feel rejected because this person cares a great deal about you and feels fulfilled just being in your presence. Enjoy the visit and don't allow yourself to feel resentful. This person will treasure the time they spend with you although they will wish that they had less work to do. Good luck is with you and you will grow closer as a result of this visit.

union card You will receive special knowledge, skills and creative ideas from an older person. This person will find delight in helping you to develop special skills that they have expertise in. For the next week, you will be able to execute your plans as you see fit.

union dues Within two days realize that you are under no obligation to behave in any way other than the way you want. Make sure no one exerts control over you to behave, speak, think or react in the way they want you to. You will be able to permanently rid yourself of someone who attempts this and this will be done with very little anxiety because of the tactful and easy way in which you handle this. You are headed in the right direction and are on the path toward a prosperous future.

union hall Make sure you keep your emotions and feelings under tight control for the next few days. You will be excluded from something you feel you should be a part of and as a result, you will become so focused on this that it could become an obsession. Do not feed into this. It was something that was simply not meant to be. Do not make matters worse by dwelling on it. Attend to matters that are far more important.

union labor Make it a point to show genuine affection toward another person. Offer more encouragement to a special person as well as the rest of your family for the next three days. You will also need to take steps to alter or avoid any negative event in this dream and try to experience only positive events in your life.

union shop It will be a major benefit to you if you make it your business to learn about the character of someone you will be dealing with within five days. Use this information as discretely as you can and keep it to yourself. You will have to do some research on this individual.

United Kingdom Although you feel certain things are impossible, anything is possible for the next seven days. You are headed for a very lucky and prosperous future. You will become extremely successful within three days with the help of someone who is relentlessly supportive of you. Proceed with confidence. This dream may also be used as a reference point in time. If you dream of this country and see its name used in any context, the dream message will occur on this day.

United Nations Someone is very eager to reenter your life for some kind of reconciliation but is unable to put this into words. This reunion will take place and both of you will come to a mutual understanding. You will enjoy a satisfactory life together and are definitely headed in the right direction. You must also remember to remain more compromising in other areas of your life. This dream is also a reference point of something wonderful that will occur in your life. You may see the United Nations mentioned in the media in some context this will mark the time for this wonderful occurrence to take place. Many blessings are with you and your family.

United States Anything is possible for you for the next week. You are in the position now to demand what you want and need from your god. Specify exactly what you want and your desires will be answered, no matter how impossible your requests may seem. This is a very powerful symbol and a promise that you will have a brilliant future. Make sure you take steps to avoid or to prevent any negative event in this dream from becoming a reality. This dream may also be used as a reference point in time. If you dream of this country and see its name used in any context, the dream message will occur on this day.

United States Air Force You will have a fantastic invitation to an extraordinary event that you will not easily forget. You will have the opportunity to speak with others about nostalgic times and you will have wonderful memories that will last a lifetime. Many blessings are with you and your family and you are headed for a prosperous future.

United States Army An exciting attractive person will have you juggling your time. Be sure you schedule some time in your life for romance and you will be able to captivate this person.

United States Marines Make sure you do not go to the extreme regarding an issue that will arise within two days and avoid crowded places during this time period.

United States Navy You will be involved with someone within three days who will develop a relationship with you where everything will seem to result in a battle of some sort. This will become a chronic state if you allow it to continue. Once you see this situation start to develop, remove yourself from the relationship. This will become an ongoing situation that will become difficult to break out of.

universal joint Within four days someone will try to violate your rights. This person will ask you to come along with them to a private area and will attempt to sexually assault you in some way. Be very aware of what is going on around you so you can keep this from taking place. Otherwise, this is a very lucky omen and you are headed for a bright future.

universe Do everything necessary to get yourself through personal hang-ups. These hang-ups are restricting you and keeping you from experiencing those things that will enhance your life. You are depriving yourself of emotional

fulfillment with another person. You will need to deal with this within two weeks because someone will come into your life who will not tolerate this behavior. You will experience deep pain if you allow this person to walk out of your life because you will be unable to get involved. Good luck is with you and do whatever is necessary to overcome this specific issue.

university Within a few days, close relatives will be scrutinizing every detail of your life. Ignore this situation even though you will experience many uncomfortable moments. You have prior notice of this and can put your best foot forward in order to prevent many of these distasteful moments. You also have enough time to take all the necessary steps to prevent any negative event you dreamed of taking place in a university from occurring in reality. You are headed for a very prosperous future and many blessings are with you and your family.

unlatch Within three days you will become very sure of relationships you thought were falling apart within the family. This cycle will promote closeness between family members.

unleash Make sure you avoid a confrontation of any kind and remain safe. Wariness and friendliness will create the atmosphere you need for yourself and your friends during this cycle.

unlock Within three days you will become involved in some unusual circumstances that will definitely improve your standard of living. Good luck is with you and many blessings will come to you and your family.

to put a key into a lock Each relationship that is important to you needs your personal attention in order to allow those you care about to know you have only the finest care and love for them. Do not allow any of your relationships to stagnate to the point where your loved ones feel deprived of your attention.

to use a key effectively to unlock It will be very important within a two day period to have a meeting with certain individuals and to make connections and the necessary requests before an important situation starts to develop. This will ensure it does not fall apart before it takes off. Stay on top of this and you will be able to make the correct adjustments in time. Pay attention to this now and everything will fall into place as you desire. Good luck is with you and your family. You are headed for a brilliant future.

to fail or see someone else fail to unlock with a key You will be dealing with someone who is very inconsiderate of the feelings of others. This individual is only interested in their own personal gratification. Do not involve yourself with this person and get on with your life without them in it.

to successfully lock or to see someone else lock You will be dealing with someone within two days who will refuse to take no for an answer. Prepare for this ahead of time and don't become stressed out behind it.

a lock that falls apart when a key enters A family member is in grave danger of being killed. If you recognize someone from this dream, make sure you warn them that their life is in danger. Otherwise, alert all family members to prevent this.

unplug Do not become unwittingly entrapped in a ménage à trois. Someone will approach you while denying involvement with anyone else. Maintain your confidence and take steps to avoid this kind of arrangement.

unruly You are definitely going in the wrong direction and you need to rethink and regroup yourself in order to focus on what you should be doing. This dream also implies that someone has devised a plot to lure you somewhere for the intent of inflicting bodily harm. Make sure you are keenly aware of what you are exposing yourself to for the next three days and take steps to protect yourself. You have prior notice of this and can make sure you take extra precautions.

unsnap A family member will take you into their confidence and ask for assistance and advice on what they can do to renew their life or to ask that you do something for them that will better their life. You will be instrumental in helping them to get on the right path and in creating a new lifestyle for themself.

unstable *structure* Take steps to avoid a real financial crisis in the family. A particular family member will bear down on your emotional and financial resources. Be alert to this for the next three days and do not put yourself in the position of being emotionally and financially drained.
   unstable person This dream implies genius and a brilliant future. Good luck is with you.

untie Within five days you will be placed in a position of leadership whether this is something you desire or not. You will have to devote much of your private time toward organizing a particular event. You will do a wonderful job and good luck is with you.

untouchable Within five days an emergency situation will come up that will definitely be out of your control. No matter what you do, things will continue to become more chaotic. Remain calm and do not panic. You will be able to solve this successfully in the best possible way.

untruthful What you feel is false in your outer world is truly an opportunity that will provide security for you. Look carefully at this and do not allow a seemingly small opportunity to escape your notice.

unwholesome Someone who has a difficult time controlling their jealousy will want to involve themselves in your life. You have prior notice of this and can take steps to limit your involvement with this person, especially for the next seven days.
up *any form* You are entering a very successful cycle. Make sure you work at a steady pace and have a detailed

plan you can follow very carefully. You will be able to reach your goals in a short period of time. By following these methods you will achieve what you are after. This is one time in your life you can accomplish just about anything you wish. Take advantage of this cycle and you will enjoy a very prosperous future. Many blessings are with you and your family.

upbringing *to hear this word* An out of the ordinary situation will occur that will require a certain amount of risks on your part. Move ahead with confidence. You will have the strength to handle this and things will work out exactly as you have envisioned. Proceed with confidence.

upholstery Do not allow any negative thoughts to rob you of your confidence. Avoid this in any way you can and dispose of any negative thoughts that come to you. Retain a positive attitude.

upper class Do not assume a personality that confuses others. Too drastic a change is more than some people can comprehend. Step back, check your behavior and avoid confusion. You will need to pay attention to your travel plans and avoid any situation that could be hazardous.

upright piano Someone from another country and of another nationality will give you a gift you will remember and cherish for the rest of your life, long after this person is no longer a part of your life.

upset *a situation that you or someone else is upset about* This episode will take place within five days. You are being made aware of this now so you can avoid the situation or change the outcome. You have prior notice of this and can handle it appropriately. Make sure anyone you dreamed of becomes aware of this situation and can handle themselves accordingly. Take steps to ensure you and anyone involved experiences only positive expressions in their life. This dream also implies that someone will talk to you about a certain situation that is going on in their life that they are very dissatisfied about and wish only to have a listening ear. Do anything you can to ease this person's stress. Do however, remain uninvolved and detach yourself. During this cycle you will also be able to determine through the heightened awareness triggered by this dream what you need to do next regarding an issue that is going on in your life. This will be very advantageous to you and will bring about a prosperous outcome. You are headed for a prosperous future.

upside down cake Stop shortchanging yourself and limiting yourself so much. Try to involve yourself in pleasurable events more and deprive yourself less. You are being too overprotective and this is keeping you from enjoying life.

upstage Someone will be very eager to satisfy your requests. Anyone you recognize from this dream will be someone who will enter your life and will profoundly affect your future in a very positive fashion.

upstairs You will receive much love and passion for the next seven days. You will enjoy luck in money and love. Use this luck to your advantage. You will also rapidly pull yourself above any troublesome situation and will perform perfectly in any area of your life that you desire. You are on the path toward a very prosperous future.

to go up You will enjoy your life fully through a variety of arranged events and amusements over the next few days. Several different people will also let you know how much they care for you and appreciate you. You will have peace and tranquility for a long period of time.

to go upstairs to an attic You will be romantically attracted to someone and you will mention this to someone else. Do not allow this person to dissuade you from pursuing this interest for the next seven days. You must also make sure you tie up all loose ends before you run into a dead end.

uptown *to hear the word* Someone will, within three days, get in touch with you and go to great lengths to involve you in their life. This is someone who, in the past, you were interested in but did not pursue. You will now be interested in this person again and everything you ever wanted from a relationship is now possible. Everyone you know will also be very excited by the possibility of this taking place. This is a very powerful cycle for you to bring about changes in those areas of your life you want to alter. Proceed with confidence. You are headed for a brilliant future.

uranium This dream is a very powerful symbol and very lucky for negotiations. You are loved beyond your imagination and many blessings will come to you and your family. You are definitely headed in the right direction.

Uranus Within three days, you will be very successful in conducting a fruitful conversation. Certain facts will be discussed between you and another person that will enlighten you and pinpoint certain issues you do not want to overlook. You are also headed for a very prosperous future and many blessings are with you and your family.

urban Within five days an emergency situation will arise that will definitely be out of your control. This dream wants to prepare you for this situation and regardless of what you do to prevent this from becoming more chaotic, nothing will work. Remain calm and do not panic and you will be able to resolve this successfully.

urchin You will misinterpret someone else's actions toward you. This person is not romantically interested in you and if you make a move, you will be embarrassed. Somehow this person has led you to believe this by their overly friendly manner. Back off for now in order to save yourself embarrassment.

urge For the next three days you will need to pay close attention to the point of view of someone you will be dealing with directly. You will need to decide on the right steps to

take for your own happiness.

Uriah *(from the Bible)* You may unintentionally sabotage someone else's plans. Be acutely aware of your actions for the next four days and make sure you do not affect other people's lives because of your behavior. Otherwise, you are headed for a brilliant future and many blessings are with you and your family.

urine/urinate *any form* You will have a variety of thoughts you will be able to mentally process, will have an irresistible impulse to include a variety of activities into your life, and will find a number of things to do in the form of recreation. You will find it difficult to resist running from one event to another. Expect this to happen within two weeks. You will find it easy to involve yourself in those things that will give you immense pleasure. This is the perfect time to involve yourself with a special person. A specific, peculiar situation will also occur within three days that will lead you to feel so much excitement you will be barely able to contain yourself. Expect good news. You are definitely headed for a prosperous future and many blessings are with you and your family.

urn The indifference you demonstrate toward someone special to you will create a quarrel. For the next three days do what you can to watch your behavior. Take steps to be more loving and do what you can to maintain happiness with those you care about.

usher Anything in this dream that you feel implies a negative connotation needs to be avoided or altered in reality. Do not allow someone else's negativity to affect the upcoming decisions you will have to make.

Utah All negotiations will result in a very successful outcome for you. A new person will also come into your life who will become a lifelong friend. This person will be very charming and will share many amusing anecdotes with you. You will also be given an important message by this person and this message will give you a completely different perspective on how to look at a particular project or concept you will be involved with. You will be able to use this knowledge to make drastic improvements in your life. Expect this to take place within three days.

utensils This dream implies that for the next month you will do everything you can to maintain harmony with those special people in your life. You will find it easy to find ways to maintain tranquility. Look up the specific utensils for a greater definition to this dream. You are headed for a brilliant future regarding love. Many blessings are with you and your family.

utilities This dream is a very lucky omen and will remain so for the next month, especially if you dream about paying your utilities. It also implies that you need to demand efficiency from others. This will help you to gain the financial security you are after. Make sure you handle these requests with tact.

Utopia Within two days acknowledge the needs of someone you care about in order to lessen their stress. Be considerate and consistent. You will find the balance you need in your life within five days.

U-turn *to be or to see someone else reluctant to make a U-turn* You should not look to the past to receive any advantages or to find any answers. Make sure you do not repeat old patterns. For the next two days you will get the feeling that something from your past has something to offer you. Instead of doing this, continue to go forward in a new direction and do not get caught up in wondering "what if".

to make a U-turn Within the next three days you need to weigh both sides before deciding to go back to the past because you feel there is some advantage you may have overlooked that you can use. You will have the intuition and clear thoughts to make the right decisions. At one time it was appropriate for you to act in a certain way and to handle yourself in a particular fashion in front of another person. Within three days, this will all change. There is no reason for you to purposely put on an act in front of this person. You will also need to make use of certain resources that you have not focused on because you are used to taking them for granted.

in any other form Within three days a situation will develop that will verify a feeling or hunch you have about a particular individual. Be keenly aware of what your intuition is telling you so you can avoid putting yourself in a situation with another person that will bring you nothing but sheer terror. Practice listening to your intuition. This will be what saves you. You must also be very detailed in all areas of your life. Your awareness will be heightened in this time period.

V

V This dream is letting you know that for the next month, you will be able to successfully conclude certain situations you are trying to resolve. This cycle will create a ripple effect from one situation to another. Each issue will trickle down to other facets of your life and you will see dramatic improvements in your life that will occur one right after the other. Also, take some time out for the next three days to choose the right person to quickly handle important tasks and back you up until your situation is successfully resolved. Do what you can, for the next three days, to encourage a special person to grow closer to you. Put love into action. You will be very successful in accomplishing the closeness you are after. Also, during this time period, do what you can to appear in front of another person in the manner you wish to appear, both physically and emotionally. You have a wish to

seem more independent. Go with your gut instincts and you will be rewarded. Trust your hunches, they are right on target and you will see much success during this time period.

vacation A situation will occur that will not work out to your satisfaction because of another person's unwillingness to work with you toward a solution. The harder you try, the more stubborn this person will become.

vaccination Analyze carefully what is bothering you physically and take steps to find the proper medical treatment for this illness. You will develop a heightened sense of awareness about this particular ailment and you will be able to find the help you need.

vacuum cleaner Do not allow your curiosity to take control and lead you into an unknown situation that goes against your better judgment. You are walking a thin line between mere curiosity and active involvement in something you have no business being involved in and you are being misled by others who desire your participation. Avoid all negative involvements, especially for the next three days.

vagina Take steps to keep any negative event in the dream from becoming a reality. You have prior notice of this and can either avoid this event entirely or change it around to a positive event. This dream also implies that someone with a mysterious lifestyle will attract your interest. This person is from another country, is very bright and will bring a tremendous amount of joy into your life. Within three days you will begin to make friends with this person. You will both share pleasurable moments together on a permanent basis. You will also enjoy a tranquil, harmonious lifestyle and you are headed for a brilliant future.

to see an exposed vagina Someone will be very eager to relentlessly help you in the areas of your life you most desire. This person will also seek involvement in your life. This individual is much younger and more charismatic than most people you are used to dealing with and will be very attentive to all your needs. Many blessings are with you and you are definitely headed for a prosperous future. Also, any negative message involving someone you recognize needs to be given to this person so they can take the necessary steps to keep it from becoming a reality. This awareness will allow them to experience a prosperous and positive future.

vagrant Make sure you are completely aware that an accident could occur and cause someone to suffer from a fall. Make sure unusual situations do not take place while you are present that could result in someone else become injured.

valedictorian For the next three days be very aware of a stranger who will come into your life in a public area. This person will create chaos by starting quarrels and disagreements. Do everything you can to remain calm and uninvolved.

valentine You will be invited to celebrate someone's wedding. You will also be inspired by an idea that will bring you a large profit in a short period of time if you choose to go this route. This dream is a very lucky omen and you will be surprised that love will come to you from a source you least expect if you choose to have this in your life.

valentine card Go for what you want out of a situation. Watch your body language because someone will think you expect less and will be firm about offering less than you deserve. Do not allow yourself to be taken for the next four days. For the next five days you must avoid getting sucked into a family vacation. Otherwise, you are headed for a prosperous future and many blessings will come to you and your family.

Valentine's Day Do everything necessary to promote closeness between yourself, family members and people you feel you should be close to. Do not assume an air of distance or coldness toward these people, especially during this time period. This is a good time to take advantage of this cycle to bring people close to you whom you want to be close to. You will also hear some very good news and achieve victory in all levels of your life within the week. Good luck will remain with you for this time period.

valet Do everything you can to regroup and rethink for the next three days in order to get some verification that the next steps you take will be the right ones at this particular time. If you don't do this, you will be making a big mistake because you will need clarity of thought in order to head in the right direction.

Valhalla This is the time to take advantage of your talents. Challenge yourself to do so and you will be able to impress others at the right time in order to see instant results and gain the career you have been wanting. You are headed in the right direction.

valium Within four days, you will experience victory because of your valiant integrity when you are required to make a decision. You will not compromise your principles but will develop a quiet conviction and relentlessness in your pursuit of money, contracts, items and agreements as well as productive conversation. Do not give up until you succeed. This dream is offering large clues that will help you with a dramatic move you are planning to undertake. This move will bring immediate and positive changes to your life. Any negative event seen in this dream needs to be prevented in reality. Take steps to experience only positive expressions in your life.

valley You will be offered the opportunity of a lifetime if you involve yourself with groups of people for the next week. This will allow you to be exposed to various opportunities you can choose from. You are entering a lucky cycle that will bring major changes that will bring you joy and expand your horizons.

valley girl This dream is alerting you to a dangerous situation that will come up within seven days. Be acutely aware that someone who demonstrates some unusual behavior will attempt to injure you. Be prepared to protect yourself at all costs and take steps to keep this from occurring.

valuables *any form* Be acutely aware of a child's status within the family to ensure their needs are being met. Within four days make sure this child is being taken care of properly and that no physical harm comes to this young person. Take steps to alter or to prevent any negative event from becoming a reality. You have prior notice of this and can take steps to change the outcome so you can be assured you only experience positive expressions in your life.

values You will be the target for someone's romantic pursuit. This will be clearly apparent to you and within four days you will make a move in this direction.

vamp Make sure you take care of your teeth. For the next few days, be careful you don't bite down on anything that could damage your teeth. You will also come up with an unexpected and surprising idea that will help you in those projects you are presently working on and enhance your productivity.

vampire Become acutely aware of what you may be doing that will limit your financial status. Do what you can to eliminate any negative actions on your part or work to discover ways you can enhance your income, especially for the next three days. Motivate yourself in order to avoid financial collapse due to your behavior or something you may be overlooking in your career. This dream is also asking you to avoid any stressful situation you may be involving yourself in. Look under Dracula for a greater meaning to this dream.

to dream of being a vampire Give others a break. Back away from a certain person and allow them the space to have their own life so they can take care of their own business. You are demanding too much of another person's time.

vampire bat Be alert, for the next three days, to the unrealistic point of view of another who will attempt to persuade you to back up a certain project you should remain uninvolved in.

van Within five days you will become caught up in a tug of war between two other people because you will fail to take care of a certain situation promptly. This will involve a promise you have made to accompany two different people to the same function. Take care of this now and avoid situations that involve squabbling.

vandal Do not underestimate yourself and do not allow yourself to become your worst enemy. Stop shortchanging yourself emotionally. Push yourself to become emotionally involved because within three days you will be entering an exciting, fulfilling cycle. You will be given the choice to become involved with someone and to enhance your life emotionally. You will be very happy that you did.

Van Dyke Be assertive in your attempts to bring a certain person closer to you. This is the perfect cycle to behave in a way that will lead this individual to feel comfortable in your presence. This will then allow them to say those words you have longed to hear. Many blessings will come to you and your family and you are headed for a prosperous future.

vane Someone wants you to enter into an agreement with them about something they are working on. At first you will not feel much interest in this but after a few days, you will realize this agreement has greater potential for you than even this person realizes. Go for it.

vanilla Make an effort to hurry because you need to meet certain deadlines. Focus on what you need to do and follow your own counsel. This dream is an extremely lucky omen and you are headed for a brilliant future.

vanilla bean Someone you are interested in will be very happy to become a part of your life. Allow your desires to become known. You will enjoy many wonderful moments, sexual satisfaction and mutually enjoyable conversations within the week. Pursue this aggressively. With encouragement, this person will make the first move. Good luck is with you and your family.

vanilla plant You will receive good news within seven days and be very pleased with the outcome of a business affair you are concerned with. This is a lucky omen for you as well as lucky for love and finances.

vanish *any form* This dream is alerting you that anything or anybody you witnessed vanishing will do so within three days and if this is something you have no desire to experience, take every precaution to ensure it does not. You will also come to an agreement with another person regarding the loan of a large amount of money to you. Once this agreement is made, this person will pull a vanishing act and will pretend this agreement never took place. You will feel like a liar and will begin to feel as though something is wrong with you. As a result, you will feel shame for bringing this matter up. At the same time this is taking place, you will have a large burden lifted from your shoulders. You will then be able to put yourself on the path toward prosperity. You will enjoy a long and healthy cycle.

vanity A long awaited proposal of marriage will finally come your way. Everyone involved will be overjoyed about this. Many blessings are with you and for everyone involved in this.

vanity fair Make the time to have an overdue conversation with someone who is special to you. This will make a definite difference in the approach both of you make regarding certain issues that will benefit both of you in the future. Pro-

ceed with confidence, you are both headed for a brilliant future.

vapor Someone will take the liberty within a few days to assign you to a volunteer position without asking you first. This will, however, turn out to your advantage if you do choose to go along with this. You will receive a large financial benefit that you do not expect.

variety *to see a variety of the same item* You have the opportunity in this cycle to pick and choose anything you desire and still be headed in the right direction.

in any other form This dream is an extremely lucky omen and you will be victorious in anything you are trying to achieve, especially for the next seven days.

variety show You are definitely headed for a brilliant future and within seven days you will be very excited about an opportunity that has presented itself to you. You will be able to grasp this at the time you recognize this as an opportunity. Many blessings are with you and your family.

varnish You will have an irresistible impulse to seek out someone you don't know and to open channels of communication and get to know them. Your desire for this will be reciprocal and you will enjoy yourself immensely with this individual. Take advantage of this cycle to bring those you care about closer to you because it will work out in the best possible way.

varsity This dream is a promise that you will find someone within three days who will bring you absolute joy, prosperity and the offer of a healthy relationship. This individual has a wealth of resources and a rich background in friends and education. You will be introduced to a new lifestyle that will offer you an abundance in a variety of ways. Should you decide to pursue this, it will be a wonderful choice and you will enjoy a beautiful life together.

vase This dream implies that you will find instant wealth when you least expect it and you will be able to tackle those tough to handle tasks that will be coming up within seven days. An emotional appeal you make for someone at a particular establishment will also bring more abundance to this person and their family. Move quickly because this cycle will last only a week. You will gain more if you act now.

vat Someone is very attracted to you and will contemplate, within the week, making a romantic overture toward you. If you choose to pursue this, you will be surprised at how quickly this will develop into a permanent union. This is a very productive cycle and will be very lucky for love matters.

Vatican You will be appointed to a very powerful position that will bring you joy. And you will have every confidence that you will be able to handle the position you are after. You will have a wonderful life and enjoy yourself immensely. This dream may also be used as a reference point in time. If you dream of this Cathedral and see its name used in any context, the dream message will occur on this day.

vaudeville You will be able to come up with a way of making some quick and easy money that will turn out to be a nightmare. Be very cautious for the next few days because you will regret becoming involved in this situation.

vault You will enter into a fantastic agreement with the object of your affections.

veal This dream is a very lucky omen for you. You will gain an unexpected abundance of health and wealth as a result of an unexpected income and you will be able to accomplish certain tasks that you felt were impossible in the past. This is a good time to tackle those big projects. Proceed with confidence, you are headed for a prosperous cycle.

vegetable oil This is an omen of continuous good luck for the next seven days. Any information you receive for the next three days also needs to be checked for authenticity. This information will make a difference between whether you fail or succeed.

vegetables Make sure you do not push yourself or allow anyone else to push you into doing something that goes against your nature. You will also successfully respond to someone's request for emotional fulfillment or for assistance.

vegetarian Make sure you do not treat those relationships that are important to you lightly and do not take them for granted. Make it a point to bond closer to those you care about and keep your relationships permanent. Demonstrate your feelings both verbally and physically, especially for the next seven days.

vehicle Someone is highly attracted to you and is contemplating making a move toward you within three days in order to bring you closer together. If you allow this to proceed, you will be surprised at how quickly this will develop into a permanent union. This is a very productive cycle and implies that you will be very lucky in love.

veil Take every precaution to change any negative event in this dream to a positive or to avoid it altogether. Any positive event portended in this dream needs to be experienced to the fullest. It will also be requested of you that you handle the care of an ill person. This person will recover quickly with tender loving care. This is a lucky cycle and you are headed for a prosperous future.

vein Do not allow resentments to build up against someone because of your own feelings of inferiority. This will lead you to take action to bring them down or to behave in a negative fashion. Check your emotions and control yourself. Be aware of what you are doing and why you are doing it.

Expect this to come up within five days. You must also take steps to keep any negative event in this dream from becoming a reality. You are entering a healthy cycle and are headed for a very prosperous future.

Velcro Think very carefully about the revenge you are seeking. This action will not bring you satisfaction and you will be very disappointed in yourself. Release these thoughts and get on with your life. Within two days, you will discover an alternative way to handle this issue.

vellum For the next three days you will achieve success in everything you attempt to do.

velour Someone in a very powerful and wealthy position will, within five days, want to do everything in their power to meet your needs in any capacity. Be very aggressive and go after what you want. This is a guarantee that you will spend your life with not only the necessities but also the finer things in life. Many blessings are with you.

velvet Someone you care about needs to know your real and special needs. This person will be more than willing to accommodate you. Don't suffer in silence. Take advantage of this cycle to go after what you really want in life and to be completely content and tranquil.

velveteen Your thoughts will be very clear and you will have a tremendous amount of clarity in your judgments. You will be able to make decisions quickly and accurately. You will feel an increase in your strength and power in ways you communicate to others so they can learn from you. Also, someone you thought had forgotten you will prove you wrong within three days. This person will come back and show you in some way that you are deeply remembered by them.

vending machine This dream implies luck for you. You will enjoy unexpected health and wealth due to an unanticipated income. You will be able to handle jobs you once felt were impossible. This is a wonderful cycle in which to take care of those big tasks. Proceed with confidence, you are headed for a prosperous future.

vendor Someone will ask you to change your behavior and attitude within the next two days. Keep this from occurring by changing your behavior yourself.

veneer Within five days someone who was cold to you in the past will unexpectedly warm up to you and will treat you with a lot more respect. This will confuse you. You have no need to be suspicious. This person has just had a change of heart and is now willing to have you be a part of their life.

venereal disease Be acutely aware of pleasure seeking activities and make sure you do not put yourself in the position that will seriously complicate your life. Also, let others know your whereabouts at all times. Play it safe. Treat your health as a precious commodity and make sure, for the next seven days, you do not expose yourself to any infection that is completely preventable. Take every precaution to change or avoid any negative event in this dream that could become a reality. Many blessings are with you and your family.

Venetian blinds Keep a very close eye, especially for the next three days, on someone you are very close to. This person's health may be poor. Look out for any peculiar behavior and refer this person to a physician. This is not serious but does need to be attended to.

Venezuela For the next three days do what you can to put your love into action. Show kindness and generosity to those young children in your family and to any child or young adult you feel close to. Make sure you eliminate all hostile behavior and provide a benign environment. Many blessings are with you and your family. This is also the best cycle for traveling in this region of the world if this is something you have been contemplating. A vast amount of luck will come with you on this trip and you will return safely. This dream may also be used as a reference point in time. If you dream of this country and see its name used in any context, the dream message will occur on this day.

Venice Within three days you will be invited on an outing by a very attractive person. For some reason you will feel this person is not sincere. This is a faulty assumption. Go along with this individual and enjoy yourself. Also, force yourself to experience the opposite of what you are experiencing now. You will also be lucky in games of chance, especially in this time frame. You are headed for a very prosperous future. This dream may also be used as a reference point in time. If you dream of this country and see its name used in any context, the dream message will occur on this day.

venison Pay no attention to what others think you may have coming in the way of finances. Let this person know what you expect and demand more than this amount.

venom You will soon meet a very charming, unusually wealthy person. You are very much attracted to each other. At first the relationship will work beautifully. For a long time you will be very spoiled and will have everything you wish for. After a while, without warning, this person will drop out of your life explaining that they were only after short term pleasure. Beware of anyone fitting this description. This person also demonstrates obsessive behavior patterns.

ventilate *to ventilate* Think ahead and regroup so you can rally those around you to help out in those tasks you need assistance in. This is the perfect cycle for you to get this help.

ventricle For you to achieve success, you need to demonstrate consistency and persistency regarding a specific situa-

tion. Aggressively pursue your goals to ensure success during this cycle.

ventriloquist Take steps to change any negative message you heard to a positive situation. Do whatever you can now to keep this from occurring. You have ample time to handle this correctly. You must also become verbally assertive with someone within two days in order to prod this person to interact with you verbally and emotionally in the manner you expect and deserve. You will be successful in your request. There is a sense of urgency to this. Proceed with confidence.

venture Be more independent in your approach to certain situations. Get your point across to another person regarding how you really feel about these issues, otherwise they will not work out.

Venus This dream is an extremely lucky cycle and you are headed for a prosperous future. This is a powerful symbol and implies that you need to associate with those who have the education and knowledge to enlighten you in such a way that you can evolve and grow. Positive attitudes will rub off on you and you can be assured that loved ones do not outgrow you. Allow closeness to grow within family circles. The deities are with you. Within three days you will experience an abundance of health and are headed for a very prosperous future.

Venus fly trap Do everything you can to stay uninvolved and to refrain from egging on any chaos that will be spawned from a small issue, especially for the next three days. This is a waste of your time and of the other person's time. Everything you thought was impossible in a relationship is also now possible. Any special relationships are headed for a mutually satisfying outcome.

verb Within five days you will be with a particular group and a stressful situation will occur. As a result, angry words will be exchanged. Do everything you can to avoid becoming involved in this chaos. Find something peaceful you can participate in.

verbalize This is the perfect cycle for you to use your communication skills to your advantage to get a point across that is very difficult to verbalize to someone. You will now be able to do this very easily and with a minimal amount of stress and anguish to you or the other person. Many blessings are with you.

verbena You will enjoy loving the same person for a lifetime.

verdict Do not attempt to strike out against anyone because it will backfire on you within the week.

verify *to verify something or have someone verify something for you* Within the week, you will have an urgent need to have something accomplished that can only be taken care of by someone else. You will need to borrow a large amount of money or have someone do such a large favor that it will seem impossible for them to deliver on this. Follow your hunches, proceed with confidence and explore your options. You will be able to locate the perfect person to help you out. As soon as a mutual agreement has been made, take immediate action before this person has a change of heart. Many blessings are with you and you are headed for a prosperous future.

to be unable to verify something for someone You will definitely experience a big victory during this cycle that will bring a wealth of opportunities to you. Position yourself with whatever power you have at your disposal and bring a completion or an agreement to your favor, especially for the next week. You have a one week period from the occurrence of this dream to motivate yourself to push this agreement through. Have no doubt that this is the best time to make this happen and it will be greeted with enthusiasm by everyone involved. You are on a very victorious path in life and many blessings will come to you and your family.

in any other form Make sure you keep anything negative you dream about from taking place in reality and do everything you can to experience any positive events in your life. This dream also implies you will achieve immediate wealth from an unusual and unexpected source. This will be something that will take place with no help from you. You will be very clear headed and will be able to direct this fortune in the appropriate direction. You are headed for a brilliant future.

vermicelli Do not waste time getting around to paperwork that needs to be promptly taken care of. Take care of this now so you can receive what you want in a timely fashion.

vermilion For the next five days make sure you do not do the investigative work necessary to clarify a situation. Another person may be more successful in getting this information for you. You are entering a very tranquil cycle. Take steps to keep any negative event in this dream from becoming a reality.

Vermont Someone will treat you in such a way that it will catch you off guard and delight you. Enjoy this fantastic treatment. Many blessings are with you and your family. This dream may also be used as a reference point in time. If you dream of this state and see its name used in any context, the dream message will occur on this day.

vermouth You are to demand extreme loyalty from those who will be helping you develop a certain situation you will be involved with in the near future. Make sure you get it across to others that you are very serious about this project. You will get the help you need and are headed for a brilliant future.

verse For the next five days you will find that many people will want to give you their input and will want to help you get to a point you wish to be in your life. This input will help you to reach your goals and to gain prosperity quickly.

vertebra Do not allow an individual to be abused by someone else. This individual needs to be protected from physical, verbal and emotional abuse by someone they least expect. Be watchful of this for the next five days.

vertigo Do not allow anyone to talk you into doing something that, at first, seems rather harmless but later will become a criminal act. You will then be involved in something you have no business being involved in. Do not involve yourself in any new situation for the next three days.

vespers Within five days someone will start making plans to create an unusual situation that will give them the chance to violate your rights for the sole purpose of their own emotional gratification. Do not allow yourself to be caught off guard. This person will do everything in their power to trap you. You have prior notice of this and can take steps to guard yourself against this distasteful situation. Proceed with confidence. Good luck is with you.

vessel Make sure you do not close doors on friendships you will later want to reopen because of the way you behave and by the manner in which you communicate through body language. Watch this carefully for the next three days and do not put off anyone that you wish to remain friends with.

vest This is a very lucky cycle for you and you must do everything necessary to enjoy yourself for the next two weeks.

vestibule Step back and decide exactly what you are trying to prove and to whom. Your success at this will enable you to develop a plan that will get you exactly what you want. Good luck is with you.

vestments A close relative will diplomatically drop hints within a three day period about a particular area of their life they feel dissatisfaction with and would like to see you take responsibility for. This person wants you to take it upon yourself to make the changes they need to improve their life. They feel they are stuck in a rut and cannot see their way through this situation. You will have the conviction and compassion needed for accomplishing this task for them. It will lead them to a far better lifestyle if you decide to take the initiative. Many blessings are with you.

Vesuvius Within five days someone will subtly attempt to manipulate you in order to get what they want and they will try a number of ways to achieve their goals. This person will use conspiratorial methods and trickery in order to succeed. This person is desperate and will latch on to anyone who seems vulnerable or easy prey. Do not set yourself up to be a target because once you become involved it will be too late. This will be a very controlling and demeaning situation. Take steps to avoid it. Many blessings will come to you and your family. This dream may also be used as a reference point in time. If you dream of this volcano and see its name used in any context, the dream message will occur on this day.

Veteran's Day Get to the meat of a certain issue. Once you determine what the missing element is, you will be able to handle yourself appropriately in certain situations.

veterinarian Do everything you can to keep problems and upsetting issues that are not yours from spilling over on to you. Keep yourself stress free and do not make other people's problems yours.

vial This dream is a good luck omen and an omen of abundance in all levels of your life. You will also be introduced to something new and exciting in this cycle.

vibration You are about to make a mistake. You are very fond of someone and are becoming impatient because this person is not coming across in the manner you wish them to. You wish to rush this person into a commitment and will, over the next three days, become demanding and mistreat this individual. Back off and use your time to develop yourself into a warmer, more positive person. This individual will then mature and develop a more meaningful relationship.

vibrator Become very aware that someone you will become attracted to within three days is mentally disabled and is unable to help themselves in their suffering. Avoid any involvement with this individual because of their inability to control their condition.

vicar Offer your assistance to someone who is special to you to help them develop their creativity. Your help will be welcomed with open arms.

vice Do not involve yourself in a situation that could turn out to be very freaky and kinky. Make sure, for the next three days, you do not become involved in something you have no business being involved in. Good luck is with you. Take steps to protect yourself.

vice president Any decision you need to make within two days should not be postponed. You must not allow yourself or others to procrastinate. Make your decisions quickly and stick by them.

viceroy Do everything you can to develop roots in a relationship. Allow growth and build a solid bond so you can have a strong foundation within this relationship if this is what you desire. You will also find the solitude you have been after for a long time.

vice squad Remain very aware of a stranger who will come into your life in a public setting to create chaos by quarreling and sparking disagreements. Do what you can to remain uninvolved, especially for the next three days. You must also be watchful of someone who will lead you to believe they can confide in you. Do not count on this person's loyal-

ty because they will let you down. Do not involve yourself with gossips.

Vichyssoise Resist all temptations to give up on a certain situation. Someone will attempt to provoke you into argumentative behaviors in order to wear you down to the point of giving in. If you do become involved in this behavior, you will allow two other people to pursue their interests. Do not compromise and do not give in to feelings of defeat. Be watchful of this for the next five days.

victim Take very special precautions to either prevent or alter any negative situation you dreamed of to keep it from becoming a reality. Do everything you can to experience only positive experiences in your life. Within two days assess your present situation so you can take the correct steps to move forward successfully.

Victorian house Although you are around many powerful and influential people, whether this is because of the position of power or the wealth they possess, there is one other person you are destined to be involved with. This will be someone of the opposite sex and this involvement will be in any capacity you choose. Leave yourself open to situations that will expose you to meeting this person. Within five days you will have the opportunity to meet this individual and conversations will flow easily between you. A sense of closeness will quickly emerge between both of you and this will allow feelings to grow. This person is well established and more secure financially than you ever expected. You are both destined for a wonderful and tranquil life. You will enjoy an abundance of health and a prosperous future.

victory A cluster of events will take place concurrently that will bring you a great amount of joy, wonder and awe because they are taking place at such a rapid pace. You will discover a powerful energy that you will be able to direct and control and at the same time this is taking place you will be able to bring others under your control. Because of your prior notice of this you will be able, within the week, to successfully direct your energy to motivate yourself to complete any task you wish in a successful manner. You will also be able to overcome any obstacle and it will now be very simple to handle any new and difficult issue. Your intuition is right on target and many blessings will come to you and your family.

video Take the necessary steps to alter the outcome or to avoid any negative event foretold in this dream. Victory is in your destiny. For the next two days, leave yourself open to any opportunity presented to you as a proposal for your involvement. Go full steam ahead. This is a very lucky cycle for you.

video cassette For the next three days, watch out that you do not blurt out anything that should not be said. This may spoil someone's surprise. Be very careful what you say in front of others.

video cassette recorder You will soon be a winner in a game of chance and you will receive congratulations for something within a short period of time. Many blessings are with you and your family and you are headed for a very prosperous future.

video game Do not allow a threatening manner from another person to keep you from organizing your life and doing what you need to do professionally. Proceed with confidence.

Vienna You will be taking big steps to raise your standard of living by focusing on your goals in a grand way. This will come about due to an unusual, joyful circumstance within five days. Everyone involved will enjoy beautiful expressions of joy and tranquility. Many blessings will be with you and your family.

Vienna sausage You will now start to reap the benefits of what you have worked a long time to accomplish. You will enjoy many abundances because of work well done in the past. Others will demonstrate a great deal of love and affection toward you and you will be surrounded by people who genuinely adore you. This dream is also a promise that something will occur within five days that is so unusual and out of the ordinary that it will bring you instant wealth. Many blessings are with you and you are definitely headed for a brilliant future.

Vietnam Do not associate with the wrong person. Someone has a history that you are not fully aware of that will injure your status in the long run. Avoid this involvement and create a stress free environment. This should be your goal for the next few days. This dream may also be used as a reference point in time. If you dream of this country and see its name used in any context, the dream message will occur on this day.

view Pay close attention to what you were viewing. If it was a negative situation, you need to take steps to alter or to prevent it from becoming a reality so you can experience only positive expressions in your life. This dream also implies that someone you admire will unexpectedly ask you to attend a function with them and you will have a terrific time. You will feel as though everything will fall into place perfectly and each moment you spend with this person will be mutually enjoyable. They will not contact you again. This is not a result of anything you did and is beyond your control. This person will simply be unable to commit because of their schedule. Get on with your life.

vigil/vigilante This dream implies that you will enjoy victory in those areas of your life you deem to be most important. Make it a point to enjoy life, love yourself and take time out to admire nature. Any negative event in this dream can also be changed to alter the outcome. You are on the path toward a brilliant future.

Viking Take extra steps to avoid any negative event or to prevent it from occurring in reality. You have prior notice of this and have plenty of time to turn these events into positive expressions in your life. This dream also implies that you need to confirm there are no obstacles between you and someone else in your life. Keep communication open so both of you can do what you need to do in order to move ahead without interference.

villa This is an extremely lucky omen and you are headed for a prosperous future. It also implies that someone will pull you aside to discuss some intimate situations. This will come to you as a big surprise. It is better that you keep all of this to yourself.

villain Someone will furnish you information about another person whom you are romantically interested in. The information you receive will be completely accurate. Good luck is with you.

vinaigrette Old situations will resurface that you need to readdress. Some of them have been outgrown. You will need to make new decisions based on these changes.

Vincent van Gogh Someone will be very irresistibly drawn to you to the point of being visibly shaken. This person will do just about anything to keep you happy and contented.

vindicate Make it a point to discard things as they have been outgrown in order to keep motivated and to keep up to date on everything.

vine This dream is an extremely lucky omen and implies that you will unexpectedly receive exactly what you want. This will come as a complete surprise to you. This dream also implies that any proposal you present to anyone in any capacity will be accepted. You will also be made an interesting offer and a proposal that you will find difficult to refuse. Many blessings are with you and you are headed for a brilliant future.

vinegar Do not listen to any gossip, especially for the next two days. Even if you do not say anything or repeat any of the gossip other people will say you were listening. This gossip will get back to the person talked about and an ugly situation will develop as a result.

vinyl Motivate other people to rally around you. You will be successful in circulating widely and encouraging a large group of people to support you. Begin this process now and you will ensure a brilliant future. You will grasp your highest ambitions.

viola A great event will be celebrated within the next few weeks that will not only surprise you but will bring you a great deal of happiness.

violate Any negative message in this dream that is connected with reality needs to be addressed now in order to prevent it from occurring in your life. Make sure you allow only positive expressions in your life. You also need to make sure you are not in the wrong place at the wrong time and get a black eye as a result.

violence Make sure you do not allow any negative event depicted in this dream to become a reality in the future. This dream also implies that you need to ask for assistance in order to get the help you need for another person. You will have better results than you ever expected. This will be a burden off your mind and you will be very pleased with the outcome.

violet Remember the mistakes you made in the past and use these to learn from, but don't dwell on them. Make sure you do not repeat the same mistakes in the future. You will also get what you are looking for in life, especially in the next seven days. You are headed for a very prosperous future.

violin This dream is an extremely lucky omen. You will receive much credit for work well done as well as a large financial settlement.

violinist This dream is a very lucky omen. Make time for yourself so you can do special things for yourself. Enjoy solitude when you need to experience it. You must also be very aware that your inattentiveness to a special plan will result in it falling apart due to your behavior. Be relentless in the pursuit of your goals.

V.I.P. Within three days you will surrender yourself sexually to someone you greatly desire. If you choose not to do this, you have enough time to prevent it.

viper In order to get the benefits that rightly belong to you, you will need to be more persuasive with those people you will be dealing with. This will be extremely important for the next three days. The week preceding this dream will be very victorious for you. Take advantage of this time period to accomplish those things you need to take care of.

viral Make sure that anything connected to this dream that should not be occurring in reality is either prevented or altered in your life. You have plenty of time to take care of this and to make sure you experience only positive expressions in your life. Anyone you recognize in this dream needs to do likewise. You must also prepare for last minute changes that will occur that need proper handling to avoid chaos.

Virgen De Guadalupe This Saint is very excited and eager to assist you. You will be provided a miracle that will bring you assistance and a speedy recovery in your financial discomforts. Your plans will quickly advance. All old burdens and issues will be resolved. Riches will come to you and you will enjoy a long and healthy life filled with prosperity.

virgin Make sure you take your complaints to the right people, especially for the next three days. Do not become confused and direct issues to the wrong people. You will be very successful in handling these situations. Take steps to avoid or to prevent any negative event you dreamed of from occurring to you or to someone you dreamed about. Make sure you forewarn this person so both of you can experience prosperity and positive expressions in your life.

Virginia This dream is a very lucky omen and implies you will develop an inner courage and strength over the next two days. Your determination and drive will motivate you to break through any invisible barriers and to rid yourself of any facet of your life that will keep you from pushing forward. Once you have overcome this barrier, you will see a clear path that will help you to develop the knowledge you need to enrich those aspects of your life you most desire. This will be the perfect cycle to develop the lifestyle you wish. You will also be treated like royalty anywhere you choose to go and will be placed on a pedestal by others. This will come as a surprise to you. You are on the path toward a brilliant future and many new opportunities will be presented to you. This dream may also be used as a reference point in time. If you dream of this state and see its name used in any context, the dream message will occur on this day.

Virgin Mary You will be provided with a miracle, a wonderful resolution regarding any issue in your life, and you will experience as a result of it a successful recovery in all areas of your life. This dream is an omen of prosperity and is asking you to focus on treatments you need to bring back a sense of normalcy and balance regarding your health. Move quickly and motivate yourself to perform the necessary tasks to move ahead in life. Victory is with you. You will retain a sense of excitement about your future and your new beginning for a long time to come.

Virgo Prepare your calendar and you can expect special and lucky situations to occur between August twenty third and September twenty second that will bring drastic improvements to your life. The changes that occur in this cycle will be absolutely unbelievable. Motivate yourself in such a way that will allow these changes to occur even earlier than they are destined to. Many blessings are with you and you are headed for a brilliant future.

visa You have prior notice to take care of any negative event foretold in this dream and to make sure you experience only positive events in your life. Within seven days you will also be able to clearly analyze someone else's behavior toward you so you can behave in the proper manner. You will have the courage and foresight to handle yourself appropriately. You are in an extremely lucky seven day cycle.

vise Lack of communication will cause you a major setback. Take steps to keep this from occurring and to improve a situation with someone you feel you need to communicate with. You will be entering a three day cycle that will allow you to easily use good communication skills and you will be able to get your point across to others successfully.

Vishnu Do not allow yourself to become overwhelmed with new responsibilities for the next three days.

vision Take steps to prevent any negative event you dreamed of from becoming a reality. You have prior notice of this and can make sure you experience only positive expressions in your life. Forewarn anyone you recognize in this dream to do the same. All of your plans will work out exactly as you want them to. All love relationships will work out well and will yield positive results.

to clearly view two separate things or people in two places at the same time Your spirit is reminding you that you have committed yourself to two events at the same time. The first thing scheduled is far more important than the second.

double vision - to see double (blurry) With the proper medical help, within a three day period you will find the solution to a recurring pain. Search relentlessly for a solution until you get the proper help. Any negative event in this dream needs to be altered or avoided. Make it a point to experience only positive expressions in your life.

visionary Pay close attention to the contents of this dream. If you see anything that is connected to anyone you recognize or to yourself that foretells a negative event, you must take steps to prevent this in reality or to avoid it completely. Forewarn this individual to do the same. This dream also implies that the connection you want to make with another person you have had difficulty connecting with will be accomplished within the week. Use this cycle to your advantage.

visions A certain group of people will be sad because of something you will say about a particular situation. You must be very careful about what you say in order to avoid injuring anyone else's feelings. Otherwise, this is a very good cycle and luck will be with you for the next two weeks. Anything portended in this dream needs to be altered or changed.

visit Anything viewed in this dream that carries a negative connotation needs to be changed or avoided in reality. Inform anyone in this dream whom you recognize to do likewise. Within five days you will also be able to grasp a once in a lifetime opportunity to meet the person who is perfect for you and you will develop a beautiful, healthy relationship. This relationship will bring great wealth and power to both of you if you choose to go this route.

visor A disagreement will break out among a group of people at an event where you will be enjoying yourself. This incident will spill over on you and you could accidentally be hurt. Take steps to avoid this for the next few days. Keep away from large crowds where this could happen.

vital signs Whatever you were emotionally deprived of in

the past with another will come to you within a few days. This person will give you everything you need because they have rediscovered how to touch someone in an emotional way.

vitamin You will have a conversation with someone within three days who will manipulate it in such a way that you will end up divulging information about your past. This will continue for as long as you allow it and at each meeting you will continually be asked about your past to the point of annoyance. You do not need to divulge this information. Your business is your business whether it is good or bad. Tactfully inform this person that you are not interested in discussing your past. You are definitely headed for a brilliant future and many blessings will come to you and your family. You can also expect a financial windfall.

vixen Within five days you will be with a group of people and have a wonderful time. You will be very popular with others. Many blessings are with you and your family. You must also execute the plans you want to implement very carefully in order to achieve success. You will be able to make the correct decisions.

vocabulary *any form* Be very aware of and take precautions against any blood infection. This could be caused by any number of things that could put toxins or bacteria into the bloodstream. Make sure you keep yourself safe for the next five days.

vocal cords Within two days start living your life to the fullest and stop depriving yourself of the spice of life. Introduce amusements into your life for more enjoyment.

vocation If you dream of any negative situation that you wish not to occur in reality, you need to take steps to prevent it or to alter the outcome. You must also take a strong stand, within five days, in your refusal to go along with someone else's plans. Do not compromise on this.

vodka You will receive the financial support you are unsure now whether you will receive from another person. Within four days you will be able to ask and receive this support from someone you care about.

voice box Pay attention to anything you heard in this dream and take steps to alter any negative message you may have heard. If this pertains to someone else you know, make sure this person takes the proper precautions. You will be tenacious in pursuing a goal until you achieve victory.

voices *to hear the voice of someone who is not there* This dream is a very lucky omen. You will need to develop a quiet conviction when going after needed services you feel you are being denied. Tactfully repeat your requests until you are clearly heard. This applies to both professional services and to emotional situations. Pay close attention to what the voice is telling you. You may be overlooking a positive situation that needs to be included in your life and embraced or a negative situation that is developing that needs to be attended to. This message will enhance your life in some capacity.

to hear a disembodied woman's voice Follow the advice given to the letter.

if you did not clearly hear the message This dream is an extremely lucky omen and you will be able to withstand any hardship that will arise within the next three days.

to hear a disembodied man's voice Pay close attention to the message given. If negative, take steps to change the outcome. If positive, take steps to incorporate it into your life. This dream also implies that someone who acts indifferently toward you is, in reality, not this way. This person actually desires very much to be involved in your life. If you choose to become involved, make the first move and let it be known that you would like more involvement. Your plans will also fall into place just as you have envisioned. Do not hold back on big projects. Tackle these projects and you will experience prosperity.

to hear a deceased person's voice You will experience victory due to your valiant integrity while engaged in making decisions. You will not compromise your principles. Develop a quiet conviction and be relentless in your pursuit of something that righteously belongs to you. This may be in the form of money, contracts, terms and agreements as well as productive conversation. Do not give up until you succeed.

void *to void a check* Watch out for the mental tapes that you are running in your mind. Do not allow yourself to get sucked into negative thoughts that will stress you out to the point of becoming ill. These thoughts will come to your mind spontaneously. Do what you can to stop them.

volcano You are heading in the wrong direction. People are depending on you and you are putting yourself in a potentially stressful situation. The plans you are making will not fall into place as they should. Step back, regroup, and rethink the different possibilities you will have to handle within the next three weeks. You can head off any problems and avoid this situation completely. Your priority now is to make sure that things fall into place correctly and to ensure you have the revenue and stability to carry them through in a stress free manner. Otherwise this will be a very prosperous situation and many blessings will come to you and your family.

volleyball Make sure the machines you are using have the proper lubrication, water, etc., they need in order to perform well at the times you need for them to be in top form. Machine maintenance should be your priority now.

volt Decide what you need to reform and act on it very quickly so everyone involved will enjoy a better lifestyle. Proceed with confidence with certain negotiations that will take place within five days.

voltage You will fail at your first try because you will at-

tempt to take care of a certain issue without all the necessary information, with the wrong tools, etc. Rethink your moves so you can get it right the first time and not waste time.

volume *to turn the volume up or down* Someone whom you feel a special closeness to is undergoing a great amount of strain that is being placed on them by another individual. They will come to you within three days in an attempt to explain this to you but will be unable to verbalize exactly what they are feeling. This person is in grave danger of having their spirit broken because of the irresponsible and abusive behavior this other person is displaying toward them. They are being controlled and are becoming very suspicious of the methods used. In actuality, there is no specific method or motive except for abusive actions toward them and they are continually remaining in this situation. This is the perfect time for this person to become more suspicious and to confront their own inability to move beyond this controlling situation. They need to be very aware that the moment they have this conversation with you, they must motivate themselves in such a way to move on. Otherwise, this could easily turn into a very distressful situation for them. They will only become aware of the amount of abuse they are under when it is too late unless they start making their moves now. You will also, within this three day period, be able to use your communication skills in such a profound way that you will be able to gain someone's absolute attention. You will be able to open their eyes in such a way that they will be able to motivate themselves and raise their standard of living to the level that suits them. By using these skills, you will be able to flush out the information you need from others and this information will prove to be very advantageous and beneficial to both of you. Many blessings are with you and you are headed for a brilliant future.

in any other form Do not allow yourself to stagnate or reach a point where you feel you are not getting anywhere. Within two days you will be focusing on what you need to do to get where you want to go. You will enjoy a vast amount of energy and the creativity it will take to turn this situation around and create the lifestyle you seek. You will be putting yourself on the right track.

volunteer Whatever you need to process within two days must be done quickly so you can get exactly what you are after. Whatever you felt was impossible is possible now. Go for it. You will also have a period where you will feel more useful, younger and will experience greater health.

vomit For the next seven days you will be motivated to bring more changes in your life and to begin work in areas that will bring about more prosperity. This will be a very lucky cycle for you.

to see yourself vomit Certain situations in your life are evolving to the point of giving others the opportunity to take advantage of you. This situation will grow to the point of being intolerable. Take control and do not allow yourself to lose power. This is especially important for the next three days.

to see someone else vomit For two days make a special effort to be kind in the manner in which you communicate with a special person in your life. Motivate this person to speak with you about their feelings, commitments and plans regarding your future. This will result in a more positive direction when dealing with this person. Good luck will be with you for the next seven days.

voodoo *to hear or use the word* Within three days you will be walking a thin line and it will be very easy for someone to steer you in the wrong direction. You will remain clear in your thoughts and will be able to grasp this situation immediately. Keep yourself going in the right direction and be very alert to this situation.

vortex Calibrate and detail your thoughts in such a way that you can put them into words and enable someone else to open up and communicate exactly what you need to know in order to tie up loose ends. This will allow you to go on with your life in the correct manner. You are headed in the right direction.

vote Follow the advice given to you very carefully. This advice will be given to you very quickly and you need to follow each word carefully in order to structure your life as you desire. If you are uncertain of what you are hearing, clarify the advice at the time this person is talking to you.

voter Within five days you will be able to perform in such a way that you will be able to meet the demands of another person, romantically and sexually.

voting machine You need to get some difficult information that will be very hard to get on your own. Within a few days this information will come to you very easily, especially if you enlist someone else to get this information for you. You also need to recall what was on the ballot. If the message implies anything negative about you or someone else, you must take the proper steps to prevent this from occurring in reality. Make sure you only experience positive expressions in your life.

voucher Loosen up your work schedule for your own health and physical well being. You are headed for a prosperous future and many blessings are with you and your family.

vow Get the professional help you need within three days in order to handle these things that need to be taken care of. Don't waste time, go for it.

vowel Do not allow anger to rule you. Take the time to regroup and to rid yourself of these feelings. Everything will fall into place as you wish.

voyage Be aware that a situation will occur within three days that will involve another person and will keep you from accomplishing what you need to take care of in a timely fashion. Several events will occur at the same time that will keep you tied up with this individual and interfere with your

schedule. Any negative event portrayed in this dream that involves you or another person you recognize also needs to be attended to and either prevented or altered in reality.

voyeur Within a few days you will be involving yourself with someone and will experience an emotional roller coaster ride. Do not allow yourself to become involved in an unfortunate sequence of events. For the next five days do what you can to avoid this completely.

V-shaped sign A big victory will come to you within five days. Be consistent and make sure that you behave appropriately in all areas of your life.

V-type engine You will find for the next ten days you will be at the peak of experience and be so together you will instinctively know you will reach the finish line before the race has really begun. You will have the feeling of confidence that comes from knowing you will succeed. You will feel the strength that comes from your inner core. Follow your goals as if you were on a mission and this will bring you to a victorious completion of your goals. Within this time frame, your sense of ethics and judgment will be intact and you are headed for a fantastic future.

Vulcan Someone will want to pay you a visit within five days. This person is living a lifestyle they do not want and wishes to visit for a few days because they know you will treat them with respect. This person will not verbalize their problems but it will be clear that something is wrong. Back off and let this person choose the right time to open up to you, otherwise you will drive them away and will be unable to offer assistance. Good luck is with you.

vulgarity Start carrying yourself in the proper way so you can handle a particular situation that will begin to evolve immediately after this dream and will escalate to the point of chaos. Get it under control within five days before it gets to the point of being out of control. Someone you recognize in this dream who is behaving in a vulgar fashion will come into your life within five days to discuss something that has them emotionally stressed out. Alert this person ahead of time so they can avoid any situation that will be distasteful to them, especially for the next few days. Someone will also attempt to involve you in a lifestyle you find very distasteful. Let this person know immediately that this lifestyle is not for you so they will not get the idea that at some point in time you will be eager to become involved. Take steps to keep any negative issue in this dream from becoming a reality and wasting your time. Otherwise, you are headed for a brilliant future and many blessings are with you and your family.

vulture This dream is a powerful omen and a promise that you will grasp the goals you are seeking. You will be very victorious and the gods will be with you for the next month. You will also be very intuitive during this time period and will be able to pinpoint those who are planning to take advantage of you. You will instinctively know those people who come to you with wrong intentions. You are headed for a brilliant future as long as you limit your involvement with those who are trying to do you harm.

vulva Take steps to keep any negative event in the dream from becoming a reality. You have prior notice of this and can either avoid this event entirely or change it around to a positive event. This dream also implies that someone with a mysterious lifestyle will attract your interest. This person is from another country, is very bright and will bring a tremendous amount of joy into your life. Within three days you will begin to make friends with this person. You will both share pleasurable moments together on a permanent basis. You will also enjoy a tranquil, harmonious lifestyle and you are headed for a brilliant future.

W

W The cycle that will be coming up for the next month will bring you a tremendous amount of prosperity because of the occurrence of many magical and wondrous happenings. You have been struggling to accomplish many tasks that have been very difficult to handle. This cycle will offer you the chance to easily take care of these tasks because you will experience what will seem to be a major breakthrough. You will feel the problems disintegrate and will be able to break through the mental block you have been struggling with. Once you begin taking care of these tasks, start focusing on other things you need to take care of. This is the perfect time to handle these jobs because you will have the energy and power to tackle them. Within five days an outstanding debt will also be unexpectedly paid for you by someone else. Attempt to locate the source of this payment during this time period. This person would also like to give you a gift of money. Motivate yourself in such a way to make yourself accessible to this gift. You are headed for a brilliant future.

wad You need to look at things from a variety of different perspectives and make sure resentments do not get in the way of having fun with a variety of people. Go ahead and enjoy a new and different style of living. Do not keep yourself from experiencing new ways of living life. Within five days you will meet a new group of people who will bring variety to your life. You will enjoy yourself immensely.

wade This dream is a very victorious omen and implies that in spite of what may be going on in your life right now, you will be focused on what you need to be doing that will enable you to grasp your goals. You will also be able to use your abilities to pull strings on your behalf. You will develop confidence and will be emotionally equipped to move ahead with success. Many blessings are with you and your family.

wading bird Someone you find attractive and appealing will, within two days, involve you in an unfortunate and dangerous event. This is because this person is still being harassed by a jealous former mate who will come after you if they learn about you. Make it clear you are interested but refuse to become involved until this is cleared up. You are also headed for a prosperous future and you will handle everything successfully.

wading pool Your energy level will run low. Do not over extend yourself, keep yourself healthy, and remain on an even keel, especially for the next five days.

wafer Within five days you will have to deal with someone who will make a big deal out of a small issue. Take an active role in order to handle this issue responsibly.

waffle Your intuition about love and money are right on target and your intuition will carry you ahead. Demonstrate patience toward another. This will allow them to open up and feel comfortable enough in your presence to communicate openly with you.

waffle iron Within three days you will be able to acquire what you want most from life. You are entering a very lucky cycle and will experience tranquility, harmony and prosperity. This is the perfect time to do those things you have been wanting to do that will bring you joy. Many blessings are with you.

wage earner Make sure that some of your clothes are not stolen within the week. Take preventive measures to ensure that this does not take place.

wages You need to avoid explosive disagreements in public places with the object of your affections. Avoid doing anything that will cause others to talk about you. Take steps to keep any negative occurrence in this dream from becoming a reality with you or anyone you recognize in the dream and do everything you can to create a stress free environment for yourself and your loved ones.

wagon This dream is a very powerful symbol and a promise to you that you will grasp the goals you are pursuing. You will be very victorious and will receive many blessings. The deities are with you. Within five days someone who formerly played an important role in your life will seek you out for the purpose of reuniting. This will be a very happy reunion for both of you. If you choose to pursue this reunion it will lead to an improved life for both of you.

wagon train *in any form* Someone is very interested in you and is very eager for you to make the first move. You will be very surprised that when you do you will be welcomed with open arms. This dream also implies that you are putting yourself on a new path that will bring you an abundance of health and healthy relationships. You are definitely headed for a prosperous future.

waif Do not waste your time scrutinizing whether a romantic situation will work out or not. You may end up talking yourself out of going on a date with this person. Things will work out wonderfully and everything will be beautiful between you if you choose this path.

Waikiki This dream is a lucky omen for love. Within three days you will clearly detail and calibrate your thoughts and put them into words in such a way that will allow someone to open their feelings up to you. This person desires you deeply. Your actions will enable this person to feel comfortable in your presence and will then be able to spark a relationship that will create a very warm union. This cycle will also allow you to tackle any situation that you have a mental block against. This block will be removed and conversations will flow easily. You must also take steps to keep any negative event in this dream from becoming a reality with you or anyone you recognize in this dream. This is a wonderful time for you to make travel plans for a vacation. If you have the opportunity to do this, take it. You will enjoy yourself and have a safe return. This dream may also be used as a reference point in time. If you dream of this beach and see its name used in any context, the dream message will occur on this day.

waist Set aside quality time to spend alone with each of your relatives and with young children who deeply love you.

waistcloth Do not be so willing to venture into the unknown. Someone has a hidden agenda that spells danger. Be aware of your surroundings, especially for the next five days and turn any negative omen in this dream to a positive experience.

waistcoat You will be passionately motivated within five days to complete a task that you find almost impossible regarding a romantic situation. You will be victorious with anything you want to accomplish that involves another person.

waistline Within three days you will be undergoing a major transformation with the help of a friend. This person will point you in a new direction and will provide you with much needed information that will successfully fulfill your desires.

wait *to wait your turn or someone else to wait for a turn* Within three days you will be able to resolve pressing responsibilities with ease. You will be surprised at how quickly this will develop and at the ease with which burdens will be lifted.

to see many people wait for you or to wait for someone else You will be dealing with someone within five days who will mislead you in a big way. This person very much wants to become involved in your life and will lead you to believe that they are well respected, have professional stability and a very credible lifestyle. You will find this person to be very believable and will be so comfortable and assured in this person's company that you will want to become involved with them. This individual will give you every reason to believe you can contact them at a moments notice and, as assurance, will give you various phone numbers, company addresses, etc. If you try to contact this person, you will find it will take hours and sometimes days for them to return your calls. You will come to the realization that this person has led you to believe they have a more impressive status than they do. If you become involved in any capacity you will be let down. Discipline yourself in order to prevent anyone from violating your emotions or insulting your intelligence. You have prior notice of this and will be able to deal with this very successfully. You are in a lucky cycle and are headed for a prosperous future.

in any other form Someone who is consistently trying to get your attention will be very aggravating. You need to make it clear from the start that you are not interested in receiving calls or in constantly being with this individual. This will reoccur within a few days and your words will not easily be erased from this person's memory. This individual will seek retaliation against you. Do what you can to avoid provoking resentments from someone you would like to have as a casual friend. Choose your words carefully and be firm but tactful. Move quickly in other areas of your life that require this behavior so things can move ahead as they should so you can reach a goal in the scheduled time. You are definitely headed for a brilliant future.

waiter/waitress Pay close attention to the contents of this dream and take steps to alter or avoid anything in this dream that foretells a negative event. All positive events should be promoted in reality. You will enjoy an abundance of health and joy and blessings will come to you and your family. All negotiations for the next seven days will also work out to your advantage. Love yourself, eat healing foods and drink plenty of water.

to wait on someone or have someone wait on you or to wait tables Make sure you are not billed for something you do not receive. If you are not careful, you will pay for something you do not own.

waiting room Take steps to prevent any negative event in this dream from becoming a reality. You have prior notice of this so you can experience only positive expressions in your life. This dream also implies that the opportunities offered to you that you expect will not work out will fall into place exactly as you desire.

wake Anything negative connected to this dream needs to be changed or avoided in reality, especially for the next five days. Alert anyone you recognize in this dream to do the same. This dream serves to mark a particular event in your life. After you have this dream, you will learn of a wake within twenty four hours or hear about one in the news, movie, etc., that is not directly connected to you.

to try to wake someone and be unable to Do everything you can to avoid any deeper involvement with a certain person you are beginning to grow closer to. Make sure you take extreme precautions. This is especially important for the next three days. This person has charm and charisma and will mislead you into believing you can depend on their loyalty and can fully confide in them. This person is clever and very skilled in deception and illusions and will have you believing in future events that will never take place. This person is secretly plotting to pursue you for some evil intent known only to them. An atmosphere of total trust will be created but if they sense you are starting to become suspicious, they will create a diversion to distract you. Once you comprehend what is going on, you will have suffered financial setbacks, emotional distress, disillusionments and disappointments. You will recover from this but it will take some time to get your life back on track. You have all the ammunition you need and enough advance notice to ensure that this does not take place. Practice common sense and you will successfully diffuse this situation. Have no dealings with this individual, do not compromise and do not allow this person to interfere in your private life. Otherwise you are headed for a prosperous future and many blessings will come to you and your family.

walk Your intuition and awareness are very keen and you will need to take advantage of this for the next five days. Your hunches will be very clear and will point you in the direction you need to be going. Also, be aware that anything negative connected to this dream can be altered so you experience only positive expressions in your life. If you see yourself or anyone else walking in this dream, this may indicate an activity you may want to encourage in your life for health purposes. Do this in a comfortable place and in a visually stimulating environment. This dream also implies that anything told to you now will be completely reliable and you are headed for a prosperous future.

to walk backwards or to see someone walking backwards You will experience new dimensions and meet new challenges with a newly hired assistant. At the first indication that this new assistant is having trouble, schedule a meeting to avoid any disruption in the work schedule.

to walk barefoot Avoid situations that expose you to bacteria. This may lead to a severe illness. Also, make sure you come to realize, within two days, you are under no obligation to behave in any way other than you choose. Make absolutely certain you are under no one else's control. You will then be able to permanently rid yourself of someone who feels they have authority over your behavior, manner of speech, thought patterns and ways of reacting. You will accomplish this with very little stress because of the tactful and easy way in which you handle this situation. You are headed in the right direction and will enjoy a prosperous future.

to walk fast Move quickly on plans you have prepared to become actively involved in, in order to bring a rapid solution and completion. Do this within five days. Do not involve yourself in any stressful situation for the next five days. You are definitely headed for a brilliant future.

to walk on fruit Make sure you drink plenty of water. You must also work toward resolving an important issue you

have lost the confidence to take care of. You will be successful within three days because you will develop new confidence. Good news is headed your way.

to walk on ice/snow This dream implies that you are putting yourself on a new path that will bring you an abundance of health and healthy relationships. You are definitely headed for a prosperous future. This dream is also an extremely lucky omen. Within three days you will be undergoing a major transformation with the help of a friend who will point you in a new direction and give you much needed information that will help you to fulfill your desires. You will also receive instant riches that will occur within a month's time. Your instincts about love will be right on target during this cycle.

to walk city blocks You will soon be paid all the money that is owed to you.

to walk at night holding a steady light or someone else holding a light You will definitely find a way out of any situation that is holding you back. An abundance of health, spiritual healing and tranquility will be yours for the next three weeks and you will enjoy a celebration within the week that will cause all those involved to rejoice. You will also find an idea, project or event you have been working on will be brought to fruition and you can expect this process to take place during the last two weeks of March and for the month of April. This project will take on a life of its own and will reach a high level of perfection. It will easily go through each channel necessary for completion and this event will be cause for a big celebration for everyone involved. You are on the path for a brilliant future.

to walk in mud You will have to decide whether to commit to a relationship. Someone else has become interested in the person you are involved with and if you do not commit, you will lose this relationship. If you do commit, this will be a very successful union. Move quickly, do not waste time, and do not allow the opinions of others to hinder your decision. You will enjoy a prosperous future because you will be able to turn a negative situation to a positive one.

to walk in the rain You will develop a fantastic idea that you will focus on completely. Your thinking patterns will be such that you will be able to pinpoint exactly what you need to do to get things going in the direction you choose in the most efficient way possible. This dream is a very lucky omen.

to walk on water A small surprise will be awaiting you. This is the perfect time to request what you desire from your higher power regardless of how impossible this request may seem. You are definitely headed for a brilliant future.

to walk on vegetables Any relationship you have that is special to you will become more special and you will both be looking forward to your future plans together. This could be a relationship in any capacity. The combination of both of you working together is an unbeatable force. The powerful force of love is working for both of you now and you will reach any goal you strive for during this cycle. Many blessings are with you and your family.

to walk through a solid wall or see someone else walk through a solid wall This dream serves as a warning that a very malicious person will come to you and present a very trustful facade. You will be led to believe that whatever you discuss will be strictly confidential. This person is really attempting to gather as much information from you as they can about a third party and will then take your words back to this individual. Be acutely aware of this because once they hear what you have said they will confront you and this could escalate to a violent episode. You have prior notice of this and can avoid this situation entirely.

to walk on a moving sidewalk or walkway This dream is an extremely lucky omen and implies you will experience an inner strength and courage as well as the drive and determination you need to motivate yourself to push beyond any physical or mental barrier that interferes with your moving ahead. Within four days you will rid yourself completely of any aspect of your life that you disapprove of. Once you do you will successfully bring a new project you are excited about into tangible form. You will also be greeted in a regal fashion and placed on a pedestal anywhere you go during this time period. You are headed for a brilliant future and many new opportunities are headed your way.

walkie-talkie Pay close attention to what you heard over the walkie-talkie and take steps to prevent any negative event foretold in this dream. Any positive event portended in the dream should be promoted to the fullest. If this dream involves someone you recognize, make sure that you forewarn them to do likewise. It also implies that you will soon hear of the birth of twins. Many blessings are with you and your family and you are headed for a prosperous future.

walking stick Do not put yourself in a situation to be sexually abused by a persistent person.

walkman Take steps to alter or avoid any negative message you heard over the walkman and bring any positive message to fruition. This dream also implies you will be entering a three day cycle that will require you give extra attention to someone you have special feelings for. You will need to express more patience and to voice your thoughts more clearly. Set aside more special time to devote to this person.

wall You are being asked to remove any mental block that keeps you from moving ahead. You need to clear yourself mentally within the next three days.

cement block Bring together creative people who will become a pool of resources you can draw from for the information you need in a business venture. The time is perfect for this now and your energies will result in life long riches.

wooden block Within a week an injury will occur to you or to your property due to inclement weather. Prepare ahead.

to do anything out of the ordinary with a wall Within five days you will definitely find the solution to any medical problem and the medical advice you will be given will be totally accurate. You will rid yourself of any mysterious ailment. Good luck is with you.

with a hole knocked in it Within three days you will be dealing with a very conniving and evil person who presents a

sweet persona and gives the impression they will do anything to keep you happy. Something, however, will be triggered inside this person that will create feelings toward you that will make them want to hurt you. This could be a result of their feelings about their mother, past experiences, etc. You will be able to identify who this person is because of a description left in the dream (i.e., the mannerisms, speech patterns, clothing, appearances, etc.) of someone you dreamed of. This person will use their winning ways and charm to play tricks on you, manipulate you and intentionally sabotage your plans. You will eventually find this out but since you know about this ahead of time you can turn it around so it can be handled appropriately. If you do not, you will be deeply hurt.

to walk through a solid wall or see someone else walk through a solid wall This dream serves as a warning that a very malicious person will come to you and present a very trustful facade. You will be led to believe that whatever you discuss will be strictly confidential. This person is really attempting to gather as much information from you as they can about a third party and will then take your words back to this individual. Be acutely aware of this because once this person hears what you have said they will confront you and this could escalate into a violent episode. You have prior notice of this and can avoid this situation entirely.

cracked or broken A close relative will lose their job. Do what you can to help. You must also take steps to empower and protect yourself by putting everything that is important to you into writing.

electric wall socket You and someone you recognize in this dream will motivate yourselves in an unusual way that will enable you to get in touch with an unknown person. You and the person in this dream will both have this experience although they will be totally unconnected. Conversations will flow easily between you and the person you have yet to meet, in a delightful way. You will both have the feeling you have not experienced this in a long time, if ever. The person you will meet possesses an artful sense of timing as well as the unusual ability to sense the feelings of other people. They are capable of bringing pleasure to others and of fully committing themself. And are also able to put themselves in a subservient role, tastefully and within limits, as well as having the capability of pampering others to the extreme, but not overly so. You will find this to be very delightful and will never have a distasteful moment. If you choose to have a relationship, it will grow as much as you want and will be a mutually satisfying and nurturing union. Expect this to occur within three days and alert the person you dreamed about to expect this as well. You are headed for a brilliant future.

wallaby You will need to gain more practice before tackling a situation you are presently involved with. Get the experience and training you need before you go any further. You will also receive old news regarding romance. This cycle will be very lucky for romance and love.

wallboard For the next three days do what you can to stay on the right side of the law in order to avoid getting a citation. Play by the rules.

wallet An unexpected romantic situation will come up out of the blue. You will feel as though you have to comply with the mood of the event. Be nice to this person but make sure you do not put out any signals that will encourage this to go on any further. Make yourself clear. If the wallet is full, this also implies that your finances will improve. If empty, start preparing now for a loss of income in the future. Many blessings are with you and your family and you are headed for a prosperous future.

wallflower You will decide to pursue a higher level of education and this will become a challenge within the month. Take care of all extraneous issues now and eliminate all negative situations so you will be able to successfully meet this challenge.

wallpaper Motivate yourself, within five days you will be able to create opportunities that will add excitement to your life and will change your life in a tremendous way. Rely on your intuition during this time period because it will lead you to the path you should take. Eat healing foods and treat yourself to something special. Many blessings are with you, you are entering a very lucky cycle and you are loved beyond your imagination.

coming off the wall Do not allow someone else to abuse your time. You should be the only one to determine what you should use your time for. Pay attention to the design or any words printed on the paper for additional clues. If negative, make every effort to change the result or to avoid it in reality. Alert anyone in the dream that you recognize to do likewise.

Wall Street Within two days you will be joyful because you will learn the intensity of someone else's involvement in your life. This dream may also be used as a reference point in time. If you dream of this street and see its name used in any context, the dream message will occur on this day.

wall to wall carpeting You have an ongoing relationship with someone who is restraining themselves from allowing this relationship to grow. Within three days do what you can to open up the lines of communication to encourage this person to grow closer to you and to stop setting so many limits in the relationship. You will be successful in this and both of you will benefit as a result.

walnut You will reach a decision with a very special person in your life. This decision will allow you both to acquire the necessities in life and you will both be mutually satisfied. This dream is an extremely lucky omen and you are entering a cycle that will allow open communication, especially regarding love. All matters involving love and romance are going in the right direction.

walrus You will have many passionate moments with the person you desire most. This will begin to develop within three days. Expose yourself to social settings where this is likely to occur. Avoid any situation during this time period that could result in an accident. Many blessings are with you and your family.

waltz You will attend an event that you will enjoy far more than you anticipated.

wampum Do not allow a persistent family member to involve you in a distasteful situation. Do everything you can to bypass this issue.

wand Do not question the feelings that are coming up between you and a special person. Go with it and allow situations to flow naturally. You will be surprised at the deep emotions you will feel. You are headed for a brilliant future, especially if it was a magic wand you dreamed of, and things you felt were impossible are now possible for the next seven days. Many blessings are with you and your family.

Wandering Jew *(plant)* A friend of a friend will introduce you to your soul mate. This person will stay with you for a lifetime and you will both find deep love with each other. You will enjoy a mutually satisfying life and will make wonderful plans for the future. Move on this now, all of your plans will work out perfectly.

want ad Take steps to keep anything negative in this dream that is connected with reality from occurring. Place a want ad for anything that could enhance your life. This is a medium you can use to bring you more prosperity. You can also use this means to advertise for a special partner in your life. This is a special cycle for you and many unusual situations can occur by you placing an ad. Many blessings are with you and your family and you are headed for a very prosperous future.

war An interesting situation will occur within two days. You will meet two different people at two different outings at separate times. You will be attracted to both of them without realizing they both share living quarters. Both are single and both will give you their phone number. Although they live in the same place, they have different phone numbers. You will call both of them, have delightful conversations, and make plans for a date with both of them not knowing they live together. Prior to the first date, you will call one of them and the other will answer the phone. This will lead to a major confusion that you will keep to yourself. Then you will call the second person and the first will answer the phone. You will hang up because of confusion both times. Both of these people are unaware of what is happening and think you are interested only in them. Be very careful because if they learn you are interested in both of them you will lose both. Decide on only one person for your own good. This will be a very exciting time for you and you will have many admirers to choose from. You are entering a very prosperous time period.

warbler This is the perfect cycle to think in terms of merging a company or a group of people together. A team effort approach will be extremely lucky. You are headed for a brilliant future.

war bonnet Within five days your thoughts will be very clear and you will be able to map out, in detail, plans for another person that will enable them to help themselves out. You will be able to give this person wonderful advice that they will be able to use. This will enable them to move on with their lives without help from others.

war chest Someone you have had a high regard for and with whom you have done business with will ask you for a loan. Although this person has always been good on their word and has always paid you back, this time they will be unable to repay this debt. This will put a lot of stress on you and on them. Do not lend money this time and you will avoid a lot of stress.

war club You will be unwittingly used and taken advantage of by another person. This individual will use deception and dishonesty regarding a certain situation with you as an innocent participant. Pay close attention to your present situation and be acutely aware of the actions of others in order to avoid being cheated.

war crime For the next five days you are being warned that you are headed in the wrong direction although your intentions are good. Those who are involved and are trying to help are playing a very selfish part by not backing off and by consistently leading you on the path toward a very stressful situation. Listen to your hunches and put a stop to this.

war cry Do everything you can for the next four days to control your temper. A distasteful situation will come up that will create suspicious and jealous feelings toward someone you are close to. These feelings will drive you into a murderous rage. Take steps to keep this from developing and do not cater to your emotions. You are putting too much importance on someone else and not enough on yourself.

ward Take every precaution to prevent any negative event you dreamed of that is connected to reality from occurring. Make sure you emphasize the positive and inform anyone in this dream whom you recognize to do likewise. For the next two weeks it is also important not to take on the responsibility of anyone else's life. Everyone needs to carry their own weight and if they are unable to, make sure they find the proper agency and assistance they need. Both of you will be glad you took this route and that you are able to free yourself from being responsible for others.

warden You will have all the verification you need, within the week, to assure yourself that the person you care about is in love with you. Because of this you will be in the frame of mind to flourish in other areas of your life. You are headed for a brilliant future.

wardrobe You will experience victory in those areas of your life you most desire and you will grasp victory in those areas you felt were impossible. You are headed in the right direction, especially for the next two weeks. Trust your intuition, your hunches are right on target.

warehouse Pay attention and concentrate for the next three days. Someone will attempt to interfere with your train of thought. This person will lead you to believe your thoughts are not that great or they will convince you that you are headed in the wrong direction and have you doubting your abilities. Otherwise this is an extremely lucky omen, especially for the next week. You will not only be able to turn this situation around but will also be able to express yourself fully to those who are important to you in a way that will bring them closer to you. Many blessings are with you.

warfare An interesting situation will occur within two days. You will meet two different people at two different outings at separate times. You will be attracted to both of them without realizing they both share living quarters. Both are single and both will give you their phone number. Although they live in the same place, they will have different phone numbers. You will call both of them, have delightful conversations and make plans for a date with both of them not knowing they live together. Prior to the first date, you will call one of them and the other will answer the phone. This will lead to a major confusion that you will keep to yourself. Then you will call the second person and the first will answer the phone. You will hang up because of confusion both times. Both of these people are unaware of what is happening and think you are interested only in them. Be very careful because if they learn you are interested in both of them you will lose both. Decide on only one person for your own good. This will be a very exciting time for you and you will have many admirers to choose from. You are entering a very prosperous time period.

war games Do everything necessary to bring more joy into your life and create a situation to release stress. You will also receive an invitation to a distant city to join someone whom you enjoy being with at this person's expense. This mini vacation will be one that you will enjoy and will treasure for a lifetime. You will enjoy a safe trip.

warhorse Any big plans you have for the next three days will be executed successfully and brought to completion. During this time frame you will have the joy of grasping your ambitions.

warlord The person you will be dealing with for the next week will require a great deal of patience on your part to have this person behave in the manner you wish. This person will finally open up and interact with you in the way you desire. Allow this person the time they need to feel comfortable enough with you to do this. Any enterprise you become involved in during this time period will also be successful.

You are headed for a prosperous future.

warm Be very attentive, especially for the next seven days, to those who are very special to you and are feeling abandoned. Although they have not expressed this to you, they are suffering in silence. This person desires more interaction with you. You will also experience many days of health and deep feelings of tranquility.

warmhearted You will be able to live up to what you have promised someone else within the week. Proceed with confidence.

warming pan All financial negotiations and transactions connected with travel will be enormously fortuitous. These negotiations will bring you a tremendous amount of joy and prosperity. Proceed with confidence.

warmonger Think ahead to the next two days. Someone who is important to you will stupidly blurt out inconsiderate and insulting remarks when you are in the presence of others. Take this person aside beforehand and state your opinions about this kind of behavior. Do this in a tactful way and you will be able to keep these thoughtless, unintentional remarks from being said.

warn Move quickly during this cycle to connect emotionally with those you feel a need to connect with. This is the perfect time for this. Not only will the opportunity present itself but your communication skills will be at their highest. You will both be able to sort out your feelings and decide on the path you want to take.
    to be warned or to warn someone For the next seven days any agreement you seek with either an individual or a group of people will reach fruition. Proceed with confidence and do not doubt yourself. Other people are now willing to compromise to get things going in the direction they should be going. Many blessings are with you.

warp Someone you care about will move to an area that will be too costly for you to communicate with them easily by phone. You will undergo feelings of deep emotional loss as a result of this. Expect this to take place within three days.

war paint Someone who is interested in you will go to great pains to make sure all your needs are taken care of, as well as the finer things in life, with no strings attached. If you choose, this relationship will develop as you wish, especially for the next two weeks. Many blessings are with you and you are headed for a prosperous future.

warpath Something is taking place behind the scenes involving another person for reasons only known to them. This individual enjoys creating chaos and disturbing events in the lives of others purely for their own pleasure. Be very aware of your surroundings and of any unusual episodes in your life. Take steps to bring balance and stability into your life.

warrant *arrest warrant* Do what you can to keep any negative event from becoming a reality. You have prior notice of this and can ensure you only experience positive expressions in your life. Make sure you forewarn anyone you recognize in this dream to do the same. You must also not allow yourself to be persuaded by someone with grandiose ideas to become involved in a scheme of theirs. Remain as you are and make no new moves to change your lifestyle or living arrangements.

warrant officer Someone who is married will be very attracted to you and will do everything in their power to lure you into a relationship with them. Do everything you can to protect yourself from this situation. It will definitely backfire on you.

warranty For the next seven days, do not become so focused on what someone else is doing. Focus yourself on what you should be doing. This person will only cause interruptions to the point of diverting you from the path you are headed. You need to be very focused and disciplined in order to accomplish your goals without any outside interference. This is especially important for the next seven days.

warren You can prevent a falling out between yourself and a close friend. This person will pull a power play because you do not have the money and power they have. You will be asked continually to perform favors for them so they can exert their control over you. Take this person aside and express your feelings. If you do not take this step, you will be forced to cut this person out of your life instead of maintaining a friendship.

warrior You will receive an abundance of health and wealth within the week. This dream also implies that a situation will occur within a five day period that will require that you demonstrate assertive behavior. You will behave accordingly and this situation will be quickly resolved.

wart This dream is an extremely lucky one. Someone wants to involve you in a project they will present to you within two days. You will not be excited by the idea but it is important that you realize that the benefits are greater than you ever anticipated. Good luck is with you.

warthog Someone will come into your life who is interested in having you share their life in any capacity. The most important thing to them is to have you share in the wealth they have recently come into. If you choose to pursue this, you will enjoy yourself with no strings attached. Many blessings are with you and your family.

war zone You have a better chance of reconciling with someone you care about if you make your move within three days. This dream also implies that you will get a quick response to your request for specific information.

wash Do everything in your power to work an agreement in your favor within the week. There is no doubt that this agreement will take place and you must motivate yourself in such a way that you will be able to push it through during this time period. Many blessings are with you.

to wash You will reach an agreement for sexual gratification with another person. This will lead to a love relationship and, eventually, to a life long union if you so desire.

white wash This dream is an extremely lucky omen and you are headed for a brilliant future.

to wash someone else Expect rewards of love, affection and financial stability.

to wash your face For the next two days make sure you are very self reliant and take pains to look at both sides of an issue. Explore the possibilities of what could occur unexpectedly prior to making any major decisions. You are loved beyond your imagination, are deeply respected and will be surrounded by those who love you a great deal. Others will show you their appreciation within seven days.

to see others wash their face Make sure that within three days you do not gravitate toward someone who has a mysterious past but does not reveal this to others. Make sure you do not involve yourself with this person or any unusual situation that could occur within the week.

if you recognize the person who was washing their face This person is very eager to involve themselves with you in any capacity. In reality they are interested in you in a deeply passionate way without your knowledge. Take the appropriate steps to bring this person closer to you or to avoid the development of a relationship as you see fit. You are headed for a very prosperous future and many blessings will come to you and your family.

to wash a car Do not deprive yourself of any intimate times that are coming to you. Do not put limits on yourself and do everything you can to feel comfortable enough to enjoy these moments. You will enjoy emotional fulfillment during this cycle.

to see laundry washed Do not allow anyone to talk you into releasing them from a promise they have made to you. You need to bear down on this person so they come through with the promise they have made for you. Do not compromise with this person. You are headed for a very prosperous future.

to flush or spray yourself, something or someone with clean water You will achieve a big victory during this upcoming cycle that will offer you an abundance of new opportunities. Position yourself by using whatever power of authority you may possess to work the completion of an agreement to your favor. This will be especially important for the next week. You have a seven day period from the time you have this dream to push this agreement through and it will be well received by everyone involved. This is the perfect cycle to take care of this task. You are on a victorious path in life and many blessings will come to you and your family.

washboard Within seven days there is a particular situation you need to give your personal attention to so it will continue to go in the direction you want it to. You will also see a def-

inite improvement in your financial affairs. You are headed for a brilliant future.

washbowl Within five days you will have a pleasurable surprise from someone you least expect. You will receive good news from them and will be asked to get involved in some capacity.

wash cloth Expect an invitation for a cozy, romantic interlude with another person whom you will find very desirable and with whom you have many things in common. If you choose, this will be a mutually satisfying relationship, filled with humor and tranquility. Expect this within the week.

washer You will become involved in a different type of lifestyle that you have never experienced before. Encourage this exploration, especially for the next two weeks. Bring new people into your environment and become more socially involved in events that will come up in this time frame. You will be exposed to many benefits that will enhance your life. This is the perfect cycle for exposure to different lifestyles. Make yourself available for this. Good luck is with you.

washer man/woman This dream is a very lucky omen and you will experience much prosperity in your life within two weeks. Things that you thought were impossible to become a part of are now possible during this two week period. Doors will be open to you and you will be welcomed with open arms. Many blessings are with you and your family.

washing machine Aggressively investigate any situation at the beginning stages so you will know how it develops if left to develop naturally. This will give you a clear picture of those aspects you want to become involved in. Do not over or underestimate any situation. Proceed with confidence.

Washington You are beginning to sense a strong emotional urge that will take up a large part of your time because you will not be able to determine the source of this drive. These urges are forcing you to focus on bringing something to reality. Expect this to continue for two weeks and you will continue to feel this deep emotional craving. Within this two week period, you will somehow arrive at the reason and source of this feeling and will then begin to act on what you feel you should be doing. This feeling is the result of heightened awareness and a psychic ability that is guiding you in the direction you should be taking. Although you have no real proof or tangible verification of this, you will know instinctively because of the intense excitement you feel, that by acting on this urge you will be granted greater benefits than you could ever anticipate. You can expect an abundance of health and a prosperous future. This is an extremely lucky omen. Your life will expand tremendously, situations will occur exactly as you have envisioned and will go in the direction you choose them to go. You are definitely headed for a brilliant future. This dream may also be used as a reference point in time. If you dream of this state and see its name used in any context, the dream message will occur on this day.

Washington, George Trust your instincts and you will motivate yourself in the direction you should be going. You will act in the appropriate way to raise your standard of living. You must also make it a point to refuse to accept unacceptable behavior from another person. Pay close attention to details about your health, be very careful, and protective of yourself for the next three days. Treat your health as a precious commodity and take steps to avoid exposure to a contagious disease. You also have detailed reliable information about a certain situation. This information should be used to cause definite improvements. Motivate groups of activists in order to focus them on certain situations that will take on a life of their own. This will bring about major improvements for all of those involved. You are in a prosperous cycle and are headed for a brilliant future.

Washington's Birthday This dream is an extremely lucky omen and you will experience an abundance of health and wealth in areas you never expected, because of an unexpected income. You will be able to accomplish those things you felt were impossible. This is the perfect cycle for this. Proceed with confidence. You are headed for a very prosperous future.

washrag Do not leave behind anything that might incriminate you and do everything you can to maintain your character in a respectable manner. Do not give others a faulty impression of yourself. For the next two days, it is important that you project yourself in the exact way you want others to perceive you.

washtub Seek an alternative answer to a situation that will begin to develop within seven days. Start preparing yourself now for different options you can take the moment you feel they are needed. This is particularly important when you begin to sense things developing along a line you do not desire. Proceed with confidence, you are headed for a prosperous future.

wasp Make sure you let someone know you are not interested in a particular lifestyle they are introducing to you. Be firm, committed and guarded so you can remain disciplined. Do not compromise yourself or your integrity with a lifestyle that is not to your liking, especially for the next five days.

WASP *(White Anglo Saxon Protestant)* Carefully consider an invitation you will receive within three days. The person issuing the invitation possesses a strangeness about them and a lifestyle that offends you. Be prepared to tactfully decline the invitation.

wassail Put yourself in a safe environment for the next five days and take extra precautions to avoid freak accidents. Make sure your environment is safe during this time period.

waste *any form* For the next five days make sure you demonstrate your best behavior and your true character to others. This will allow them to feel comfortable and nourished enough in your presence to include you in their plans whether financial, romantically or in any other capacity. During this five day period other people will also feel a need to be nourished and may need attention and affection from you. You may also be in contact with someone who has a disability and will approach you with benefits in some capacity. Make sure anything you see wasted in this dream is not wasted in reality. You are headed for a prosperous future.

wasteland Pay close attention to someone who is very immoral and wicked. Take steps to avoid any contact with the person.

wastepaper basket Within three days you will become aware of the deep emotional feelings you have for another. Because of this enlightenment you will quickly want to surrender yourself to this person. Expect nothing but the best from this relationship. You will be emotionally fulfilled in this union. Tranquility and mutual understanding will be yours if you choose to go this route. Pay attention to the contents of the wastepaper basket and if it portends a negative event, take steps to alter the outcome or to avoid the event altogether. Proceed with confidence. Many blessings are with you and your family.

watch *to watch or to be watched* Make sure, for the next five days, before you commit to something that you know you will not back out, otherwise do not make promises you cannot keep.

watch *(time piece)* All negotiations will have good results for the next week. Think ahead, someone you hire to do repair work will give you a different estimate than what was originally agreed upon. Get this in writing within two days and refuse to accept verbal agreements. Do not behave rudely to others or continually check the time when in the presence of another person. This person will be insulted. This dream is a lucky omen.

to hear a watch tick This dream indicates that you should not waste time when pursuing a project.

to look at a watch and note the time This dream is a lucky omen. If you have an important event scheduled within seven days, attempt to reschedule it at the time you dreamed about for greater success. Any hurdle you wish to resolve will be worked out in this time frame and an anticipated great event will occur at this specific hour. An unexpected romantic interlude will also occur within five days and will leave a lasting memory.

pocket watch You will accidentally stumble upon a brilliant opportunity within four days, especially if you put yourself in a position that will leave you open for this. You will know how to motivate yourself to grasp this opportunity. Many blessings are with you.

watchband Within three days someone will be eager to demonstrate their feelings for you and will reveal how deeply they want to become involved with you. This person will perform a series of chores and favors for you in the hopes of attracting your attention. Your every desire will be fulfilled. Openly demonstrate your affection and consideration to this person for their generosity and efforts. Be very cautious and do not hurt this person's feelings or become suspicious of this person's motives.

watch cap This dream is a very lucky omen. As a result of an unexpected income, you will gain an abundance of health and wealth in areas you least expect. You will also be able to take on those tasks you once felt were impossible. Take advantage of this cycle. Proceed with confidence. You are on the path for a prosperous future.

watchdog Someone you are working very hard with on a certain project that you both want to complete will be as tenacious as you in reaching your goal. Both of you will experience, in the near future, an increase in finances like you never imagined. You will both flourish because of this project in ways you never envisioned. Many blessings are with you and you are headed for a brilliant future as well as everyone else involved in this project.

watchmaker For the next week it will be extremely important to make sure you are handling tools correctly and you are using the proper tools for the job.

water *fresh* For a five day period your thoughts will be illuminating. This will be a gift from the divinities. You will be able to precisely detail those things that are important to do in your life. Once these plans are set in motion, you will experience grand changes in your way of living. You are headed in the right direction. Eat healthy foods, drink plenty of water and love yourself.

tainted in an unusual way Prepare yourself for the next seven days so you can handle any potential negative event that will develop in this time period. Turn this around quickly so you can experience only positive events in your life.

to flush or spray yourself, something or someone with clean water You will achieve a big victory during this upcoming cycle that will offer you an abundance of new opportunities. Position yourself by using whatever power of authority you may possess to work the completion of an agreement to your favor. This will be especially important for the next week. You have a seven day period from the time you have this dream to push this agreement through and it will be well received by everyone involved. This is the perfect cycle to take care of this task. You are on a victorious path in life and many blessings will come to you and your family.

body of water covered with scum Certain events will occur within three days that you must make a point of not dwelling on. This will only make situations worse. Motivate yourself to get busy on new ideas you need to work on.

to see water falling or spilling in any form All joint investments made within three days will be very successful. Glorious days are ahead. Enjoy yourself.

water bag Do not lend any articles of clothing or tools. They will not be returned in the same condition.

water barrel *empty* A serious move against your co-workers will be made by a supervisor. Co-workers will want you to testify for them. Stay neutral for the next three days.

full You will finally be asked out by someone you desire. Good luck is with you.

water beetle Give yourself some time within five days to contemplate and reflect on your feelings and ideas. This will enable you to connect with those aspects of your life that you wish to improve. You will be better able to do this by giving yourself the time to mull over those decisions you will be making.

water bird Within five days you will receive old news regarding romance. This cycle will be very lucky for romance and love.

water boy Do everything you can to tie up loose ends regarding all negotiations that will have to be dealt with within five days.

water buffalo This is the perfect time for you to pull strings to get the financial backing you are after in order to bring about what you really desire. This cycle will last for three days.

water chestnut All written plans, proposals, etc., will be very lucky for you now.

watercolor paintings Pay attention to what was represented in this painting. This will offer you a clue to something you need to pursue or an event or opportunity that needs to be investigated. You will find this will enhance your life and give you an advantage in the direction you are going. Anything negative in this dream that could become a reality needs to be altered or prevented in reality. Take steps to ensure you experience only positive expressions in your life. This dream also implies that this is the perfect time for you to carefully evaluate the choices you will have to make within three days. You will be able to take the thoughts you have been developing and devise ways to generate a larger income than you imagined. As a result, you will gain prestige and respect from your endeavors. Your motivation will rapidly spur this on. You will be put in a position of authority on a large scale situation at a low salary. This will rapidly grow into a position that you anticipated and prestige and a large salary will be the result. Expect this to take place soon.

watercolors You are definitely headed for a brilliant future. Look up the specific color for a more detailed definition of this dream.

water cooler Do everything necessary to unload some unusual responsibilities that are coming your way. If they are not rerouted or delegated out to others, you will find yourself fully responsible for these unusual issues. Do not leave yourself available for any added burdens or responsibilities.

watercress This dream is an extremely lucky omen. Within five days you will receive a financial windfall that will enable you to release yourself from all debts within the month. You must also make sure you eat foods, drink liquids, or take supplements to bring more calcium into your body. Many blessings are with you and you are headed for a brilliant future.

waterfall You will experience long lasting love and many moments of joy from those you were never aware existed before. You will also experience a new spiritual enlightenment and undergo some unusually extraordinary changes in your life that will not be the result of anything you do. These changes will occur quickly and will vastly improve your lifestyle. You will enjoy a busy social life and meet many wonderful new people. Live it up. Many blessings will come to you and your family. You are headed for a brilliant future.

water fountain You will receive good news within three days and be very pleased with the outcome of a business affair you are concerned with. This is a lucky omen for you as well as for love and finances.

Watergate Do everything necessary to bring more amusements into your life and to create a stress free environment. This will enable you to remain mentally healthy as well as allowing you to maintain mental clarity. Do not overload yourself with the problems of others. Keep yourself free from their demands and responsibilities and do not allow yourself to create extra burdens and responsibilities for yourself. Take a mini vacation for rest, reading, listening to good music, eating well and being good to yourself. This dream may also be used as a reference point in time. If you dream of this place and see its name used in any context, the dream message will occur on this day.

water gun Do not make yourself available to someone who may have a hidden agenda. This could result in an unusual kinky experience that will bring many uncomfortable and distasteful moments to you. Avoid this for the next three days. This will be someone you feel comfortable with who will turn on you the moment they sense your vulnerability. Keep yourself safe.

water heater Do not allow yourself to be verbally chastised by someone who wants you to enter into an agreement you have no wish to be involved in. Expect this to occur within three days and once it does, cut the conversation short because it could easily escalate into a very violent argument.

watering can This dream implies that you are entering a very lucky cycle and will experience an abundance of health and wealth in areas you least expect. This will be as a result of an unexpected income. You will also be able to take care of these tasks you once felt were impossible. Take advantage of this cycle to tackle those big tasks. Proceed with confidence. You are headed for a prosperous future.

watering hole You will expand your mental powers and be very clear on the direction you want to go. Proceed with confidence. Good luck is with you.

water lily You will become involved with someone you are very attracted to. Make sure, for the next five days, that you conduct yourself appropriately in front of this person so you can leave the impression you want.

Waterloo Make sure, at any cost, you do not put yourself in the position to allow things to happen that you do not want.

watermark Within a three day period make sure all your acquaintances know how you feel about a special person. This will ensure that there will be no misunderstandings and that everyone will treat this person with respect.

watermelon An unusual situation will occur within five days with a person who is unknown to you. This person will point things out to you that you have never known or experienced before. It would be advantageous to you to add these enlightenments to your life. Be very attentive to the suggestions made by others. By becoming involved, you will allow certain things to occur very rapidly that will bring about the changes you are destined for. You are definitely headed for a brilliant future.

water moccasin Protect what is precious to you at this moment. You must become very protective over anything that could become sour or negative, especially for the next seven days. You must be protective of everything you value in all levels of your life.

water nymph Someone has a conspiracy going on against you and has done a good job of concealing it. Be aware of this and do whatever is necessary to protect yourself.

water pipe You will be taken in easily by a conniving friend. This person will become a very clever enemy and will go to great lengths to sabotage an important opportunity just before you gain knowledge of it. Since you have prior notice you can determine who this person is and take care of this situation correctly. You will be able to turn this around to your advantage.

water polo Do not give in on a situation you have been resisting, especially for the next three days. You will find yourself placed in a position that you will find difficult to extricate yourself from and will find yourself surrendering because of your precarious position. You have prior notice of this and can take steps to avoid this completely.

waterproof You will find it easy to resist those situations that, in the past, you easily involved yourself in and that always produced negative results. This is a very good cycle to rid yourself of the habit of getting involved in negative situations. You will be able to move confidently ahead in your life.

water repellent Prosperity is in your destiny within five days. You will also have many admirers to choose from and to involve in business transactions that will quickly bring you major benefits. This cycle will bring you many changes in financial and business negotiations.

water ski Do not overlook an important event that is scheduled for the upcoming week. If you do, someone's feelings will be deeply injured. Prepare a gift in advance and take every precaution to ensure this event runs smoothly. You will then be able to prevent disappointments. You must also make sure any negative event witnessed in this dream does not become a reality.

water softener Anything that was not possible in past relationships is now possible. If you decide to reinvolve yourself, you will have the perfect opportunity to do so. You will also enjoy fruitful interactions in all business dealings that will pan out perfectly for you.

waterspout Use this cycle to bring those you care about closer to you. Devote more time to special people in your life to assure them that they are still special to you.

water sprite Someone will attempt to involve you in a relationship within the week. At first you will have mixed feelings about this person but your hesitation will be unwarranted. You will enjoy yourself immensely if you choose to pursue this. Involve yourself totally and you will experience joy on every level you desire.

waterwheel Every resource you need will be available to you for the next seven days. Motivate yourself now to acquire the knowledge and means to put yourself on the correct path. Wealth and riches will come to you very rapidly. You will have a long and healthy life and are headed for a brilliant future.

water wings You will be witness to a situation regarding someone's ability to create chaos because of their behavior. You will discuss a business arrangement you have made with a certain person that involves a task they have been hired to do. An opposite sexed person will enter the scene and start making changes in your arrangements to suit their purposes and their feelings on how things should be handled. This person will bully themself into the conversation in such a way that it will be difficult for you to maintain control. Do everything you can to avoid compromise. You have prior notice and can successfully keep this from taking place.

watt The person you will be involving yourself with within seven days will claim they have certain skills. This person does not have the expertise they claim to have. Take steps to protect yourself from this kind of manipulation.

wave *ocean* This dream is telling you of a situation that will come up within the week. Someone will say they will do one thing but will then turn this around and claim their intentions were otherwise. This person will wait until the last moment to make you aware of this. Be very alert so you can plan ahead of time how to handle yourself appropriately.

wave *to wave at someone or have them wave at you* This dream signifies that you will have an urgent need to have something accomplished within the week that can only be taken care of by someone else. This could be anything in the way of a financial loan or a big favor, etc., that needs to be given to you immediately and hassle free. It will be such a large request that it will be difficult for you to imagine it can be accomplished. Your intuition will lead you to the right person to approach. Proceed with confidence and explore all of your options until you locate the right person to ask. As soon as a mutual agreement has been made you need to take immediate action so this matter can be concluded before this person has a change of heart. Many blessings are with you and you are headed for a prosperous future.

signal by moving hand, to wave a light, etc. Be very careful for the next three days. Make sure you do not become more involved with someone you are beginning to grow close to, unless you take extreme precautions. You will be led to believe you can give your full confidence to this individual and can rely on their loyalty. This person is very cunning and devious and is very skilled at creating illusions and deceptions. You will fully believe that certain events and situations will occur in the future that will never take place and an air of trust will develop that will leave you with no suspicions. This person has a hidden agenda that involves pursuing you for reasons known only to them and, because of their charm and charisma, they will easily be able to create diversions if they think you are becoming suspicious of them. By the time you realize what is going on you will have suffered disappointments, disillusionments, and financial setbacks. You will be able to get your life back in order but it will take some time. You have enough advance notice and all the ammunition you need to ensure this does not take place. Practice common sense and you will be very successful in diffusing this. Refuse to become involved, do not compromise and do not allow this person to pry into your affairs. You will develop the confidence you need to put yourself on the path toward a prosperous future. Many blessings are with you and your family.

wax Someone will lead you to believe they are capable of handling a large responsibility. This person will let you down in a big way after you have put your trust in them. Seek an alternative way beforehand to deal with this before you risk placing a heavy responsibility on someone who will let you down.

wax bean Do not allow yourself to be taken in by someone's persuasive techniques. Trust your own instincts and do not compromise yourself so easily for another.

wax museum Take steps to turn any negative event that was foretold in this dream into a positive. Alert anyone you recognize to do likewise. For the next week it will also be important to include more order and organization in your life. Divorce yourself from any situation or hang up you have outgrown and you will experience more tranquility in your life.

wax paper Do not over or underestimate any situation that will develop within five days. Weigh both sides of this situation before you involve yourself in any capacity.

waxwing Something you are taking on a daily basis that you think is good for you will have the opposite effect. If this behavior is not halted within five days, you will have a reaction to this substance. Otherwise, you are headed for a very healthy and prosperous future.

waxworks You will definitely be making the correct decisions within the week involving business, finances and love. You are on the path toward prosperity. Make sure you pounce on anything that seems unusual and out of the ordinary; this will be your key to success.

way *to look for a way out* Take every precaution you can to prevent any negative event in this dream from becoming a reality to you or to someone else. Maintain a low profile and keep your mind on your regular routine tasks. Focus on any mistake that could come up within three days. Make sure you take care of all mistakes immediately so everything will fall into place as you desire. Many blessings will come to you and your family and you will enjoy an abundance of health.
to look for a way out and not be able to get out Do not lose your sense of alertness, especially for the next three days and make sure you do not let down your guard. Do not permit yourself to be persuaded into going someplace that could represent a hazard to you and do not become involved in new situations with another person who could unwittingly cause injury to you. For this three day period, it will be extremely important that you choose wisely what you will or will not involve yourself in.
to hear the phrase - look for a way out Become very aggressive with upcoming situations. Work to solve problems immediately before they reach a crisis. Aggressive, relentless action is the only way to handle any personal crisis.
someone else is looking for a way out You will have to assist with upcoming situations before they reach a crisis. Aggressive, relentless action will be the only way you can handle this crisis for this person.
to find a way out You will be able to empower yourself and achieve victory within three days because you will see things clearly enough to change gears and put yourself in the direction you should be going. Good luck is with you for the next seven days.

someone else looking for a way out and finding a way out Within three days you will be asked for a loan. Do not involve yourself in this situation, it will not work to your advantage. You will also enjoy many days of dancing and social entertainment. This is a wonderful social cycle and you will have many opportunities for entertainment.

weak *to weaken or to see someone else weaken* For the next seven days do everything necessary to promote a healthier environment as well as healthier eating habits. Drink plenty of water and dress appropriately.

wealth You are being told beforehand that anything connected to this dream needs to be addressed immediately, especially if it was a negative situation. Take this and work to turn it around to a positive situation. If positive, do everything you can to bring it to fruition. You will also experience riches that will come to you through an unusual and unexpected circumstance. This will occur within the month. You are definitely headed for a brilliant future.

wean *to wean* Something you have long desired to possess will be within your grasp within seven days.

weapon Within the week you will involve yourself in an unusual situation. Because you have prior notice of this, you will be able to handle yourself properly and conduct yourself appropriately. You will perform successfully in any capacity that this particular situation demands of you.

wear *to hear the word in any form* Do everything necessary to avoid a squabble or disagreement with someone who is special to you, especially for the next seven days.

weasel Back off from someone who is special to you. Be more of a lover instead of a parent or authority figure. Restrain yourself and behave in a better way to someone you care about, especially for the next week.

weather This dream will offer you a clue to the weather that you will soon be dealing with in reality or of how situations will go with a special person within the week. Look up the particular type of weather for additional clues.

weatherboard Make sure you do not allow someone to be a financial drain to you, especially for the next five days.

weather bureau Within five days someone whom you originally did not have romantic feelings for will begin to interest you. You have prior notice of this and can either avoid this situation completely or allow it to happen. You will find that this person does not have the same intentions you do. Since you are aware of this ahead of time you will be able to handle yourself appropriately.

weatherman Someone is already spending your money and is devising a way to manipulate you into spending more than you should. Be aware of this for the next week so you can handle this appropriately.

weatherproof Avoid suspicious feelings about those who are close to you. These people are very loyal and will do everything in their power to make you happy and fulfill your desires. Proceed with confidence.

weather stripping Whatever hopes you had in the past and have given up on are now within reach. Proceed with confidence in the direction you are now heading.

weather vane You will have a very successful conversation with someone who has been very hard to pin down. This person will avoid contact with other people at any costs. Within five days you will have the opportunity to openly converse with this person. Prepare yourself now so that when the opportunity arises you will be able to say what you need in the allotted time and score a major victory on your behalf. Good luck is with you.

weave You will definitely experience, within the month, a major change that you would have never imagined would take place in your life. You are headed for a brilliant future.

weaver You are headed for a prosperous future. Take steps to have those you care about more involved in your life in ways that everyone will find enjoyable and tranquil. Many blessings are with you and your family.

web Do everything necessary to avoid any disagreement or confrontation that will destroy a relationship that is special to you, especially for the next five days. Do not say anything to anyone that will create a major uproar. You will be unable to correct this and it will leave the relationship very fragile and tenuous. You have prior notice and can prevent any negativity.

webbed feet Be very careful that the children and young adults you are involved with do not put themselves on a path of life that will be very difficult to change at a later date. You have prior notice of this and can address emotional hang ups and attitude problems early on so they will not disrupt this young person's future. This person will be very grateful to you in the future.

wed *to wed* You will be surrounded by those who are loyal to you and love you. You will experience more respect, appreciation and consideration from others. Many blessings are with you.

wedding You will experience victory because of your valiant integrity when you are required to make a decision. You will not compromise your principles but will develop a quiet conviction and relentlessness in your pursuit of money, contracts, items and agreements, as well as productive conversation. Do not give up until you succeed. This dream is offering large clues that will help you with a dramatic move you are planning to undertake. This move will bring immediate

and positive changes to your life. Any negative event seen in this dream needs to be prevented in reality and you will need to take steps to experience only positive expressions in your life.

wedding dress A cluster of unexpected events will start to take place concurrently and you will receive a flood of invitations that you can pick and choose from. It is important that you not miss one specific event. This one will be far more exciting and glamorous than the others and you will need to prepare yourself ahead of time because it will require formal attire and you will want to look your best. Make sure you attend this enjoyable event because not only will you have a wonderful time but you will also meet many powerful and influential people who will become friends for a lifetime. You will win a door prize at this event and/or receive a gift. You will also, during this cycle, become aware that the person you desire cares about you in the same way. You will both share many affection moments and you will both be very excited about this new development. You are headed for a prosperous and brilliant future.

wedding march Within a few days you will be with someone who will promise you many things in a desperate attempt to hold on to you. In reality, this person is going through many changes and is undergoing a great deal of stress. It would be impossible for them to deliver on any of these promises and although you can see through this you need to step back if you are interested in this individual. Within two weeks, this person will recover from this chaotic time in their life and will be able to deliver on these promises. They will be in great financial and emotional form in the near future. All things will work out exactly as they have envisioned and you will both enjoy a brilliant future and an abundance of health.

wedding ring You are headed for a brilliant future and will experience riches within the month, not only in finances but also in love and business negotiations. Any negative event occurring in this dream that you do not want to become a reality can also be changed or avoided entirely. Take steps to ensure you experience only success in your life.

wedge Face up to situations that need to be handled by you within the week and bring them to a successful resolution. You are entering a successful cycle and will be able to accomplish this easier at this time.

Wednesday This dream is an extremely lucky omen. You are entering the best cycle possible to accomplish about anything your heart desires. You will be very victorious and are headed for a brilliant future.

weed Someone will come to you with an unrealistic story. Follow your instincts and you will find you are being told an outright lie. No matter how well this lie is put together and how credible it seems, it will be an untruth.

weed killer Do everything you can to keep any negative event in this dream from becoming a reality, especially for the next seven days. It is also alerting you to handle poisonous substances carefully and keep them out of the reach of those who do not know how to handle them properly. Take steps to protect yourself from toxic substances: food, chemicals, or otherwise. It is also important not to rely on someone who is completely unreliable. This person will let you down.

week Make sure you get your point and thoughts across to others, especially when it comes to your emotions. You need to get this across to the person you feel will give you emotional gratification during this cycle. You will feel a tremendous amount of relief once you have gotten this out of your system. Stop depriving yourself. Many blessings are with you.

weekend Do not overwhelm yourself by allowing your imagination to run wild. Do not overextend yourself, physically, emotionally, or mentally. Something good will occur to you either by way of a gift or good news over the coming weekend. Many blessings are with you and your family.

weep *to cry* This dream implies victory. All things you thought were impossible will now be possible. You will also receive verification of the love someone has for you within five days. This will lead to emotional fulfillment in some capacity.

someone else crying You will enjoy happy reunions. A love reconciliation will also be possible during this cycle, if you choose, and new financial agreements will be made with a special person. This is a lucky cycle for you.

baby crying A hot financial tip will lead to riches.

man crying You will be charged for services never received. Be careful of con artists and lawsuit charges. This will occur within a few days.

woman crying You will have to put away money because a situation will arise within a few weeks that will require extra finances.

in any other form You will receive massive support in those areas in which you seek support. Certain situations will take place within five days that will appear they are unfolding in a way you neither desire nor expect. Overall, things will develop to your advantage. As a result you will experience dramatic changes and improvements in your life. You will then experience an uplifting of emotional and financial status.

weeping willow You will travel extensively within six months. You will enjoy your travel and will return safely. You also have prior notice to prevent anything negative connected to this dream from becoming a reality. Make sure you experience only positive expressions in your life.

weevil Proceed with confidence. You will be able to handle those tasks you feel are overwhelming you and you will be able to find the ways and means to tackle them and to contin-

ue your life in prosperity.

weigh *to weigh yourself or to see someone else weigh themselves* Take steps to prevent any negative event portrayed in this dream from becoming a reality. This dream also implies that you will receive a proposal that you will not want to turn down. You will be victorious and expand your life in ways you never thought possible. This may also include a marriage proposal. If you choose to involve yourself this will become a reality within the month.

in any other form Do not waste your time coming up with a plan to get even with somebody because you are seeking emotional gratification. This will be counterproductive to your welfare and will backfire within five days.

weight *overweight* You need to be keenly aware of what you eat and drink in order to avoid allergies, toxic reactions and food poisonings.

weight lifting Make sure the assignments you are responsible for are completed on time.

weird *any form* This dream implies that some news coming to you will be very hard to comprehend. Don't even try. You have prior notice of this and will be able to emotionally handle any strange news that will invade your happiness, especially for the next seven days. Don't be taken and refuse to be a participant to this conversation.

weirdo You have been led by someone to believe you can entrust them with heavy responsibilities. Once you allow this person to take on these tasks, you will be let down in a big way. This individual fully believes they are capable of handling these big responsibilities but their ego is larger than their ability. Be aware of this and do not risk anything of importance.

welcome mat This dream is an extremely lucky omen and is a promise that you will enjoy an abundance of health, wealth and finances, as well as an improved standard of living. You will also experience a greater sense of protectiveness from a special person. This will lead to a sense of excitement because you will know that someone cares so much for your well being. You are headed for a brilliant future.

weld *to weld or to see others weld* Someone will come to you within two days with a certain situation. Back off, this person is too stubborn to handle this issue in any way but their own. Spare yourself and your emotions by refusing to deal with this. This will be a very stressful situation if you try to convince them to handle this in any other way. Get on with your life without dealing with this issue, especially for the next seven days.

welfare This is the perfect cycle for being granted just about anything you ask for and felt was impossible to grasp. Demand from your gods what you feel is important in your life. They are with you and any request made will be granted. Many blessings are with you and you are definitely headed for a brilliant future.

to be the recipient of a welfare check Be very attentive because an unusual occurrence will develop regarding a person, project or position that will lead to a financial windfall. You may marry someone who will leave you a monthly pension, develop a project that will deliver you monthly royalties, or secure a position that will offer you monthly provisions for a lifetime. You are in a sound position to receive this in the near future. Develop your curiosity, especially for the next week, to ensure you do not miss out on these benefits. You will receive an abundance of health, many blessings and are headed for a brilliant future.

welfare state Each event connected to this dream that is positive needs to be converted into a reality as quickly as possible. Each negative event may be altered. This dream is a lucky omen and you will magically possess the inner strength to handle forthcoming situations. You will enjoy prosperity, balance and tranquility in your life. You will also be blessed with the clarity of thought needed to develop a plan and execute it successfully. This plan will bring about the changes you desire to experience in your present life. Luck will be with you, especially for the next seven days.

well This dream is an extremely lucky omen. You are being told to involve yourself in anything that seems unusual and out of the ordinary. This will result in an increase in finances and in your emotional well being. Many blessings are with you and you are headed for a brilliant future.

well groomed You will have your higher power's protection and the help you need to develop an emotional and financial balance. This will be a lucky and tranquil time. You have many admirers but the one you desire most will return your love and affection.

Welsh You are entering an extremely awesome cycle. Anything you felt was impossible to grasp is now within your reach. This is a good time to involve yourself in those tasks you felt were overwhelming and that you lacked the confidence to handle. Take advantage of this cycle to bring these tasks to completion and they will bear fruit in the way you want them to.

werewolf Become acutely aware of what you may be doing that will limit your financial status. Eliminate any negative actions on your part or work to discover ways you can enhance your income, especially for the next three days. Motivate yourself in order to avoid financial collapse due to your behavior or something you may be overlooking in your ca-

reer. This dream is also asking you to avoid any stressful situation you may be involving yourself in.

west You are headed for a very prosperous future, longevity, health and mental well-being. You will also develop the tenacity to complete a certain task and will explore various ways of achieving this.

westerly For the next seven days you will be spending much more than you should. Curb your spending and find ways to allocate less money to certain expenditures. You will find you will have as much fun and spend less money than you had planned to spend. Many blessings are with you.

westerner Pay close attention to the energy and fury you are putting into a certain situation. You are taking this issue far too seriously. Look at this closely for the next seven days so you can back off and stop spinning your wheels. Stop being so overly involved, especially during this time period.

western movies A certain situation is about to occur within two weeks. Take time out now to make sure you get as much accomplished as you can to prepare yourself for this situation. This way you will have a list of things that have priority at the time these other things are occurring. Proceed with confidence. Any negative event from this dream needs to be avoided or changed into a positive experience.

western saddle Look very carefully at something over the next three days before you reject it. There is something developing that you should retain. Keep your eyes and ears open.

Westminster Abbey You will run up against obstacles from some people who wish to put a stop to what you want to put into motion. Don't waste time on this. Move ahead with other things that are more important in your life. This dream may also be used as a reference point in time. If you dream of this cathedral and see its name used in any context, the dream message will occur on this day.

West Point Make sure, for the next five days, you are in perfect control when you encounter certain things that will throw you off balance. Do not allow yourself to get into a conflict with yourself at this specific moment. You need to focus on issues that are far more important instead of allowing yourself to become sidetracked by suppositions and suspicions that are unfounded and not based on fact.

West Virginia You will feel joy because someone you know is unexpectedly back in town and will request your company. You are loved beyond your imagination and you are definitely headed for a brilliant future. This dream may also be used as a reference point in time. If you dream of this state and see its name used in any context, the dream message will occur on this day.

wet Be very attentive to someone who does not easily show emotions but implies through body language that something is not quite right. This individual is considering suicide and needs help in getting back on the right track. You will be successful in putting a stop to this situation and in giving help to someone who is emotionally vulnerable right now. This will occur within three days.

to be drenched with anything You will be hearing pleasing words you have longed to hear within three days.

to wet on yourself or to see someone wet themselves You will be ecstatically happy about an unexpected opportunity that will present itself at an odd moment. You will be able to pounce on this opportunity, grasp it and benefit greatly from it.

wet blanket Someone who loves you but is not in verbal contact with you misses you a great deal and has intentions to contact you soon to involve you in an enjoyable event within the week.

wet dream Within seven days you will make an emotional appeal to someone who is in the position to help out in any way you wish. This person is able to help out financially and pull strings on your behalf. You will empower yourself, because of this occurrence, in ways you will find beneficial in your life. Move quickly on this. You will be able to position yourself in life in ways you were never able to before. Many blessings are with you and you are headed for a brilliant future. You are also loved by someone beyond your imagination and will have verification of this within seven days.

wet nurse You can proceed with confidence with what you have in mind to develop within five days. Everything will work out exactly as you have envisioned.

wet suit You are overextending yourself to the point of exhaustion. For the next week, do everything you can to maintain and improve your health. Eat healthy foods, drink plenty of water and set limits on what you are willing to do for others. For this coming week, all requests you make will also be granted, no matter how impossible they may seem.

whale You are getting a variety of mixed emotions at the same time. You have not yet determined a specific pattern in someone's behavior that you are interested in. Do not proceed with any involvement with this person. This person represents danger. Move on with your life without this person in it. Do not encourage this person in any way or leave an opening that will enable them to reenter your life at a later date. This dream is alerting you to avoid any involvement that could lead to a dangerous situation. Otherwise you are headed for a brilliant future and you will be able to tackle a situation you recently felt was impossible. Proceed with confidence, your special deity is with you.

blue whale For the next week, you will be motivated to make changes in your life and to work in those areas that will bring you prosperity. This will be a very lucky cycle for you.

whaleboat Within seven days you will receive verification of someone's true feelings for you. You will enjoy a long relationship that you will find mutually satisfying. If you choose to go this route, you will have a wonderful life with this person.

whalebone This dream is an extremely lucky omen and is also letting you know you are loved beyond your imagination. This love will be reciprocal on your part and you will be definitely treated with respect.

whaler Someone will come into your life and involve you in an unusual and kinky situation. Do not allow yourself to be caught off guard, especially for the next seven days. Maintain a safe environment at all times.

wharf Keep an eye on what will be unfolding within the week in order to immediately take care of something that will develop that should not be taking place.

whatnot Do everything necessary to avoid any unnecessary travel for the next three days. You will also experience an increase in your finances within the week.

"what's up" *(slang phrase)* Do everything necessary, within four days, to prevent someone from carrying out a plot against you that includes deception. Be very alert and pay close attention to the behavior of others. You will become aware of who this person is because you have prior notice of this and can monitor all suspicious behavior. Do not allow yourself to be deceived during this time period.

wheat Within three days your determination, confidence and belief in yourself will be the main ingredient that will enable you to get through what you need to and emerge victorious. Proceed with confidence.

wheat bread A business involvement you will have in three days should be kept strictly business. Do not become overly friendly. This behavior would not be appropriate during this time period.

wheat cake Within the week you will have the chance to begin all over again. This time you will definitely be able to get it right. Good luck is with you.

wheel You can proceed with confidence. You do have the competence and the confidence in yourself to make the right decision to develop the future you want to experience. Expect this to evolve within three days. You are definitely headed for a brilliant future and will experience an unexpected financial windfall just when you need it.

two wheeler You are making all the correct moves and are motivating yourself to achieve victory. You will also finally connect within the week, with a certain person whom you have been unable to contact in the past. It would also be a good idea to take steps to schedule a small vacation to a quiet get away spot. This will leave you with many pleasurable memories. All things that were impossible in the past are now possible and you are headed for a brilliant future.

three wheeler Make sure you do not challenge the ideas of another. Everything will come down heavily on you and it will seem impossible to get out of this situation. Get on with your life without this involvement. You are headed for a prosperous, fortunate future. For the next three days you will find everything will work to your advantage.

wheel and axle Do not leave something behind that you do not want anyone else to go through because they will find information that is meant only for you. Be very cautious with your personal belongings as well as your personal business for the next five days.

wheelbarrow Do everything necessary to become more socially involved, especially for the next five days. Several events will be coming up that you can involve yourself with to bring more entertainment to your life. You will meet with a joyous surprise at one of these events. Many blessings are with you.

wheelchair For the next four days you will be able to affect changes that will vastly improve your life. All of your goals will be realized in the exact manner you have planned. This dream is a very lucky omen.

wheeze *to wheeze* Within three days a certain situation will occur that will leave you with some very negative and depressing thoughts. This will reach the point of losing confidence in a certain situation that you know you can handle with ease. Your own thoughts, however, will give you the idea that you are unable to handle this. Stop these thoughts and put yourself in a better frame of mind. Proceed with confidence, especially if it involves someone you are interested in. Many blessings are with you. You must also take steps to keep any negative event in this dream from becoming a reality for you or for anyone you recognize.

whetstone Make sure you do not assume anyone else's responsibilities, even if it is only one time. Before you know it, this responsibility will become a burden and will be difficult to get away from. Make sure you do allow this process to begin.

whey You will be the recipient of a rare and unusual offer within five days. Pounce on this and be grateful you have the opportunity to grasp it.

whimper You will quickly develop a support system and will be able to move quickly ahead in the direction you desire, especially for the next five days.

whine *any form* Be very aware of your attitude and do what you can to avoid becoming so bored with something that you abandon it. Be especially careful of this over the next three days.

whip *to be whipped, to see someone whipped, or to hear the sound of a whip* You will be asked to provide shelter for a family with children until they are able to become more financially secure. This will be short term and you will be richly rewarded once they have moved.

whiplash Take precautions for the next seven days to make sure that does not take place in reality. This is the perfect time to treat someone who has been very special to you or has treated you in a special way to something they would never imagine. This implies that your divinity is with you and many blessings are with you and your family.

whipped cream Circumstances will occur that will create a lot of eroticism in your life for the next five days. This may come through books, films or pleasures of the flesh. You will enjoy this time period tremendously. You are headed for a brilliant future and will enjoy a financial windfall that will come in an unexpected way from an unexpected place.

whipping post Make sure you do not come into contact with or fall prey to an extremely dangerous person. Make sure, for the next three days, you keep yourself and your environment safe. Do not trust anyone during this time period. Do not leave yourself vulnerable and do not frequent unfamiliar places. Do everything you can to protect yourself from a random act of violence that will come from someone you least expect.

whippoorwill Protect your belongings from fire, especially for the next four days.

whirlpool Within three days you will have to develop a certain amount of patience. You will find yourself caught up in a cycle with too much to do. You will find yourself going from one thing to another in an attempt to take care of many issues at the same time. This will be a big waste of time for you. Prepare yourself ahead of time and learn to develop patience, otherwise you will feel emotionally depleted and on the verge of tears. Remain calm and you will be able to take care of what you need to take care of.

whirlwind Do everything necessary to keep stress from playing a major role in your life and effecting your emotions for the next three days. It will seem as though everything will begin to happen at once. Remain calm and handle each issue one at a time.

whisk broom Start now to work on a way to increase your cash flow. You will need extra income within three weeks to make ends meet. Certain situations will come up that will require extra cash. You have prior notice of this and can take steps now to ensure your needs are met.

whisker Detail your thoughts in such a way that you will be able to navigate yourself through certain situations that will come up within the week. Step back each time you need to think things over and you will be able to guide yourself through everything with ease. Remain free from stress by bringing more joy and entertainment into your life. Treat your body like a sacred vessel by eating correctly and getting plenty of rest. Drive defensively and make sure your transportation is in good repair.

whiskey Be very careful of accidental injuries, especially of painful blows to the body caused by yourself. It is especially important for the next three days.

whisper Pay close attention to the words whispered in this dream. This will offer you a clue to the meaning to this dream. If it is a negative message, take steps to change or alter this forthcoming event. If this is something that must be encouraged, take steps to do so. This dream is an extremely lucky omen for you. Within three days, certain events will begin to develop very quickly. Take steps to put a lid on those situations that do not need to escalate and that you do not want to deal with. Many blessings are with you and you are headed for a brilliant future.

whistle *any form* This dream is a warning that you need to pay attention to a certain situation to ensure it does not spiral downward. Do what you can to head off any potentially negative event that will lean in a direction you do not wish it to go. Listen to your hunches. Your instincts will alert you to avoid the company of certain individuals you do not need to associate with. Other people will attempt to do you harm in a subtle and conniving way at a time you leave yourself unguarded. Protect yourself and everything you find emotionally precious to you. You have prior notice of this and will be able to handle yourself appropriately for the next three days.

whistling swan Do everything necessary to protect children and young adults who need closer supervision, especially for the next three days. Make sure they do not come to any physical harm. Many blessings are with you and your family. You have prior notice and can keep any negative event from occurring.

white This dream is an extremely lucky omen and you are definitely headed for a brilliant future. You will receive a proposal that will be very difficult for you to refuse. If you choose to involve yourself in this, you will find you will enjoy a better lifestyle than you ever envisioned. Proceed with confidence. The powers of the Gods are with you. You will also have the creativity you need to accomplish what you want for at least a month. Do not talk yourself out of achieving because of your feelings of intimidation. Go for the big plans.

off white Your intuition will be right on target when it applies to financial matters and business negotiations. You will be tremendously successful if you follow your own counsel, especially for the next three days.

white blood cell Do everything necessary to remain physically healthy and do not expose yourself to any infectious diseases. Eat healthy foods, drink plenty of water, get plenty of rest and avoid stress. Take steps to avoid any negative event foretold in this dream.

white bread Something unusual will occur within five days. You will locate someone who will be willing to help you and will relentlessly stick to their goals until your needs are met.

white elephant This is an exceptionally lucky omen and you will experience a rapid increase in wealth within three weeks due to an unusual occurrence. Success will abruptly come to you at a time you least expect.

white flag .For the next three days move slowly in the correct direction so you do not miss any important details that are necessary for future decisions on your behalf.

whitefly A certain possession needs to be more protected. Take stock of what you own and make sure a certain possession does not get lost, stolen or destroyed due to your neglect. Cover your bases for the next three days to make sure this does not occur.

white horse This dream is an exceptionally lucky omen and you will experience a rapid increase in wealth within three weeks due to an unusual occurrence. Success will abruptly come to you at a time you least expect.

white lightning Be careful you do not allow yourself to be vulgarized by others who would take advantage of you financially, physically, and emotionally. Set limits and keep others from demanding you meet their needs. Make sure your needs take priority for the next five days, and that you do not overextend yourself. Especially, watch out for one person who is demanding of you. A very prosperous cycle is heading your way.

white rat Someone with a subtle yet somewhat conniving attitude will become financially and emotionally draining. This will be someone you respect and like a great deal. This dream is a warning to back off and become aware of how the relationship is developing between you and your friend in order to protect yourself and your interests.

whitewall tires Within five days you will find yourself caring for someone who is unable to care for themselves. This person will improve physically and achieve the quality of life they need in order to reach social personal acceptance. You will also be swamped with many social engagements and must make an effort to maintain your appearance and keep your attire in the best possible condition during this time period. This will be a very successful cycle for you.

whitewash This dream is an extremely lucky omen and you are headed for a brilliant future.

wholesale Do everything you can to drive a hard bargain when you set out to purchase a luxury item, a large ticket item or food items. You are definitely headed for a prosperous future.

whooping cough Take every possible step to keep a negative event in this dream from becoming a reality and do what you can to turn it around to a positive situation. You must also not use any of the authority or power you possess to disadvantage another individual or to force them to behave in some way that you desire. This will definitely backfire. Back off and correct your behavior, especially for the next three days.

whooping crane Watch your behavior. You will have to control your anger for the next three days because you will be treated rudely by someone for some unknown reason and this will bother you tremendously. You have prior notice of this and can take steps to avoid a situation that poses danger to you because of the way you are treated. Just remind yourself that this person has a problem dealing with you and remove yourself from the situation.

whore *to hear the word* Someone who will come into your life within three days will do everything in their power to remain an enigma to you. The moment you try to figure this person out, ask yourself if there isn't something you would rather be doing instead of focusing so much time on this person. Control your thoughts and move on with your life by doing something that is more important to you.
    to be a whore or to pretend to be one Someone is trying to persuade you, within three days, to enter into an arrangement that seems to be very attractive. This project will seem more attractive because this offer will be limited. You are going in the wrong direction and once you become involved it will take years to get out and it will be very distasteful to you. Otherwise, you are headed for a brilliant future and, within three days, you will be given a small gift that will give you joy. You are definitely entering a lucky cycle.

whorehouse You will see clearly within five days, what you need to do because you will learn from an example set by another person. Keep your eyes and ears open for this so you can see and determine what you choose not to have going on in your life for the next two weeks. Do what you can now to stop this before it becomes an issue. Many blessings are with you.

wick Speak up for your rights and make sure you know all the facts so you can deal with the situation in a way that it should be dealt with. Encourage others to do the same, especially for the next three days.

wicker You will feel a conspiracy is going on because, within three days, more than one person will tell you the same thing. You know, within yourself, you are correct in spite of what others are saying. Deal with conspirators by seeking advice from a professional who is not a member of this group. Get to the bottom of this issue and deal with what you need to deal with.

widow/widower Someone is very eager to involve themselves in a new life, new relationship and new experiences. This person is one who has raced to the challenge and has the capacity to involve themselves with someone new, the ability to be very loving and the capacity to bring a fresh approach to a relationship. You can also learn from this person's experiences if you choose to become involved. This would be a wholesome, caring, loving, financially stable relationship for a lifetime. Anything in this dream that you felt was negative that should not be allowed to occur in reality must be avoided or altered in reality. It is in your power to change any aspect of your future that you want to change. You are headed for a prosperous future.

widow's peak Make sure you do not put yourself in the position to have to do any heavy physical labor for the next three days. Back off. Take it slow and easy in order to prevent any injury due to heavy exercise. You are definitely headed for a prosperous future.

widow's walk Someone will ask you to do something for them that in your heart you know you really want to do, but you are also aware this is a situation that will be ongoing for a long time to come. You will have to compromise your lifestyle in order to grant this person this favor. Be selfish and get on with your life without committing to this in spite of any guilt trip that anyone would want to place on you. This favor can be handled without you taking full responsibility.

wiener Do not take too long in making up your mind determining the course of action you want to take involving a particular situation you must deal with within three days. Many blessings are with you and you are definitely headed for a brilliant future.
    if the wiener is used as a sexual object or tool A request you make to another will definitely be granted, especially for the next five days. Many blessings are with you and you are definitely headed for a brilliant future.

Wiener schnitzel You are grossly underestimating a situation you will be involved with in a five day period. Move quickly on this before it slips through your fingers. This will be your golden opportunity.

wife Anything in this dream that depicted a negative event needs to be prevented in reality or altered in such a way that you and anyone you recognize experiences nothing but positive experiences in reality. Alert this person to this potential negative experience as well as any positive event foretold in this dream. Someone will also be selected by your deity to come into your life in order to involve themselves with your interests and offer assistance in helping you reach levels you thought were impossible. You will be able to expand your horizons and live a fuller life on a grander scale. Pay close attention to those you come into contact with so you will be able to determine who this person is. You will learn who this person is because of their obvious interest in your goals and their willingness to point you in the right direction. This person will be there for you in many different capacities as an instrument to use in many different ways and to enjoy as a support system. You are definitely headed for a brilliant future.

housewife Be very aggressive when dealing with a situation that will come up within three days in order to maintain control and handle it correctly. Avoid any negative event portrayed in this dream and promote any positive expressions in your life.

wig For the next week a number of different opportunities will be presented to you that you can involve yourself in. Any of these could make you a very wealthy person. This is a time when conversations will be very productive in business and love relations. You will find various ways of promoting yourself for success and will meet many people with the wealth and resources to further your goals. You are in a very prosperous cycle and are headed for a brilliant future. From this point on you can expect an increase in finances and situations will take place one right after the other. Your life will change for the better in any way you desire.

wigwam You are in a lucky cycle and you need to move on your hunches and intuition. You are going in the right direction.

wild boar Think on a grander scale. Do not limit your plans and find ways of getting them out there in a more expanded form. You are definitely headed for a brilliant future.

wild card All communications you have had difficulty getting through to the right person will be successful within three days. Move quickly on this.

wildcat Someone will be very manipulative in their attempt to get what they want. They will be very subtle and will try various ways to achieve their goals. This person will use trickery, conspiratorial methods and just about anything at their disposal to succeed. This will be a very desperate individual who will latch on to any vulnerable person who is easy prey. It is extremely important that you do not allow yourself to be the target. After you become involved, it will be too late. This will be a very draining, controlling and demeaning situation. You have prior notice of this and can take steps to keep this from taking place. Many blessings and good luck are with you.

wildebeest Become centered and determine the reasons why you refuse to hear the words of others. Many people are telling you the same thing and they cannot all be wrong. Face facts and decide why you are unwilling to deal with this issue in the correct manner so you can move beyond this and take care of what you need to put yourself on the right path. This is especially important for the next three weeks.

wilderness You will enjoy a great deal of passion in your life and will live life to the fullest. This is the perfect time to

do those things you have never had a chance to do because you lacked either the finances or the time. You can be selfish and treat yourself to elaborate and fancy things and to events you either attend alone or with someone else. Take steps to alter or to prevent any negative event in this dream from becoming a reality. It is important that you do this within three days. Alert anyone you recognize in this dream to do likewise and take steps to experience only positive expressions in your life. You are headed for a prosperous future and will begin to see this unfold within two weeks.

wildfire Take precautions to avoid anything in this dream that should be avoided in reality and turn events around so you experience only positive expressions in your life. Forewarn anyone in this dream whom you recognize to do the same. Someone also needs to know you are willing to grant them their emotional and passionate desires. This is a time when you will not have to compromise. You will have all of your emotional desires fulfilled and will immerse yourself in a fulfilling deep felt relationship.

wildflower This is the time, within three days, to arrange your life in such a way that you will automatically have the power you need in certain situations and will have your wishes granted in the manner you desire. You will have no limitations, especially for the next seven days.

wild goose chase A wild goose chase is exactly what you want to avoid, especially for the next three days. Someone will accidentally put you in the position that will lead you on a wild goose chase because you have been given the wrong address, information, directions, etc., that you need in order to accomplish a particular task. For the next five days, double check everything before you take action. This dream also implies that your affections will be in demand during this time period.

wild oats Take steps to ensure that someone's power and authority over you does not exceed acceptable limits and become abusive, especially for the next three days. Be very alert to this and do not allow yourself to be abused in any way. Otherwise, this is an extremely lucky omen and the next three days will be so lucky it would be a good idea to take a small risk in a game of chance for big returns.

wild rice This dream is an extremely lucky omen and you will be surprised when you receive a very luxurious and unexpected gift.

Wild West Do everything necessary to apply yourself personally to handle certain tasks that need to be taken care of. Some changes will also occur within the week between you and someone else. A plan that both of you develop will enable you to experience a much more sophisticated and luxurious lifestyle and you will be able to afford extensive travel. Many blessings are with you and your family. This is a very prosperous and lucky cycle for you.

William Tell This dream is a very lucky omen. Within two days you will overhear a deep confidential secret about another person. This will be an unexpected occurrence and this person will seek you out to speak about this matter. Keep all information to yourself.

willow Make sure you do not overtly demonstrate your emotions to someone else, especially for the next three days.

willpower Do not make excuses for those aspects of your life in which you know you are not conducting yourself properly. Face facts and discipline yourself in such a way that you become the person you want to be. This cycle will permit you to make these changes with ease if you act quickly. During this three day cycle, you will want to demonstrate that special personality that you want others to see and you will leave a positive impression with others. Prioritize your desires in other areas of your life. This cycle will allow you to accomplish this. Take steps to keep any negative event in this dream from becoming a reality and make sure you alert anyone you recognize to do likewise.

wilt Do not make any major decisions for the next three days. Give yourself some time to think over the decisions you feel need to be made immediately. Back off and give yourself the time you need to make the right choices.

win/winner You will be so successful in diffusing a plot against you that it will be impossible for it to be carried out. This plot will involve someone's desire to bring chaos and discomfort into your life. You will be able to use whatever power you may possess to keep this from taking place in a responsible, efficient and effective manner. You will also be repaid, during this cycle, for any generosity you demonstrated toward others in the past. You will receive many gifts, score some major wins and are headed for a brilliant future. Any negative event you saw in this dream needs to be prevented in reality. Do everything you can to experience only positive events in your life.

to win the pot You will receive a great deal of money. A carefully worded plea will bring a reconciliation with someone who is important to you.

to win a race Circumstances that will be coming up within a few days will create a great deal of stress. Prior notice of this will give you the opportunity to develop a calm demeanor and will lessen the impact of the stress.

to win money This dream implies that, if you desire, you will marry someone who will provide you with a great life. It is also important that you do not linger on any decision. Take care of what you can now instead of procrastinating. You will enjoy a prosperous future. If you recall any numbers or denominations of bills, use this knowledge for games of chance. Small risks will yield large benefits.

to win a sweepstakes Someone you desire will fall in love with you. This will lead to a very successful marriage.

someone else win a sweepstakes You will soon win a prize. Luck is with you.

to hear this phrase "be a winner" Do everything neces-

sary to prevent any physical harm from coming to you because of a tool or vehicle you will be operating. Be acutely aware of your surroundings for the next three days.

to fail to be a winner Be aware of your involvements with others for the next three days and control what you will and will not allow to happen in your life.

to see someone else fail to be a winner Do everything necessary to put yourself in the position to gain the upper hand in a situation that will be presented to you by another person. Make sure you have the advantage and do not compromise yourself.

to be the winner Whatever you dreamed of that is positive will come to pass in reality. If it was negative you need to do what you can to alter the outcome. Someone will also go to great lengths to assist you in every way they can to make sure you grasp your goals.

in any other form You will have the opportunity within three days to express your hidden desires that until now, you have not had the chance or the means to express. You will receive instant gratification and those tasks you felt were impossible to tackle are now possible. Many blessings are with you and your family.

wind Within the week you will be placed in some unusual circumstances that will require you to take on the character of a leader and to assume a leadership role. You will lead others to believe you have the power and authority to handle certain situations that need to be taken care of within this time frame. Carry yourself in such a way that will give others the confidence to rely on you. Ask specific questions and get specific answers so you come across clearly. Prepare yourself in the beginning in such a way that you can take charge. Look forward to someone handing over certain responsibilities to you. Any situation you view as being negative needs to be turned around in reality. Anyone you recognize in this dream needs to be alerted to do the same so both of you can experience only positive experiences in your life. You are headed for a prosperous future.

strong wind Focus on those benefits that are due you that you may not even be aware of. For the next three days, investigate this in detail to ensure you receive what you need during this time in your life. You are headed in the right direction.

windbag Do not permit yourself to get caught up in game playing. Someone will attempt to draw you into this and you will only find stress and discomfort. Work to keep this from taking place, especially for the next three days.

windbreaker A situation that has always been difficult for you to become involved in will now be open to you and others will respond very favorably toward you. You will now be allowed to be involved in something that in the past you were not allowed to take part in. You and another person will also discuss plans between the both of you. These plans will build a solid foundation for your future and will mutually satisfy both your desires. Look forward to this evolving within the week.

wind chill Make it a point not to miss out on a scheduled event within the week. You will enjoy the company of an admirer who will take great steps to win your affections. Although it is not apparent to you, this person is powerful and in a position of authority. You will find this person to be agreeable and charming and a joy as a lifetime partner. Go with confidence. You will enjoy a very prosperous future.

wind chime You are being led by someone to believe that you can trust them to handle heavy responsibilities. Once you permit this person to take on these tasks, you will be let down in a big way. This individual fully believes they are able to handle big responsibilities but their ego is larger than their abilities. Be aware of this and risk nothing of importance.

windflower Someone will come to your assistance in the nick of time. Help is on the way.

wind gauge Do not give up any of the private moments you spend intimately with another person you desire in your life, especially for the next three days.

wind instrument Get more rest and provide a more tranquil and stress free environment for yourself. Eat healthy foods and drink plenty of water. Many blessings are with you.

windmill Your intuition regarding matters of the heart will be very clear, especially for the next three days. You will be able to communicate with others in such a way that will bring them closer to you in the way you desire.

window Within three days someone will become openly affectionate in a way you find appealing. In the past, this person's attitude toward you was very cold. You will also be received with open arms by those who request your presence. Anything you saw in this dream that portended a negative event can be altered or avoided in reality. Allow only positive experiences into your life, especially for the next five days. Forewarn anyone you recognize to do the same.

to look out of the window You will experience an unexpected reconciliation when you thought all was lost. Expect this within the week.

to see someone else looking out of a window You will receive a gift of mental inventiveness within the week. If you jot down your thoughts and develop them at a later time, you will be amazed at how quickly you will receive benefits from this. Good luck is with you.

to see someone through a window You will be touched very sensually and romantically in just the way you wish to be touched. You will find emotional fulfillment, if this is something you desire. You will have the opportunity to do this with someone you are very attracted to within three days.

to open a window You will have verification of love within five days and will find you are loved beyond your imagination. You are headed for a prosperous future. If you recognize anyone in this dream, this will be someone who is very eager to grant you your wishes.

to be unable to open a window Avoid any group activities that could result in an injury that will keep you from living your life fully. It is especially important that you attend to this for the next three days. Someone will also request a sexual liaison with you when you least expect it. It is up to you whether to pursue this or not.

broken window glass Prevent a falling out between yourself and a dear friend. This other person will pull a power play because you lack the finances and power they have. They will continually ask you to perform favors for them in order to keep you in control. Take this person aside and express your feelings. If you don't, you will be forced to cut this person out of your life instead of maintaining a friendship.

broken car window Remain calm and centered for the next three days. A situation will come up that you will be very tempted to become involved in. Do not allow another person's problems to cause you to become so desperate that you compromise yourself and become entangled in this issue. Once you involve yourself, it will be very difficult to pry yourself loose and it will become progressively worse as time goes by. You are seeing only the tip of the iceberg. Remain uninvolved.

to see your reflection in a window pane You will rapidly advance to a higher plane in life than you had ever imagined within a two week period. You will enjoy an increase in productivity, income, productive conversations, and more affection and loyalty from others. Other people will express their desire to be a part of your plans. You are headed for a brilliant future and will enjoy an abundance of health. All of this will occur in a shorter period of time than you ever anticipated.

to see a reflection of another's face in a window pane Look ahead, someone will write a check to you and there will be insufficient funds to cover it.

bay window You will need a quiet stress free space. Meditate and think through future decisions for the next three days.

drive through window Focus on someone who carries themselves in a simple and quiet fashion. Do not overlook the importance of this person. This individual possesses a great deal of knowledge relating to an issue you are handling now. Listen carefully to this wealth of information in order to ensure a prosperous outcome.

window pane/shield You are on the right path and are headed for a brilliant future. You are also promised wealth in the near future.

to see window pane shatter You will need to be aware of another's irresponsibility. This will catch you off guard. Be prepared and do not allow yourself to be taken.

to close a window Be keenly aware of where you are allowing someone to lead your feelings. This person will, for reasons known only to them, mislead you into believing they are completely in love with you. Words of love may or may not be used at this time but an atmosphere of romance will be created by this individual (i.e., flowers, gifts, romantic outings, etc.). Your feelings will grow very deep for this person but if you allow this individual to make love to you they will not touch you in a way that suggests love. You will feel very empty and cold as a result of this. You will not be able to connect on the level of love you felt was there and you will not be loved, touched or kissed in any way that is special although this person will make an attempt to fulfill this need. Rather than put yourself through this, you have enough notice to avoid this scenario completely. Get on with your life without this person in it and the emotional upheaval that will go along with this situation. A hidden agenda is at play here that will require you to do something for this person that only they are aware of. Avoid this because it will only lead to unhappiness. Otherwise, within the week you will start on a path toward a prosperous future.

in any other form You will have the strength and inner courage to make unusual and extraordinary choices. Many blessings will be yours.

window box Control your sexual urges when in the presence of someone you desire, especially for the next week.

window dressing You will enjoy a long and healthy life.

window seat You will gain instant wealth within seven days. This will completely overwhelm you.

window shade *to raise or try to raise a window shade* Your aggressiveness will put an end to a potential problem that will arise within the week.

to put down or try to put down a window shade Do not allow yourself to be put on an emotional roller coaster by someone else. The moment you see this start to develop, get busy with something else in your life for the sake of your health.

in any other form You will receive a positive response to an agreement that you felt you would get a negative response to. Good luck is with you.

window shop A variety of opportunities will present themselves and you will enjoy a myriad of choices to events from which you can choose to attend. You will savor experiences that will enhance your life. You are loved beyond your imagination by all those who are special to you. You are headed for a prosperous future.

windowsill Be very selfish with your time for the next two days.

windshield *to see a windshield fogged up by heavy breathing* Within the week you will be entering an extremely lucky cycle and anyone involved in your life will share this luck. You will also be offered services that will help you to successfully accomplish your goals. You will reach a higher level of success than you thought possible, particularly with anything you deem important and of high priority. You can expect to make many amazing and wonderful connections that will assist you in grasping and meeting your goals. You can also expect a mega merger and the synergism working

between you and those you will be working with will bring you to a higher level of success than you ever anticipated. This dream also implies that you will receive many benefits by attending a festive event, by participating in an educational event or by attending an event in which one person will take an interest in promoting you and your plans. Following this you will enjoy a long period of tranquility and a prosperous future. Anything negative witnessed in this dream may be changed in reality and you must make it a point to forewarn anyone you dreamed about to do the same.

windstorm Be acutely aware of the behavior of those you come in contact with for the next seven days. This will give you a clue of how you should be handling yourself.

windsurf Push yourself to bring certain issues to a conclusion. Your efforts will create an improved lifestyle for yourself and everyone involved. Make the final moves within seven days.

wine This dream is an extremely lucky omen for you and everyone involved in your life. Expect an amazing and wonderful situation to take place, especially for the next five days.

red wine When someone consistently uses negative statements to belittle you, make it a point to turn them into positive statements while still in the presence of the other person. Good luck is with you and you are deeply loved by others.

wine bottle *broken* Make sure you do not allow someone to take you on an emotional roller coaster ride. This will be a very painful, hurtful situation for you. Be acutely aware of this for the next three days. Take control of your life to the point that someone does not suck you in emotionally. Any negative event connected to this dream must be altered in such a way that you experience only positive expressions in reality. Alert all those you recognize in this dream to do the same, especially for the next seven days.

wine cellar Make sure you are not caught off guard by someone who will unexpectedly drop in within two days. Place more importance on your personal appearance so you will be seen in your best light.

wine cooler Pay close attention to children and make sure their needs are being met. Place more importance on your personal appearance and budget your time to ensure that others are not wasting it.

wineglass Do not involve yourself in any group that is out to fight a cause. You will be given the wrong information and will regret joining this group at a later time.

winemaker Make sure someone does not verbally abuse you in front of others to the point of embarrassment. You have prior notice of this and can take steps to prevent this occurrence.

winepress You will become very excited about a new product that will be on the market in about six weeks. This product will assist you greatly on a project you are now working on. You will then be able to achieve your goals in a much more efficient manner. As a result, you will be offered many new opportunities and will experience an increase in wealth. Good luck is with you.

wine sap You will have a terrific opportunity to enjoy life to the fullest for the next three days. You will enjoy tranquility and harmony in your life. Many blessings are with you and your family.

wineskin Step back and determine exactly what you are trying to prove to others. You will then be able to develop a plan that will get you exactly what you want. Good luck is with you.

wine taster Someone will let you know, within three days, that they are interested in letting you have something they own. It is in your best interest to follow this through as soon as it is offered to you, otherwise this person may change their mind. Take advantage of this before the offer is rescinded. A dangerous undertone will become apparent regarding an issue that will involve a member of the opposite sex. This person is dangerous and evil and will try to catch you off guard in order to gauge your reactions at an unexpected time. For the next three days, take steps to protect yourself and stay in a safe environment.

wing The choice you will be making within three days to involve someone in your life will be the correct choice. You will receive benefits in many areas of your life that you want to involve yourself and this person in.

wink *to wink at someone* You will enjoy pleasurable moments with a person you desire in your life. For seven days, the cycle will be perfect to bring someone much closer to you. This person is kind, demonstrative, giving and very affectionate. Good luck is with you.
    to be winked at Pay attention to the messages coming from someone else for the next seven days. These messages will offer suggestions that will alter your life for the better. Pay close attention to matters that should not be overlooked and pay close attention to your dreams during this cycle. Your intuition is right on target and a prosperous future is headed your way.
    in any other form Within two days you will unexpectedly experience an abundance of productivity, an increase in income and productive conversation. You will be surrounded by loyal and affectionate people who will offer their assistance in any area or form you desire. You are headed for a very prosperous future.

wino A distasteful and uncomfortable situation is coming your way. Within three days you will need to take steps to keep this from taking place. The moment you see this situation start to develop, begin working on it because it will rapidly escalate out of control.

winter Leave yourself open so others will feel they can approach you with situations that will be advantageous to you. You are headed for a bright future.

wintergreen Within the week, you will be given the chance to cater to others from a different ethnic background. Your hard work, eagerness to please and ability to handle certain issues with diplomacy and tact will open doors for you on a permanent basis. As a result, you will be offered many new opportunities and will experience an increase in finances. Good luck is with you.

wipe *to wipe* You can expect a long standing burden to be lifted off your shoulders. Your difficulties will end very quickly.
    to wipe clean Take any steps within your power to bring more romance into your life and to bring someone into your life who can provide you with emotional fulfillment. Make your move now and you will be able to experience this fulfillment within seven days. This is the perfect cycle to pursue this if it is something you want in your life. Make yourself more accessible to those who are eager to be in your company. Many blessings are with you and your family.

wipers Remain focused for the next three days in order to avoid an emotional situation that will escalate to the point where you will be unable to bring it back to normality.

wire Within five days make a list of your priorities in order to receive greater benefits from the opportunities that will be presented to you within this time frame.
    man working with wires (any) Someone is plotting your murder. Be aware of your surroundings and the people around you for the next seven days.

wirehaired terrier Someone is feeling very abandoned by you. As soon as you can, let this person know they are very special to you and give them a tangible representation of your appreciation (i.e., flowers, gifts, etc.). This will surprise this individual and will also let them know you are deeply involved with them. Demonstrate your love with words and actions in order to create a deeper bond between you. This is the perfect cycle to put love into your life on a permanent basis. You are headed for a very prosperous future.

wireless Get to the bottom of a particular situation. Once you determine what the missing element is, you will be able to handle yourself appropriately.

wireman Be extremely careful of your surroundings and of your environment in order to prevent anything of danger from occurring to you, especially for the next five days. This will involve someone trying to physically harm you in some way.

wiretap Become very focused, especially for the next seven days, in order to pinpoint those situations you need to be determined to rid yourself of. Motivate yourself to take care of these issues. You will then enjoy the lifestyle you choose to experience. You are headed for a prosperous future. You need to be very aggressive in pouncing on those aspects of your life you wish to make changes in. You will be able to accomplish this much easier during this time period.

wireworm Dig deeply to determine exactly what your financial status is now and make projections about where you will be in the future. Use your drive and ambition to determine what you need to do now in order to make ends meet for the next three weeks. This is the perfect cycle to do this in order not to be caught off guard.

Wisconsin Prepare yourself for an event that will be very unusual and remarkable. This will take place within three days. At the same time that this is going on, you will be able to think through each step you need to take in order to comfortably get through this cycle. Your curiosity will be particularly high during this three day period and you will need to be firm and disciplined in order to keep your curiosity in check. Expect an abundance of health during this cycle. This dream may also be used as a reference point in time. If you dream of this state and see its name used in any context, the dream message will occur on this day.

wisdom *any form* You need to give more of yourself to a relationship that means a lot to you and make sure it remains strong. By doing this you will enjoy beautiful moments in those relationships that are special to you. Apply yourself to this for the next seven days.

Wisdom of Solomon *(from the Canonical Bible)* Within five days you will enjoy a new sense of confidence, balance and a sense of being solidly grounded. As a result, you will be able to handle each issue that requires this facet of your personality. Use this time period to work on those aspects of your life that you desire changes in. You will have the opportunity to bring prosperity into your life at the level you desire. You are on the path toward a brilliant future.

wisdom tooth Within five days you will have an urgent need to have something taken care of that requires assistance from someone else, whether this is in the nature of a large loan or a big favor that you need immediately with no hassles. This request will be so big it will be difficult to imagine that it will be granted to you. Follow your intuition and it will lead you to the right person who will come through for you. Act with confidence and explore all your options until you find the perfect one. As soon as you reach an agreement, be sure to take immediate action so the situation will be concluded before this person has a chance to change their mind. Many blessings will come to you and you are on the path toward a prosperous future.

wise *any form* Do not give others the impression that you are limiting your feelings, especially for the next two days. Reveal your feelings accurately to someone you need to express them to.

wise guy Do everything necessary to protect your own values and morals and make sure others respect you and treat you in ways you should be treated, especially for the next seven days.

wish *to dream of making a wish* You will be granted your deepest desires.

to hear yourself wish someone good luck This dream is a powerful symbol and is a promise that you will grasp the goals you are pursuing. You will be in a very victorious cycle for the next two weeks. Anything negative portended in the dream needs to be altered or changed. Make sure you experience only positive expressions in your life. The gods are with you.

in any other form Before you commit yourself to being with someone, make sure you do not allocate too much time to this person. At first, you will feel excited to be with this individual but after some time in their presence you will find you do not enjoy their company that much and will wish to find a way out. Think about this ahead of time and allocate only enough time to find out if you will be comfortable in their presence. Take special steps to avoid or to alter anything in this dream that you perceive as negative from becoming a reality. You have prior notice of this and can ensure you experience only positive expressions in your life. Be sure to forewarn anyone in this dream whom you recognize to do the same. Take each positive event in this dream to fruition.

wishbone Within three days an unusual situation will occur that involves another person. The look, voice or mannerisms of this person will not match your perception of who they are and after being in their presence you will find they are much more pleasant and delightful than you anticipated. Seek more time for this person. Good luck is with you.

wisp Within seven days someone will go to great lengths to extend themselves to you in a very special way. This person will surprise you with either a party or a special gift to express their appreciation for who you are.

wisteria This is the time to make sure that the way you carry yourself, your mannerisms and your attitude is proper and accepted by your family and loved ones, especially for the next three days.

witch This dream implies that you are entering a victorious cycle and this sense of power will stay with you for an eight week period. You will begin to reap benefits within four days. Someone will also come into your life who will resemble someone seen in the dream whom you may or may not recognize in reality. This person will repeat patterns of behavior that are evidenced in this dream. Think carefully about whether you wish to become involved with this person based on whether these behavior patterns are positive or negative. You will also receive services from someone who is in the same line of work or in the same profession as you. This person will help advance you to a higher level of success than you ever thought possible. You will also find something very important to you at one time will take on a new priority in your life and will introduce more positive expressions in your life. No matter what else occurs you will develop a higher awareness, greater intelligence and maintain higher ideals in life.

to put a spell on someone Watch your actions. If they are negative, stop the behavior. If positive, continue. This dream is a very lucky omen for you. You will also recover quickly from an emotionally draining situation.

to see someone have a spell cast on them The person you see will come to emotional harm within three days. If you recognize this person, take steps to alert them to this potential damage.

in any other form Be very careful when engaged in pleasure seeking activities. Also, do not allow someone to usurp your power and authority. This individual wants to gain control of something you presently have control of and will attempt to manipulate you in order to gain power over you and a certain situation you are dealing with. Make sure you do not fall prey to this person. Prepare yourself in such a way to avoid this occurrence. You will have the strength and ability to handle this situation. Good luck will be with you.

witchcraft An unusually lucky circumstance will take place within four days that will influence what you hold to be your highest priority. This will enable you to achieve your highest level of success. Any negative event depicted in the dream should be attended to and changed into a positive event. Should you also see someone placing a spell on you in your dreams, become very aware of who this person is. They are very immoral and wicked. If you do not recognize the face, it will represent someone who will shortly come into your life. This person will cause you great emotional harm. Avoid this individual at all costs. You will have the ability and strength to endure anything you need to handle. Victory is with you.

witch doctor Watch your actions. If they are negative, stop the behavior. If positive, continue. This dream is a very lucky omen for you. You will also recover quickly from an emotionally draining situation.

witches' brew Someone is trying to involve you in petty game playing. If you do involve yourself, it will prove costly to your reputation. Stay alert for the next three days. You must also not allow your opinions to become common knowledge in spite of how hard others try to convince you to voice them. Your words will later be held against you and another individual will betray you by telling others what you say. This is likely to take place within two days. Otherwise you are entering a lucky three week cycle and will be able to accomplish much toward your goals. Any negative event

foretold in this dream can be avoided or altered in reality.

witches' Sabbath You will experience an extraordinarily lucky circumstance within three days that will influence what you hold to be your highest priority. You will then be able to achieve your highest level of success. You must also attend to any negative event depicted in this dream and change it into a positive. Any positive event needs to be brought to full bloom. You must also remain alert, someone whom you may or may not know will focus on you in order to bring you bodily harm once they catch you alone and vulnerable. Make sure you are acutely aware of your surroundings, especially for the next three days.

witch hazel Do everything necessary to keep someone from placing demands on you that you will very much regret later on. Make sure you refuse in such a way that there is no chance this person will think you may concede later on. Insulate yourself from this situation completely.

witch hunt Be acutely aware of someone who acts overly enthusiastic toward you when in your presence. The moment your back is turned, this person will behave in an entirely different manner and will act as though you are pushing yourself on them. This person will tell others that they don't know how to tell you they do not want any involvement with you. Do everything necessary to avoid this scenario completely and to avoid hurt feelings entirely. Do this soon and get on with your life.

witness You will be the one who has the last word regarding a particular situation, even if it does not seem so at the time. Be aware that this is just the way things will work during this cycle.

witness stand You will get to the bottom of a certain situation and will be able to determine the facts within three days. This will keep you from making a mistake because you have reached the wrong conclusion. Give yourself several alternative ways of handling a situation that you will be dealing with during this time period. This approach will give you many different avenues to fully develop and at the same time you will be able to develop a way to bring prosperity into your life. Many blessings are with you and your family. You are definitely headed for a brilliant future.

wizard You will have the intelligence and ability to bring those issues you want to resolve to a conclusion very quickly and successfully. This will allow you to get a fresh start and to move on to fresh horizons. Many blessings are with you and you are headed for a brilliant future.

wok Display your charming personality, proper upbringing and education. You will then be admired by many influential people within a five day period. Do not allow yourself to be timid.

wolf Do not depend so heavily on the current way you are doing things. Develop different avenues to bring in extra income. Aggressively motivate yourself to increase your flow of finances and to enjoy more abundances in your life. Prepare yourself for what may come up within three weeks and do everything necessary to make ends meet. This is the perfect cycle for this.

wolf call *to hear a wolf call from a man or woman* You will receive some terrific news within the week. Someone will bring you information you have been wanting to hear for a long time. You have been asking someone to complete or to commit to something and it will come as a pleasant surprise when they do. Many blessings are with you and your family.

to hear a wolf call from a wolf Prepare yourself. You will have to make changes and relocate. This will come up unexpectedly and without your prior knowledge. Accept this calmly and you will find this to be a prosperous and delightful change in your life. You will have to maintain an aggressive attitude during this cycle.

wolf cub You will receive advice from someone who is right on target and will steer you in the direction you should be going if you choose to take this advice. Any professional help that comes your way will work for you successfully, especially for the next seven days. You also need to take steps to change or to avoid any negative event in this dream that could become a reality and make sure any positive event reaches fruition. Within seven days you will have to express your true feelings to someone. This will change this person's mind and keep them from doing something that may be damaging to the relationship. Maintain an aggressive approach to life and do not take even the ordinary things for granted.

wolfhound Within three days you will get hold of some hard to get information. You will be very surprised at the source you received this information from. This will definitely give you a brighter easier way of handling things and a new outlook on life you had not previously had.

wolfs bane Do everything in your power to protect yourself from any unusual situation that may occur within seven days. You will definitely have the courage and confidence it takes to deal with certain situations that will occur within three days and you will make the right decision.

wolverine Be sure you do not expose yourself to any contagious illnesses. Surround yourself with tranquility, harmony and joyful experiences for the next seven days. Also, for the next two weeks you will have to be verbally and physically helpful to another. This person feels neglected and you need to make sure their needs are being met.

woman Be sure you play a very active role in having your emotional needs met. Within five days you will be able to visualize the path you need to take for a brilliant future. Good luck is with you.

angry Do not gamble or take chances with your plans and with people who do not have the expertise to implement your proposed changes.

beautiful Your intuition is on target concerning money and love. Move on this quickly.

black This dream implies victory with your plans and they will work themselves out through an agreeable conversation.

black-dressed You will need to keep your confidence up despite misfortune, and all your plans will have a positive outcome.

crying You will have to put away money. A situation will occur within a few weeks that will require extra finances.

deranged You will be granted a favor.

happy A romantic lover will return to you after a quarrel. There will be an agreement and plans for mutual happiness in your lives.

to hear a disembodied woman's voice Follow the advice given in this dream to the letter. If you do not clearly hear the message, this is an extremely lucky omen. You will be able to withstand any hardship that will arise within the next three days.

homeless You will be misled by a person who goes along with your ideas only to undermine them.

horrifying You are overextending yourself to the point of physical burn out. Within the week, take steps to maintain and improve your health. Eat healthy foods, drink plenty of water and place limits on what you will do for others. You will also receive all requests that you make from your special deity within the week, no matter how outrageous these requests may be.

murdered woman You need to select a new doctor.

muscular You will have a pleasurable luncheon date with a new and flirtatious person. This may lead to a romantic relationship for a duration.

older You will enjoy victory with your plans. An older person will delight your life by helping out financially. You are loved beyond your imagination.

overweight There will be gossip accusing you of physical or sexual abuse of a child. Take steps to prevent this.

perfect female figure Within five days you will find yourself in the position of caring for someone until they are able to improve their life and physical well being to the point of social and personal acceptance. This dream also implies, for the next five days, you will be overwhelmed with social activities. You will need to take extra pains to keep your appearance up and your attire in good condition. This will be a successful cycle for you.

police Remain free for a while. Someone else will come into your life.

professional group (or conversation with a professional woman) You will find a balanced relationship and you will both want to work together to keep the relationship alive.

red-haired You will witness the downfall of a cruel person who has taken advantage of your efforts. This person will lose any power or authority they may have over you and any control you feel they have will come to an immediate halt. You are headed for a prosperous future. Health is yours. You must also become very aware of something you are doing now that will cause financial damage later on. You will not be aware of the extent of this damage for some time. Protect your expenditures now.

skinny Take an independent stand and make a bold move to help a younger person or child to achieve a better way of life.

sleeping This dream is a promise of a good solution to a bad situation.

sloppy You will be in the company of immoral people who have no concern for your well being. Avoid the company of those with loose morals.

strange Do not put yourself in a situation to be deceived by a roommate.

suicidal Celebrations will be made connected with a long -awaited sum of money that will be received within seven days. This will be the solution to present problems.

tall Do not be persuaded to return to a former relationship by an emotional plea. Go on with your life.

washer woman This is a very lucky omen and you will be experiencing much prosperity in your life within two weeks. Things that you thought were impossible to become a part of are now possible during this two week period. Doors will be open to you and you will be welcomed with open arms. Many blessings are with you and your family.

to see a woman's head on another body You need to be acutely aware of the person you dreamed about because they will attempt to bring some harm to you, either emotional or physical. Do everything you can to keep yourself safe. Get on with your life without this person in it because they are serious. Although this person will present a very kind and nice demeanor, they are very evil and cunning. Within three days make sure you disassociate from this person, move on with your life, and take steps to turn this situation around. Make sure you take steps to turn any negative event you dreamed of around so you can experience only positive expressions in your life.

to be a woman in delivery You will begin receiving money from a billed source. Because of circumstances over the next week, you will receive less than anticipated. Be patient, but relentless. In time you will receive the full amount. You will also perform physical labor without pay.

to see a delivery You will hear of a birth of twins.

woman's clinic You will be in the presence of someone within a few days who will promise many things to you in order to hold your interest. This person is desperate to keep you close to them. In reality they are going through many transitions and stresses in their life and it would not be possible for them to deliver on these promises. Although you can see through this ploy, hold back if you are interested in this person. They will recover from this episode within two weeks and will soon be in great shape both emotionally and financially to deliver on these promises they have made. Everything will work out exactly as they have envisioned and you will both enjoy an abundance of health and a brilliant future. Any negative event you saw in the dream needs to be avoided or altered in reality. Be sure you forewarn anyone in the dream whom you recognized to do the same. Take steps to ensure you experience only positive events in your life.

woman's rights Situations will occur that will definitely raise the level of your love life in a grand and passionate manner. Your love relationship will bring you a more prosperous and brilliant future than you ever imagined.

womb You will be very lucky and will experience victory for the next month. You will also receive abundances in areas of your life you most desire. Someone will also verify the love and deep passion they have for you. This will bring you a tremendous feeling of joy because it will catch you off guard and it will come from a person you deeply desire to have in your life. From this moment on you will both conduct your lives and make plans together in such a way that you will enjoy harmony and drastically improved changes that will bring you joy for a lifetime.

wonderland You will enjoy emotional gratification, realize your ambitions and maintain luck for the next month. This dream also implies that you will be able to communicate in a profound and direct way to get your feelings across to another. This will be reciprocal and you will be welcomed with open arms. You are definitely headed for a brilliant future.

Wonder Woman Within three days you will receive the gift of greater healing and heightened psychic abilities by the gods. As a result, you will develop greater organizational skills and will be able to put these gifts and your talents to use in a dynamic way. Many blessings will be with you for a lifetime and you are headed for a brilliant future.

wonton Within seven days you will be very excited about an opportunity that will present itself and you will gain the information and the means to grasp this opportunity. You will be fully able and emotionally equipped to retain this opportunity and it will give you a new start in those areas of your life where you desire change. A difficult situation will also be resolved in this time frame if you make the effort to expedite it. You are entering a cycle that will offer you a tremendous amount of future prosperity.

wood Within seven days you will acquire a long desired possession and will rejoice over finally possessing this item.

firewood You are entering a very lucky cycle for the next four days. Your intuitions and thoughts are very clear and you will be able to use this to your advantage to conclude a situation that has been very difficult for you. You will also be able to say something that has been difficult to someone in such a way that will not create any extra chaos. You will be able to get your point across. Many blessings are with you.

to burn wood Relationships that are close to you will grow only as much as you are willing to invest yourself. There are things that you can either do or avoid doing that will bring more closeness into the relationship. You will also need to watch young children in your family who are in need of more supervision. Many blessings are with you and your family.

burn marks on wood Within three days someone will diplomatically drop subtle hints about a particular area of dissatisfaction in their life that they would like to see you become responsible for. This person wants you to take it upon yourself to make the necessary changes to improve their life. They feel they are stonewalled and cannot get through this situation. You will have the conviction and compassion to do this for them and it will lead them to a better lifestyle if you take the initiative. Many blessings are with you.

woodwork You will definitely have clarity of thought and will enjoy harmony in your life. Many blessings will come to you and your family and you will celebrate the realization of your ambitions.

wood alcohol Do not become anxious for the next seven days over changes that will occur. Any changes that take place during this time period will be positive and will bring an enormous amount of tranquility and prosperity into your life.

wood bin This dream is alerting you to make yourself available for the next three days when an unusual invitation unexpectedly comes to you. This is one that should not be missed. Take full advantage of this and you will bring into your life a wonderful situation that you never imagined was possible. You will bring this situation into your life quickly and will enjoy a fantastic life as a result. Go for it.

woodblock Be aware. Within five days you will see several situations automatically emerge in your life. You will also be able to choose from a variety of situations that will come up and each will offer you a way to expand and improve your lifestyle. You are definitely headed for a brilliant future.

wood carving You will have a golden opportunity to speak with someone in such a way that will bring this person closer to you. This cycle will offer you the best chance for this to occur. You have prior notice of this and can take full advantage of this opportunity to bring that special person closer to you in the manner you desire. You will both be able to discuss future plans that you will be able to put into action immediately. Take steps to keep any negative event in this dream from becoming a reality. Forewarn anyone you recognize to do likewise.

woodchuck For the next three days someone you know will be sending mixed messages. This person will be friendly yet will act as though they are eager to leave your company. They will give you valuable information yet will act as though they desire no involvement with this. Do not feed into this behavior and do not attempt to sort it out. Get on with your life.

woodcraft Treat yourself in ways you have never been treated before. Enjoy yourself by attending some wonderful, enjoyable events. Consider different lifestyles that will enable you to enjoy yourself. Eliminate stress and eat healthful and healing foods, drink plenty of water and do things that will make you feel very relaxed.

woodcut Do not create suspicions, do not allow your imagination to run wild and do not jump to conclusions about a special person. Back off, regroup, and stay firmly in control of your thoughts. Nothing underhanded is going on. You are headed for a brilliant future and many blessings are with you and your family.

woodcutter For the next three days do not allow old festering, hurtful, painful feelings to surface. The moment these feelings start to come to you, replace them with something that will make you feel good about yourself.

wooden horse This dream is an extremely lucky omen and is letting you know that, within three days, you will have a great opportunity to involve yourself in a very loving, romantic relationship. If you choose to go this route, you will enjoy a terrific wonderful life. Any negative event connected to this dream can be changed or avoided completely. Any positive event needs to be brought to fruition.

wooden Indian Something very unusual and peculiar will occur within three days. At the same time this is taking place, you will have the clarity of thought needed to take you through each step to get through this cycle comfortably. Your curiosity will be at an all time high during this time period and you will need to be very firm and disciplined in order to keep this curiosity at bay. You will enjoy an abundance of health during this cycle.

woodland You will be able, within five days, to promote yourself and to rally around you a group of people who will support you financially with a particular idea you want to develop. This will be a very promising situation and the alternatives that come up will be beneficial as well.

wood nymph Make sure you do not underestimate yourself. Do not short change yourself and do not become your own worst enemy. Do everything you can to become emotionally involved. Within three days you will enter a very fulfilling cycle and find a way to involve yourself in situations that will emotionally enhance your life. Love is waiting for you.

woodpecker Do not allow yourself to overextend your energies by trying to keep up with someone else's demands and wishes, especially for the next five days. You will be able to make a profound and successful move. Many blessings are with you and your family.

wood pulp Prepare ahead. You will have a greater number of guests than you anticipated. This situation will require that you have more provisions than you have. Take steps to make sure you have enough to make everyone comfortable.

woodshed An unusual situation will occur and you will have the clarity of thought to make a wise decision regarding certain investments. This clarity of thought will lead you to rapid wealth. You are headed for a very prosperous future.

wood shop Within three days someone will attempt to force their way into your company by using tact and a sweet manner. This will create a feeling of uneasiness and suspicions about this person's motives. Follow your instincts and do not compromise your feelings. Your hunches are on target and by following these hunches you will not make a mistake, especially for the next three days.

woodsman/woman Be alert for the next two weeks. You will have to make drastic changes in order to remain out of a very stressful situation. Others will want you to get involved and you need to make sure you stay clear of this. Seek tranquility, peace and a stress free lifestyle. Proceed with confidence. You must also be very watchful for the next three days of someone's irritable manner. Back off so an explosive disagreement does not take place.

woodwind Someone will ask you to assist them in very tedious time consuming paperwork that will require you to be in contact with an agency, etc. Step back and assess every move so you do not become bogged down with unnecessary work or waste your time. Ask detailed questions so you can move rapidly ahead. Many blessings are with you and your family.

woodwork You will definitely have clarity of thought and will enjoy harmony in your life. Many blessings will come to you and your family and you will celebrate the realization of your ambitions.

wool Someone will verify the love and passionate feelings they have for you. This will catch you off guard and will come from someone you deeply desire. From here on out both of you will take all of the right steps to ensure a lengthy and fulfilled relationship. These new and wonderful changes will fill you with joy for a lifetime.

wool gathering For a five day period your thoughts will be illuminating. This will be a gift from the deities. You will be able to precisely detail those things that are important to do in your life. Once these plans are set into motion you will experience grand changes in your way of living. You are headed in the right direction. Eat healthful foods, drink plenty of water and love yourself.

Worcestershire Sauce Pay close attention to messages that will be coming from someone else for the next week. These messages will offer you suggestions that will change your life for the better. Make sure you attend to matters that should not be overlooked. You will also need to pay close

attention to your dreams during this time period. Your intuition is right on target.

word You will do your best work at the top level of your capacity. Riches are coming your way and this dream is a guarantee that you can expect this with confidence. Many blessings are with you and your family.

Word of God This dream is a reminder to reaffirm your beliefs and faith. Brilliant events will begin to happen suddenly and surely. Whatever was revealed to you in this dream must not be revealed to another person until it has been manifested in reality. Any message revealed about another person should be given to this individual so they will have the time to change any forthcoming negative event or work to enhance any future positive event. This applies to the dreamer as well. You will also receive a sense of optimism and confidence that will allow you to turn your life around. You are headed for a brilliant future. This feeling of excitement will stay with you for a long period of time and will assist you in the task of turning your life around more rapidly. Many blessings will be with you and your family.

word processor Every issue you are involved with will be successfully resolved within the week. You will also be inspired to seek a new way of living in a specific area of your life. You need to work slowly and on a day by day schedule until you reach the heights you desire. Expect this to occur this month. Victory is yours.

work You will be victorious over an illness and will recover rapidly. You will see a major improvement within the week and are headed for a brilliant future.

homework For the next three days you will be successful in tackling any situation that appears complicated. You will develop the confidence you originally lacked and you will be able to handle any situation that seemed impossible. Good luck is with you. Be sure that you bring any positive message in this dream to full bloom and make sure you prevent the occurrence of any negative event.

overwork Within two days you will find assistance with an ongoing situation that you feel at the moment is almost impossible to turn around positively. This also implies that someone you have been wanting to see will surrender to you and grant you this wish within four days.

woodwork You will definitely have clarity of thought and will enjoy harmony in your life. Many blessings will come to you and your family and you will celebrate the realization of your ambitions.

workaholic Someone will do everything in their power to manipulate you out of something that is righteously yours. Be very watchful during this cycle but investigate closely to locate the source. This will be a very lucky cycle for you and you will accomplish what you had doubts that you would accomplish.

workbench Someone with a dynamic reputation will back

you up on a business plan. Good luck is with you and you are headed in the right direction.

workbook Someone, within five days, will lead you into a new career that will prove to be very successful and will provide a solid foundation for a lifetime. This will be a same sexed person who will be very tenacious in making sure you are headed in the right direction.

work camp Someone will not deny you the affections you request from them, especially for the next three days. You are deeply loved and appreciated by others.

worker Pay close attention to what you are being told by others for the next three days. This message will be very instrumental in swaying you in the right direction concerning those decisions you have to make in life.

road worker Do not make any major decisions for the next three days. Give yourself time to think about this very carefully.

worker's compensation This is the perfect time for seeking the information you need for making all the correct decisions in life.

work gloves *cotton* It will become necessary because of a situation that will occur within three days to determine whether someone you are working with on a particular project is pulling their load. This person may be having you do the work of two people if you are not alert to this. Focus on this so you can get the help you need without taking over extra responsibilities or extra stress. Speak up and demand that this person pull their own weight. Many blessings are with you and you will enjoy a prosperous future through your senior years.

workplace You will be able to competently handle rough tasks. You will develop a relentless character during this time frame and get your rewards because you will do away with errors.

work table You are definitely headed for a prosperous future and you will have a lucky month long period to take care of what you need to take care of. You also need to provide yourself with the solitude you need in order to clear your thoughts, especially for the next seven days. Proceed with confidence, you are headed for a brilliant future.

world Your thoughts will be magically illuminated and you will be able to clearly communicate ideas that will enhance your life. You will feel solid and whole and will be able to handle problems quickly and confidently. Others will see these changes. You will be blessed for many years and the knowledge you have gained will always remain with you. You will be able to tap into this knowledge for future benefits. You can expect this to come into a very clear pattern within the week.

to dream of two different worlds Someone will behave toward you in ways that are completely unexpected and will express their feelings toward you beautifully. This person will also make a proposal to you that will fill you with joy and will be impossible to refuse. You are definitely headed for a brilliant future.

to dream of a world in the process of destruction Within three days you will associate with a very forceful person who will skillfully use their words in such a way that you will feel compelled to surrender to their desires, behave in the way they want you to, and speak in the manner they wish. Be very wary of this because they will do everything they can to get their way. This person also has a bad habit of using every means at their disposal to avoid responsibilities. They will hide behind the little things you do to evade their responsibilities. You have prior notice of this and can take the appropriate steps to avoid this situation.

World Series Power and authority will be given to you and you will have the competency you need to take on this leadership position. You will give others the confidence to believe that you will be able to handle these tasks. You will also need to allocate a certain amount of time to certain agendas you will be developing within seven days so situations are resolved in the proper time and order.

World's Fair A variety of situations will be developing within the week. You will have to be on your toes so you can give these issues your attention as they are developing. You can use the proper procedure to handle each one and ignore those that are not worth developing any further. You are on the right path toward prosperity. Proceed with confidence.

World War I You will have to bear down relentlessly on someone until things develop as you want them to, especially for the next five days. Many blessings are with you and your family and you are headed for a prosperous future.

World War II Someone will focus on you and attempt to force you to feel feelings that you do not have for them. Because of this focus on you, you need to do everything you can to avoid a very distasteful episode. Remain free of stress and protect yourself as best you can. This should be your priority for the next three days. You have prior notice of this and can position yourself in such a way that no one can take advantage of you in any manner.

worm Several situations will take place within the week that you can expose yourself to. Motivate yourself to take advantage of this because these will be once in a lifetime opportunities. Do not procrastinate and take steps to grasp these. Expose and mobilize yourself so you will not miss any of them. Otherwise, you are headed for a brilliant future.

wormhole You will be victorious, are headed for a brilliant future and can expect to turn any negative situation into a positive one within the month. Proceed with confidence.

cabbage worm Do not allow someone to harass you to the point of giving up something you cherish. Be very firm about putting an end to someone's abusive behavior, especially for the next week.

hookworm Be very disciplined with your behavior, especially around children. Do not allow yourself to be irresponsible or to act on impulse when in the company of young people. Control your emotions, do nothing inappropriate for the next three days.

meal worm Do not allow your moods to control your behavior. Avoid this for the next three days. You may scare someone away permanently whom you want very much in your life.

silk worm Avoid peer pressure and do what you want in order to enjoy life more.

tape worm This dream is a warning to avoid all exposure to disease or to avoid any contact that would spread an infection. Avoid all sexual contact for the next two days. You also need to do everything necessary to avoid forcing yourself on another person. You will be tempted to do so within seven days but in spite of the appearance that this is acceptable behavior on your part toward this person, refrain from acting this way. The other individual will be repulsed by your actions and you will find it difficult to forgive yourself later. You must also make sure your environment is free of toxins.

wire worm Dig deeply to determine exactly what your financial status is now and make projections about where you will be in the future. Use your drive and ambition to determine what you need to do now in order to make ends meet for the next three weeks. This is the perfect cycle for you to do this in order not to be caught off guard.

worm wood Possessions of yours that are semi abandoned are in danger or being damaged or lost. Do everything in your power to make sure your property is well cared for and kept safe, especially for the next three days.

worn *any form* Make certain you are not put in the position of being taken advantage of by someone who refuses to see any way but their own. This person is determined to force you to be the one who will carry out their wishes. Be very clear and do not allow empathy to sway you to offer help without grasping the magnitude of the responsibilities. You will come up with the successful solution. Good luck is with you.

worry Anything connected with this dream that you feel should be eliminated in reality can be taken care of and you can avoid any negative event from taking place. For the next seven days when you catch yourself worrying, you will also need to take steps to avoid getting caught up in this negativity. This dream is a guarantee you will be victorious in whatever you want to accomplish for the next month. You are definitely headed for a brilliant future. Do everything you can to create a stress free environment and continue to remind yourself that you will remain victorious. Proceed with confidence.

worry beads You definitely have the capabilities and means to be victorious in situations that will come up within the

week that you felt you were unable to grasp. Many blessings are with you and you are headed for a brilliant future.

worship For a three week period, make it a point to meditate in your favorite way.

wound Do everything necessary to protect yourself from any wounds, especially for the next seven days. Alert those you recognize in this dream to do the same. Do whatever you can to avoid negative experiences in your life and take steps to experience only the positive. Do everything necessary to avoid any situation that will lead to your feelings being hurt because you insist on behaving in a way that someone has asked you not to.

wraith Any negative festering hang ups that are keeping you from moving on the path you desire will completely disappear. You will clear your mind and take all the correct steps to put yourself on the path toward prosperity.

wrangler For the next three days be very strict with another person and demand that a certain behavior of theirs stops. You will be able to use this cycle to accomplish this task and come out very successfully.

wrap You will be able to pin down someone who is very difficult to pin down. State to this person exactly what you need and want from them. Use this cycle to have your needs met by this person. You will be successful.

wraparound Do everything you can to determine your next move with a special person. Victory is yours. You will make the correct decision.

wrapper Make it your business to talk to a special person about your needs for the next two days. This person will be eager and willing to accommodate you. You need to verbalize what you need because no one can read your mind. You will be able to successfully resolve all issues.

wreath Do not allow yourself to become so curious that you are unable to use good judgment and venture into the unknown. There is a very thin line between mere curiosity and an active participation in something you should avoid. You are being misled by others who desire your participation. Stay uninvolved. You have prior notice of this and can avoid all negative involvements, especially for the next three days. Make sure you only experience positive expressions in your life.

wreck *to see a wreck* Do everything within your power to keep yourself safe and to avoid an accident of any sort. Any event in this dream that is connected to you or to someone else needs to be avoided at all costs. Take steps to change any negative event to a positive one in reality.

in any other form Do everything in your power to ensure you do not verbally wreck anything for yourself. For the next three days do everything you can to create a very harmonious and stress free environment for those whom you feel are special to you. Many blessings are with you and you can proceed with confidence.

wrecker's ball Someone you have known for a long time will unexpectedly call you out of the blue and ask you subtle personal questions throughout the conversation. The conversation will end with a proposal of marriage. Until now, this person has not had the time for a commitment and is now ready to look for the proper mate. If you choose to go this route, you will enjoy a wonderful, stable and successful union. Many blessings are with you and you are headed for a brilliant future.

wrecking yard An older, loving person will bequeath you a collection they have acquired over a lifetime.

wren You are making the correct decisions. Do not create doubt and suspicions, especially for the next three days. You are headed for a prosperous future and you will be able to make all the correct decisions in this time period.

wrench Make sure you rally people around you who will be enthusiastic about your cause. You will then be able to get things going in the direction you desire in a much quicker fashion. This is the perfect cycle for you to move on this. You will be expanding your lifestyle in a way that would be impossible unless you take these steps.

wrestle Take steps to keep any negative event in this dream from becoming a reality, especially for the next two days. Make sure that anyone you recognize from this dream avoids any forced wrestling situation that could occur in their life. You have prior notice and can keep it from occurring. This dream also implies that someone will focus on you for the purpose of sexual favors and will do everything they can to interest you in physical involvement. If you choose to do this, you will find you will regret it. Many blessings are with you and you will correctly choose your destiny.

wriggle Do everything you can to avoid being in the company of someone who wears on your patience and will irritate you to the point that you will regret any involvement. If you know someone with this personality, do everything you can to avoid their company, especially for the next three days.

wring Be very realistic about the situation that you know will develop within the next three days. Someone will start trying to earn your confidence in order to have you give them a large responsibility. This person has let you down in the past. There will be no time to start looking for alternatives once they have decided to back out of the original agreement. Do not allow this to occur, especially during this time frame.

wrinkled Get your act together. A very special and unusual event will occur very unexpectedly that you need to start anticipating now. This will give you the time to ready your-

self properly in case you get a sudden call. You will then be able to throw yourself together quickly so you will not miss a once in a lifetime event. This should be your priority now.

wrinkles Someone will give you very specific signs about how they truly feel about particular issues that you are taking for granted regarding everyday situations. You are very comfortable with this but this other person is not. This individual does not wish you to have any involvement in this particular situation but does not have the capabilities to express this to you verbally. Pay close attention to anything that may need to be handled in a totally different manner. Make yourself available to interact with this person until you are able to resolve this issue to everyone's satisfaction. You will find this to be the most advantageous route to take. This dream also implies that, in spite of anything else that is going on in your life now, you will have a brilliant future in ways that you never imagined.

wrist It is essential for the next three days that you devote your time to positioning yourself in such a way that you can create excitement and generate a greater interest regarding a new situation. You will be able to segment more success about a new product, plan, idea or conversation. You will gain excellent feedback that will bring about more productivity, more fun and will create a non stressful outcome to what is a priority to you now. You will be able to bring everyone involved together in building a common understanding. You will determine what, where, and how to effectively achieve a chief victory on a grander scale than you anticipated. Your goal is to make the world aware of these exciting ideas, etc., and you will find that they are well received by others.

if you dream of anything distasteful around your wrist that should not be there Make sure anything negative you dreamed of that concerns your wrist does not take place, especially for the next three days. Anything you dreamed of that concerns your wrist in a positive way should be allowed to happen during this time frame.

if you dream of something attractive around your wrist This dream is a guarantee that you will receive good news and will receive something that will please you during the same time frame. Alert all those you recognize in this dream to expect the same thing so they can take the necessary steps to allow anything positive to blossom or to prevent any negative event from taking place. This dream also implies that someone will take you by surprise by expressing their deep emotional feelings and passion for you. It is your choice whether you want to become involved or not. Many blessings are with you and you are headed for a very prosperous future.

wristband Do everything necessary to set aside some time to enjoy quiet and tranquility. You will also find that someone who is special to you needs to work out an agreement and a compromise so you can develop a better way of treating each other. Schedule events together as well as planning unusual places you can visit together. You will find this time together to be very instrumental in laying the foundation for many wonderful years for both of you.

wristwatch You will unexpectedly receive a windfall and a gift of money. The more glamorous the wristwatch you dreamed about, the better the gift will be. This is also the perfect time to begin collecting the money that is owed to you. These next two days are the best time to receive money.

write Pay close attention to what was being written. If this portended a negative event, you have prior notice so you can avoid this entirely or alter it in reality. You must also alert those you recognize from this dream to do likewise. This dream also implies that any documents, conversations or agreements concerning other people need to be worked out by everyone involved. This is a time when you will see money come from different sources and different areas and you will definitely see an increase in finances. This is also a time when you will see an increase in other people's interest in the completion of those issues you need to take care of.

to write in stone Take steps to develop a clever plan that will allow you to work independently on a situation that will develop within three days. You will then be able to work without the interference of others. This plan will come to you with great clarity and you will be able to successfully resolve this situation.

writer This dream is a verification that you will get your product, art form, etc., on the market. You will reach the level you are seeking. You will realize your ambitions and you will flourish.

writer's cramp You will definitely find the financial stability you need in the areas you are working on. This is definite verification that your ambitions will be realized. You are headed for a brilliant future.

writing *scrawled* For the next three days be very aware and do not become any more involved with someone except with extreme caution. This person is someone you are beginning to develop a sense of closeness to and they will lead you to fully confide in them and depend on their loyalty. This person is very skilled in creating illusions and will lead you to believe that certain events will take place that will never occur. This person has a devious hidden agenda that involves pursuing you for purposes known only to them and will go to great lengths to create a suspicion free and trusting environment. This individual is very charming and charismatic and will, if they think you are becoming suspicious, create a crisis to divert you from your suspicions. By the time you realize what is taking place, you will have suffered disappointments, disillusionments and financial distress. It will take you a long time to recover from this and get back to a normal life. You have prior notice of this and all the means necessary to successfully diffuse this situation. Practice common sense and refuse to become involved. Do not compromise and do not allow this person to pry into your personal life. You will have the confidence you need to put yourself on the path toward a prosperous future. Many blessings will come to you and your family.

writing desk The head of your household will make an emotional appeal to someone in power. This will bring an abundance of wealth to the family. Move quickly, this cycle will last for seven days and will be a good luck omen for this period of time.

writing paper It is very important that you attend a specific function because it will be very glamorous and exciting. Be sure to prepare for this ahead of time because it will require formal attire and you will want to look your best. You will meet many influential people who will become friends for life and you will enjoy yourself tremendously. During this time period you will also become very aware that the person you most desire feels the same way about you. You will develop many affectionate feelings toward each other and you will be very excited about this new development. You are on the path for a prosperous and brilliant future.

writing pen This dream is a lucky omen. You are in a powerful cycle for achievement and you will accomplish everything you attempt.

felt tip pen Someone you have known for a long time will call unexpectedly and ask subtle questions to draw information from you. After a short period of time, this person will bluntly ask you to marry. This will be prefaced by the statements that they have known you for a long time, have no one in their life and you would be a good couple. It is your choice whether to pursue this or not. This person has an income and property but is neither rich nor poor. If you choose this route, you will find it is the right and proper path for you.

written exam *to pass a written exam* Within three days you will suddenly be free of a long standing burden. You will not have to go through a difficult and lengthy process to achieve this.

wrong *to hear this word* A very evil conniving person will manipulate you into conforming to their wishes within five days. Remain uninvolved, especially when it comes to someone offering to do you a favor. Do everything you can to turn any negative event around to a positive expression, especially for the next three days. Anyone you recognize from this dream will be someone you need to be alerted to. This person will try to take advantage of you. Move on with your life without this person in it.

wrought iron Remain calm and non argumentative when discussing an extremely delicate issue that will come up between family members. Do everything you can to stay uninvolved, especially for the next week.

Wyoming You will enjoy yourself fully if you allow your-to accept an invitation that will be extended to you within two weeks. You will be invited to an exotic place, have a wonderful time and have wonderful memories to bring home with you. You will have a safe trip and return home exhilarated. You are headed for a prosperous future and will also receive a gift that will make you ecstatically happy. This dream may also be used as a reference point in time. If you dream of this state and see its name used in any context, the dream message will occur on this day.

X-ray tube Stay clear of petty, negative gossiping people. Keep your opinions to yourself. You also need to realize that you are a sacred vessel and should take steps to nurture yourself in the best possible way. Any negative event in this dream needs to be taken care of. Do not allow it to become a reality for you or anyone you recognize in this dream. Otherwise, you are headed for a very prosperous future.

X

X Persevere in matters concerning any child's education. A past skill or creative streak will be rekindled and will also become profitable. This dream implies grandness, power and victory in each aspect of your life. It also implies that you will be undergoing some very exciting changes in your way of living. You will also meet someone very soon who has a flair for drama. If you choose, this is the perfect time to add style and drama to your appearance. This will result in a very pleasurable meeting with a larger income flow within five days.

Xerox Negotiations between yourself and someone in power will be successful.

XL/extra large *any form* An event will occur within seven days that you must attend. You will be in the company of two admirers who will subtly attempt to win over your affections. Both of these people will be very agreeable and charming but one of them possesses a great deal of power and authority. It would be to your advantage to choose one of them as a life long partner. You can be confident that you are on the path of a prosperous future.

Xmas *any form* It is a lucky omen to have this dream. A secret or mystery will surface. You will also receive one thrilling gift. The outcome will be the same if you have this dream during any time of the year. You will also be presented with a new opportunity and will now have the means to grasp it. This will enable you to make a new start in those areas of your life that you desire changes in. All old issues and burdens that have been plaguing you will come to an immediate halt and big changes will occur that will leave you with a new zest for life. You will enjoy success regarding all negotiations that will take place within this week and everyone involved will help bring these plans to completion.

X-ray A soft manner will give you the position desired in a relationship. You will also find that whatever you saw in the x-ray will show up in an x-ray result in reality. Take every step you can to practice preventive medicine. Alert anyone you recognized in the dream to do likewise.

Y

Y You will need to motivate yourself to create situations that you have never thought of becoming involved in. You are destined to receive two different gifts at the same time that will provide two different paths. You will need to become active in such a way that you will allow your destiny to take over. Develop your creativity and follow your hunches. This needs to take place within three months of having this dream. Either path you take will be successful and you will grasp what you want, whether this is a tangible material goal or something far more abstract. One of them, however, is far superior than the other and the resulting goal will be greater. Whichever one you choose must be decided on and grasped within a three month period and you will need to start motivating yourself in this direction now. This will be guaranteed major victory for you and you are definitely headed for a brilliant future.

yacht Remain focused and stay on your destined course, especially for the next three days. This must be your priority now. You will definitely grasp your goals. Any negative event foretold in this dream also needs to be altered or avoided in reality. Take steps to experience only positive events in your life. Make sure you advise anyone you recognize in this dream to do likewise. You must also be very cautious not to involve yourself, for the next three days, with anyone who will cause you a great deal of embarrassment because of their socially unacceptable behavior. Otherwise, you are definitely headed for a prosperous future.

yacht club Within the week you will agree to wed someone you deeply desire. You will enjoy many years of happiness with someone you care deeply about. Luck and blessings will be with you and your family.

yam You will have an irresistible impulse to win over someone you have just been introduced to or will meet on your own within seven days. If you choose to pursue this, you will find this relationship to be emotionally rewarding and satisfying. You are headed for a prosperous future.

Yankee Within three days you will focus on yourself and will be able to project to others the character you most want. You will see far more exciting and developed personal characteristics in yourself at the end of a two week period.

Yankee Doodle Within two days you will relentlessly go after those needs you want to have satisfied. You will be able to accomplish this and will feel very exuberant and excited because of it. You must also take steps to prevent any negative event in this dream from becoming a reality and make sure you warn anyone else involved to do the same.

yard Because of your loving nature, you will be able to bring anyone you choose closer to you within three days. You will be able to draw out the best in this person and will be treated in a very special way for the next five days.

junk yard Take care of only one thing at a time to ensure each situation is brought to a satisfactory conclusion.

wrecking yard An older, loving person will bequeath you a collection they have acquired over a lifetime.

yard sale A tremendous opportunity will open up for you if you place yourself at the right place at the right time. You will grasp exactly what you are after and will see an increase in the benefits you are seeking. Many blessings are with you and your family.

yard work A situation will occur within the next five days involving a certain individual whom you felt was very special to you. This situation will leave you thinking about this person in a very different way than you have before.

yardage Within three days you will have to prepare yourself to act in a certain manner to enlist someone you are interested in involving yourself with in some capacity. You have prior notice of this and can make preparations to handle yourself in an appropriate manner.

yardarm Someone you will involve yourself with during the next week will be so stubborn and narrow minded they will mislead you with incorrect information rather than checking to see if they are giving you the facts. Make it clear to this person that you wish to verify whether there are more options than the ones they introduced.

yard bird Many blessings are with you and what you felt was impossible in the past will be very possible now, especially for the next three days. Proceed with confidence.

yard sale A tremendous opportunity will open up for you if you place yourself at the right place at the right time. You will grasp exactly what you are after and will see an increase in those benefits you are seeking. Many blessings are with you and your family.

yardstick You will come across some privileged information within three days. Expand your horizons.

yard work A situation will occur within five days involving a certain individual whom you felt was very special to you. This situation will leave you thinking about this person in a very different way than you have before.

yawn Conduct yourself properly when you receive information about a certain situation. Do not jump to conclusions. This information will be incorrect. Expect this to occur within three days.

to see yourself or anyone else yawn Do not procrastinate or hesitate too long. Move quickly and motivate yourself to push things along in the direction you feel they should be going. Do this within five days to ensure you get exactly what you are after. You will be victorious.

year If you dream about a specific year that brought you joy or distasteful moments you must, within five days, take steps to ensure that these distasteful events do not reoccur. Take steps to bring the pleasant ones to fruition. Victory will be yours and you will have a guarantee that, if you remain focused and disciplined, you will meet your goals and complete your mission within a one year period.

yearbook Do not allow someone else's influence to cause you to switch gears. Listen to your own counsel and advice, and follow your own hunches. Your intuition is correct. Anything you dreamed of in the yearbook that you perceive as negative must be altered or avoided in reality and make sure that all positive things you saw are brought to fruition. You have five days in which to do this. You are headed for a brilliant future.

recognizable face This person will be a major player in helping you to shape the type of future you most desire in life.

yearn A family member will ask you for a specific favor that at this time in your life you will find extremely difficult to grant. This dream is letting you know that in spite of anything else that is going on in your life, if you choose to help, everything will work out successfully with very little stress. Proceed with confidence and handle this quickly. Many blessings are with you and you are headed for a prosperous future.

yeast Within five days you will be very successful, especially if you use the art of skill and diplomacy.

yeast infection Do whatever is within your power to avoid any negativity connected to this dream concerning you or anyone else you recognize in this dream. You have prior notice of this and can take all the necessary steps to handle this correctly. Also avoid putting yourself in a position where your feelings will be hurt by expecting too much from a certain individual you are expecting to come through for you. Avoid this by not setting yourself up for hurtful feelings during this time frame.

yell *to yell out or to hear someone else yell out a recognizable name* This name represents the person you will need on your side when certain situations start to evolve. This situation could be very abusive and if you have this person with you, you will be saved just in time. Depending on the contents of this dream you can determine whether the significance of what was yelled needs to be attended to. If it was a negative message, take steps to ensure that all of your bases are covered.

to yell/scream out someone's name whom you do not recognize Make sure, for the next three days, you do not go anywhere without the company of someone else, especially if you are going out with someone or are meeting with someone you do not know well. This could be a potentially abusive situation. Having someone with you will save you from this. Depending on the contents of this dream you can determine whether the significance of what was yelled needs to be attended to. If it was a negative message, take steps to ensure that all your bases are covered.

if you recognize the person yelling out a name You will need to alert this individual that certain situations will begin to evolve that could be very abusive. Warn this person that if they have someone with them they will be saved just in time. The person they need to have with them is the person whom they called out for. Make sure you alert this person not to go out alone because it will be a potential dangerous situation.

to see yourself or someone else yell for no reason You are beginning to feel a strong emotional wave that will consume a great deal of your time because you have no knowledge of where this drive is coming from. This drive is causing you to focus on bringing something to reality. This will go on for two weeks and you will continue to feel this deep emotional craving. Within this two week period you will somehow arrive at the reason and source of this feeling and will then begin acting on what you think you should be doing. This powerful craving is a result of a heightened awareness and psychic ability that is driving you in the direction you need to go. Although you will have no tangible proof or verification you will instinctively know because of the intense excitement you feel, that by acting on this urge you will reap grander benefits than you ever felt possible. If you deem this to be socially unacceptable or incorrect, you have the time and enough notice to seek the professional help you need to come to grips with your desires and live at peace with yourself and your urges. The moment you sense this emotional wave, seek help. This is the perfect cycle for you to find just the right person who is equipped to handle this issue. It will be properly addressed and you will once more feel as though you are in control of your emotions in a healthy way. Otherwise, you are headed for a brilliant future.

yelling *any form* Be very wary for the next three days and move forward with someone else only with extreme caution. This person and you are beginning to develop a sense of closeness and you will get the feeling you can confide fully in this individual and can depend on their loyalty. This person is very crafty and skilled in creating deception and illusion and will lead you to believe that certain events will take place in the future that will never occur. This person has a very diabolical hidden agenda that involves pursuing you for reasons only known to them. They will go to great lengths to create an atmosphere that will leave you trusting them totally with no suspicions of their plans. They will, however, because of their charm and charisma, be able to create diversions if they sense you are becoming suspicious. By the time you realize what is taking place, you will suffer disappointments, disillusionments and financial distress. It will take a long time to recover from this and get your life back to normal. You have prior notice of this and the means to ensure this does not occur. Practice common sense and you will successfully diffuse this issue. Do not compromise yourself, do not become involved and do not allow this person to pry into your affairs. You are on the path toward prosperity and many blessings will come to you and your family.

yellow This is an extremely victorious color to dream about. You can breathe easily and take it slowly in business and love matters. Everything will turn out exactly as you have envisioned and will fall into place exactly as you want. You will receive verification about what you are expecting within seven days. You will also see the realization of your ambitions.

yellow belly You will become the beneficiary of something you least expect within three weeks.

yellow cake Relax, certain situations that will soon evolve will fall in your favor. Go for it and do not question this development.

yellow daisy You will definitely get the opportunity you want and desire with the person of your choice. If you choose to go this route, this opportunity will be presented to you within two days. This is an extremely lucky cycle.

yellow fever This is the wrong time to move on proposals in any capacity. Stay uninvolved and step back, especially for the next seven days.

yellow jacket Be extremely careful with young adults and young children. Make sure they remain safe and accident free, especially for the next three days. You will also need to use relentless persistence to grasp what you want to achieve your goals.

yellow pages This is an extremely lucky omen and you will be very victorious in anything you involve yourself with for the next seven days. You will need to be persistent in getting the information you need. It will be easier to come by in this time frame. You will also need to turn around anything negative that you dreamed you saw in the yellow pages and take steps to turn any positive information you received into a reality. If anyone you recognized was in this dream, advise them to do the same. Many blessings are with you and you will enjoy a very victorious future.

Yellowstone Park Any negative response you were expecting to receive within five days will be positive. Proceed with confidence, you are headed for a prosperous future. This dream may also be used as a reference point in time. If you dream of this park and see its name used in any context, the dream message will occur on this day.

yellowtail Allow that special person in your life to express their opinion, especially for the next three days. You are loved beyond your imagination.

yen Allow the special people in your life to have the space they need to take care of the special needs they have without the guilt of feeling they have to be responsible for your needs. Do what you can to open up conversations and allow more understanding in this area. Many blessings are with you and your family.

yeoman Do not allow someone else's sense of uncomfortableness and perception of life affect you. Do not allow your mood to change in response to this individual's behavior. Maintain your confidence and get on with your life without this person's influence.

yes You will receive a yes answer to what you are requesting, especially for the next seven days. Remain confident and firm. You are headed for a brilliant future.

yesterday Make sure you do not repeat any past negative patterns. Do everything in your power to make sure your loved ones do not outgrow you. Do what you can to grow and evolve so those you care about do not become bored because of your unwillingness to move forward. Live life to the fullest and proceed with confidence.

yew Protect yourself by refusing an unusual request, especially for the next seven days. You must also do everything necessary for the next three days to ensure you do not put out negative feelings toward someone else. Let bygones be bygones and do not harbor grudges or the feelings of revenge. Release those feelings and get on with your life. You are headed for a brilliant future.

Yiddish Within a short while you will have a conversation with a total stranger that will lead to wonderful events in the future. Both of you have a great deal in common and will develop a strategy that will provide you both with a lavish lifestyle. You are headed in the right direction. Proceed with confidence.

YMCA This dream is alerting you that within seven days you will have to make a lot of calls to verify information about a certain person. You have prior notice of this and can take steps now to avoid having to do more investigative work later on. You are headed for a very prosperous life and many blessings will come to you and your family.

yodel *to yodel* Make sure you double check your schedule. You have scheduled two different events at the same time. One of them is more important than the other. Take care of this now so you have plenty of time to cancel the least important one or to reschedule.

yoga Meditate in your favorite form. You are definitely in the position to move ahead confidently in that area of life that you are interested in involving yourself. You will also have clarity of thought and be able to make all the right decisions in this time period. Make sure you take time to enjoy the marrow of life. Eat healthy foods, drink plenty of water and exercise in your favorite form.

yogurt Be prepared. Within five days, a large victory will come your way. Be consistent and be sure that you behave appropriately in all areas of your life.

yoke You will fall deeply in love with someone who is much younger than you. If you choose to go this route, you will find that this person will have a deep respect and love for you. Many wonderful moments are headed your way and you will enjoy mutual understanding and a tranquil life.

yolk Do everything you can to allow certain individuals in your life to develop and grow properly. Desperately seek ways that young ones can develop and grow and transform into someone they can be proud of. Make sure they have a clear path to develop into productive good people. You also have the chance to grasp victory in every level of your life that you desire. Proceed with confidence. Everything you felt was impossible is now very much a possibility. You are headed for a brilliant future.

Yom Kippur A certain situation that has been draining you emotionally will rapidly stabilize and you will see big improvements in your life within four days. Take time to recover from this situation and do not take on another troublesome problem. Enjoy life and keep yourself safe.

Yorkshire pudding You will develop some well formed ideas within two days. If you take the time to execute these plans, you will receive what you need to meet your goals.

Yorkshire terrier Be very attentive to someone who has a difficult time showing their emotions. This person will demonstrate, through body language, that something is amiss. They are thinking about committing suicide and need help getting on the right track. You will have success in putting a stop to this situation and in offering help to someone who is emotionally vulnerable right now. Expect this to take place within three days.

Yosemite You will become very successful in the eyes of others in an area you will specialize in. You will begin to develop this within three weeks. You will receive everything you ever wanted and will position yourself well in life. You will enjoy a very financially stable lifestyle and are definitely headed for prosperity. This dream may also be used as a reference point in time. If you dream of this park and see its name used in any context, the dream message will occur on this day.

young *to see the face of someone you recognize as a bit* *younger than in reality* If this individual represents a time period in your life when certain patterns occurred that you do not want to repeat and/or people you do not want to be involved with now, you have prior notice and can take steps to prevent it. These could be the same episodes and people, or similar events and people with the same characteristics. This dream could also represent a time period when you enjoyed many wonderful experiences and want to repeat them in your life now. Think back to something you want to recreate in order to gain the benefits and advantages these experiences offered. You may also want to include someone with the same character whom you remembered in this time frame as having a positive influence on you. Make the person you recognized aware of your dream so they can do likewise. You may also, within the month, see this particular person or someone they were associated with during the time period you dreamed about who will talk about them. You may also run into someone who was in your life during this time period whom you may or may not want to include in your life. Any negative situation you dreamed of concerning this person needs to be prevented and any positive expression will become a reality because your spirit is alerting you that what you dreamed of will occur when you see this person in reality. Your plans will work out on a grander scale than you ever anticipated if you approach everything on a larger scale. You are headed for a prosperous and brilliant future.

to see the face of someone you know as a baby or as far younger than they are in reality Think back to important events that were occurring during the time period that this individual was a part of your life. These events will supply you with clues of a forthcoming event that will occur within four days. You may desire to include this in your present life or take steps to ensure that it does not occur. You must also focus on your health as well as on everyday situations that you take for granted. This person or someone with similar traits will require extra help and protection from freak accidents. This dream also implies that someone has difficulty expressing their true feelings for you. This is the perfect time for you to become aware that it is important to allow this person to be comfortable enough to open up and express their true feelings. Any negative event depicted in this dream needs to be avoided in reality, and alert those who need to be forewarned of events that were depicted in this dream. Remain alert and open to all messages for the next four days that will bring you good news. Otherwise, you are headed for a prosperous future.

to see yourself as a baby or far younger than you are in reality Avoid any accidents and illnesses that are within your power to prevent. Pay attention to the people who were most important to you during this time frame. Be sure to involve someone in your life who shares similar traits to someone who, in the past, brought you much happiness. Make sure you avoid anyone who shares the same behavior as someone who caused you distress and despair. Any positive experience you had during that time period can be reproduced in the present. Keep all old patterns and hang ups that you were going through during that time period from reoccurring during this cycle.

in any other form Within the week an exceptional person will enter your life and you will become involved with them in spite of the fact that they do not fit the type you are usually interested in. This will be a very blessed union and much luck will come to you. You will find your true self. Good luck is with you.

youngster *to hear the word* You are headed in the right direction and will be greatly rewarded for a favor that you will do for someone within three days. Many blessings are with you and your family.

youth A blissful feeling will come over you within seven days because of a feeling of completeness and wholeness. Many blessings will come to you and your family.

Yo-yo Make sure you do not allow someone to take you on an emotional roller coaster ride, especially for the next three days. Get control of your life to avoid becoming sucked into this type of abuse. If this dream portends a negative event, take extra steps to prevent its occurrence in reality.

Yucatan Conduct yourself in such a way that you can incorporate a number of different events into your life so you can enjoy the spice of life. Do as many enjoyable things as you can in a short period of time and collect as many wonderful moments as possible. You are destined to experience many grand and awesome changes in your life within the week. This dream may also be used as a reference point in time. If you dream of this peninsula and see its name used in any context, the dream message will occur on this day.

yucca You must make it a point to seem forthright and settled to someone who has the power and authority to pull strings on your behalf. Proceed with confidence and you will be very successful in accomplishing what you need to accomplish within the week.

Yugoslavia Something that has caused you anguish for some time will suddenly be resolved. You will be freed of this burden. This dream also implies that you will receive some terrific news that will lead to rejoicing. This dream may also be used as a reference point in time. If you dream of this country and see its name used in any context, the dream message will occur on this day.

Yukon You are on the right path. Within three days you will be richly rewarded for a favor you do for another person. Many blessings will come to you and your family. This dream may also be used as a reference point in time. If you dream of this territory and see its name used in any context, the dream message will occur on this day.

Yule Someone will try to convince you within the week that something you are about to receive does not belong to you and you should return it. Make sure you do not allow yourself to be taken advantage of.

Yule log Do not allow yourself to become so phobic about a situation that will present itself within the week. You have prior notice of this so you can conduct yourself appropriately and not miss out on opportunities that could benefit you.

Yuletide Make sure the person you are depending on to provide you with certain information is not just giving you their perception of what they think you should know. Make sure you are getting all the facts, especially for the next five days.

yuppie Start preparing yourself now for a very high profile glamorous event that will take place within three weeks. If you choose to go, this event will be talked about for a long time to come. It will be good for you to involve yourself in this wonderful event.

YWCA Do whatever you can to remain equal, in your eyes, to everything you are exposed to for the next seven days. Expose your mental abilities and personality to as many opportunities as possible. Remain balanced as you go through these life events. This will provide you the opportunity to mold the remainder of your life and you will experience a prosperous future.

Z

Z This dream implies luck. You will gain an increase in good health as well as wealth in unexpected areas of your life due to an unanticipated income. You will also be able to accomplish tasks that you once felt were impossible to handle. This is a good time to tackle those big projects and to ask pointedly for your finances to be bettered. You will be granted these requests. Proceed with confidence. You are headed for a prosperous future.

Zacharias *(from the Bible, the father of John the Baptist)* An adversary has laid a trap in order to cause you injury. Be careful of this. Maintain your sense of alertness, especially for the next three days and make sure you keep your guard up. Do not allow yourself to be talked into going anywhere or becoming involved in new situations with another person who could accidentally cause you harm. It is very important, for this time period, to choose carefully what you are willing to become involved in.

zealot Do not become too deeply involved in a new relationship because the other individual will be unable to commit and will be fickle.

zebra Focus on keeping problems out of your domestic life that you do not want to experience. Do this now to avoid unpleasant situations at a later time.

zebra fish You will realize a fantastic creative opportunity.

zenith Tone down your authority.

Zephaniah *(from the Canonical Bible)* Keep a very low profile and focus on regular routine tasks. Focus on any error that could come up within three days and take care of them at once so everything will fall into place exactly as it should. Do everything you can to avoid any negative event in this dream concerning you and another person that could become a reality. Many blessings are with you and your family and you will enjoy an abundance of health.

zero You are now entering a very lucky cycle and it would be advantageous to you to maintain your relationships at the highest possible level. By doing your part in keeping relationships close, you will save energy and this will give you the time to focus on those issues that are important to you. This is also a perfect time to make an important decision. You have been procrastinating but if you make this decision now, victory will be yours. You are both headed for a brilliant future.

Zeus *(Greek mythology)* An older person will offer assistance just in time to resolve difficulty with money.

zinc Do everything necessary to maintain a clear complexion. Avoid skin infections.

zip code Do not attempt a new diet, this will cause health problems.

zipper Give others a break.

zircon You will enjoy a very financially secure love relationship. Extra clues can also be gained by looking up the colors of the zircon. You will enjoy great psychic clarity and excellent decision making abilities regarding the new dimension you are pointing yourself toward. This will bring you tranquility and pleasure beyond your belief.

zodiac Give your affections to a deserving person. Avoid those who do not like you. Dig for further clues by looking up the particular sign and symbols seen in the dream. You are headed for a brilliant future.

zombie Do not rely on sleep inducers or become addicted to any prescription medication.

zone Pay attention to the zone you dreamed about. Depending on the contents of this dream, this is a particular zone you will either need to avoid or to place yourself in, especially for the next three days. A rude and abrasive attitude is the proper attitude to take now so you will not compromise yourself. Someone will attempt to coerce you into doing something you do not want to do.

twilight zone You will receive a fantastic gift that you least expect at a time you least expect it from someone who feels a deep gratitude toward you. You must also do everything you can to make sure you are not going in the wrong direction, especially for the next three days. Make sure you carefully investigate the situation to ensure you are on the right path.

zoo You will develop great clarity of thought regarding the new dimension you are aiming for. This will bring you tranquility and pleasures greater than you ever believed possible. Until now you felt it was beyond your abilities to move in the direction you chose but you now have a new confidence in your abilities. You will move quickly to achieve what you are after. Within the week, you will have a feeling of being solidly grounded and you will enjoy a new sense of balance and confidence. You will then be able to take care of those issues that require this aspect of your personality. Use this cycle to change those areas of your life you wish to change. You will be able to bring prosperity into your life on the level you desire. You have a brilliant future in front of you.

zoologist Circulate and enjoy yourself.

Zulu *any form* It is very important not to miss an event that has been scheduled within the week. You will enjoy the company of two admirers who will subtly attempt to win over your affections. Although it will not be easily apparent to you, one of them possesses a great deal of power, wealth and authority. Both will be charming and very agreeable and you would enjoy having one of them in your life. You are on the path toward a prosperous future. You must also make sure you get to the heart of a certain matter. Once you determine what the missing element is, you will be able to resolve this in an appropriate way. Discuss changes that others want to implement and you will enjoy a successful venture.

About the Author

Briceida Ryan has been involved in dream interpretation for over twenty-eight years beginning at the age of nineteen. At the age of twenty-four she began keeping a journal of dreams and their interpretations. She has learned from family members that she demonstrated psychic abilities from the moment she could speak, and has also experienced premonitional dreams from an early age. She has had the ability to precisely predict future events based on the dreams of others. Work on this book began in 1991 and steady, uninterrupted work progressed until publication. She is self taught in the method used to produce this material for precise definitions of dreams for herself and others, and has interpreted dreams for people all over the world and from all walks of life. She is bilingual in Spanish and English and this has enabled her to work with a broad spectrum of ethnic groups.

She has also pursued other unrelated fields, and worked extensively as a health educator in prenatal and postnatal maternity and infant care for the Department of Obstetrics and Gynecology at the University of California in San Francisco. This work extended to St. Luke's Hospital and San Francisco General. She was a member of the staff at UCSF that introduced the midwifery program for mothers and babies as well as WIC (a subsidized food program).

The author is the owner of successful real estate investments in the heart of San Francisco. She presently resides in Pacifica and raised, as a single parent, four children and is a grandmother of six.

In addition, she has done freelancing art design in San Francisco, Pacifica, Santa Cruz and Half Moon Bay. She is a serious orchid enthusiast and a member of the American Orchid Society.

You may contact the author at *Breryan01@aol.com* or visit her at *www.dreamsos.com.*